THE BEGINNING TRANSLATOR'S WORKBOOK

or the ABCs of French to English Translation

REVISED EDITION

Michele H. Jones

University Press of America,® Inc.
Lanham · Boulder · New York · Toronto · Plymouth, UK

British Library Cataloging in Publication Information Available

Library of Congress Control Number: 2013956578
ISBN: 978-0-7618-6316-8 (paperback : alk. paper)
eISBN: 978-0-7618-6317-5

Contents

Chapter 3   **Deceptive Cognates**

Chapter 4   **Translation Techniques**

Chapter 5   **Borrowings**

Chapter 6   **Calques**

Chapter 7   **Literal Translation and Structural Obstacles to Literal translation**

Preface

Why a textbook on translation?

Necessity is the mother of invention. This book was born of the need for adequate material to be used in a translation course for beginners with a proficiency in French ranging from intermediate to advanced. Unlike most books on the subject which either focus on theory and method and target professionals, or focus on practice and only provide texts with their finished translation without indicating how to get there, this manual offers methodology and practice concurrently.

Each of the beginning eleven chapters defines a particular translation problem, introduces a method of dealing with it, provides examples to illustrate the point, and concludes with practice exercises consisting of short sentences designed to make the student think about the difficulty and select the proper translation strategy. The advantage of this methodological approach is that even a novice translator will quickly learn how to identify the various pitfalls of translation and will react with the proper response.

It has been my experience as an instructor that students new to translation shy away from idiomatic translation and instead stick stubbornly to the text word for word. The proposed method, through a progressive framework, will enable them to move beyond literal translation to a fluid and idiomatic rendition of the source text by building up confidence and savoir-faire.

After students become familiar with the translation environment, and attain a solid level of proficiency through the use of the various strategies put at their disposal, the final chapters are intended to provide a global application of the principles taught by guiding them through the actual process of literary and non-literary translation. Suggested translations are offered alongside the texts as illustrations of what a finished translation can be, but by no means as the one and only solution and model.

Throughout the book, particular care has been taken to provide material for both literary and business or technical translation, in order to make the apprentice translator aware of the semantic and structural differences involved. Guidelines have also been provided delineating the different approaches to follow and the different expectations to be met on both counts.

If classes meet for three hours per week, the various translation techniques and corresponding exercises can be covered in half a semester, leaving the remainder of the semester for practice on full length newspaper or magazine articles as well as novel and play excerpts. A selection of texts for translation practice has not been included, so as to leave freedom of choice to the course instructor. Everyone tends to have particular favorites and it is advisable to renew the texts in subsequent courses in order to keep them current and make sure that students are challenged with new material for which there is no available correction.

Translation is both an art and a skill, a discipline with rules, do's and don'ts. The recently coined words of "*traductique*" and "*traductologie*" in French emphasize the scientific aspect of modern translation. It is a difficult and demanding process. To attain a high proficiency level will require years of practice. But what a wonderful exercise for the mind and what great intellectual benefits it yields: from the sharpening of analytical powers and the sheer enjoyment of being able to convey a message by watching thoughts take shape in different words, right down to the thrill and sense of accomplishment which accompanies the finding of solutions to puzzling semantic or structural problems. Translation can be a discipline as well as a pastime. And even though computer scientists and linguists have been working for some fifty years now on "robot translators' or automatic translation in the hope of one day replacing the human translator, technology is still light years away from being able to produce the software which will translate Molière, Baudelaire or Proust. Let's be thankful for that, for it would deprive us of using and developing that great machine of ours, our brain.

This revised edition has been enlarged to include clarifications of some of the finer points of the translation techniques introduced in the first edition and to provide additional illustrations of the various problems encountered in translation with their solutions. Extra exercises have also been provided to practice the theory of translation explained in each chapter. New texts are presented with model translations. A list of free online resources for translation in specialty fields, such as business, medicine, the law, computer science, science and technology, slang and idiomatic expressions, has been included in the Translator's Tools chapter at the end of the book.

Finally a support website summarizing the various translation techniques and featuring more examples and exercises is now available for use in class for instructors who have access to a computer podium at: http://facpub.stjohns.edu/~jonesm/BTW_WebSupport.htm

Lastly, I would like to add a word of thanks for my students, who have provided the experimental field without which this book would not have been possible, and particularly Walter Schaap for allowing me to reproduce the poem translations found in this book. I also thank the weekly magazine *Evènement du Jeudi*, and the newspapers *France Amérique* and *Journal de Genève-Gazette de Lausanne* for their gracious permission to reprint the articles found in chapter 17.

The Beginning Translator's Basic Terminology

Source language (S.L.): language from which one translates (Fr. langue de départ, L.D.)

Target language (T.L.): language into which one translates (Fr. langue d'arrivée, L.A.)

Sign versus concept: a linguistic sign is formed of an acoustic sound (in speech) or a visual image (in writing) representing a concept. E.g. *arbre* and *tree* are two signs and one concept.

Translation unit (T.U., Fr. unité de traduction, U.T.): a unit of thought in the language, the smallest portion of a message whose elements cannot be translated separately without resulting in mistranslation or even nonsense. E.g. *faire un clin d'oeil* (*to wink*), or *to put on weight* (*grossir*).

Delineation of translation units: structural analysis of the text to be translated in order to determine the translation units it encompasses.

Mistranslation: erroneous or incorrect translation which may or may not make sense in the TL and results from a lack of sufficient knowledge or a misinterpretation of the SL; can occur in one word or a whole sentence.

Barbarism: the use of words or expressions not in accordance with the classical standard of a language, especially such as are of foreign origin. A mistake made in translation by inventing or deforming a word, or using a word to mean something it does not. An example of barbarism would be to say *Romantism* after the French *Romantisme* instead of *Romanticism.*

Inventing a grammatical structure, often by copying the SL, is also considered a barbarism. E.g. the use of the definite article for general terms and concepts being the rule in French, but not in English, a barbarism in English would be incurred by saying: *The beauty is fleeting* to translate *La beauté est éphémère.*

Solecism: a specific type of barbarism involving a violation of the rules of grammar and syntax.

Overtranslation: occurs when the translator sees several translation units when only one exists. Elements absent from the source text are added and the translation is longer than it should be; i.e. *petits pois* constitutes one translation unit rendered as *peas* rather than *small peas,* which would be the equivalent of *petits pois extra fins.*

Undertranslation: occurs when the translator sees fewer translation units than actually exist by overlooking one or several of the elements of the original message and failing to translate them.

Retranslation: is a checking device in translation. The translator retraces his steps from the TL back to the SL and then compares this retranslation with the original text to verify translation accuracy.

Deficiency versus compensation: a deficiency occurs when a particular semantic or grammatical concept does not exist in either the SL or the TL. A compensation, on the other hand, is an attempt to make up for that deficiency through some other means; i.e the lack of the *tu* form of address in English can be compensated with the use of the person's nickname to indicate familiarity; or the lack of phonetic emphasis in French can be compensated by stylistic emphasis: *I told you, not he* may be rendered as *C'est moi qui te l'ai dit, ce n'est pas lui.*

Loss versus gain: a loss in translation occurs when a semantic or structural deficiency in the TL cannot be compensated for; whereas a gain occurs when an element which did not exist in the SL is added whenever the TL is semantically richer. E.g. When the sentence *Le taux de chômage est passé à 5,8 pour cent en avril de 5,5 pour cent en mars* is translated as *The unemployment rate jumped to 5.8 per cent in April from 5.5 percent in March*, we have a gain in English with the verb *jumped* indicating a sudden upward trend absent from the SL word *est passé*.

Saving versus padding: saving is when the S.L. message can be translated in fewer words, and padding when it has to be expressed in more words. An example of saving in English: *Il a prit sa retraite, He retired*; an example of padding: *Tu es insortable, You are not fit to be taken out.*

Language levels: they determine the type of language to be used in translation: poetic vs. prosaic, literary vs. colloquial, refined vs. vulgar, ancient vs. modern, aesthetical vs. functional, philosophical vs. technical etc. The translator has to adopt the tone of the SL as well as its register, whether formal or informal, and target the audience targeted by the SL. One does not translate *Je vous prie de bien vouloir quitter ces lieux* (*I ask you to please leave these premises*) and *Foutez moi le camp!* (*Get the hell out!*) quite in the same language register.

Literal versus figurative sense: many words have both a concrete meaning and an abstract one. E.g. Fr. *ivresse*: (literal sense) *drunkenness*; (figurative sense) *rapture*.

False cognates (Fr. faux amis): words with the same linguistic origin in the SL and TL whose meanings have evolved differently over the years. E.g. Fr. *actuellement*: *at present*, and Engl. *actually*: *en réalité*.

Translation techniques: these are the various strategies at the disposal of a translator when confronted with structural, semantic or metalinguistic obstacles.
There are three literal translation techniques: borrowing, calque and word for word translation, and four non literal ones: transposition, modulation, equivalence and adaptation.

Borrowing: when a concept first exists in the SL but not in the TL it is often borrowed in its original form by the TL without any form of translation. Example of English borrowing from French: *mayonnaise*; of French from English: *steak*.

Calque: occurs when instead of being borrowed in its original form a new concept from the SL is translated literally, "copied" by the TL. E.g. from English to French: *the cold war, la guerre froide*; from French to English: *secrétaire général, secretary general*.

Literal translation: when there are no structural or semantic obstacles for doing so, the words in the SL and in the TL can be translated word for word and in the same order. E.g. *Où est le chat? Where is the cat?*

Transposition: is a change in grammatical categories between SL and TL so as to surmount a structural obstacle and remain idiomatic, i.e. *Maison à vendre: House for sale* (in this case the change is from a verb to a noun).

Modulation: occurs when the SL and the TL see the same concept from different angles. There can be word modulations (found in dictionaries), e.g. *un logiciel* (abstract viewpoint): *software* (concrete); preposition modulations (found in grammar books), e.g. *J'ai vu une émission intéressante à la télé, I saw an interesting show on TV*; or message modulations, e.g. *On m'a appris la nouvelle, I was told the news*.

Equivalence: when the translation unit is an idiomatic expression, a cliché, a reflex formula, a greeting formula, slang, a proverb or saying, a cultural reference, the translator must first understand the situation from the context and then give the appropriate equivalent expression used in a similar situation in the TL. For instance, in the situation of a child asking another about what has been going on during his absence: *Quoi de neuf? What's up?* would be the equivalent in English.

Adaptation: when there are obstacles to translation resulting from cultural differences, *i.e.* different institutions, customs or traditions which the readers in the TL cannot well comprehend for lack of a ready equivalent, the translator must resort to adaptation. One form of adaptation is compensation, another might be an explanatory periphrasis, yet another, some similar concept in the TL. For example: *Le musée se trouve à 200 mètres d'ici, The museum is about 200 yards away.*

Preliminary Remarks
Linguistics and Metalinguistics

Reality, in the creative process required to give a language its vocabulary and syntax, can be seen under many different angles. In apprehending a particular concept each language tends to focus on different aspects of the same reality, and to see things slightly or even very differently from what other languages may perceive. This is true at the semantic level, in the creation of vocabulary and idioms. It is also true at the syntactic and grammatical level, in the delivery of the message.

A few examples:

Semantically

Where Anglophones see:	Francophones see:
a goldfish	a red fish (un poisson rouge)
a fireman	a (water) pumping man (un pompier)
a keyhole	a lockhole (un trou de serrure)
a moving sidewalk	a rolling carpet (un tapis roulant)
a life threatening disease	a mortal disease (une maladie mortelle)
W (double U)	W (double V)

Grammatically

Whereas English favors the passive voice in certain constructions, French favors the active voice:

I've been told that he is feeling better

translates best as *On m'a dit* qu'il va mieux.

Modulation can occur in the use of the auxiliary verb in common expressions:

"She *is* 20 years *old*"   becomes   "Elle *a* 20 *ans*"

Syntactically

Syntax is yet another field in which variations are frequent. English has a propensity to be more synthetic and favor the use of compound words, French, more analytic and favor the use of articulations:

business French	le français *des* affaires
a customer oriented company	une firme tournée vers le client/
	une firme qui donne la priorité au client

Importance of culture and civilization in the formation of languages

Metalinguistics (from the Greek *meta*, beyond), *i.e.* all the elements which beyond the language encompass the civilization and culture of a particular linguistic group, has a profound influence over the formation of the language.

Concepts as French as the 14th of July, cafés, croissants, the baccalauréat, the legion of honor are steeped in history and culture. A serious translator must therefore have a very good knowledge of the culture and civilization of the language from which he or she is translating in order to be able to pick up historical and literary references which would elude a less informed amateur. Expressions such as *l'homme du 18 juin*, a reference to Charles de Gaulle, the man responsible for the famous London broadcast of June 18th 1944 calling to rally all the forces of Free France to continue fighting the Nazi regime which had just overtaken France; or *Revenons à nos moutons*, a saying taken from a popular medieval play, *La Farce de Maître Pathelin*, in which a judge, overwhelmed by an onset of confusing complaints, pleads to have the plaintiff stick to one complaint at a time: the loss of some sheep. The expression has eventually passed into everyday speech with the meaning of *Let's stick to the point.*

Differences in concept focus between English and French in the creation of words

The following are sample categories in which metalinguistics and different perceptions of the world have resulted in diverging messages for the same concept. The list is by no means exhaustive but meant only as an illustration of this point.

Greetings and salutations
Different ways of dividing the day:
  Good morning!/ good afternoon!   Bonjour!

Reflex formulas
Different perspectives. The English exclamation below is concrete and involves the eyesight while the French one is abstract and involves the mind:
  Watch out!   Attention!

Public signs
Different approaches in the delivery of the message. Here is an informal communication in English and a more formal and authoritative French counterpart:
  Keep off the grass   *Défense* de marcher sur les pelouses

Idioms and clichés
Different priorities and values in life. The importance of sports and the outdoors in the English speaking world versus the importance of anything having to do with cooking in French speaking countries are reflected in these two equivalent clichés:
  Let's not beat around the bush   Ne tournons pas autour du pot

Vocabulary related to architecture
Different ways of defining space:
  a first floor (U.S.)   un rez de chaussée (U. K. ground floor)

Vocabulary related to measures
Different ways of visualizing measuring units:
  a yard
  un mètre (a unit created during the French Revolution in a concerted effort
  to improve on the confusing measure system then existent throughout France)

Vocabulary related to professions
Different ways of delineating areas of specialization in professions.
  A lawyer (U.S.) who may specialize in litigation, tort law, estates and wills etc.
  is the equivalent of two French professions:
  avocat (U.K. barrister) and notaire (U.K. sollicitor)

We will see more of these metalinguistic divergences as we go along, because metalinguistics cannot be dissociated from the creative process involved in linguistics.

Chapter 1 **Translation Units**

What are translation units and what is their purpose?

After reading the text to be translated, the basic task of the translator, in the transcoding process from the source language to the target language that follows, is to go beyond words to the concepts behind those words. In that particular phase of translation and for a split second, the translator is actually transcending words, languages, navigating in a world of pure thought, before giving back the message in a new shape, a new code.

Literal or word for word translation occurs whenever there are no semantic or grammatical obstacles, *i.e.* when one noun in the S.L. corresponds to one noun in the T.L., one verb to one verb, one grammatical construction to a structurally similar grammatical construction and when the word order also is identical. Needless to say, such ideal conditions generally do not exist, except perhaps in sister languages originated from a common tongue with a similar grammar and syntax such as Romance languages, which are derived from Latin.

In the case of English and French however, we cannot speak of sister languages, for, although they are often close semantically due to a common vocabulary stock derived from Latin, ancient Greek, old French, and mutual borrowings over the centuries, they both differ considerably in grammar and syntax, English belonging to the family of Germanic languages and French to the Romance language group. Between English and French, therefore, literal translation may occur in very simple and short sentences, sentences such as: *The cat eats the mouse, Le chat mange la souris*, but never in complex structures. In French, or in English, a concept may not always coincide with one word, and so one word in one language may correspond to several words in the other and vice-versa.

Both languages have different characteristics. French tends to be more analytical and to expand its concepts with the use of articulations. English tends to be more synthetic, using concise compound expressions. A translation into English from the French will typically run much shorter than the original without any loss in the global message.

The translator must then learn what constitutes a concept, a unit of thought in the S.L., delineate the message to be translated into as many translation units as there are concepts, and finally translate them into their T.L. counterparts.

This is how we may therefore define a translation unit:

> **A translation unit [T.U.] is the smallest portion of a sentence whose words cannot be translated separately without resulting in nonsense or mistranslation.**

A. Lexical translation units

These translation units may be lexical, based on words or expressions which can be found in a good dictionary.

Overtranslation is a common mistake made by beginners: several translation units are seen where only one exists and the end result is either nonsense or mistranslation, that is to say an erroneous interpretation of the SL

Let's take two examples:
1. **the adverbial phrase** *de bonne heure*: if the translator does not see a single translation unit here, the phrase will be divided into 3 parts and translated literally as *of good hour*, which would result in total nonsense in the T.L, or as *at a good hour* which would be a mistranslation instead of the correct meaning *early*.
2. **the nominal phrase** *poids lourd* in the context *Ce poids lourd me barre la route*: again, if the translator, due to lack of semantic knowledge, sees two units of translation where in fact only one exists,

the concept will be translated as *heavy weight*, also a mistranslation, since the message in the T.L. would read *heavy weight* as in *heavy weight champion* instead of *truck*.

The following are representative examples in both languages of what may constitute a lexical translation unit:

French (group of words) to English (one word):

Nominal phrases: un hôtel de ville: a townhall; un chef d'orchestre: a conductor

Verbal phrases: montrer du doigt: to point (at); donner un coup de pied: to kick; émettre une hypothèse: to hypothesize

Adverbial phrases: à toute vitesse: speedily; quand même: anyway; dans tout le pays: nationwide

Adjectival phrases: mal à l'aise: awkward/ uncomfortable

Prepositional phrases: le long de: along; au dessus de: above

Conjunctional phrases: au fur et à mesure que: as; du temps où: when

French (one word) to English (group of words):

Nouns: une standardiste: a (female) switchboard operator; un percepteur: a tax collector; l'équitation: horse back riding; un bilan: an outcome assessment

Verbs: vieillir: to get old; rentabiliser: to make profitable; déconseiller: to advise against; s'immobiliser: to come to a standstill

Adjectives: influençable: easily influenced; fragilisé: rendered more precarious

Adverbs: péniblement: with difficulty; dorénavant: from now on

Standard expressions:

Global expressions which are standard and idiomatic in the language also constitute units of translation. They can involve a verb and a direct object, such as:

établir une comparaison: **to draw** a comparison; **faire face à** une obligation: **to meet** an obligation; **faire** une objection: **to raise** an objection; **réaliser** un bénéfice: **to make** a profit etc...

or a nominal group, such as:

un cas de force majeure: circumstances beyond one's control; un délit d'initié: insider trading; un travail de longue haleine: long and hard work, etc...

or even a group adjective-noun:

un **pauvre** type: a loser; une **mauvaise** réponse : a **wrong** answer; un **gros** rhume: a **bad** cold *etc...*

B. Grammatical translation units

These translation units may also be grammatical, based on different grammatical or syntactical structures between the two languages, structures giving cohesive unity to a global concept.

For example:

Verbs followed by prepositions:
Verbs whose construction requires that they be followed by a special preposition before a noun or another verb constitute translation units:

Cela ne *dépend* pas *de* moi: That does not *depend on* me.

Sometimes the prepositions coincide in the two languages; but sometimes also they can be different, or there can be a preposition in one language and none in the other. Good grammars will offer lists of such prepositional constructions. Otherwise, check in your dictionary.

Examples of prepositional structures which coincide:
s'habituer *à*: to get used *to*; voter *pour*: to vote *for*
Which do not coincide:
commencer *par*: to start *with;* décider *de*: to decide *to*
Instances in which there is a preposition in English but none in French:
to look *at*: regarder; to ask *for*: demander
A preposition in French/ none in English:
assister *à*: to attend; discuter *de* : to discuss

Active/ passive voice:
Very often an active voice in French will be translated as a passive voice in English. The corresponding structure constitutes a translation unit.

On nous avait prévenus: *We had been forewarned.* Instead of an awkward literal rendition contrary to English usage (one had forewarned us...) the use of the passive voice will yield an idiomatic translation.

Articulated expressions vs. compound expressions:
French like all Romance languages is an analytic language, that is to say one which often makes use of connective prepositions between the various components of a concept, whereas English is a synthetic Germanic language which tends to juxtapose these same elements without connectors. Therefore articulated expressions in French will constitute units of translation often to be rendered as compound expressions in English with an accompanying change in word order:

> *Des jeans qui serrent au corps*:   *tight fitting jeans*
> *Une compagnie en plein essor*:   *a fast growing company*
> *Une crème soins de jour pour le visage:*   *a day care face cream*

C. Extended translation units

Translation units are not necessarily limited to phrases, small groups of words, or different grammatical constructions: they can encompass entire sentences or even entire messages. Idioms and slang, greetings and reflex-formulas, clichés, proverbs and sayings, public signs and regulations, all constitute complex translation units whose elements cannot be translated separately:[1]

> *A la prochaine*! *See you soon*!
> *Non mais alors*, vous ne pouvez pas faire attention! *Look here*, can't you be *more* careful!
> J'étais *dans mes petits souliers*: I was *on tenterhooks*.
> Votre enfant est *sage comme une image*:Your child is *as good as gold*.
> Tandis qu'il parlait, *j'avais la moutarde qui me montait au nez*: As he spoke, *I was getting miffed*.
> *Comme on fait son lit on se couche*: *As you sow, so shall you reap*.
> *Sens interdit*: *One way street*.

D. Delineation of translation units

It is good practice for the student translator to learn how to delineate translation units, *i.e.* make a semiological analysis of the

---

[1] We will deal with these at length in the chapter on equivalence.

text, by cutting out and pairing the words which constitute single concepts in order to translate them into their proper counterparts. Experienced translators will automatically do a quick mental delineation of translation units before a translation, and after some practice this procedure should become second nature.

Make sure that all nominal, verbal, adverbial, prepositional and conjunctional phrases are correctly recognized, as well as grammatical TUs such as active/passive constructions, prepositions attached to verbs, and all the idiomatic expressions which we grouped under the heading *Extended T.U.s*.

Examples:

Tout le monde me dit que je ressemble comme deux gouttes d'eau à mon grand-père.
[1   ] [2] [3] [4] [5] [6   ] [7]
[8   ]
Everyone tells me that I   am the spitting image of my grand father.
[1   ] [3] [2] [4] [5] [6   ] [7] [8   ]
The difficulty here lies in the proper recognition of *ressembler comme deux gouttes d'eau à* as one concept, therefore as one TU.

On   nous a demandé de repasser dans une semaine.
[1-2] [3] [1-2   ] [4] [5] [6] [7] [8] [9   ]
We were asked   to come back in one week.
[3] [1-2   ] [4] [6] [5] [7] [8] [9]
The verb *a demandé* has to be understood as two TUs: one for the verb itself and one for the past tense. The verb *repasser* also corresponds to two concepts: *re-* and *passer*.

Ça par exemple, tu   as   encore fait la grasse matinée!
[1   ] [2] [3-4] [5] [3-4   ]
My goodness, you've been sleeping late again!
[1   ] [2] [3-4   ] [5]
Ça par exemple has to be recognized as a set expression, therefore as one TU, and so does the idiom *faire la grasse matinée* even though it is interrupted by the adverb *encore* which has to be repositioned in English. Also: *Tu as fait* encompasses two TUs: one for the verb concept and the other for the past tense.

Défense de stationner.
[1   ]
No parking.

[1   ]

Aide-toi le ciel t'aidera.
[1   ]
Heaven helps those who help themselves.
[1   ]
Public signs and regulations, proverbs and sayings, which are set in the language, constitute one TU each.

Overtranslation and undertranslation are standard translation mistakes resulting from improper T.U. delineation:

- **Overtranslation** occurs when the translator sees more TUs in the source text than actually exist.
- **Undertranslation**, when the translator sees fewer TUs than actually exist.

> **Example one: Que veux-tu dire?**
> If the translator sees two TUs in the verb *vouloir dire* (to want to say) instead of only one (to mean), as is correct, the result will be an overtranslation: *What do you want to say*? instead of *What do you mean?* The first translation is erroneous because it introduces an intent absent from the source text, and would be more the equivalent of *Tu veux dire quelque chose*?
>
> **Example two: Quand vous reverrai-je?**
> If the translator fails to recognize that the verb *revoir* actually constitutes two TUs (to see/ again) the result will be an undertranslation: *When shall I see you?* instead of *When shall I see you again?*

In summary, the main purpose behind the delineation of a text into translation units is to remind the novice translator to work with concepts rather than words: you must get to the message behind the signs in order to avoid error, nonsense or just plain non-idiomatic translation.

Exercices: Les Unités de traduction

> *Une unité de traduction [U.T.] est le plus petit segment d'une phrase dont les éléments ne peuvent être traduits séparément sans tomber dans le non-sens ou le contresens (synonyme: unité de pensée, concept)*
> *Dans l'unité de traduction le concept peut être un mot, un groupe de mots ou même une phrase .*
> *Un mot dans la langue de départ [LD] peut coïncider avec un groupe de mots dans la langue d'arrivée [LA] ou vice versa.*

A. Les Unités de traduction lexicales

I. Les locutions suivantes en français constituent des unités de traduction qui se traduisent par un mot simple en anglais. Retrouvez-en le sens.

1. Locutions nominales:

Un ancien combattant; un ancien élève; un chef de gouvernement; un exploitant agricole; un franc-tireur; un homme politique; un metteur en scène; une personne du troisième âge; un sans-abri; un sans emploi.
Un animal domestique; le bout des doigts; un chef d'oeuvre; un chemin de fer; un coup de pied; un courant d'air; le cuir chevelu; une grande surface; un hôtel de ville; la main d'oeuvre; des petits pois; un poids lourd; une pomme de pin; une pomme de terre; une tenue vestimentaire; une vente aux enchères.
Un chiffre d'affaire; une expression idiomatique; un fil de fer; un jour férié; une manchette de journal; un manque de considération; une matière plastique; une mise au point; une mise en oeuvre, un mode d'emploi; une pension alimentaire; un point de repère; un titre de propriété; une tranche horaire.

2. Locutions verbales:

Avoir affaire (à); donner une autorisation; donner des leçons particulières; donner sa démission; faire allusion (à); faire appliquer (une loi); faire confiance à; faire état de; faire mention de; faire peur à; faire de la publicité; faire un procès; jouer un mauvais tour; lancer des représailles; mettre en cause; mettre en question; mettre (une lettre) à la boîte; mettre en oeuvre; montrer du doigt; prendre sa retraite; remettre (quelque chose) à plus tard; se mettre d'accord ; traduire en justice; tirer un coup de fusil; vouloir dire.

3. Locutions adverbiales:
(Comparer) à l'échelle mondiale; (faire quelque chose) sans effort; (parler) en connaissance de cause; (partir) de manière précipitée; (prendre) au sérieux; (regarder) en silence; (se lever) de bonne heure; (venir) tout de suite.

4. Locutions adjectivales:
(Etre) à bout de forces; (être) transporté de joie; (un accord) sans conditions ; (un produit) sans matière grasse.

5. Locutions prépositionnelles:
A côté de; à destination de; à la différence de; au-dessus de; dans la direction de; de la part de; en ce qui concerne; en provenance de; le long de; par le moyen de; pour ce qui est de.

6. Locutions de conjonction:
A l'endroit où ; à l'époque où; au fur et à mesure que; au moment où; de telle sorte que.

II. Les mots français suivants correspondent à des groupes de mots en anglais: traduisez.

1. Substantifs:
Un arriéré (de paiement); un récidiviste; un charcutier; la cohabitation (politique); la conjoncture (économique); une fermière; une gentilhommière; une journaliste; une mévente; un particulier; une pâtissière; un restaurateur; une standardiste; un vieillard .

2. Verbes:
Arrondir; élargir; grossir; lâcher; maigrir; rajeunir; culpabiliser; déconseiller; rentabiliser; redémarrer; refaire; revoir; s'agrandir; s'assouplir; se désintéresser; s'entendre (avec quelqu'un).

3. Adjectifs:
Influençable; insortable; indissociable; frileux; travailleur.

B. Les Unités de traduction grammaticales

> *Les verbes auxquels sont rattachées des prépositions constituent des unités de traduction. Parfois les prépositions coïncident dans les deux langues, parfois elles sont différentes, et parfois il y a une préposition dans une langue mais pas dans l'autre.*

Traduisez.

1. Il faut téléphoner *à* la compagnie aérienne pour confirmer notre retour.
2. Le résultat ne dépendra que *de* toi.
3. Dans une dissertation on doit toujours commencer *par* une introduction.
4. Pourquoi étais-tu en colère *contre* moi?
5. Il vient de se faire opérer *d*'un kyste.
6. Etudions pour éviter *d*'échouer *à* cet examen.
7. Quand t'intéresseras-tu *à* quelque chose qui en vaille la peine?
8. Le commandant de la milice donna l'ordre de tirer *sur* la foule.
9. Il me semble que je commence à m'habituer *à* ma vie d'étudiant.
10. Attends-moi!
11. Je cherche mes lunettes.
12. Mais je n'ai pas ri *de* toi, seulement *de* ton chapeau!
13. *A* quels cours vous êtes-vous inscrits ce semestre?
14. Pour le physique il tient *de* son père.
15. Nous préférons écouter de la musique classique.
16. Il serait désormais difficile de se passer *d*'électricité.

C. Les Unités de traduction: découpage

I. Combien d'unités de traduction (U.T.) dans les mots et expressions suivantes ?

(Une) pomme de terre ; (des) pommes de terre ; (une) co-équipière ; le travail ; les travaux

Prendre sa retraite; déconseiller; refaire; (nous) viendrons ; (nous) reviendrons; (tu) aurais regardé; (ils) sont partis

Au fur et à mesure que ; bien que ; tandis que ; de côté ; là-bas ; aujourd'hui ; ne…pas encore; ne…que

II. Découpez les phrases suivantes en unités de traduction.

1. Le succès de l'entreprise ne dépend que de toi.
2. De temps à autre je me fais des idées noires, ce que mon petit ami met en question avec désinvolture.
3. L'homme politique eut tout de suite l'idée qu'il s'agissait d'un piège.
4. Bien qu'elle eut très peur, la petite fille ne poussa pas un cri.
5. Je n'avais pas le coeur serré à la pensée de quitter l'endroit qui m'avait vu naître.
6. On nous montra du doigt le musée qui se trouvait juste en face de l'hôtel de ville.
7. Au fur et à mesure que la soirée avançait les invités s'éclipsaient jusqu'à ce qu'il ne reste plus que nous.
8. Le président directeur général va prendre la parole pour établir une comparaison entre le chiffre d'affaire de cette année et celui de l'année dernière.
9. Tout le monde s'attend à ce que l'inculpé soit traduit en justice dans les jours qui viennent.
10. Une fois par an nous faisons une grande fête de famille qui commence par un banquet et se termine par des embrassades.

D. Les Unités de traduction: le contexte

> *La distinction entre les groupes de mots qui constituent des locutions, donc des unités de traduction simples et les groupes de mots qui n'en sont pas est quelquefois difficile à faire. Elle dépend du contexte, ou bien encore de petits indicateurs morphologiques, syntaxiques ou lexicaux, tels les changements d'articles ou de prépositions, mots composés, sens propre contre sens figuré, etc..*

Dans les phrases suivantes indiquez si les groupes de mots similaires constituent une seule U.T. (en tant que locutions) ou plusieurs U.T (en tant que concepts séparés).

1. Please set out the *tea cups*.
2. Would you like another *cup of tea*?
3. Come tomorrow morning at 9 *without fail*.
4. I *won't fail* this exam.
5. They are not *in the know*.
6. They are not *to know*.
7. Concerning this matter, we are all in *the same boat*.
8. *The same boat* took them to the other side of the lake.
9. There's a *man in the street* standing in front of our door.
10. How does the *man in the street* feel about this issue?
11. *Serve you right*!
12. Guests must be *served* first.
13. One *can never tell* you anything for fear of having it broadcast everywhere.
14. You *never can tell*!
15. That *takes the cake*!
16. *Take the rest of the cake* with you, we're on a diet.
17. I got this antique chest *for a song* at a flea market.
18. *For this song* you'll get a kiss.
19. There's no need to *rub it in*.
20. The instructions say: first *rub the paste in*, let it dry, then buff it to a polish.
21. You are going about it *the wrong way*.
22. We drove up the street *the wrong way*.

23. There you go again: you *spilled the beans*!
24. Be careful not *to spill any beans* on the floor.
25. The prisoner *was shot in the arm* while trying to escape.
26. Lower interest rates have given the economy a *shot in the arm*.

E. Les Unités de traduction complexes

> *Les formules-réflexes, les salutations, les clichés, les expressions idiomatiques et argotiques, les affiches officielles, et les proverbes et dictons sont des cas particuliers d'unités de traduction.*

Retrouvez les équivalents anglais des unités suivantes.
1. *Bon appétit!*
2. *Comment ça va?*
3. *Dites donc*, comme votre fils a grandi!
4. *Tant pis pour toi*!
5. *Allons*, tu ne vas pas me faire croire ça!
6. *Voyons*, ce n'est pas sérieux!
7. *Défense de marcher sur les pelouses.*
8. *Attention: travaux.*
9. *Défense de stationner.*
10. Elle est jolie *comme un coeur.*(Elle est très jolie)
11. Tu fumes *comme un pompier.*(Tu fumes beaucoup)
12. *J'ai pris mes jambes à mon cou.*(J'ai vite couru)
13. *Ne va pas chercher midi à quatorze heures!*(Ne fais pas de difficultés)
14. *Occupe-toi de tes oignons!* (Occupe-toi de tes affaires)
15. *22, v'la les flics!* (Attention voilà la police!)
16. *L'habit ne fait pas le moine.* (Il ne faut pas juger les gens sur l'apparence)
17. *Plus on est de fous, plus on rit.* (Plus il y a de gens, plus on s'amuse)

F. Traduction de texte

Le dialogue suivant contient un certain nombre d'expressions idiomatiques et de clichés (en gros caractères dans le texte) qui constituent des unités de traduction, et, de ce fait, ne peuvent pas être traduits littéralement. En voici les équivalents (dans le désordre) en anglais.

if you think I'm gonna fall for this	**buddy**
for goodness sake	**a scam**
you must be kidding	**keep trying**
a strange thing happened to me	**to be busy reading**
sweepstakes	**congratulations**
O.K., I get it	**speaking**

Traduisez le passage ci-dessous en choisissant les expressions équivalentes en anglais.

Il m'est arrivé une drôle d'histoire l'autre jour. J'étais **plongé dans la lecture de** mon journal juste avant de partir pour le bureau, quand le téléphone a sonné. « **Ça par exemple**, qui peut bien téléphoner de si bonne heure? » J'ai décroché. Une voix à l'autre bout du fil s'est fait entendre:

« -Allô, ici Jean Dupont de la firme Bouquins et cie, j'aimerais parler à M. Jacques Legrand.

-*C'est lui-même à l'appareil.*

-Monsieur, j'ai le grand plaisir de vous annoncer que vous êtes l'heureux gagnant de notre **tirage au sort. Toutes mes félicitations**!

-Que voulez-vous dire?

-Vous avez gagné l'un de nos premiers prix: un magnifique baladeur d'une valeur de cent euros.

-*Vous voulez rire*! »

Ce type me prenait par surprise, je n'avais jamais rien gagné de ma vie auparavant.

« -Mais pas du tout! Il n'y a qu'une petite condition pour que vous puissiez recevoir ce prix exceptionnel: vous engager à souscrire à un abonnement de 3 ans au magazine...

-*Ça y est, je comprends*. **Un attrape-sot**, ai-je pensé, **mon vieux**, si tu crois que **je vais me laisser prendre comme ça, tu peux toujours courir**! »

Et j'ai raccroché.

Chapter 2   **Words in Context**

Polysemy: Words and their semantic range

Except in the fields of science and technology, where accuracy is a must, very few words are monosemous in any given language, *i.e.* have one meaning only. The words one uses on a daily basis are all polysemous, carrying multiple meanings.

Let's examine some of the various categories these meanings fall into.

First there is the concrete versus the abstract level:

> On passe un bon film en ce moment au *cinéma* du quartier. (Concrete)
> L'industrie du *cinéma* est importante aux Etats Unis. (Abstract)

The literal versus the figurative level:

> Le *chou* est un légume crucifère. (Literal)
> Mon petit *chou,* réveille-toi! (Figurative)

The restricted versus the extended meaning:

> Posez donc ces dossiers sur mon *bureau*! (Restricted)
> Je ne vais jamais au *bureau* le samedi ni le dimanche. (Extended)

The ancient versus the modern meaning:

> Les mauvais *succès* sont les seuls maîtres qui peuvent nous reprendre utilement. (Bossuet) (ancient meaning: prior to the XVIIIth century: "succès" meant both the good or bad result of an action)
> Notre entreprise a été couronnée de *succès*. (Modern meaning)

The meaning of a word in the standard language versus its meaning in a language of specialty:

> La *poire* est un des fruits que je préfère. (Standard)
> Ce type est une vraie *poire*. (Slang, as a language of specialty)

In none of the above-listed sentences will the same word in French be translated with the same counterpart in English.

Words cannot be separated from their context. Far from being separate entities, they are flavored by their surroundings. The context will give a word a particular twist, a particular shade of meaning. As we have just seen, the range of meaning of most words offers a certain number of variations, and different contexts will highlight anyone of these variations, for instance the concrete versus the abstract meaning of the word, or the standard meaning of the word versus its meaning in a specialty context, etc...

As a result, polysemy is one of the major problems a translator has to face, due to the fact that words in the S.L. and in the T.L. generally have semantic ranges which do not totally coincide in all of their various meanings: a word in the S.L. may have one (or several) of its shades of meaning covered by one counterpart in the T.L., while other extensions or variations of meaning of the same S.L. word require the use of totally different counterparts in the T.L.

The following diagram tries to illustrate how the semantic range of two words may coincide:

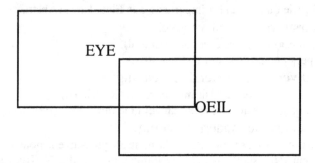

Two examples.
Looking up the French equivalent for the word *eye* in a bilingual dictionary will yield:

> **eye:**   1. *oeil* as in the eye of the master (concrete): l'oeil du maître
> 2. *chas* the eye of a needle (figurative): le chas d'une aiguille
> 3. *en vue* to be in the public eye (idiom): être en vue

Conversely, looking up the English equivalent for the French word *innocent* also gives diverse translations:

innocent: 1. pure, sinless, blameless as in le massacre des Saints *innocents,* the slaughter of the Holy *Innocents*
2. simple, guileless, simpleton as in l'*innocent* du village: the village *idiot.*

In both examples only the first meaning of the word coincides in the S.L. and in the T.L. The other meanings, being extensions of the first, no longer coincide in the T.L. and have to be rendered by the equivalent required by the context.

Literal vs. figurative meaning

Due to extended semantic ranges many words have both concrete and abstract or literal and figurative meanings. It may happen that the two coincide in the SL and TL. One can speak of a *hole* in the sleeve of a sweater and a *hole* in the budget, *un trou dans la manche d'un chandail* and *un trou dans le budget*, but such coincidences are rather rare. Here are a few examples taken from different grammatical categories which illustrate differences between literal and figurative meanings, with the former requiring one word and the latter a different word in the TL:

literal:	se mordre *la langue*	to bite one's *tongue*
figurative:	être une mauvaise *langue*	to be a *scandalmonger*
literal:	*faire face à* une foule en colère:	*to face* an angry crowd
figurative:	*faire face à* une obligation:	*to meet* an obligation
literal:	être *ivre:*	to be *drunk*
figurative:	être *ivre de joie*	to be *ecstatic*

Standard language vs. language of specialty

Language levels are an example of the importance of the context in determining word significance. Words are chosen in function of the public they target. Other than standard French or standard English there are many other language levels: technical, poetic, or slang, to name just a few.

Thus a word may mean one thing in standard French and quite another in a language of specialty. In theatrical jargon for instance *la douche* does not refer to a *shower* but to the spotlight focusing on the actors on the stage, and *le torchon* not to any rag but to the curtain. Likewise in the language of oil drillers *une carotte* is no longer a vegetable but a core sample.

Whereas the word *les méninges* anatomically refers to the meninges, the colloquial expression *se creuser les méninges* means *to think hard.* *La peau* may signify *the skin* in standard French. In slang, however, *une vieille peau* has more of the connotation of the English expression *an old bat.*

The language used in poetry is yet another one of these levels: *les palmes d'un arbre* refers to the branches of a tree, *l'azur* to the sky and not just to the color blue, while *the main* in a poetic context in English designates the sea.

Gender problems

French being a language which assigns genders to all nouns, some specific problems in translation may arise from overlooking the gender of words identical in everything but gender:

le chèvre (goat cheese)	la chèvre (goat)
le critique (the critic)	la critique (criticism)
le livre (book)	la livre (pound)
le manche (handle)	la manche (sleeve)
le mode (mode)	la mode (fashion)
le parti (party)	la partie (part/ game)
le poste (position/set)	la poste (post office)
le tour (tour)	la tour (tower)
le voile (veil)	la voile (sail)

Let's examine the following sentence:

> A l'horizon un petit vapeur est passé et j'en ai deviné la tache noire au bord de mon regard.   (Albert Camus, L'Etranger)

A mistranslation would arise should the gender of *vapeur* be overlooked and the word taken in its usual meaning of *steam*, a feminine word in French (*la vapeur*), instead of the masculine *le vapeur*, the *steamboat*.

On the horizon a small steamboat went by and I could make out its dark patch from the corner of my eye.

Dictionaries and thesauri

Given the extreme importance of the context in determining the exact significance of a particular word, here is one piece of advice: beware of dictionaries, especially small dictionaries which do not show the various meanings of a word in a sentence. Do not be a slave to them. Even the best of dictionaries will not always give you the exact equivalent required by the context, since they can only provide a limited number of illustrations. In this respect a thesaurus, which lists synonyms and the subtle nuances encompassed by one concept, will prove of more help in your search for the right word. For certain semantic fields in which the English language is richer, such as the field of sensorial perceptions, resorting to a thesaurus will enable you to select the proper word in light of the context.

Computer translation and the problem of polysemy

Polysemy is the reason computer-based translation is not as successful as it should be, given the amount of effort that has been put into the venture. Computers or translation software are unable to read a word within its context and therefore select the meaning that is appropriate in that context. Everyone has heard hilarious stories of instant Web translations done through artificial intelligence. One such story is about the translation into English of the standard French expression *"Le ministre des Affaires étrangères'*, which was churned out as *"The Alien Business Minister"*, or a reference in the news to a lawsuit filed by a grocer as "un *costume* d'épicier".

Polysemy is also the source of obvious mistakes in amateurish translations from one's native tongue into a foreign tongue. An example is the following sign spotted in a tailor shop abroad, with an unintentional pun resulting from ignorance of polysemy and the selection of the wrong word for the context:

"Order your suits here. Because of big rush we will *execute* customers in strict rotation".

Executing orders and executing customers are indeed two different things.

In conclusion, remember this rule:

There is no single permanent equivalent for any given word.

Exercices: Les Mots en contexte

Il est assez rare qu'un mot puisse être traduit d'une seule façon. Le sens des mots est influencé par le contexte dans lequel ils se trouvent. Un mot peut ainsi avoir des traductions tout à fait différentes selon son contexte.

A. Les Mots en contexte

Traduisez les phrases suivantes en changeant la traduction des mots en italique en fonction de leur contexte.

1. **Aller:**
   Ça *va*? -oui, ça *va*.
   Nous *allons* déjeuner dans 10 minutes.
   Ce pull te *va* à ravir!
   Ne te trompe pas: les fourchettes *vont* dans le tiroir de gauche.
   Mon père *va* sur la quarantaine.
   Allons, dépêchez-vous, sinon nous serons en retard!

2. **Faire:**
   Il *fait* beau aujourd'hui, vous ne trouvez pas?
   Pour rester en forme il faut *faire* du sport.
   Tu *as fait* quelque chose d'intéressant hier?
   Ma soeur *fait* mieux la cuisine que moi.
   Cette robe te plaît? C'est moi qui *l'ai faite*.
   Il est assez grand, il *fait* un mètre 80.
   Je prends une livre de pommes. Combien ça *fait*?
   Tu devrais aller te *faire* couper les cheveux.
   Elle ne dormait pas. Elle *faisait* seulement semblant.

3. **Lever:**
   Levez la main lorsque vous aurez la réponse.
   Il est 10 heures du matin; il est grand temps de *vous lever*.
   Levez-vous lorsque le principal entrera dans la classe.

La séance *est levée.*

Un corps d'armée de 50 000 hommes *a été levé.*

L'O.N.U. cherche à faire *lever* le siège de Sarajevo.

4. **Mettre:**

C'est l'heure du dîner. *Mets* vite la table!

L'hôtesse *avait mis* sa plus belle robe pour faire impression sur ses invités.

On ignore qui *a mis* le feu au bâtiment.

Mettez-vous dans ce fauteuil, il est beaucoup plus confortable que la chaise.

Mets-toi là pour arrêter la balle!

Jeanne d'Arc *mit* le siège à la ville d'Orléans pour la délivrer de l'emprise anglaise.

Son patron vient de le *mettre* au courant de la situation.

5. **Passer:**

Il faut que je *passe* un examen de chimie.

Quand on s'amuse le temps *passe* vite.

Par mesure de sécurité personne n'a le droit de *passer.*

Que *passe*-t-on au cinéma du quartier cette semaine?

Le docteur Girod *passe* pour être le meilleur cardiologue de la région.

6. **Tenir:**

Il *tient* le coup (idiomatique).

Votre fils *tient* de vous, c'est frappant!

Elle *tenait* beaucoup à ce collier qui lui venait de sa grand-mère.

Les chiens doivent être *tenus* en laisse dans le parc.

Vous voulez que je *tienne* tête au P.D.G.?

Tenez, vous ne savez pas ce que vous dites!

7. **S'agir:**

Dans ce film, il s'*agit* d'une petite fille qui essaie de surmonter la mort de sa mère.

Ne faites pas de bêtises, c'est de votre intégrité professionnelle qu'il s'*agit.*

Il *s'agit* de faire attention, si nous ne voulons pas être grondés par nos parents. (colloquial)

8. Chez:

Les Durand m'ont invité à venir passer le week-end *chez* eux à la campagne.

On retrouve souvent *chez* Balzac les mêmes personnages d'un roman à l'autre.

Chez un animal qui doit fuir ou combattre, le coeur s'accélère et la tension artérielle s'élève.

9. Plein:

As-tu fait le *plein* d'essence?

Ce devoir est *plein* de fautes d'orthographe!

La nuit de la Saint Jean, en Scandinavie, il fait clair comme en *plein* jour.

En *plein* milieu du concert quelqu'un s'est mis à éternuer.

10. Coup:

Passe-moi un *coup* de fil demain!

L'homme donna un *coup* de pied au chien.

Ils furent réveillés dans la nuit par de grands *coups* à la porte.

Pouvez-vous me donner un *coup* de main pour changer cette table de place?

11. Ennui:

L'*ennui* est source de bien des maux.

Qui ne connaît actuellement des *ennuis* financiers?

Je voudrais bien t'aider. L'*ennui* c'est que je n'ai pas beaucoup de temps.

12. Etat:

"L'*état*, c'est moi" aurait dit Louis XIV.

Tu es fort enrhumé: tu n'es vraiment pas en *état* de sortir.

Pour un acte de naissance il faut s'adresser à l'*état* civil.

Un propriétaire, avant de louer son appartement, fait en général faire un *état* des lieux.

Le tiers *état*, groupe auquel appartenait la bourgeoisie, participa activement à la révolution française de 1789.

B. Sens propre ou figuré?

Déterminez si le sens des mots en italique est concret ou abstrait en fonction du contexte, puis traduisez les phrases dans lesquelles ils se trouvent.

1. Des champs de tournesol *s'étendaient* à perte de vue.
2. Il n'est pas assez de toute une vie pour *étendre* son savoir.
3. Les enfants s'étaient amusés à *jouer* aux gendarmes et aux voleurs.
4. Il *joue* régulièrement de grosses sommes dans l'espoir de devenir un jour millionnaire.
5. La porte du café *s'ouvrit* et un inconnu s'avança vers le zinc.
6. Si tu as des craintes au sujet de ce traitement, *ouvre-t-en* à ton médecin traitant.
7. Connaissez-vous l'expression "*doux* comme une peau de bébé"?
8. En dépit des prédictions pessimistes l'hiver s'est révélé très *doux*.
9. Pour être plus crédible vous devez *étayer* votre thèse.
10. Les murs d'une cathédrale gothique *sont étayés* par des arcs boutants.
11. Il est interdit de parler à *voix* haute dans la salle de lecture de la bibliothèque.
12. Le candidat donné comme favori par les sondages n'a été élu qu'à quelques *voix* de majorité.
13. Le développement des *transports* en commun serait une solution pour soulager la congestion urbaine.
14. Dans un *transport* de colère je me saisis du vase et le lançai violemment à terre.
15. Sa *démarche* était horriblement bancale, ce qui lui avait valu le surnom de Bamban (Alphonse Daudet, Le Petit Chose)
16. Le gouvernement ne sait quelle *démarche* adopter pour désamorcer les tensions sociales.

17. Ses *freins* ayant lâché, la voiture dévala la pente et alla s'écraser contre un arbre.

18. En France le coût du licenciement est longtemps demeuré un *frein* à l'embauche.

19. Avec une telle blessure il ne faut pas que le bandage *touche* à la peau.

20. Nous devrions nous mettre d'accord pour ce qui *touche* à cette question.

21. La bonne nouvelle nous a rendus *ivres* de joie.

22. Les invités avaient trop bu. A la fin de la soirée, la plupart étaient *ivres*.

C. Les Champs sémantiques

Pour les champs sémantiques tels que les perceptions sensorielles, la langue anglaise se révèle plus riche que le français. Utilisez un thésaurus anglais[1] pour trouver les mots qui rendent au mieux le sens des mots en italique dans les phrases ci-dessous.

Champ sémantique des sons *(consultez: sound, sonance, faint sounds, loud sounds, explosive sounds, resonance).*

1. Au loin une cloche *tinte* dans l'air du soir.

2. Je pensais à la source fraîche derrière le rocher. J'avais envie de retrouver *le murmure* de son eau. (Albert Camus, L'Etranger)

3. Seul *le murmure* des conversations d'élèves parvenait au professeur derrière sa chaire.

4. C'était une magnifique journée de printemps. Les oiseaux *chantaient* dans les arbres.

5. Nous entendîmes *un bruit sec,* semblable à celui d'un coup de fusil.

6. *Le bruit* des vagues lui parvenait à intervalles réguliers.

7. Aimes-tu *le bruit* de la pluie sur les toits?

8. Il y eut deux *coups brefs* à la porte, puis plus rien.

---

[1] See Appendix pp.278 and 286 for a list of thesauri.

Champ sémantique de la lumière *(consultez: light).*

9. Après que le soleil eut disparu à l'horizon, une *lueur rouge* continua à embraser le ciel.

10. Seule *la lueur* d'une chandelle éclairait la chambre où il travaillait.

11. Il y a peut-être encore *une lueur* d'espoir.

12. J'aperçois *une lueur* de malice dans tes yeux.

13. La surface du lac *miroitait* sous la lune.

14. Vois-tu l'étoile polaire qui *brille* là-haut dans le ciel?

15. Toute la maison *brillait* de propreté.

Champ sémantique de la chaleur *(consultez: heat, hotness).*

16. La plage était *brûlante* de soleil.

17. Le soleil *avait complètement brûlé* les récoltes.

18. Attention, tu risques de *te brûler* avec cette eau chaude!

19. Ces petits pains sortent du four: ils sont *brûlants*.

20. *La chaleur* de l'été nous engourdissait.

21. Ce qui frappait le plus chez lui, c'était *la chaleur* de son regard.

Champ sémantique des vibrations *(consultez: vibration, shaking).*

22. Sous le coup de la peur, mon coeur se mit *à battre à grands coups* dans ma poitrine.

23. On pouvait voir ses veines qui *battaient* à fleur de peau.

24. L'oiseau *battit* des ailes, puis s'envola.

25. *Un tremblement* nerveux au coin de l'oeil trahissait son agitation intérieure.

26. La voix de l'enfant *tremblait* d'émotion.

27. Sur le chemin de la guillotine, Bailly, le maire de Paris déclara: "Si je *tremble,* c'est de froid et non de peur."

28. Son image *dansait* devant mes yeux.

Chapter 3   **Deceptive Cognates**

Faux amis

> **Deceptive cognates are what French linguists refer to as "*faux amis*", that is to say words which you think you might trust to mean exactly the same thing as similar looking target language words, but should not.**

Cognates and deceptive cognates

Cognates in English and French are words that look and sound similar, share the same etymology and have the same meaning. They are usually derived from a common Latin, ancien Greek or old French source. These are words such as revolution/révolution, classicism/classicisme, biography/biographie, clear/clair, to descend/descendre , reality/réalité, archaic/archaïque etc. Due to a long history of political, social and cultural interaction between the English and French speaking worlds, they are many.

However, the meaning of words does not necessarily remain static and many undergo significant changes. Over centuries of use, some of these French and English cognates have evolved in different semantic directions by extension or restriction of the original sense, to the point of yielding now very divergent meanings. Let us compare for instance *achever* (to finish) and *to achieve* (accomplir): English, in this case, has focused on what remains, the accomplishment, after the task is finished while French has left it at that. With *hasard* (chance) and *hazard* (danger);   *malicieux* (mischievous) and *malicious* (méchant), English in both cases has elaborated on the negative elements of the concept.

Occasionally cognates can be so deceptive as to carry diametrically opposed meanings. Be the judge:

Fr. *chiffon* (rag)	**Engl**. *chiffon* (gauze material as in a "chiffon" dress)
clinique (hospital for private patients)	*clinic* (hospital for the indigent)

Partial faux amis

In addition and to confuse the translator further, there are so-called "partial false cognates" which occur in the case of polysemous words (words carrying several meanings). In such words, one meaning might coincide between the French and the English cognate while others do not.

For example:
French to English
faculté: 1. faculty, ability, as in
> *Il a la faculté de voir clairement les choses* (cognate)
2. faculty, college, as in
> *Ses enfants vont à la faculté de lettres de la ville* (cognate)

However the French word never assumes the meaning of *faculty* in the sense of *a teaching body at a school or college*. This last meaning is a false cognate, and a different counterpart, *le corps enseignant*, must be resorted to in translation.

English to French
to assume: 1. assumer, as in
> *Assumer une fonction*, *to assume a function* (cognate)
2. supposer, as in
> *Qu'allez-vous supposer? What are you assuming*? (false cognate)

The word is a partial false cognate due to the second meaning of the English word which has a different French counterpart.

Unrelated similar looking words

Not to be confused with true or false cognates are a certain number of words of totally unrelated origin which only look the same out of sheer coincidence. Such words can easily be spotted due to the fact that they usually belong to different grammatical categories. Let's mention:

Fr. une *averse*: shower (noun)	and	Eng. *averse*: opposé à (adjective)
fond (m.): bottom (noun)		*fond*: affectueux (adjective)
if (m.): yew tree (noun)		*if*: si (conjunction)
lame (f.): blade (noun)		*lame*: boiteux (adjective)
legs (m.): legacy (sg noun)		*legs*: jambes (plural noun)
lent: slow (adjective)		*Lent*: le Carême (noun)
or: now (adverb)		*or*: ou (conjunction)
sale: dirty (adjective)		*sale*: vente; soldes (noun)

but also, belonging to the same grammatical category, we may list:

Fr. *bride* (f.): bridle	Eng. *bride*: mariée (f.)
dot (f.): dowry	*dot*: point (m.)
nappe (f.): tablecloth	*nap*: sieste (f.)
pin (m.): pine tree	*pin*: aiguille (f.)
pain (m.): bread	*pain*: douleur (f.)
rein (m.): kidney	*rein*: rêne (m.)
ride (f.): wrinkle	*ride*: promenade (f.) (à cheval, à bicyclette ou en voiture)

Never underestimate the importance of learning about false cognates. Failure to do so may put you in some very embarrassing situations. Suppose for a minute that you are at a dinner table in a French speaking country and wish to convey to your hosts that you appreciate fresh, natural food in which there are no *preservatives*. If unaware that the term is a *faux ami*, you will be tempted to use the French cognate *preservatif*, only to find out, after the company has burst out laughing with much damage to your dignity, or worse, stiffened into a deadly silence, that you have been speaking about food in which there are no *condoms* instead of using the correct term, *agent de conservation*!

The following is a list of some of the most common deceptive cognates:[1]

French	English
Abuser de quelque chose: to overdo, overuse (quelqu'un) to fool (s.o)	to abuse: maltraiter, insulter
achever: to complete, to finish	**to achieve**: accomplir, réaliser
accomoder: to accommodate, (part.) to arrange (food)	**to accommodate**: (part.) loger
actuel: present, current, up to date	**actual**: réel, véritable
actuellement: at present, now	**actually**: en réalité
agenda: memo book	**agenda**: ordre du jour
agréable: pleasant	**agreeable**: consentant
amateur: fan, lover	**amateur**: non-professionnel, dilettante
ancien: ancient, (part.) former	**ancient**: ancien, antique
anniversaire : birthday	**anniversary** : anniversaire (other than birthday)
antique:(adj.) ancient	**antique**: (noun) antiquité
anxieux: worried	**anxious**: désireux
apologie: apology, defence	**apology**: apologie, (part.) excuses
application: application, diligence	**application**: (part.) demande (sur formulaire)
arguer : to infer	**to argue** : soutenir, disputer
argument: raison, justification	**argument**: forte discussion, querelle, dispute
arrêt: stop	**arrest**: arrestation
assister à: to attend	**to assist**: aider
assumer: to assume, to take on	**to assume**: (part.) présumer, supposer
attendre: to wait for	**to attend**: assister à (an event), fréquenter (a place)
	to attend to: s'occuper de
attirer: to attract	**to attire**: vêtir
audience: hearing, session	**audience**: auditoire, assistance, public

---

[1] Entries marked (part.) are partial false cognates for the meaning of the word indicated. For a more comprehensive study refer to any of the dictionaries of false cognates listed in the appendix, p.279.

avertir: to inform, to warn

avertissement: warning

avis: opinion, notice

axe: axis

bachelier: holder of the baccalaureate

bail: lease

banc : bench

baraque: shack, hut

blamer: to criticize

blesser: to wound, to hurt

bond: bound, leap, jump

bouquet bunch (of flowers)

bribe: fragment, scrap

caractère: character, personality

brigadier: corporal

caméra: movie camera

canapé: couch, sofa

candide: ingenuous

canot: rowboat

cap: cape (i.e of Good Hope)

car: coach, intercity bus

caractère: nature, temperament

cargo: cargo-ship, freighter

carte: card, map

carton : cardboard

casserole : saucepan

caution: deposit, bail

cave: cellar

chair : flesh

chance: luck

chandelier: candlestick

change : exchange rate

charge : load, burden

charte: charter

chasser : to hunt

chat : cat

chauffeur : driver

chef : chief, boss

to avert: prévenir, empêcher, éviter

advertisement: réclame, publicité, annonce

advice: conseil

axe: hache

bachelor: diplomé universitaire, (part.) célibataire

bail: liberté sous caution

bank : banque

barracks: caserne

to blame: render responsable

to bless: bénir

bond: lien, (fin.) obligation

bucket: seau

bribe: pot de vin

character: (part.) personnage (in a play)

brigadier: général de brigade

camera: appareil-photo

canopy: dais, baldaquin

candid: franc, sincère

canoe: pirogue

cap: (with visor)casquette, (without) bonnet

car: automobile, voiture

character: personnage

cargo: cargaison

cart: charrette

carton : boîte (en carton)

casserole : plat cuit au four

caution: précaution, prudence

cave: caverne, grotte

chair : chaise

chance: occasion, possibilité

chandelier: lustre

change : monnaie

charge : accusation, prix à payer

chart: carte, graphique

to chase : poursuivre

chat : bavardage, causerie

chauffeur : chauffeur privé

chef : chef cuisinier

clamer : to loudly proclaim

to claim : réclamer, prétendre

coin : corner

coin : pièce de monnaie

collège: junior high school

college: faculté, université

complainte: lament (poetry, music)

complaint: plainte, réclamation

complexion: disposition, constitution

complexion: teint

compréhensif : comprehensive ; (part.) understanding

comprehensive: compréhensif, total, complet, exhaustif

concerné: involved,

concerned: inquiet, soucieux

conducteur: driver

conductor: chef d'orchestre, chef de train, contrôleur

confection: making, ready to wear

confection: confiserie

conférence: lecture, speech

conference: congrès

confidence: secret

confidence: confiance

confus: embarrassed

confused: embrouillé

contrôler: to check, to verify

to control: diriger, maîtriser

conjurer: to beseech

to conjure: faire apparaître

convention: agreement

convention: congrès

copie: copy

copy: (part.) exemplaire (of magazine etc.)

corporation : guild

corporation : société par actions

corps : body

corpse : cadavre

couramment : frequently , fluently

currently : actuellement

courrier: (part.) mail

courier: messager, courrier (person)

cours : lesson, lecture

course : série de cours

courtier: broker

courtier: courtesan

crayon: pencil

crayon: crayon de couleur

crier: to scream, to shout

to cry: pleurer

cure: course of treatment

cure: remède

décade: ten days

decade: décennie

décevoir: to disappoint

to deceive: tromper

déception: disappointment

deception: tromperie, duperie

défendre: to defend, (part.) to forbid

to defend: défendre, protéger

défiance: distrust

defiance: défi

défiler: to parade

to defile: souiller

définitivement: permanently, for good

definitely: à coup sûr, sans aucun doute

déguster : to taste, to savor

to disgust: dégoûter

délai: delay, (part.) time limit

delay: retard

délivrer: to rescue, to set free

to deliver: distribuer, livrer

demander: to ask

to demand: exiger, réclamer

demande: request

demand: exigence

démonstration : presentation

demonstration : manifestation

denture : set of teeth

député: (U.S.) assemblyman, (G.B.) M.P.

dérober: to steal

désagrément: annoyance, unpleasantness

désespéré: without hope

déterrer: to unearth

dévotion: piety

disposer de: to have at one's disposal

dispute: quarrel

dissertation: essay

distraction: entertainment

divertir: to entertain

donjon: (castle) keep

dot: dowry

dresser: to set up (sthg), to train (animals)

éditer: to publish

éditeur: publisher

embrasser: to kiss

énervant : annoying, irritating

enfant: child

engagé; committed

engagement: commitment

engin : contraption, device

ennuyer: to bore, to trouble, bother

entrée: (in a menu) appetizer

étiquette: etiquette, (part.) label,

errer : to wander

éventuellement: possibly

évidence: obvious fact

évincer : to oust, unseat

excitant : stimulating, exhilarating

excuse: apology

expérimenté: experienced, skilled

extra: first rate

fabrique: factory

faculté: faculty, college

faillir: (to) almost (do)

publique

denture : dentier

deputy: sous-chef, adjoint suppléant, délégué

to disrobe: se dévêtir

disagreement: désaccord

desperate : prêt à tout

to deter: dissuader

devotion: dévouement

to dispose of: se débarrasser de

dispute: controverse, contentieux

dissertation: mémoire

distraction: détournement d'attention

to divert: dévier, détourner

dungeon: cachot, oubliettes

dot: point

to dress: habiller/ s'habiller

to edit: corriger, retoucher

editor: rédacteur

to embrace: serrer dans ses bras. Etreindre

enervating : débilitant

infant: nouveau-né

engaged: occupé, fiancé

engagement: rendez-vous, fiançailles

engine : moteur

to annoy: irriter

entrée: plat principal

étiquette : étiquette, protocole

to err : se tromper

eventually: finalement, tôt ou tard

evidence: preuve, témoignage

to evince : faire preuve de

exciting : passionnant

excuse: prétexte

experimented: testé

extra: supplémentaire

fabric: tissu, étoffe

faculty: faculté, (part.) corps enseignant

to fail: échouer

fantaisie: whim, fancy
fastidieux: tedious, boring
faute: fault, (part.) mistake
figure: face

file : waiting line, lane
filer: to spin,(coll.) to run away

formel: definite, strict, categorical

formidable: formidable, (part.) great

forfait : felony, package deal
forme: shape, form
formidable: great, fantastic

fournitures: supplies
glace: mirror, ice, ice cream
grief: grievance
grand: big
habileté : skill
habit: costume
hasard: chance
heurter: to knock
humeur: mood
hurler: to yell
ignorer: not to know, to be unaware of

inconvénient: (noun) disadvantage

informations (pl.): the news
inhabité: uninhabited
injure: insult
intoxiqué: poisoned
issue: end, exit

joli: pretty
journée: whole day
labourer: to plough
large: wide
lecture: reading

fantasy: fantasme
fastidious; maniaque
fault: faute, (part.) défaut, vice
figure: silhouette, personnage, chiffre
file : fichier
to file: limer (nails), classer (documents)
formal: cérémonieux, de cérémonie, officiel
formidable: formidable, redoutable
forfeit : confiscation, gage
form: forme, (part.) formulaire
formidable: redoutable, impressionnant
furniture: mobilier, meubles
glass: verre
grief: chagrin
grand: grandiose
ability : aptitude, capacité
habit: habitude
hazard: danger, risque
to hurt: blesser, faire mal
humor: humour
to hurl: lancer violemment
to ignore: ignorer, faire semblant de ne pas voir (person), (part.) ne pas tenir compte de, négliger (facts)
inconvenient: (adj.) gênant, incommode
information: renseignement
inhabited: habité
injury: blessure, dommage
intoxicated: ivre
issue: résultat, question, émission (banknotes), numéro (magazine)
jolly: enjoué
journey: voyage, trajet
to labor: travailler péniblement
large: grand, gros
lecture: conférence

librairie: bookstore
licence: permis, (part.) bachelor's degree
licencier: to lay off, to dismiss
limonade: lemon soda
location: rental
lunatique: moody, fickle
malicieux: mischievous
mémoire:(f.) memory, (m.) memoir

messe: mass (religious office)
misère: extreme poverty or misfortune
monnaie: currency, (small) change
note: note, (part.) (school)grade, bill
nouvelle: piece of news, short story
ombrelle: parasol, sun umbrella
opportunité: timeliness
or: gold
outrageant: offensive, insulting
pair (m.): peer
passer: (exam) to sit for, to take
pâte: paste, (part.) dough
pathétique: moving, touching
patron: boss
part: share, portion
pasteur: shepherd, (protestant) minister
peuple: nation, people
photographe: photographer
phrase: sentence
physicien: physicist
place: seat, (town) square
plat: dish
préjudice: damage, wrong
préservatif: condom

prétendre: to claim
prévenir: to warn
procès : trial
professeur : (part.) teacher ; professor
propre: clean, own

prune: plum
questionner: to question (someone)

library: bibliothèque
license: licence, permis
to license: accorder un permis
lemonade: citron pressé
location: situation, emplacement
lunatic: fou
malicious: méchant, malveillant
memory: mémoire (f.), (part.) souvenir
mess: désordre
misery: souffrance, détresse
money: argent
note: note, (banknote) billet
novel: roman
umbrella: parapluie
opportunity: occasion
ore: minerai
outrageous: révoltant, scandaleux
pair: paire
to pass: (exam) réussir à
paste: colle
pathetic pitoyable, lamentable
patron: mécène
part: partie
pastor: prêtre, curé
people: peuple, (part.) les gens, on
photograph: photo(graphie)
phrase: locution, expression
physician: médecin
place: endroit, lieu
plate: assiette, plaque
prejudice: préjugé, parti pris
preservative: agent de conservation
to pretend: faire semblant
to prevent: empêcher
process: procédé, processus
professor: professeur universitaire
proper: comme il faut, convenable
prune: pruneau
to question: (part.) mettre en question, contester (sthg)

raisin: grape

réaliser: to realize, (part.) to achieve

récupérer: (coll.) to recover (health),

recycler: (part.) to retrain (s.o.); to recycle

regard: look, glance

relaxer: to free (a prisoner)

relief: (geographic) surface

rente: unearned income

rentable: profitable

reporter: to postpone

(se) résigner à: to be resigned to

rester: to stay, to remain

résumer: to summarize

résumé: summary

réunion: meeting

révoquer: to revoke (decree), (part.) to fire, to dismiss (s.o.)

schéma: diagram, sketch

sensible: sensitive

sensiblement: appreciably

sentence: sentence, judgment

site: picturesque site

souvenir: (part.) memory, souvenir

spirituel: spiritual, (part.)witty

store: shade, venitian blind

supplier: to beg, to beseech

supporter: to support, to prop, (part.) to tolerate, to bear

sympathique: likeable, personable, nice

trafic: traffic (goods), (part.) illicit trade

transpirer: to transpire (news), (part.) to perspire

unique: sole, single, only

usage: custom

user: to wear out

voyage: trip (by sea, air, or land)

vent: wind

veste: jacket

wagon: (railroad) car

raisin: raisin sec

to realize: se rendre compte

to recuperate: se rétablir (part.) to recover (sthg)

to recycle: recycler, récupérer

regard: considération, égard

to relax: se détendre

relief: soulagement, secours

rent: loyer

rentable: qui peut se louer

to report: rapporter

to resign: démissionner

to rest: faire reposer, se reposer

to resume: continuer, reprendre

résumé: curriculum vitae

reunion: retrouvailles

to revoke: révoquer, annuler

scheme: agencement, intrigue

sensible: sensé, raisonnable

sensibly: raisonnablement

sentence: sentence; (part.) phrase

site: emplacement

souvenir: souvenir

spiritual: spirituel, de l'esprit

store: magasin, boutique

to supply: fournir

to support: soutenir (sth or s.o.), faire vivre (s.o.)

sympathetic: compréhensif, compatissant

traffic: circulation (transports)

to transpire: transpirer, (part.) se passer, avoir lieu (events)

unique: sans pareil, seul en son genre

usage: emploi

to use: utiliser

voyage: voyage en bateau

vent: passage, trou d'aération

vest: gilet

wagon: charrette, chariot (in a supermarket)

Exercices: Les Faux Amis

A. Les Faux Amis

Traduisez les phrases suivantes en anglais: attention au sens des mots en italiques. Aidez-vous du lexique sur les faux amis pp.30-6.

1. Cet *enfant* est de *complexion* fragile, mais il a un *regard malicieux.*
2. Regarde ta *figure* dans la *glace:* tu es *joli* ainsi tout barbouillé!
3. Les *prunes* et les *raisins* qu'on nous a servis au dessert étaient *extras*!
4. Le *hasard* fait parfois bien les choses.
5. Le film nous *a* beaucoup *ennuyés*: il y avait trop de bavardage et pour ainsi dire pas d'intrigue.
6. Une personne *sympathique* vous attire par son caractère sociable, une personne *sensible* par son émotivité et une personne *spirituelle* par son *esprit.*
7. Je viens de rencontrer un de mes *anciens professeurs* que j'ai à peine reconnu tant il avait changé.
8. De mes études de latin il ne me reste que des *bribes.*
9. Dépêche-toi si tu veux *assister* au début de la conférence!
10. Le médecin a été *formel*: tu dois garder le lit pendant deux jours jusqu'à ce que tu ailles mieux.
11. Ce livre vient de sortir. Vous pouvez dès aujourd'hui le trouver en *librairie.*
12. La *lecture* est un des passe-temps favoris des personnes du troisième âge.
13. L'*éditeur* vient de lui accorder un contrat très avantageux pour son nouveau livre.
14. Le jeu des portraits consiste à décrire une personne en quelques *phrases* pour permettre aux joueurs de deviner.
15. Cet ambitieux est arrivé dans la vie, non par ses propres moyens, mais grâce à ses *relations.*

16. Dans cinq minutes on passe les *actualités* à la télé.

17. Il y a plusieurs années que ces bidonvilles restent *inhabités*.

18. Tout étranger résidant en France peut *éventuellement* requérir la nationalité française après un certain temps.

19. La cérémonie d'inauguration aura lieu dès l'*achèvement* des travaux.

20. Les manifestants ont *hurlé* des *injures* aux contre-manifestants.

21. L'inspecteur de police *a dressé* un procès-verbal.

22. Après avoir été appréhendé par la police pour vol avec effraction, il a dû verser une *caution* de 10.000 euros.

23. L'inculpé *prétend* qu'il est totalement innocent.

24. En raison du manque de preuves à charge le prisonnier a été *relaxé*.

25. Le procureur de la République *a réclamé* la *peine* maximale contre l'accusé durant le *procès*.

26. Il faisait une chaleur étouffante. Les marcheurs *transpiraient* par tous les pores de leur peau.

27. Le bétail est acheminé par train dans des *wagons* de marchandise.

28. En 1814 Louis XVIII a accordé aux Français une *charte* constitutionnelle.

29. Victor Hugo dans son roman "Les *Misérables*" nous donne une fresque historique et humaine tout à fait *pathétique*.

30. Pierre et Marie Curie furent des *physiciens* renommés du début du XXème siècle.

31. Peux-tu me *résumer* brièvement l'intrigue du roman policier que tu viens de lire et qui t'a tant plu, sans m'en dire la fin?

32. Comment pouvez-vous *supporter* cet individu: ne voyez-vous pas qu'il est menteur et arrogant?

33. L'entreprise connaît *actuellement* des difficultés passagères mais espère pouvoir les surmonter à brève échéance.

34. Les actionnaires *ignorent* les termes du contrat passé entre le patronat et les syndicats.

35. Le conseil d'administration doute de l'*opportunité* de cette motion.

36. Avec la chute des taux d'intérêt les personnes vivant de leurs *rentes* sont les plus *touchées*.

37. La firme garantit la réception de la marchandise dans un *délai* d'une semaine.

38. Le *patron* est *actuellement* en congé de maladie à la suite d'une opération chirurgicale.

39. L'entreprise a dû *licencier* du personnel en raison de la crise économique.

40. La banque exige que toutes les transactions soient *régulières*.

41. Le projet a été *sanctionné* par le conseil des ministres.

42. L'administration va l'*affecter* à un nouveau *poste* en province.

43. Le chef du gouvernement a fait une *grande* faute en n'acceptant pas de dialoguer avec les représentants des grévistes.

44. Il est *formellement* interdit d'apposer des affiches dans les endroits publics.

B. Vrai ou faux ami?

Donnez le mot français qui correspond au mot anglais.

1. I am still a novice at this game but I will *eventually* get the hang of it.

2. Oil painting is *actually* easier than you might think.

3. Must you always *pretend* to have the answer to everything?

4. The driver *realized* too late that he had taken the wrong turn.

5. I *assume* that you know what you are doing.

6. Do you plan to *attend* the lecture?

7. As soon as he gets better, the patient may *resume* all his former activities.

8. The chairman of the board was forced *to resign* after the scandal.

9. How do you intend to *achieve* your proposal?

10. Eight hours of sleep a night are generally *regarded* as necessary for the body's equilibrium.

11. Running out without a raincoat in this weather, is that *sensible*?

12. There was *malicious* intent in this so-called accident.

13. Do you have any *relevant* material to show me?

14. Experts seem very *confident* that the economy is on an upturn.

15. Pride and *Prejudice*, *Sense* and Sensibility are two of Jane Austen's best loved novels.

16. Do not add insult to *injury*!

17. To prevent any mishap please put the *camera* back in its case.

18. Only a *lunatic* could reason in this way.

19. A compromise was reached to settle the *argument*.

20. *Figures* do not lie: the budget is not balanced.

21. January 1st is the deadline for filing all *applications*.

22. During the holidays a *delay* in the processing of packages is inevitable.

23. We need some *information* about train schedules.

24. Staff loyalty, for *decades* a matter of immense pride, has been shaken.

25. A research *executive* for the company was dispatched to a second tier job in Asia.

26. The candidate's *accomplishments* are *significant*.

27. You have the bad *habit* of interrupting people when they speak.

Chapter 4   **Translation Techniques**

Main problems in translation:
What strategies do translators have at their disposal?

In the transcoding process of the S.L. message, the translator will be faced with many problems. To counter these problems one can resort to a certain number of techniques which will help achieve an idiomatic and satisfactory result, one which will not feel like a translation. Remember that among the worst criticisms which can be leveled at you, the translator, is the following kind of reaction: "I understand what you are trying to convey, but it sounds too much like a translation. No one speaks or writes like that in good English." In other words, you have not been idiomatic enough and here are the tools at your disposal to help redress the situation.

> **Problems in translation stem from one of three things: semantic, structural or metalinguistic obstacles standing in the way of a word for word translation.**
> **A translation technique is a specific strategy to help translators find a solution to a particular problem.**

What are the main problems in translation?

- Polysemy and trying to translate words outside of their context

- Faux Amis (deceptive cognates) and partial Faux Amis

- Concepts which exist in one language but not in the other

- Different grammatical structures and word order and the S.L. and the T.L.

- Stylistic preferences for certain grammatical structures in one language over others in the second language

- Idiomatic expressions and set phrases

- Metalinguistic obstacles stemming from cultural differences

The various translation techniques

The following examples are representative of the seven translation techniques described by Jean-Paul Vinay and Jean Darbelnet in their groundbreaking work *La Stylistique Comparée du Français et de l'Anglais,*[1] which are generally accepted as standard by linguists and translators.

They are at the word level in the first column, and at the message level in the second column, while the various techniques (from borrowing to adaptation) are listed in order of increasing remoteness from the S.L. original.

Borrowing

French-English: mayonnaise   French-English: C'est la vie
English-French: un steak   English-French: Okay

Calque

A.I.D.S: used cars:
S.I.D.A.   chars usagés (Canada)

Literal translation

un jeune homme   Où sommes-nous?
a young man   Where are we?

---

[1] Paris: Didier, 1958.

Transposition	
faillir:	Comment vous appelez-vous?
(to) almost (do)	What is your name?
Modulation	
une assurance-maladie:	On m'a embauché
health insurance	I have been hired
Equivalence	
une pomme de discorde	L'habit ne fait pas le moine
a bone of contention	You can't tell a book by its cover
Adaptation	
l kilogramme	Nous nous tutoyons
2.2 lbs	We are on a first name basis

Three of these techniques will yield a literal translation:

- borrowings
- calques
- word for word

The other four, a non-literal translation:

- transpositions
- modulations
- equivalences
- adaptations

Here is a summary of how to solve the main translation problems enumerated above:

- **Polysemy** can be dealt with by watching out for the context, checking to see whether a word is taken in its concrete or abstract meaning, standard meaning or specialty meaning; checking for the gender of nouns; by being careful with dictionaries and using a thesaurus to make sure you have the exact nuance of a word.

- **Deceptive cognates:** by resorting to a bilingual dictionary or, better still, to dictionaries specializing in deceptive cognates.

- **Linguistic deficiencies**: by using borrowings or calques.

Concepts which exist only in the S.L. can be borrowed in their original form or else copied in translation for more of a "native" touch (as semantic or structural calques, *i.e.* translated borrowings).

- **Structural problems or impossibility to translate word for word** can be dealt either with transpositions or modulations.

- **Idiomatic expressions and set phrases** can be translated with equivalences. You may resort to dictionaries specializing in idioms.

- **Metalinguistic obstacles,** which stem from cultural differences, require adaptation.

We are going to examine all seven translation techniques in detail in the following chapters. Meanwhile, here is a word of general advice for a faithful and good translation:

> **Be as literal as possible and as idiomatic as necessary.**

Therefore stick to literal translation whenever meaning and structure allow it, but do not be afraid to resort to a non-literal translation whenever needed.

> **Resort to non-literal translation whenever the message if translated literally into the T.L.:**
> 1. makes no sense
> 2. makes some sense but does not sound idiomatic
> 3. is structurally impossible to translate word for word
> 4. gives a meaning different from the one in the S.L.
> 5. cannot be translated as such, due to lack of an equivalent concept, custom or institution in the T.L.

Chapter 5 **Borrowings**

What is a borrowing and what is its purpose?

> **A linguistic borrowing is a translation strategy born of a linguistic deficiency in the T.L.**
> **This deficiency may result from one of two factors:**
> * **cultural**
> * **technological**

When a particular concept -be it expressed as a noun, verb, adjective or even phrase-, which is the result of a way of life or of a technological advance, exists in one linguistic group only, and then through communications and exchanges is introduced to other linguistic groups, an immediate need for a sign to convey it arises in the target languages. When there is lack of an immediate and ready equivalent, it is often borrowed from the S.L. in its original form without incurring any change in spelling. However, when the borrowing goes against the etymological characteristics of the T.L. (as in the case of borrowings between English and French), modifications usually occur in pronunciation, and over the years significant changes may even develop in spelling and meaning as exemplified in the word *redingote,* a nineteenth century corrupted borrowing from the English word *riding coat.*

Let's take two examples, one from the field of culture and the other of science:

> **A café,** a public place where one may order alcoholic or non-alcoholic beverages and even snacks while sitting out on a terrace watching other

people stroll by, is a concept developed in Mediterranean countries where the sun shines and outdoor public life plays an important role. When at the onset of mass tourism northern Europeans and Americans discovered the café and started enjoying its relaxing effects they borrowed both the institution and the word.

A pacemaker, on the other hand, is a 20th century American invention, a technological advance which, when it came out, revolutionized the field of health and therefore was immediately accepted worldwide. At any rate, for lack of linguistic creativity no French word was available at the time and so the S.L. word was adopted in its foreign form (although since then, the more French sounding word of *stimulateur cardiaque* has been officially substituted).

Examples of linguistic deficiencies

When the need for a borrowing is not felt in the T.L., a real linguistic deficiency occurs and one must resort to a periphrasis. In French for instance, the word "*privacy*" can only totally be conveyed by the phrase "le sentiment d'être abrité des regards indiscrets", "a *commuter*" ,"une personne qui travaille en ville et habite à la campagne" or "a *shallow* river", "une rivière peu profonde". Conversely in English, the French concept of "*être débordé*" must be rendered by several words: "to be overwhelmed with work or cares", and "un *acharnement*" by "a relentless and desperate attempt at doing something". One can only point out that such concepts are truly representative of a particular culture and do not translate well.

French and English: a history of mutual borrowings

Ever since the fateful date of 1066 which marks the Norman conquest of England by William the Conqueror, duke of Normandy, the two linguistic groups have been borrowing extensively one from the other.

The Norman conquest indeed changed forever the character of the English language, and from that time it is roughly estimated that half the English vocabulary has evolved from French borrowings. This explains the wealth of the English language: a bilingual English to French dictionary is typically twice as big as its French to English counterpart. Often two terms coexist, one of Anglo-Saxon and the other of French origin, pairs such as *to come in* and *to enter* (from the French *entrer*), *lovely* and *pleasant* (from *plaisant*), *tastily* and *deliciously* (from *délicieusement*), *by the side of* and *along* (from *le long de*) etc.

French, on the other hand, only started borrowing heavily from English in the mid-19th century when an appeasement took place after centuries of bitter political rivalry between the two countries and anglomania overtook the affluent classes of France during the reigns of Louis-Philippe and Napoleon III. Since then it has made up for lost time and the trend started accelerating right after the first World War as English began to be considered the world's most influential language. Since World War II, even where at times a perfectly good French equivalent already existed, fashionable but indiscriminate borrowing in many fields has taken place and given alarm to the formidable French *Académie*, the long time cultural watchdog over the French language and grammar. Fearing irretrievable damage to the tongue of Molière, Voltaire and Victor Hugo, and in an effort to prevent it from turning into unrecognizable "*franglais*", a special branch has been created at the Ministry of Culture, a *Délégation Générale à la Langue Française* whose function is to come up with a new nomenclature of French equivalents to English concepts based on roots closer to French etymology.[1] The linguists who head this delegation have indeed been responsible for various strikes, such as *ordinateur, logiciel* and *matériel* which have managed to supersede *computer, software* and *hardware,* no small feat in a world dominated by American computer terminology. But ultimately the public remains

---

[1] Since most of the French government's main divisions have their own terminology commissions to deal with anglicisms, a Commission générale de Terminologie et de Néologie was recently created (decree of July 3rd, 1996) which answers directly to the prime minister. Its purpose is to harmonize the findings, and, after approval by the French Academy, publish them in the Journal Officiel.

the final judge, as some replacements are easily accepted while others continue to be dismissed in favor of English borrowings. Only time will tell. In any case, after twenty years of research, an official dictionary was published in 1994 listing 3,500 terms or technical expressions to replace common English borrowings,[2] and a very controversial law was passed, the Toubon law, named after the minister of culture who introduced it, in order to impose use of the new terminology by administrative public services.

Here is a representative sample, with some clever replacements for borrowings that sound too Anglo-Saxon to a French ear, and a few potential flops:

Le brainstorming: le remue-méninges
un cameraman: un cadreur
un compact disk: un disque audionumérique
la médecine préventive: la préventologie
le design: la stylique
un jumbo jet: un avion gros porteur
le hit parade: le palmarès
hot money: des capitaux fébriles
un leader: un meneur
le leasing: voiture louée avec option
            d'achat
le marketing: la mercatique

un one man show: un spectacle solo
un play back: un rejeu
un scoop: une primeur
un restaurant fast food: un restovite
une speakerine: une annonceuse
sponsoriser (to sponsor): parrainer
un tennisman: un joueur de tennis
un tie-break: un jeu décisif
un tour operator: un voyagiste
un walkman: un baladeur

Lexical fields of borrowing

Borrowing occurs when one linguistic group proves culturally more creative or technologically more advanced than another. For instance when, in the seventeenth century, France was the number one military power in Europe and its army a model for other nations, many of its military terms were borrowed. But by the eighteenth century, French supremacy had switched to the fields of art, philosophy and social life, which in turn led to borrowings by England in those domains. Today most borrowings are one way,

---

[2] <u>Dictionnaire des termes officiels de la langue française</u>, Journal officiel, 1994.

from English into French, and pertain to the fields of sports, entertainment, finance and above all technology.[3]

Some examples of borrowings in a list that is far from exhaustive:

English from French
army: general, brigadier, colonel, lieutenant, major, sergeant (sergent), corporal (caporal), grenadier, cavalry (cavalerie), artillery (artillerie), infantry (infanterie), battalion (bataillon), canteen (cantine), bivouac, reconnaissance, corps, legionnaire, maneuver (manoeuvre), surveillance, camouflage, fatigues

gastronomy: cuisine, restaurant, café, hotel, chef, gourmet, maître d', hors d'oeuvre, sauce, casserole, dessert, champagne, eau de vie, mayonnaise, omelette, soufflé, mousse, sorbet, filet mignon, à la carte, prix fixe dinner, (to) sauté

politics and diplomacy: diplomat, attaché, envoy (envoyé), vice-roy, aide, partisan, informant, protégé, coup (d'état), détente, impasse, communiqué, accord, clause, laissez-faire, sabotage

economy and finance: financier, entrepreneur, millionaire, arbitrage, franchise

architecture and fine arts: architect, arcade, façade, balustrade, cornice (corniche), frieze (frise), niche, bas relief, dome, suite, apartment, garage, baroque, rococo, palette, crayon, pastel

fashion: haute couture, boutique, béret, culotte, lingerie, négligé, brassiere, chic, elegant, coiffure, brunette, blond, beige, ecru, rouge

society: étiquette, savoir faire, flair, finesse, expertise, gaffe, faux pas, malaise, routine, penchant, liaison, affair, tête-à-tête, rendez-vous, matinée, soirée, encore, salon, élite, bourgeois, cachet, cliché, connaisseur, amateur, fiancé, divorcé, chauffeur, habitué, clairvoyance, osé, risqué, grotesque

medicine: curettage, ligature, malaise, massage

and many phrases: au courant, c'est la vie, la crème de la crème, coup de grace, tour de force, pièce de résistance, double entendre, mot juste, carte blanche, déjà vu, ménage à trois, fait accompli, bête noire, en masse, bon voyage, bon appétit.

French from English
More than half of all borrowings from English to French are of Anglo-American origin:[4]

---

[3] For a more exhaustive study please refer to dictionaries on borrowings from English to French and French to English listed in the appendix pp.279 and 286.

sports and leisure: football, basketball, volleyball, rugby, tennis, golf, bowling, footing, aerobic, yatching, surf, camping, match, score, goal, shooter (verb), penalty, handicap, corner, tennisman, recordman, jockey, autostop, hobby

entertainment: night club, rock, swing, twist, bee-bop, blues, negro spiritual, jazz, folklore, film, western, script girl, camera, cameraman, travelling, suspense, star, cover girl, vamp, pin up, strip tease, sex, media, box office, hit parade, bridge, club

journalism: magazine, scoop, racket, hold up, revolver, reporter, freelance, flash, interview, copyright, best seller

everyday life: shopping, parking, motel, leader, stress, slogan, label, week end, design, living (room), baby sitter, shampoing (from shampoo), brushing, lifting

clothing: tweed, short, tee shirt, blue jeans, sweat shirt, pull over, cardigan, smoking (tuxedo), duffle coat, loden, tennis (sneakers)

food: cocktail, lunch, fast food, grill room, barbecue, steak, hot dog, hamburger, ketchup, chewing gum, sandwich

technology: by far the largest and most active field of borrowing, most terms being the reserved domain of specialists and having no impact on the general public. Let us just mention some terms in aviation: stewart, jet, cockpit; in heavy industries: pipeline, bulldozer, derrick, tank; in medicine: laser, pacemaker, by-pass; in economy and finance: dumping, cash flow, Dow Jones.

Creative borrowing

The term "creative borrowing" may seem like an oxymoron, but in the process of transfer from one language to the other it can happen that the original word undergoes slight or even significant variations in meaning.

What the French refer to as *le camping* (campsite), *le brushing* (blow drying), *le dancing* (dance hall) , *le shampoing* (shampoo) or *le smoking* (tuxedo) are nothing less than "faux amis". They are of the same order as the following English borrowings from the French: *citron* (cédrat), *chiffon* (voile), *clinic* (dispensaire), *amateur* (non-professionnel) and *boutonnière* (fleur à la boutonnière).

Borrowing indeed does not preclude creativity. Nouns constitute the vast majority of borrowings due to problems presented by verb

---

[4] Out of the 35,000 words considered representative of modern French, about 4,200 are of foreign origin, of which 25% or 1053 come from the English or American English language.

conjugation, but occasionally a language may coin other words from a borrowed stem. Thus French has patterned a few verbs after its first conjugation: *boycotter, loguer, surfer, shooter* (or *chouter), lifter, scanner* and *faxer*; and has created additional nouns with the standard French suffixes *-tion, -eur* and *-ine*: *gadgétisation, boxeur, speakerine*. It has even gone as far as to coin new terms with the English suffixes *-man* and *-ing*: *tennisman* (for tennis player), *recordman* (for record holder), *barman* (for bar tender), *footing* (for jogging), *parking* (for parking lot), *caravaning* (for going camping with a caravan or trailer) etc..; while English has coined verbs from French past participles, as in *to sauté*, or from nouns, as in *to camouflage* or *to arbitrage*.

Some borrowings are even shuffled back and forth between the two languages. *Rail*, an English adaptation of the old French word *reille*, itself derived from the latin *regula* meaning a straight piece of wood, was borrowed back by the French in its English form in the second part of the nineteeth century with the advent of the railroad. *To flirt*, came from the French mediaeval word *fleuretter* or *conter fleurette*, and in turn gave *flirter* when it was borrowed back in the twentieth century with its English accent. *Chalenge*, another French mediaeval word, had become obsolete by the sixteenth century, but made it back to its homeland after World War II under the English spelling, *challenge*. And one of the most noteworthy examples is the linguistic history of *tennis*: the sport's English name, also returned after a lapse of about a hundred years to the land of its ancestor, the *jeu de paume*, a game originally played with the palm of the hand without a racket from the sixteenth century to the time of the French Revolution. One player would warn the other to catch at the call of "Tenez!", corrupted into *tennis* when the game took hold in England.

Unnecessary borrowing

The very purpose of a borrowing is defeated when a term already exists to designate a particular concept in the TL. And yet unnecessary borrowings do take place for reasons which may range from politics to snobism. We have already seen that, since the days of the Norman conquest, part of the English vocabulary is comprised of synonymous pairs consisting of one native term and one French borrowing (*to go down* and *to descend, fickle* and *versatile* etc.). As for French, in its long twentieth century borrowing phase, it has succumbed to snobbish appeal. Thus *une star* coexists with *vedette* which has given it its feminine gender, and *un smoking* with *habit de soirée*. Sometimes also, languages borrow to extend the semantic range of some existing words, as in the case of *réaliser* which, until around 1895 only signified *to accomplish* when the meaning of its English (false) cognate *to realize* was added to it, even though *se rendre compte* already served the purpose.

Use of borrowings

In conclusion be aware that borrowings are steeped in the civilization of the country they come from and therefore particularly reflect the culture of the SL.

Use them to add a touch of local color to your literary translations. A sentence like "C'était un *gentleman farmer*" replaces the story in its social British context, while in "After their arduous game of *pétanque* the players were resting in the shade at the terrace of the old *café*, sipping the local *pastis*" the borrowings help convey the atmosphere of a southern French village.

Use borrowings:
      1. in case of linguistic deficiency in the target language, especially in non-literary, technical translation.
      2. for local color in literary translation.

Exercices: **Les Emprunts**

A. **Emprunts et faux amis**

Traduisez les phrases suivantes en anglais en tenant compte du fait que les emprunts à la langue anglaise ont pu subir une variation de sens dans le processus de transfert. Essayez d'en retrouver le sens véritable.

1. J'ai laissé ma voiture au *parking* de la gare pour faire mon *shopping* en ville.

2. -Qu'est-ce que tu utilises? Un *shampoing* pour cheveux secs ou pour cheveux gras?

-Pour cheveux secs: mes cheveux sont devenus cassants avec tous ces *brushings*.

3. Tu ne trouves pas qu'il y a maintenant trop de *spots* publicitaires à la télé?

4. C'est ma *speakerine* préférée qui va annoncer le programme de ce soir à la télé.

5. Vous pouvez vous fier à ce *label* de qualité: il est reconnu par tous les *clubs* de consommateurs.

6. Avez-vous vu Mme Dubois récemment? Ne pensez-vous pas qu'elle a rajeuni? On dirait qu'elle s'est fait *lifter*!

7. L'invitation précise "tenue de soirée de rigueur". Ton *smoking* a besoin d'être nettoyé. Porte le donc au *pressing*!

8. Après considération les jeunes gens ont décidé d'aller passer la soirée au *dancing* plutôt qu'au *night club*.

9. Le *barman* du Ritz se souvient encore d'un habitué célèbre: l'écrivain Ernest Hemingway.

10. Situé au bout d'une allée de tilleuls le terrain de *camping* était d'aspect accueillant.

11. Lors du *match* de *football* le *goal* de l'équipe locale a laissé marquer un but qu'il aurait pu arrêter.

12. Les *supporters* de l'équipe de France de *volleyball* étaient venus en masse assister au championnat.

13. Savez-vous qui est le *recordman* du monde pour le saut à la perche?

14. *Le doping*, qui s'est révélé un problème majeur dans les courses de chevaux, fait désormais l'objet de contrôles très stricts.

15. Selon un récent sondage le *leader* socialiste a amélioré son *score* de 2% contre le candidat de la droite. Il recueillerait 38% des intentions de vote.

B. Les Emprunts français

Choisissez l'emprunt français approprié pour traduire le mot en italique dans chaque phrase.

1. Le personnage principal du Bourgeois Gentilhomme de Molière est le type même du *parvenu* qui cherche à singer les belles manières.
a. bourgeois   b. nouveau riche   c. connaisseur

2. Ce paysage nous laissait une impression *familière*. C'était comme si, tant de fois reproduit et disséminé par les magazines et les cartes postales, nous le connaissions depuis toujours.
a. naïve   b. baroque   c. déjà vu

3. Selon le dernier dictat de la mode le beige sera *essentiel* pour le printemps et les fournisseurs de mode viennent de déverser des flots de khaki, écru et crème sur le marché.
a.de rigueur   b. chic   c. à la mode

4. Aux Etats Unis le nombre des femmes *chefs d'entreprise* s'élève à 6.5 millions.
a. concessionnaires   b. rapporteurs   c. entrepreneurs

5. Il est important que vous utilisiez toutes les *possibilités* qui s'offrent à vous en vue de résoudre ce problème.
a. avenues   b. echelons   c. cartes blanches

6. Avec la Mazda Miata, Honda a trouvé un *créneau*: celui des petites voitures de sport à prix abordable.

a. cache   b. sinecure   c. niche

7. La *maîtrise technique* de votre activité vous permettra d'évoluer de façon significative dans notre entreprise.

a. your technical tour de force   b. your technical expertise
c. your technical flair

C. Phrases originales

Faites des phrases originales en anglais avec les emprunts français suivants (consultez un dictionnaire pour les mots que vous ne connaissez pas).

Substantifs: amateur, protégé, élite, cliché, gaffe

Adjectifs: gauche, blasé, banal, risqué

Verbes: to sauté, to camouflage

Expressions figées: c'est la vie! bon appétit! savoir-faire, coup de grâce, rendez-vous

Chapter 6   **Calques**

What is a calque? Semantic and structural calques

According to the Oxford English dictionary *to calque* (or calk) from the French *calquer* means "to copy a design by rubbing the back with a coloring matter and drawing a blunt point along the outlines so as to trace them in the color on a surface placed beneath." Or, if this definition seems a bit confusing, remember the game that children sometimes play: they take a coin, place a piece of paper over it and transfer the coin's design by rubbing a pencil over the paper. That's a calque. In other words, a copy of an original, a blueprint.

A linguistic calque is also a copy of an original. It is a translated borrowing: the borrowing of a foreign word or group of words by literal translation of its components.

Like borrowings, calques are a translation solution in case of a linguistic deficiency in the T.L., but whereas borrowings tend to be confined to single words, calques tend to involve a group of words. There are two sorts of calques:

- **semantic calques** which respect the structure of the T.L., *i.e.* its syntax and grammar, such as word order and the use of articulations in French or compound words in English.

    For example: *une conférence au sommet* (articulated group of words following French syntactic characteristics) for *summit meeting* (a typical English compound word)

- **structural calques** which even keep the structure of the S.L. by going against the traditional T.L. rules of syntax and grammar:

  For example: *ambassador extraordinary* which copies the French word order (adjective following noun) from *ambassadeur extraordinaire,* or *surprise-partie* which copies the English compound word order.

To sum it up: semantic calques are good translations of borrowings, while structural calques are nothing more than faulty translations.

Calques and neologisms

Like borrowings, calques are a strategy currently much in use in the creation of new words. The need for them is accelerating as new words are being coined almost daily in our era of technological and scientific discoveries, of global and instant communications. As a new concept emerges in one particular nation in the world, it is avidly borrowed or copied by the rest. The more trend-setting the nation, the less it will have to resort to borrowings and calques itself and the more others will try to borrow or copy its terminology. Today, at the dawn of the third millenium, English, the predominant language in the world, is the original from which copies are being made.

We find calques in various fields, particularly in politics, science, technology, and economics. And the media, which deal in the shuffling of concepts across countries, naturally play a very important role in their dissemination and acceptance by the general public.

Some of these calques are unwarranted, like *réaliser* calqued after *to realize* and used in the sense of *se rendre compte*, while prior to 1895, *réaliser* only had the sense of *to accomplish, to execute*; or *étoile* patterned after *star* when *vedette* would have done as well.

But in the field of nation nomenclature calques have proven very useful:

  the United States of America: les Etats Unis d'Amérique

the United Kingdom:	le Royaume Uni
the Commonwealth	la Communauté
of Independent States	des Etats Indépendants
the Middle East:	le Moyen Orient
the Near East	le Proche Orient
the Third World	le Tiers Monde.

As well as in politics:

the cold war:	la guerre froide
the iron curtain:	le rideau de fer
anti-ballistic missiles	les missiles anti-ballistiques
D-Day	le jour J (a set term which allowed military planners during W W II to prepare and disseminate detailed plans much ahead of the date later decided upon: June 6, 1944).

Calques and acronyms

We find calques in many acronyms, in an age when acronyms are ubiquitous[1]:

AIDS (Acquired Immuno Deficiency Syndrome)	SIDA (Syndrôme Immuno Déficitaire Acquis)
EMS (European Monetary System)	SME (Système Monétaire Européen)
WHO (World Health Organization)	OMS (Organisation Mondiale de la Santé)
WTO (World Trade Organization) etc.	OMC(Organisation Mondiale du Commerce).

Calque vs. borrowing

A calque, particularly a semantic calque, manifests a will on the part of the nation that resorts to it to keep the borrowing of foreign sounding words in check so as not to alter the characteristics of its language.

---

[1] For a dictionary of acronyms used in France see: http://acronymes.info/

Among French speaking countries the province of Quebec is particularly prone to resorting to calques from English, due to its linguistic isolation in the midst of English speaking territories and the overwhelming influence of English in the media. Only in Canada will you hear expressions such as *tomber en amour* (to fall in love) for *tomber amoureux, chiens chauds* for *hot dogs, chars usagés* (used cars) for *voitures d'occasion.* Such calques give the language of Quebec a flavor all its own.

It must be also noted that at times French Canadians have proved more linguistically creative than the French themselves in their use of calques: an example is the coinage of the word *vivoir* (living room) for *salle de séjour,* and another, the word *courriel* (e-mail) for *courrier électronique* while France has resorted to a more or less direct borrowing from English with *le mel* or *mail.*

Exercices: Les Calques

> Le calque est un emprunt de la L.D. traduit en L.A.
> Il existe deux catégories de calques: les calques sémantiques qui respectent la syntaxe de la L.A. c'est à dire l'ordre des mots et la structure grammaticale, et les calques de structure qui conservent la syntaxe de la L.D.

A. Calques sémantiques ou de structure?

Déterminez si les calques suivants sont sémantiques ou de structure.

1. **Anglais-Français** :   Un cessez-le-feu;   une conférence-au-sommet; une division aéroportée; une fin de semaine; une frappe aérienne; un gratte-ciel; la maladie des vaches folles; le papier-monnaie;   les radicaux libres;   la science-fiction;   la Sécurité Sociale;   le statut de la nation la plus favorisée;   une surprise-partie; des cellules souches, un char usagé (Québec);   un chien chaud (Québec); compliments de la saison (Québec).

2. **Français-Anglais**: A chamber of commerce; an editor-in-chief; an envoy extraordinary;   the Estates general;   a head of state; Prince charming; a secretary general; the Third World.

B. Les Sigles

Le procédé du calque est très employé actuellement dans la composition des sigles (acronyms). Essayez de retrouver les sigles anglais qui correspondent aux sigles français suivants.

L'A.D.N. (Acide Désoxyribo Nucléique)
L'A.G.E.T.A.C. (Accord GÉnéral sur les TArifs douaniers et le Commerce)

L'A.L.E.N.A. (Accord de Libre Échange Nord Américain)
L'A.M.F. (Autorité des Marchés Financiers)
La B.C.E. (Banque Centrale Européenne)
La C.E.D.E.A.O. (Communauté Economique Des Etats de l'Afrique de l'Ouest)
La C.E.I. (Communauté des États Indépendants)
La C.J.I. (Cour de Justice Internationale)
Un D.A.B. (Distributeur Automatique de Billets)
L'E.E.E. (Espace Économique Européen)
Le F.M.I. (Fond Monétaire International)
Un O.G.M. (Organisme Génétiquement Modifié)
L'O.M.S. (Organisation Mondiale de la Santé)
L'O.M.C. (Organisation Mondiale du Commerce)
Une O.N.G. (Organisation Non Gouvernementale)
L'O.N.U. (Organisation des Nations Unies)
L'O.P.E.P. (Organisation des Pays Exportateurs de Pétrole)
L'O.T.A.N. (Organisation du Traité de l'Atlantique Nord)
Le P.N.B. (Produit National Brut)
Le S.I.D.A. (Syndrome Immuno-Déficitaire Acquis)
La T.V.A. (Taxe à la Valeur Ajoutée)
L'U.E. (Union Européenne)

C. Les Sigles français spécifiques

Les sigles suivants sont des mots français spécifiques sans sigles qui leur correspondent en anglais. Essayez de leur trouver une traduction satisfaisante.

(Être) B.C.B.G. [Bon Chic, Bon Genre]
Une B.D. [Bande Dessinée]
L' E.D.F. [Electricité de France]
Un P.V. [Procès Verbal]
Le R.E.R. [Réseau Express Régional]
Le S.A.M.U. [Services d'Aide Médicale Urgente]
Un S.D.F. [Sans Domicile Fixe]
La S.N.C.F. [Société Nationale des Chemins de Fer]

S.V.P. [S'il Vous Plaît]
Le T.G.V. [Train à Grande Vitesse]
Les W.C. [Water Closet]

D. Le Vocabulaire de l'informatique et de l'internet

Les mots suivants sont-ils des calques de l'anglais ou des mots originaux?

L'autoroute de l'information (information superhighway); une banque de données (database); convivial (user-friendly); un coupé-collé (cut and paste); une corbeille de départ/ d'arrivée (outbox/inbox); le courrier électronique (e-mail); le disque dur (hard disk); un espace-dialogue (chat-room); une fenêtre (window) ; la Foire Aux Questions (Frequently Asked Questions); un fouineur (a hacker) ; un fournisseur d'accès internet (an Internet service provider); un logiciel (software); la messagerie instantanée (instant messaging); la messagerie vocale (voice mail) ; un moteur de recherche (search engine); un mouchard (a cookie) ; un navigateur (browser); un Numéro d'Identification Personnel, NIP (Personal Identification Number, PIN); un ordinateur (computer); une page d'accueil (homepage); sauvegarder (to save); un signet (a bookmark) ; une puce électronique (a microchip); le réchauffement de la planète (global warming) ; un site sur la toile (website); une souris (mouse); télécharger (to download), un texto (a text message)

E. Traduction

Traduisez les phrases suivantes en essayant de retrouver les équivalents anglais des calques français indiqués en italiques.

1. Après les Etats Unis, la France lance le chantier des *autoroutes de l'information* pour faire circuler rapidement et facilement de grandes quantités d'images, de communication et de données informatiques dans des *cables en fibre optique* de l'épaisseur d'un cheveu. (France-Amérique, 5-11 mars 1994, no. 11334)

2. Avec une *souris*, l'utilisateur d'un ordinateur peut facilement *cliquer les icônes* de son écran pour avoir accès à différents *programmes d'application*.   Il peut également faire appel à un *fournisseur de services Internet* pour *se connecter* avec l'Internet et pouvoir *naviguer* de *site* en site dans *l'espace cybernétique*.

3. Pendant la *deuxième guerre mondiale* les *forces alliées* débarquèrent sur les côtes normandes au petit matin du *jour J* tandis que des *divisions aéroportées* américaines et britanniques étaient larguées à l'intérieur des terres.

4. Plus de trois cents hémophiles sont morts en France et plus de douze cents ont été contaminés par le *virus de l'immuno déficience humaine* entre 1984 et 1985. (France-Amérique, 25 juin-1er juillet 1994)

5. La France dont les soldats sont en première ligne face aux belligérants en Bosnie Herzégovine a ouvertement reproché à *l'O.N.U.* les hésitations et les retards dans l'emploi de *frappes aériennes* en risposte à des tirs contre les casques bleus. (France-Amérique, 19-25 mars 1994)

6. AOL a réussi à se vendre à des millions de novices comme le moyen le plus facile de *se brancher* sur *la Toile*. La société a offert une   gamme   croissante   de   services   (*espaces-dialogue, communautés virtuelles, courrier électronique*).   (Le Monde diplomatique, février 2000)

7. Les prix de la laine, du café arabica, du nickel sont *en chute libre* depuis des mois. Ils ont perdu en moyenne 17,6% entre juillet 1997 et 1998, selon l'indice mensuel de *l'Insee*. (Le Revenu Français, 28 août 1998)

8. Dans une *transplantation cardiaque*, on appelle *temps ischémique* le temps qui s'écoule entre le *clampage* aortique lors de l'extraction de l'organe chez le *donneur* et le *déclampage* aortique lors de l'*implantation* chez le *receveur*.

Chapter 7   **Literal Translation**
Structural Obstacles to Literal Translation

What is a literal translation?

> **One may speak of a literal translation when the sentence or message of the SL can be translated word for word into the TL, without a change in the word order or grammatical structure, while remaining both correct and idiomatic.**

Literal translation is possible when there are no structural (grammatical and syntactic) obstacles and no metalinguistic (cultural) obstacles. Such ideal conditions mainly exist between languages of the same linguistic family which share a similar syntax and grammar but this can hardly be the norm between languages belonging to different backgrounds, as in the case of English and French. However, a long history of mutual borrowing, both in word formation and thought patterns, has brought them close enough to allow for literal translation in very simple sentences, sentences like:

> Où est le propriétaire de ce chien? Where is the owner of that dog?
> Nous arrivâmes épuisés à l'hôtel après un pénible voyage. We arrived exhausted at the hotel after a taxing journey.

And even in a number of idiomatic expressions.

Some examples of identical verbal expressions:

> avaler la pilule: to swallow the pill
> avoir un mot sur le bout de la langue: to have a word on the tip of one's tongue

avoir un pied dans la tombe: to have a foot in the grave

chercher une aiguille dans une botte de foin: to look for a needle in a haystack

connaître toutes les ficelles: to know the ropes

donner le feu vert à quelqu'un: to give someone the green light

dorer la pilule: to gild the pill

envoyer en chute libre: to send into a free fall

être au septième ciel: to be in seventh heaven

être pris entre deux feux: to be caught between two fires

jouer avec le feu: to play with fire

jouer un jeu dangereux: to play a dangerous game

laisser quelqu'un mijoter dans son jus: to let someone stew in his own juice

mordre la poussière: to bite the dust

prendre le taureau par les cornes: to take the bull by the horns

remuer ciel et terre: to move heaven and earth

se casser le cou: to break on's neck

tenir sa langue; to hold one's tongue

trembler comme une feuille: to tremble like a leaf

verser des larmes de crocodile: to shed crocodile tears.

Identical ways of looking at a concept in a verbal expression:

attacher de l'importance à: *to attach* importance to

courir un risque: *to run* a risk

être *en cours*: to be *in progress*

faire une scène: *to make* a scene

jouer un *sale* tour: to play a *dirty* trick

peser ses paroles: *to weigh* one's words

prêter l'oreille à quelqu'un: *to lend* someone an ear

savoir *par coeur*: to know *by heart*

tirer à sa fin: *to draw* to an end

voir rouge: *to see* red.

Identical phrases:

avec de l'huile de coude: with elbow grease

sans l'ombre d'un doute: without the shadow of a doubt.

Identical proverbs:

Il faut battre le fer pendant qu'il est chaud: you must strike the iron while it is hot

Pierre qui roule n'amasse pas mousse: a rolling stone gathers no moss

Nominal expressions: (most of them calques)

le libre-échange: free trade

le prêt à porter: ready-to-wear
le tiers monde: the third world.

Sometimes the SL and TL words share their semantic range including figurative meanings which can be translated literally:

ex. un requin: a shark (1. fish, 2. swindler).

What are some structural obstacles to a literal translation?

Let us now examine some of the structural differences which stand in the way of literal translation between the two languages.[1]

A. Differences in word order

The following will interfere with a word for word translation.

Respective position of adjectives and adverbs
Adjectives in French are generally placed after, not before, the noun they modify, except for a handful expressing Beauty, Age, Goodness, and Size (BAGS) and those which reflect the subjective opinion of the narrator, while adverbs of time, such as *bientôt, souvent, toujours, rarement, encore, enfin, déjà*, and manner, *bien, mal, vite* etc. are positioned after a verb in simple tenses and between the auxiliary and the past participle in compound tenses:

Ainsi finit notre expérience *américaine*. Thus ended our *American* experience.

Ils manquent *souvent* leur train. They *often* miss their train.

Mange *vite* ta soupe! *Quickly* eat your soup!

Position of direct and indirect object pronouns
Before the verb in French, after in English:

Je *te l'*ai déjà donné. I already gave *it to you.*

Position of interrogative adverbs in a prepositional construction
In French the preposition must precede the interrogative adverb

---

[1] It is not our purpose here to list all diverging structures, which one can find in any good grammar, only to list the most representative ones.

whereas in English it has a tendency to be thrown to the end of the question:

> *Pour* qui as-tu acheté ça? Whom did you buy this *for?*
> *Par* quoi voulez-vous commencer? What do you want to start *with?*

Position of direct objects in relation to verbs
English does not like to separate a direct object from the verb it relates to.   French does not mind interpolating adverbs, or adverbial phrases:

> Tu *fais* bien *ton travail*. You *do your work* well.
> Ma mère *m'offrit*, contrairement à mon habitude, *une tasse de thé*.
> (Marcel Proust, A la Recherche du temps perdu). My mother, contrary to custom, *offered me a cup of tea*.

Inversion verb-subject with adverbs
In English and French literary texts certain adverbs may be placed in an initial position in a sentence for stylistic emphasis, but require an inversion verb-subject. Unfortunately these adverbs do not correspond between the two languages, and, with a couple of exceptions, the order in translation will differ.

We find such a construction in French with adverbs *peut-être,* and *aussi* (bear in mind that these sentences are statements not to be confused with questions formed by inversion.):

> *Peut-être était-il* innocent. He *may* have been innocent.
> Nous travaillons dur, *aussi réussirons-nous*. We work hard, *therefore* we will succeed.

In English we find this inversion after adverbs such as *no sooner,* and *never*:

> *No sooner did we arrive* than the show began. Nous n'étions pas plus tôt arrivés que le spectacle commença.
> *Never have I seen* anything like this! Je n'ai jamais rien vu de tel!

No sooner ...than may be translated as *à peine...que,* in which case the order remains the same:

> A peine se furent-ils rendu compte de leur erreur, qu'ils s'excusèrent.
> *No sooner had they realized* their mistake *than* they apologized.

Analytic versus synthetic language
One of the basic causes of difference in word order between English and French is due to the fact that French is an analytical

language which likes to make use of articulations (prepositions, conjunctions and even relative pronouns) in expressions, while English, a synthetic language like all Germanic languages, prefers juxtaposition.

Many French articulated nominal expressions will become nominal compounds in translation:

un lieu *de* travail:	a workplace
un mur *en* brique:	a brick-wall
un nid *à* poussière:	a dust nest
une assurance *contre* le vol:	theft insurance

French adjectival expressions may likewise become English adjectival compounds:

adepte en informatique:	computer savvy
tranchant comme un rasoir:	razor sharp

Nominal expressions involving past participles will be turned into multiple compounds:

des produits *destinés à l'exportation*:	*export oriented* merchandise
une grève *voulue par les syndicats*:	a *union driven* strike

And finally many short relative clauses in French can be rendered by a verbal adjective in the *-ing* form in English preceding the antecedent they refer to:

les mères *qui travaillent*:	*working* mothers
une tâche *qui prend du temps*:	a *time consuming* assignment
des facteurs *qui agravent la situation*:	*aggravating* factors

The English possessive case

This is another instance of the love of synthetic structures in English. The possessive case is essentially a genitive establishing a relation of possession between animate beings or animate beings and inanimate objects. French has no such structure and must articulate the possessive relation with the use of preposition "de":

le père *de* mon ami:	my friend's father
le dernier roman *de* Flaubert:	Flaubert's last novel
la maladie *de* Parkinson:	Parkinson's disease

B. Ellipses

Sometimes it is contrary to usage for the T.L. to translate all the S.L. words (a case of economy in translation), and again sometimes one must add to the message in order to remain idiomatic (a case of amplification).

Ellipses in English are an example of economy in translation.

The French definite article in general concepts
Thus, the definite article which precedes all general concepts in French is done away with in translation:

> *La* vie est courte.   Life is short.

Other examples of ellipses in English:

Invariable pronoun "le" which can replaces one or several adjectives, or a direct object clause
Pronoun of location "y" when referring to a place already mentioned along with verb *aller*
Indefinite pronoun "en" when used with an expression of quantity:

> Les Français sont-ils *chauvins*?   -Certains *le* sont.
> Are the French chauvinistic?   -Some of them are.
> La ligne est occupée.   -Je te *l'*avais dit.
> The line is busy   -I told you (*that it is busy*).
> On nous avait recommandé la rétrospective Matisse, alors, nous *y* sommes allés. We had been told about the Matisse retrospective and so we went.
> Combien de revers ont-ils subis?   -Ils *en* ont subi plusieurs.
> How many set-backs have they had?   -They have had several.

Ellipses of prepositions, conjunctions and possessive or demonstrative adjectives in a list:

> *Quand* j'étais petit et *que* j'allais à l'école...*When* I was little and going to school...
> Elle l'a fait *par* devoir plutôt que *par* intérêt. She did it *out of* duty rather than self- interest.
> La société a une responsabilité *envers ses* clients et *ses* actionnaires. The company has a responsibility *towards its* clients and shareholders.
> Il arriva avec toute *sa* famille: *son* père, *sa* mère, *ses* frères et soeurs.
> He arrived with *his* entire family: father, mother, sisters and brothers

Optional ellipses in English: these occur in the case of relative pronouns which are direct objects, and conjunctions introducing an object clause:

> Voici l'article que j'ai lu. Here is the article (which/that) I read.
> C'est la personne à qui je fais le plus confiance. He/she is the person (whom) I trust the most.
> Je lui ai dit que je le rappellerais. I told him (that) I would call back.

Ellipses in French: these, on the other hand, are an example of amplification of the message in English.

Positive or negative answers to a question

> Tu n'as pas oublié notre rendez-vous? *-Non.*
> You did not forget our appointment? *-No, I didn't.*
> Ne préféreriez-vous pas prendre le dessert plus tard? *-Si.*
> Wouldn't you prefer to have dessert later? *-Yes, we would.*

C. Gallicisms and anglicisms

A gallicism is a mode of expression which is a characteristic feature of the French language and conversely an anglicism, one characteristic of the English language. Being idiomatic, they stand in the way of a literal translation.

Some examples of gallicisms

1. Emphatic pronouns and emphatic constructions:

> *Moi*, ça m'est égal! *Personally*, I don't care!
> *C'est nous qui* sommes responsables. *We are the real culprits.*
> *C'est à toi que* je veux parler. *You are the one* I want to talk to.
> Où est-*elle, cette récompense*? Where *on earth* is that reward?

2. Indefinite pronoun "*on*" which, when it does not stand for "*nous*", is best rendered as an English passive, or alternately as an indefinite "*they*", or even as a general "*you*" in sayings and axioms:

> *On ne le revit* jamais plus. *He was* never *seen* again.
> *On dit* que tu es dur avec les gens. *They say* that you are hard with people.
> *On* n'attrape pas les mouches avec du vinaigre. *You* can't catch flies with vinegar.

Some examples of anglicisms
Emphatic auxiliary verbs:

> We *did* send you a postcard. It must have gotten lost. Nous vous avons *pourtant* envoyé une carte postale. Elle a dû se perdre.
>
> You will close the door after you, *won't you*? Fermez la porte derrière vous, *vous voulez bien*?
>
> You wanted to go and see that movie? Well, *don't!* Vous vouliez aller voir ce film? *Gardez-vous en bien!*

D. Special problems with verb tenses

The French historical present
One of the functions of the French present allows it to be used in a context clearly marked as belonging to the past in order to make the actions more vivid, more real. This is the so-called historical present. Even though this usage also exists in the English language, it is more restricted. Most of the time, the French historical present is best translated as a simple past. Also, certain business practices must be kept in mind: it is customary, for instance, to record the minutes of a meeting in the present tense in French whereas those same minutes must be translated into English using the simple past.

> Napoléon *naît* en 1769, *devient* empereur en 1804 et *meurt* en 1821.
>
> Napoleon *was born* in 1769, *became* emperor in 1804 and *died* in 1821.
>
> M. le Président *expose* que le conseil *s'est réuni* pour délibérer et statuer sur l'ordre du jour suivant.
>
> The Chairman *stated* that the Board *met* to deliberate and issue resolutions on the following agenda.

Special use of the conditional in French
To indicate an action or a situation not officially verified, French uses the conditional present.   There is no such use of the conditional in English so that one has to resort to a periphrasis in translation to express the fact that it is only a seeming possibility.

> Selon le journal, *il y aurait* une grève des aiguilleurs du ciel la semaine prochaine.
>
> According to the newspaper *it seems* that air traffic controllers *will be* on strike next week.

The English progressive form

The progressive form, which is used to express an action in progress, is a structural form specific to English. Present and future progressives find an equivalent in the regular French present and future while the past progressive finds an equivalent in the imparfait:

> *Are you leaving?*   *Partez-vous?*
> I *shall be working* all summer.   Je *travaillerai* tout l'été.
> Il *neigeait.*   It *was snowing..*

As for the present perfect progressive, it translates the French present tense when the action started at some stated time in the past and is still going on:

> Il y a dix ans que j'*habite* ici. I *have been living* here for ten years.
> Voilà deux heures que nous vous *attendons*: We *have been waiting* for you for two hours.
> Il *pleut* depuis ce matin. It *has been raining* since this morning.

And the past perfect progressive translates a French imparfait under the same conditions:

> Cela *faisait* déjà longtemps que les gens *jasaient* sur l'origine de sa fortune.
> Already people *had* long *been gossiping* about the origin of his wealth.

Translating a passé composé: simple past or present perfect?

Whenever the action is completed, the simple past is to be used. Whenever the verb conveys a past continuous action or situation which is still linked to the present, the present perfect is to be used. Compare:

> J'*ai vu* ce film la semaine dernière. I *saw* this movie last week.
> Je *n'ai pas* encore *vu* ce film.   I *have not seen* this movie yet.
> Hier, son état *s'est aggravé.*   Yesterday, his condition *deteriorated.*
> Son état *s'est aggravé* depuis hier. His condition *has deteriorated* since yesterday.

The iterative imparfait

Beside expressing a past progressive, *i.e.* an action in progress in the past, the French imparfait can have an iterative or repetitive function rendered by "used to" or the more literary "would" of habit:

> Quand j'étais petit je *faisais* de la bicyclette.

When I was young I *used to go cycling/* I *would go cycling.*

Durative versus punctual aspects of French semi-auxiliaries

The imparfait expresses an action in its continuity or duration (the so-called durative aspect rendered by the English past progressive). This aspect stands in contrast with the function of the passé composé and the passé simple which is to express an action in its completion, that is to say with a beginning and an end without any notion of duration (the punctual aspect of the verb rendered by the simple past: the action is viewed as a point in time). However, some English verbs, particularly modal auxiliaries, cannot be expressed in the progressive form and, consequently, corresponding French verbs must be translated with different counterparts in the imparfait and passé composé to render these variations of aspect.

Il *savait* qu'il avait tort. He *knew* he was wrong (continuous).
J'ai su la nouvelle par Georges. I *heard* the news through George (limited).

Ils *se connaissaient* depuis longtemps. They *had known each other* for a long time.
Nous nous sommes connus en vacances. We *met (each other)* while on vacation.

Voulais-tu m'accompagner? *Did you want* to come with me?
Je *voulus* m'arrêter mais les freins de la voiture lâchèrent. I *tried* to stop but the car brakes gave way.

Ne *pouviez-vous* pas faire attention? Couldn't you be careful?
J'ai pu dormir une heure ou deux dans l'avion. *I was able* to sleep for a couple of hours on the plane.

Tu devais être là à dix heures. *You were supposed* to be here at 10.
Elle a dû renoncer à son projet. *She had to* abandon her plan.

Nous *avions peur* que vous ne vous soyez égarés. We *were afraid* that you had gotten lost.
L'enfant *eut peur* en entendant la grosse voix de l'homme. The child *became frightened* at the sound of the man's loud voice.

The future in temporal clauses

Don't forget that sometimes a French future has to be rendered as a present after conjunctions of time (*quand, dès que, aussitôt que, tant que, pendant que*):

> Aussitôt que nous *serons* prêts nous partirons. As soon as we *are* ready, we will leave.

The subjunctive

The subjunctive mood, practically inexistent in English, presents special difficulties in translation. Strict rules govern tense sequence in the subordinate clause depending on whether there is a relation of anteriority, simultaneity or posteriority between the action in the main clause and the action in the subordinate clause. Consequently, a present subjunctive may correspond to an English future even though the verb in the main clause is present, and to a conditional present representing a future in the past even though the main clause verb is in the past; and since tense sequence also dictates the use of the present subjunctive in a subordinate clause when its action is concurrent with a past action in the main clause, a present subjunctive can, in addition, be the equivalent of a past tense.

> Etes-vous sûr qu'il *vienne*? Are you sure that he *will come*?
> Nous avions peur qu'ils ne *nous reconnaissent* pas. We were afraid that they *would not recognize us*.
> Je craignais qu'ils ne *soient* en danger. I feared that they *were* in danger.

E. Problems with French pronominal verbs

Pronominal verbs are a feature specific to Romance languages. Most of the time, translating them literally runs counter to an idiomatic translation in English. Here are various ways of dealing with them.

Pronominal verbs can be the expression:
1. of a reflexive action (done by an animate subject upon himself)
2. of a reciprocal action (when two or more subjects interact)
3. of an action done upon an inanimate passive subject.

- In the first case, the French reflexive pronoun can be rendered by the equivalent English reflexive pronoun, although this is not necessary when the action is a customary one:

  Tu *t'es fait* mal? Did you *hurt yourself?*
  Le matin je *me lève*, je *me lave* et je *m'habille.*
  In the morning, I *get up*, I *wash* and I *get dressed.*

- In the second case, reciprocal pronouns are used, but sometimes the reciprocity is only implied in English:

  Ils *se téléphonent* tous les jours. They *phone each other* every day.
  Nous nous sommes querellés. We *quarreled (with each other).*

- In the third case, a passive voice is often resorted to in translation:

  Ce vin *se sert* chambré. This wine *is served* at room temperature.

Many French pronominal verbs are therefore translated as simple verbs or as passive verbs in English.

Here is a representative list:

s'agir de: to be a question of, to be about
s'attendre à: to expect
s'accroître: to increase
se convaincre de: to become convinced of
se décourager: to become discouraged
se demander: to wonder
se déplacer: to travel, to move
se dire: to think to oneself
se douter de: to suspect
se dérouler: to take place
s'engager à: to agree to
s'ennuyer: to be bored
s'entendre dire que: to be bluntly told

se féliciter: to be very pleased
se mettre à: to begin to
se mobiliser: to rally
se moquer de: to make fun of/
s'occuper de: to take care of
se passer de: to do without
se plaindre: to complain
se prononcer: to pass judgment
se réfugier: to take refuge
se rendre compte: to realize
se transformer: to turn into
se tromper: to make a mistake
se trouver: to be (in a place). to be located

Additional structural or linguistic obstacles shall be dealt with in the coming chapters.

Exercices: La Traduction littérale

A. Les Aphorismes

Traduisez en anglais les aphorismes suivants.

La Rochefoucauld

1. Tout le monde se plaint de sa mémoire, et personne ne se plaint de son jugement.
2. L'hypocrisie est un hommage que le vice rend à la vertu.
3. Nous pardonnons souvent à ceux qui nous ennuient, mais nous ne pouvons pardonner à ceux que nous ennuyons.
4. L'amour-propre est le plus grand de tous les flatteurs.
5. C'est une grande folie de vouloir être sage tout seul.
6. Nous avons tous assez de force pour supporter les maux d'autrui.
7. Si on juge de l'amour par la plupart de ses effets il ressemble plus à la haine qu'à l'amitié.
8. L'absence diminue les médiocres passions et augmente les grandes comme le vent éteint les bougies et allume le feu.

Boileau

9. Ce que l'on conçoit bien s'énonce clairement
   Et les mots pour le dire arrivent aisément.

Pascal

10. L'homme n'est qu'un roseau, le plus faible de la nature, mais c'est un roseau pensant.
11. Le nez de Cléopâtre, s'il eût été plus court, toute la face de la terre aurait changé.
12. -Pourquoi me tuez-vous? Je n'ai pas d'armes.

    -Eh quoi! ne demeurez vous pas de l'autre côté de l'eau? Mon ami, si vous demeuriez de ce côté, je serais un assassin et cela serait injuste de vous tuer de la sorte, mais puisque vous demeurez de l'autre côté, je suis un brave et cela est juste.

La Bruyère

13. Les femmes sont extrêmes: elles sont meilleures ou pires que les hommes.

14. L'amour et l'amitié s'excluent l'un l'autre.

Vauvenargues

15. Les grandes pensées viennent du coeur.

16. La raison nous trompe plus souvent que la nature.

17. Pour exécuter de grandes choses, il faut vivre comme si on ne *devait jamais* mourir.

Lamennais

18. N'aimer que soi, c'est haïr les autres.

B. Articulation et juxtaposition

En vous référant aux explications des pages 68-9 (analytic vs. synthetic language) traduisez les phrases suivantes en anglais en utilisant le procédé de juxtaposition au lieu de l'articulation pour les expressions en italique.

1. Je préfère *les boissons sans caféine.*

2. C'est un sacrifice *qui en vaut la peine.*

3. Voilà *une personne à l'aspect qui n'augure rien de bon.*

4. Nous venons de vivre *une expérience à vous faire dresser les cheveux sur la tête.*

5. Je vous conseille de traiter avec *une société qui soit orientée vers le client.*

6. Il a *une voix aux sonorités jeunes.*

7. Le musée de la ville est fier de sa *collection de tableaux du XIXème siècle.*

8. *Un livre qui donne à penser,* voilà la qualité principale de cette critique de la société actuelle.

9. Grâce à la détection précoce *d'un cancer du colon*, le malade put subir *une opération qui lui sauva la vie.*

10. *Le domaine de l'industrie de la santé* a subi de fortes pressions en raison *d'une concurrence globale qui s'accentue.*

11. *Les maladies causées par le tabac* sont en nette progression dans tous les pays développés.

12. *Des augmentations de prix, prévues depuis longtemps,* viennent d'être mises en place.

13. *Des changements de fond en comble* vont être nécessaires pour l'assainissement des *finances de la société.*

14. Les obligations émises par l'état pour financer les travaux d'infrastructure du projet seront *exonérées d'impôts.*

15. Les progrès faits récemment en recherche génétique vont avoir *des conséquences de grande portée* pour l'avenir de la médecine.

C. Traduction littérale ou non-littérale?

Une traduction littérale des phrases suivantes est-elle possible? Sinon définissez le problème. Ensuite traduisez.

1. Pourquoi attacher tant d'importance à ce détail?
2. La guerre éclata vers le milieu de l'été.
3. Les syndicats avaient accusé la direction de chantage.
4. Dans les années qui viennent, le débat sur l'avenir de l'Europe va devenir crucial.
5. Le rouge est ma couleur préférée, et toi? Il l'est aussi.
6. Ce ne sont pas de vraies larmes que tu verses mais des larmes de crocodile.
7. La formule "L'existence précède l'essence" est au coeur de la philosophie de Sartre.
8. Comme nous n'étions pas sûrs qu'il fasse beau, nous avons reporté l'excursion que nous avions projetée.
9. Quand tu auras terminé ton rapport, montre-le-moi.
10. C'est lui qui veut démissionner, ce n'est pas moi qui l'y force.
11. Ne sait-on pas encore qui va gagner l'élection? Si.
12. Lorsque j'ai voulu expliquer ce qui s'était passé, on ne m'a pas cru.
13. Voilà deux heures qu'il joue le même morceau de musique!

14. Autrefois, en été, nous allions en pique-nique presque tous les dimanches.

15. Parce qu'il fait trop chaud et que tu es fatigué, nous allons nous arrêter pour nous reposer.

16. Par sa détermination, par son ambition et son énergie cette personne ira loin.

D. Les Verbes pronominaux

S'agit-il de verbes simples, réfléchis, réciproques ou de voix passive en anglais? Traduisez.

1. [Les années] *s'additionnent* si promptement...elles *s'évanouissent* si complètement qu'en *se retournant* pour voir le temps parcouru on n'aperçoit plus rien et on ne comprend pas comment il *se fait* qu'on soit vieux. (Guy de Maupassant, Contes du jour et de la nuit)

2. M. Seguin *se trompait*. Sa chèvre *s'ennuya*. Un jour, elle *se dit* en regardant la montagne: "Comme on doit être bien là-haut!" (Alphonse Daudet, La Chèvre de M. Seguin)

3. "Elle a toutes les griffes cassées, dit-il en *se parlant* à lui-même, elle *s'est retenue*, accrochée..." Il *s'interrompit*, prit sans un mot de plus la chatte sous son bras et l'emporta dans la salle de bains. (Colette, La Chatte)

4. Je *me mettais* quelquefois à penser à ma chambre. Je *me souvenais* de chaque meuble et, pour chacun d'entre eux, de chaque objet qui *s'y trouvait*. (Albert Camus, L'Etranger)

5. Il *se tuera*, pensa Kyo. Il avait assez écouté son père pour savoir que celui qui cherche aussi âprement l'absolu ne le trouve que dans la sensation. (André Malraux, La Condition humaine)

6. Mon père *se pencha* un peu vers lui et déclara: "J'ai une nouvelle, mon vieux. Anne et moi, *nous nous marions* le 5 octobre." (Françoise Sagan, Bonjour tristesse)

7. Mon grand-père saisissait l'occasion de montrer sa faiblesse: il prenait parti contre sa femme qui *se levait* outragée pour aller *s'enfermer* dans sa chambre. (J.P. Sartre, Les Mots)

8. L'homme d'action ne *se conçoit* guère sans une forte dose d'égoïsme, d'orgueil, de dureté, de ruse. (Charles de Gaulle, Le Fil de l'épée)

9. Elle *se regarde*. Elle *s'est approchée* de son image, ne *se reconnaît* pas bien. (Marguerite Duras, L'Amant)

10. Il en est ainsi, Mademoiselle. Ça ne *s'explique* pas. Ça *se comprend* par un raisonnement mathématique intérieur. (Eugène Ionesco, La Leçon)

Chapter 8 **Transposition**

What is transposition?

Transposition is the first of the non-literal translation techniques. It is also the most used technique in translation. Resort to it when an obstacle in the process of translation occurs due to different grammatical structures in the S.L. and T.L. As we have seen in the chapter on literal translation, English and French have particular preferences for certain constructions which are at variance one with the other.

The following diagram will help you understand how a transposition works:

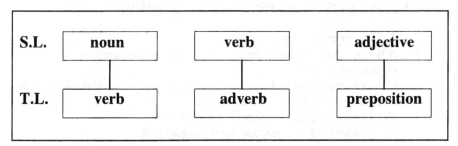

S.L.	noun	verb	adjective
T.L.	verb	adverb	preposition

> **A transposition is a translation technique which involves a switch in grammatical categories (*i.e.* nouns, verbs, adjectives, adverbs and prepositions) from the S.L. to the T.L., this without affecting the meaning of the message.**

It remains at the grammatical level without affecting the semantic level: the message stays exactly the same.

With a transposition, while the original and its translation remain literally close and semantically identical, a verb in the S.L. might become a noun in the T.L.; or a noun, a verb; a verb, an adverb or an adjective; a past participle, a preposition or an adjective etc. The possibilities are many, even though some types of transpositions are more commonly used than others, as is the case with the change verb into adverb, or noun into verb.

When should you resort to a transposition?
When the message, if translated literally, is either nonsensical, a mistranslation, or understandable to the T.L. speaker without sounding idiomatic or correct, while the cause of the problem is only structural.

Some transpositions are absolutely necessary (*i.e.*, when there is no other way of dealing with the structural problem), while others remain optional, as alternatives to a literal translation. In the latter case, a literal translation tends to be more literary whereas the use of a transposition will give a more colloquial flavor.

Some examples of necessary transpositions

1. **Est-ce que Jean est *de retour*?**
A literal translation has to be ruled out as being nonsensical.
(Is John *of return*?)
Only a transposition will retain all the elements of the original message and convey them in an idiomatic way:
Has John *come back*? transposition noun-verb
Or: Is John *back*?   transposition noun-adverb.

2. **Tu *as raison* de croire Marie.**
A literal translation (You have a reason to believe Mary) would result in a mistranslation, that is to say a mistake in the interpretation of the original message.
In this case only a transposition noun-adjective along with a change in auxiliaries will yield the correct translation:
You are right to believe Mary.

3. **Maison *à vendre***

Here a literal translation would make sense (house to sell), but has to be dismissed as not being idiomatic.

House for sale is the expression sanctioned by usage, and we need to resort to a transposition verb-noun.

Examples of optional transpositions

1. *Réduction de **25%** sur tous les articles*

A literal translation (25% *reduction* on all articles) as well as a transposition noun-preposition (25% *off* all articles) are both correct.

2. *Après la reprise des combats* **la guerre parut s'éterniser.**

Both a literal and a noun-verb transposition are possible:

After resumption of the fighting the war seemed to drag on.

After the fighting resumed the war seemed to drag on.

However the two translations are not quite on a par stylistically: the first one, calqued after the French nominal expression, being more literary; and the second, which follows English preference for verbs, more colloquial.

Noun-verb transposition

This is one of the most common types of transposition between French and English, and it is due to the fact that French very often prefers nouns in structures in which English uses verbs. Such structures include temporal clauses introduced by prepositions: *dès, au fur et à mesure de, après, avant, lors de, au moment de.*

> *Dès mon arrivée* à l'hôtel, j'ai pris un bain, je me suis habillé et je suis sorti faire une promenade. *As soon as I arrived* at the hotel, I took a bath, got dressed and went out for a walk.
> Nous nous trouvions à Paris *lors des grèves* des syndicats. We were in Paris *when* the unions *went on strike.*
> Quelques jours *après sa mort*, la presse fit des révélations sur la vie privée du président. A few days *after he died*, the press leaked out information on the president's private life.
> Mettez le fichier à jour *avant votre départ* en vacances. Bring the file up to date *before you leave* for your vacation.
> *A la vue* des problèmes qui s'accumulaient, nous avons renoncé au projet. *When we saw* problems accumulating, we gave up on the plan.

Au fur et à mesure de la montée du chômage, l'inquiétude s'accroît dans toutes les couches de la société. *As unemployment rises*, all strata of society become increasingly worried.

Transpositions with postpositional adverbs

As we have just seen, English is a dynamic language which often favors the use of verbs over nouns. As a result, it has developed verb structures which simply do not exist in French. One such structure involves the use of postpositional adverbs as mark of an incipient (*away, off*), gradual (*away, down*), continual (*on*), or final action (*out, up, off, through, down*). The English speaking translator must not forget to make use of their possibilities.

Continuons à marcher! *Let's walk on*!

Le bruit *s'estompa*, puis *s'arrêta tout à fait*. The noise *faded away* and *died out*.

La fabrique *a fermé ses portes*. The factory *closed down*.

Il faut *mettre fin* à nos relations. We must *break off* our relationship

Tu *te sortiras de cette situation*. You *will pull through*.

Sampler of transpositions across various grammatical categories

S.L. noun - T.L. verb:

    C'est quand ton *mariage*?   When are you *getting married*?

S.L. verb – T.L. adverb:

    Cela *reste* à démontrer.   This is *still* to be proven.

S.L. adjective - T.L. preposition:

    Le village est *privé* d'eau.   The village is *without* water.

S.L. adverb - T.L. adjective:

    Je donne une fête *de temps en temps*. I give an *occasional* party.

S.L. adverb - T.L. verb:

    Tu as *peut-être* raison.   You *may* be right.

S.L. verb - T.L. adjective:

    Vous *vous trompez* de numéro!   You have the *wrong* number!

S.L. verb -T.L. preposition:

    Il faut envoyer *chercher* le médecin. We must send *for* the doctor.

S.L. noun - T.L. adjective:
> Je pars *fin* juin.   I am leaving *late* June.

S.L. noun - T.L. preposition:
> Ce train est à *destination* de Bruxelles. This is the train *to* Brussels.

S.L. conjunction - T.L. verb:
> *A force de* crier tu vas avoir mal à la gorge! If you *keep* screaming
> you'll have a sore throat!

Remember that an English thesaurus, which lists concepts across the various grammatical categories, can be an invaluable resource and will help you with this sort of exercise in grammatical switching.

Cross transposition

A cross transposition is a special type of transposition. It is a double transposition with a change in word order, the two transposed words in the T.L being switched around in relation to the order in the S.L.

e.g.. Je descendis l'escalier en courant

A literal translation (I went down the staircase running) would fail to be idiomatic. Instead let's try a double transposition verb-preposition, and verbal adjective-verb in a cross pattern:

Je descendis l'escalier en courant

I ran down the staircase

Generally cross transpositions are *de rigueur* with actions involving motion when the means or manner of this motion are also expressed:

mean: *Nous nous rendrons* à New York *par avion.*
    We will *fly to* New York.

manner: *L'animal s'éloigna en boitant.*
     The animal *limped away.*

In this category, the manner or the means will be expressed as a verb in English, while the French verb of motion will be rendered as a preposition or adverb of motion (*up, down, to, across, by, on, off, out, through, away, forth etc.*).

It is not rare to find incomplete cross transpositions in French, since this particular type of construction is more awkward than in English.

For example: "Les enfants *s'éloignèrent*" may be translated as "The children *moved away, walked away, rode away, drove away.*" This is a case of translation gain, since the manner of motion, while being specified in English, is absent from the French message.

Sometimes also cross transpositions are used when the end result of a situation is mentioned along with the reason for this result:

    e.g.. Je suis *mort de faim*   I am *starving to death.*

The difference in word order between English and French which necessitates the use of a cross transposition in translation stems from a basic divergence of approach in apprehending reality:

- **French, a more abstract and intellectual language, favors the order:**

        results first, means or manner later.

- **English, more concrete and logical, follows the action through the visual order of events:**

        means or manner first, results subsequently.

Exercices: **La Transposition**

> *La transposition est un procédé de traduction non littérale par lequel un mot change de catégorie grammaticale en passant de la L.D. à la L.A. Ainsi un verbe peut devenir un nom, ou un participe passé une préposition, ou un verbe un adverbe, ou encore un nom un adjectif, etc.*
>
> *Utilisez un thésaurus anglais pour vous familiariser avec la pratique de remplacement d'un nom par un verbe ou d'un verbe par un adverbe, ou bien d'un nom par un adjectif et vice-versa.*

A. La Transposition

L'exercice suivant est destiné à familiariser l'apprenti traducteur avec le procédé de la transposition, c'est à dire avec le passage d'une catégorie grammaticale à une autre. Utilisez le thésaurus anglais pour trouver le même concept dans une autre catégorie grammaticale.

Verbe en substantif (noun):
To cease; to come back; to come close; to confide; to feel;   to get over (something); to give back; to leave/ to go away; to go up; to own, to take away.

Verbe en adjectif:
To advise; to appear; to comprehend; to finish; to hold; to start; to run away.

Verbe en adverbe:
To be used to (do something); to end; to keep (doing something); (I) may (in the sense of a possibility); to proceed (to do something); to remain; to result; to win.

Substantif en adjectif:
Effect; habit/custom; memory; mistake; novelty.

Substantif en verbe:
Affection; agent; domicile; duration; incantation; inception; sensibilité.

Verbe en préposition:
To follow; to precede.

B. La Transposition

Traduisez les phrases suivantes en changeant la catégorie grammaticale des mots en italique selon les directives.

Verbe en adverbe

1. Bien qu'on nous ait demandé de garder le secret nous *avons failli* tout révéler.
2. Si on le leur répète, ils *finiront* bien *par* comprendre.
3. Je *n'arrive pas à* vous entendre, la communication est brouillée, parlez plus fort!
4. Il *arrive à* tout le monde de se tromper.
5. Ça *va* faire un an que nous habitons ici.
6. Il *suffit* de lire ce livre pour se convaincre de l'originalité de son auteur.
7. Patientons un peu, les invités *ne vont pas tarder à* arriver.
8. Il *ne cesse de* pleuvoir depuis deux jours.
9. Le chien *n'arrêtait pas* d'aboyer.
10. Nous ne partageons plus les mêmes idées politiques mais je lui *conserve* toute mon estime.
11. Pendant que sa mère le grondait l'enfant *se contentait de* baisser la tête.
12. *Il paraît* que le premier ministre va démissionner.
13. En dépit de la baisse des taux d'intérêt l'affaire *demeure* rentable.

Substantif en verbe

1. *Quelle est la date de votre départ?*
2. Il y a beaucoup à faire avant *la rentrée* des classes.
3. Le diner commencera dès *l'arrivée de* l'invité d'honneur.
4. La foule a applaudi *au passage du* cortège présidentiel.
5. Les animaux se sauvèrent *à l'approche des* chasseurs.
6. Le client est remboursé intégralement en cas *de non-satisfaction.*
7. Les hostilités cessèrent après *la signature du* traité d'autonomie.
8. *A la vue de* l'ampleur de la catastrophe les sauveteurs furent épouvantés.
9. *Par mesure d'économie* la société a décidé de licencier du personnel.
10. *L'erreur* est humaine.

Substantif en adjectif

1. La Révolution française a mis l'accent sur les droits *de l'homme* et *du citoyen*

Verbe en substantif

1. *Comment vous appelez-vous?*
2. Tiens, j'ignorais que la maison d'en face était *à vendre*!
3. *Il s'agit* maintenant de trouver une solution à ce problème.
4. Beaucoup de gens pensent que l'Europe peut aider *à lutter* contre le chômage en recourant au protectionnisme.
5. En politique le public exige *que cessent* les mensonges et la langue de bois.

Adverbe en verbe

1. Ils sont en retard: ils ont *peut-être* eu un accident de voiture.
2. *Certes*, les jeunes sont souvent égoïstes et intransigeants, mais ils sont l'avenir de la planète.

Verbe en adjectif

1. Le 34-25-69? Désolé, vous *vous trompez* de numéro!
2. *Ai-je réussi* à te faire changer d'avis?

Conjonction en verbe

1. *A force de* lire dans la pénombre tu vas finir par t'abîmer la vue.

Substantif en adjectif

1. La séparation de l'Eglise et de l'Etat a eu lieu au *début du* XXème siècle.
2. Le mariage sera célébré à *la fin du mois de* mai.
3. Nous comptons prendre nos vacances *au milieu de* l'été.

Participe passé en adverbe

Utilisez les adverbes post-positionnels anglais suivants: on, off, over, out, away, up, down, back etc. pour remplacer les participes passés en italique.

1. Le match a été *annulé* en raison du mauvais temps.
2. Le four est-il *allumé* ou *éteint*?
3. Le voisin? Désolé, il est *parti* en voyage.
4. Non, Sabine n'est pas *sortie*. Elle n'est même pas encore *levée*.
5. Pierrot devrait bientôt être *rentré* de l'école.
6. Ces soldes d'hiver sont intéressantes: les prix sont *réduits* de 50%.
7. Le film *fini,* nous allâmes flâner le long des Champs Elysées.
8. Loulou, notre chien, est *déprimé* en ce moment. Il ne veut même plus sortir.

Substantif en préposition

1. Embarquement immédiat porte no 6 pour les passagers *à destination de* New York.
2. La livraison des marchandises sera effectuée *dans un délai de* cinq jours.

Adjectif en préposition

1. *Privé de* l'appui de la chambre des députés, le chef du gouvernement a dû démissionner.

Verbe en préposition

1. Son état empire. Il faut envoyer *chercher* l'ambulance.
2. N'as-tu jamais entendu *parler de* cette histoire?

C. L'adverbe post-positionnel anglais

Pour les traductions suivantes remplacez les mots en italique par un adverbe post-positionnel (voir p.86: Transposition with post-positional adverbs).

1. Il a gaspillé *tout* son argent.
2. *Continuez de* lire!
3. Tiens-toi *à l'écart!*
4. J'ai usé ces vêtements *jusqu'au bout.*
5. Il faut *continuer à* suivre les évènements.
6. Nous nous sommes mis *en route.*
7. *Au commencement*, quand j'ai débuté dans cette carrière, j'étais très inexpérimenté.
8. Elle était gaie comme un pinson et chantait *sans s'arrêter.*

D. Transposition nécessaire ou facultative?

Déterminez si la traduction des phrases suivantes nécessite une transposition nécessaire ou facultative.

1. Ils sont toujours *en retard!*
2. Tu ne peux pas prendre de décision aussi importante sans *une consultation avec* le reste de la famille.
3. On me dit que je *ressemble* à ma soeur *de manière frappante.*
4. Je *viens* de rater mon train.
5. *Défense de stationner.*
6. Je vais trouver le temps long après *ton départ*!
7. Les spectateurs applaudirent *dès l'entrée* des joueurs de l'équipe locale sur le stade.
8. La petite grelottait de froid. Elle *ne* portait *qu'*un vieux châle élimé par-dessus sa robe mince.

9. De la fenêtre de ma chambre j'entendais *le chant* des oiseaux.

10. *Il y eut un coup de sonnette* à la porte.

11. *Aidé de* ses proches, il put surmonter ses difficultés.

12. Le facteur est arrivé juste *au moment où* je partais.

13. Voilà la raison *pour laquelle* je me suis abstenu de donner mon avis.

14. *A l'arrivée de* la diligence il se fit un brouhaha dans l'auberge.

15. Les gens *qui en ont* les moyens peuvent s'offrir des vacances de neige.

16. *A chacun de nos voyages* en Italie, nous nous arrêtons à Venise.

17. Le chauffeur de la voiture *continua sa route sans s'arrêter devant* moi.

18. On a diagnostiqué *une rupture* de disque chez ce malade.

19. *Au sein de* l'Union Européenne l'unanimité n'est pas toujours de mise.

20. *Etant donné* vos capacités, vous ne devriez avoir aucun problème dans votre nouvel emploi.

21. De profondes réformes vont être *nécessaires* pour éviter une fracture du tissu social.

22. Le président a *ensuite* déposé une gerbe de fleurs sur la tombe du soldat inconnu.

23. *On peut estimer* que l'enquête devrait contribuer à faire la lumière sur la vérité historique.

Exercices: **La Transposition croisée**

> *La transposition croisée est un cas particulier du procédé de transposition.*
> *Dans une transposition croisée le changement grammatical est double et s'effectue par un changement d'ordre des mots entre la L.D. et la L.A. en forme de croisement.*
> *En général ce sont des actions indiquant des mouvements ainsi que le moyen ou la manière de ce mouvement qui nécessitent des transpositions croisées. Parfois aussi ce sont des résultats de situations lorsque la cause ou la raison en est mentionnée.*

A. Les Verbes de mouvement

Traduisez les phrases suivantes en utilisant une transposition croisée pour les mots en italique.

1. Les enfants *sont entrés* dans la chambre *sur la pointe des pieds* pour voir si leurs parents dormaient encore.
2. Le chat *traversa* la rue *à toute vitesse* juste devant la voiture.
3. En été, les touristes *remontent* l'avenue de l'Opéra *en flânant* et en regardant les devantures des magasins.
4. Nous *avons chassé* les intrus *à coups de pied.*
5. Au lieu de prendre le train par l'Eurotunnel nous *irons* à Londres *par avion.*
6. Christophe Colomb fut le premier à *traverser* l'Atlantique *en bateau.*
7. Après les embrassades et les promesses de se revoir toute la petite troupe *disparut en voiture.*
8. Entendant un bruit étrange dans la chambre au-dessus, le locataire *monta* l'escalier *à la hâte* pour voir quelle en était la cause.
9. L'autre jour je *suis tombé par hasard* sur un de mes amis d'enfance.

10. Le jardinier doit *couper* la grosse branche du pommier *avec sa scie*.

11. Nous *avons longé* la rivière *à pied*, puis nous *avons continué notre chemin*.

12. L'étranger entra dans la cabane et *ferma* la porte *d'un coup de pied*.

13. Notre groupe *a sillonné* la France *en voiture*.

14. Il n'y avait pas de pont. Le régiment dut *traverser* la rivière *à la nage*.

15. Pris sur le fait le voleur *se retourna d'un bond*.

B. Résultats d'actions ou de situations

1. Papa *a achevé de payer* l'hypothèque de la maison.

2. Allons ! Dépêche-toi, *finis de boire* ton café !

3. A la fin de la soirée les invités *étaient morts d'ennui*.

4. Si nous restons plus longtemps dans cet endroit glacé nous allons *périr de froid*.

5 Je *suis mort de peur* à l'idée de devoir parler en public.

Chapter 9 **Modulation**

What is modulation?

Two languages may view the same concept from different points of view, different angles. When this happens we have a modulation.

> **A modulation involves a change, not in grammatical categories as with transposition, but in the way of thinking, in categories of thought.**

A change in categories of thought may mean a switch from concrete to abstract, cause to effect, means to result. It may involve viewing one part for the whole, and vice-versa, or one part for another part. It may also involve a difference in the sensorial perceptions of reality, a switch to opposites, the use of learned terms for popular ones *etc*. A few modulations, at the message level, do involve grammar with a change from positive to negative, active to passive, or even singular to plural and vice-versa.

The underlying causes for such different points of view are to be found in the characteristics of the language, in its particular genius. We have already seen that English tends to be more logical, more sensorial in its apprehension of reality, whereas French usually manifests a more abstract and intellectual approach. In this chapter, we will come across other specific traits of the two languages.

There are various types of modulations:

- **word modulations**, affecting one word or set of words which cannot be dissociated from each other, such as verbal or nominal expressions. Such modulations are set in the language and found in dictionaries, and therefore, with the exception of newly coined words, pose no particular challenge to the translator.
- **grammatical modulations**: which can be found in a good grammar and are set in the language by usage and rules. They can also be an expression of the stylistic differences between two languages.
- **message modulations**: which affect a whole phrase, sentence or message. These, like transposition, may be necessary, or optional as one solution among others. Since they will not be found in a dictionary, they are the real touchstone of a good and experienced translator, one who has learned to recognize when a change of focus is needed in order to give the message an idiomatic turn.

Word modulations

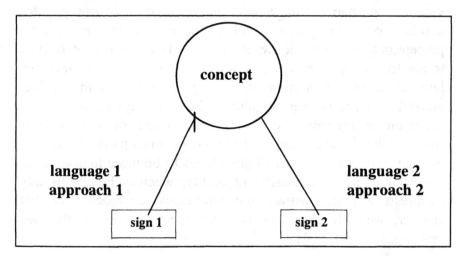

Perhaps one of the most striking examples of a word modulation is the duo *pompier-fireman* mentioned by Vinay and Darbelnet in *La*

Stylistique comparée du français et de l'anglais: the French word viewing the concept from the angle of the man whose task is to pump water leaving out the eventual duty of extinguishing the fire, while English only sees the man who fights the fire. Between the two words the emphasis switches from the preparation for the task to the relation person-task.

Among the many word modulations which can be found in dictionaries, the following are worthy of note:

Concrete to abstract

la saison *creuse*:	the *off* season
un sans *abri*:	a *home*less
le siècle des *Lumières*:	the Age of *Enlightenment*
un *train* de vie:	a life*style*
les *verts*:	the *environmentalists*
des vacances *de neige*:	a *winter* vacation
donner *un coup de fil*:	to give *a call*
de mon *côté*	for my *part*

Abstract to concrete

un avant-*projet*:	a first *draft*
l'esnseignement *supérieur*	*higher* education
des fonds *alternatifs*	*hedge* funds
les heures *de pointe (peak)*:	*rush* hours
des *licenciements*:	*lay offs*
un *logiciel*:	*software*
des matières *premières*:	*raw* material
un tableau *d'affichage*:	a *bulletin* board
être *à court* d'argent	to be cash *strapped*
parler *haut*:	to speak *loud*
réduire les effectifs:	*to downsize*
rire *tout bas*:	to laugh *in one's sleeve*

Means-result

en venir *aux mains*:	to come to *blows*

Result-means

un cours de *rattrapage*:	a *remedial* class
un *libre* service:	a *self*-service
un témoin *à charge*:	a witness *for the prosecution*

Cause-effect

un *bourreau* de travail: a work*oholic*

(Fr.: one who is his own *executioner* through too much work.
Eng.: patterned after the word "alcoholic", one who suffers the
consequences of too much work)

Effect-cause

une maladie *mortelle*:   a *life threatening* disease
des prêts hypothécaires *à risque*   *sub-prime* mortgages

Part-whole

une maison *mère*:   a *parent* company
du *matin au soir*:   *all day* long
du *jour au lendemain*   *overnight*
un *organe* exécutif: an executive *body*

Whole-part

le *billet* vert: the green *back*
de mon *temps*:   in my *day*
oublier son *texte*:   to forget one's *lines*
se laver *la tête*:   to wash *one's hair*

Part for other part

une brûlure d'*estomac*:   a *heart* burn
des *écouteurs*:   a *headset*
un *pied* de laitue: a *head* of lettuce
casser *les pieds* (à quelqu'un):   to be a pain *in the neck*
fermer la porte au *nez* de qqun   to slam the door in someone's *face*
crier à tue-*tête*   to shout at the top of one's *lungs*

Different images

une *pomme de discorde*   a *bone of contention*

(the first, a cultural allusion to Greek mythology: Paris's judgment,
which, by awarding the apple to Aphrodite for her superior beauty
aroused the jealousy of Athena and Artemis and led to the Trojan war;
and the second, an evocation of the concrete and realistic image of a
pack of dogs fighting over a bone)

avoir la *chair de poule*   to have *goosebumps*
faire chanter: *to blackmail*
un *dépliant* (which you unfold):   a *flier*
un *embouteillage* (bottle neck traffic flow): a traffic *jam*
des obligations *pourries/*   *junk* bonds

des obligations de pacotille
un *rouge* à lèvres: a lip*stick*
une station *balnéaire* (where one goes bathing): a *seaside* resort

Different sensorial perceptions

avoir des idées *noires*   to have the *blues*
le fossé s'est *creusé*:   the gap has *widened*
un poisson *rouge*:   a *gold*fish
un repas *lourd*:   a *rich* meal

Different intellectual perceptions

une chance *sur deux*:   a *fifty-fifty* chance
j'ai dit *plus haut*:   I said *earlier...*
sans caféine: caffein *free*
du jour au lendemain   *overnight*
le *troisième millénaire*:   the *twenty first century*
l'heure d'été   *daylight saving time*

Opposites

une assurance-*maladie*:   *health* insurance
en chômage: *out of work*
la *vente* par correspondance: mail *order* business

Learned-popular

l'agriculture: farming
un *auto*portrait: a *self* portrait
une *congestion cérébrale*:   a stroke
un *infarctus du myocarde*:   a heart attack
un *oléoduc*:   a pipeline
*ostréi*culture: oyster breeding
un *otorhinolaryngologiste*:   an ear throat and nose doctor
une *radiographie*:   an X-ray
un système *acoustique*:   a *sound* system

Word modulations can be found in lexical units working as affinity groups. The following is a short list of some set word modulations found in common expressions:

Word modulations in verbal expressions

accuser réception: to *acknowledge* receipt
aiguiser l'appétit   to *wet* the appetite
avoir lieu: to *take* place
avoir quelque chose *à voir* avec: to have something *to do* with

battre un record:	to *set* a record
céder le pas:	to *give* way
distribuer le courrier:	to *deliver* the mail
faire face à une obligation:	to *meet* an obligation
lancer un emprunt:	*to float* a loan
lever une séance:	*to adjourn* a meeting
marquer un point:	*to score* a point
percevoir des impôts:	*to collect* taxes
poser une question:	to *ask* a question
soulever une question	to *raise* an issue
poser un problème:	*to create* a problem
prendre *parti pour*:	to take *sides in favor of*
rallier des suffrages:	*to pick up support*
rattrapper le temps perdu:	*to make up for* lost time
redresser un tort:	to *right* a wrong
régler une facture:	*to pay* a bill
remporter une victoire:	*to win* a victory
rendre hommage:	*to pay tribute*
répondre à un défi:	*to meet* a challenge
resserrer des liens:	*to strengthen* ties
se mettre au travail:	*to set* to work
se tailler la part du lion:	*to grab* the lion's share
suivre un cours:	to *take* a course
toucher un chèque:	to *cash* a check

Word modulations in nominal expressions

un *cheval de bataille*:	a *pet argument*
un *coup* de rouge:	a *shot* of red wine
la *fourchette* des prix:	a price *range*
l'*offre* et la demande:	*supply* and demand
la société de consommation:	*consumerism*
une *tranche* d'imposition:	a tax *bracket*
le travail au noir:	*working off the books*
donner *la parole* à quelqu'un	to give someone *the floor*
prendre *parti*	to take *sides*

Word modulations on adjectives and adjectival expressions

donner la *mauvaise* réponse:	to give the *wrong* answer
des prix *cassés*:	*rock bottom* prices
des fonds *bloqués*	*frozen* assets
un jour *ouvrable*:	a *working* day
un modèle *haut de gamme*:	*a top of the line* model
une phrase *affirmative*:	a *positive* sentence

un poste *vacant*:	an *open* position
des rapports *étroits*:	a *close* relationship
être en *pleine* forme	to be in *great* shape

Word modulations on adverbial expressions

autrement dit:	*in other words*
en franchise:	*duty free*
expliquer *à fond*:	to explain *thoroughly*

Other word modulations

après réflexion:	*on second thought*
il n'en reste pas moins que:	*the fact remains that*

Clichés

Clichés theoretically belong in the chapter on equivalence. But an equivalence being an off-shoot of modulation, here are a few clichés which illustrate the principle of modulation:

joli comme un *coeur*:	pretty as a *picture*
laid comme un *pou*:	ugly as *sin*
sage comme une *image*:	as good as *gold*
avoir d'autres *chats à fouetter*:	to have other *fish to fry*
boire comme un *trou*:	to drink like a *fish*
couper l'herbe sous les pieds de quelqu'un:	*to pull the rug from* under someone's feet
fumer comme un *pompier*:	to smoke like a *chimney*
pleuvoir *des cordes*:	to rain *cats and dogs*

Grammatical modulations

The following are only a sampler of modulations which can take place at the grammatical level. Like word modulations these are compulsory, since they are set by grammatical rules and usage.

Preposition modulations

Two languages may differ in the way they view things right down to the use of prepositions.

Let's examine the following sentence in French. Translating it literally without any modulation on prepositions would result in barbarisms:

L'homme *de* la rue qui voyage *dans* le métro se met en colère *contre* tout retard des trains.

In English one sees a man as being *in* the street rather than *of* the street, as traveling *on* the subway instead of *in* the subway and being angry *with* delays, certainly not *against* them!

A few other examples for good measure:

un enfant *aux* yeux bleus:	a child *with* blue eyes
une personne *sur* trois:	one person *out of* three
à l'émission de ce soir:	*on* tonight's program
en moyenne:	*on* average
par pure chance:	*out of* sheer luck
consulter *sur* rendez-vous:	to see (a patient) *by* appointment
envoyer *par* la poste:	to send *through* the post
être *en* vacances:	to be *on* vacation
ouvrir *sur* le jardin:	to open *into* the garden
parler *du* nez:	to speak *through* one's nose
regarder *vers* l'avenir:	to look *to* the future
sauter *de* joie:	to jump *for* joy
aller *chez* le dentiste:	to go *to* the dentist
être *chez* le dentiste:	to be *at* the dentist's

(Note that French here makes no difference between motion and non-motion in its use of the preposition.)

Most preposition modulations are lexical and can be found in dictionaries. Many involve verbs which are constructed with one sort of preposition in French and another, different from its literal translation, in English:

comparer *à* (to compare *with* or *to*), être intéressé *par* (to be interested *in*) être surpris *de* (to be surprised *at*), dépendre *de* (to depend *on*), faire feu *sur* (to fire *at*), remercier *de* (to thank *for*), remplacer *par* (to replace *with*), se détacher *sur* (to stand out *against*), substituer *à* (to substitute *for*), veiller *sur* (to look *after),* etc.

Grammatical modulations involving verb tenses or modes

An example is the use of the present in English instead of the future in French after conjunctions of time (*quand, dès que, pendant que etc.*):

Quand tu *seras* prêt, nous pourrons partir.
When you *are* ready, we will be able to leave.

Or the use of the French conditional instead of the English present after "*au cas où*" (in case), French seeing it as a possibility warranting the use of the conditional:

> Au cas où tu *serais* absent, laisse la clé sous le paillasson
>
> In case you *are* not there, leave the key under the mat.

Or the use of the imperative in English to replace the infinitive in French for general directions:

> *Prendre* un oignon et trois carottes, les *éplucher* et les *mettre* dans la poêle avec un peu d'huile.
>
> *Take* one onion and three carrots, *peel* them and *put* them in a skillet with a little oil.

Expression of the concept of duration of an action with a link past-present or with a link past-remote past

This concept of duration of an action with a link past-present is expressed with the present and the use of additional words in French, such as "*il y a...que...*" or "*depuis'*. It is expressed with the present perfect progressive in English:

> Il y a longtemps *que je t'attends*. (or) *Je t'attends depuis* longtemps.
>
> *I have been waiting* for you *for* a long time.

The concept of duration with a link past-remote past is expressed with the imparfait in French and with the past perfect progressive in English:

> Il y *avait* longtemps *que je t'attendais.*
>
> *(or) Je t'attendais depuis* longtemps.
>
> I *had been waiting for* you *for* a long time

Grammatical modulations involving number

Some concepts will be singular in French (as determined by the article) whereas they are plural in English, as in the case of "*la famille, la police*", or vice-versa, as with "*the news*" (les nouvelles)

> Ces vacances ont été trop courtes :   *That vacation was* too short.
>
> The news *is* alarming: *Les* nouvelle*s sont* alarmante*s*.

Message modulations

Here are various categories of thoughts for message modulations along with some examples:

Positive-negative

Le président *ne se rend pas compte* de la gravité de la situation. The president *fails to realize* how serious the situation is.

Qu'il va y avoir une reprise de l'inflation *ne fait aucun doute*. That inflation is going to come back *is perfectly clear.*

Personne n'ignore que ces mesures ne sont qu'un expédient. *Everyone is fully aware* that these steps are only a makeshift arrangement.

Tu n'arrêtes pas de tousser: prends du sirop contre la toux! *You keep* coughing: take some cough syrup!

Cet article est bon marché, *à la différence de* celui que tu as choisi. This article is cheap, *unlike* the one you chose.

Active voice-passive voice

Ici *on parle français*:	*French spoken* here.
Ce livre *se trouve* partout en librairie	This book *is found/ can be purchased* in all bookstores.

Singular-plural

La police *a* appréhendé le voleur:	Tthe police *have* caught the thief.
Les hommes sont méchants:	*Man is* wicked.
*Des recherches von*t être nécessaires:	*Research is* going to be needed.

Abstract-concrete

Nous *avons appris* qu'il allait y avoir un orage à la radio:	We *heard* of an impending storm on the radio.
Parlez plus fort, je ne vous *comprends* pas	!Speak louder I can't *hear* you!
Savez-vous nager?	*Can* you swim?

Personal-impersonal

Il se peut que nos invités arrivent en retard	*Our guests may* arrive late
Il faut nous dépêcher	*We must* hurry
Il arrive qu'on se trompe	*One can* make a mistake

Opposite points of view

Pouvez-vous patienter?	*Are you in a hurry?*
Comme vous avez la figure rouge!	*How red your face looks!*

Tais-toi!   *Don't speak!*

Necessary and optional modulations

Message modulations may be necessary or optional just like transpositions.

- **Necessary** when diverging structures or usage demand it.

Many message modulations involve a switch from the active voice (favored by French) to the passive voice (favored by English). Grammatically French is more limited in its use of the passive voice than English, since an indirect object may never become a passive subject. English, on the other hand, is reluctant to use the indefinite pronoun "one", contrary to French:

> *On lui promit* de *prendre sa demande* en considération.
> *He was promised* to *have his request taken* into consideration. (The modulation active to passive voice is the only possible solution.)

French use of pronominal verbs with an inanimate subject often has no counterpart in English except for the passive voice:

> En France les télécartes *se trouvent* dans tous les bureaux de tabac.
> In France phone cards *can be found* in all tobacco shops.

Other modulations may involve metalinguistics, usage rather than grammar:

> *J'ai appris* le résultat des élections *par* le journal.
> *I read* the results of the election *in* the newspaper. (Abstract to concrete.)
> L'hôtel *affiche complet*   The hotel *is booked out.*

- **Optional** when modulation is only one way of translating the message.

> **Elle *n'a pas cessé* de me regarder pendant tout le trajet**
> This sentence can be translated three ways:
> 1. She did not stop looking at me during the whole trip (literal)
> 2. She *kept* watching me during the whole trip (modulation negative-positive)
> 3. She looked at me *continuously/ incessantly/ without stopping* during the whole trip (transposition verb-adverb).

Modulation with transposition

Modulation can be closely interrelated with transposition.

This is true of all verbal expressions which take one auxiliary in one language and another in the second language, expressions such as *avoir* chaud, froid, faim, soif, sommeil, raison, de la chance *etc.*: *to be* hot, cold, hungry, thirsty, sleepy, right, lucky etc. They require a modulation active voice - passive voice as well as a transposition noun - adjective.

> Ce chanteur *a* beaucoup de *succès*: This singer *is* very *popular.*
> Vous *avez* de la *chance*: You *are lucky* (transposition-modulation)
> as opposed to: *You're in* luck (modulation only).

Other examples:

> *Autrement dit*, cela ne t'intéresse pas: I*n other words* you're not interested.
> Louis XIV vécut *jusqu'à un âge avancé*: Louis XIV lived *to be very old.*
> *Quelles que soient* ses opinions politiques on ne peut rester insensible au problème du chômage: *Regardless of* your political opinions you cannot remain insensitive to the problem of unemployment.

Exercices: **La Modulation**

Lorsque deux langues expriment le même concept ou le même message selon un angle ou un point de vue différent, on parle de modulation. La modulation ne nécessite pas un changement de catégories grammaticales comme la transposition, mais plutôt un changement de catégories de pensée: par exemple la langue aborde le concept d'un point de vue concret ou abstrait, du point de vue de la cause ou de l'effet, du moyen ou du résultat. Elle considère une partie au lieu d'un tout, ou une partie à la place d'une autre partie, etc.

On trouve des modulations en anglais et en français à trois niveaux:

- *au niveau des mots et expressions nominales ou verbales dans des unités de traduction (groupes de mots qui ne peuvent pas être dissociés les uns des autres). Ce genre de modulation est figé et se trouve dans les dictionnaires bilingues.*
- *au niveau de la grammaire (usage également figé et consacré par les règles de grammaire).*
- *au niveau du message (ce type de modulation peut être nécessaire ou facultatif). Il est plus complexe et requiert l'ingéniosité du traducteur.*

A. La Modulation de termes

I. La modulation d'unités lexicales
Essayez de retrouver la modulation en anglais pour les unités lexicales suivantes.

Un ayant-droit; une carte de visite professionnelle; un contribuable; des cours de rattrapage; une date butoir; dédouaner des marchandises;. un mal-entendant; un mal-voyant; un numéro vert; un paradis fiscal; un parc d'attractions; le parrainage; des petits-enfants; une plus-value; un (téléphone) portable; un sans-abri; un sans-papiers; un tapis roulant; un test d'orientation; un vélo tous terrains (VTT).

II. La modulation de termes en contexte

Traduisez les phrases suivantes en faisant une modulation sur le ou les mots en italique.

1. Tu te trompes, ce n'est pas la *bonne* clé.
2. Mon patron est un *gros* fumeur.
3. Désirez-vous votre steak *saignant* ou *à point*?
4. Les exercices de notre livre de travaux pratiques sont d'un niveau *supérieur* plutôt que *moyen*.
5. Pendant la saison *creuse* il est possible d'obtenir des tarifs avantageux dans les grands hôtels de la Côte d'Azur.
6. Aux heures *de pointe* la circulation en ville est un véritable cauchemar.
7. L'usine utilise une technologie *de pointe*.
8. L'acteur avait oublié une partie de son *texte*.
9. Il n'y a de *distribution* de courrier ni le dimanche ni les jours fériés.
10. La *fraude fiscale* est un problème de nos sociétés modernes.
11. Quand nous avons fait cette suggestion au chef de service pour améliorer la productivité, il nous a ri *au nez*.
12. Avant l'utilisation du produit veuillez lire soigneusement *le mode d'emploi*.
13. La production se règle par la loi de *l'offre* et de la demande.
14. Le fournisseur n'ayant pas respecté les délais de livraison, le client a déclaré qu'il y avait *rupture* de contrat.
15. Les *droits* de douane ont été abolis entre tous les pays de l'Union Européenne.
16. La situation n'est pas désespérée: persévérez. *De mon côté* je vais voir ce que je peux faire pour vous venir en aide.

III. La modulation de locutions verbales

Traduisez les phrases suivantes en faisant une modulation sur les verbes en italique.

1. Est-ce que tu *as* déjà *pris* une décision?

2. Si nous prenons cette route, nous *gagnerons* du temps.

3. Cette vieille photo ne lui *rend* vraiment pas justice.

4. Au lieu de *faire la queue* pour aller voir un film idiot, il vaudrait mieux *faire une promenade* dans le parc.

5. Pour le désarmer, *fais*-lui un joli sourire!

6. Dans le noir je heurtai quelque chose et *poussai* un cri.

7. L'orateur *prononça* son discours d'une voix monotone.

8. Le comité est chargé de *réunir* les fonds nécessaires pour le projet.

9. Le P.D.G. *a établi* une comparaison entre le chiffre d'affaire de l'année dernière et celui de cette année.

10. Les autorités compétentes vont vous *délivrer* un passeport.

11. Si vous avez été victime d'une agression, allez *porter* plainte au commissariat de police.

12. Les pays membres de L'Union Européenne veulent *resserrer* les liens qui les unissent.

13. Les représentants des syndicats et du patronat ont *jeté les bases* d'un accord durable.

14. Ces derniers temps un fossé *s'est creusé* entre les deux pays qui affecte de façon négative leurs relations diplomatiques.

15. Les politiciens *commettent* une grave erreur en ne tenant aucun compte de la majorité silencieuse.

16. Le service de publicité assure que le nouveau produit va *connaître* un gros succès.

B. La Modulation grammaticale

I. La modulation de prépositions liées à des substantifs ou à des pronoms

Traduisez les phrases suivantes en faisant une modulation sur les prépositions en italique.

1. Les nouvelles *à* la radio sont catastrophiques.

2. Les trains en France sont toujours *à* l'heure.

3. C'est *à* moi de trouver une solution à ce problème.

4. Vous voyez la maison *aux* volets rouges là-bas? C'est la mienne.

5. Il y avait un tableau de maître *au* mur de la chambre.

6. Il lui a fait sa demande en mariage *à* genoux.

7. *A* l'avenir il faudra que tu fasses plus attention.

8. Il est exactement 10 heures et quart *à* ma montre.

9. Napoléon est resté *au* pouvoir pendant quinze ans.

10. Nous ne savons que faire: *d'*un côté nous ne pouvons pas demander au patron de s'arrêter de fumer et *de* l'autre nous ne voulons pas subir les effets nocifs de ses cigarettes.

11. Pouvez-vous m'indiquer le chemin *du* musée d'Orsay?

12. Il faut voir Paris *de* nuit.

13. Lis donc ce roman *de* Stendhal!

14. Son frère est plus âgé que lui *de* 3 ans.

15. Doit-on se fier à l'opinion de l'homme *de* la rue?

16. Entre 1939 et 1945 presque tous les pays du globe étaient *en* guerre.

17. La secrétaire est actuellement *en* congé de maladie.

18. Il lui semblait qu'elle avait le visage *en* feu.

19. La maison vend uniquement *sur* catalogue.

20. Nous n'avons qu'une chance *sur* plusieurs millions de gagner à la loterie.

21. J'aimerais attirer votre attention *sur* un détail.

22. Il fallut faire le trajet à pied *sous* la pluie.

23. Pour contrôler la maladie le malade doit se mettre *au* régime..

24. Faisons-le *par* devoir sinon *par* intérêt propre.

25. L'oiseau pénétra dans la chambre *par* la fenêtre qui était grande ouverte.

26. Es-tu toujours en colère *contre* moi?

27. Je suis prêt à parier dix *contre* un que tu te trompes.

28. Ça se voit que vous n'avez jamais travaillé *dans* une ferme.

29. Ne bois pas *dans* ce verre, il n'a pas été lavé!

30. J'étais *hors de* moi.

31. A trente ans il vit toujours *chez* ses parents.

32. Certains d'*entre* vous se demandent pourquoi cette réunion a été organisée.

33. Il va falloir mettre cet enfant *sous* antibiotiques pendant deux semaines.

34. La guerre d'indépendance américaine a eu lieu *sous* le règne de Louis XVI.

II. La modulation de prépositions liées à des verbes

Traduisez les phrases suivantes en faisant une modulation sur les prépositions en italique.

1. Je vous remercie *d*'avoir pensé à moi.

2. *De* quoi parlez-vous?

3. Ayez pitié *de* moi!

4. Etes-vous content *de* votre nouvelle voiture?

5. Cet enfant tient *de* son père, c'est évident.

6. Inscrivez-vous dès maintenant *aux* cours d'été.

7. Le dîner a été superbe: nous avons commencé *par* des huîtres et nous avons fini *par* une mousse glacée aux framboises.

8. Ma fille a été opérée *de* l'appendicite le mois dernier.

9. L'un des devoirs des enfants est de veiller *sur* leurs parents lorsque ceux-ci sont incapacités par l'âge.

10. La décision ne dépend que *du* chef de service.

11. T'intéresses-tu vraiment *à* tes études?

12. Je suis fâché *contre* Jean parce qu'il a ri *de* mes problèmes.

13. Il est temps de remplacer le canapé du salon *par* quelque chose de plus moderne.

14. Nous avons été surpris *de* sa violente réaction.

15. Pour les régimes sans cholestérol il est préférable de substituer des huiles végétales *au* beurre.

16. Les tourelles sombres du manoir se détachaient *sur* un ciel d'orage.

17. Si l'on compare ce tableau *de* Lancret *à* celui-ci *de* Watteau, l'influence du maître *sur* le disciple est nette.

III. La modulation de temps et de modes

Traduisez les phrases suivantes en faisant les modulations nécessaires sur les temps ou les modes des verbes.

1. Au cas où l'ordinateur *tomberait en panne* au cours de l'année suivant l'achat, la garantie couvrirait entièrement les frais de réparation.

2. La voisine a accepté d'arroser les plantes pendant que *nous serons* en vacances.

3. Tant que *vous refuserez* d'accepter le compromis, il sera impossible de parvenir à un accord.

4. Aussitôt que *vous aurez terminé* vos devoirs, les enfants, vous pourrez regarder la télé.

5. Je transmettrai votre message à Jean lorsqu'*il sera* de retour.

6. *Il y a* longtemps *que je me pose* cette question.

7. *Il y avait* des années *que* Cendrillon *attendait* son prince charmant.

8. Il n'est guère probable que *tu te sois trompé.*

9. Nous regrettons infiniment que *vous ne puissiez* venir.

10. Vous voulez que *nous fassions* le devoir écrit pour lundi?

11. Directives pour retirer de l'argent d'un distributeur automatique de billets: 1. *introduire* la carte , 2. *taper* le code secret, 3. *choisir* le compte à débiter, 4. *taper* le montant désiré, 5. *attendre* que la banque traite la demande, 6. *retirer* l'argent.

C. La Modulation de message

Traduisez les phrases suivantes en faisant une modulation sur les passages en italique. Si possible indiquez de quel changement de catégorie de pensée il s'agit.

1. *Mets le couvert!*

2. *Vous désirez?* [situation: le vendeur au client au magasin]

3. *Ce dessin te plaît?*

4. Qu'est-ce qui *ne va pas?*

5. *On m'a dit* que tu me cherchais.

6. C'est l'heure! *Rendez* vos devoirs! [situation: le professeur aux étudiants à la fin d'une interrogation écrite]

7. Ce modèle de chaussure *a beaucoup de succès*.

8. *Vous avez un rire communicatif!*

9. *As-tu encore mal au genou?*

10. Il faut aller au supermarché: on *n'a plus de lait* à la maison.

11. *Avez-vous un emploi* ou *êtes-vous toujours étudiant*?

12. *Ne quittez pas!* Je vous passe le responsable du service. [situation: au bureau]

13. Ma soeur est ravie: *on vient de l'embaucher*.

14. *J'ai appris par* le journal qu'il y avait une grève des chemins de fer.

15. Pourriez-vous m'expliquer ceci encore une fois? *Je ne vous suis plus!*

16. Après une telle mésaventure il serait préférable *que vous ne vous fassiez pas remarquer* pendant quelque temps.

17. Avec l'essor prodigieux de la science et de la technologie des dernières décennies notre conception de l'avenir *se trouve profondément modifiée*.

18. Le candidat à l'élection *ne s'était pas rendu compte* que les priorités des électeurs *avaient changé*.

19. La situation économique a tendance à s'améliorer. *Il n'en reste pas moins* que le chômage stagne à un niveau trop élevé pour être acceptable.

20. Je songerai à changer d'emploi quand *il se présentera une offre* qui en vaille la peine

21. Nous sortons *tous les jours* nous promener.

D. La Transposition-modulation

Faites une transposition-modulation (changement de catégories grammaticales plus changement de catégories de pensée) pour la traduction des phrases suivantes.

1. Où peut-on se procurer ce produit?

2. C'est un chanteur qui a beaucoup de succès en ce moment.

3. Vous n'avez vraiment pas de chance!
4. Je n'ai pas sommeil: j'ai trop froid aux pieds.
5. Tiens, il y a une panne de courant!

Chapter 10   **Equivalence**

What is equivalence?

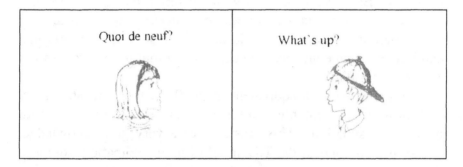

Some linguists question the validity of equivalence as a category and consider it an off-shoot of modulation.

Equivalence is indeed a modulation, given the fact that it views a concept from a distinctive angle, often as an image which expresses the particular values of the language, or a reflection of particular trends common to a linguistic group.

However, an equivalence is also a set message, something which cannot be altered and must be used as such.

An equivalence is a special type of modulation: it is a set message modulation. The translator will recognize the need for an equivalence from the situation which has brought about the message. It is therefore inseparable from its context.

For instance the meaning of the simple phrase "*C'est à moi*" will be dependent on the situation which has elicited it. "*C'est à moi de jouer*" (*It's my turn*) translates differently from "*C'est à moi de* trouver une solution à ce problème" (*It's up to me* to find a solution to this problem), or even from "Ne touche pas! *C'est à moi!*" (Don't touch, *that's mine!*").

An equivalence must replace a global message. It encompasses a translation unit whose elements cannot be translated separately. Failure to realize this would lead to nonsense or mistranslation. The literal translation of a colloquial expression such as "Notre chanson a eu *un succès boeuf*" would undoubtedly bring a puzzled look on the face of an Anglophone until realized that it just means *a tremendous success*. Conversely, trying to see two translation units in the English phrase *a home run*, taken in its figurative sense as in "the new product was a definite *homerun*", would lead to a mistranslation. "Une course à la maison" just won't do, and the solution lies in an equivalent concept, something in the order of *un succès incontestable*.

To come up with an equivalent in the T.L., the translator must think of what is commonly said under the same circumstances, and in the same situation. This presupposes a very good knowledge both of the S.L. and of the T.L. in all of their idiomatic resources. The result can be stylistically and structurally very different from the S.L. since the message in an equivalence is never equal to the sum of its parts. Messages requiring the use of an equivalence in translation are an expression of conformity with the standard formulas, idioms and catch phrases of a linguistic group. They would be meaningless if translated literally, since they are steeped in the culture and traditions of that particular language.

We find equivalences in the following categories of situations.

Exclamations and reflex-formulas

These are ready-made words or groups of words used in set situations to express particular feelings and emotions.
For instance:

when surprised: Ça par exemple! Ça alors!: You don't say! Unbelievable!
                    Tiens!:   Hey!/ Look!

in disbelief:	Voyons!:	Come on!/ Are you kidding?
	Allons donc!:	Nonsense!
annoyed	Dis donc!:	Hey1
in denial:	Pensez vous!:	Come off it!
in agreement	D'accord!:	O.K./agreed
defiant:	Et alors!:	So what!
in pain:	Aïe!:	Ouch!
thankful:	Dieu merci!:	Thank goodness! Thank God!
appreciative:	Formidable!:	Great! Super!

etc.

In this category belong all popular expletives from the meekest (*Flute! nuts! Zut! darn!*) to the strongest.

Prop words

Prop words are words used in conversation to add nuances to the general meaning of a message. Very often these are adverbs such as :

donc , used to soften any request: "Venez *donc* diner chez nous" "*Why don't you* come and have dinner with us?", or to show impatience "Que faites vous *donc?*" "What *on earth* are you doing?"

bien, used for emphasis: "Tu vas *bien* prendre un petit verre avec moi!" "*Aren't you* going to have a drink with me?"

alors used to show impatience: "*Alors*, vous vous dépêchez?" "Are you hurrying *or not*?"

Or they can be locutions such as *n'est-ce pas*? used to elicit approval or confirmation: "Vous me préviendrez, *n'est-ce pas*?" "You will let me know, *won't you*?"

Greetings and letter closings

Greetings and forms of address are standard expressions of conformity to social protocol and usage. Their translation must reflect the tonality of the original.

Bonjour!: Hello! *or* Good morning! Good afternoon!

Salut!: Hi! *or* So long! depending on whether one is coming or leaving)
A bientôt! A un de ces jours! A la prochaine!: See you soon! *or* I'll see you!
Enchanté de faire votre connaissance!: Pleased to meet you!
Bonnes fêtes de fin d'année!: Happy holidays!

Follow the same rules for epistolary customs, opening and closing formulas such as:

Je vous prie d'agréer, Monsieur/ Madame/ Mademoiselle, l'expression de mes sentiments distingués: Yours sincerely.
Dans l'attente de vous lire..: We look forward to hearing from you.
Veuillez croire, Monsieur, à l'assurance de nos sentiments dévoués: We remain at your service.
Bien des choses de ma part à...: Please give my best to...
Grosses bises: hugs and kisses.

Clichés and idioms

We find these hackneyed phrases under many guises:
In adverbial expressions

après coup: after the fact
dans une certaine mesure: to a certain extent
de toutes ses forces: with all one's might
étant donné que: in view of the fact that...

In nominal expressions

une affaire classée: case closed
un cercle vicieux: a catch 22 situation
un délit d'initié: insider trading
le démon de midi: the seven year itch
un feu de paille: a flash in the pan
une fièvre de cheval: a raging fever
une formation préalable: prior training
un gros mot: a four letter word
Monsieur tout le monde: the man in the street
le mot de la fin: the punch line
un moulin à paroles: a chatterbox
une occasion rêvée: a golden opportunity
un panier percé: a spendthrift
une planche de salut: a lifesaver
le premier venu: just anybody
un produit haut de gamme: a top of the line product

un rire communicatif:	a contagious laugh
le secret de polichinelle:	everybody's secret
une solution de rechange:	an alternative solution
une tête de linotte:	a scatterbrain
un train d'enfer:	a hectic pace
un vieux de la vieille:	an old timer
une voie sans issue:	a dead end

In verbal expressions

Many of these use food imagery, an essential preoccupation for the French:

avoir du pain sur la planche:	to have a lot to do
battre à plate couture:	to beat to a frazzle
être dans de beaux draps:	to be in hot water
faire bouillir la marmite:	to bring home the bacon
mettre les bouchées doubles:	to work twice as hard
ne pas se sentir dans son assiette:	to feel under the weather
s'occuper de ses oignons:	to mind one's own business
tomber dans les pommes:	to faint.[1]

Slang and slang expressions

The French "*langue verte*" or slang is a language by itself and many of its colorful expressions find equivalents in English slang:

C'est pas de blague?:	No kidding?
Il a piqué une rogne:	He got hot under the collar.
Les flics ont fini par l'épingler:	The cops finally nailed him.[2]

Proverbs and axioms

In striking little pronouncements proverbs contain the popular wisdom of nations, essentially the same the world over, and consequently most French proverbs do have equivalents in English. We will just list two here:

Il faut hurler avec les loups.   When in Rome do as the Romans do.

---

[1] For an extended list of such expressions please refer to the appendix under dictionaries of French idioms, colloquialisms and slang, pp.279-80, and 286.

[2] See appendix pp.279-80 and 286 for dictionaries on French slang.

Honni soit qui mal y pense!   Evil to him who evil thinks!

Official signs and warnings

Signs and warnings constitute ideal material for equivalences, for
they sum up a message in a stereotypic situation:

attention à la peinture:	wet paint
fermeture pour cause de travaux:	closed for renovation
inauguration du magasin:	grand opening
priorité à droite:	yield to the right
travaux en cours:	men at work

and so on.

References to a common socio-cultural heritage

There is a very vast reservoir consisting of references to sociocultural facts well known to the linguistic group of the S.L., people
who share a common education, a common history and culture, and
common institutions; but allusions cryptic to the speakers of the
T.L. unless they, too, are familiar with the culture and civilization
of the S.L.   In any case, the translator, in order to catch their
meaning will have to be very well acquainted with French
civilization.

References to *les personnes du troisième âge* (senior citizens),
l'hexagone (France, whose shape is hexagonal), *l'hémicycle* (the
house of representatives shaped in a semi-circle), *la Côte d'Azur*
(the French Riviera, famous for its azure blue sky and waters), *le
débarquement* (the allied landing of D day), *les trente glorieuses*
(the economic boom of the 30 years which followed World War
II), *Marianne* (the representation of the French Republic as a young
woman found in every French town hall -actress Catherine
Deneuve sat for the bust-), *la ville lumière* (Paris, the city of lights)
to name but a few, along with covert allusions to a literary heritage,
such as "C'est un vrai *Harpagon*" or "Nous ne sommes que des
roseaux pensants" are all meaningful to people living in France but

constitute a sort of coded language which needs deciphering for an English speaking public.[3]

> **Equivalence as a translation technique is often resorted to in the translation of dialogues and plays (for exclamations, reflex-formulas and colloquialisms) as well as in the translation of ads, newspaper and magazine articles which make frequent references to socio-cultural facts and situations.**

---

[3] Beginners may find some help in the dictionaries on French cultural references listed in the appendix, p. 280.

Exercices: L'Equivalence

Exclamations, formules-réflexe, expressions idiomatiques et argotiques, clichés, proverbes, avis officiels, formules de salutation, allusions culturelles figées nécessitent des équivalences dans la L.A.

La difficulté pour le traducteur consiste à savoir reconnaître la partie du texte qui nécessite une équivalence comme un message global, comme une unité de traduction dont les éléments sont indissociables les uns des autres, et de ce fait, ne peuvent être traduits séparément.

A. Les Diverses Catégories d'équivalence

Traduisez les phrases suivantes en donnant une équivalence pour les expressions en italique.

I. Formules-réflexe

Dans l'exercice suivant, laissez-vous guider par la situation et par l'émotion que vous essayez d'exprimer (cette émotion est donnée entre crochets)

1. *Aïe*, je me suis fait mal ! [expressing pain]
2. *Dites donc*, vous ne pouvez pas faire attention, vous venez de renverser du jus d'orange sur ma veste! [expressing annoyance]
3. *Ça par exemple,* il a réussi à son examen! [expressing surprise]
4. *Allons donc*, tu ne vas tout de même pas me faire croire cette histoire! [expressing disbelief]
5. Ça te dérange, *et alors*? [expressing challenge]
6. Attendez une minute: vous *voyez bien* que je suis occupé! [expressing annoyance]
7. *Rien à faire*, il refuse absolument de venir. [expressing giving up]
8. Tu crois pouvoir me battre au tennis? Essaie *un peu*! [expressing defiance]

9. *Ça suffit*, les enfants, arrêtez de vous chamailler! [expressing impatience and authority]

10. *Vivement* les vacances pour que je puisse enfin me reposer! [expressing a wish]

11. Tu ne veux vraiment pas venir avec nous au cinéma, *tant pis pour toi*! [expressing lack of interest]

II. Clichés

1. Vos enfants grandissent *à vue d'oeil!*

2. Ecoute, arrête de parler *à tort et à travers*!

3. Ce gosse est insupportable, il réclame des jouets *à tout bout de champ*!

4. Tu te plains sans arrêt, tu ne fais pas ton travail, et *par-dessus le marché* tu es exigeant avec tout le monde.

5. *Par les temps qui courent* il ne fait pas bon d'avoir sur soi beaucoup d'argent liquide.

6. La mère et la fille se ressemblent *comme deux gouttes d'eau*.

7. Cet ensemble vous va *comme un gant*.

8. Nous avons acheté ce terrain *pour trois fois rien*.

9. C'est un monsieur *comme il faut*.

10. Ça ne m'ennuie pas *le moins du monde* de vous déposer chez vous.

11. *Chacun à son goût*.

III. Expressions idiomatiques

1. Pose la question à ton patron *pour en avoir le coeur net*!

2. Aujourd'hui, impossible de sortir, *je regrette, je ne suis pas dans mon assiette*.

3. Jacques Dupont? Non, ce nom *ne me dit rien*.

4. C'est difficile, mais *il faut faire contre mauvaise fortune bon coeur*.

5. *Trouvez-vous quelque chose à redire à* mon exposé?

6. Georges *a le verbe facile*, mais moi pas.

7. Nous ne nous en sortirons pas, c'est *un cercle vicieux*.

8. J'ai un voyage d'affaires le mois prochain à Paris: c'est *une occasion rêvée* pour aller découvrir les grands restaurants parisiens.

IV. Avis officiels

1. *Défense de fumer.*
2. *Défense de jeter des ordures.*
3. *Ne pas se pencher par la portière.*
4. *Ne pas marcher sur les pelouses.*
5. *Réservé à la clientèle.*
6. *Fermeture annuelle.*
7. *Passage interdit.*
8. *Sens unique.*
9. *Voitures d'occasion.*
10. *A louer.*

V. Souhaits, salutations, excuses et formules épistolaires

1. *Enchanté!*
2. *Bon voyage!*
3. *A la prochaine!*
4. *Tous mes souhaits pour un prompt rétablissement!*
5. *Je vous prie d'agréer, Monsieur, l'expression de mes sentiments distingués.*
6. *Nous vous présentons toutes nos excuses. -Mais je vous en prie!*
7. *Je t'embrasse affectueusement.*
8. *Veuillez me faire parvenir* un exemplaire de votre brochure sur les croisières en Méditerranée.
9. *Ayez la gentillesse de me rappeler au bon souvenir de* vos parents.

VI. Argot et expressions argotiques

Le mot standard en français est indiqué entre crochets, essayez de retrouver l'équivalent argotique en anglais.

1. Depuis que son *mec* [petit ami] l'a *plaquée* [quittée] elle ne fait que *chialer* [pleurer].
2. Les *flics* [policiers] l'ont *flanqué* [mis] en *taule* [prison].
3. Je n'ai *pigé que dalle* [rien compris] à ce *polar* [roman policier].
4. Ne te *fais pas de bile* [ne t'inquiète pas], c'est *du gâteau* [c'est très facile].

5. Ce *zigoto* [cet individu] a un *sacré culot* [a beaucoup d'insolence] pour *faire du grabuge* [faire une scène] comme ça en pleine nuit.

6. Tu *déménages* [tu es fou]! Ne me *pique* [vole] pas mon *bouquin* [livre]!

7. *Casse-toi* [va-t-en] , *pauvre con* [pauvre idiot]!

VII. Proverbes et dictons

1. Venez donc à notre soirée samedi! *Plus on est de fous, plus on rit.*

2. Je peux bien me permettre un petit écart, *une fois n'est pas coutume.*

3. Il faut choisir: tu ne *peux pas avoir le beurre et l'argent du beurre.*

4. Ne soyez pas imprudents. *Si vous misez tout sur le même cheval,* vous risquez d'*y laisser votre chemise.*

VIII. Allusions culturelles

L'explication des mots en italique est donnée entre crochets, trouvez l'équivalent anglais

1. *La belle époque* [les années 1900] en France a été une période d'insouciance et de prospérité pour les classes aisées.

2. Au sortir de la première guerre mondiale, *pendant les années folles,* [1920-26] la mode pour les femmes fut aux cheveux courts et aux robes sans corset.

3. *La pucelle d'Orléans* [Jeanne d'Arc], *le vert galant* [Henri IV], *le roi soleil* {Louis XIV}, *l'ogre de la Corse* [Napoléon] *et l'homme du 18 juin* [De Gaulle] comptent parmi les figures les plus hautes en couleur de toute l'histoire de France.

4. A la veille de la Révolution de 1789 Camille Desmoulins ameuta le peuple de Paris au Palais Royal en lui faisant craindre que le roi préparait *une Saint Barthélémy* [terrible massacre de protestants par les catholiques au 16e siècle] des patriotes.

5. En période de conflit social, l'atmosphère au *Palais Bourbon* [siège de l'assemblée nationale française] est fiévreuse.

6. L'essor économique des années soixante et soixante-dix a profité à *la génération née après la guerre* [la deuxième guerre mondiale].

7. *L'hexagone* [quel pays a la forme d'un hexagone?] arrive en tête des destinations touristiques à l'échelle de la planète.

8. Si vous le voulez bien, *revenons à nos moutons* [phrase célèbre d'une comédie du Moyen Age, *La Farce de Maître Pathelin*]!

9. *La guerre de Sécession* a opposé les états du nord aux états du sud en Amérique sur la question de l'esclavage de 1861 à 1865.

B. Les Locutions verbales idiomatiques

Retrouvez les expressions idiomatiques équivalentes en anglais (la signification des expressions idiomatiques françaises est donnée entre crochets).

1. arriver comme un cheveu sur la soupe [arriver à un mauvais moment]
2. avoir la gueule de bois [être malade après avoir trop bu]
3. avoir la langue bien pendue [parler beaucoup et facilement]
4. avoir quelque chose pour une bouchée de pain [pour presque rien]
5. ne pas avoir un rond [ne pas avoir d'argent]
6. broyer du noir [être déprimé]
7. couper les cheveux en quatre [chercher des difficultés]
8. dormir à poings fermés [dormir d'un profond sommeil]
9. en avoir plein le dos [en avoir assez, être fatigué de tout]
10. être aux anges [être absolument ravi]
11. être dans ses petits souliers [être dans une situation difficile]
12. être du pareil au même [être exactement la même chose]
13. faire l'école buissonnière [manquer l'école et aller se promener]
14. faire le grand saut [passer dans l'autre monde]
15. faire quelque chose en cinq sec [faire quelque chose très vite]
16. jouer double jeu [être hypocrite]
17. manger sur le pouce [manger quelque chose de simple très vite]
18. mettre de l'eau dans son vin [s'accommoder d'une situation]
19. mettre du beurre dans ses épinards [profiter financièrement d'une situation]
20. mettre les pieds dans le plat [intervenir maladroitement]
21. ne pas savoir sur quel pied danser [ne pas savoir quoi faire pour arranger la situation]

22. ne faire ni chaud ni froid à quelqu'un ["ça ne me fait ni chaud ni froid" = ça m'est égal]

23. parler à tort et à travers [dire des choses qui n'ont pas de sens]

24. passer l'éponge [pardonner une offense]

25. perdre les pédales [devenir fou]

26. promettre monts et merveilles [faire des promesses impossibles à tenir]

27. rendre à quelqu'un la monnaie de sa pièce [se venger de quelqu'un]

28. retourner le couteau dans la plaie [aggraver les choses]

29. se mettre sur son trente et un [mettre ses plus beaux habits]

30. s'occuper de ses oignons [s'occuper de ses propres affaires]

31. se porter comme un charme [être en excellente santé]

32. tourner autour du pot [éviter d'aller à l'essentiel]

33. travailler/ se battre pour le roi de Prusse [ne tirer aucun avantage d'une situation]

34. vendre la mèche [révéler le secret]

35. vouloir décrocher la lune [vouloir l'impossible]

36. y perdre son latin [ne rien comprendre]

C. Les Locutions verbales idiomatiques (suite)

Faites correspondre les locutions verbales idiomatiques suivantes avec leur équivalent anglais.

1. jouer avec le feu   ____ to add fuel to the fire

2. vivre au jour le jour   ____ to shout at the top of one's lungs

3. remuer ciel et terre   ____ to take something literally

4. prendre quelqu'un en grippe ____ to sleep late

5. faire d'une pierre deux coups ____ to bite off more than you can chew

6. passer une nuit blanche   ____ to court danger

7. être né coiffé   ____ to kill two birds with one stone

8. en avoir le coeur net   _____ to live from hand to mouth

9. faire la grasse matinée   _____ to take a dislike to someone

10. dormir à la belle étoile   _____ to spend a sleepless night

11. crier à tue-tête   _____ to catch someone in the act

12. prendre quelque chose au pied de la lettre_____ to have been born under a

lucky star

13. prendre ses jambes à son cou   _____ to move heaven and earth

14. prendre quelqu'un sur le fait _____ to take to one's heels

15. verser de l'huile sur le feu   _____ to walk out on a job

16. tuer la poule aux oeufs d'or   _____ to get to the bottom of things

17. avoir les yeux plus grands que le ventre _____ to kill the goose with the

golden eggs

18. rendre son tablier   _____ to sleep outdoors

D. Les Proverbes

Retrouvez les équivalents anglais des proverbes français suivants.

Il faut savoir laver son linge sale en famille.
Une hirondelle ne fait pas le printemps.
Ne réveillez pas le chat qui dort.
Un malheur n'arrive jamais seul.
Il faut battre le fer pendant qu'il est chaud.
Mieux vaut tard que jamais.
Il y a loin de la coupe aux lèvres.

E. Les Proverbes (suite)

1. Faites correspondre les proverbes ou dictons de la colonne de droite avec ceux de la colonne de gauche.

1. Aide-toi le ciel t'aidera   _____ a rolling stone gathers no

moss

2. L'habit ne fait pas le moine   ____ the more, the merrier

3. Comme on fait son lit on se couche   ____ spare the rod and spoil the

                child

4. Un tiens vaut mieux que deux tu l'auras   ____ when in Rome, do as the

                Romans do

5. On ne peut pas avoir le beurre et   ____ don't count your chickens

 l'argent du beurre   before they hatch

6. Tel est pris qui croyait prendre   ____ catchers may find the tables

                turned

7. Qui aime bien, châtie bien   ____ when the cat is away, the

                mice will play

8. Oeil pour oeil, dent pour dent   ____ dead men tell no tales

9. Paris ne s'est pas fait en un jour   ____ tit for tat

10.Qui se ressemble, s'assemble   ____ you can't have your cake and

                eat it too

11. Plus on est de fous, plus on rit   ____ you must not put the cart

                before the horse

12. Quand on veut, on peut   ____ the devil you know is better

                than the one you don't

13. A quelque chose malheur est bon   ____ once bitten, twice shy

14. A trompeur, trompeur et demi   ____ as you sow, so shall you reap

15. De deux maux il faut savoir choisir   ____ a bird in the hand is

 le moindre   worth two in the bush

16. Pierre qui roule n'amasse pas mousse   ____ half a loaf is better than no

                bread at all

17. Loin des yeux, loin du coeur   ____ birds of a feather flock

                together

18. Il faut hurler avec les loups   ____ where there's a will there's a

                way

19. Quand on parle du loup, on en voit   _____ what goes around comes
    la queue   around

20. Chat échaudé craint l'eau froide   _____ out of sight, out of mind

21. Quand le chat n'est pas là, les souris   _____ heaven helps those who help
    dansent   themselves

22. Il ne faut pas vendre la peau de l'ours _____ you can't tell a book by its
    avant de l'avoir tué   cover

23. Il ne faut pas mettre la charrue devant _____ talk of the devil and
    les boeufs   he's sure to appear

24. Faute de grives on mange des merles   _____ Rome was not built in a day

25. Morte la bête, mort le venin   _____ it's a blessing in disguise

*2.   Parmi les traductions de proverbes de la section D et de la
section E relevez-en une qui soit:*

- *une traduction littérale*

- *une transposition*

- *une modulation*

- *une équivalence*

Chapter 11   Adaptation

What is adaptation?

quatre litres   one gallon

> **Adaptation, our last technique, is the furthest removed from literal translation. Rather than a definite technique, it is more of a bag of tricks translators have at their disposal when all else fails. Consequently, one can possibly consider it the least satisfactory of all translation techniques, since some loss is incurred in the rendition of the message.**
>
> **Unlike the other translation techniques which address structural problems, it addresses cultural ones.**

So far, the obstacles we have encountered were linguistic obstacles, either structural or semantic. There remains a more formidable category: metalinguistic obstacles, which go beyond the language and arise from cultural discrepancies between the S.L. and the T.L.

When one concept, linked to cultural factors, is untranslatable as such into the T.L. because it does not exist, or does not exist exactly in the same way, an adaptation must be resorted to.

The above picture gives an illustration of this last technique. The example of the four liters versus the gallon points to the lack of a common measuring system. What the translator can give then is an approximation, something that the speakers of the T.L. can understand and relate to.

Let us use a simile to better understand the purpose of adaptation. Suppose for a moment that you have undertaken the task of translating an African fable for the benefit of a remote Eskimo tribe. In this fable a silk-cotton tree plays a symbolic key role. Now in all likelihood the Eskimo language will have no equivalent for the tree since its very concept is unknown to the speakers of that language, and it will be up to you to come up with a solution to this problem. The silk cotton tree being important only inasmuch as it is a symbol, any tall bush growing on the tundra and known to your audience will serve the purpose. This, in essence, is what adaptation is all about: carrying a concept over and across the barriers of language and culture, trying to make sense out of something that is totally foreign to the linguistic group you are translating for.

Differences in geography, customs, conceptions of the world, values, institutions *etc.*, between nations, lead to appreciable difficulties when translating from one language to another, and the greater the divergence between the cultures, the greater the difficulty.

Even though English and French have had centuries of a closely interrelated history to prevent total incompatibility between their linguistic systems, there are still areas of major differences between the two. Common problems in translation arise from different greeting customs, such as the lack of the familiar form of address in English to render the French "*tu*"; or the physical ways of greeting people, from differences in honorific titles, epistolary etiquette, the delineation of time and space, to differences in money and measure units, meals, shops, occupations, and institutions, whether educational, social or political.

Linguistic deficiency and compensation

Let us first see how the structural problem created by the lack of a *tu* form in modern English may be compensated for in translation. Even though a verb like *tutoyer*, *se tutoyer* has no equivalent in the English speaking world, people still make a sharp distinction between those with whom they are on a familiar basis -family and friends- and those with whom they are not -superiors, strangers, mere acquaintances-. Consequently, one way of making the sentence "*Nous nous tutoyons maintenant*" understandable to an English speaking public might be "*We are now on a first name basis*", and one way of translating "*Viens-tu?*" when the speaker has just switched from a previous *vous* to show that the two are now friends, could possibly be "*Bob (or Johnny etc.), are you coming?*"

Adaptation in traditions, usages and institutions

Differences in greeting customs

Greetings often necessitate the use of adaptation in order to prevent misunderstanding or even mistranslation.

For instance, handshaking in Anglo-Saxon and French speaking countries follow different rules of etiquette. In the former, you shake someone's hand once only, when first introduced to that person. In France on the other hand, people would consider it very odd, if not downright rude or at least very informal, if you did not shake an acquaintance's hand each time upon meeting or parting. And thus "*Il me serra la main avec effusion*" may be translated as "*He greeted me warmly*" or "*We said an effusive good-bye*" depending on whether the handshake is an expression of greeting or leaving.

The custom of kissing for men of the same family or for long time friends is a Mediterranean one, not shared by Anglo-Saxon nations. Therefore in order not to send the wrong message a translator will have to change a sentence such as "*Les deux hommes se sont embrassés"* into *"The two men gave each other a hug."*

Differences in forms of address and titles

French is far more formal than English when it comes to forms of address and use of titles. *"Hello, Mrs. Smith!"* or just plain *"Hello!"* can be considered the equivalent of *"Bonjour Madame!"*, which certainly does not translate as *"Good morning, Lady!"*, the patronizing implication of the English phrase being far off the mark of the very polite French form of address.

Greeting formulas in letters follow the same pattern: *Dear Sir* to a person you do not know well or do not know at all becomes *Monsieur*. Honorific titles follow rules of their own. Use of the possessive is the norm for army and navy titles: *Mon général, Mon commandant, Mon lieutenant*; while political or administrative titles use the regular civilian title followed by the description of the office held: *Monsieur le président, Madame le juge, Monsieur le maire etc.*

University professors are never addressed as *Professeur X* but simply as *Monsieur* or *Madame*, and certainly never as *Docteur*, a title reserved for physicians, while *le professeur X* designates a teaching physician at a medical university, or just any teacher at the high school or college level.

Differences in measure units

Measure units may at times necessitate an adaptation. Depending on the public targeted and the context, a translator will have to debate whether or not to give an approximate conversion of French francs, or now euros, into dollars, kilometers into miles, kilos into pounds, or liters into quarts and gallons. The rule is: convert whenever this is considered essential to the readers' understanding. Obviously *"Il mesure un mètre quatre-vingt"* has to be rendered as *"He is six feet tall"*, *"Va me chercher un litre de lait"* as *"Go and get me a quart of milk"* and *"Le village le plus proche était à trois kilomètres de là"* as *"the nearest village was 2 miles away"*. Sometimes, however, keeping the S.L. measure unit may be preferable, to add local color to the message for instance, or to be accurate if dealing with a scientific translation.

Differences in the division of time and space

This becomes obvious in the way the two languages delineate the periods of the day for greeting purposes or for social use: "*Bonjour!*" can mean "*Good morning*" or "*Good afternoon*" depending on the time of day, and whereas *bonsoir* means *good evening*, *ce soir* refers to *tonight* and *la nuit dernière* to *last night*. The 24 hour clock is also scrupulously adhered to in public life, from the media and entertainment industry to train and plane schedules. References to "*Le journal télévisé de 20 heures*" or "*Le train partira à 21 heures 35*" have to be adapted for English speakers.

Even the delineation of weeks is at odds. The French like to illogically refer to a week's time as eight days and two weeks' time as fifteen days. Taking literally the sentence "*Je vais aller passer huit ou quinze jours à la campagne*" would indeed be a mistranslation. And not just week delineation but French ways of counting in cliché expressions are at variance with English usage. "Nous sommes sortis ensemble *deux ou trois fois* le mois dernier" is in fact the equivalent of "We went out *a couple of times* together last month" and "Je ne vais pas te le répéter *trente-six fois*" of "I am not going to repeat it to you *a hundred times*".

A French speaker will also use different bearings for space. "Le musée se trouve à deux *rues* d'ici" translates as "The museum is located two *blocks* from here" and "Vous trouverez les chaussures pour dames au *premier* étage" as "You will find ladies shoes on the *second* floor" since the first floor in the U.S. corresponds to the British *ground floor* or French *rez de chaussée*.

Differences in shops and stores

They do not always correspond either. A *charcuterie* is not quite a delicatessen, but rather, the shop of a pork butcher who very often doubles up as a caterer: there you can find not only pork chops, sausages, ham and cold cuts but also prepared dishes to take out as well as appetizers and salads. In a *bureau de tabac* newspapers, paperbacks, cigarettes can be purchased as well as lottery tickets, stamps and phone cards. And a *grande surface* will combine fish, dairy, meat, deli and bakery-pastry departments along with a liquor aisle, electric appliances, kitchen utensils and sometimes also books, lamps and articles of clothing.

Differences in meals

Let's now compare meals: *le petit déjeuner*, sometimes referred to in this country as *continental breakfast*, and an English type of *breakfast* can hardly be called similar. The difference is even greater between *le déjeuner*, traditionally the main three or four course meal in France, and *lunch*. Dinner, on the other hand is the main meal in Anglo-Saxon countries while *le diner* is very often nothing more than a light supper consisting of a soup, cold cuts and a quick dessert. How is one then to translate a sentence like *"Venez donc déjeuner chez nous dimanche?"* *"Why don't you come have dinner with us Sunday!"* seems the appropriate answer.

Translating the names of dishes in a country famed for its culinary inventiveness and savoir-faire is a very special problem. One way of dealing with it is simply to borrow. *Hors d'oeuvre, foie gras, mousse* and *champagne* have indeed passed into the English language. But unless one is looking for local color, adaptation is sometimes advisable and a *tarte aux pommes* may just have to become an apple pie.

Differences in occupations

Occupations in French and English speaking countries do not necessarily match. A *nanny* for instance is not a must in France, where day care centers for young mothers are both numerous and affordable, and therefore the concept has no real equivalent; although the term *baby sitter*, a recent borrowing, has replaced grandmothers or other relatives who traditionally took care of young children until the politics of economic change sent families in all directions. The function of a *concierge*, essentially a woman's job in Parisian apartment buildings, can hardly be construed as similar to the duties of a janitor or custodian. Brokers and *courtiers* do not cover the same realities since investments are a standard service offered by most French banks. *Les cadres*, an often used and vague collective denomination, encompasses technicians and engineers, as well as administrators, teachers, researchers, commercial agents and civil servants. According to the 1946 Parodi-Croizet decree: "are considered as *cadres*, agents who possess technical, administrative, legal, commercial or financial training and who as proxy of their employer, exert authority over collaborators." In view of this definition, the adaptation which seems to impose itself is the term *middle management*, keeping in mind that a scale exists within this very frame and that *cadre débutant* and *cadre supérieur* may be best rendered as *junior* and *senior executive*.

The legal profession is perhaps the best example of discrepancy in the matter. *Avocats*, *notaires* and *avoués* are all lawyers by U.S. definition but specialize in different areas of the law, and respectively correspond to the British terminology of *barristers*, *solicitors* and *attorneys*. One way of dealing with this problem in translation would be perhaps to borrow the foreign term both for local color and accuracy.

Differences in institutions

State and local institutions may require adaptations in translation for the message to be intelligible to the target audience.

The French educational system with its rigid system of diplomas and different grading system could prove baffling to English speakers. The *baccalauréat*, which sanctions the end of secondary education, is not quite the equivalent of a high school diploma in the United States since it also grants admission to college and has in fact been given as the academic equivalent of two years of a U.S. college education. In a digital grading system which goes from 0 to 20 the passing grade or D is therefore 10. In addition, French teachers are traditionally hard graders and a very good grade or 15 out 20 could be construed as the equivalent of an A in the U.S, since a "mention très bien" or 15/20 and above corresponds to a diploma *summa cum laude*.

Social and political institutions deserve a special mention. *La Sécurité sociale*, a false friend, refers to the French national health and social benefit plan, the same for all French citizens. The *allocations familiales* are a more difficult concept to comprehend this side of the Atlantic where this benefit, which refers to family supplemental income given to all parents whether rich, poor or middle class to help them raise their children, simply does not exist. And what of all those acronyms which are part of daily life in France, *S.N.C.F., E.D.F., P.et T.*? and which truly have no U.S. equivalents?

What of the administrative and political institutions? The administrative division of a country equal to only 1/50th of the United States cannot possibly be the same. A *région* just is not a state, nor a *département* a county; a *préfet* though he may have some of the attributes of a governor is not elected but nominated by the government. France, traditionally more centralized than the United States, requires an official *carte d'identité* with photo and particulars to be carried by all its citizens, while a simple driver's license is the standard I.D. needed in America.

Political and institutional references well-known to a French audience doubtless will need to be adapted. The literal translation of a message such as *"L'Elysée a fait pression sur Matignon pour une prompte résolution de l'impasse"* would indeed sound very cryptic to an Anglo-Saxon reader unaware that the Elysée palace is the dwelling place of the French president or the Hôtel Matignon the seat of the prime minister.

Political parties themselves are not divided along the same lines as in American politics but offer a wide range of variations, some nine different tendencies from the communist party to the extreme right or *Front National*, including two parties for environmentalists, although polarization, U.S. style, seems more and more to have become the order of the day. Thus *"Etes-vous de gauche ou de droite?"* could be transcoded as *"Are you a liberal or a conservative?"*

Those are just a sample of the difficulties awaiting the translator along the path. Let me give an example of the resourcefulness to which a translator may have to resort, when confronted with the necessity of finding a satisfactory solution to the translation of a concept foreign to the linguistic group targeted. During the 1994 United Nations Cairo Conference on Population Growth, newly coined phrases such as *female empowerment, reproductive health, family leave, reproductive rights*, all relatively new American concepts without any foreign counterparts, created massive problems when the original English drafted document had to be translated into the five other official languages of the U.N., Arabic, Chinese, Russian, Spanish and French. French translators, for instance, had to dig up a word which had been obsolete since the nineteenth century, *santé génésique*, in order to render the concept of *reproductive health.*[1]

Remember that when all else fails and even adaptation proves impossible, a short translator's note explaining the concept or situation is your very last resort. But keep in mind that concision here is the key, for it is the duty and responsibility of any good translator to appear as invisible as possible.

The following is a list of the various strategies one may consider when faced with cultural obstacles to translation:

- Compensation e.g. *"se vouvoyer"*:not to be on a first name basis
- Borrowing   a *"soufflé"*
- Calque   *"un litre"*: a liter
- Approximation   *"un litre"*: a quart
- A succinct explanation of the S.L. concept in the T.L.
  e.g. *"La sécurité sociale"*: the French National Health and Social Benefit Plan
- A translator's note

---

[1] Waldman, Peter. "Lost in Translation: How to Empower Women in Chinese." *Wall Street Journal* Sept. 13 1994.

In summary, it is not sufficient for a translator to know the S.L. thoroughly.   The knowledge and understanding of its underlying civilization and culture is also a must.   This knowledge must constantly be kept up to date by taking trips to the country, reading its papers, magazines and literature, going to see its movies, watching its TV shows, surfing its internet sites. A language is steeped in the culture which has given birth to it, and you cannot claim to know one while ignoring the other.

Exercices: **L'Adaptation**

Dans tous les cas où le concept, la coutume ou l'institution à laquelle se réfère le message à traduire n'existent pas dans la L.A. le traducteur se voit obligé de faire appel à une adaptation, c'est à dire à la re-création d'un concept, d'une coutume, d'une institution équivalente, ou dans les cas extrêmes à une explication succincte qui soit intelligible au groupe linguistique de la L.A.

A. L'Adaptation

Faites les adaptations nécessaires à la traduction correcte des messages suivants.

1. *Nous nous tutoyons* depuis toujours.
2. *Je lui ai serré la main* et nous nous sommes séparés.
3. Se retrouvant par hasard après des années les deux hommes *s'embrassèrent* avec effusion.
4. Il est grand et mince: il *mesure un mètre quatre-vingt* et *pèse soixante-quinze kilos.*
5. En France la réglementation de la vitesse sur les routes est la suivante: une vitesse maximum de *50 km* à l'heure est permise dans les *agglomérations*, de *90 km* heure en *zone rurale* et de *130 km* heure sur les autoroutes.
6. Va à *l'épicerie du coin* et rapporte-moi *un litre* de lait et *un kilo* de pommes.
7. Le capital de cette *société anonyme* est de l'ordre de *un milliard d'euros.*
8. Cet été nous comptons rester *huit ou quinze jours* chez nos amis qui ont *une résidence secondaire* en Normandie.
9. L'an dernier j'ai été tellement occupé que je n'ai eu le temps d'aller au cinéma que *deux ou trois fois.*
10. Il n'y a pas *trente-six façons* de s'y prendre. Seule celle-ci est la bonne.

11. Venez donc *déjeuner* chez nous *dimanche en huit*! Ce sera à la fortune du pot!

12. *La Comédie Française* donne une représentation de "L'Avare" *ce soir à 21 heures.*

13. Après demain c'est *ta fête.* Qui veux-tu inviter?

14. Le rayon des produits de beauté se trouve *au rez-de-chaussée* à gauche de l'escalier roulant.

15. Je vous offre *l'apéritif* à la maison ou au café du coin?

16. Ce bourgogne est délicieux bien que nous l'ayons acheté dans *une grande surface.*

17. Mes plats préférés en hiver? Un bon *pot au feu* avec comme dessert *une tarte Tatin.*

18. Il a voulu nous éblouir en nous emmenant déjeuner dans un restaurant *trois étoiles.*

B. L'Adaptation (suite)

Faites les adaptations nécessaires à la traduction correcte des messages suivants.

1. J'ai réussi de justesse à mon examen de maths. Je n'ai eu que *la moyenne.*

2. Tu as fait beaucoup de progrès en anglais ce semestre. *Ta moyenne est passée de 11 à 14.*

3. *Elle vient de passer son baccalauréat et va sans doute préparer un diplôme d'études supérieures.*

4. Son fils a reçu sa maîtrise *avec la mention très bien.*

5. En France *les écoles libres* reçoivent des subsides de l'Etat tout comme *les écoles laïques.*

6. En France *les instituteurs* de l'enseignement primaire et *les professeurs* de l'enseignement secondaire sont *fonctionnaires d'état.*

7. Nous étions en infraction, aussi l'agent de police nous a-t-il réclamé notre *carte d'identité.*

8. Après la victoire de l'équipe régionale au championnat ce fut une atmosphère de fête par toute la ville. On se serait cru *au 14 juillet.*

9. *Le préfet* a envoyé ses nouvelles directives dans tout *le département.*

10. Hier*, au Palais Bourbon, les députés* se sont réunis pour voter *la motion de censure.*

11. *La Sécurité Sociale* fut accordée aux Français sous la quatrième République.

12. Le but des *allocations familiales* mises en place à la Libération fut d'encourager une recrudescence de la natalité.

13. La *S.N.C.F.* consent des tarifs spéciaux aux étudiants, aux personnes du troisième âge ainsi qu'aux *familles nombreuses.*

14. L'un des services des *P. et T.* est celui des chèques postaux.

15. Connaissez-vous les *DOM TOM*?

16. Historiquement *la bourgeoisie* française détient le pouvoir depuis le règne de Louis-Philippe.

17. A quelle tendance politique appartenez-vous, au *P.S.* ou à *l'U.M.P.*?

18. Mon gendre est *cadre* chez Renault.

19. *Un notaire* s'occupe des affaires de succession, *un avocat* représente un client lors d'un procès et est chargé de la plaidoirie, tandis qu'*un avoué* doit préparer la procédure du procès.

20. C'est le *professeur* Montagnier qui a le premier découvert le virus du SIDA.

21. *Chère Madame* (formule épistolaire à une connaissance, Mme Dupont).

22. *Monsieur* (formule épistolaire à une personne que vous ne connaissez pas bien).

Chapter 12 Applying Translators' Techniques To Literary Texts

The following pages are intended to acquaint the student with literary translation by offering, side by side with their suggested translation, sample sentences taken from masterpieces of French or Francophone literature in various genres and time periods. Each sentence contains a particular translation problem which is dealt with by using one of the four non literal translation techniques introduced in previous chapters.

Transposition

1. Que l'homme contemple donc la nature entière dans sa haute et pleine majesté, *qu'il éloigne sa vue des* objets bas *qui l'environnent.* (Blaise Pascal, Pensées)

Let man therefore contemplate the whole of nature in its great and full majesty, let him *look away* from the lowly objects *around him.*

2. Je fus hier au Buron, j'en revins le soir. Je pensai pleurer *en voyant* la dégradation de cette terre. (Mme de Sévigné, Lettres)

I went yesterday to Buron and came back at night. I could have wept *at the sight of* the damage done to that land.

3. Tout le reste d'une conversation si désirée ne pouvait *manquer* d'être infiniment tendre. La pauvre Manon me raconta ses aventures, et je lui appris les miennes. (Abbé Prévost, Manon Lescaut)

The remainder of a conversation I had so desired could not *but* be infinitely loving. Poor Manon gave me an account of her adventures and I shared mine.

4. Ami, rire d'un vieillard *désespéré*, cela porte malheur; [mais] si tu dis *vrai, à l'action*! (Alfred de Musset, Lorenzaccio)

Friend, making fun of an old man *in despair* brings bad luck; but if you speak *the truth*, then *act on it*!

5. On était *au commencement d'avril* quand les primevères sont *écloses*, un vent tiède se roule sur les plates-bandes labourées, et les jardins, comme des femmes, semblent faire leur toilette pour les fêtes de l'été. (Gustave Flaubert, Madame Bovary)

It was *early April* when primroses are *out*, a warm wind wafts over tilled flower-beds and gardens, like women, seem to be dressing up for the summer parties.

6. *Il pleure* en mon coeur
   Comme *il pleut* sur la ville.   (Verlaine, Romances sans paroles)
   Tears fall within my heart
   As *rain* upon the town.

7. *Aux approches de la guerre*, tous les évènements revêtent un nouveau vernis, qui est *le mensonge*. (Jean Giraudoux, La Guerre de Troie n'aura pas lieu)

As war draws near, every event assumes a new tone, everything *lies.*

8. Florent: Mais tu ne peux pas me reprocher éternellement cet argent. Qu'est-ce que tu veux que j'en fasse?
   Thérèse: Oh rien, Florent. Tu *aurais beau* le jeter tout entier au vent, par la fenêtre, en riant, comme l'autre jour, que ma peine ne s'envolerait pas avec lui. (Jean Anouilh, La Sauvage)

Florent: But you can't hold this money against me forever. What do you want me to do with it?

Thérèse: Oh nothing, Florent. *Even if* you threw it all out the window to the wind with a laugh, as you did the other day, my grief would not fly away with it.

9. Les Français sont *peut-être* des maîtres de la conversation, mais ce sont des enfants lorsqu'il s'agit de parler du temps. C'est là une spécialité dont les

Anglais *sont les rois* incontestés.   (Pierre Daninos, Les Carnets du major Thompson)

The French *may* be master conversationalists, but they are neophytes when it comes to discussing the weather.   That is a domain in which the English *reign* unchallenged.

10. On ne meurt pas d'être né, d'avoir vécu, ni de vieillesse.   On meurt de quelque chose [...] un cancer, une embolie, une congestion pulmonaire: c'est aussi brutal et imprévu que *l'arrêt* d'un moteur en plein ciel.   (Simone de Beauvoir, Une Mort très douce)

You don't die from being born, from having lived, or from old age.   You die from something, cancer, thrombosis, pneumonia: it is as brutal and unforeseen as an engine *coming to a stop* in mid-air.

11. "Les épines, à quoi *servent*-elles?"   Le petit prince ne renonçait jamais à une question, une fois qu'il l'avait posée.   J'étais irrité [...] et je répondis n'importe quoi: "Les épines, ça ne *sert* à rien.   C'est de la pure méchanceté de la part des fleurs."   (Antoine de Saint-Exupéry, Le Petit Prince)

"Thorns, what are they *for*?"   The little prince never gave up after he had asked a question.   I was annoyed and answered whatever came to mind: "Thorns, they have no *use*.   It's pure wickedness on the flowers' part."

12. *Il m'est arrivé* de penser que tout ce travail [...] mon père l'eût aussi bien confié à l'un ou l'autre de ses aides.   Ceux-ci ne manquaient pas d'expérience [...].   Quand enfin l'or entrait en fusion [...] je tressaillais en regardant mon père remuer la pâte encore lourde où le charbon de bois *achevait de se consommer*.   (Camara Laye, L'Enfant noir)

The thought has *sometimes* crossed my mind that this operation might as well have been entrusted to anyone of my father's aides.   They had plenty of experience.   When finally the gold metal reached the melting stage, I would shudder, as I watched my father stir the paste, still quite heavy, in which the charcoal *was burning off*.

13. Joyeuse Pitou *entourée de* sa marmaille hurlante et sale, vociféra jusqu'à en perdre le souffle, et, de désespoir et d'épuisement, *finit par* s'effondrer sur le sol.   (Jacques Stephen Alexis, Les Arbres musiciens)

Joyeuse Pitou, her dirty and howling brood *all around* her, screamed until she ran out of breath, and, from despair and exhaustion, *finally* collapsed on the ground.

14. Quand au sortir de la première guerre mondiale on en vint à oublier les griefs que l'on nourrissait à l'encontre des [noirs du] Congo, le jeune homme put louer un petit local sur la Rue-Derrière qui *ne tarda pas* à prospérer, et cela sans l'aide d'aucun maléfice. (Raphaël Confiant, Eau de café)

When at the end of World War I the grievances which had been nurtured against blacks from the Congo were eventually forgotten, the young man was able to rent in the Rue-Derrière a small shop which *soon* prospered, and quite without the help of any evil spell.

Modulation

1. Toute *leur vie était employée* non par lois, statuts ou règles mais selon leur vouloir et franc arbitre. (Rabelais, Gargantua)

Their whole *life was spent* not following laws, statutes or rules but according to their own desires and free will.

2. Ce que nous appelons ordinairement amis et amitiés ne sont qu'*accointances et familiarités nouées* par quelque occasion ou commodité. (Michel de Montaigne, Essais)

What we commonly call friends and friendships are no more than *acquaintances and close associations contracted* by chance or for convenience.

3. Un après-midi j'étais là, regardant beaucoup, parlant peu et écoutant le moins que je pouvais, lorsque je fus abordé par l'un des plus bizarres personnages de ce pays *où Dieu n'en a pas laissé manquer.* (Denis Diderot, Le Neveu de Rameau)

One afternoon I was there, observing a lot, not saying much and listening as little as possible, when I was accosted by one of the most bizarre characters in this land *where God saw to it that there should be no lack of them.*

4. Ou tu ne penses pas ce que tu dis, ou bien *tu fais mieux* que tu ne penses. (Montesquieu, Les Lettres persanes)

Either you don't believe what you are saying, or *you are more successful* than you think.

5. Au loin, par intervalles, *on entendait* les sourds mugissements de la cataracte du Niagara qui dans le calme de la nuit se prolongeaient de désert en désert et expiraient à travers les forêts solitaires. (François-René de Chateaubriand, Le Génie du christianisme)

Intermittently, in the distance, the dull roar of Niagara Falls *could be heard*, which in the stillness of the night echoed from wild to wild and died away through the lonely forests.

6. *Je me fis un plaisir* de lui apprendre [...] que Chopin, bien loin d'être démodé, était le musicien préféré de Debussy. "Tiens, c'est amusant" me dit en souriant

finement [Madame de Cambremer-Legrandin]. (Marcel Proust, Sodome et Gomorrhe)

It gave me pleasure to inform her that Chopin, far from being out of fashion, was Debussy's favorite composer.   "Well, that's funny." Madame de Cambremer-Legrandin replied with a subtle smile.

7. Tout compte fait, mieux valait que Thérèse disparût, on l'oublierait *plus vite*, les gens *perdraient l'habitude* de parler d'elle. (François Mauriac, Thérèse Desqueyroux)

All things considered, it was better that Thérèse should go away, she would be forgotten *sooner,* people *would stop* talking about her.

8. On a tout à se dire, mon prince. *L'occasion ne se présentera peut-être pas deux fois.* (Jean Anouilh, Beckett)

We have a lot to talk about, my Lord. *This opportunity might not be found again.*

9. *La brûlure du soleil gagnait* mes joues et j'ai senti des gouttes de sueur s'amasser dans mes sourcils. [...] A cause de cette brûlure que je ne pouvais plus supporter [...] *j'ai fait un pas*, un seul pas en avant. [...] *La mer a charié un souffle épais et ardent.* (Albert Camus, L'Etranger)

The sun was now beginning to scorch my cheeks and I felt beads of sweat gathering in my eyebrows. Because of this sensation which I could no longer bear *I took one step*, one single step forward. *A heavy and burning gust of wind drifted from the sea.*

10. *Tout est permis aux héros.* (Jean-Paul Sartre, Huis clos)

Heroes can do no wrong.

11. Je ne crois pas du tout que j'ai cherché en [l'homme que j'aimerais un jour] un succédané de mon père; *je tenais à mon indépendance*, j'exercerais un métier, j'écrirais, j'aurais une vie personnelle. (Simone de Beauvoir, Les Mémoires d'une jeune fille rangée)

I do not at all believe that I was looking for a father image in the man whom I would love one day; *I valued my independence*, I would hold a job, write, have a life of my own.

12. *Après avoir dépassé le milieu du pont*, [le colonel Nicholson] se pencha au-dessus de la balustrade, comme il le faisait tous les cinq ou six mètres [...]. L'oeil du maître avait aperçu du premier coup le bourrelet d'eau prononcé causé à la surface par une charge. (Pierre Boulle, Le Pont de la rivière Kwaï)

After he was more than half way across the bridge, Colonel Nicholson leaned over the parapet, as he had done every five or 6 yards. The master's eye had at once noticed the marked ripple caused on the surface by an underwater load.

13. Mon camarade suit [le requin], l'approche, le prend par la queue, *partagé entre* le désir de tirer fort [...] et la crainte qu'il ne se retourne pour mordre. (Jacques Cousteau, Le Monde du silence)

My friend follows the shark, swims up to it, grabs it by the tail, *torn between* the desire to pull hard and the fear that it should turn around and bite.

14. Je sentais la sueur dégouliner sur mon front, le long de mon nez, sur mes joues et se former en gouttelettes à la pointe de mon menton *tellement m'échauffait la colère.* (Mongo Beti, Le Pauvre Christ de Bomba)

I could feel sweat trickling down my brow, along my nose, over my cheeks and form droplets at the tip of my chin, *I was burning so with anger.*

Equivalence

1. Si je compare tout le reste de ma vie, quoiqu'avec la grâce de Dieu *je l'ai passée douce* et sauf la perte d'un tel ami exempte d'affliction [...] si je la compare toute aux quatre années qu'il m'a été donné de jouir de la douce compagnie de ce personnage, ce n'est que fumée, ce n'est qu'une nuit obscure et ennuyeuse. (Michel de Montaigne, Essais)

When I compare all the rest of my life, although by the grace of God *it has been kind to me* and, save the loss of such a friend, free from affliction, when I compare it with the four years during which I was given the opportunity to enjoy the sweet company of this man, all is nothing but smoke, nothing but a dark and tedious night.

2. *Qui ne fait des châteaux en Espagne?*
   Picrochole, Pyrrhus, la laitière, enfin tous,
   Autant les sages que les fous. (Jean de la Fontaine, Perrette et le pot au lait)
   Who has not built castles in the air?
   Picrochole, Pyrrhus, the milkmaid, everyone,
   The wise and the foolish.

3. Elle a des façons de parler qui *me mettent hors de moi*. (Marivaux, Le Jeu de l'amour et du hasard)
   She has a way of speaking which *infuriates* me.

4. On s'ennuie de tout, mon ange, c'est une loi de la nature; *ce n'est pas ma faute*.[...] Si, par exemple, j'ai eu juste autant d'amour que toi de vertu, et c'est sûrement beaucoup dire, il n'est pas étonnant que l'un ait fini en même temps que l'autre. *Ce n'est pas ma faute*. (Pierre Choderlos de Laclos, Les Liaisons dangereuses)

One tires of everything, my angel, it is a law of nature; *I cannot help it*. If, for instance, I had only as much love as you, virtue, and that is probably saying much, it comes as no surprise that they should both end at the same time. *I cannot help it.*

5. Lequel de vous, messieurs, demanda le magistrat [...] s'appelle Andréa Cavalcanti? -Mais quel est *donc* cet Andréa Cavalcanti, demanda Danglars presque égaré. -Un ancien forçat échappé du bagne de Toulon. -Et quel crime a-t-il commis? -Il est prévenu, dit le commissaire de sa voix impassible, d'avoir assassiné le nommé Caderousse, son ancien compagnon de chaîne, au moment

où il sortait de chez le comte de Monte Cristo. (Alexandre Dumas, Le Comte de Monte Cristo)

-Who among you, gentlemen, answers to the name Andrea Cavalcanti? asked the magistrate. -Who *on earth* is Andrea Cavalcanti? asked Danglars almost distraught. -A former convict who ran away from the Toulon forced labor camp. -What's his crime? -He is charged, replied the police superintendent in his calm and collected voice, with having murdered the said Caderousse, his former chain companion, as he was leaving the house of Count Monte Cristo.

6. [Musset] *avait fait des niches* aux *classiques à perruques* de 1830; il aimait les grands classiques de 1660, y compris Racine, *la bête noire* en ce temps-là des *esprits larges.* (Gustave Lanson, Histoire de la littérature française)

Musset *had played pranks* on the *unconditionals of classicism* in 1830; he loved the great classics of 1660, including Racine, who, at the time, was the *pet aversion* of *progressive minds.*

7. "Cette enfant est surchargée de travail, elle se fatigue beaucoup. De plus on lui fait trop sentir, je crains, sa pauvreté. "[...] -"Hélas, me répondit maître Mouche, *il faut bien* la préparer à la vie. On n'est pas sur terre pour s'amuser et pour *faire ses quatre cents volontés.*" (Anatole France, Le Crime de Sylvestre Bonnard)

"The child is overworked, she is tiring herself out. In addition, I fear, she is made to feel too conscious of her poverty." "Unfortunately, replied Schoolmaster Mouche, *we do have to* prepare her for life. You are not here on earth to have fun or *do as you please.*"

8. Le renard était assis au pied de l'acacia. Il regardait le coq perché sur une haute branche et il voulait le manger [...] Le coq ne voulait pas descendre. Il disait qu'il aimait mieux être mangé par ses maîtres que par le renard. "-Je préfère mourir de ma mort naturelle". "-*Qu'il est bête*, mais la mort naturelle, *ce n'est pas ça du tout.*" "-Tu ne sais pas ce que tu dis, renard. Il faut bien que les maîtres nous tuent *un jour ou l'autre.* C'est la loi commune, il n'y a personne qui puisse y échapper. Le dindon lui-même, qui *fait tant son rengorgé, y passe* comme les autres. *On le mange aux marrons.*" (Marcel Aymé, Contes du chat perché)

The fox was sitting at the foot of the acacia. He was watching the rooster nested high up on a branch and planned to eat him. The rooster refused to come down. He said that he would rather be eaten by his masters than by the fox. "-I prefer to die a natural death". "-But, *silly, that's not what a natural death is about*." "-You don't know what you are saying, fox. Our masters must kill us *sooner or later*. It's our common fate, none of us can escape it. Even the turkey, who *likes to give himself airs, has to face the music. They accomodate him with chestnut stuffing*."

9. *Pour moi c'était une histoire finie*, et j'étais venu là *sans y penser*. (Albert Camus, L'Etranger)

　　As far as I was concerned the matter was closed, and I had come there *without giving it another thought*.

10. [Balducci] se leva et se dirigea vers l'Arabe en tirant une cordelette de sa poche. "Qu'est-ce que tu fais?" demanda sèchement Daru. Balducci, interdit, lui montra la corde. "-*Ce n'est pas la peine*". (Albert Camus, L'Exil et le royaume)

　　Balducci got up and walked toward the Arab taking a small rope from his pocket. "What are you doing?" Daru asked dryly. Balducci, disconcerted, showed him the rope. "-*There's no need*."

11. Oui, tu connais le prix du mal, et si tu dis que je suis un lâche c'est *en connaissance de cause, hein*? (Jean-Paul Sartre, Huis clos)

　　Yes, you know what evil costs, and when you call me a coward *you know from experience, isn't that so?*

12. Monsieur: Je n'ai pas besoin de vos services, Madame.

　　La concierge: *Ça c'est trop fort*! C'est *pourtant* vous qui m'avez priée, *c'est malheureux*, j'ai pas eu de témoins, *je vous ai cru sur parole, je me suis laissée faire*. Je suis trop bonne. (Eugène Ionesco, Le Nouveau Locataire)

　　Gentleman: I don't need your services, Madam.

　　Caretaker: *Well, how do you like that? And* you're the one who begged me! *Pity* I got no witnesses, *I took you at your word, and let you take advantage of me*. I'm too kind.

13. *Je prétends* que *le tout* n'est pas *encore* de se marier, mais de rester ensemble *devant le changement des saisons*. (Simone Schwarz Bart, Pluie et vent sur Télumée Miracle)

In my opinion getting married *is one thing* but *what counts* is sticking it out together *when the wind turns*.

14. Le Chinois dit: "Je vais à Sadec cette nuit, je suis obligé, je reviens dans deux jours. Le chauffeur va t'apporter le repas. On te reconduira à la pension avant de partir." Ils se douchent. Elle lui parle de la quarantaine dont elle est l'objet au lycée. Elle rit. "-On ne me parle plus au lycée à cause de toi" "-C'est *une idée que tu te fais*." "-Non, il y a eu des plaintes de mères d'élèves." Il rit avec elle. Il demande de quoi a peur cette société. (Marguerite Duras, L'Amant de la Chine du nord)

The Chinese man says: "I'm going to Sadec tonight, I have to, I'll be back in two days. The chauffeur will bring you your meal. We will drive you to the boarding school before leaving." They take a shower. She tells him of her being ostracized at school. She laughs. "-No one speaks to me at school anymore, because of you." "-*You're imagining things*." "-No, there were complaints from some students' mothers." He laughs with her. He wants to know what these people are afraid of.

Adaptation

1. Maître de philosophie: La voix A se forme en ouvrant fort la bouche: A.
   M. Jourdain: A, A, oui.
   M.P.   *La voix E se forme en rapprochant la mâchoire d'en bas*
                     de celle d'en haut: A, E.
   M.J.   A, E, A, E. Ma foi, oui. Ah que cela est beau!
   M.P.   *Et la voix I, en rapprochant encore davantage les machoi-*
                     res l'une de l'autre, et écartant les deux coins de la bou-
                     che vers les oreilles. A, E, I.

                              (Molière, Le Bourgeois gentilhomme)

English vowels in the alphabet being sounded quite differently
from French vowels, an adaptation of Molière's text to fit English
phonetics seems inevitable.

   Philosophy master: Vowel A is formed by opening your mouth
wide: A.

   Mr. Jourdain: A, A, yes.

   P.M.   *Vowel E is formed by bringing the lower jaw closer*
to the upper jaw while pulling the corners of your mouth sideways:
A, E.

   M.J.   A, E, A, E,. My word, yes. How beautiful!

   P.M.   *And vowel I by bringing the jaws even closer*
together with your tongue rising toward your palate. A, E, I.

2. La façade de la pension donne sur un jardinet [...]. Le long de cette façade,
entre la maison et le jardinet, règne un cailloutis en cuvette large *d'une toise*,
devant lequel est une allée sablée bordée de géraniums. (Honoré de Balzac, Le
Père Goriot)

The problem in this excerpt is the conversion of measure units used
in nineteenth century France before the acceptance of the metric
system. Since most dictionaries will not list such obsolete words,
you will have to resort to a French monolingual dictionary to
figure out the metric system equivalent before you can do the
conversion.

   The front of the boarding house overlooks a small garden. Along
the front, between the house and the garden runs a sunken cobbled
space, some *6 feet* wide, and beyond, a sanded path lined with
geraniums.

3. Se dénoncer, grand Dieu! se livrer! [...] A son âge, après avoir été ce qu'il était! Si encore il était jeune! Mais vieux, *être tutoyé* par le premier venu, être fouillé par le garde-chiourme, recevoir le coup de bâton de l'argousin, avoir les pieds nus dans des souliers ferrés! (Victor Hugo, Les Misérables)

The lack of distinction between "tu" and "vous" in addressing others in English often creates a problem in translation. Since the familiar "tu" form can be used as a means of disrespect by a superior to an inferior, as in this context, compensation in the form of a verb indicating disparagement may be substituted.

To confess, good God, to turn himself in! At his age, after what he had become! If only he were young! But, an old man, *to be talked down to* by anyone, to be searched by the warder, hit by the turnkey's club, with bare feet in hobnailed shoes!

4. Madame Alvarez mit une main sur son sein. -En mon âme et conscience, Gaston, si ça n'était que pour vous et pour moi je vous dirais: "Emmenez Gilberte où vous voudrez, je vous la confie les yeux fermés". Mais il y a les autres...Vous êtes connu mondialement. Sortir en tête à tête avec vous, pour une femme, c'est...

Gaston Lachaille perdit patience. -Bon, bon j'ai compris! Vous voulez me faire croire que de *goûter* avec moi, voilà Gigi compromise. (Colette, Gigi)

Meals do not always quite correspond between French and Anglo-Saxon cultures. Here a "goûter" refers to a late afternoon snack taken by children after school which usually consists of hot chocolate, tea or milk and pastries or bread and butter with jam. English tea, which is a late afternoon light meal for both children and adults in England seems a close enough equivalent.

Madame Alvarez placed her hand over her breast. Upon my soul, Gaston, if we were the only two people concerned I would say to you: "Bring Gilberte wherever you want, I entrust her to you with my eyes closed." But there are others... You are known the world over. For a woman to go out with you alone is...

Gaston Lachaille lost his patience. Oh, all right, I see what you are getting at! You want me to believe that by *having tea* with me Gigi will be compromised.

5. Les Puybaraud étaient les derniers devant qui [Brigitte] eût consenti volontiers à montrer quelque faiblesse. "Ils vont me prendre pour *une commerçante*" se disait-elle. (François Mauriac, La Pharisienne)

In this context the term "commerçant", "shopkeeper" has a negative social connotation: someone materialistic with intellectual limitations. A simple translation of the word would prove inadequate and an explanatory adaptation is necessary.

The Puybarauds were the last people to whom Brigitte would have wanted to show any weakness. "They will take me for *some petty bourgeois*" she would say to herself.

6. J'entendis un chuchotement qui disait: "-En quelle section es-tu?" D'abord je ne compris pas que c'était mon voisin qui me parlait car il restait parfaitement impassible, le regard fixé sur son emploi du temps. Mais je vis tout à coup le coin de sa bouche remuer imperceptiblement, et il répéta sa question. J'admirai sa technique, et en essayant de l'imiter, je répondis: "-Sixième A2." "-Chic! dit-il. Moi aussi. [...] A cause du latin, je *redouble la sixième*." Je ne compris pas ce mot, et je crus qu'il voulait dire qu'il avait l'intention de *redoubler d'efforts*. (Marcel Pagnol, Le Temps des secrets)

The adaptation problem here is not the grade conversion since "la sixième" does correspond to "sixth grade", although "septième" and "cinquième" would respectively be fourth and seventh grade, but it is the translation of a play on words: "redoubler une classe" and "redoubler d'efforts", the latter being an idiomatic expression meaning "to try twice as hard." A solution can be found in a similar play on words with "to repeat", the objective for the translator being to convey the idea that the narrator is a naïve and inexperienced young boy.

I heard a whisper saying: "-In what section are you?" At first I did not realize that it was the boy sitting next to me who was speaking, since he remained perfectly impassive and kept his eyes on his study schedule. But all of a sudden I noticed the corner of his mouth moving imperceptibly as he reiterated his question. I admired his technique, and trying to imitate him replied: "-Sixth A2" "-Great! he said, me too! I'm *repeating sixth grade* because of latin." I did not understand that phrase and thought that he meant he wanted *to repeat his lessons*.

7. L'été de mes quinze ans, à la fin de l'année scolaire, j'allai deux ou trois fois canoter *au bois* avec Zaza et d'autres camarades.   (Simone de Beauvoir, Mémoires d'une jeune fille rangée)

To Parisians "le bois" refers to the bois de Boulogne, a large wooded space west of the city. A translation would have to make this explicit to Anglophone readers unfamiliar with this fact.

The summer I turned fifteen, at the end of the school year, I went boating in *the Bois de Boulogne* on a couple of occasions with Zaza and a few other friends.

8. L'asile de vieillards est à Marengo, *à 80 kilomètres* d'Alger. (Albert Camus, L'Etranger)

Conversion of distances are essential for an American public to understand.

The old people's home is in Marengo, *some 50 miles* from Algiers.

Exercices Généraux:
Les Procédés de Traduction non Littéraux

A. *Lisez les extraits littéraires suivants ainsi que leurs traductions. Déterminez si, pour les passages en italique traduits, vous avez affaire à une transposition, une modulation, une équivalence ou une adaptation.*

1. Pathelin: Je m'en veux aller à la foire [...]
   Guillemette: Mais *vous n'avez ni sou ni maille*. Qu'y ferez-vous?
   Pathelin: C'est mon secret. Si je n'apporte assez de drap pour vous et moi, alors traitez moi de menteur. Quelle couleur préférez-vous? [...]
   Guillemette: Apportez ce que vous pouvez. *Un emprunteur ne choisit pas.*
   (La Farce de Maître Pathelin)

   Pathelin: I intend to go to the fair.
   Guillemette: But *you don't have a penny*. What will you do there?
   Pathelin: The secret's mine. If I don't bring back enough cloth for you and me, then call me a liar. What color do you prefer?
   Guillemette: Bring what you can. *Beggars can't be choosers.*

2.   Le meunier repartit:
   "Je suis âne, il est vrai, j'en conviens, je l'avoue.
   Mais que dorénavant on me blâme, on me loue,
   Qu'on dise quelque chose, ou qu'on ne dise rien
   J'en veux faire à ma tête."
   (Jean de La Fontaine, Le Meunier, son fils et l'âne)

                And the miller replied:
   "I'm an ass, it is true, I admit, I confess,
    But whether hereafter they give me blame or praise
    Speak their mind, hold their peace
    I shall do as I please."

3. Le génie et les grands talents manquent souvent; quelquefois aussi les *seules* occasions: tels peuvent être loués de ce qu'ils ont fait, et tels de ce qu'ils auraient fait. (La Bruyère, Les Caractères)

There is often a lack of genius and great talent; sometimes, too, of opportunity *only*: some may be praised for what they have achieved, others for what they might have achieved.

4. *Il se fit* alors un grand silence; *on cessa de danser* et les violons *ne jouèrent plus, tant on était attentif à contempler* les grandes beautés de cette inconnue. *On n'entendait qu'un bruit confus*: "Ah, qu' *elle est belle!*" Le roi même, *tout* vieux qu'il était, *ne laissait pas* de la regarder, et de dire tout bas à la reine qu'il y avait longtemps qu'il n'avait vu une si belle et si aimable personne. (Charles Perrault, Cendrillon)

Then a great silence *fell upon the assembly*; *all dancing stopped* and the violins *came to a halt, so intense was the attention bestowed upon* the great charms of this stranger. *Only a confused rumor could be heard*: "Oh, what *a beauty!*" Even the king, old *though* he was, *could not help* looking at her, whispering to the queen that it was a long time since he had seen such a beautiful and lovable person.

5. *Il me faut* des torrents, des rochers, des sapins, des bois noirs, des montagnes, des chemins raboteux à monter et descendre." (Jean Jacques Rousseau, Confessions)

I need torrents, rocks, fir-trees, dark woods, mountains, bumpy paths to follow up and down.

6. Le lendemain à neuf heures [...] Julien descendit de sa prison pour aller dans la grande salle du *palais de justice. [Il] avait bien dormi*, il était fort calme, et n'éprouvait d'*autre* sentiment *qu*'une pitié philosophique pour cette foule d'envieux qui, sans cruauté, *allait* applaudir à son arrêt de mort. [...] *On eût dit* ce jour là *qu'il n'avait pas vingt ans*. (Stendhal, Le Rouge et le noir)

The following day at nine, Julien came from his prison cell down to the main hall of the *Law Court. He had had a good night's sleep*, was quite composed, and felt *nothing beyond* philosophical pity toward the envious crowd *about to* applaud, without cruelty, his death sentence. On that day *he barely looked twenty*.

7. *Si* la crise industrielle tirait à sa fin, si les usines rouvraient une à une, l'état de guerre *n'en restait pas moins déclaré, sans que* la paix fut désormais possible. (Emile Zola, Germinal)

Even though the industrial crisis was drawing to an end, and the factories were reopening one by one, the state of war *was still on*, and peace no longer possible.

8. Deux hommes restaient encore, les mains dans les poches [...], le bonnet de laine *enfoncé* jusqu'aux yeux. (Guy de Maupassant, Contes du jour et de la nuit)

Two men stayed on, hands in their pockets, their woolen cap *down* to their eyes.

9. Chère imagination, ce que j'aime *surtout* en toi, c'est que tu *ne pardonnes pas*. (André Breton, Manifeste du surréalisme)

Dear imagination, what I like *best* about you is that you *leave no room for error*.

10. A quoi faire servir cette force que je sens *en moi*? Comment *tirer le meilleur parti* de moi-même? Est-ce en me dirigeant vers un but? Mais ce but, comment le choisir? Comment le connaître, aussi longtemps qu'il n'est pas atteint? (André Gide, Les Faux monnayeurs)

How am I to use the strength I feel *inside*? How *make the best* of myself? By heading for a goal? How am I to select that goal, know what it is, as long as it has not been reached?

11. En été deux fois par semaine, Adrienne allait au jardin cueillir des fleurs *sous les yeux attentifs* de son père [...]. Le reste du temps, sa tâche *se réduisait à* parcourir la maison [...] et à s'assurer que tout était en ordre. (Julien Green, Adrienne Mesurat)

In the summer twice a week, Adrienne would go and pick flowers in the garden *carefully watched* by her father. The rest of the time her *only* duty was to go through the house and see to it that everything was tidy.

12. *Ce qui me plaît surtout en lui* c'est qu'il *possède* et cultive une voix agréable, grave et mélodieuse. (Jean Giono, Naissance de l'Odyssée)

What I like most about him is this pleasant, deep and melodious voice *of his* which he cultivates.

13. Estragon: Qu'est-ce que nous avons fait hier?
    Vladimir: Ce que nous avons fait hier?
    Estragon: Oui.
    Vladimir: *Ma foi...* (se fâchant) Pour jeter le doute, *à toi le pompon. Pour moi, nous étions* ici. (Samuel Beckett, En attendant Godot)

Estragon: What did we do yesterday?

Vladimir: Yesterday? What did we do?

Estragon: Yes.

Vladimir: *Well...* (getting angry) When it comes to raising doubts, *you take the cake. We must have been* here.

14. Je passai des vers à la prose.[...] A peine eus-je commencé d'écrire, je posais ma plume *pour jubiler.* Rien ne me troublait plus que de voir mes *pattes de mouche* échanger peu à peu leur luisance de feux follets *contre* la terne consistance de la matière: *c'était la réalisation de l'imaginaire.* (Jean-Paul Sartre, Les Mots)

I went from verse to prose. No sooner did I start writing when I would put down my pen *in exultation.* Nothing moved me more than to watch my *chicken scratch* exchange, little by little, its will o' the wisp gleam *for* the dull consistency of matter: *fantasy had come into being.*

B. Select sentences from a French literary text or magazine and in your translation give:
- *one transposition*
- *one modulation*
- *one equivalence*
- *one adaptation*

Chapter 13   **Translating Titles**

General advice

A title is very important to a translation. Unfortunately it is all too tempting for the novice translator to start an assignment by translating the title right away, usually dismissing it with a word for word translation, and then move on to the rest of the text as being alone worthy of any effort.

Titles serve a double purpose. Their first function is that of an abstract, insofar as they must reflect the theme of the excerpt, book or article to be translated in order to prepare the reader for what is to follow. At the same time they must be tantalizing and try to make an impact on the potential reader. Authors and publishers are very aware of the fact that the title of any written material, coupled with the design of the book cover, serves as an ad to catch the readers' eye and entice to further reading. Therefore it is ultimately the title which will promote the book, and very special care should be given to its translation.

In addition, a distinction must be made between translating the title of a novel, play or movie and translating the headline of a newspaper; magazine or article. The conventions governing the latter category will be covered in chapter 17.

Here are a few tips on translating titles:

- **Titles should be translated last**, only after you have reached a thorough understanding of the text. You should be able to summarize the main lines of the text before you even attempt to decide on its title. After all, a title serves as the key that opens the door to a story.

- **You can afford to be freer with the translation of a title than with the text itself.** At your disposal you also have the same tools: literal translation, when there are no structural or cultural obstacles; transposition, if a more idiomatic touch is needed; modulation, to give the title an interesting twist and focus, both for stylistic and semantic reasons; equivalence to render idioms; or even adaptation, for all cases in which the original title is untranslatable due to metalinguistic obstacles.

- **Be aware that English and French favor different approaches when it comes to titles**.
  French has a marked preference for brief titles, usually nouns preceded by an article:

  e.g.. *Les Essais* (Montaigne), *Les Méditations* (A. de Lamartine), *Les Misérables* (V. Hugo), *L'Education sentimentale* (G. Flaubert), *Le Rouge et le noir* (Stendhal); *L'Assommoir* (Zola), *Une Vie* (G. de Maupassant), *Le Rire* (H. Bergson), *Colline* (J. Giono), *Les Mandarins* (S. de Beauvoir), *La Nausée* (J.P. Sartre), *La Peste* (A. Camus), *L'Espoir* (A. Malraux), *Le Petit Prince* (A. de Saint Exupéry), *L'Oeuvre au noir* (M. Yourcenar), *L'Amant* (M. Duras), *Le Procès verbal* (J. M. Le Clézio), *Le Rivage des Syrtes* (J. Gracq), *Belle du Seigneur* (A. Cohen), *etc.*

  Whereas English loves verbs and does not mind entire sentences:

  e.g.. *She Stoops to Conquer* (Goldsmith), *The Importance of Being Earnest* (Oscar Wilde), *Where Angels Fear to Tread* (E.M. Forster), *For Whom the Bell Tolls* (E. Hemingway), *Brideshead Revisited* (E. Waugh), *The Lady's not for Burning* (Christopher Frye), *The Iceman Cometh* (E. O'Neil), *The Mirror Cracked* (A.Christie), *Rosencrantz and Guildenstern are Dead* (Tom Stoppard), etc.

  This noun versus verb preference should be kept in mind for transpositions whenever possible, that is to say whenever a noun in the French title has a corresponding verb in English. "Choosing a Husband" and "Educating the Masses" to translate "Le Choix d'un mari" and "L'Education des masses" sounds better and more dynamic in English than "The Choice of a Husband" or "The Education of the Masses".

Translation techniques applied to the translation of titles

The following list of titles in translation contains some interesting ideas for the would-be translator.

1. **Remembrance of Things Past**: with its title borrowed from Shakespeare, the landmark English translation of Marcel Proust's *A la Recherche du temps perdu* by C.K. Scott Moncrieff is nothing short of a modulation-adaptation, albeit one with a real catch and a poetic ring. *A Search for Lost Time* a more recent translation by James Grieve has tried to remain more literal and faithful to the original, without managing to be as fetching.

2. **She Came to Stay**: which translates Simone de Beauvoir's first novel *L'Invitée* is one of those rare examples in which a translation can actually improve on the original. It does so by cleverly anticipating on the plot with the use of a sentence-title in the English way, while the French title remains non-committal and more cryptic.

3. **No Exit**: the English rendering of Jean-Paul Sartre's famous play *Huis clos* in which, after their death, three villainous protagonists find themselves locked in a room symbolizing hell with no hope of escape and no future except tormenting one another, is also an adaptation derived from the plot, since *huis clos*, a legal term meaning *trial behind closed doors*, is not a concept altogether well-known in Anglo-Saxon countries.

4. **Lucifer and the Lord**: for Sartre's *Le Diable et le bon Dieu*, has the merit of retaining both the original's alliteration and antithetical rythm.

5. **Around the World in Eighty Days** is an adept transposition of Jules Verne's *Le Tour du monde en 80 jours* which manages to remain both close to the French title and idiomatic.

6. **The Would-be Gentleman** is an interesting modulation-adaptation of Molière's challenging title *Le Bourgeois gentilhomme*. In this version, the translator, Morris Bishop, does away with the concept of bourgeois and middle class to concentrate

instead on the English calque for *gentilhomme* and tabulate on the main character's chief fault, his vain and unreasonable desire to be better than he actually is in the social scale.

Adaptations in titles: Many adaptations are in fact nothing but re-creations of titles. Here poetic license can take over, especially when the translator is himself a celebrated writer, as in the case of Christopher Fry, whose *Tiger at the Gates* for Giraudoux's *La Guerre de Troie n'aura pas lieu* or *Rings Around the Moon* for Anouilh's *L'Invitation au château* stray very far from the original.

So do titles which, by breaking away from either too bland or abstract French counterparts, are more explanatory in translation than in the SL, a gimmick deemed necessary to entice an Anglo-American readership, titles such as *The Lost Domain* or *The Wanderer* for Alain Fournier's *Le Grand Meaulnes*, or *Wind, Sand and Stars* for Saint-Exupéry's *Terre des hommes*, *Red gloves* for Sartre's *Les Mains sales*, or *A Change of Heart* for Michel Butor's *La Modification*, and *The Order of Things* for Michel Foucault's *Les Mots et les choses*.

Another example of title adaptation that comes to mind concerns Maryse Condé's *La Migration des coeurs*, a re-writing of Emily Brontë's *Wuthering Heights*, transposed to a Caribbean setting. The title translation makes the connection clear for an English-speaking public: *Windward Heights*.

Word modulation in titles: Sometimes all that is needed is a word modulation, be it a preposition, adjective or noun modulation, as made evident by the following renditions.

> The School *for* Wives: L'Ecole *des* femmes (Molière)
> The Roads *to* Freedom: Les Chemins *de* la liberté (Sartre)
> A Very *Easy* Death: Une Mort très *douce* (Beauvoir)
> *Masters'* of the Dew: Les *Gouverneurs* de la rosée (Jacques Roumain)
> Death of a *Nobody*: Mort de *quelqu'un* (Jules Romains)
> Four*some*: *Scène* à quatre (Ionesco)

A modulation may help keep the translation close to the original phonetically if not semantically.

> The Vipers' *Nest*: Le *Noeud* de vipères (Mauriac)
> The Satin *Slipper* : Le *Soulier* de satin (Paul Claudel)

The following modulation is double, abstract to concrete and plural to singular.

> The S*eed* and the F*ruit*: Les S*emailles* et les *moissons* (Henri Troyat)

A modulation may be able to save a pun.

> L'Importance d'être *constant*: The Importance of Being E*arnest* (Oscar Wilde).

Here the word modulation is crucial since the title is a play on the words earnest and Ernest, favorite name of the two main characters, but the French translator has saved the day by substituting a corresponding first name and adjective in the target language. More often than not, however, a play on words just cannot be saved, as in the case of Patrick Modiano's *La Place de l'Etoile* which refers both to the famous Parisian square where the Arch of Triumph stands, and to the spot on a coat where Jews had to display the yellow star of David during the occupation of France by the Nazis. The English title simply reads *A Jewish Story*.

Transposition-modulation in titles: this might solve a translation problem.

> as in Malraux's *Man's Fate* for *La Condition humaine*.
> *Fruits of the Earth* for André Gide's *Les Nourritures terrestres*.

Equivalence in titles: an equivalence will work for idioms.

> *Death on the Installment Plan* for Céline's *Mort à crédit*.

Or cliché-titles.

> *The Prime of Life*: *La Force de l'âge* , and *The Force of Circumstance*: *La Force des choses* (Beauvoir).

Literal translation in titles: sometimes, quite simply, a literal translation is just about the best thing.

> *The Flowers of Evil*: Baudelaire's *Les Fleurs du mal*; *Heartbreak*: Louis Aragon's *Le Crève-coeur*; *The Bald Soprano*: Ionesco's *La Cantatrice chauve*; *Being and Nothingness*: Sartre's *L'Etre et le* néant; *The Stranger*: Camus' *L'Etranger*; *Waiting for Godot*: Beckett's *En attendant Godot*.

But one must beware of literal translation when the phrase to be translated is in fact an idiom, as happened in the case of François Truffaut's *nouvelle vague* film *Les 400 Coups*, inaccurately rendered as *The 400 Blows* in the English version. The French title should have been replaced within its proper context, the idiomatic expression *faire les 400 coups* which, in English, is the equivalent of *to sow one's wild oats* or *to run wild*. A more fitting title perhaps would have been *Wild Oats*, or *Running Wild*.

On the other hand the British movie *Room at the Top* was very adequately translated into French with an equivalence as *Les Chemins de la haute ville,* since, historically, *la haute ville* was the part of town where upper classes would reside leaving *la basse ville* to the lower classes closer to the river and therefore subject to the risk of flooding.

And occasionally a translation may even be superior to the original, proving the old adage "*traduttore, traditore*" false, as in the French version of the American movie title *The Truth about Cats and Dogs, Comme un chien dans un jeu de filles* which cleverly plays on words around the expression "*comme un chien dans un jeu de quilles*".[1]

Lastly, mention must be made of the different conventions governing the capitalization of titles in English and in French. Whereas all nouns and verbs are capitalized in English titles , only the first article and noun are capitalized in French, except if an adjective is placed between the article and the noun, in which case the adjective is also capitalized.

---

[1] For the treatment of titles in non-literary material, such as newspaper headlines, and titles in magazine and review articles, see chapter on "*Guidelines for the Translation of Non-Literary Texts*", Conventions in Newspapers and Magazines, pp.241-2.

Exercices: **Les Titres**

Traduire le titre d'un article ou d'un livre n'est pas quelque chose de secondaire: n'oubliez pas que c'est le titre qui va accrocher ou rebuter votre lecteur potentiel. En général les titres se traduisent en dernier, après que le traducteur connaisse son texte à fond. C'est seulement à ce moment-là qu'il sera en mesure de décider s'il faut garder le titre original en faisant une traduction littérale, faire une transposition qui sonne de façon plus idiomatique dans la L.A., risquer une modulation qui soit stylistiquement et sémantiquement plus intéressante, ou même s'il faut carrément se lancer dans une adaptation au cas où le titre de la L.D. serait intraduisible.

A. Le Jeu des titres

Connaissez-vous les titres anglais de ces oeuvres littéraires françaises ou francophones? Sinon, essayez de les traduire au mieux.

1. Le Malade imaginaire (Molière)
2. L'Esprit des Lois (Charles de Montesquieu)
3. Les Liaisons dangereuses (Pierre Choderlos de Laclos)
4. Le Jeu de l'amour et du hasard (Marivaux)
5. Les Confessions (Jean-Jacques Rousseau)
6. Les Mémoires d'outre-tombe (François-René de Chateaubriand)
7. Les Travailleurs de la mer (Victor Hugo)
8. L'Homme au masque de fer (Alexandre Dumas)
9. On ne badine pas avec l'amour (Alfred de Musset)
10. La Mare au diable (George Sand)
11. Le Père Goriot (Honoré de Balzac)
12. Le Rouge et le noir (Stendhal)
13. Un Coeur simple (Gustave Flaubert)
14. La Parure (Guy de Maupassant)

15. Les Fleurs du mal (Charles Baudelaire)

16. Le Petit Chose (Alphonse Daudet) (*chose* est le mot qu'on emploie quand on ne peut pas se rappeler le vrai nom d'une personne)

17. L'Assommoir (Emile Zola)

18. Les Dieux ont soif (Anatole France)

19. A l'Ombre des jeunes filles en fleurs (Marcel Proust)

20. Le Diable au corps (Raymond Radiguet)

21. Les Enfants terribles (Jean Cocteau)

22. Voyage au bout de la nuit (Louis-Ferdinand Céline)

23. Le Bal des voleurs (Jean Anouilh)

24. La Folle de Chaillot (Jean Giraudoux)

25. L'Etre et le néant (Jean -Paul Sartre)

26. L'Homme révolté (Albert Camus)

27. Le Deuxième Sexe (Simone de Beauvoir)

28. Des Chênes qu'on abat (André Malraux)

29. Le Fil de l'épée (Charles de Gaulle)

30. Oh! les beaux jours (Samuel Beckett)

31. Tueur sans gages (Eugene Ionesco)

32. Les Bonnes (Jean Genêt)

33. L'Emploi du temps (Michel Butor)

34. Pieux Souvenirs (Marguerite Yourcenar)

35. Les Particules élémentaires (Michel Houellebecq)

36. Les Bouts de bois de Dieu (Ousmane Sembène)

37. La Rue Cases-nègres (Joseph Zobel)

38. Antan d'enfance (Patrick Chamoiseau)

39. La Traversée de la mangrove (Maryse Condé)

40. L'Enfant de sable (Tahar Ben Jelloun)

B. Classiques français et leurs traductions anglaises

Faites correspondre les titres originaux avec leurs traductions.

1. Le Bourgeois gentilhomme (Molière)   ____ Endgame
2. Notre Dame de Paris (V. Hugo)   ____ Exit the King
3. Le Tour du monde en 80 jours (J. Verne)   ____ Man's Fate
4. A la recherche du temps perdu (M. Proust)   ____ Strait is the Gate
5. Le Blé en herbe (Colette)   ____ No Exit

6. La Porte étroite (A. Gide)   ___ The Would be Gentleman

7. Partage de midi (P. Claudel)   ___ The Ripening Seed
8. L'Alouette (J. Anouilh)   ___ The Sea Wall
9. Les Mémoires d'une jeune fille rangée (S. de Beauvoir)   ___ Around the World in Eighty Days
10. Huis clos (J. P. Sartre)   ___ Remembrance of Things Past

11. La Condition humaine (A. Malraux)   ___ The Hunchback of Notre Dame

12. Fin de partie (S. Beckett)   ___ Memoirs of a Dutiful Daughter

13. Le Roi se meurt (E. Ionesco)   ___ Noontide
14. L'Ere du soupçon (N. Sarraute)   ___ The Lark
15. Un Barrage contre le Pacifique (M. Duras)   ___ The Age of Suspicion

C. Titres français de classiques anglo-américains

Essayez de retrouver les titres originaux des traductions françaises suivantes.

1. Beaucoup de bruit pour rien (William Shakespeare)
2. La Mégère apprivoisée (William Shakespeare)
3. Le Songe d'une nuit d'été (William Shakespeare)
4. Peines d'amour perdues (William Shakespeare)
5. L'Ecole de la médisance (Richard Brinsley Sheridan)
6. Les Hauts de Hurlevent (Emily Brontë)
7. Les Grandes Espérances (Charles Dickens)
8. La Foire aux vanités (William Thackeray)
9. Alice au pays des merveilles (Lewis Carroll)
10. L'Importance d'être constant (Oscar Wilde)
11. Gens de Dublin (James Joyce)
12. La Case de l'oncle Tom. (Harriet Beecher Stowe)
13. Le Tour d'écrou (Henry James)
14. La Conquête du courage (Stephen Crane)
15. Au Temps de l'innocence (Edith Wharton)
16. L'Envers du paradis (F. Scott Fitzgerald)
17. L'Adieu aux armes (Ernest Hemingway)

18. Pour qui sonne le glas (Ernest Hemingway)
19. Un Tramway nommé désir (Tennessee Williams)
20. La Chatte sur un toit brûlant (Tennessee Williams)
21. Les Raisins de la colère (John Steinbeck)
22. L'Attrappe-coeur (J.D. Salinger)

D. Titres de films

I. Retrouvez les titres originaux des films anglo-américains suivants. (Consultez un moteur de recherche français, tel que http://www.yahoo.fr, ou www.google.fr)

1. La Ruée vers l'or
2. Le Magicien d'Oz
3. Autant en emporte le vent
4. Le Train sifflera trois fois
5. L'Homme qui en savait trop
6. Fenêtre sur cour
7. Bons Baisers de Russie
8. Blanche neige et les sept nains
9. La Belle et le clochard
10. La Panthère rose s'en mêle
11. Vol au dessus d'un nid de coucou
12. Les Dents de la mer
13. S.O.S. fantômes
14. L'Empire contre attaque
15. Retour vers le futur
16. Les Aventuriers de l'arche perdue
17. Le Cercle des poètes disparus
18. Maman, j'ai raté l'avion!
19. La Famille Pierrafeu
20. L'Arme fatale
21. Sur la route de Madison
22. Qui veut la peau de Roger Rabbit?
23. Les Vestiges du jour
24. La Planète des singes

25. Le Seigneur des anneaux:
26. Harry Potter à l'école des sorciers
27. La Chute du faucon noir
28. Orgueil et préjugés
29. Le Discours d'un roi
30. Le Bon Côté des choses

II. Retrouvez les traductions en anglais de ces titres de films français.

1. La Règle du jeu
2. Les Enfants du paradis
3. A Bout de souffle
4. Les Diaboliques
5. Les Quatre cents coups
6. Ascenseur pour échafaud
7. Le Salaire de la peur
8. Les Parapluies de Cherbourg
9. Au Revoir les enfants
10. Le Retour de Martin Guerre
11. Diabolo-menthe
12. Le Hussard sur le toit
13. Le Dîner de cons
14. La Vie rêvée des anges
15. Le Placard
16. Le Fabuleux Destin d'Amélie Poulain
17. La Marche de l'Empereur
18. Stupeur et tremblements
19. La Môme
20. Coco avant Chanel
21. Entre les murs
22. Des Hommes et des dieux

III. Parmi les titres des exercices I et II de la section D, indiquez lesquels sont des traductions littérales, des emprunts, des calques, des transpositions, des modulations, des équivalences ou des adaptations.

Chapter 14
Guidelines
For the Translation of Literary Prose

Sticking to the text vs. demonstrating originality

One of the first questions a beginning translator will probably ask is: how much leeway do I have with the translation of a text? The answer is easy to formulate but more difficult to adhere to: try to strike a happy balance between not keeping enough distance and keeping too much distance from the source text. There are dangers in being extreme. Remaining too close to the source text and its wording might blind the translator to its ideas and spirit and lead to paraphrasing, the result being a version which could sound too much like a translation. On the other hand, straying too far from the source text by attempting to be overly creative and idiomatic could lead to losing sight of the original message with all its nuances and result in an adaptation more than a translation.

What are the basic guidelines to follow for a successful literary translation?

1. Difference between literary and non-literary translation
Literary translation essentially differs from non-literary translation in that accuracy alone will not be sufficient. Of equal importance with the message are the spirit of the text and the author's style. Those qualities, too, must be rendered.
2. Adapt to tone of text

Determine the tone of the text: is it prosaic, poetic, philosophical, didactic, classical, romantic, modern, old fashioned, confidential *etc*.? And adapt your translation to it.

3. Adapt to language level

Determine the language level from the social context: are we dealing with a highly refined language register, one that reveals education, erudition and sophistication; or are we dealing with a simple, colloquial approach, one characteristic of everyday conversation; or still, with a vernacular, such as adolescent or proletarian speech, slang, or one of the languages of the various ethnic groups within the Francophone community?

4. Adapt to author's style

Determine the style used by the author and remember that translators must not have a style of their own, but be versatile like the chameleon. If an author has a convoluted style (such as Proust's), writing quirks (such as the synonymous word pairs in Rabelais and Montaigne), makes ironical quips (such as Voltaire), resist the impulse to change anything in an effort to "improve" on the original. These are distinctive characteristics which are the hallmark of well-known authors, and make them instantly recognizable. You, as a translator, have the duty to keep behind the scene and resist any temptation to edit, modify, add or delete words or groups of words, in short, act as a co-author. Your task is not to make an adaptation or re-write the book, but rather to faithfully render a message, style, tone, and atmosphere.

5. Necessary and unnecessary changes

Watch out for words or phrases which are placed in emphatic positions. Do not alter sentence structure, word order, or punctuation unless these run counter to English usage. In case modifications become absolutely necessary in order to yield an idiomatic translation, or for unequivocal understanding, you may take liberties with the grammatical categories and structures as required by the various translation techniques. But do not take liberties with tenses. Keep the tense the author intended for the story, except in those cases which are covered in chapter seven on *Literal Translation.*[1]

6. Adapt to the time period

Unless you have been specifically commissioned to give the modern version of a particular work in translation, adapt your vocabulary to the time period of the source text. For the translation of an old text you will obviously not be required to create a pastiche, but the carefully metered use of period vocabulary will add a touch of atmosphere and replace the piece in its historical context. After all, an eighteenth century novel or short story should not sound like a twentieth century one.   Here, recourse to comparative literature can be of invaluable help. Read French and English or American authors of the same time period, genre and style to establish affinities, and to glean ideas for the re-creation of the proper atmosphere through the use of similar words and syntax. There are similarities between Choderlos de Laclos and Richardson, Victor Hugo and Charles Dickens, George Sand and George Eliot, Marcel Proust and Virginia Woolf to mention just a few.

Working method

You have been assigned a particular text to translate. How should you proceed?

1. Getting acquainted phase: if you know nothing about the author and his or her work, now is the time to do a little research. Find out what century, what school of writing he or she belongs to, what his or her claim to fame is. Read the text to be translated right through once to get its overall message and tone. Do a quick textual analysis reviewing all the elements mentioned earlier. What writing techniques are used? Is it a narration, a description, a dialogue? What focalization is resorted to? Is the narration in the first or third person? Is the narrator an omniscient one, a specific

---

[1] See pp.72-5, special problems with tenses.

character, or the author himself? Does the text have a psychological, sociological, philosophical or educational interest? What kind of style is used, what sort of language? When was it written? Be aware of all the implications. You may even have to read between the lines if the text is cryptic.

2. Deciphering phase: read the text a second time for a close semantic and structural analysis. Delineate translation units, underline all words and expressions that remain obscure or present a problem and resort to a monolingual dictionary in the S.L. to determine their meaning. Study words in their context. If the text is stylistically very complex, watch out for separators such as colons, semi-colons, and commas. Also watch out for verbs and verb endings to determine the proper tenses.

3. Transcoding phase: this is the most important and difficult part of the translating process, the passage from the S.L. to the T.L. in thoughts and words. For a correct semantic transfer watch out for the proper lexical register, for false cognates, abstract meanings, words in context, and idioms. Apply the various translation techniques as needed for an accurate and idiomatic rendition. For a correct syntactic transfer, watch out for proper word order, necessary ellipses and structural changes brought about by the use of translation techniques. In your search for the right word or expression, use a thesaurus, a good bilingual dictionary, and a monolingual dictionary in the T.L. as necessary.[2] Translate the title now.

4. Finishing phase: the rough product or first draft of phase three must be worked into a satisfactory and harmonious translation, one that reads as smoothly as the original. A subtle balance must now be struck between remaining as literal and close to the S.L. text as possible, and departing from it as required by idiomatic usage in the T.L., so as not to give readers the feeling that they are dealing with a translation. In case several solutions are possible in the translation of a particular phrase or sentence, retain the one which

---

[2] See appendix pp.278-80 for a list of mono and bilingual dictionaries.

will fit best in the context. This phase is the icing on the cake and the overall success of the project depends upon it. It is usually best tackled after a certain lapse of time, preferably a day or two, allowing you to put a little distance between yourself and the text, and view everything more critically.

5.Checking phase: this entails a final proofreading of the translation in comparison with the original text to correct mistakes and oversights.

The following chart summarizes the whole process:

1	2	3	4	5
getting acquainted with text: research and text analysis	deciphering: structural and semantic analysis	transcoding SL-TL: actual translation	finishing touch: stylistic corrections	proofreading: comparison with original

We shall now apply these guidelines to a sample of literary texts by well-known French authors from different time periods and offer suggested translations as examples of the finished product which is to be aimed at. A comparison of the source text with its translation should give the student some idea about the degree of freedom allowed in such undertakings.

Prose Text 1   **Il faut cultiver notre jardin**

---

*The following excerpt is the conclusion to Voltaire's philosophical tale,
Candide. The hero, a young man, has been influenced by the teaching of his
master Pangloss, a philosopher who professes that "everything is for the best in
the world". He has scoured the world in pursuit of happiness and of his beloved
Cunégonde, yet has found instead nothing but evil, man-made disasters as well
as metaphysical ones, in the guise of intolerance, cruelty, cheating, exploitation,
wars, storms, illness and earthquakes. What then is the purpose of life? And
what practical attitude is one to adopt?*

Il y avait dans le voisinage un derviche[1] très fameux, qui passait pour le meilleur
philosophe de [2] la Turquie; [Candide, Pangloss et Martin] allèrent le consulter;
Pangloss porta la parole[3] et lui dit: "Maître, nous venons vous prier de nous dire
pourquoi un aussi étrange animal que l'homme a été formé." "-De quoi te
mêles-tu? dit le derviche, est-ce là ton affaire?"[4] "-Mais, mon révérend père,[5] dit
Candide, il y a horriblement de mal sur la terre.[6] "-Qu'importe, dit le derviche,
qu'il y ait du mal ou du bien?[7] Quand sa Hautesse[8] envoie un vaisseau en
Egypte, s'embarrasse-t-Elle[9] si les souris qui sont dans le vaisseau sont à leur
aise ou non?" "-Que faut-il donc faire? dit Pangloss." "-Te taire" dit le
derviche. "-Je me flattais,[10] dit Pangloss, de raisonner un peu avec vous des
effets et des causes, du meilleur des mondes possibles, de l'origine du mal, de la
nature de l'âme et de l'harmonie préétablie."[11] Le derviche, à ces mots, leur
ferma la porte au nez.[12]

Pendant cette conversation, la nouvelle s'était répandue qu'on venait
d'étrangler à Constantinople deux vizirs du banc et le mufti,[13] et qu'on avait
empalé plusieurs de leurs amis.[14] Cette catastrophe faisait partout un grand
bruit[15]pendant quelques heures. Pangloss, Candide et Martin, en retournant[16] à
la petite métairie,[17] rencontrèrent un bon vieillard qui prenait le frais[18] à sa porte
sous un berceau d'orangers. Pangloss, qui était aussi curieux que raisonneur,[19]
lui demanda comment se nommait le mufti qu'on venait d'étrangler. "-Je n'en
sais rien,[20] répondit le bonhomme, et je n'ai jamais su le nom d'aucun mufti ni
d'aucun vizir. J'ignore[21] absolument l'aventure dont vous me parlez; je
présume qu'en général, ceux qui se mêlent des affaires publiques périssent
quelquefois misérablement, et qu'ils le méritent; mais je ne m'informe[22] jamais
de ce qu'on fait[23] à Constantinople; je me contente d'y envoyer[24] vendre les
fruits du jardin que je cultive." Ayant dit ces mots, il fit entrer les étrangers dans
sa maison; ses deux filles et ses deux fils leur présentèrent plusieurs sortes de
sorbets qu'ils faisaient eux-mêmes, du kaïmak[25] piqué d'écorces de cédrat confit,

des oranges, des citrons, des limons, des ananas, des dattes, des pistaches, du café de Moka [...]. Après quoi les deux filles de ce bon musulman parfumèrent les barbes de Candide, de Pangloss et de Martin.

"Vous devez avoir, dit Candide au Turc, une vaste et magnifique terre?" "-Je n'ai que vingt arpents,[26] répondit le Turc, je les cultive avec mes enfants; le travail éloigne de nous trois grands maux, l'ennui, le vice et le besoin.[27]"

Candide, en retournant dans sa métairie, fit de profondes réflexions[28] sur le discours du Turc. Il dit à Pangloss et à Martin: "Ce bon vieillard me paraît s'être fait[29] un sort bien préférable à celui des six rois avec qui nous avons eu l'honneur de souper." "Les grandeurs, dit Pangloss, sont fort dangereuses, selon le rapport de tous les philosophes; car enfin [   ] vous savez comment périrent [...] Richard II d'Angleterre, Edouard II, Henri VI, Richard III, Marie Stuart,[30] Charles Ier, les trois Henri de France, l'empereur Henri IV? Vous savez..." "-Je sais aussi, dit Candide, qu'il faut cultiver notre jardin." "-Vous avez raison, dit Pangloss; car, quand l'homme fut mis dans le jardin d'Eden, il y fut mis [...] pour qu'il travaillât, ce qui prouve que l'homme n'est pas né pour le repos" "-Travaillons sans raisonner, dit Martin, c'est le seul moyen de rendre la vie supportable.[31]"

Toute la petite société entra dans ce louable dessein,[32] chacun se mit à exercer ses talents. La petite terre rapporta beaucoup. Cunégonde était à la vérité bien laide; mais elle devint une excellente pâtissière; [...] et Pangloss disait[33] quelquefois à Candide: "-Tous les évènement sont enchaînés dans le meilleur des mondes possibles; car enfin, si vous n'aviez pas été chassé d'un beau château à grands coups de pied dans le derrière[34] pour l'amour de Mademoiselle Cunégonde, si vous n'aviez pas été mis à l'Inquisition, si vous n'aviez pas couru l'Amérique à pied, si vous n'aviez pas donné un bon coup d'épée[35] au baron, si vous n'aviez pas perdu tous vos moutons du bon pays d'Eldorado, vous ne mangeriez pas ici des cédrats confits et des pistaches." "-Cela est bien dit, répondait Candide, mais il faut cultiver notre jardin."

(Voltaire, Candide)

Guiding notes

The above text is a narrative which includes some drama in the form of dialogue inserts. The style is distinctive of its author, classical and concise; the tone, full of irony and satire. The rhythm is lively and swift and tends to the quick demonstration of Voltaire's philosophical tenets. In order to be faithful, the translation must respect these characteristics, render the irony while keeping to the rhythm by taking particular care not to weigh down the sentence with heavy grammatical structures or unnecessary padding. It is also advisable to maintain the eighteenth century flavor whenever possible by giving preference to words of that period, *i.e.* words of Latin derivation, over newer terms.

---

[1] **Derviche**: keep this Turkish borrowing to add a touch of exoticism as Voltaire intended.

[2] **Le meilleur philosophe de la Turquie**: avoid a barbarism by keeping in mind that the use of a superlative in English entails a preposition modulation when followed by the name of a place.

[3] **Porta la parole**: an eighteenth century turn of phrase meaning "fut le porte parole."

[4] **De quoi te mêles-tu? Est-ce là ton affaire?**: keep the tone of informal conversation; use an equivalence.

[5] **Mon révérend père**: customs in titles differ between English and French; no possessive adjective in English is used when the person is addressed directly.

[6] **Il y a horriblement de mal sur la terre**: a literal translation is simply impossible here; "horriblement" implies both degree in horror and amount: try a transposition with an adjective and a noun instead.

[7] **Qu'importe...que...ou**: keep the parallel construction with the proper conjunction to introduce alternative possibilities.

[8] **Sa Hautesse...Elle**: again involves usage in titles; certain titles are always feminine in French regardless of the sex of their holder when referring to the third person, *i.e.* Sa Hautesse le sultan..., Sa Majesté le roi..., Sa Sainteté le pape.... This involves use of the feminine personal pronoun. Watch for the appropriate gender in English.

[9] **S'embarrasse-t-elle?**: se soucie-t-elle?

[10] **Je me flattais**: eighteenth century phrase meaning "j'espérais."

[11] **De raisonner un peu...harmonie préétablie**: this is an ironical and condensed summary of Leibnitz's philosophical theories which Voltaire has tried to prove wrong throughout his tale. Keep to a literal translation.

[12] **Leur ferma la porte au nez**: a word modulation will be necessary for this idiomatic expression.

[13] **Vizir...mufti**: see note 1.

[14] **On venait...on avait... amis**: a message modulation using the passive voice will avoid the awkward use of the indefinite English pronoun "one."

[15] **Faisait un grand bruit**: use a verb and a noun modulation for this idiom.

[16] **En retournant**: several translations are possible here; "while" followed by the gerund as in the text, or a noun transposition.

[17] **Métairie**: check the meaning of this term in a French monolingual dictionary before deciding on a translation since this is not a concept prevalent in America.

[18] **Qui prenait le frais**: qui prenait l'air frais.

[19] **Raisonneur, raisonner**: in this text, used as false cognates in the sense of argumentative, to argue.

[20] **Je n'en sais rien**: give an equivalence.

[21] **J'ignore**: false cognate meaning "je ne sais pas."

[22] **Je ne m'informe jamais**: je ne demande jamais de renseignements.

[23] **Ce qu'on fait**: ce qui se passe.

[24] **Je me contente d'y envoyer**: do not translate literally as "I am content to send there...," this would fail to understand the nuances of the verb "se contenter de" which are closer to "to be satisfied." Try an adverb transposition instead: "J'y envoie simplement."

[25] **Kaïmak**: see note 1.

[26] **Arpent**: an old French measure now obsolete, roughly the equivalent of one acre.

[27] **L'ennui, le vice et le besoin**: remember that general terms take the definite article in French but not in English.

[28] **Faire une réflexion**: one T.U. meaning "réfléchir."

   Fit de profondes réflexions: make an adverb transposition on the adjective "profondes."

[29] **S'être fait**: do not overlook the reflexive aspect of this verb and keep it in mind for your translation.

[30] **Marie Stuart**: English speakers do not refer to this queen of Scotland by the same name.

[31] **Supportable**: false cognate.

[32] **Entra dans ce dessein**: eighteenth century phrase meaning "se rallia à ce projet."

[33] **Pangloss disait à Candide**: the iterative aspect of the imparfait must not be overlooked, Voltaire does not say "Pangloss dit à Candide."

[34] **Chassé à grands coups de pied dans le derrière**: "chassé à coups de pied" would be simple to render as a cross transposition: "kicked out". But the difficulty here lies in translating the manner in which Candide was kicked out and which Voltaire intended to be both comical and shameful: with hard kicks in the backside. An English translation fails to be as fluid as the French expression and a loss is incurred.

[35] **Donner un coup d'épée**: one T.U.; donner un *bon* coup d'épée: introduces a connotation of finality with a comical note, the sword thrust that did the baron in.

Let's Tend Our Garden

There lived in the vicinity a very famous dervish, reputed to be the best philosopher in Turkey. Candide, Pangloss and Martin went to consult him. Pangloss acted as spokesman and said: "Master, we have come to beg of you to tell us why such a strange animal as man was created." "-Why stick your nose into this? replied the dervish, what business is it of yours?" "-But, Reverend Father, said Candide, there is a horrible amount of evil on earth." "-What does it matter, the dervish said, whether there is good or evil? When His Highness sends a vessel to Egypt, does He worry that the mice on board are comfortable or not?" "-What are we to do then?" said Pangloss. "-Hold your tongue" replied the dervish. "-I was hoping, said Pangloss, to be able to argue with you for a while about effects and causes, the best of possible worlds, the origin of evil, the nature of the soul, and pre-established harmony." The dervish, upon this, slammed the door in their faces.

During this conversation, the news had spread that two viziers of the sultan's council and the mufti had just been strangled in Constantinople, and that several of their friends had been impaled. This catastrophe created a big stir everywhere for a few hours. Pangloss, Candide and Martin, on their way back to the small farm they sharecropped, came upon a good old man who was taking the fresh air on his doorsteps under an arbor of orange trees. Pangloss, who was as curious as he was argumentative, inquired after the name of the mufti who had just been strangled. "-I have no idea, replied the old man, and I have never known the name of any mufti or vizier. I know absolutely nothing of the event to which you are referring; I presume that generally people who meddle in public affairs sometimes come to a miserable end, and that they deserve to, but I never enquire about what goes on in Constantinople; it's enough for me to send the fruit of the garden I farm to be sold there." Having said this, he ushered the strangers into his house; his two daughters and his two sons offered them several sorts of home-made sherbets, some Kaïmak flavored with candied citron peel, oranges, lemons, limes, pineapples, dates, pistachios and Moka coffee. After which, the two daughters of this good muslim perfumed the beards of Candide, Pangloss and Martin.

"-You must, Candide said to the Turk, be the owner of a vast and magnificent estate?" "-I only have twenty acres, the Turk replied; I farm them with my children; work keeps at bay three great evils, boredom, vice and want." Candide, on his way back to his farm, reflected deeply upon the Turk's remarks. He said to Pangloss and Martin: "-This good old man seems to me to have made for himself a life far preferable to that of the three kings with whom we had the honor of having supper." "-Greatness, said Pangloss, is a very dangerous thing, in the recorded opinion of all philosophers; for, after all, you do know how Richard II of England, Edward III, Henri VI, Richard III, Mary Queen of Scots, Charles Ist, the three Henri of France, the emperor Henry IV perished? You do know..." "-I also know, said Candide, that we must tend our garden." "-You're right, said Pangloss: for when man was put in the garden of Eden, he was put there to work; which proves that man was not born to be idle." "-Let's work without arguing, said Martin, that's the only way to make life bearable."

The entire company joined in this praiseworthy venture, each started exerting his talents. The small landholding yielded plenty. Cunegonde was indeed quite ugly; but she became an excellent pastry cook; and Pangloss would sometimes say to Candide: "-All events are linked together in the best of possible worlds; for, after all, had you not been driven away from a beautiful castle by hard kicks in your backside for the love of Mademoiselle Cunegonde, had you not suffered at the hands of the Inquisition, had you not scoured America on foot, had you not run the baron through with your sword, had you not lost all your sheep in the good land of Eldorado, you would not be here eating candied citron and pistachios." "-Quite so, Candide would reply, but let's tend our garden."

Prose Text 2   **La Vieille servante**

The passage below is an example of Flaubert's esthetics of realism, the portrait of a woman who has given her whole life to service and hard work. It is incidental in the unfolding of the novel, Madame Bovary, from which it is taken, but stands in sharp contrast to the life and aspirations of the heroine, Emma, a romantic who finds no place in a petty and materialistic world. It is meant as a social comment on the life of the working poor during the July Monarchy in contrast to the increasing prosperity of the bourgeois class.

"Catherine Nicaise Elizabeth Leroux, de[1] Sassetot-la-Guerrière, pour cinquante-quatre ans de service dans[2] la même ferme, une médaille d'argent -du prix de vingt-cinq francs![3] "

"-Où est-elle, Catherine Leroux?[4] " répéta le conseiller.[5] Elle ne se présentait pas,[6] et l'on entendait des voix qui chuchotaient:[7]

-Vas-y![8]

-Non.

-A gauche!

-N'aie pas peur!

-Ah! qu'elle est bête![9]

-Enfin[10] y est-elle? s'écria Tuvache.

-Oui, la voilà!

-Qu'elle approche donc![11] "

Alors on vit s'avancer sur l'estrade une petite vieille femme[12] de maintien craintif, et qui paraissait se ratatiner dans ses pauvres[13] vêtements. Elle avait aux pieds[14] de grosses galoches[15] de bois, et, le long des hanches,[16] un grand tablier bleu. Son visage maigre, entouré d'un béguin[17] sans bordure, était plus plissé de rides[18] qu'une pomme de reinette[19] flétrie, et des manches[20] de sa camisole rouge[21] dépassaient[22] deux longues mains, à articulations noueuses. La poussière des granges, la potasse des lessives et le suint des laines les avaient si bien encroûtées, éraillées, durcies,[23] qu'elles semblaient sales quoiqu'elles fussent rincées d'eau claire,[24] et, à force d'avoir servi,[25] elles restaient entr'ouvertes, comme pour présenter d'elles-mêmes l'humble témoignage[26] de tant de souffrances subies. Quelque chose d'une rigidité monacale relevait[27] l'expression de sa figure. Rien de triste ou d'attendri n'amollissait ce regard pâle. Dans la fréquentation des animaux,[28] elle avait pris[29] leur mutisme et leur placidité. C'était la première fois qu'elle se voyait au milieu d'une compagnie si nombreuse; et, intérieurement effarouchée par les drapeaux, par les tambours, par les messieurs en habit[30] noir et par la croix d'honneur[31] du conseiller, elle demeurait tout immobile, ne sachant s'il fallait s'avancer ou s'enfuir,[32] ni pourquoi la foule la poussait et pourquoi les examinateurs[33] lui souriaient. Ainsi se tenait, devant ces bourgeois épanouis, un demi-siècle de servitude.[34]

"Approchez, vénérable Catherine Nicaise Elizabeth Leroux!" dit M. le conseiller,[35] qui avait pris des mains du président la liste des lauréats.[36] Et tour à tour examinant la feuille de papier, puis la vieille femme, il répétait[37] d'un ton paternel:

"Approchez, approchez!"

"-Etes-vous sourde?[38] " dit Tuvache, en bondissant sur son fauteuil. Et il se mit à lui crier dans l'oreille: "Cinquante-quatre ans de service! Une médaille d'argent! Vingt-cinq francs! C'est pour vous."

Puis, quand elle eut sa médaille, elle la considéra. Alors un sourire de béatitude[39] se répandit sur sa figure[40] et on l'entendait qui marmottait[41] en s'en allant:[42] "-Je la donnerai au curé[43] de chez nous, pour qu'il me dise des messes."

"-Quel fanatisme!" s'exclama le pharmacien, en se penchant vers le notaire.[44]

La séance était finie;[45] la foule se dispersa,[46] et, maintenant que les discours étaient lus, chacun reprenait son rang et tout rentrait dans la coutume:[47] les maîtres rudoyaient[48] les domestiques, et ceux-ci frappaient les animaux, triomphateurs indolents qui retournaient à l'étable, une couronne verte entre les cornes.[49]

(Gustave Flaubert, *Madame Bovary*)

Guiding notes

This nineteenth century excerpt makes use of three different writing techniques: narration, description and dialogue. The tone between these sections varies greatly and proper care must be taken to adopt a familiar register for the dialogues and a literary one for the detailed descriptions. An essential element of Flaubert's style is the proper selection of the "*mot juste*", the right word. This also has to be kept in mind in the translation, particularly where descriptions are concerned, and use of a thesaurus is strongly recommended.

---

[1] **De Sassetot la Guerrière**: choose a preposition indicating origin.

[2] **Dans une ferme**: a preposition modulation is needed here.

[3] **Du prix de vingt-cinq francs**: various translations are possible, one of which involves a transposition with an adjective. In a literary context do not convert francs into dollars, it is best to keep the French currency for local color in order

to situate the story in its geographical and historical context, especially now that francs have been replaced by euros.

[4] **Où est-elle, Catherine Leroux**?: the use of the name along with the personal pronoun is a gallicism with which English usage is at variance.

[5] **Le conseiller***: i.e.* "conseiller de prefecture," a member of the "conseil du préfet" or council of the highest executive official in the region.

[6] **Elle ne se présentait pas**: avoid an unidiomatic reflexive verb in English; find a message modulation instead.

[7] **On entendait des voix qui chuchotaient**: use the passive voice to render the construction with the indefinite pronoun "on."

[8] **Vas-y**: use a speech equivalent.

[9] **Qu'elle est bête**: use a speech equivalent.

[10] **Enfin, y est-elle**?: the adverb "enfin" is used here in a conversational context and does not carry the same meaning as in a demonstrative context. It denotes impatience on the part of the speaker. Find an equivalence.

[11] **Qu'elle approche donc**!: a subjunctive used as an imperative for the third person; "donc" here is a prop word used in familiar conversation and does not have its usual meaning of "therefore." Find a speech equivalent.

[12] **Alors on vit s'avancer**...: use a passive construction.

[13] **Ses pauvres vêtements**: is the adjective taken in a concrete or abstract sense? Choose your translation accordingly.

[14] **Elle avait aux pieds**: use a preposition modulation.

[15] **De grosses galoches**: look up meaning in a French monolingual dictionary to help you figure out the English equivalent.

[16] **Le long des hanches**: use a preposition modulation.

[17] **Un béguin**: a bonnet.

[18] **Etait plus plissé de rides**: is it possible to economize words in the translation?

[19] **Une pomme de reinette**: a russet apple.

[20] **Des manches**...: use a preposition denoting origin.

[21] **De sa camisole rouge**: look up "camisole" in a monolingual dictionary to determine the proper equivalent.

[22] **Dépassaient**: visualize the image in order to find the right message modulation in English.

[23] **Les avaient si bien encroûtées, éraillées, durcies**: look up unknown words in a bilingual dictionary, then go to a thesaurus for the right words in this context.

[24] **Quoiqu'elles fussent rincées d'eau claire**: use of the subjunctive imperfect is dictated by conjunction "quoique;" a pluperfect seems appropriate in English to express anteriority of the action in relation to the previous clause.

[25] **A force d'avoir servi**: most dictionaries give "by dint of" as an equivalent to "à force de." The main difference is that "by dint of" is now obsolete, unlike "à force de" which is still very much in use and connotes the constant repetition of

an action; find a solution in a message modulation, a transposition or a different preposition.

[26] **Comme pour présenter d'elles mêmes**...: find a non literal translation.

[27] **Relevait**: abstract meaning.

[28] **Dans la fréquentation des animaux**: a literal translation is not possible; the phrase means "du fait qu'elle avait tant vécu au milieu des animaux ;" a transposition or a modulation can be resorted to.

[29] **Elle avait pris**: the verb is used in an abstract sense.

[30] **En habit noir**: false cognate.

[31] **La croix d'honneur**: the cross of the Legion of Honor created by Napoleon the First to reward those having provided exceptional services to the State.

[32] **Ne sachant s'il fallait s'avancer ou s'enfuir**: use a personal construction instead of this impersonal one.

[33] **Les examinateurs**: false cognate; here we are not dealing with an exam but with a contest, and with the awarding of prizes by judges.

[34] **Ainsi se tenait, devant ces bourgeois épanouis, un demi-siècle de servitude**: try and find the proper words to render this concise and striking formula.

[35] **M. le conseiller**: *i.e.* Monsieur le conseiller; this very formal form of address cannot be rendered in English.

[36] **Lauréats**: false cognate; think of the situation: who are these lauréats? what do they stand to win?

[37] **Il répétait**: do not overlook the iterative aspect of this past tense.

[38] **Etes-vous sourde?**: a modulation using a negative expression would probably be the best idiomatic way of translating this question.

[39] **Un sourire de béatitude**: use a transposition with an adjective.

[40] **Se répandit sur sa figure**: use a message modulation; think of the concept.

[41] **Qui marmottait**: the relative pronoun can be economized in the English translation without incurring any loss when the imparfait is rendered as a gerund.

[42] **En s'en allant**: use a noun transposition.

[43] **Au curé**: false cognate; the French word may be borrowed for local color.

[44] **Le notaire**: false cognate; a "notaire" takes care of wills and estates.

[45] **La séance était finie**: use an adverbial transposition for the verb.

[46] **La foule se dispersa**: avoid a reflexive verb in English.

[47] **Tout rentrait dans la coutume**: find an equivalent.

[48] **Les maîtres rudoyaient**...: the following list of imparfaits must be rendered as past progressives.

[49] **Entre les cornes**: English usage requires the use of the possessive adjective before parts of the body.

The Old Servant

"To Catherine Nicaise Elizabeth Leroux from Sassetot-la-Guerrière, for fifty four years of service on the same farm, a silver medal, worth twenty five francs!"
"Where is Catherine Leroux?" repeated the councilor.
There was no sign of her, and voices could be heard whispering:
  -Go ahead!
  -No
  -To the left!
  -Don't be afraid!
  -What a fool!
  -Is she here or isn't she? cried Tuvache.
  -Yes, there she is!
  -Let her step forward then!
    At that moment a little old woman of frightened appearance who seemed to have shriveled up inside her shabby garments, was seen coming onto the platform. She had clumsy wooden clogs on her feet and a big blue apron around her hips. Her skinny face, framed in a peasant's coif without edges, was more wrinkled than a withered russet apple, and from the sleeves of her red jacket hung her long gnarled hands. The dust of barns, the lye of washings and the grease of raw wool had left them so scabby, chafed and hardened that they looked dirty, even though they had been rinsed out in clear water; and from years of service they remained half open, as if to bring their own humble testimony to the many hardships endured. A touch of monastic austerity enhanced her countenance. Nothing sad or tender softened her pale eyes. Living as she did among the animals, she had assumed their silence and placidity. It was the first time she found herself in the midst of such a large crowd, and scared deep down by the flags, the drums, the gentlemen in black coats and the councilor's badge of honor, she stood transfixed, not knowing whether she should proceed or turn around and flee, or why the crowd was urging her on and the judges smiling at her. Thus stood, before those beaming bourgeois, half a century of bondage.
    "-Step forward, venerable Catherine Nicaise Elizabeth Leroux!" said the councilor who had taken the list of award recipients from the chairman's hands. And looking now at the sheet of paper, now at the old woman, he kept repeating in a fatherly tone: "Step forward!"
    "-Can't you hear?" said Tuvache springing from his chair. And he began to shout in her ear:
    "-Fifty four years of service! A silver medal! Twenty five francs! It's for you."

After she got her medal, she examined it. Then her face broke into a blissful smile and she could be heard mumbling on her way out: "I'll give it to the priest back home, to say masses for me."

"-Such fanaticism!" exclaimed the pharmacist leaning toward the lawyer.

The show was over. The crowd dispersed; and now that the speeches had been read, everyone resumed his former rank, everything reverted to the old order: masters were bullying their servants, and servants were beating the animals, placid in their triumph, returning to their barn with green wreaths between their horns.

Prose Text 3   **Un Univers dans une tasse de thé**

This is the central passage of Proust's Remembrance of Things Past.   It recounts the magical moment when Marcel, the narrator, unexpectedly finds a way to recapture his past, the nostalgic days of his boyhood.

Il y avait déjà bien des années[1] que, de Combray, tout ce qui n'était pas le théâtre et le drame[2] de mon coucher n'existait plus pour moi, quand un jour d'hiver, comme je rentrais à la maison, ma mère, voyant que j'avais froid, me proposa de me faire prendre,[3] contre mon habitude,[4] un peu de[5] thé. Je refusai d'abord et, je ne sais pourquoi, me ravisai.[6] Elle envoya chercher[7] un de ces gâteaux courts et dodus appelés petites madeleines[8] qui semblent avoir été moulés dans la valve rainurée d'une coquille de Saint-Jacques.[9] Et bientôt, machinalement,[10] accablé par la morne journée et la perspective d'un triste lendemain, je portai à mes lèvres une cuillerée du thé où j'avais laissé[11] s'amollir un morceau de madeleine. Mais à l'instant même où[12] la gorgée[13] mêlée des miettes du gâteau toucha mon palais,[14] je tressaillis, attentif à ce qui se passait d'extraordinaire en moi.[15] Un plaisir délicieux[16] m'avait envahi, isolé, sans la notion de sa cause. Il m'avait aussitôt rendu les vicissitudes de la vie indifférentes, ses désastres inoffensifs, sa brièveté illusoire [...]. J'avais cessé de me sentir médiocre, contingent,[17] mortel. D'où avait pu me venir cette puissante joie?[18] Je sentais[19] qu'elle était liée au goût du thé et du gâteau, mais qu'elle le dépassait infiniment, ne devait pas être de même nature. D'où venait-elle?[20] Que signifiait-elle ? Où l'appréhender?[21] Je bois une seconde gorgée où je ne trouve[22] rien de plus que dans la première, une troisième qui m'apporte un peu moins que la seconde. Il est temps que je m'arrête, la vertu du breuvage[23] semble diminuer.[24] Il est clair que la vérité que je cherche n'est pas en lui,[25] mais en moi [...]. Je pose la tasse et me tourne vers mon esprit.[26] [...]

Et tout d'un coup le souvenir m'est apparu. Ce goût, c'était celui[27] du petit morceau de madeleine que le dimanche matin à Combray [...] quand j'allais lui dire bonjour dans sa chambre, ma tante Léonie m'offrait[28] après l'avoir trempé[29] dans son infusion de thé ou de tilleul.[30] La vue de la petite madeleine ne m'avait rien rappelé avant que je n'y eusse goûté,[31] peut-être parce que, en ayant souvent aperçu depuis, sans en manger,[32] sur les tablettes des pâtissiers, leur image avait quitté ces jours de Combray pour se lier à d'autres plus récents; peut-être parce que, de ces souvenirs[33] abandonnés si longtemps hors de la mémoire, rien ne survivait, tout s'était désagrégé [...]. Mais, quand d'un passé ancien[34] rien ne subsiste, après la mort des êtres, après la destruction des choses,[35] seules, plus frêles mais plus vivaces, plus immatérielles, plus persistantes, plus fidèles, l'odeur et la saveur restent encore longtemps, comme les âmes, à se rappeler, à attendre, à espérer, sur la ruine de tout le reste, à porter[36] sans fléchir, sur leur gouttelette presque impalpable, l'édifice immense du souvenir.[37]

Et dès que j'eus reconnu le goût du morceau de madeleine trempé dans le tilleul que me donnait[38] ma tante [...] aussitôt la vieille maison grise sur la rue, où était sa chambre, vint comme un décor de théâtre s'appliquer au petit pavillon donnant sur[39] le jardin, qu'on avait construit[40] pour mes parents [...] et avec la maison, la ville [...], la Place[41] où on m'envoyait avant déjeuner, les rues où j'allais faire des courses, les chemins qu'on prenait[42] si le temps était beau. Et comme dans ce jeu où les Japonais s'amusent à tremper dans un bol de porcelaine rempli d'eau, de petits morceaux de papier jusque-là indistincts qui, à peine y sont-ils plongés,[43] s'étirent, se contournent, se colorent, se différencient,[44] deviennent des fleurs, des maisons, des personnages consistants et reconnaissables, de même[45] maintenant toutes les fleurs de notre jardin [...], et les nymphéas de la Vivonne, et les bonnes gens du village et leurs petits logis et l'église et tout Combray et ses environs, tout cela[46] [...] est sorti, ville et jardins, de ma tasse de thé.[47]

(Marcel Proust, *Du côté de chez Swann*)

Guiding notes

The passage is an introspective narration written in the first person and delving into things psychological: the author has been searching his memory to find the key to an unexpected and powerful feeling of joy which occurred as he was eating a French cookie and drinking tea.

Translation difficulties here arise mostly from the choice of vocabulary and from the grammatical and syntactical structure. The language is refined and literary and Proustian style is famous for its long winded and balanced sentences which can unfurl into an entire paragraph. Any attempt on the translator's part to cut them for the sake of clarity would interfere with a stylistic effect, for Proust's long sentences show the progress of thoughts as they arise and develop in the mind of the narrator. Let yourself be guided by their structure. Word order is also important since certain groups of words are placed in positions of emphasis in order to catch the reader's attention. Particular care should be taken to keep them in the limelight, at the beginning or at the end of the sentence.

---

[1] **Il y avait déjà bien des années**: there is no need to keep the impersonal construction in the translation.

[2] **Le théâtre et le drame**: these terms are to be taken in the abstract; Proust refers to the scenes that used to accompany his going to bed when he was a child at Combray.

[3] **Proposa de me faire prendre**: the function of verb "faire" here is causative.

[4] **Contre mon habitude**: go beyond a literal translation to remain idiomatic.

[5] **Un peu de thé**: this direct object is separated from its verb by the phrase "contre mon habitude" as permitted by French syntax; can a verb be similarly separated from a direct object in English?

[6] **Je me ravisai**: je changeai d'avis.

[7] **Elle envoya chercher**: use a preposition transposition in place of the second verb.

[8] **Appelés petites madeleines**: borrow the French word since there is no English equivalent: Proust has made them famous even outside France.

[9] **Une coquille de Saint Jacques**: the shell of a scallop; the French term is named after St James because pilgrims on their way to the shrine of St. James of Compostella have been wearing it as a badge since the Middle Ages.

[10] **Machinalement**: go beyond a literal translation; think of the idea beyond the words.

[11] **Où j'avais laissé**: dans laquelle j'avais laissé; English needs to turn "où" into a relative pronoun.

[12] **A l'instant même où**...: constitutes one T.U.; "où" here serves the function of a relative pronoun referring to its antecedent "instant;" "où" as a relative pronoun in French can be indiscriminately linked to expressions of place or time; where expressions of time are concerned in English a modulation becomes necessary: "où" has to change to "when."

[13] **La gorgée**: implies the intake of liquid food contrary to solid food as with "bouchée."

[14] **Mon palais**: polysemous word; select the proper meaning given the context.

[15] **A ce qui se passait d'extraordinaire en moi**: aux choses extraordinaires qui se passaient en moi.

[16] **Délicieux**: a false friend in this context; "delicious" in English only refers to food.

[17] **Contingent**: look up the meaning of this word in a French monolingual dictionary before deciding on a translation.

[18] **D'où avait pu me venir cette puissante joie**?: does English follow the French preposition order here?

[19] **Je sentais**...: one T.U. which can be padded in translation.

[20] **D'où venait-elle**?: see note 18.

[21] **Appréhender**: a partial false cognate here since this particular meaning of the verb "to apprehend" is now obsolete in English; a synonym in French would be "saisir," "capturer."

[22] **Où je ne trouve**...: notice the change of tense with this verb and the following; what is the author's purpose? Can the same stylistic effect be achieved in English? For a translation of "où" see note 11.

[23] **Breuvage**: false cognate; does not refer to "beverage" whose French equivalent is "boisson non alcoolisée."

[24] **Diminuer**: whereas the French language likes abstract words, English prefers concrete ones; find a more expressive way of translating this concept.

[25] **En lui**: what preceding noun does this pronoun refer to? Watch for the proper gender in English.

[26] **Je me tourne vers mon esprit**: a literary turn of phrase; go to the idea beyond the words to find a translation.

[27] **Ce goût, c'était celui**...: gallicism; emphatic construction to place the word "goût" in the limelight; a literal translation being impossible, find another way of emphasizing this particular word in English.

[28] **Quand j'allais...m'offrait**...: what is the value of these imparfaits? How should you render them?

[29] **Après l'avoir trempé**: conjunction "après" is always followed by the past infinitive in French: is English usage the same?

[30] **Son infusion de thé ou de tilleul**: "thé" referring to "tea" and "tilleul" to a kind of herbal tea called "linden tea", the problem here arises from the repetition of the word "tea" within a short interval, an awkward effect; find a circumlocution.

[31] **Avant que je n'y eusse goûté**: conjunction "avant que" necessitates use of the pluperfect subjunctive; can English simplify the translation here? What does pronoun "y" refer to?

[32] **Sans en manger**: do not overlook the translation of indefinite pronoun "en"; what word does it refer to?

[33] **Ces souvenirs**: false cognate.

[34] **Un passé ancien**: "ancien" is not the equivalent of "ancient' here; give a word modulation.

[35] **Après la mort des êtres, après la destruction des choses**: use verb transpositions instead of nouns.

[36] **A se rappeler, à attendre, à espérer...à porter**: in a parallel construction prepositions are repeated in front of each word in French; does English follow the same syntactical rule?

[37] **L'édifice immense du souvenir**: key expression placed in an emphatic position at the end of the sentence; keep it there in your translation and try to find an equally striking formula.

[38] **Donnait**: iterative or progressive aspect?

[39] **Donnant sur**: one word in English.

[40] **Qu'on avait construit**: use a passive construction.

[41] **La Place**: false cognate.

[42] **Les chemins qu'on prenait**: can a passive construction be used here? Who does this "on" stand for, someone indefinite or someone more specific?

[43] **A peine y sont-ils plongés**: why is there a word inversion here?

[44] **S'étirent, se contournent**...: is it necessary for these verbs to remain reflexive in the translation?

[45] **De même**: de la même manière.

[46] **Tout cela**: padding is needed in English.

[47] **Tasse de thé**: be aware of the semantic difference between "tasse de thé" and "tasse à thé," which one refers to contents and what is the proper translation here?

A Whole World in a Cup of Tea

Many years had elapsed during which nothing of Combray beyond the stage and tribulations of my bedtime existed for me any longer, when, coming home one winter day, my mother, who saw that I was cold, offered to have me take some tea, something I didn't usually do. I declined at first, and then, for no particular reason, changed my mind. She sent for one of those short and plump little cakes called "*madeleines*" which look as though they have been molded from the grooved shell of a sea scallop. And soon, without thinking, disheartened by that dreary day and the prospect of another bleak day to come, I took to my lips a spoonful of tea in which I had let a piece of madeleine soften. But just as the sip of liquid with the cake crumbs touched my palate, I shuddered, fascinated by the extraordinary changes taking place within me. A delightful feeling had come over me, disconnected, with no notion of what had brought it about. At once it had made the vicissitudes of life indifferent to me, its disasters, harmless, its brevity, an illusion. I had ceased to feel ordinary, unessential, mortal. Where could this powerful feeling of joy have come from? I had a feeling that it had something to do with the taste of tea and cake, but that it went infinitely beyond, that it had to be of a different nature. Where was it coming from? What was its significance? Where was I to capture it? I take a second sip in which I find nothing more than in the first, a third which brings even less. It is time for me to stop, the magic of the potion seems to be wearing out. It is clear that what I am looking for does not rest in it but in me. I put down the cup and begin to concentrate.

And all at once the memory resurfaced. This was the taste of the little piece of madeleine which, on Sunday mornings at Combray when I went to her room to say hello, my aunt Leonie used to offer me after she had dipped it in her tea or linden infusion. The sight of the little madeleine had recalled nothing before tasting it; perhaps because, having often seen such cakes since, without eating any, on the shelves of pastry shops, their image had left those Combray days to fix itself to more recent ones; perhaps because, of all those memories so long foregone and put out of mind, nothing survived, everything had disintegrated. But when of a distant past nothing remains, after people are dead, after things are destroyed, alone, more frail yet more enduring, more immaterial, persistent and faithful, smell and taste stay on like souls to remember, wait, hope when all else lies in ruin, and to carry unflinchingly, in their almost impalpable droplet, the gigantic monument of recollection.

And as soon as I had recognized the taste of the piece of madeleine dipped in tea which my aunt used to give me, at once the old grey house on the street where her bedroom was, came like a stage backdrop right next to the little pavilion overlooking the garden which had been built for my parents; and along with the house, the town, the square where they used to send me before lunch, the streets where I ran errands, the country lanes where we walked in fair weather.   And just as in that Japanese game in which you dip small indistinguishable pieces of paper into a porcelain bowl filled with water, and no sooner are they in the water than they stretch, assume shapes, color, characteristics, become flowers, houses, substantial and recognizable people, in the same way at that very moment all the flowers of our garden, the water lilies on the Vivonne, the good folk of the village, their little dwellings, the church, and Combray with its surroundings, all of that, town and garden, came out of my cup of tea.

Chapter 15
Guidelines
For the Translation of Dialogues and Plays

The translation of plays, as well as the translation of dialogues which are to be found in novels and short stories, is of a specific kind. It calls for a slightly different approach from the one which generally applies to literary prose.

An oral text is essentially different from a written one in that a different sort of language is used, different dynamics apply: no one speaks as one writes. Therefore, for this act of communication to sound true, the translation of a dialogue will have to try and reproduce the direct speech of conversation.

Problems specific to the translation of dialogues and plays

There are specific difficulties and problems involved in the process. In the translation of dialogues and plays, as in prose translation, a preliminary textual analysis is a must:

- Look into the dramatic context, the circumstances, the time, place and atmosphere.
- It is important to study the social and historical background in order to select the level of language that is most suitable for the translation. One crucial prerequisite will be to determine the language register of the character or characters who are speaking, so as to adapt to it in the T.L. Who is speaking?

What is his or her station in life?   To whom is the message addressed? Is the speaker using informal, popular language? slang? or highly refined speech? Is it contemporary French or is it the tongue of Molière, Marivaux or Musset's time?

- Sometimes various levels of language will have to be used within the same play to reflect the different social status of the characters. As an example, the valets and maids in Molière's plays do not express themselves as do their masters and mistresses. And among the masters and mistresses themselves the range is wide, from simple and uneducated bourgeois such as M. Jourdain, to the literary circles of the *précieuses* and the noble courtiers of the Sun King.   The social rank of all characters must be mirrored in the way they speak. For samples of appropriate cues and repartees in period plays one can turn to comparable English plays of the same era, e.g. Restoration drama in the case of Molière's plays, or Oscar Wilde and G.B. Shaw as well as Eugene O'Neil and Tennessee Williams in the case of Paul Claudel, Jules Romain, Jean Giraudoux, Jean Anouilh *etc.*   For T.L. samples of the various registers in contemporary speech, one can turn to television, the radio, the movies, or other plays.

Equivalence as the preferred translation technique for dialogues

The translation of dialogues, more than any other translation, demands that one goes beyond words, grammar and syntax to the meaning of the original message. Conversation is unquestionably the domain of interjections, colloquial expressions, idioms, set phrases, clichés and reflex formulas as well as cultural references, all impossible to translate literally. Moreover, since the text to be translated is also intended to be acted out on the stage, a certain rhythm, a certain fluency must be maintained in accordance with the rhythm of the S.L. Reading the text aloud will help to get a feel both for intonation and flow.   Also sometimes, what is not verbalized but rather implied can be as important as what is actually said. Consequently, equivalence, a technique which goes to the spirit rather than the letter of a message, will be the preferred strategy for the translator of plays. And the goal to keep in mind will be to strive for the same effects as the original: alliterations, onomatopoeic effects, repetition of certain words for emphasis for instance.

Use of a specific vocabulary

In dialogues, language reflexes play a prominent role, particularly the use of prop words and tags which help the speaker along a sentence. Answer-words like *bon*, *mais oui*, *voilà*, or reinforcing words such as *bien*, *donc*, *alors*, *mais*, *surtout*, as well as words that reiterate a question for rhetorical emphasis at the end of a sentence such as *hein* and *n'est-ce pas* are typical of an oral text.[1] Just remember that in a conversational context these adverbs will have a meaning different from the one they would assume in a prose context, and that whereas "Je me sens *bien*" may mean "I feel *well*", "Vous viendrez *bien* nous voir!" is the equivalent of "You will come and see us, *won't you?*". Likewise, *donc* in "Je pense, *donc* je suis" (I think *therefore* I am), does not have the same function as the *donc* in "Tu ne vois *donc* pas que je suis occupé?" *(Can't* you see that I am busy?) or even the *donc* in "Repasse *donc* demain!" whose purpose is to soften a request (*Why don't you* come back tomorrow?). *Surtout* in the following context "*Surtout* n'allez pas croire qu'il s'agit d'une critique" no longer means *above all* but is closer to *please*: (*Please* do not construe it as a criticism), while *mais* cannot be translated as *but* in "*Mais* je le ferai avec plaisir!" (*Of course*, I'll gladly do it!)

The beginning translator who intends to become serious about dialogue translation will also have to develop glossaries of common reflex formulas and clichés in conversation, many of which are not recorded in standard dictionaries and presuppose a

---

[1] See chapter on equivalence: exclamations and reflex formulas, prop words.

good spoken mastery of the S.L. Expressions such as *"Vous voulez rire!"* (*You must be joking!*), *"Mon vieux"* (*Old buddy*), *"Ne te dérange pas"* (*Don't bother*) etc. And never forget that the context or situation is of prime importance in determining the final significance of one such phrase or sentence. For example, an insignificant little *Dites donc!* may mean *Listen* as in *"Dites donc, n'oubliez pas de me téléphoner"*; *Go ahead!* as in *"Dites donc, ne vous gênez pas!"*; or even *And how!* as in "Votre fils a grandi, *dites donc!*". Specialized dictionaries, dictionaries of colloquialisms in particular, will prove of great help in that respect.[2]

Finally, do not forget to make use of English speech contractions, particularly verbal contractions, which speed up the flow of speech, such as *it's, I'm, we're, don't, won't, etc.*

---

[2] For a list of such dictionaries see appendix pp.281-2.

Play Excerpt 1   **L'Education d'un parvenu**[1]

Mr. Jourdain is a rich but uneducated bourgeois with rather coarse manners who has decided to emulate the sophisticated ways of noblemen of his time. To this end he has secured the services of various masters who will be teaching him music, dancing, fencing and philosophy.   Here is part of the "philosophy" lesson.

M. Jourdain: Il faut que je vous fasse une confidence.[2] Je suis amoureux d'[3] une personne de grande qualité,[4] et je souhaiterais que vous m'aidassiez[5] à lui écrire quelque chose dans un petit billet que je veux laisser tomber[6] à ses pieds.
Le maître de philosophie: Fort bien.[7]
M. Jourdain: Cela sera galant, oui.[8]
Le maître: Sans doute. Sont-ce des vers[9] que vous voulez écrire?
M. Jourdain: Non, non; point de vers.
Le Maître: Vous ne voulez que de la prose?
M. Jourdain: Non, je ne veux ni prose ni vers.
Le maître: Il faut bien que[10] ce soit l'un ou l'autre.
M. Jourdain: Pourquoi?
Le maître: Par la raison, monsieur, qu'il n'y a pour s'exprimer que la prose ou les vers.[11]
M. Jourdain: Il n'y a que la prose ou les vers?
Le maître: Oui, monsieur. Tout ce qui n'est point prose est vers, et tout ce qui n'est point vers est prose.
M. Jourdain: Et comme l'on parle, qu'est-ce que c'est donc[12] que cela?
Le maître: De la prose.[13]
M. Jourdain: Quoi? quand je dis, "Nicole, apportez-moi mes pantoufles et me donnez mon bonnet de nuit", c'est de la prose?
Le maître: Oui, monsieur.
M. Jourdain: Par ma foi,[14] il y a plus de quarante ans que je dis de la prose[15] sans que j'en susse[16] rien, et je vous suis le plus obligé du monde[17] de[18] m'avoir appris cela. Je voudrais donc lui mettre dans un billet: Belle marquise,[19] vos beaux yeux me font mourir d'amour; mais je voudrais que cela fût mis d'une manière galante,[20] que cela fût tourné gentiment.
Le maître: Mettre que les feux de ses yeux réduisent votre coeur en[21] cendres, que vous souffrez nuit et jour pour elle les violences d'un...
M. Jourdain: Non, non, non; je ne veux point tout cela. Je ne veux que ce que je vous ai dit: Belle marquise, vos beaux yeux me font mourir d'amour.
Le maître: Il faut bien étendre[22] la chose.

M. Jourdain: Non, vous dis-je; je ne veux que ces seules paroles-là[23] dans le billet, mais tournées à la mode, bien arrangées comme il faut.[24] Je vous prie de me dire un peu, pour voir,[25] les diverses manières dont on les peut mettre.

Le maître: On les peut mettre, premièrement, comme vous avez dit: Belle marquise, vos beaux yeux me font mourir d'amour. Ou bien: D'amour mourir me font, belle marquise, vos beaux yeux. Ou bien: Mourir vos beaux yeux, belle marquise, d'amour me font. Ou bien: Me font vos beaux yeux mourir, belle marquise, d'amour.[26]

M. Jourdain: Mais, de toutes ces façons-là, laquelle est la meilleure?

Le maître: Celle que vous avez dite: Belle marquise, vos beaux yeux me font mourir d'amour.

M. Jourdain: Cependant je n'ai point étudié, et j'ai fait cela tout du premier coup. Je vous remercie de tout mon coeur, et vous prie de venir demain de bonne heure.

Le maître: Je n'y manquerai pas.

(Molière, *Le Bourgeois gentilhomme*)

Guiding notes

The greatest difficulty here lies in the choice of proper vocabulary and grammar to convey the atmosphere of a seventeenth century conversation between a philosophy master who knows how to turn a phrase and his pupil, a rich bourgeois who has had very little education and tries to mimic the genteel ways of the nobility. The discrepancy in the manner of their speech should be felt in the translation.

---

[1] **L'Education d'un parvenu**: the title needs some special attention. Education: the gerund would be preferable to a noun. Parvenu: refers to a person who has reached an important social position in life without having had time to acquire the proper manners that should go along with it. Find a French borrowing which means just that.

[2] **Faire une confidence**: dire un secret.

[3] **Je suis amoureux de**: a preposition modulation is needed.

[4] **De grande qualité**: a seventeenth century way of saying "de haute noblesse."

[5] **Je souhaiterais que vous m'aidassiez**: the tense sequence is very complex here. According to classical rules of grammar, the use of a conditional in the main clause brings about an imperfect subjunctive in the subordinate clause. This is no longer the case in modern French, in which a simpler present subjunctive has replaced the imperfect subjunctive of the age of Molière. However the message is that Monsieur Jourdain, whose French is not always the

best, is trying to mimic the speech of the high society he is now rubbing elbows with. Due to the lack of subjunctive in English (let alone a subjunctive imperfect) the English translator will have to try and duplicate the effect of a very fancy phraseology through some other means.

[6] **Laisser tomber**: one T.U.

[7] **Fort bien**: elegant seventeenth century way of agreeing with someone; find an equivalent.

[8] **Cela sera galant, oui**: find a less literal way of reiterating the first part of the sentence than "yes."

[9] **Sont-ce des vers**?: a very refined way of saying "Est-ce que ce sont des vers...?" Des vers: de la poésie.

[10] **Il faut *bien* que**: the adverb here emphasizes the idea of necessity; find an equivalent.

[11] **Il n'y a pour s'exprimer que la prose ou les vers**: impersonal construction which would be better personalized in English: try a modulation by reversing the order and making the direct object the subject of the sentence.

[12] **Donc**: alors.

[13] **De la prose**: can the partitive article be rendered in translation?

[14] **Par ma foi**: a seventeenth century exclamation; find an equivalent which also has an obsolete flavor.

[15] **Il y a plus de quarante ans que je dis de la prose**: when a situation or action has been going on for a specific amount of time and is still going on as we speak, the tense of the main verb is the present in French; what is it in English?

[16] **Sans que j'en susse rien**: imperfect subjunctive of verb "savoir."

[17] **Je vous suis le plus obligé du monde**: refined expression of politeness; find an equivalent.

[18] **De m'avoir appris cela**: a preposition modulation is needed.

[19] **Marquise**: a French title of nobility for a lady; it is best to borrow the term since "marchioness" would place the dialogue in an English context.

[20] **D'une manière galante**: one T.U.; one adverb in English.

[21] **En cendres**: use a preposition modulation.

[22] **Étendre**: used in its figurative meaning, "élaborer."

[23] **Je ne veux que ces seules paroles-là**: Mr. Jourdain's phraseology is redundant; "ne...que" and "seules" serve exactly the same purpose. This lack of grammatical correctness should be felt in the translation.

[24] **Comme il faut**: one T.U.

[25] **Pour voir**: find a speech equivalent.

[26] **On les peut mettre...d'amour**: faced with his pupil's intransigence the philosophy master takes the request to the letter and switches the order of the various components of the sentence; each new version must progressively offer a more bizarre syntax in order to end with the most outlandish suggestion.

Educating a Nouveau Riche

Mr. Jourdain: I must tell you something in confidence. I am in love with a lady of the best quality, and I should like you to help me write her a note which I want to drop at her feet.

Philosophy master: Very well.

Mr. Jourdain: It will be gallant, won't it?

Master: Certainly. Is it verse you wish to write her?

Mr. Jourdain: No, no; no verse.

Master: You only want prose?

Mr. Jourdain: No, I want neither prose nor verse.

Master: It must be one or the other.

Mr. Jourdain: Why?

Master: For the reason, Sir, that prose or verse are the only means of expression we have.

Mr. Jourdain: Only prose or verse?

Master: Yes, Sir. All that is not prose is verse and all that is not verse is prose.

Mr. Jourdain: And the way we speak, what's that then?

Master: Prose.

Mr. Jourdain: What? When I say "Nicole, bring me my slippers and give me my nightcap", that's prose?

Master: Yes, Sir.

Mr. Jourdain: Upon my word, I have been talking prose for over forty years and did not even know; and I am most obliged to you for telling me. So, I would like to put in a note: Beautiful Marquise, your pretty eyes make me die of love", but I would like it to be gallantly put, nicely turned.

Master: You want to put down that the fire in her eyes reduces your heart to ashes, that for her, night and day you suffer the torments of...

Mr. Jourdain: No, no, no, I don't want any of that. I only want what I've told you: Beautiful marquise, your pretty eyes make me die of love.

Master: We should elaborate on the matter somewhat.

Mr. Jourdain: No, I tell you; I want nothing but those words by themselves in the note, fashionably turned though, properly arranged. Why don't you please tell me, just to get an idea, the various ways in which it can be done.

Master: First of all, we can write, as you said: Beautiful Marquise, your pretty eyes make me die of love. Or else: Of love, beautiful Marquise, your pretty eyes make me die. Or else: Die your pretty eyes, beautiful Marquise, of love make me. Or else: Die make your pretty eyes me, beautiful Marquise, of love.

Mr. Jourdain: But of all those ways, which is the best?

Master: The one you chose: Beautiful Marquise, your pretty eyes make me die of love.

Mr. Jourdain: Yet I have never studied, and I did it on my very first try. I thank you with all my heart, and pray come again tomorrow early.

Master: I shall, without fail.

Play Excerpt 2   Le Mariage de Figaro

The Marriage of Figaro, the sequel to The Barber of Seville, stages Count Almaviva, Figaro, the former barber of Seville who has now become the count's indispensable valet, and Rosine, the count's lady, whose love he courted in the previous play, now his wife. But the count is fickle. He has turned his attention to his valet's fiancée, Suzanne, and what is more, is claiming the lord's prerogative. What is Figaro to do, for the political system is still based on feudal order? Even though Beaumarchais, to foil royal censorship, sets his play in Spain,, no one is a dupe: the issues are those of pre-revolutionary France. The verbal sparring between master and valet echoes the grievances of the Third Estate against the privileged classes, and announces the sweeping changes that are going to take place in the social order.

Le comte: Quel motif avait la Comtesse, pour me jouer un pareil tour[1]?

Figaro: Ma foi, Monseigneur, vous le savez mieux que moi.

Le comte: Je la préviens sur tout[2] et la comble de présents.

Figaro: Vous lui donnez, mais vous êtes infidèle. Sait-on gré du superflu à qui nous prive du nécessaire?

Le comte: Autrefois[3] tu[4] me disais tout.

Le comte: Et maintenant je ne vous cache rien

Figaro: Combien la comtesse t'a-t-elle donné pour cette belle association?

Le comte: Combien me donnâtes-vous[5] pour la tirer des mains du Docteur[6]? Tenez, Monseigneur, n'humilions pas l'homme qui nous sert bien, crainte d'en faire un mauvais valet.

Le comte: Pourquoi faut-il qu'il y ait toujours du louche en ce que tu fais?

Figaro: C'est qu'on en voit partout[7], quand on cherche des torts.

Le comte: Une réputation détestable!

Figaro: Et si je vaux mieux qu'elle? Y a-t-il beaucoup de seigneurs qui puissent en dire autant?

Le comte: Cent fois je t'ai vu marcher à la fortune[8], et jamais aller droit.

Figaro: Comment voulez-vous[9]? La foule est là; chacun veut courir, on se presse, on pousse, on coudoie, on renverse, arrive qui peut; le reste est écrasé. Aussi c'est fait; pour moi j'y renonce.

Le comte: A la fortune? (*A part*) Voici du neuf.

Figaro: (*A part*) A mon tour, maintenant. (*Haut*) Votre Excellence m'a gratifié de la conciergerie du château[10]; c'est un fort joli sort: à la vérité je ne serais pas le courrier étrenné[11] des nouvelles intéressantes; mais, en revanche, heureux avec ma femme au fond de l'Andalousie[12].

Le comte: Qui t'empêcherait de l'emmener à Londres?

Figaro: Il faudrait la quitter si souvent, que j'aurais bientôt du mariage par-dessus la tête[13].

Le comte: Avec du caractère et de l'esprit, tu pourrais un jour t'avancer dans les bureaux.

Figaro: De l'esprit pour s'avancer?   Monseigneur se rit du mien. Médiocre et rampant, et l'on arrive à tout.

Le comte: Il ne faudrait qu'étudier un peu sous moi la politique.

Figaro: Je la sais[14].

Le comte: Comme l'anglais: le fond de la langue![15]

Figaro: Oui, s'il y avait ici de quoi se vanter; mais feindre d'ignorer ce qu'on sait, de savoir ce qu'on ignore, d'entendre ce qu'on ne comprend pas, de ne point ouïr ce qu'on entend, surtout de pouvoir au-delà de ses forces; avoir souvent pour grand secret de cacher qu'il n'y en a point, s'enfermer pour tailler des plumes[16] et paraître profond quand on n'est, comme on dit, que vide et creux, jouer bien ou mal un personnage, répandre des espions et pensionner des traîtres, amollir des cachets[17], intercepter des lettres, et tâcher d'ennoblir la pauvreté des moyens par l'importance des objets: voilà toute la politique, ou je meure!

Le comte: Eh! C'est l'intrigue que tu définis!

Figaro: La politique, l'intrigue, volontiers, mais comme je les crois un peu germaines[18], en fasse qui voudra.

(Beaumarchais, Le Mariage de Figaro)

Guiding notes

Figaro, the ingenious and cocky valet, embodies the spirit of the times, which is challenging the prevailing order and claiming a share of the pie proportionate to one's skills and contributions to the wealth of the State.

The count, on the other end, is a member of the aristocracy and consequently deems himself superior. However, in growing frustration, he has to listen to his arguments being countered one by one by his valet. This cat and mouse play must be rendered in the tone of the translation and the tit for tat exchange, which is reminiscent of dueling, kept in the rhythm.

Unlike the plays of Molière, in which different language registers were used to separate servants and masters, Figaro's speech is grammatically and verbally undistinguishable from the count's, thereby indicating an intention on the part of the author to phase out linguistic distinction as a preliminary to phasing out rank distinction.

---

[1] **Pour me jouer un pareil tour**: the count believes his wife to be unfaithful. To get even with his master, Figaro has told him falsely that someone is interested in the countess.

[2] **Je la préviens sur tout**: an obsolete use of the verb *prévenir*. Here it means "je suis prévenant avec elle en tout."

[3] **Autrefois**: use a transposition.

[4] **Tu me disais tout**: the switch from the "tu" to the "vous" form of address in this dialogue is an example of translation loss, since "thou" has disappeared from modern English. One might try to compensate for this loss by adding prop words here and there showing that the count is the social superior of Figaro.

[5] **Combien me donnâtes-vous...**: use of the subjunctive imperfect, now obsolete in modern French, is proof of Figaro's high language register. However this indication is lost in the English translation. Try to compensate, not necessarily here, but whenever the translation gives you the choice between a high register and a lower one.

[6] **Pour la tirer des mains du Docteur**: Figaro is referring to Doctor Bartholo, Rosine's guardian in The Barber of Seville, who was keeping his ward a virtual prisoner to prevent her from meeting young suitors so that he could eventually marry her. Use an equivalence.

[7] **On en voit partout**: what word does the indefinite pronoun "en" refer to?

[8] **Marcher à la fortune**: "*fortune*" is false cognate here. The expression means "réussir dans tes entreprises."

[9] **Comment voulez-vous?**: an elliptical and idiomatic expression meaning "Comment voulez-vous que je fasse? Comment cela serait-il possible?"

[10] **Château**: rather than borrow the French term, use the word "*castle*" here since the play takes place in Spain, not in France.

[11] **Je ne serai pas le courrier étrenné**: an obsolete and arcane expression meaning "Je ne serai pas le premier à apprendre des nouvelles intéressantes ni à les transmettre." "*Les étrennes*" refer to an old French custom, the first gift – usually money- that children receive from family members in the New Year.

[12] **Au fond de l'Andalousie**: use a preposition modulation to convey the idea that he will be far away from where the action is.

[13] **J'aurais bientôt du mariage par-dessus la tête**: idiomatic expression meaning "Je serais vite fatigué d'être marié."

[14] **Je la sais**: the use of "*savoir*" in preference to "*connaître*" is indicative of thorough knowledge of a subject matter. Express that in your translation.

[15] **Comme l'anglais, le fond de la langue!:** the count is making fun of Figaro, who had claimed earlier in the discussion that he knew enough English to get by.

[16] **Pour tailler des plumes**: the play is set circa 1780. People then used quills to write, which had to be sharpened periodically.

[17] **Amollir des cachets**: to soften seals in order to open other people's letters secretly without appearing to have done so.

[18] **Je les crois un peu germaines**: the exact expression is "*cousines germaines,*" *i.e.* "first degree cousins." The simile points to a close family relationship.

The Marriage of Figaro

The Count: What was the Countess's motive for playing such a trick on me?

Figaro: Truthfully, my Lord, you know better than I.

The Count: I am attentive to her in everything and shower her with presents.

Figaro: You are generous but unfaithful. Can you thank the one who deprives you of the essential when you are given the superfluous?

The Count: You used to tell me everything.

Figaro: And now I hide nothing from you.

The Count: How much did the Countess pay you for this fine partnership?

Figaro: How much did you give me once to snatch her from the Doctor's hands? Look, my Lord, let's not humiliate the man who serves us well, lest it should turn him into a bad valet.

The Count: Why must there always be something devious in what you do?

Figaro: Because that's what you find everywhere when you look for faults.

The Count: [You have} a detestable reputation!

Figaro: And if I deserve better? Can many noblemen say as much?

The Count: I have watched you a hundred times on your way to success, and that was never in a straight line.

Figaro: How could I? There is a crowd. Everyone wants to have a run. There's a press. You push, you shove, you knock down, gets there who can, the rest is trampled. So it's over. So far as I am concerned, I give up.

The Count: On success? (*Aside*) That's something new.

Figaro: (*Aside*) My turn now. (*Loud*) Your Excellency has gratified me with the caretaking of the castle; that's a very enviable lot. Indeed I won't be the first to hear or bear interesting news, but, on the other hand, I will be happy with my wife, out of the way, in Andalusia.

The Count: Who would stand in the way of your bringing her along to London?

Figaro: I'd have to part from her so often that I would soon have my fill of marriage.

The Count: With character and wit you could one day get ahead in the administration.

Figaro: Wit to get ahead? Your Lordship makes fun of my wit. Be mediocre and fawn and you'll get anywhere.

The Count: You'd only have to study politics a little under my guidance.

Figaro: I know politics well.

The Count: As you do English: the fundamentals of the language!

Figaro: Yes, if there was something here to boast about.   But pretending not to know what you know, to know what you don't know, to hear what you don't understand, not to perceive what you hear, and above all to be able to do above and beyond what you possibly can; holding as your foremost secret the fact that you are hiding that there is none; locking yourself up to sharpen quills and looking profound when you are, as they say, only empty and superficial; playing a role successfully or unsuccessfully; sending out spies and paying off traitors, melting seals, intercepting letters, and trying to glorify the poverty of the means with the importance of the goal: that's politics in a nutshell, cross my heart and hope to die if I'm wrong!

The Count: Hey! That's intrigue you are defining!

Figaro: Politics, intrigue, as you wish; but as I believe them to be somewhat akin, let others play their game.

Play Excerpt 3   La Guerre de Troie n'aura pas lieu

The theme of this play is the inevitability of war. Using the Trojan war as a metaphor, Giraudoux, who is writing in 1935, draws a parallel between the Trojan war and the war that is fast approaching in Europe and which seems just as absurd. The following dialog takes place between Helen, whose abduction by Paris is the cause of the Trojan war, and Andromache, wife of Hector. For Giraudoux, Andromache is the real heroin. She is in love with her husband. She is sensitive, intelligent, and ready to make sacrifices, provided they are in support of a worthy cause; whereas Helen, the archetype of the "femme fatale", seems to take interest in no one and nothing but herself. What is absurd about this impending war is the fact that Helen and Paris do not even appear to truly love each other. The disparity in the protagonists' discourse is meant to emphasize everything that separates them and the impossibility to find a common ground: Giraudoux, to update the ancient story and show its relevance in a modern context, does not recoil from the use of anachronisms and purposely turns to popular language: his Andromache speaks in a poetic, lyrical and moving way and his Helen, like a common, superficial call girl.

In the following passage, Andromache makes an ultimate appeal to Helen, begging her to give a reason for the fight, making the war a just cause, while sensing from the start that her attempt is doomed to failure. The war will be absurd.

Hélène: Si vous avez découvert ce qu'il veulent, les dieux, dans toute cette histoire[19], je vous félicite[20].

Andromaque: Je ne sais si les dieux veulent quelque chose. Mais l'univers veut quelque chose. Depuis ce matin, tout me semble le réclamer[21], le crier, l'exiger, les hommes, les bêtes, les plantes... Jusqu'à cet enfant en moi...

Hélène:- Ils réclament quoi?

Andromaque: Que vous aimiez Pâris[22].

Hélène:- S'ils savent[23] que je n'aime point Pâris, ils sont mieux renseignés que moi[24].

Andromaque: Vous ne l'aimez pas! Peut-être pourriez-vous l'aimer. Mais, pour le moment, c'est dans un malentendu que vous vivez tous les deux.

Hélène: Je vis avec lui dans la bonne humeur, dans l'agrément, dans l'accord. Le malentendu de l'entente[25], je ne vois pas très bien ce que cela peut être.

Andromaque: Vous ne l'aimez pas! Peut-être pourriez-vous l'aimer. On ne s'entend pas, dans l'amour. La vie de deux époux qui s'aiment, c'est une perte de sang-froid perpétuelle. La dot[26] des vrais couples est la même que celle des couples faux: le désaccord originel[27]. Hector est le contraire de moi. Il n'a aucun de mes goûts. Nous passons notre journée[28] ou à nous vaincre l'un l'autre ou à nous sacrifier. Les époux amoureux n'ont pas le visage clair.

Hélène: Et si mon teint était de plomb[29], quand j'approche Pâris, et mes yeux blancs, et mes mains moites, vous pensez que Ménélas en[30] serait transporté, les Grecs épanouis!

Andromaque: Peu importerait alors ce que pensent les Grecs!

Hélène: Et la guerre n'aurait pas lieu?

Andromaque: Peut-être, en effet[31], n'aurait-elle pas lieu! Peut-être, si vous vous aimiez, l'amour[32] appellerait-il à son secours l'un de ses égaux, la générosité, l'intelligence… Personne, même le destin, ne s'attaque d'un coeur léger à la passion… Et même si elle avait lieu, tant pis[33]!

Hélène: Ce ne serait sans doute[34] pas la même guerre?

Andromaque: Oh! Non[35], Hélène! Vous sentez bien[36] ce qu'elle sera, cette lutte. Le sort ne prend pas tant de précautions pour un combat vulgaire. Il veut construire l'avenir sur elle, l'avenir de nos races, de nos peuples, de nos raisonnements. Et que nos idées et notre avenir soient fondés sur l'histoire d'une femme et d'un homme qui s'aimaient, ce n'est pas si mal. Mais il ne voit pas que vous n'êtes qu'un couple officiel[37]… Penser que nous allons souffrir, mourir, pour un couple officiel, que la splendeur ou le malheur des âges, que les habitudes des cerveaux[38] et des siècles vont se fonder sur l'aventure de deux êtres qui ne s'aimaient pas, c'est là l'horreur.[39]

Hélène: Si tous croient que nous nous aimons, cela revient au même[40].

Andromaque: Ils ne le croient pas. Mais aucun n'avouera qu'il ne le croit pas[41]. Aux approches de la guerre, tous les êtres secrètent une nouvelle[42] sueur, tous les évènements revêtent un nouveau vernis, qui est le mensonge. Tous mentent. Nos vieillards n'adorent pas la beauté, ils s'adorent eux-mêmes, ils adorent la laideur. Et l'indignation des Grecs est un mensonge. Dieu sait s'ils se moquent[43] de ce que vous pouvez faire avec Pâris[44], les Grecs! Et leurs bateaux qui accostent là-bas dans les banderoles et les hymnes, c'est un mensonge de la mer. Et la vie de mon fils, et la vie d'Hector vont se jouer sur[45] l'hypocrisie et le simulacre, c'est épouvantable!

Hélène: Alors?

Andromaque: Alors je vous en supplie, Hélène. Vous me voyez là pressée contre vous comme si je vous suppliais de m'aimer. Aimez Pâris! Ou dites-moi que je me trompe! Dites-moi que vous vous tuerez s'il mourrait! Que vous accepterez qu'on vous défigure pour qu'il vive!… Alors la guerre ne sera plus qu'un fléau, pas une injustice. J'essaierai de la supporter[46].

(Jean Giraudoux, *La Guerre de Troie n'aura pas lieu*)

Guiding notes

What characterizes this exchange is the contrast in the poetic tone of one protagonist and the common tone of the other. The first character, Andromache, speaks in an impassioned and lyrical way, trying to convince the other, Helen, of doing her part in order to give meaning to the approaching war, while Helen barely pays attention and shows her lack of interest and personality through commonplace repartees. To remain true to Giraudoux's intention, as far as character development is concerned, it is essential to maintain this double tone in the translation.

---

[19] **Dans toute cette histoire**: remember that Helen's way of speaking is colloquial, even prone to lapsing into slang at times. Give an equivalence for all the idiomatic expressions and clichés the author puts in the mouth of his character.

[20] **Je vous félicite**: give an equivalence.

[21] **Réclamer**: false cognate.

[22] **Que vous aimiez**: here, the subjunctive mood is an expression of will, request, which should be expressed in English through some other means, given the fact that the subjunctive does not really exist in modern English any more.

[23] **S'ils savent**: expand the meaning.

24 **Ils sont mieux renseignés que moi**: a familiar cliché, give an equivalence

[25] **Le malentendu de l'entente**: the play on words must be rendered.

[26] **La dot**: literally "the dowry;" the money or chattels which a bride would bring into the marriage; the image is probably best rendered through a more abstract concept : use a modulation.

[27] **Originelle**: des origines; use a transposition adjective-noun.

[28] **Notre journée**: the ending –ée indicates that the day is considered in its duration, as opposed to "jour" which is just a concept of time.

[29] **Un teint de plomb**: a complexion which is indicative of illness, as opposed to "un teint frais et rose."

[30] **En**: pronoun meaning literally "by it;" which is superfluous in English.

[31] **En effet**: in dialogues this expresses agreement with the previous speaker's utterance.

32 **L'amour**: use *Eros* to avoid repetition since *Love* here is personified.

[33] **Tant pis!**: a familiar expression, give an equivalence.

[34] **Sans doute**: Helen is making fun of Andromache. Give an equivalence.

[35] **Oh, non**: In English there are other ways of disagreeing beside "no;" use a more idiomatic expression..

[36] **Vous sentez *bien***: give an equivalence for the prop word *bien*.

[37] **Un couple *officiel***: a couple only in appearance, as opposed to a real one: use a modulation such as "a couple *on paper*."

[38] **Les habitudes des cerveaux**: literally "the habits of brains"; a modulation concrete-abstract might be a good idea for the accurate and idiomatic rendition of this phrase.

[39] **C'est là l'horreur**: give an equivalence.

[40] **Cela revient au même**: give an equivalence.

[41] **Aucun n'avouera qu'il ne le croit pas**: English can be more concise than French here.

[42] **Nouvelle**: use a word modulation.

[43] **Ils se moquent**: the verb here is used in its idiomatic meaning of "not to care"; do not translate literally. A current published translation renders this phrase as "*they are amused enough,*" a mistranslation.

[44] **De ce que vous pouvez faire avec Pâris**: an idiomatic expression, give an equivalence.

[45] **Se jouer sur**: use a preposition modulation.

[46] **J'essaierai de la supporter**: give an equivalence bearing in mind that "supporter" and "to support" are false cognates.

The Trojan War Shall be Called off

Helen: -If you've found out what the gods want in this whole thing, congratulations!

Andromache: -I don't know that *they* want anything. But the whole world wants something. Since this morning I have felt that everyone and everything is clamoring for it, crying for it, that they demand it, humans, beasts and plants...even this child within me...

Helen: -They're clamoring for what?

Andromache: -That you should love Paris.

Helen: -If they're convinced that I don't love Paris, they know more than I do.

Andromache: -You don't love him! Perhaps you could. But right now, you are both living a misunderstanding.

Helen: -I live with him in good cheer, in pleasure and harmony. To misunderstand and still get along, I don't quite see how that could be.

Andromache: -You don't love him. In love, you don't get along. The life of a husband and wife who are in love is a constant battle of nerves. The lot of real couples is the lot of fake ones: absence of harmony as it was at the beginning of times. Hector is my exact opposite. He shares none of my tastes. We spend our time trying to get the better of each other or making sacrifices for each other. People in love don't put on a serene face.

Helen: -And if my complexion turned sallow each time I go near Paris, if my eyes rolled in my head and my hands got clammy, do you think that Menelaus would be thrilled and the Greeks ecstatic?

Andromache: -It would matter little, then, what the Greeks thought!

Helen: - And there wouldn't be any war?

Andromache: - May be, yes, there wouldn't be any war. May be, if you were in love, Eros would call one of his peers to the rescue: generosity, intelligence...No one, not even Fate likes to challenge passion in a careless way... And even if there was a war, it would not matter!

Helen: -And it actually wouldn't be the same war?

Andromache: -Oh Helen, it wouldn't! You do realize what this fight will be like? Fate does not take so many precautions for an ordinary conflict. It intends to build the future on it, the future of our races, our people, our ways of thinking. And if our thoughts and future are based on the story of a man and a woman in love, that's not so bad. But Fate does not see that you're only the image of a couple. To think that we are going to suffer, die for an image, that the splendor or misfortune of all ages, the ways of humanity and of centuries are going to be determined by the fortunes of two people who were not in love, that's what's so awful.

Helen: -If everyone believes that we're in love, it makes no difference.

Andromache: -They don't believe it. But no one will admit to it. As war draws near, they all sweat in a different way, everything puts on a different coat, the coat of falsehood. They all lie. Our old men do not worship beauty, they worship themselves, they worship ugliness. And the Greeks' indignation is a lie. God knows they couldn't care less what your business with Paris is. And their ships, setting anchor over there amid banners and anthems, that's the sea deceiving us. And my son's life, and Hector's life are going to be staked against hypocrisy and pretense, that's horrendous!

Helen: -So?

Andromache: -So, I beg of you, Helen. You see me here, pressed against you as if to beg you to love me. Love Paris! Or tell me I am mistaken! Tell me that you would kill yourself if he died! Accept to be disfigured so that he might live!... Then, war will only be a scourge, not an injustice. I will try to live with that.

Chapter 16
Guidelines for the Translation of Poetry

Poetry translation: a difficult but creative enterprise

The translation of poetry is the most difficult of all translations. Why? Because in this process, contrary to the process involving prose translation, rendition of the meaning behind the words is no longer the one and only important consideration. In the configuration of a poem other factors come into play: form, rhythm, sounds, harmony, tone, all contributing in no small part to the global impact on the reader and listener.

But poetry translation is also the most creative of all translations, for, very often, translating a poem is nothing short of re-creating the poem. There will be losses, additions, alterations to the original in order to keep some of its vital elements. Between freedom and submission the translator must strive to find a happy medium, to respect the spirit of the poem while avoiding to remain a slave to the letter of its content.

Is poetry translation the reserved domain of poets?

Many poets have translated other poets. Several of Ronsard's and Du Bellay's most famous pieces are re-creations of poems by Horace or Petrarch. Baudelaire set out to translate Edgar Allan Poe, and we also have, among others, Paul Valéry's translations of Thomas Hardy, Saint-John Perse's translations of T.S. Eliot and vice versa, Marianne Moore's translations of the fables of La

Fontaine and Yves Bonnefoy's translations of Shakespeare and Yeats. Should we say then that it takes a poet to translate the works of another poet? It probably does, for not only do you have to be aware of the music and pattern of the sounds, of the rhythm and flow of the poem, the power of suggestion of the words, the images, metaphors and symbols, but you also have to try and reproduce the same effects in the T.L. However, even if you are not a poet, poetry translation can yield much fun as an exercise in style, provided you are armed with patience and willing to let your ideas simmer a while, for several days if necessary, until a solution finally surfaces. You can be aided in your attempts by the various books on prosody and the rhyming dictionaries on the market. Of course not all poetry is equally difficult to translate, and a descriptive or narrative poem in blank verse will be easier than a sonnet with its rhyme constraints, or a surrealistic poem with its disruption of conventional syntax, thought patterns, words and image associations which aim at re-creating a language.

The different levels of poetry translation

There are four great categories of poetry translation depending on the degree of faithfulness to the original.

1. **A literal translation** will remain faithful to the meaning of the poem in the S.L. while maintaining its complete poetic integrity. Needless to say, this is rarely possible, due to differences in word sounds, especially vowel sounds which are essential to the music of a poem, and due to differences in syntax between English and French. To illustrate the difficulty let's take the case of nasal sounds, which do not exist in English: how is one then to translate a poem like Verlaine's *Chanson d'automne* in which nasals play a crucial part in conveying a melancholy mood?

2. **An approximation**, while trying to remain faithful and keeping some of the source elements such as sense, structure, rhyme scheme *etc.*, will take more liberties, due to the

difficulties mentioned above and other considerations like rhyme constraints.

3. **An adaptation** will be more remote from the source both in sense and structure.

4. **An imitation** will be a re-creation of the poem: other than borrowing the theme, the mood, and may be some of the symbols and metaphors from the source of inspiration, the new poem will have a life and originality of its own.

In short, do not expect to be able to render the poem in its entirety. Depending on the degree of difficulty, the yield may vary from three quarters to half or even less, although every rule has its exceptions, and in the history of literature there have been documented cases in which the translation or imitation has proved superior to the original. Which allows us to maintain, despite Robert Frost's affirmation to the contrary, that poetry is not "what gets lost in translation".

How to proceed with the translation of a poem

The following steps summarize the process involved in the translation of a poem

1. An indispensable preliminary step will be a semantic, structural, and phonetic analysis of the poem

- For meaning (theme, message, obvious and hidden ideas, metaphors and symbols). Look up all the words you are not familiar with.

- For form (type of poem: *i.e.* sonnet, ode, ballad etc., meter, rhyme scheme, stanzas, rhetorical figures, time period).

- For rhythm and structure (run-on lines, repetitions and parallel constructions, pauses, anaphors and words placed in an emphatic position).

- For poetic sound effect (alliterations, rhymes and internal rhymes, music and harmony of sounds: are they sharp or deep? Are they important? Do they convey a cheerful or a pensive

and melancholy mood? Are there special correspondences and modulations between them?)
- And finally don't forget that a poem is meant to be read or recited out loud in order to fully appreciate its rhythm, music and harmony.

2. Make a first draft concentrating just on the translation of ideas and images and keeping to the structure of the model as a framework without concern for artistry.

3. Put the translation into verse
- Determine what meter is best to convey the atmosphere and rhythm of the poem. Here, a major difficulty lies in the fact that prosody for romance languages uses a syllabic count whereas Anglo-Saxon languages, with very few exceptions, use a stress count. Keep in mind that alexandrine verse (twelve syllables in the line) is best rendered by pentameters (five stress counts), but also sometimes by tetrameters (four stress counts), which are generally used respectively for decasyllabic (ten syllable) and octosyllabic (eight syllable) verse. And on occasion, octosyllables have been successfully translated as tri-meters when padded with extra unstressed words (which may even be foreign to the original text).
- Determine what sounds to keep for the rhymes and stick to the original rhyme scheme. Many rhyming dictionaries are available to make the task less daunting,[1] but you will have to do some juggling around to keep to the limits imposed by the rhymes.
- Select words on the basis of both meaning and music and try to rescue the internal rhymes, alliterations and other poetic effects. Use language that is appropriate for the period of the poem. Do not use twentieth century language for an ancient

---

[1] The rhyming dictionaries found in the appendix p.283 should be especially helpful.
Also useful: *Roget's Thesaurus* when looking for the right word, or for a specific sound in a word (as for alliterations).

poem if it can be avoided so as not to betray the original atmosphere. And do not forget to pay particular attention to the last line of a short poem, especially in the case of a sonnet, for the last line is usually the most crucial and the most artistic, the one which recaps the tone of the poem and often its central idea.

French rules of prosody

A prerequisite to poetry translation is, of course, a basic knowledge of the rules of French and English prosody,[2] that is to say of the science and art of versification, an understanding of the various forms and structures of poems, meters, rhymes and rhyming patterns, types of stanzas, etc. There are also a certain number of conventions in French versification of which one must be aware before tackling the process of textual analysis.

The first of these conventions is that all compulsory as well as optional liaisons must be made when reciting the poem to better emphasize the sounds, for greater musicality, and also to help in delineating the syllable count. Thus the following line from José Maria de Hérédia's poem *"Le Conquérant"*:

> Et les vents alizés inclinaient leurs antennes

must be pronounced as follows:

> Et les vents zalizés zinclinaient leurs zantennes

whereas in standard French only the last of these liaisons would be a compulsory one.[3]

Another convention affects the sounding of unaccented vowel *e*, which can be pronounced or mute depending on its position in the

---

[2] For more on the English and French rules of prosody refer to the books listed in the appendix p.283.

[3] Compulsory liaisons in standard French are made between words with a close syntactic connection, such as between article and noun, possessive or demonstrative adjective and noun, or pronoun and verb. Optional liaisons are all of the others, except for the very rare cases in which a liaison is forbidden, such as after the conjunction "et".

line and depending on the word that follows. When found inside the line before a consonant or aspirate *h*, *e* is pronounced and counts as a syllable (unlike standard French). When placed before a vowel or mute *h*, it is mute and does not count as a syllable (as in standard French). When found at the end of the line, it may or may not be pronounced, but does not count as a syllable.

Finally, the delineation of a line into syllables to determine the type of verse will take a little practice.

A syllable is a basic phonetic unit formed according to the following pattern:

> 1. sounded consonant   +   sounded vowel (or nasal vowel: an, on, in, un)
>
> 2. or sounded consonant   +   sounded vowel   +   sounded consonant (provided   the next consonant in the word or following word is different)

Let's take an example from one of Ronsard's *Sonnets à Marie*:

Comme on voit sur la branche au mois de mai la rose

Co	mon	voi	sur	la	bran	chau	moi	de	mai	la	roz
1	2	3	4	5	6	7	8	9	10	11	12

The first two *m*'s count only as one consonant since they are the same sound. Nasal vowels *an* and *on* count as regular vowels. Unsounded final consonants *t* and *s* in *voit* and *mois* do not count. The syllabic pattern is therefore mostly of the consonant + vowel type, except for syllables 4 and 12 which end in sounded consonants. Vowel *e* in *comme* and *branche* disappears before vowels *on* and *au*, whereas in *de* the sound is maintained because followed by a word starting in a consonant, *mai*. In the last word *rose* the *e* is mute since it is in the final position, and consequently only gives a single syllable: *roz*. This yields a twelve syllable count, the so-called alexandrine verse, named after a mediaeval poem on Alexander the Great, which for the first time used the twelve syllable count.

The alexandrine is the longest verse. There are eleven other lengths from the monosyllabic (1) to the hendeca syllabic verse (11). All are not equally popular with poets and, generally speaking, the alexandrine, decasyllabic (10), octosyllabic (8) and tetrasyllabic (4) are the most widely used.

Poem 1   Ode à Cassandre

Mignonne, allons voir si la rose
Qui ce matin avait déclose
Sa robe de pourpre au soleil,
N'a point perdu cette vesprée
Les plis de sa robe pourprée,
Et son teint au vôtre pareil

Las! voyez comme en peu d'espace,
Mignonne, elle a dessus la place,
Las! las! ses beautés laissé choir!
O vraiment marâtre nature
Puisqu'une telle fleur ne dure
Que du matin jusques au soir!

Donc, si vous m'en croyez, mignonne,
Tandis que votre âge fleuronne
En sa plus verte nouveauté,
Cueillez, cueillez votre jeunesse:
Comme à cette fleur la vieillesse
Fera ternir votre beauté.

(Pierre de Ronsard)

Guided translation:

Step one: translation in prose:

My little beauty, let's go see if the rose
Which this morning had displayed

Its crimson dress in the sun
Has by these vespers lost none
Of the folds of its crimson gown,
And of its complexion so much like yours.

Alas! see how in so short a space,

Ode to Cassandra

Step two: translation in verse:

See if the rose, my pretty maid,
Which to morning's sun had dis-
                              -played
The gorgeous crimson of its dress
Has kept the beauty of its prime
Or lost that tint by vesper time
Which could rival your loveliness.

Alas! see how in so short a space

Pretty one, it has upon the spot,
Alas! alas! let its beauties drop!

Petals dropped all over the place.
Their transient beauty makes us
                                    grieve!

O Nature, you truly wicked stepmother,
Since such a flower only lasts

Nature, o cruelest stepmother,
Your child's bloom so soon to
                                    smother

From morning till evening!

That it can't last from morn to eve!

So, if you believe me, pretty one
As long as your tender age is in bloom
In its freshest novelty
Gather, gather the blossom of your youth,
For old age, as it did this flower,
Shall tarnish your beauty too.

My pretty girl, believe this truth:
Make the most of your lovely youth
Think of the rose's crimson bloom.
Time flies! so always remember:
May gives way to bleak December.
Age one day shall your beauty
                                    doom.

Notes

We owe the translation of this sixteenth century odelette, Ronsard's most famous, to Walter Schaap who has converted the octosyllabic verse to an iambic tetrameter. Perhaps the most extraordinary feature of this poem is the osmosis which the poet has achieved between the flower and the young girl by dressing one with the normal attributes of the other and vice versa. The tone is light and gallant, and music plays a role through sound harmony, internal rhymes and alliterations.

A closer examination of the differences between the original and its translation reveals some loss, namely in the obsolete flavor which permeates Ronsard's piece, due to words such as *choir*, *fleuronne*, and particularly *marâtre*, a word which is evocative of fairy tales. Yet, the translation, while more modern in tone and taking liberties with the text, particularly in the last stanza, maintains Ronsard's a-a-b-c-c-b rhyme scheme, and keeps the theme of "seize the day while you may" characteristic of Ronsard's poetry.

Poem 2 **Rondeau**

Le temps a laissé son manteau
De vent, de froidure et de pluie,
Et s'est vêtu de broderie,
De soleil luisant, clair et beau.

Il n'y a bête ni oiseau,
Qu'en son jargon ne chante ou crie:
Le temps a laissé son manteau
De vent, de froidure et de pluie.

Rivière, fontaine et ruisseau
Portent en livrée jolie
Gouttes d'argent, d'orfèvrerie;
Chacun s'habille de nouveau
Le temps a laissé son manteau.

(Charles d'Orléans)

Roundel 1

The weather's cast his cloak away
Of nasty wind and chill and rain,

To don princely raiment again,

Of shining sun radiant and gay.

Furry beast and feathered blue jay
Proclaim all around in happy strain:
The weather's cast his cloak away
Of nasty wind, and chill and rain.

Fountains, brooks, rivers on this day
Are wearing in their pretty train

Roundel 2

Cast off is Nature's winter gear
Her cloak of cold, of wind and
                      rain,
She's donned her springtime
                clothes again,
Her bright sunlight, so fine and
                  clear.

To every beast and bird give ear.
They all rejoice in sweet refrain:
Cast off is Nature's winter gear
Her cloak of cold, of wind and
                      rain.

Each brook, river and placid mere
Splashes like silvery, golden rain

Beads of silver and golden chain;	In jeweled gown and glittering train;
Everyone's clothed in new array	How dazzling does the world appear!
The weather's cast his cloak away.	Cast off is Nature's winter gear. (Walter Schaap)

Notes

The *rondeau*, a fixed lyrical form of French origin used in the Middle Ages, runs on two rhymes and usually consists of thirteen lines, a refrain or burden taken from the first line, and a set rhyme scheme: abba, abab, abbaa.

The spelling of the original fifteenth century poem has been modernized for easier reading. This is a simple piece, with a merry tone, in tribute to the coming of Spring after a long and nasty winter. Music here plays an essential role and accordingly, sounds in the translation must be carefully selected in order to render this cheerfulness and vivacity, this feeling of coming back to life after a hibernating pause, and of celebrating the renascence of nature after the dreary winter months.

Two translations are offered as an exercise in stylistics to show the various effects which can be achieved with contrasting figures of style, and a variety of rhymes. Their chief disparity lies in the choice of a different personification as a central figure for the poem.

Both manage to remain pretty close to the original in spite of the constraints of the rhyme scheme which has led to some divergences (*radiant and gay* for *clair et beau*; *on this day* for *fontaine*; *train* for *livrée*; *golden chain* for *orfèvrerie*), and to some necessary padding in order to maintain the meter (*bête ni oiseau* is expanded into: *furry beast and feathered blue jay* in the first version, and *fontaine* into *placid mere*, *portent en livrée jolie* into *their jeweled gown and glittering train* in the second). The second English version is somewhat less literal due to the choice of a different metaphor and departs slightly from the original poem in the last stanza.

Poem Three **Demain dès l'aube**

Demain dès l'aube, à l'heure où blanchit la campagne
Je partirai. Vois-tu, je sais que tu m'attends.
J'irai par la forêt, j'irai par la montagne,
Je ne puis demeurer loin de toi plus longtemps.

Je marcherai les yeux fixés sur mes pensées
Sans rien voir au dehors, sans entendre aucun bruit,
Seul, inconnu, le dos courbé, les mains croisées,
Triste, et le jour pour moi sera comme la nuit.

Je ne regarderai ni l'or du soir qui tombe
Ni les voiles au loin descendant vers Harfleur
Et quand j'arriverai je mettrai sur ta tombe
Un bouquet de houx vert et de bruyère en fleur.

(Victor Hugo, Les Contemplations)

Guided translation

Step one: our first task is to decipher the poem, to make a close translation without regard for meter, music or rhyme, just to get familiar with the structure, themes, images, symbols and general mood. This is a lyrical poem, typical of the romantic manner, which uses simple, direct language and closely associates emotions with images of nature. It evokes the annual pilgrimage made by the poet to the grave of his daughter, a young bride of several weeks who tragically drowned while taking a boat ride on the Seine river with her husband.

Tomorrow, at dawn, when the countryside turns white
I shall set out. You see, I know thou art awaiting me
I shall go through forest and mountain
I cannot stay away from thee any longer.

I shall walk with my eyes set upon my thoughts
Without seeing anything outside, without hearing any sound
Alone, a stranger, shoulders bent, hands folded

Sad, and the day to me shall be like the night.

I will not look at the gold of the sunset
Nor the sails in the distance heading towards Harfleur
And when I arrive, I shall place on thy tomb
A bouquet of green holly and heather in bloom.

Step two: this step involves recreating the poem in translation by working with meters, alliterations, rhymes, rhyme scheme, rhythm, parallel constructions, run-on lines and the music of sounds.

The fixed form here is the sonnet. The original alexandrine verse (twelve syllable count) is best rendered as an iambic pentameter. The rhyme scheme: abab, cdcd, efef has to be maintained. The run-on-lines of the first-second and eleventh-twelfth lines also have to be kept, as well as the parallel construction of the sixth line. However, the symbolic image of the green holy and blooming heather probably has to be sacrificed to rhyme constraint and Harfleur, a port in Normandy, which would evoke nothing to an Anglo-Saxon reader can be done away with. One major divergence (and betrayal) with the source poem in the following translation is the special emphasis given to the last word through its position: whereas Hugo chose to end his poem on an image of life and beauty (*en fleur*), the translation insists on an image of death (*grave*) although it manages to maintain until the very end the unexpected shock, to the reader, of the death of the loved girl.

Tomorrow as the dawn grows bright over the land
I will set out. Thy sweet call's come to me.
Mountains and woods I shall withstand
No longer can I be separated from thee.

This journey will take me wrapped in a pensive state,
Deaf to the sounds of life, blind to a world of light,
Walking lone, a stranger, hands folded and prostrate,
Sad, and the day shall seem just as the night.

With the golden sunset and the sails in the bay
The beauty of the earth now must my senses waive
And before I reach thee, I'll pick along the way
The bouquet I shall place quietly on thy grave.

Chapter 17
Guidelines
For the Translation of Non-Literary Texts

Content vs. style

Non-literary texts constitute a vast and multifaceted category. From highly specialized reviews, magazines and documents on the law, science, economics, business, and technology, from works of vulgarization, company catalogs and publications, marketing documentation on export-oriented products, down to newspaper and magazine articles on current events and to public relations brochures and ads, non-literary texts offer an increasingly large source of material for translation which has given rise to the development of an important translation industry.

The main difference in the treatment of literary and non-literary translation can be summed up in a few words: whereas in literary translation the translator's responsibility lies with the author (*i.e.* faithfulness to the original meaning, form and spirit), in non-literary translation it lies with the reader (*i.e.* keeping the integrity of the message and making it clear). Non-literary translation is basically a utilitarian act of communication in which stylistics does not play a great role. Of paramount importance is accuracy, not artistry. Information, data, facts and ideas are what counts, not style, structure, art or atmosphere.

The translator of non-literary material can therefore, with an easy conscience, indulge in taking liberties with the form and structure of the text, if the accuracy and clarity of the message being passed along stand to benefit by it, and if a final check is run to verify that none of the ideas and nuances of the source text have been overlooked.

Non-literary and specialty languages

The language used in non-literary texts is a language different from the one used in literature or in conversation. It is a structured and dense language packed with information. For legal, technical and scientific material, a highly specialized vocabulary is used, often understandable only to experts in the field. Even specialized dictionaries will sometimes fail to provide a T.L. equivalent. Since new concepts are constantly emerging due to discoveries and inventions in every domain, new words referring to them must also be coined, and given the fact that it takes years to put a hard copy dictionary together, it is easy to understand why traditional dictionaries cannot keep up with neologisms, and why now they are being put in an online form. Inventions such as fax machines, word processors, VCRs and cellular phones, which have now been around for a while, have only just recently found their way into standard bilingual dictionaries.

However it is relatively easy to determine new French–English counterparts given the proper context, and translators in a specific field of expertise compile their own data and make their own glossaries of specialized terms. They do this by consulting with experts and by making a habit of reading specialized reviews in both the S.L. and the T.L. in order to figure out equivalents. They also often join a network of professional translators and tap into their resources. And last but not least, the web is increasingly becoming a great and widely used research tool for the translation of non-literary material: surfing the web and searching for subject-related documents in reliable sources in the T.L will yield the correct terminology. Already quite a number of good multi-lingual dictionary databases and translators' blogs exist online which may be resorted to[1].

The language used in non-literary texts is a strong indicator of all the changes which are occurring in the tongue of a linguistic group both semantically and morphologically due to sociological and technological factors. Newspapers, magazines and reviews will show all the trendy phrases and buzz words of the moment, many of which are newly coined and therefore present special difficulties for the translator.

Finally, knowing the kind of audience being targeted is especially important in the translation of a non-literary text in order to adopt the appropriate tone and vocabulary. Is the text intended for a scholarly readership with a view to research or is it a work of vulgarization aimed at the general public? Is the main purpose to inform, as with technical material and journalism, or to proffer an opinion as with editorials, or even to persuade as with marketing documentation and ads?

Taking liberties with sentence structure

In the development of a logical thought French and English tend to adopt opposite approaches: while French goes from the circumstantial to the essential, English favors the reverse sequence.[1]

Let us give one example:

> Avec le fulgurant essor des techniques spatiales et électroniques - les premières ont permis d'explorer les mondes proches; grâce aux secondes, les observatoires terrestres sont devenus des dizaines de fois plus performants -, notre image du cosmos s'est trouvée, en quelques décennies, profondément modifiée. (*France-Amérique*, Terre-Lune: un couple de 4,5 milliards d'années, 31/8/91)

We suggest the following as a translation closer to the reasoning pattern of the English language. The cause-effect sequence of the

---

[1] See Appendix, pp.287-8

[1] Vinay, J.P. and J. Darbelnet. *La Stylistique comparée du français et de l'anglais.* Paris: Didier, 1958, pp.202-3.

French sentence is turned around into an effect-cause statement with a breakdown of the sentence for more clarity:

> Our vision of the cosmos has undergone deep changes within a few decades due to the prodigious advance in space and electronic technologies. The first have allowed man to explore neighboring planets and the second, doubled or tripled the performing power of observatories on earth.

Thus, in French, sentences aiming at the demonstration or illustration of an idea will very often start with a delineation of the circumstances in the form of a participial clause introducing a relationship of relativity, time, cause or condition and will end with the essential point, the main clause. When rendered literally into English with the same clause order, the result sounds very awkward and very much like a translation. A more satisfactory solution consists in reshuffling the clause sequence in the sentence and making the participial clause explicit by means of a relative pronoun or a conjunction of time, cause or condition followed by a conjugated verb.

For instance:

> Les femmes formant aujourd'hui 44% de la population active, la France paraît se diriger vers le modèle scandinave. (*Bilan Economique et Social*, Les Femmes au premier plan, 1991)

The present participle *formant* introduces a relationship of cause and effect between the subordinate and main clauses and the sentence reads better if this is made explicit in English:

> France seems to be headed towards a Scandinavian type of society given the fact /(or) if you consider that women today account for 44% of the workforce.

In a second example the message of the text involving an opening clause with a past participle is made clearer in English when the participial clause is developed into a full relative clause and when the main nominal group starts the sentence:

> Voulu par Georges Pompidou peu avant sa mort en 1974, maintenu par Valéry Giscard d'Estaing qui ne l'aimait guère, le TGV fut inauguré par François Mitterrand quelques mois après son premier septennat, le 22 septembre 1981. (*Bilan Economique et Social*, 1991)
>
> The French high speed train, which had been commissioned by President Georges Pompidou just before he died in 1974, and maintained by his successor, Valery Giscard d'Estaing, who was not

much in favor of it, was finally inaugurated by François Mitterrand on September 22, 1981, at the beginning of his first term.

Improving on the original

Improving on an original text would be anathema in any literary translation. However, non-literary material, and especially newspaper and magazine articles as well as research material or technical documents, can be poorly written because put together with deadlines in mind. Reporters and researchers cannot afford to agonize like Flaubert over *le mot juste* or the right word. Often, sentence construction will leave much to be desired. At worst, there will be typographical errors or even missing words. Whenever confusion is likely to occur in the mind of the intended reader, do not hesitate to clarify the text by making the idea explicit or by rewriting the sentence so that it is correct. Instead of sticking blindly to the structure, follow the ideas behind the words.

French journalists have a particular idiosyncrasy: the use of ellipses. The main verb for instance will be missing from a sentence. For a better comprehension and a more flowing style it is advisable to put it back in English along with the proper tense.
An example:

> Troisième volet de l'avance nipponne que les occidentaux comprennent aujourd'hui: la conception rapide des nouveaux modèles. (*Bilan Economique et Social*, Une Course mondiale derrière les Japonais, 1991)

Suggested translation:

> The third facet in the Japanese lead which Western countries are now beginning to take into account is their ability to quickly develop new models.

Remember, the translation of a non-literary text must strive to make the reading as easy as possible, especially if the text targets the average reader. Always adapt your style to the intended audience.

Conventions in newspapers and magazines

A. Conventions in headlines and titles

When it comes to headlines and the titles of articles, customs are different between English and French. English headlines recap the gist of the story, telegram style, in a whole sentence without definite or indefinite articles.

One illustration:

> Rights to Life: Some Fear U.S. Efforts to Patent Genes May Inhibit broader Research. (*Wall Street Journal*, 4/17/1992)

Not so in French. A similar article in *Le Monde* (12/7/1991) reads:

Le commerce du génome humain condamné par le Comité d'éthique.

Or compare two other related articles, the first taken from the *Wall Street Journal* (10/1/ 1992), the second from *Le Bilan Economique et Social,* 1991:

> Importing Solutions: Car Makers Fight Japanese by Copying Them.
> Une course mondiale derrière les Japonais.

French titles tend to be more succinct. And although the story-recap in imitation of the English trend is seen more frequently, a nominal group still is often the preferred form. A random selection of headlines from *Le Monde* has yielded the following:

> Le rêve d'Albertville
> L'Occident gorbimaniaque
> Les trois Europes
> La Saga du chocolat

for which possible translations might be:

> Albertville has a dream
> West suffers from Gorbimania
> Are there three Europes?
> How to make chocolate.

B. Conventions in the use of tenses

French journalistic style sometimes makes a special use of the present, future perfect and conditional tenses.

1. The historical present: this is a stylistic device designed to bring more reality and life into the narration. The historical present is not nearly as prevalent in English as in French. In a context clearly marked as belonging to the past it is best to revert to the past tense in your English translation.

> En 1884 le colonel Sandherr, chef des Renseignements militaires, *reçoit* de l'un de ses agents alsaciens une lettre dénonçant le capitaine [Dreyfus] comme un espion allemand. (*L'Express*, 3/17/1994)
>
> In 1884 Colonel Sandherr, chief of military Intelligence *received* from one of his Alsatian agents a letter denouncing Captain Dreyfus as a German spy.

2. <u>The future perfect (*futur antérieur*)</u>: the grammatical function of the future perfect is to anticipate on the actual occurrence of a future action or situation in relation to a time marker connoting the future. It presents that action or situation as accomplished by a certain time in the future. After a conjunction of time (*quand, lorsque etc.*) the *futur antérieur* in French also serves to indicate that a future action or situation will take place prior to another future action or situation, although, in this case English uses a present perfect.

> Demain, à cette heure *je serai arrivé* à Paris. Tomorrow, at this time *I will have arrived* in Paris.
>
> Quand *tu auras terminé* tes devoirs, nous dinerons. When *you have finished* your homework, we will have dinner.

In journalism, an additional use is made of the *futur antérieur*. It is often applied to past actions or situations in a sort of retrospective over a rather exceptional course of events, for instance when taking stock of someone's achievements by examining the situation from a vantage point of view, such as at that person's death. In such a context only a past tense can be used in English.

> Le président Mitterrand *aura dirigé* son pays pendant deux septennats. (*Journal de Genève-Gazette de Lausanne*, 9 janvier 1996)
>
> President Mitterrand *led* his country for two consecutive terms.

3. <u>The present and past conditional</u> in French are often used to pass on information that is unverified. By using the conditional the journalist or person giving the information indicates that there is no proof as yet that the reported fact is accurate and declines responsibility should the statement prove to be false. Since there is no such function or use of the English conditional, the translator will have to circumvent the problem by compensating with a short indication that the information is unverified:

> Selon Oliver Stone le président Kennedy *aurait été* victime d'un complot organisé par le complexe militaro-industriel américain inquiet

de l'intention prêtée au président de rappeler les troupes engagées au Vietnam (*Le Monde*, 12/21/1991)

Oliver Stone's *theory* is that President Kennedy *was* the victim of a plot engineered by the American military industrial complex worried about the president's alleged intention of recalling the troops from Vietnam.

La vie sur notre planète *serait* née grâce à une molécule arrivée d'au-delà du système solaire. (*L'Express*, 16-22 mai 1996)

It appears that life on Earth was born of a molecule originated from beyond the solar system.

Le meurtrier *aurait* avoué.

The murderer *allegedly* confessed.

Cultural references in newspapers and magazines

Newspapers and magazines target a linguistic group with a specific culture and civilization in common. Consequently they make constant references to particular facts, events, or people, which their readers are able to recognize instantly. Translating such articles presupposes an adequate knowledge of the cultural heritage of the S.L. on the part of the translator, first to recognize cultural references and second to make them intelligible to the readers of the T.L. In America, for instance, everyone knows what *the big apple* stands for, but would it be the same in France? Conversely in France, a reference to *l'homme du 18 juin* immediately conjures up General de Gaulle and his June 18th 1940 BBC broadcast calling for the rally of Free France against the Nazi invaders, but in order to make it clear to an English speaking readership a translator would have to substitute the General's name for the epithet.

Many of these references are not only historical, political, sociological, they are also literary. Allusions to a repertory of the great French classics, Montaigne, Corneille, Racine, Molière, La Fontaine, Voltaire *etc.* or to a repertory of the world's great classics, will pop up even in a non-literary context.

We shall quote as an example an article from *Le Monde* (12/26/1991) on the enthusiastic welcome by Mrs. Thatcher, then prime minister of England, of Michael Gorbachev, then leader of the USSR just before the end of the cold war:

> Chaque fois que [Mrs. Thatcher] reçut [Mr. Gorbachev] à Londres, elle avait pour lui les yeux de Chimène.

clearly an allusion to Corneille's seventeenth century play *Le Cid*:

> Tout le monde pour Rodrigue a les yeux de Chimène.

But it is one thing to recognize the allusion, and quite another to translate it. Since Corneille's heroine and her dilemma of love versus honor will most likely mean nothing to an Anglophone public, the translator will have to choose between finding an equivalence in the Anglo-American literary repertory, or making the author's intention explicit in a more prosaic way, for instance by showing that Mrs. Thatcher is torn between her "honor", her allegiance to her western allies, and her "instinct", her confidence in this Russian leader with a new style. This will necessitate a circumlocution which will have to be kept as short as possible.

Another article in *France-Amérique*, entitled *En attendant les Russes*, is an obvious allusion to Samuel Beckett's play *En attendant Godot*. The translator here is luckier, for *Waiting for Godot* is also well known this side of the Atlantic. No explanation will therefore be necessary and it is up to the reader to catch the implication.

The phrase *Dallas au pays des merveilles* found in a review of Oliver Stone's film *JFK* in *Le Monde* is clearly an allusion to Lewis Carroll's *Alice in Wonderland*. Examples of such cultural hints in a non-literary context are many.

Let yourself be guided by this general rule: when the cultural reference or the figure of style is not essential to the understanding of the text, it is perhaps best to leave it alone or at least to simplify it.

Article 1
Mitterrand: la fin d'un combat honorable mené contre soi-même[1]
Mitterrand: un homme libre qui avait trop souvent tutoyé la mort pour la craindre[2]

François Mitterrand est mort,[3] selon l'annonce officielle, lundi 8 à 8h.30 au siège de son bureau[4] avenue Le Play près du Champ-de-Mars[5] à Paris.[...] Mitterrand, quatrième président de la Ve République créée par le général de Gaulle, aura dirigé[6] son pays pendant quatorze ans, soit deux septennats,[7] longévité présidentielle sans précédent.[8] L'ancien[9] chef de l'Etat était atteint depuis 1992 - une intervention chirurgicale[10] l'avait alors rendu public- d'un cancer de la prostate.[11] Il avait réussi à poursuivre son mandat[12] jusqu'au bout malgré des épisodes de souffrance aiguë. Les Français, classe politique comprise,[13] lui étaient reconnaissants de la bonne grâce avec laquelle il avait supporté sa maladie.

Le respect d'Helmut Kohl
En cette matinée[14] d'hiver [...] les Français auront été cueillis à froid[15] par la nouvelle. [...] Mitterrand, qui s'était sportivement[16] retranché de la vie publique depuis sa retraite,[17] avait été aperçu il y a quelques jours en Egypte où il aimait passer les fêtes de fin d'année[18] sous le soleil du Nil.[19] Dans la rue, avec ce mélange de pudeur affective et de volonté de paraître qui les caractérise,[20] les Parisiens exprimaient de la surprise et des commentaires convenus devant un évènement qui avait été peut-être un peu trop préparé pour laisser de la place à la spontanéité. Tous manifestaient cependant peine et estime.[21]

A l'étranger comme dans les rédactions de presse se mettait en place un énorme flux d'hommages dont celui du chancelier Kohl fut probablement le plus senti.[22] Le chancelier avait déjà eu l'occasion[23] d'écrire, au moment de la retraite du président, son respect pour cet improbable mais fidèle compagnon de route d'une décennie.[...]

Au siège du bureau présidentiel, familiers et notables se pressaient immédiatement pour rendre un dernier hommage[24] au président, en présence de la famille. Au début de l'après-midi,[25] les proches[26] annonçaient que, conformément au voeu de l'ancien président, ses obsèques n'auraient pas lieu à Paris mais à Jarnac (Charente-Maritime) [où étaient ses racines familiales] et dans l'intimité.[27] [...]

"C'est une oeuvre"

A la télévision, c'est sur un ton très personnel que le président Jacques Chirac[28] a rendu hommage hier soir à son prédécesseur: "François Mitterrand, a-t-il dit, c'est une oeuvre.[29] "

Mitterrand aura en effet marqué l'espace français de sa personne comme il en aura imprégné la durée.[30] Sa fameuse affiche électorale de 1981, où l'on voit un village serré autour du clocher au coeur de labours[31] fumants, n'était pas qu'une image mais un programme. Pour cet homme qui fut un véritable maître de la politique, c'est à dire quelque part entre les pôles de l'opportunisme et de la clairvoyance, il y avait des fidélités.[32] La terre en était une; il sut non seulement l'évoquer dans ses livres mais la chérir par la pratique assidue du jardinage. Contre son itinéraire personnel de provincial monté à Paris[33] et contre presque toute évidence, il évoquait encore dans les années récentes le caractère irrécusablement rural de la France, à l'opposé des grandes villes. En[34] pélerinage à la roche de Solutré ou ailleurs, il faisait cas de[35] ses origines paysannes, en réalité relativement lointaines.

Sens de l'opportunité

Quant au temps, on connaît son fameux aphorisme -il faut laisser du temps au temps[36] - par lequel il ressemble au général de Gaulle et à Mao Tsé-toung, occasionnels amateurs et émetteurs[37] comme lui de sonores platitudes. Par là comme par sa mort si méticuleusement préparée, il manifeste son sens de l'opportunité, de la durée, de la persévérance.[38] Et plus attachant que tout, la fréquentation de la mort[39] l'intéresse de plus en plus, par curiosité autant intellectuelle que spirituelle, à mesure qu'il vieillit. Il décrit la maladie comme un combat honorable à mener contre soi-même. A une époque où[40] rares sont les gens qui savent (ou peuvent) mourir dignement, l'ultime cadeau aux Français de son départ impeccable n'est peut-être pas le moindre.

(Antoine Maurice, *Journal de Genève et Gazette de Lausanne*, 9 janvier 1996)

Guiding notes

The above article is a representative sample of the journalistic treatment of a news item. It appeared the day after President Mitterrand's death and, being written from a foreign albeit French speaking country's point of view, gives a non-partisan tribute to the former head of state. The prose is dense and informative and the vocabulary is non-specialized but makes use of "in" phrases and stylistic features which pertain to newspaper writing: this is manifested in the love of nominal groups (e.g. *le siège du bureau présidentiel, la fréquentation de la mort*), the importance of set idiomatic expressions from the spoken language (*la volonté de paraître, cueilli à froid, faire cas de*), neologisms which may need defining (*l'espace français*) and the special use of tenses which have no counterpart in English (here: the use of the futur antérieur: *aura dirigé, aura marqué, etc.*)

---

[1] **Title**: after translating the article find a title which can best sum up its contents and write it English headline style using verbs.

[2] **Subtitle**: the main problem here is the translation of "*tutoyer*" a concept which no longer exists in the English language; to help you along the way of a suitable translation ask yourself: is the verb used here in a literal or figurative meaning? What does the use of "*tu*" to a person imply about the relationship?

[3] **Est mort**: does this verb express a situation or an action here? Consequently is it a present passive or a passé composé?

[4] **Au siège de son bureau**: simplify.

[5] **Près du Champ de Mars**: ask yourself whether this landmark, which is well known to French speakers, is also well known to your audience; if not, substitute a better known landmark.

[6] **Aura dirigé**: the use of the futur antérieur (future perfect) is widespread in journalistic parlance; in regular literary prose its function is to anticipate on the occurrence of a future action or situation (e.g.. *Demain à cette même heure nous serons arrivés à destination*: Tomorrow at this hour we will have reached our destination); here however it is clearly not a future since the former president just passed away: the purpose of the journalistic futur antérieur is to look back upon a whole course of events (in this case Mitterrand's career) and take stock; what tense then seems best suited in English?

[7] **Deux septennats**: a "*septennat*" is a period of seven years; it is generally used to designate the seven year term a French president served at that time (it has now been reduced to 5 years) .

[8] **Longévité présidentielle sans précédent**: a modulation will be necessary here; be sure not to overlook all the information contained in these few words.

[9] **L'ancien chef de l'Etat**: the adjective is a false friend.

[10] **Une intervention chirurgicale**: simplify.

[11] **Etait atteint d'un cancer de la prostate**: use a verb and a preposition modulation; watch out for the proper tense in English since this is a continuous situation in the past.

[12] **Son mandat**: what word is used in English for this specific sort of "mandate", a presidential "mandate"?

[13] **Classe politique comprise**: the term "*classe politique*" is a rather recent one and refers to all politicians, from the left to the right; find a phrase.

[14] **En cette matinée**: use a preposition modulation.

[15] **Auront été cueillis à froid**: a highly idiomatic expression not to be taken literally; look up its meaning in a French monolingual dictionary such as *Le Petit Robert* before deciding on a translation.

[16] **Sportivement**: false friend; *"sportivement"* has a very specific meaning: in an attitude of fair play.

[17] **Retraite**: false friend in this context.

[18] **Les fêtes de fin d'année**: refers to the Christmas and New Year's holidays.

[19] **Sous le soleil du Nil**: a possible literary allusion to and stylistic reproduction of the title of Georges Bernanos's novel *"Sous le soleil de Satan;"* modulate.

[20] **Avec ce mélange...qui les caractérise**: analyze all the elements of the sentence and rephrase them in an idiomatic way.

[21] **Tous manifestaient peine et estime**: a change of focus to the passive voice would work best.

[22] **Le plus senti**: the past participle needs some padding in English.

[23] **L'occasion**: false friend.

[24] **Pour rendre un dernier hommage**: both a verb and noun modulation are needed.

[25] **Au *début* de l'après midi**: use an adjective transposition.

[26] **Les proches**: an adjective turned into a noun meaning *"ceux qui étaient proches de lui," "ses intimes."*

[27] **Dans l'intimité**: one T.U.

[28] **Le président Jacques Chirac**: remember that the translation is from a non-French point of view; the nationality of the president needs to be made explicit for the target audience.

[29] **Une oeuvre**: refers to one's achievements, whether literary or otherwise.

[30] **Aura marqué l'espace français...durée**: see note 6 for the use of the futur antérieur; *"l'espace français"*: a neologism with no English equivalent. One hears more nowadays about *"l'espace francophone" i.e.* all the French speaking countries of the world. The sentence seems rather cryptic at first. It plays on the double factor of space and time and how both were affected by Mitterrand's tenure. It is obvious that no literal translation will do.

[31] **Labours**: *i.e. champs labourés.*

[32] **Pour cet homme...fidélités**: simplify the construction.

[33] *Monté* **à Paris**: the consecrated phrase for French people who leave their native province to make a career in Paris, since most of them come from regions of France located south of Paris; can the image be kept for a non-French public?

[34] **En pélerinage**: use a preposition modulation.

[35] **Il faisait cas de**: il se vantait de...

[36] **Il faut laisser du temps au temps**: work on that formula; what does Mitterrand mean?

---

[37] **Amateurs et émetteurs**: the play on words with an internal rhyme for stylistic effect is perhaps best left out of the translation but remain concise in your rendition.

[38] **Par là comme par sa mort...persévérance**: for the structure of this sentence follow the approach favored by the English language, essential argument first, circumstancial details second.

[39] **La *fréquentation* de la mort**: use a word modulation.

[40] ***A une époque où:*** use a preposition modulation and an adverb-conjunction transposition.

Mitterrand's Death or the End of a Remarkable Struggle against Terminal Illness
He had been living with death too long to fear it

According to official news François Mitterrand died at 8:30 am, Monday the 8th in his Paris office on the Avenue Le Play near the Eiffel Tower. Mitterrand was the fourth president of the Fifth Republic founded by General de Gaulle and led his country for fourteen years, two consecutive terms - a record. The former head of state had been suffering from prostate cancer since 1992 when his undergoing surgery first brought it to public attention. He had managed to reach the end of his second term in spite of periods of severe pain. The French people, including politicians from all parties, were grateful to him for bearing his illness so gracefully.

Chancellor Kohl pays his last respects

The news took France by surprise on that winter morning. Mitterrand, who, like a good sport, had withdrawn from public life after leaving office, had been seen a few days before in Egypt where he enjoyed spending the Christmas holidays in the sunny valley of the Nile. Parisians interviewed on the street, with the typical mixture of emotional reserve and propensity to show off which is a characteristic of theirs, expressed surprise along with suitable comments on an event which, perhaps, had been anticipated too long to leave any room for spontaneity. Nonetheless, all manifested sorrow and appreciation.

An impressive flow of tributes started pouring in from the editorial staffs of newspapers in France and abroad. Among those, chancellor Kohl's was probably the most heartfelt. Already, at the time of the president's retirement, the chancellor had taken the opportunity of writing to convey his best wishes to the man who, for a decade, had proved an unlikely but loyal traveling companion.

Friends and VIPs immediately crowded the presidential office to pay their last respects to the late president and express sympathy to his family. In the early afternoon it was announced by people close to him that, in compliance with François Mitterrand's last wish, the funeral would be held privately, not in Paris but in the small town of Jarnac in south western France where he had family roots.

François Mitterrand: "A sum of achievements"

Last night on television French president Jacques Chirac paid tribute to his predecessor in a very personal way. "The life of François Mitterrand, he declared, has been a sum of achievements."

Mitterrand certainly has left his personal mark on France through his long presidency. His famous 1981 campaign poster, which showed a village huddling around a church steeple in the middle of misty ploughed fields, was not just a picture but a whole program. The man, a master politician who maneuvered between the poles of opportunism and clear sightedness, remained faithful to a few ideals. Land was one of them. Not only did he succeed in bringing it to life in his books, but he was also able to show his love for it through the regular practice of gardening. In recent years in spite of his own personal itinerary (he had gone "up" to Paris as a country lad) and in spite of much evidence to the contrary, he kept alluding to the irrefutably rural character of France, in contrast to the big cities. While on a pilgrimage to Solutré or elsewhere he would emphasize his peasant origins, actually quite remote.

A sense of timeliness

We all know his aphorism on time: "You must let time take its time", in the tradition of General de Gaulle and Mao Zedong, also occasional amateurs and dispensers of resounding truisms. His sense of timeliness, endurance, and perseverance shows through such a pronouncement, as well as in the manner of his death, so meticulously prepared. And most endearing of all, as he advanced in years and got acquainted with death, he showed signs of a curiosity both spiritual and intellectual. He described illness as an honorable fight against the self. In an age when those who know how to die or can do it with dignity are few, his impeccable departure may be his last but not his least gift to France.

Article 2
GATT: Pourquoi il faut absolument un accord
Le Mythe de la France seule[1]

Les négociations sur le Gatt arrivent à échéance,[2] et la France paraît un peu seule dans la défense de ses intérêts agricoles et dans la proclamation[3] de son "exception culturelle."[4] Cette double cause[5] rassemble une majorité de Français et, sans doute, le combat actuel[6] du gouvernement ne manque-t-il pas de bons arguments. Moins acceptable, plus inquiétant, est le retour insidieux, au milieu de cette bataille diplomatique, de l'esprit protectionniste.

Celui-ci[7] a dominé notre pays,[8] toutes classes confondues,[9] pendant si longtemps, que ses marques restent indélébiles.[10] Napoléon III avait imposé un libre-échange en 1860 contre sa classe dirigeante:[11] on parla de *"coup d'état[12] douanier."*

Au début des années 1880, quand la dépression économique mondiale atteignit la France, on n'eut de cesse de[13] vouloir rétablir la protection douanière. Un républicain modéré s'en fit alors le champion[14] et le législateur: Jules Méline, futur auteur d'un *Retour à la terre*, ouvrage dont le titre est à lui seul[15] un vaste programme. Il satisfaisait aussi bien la France des "petits" que la France des "gros":[16] la démocratie rurale des laboureurs,[17] des vignerons et des bûcherons s'alliait[18] aux manufacturiers pour réclamer le cadenassage[19] des frontières.

Ces tarifs douaniers donnèrent sans doute un peu d'air[20] à tous ces petits propriétaires, mais à la longue,[21] ils contribuèrent à maintenir des structures archaïques, donc des coûts élevés, lesquels, par un effet de retour,[22] impliquaient la fermeture. Résultat: une agriculture médiocre sur laquelle vivait mal un monde rural surabondant.[23] La modernisation des années 60 fut d'autant plus brutale. Elle était nécessaire, elle se fit[24] à coups de[25] subventions massives et, pour les paysans[26] transformés en patrons de PME,[27] à coups d'endettements écrasants. La situation actuelle de l'agriculture française est encore tributaire de ce passé protectionniste, quand bien même[28] elle n'a de respiration que par les ventes à l'étranger.

L'exception culturelle est en soi une formule risible. La France est le pays de l'universalisme. J'entends bien[29] qu'on doit défendre le cinéma français et le reste! Mais d'abord par des oeuvres à portée universelle, où la France de Voltaire et de Diderot, où la France de Balzac et de Victor Hugo, où la France d'Auguste et de Jean Renoir[30] s'y reconnaisse.[31] Le reste n'est que bataille corporatiste. La défense de la sub-culture "bien de chez nous"[32] ne présente aucun intérêt, ni pour l'avenir de la France, ni pour celui de l'humanité.

Il y a toujours eu dans notre pays une tendance au repli sur soi.[33] Charles Maurras, en son temps, a fort bien exprimé cette psychologie et cette idéologie de la société close [...] horrifiée par tout ce qui est étranger et qui par définition, altère sa quintessence. Après la défaite de 1940, ce fut le slogan de "la France seule" sous le bâton du Maréchal.[34] L'illusion fut de courte durée.[35]

La France est la quatrième puissance exportatrice du monde: il ne faudrait pas parler du Gatt comme si nous pouvions ruminer sur notre pré carré,[36] derrière des fils barbelés, en attendant l'abattoir.

(Michel Winock, L'Evènement du Jeudi, 2-8 décembre 1993)

Guiding notes

This editorial from a weekly magazine on the occasion of the 1993 GATT negotiations gives a historical perspective of the French position on trade tariffs and like all editorials advocates a certain stance. Although aimed at a general readership, some of its vocabulary may be somewhat arcane from a T.L. point of view and words from the field of business and economics may require the use of a specialized dictionary. The translator will also have to be familiar with some of the expressions common to French political discourse (*i.e.* "*la France des petits et la France des gros*," "*la classe dirigeante*")   with neologisms ("*l'exception culturelle*," "*Une bataille corporatiste*," "*une subculture*") and with modern French history, literature and art to recognize some of the less transparent cultural references.

---

[1] **Subtitle**: a nominal title is not a characteristic feature of English headlines; find a more suitable formula which would keep all the elements implied in the original. Remember that a "myth" implies something not quite in touch with reality. It is best to select a title and subtitle after having translated the whole article for a thorough understanding of its contents.

[2] **Les négociations sur le GATT arrivent à échéance**: arrivent à leur fin; give an adverb transposition for the noun. Notice that the English acronym GATT instead of the French one AGETAC is used.

[3] **Dans la défense et dans la proclamation**: using verbs instead of nouns would be closer to the English stylistic approach;   also remember that English simplifies by dropping all prepositions but the first in a list.

[4] **Son "exception culturelle":** the use of inverted commas in the text indicates that the term is new and not yet a household word (it was coined for the negotiations). It refers to France's determination not to include the products of its movie and television industry among the business and trade brought to the negotiation table and to impose quotas on U.S.-made films in an effort to protect its own culture from Hollywood's overwhelming influence. Since the concept was born in France of a specific situation there can be no English equivalent: use a calque.

[5] **Cette double cause:** give a modulation.

[6] **Actuel:** false friend.

[7] **Celui-ci:** the use of this demonstrative pronoun is frequent in French to refer to previously mentioned persons or facts; "the latter" is often suggested as an English equivalent, but makes the sentence sound too much like a translation; a preferable course of action would be to determine what word the pronoun refers to and simply repeat it.

[8] **Notre pays:** from whose point of view is the article written? Some clarification will be necessary for the T.L. public.

[9] **Toutes classes confondues:** toutes classes sociales mélangées.

[10] **Ses marques restent indélébiles:** give a message modulation (a different perspective).

[11] **Sa classe dirigeante:** la classe qui gouverne; a common phrase in political discourse; find an English equivalent.

[12] **Coup d'état:** the word has been borrowed in English with a slight modification.

[13] **On n'eut de cesse de...:** an old fashioned expression meaning "on ne s'arrêta pas avant de...;" rephrase the sentence.

[14] **S'en fit le champion:** headed the movement.

[15] **A lui seul:** en soi

[16] **La France des "petits" et la France des "gros":** in this phrase the adjectives are taken as nouns; the antithetical and metaphorical terms designate the two economic poles of French society; find an English equivalent

[17] **Laboureurs:** false friend.

[18] **S'alliait:** a past perfect seems more appropriate in translation than a past progressive.

[19] **Le cadenassage:** a word coined by the author from "cadenas" (lock) plus suffix -age (which indicates the action of...); use a gerund.

[20] **Donnèrent un peu d'air:** permirent de respirer; the expression is used in a figurative sense; keep the image in English in your search of an equivalent.

[21] **A la longue:** use a preposition modulation and pad.

[22] **Par un effet de retour:** try to visualize the concept by following the author's argument closely to be able to come up with an equivalent.

[23] **Résultat...surabondant**:   sentence without a main verb which is not uncommon in French journalism; replace the implied verb in your translation.

[24] **Elle se fit**: false reflexive verb meaning "elle eut lieu."

[25] **A coup de**: avec beaucoup de.

[26] **Les paysans**: this term in French does not carry the pejorative connotation of its English counterpart, it is simply a synonym of "*fermiers.*"

[27] **PME**: an acronym which stands for "*Petites et Moyennes Entreprises.*"

[28] **Quand bien même**: (literary) même si.

[29] **J'entends bien que...**: a not so well known meaning of "entendre." In this context: "*je suis d'accord,*" "*j'admets.*"

[30] **Auguste et Jean Renoir**: the former is one of the major painters of the famous impressionist group, the latter, his son, a movie director who created some of France's great movie classics.

[31] **S'y reconnaisse**: se retrouve.

[32] **La sub-culture "bien de chez nous"**: typiquement française.

[33] **Le repli sur soi**: use a verb transposition for the noun.

[34] **Le Maréchal**: a historical allusion to Marshall Pétain who led the Vichy government during the Nazi occupation of France between 1940 and 1944; obviously this allusion will fail to be clear to a T.L. public; an explanation is therefore necessary in the translation.

[35] **Fut de courte durée**: use a verb transposition for the noun.

[36] **Pré carré**: idiomatic expression meaning "*reserved domain.*" Obviously here the image of the meadow gets lost in translation.

GATT:
Why an Agreement Is a Must
Can France really go it alone?

GATT negotiations are coming up and France appears somewhat isolated in defending her farming interests and proclaiming her "cultural exception." The French in their majority are behind these two issues and the government's current battle certainly does not lack for good reasons. But less acceptable and more worrisome is the insidious come-back of the spirit of protectionism in the midst of this diplomatic fight.

Protectionism in France has been prevalent for so long in all strata of society that it has left a permanent impression over the country. In 1860 when Napoleon III imposed a free trade agreement against the wish of the ruling class of the time, it was referred to as a "trading coup."

In the early 1880's, as a world economic depression reached France, a return to tariffs was urgently advocated. A moderate republican, Jules Meline, who later was to write "Back to the land" a book whose title is in itself a vast program, became the champion and legislator of this movement. It was an answer to the expectations of both the working class and the ruling class: the rural democracy of farmers, vintners and woodcutters had concluded an alliance with factory owners to require a tight closing of the borders.

Trade tariffs undoubtedly gave all small landowners a breather, but in the long run, were partially responsible for keeping archaic structures, therefore high costs, which, through a boomerang effect led to closed borders. The result was an agriculture which left much to be desired and barely managed to feed a rural overpopulation. Modernization in the sixties proved all the more brutal. It had become necessary, was carried out through massive subsidies and turned farmers into small firm owners at the cost of overwhelming mortgages. The present state of French farming is still linked to this protectionist past, even though exports are its only life saver.

Deep down the idea of a "cultural exception" is laughable. France is the land of the universal. Certainly the French movie industry should be protected, along with the rest! But first through works of universal value, which the France of Voltaire and Diderot, the France of Balzac and Victor Hugo, the France of Auguste et Jean Renoir could call her own. The rest is nothing but a corporate fight. The defense of a Gallic subculture offers no interest, either for the future of France, or of humanity.

The country has always had a tendency to look inward. In his day, Charles Maurras was a good exponent of the psychology and ideology of a closed society, a society horrified by anything foreign which by definition would alter its quintessential purity. In the wake of the 1940 defeat came the slogan "France on her own" under the rule of Marshall Petain. It proved to be a short-lived illusion.

France is the fourth largest exporting nation in the world: we should not be talking about GATT as if we were chewing our cud on our reserved pasture behind barbed wire, while waiting for the slaughter-house.

Article 3
Sida:[1]   Une Découverte française majeure
Une équipe de chercheurs de[2] l'institut Pasteur, dirigée[3] à Paris par le Professeur[4] Hovanessian, met en évidence[5] un mécanisme essentiel de l'infection

---

Probablement capitale, cette découverte[6] devrait, à terme,[7] permettre aux chercheurs de trouver un moyen d'attaquer le virus. [...] Les résultats complets de ces travaux[8] ont été présentés officiellement mardi 26 octobre lors[9] d'un colloque consacré à la recherche sur cette maladie qui rassemblait les plus grands noms de la recherche mondiale.[10]

Les virologues pensaient jusqu'à présent qu'il existait sur les cellules un seul récepteur, la molécule CD4,[11] qui permettait au virus de pénétrer dans l'organisme. "En fait, nous avons découvert qu'il fallait, non pas un seul récepteur, mais deux, les CD4 et les CD26, pour permettre au virus d'infester cette cellule," a expliqué le Pr. Hovanessian.

Schématiquement,[12] on peut comparer le virus à la cargaison d'un cargo,[13] et la cellule cible[14] au quai de débarquement. Pour que le déchargement du bateau puisse être effectué,[15] il faut, premièrement, une amarre pour immobiliser le navire à quai et, deuxièmement, une grue pour extraire la cargaison de la cale et l'entreposer. Les molécules[16] CD4 qui fixent le virus servent en gros d'[17] amarre et les CD26 représentent la grue. De la même manière que[18] le déchargement n'est possible que si un bateau est immobilisé et si on dispose d'[19] une grue, l'infection ne peut se produire qu'au terme de[20] deux étapes, l'accrochage[21] du virus et l'entrée. "Il s'agit d'[22] un mouvement en deux temps[23] qui fait de ces deux protéines des éléments indissociables,[24]" indique le Pr. Hovanessian. "S'il n'y a pas de CD4 à la surface des cellules cibles, le virus du SIDA ne peut pas y pénétrer et, inversement, si les cellules visées par le virus sont dépourvues de protéines CD26, le virus reste errant autour de la cellule."

Le Pr. Hovanessian et ses collaborateurs ont en outre découvert que les CD26 savent reconnaître, sur une des parties les plus importantes du virus, des "clefs" qui restent constantes[25] chez tous les virus et permettent d'ouvrir la "porte" CD26. Il suffira donc de brouiller la serrure pour empêcher le virus de passer[26] "Même si le virus du SIDA change -ce qu'il fait constamment-, les clefs restent identiques," souligne le Pr. Hovanessian. Selon ce dernier,[27] cette constance, particulièrement importante, montre qu'il existe un point commun à tous les types de virus. Jusqu'à présent, en raison de la versatilité du virus du SIDA et faute de[28] trouver un point commun aux différents virus, les chercheurs n'étaient même pas sûrs de parvenir à créer un vaccin polyvalent.

Ils redoutaient au contraire de devoir lutter au coup par coup,[29] contre le virus africain ou asiatique par exemple, et de devoir adapter leur formule vaccinale en fonction de[30] variations de virus. Au contraire, l'existence d'un dénominateur commun à tous les virus du SIDA devrait donner aux chercheurs un objectif de choix.[31] En théorie, il suffirait de trouver un moyen de bloquer l'interaction entre les clefs et les CD26 ou d'utiliser des molécules bloquant directement l'activité des CD26 pour empêcher le virus d'infecter les cellules.

"Ce sera un travail de longue haleine[32] " a estimé le Pr. Hovanessian. "Le rôle du CD26 a été démontré et nous disposons d'inhibiteurs efficaces utilisables comme modèles. Mais il nous faut encore parvenir à augmenter leur activité avant de pouvoir les injecter aux malades, dans deux ans si tout marche bien."

[...]

Directeur de recherches au CNRS[33] et chef de l'unité de virologie et d'immunologie cellulaire à l'Institut Pasteur (associé au CNRS) le Pr. Hovanessian a mené ses recherches en coopération avec trois autres chercheurs. [...]"Nous avons gardé nos travaux confidentiels jusqu'à ce que tout ait été démontré de façon irrévocable," a-t-il précisé à l'AFP.[33] [...] Le Pr. Luc Montagnier, responsable de l'équipe française de l'Institut Pasteur qui a découvert le virus de l'immuno-déficience humaine (VIH), a souligné l'importance du travail du Pr. Hovanessian qui constitue une percée nouvelle qui permettra peut-être de mettre au point de nouvelles thérapeutiques ou un vaccin contre le SIDA.

(Reprinted with the permission of the newspaper *France-Amérique*.
Philippe Coste, AFP, *France-Amérique*, 30 octobre-5 novembre 1993)

Guiding notes

This last article from the medical column of a weekly newspaper does not target specialists in the field but the general public. Its purpose is to vulgarize the latest medical findings in research on AIDS, that is to say make them understandable to non-experts. Nonetheless its vocabulary is in part specialized, and as such requires the use of a medical or scientific bilingual dictionary. The article also makes frequent quotations, which will provide good practice for the student translator to adapt the phrasing of the sentences leading to these quotations to English usage, interpolated sentences like *"indique le professeur,"* *" souligne le professeur,"* *"a-t-il estimé,"* etc.

[1] **SIDA**: acronym for Syndrôme Immuno-Déficitaire Acquis; find the English acronym from which it is a calque.

[2] **De l'Institut Pasteur**: choose a preposition connoting origin.

[3] **Dirigée**: an example of French love of abstract concepts where English prefers concrete ones.

[4] **Le Professeur Hovanessian**: in France, this is the title of a physician teaching at a medical school. May be referred to as Professor or Doctor in English.

[5] **Met en évidence**: one T.U.

[6] **Probablement capitale, cette découverte**: restructure the beginning of this sentence by expanding it into a full clause, and remember that you can use a transposition or a modulation to convey the meaning of "*probablement.*"

[7] **A terme**: (literary) *au bout, à la fin* (don't forget to make use of a French monolingual dictionary to clarify the meaning of words or expressions you are not familiar with).

[8] **Ces travaux**: *i.e.* ces travaux de recherche, ces recherches.

[9] **Lors d'un colloque**: a preposition modulation is advisable here, shift from a concept of time to a concept of place.

[10] **De la recherche mondiale**: a nominal group with adjective in French which becomes a compound noun in English; preposition modulation on "de."

[11] **La molécule CD4**: scientific neologisms are almost always calques from the language which made the discovery and first came up with the word. The only difference in English will be one of word sequence: we are dealing with a semantic calque, not a structural one.

[12] **Schématiquement**: an adverb patterned after a noun which is a false friend in English "*un schema,*" meaning not a scheme, but a diagram, a sketch. There is no equivalent adverb in English; modulate.

[13] **Un cargo**: a false friend; refers to the ship transporting the cargo (Fr. *cargaison*).

[14] **La cellule cible**: a semantic calque.

[15] **Effectuer un déchargement**: one T.U.

[16] **En gros**: means « *en substance, sans entrer dans les détails.* »

[17] **D'amarre**: preposition modulation.

[18] **De la même manière que**: one T.U.

[19] **On dispose de**: false friend; means "*on a à sa disposition.*"

[20] **Au terme de** : see note 7.

[21] **L'accrochage**: a noun patterned after "*accrocher*" (to hook) meaning the action of hooking; use an English gerund.

[22] **Il s'agit de**: an impersonal expression synonymous with "c'est."

[23] **En deux temps**: en deux étapes.

[24] **Indissociables**: the adjective does not exist in English; use a padded expression.

[25] **Restent constantes**: *restent les mêmes.*

---

[26] **Il suffira...passer**: transpose on "*il suffira*" and "*brouiller la serrure.*"

[27] **Ce dernier**: like "*celui-ci*" a French stylistic idiosyncrasy referring to the last person mentioned; find another solution beside using "the latter".

[28] **Faute de**: *par manque de.*

[29] **Au coup par coup**: *par une suite d'actions séparées.*

[30] **En fonction de**: *selon.*

[31] **Un objectif de choix**: *un objectif numéro un.*

[32] **Un travail de longue haleine**: literally, "work that will take a long breath", meaning "that will take a long time."

[33] **CNRS, AFP**: acronyms not intelligible to an Anglophone public; shortly explain what they stand for in your translation.

AIDS: A Major French Discovery

Headed in Paris by Dr. Hovanessian, a research team from the Pasteur Institute demonstrates one of the infection's main mechanisms

The discovery appears to be of primary importance and should in time give researchers the means to fight the virus. The final results of this undertaking were officially presented on October 26 at a colloquium which brought together the most famous names in world research on the virus.

Up until now virologists thought that only one receptor on the cells, the CD4 molecule, enabled the virus to enter the system. Dr. Hovanessian shed light on his findings: "We have discovered that not one but two receptors, CD4 and CD26, are actually necessary to let the virus take over the cell."

In a simplified illustration of the procedure the virus may be compared to the cargo of a ship and the target cell to a landing dock. For the ship cargo to be unloaded, first, moorings are needed to secure the ship to the wharf, then a crane to remove the cargo from the hold and store it in the warehouse. The CD molecules which fix the virus roughly serve as moorings and CD26 plays the role of the crane. Just as the unloading becomes possible only when the ship is moored to the wharf and a crane is on hand, the infection can take place only after two steps are completed: after the virus has fixed itself onto the cell and after it has penetrated the cell. In the words of Dr. Hovanessian "this is a two-step process by which the two proteins become elements that cannot be dissociated. If there are no CD4 on the surface of target cells, the AIDS virus cannot enter, and conversely if the cells targeted by the virus have no CD26 proteins, the virus is kept wandering outside the cell."

In addition, Dr. Hovanessian and his collaborators have discovered that, on one of the most important parts of the virus CD26 can recognize "keys" which are found in all the viruses. With these keys it is possible to open the CD26 door. Therefore a simple jamming of the lock will prevent the virus from entering. Dr. Hovanessian pointed out that "even if the AIDS virus changes, as it keeps doing, the keys remain the same." In his opinion, this extremely important consistent pattern shows that there is a factor common to the various virus types. Up until now in the absence of a common factor between the different viruses, researchers were not even sure of being able to come up with a polyvalent vaccine due to the ever changing character of the AIDS virus. They were afraid of having to fight the various strains of the virus, such as the African or Asian strains, one by one, and of having to adapt their vaccine formula to the variations of the virus. Now on the contrary, the existence of a denominator common to all AIDS viruses should provide researchers with a prime objective. Theoretically all that is needed is the means to block the interaction between the keys and CD26 or to use molecules which would directly block the activity of CD26 in order to prevent the virus from infecting the cells.

In Dr. Hovanessian's estimation this will take some time. "The role of CD26 has been demonstrated. We have efficient inhibitors at our disposal to use as models. But we still have to increase their activity before we can inject them into patients, in two years' time if all goes well."

Dr. Hovanessian, head of research at the French National Center for Scientific Research (CNRS) as well as head of virology and cellular immunology at the Pasteur Institute (which is associated with CNRS) has carried out this experiment with the help of three other research assistants. He disclosed to Agence France Presse, the French news agency, that the undertaking was kept a secret until everything could be demonstrated in an irrefutable way. Dr. Luc Montagnier, chief of the French team who discovered the human immunodeficiency virus (HIV) at the Pasteur Institute, has emphasized the importance of Dr. Hovanessian's work as a new advance which may lead to new therapies or to a vaccine against AIDS.

Chapter 18
Guidelines for the Translation of Ads

Ads and cultural references

Next to translating poetry, translating advertisements is perhaps the most creative and the most difficult task a translator can undertake. Creative, because of the impossibility to remain literal, and difficult because of the extensive use the ad industry makes of cultural references in targeting potential customers.

The use of cultural hints is widespread in French advertising. It is a way of letting the ad reader know that he or she belongs to a sociological group with a common education and common traditions. Many ads read like little riddles with codes of their own which try to appeal to the readers' taste for puzzles while comforting them with a sense of cultural identity.

I will give three examples of French ads making cultural references the focal point of their argument. One will quickly see why such ads are on the borderline of translatability.

The first, a poster in the Paris metro, read:

Carpaccio à volonté: ils sont fous, ces bistros Romains!

The message, flaunting the generosity of a chain of Parisian bistros in indulging their clients with as much *carpaccio* as they wished, appears rather ordinary and disconnected to an English speaker. To a French person on the other hand, whose education would not be complete without having read the very popular comic strip *Astérix*, the quip evokes the vision of a wily and endearing little Gaul who, with the help of his friends and a magic potion concocted by the village druid, undertakes to keep Caesar's Roman legionnaires in check. When faced with some puzzling behavior on the part of the enemy, he always lets out his leitmotiv phrase: "Ils sont fous, ces Romains!"

It is clear that a literal translation of the ad would only yield half of the message and destroy its spirit. The obstacle being a metalinguistic one, only adaptation can rescue some of the original intention. The translator would be well advised to keep to the T.L. cultural field and find a solution in, for instance, one of Charlie Brown's favorite sayings or a catch phrase by some other well-known U.S. cartoon character.

A second ad, vaunting a shuttle service, goes as follows:

> Orlyval: Paris-Orly en 30 minutes pour que votre avion ne soit pas un mirage.

The pun here revolves around a *double entendre* on the word *mirage*. The translator has to be aware, first, that Orly refers to one of the two Paris airports, and second, that a mirage, beyond the primary meaning of the word, refers to a specific French plane prototype well known to anyone with a French background. Even though people abroad may have heard of the plane, the message still is not as clear outside the S.L. when translated literally.

In fact French ads revel in playing on words, making them untranslatable as such. Indeed, how is one to translate the following ad from a restaurant offering each prospective client a pair of sunglasses during the summer months?

> Des lunettes à l'oeil: des lunettes de soleil avec notre menu.

"Sunglasses on the house", which is what is meant, loses both pun and image.

Finally, in *France-Amérique* (10/23-29/93), an ad for AT & T pitching savings on international calls features the picture of a human-looking well-clad and evidently well-nourished ant who is turning away from her doorstep and into the cold weather a famished looking grasshopper carrying a guitar, with the caption:

> Cet automne, chantez comme la cigale à des prix de fourmi.

The ad refers to a very popular fable by seventeenth century beloved fabulist Jean de la Fontaine. Since the complete education of any French school boy or girl entails the memorization of this particular fable, its moral message will instantly come to mind: in France the hard-working and provident ant has long been a symbol of rewarded labor and frugality while the insouciant, fun-loving and lazy grasshopper personifies the loser left to die when hard times finally arrive. But the ad cleverly gives a new twist to the story and its morality by implying that readers can have the best of both worlds: have fun while enjoying the savings offered by the company. A translation into English, however, is near impossible unless situation equivalence can be found in a book more familiar to an English speaker, a tale with overtones of moralization, perhaps Mother Goose or some other nursery rhyme.

Advice for the translation of ads

When translating ads, keep in mind the following:

- Writing or translating an ad is not unlike writing a title or headline. It is doing a bit of marketing, for you must grab a potential client's attention with catchy phrases, trendy expressions, striking formulas, and punch lines.

- Concision, short sentences, and going straight to the point are your best bets.

- Since making a point or pitching a product is what matters most, you can be free with the wording of your translation. Keep to the ideas, but use idiomatic language and clichés, and remember that syntactically French is analytical and English synthetical: whereas French will say "*Ceci ne prend pas beaucoup de temps*", English will say "*this is not time-consuming*".

- You will most likely have to resort to an equivalence or an adaptation in order to render the spirit of the original message, since cultural barriers will probably stand in the way of comprehension for the T.L. audience.

Ad One

Dans les yeux des enfants brillent les plus belles visions du monde de demain.
Alors nous avons conçu un téléviseur qui transforme votre salon en salle de cinéma.

Avec son format 16/9, ce téléviseur Thomson vous permet de voir les films dans leurs vraies dimensions. Et cela dans les meilleures conditions de confort pour les yeux. Comme au cinéma. Il vous assure une qualité visuelle et sonore tout à fait exceptionnelle. Le système acoustique Cabasse 2 x 50 watts apporte au son des films un relief saisissant.
Ce téléviseur est vraiment conçu pour être à la mesure de votre imagination.

Thomson: autant voir grand.

Notes

In this ad the stylistic emphasis is concentrated on the opening sentence and the closing punch-line. Therefore devote most of your attention to their translation for maximum impact on the reader. A modulation direct object-subject in the first sentence will allow you to keep the image. Amplification will also be necessary for the sentence connector *alors* which, in this context, serves to draw a conclusion and just cannot be translated literally as *then*.
The body of the ad merely gives information. Again a modulation object-subject on the verb *vous permet/ you can* as well as a transposition on *visuelle et sonore* will make the message more idiomatic. Some imagination will be required to render the word *relief*, a false friend for which there is no real English counterpart, and which means something like *contrast sharpness*. Find an equivalent for the idiomatic verbal locution *être à la mesure de*.

The eyes of children mirror the most beautiful visions of the future.

That's why we have designed a TV set that will turn your living room into a movie theater.

With the Thomson 16/9 TV screen you can see films true to size and in the best conditions of comfort for your eyes. Just like at the movies. You will enjoy an exceptional quality of sound and picture. And Thomson's Cabasse 2 x 50 watts acoustic system gives the sound track amazing reality.

A TV set truly designed to live up to your imagination.

Thomson. Why not see big?

Ad Two

Avec le four multi-fonctions Dimension 4 la grande cuisine devient enfin accessible à tous.

Un four qui, d'une seule touche, calcule lui-même la puissance, la température ainsi que la cuisson nécessaire, vous connaissez plus simple? Et c'est bon. Très bon même, car le four Dimension 4 est un vrai four, vraiment multi-fonctions: parois en émail, 36 litres, neuf modes de cuisson combinant micro-ondes, convection, chaleur tournante, gril ou gril pulsé pour réussir une cuisson traditionnelle.

Alors, qui a dit que la grande cuisine était difficile?

Panasonic, Quel bonheur!

Notes

A reversal in the order of the presentation of ideas will help with the translation of the first sentence. While French favors the approach: circumstantial details first and essential argument second, English likes to turn things around. Certain concepts such as *la grande cuisine* cannot be translated literally, a modulation is needed to render the same. Also remember to use some cliché expressions such as *cooking time, featuring* etc. A conversion to cubic feet will be necessary to make the capacity of the oven intelligible to your English speaking public, who, most likely, will have no idea how much is one liter . Use your creativity for the closing formula in the form of a pun, and keep in mind that you do not need to stick to the original.

Now gourmet cooking within everyone's reach with the multiple features of the Dimension 4 oven.

An oven which figures out the right power, temperature and cooking time, all at the touch of a button, what could be easier? And with absolutely delicious results, since Dimension 4 is a real oven, featuring enamel walls, a nine cubic foot capacity, nine cooking combinations with microwave, convection heat, turntable, broiler and pulsating broiler, for you to turn out a great traditional dinner anytime.

So, who still says that gourmet cooking is a hassle?

Thank goodness for Panasonic!

Ad Three

Paul-Loup Sulitzer, votre prochain manuscrit, vous l'enverrez en Distingo.

Vous avez certainement déjà constaté que certain courriers sont plus importants que d'autres: un manuscrit original, par exemple. Et dans ce cas, vous aimeriez que tout le monde le comprenne. La Poste comme votre destinataire. C'est pour répondre à ce besoin que nous avons créé un service nouveau: Distingo.
En Distingo, votre courrier se distingue:
-Par son traitement particulier: transporté de manière privilégiée dans son enveloppe indéchirable en "Tyvek", Distingo est remis chez votre destinataire. En cas d'absence, le courrier Distingo est déposé dans la boîte aux lettres tandis qu'un avis signalant le passage spécial du facteur est glissé sous la porte.
-Par sa simplicité: selon le volume de votre envoi, l'enveloppe Distingo existe en deux formats prétimbrés (A4 et demi A4). Vous n'avez même plus besoin de la peser avant de la glisser dans la boîte.

Distinguer le courrier important, c'est nouveau, c'est Distingo.
Pas de problème. La Poste est là.

Notes

This is an example of cultural reference in advertising. If translated literally, the opening sentence would be totally meaningless to an English speaking audience. Who, this side of the Atlantic, has ever heard of Paul-Loup Sulitzer? To a French public, on the other hand, the name conjures up the figure of a popular best-selling novelist. Clearly an equivalent has to be found to suit the English speaking culture: someone on top of the best seller list. In addition, some words present a semantic problem: *courrier* and *destinataire* for instance are difficult to translate in this context: English simply does not make use of *mailing* and *addressee* as much as French does.

Keep the parallel construction of the ad to emphasize the dual point of the message: distinctive treatment and simplicity of use. And try to find an attention getter for the closing lines.

J. K. Rowling, trust your next manuscript to Distingo!

It's obvious that some mail takes priority, an original manuscript for instance. And if that's the case, you would like everyone to know, the Postal Service as well as your recipient. In response to this need we have created a new service: Distingo.

With Distingo your mail stands out.

It receives special treatment. We deliver it in a special non-tearable "Tyvek" envelope. If no one is at home, the carrier will leave it in the mailbox and slip a notice under the door to indicate special delivery.

Distingo is simple to use. Envelopes come in two pre-stamped sizes (A4 and half size). They don't even have to be weighed before you drop them into the mailbox.

Give your priority mail distinction, give it to Distingo.

No problem. We deliver.

Appendix   The Translator's Tools

If, ideally, a professional translator should be bilingual, in practice things tend to be different, and the history of translation has many records of translators actually learning the source language they were translating from as they were doing a particular translation, from Baudelaire deciphering Edgar Allan Poe to Proust interpreting Ruskin.

Thus translators, even professional ones, must rely on an array of tools to help them in their undertaking, and, so must, all the more, apprentice-translators.

On top of the list are dictionaries, both mono- and bilingual; the first, to assist you in your comprehension of a difficult and unusual SL concept or to fine tune your mastery of a TL one; the second to bring you the TL counterpart. Next are thesauri, whose importance cannot be stressed enough, since they are "analogy" dictionaries that bring you concepts by semantic fields instead of separately, allowing you to search for just the right word, once you understand the original concept but are not completely satisfied with the TL counterparts found in the bilingual dictionary. They offer a wide range of choices not available in even the most detailed bilingual dictionaries.

Of great help also are dictionaries of synonyms, idioms and colloquialisms, false cognates, slang as well as dictionaries of quotations and books on cultural references.

For technical translation resort to specialized glossaries and dictionaries and to encyclopedias: medical, scientific, legal, financial and so forth. Translators of texts that are on the cutting edge of technology and science will have to turn to experts in the field and specialized reviews for help, or resort to borrowings or neologisms, since no dictionary can claim to be up to date in that respect.

Last but not least, you can conveniently in this computer age access free online data bases for translations in specialty fields. since these are regularly updated to include the translation of new terms, they are even more reliable than any dictionary in hard copy form and a god-sent for the translation of legal, medical, scientific, and technical documents.

Bilingual Dictionaries

Considered the most indispensable tool, they can also prove the most frustrating and disappointing. But there are only "bad" bilingual dictionaries insofar as they are misused. Paradoxically, people who are beginning to learn a language tend to use pocket size dictionaries which only give few entries for each word and most of the time not even in context, so that mistakes are easily made by misjudging the semantic range of words. Instead, since new learners are not yet aware of the problems involved in translation, they should be the ones using the most detailed bilingual dictionaries, which show the polysemy of words by illustrating their various nuances in context.

The following are some of the very good medium and large size bilingual dictionaries on the market (all are French to English and vice versa).

Citron, Sabine et al. *Dictionnaire Le Robert et Collins français/anglais-anglais/français..* HarperCollins, 2010.

Collins-Robert French College Dictionary. 7th ed. HarperCollins Publishers, 2008 (Over 350,000 entries and translations including thousands of contemporary technical, political and business terms for students and professionals).

Corréard Marie Hélène, Valérie Grundy, & Jean-Benoît Ormal-Grenon ed. *The Oxford Hachette French Dictionary.* Oxford,   New York,   Toronto: Oxford University Press, 2007. (fully   updated fourth   edition with better coverage of the language   than ever before,   and improved treatment of acronyms   and EU terminology, as well as thousands of new words in both English and French.

Duval, Alain, & Vivian Marr, general editors. *Le Robert & Collins Super Senior. Français anglais.* 1 vol. *Anglais-français.* 1 vol. Paris: Dictionnaires Le Robert, 2002. (400,000 references).

Harper Collins Robert French Unabridged Dictionary, 7th ed. Dictionnaires Le Robert, 2005. (Over 300,000 entries and 50,000 translations. Fully re-vised and updated "Language in use" section. Comprehensive treatment of current French and

English, including thousands of technical, political and business terms).

Harrap's Unabridged PRO French/English-English/French. Laurier Books Ltd, 2007.

Harrap's French and English College Dictionary. McGraw-Hill Education, 2000.

Larousse Unabridged English-French/French-English Dictionary. Larousse, 2010 (Over 850,000 words. Phrases and translations with abbreviations and acronyms – the most comprehensive title in the French bilingual line, an in-depth reference specially designed to help translators, students and teachers translate into or from either language clearly and easily).

Merriam-Webster French-English Dictionary/Dictionnaire Anglais-Français. 2000. This dictionary provides up-to-date coverage of French words and phrases as spoken in France and in other European countries, including the terminology of French-speaking Canada.

NTC's New College French and English Dictionary. Lincolnwood: National Textbook Company, 1997.

Urwin, Kenneth, ed. *Langenscheidt's Standard French-English/English-French Dictionary.* New York, Berlin and Munich: Langenscheidt, 1988. Over 80,000 references on 1278 pages. A broad range of entries with many new words and a wealth of idiomatic expressions.

On CD-ROM

Let's not forget bilingual dictionaries on CD-ROM for both Windows and Macintosh which make consulting an entry as expedient and easy as a click of the mouse:

Collins French CD-Rom Dictionary

Dictionnaire Larousse bilingue de la langue anglaise (contains a general bilingual French-English dictionary with 90,000 words and expressions, as well as a bilingual business dictionary of 40,000 words and a bilingual computer science dictionary of 30,000 words).

Grand dictionnaire Larousse anglais-français/français-anglais (boasts 350,000 words and expressions, acronyms and proper nouns, historical and cultural articles and the conjugation of the French verbs).

McGraw-Hill's French Student Dictionary for your iPod gives you access to 3,500 essential words   Over 500,000 translations

Oxford Hachette. French Dictionary. Over 350,000 words and phrases.

French Monolingual Dictionaries
Le Robert College 2013 : Monolingual French Dictionary for Secondary School (French Edition). Le Robert, 2013. 40,000 head words and 75,000 definitions

Analogical Dictionaries
Berube, Margery S., et al. *Roget's II: The New Thesaurus.* 3rd edition. Boston, New York: Houghton Mifflin Co., 1995.

Boussinot, Roger. *Dictionnaire Bordas des synonymes, analogies, antonymes.* Paris: Bordas, 1988.

Chapman, Robert L., ed. *Roget A to Z.* New York: Harper Perennial, 1994.

Dictionnaire des termes officiels de la langue française. Paris: Journal Officiel, 1996.

Gove, Philip B., ed. *Webster's New Dictionary of Synonyms.* Springfield: Merriam-Webster, 1984.

Mairé-Weir, Kay, ed., et al. *Webster's Collegiate Thesaurus.* Springfield: Merriam-Webster, 1988.

McCutcheon, Marc. *Roget's Super Thesaurus.* Cincinnati: Writer's Digest Books, 1995.

Niobet, G. *Dictionnaire analogique.* Paris: Larousse, 1992.

Péchouin, Daniel. *Thésaurus Larousse.* Paris: Larousse, 1991

Roget, Peter & Paul. *The New Roget Thesaurus in Dictionary Form.* Berkley Trade. 1990

Urdang, Laurence. *The Oxford Thesaurus.* American Edition. Oxford, New York, Toronto: Oxford University Press, 1992.

Ward-Pitha, Elizabeth, chief ed., et al. *Barlett's Roget's Thesaurus.* Boston, New York, Toronto, London: Little Brown and Company, 1996.

Dictionaries of False Cognates
Colignon, Jean Pierre, and Pierre-Valentin Berthier. *Lexique des faux amis.* Paris: Hatier/Profil, 1985.

Kirk-Greene, C.W.E. *NTC's Dictionary of Faux Amis.* Lincolnwood: National Textbook Company, 1996.

Thody, Philip, and Howard Evans. *Mistakable French: A Dictionary of Words and Phrases easily Confused.* New York: Charles Scribner's sons, 1985.

Thody, Philip. *Mistakable French : Faux anis and Key Words*. 2nd ed. Hippocrene Books, 1998

Van Roey, Jacques et al. *Dictionnaire des faux amis français-anglais*. 3ème édition. Gembloux: Duculot, 2001.

Borrowings, English to French

Colpron, Gilles. *Dictionnaire des anglicismes*. Chomedey Laval: Beauchemin, 1982.

Deak, Etienne. *Grand Dictionnaire d'américanismes américain-français*. Paris: Dauphin, 1981.

Etiemble, René. *Parlez-vous franglais?* Paris: Folio-Actuel, 1991.

Leprat, Henri. *Dictionnaire de franglais*. Paris: Livre de Poche, 1980.

Rey-Debove, J., and G. Gagnon. *Dictionnaire des anglicismes: les mots anglais et américains en français*. Paris: Dictionnaires Le Robert, 1990.

Dictionaries for French Idioms, Colloquialisms and Slang

Blum, G., and N. Salas. *Les idiomatiques français-anglais*. Paris: Seuil, 1989.

Brunet, François, and Dedan McCavana. *Dictionnaire bilingue de l'argot d'aujourd'hui: Bilingual Dictionary of Today's Slang*. Paris: Langues pour tous, 2000.

Burke, David. *Street French: How to Speak and Understand French Slang*. John Wiley, 1988.

_____. *More Street French Slang, Idioms and Popular Expletives*. New York: John Wiley, 1990.

Colin, Jean Paul, and Jean Pierre Mével, with the collaboration of Christian Leclère. *Dictionnaire de l'argot*. Paris: Larousse, 1996.

Deak, Etienne, and Simone Deak. *A Dictionary of Colorful French Slanguage and colloquialisms*. New York: E.P. Hutton, 1961.

Denoeu, François, David Sices, and Jacqueline B. Sices. *2001 French and English Idioms*. 2nd edition. New York: Barron, 1996.

Fréchette, Denis. *Dictionnaire d'expressions anglaises*. [50,000 English expressions and their French equivalents]. Canada : éditions Olographes, 2005.

_____. *Le traducteur instantané: Français-Anglais*. [20,000 literally untranslatable French expressions and their English equivalents]. Canada: éditions Olographes, 2005.

Hérail, René James, and Edwin A. Lovatt. *Dictionary of Modern Colloquial French.* London: Routledge, 1984.

Kettridge, J.O. *French Idioms and Figurative Phrases with Many Quotations.* New York: French and European Publications.

Levieux, Michel, and Eleanor Levieux. *Cassell's Colloquial French: a handbook of idiomatic Usage.* London: Macmillan, 1980.

Lupson, Peter, and Michel Pelissier. *Guide to French Idioms.* Lincolnwood: Passport Books, 1987.

Marks, Georgette, and Charles Johnson, revised by Helen Knox. *Harrap's Slang: Dictionnaire d'argot anglais-français/français-anglais.* Edinburgh: Harrap, 1994.

Strutz, Henry. *Dictionary of French Slang and Colloquial Expressions.* Barron's Educational Series, 2009

Books on French Cultural References

Bologne, Jean Claude. *Les allusions littéraires: Dictionnaire commenté des expressions d'origine littéraire.* Paris: Larousse, 1989.

Dournon, Jean-Yves. *Le dictionnaire des proverbes et dictons de France.* Paris: Livre de Poche, 1986.

_____. *Le grand dictionnaire des citations françaises.* Paris: Belfond, 1992.

Goursau, Henri. *Dictionnaire anglais-français des phrases et expressions usuelles.* Editions Goursau, 2010.

Guterman, Norbert. *The Anchor Book of French Quotations with English Translations.* New York: Doubleday, 1990.

Maloux, Maurice. *Dictionnaire des proverbes, sentences et maximes.* Paris: Larousse, 1992.

Montreynaud, Pierron and Suzzoni. *Dictionnaire de proverbes et dictons.* Paris: Dictionnaires Le Robert, 1993.

Oster, Pierre. *Dictionnaire des citations françaises.* 2 vols. Paris: Dictionnaires Le Robert, 1993.

Rey, Alain, ed. *Le Petit Robert dictionnaire universel des noms propres.* New ed. under Thieri Foulc. Paris: Dictionnaires Le Robert, 1996.

Rhyming Dictionaries and Books on English and French Prosody

Abercrombie, Ascelles. *Principles of English Prosody.* New York: AMS Press, 1976.

Allen, Gay Wilson. *American Prosody*. New York: Octagon Books, 1966.

Espy, Willard R. *Words to Rhyme with*. New York: Facts on File Publication, 1986 (includes a primer of English prosody).

Fergusson, Rosalind. *The Penguin Rhyming Dictionary*. New York: Viking, 1985.

Grammont, Maurice. *Petit traité de versification française*. Paris: Armand Colin, 1966.

Johnson, Burges. *New Rhyming Dictionary and Poet's Handbook*. New York: Harper, 1957.

Packard, William. *The Poet's Dictionary: a Handbook of Prosody and Poetic Devices*. New York: Harper & Row, 1989.

Shapiro, Karl, and Robert Beum. *A Prosody Handbook*. New York: Harper & Row, 1965.

Wood, Clement. *Wood's Unabridged Rhyming Dictionary*. New York: The World Publishing Company, 1943.

Young, Sue. *The New Comprehensive American Rhyming Dictionary*. New York: William Morrow & Co., 1991.

Specialized Bilingual Dictionaries
Business, Finance and Marketing

Baleyte, Jean, et al. *Dictionnaire économique et juridique*. Paris: Navarre, 1992.

Harrap's Business French. Englewood Cliffs: Prentice Hall, 1991.

Bernard, and Colli. *Vocabulaire économique et financier*. Paris: Seuil, 1989.

Collin, P-H., et al. *Dictionary of Business*. Teddington: Peter Collin, 1990.

Duvillier, Fabienne. *Dictionnaire bilingue de la publicité et de la communication*. Paris: Dunod, 1990.

Echaudemaison, C.D. *Dictionnaire d'économie et de sciences sociales*. Paris: Nathan.

Gillmann, Bernard, and Martin Verrel. *Mastering French Business Vocabulary*. Barron's, 1996. (A thematic approach)

Harrap's French-English Business Dictionary. McGraw-Hill, 2005

Kettridge, J.O. *French-English and English-French Dictionary of Commercial and financial Terms, Phrases, and Practice*. London: Routledge, 1992.

La Rocque, G. de, and Y. Bernard. *Dictionnaire de l'anglais des affai- res.* Paris: Livre de Poche, 1988.

Lenoir, Robert. *Dictionnaire commercial et économique bilingue fran- çais-anglais et anglais-français.* Paris: Editions Economica, 1989.

Marcheteau, Michel et al. *Dictionnaire de l'anglais économique, commercial et financier: Dictionary of Economics, Business & Finance.* Paris: Langues pour tous, 1995.

Marcheteau, Michel, et al. *NTC's French & English Business Dictionary.* Lincolnwood: National Textbook Company, 1996.

Ménard, Louis et coll. *Dictionnaire de la comptabilité et de la gestion financière: anglais-français avec index français-anglais.* Toronto: L'Institut Canadien des Comptables Agréés, 1994.

Péron, Michel, et al. *Le Robert & Collins du management: commercial, financier, économique et juridique.* Paris: Dictionnaires Le Robert, 1995.

Ritchie, Adrian C. *Newspaper French: A Vocabulary of Administrative and Commercial idiom with English Translation.* Cardiff: University of Wales Press, 1990.

Routledge. *French Dictionary of Business, Commerce and Finance.* Routledge, 1996. (for French-English/English-French terminology on banking, accounting, computing, correspondence, patents, insurance, media, marketing, import-export, the stock market and taxation, contains 50,000 words and 4,000 abbreviations)

Saxcé, Frank de. *Dictionnaire comptable, fiscal et financier: Accounting, Tax, and Financial Dictionary.* Cabinet Saxcé, 1986.

Stevenson, Anna, ed. *Harrap's Marketing: Dictionnaire anglais-français/français-anglais.* Edinburgh: Chambers Harrap Publishers, 1999.

Computer Science Dictionaries

Collin, S.M.H., et al. *Dictionary of Computing and Information Technology.* Teddington: Peter Collin, 1991.

Dictionnaire de l'informatique. Paris: Afnor, 1989.

Fisher, Renée. *Dictionnaire informatique français-anglais.* Paris: Eyrolles, 1986.

Ginguay, Michel. *Dictionnaire d'informatique français-anglais*. Paris; Masson, 1993.

Harrap's Data Processing French Dictionary. Englewood Cliffs: Prentice Hall, 1986.

Hildebert, Jacques. *Dictionnaire des technologies de l'informatique: Dictionary of Information Technology*. Paris-New York: La Maison du Dictionnaire/Hippocrene Books, 1998, 2 vol.

Larousse. *Dictionnaire de l'informatique*. Paris: Larousse, 1996.

Pyper, T.R. *French Dictionary of Information Technology*. London: Routledge, 1989.

Virgatchik, I. *Dictionnaire bilingue d'informatique*. Paris: Marabout, 1990.

Wiard, A., and I. Virga. *Dictionnaire bilingue d'informatique*. Paris: Hachette, 1995.

Legal Dictionaries

Baleyte, Jean, et al. *Dictionnaire économique et juridique*. Paris: Navarre, 1992.

Bridge, F.H.S.. *The Council of Europe French-English Legal Dictionary*. Council of Europe Press, 1994.

Dahl, Henry S. *Dahl's Law Dictionary/Dictionnaire juridique Dahl French to English/English to French*. 3rd edition. Fred B. Rothman $ Co., 2007

Hachette. *Dictionnaire de l'anglais économique et juridique*. Paris: Hachette, 1996.

Harrap's Dictionnaire juridique/Law Dictionary.Educa Books/Dalloz, 2004

Herbst, Robert, and Alan G. Readett. *Dictionary of Commercial, Financial and Legal terms*. English, German, French. Bergh Publishing, 1990.

Kahn-Paycha, Danièle. *Lexique d'anglais juridique*. Paris: Ellipses, 1993.

Le Docte, E. *Legal Dictionary in four Languages: English, French, German, Dutch*. Maklu, 1988.

Medical Dictionaries

Dorland Dictionnaire médical bilingue français/anglai et anglais/français. Elsevier, 2008

Garnier, Marcel and Jacques Delamare, eds. *Dictionnaire des termes de médecine, français-anglais, anglais-français.* 27eme édition revue et augmentée. Paris: Maloine, 2000.

Gladstone, William J. *English-French Dictionary of Medical and Paramedical Sciences.* 4th ed. Edisem, 1996.

Gordon, Alfred. *French-English Medical Dictionary.* Forgotten Books, 2012

Lepine, P. *Dictionnaire des termes médicaux et biologiques.* Paris: Flammarion, 1974.

Lexique médical anglais-français/français-anglais. 2nd ed. Paris: Masson, 1991.

Zemback, A.H. *English-French Medical Dictionary & Phrasebook. French-English.* CreateSpace Independent Publishing Platform, 2010

Sciences and Engineering Dictionaries

Bucksch, Herbert. *Dictionnaire pour les travaux publics, le bâtiment et l'équipement des chantiers de construction.* Paris: Eyrolles, 1982.

Chapin, Marie Madeleine. *Dictionnaire technique du français et de l'anglais.* Paris: Marabout.

Collin, P.H., and M. Schuwer. *Dictionary of Ecology and Environment.* Teddington: Peter Collin, 1992.

Ernst, Richard. *Dictionnaire général de la technique industrielle français-anglais.* Brandsletter, 1982.

Forbes, J.R. *Dictionnaire des techniques et technologies modernes.* Paris: Lavoisier, 1993.

Goursau, Henri. *Dictionnaire technique et scientifique/ Dictionary of technical and scientific terms anglais/français-/English/French.* Editions Goursau 1995.

_____ *Dictionnaire de l'aéronautique et de l'espace/ Dictionary of Aeronautics and Space Technology anglais/français -English/French.* Editions Goursau, 1982.

Lydersen, Aksel L. *Dictionary of Chemical Engineering: English, French, German, Spanish.* Chichester, New York: John Wiley, 1992.

Malgorn, Guy. *Dictionnaire technique français-anglais.* Montrouge: Gauthier-Villars, 1975.

Michel, J.P., and R.W. Fairbridge. *Dictionary of Earth Sciences.* Chichester, New York: John Wiley, 1992.

Piraux, H. *Dictionnaire des termes relatifs à l'électronique, l'électrotechnique et l'informatique français-anglais.* Paris: Eyrolles, 1984.

Online Bilingual Dictionaries, Encyclopedias and Resources

The following are free online databases of French-English words:

A very useful and easy to use multilingual dictionary giving words in context which also provides a discussion forum for specific translation problems:

> http://www.wordreference.com

From Quebec, Le Grand Dictionnaire Terminologique (–GDT– for commercial, legal, medical, technical and scientific terminology):

> http://gdt.oqlf.gouv.qc.ca/

Eurodicautom (Translation database of the European Union)

> http://iate.europa.eu/iatediff/SearchByQueryLoad.do;jsessionid=
> 9ea7991c30d586a579b30ba941d8be72cd6c82e43837.e3iLbNeK
> c3mSe3aNbxuQa3qLb40?method=load

French encyclopedias: the first is a database of 50,000 articles, with a dictionary of 65,000 definitions, photos, maps and videos. Regularly updated. The second, the most popular French encyclopedia:

> http://encyclo.voila.fr/
> http://www.larousse.fr/encyclopedie/

Online French grammar:

> http://grammaire.reverso.net/

French monolingual dictionary:

> http://www.larousse.com/en/dictionaries/french

French-English/ English-French bilingual dictionary:

> http://www.larousse.com/en/dictionaries/english-french
> http://www.larousse.fr/dictionnaires/francais-anglais
> http://www.merriam-webster.com/dictionary/french

French-English business dictionary:

> http://dictionnaire.reverso.net/business-anglais-francais/

French-English computer science dictionary:

> http://dictionnaire.reverso.net/informatique-anglais-francais/

French-English dictionary for idiomatic expressions:

> http://dictionnaire.reverso.net/francais-
> anglais/expression%20idiomatique

French-English legal dictionary:
>   http://dictionnaire.reverso.net/francais-anglais/juridique
>   http://www.freelang.com/dictionnaire/anglais_juridique.php

French-English medical dictionary:
>   http://dictionnaire.reverso.net/medical-francais-anglais/

French-English dictionary for the sciences:
>   http://dictionnaire.reverso.net/francais-anglais/scientifique

French-English dictionary for slang:
>   http://dictionnaire.reverso.net/anglais-francais/argot

Dictionary of French proverbs into English:
>   http://www.anglaisfacile.com/free/proverbes.php

On French- English false cognates:
>   http://french.about.com/od/vocabulary/a/fauxamis-a.htm
>   http://www.oxfordlanguagedictionaries.com/Public/PublicResou
>   rces.html?direction=b-fr-
>   en&sp=S/oldo/resources/fr/Difficulties-in-French-fr.html

On borrowings from English to French:
>   http://fr.wiktionary.org/wiki/Annexe:Mots_fran%C3%A7ais_d
>   %E2%80%99origine_anglaise

French dictionaries of synonyms and antonyms:
>   http://www.synonymes.com/
>   http://www.cnrtl.fr/synonymie/
>   http://dictionnaire.reverso.net/francais-synonymes/
>   http://www.crisco.unicaen.fr/des/synonymes/

Merriam-Webster English dictionary and thesaurus:
>   http://www.merriam-webster.com/dictionary/thesaurus

Roget's English Thesaurus:
>   www.Thesaurus.com

English rhyming dictionary:
>   http://wikirhymer.com/

Online Machine Translators

These sites use the same translating software and yield the same results. A word of caution: even though computer translations have made great progress in the past 10 years, do not expect a flawless and trustworthy translation, especially when dealing with literary and advertising translations which require understanding of a cultural background. You will get an approximation with, in the worst of cases, grammatical mistakes, mistranslations and even nonsensical sentences that will have to be reworked word by word by a human translator.

http://ww.babelfish.com
http://translate.google.com/
http://translateye.com/download/

The following are suggested readings on the methodology of French to English translation

Baker, Mona. *In Other Words: A Coursebook on Translation.* London: Routledge, 1992.

Ballard, Michel, *La Traduction de l'anglais au français*, 2nd ed. Armand Collin, 2005

    Le Nom propre en traduction anglais-français. Ophrys, 2002

Benjamin, Walter. "The Task of the Translator" in *Illuminations.* Harry Zohn, trans. London: Fontana, 1992: 70-82.

Bensimon, Paul, chief ed. *Palimpsestes.* Number 1: *Traduire le dialogue, traduire les textes de théâtre.* Paris: Presses de la Sorbonne Nouvelle, 1987.

_____. *Palimpsestes.* Number 2: *Traduire la poésie.* Paris: Presses de la Sorbonne Nouvelle, 1990.

_____. *Palimpsestes.* Number 3: *Traduction/ Adaptation.* Paris: Presses de la Sorbonne Nouvelle, 1990.

_____. *Palimpsestes.* Number 8: *Le traducteur et ses instruments.* Paris: Presses de la Sorbonne Nouvelle, 1993.

_____. *Palimpsestes.* Number 10: *Niveaux de Langue et registres de la traduction.* Paris: Presses de la Sorbonne Nouvelle, 1995.

Chuquet, Hélène, and Michel Paillard. *Approche linguistique des problèmes de traduction anglais-français.* Gap: Ophrys, 2002

Chuquet, Hélène. *Pratique : Traduction anglais-français.* Ophrys. 2002

Delisle, Jean. *L'Analyse du discours comme méthode de traduction.* Ottawa: Ottawa University Press, 1980.

Gabilan, Jean-Pierre . *L'Imparfait français et ses traductions en anglais: Approche méta-opérationnelle.* P.U de Savoie, 2011

Gallix, F., and M. Walsh. *Pratique de la traduction: la presse économique, versions et thèmes anglais.* Paris: Hachette, 1993.

Gile, Daniel. *Basic Concepts and Models for Interpreter and Translator Training.* Philadelphia: John Benjamins, 1995

Gouadec, Daniel. *Le traducteur, la traduction et l'entreprise.* Paris: Afnor, 1990.

Guillemin-Flescher, J. *Syntaxe comparée du français et de l'anglais: problèmes de traduction.* Gap: Ophrys, 1981.

Hervey, Sendor and Ian Higgins. *Thinking French Ttranslation,: A*

Course in Translation Method, French to English. 2nd ed.. London: Routledge, 2002.

Hiernard, Jean-Marc. *Les Règles d'or de la traduction anglais/français-français/anglais.* Ellipses, 2009

Kussmaul, Paul. *Training the Translator.* Philadelphia: John Benjamins, 1995.

Lefevere, André. *Translating Literature: Practice and Theory in a Comparative Literature Context.* New York: The Modern Language Association of America, 1992.

Merteens, René. *La Pratique de la traduction d';anglais en français.* Chiron, 2011

_____ *Guide anglai-français de la traduction.* Chiron, 2012

Merle, Jean-Marie. *Etude du conditionnel français et ses traductions en anglais.* Ophrys, 2002

Mounin, Georges. *Les problèmes théoriques de la traduction.* new ed. Paris: Gallimard, 1976.

_____. *Linguistique et traduction.* Bruxelles; Dessart and Mardaga, 1978.

Thompson, Jean-Max. *From and Into English.* Paris: Dunod, 1993.

Vinay, J.P., and J. Darbelnet. *Stylistique comparée du français et de l'anglais.* new edition. Paris: Didier, 1977.

_____. *Stylistique comparée du français et de l'anglais: cahier d'exercices/workbook.* Chomedey Laval: Beauchemin, 1990.

Watson Rodger, Valentine. *Apprendre à traduire.* 3rd ed. Toronto: Canadian Scholar's Press, 2004. (English and French edition. For French-English/English-French translation)

Traduire le thème, la version. Toronto: Canadian Scholar's Press, 2005 (English and French edition)

Index

CPSIA information can be obtained
at www.ICGtesting.com
Printed in the USA
LVHW012055280822
727031LV00005B/269

9 780761 863168

Business

A Changing World

Business

Fifth Edition

A Changing World

O. C. Ferrell
Colorado State University

Geoffrey Hirt
DePaul University

Linda Ferrell
University of Wyoming

McGraw-Hill
Irwin

Boston   Burr Ridge, IL   Dubuque, IA   Madison, WI   New York
San Francisco   St. Louis   Bangkok   Bogotá   Caracas   Kuala Lumpur
Lisbon   London   Madrid   Mexico City   Milan   Montreal   New Delhi
Santiago   Seoul   Singapore   Sydney   Taipei   Toronto

The McGraw-Hill Companies

McGraw-Hill Irwin

BUSINESS: A CHANGING WORLD
Published by McGraw-Hill/Irwin, a business unit of The McGraw-Hill Companies, Inc., 1221 Avenue of the Americas, New York, NY, 10020.

Some ancillaries, including electronic and print components, may not be available to customers outside the United States.
This book is printed on acid-free paper.

1 2 3 4 5 6 7 8 9 0 DOW/DOW 0 9 8 7 6 5 4

ISBN   0-07-297358-7

Editorial director: *John E. Biernat*
Sponsoring editor: *Ryan Blankenship*
Senior developmental editor: *Christine Scheid*
Executive marketing manager: *Ellen Cleary*
Media producer: *Benjamin Curless*
Lead project manager: *Mary Conzachi*
Senior production supervisor: *Sesha Bolisetty*
Lead designer: *Pam Verros*
Photo research coordinator: *Ira C. Roberts*
Photo researcher: *Mike Hruby*
Media project manager: *Joyce J. Chappetto*
Supplement producer: *Gina F. DiMartino*
Developer, Media technology: *Brian Nacik*
Cover/interior design: *Maureen McCutcheon*
Typeface: *10.5/12 Minion*
Compositor: *Carlisle Communications, Ltd.*
Printer: *R. R. Donnelley*

Library of Congress Cataloging-in-Publication Data

Ferrell, O.C.
    Business : a changing world / O.C. Ferrell, Geoffrey Hirt, Linda Ferrell.—5th ed.
      p. cm.
    Includes index.
    ISBN 0-07-297358-7 (alk. paper)
    1. Business. 2. Management—United States. I. Hirt, Geoffrey A. II. Ferrell, Linda. III.
Title.
HF 1008.F47 2006
650--dc22

                                     2004042321

www.mhhe.com

To Kathlene Ferrell

To Linda Hirt

To Norlan and Phyllis Nafziger

Welcome to

Where other authors entered the essentials market with "ground down" versions of their hardback editions, we entered it with a book developed from the "ground up" to effectively and efficiently teach Introduction to Business. We focused on the needs of the essentials market from the very beginning. There is so much information available to students today: the Internet, magazines, newspapers, television, radio, encyclopedic textbooks, trade books—the list is endless. You can overwhelm a student with too much information too soon in providing an understanding of the world of business. Our goal is too selectively provide the right balance of content and application to engage students and heighten their interest in studying about business concepts.

Our book has been successful because we provide a real-world, comprehensive framework in a compact format. Examples, boxed features, and video cases are up to date and make business come alive for students. Our Web site and supplementary classroom teaching materials provide support to enhance the learning experience. When we started revising the fifth edition, 24 Introduction to Business instructors were asked to provide reviews of each chapter. This analysis yielded strong praise for the previous edition, but also provided directions for continued improvement. The consensus indicated the need for greater balance in coverage of topics, avoiding the overemphasis of trendy business fads. We gained insight into the types of companies and nonprofit organizations to focus on in the boxes, examples, and cases that are most useful in the classroom.

We would like to welcome Linda Ferrell, University of Wyoming, to the author team. Linda brings a rich background of business experience as well as a successful academic career to the team. As an advertising account executive on the Pizza Hut and McDonald's accounts, her experience in working with franchisees, agencies, and corporations has filtered into the book. Her small business experience working with small retailers has broadened our perspective and appreciation of this area. She also pioneered and co-developed the role-playing exercises at the end of each part. With her Ph.D. in management from the University of Memphis, she complements the author team in content specialization.

"ground up"

the Fifth Edition

There have been many dramatic changes in business since the fourth edition was published. We have learned that **the Internet and e-business** continue to evolve, but have not completely reshaped the world of business. We explore Google's success in e-commerce and its "dutch auction" method of selling its stock. The interface between business and government has become even more significant as government policies have affected interest rates, regulations, and entire industries (such as accounting). The ramifications of the **Sarbanes-Oxley Act and corporate governance** are integrated at the appropriate level for this course. At the moment, the dramatic **growth of developing countries** such as China is having a tremendous impact on the prices of commodities and on global competition. **Outsourcing** has become a popular way for businesses to stay competitive, but is controversial among workers and communities negatively affected by such decisions. Companies such as IBM are examined to understand the business rationale on outsourcing as well as the role of countries such as India in the outsourcing debate. These as well as many other evolving issues are carefully addressed in the fifth edition.

One thing we've learned over the last few years is that business has to be open and fair to all stakeholders, including investors, employees, customers, and members of society. We explore the **Enron, WorldCom, and Parmalat business failures** that affected many of us. On the other hand, we look at the **highly responsible acts of companies such as Hershey Foods, Starbucks, and Home Depot.** Introduction to Business students need to understand that most businesses are responsible and have value systems that encourage and even require ethical and responsible conduct. On the other hand, the conduct of some business leaders and their organizations has damaged the reputation of the world of business. Students need to discuss and understand these events to be able to defend business and develop as ethical business leaders. The fifth edition integrates these concerns into every chapter in content, examples, and boxes. We have written a supplement for instructors on teaching business ethics in Introduction to Business.

Our hope is that all of our readers, students and instructors alike, find *Business: A Changing World* to be what we have striven to make it: the best value available for helping to teach — and learn — **Introduction to Business.**

–O.C., Geoff, Linda

Created from the ground up,

The best selling paperback text on the market, *Business: A Changing World* was built from the ground up—that is, developed and written expressly for faculty and students who value a brief, flexible, and affordable paperback with the most up-to-date coverage available.

Conversely, most brief Intro to Business textbooks on the market today are simply "ground-down" versions of much longer hardcover books. None of these books is truly designed to meet the needs of students or instructors; they're afterthoughts, products chiefly designed to leverage existing content, not to help you teach your course.

With market-leading teaching support and fresh content and examples, *Business: A Changing World* offers just the mix of currency, flexibility, and value that you need. It is the fastest-growing book—and the best value available—in the brief Introductory Business market.

What sets Ferrell/Hirt/Ferrell apart from the competition? An unrivaled mixture of current content, topical depth, and the best teaching support around.

The Freshest Topics and Examples

Because it isn't tied to the revision cycle of a larger book, *Business: A Changing World* inherits no outdated or irrelevant examples or coverage. Everything in the fifth edition reflects the very latest developments in the business world, from Google's "dutch auction" approach to selling its stock, to the controversy over outsourcing. In addition, ethics continues to be a key issue and Ferrell uses "Consider Ethics and Social Responsibility" boxes to instill in students the importance of ethical conduct in business.

Just Enough of a Good Thing

It's easy for students taking their first steps into business to become overwhelmed. Longer books try to solve this problem by chopping out examples or topics to make ad hoc shorter editions. *Business: A Changing World* carefully builds just the right mix of coverage and applications to give your students a firm grounding in business principles. Where other books have you sprinting through the semester to get everything in, Ferrell allows you the breathing space to explore topics and incorporate other activities that are important to you and your students.

Teaching Assistance that Makes a Difference

The first and often most serious hurdle in teaching is engaging your students' interest, making them understand how textbook material plays a very real role in real business activities. The instructor's material for *Business: A Changing World* is full of helpful resources that enable you to do this, including detailed teaching notes and additional material in the Instructor's Manual, even for each text part's role-playing exercises. Furthermore, the new **Active Classroom Resource Manual** is loaded with additional team projects, cases, and exercises.

There's much more to *Business: A Changing World,* and much more it can do for your course. To learn about Ferrell's great pedagogical features and top-notch ancillaries, keep reading.

not ground down

Getting a Handle on Business

Business: A Changing World's pedagogy helps your students get the most out of their reading, from handy outlines at the beginning of the chapter to a range of questions and exercises at the end of it.

Chapter Outlines

These provide a useful overview of all the topics covered in the chapter, giving students a sneak preview of what they'll be learning. Special expanded outlines are available on the book's Online Learning Center (see page xvii).

CHAPTER OUTLINE

Introduction

Organizational Culture

Developing Organizational Structure

Assigning Tasks
Specialization
Departmentalization

Assigning Responsibility
Delegation of Authority
Degree of Centralization
Span of Managment
Organizational Layers

Forms of Organizational Structure
Line Structure
Line-and-Staff Structure
Multidivisional Structure
atrix Structure

Organization, Teamwork, and Communication

OBJECTIVES

After reading this chapter, you will be able to:

- Define organizational structure and relate how organizational structures develop.
- Describe how specialization and departmentalization help an organization achieve its goals.
- Distinguish between groups and teams and identify the types of groups that exist in organizations.
- Determine how organizations assign resp~~~~~~~~~~~~~
  ~~~~~~hority.

OBJECTIVES

After reading this chapter, you will be able to:

- Define organizational structure and relate how organizational structures develop.
- Describe how specialization and departmentalization help an organization achieve its goals.
- Distinguish between groups and teams and identify the types of groups that exist in organizations.
- Determine how organizations assign responsibility for tasks and delegate authority.
- Compare and contrast some common forms of organizational structure.
- Describe how communication occurs in organizations.
- Analyze a business's use of teams.

Chapter Objectives

These appear at the beginning of each chapter to provide goals for students to reach in their reading. The objectives are then used in the "Review Your Understanding," the summary at the end of each chapter, and help the students gauge whether they've properly learned and retained the material.

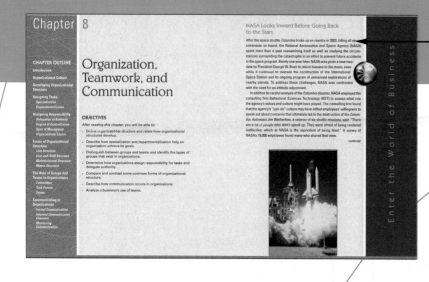

Chapter-Opening Vignette

These anecdotes neatly illustrate the real-world implications of the business issues students will encounter in their reading. A "Revisit the World of Business" segment at the end of the chapter requires students to return to the Opening Vignette to answer follow-up questions, calling on the insight they've gained from reading the chapter.

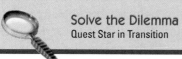

Solve the Dilemma

These boxes give students an opportunity to think creatively in solving a realistic business situation.

Solve the Dilemma
Quest Star in Transition

Quest Star (QS), which manufactures quality stereo loudspeakers, wants to improve its ability to compete against Japanese firms. Accordingly, the company has launched a comprehensive quality-improvement program for its Iowa plant. The QS Intracommunication Leadership Initiative (ILI) has flattened the layers of management. The program uses teams and peer pressure to accomplish the plant's goals instead of multiple management layers with their limited opportunities for communication. Under the initiative, employees make all decisions within the boundaries of their responsibilities, and they elect team representatives to coordinate with other teams. Teams are also assigned tasks ranging from establishing policies to evaluating on-the-job safety.

However, employees who are not self-motivated team players are having difficulty getting used to their peers' authority within this system. Upper-level managers face stress and frustration because they must train workers to supervise themselves.

1. What techniques or skills should an employee have to assume a leadership role within a work group?
2. If each work group has a team representative, what problems will be faced in supervising these representatives?
3. Evaluate the pros and cons of the system developed by QS.

Explore Your Career Options

These end-of-chapter features offer valuable advice on a wide spectrum of business career choices.

Explore Your Career Options
Flexibility First!

Most business school students major in marketing, finance, accounting, management information systems, general management, or sales. Upon graduation, they generally expect to be hired by a company to do more of whatever it is they were trained to do as a student. For example, an accounting major expects to be an accountant. However, depending upon the way the company is organized, the roles played by the employees will differ.

If you are hired by a large, divisionalized company, you might expect to practice your profession among many others doing the same or similar tasks. You are likely to learn one part of the business fairly well but be completely uninformed about other departments or divisions. A wise e_____ in this situation ____ ll learn to request occ_____ional ____ div_____ ___rn all as ____ ___r-

may find that you ar_
for which you were _
employees are often _
to make the organiz_
can come as a shoc_
cover that, in additio_
doing bookkeeping, _

Likewise, employ_
heavy use of teams _
may find that the cor_
skills learned in sch_
you may find that yo_
and expertise, but yo_
eng_____ring, comput_

Getting a Handle on Business

These features, scattered liberally throughout the book, use real and often familiar companies to highlight various issues of importance in business today.

Consider Ethics & Social Responsibility

Consider Ethics & Social Responsibility

Ethics in business continues to be a major public concern, and it is vital for students to understand that unethical conduct hurts investors, customers, and indeed the entire business world. These features highlight the importance of ethical conduct and show how businesses can serve a vital, positive function in their communities.

Think Globally

Think Globally

The global economy is important to more than large multinationals these days: issues of economics, culture, language and more can affect all levels of domestic business, and Think Globally boxes encourage students to keep their eyes on the big picture.

Embrace Technology

Business technology means more than computers. From cell phones and PDAs to sophisticated project management and inventory tracking systems, Embrace Technology boxes teach students just how pervasive technology is throughout the business world.

Embrace Technology

Growing a Business

New to the fifth edition, this feature highlights entrepreneurial opportunities, showing the issues and obstacles in building a venture from the ground up.

Responding to Business Challenges

These boxes illustrate how businesses overcome tough challenges and provide an excellent vehicle for stimulating class discussions.

Enchance Business Productivity

Valuable tips and insights on one issue that's vital to everyone at all levels of business.

End-of-Chapter Material

Whether your students discover it on their own or you make it an integral part of your classroom and homework assignments, the end-of-chapter material provides a great opportunity to reinforce and expand upon the chapter content.

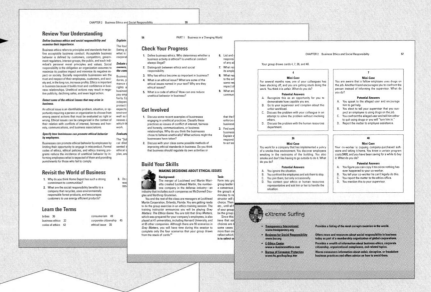

Review Your Understanding

Define marketing and describe the exchange process.

Marketing is a group of activities designed to expedite transactions by creating, distributing, pricing, and promoting goods, services, and ideas. Marketing facilitates the exchange, the act of giving up one thing in return for something else. The central focus of marketing is to satisfy needs.

Specify the functions of marketing.

Marketing includes many varied and interrelated activities: buying, selling, transporting, storing, grading, financing, marketing research, and risk taking.

Explain the marketing concept and its implications for developing marketing strategies.

The marketing concept is the idea that an organization should try to satisfy customers' needs through coordinated activities that also allow it to achieve its goals. If a company does not implement the marketing concept by providing products that consumers need and want while achieving its own objectives, it will not survive.

whose needs and wants a company focuses its marketing efforts). Some firms use a total-market approach, designating everyone as the target market. Most firms divide the total market into segments of people who have relatively similar product needs. A company using a concentration approach develops one marketing strategy for a single market segment, whereas a multisegment approach aims marketing efforts at two or more segments, developing a different marketing strategy for each.

Investigate how marketers conduct marketing research and study buying behavior.

Carrying out the marketing concept is impossible unless marketers know what, where, when, and how consumers buy; marketing research into the factors that influence buying behavior helps marketers develop effective marketing strategies. Marketing research is a systematic, objective process of getting information about potential customers to guide marketing decisions. Buying behavior is the decision processes and actions of people who purchase and use products.

Summarize the environmental forces that influence decisions.

Review Your Understanding

Are your students sometimes unsure whether they've properly absorbed the chapter material? This feature resummarizes the chapter objectives, leaving students in no doubt of what they're expected to remember.

Revisit the World of Business

These exercises refer to the chapter opening vignettes (see page xi) and ask students to answer more in-depth questions using the knowledge they gained in their reading.

tional line relationship between superiors and subordinates, and specialized staff managers are available to assist line managers. A multidivisional structure gathers departments into larger groups called divisions. A matrix,

attempting to restructure to a team env
the material presented in this chapter,
to evaluate the firm's efforts and make
for resolving the problems that have de

Revisit the World of Business

1. Which organizational factor contributed most to the *Columbia* disaster at NASA?

2. In what way did the organizational culture contribute to the disaster?

3. How can NASA harness its "can-d succeed to create safer missions and beyond?

Learn the Terms

accountability 236
centralized organization 237
committee 243
custom— departmentalization
d—

group 242
line-and-staff structure 239
line structure 239
matrix structure 241
multidivisional 240

project teams 24
quality-assurance
circles) 245
responsibility 236
—ted work

Build Your Skills

MANAGING MONEY

Background:
You have just graduated from college and have received an offer for your dream job (annual salary: $35,000). This premium salary is a reward for your hard work, perseverance, and good grades. It is also a reward for the social skills you developed in college doing service work as a tutor for high school students and interacting with the business community as the program chairman of the college business fraternity, Delta Sigma Pi. You are engaged and plan to be married this summer. You and your spouse will have a joint income of $60,000, and the two of you are trying to decide the best way to manage your money.

Task:
Research available financial service
area, and answer the following quest

1. What kinds of institutions and se
   to help manage your money?
2. Do you want a full service finance
   can take care of your banking, in
   investing needs or do you want
   business among individual spec
   you made this choice?
3.

(at top:) NOW accoun... egular checking accounts. In which type of account and in what institution would you deposit your money? Why?

Build Your Skills

These activities are designed to be carried out in teams, giving you a launching pad for a lively in-class discussion.

e-Xtreme Surfing

This feature points out Web sites that elaborate on the chapter content. All eXtreme Surfing sites can be linked at your discretion from the book's Online Learning Center (see pages xvi–xvii).

e-Xtreme Surfing

- **Leading Concepts**
  www.leadingconcepts.com/

  Provides information about t
  companies improve commun

- **Model Electronic Privacy Act**
  http://archive.aclu.org/issues/
  worker/legkit2.html

  Offers information from the A
  legislation regulating electr

- **NASA's organizational chart**
  www.hq.nasa.gov/hq/orgchart.htm

  Presents the organizational

See for Yourself Videocase

FISHING FOR SUCCESS: THE PIKE PLACE FISH MARKET

It has been almost 100 years since the Pike Place Market opened in Seattle. In response to rising produce costs and concerns that farmers were being deprived of their just return by middlemen—a pound of onions rose from 10 cents to $1 in just one year—the market opened so that consumers could buy directly from farmers. On opening day, eight farmers merged on the corner of First and Pike, and more than 10,000 eager buyers showed up to choose from their wares.

Today, the Pike Place Market is much more than its name suggests. Covering roughly nine acres, the market comprises food stores (bakeries, dairies, fish/seafood, commercial produce stands, meat and butcher shops, produce stands, specialty food stores as well as restaurants, cafés, and fast-food businesses) and mercantile shops (antiques and collectibles, art galleries, books, stationery and cards, clothing and shoes, cookware, and flowers) with over 100 vendors operating each day. One of the more

counter banter and shout, "Anyone
Tourists and shoppers cheer and c

Perhaps the most unique chara
Fish Market is the fact that, excep
never advertised. If you look on the
you can read numerous articles
about the company in local new
newspapers, magazines, and trave
mer's. The fish market also receives
time it is featured on a Food TV ch
fact, the company receives more
most large companies that spend

See For Yourself Videocase

Stimulate your students with these engaging case videos, all of which are new to this edition.

Part 4 Role-Play Exercise*

eQuality Assured

Quality Assured (QA), a nonprofit organization, was started in 1977 to promote the establishment, development, and preservation of high professional standards and audit the social responsibility of companies in the United States. The audits could be used to promote the company's good corporate citizenship and determine areas that need improvement. Of the four issues of social responsibility (voluntary, ethical, legal, and economic), it had always focused most on the voluntary and ethical aspects. During the early years, QA dedicated a majority of its resources to environ-

eQuality has a full-time staff of 50 emplo
core workers are responsible for all the fu
formed at the organization. Most are not expe
cation, but carry out functional responsibili
accounting and technology. Some important
monitoring the business environment, deter
issues need to be addressed, interacting wi
profit organizations, recruiting volunteers, a
all aspects of the projects. Because of the
deadline, a majority of the paid staff feels ove

Role-Play Exercises

at the end of each part give students the opportunity to assume organizational roles and make decisions through application of the text concepts.

Instructors Supplements

Instructor's Resource CD-ROM

Everything you need to get the most from your textbook, including:

Instructor's Manual. Includes learning objectives; lecture outlines; PowerPoint
notes; supplemental lecture; answers to discussion questions and end-of-chapter exercises; notes
for video cases; term paper and project topics; suggestions for guest speakers; and roles and
options for implementing the role playing exercises in each text part.

Computerized Test Bank. Includes hundreds of multiple choice, true/false and
essay questions.

PowerPoint Presentations. Organized in outline format, there are 20-25
slides per chapter. Additional figures and tables from the text may be found on the CD-ROM in
the "Image Bank."

Link to Online Learning Center
(www.mhhe.com/ferrell5e)

Online Learning Center (OLC) with Premium Content
www.mhhe.com/ferrell5e
Access everything you need to teach a great course
through our convenient online resource. A secured
Instructor Resource Center stores your essential course
materials to save you prep time before class. The
Instructor's Manual, Solutions, PowerPoint™, and
sample syllabi are now just a couple of clicks away;
you'll also find useful packaging information and notes.

A Guide for Introducing and Teaching Ethics in Introduction to Business

Written by O.C. Ferrell and Linda Ferrell, this is your one-stop guide for integrating this
important issue into all aspects of your course. It helps you to demonstrate how business ethics
lead to business success and offers a wide range of business ethics resources, including
university centers, government resources, and corporate ethics programs.

Active Classroom Resource Guide

An Additional collection of team projects, cases, and exercises that instructors can choose from
to be used in class or out.

Student Supplements

Study Guide

Each chapter of the Study Guide includes a chapter summary, learning objectives, and plenty of true/false, matching, and multiple-choice questions to practice.

Interactive Study Guide on CD-ROM

Each chapter of this powerful review tool includes sample quizzes, along with activities from McGraw-Hill/Irwin's self-assessment series "Build Your Management Skills."

Online Learning Center (OLC) with Premium Content

www.mhhe.com/ferrell5e

More and more students are studying online. That's why we offer an Online Learning Center (OLC) that follows *Business: A Changing World* chapter by chapter. It doesn't require any building or maintenance on your part, and is ready to go the moment you and your students type in the URL.

As your students study, they can refer to the OLC Web site for such benefits as:

- Internet-based activities
- Self-grading quizzes
- Learning objectives
- Extended chapter summaries
- Additional video and related video exercises

The fifth edition includes an **online running video case** highlighting entrepreneur Todd McFarlane, who parlayed his artistic ability (and a passion for sports) into a multimillion dollar business that straddles film and television production, toys, comic books, sports licensing and games. Students watch and learn as McFarlane explains how he leads his company across all functional areas of business, illustrating how firms deal with the problems and opportunities of today's business world. With one video case for each part of the textbook highlighting this fun and unique company, students and instructors are provided a complete context for discussing every aspect of introductory business.

Create an Online Course

For the instructor needing to educate students online, we offer *Business: A Changing World* content for complete online courses. To make this possible, we have joined forces with the most popular delivery platforms currently available. These platforms are designed for instructors who want complete control over course content and how it is presented to students. You can customize the *Business: A Changing World* Online Learning Center content and author your own course materials. It's entirely up to you.

Products like WebCT, Blackboard, and eCollege all expand the reach of your course. Online discussion and message boards will now complement your office hours. Thanks to a sophisticated tracking system, you will know which students need more attention—even if they don't ask for help. That's because online testing scores are recorded and automatically placed in your grade book, and if a student is struggling with coursework, a special alert message lets you know.

Remember, *Business: A Changing World's* content is flexible enough to use with any platform currently available. If your department or school is already using a platform, we can help. For information on McGraw-Hill/Irwin's course management supplements, including PageOut, Instructor Advantage, and Knowledge Gateway, see "Knowledge Gateway" on the next page.

Managing an Online Course

Knowledge Gateway
mhhe.eduprise.com/home.nsf

Developed with the help of our partner, Eduprise, the **McGraw-Hill Knowledge Gateway** is an all-purpose service and resource center for instructors teaching online. While training programs from WebCT and Blackboard will help teach you their software, only McGraw-Hill has services to help you actually manage and teach your online course, as well as run and maintain the software. **Knowledge Gateway** offers an online library full of articles and insights that focus on how online learning differs from a traditional class environment.

The First Level of **Knowledge Gateway** is available to all professors browsing the McGraw-Hill Higher Education Web site, and consists of an introduction to OLC content, access to the first level of the Resource Library, technical support, and information on Instructional Design Services available through Eduprise.

The Second Level is password-protected and provides access to the expanded Resource Library; technical and pedagogical support for WebCT, Blackboard, and TopClass; the online Instructional Design helpdesk; and an online discussion forum for users. The **Knowledge Gateway** provides a considerable advantage for teaching online—and it's only available through McGraw-Hill.

To learn how these platforms can assist your online course, contact your McGraw-Hill/Irwin representative.

PageOut

PageOut is McGraw-Hill/Irwin's custom Web site service. Now you can put your course online without knowing a word of HTML, selecting from a variety of prebuilt Web site templates. And if none of our ideas suit you, we'll be happy to work with your ideas.

If you want a custom site but don't have time to build it yourself, we offer a team of product specialists ready to help. Just call 1-800-634-3963 and ask to speak with a PageOut specialist. You will be asked to send in your course materials and then participate in a brief telephone consultation. Once we have your information, we build your Web site for you, from scratch. Best of all, PageOut is free when you adopt *Business: A Changing World*! To learn more, please visit www.pageout.net.

Instructor Advantage and Instructor Advantage Plus

Instructor Advantage is a special level of service McGraw-Hill offers in conjunction with WebCT and Blackboard. A team of platform specialists is always available, either by toll-free phone or e-mail, to ensure everything runs smoothly through the life of your adoption. Instructor Advantage is available free to all McGraw-Hill customers.

Instructor Advantage Plus is available to qualifying McGraw-Hill adopters (see your representative for details). IA Plus guarantees you a full day of on-site training by a Blackboard or WebCT specialist, for yourself and up to nine colleagues. Thereafter, you will enjoy the benefits of unlimited telephone and e-mail support throughout the life of your adoption. IA Plus users also have the opportunity to access the McGraw-Hill Knowledge Gateway (see above).

Superior Service

No matter which online course solution you choose, you can count on the highest level of service. That's what sets McGraw-Hill apart. Once you choose *Business: A Changing World*, our specialists offer free training and answer any question you have through the life of your adoption.

Acknowledgments

The fifth edition of *Business: A Changing World* would not have been possible without the commitment, dedication, and patience of Gwyneth Walters. She assisted the authors in developing and coordinating all of the content in the text, ancillaries, and the Online Learning Center. Barbara Gilmer made significant contributions to the content of the previous edition. Ryan Blankenship, Sponsoring Editor, provided leadership and creativity in planning and implementing all aspects of the fifth edition. Christine Scheid, Senior Developmental Editor, did an outstanding job of coordinating all aspects of the development and production process. Mary Conzachi was the Project Manager. Mark Molsky managed the technical aspects of the Online Learning Center. Others important in this edition include Joyce Chappetto (Supplements), Ellen Cleary (Marketing Manager), Pam Verros (Design) and Dan Wiencek (Advertising).

Liza Hann and Nori Comello contributed several boxes to this edition. Sarah Scott contributed boxes, cases, and assisted in the overall revision process. Michael Hartline developed the Personal Career Plan in Appendix C and assisted in developing the Business Plan in Appendix B. Vickie Bajtelsmit developed Appendix D on personal financial planning. Eric Sandberg of Interactive Learning assisted in developing the interactive exercises and "Business Around the World" on the CD. Anthony Chelte of Western New England College helped us with the Student CD Chapter Quizzes and Outlines.

Many others have assisted us with their helpful comments, recommendations, and support throughout this and previous editions. We'd like to express our thanks to the reviewers who helped us shape the fifth edition:

James Bartlett
University of Illinois

Stephanie Bibb
Chicago State University

Alka Bramhandkar
Ithaca College

Michael Cicero
Highline Community College

Debbie Collins
Anne Arundel Community College—Arnold

Laurie Dahlin
Worcester State College

Tom Diamante
Adelphi University

John Eagan
Erie Community College/City Campus SUNY

Robert Ericksen
Craven Community College

Art Fischer
Pittsburg State University

Toni Forcino
Montgomery College—Germantown

Chris Gilbert
Tacoma Community College/University of Washington

Ross Gittell
University of New Hampshire

Gary Grau
Northeast State Tech Community College

Claudia Green
Pace University

David Gribbin
East Georgia College

Peggy Hager
Winthrop University

Verne Ingram
Red Rocks Community College

Steven Jennings
Highland Community College

Eileen Kearney
Montgomery County Community College

Craig Kelley
California State University—Sacramento

Arbrie King
Baton Rouge Community College

John Knappenberger
Mesa State College

Anthony Koh
University of Toledo

Dorinda Lynn
Pensacola Junior College

Larry Martin
Community College of Southern Nevada—West Charles

Kristina Mazurak
Albertson College of Idaho

Mary Meredith
University of Louisiana at Lafayette

Michelle Meyer
Joliet Junior College

Fred Nerone
International College—Naples

Michael Nugent
SUNY—Stony Brook University New York

Wes Payne
Southwest Tennessee Community College

Dyan Pease
Sacramento City College

John Pharr
Cedar Valley College

Shirley Polejewski
University of St. Thomas

Daniel Powroznik
Chesapeake College

Krista Price
Heald College

Larry Prober
Rider University

Kathy Pullins
Columbus State Community College

Tom Reading
Ivy Tech State College

Susan Roach
Georgia Southern University

Dave Robinson
University of California—Berkely

Marianne Sebok
Community College of Southern Nevada—West Charles

Cheryl Stansfield
North Hennepin Community College

Ron Stolle
Kent State University—Kent

Jeff Strom
Virginia Western Community College

Cheryl Stansfield
North Hennepin Community College

Steve Tilley
Gainesville College

Lawrence Yax
Pensacola Junior College—Warrington

We extend special appreciation to the following people who reviewed previous editions:

Linda Anglin, Mankato State University

John Bajkowski, American Association of Individual Investors

Barbara Boyington, Brookdale County College of Monmouth

Suzanne Bradford, Angelina College

Eric Brooks, Orange County Community College

Nicky Buenger, Texas A&M University

Anthony Buono, Bentley College

William Chittenden, Texas Tech University

M. Lou Cisneros, Austin Community College

Karen Collins, Lehigh University

Katherine Conway, Boro of Manhattan Community College

Rex Cutshall, Vincennes University

Dana D'Angelo, Drexel University

John DeNisco, Buffalo State College

Joyce Domke, DePaul University

Michael Drafke, College of DuPage

Thomas Enerva, Lakeland Community College

Joe Farinella, DePaul University

James Ferrell, R. G. Taylor, P.C.

Jennifer Friestad, Anoka—Ramsey Community College

Bob Grau, Cuyahoga Community College—Western Campus

Jack K. Gray, Attorney-at-Law, Houston, Texas

Catherine Green, University of Memphis

Phil Greenwood, University of St. Thomas

Michael Hartline, Florida State University

Neil Herndon, University of Missouri

James Hoffman, Borough of Manhattan Community College

Joseph Hrebenak, Community College of Allegheny County—Allegheny Campus

Stephen Huntley, Florida Community College

Rebecca Hurtz, State Farm Insurance Co.

Roger Hutt, Arizona State University—West

Scott Inks, Ball State University

Carol Jones, Cuyahoga Community College—Eastern Campus

Gilbert "Joe" Joseph, University of Tampa

Norm Karl, Johnson County Community College

Janice Karlan, LaGuardia Community College

Ina Midkiff Kennedy, Austin Community College

Daniel LeClair, AACSB

Frank Lembo, North Virginia Community College

Richard Lewis, East Texas Baptist College

Corinn Linton, Valencia Community College

Corrine Livesay, Mississippi College

Thomas Lloyd, Westmoreland Community College

Terry Loe, Kennerow University

Isabelle Maignan, ING

Debbie Thorne McAlister, Texas State University—San Marcos

John McDonough, Menlo College

Tom McInish, University of Memphis

Noel McDeon, Florida Community College

Glynna Morse, Augusta College

Fred Nerone, International College of Naples

Laura Nicholson, Northern Oklahoma College

Stef Nicovich, University of New Hampshire

Constantine G. Petrides, Borough of Manhattan Community College

Stephen Pruitt, University of Missouri—Kansas City

Charles Quinn, Austin Community College

Victoria Rabb, College of the Desert

Marsha Rule, Florida Public Utilities Commission

Carol A. Rustad, Sylvan Learning

Martin St. John, Westmoreland Community College

Nick Sarantakes, Austin Community College

Elise "Pookie" Sautter, New Mexico State University

Dana Schubert, Colorado Springs Zoo

Jeffery L. Seglin, Seglin Associates

Daniel Sherrell, University of Memphis

Nicholas Siropolis, Cuyahoga Community College

Robyn Smith, Pouder Valley Hospital

Wayne Taylor, Trinity Valley Community College

Ray Tewell, American River College

Jay Todes, Northlake College

Amy Thomas, Roger Williams University

Ted Valvoda, Lakeland Community College

Sue Vondram, Loyola University

Elizabeth Wark, Springfield College

Emma Watson, Arizona State University—West

Jerry E. Wheat, Indiana University Southeast

Frederik Williams, North Texas State University

Pat Wright, Texas A&M University

Timothy Wright, Lakeland Community College

O.C. Ferrell
Geoffrey Hirt
Linda Ferrell

— July 2004

Authors

O.C. Ferrell

O.C. Ferrell is Chair of the Department of Marketing and the Ehrhardt, Keefe, Steiner, and Hottman P. C. Professor of Business Administration at Colorado State University. He also has held faculty positions at the University of Memphis, University of Tampa, Texas A&M University, Illinois State University, and Southern Illinois University, as well as visiting positions at Queen's University (Ontario, Canada), University of Michigan (Ann Arbor), University of Wisconsin (Madison), and University of Hannover (Germany). He has served as a faculty member for the Master's Degree Program in Marketing at Thammasat University (Bangkok, Thailand). Dr. Ferrell received his B.A. and M.B.A. from Florida State University and his Ph.D. from Louisiana State University. His teaching and research interests include business ethics, corporate citizenship, and marketing.

Dr. Ferrell is widely recognized as a leading teacher and scholar in business. His articles have appeared in leading journals and trade publications. In addition to *Business: A Changing World*, he has two other textbooks, *Marketing: Concepts and Strategies* and *Business Ethics: Ethical Decision Making and Cases*, that are market leaders in their respective areas. He also has coauthored other textbooks for marketing, management, business and society, and other business courses, as well as a trade book on business ethics. He chaired the American Marketing Association (AMA) ethics committee that developed its current code of ethics. He was the vice president of marketing education and president of the Academic Council for the AMA.

Dr. Ferrell's major focus is teaching and preparing learning material for students. He has taught the introduction to business course at Colorado State University using this textbook. This gives him the opportunity to develop, improve, and test the book and ancillary materials on a first-hand basis. He has traveled extensively to work with students and understands the needs of instructors of introductory business courses. He lives in Fort Collins, Colorado, and enjoys skiing, golf, and international travel.

Geoffrey A. Hirt

Geoffrey A. Hirt is currently Professor of Finance at DePaul University and a Mesirow Financial Fellow. From 1987 to 1997 he was Chairman of the Finance Department at DePaul University. He teaches investments, corporate finance, and strategic planning. He developed and was director of DePaul's M.B.A. program in Hong Kong and has taught in Poland, Germany, Thailand, and Hong Kong. He received his Ph.D. in Finance from the University of Illinois at Champaign–Urbana, his M.B.A. from Miami University of Ohio, and his B.A. from Ohio-Wesleyan University. Dr. Hirt has directed the Chartered Financial Analysts Study program for the Investment Analysts Society of Chicago since 1987.

Dr. Hirt has published several books, including *Foundations of Financial Management* published by Irwin/McGraw-Hill. Now in its tenth edition, this book is used at over 600 colleges and universities worldwide. It has been used in over 31 countries and has been translated into over 10 different languages. Additionally, Dr. Hirt is well-known for his text, *Fundamentals of Investment Management,* also published by Irwin/McGraw-Hill, and now in its seventh edition. He plays tennis and golf, is a music lover, and enjoys traveling with his wife, Linda.

Linda Ferrell

Dr. Linda Ferrell is Assistant Professor in the Management & Marketing Department at the University of Wyoming. She completed her Ph.D. in Business Administration, with a concentration in management, at the University of Memphis. She has taught at the University of Tampa, Colorado State University, University of Northern Colorado, and the University of Memphis. She also team teaches a class at Thammasat University in Bangkok, Thailand.

Her work experience as an account executive for McDonald's and Pizza Hut's advertising agencies supports her teaching of advertising, marketing management, marketing ethics and marketing principles. She has published in the *Journal of Public Policy and Marketing, Journal of Business Research, Journal of Business Ethics, Journal of Marketing Education, Marketing Education Review, Journal of Teaching Business Ethics, Case Research Journal,* and is co-author of *Business Ethics: Ethical Decision Making and Cases* (6th edition) and *Business and* Society (2nd edition). She is the ethics content expert for the AACSB Ethics Education Resource Center (www.aacsb.edu/eerc) and was co-chair of the 2004 AACSB Teaching Business Ethics Conference in Boulder, CO.

Dr. Ferrell has served as Vice President of Development for the Academy of Marketing Science and is on the Board of Directors of the Marketing Management Association. She frequently speaks to organizations on "Teaching Business Ethics," including the Direct Selling Education Foundation's training programs and AACSB International Conferences. She has served as an expert witness in cases related to advertising, business ethics, and consumer protection.

Brief Contents

Contents

Part 1

Business in a Changing World

Chapter 1

The Dynamics of Business and Economics

OBJECTIVES

After reading this chapter, you will be able to:

- Define basic concepts such as business, product, and profit.

- Identify the main participants and activities of business and explain why studying business is important.

- Define economics and compare the four types of economic systems.

- Describe the role of supply, demand, and competition in a free-enterprise system.

- Specify why and how the health of the economy is measured.

- Trace the evolution of the American economy and discuss the role of the entrepreneur in the economy.

- Evaluate a small-business owner's situation and propose a course of action.

Satellite Radio Offers More Choices

Radio broadcasts have long been available to anyone with a receiver, but two companies are gambling that consumers will pay for satellite radio. The satellite radio industry has already gained millions of subscribers. Satellite radio offers hundreds of diverse channels of music, news, comedy, and talk, including full-time channels devoted to classical, blues, rock, electronica, reggae, country, and Broadway show tunes. Some channels offer types of music or comedy that typically do not attract enough listeners to justify a traditional radio station in most markets. Moreover, the private services offer somewhat racier material than commercial stations.

Sirius offers commercial-free channels with little interruption from announcers. XM's channels, sound more like traditional radio stations with live announcers. Although XM included a sprinkling of concentrated commercials when it began, it is now commercial-free. Customers love the fact that they can receive their favorite channel even in rural areas where traditional radio stations are few and far between.

Neither company has yet to show a profit. Initial growth may have been slow due to the bulky and expensive receivers required to use them. Now, XM and Sirius both offer reasonably priced "plug and play" devices that subscribers can take from their car to home or office. Moreover, exclusive deals with automakers mean that an increasing number of new vehicles come equipped with satellite radio receivers.

Both XM and Sirius face competition from traditional commercial FM radio, which most consumers continue to access for free. However, some contend that satellite radio offers greater choices in markets increasingly

continued

dominated by a single media company. For example, Clear Channel Communications, which owns more than 10 percent of the nation's radio stations, has been accused of owning so many stations in certain large markets that it effectively operates as a monopoly and limits consumer access to new music. In addition, XM and Sirius also face competition from MP3 players, which allow users to play music they download from the Internet.

Although XM and Sirius have their skeptics, many investors have been willing to bet on the continuing growth of satellite radio. With more than 100 million households and 200 million cars (not to mention boats, RVs, and other vehicles), the prospects for growth appear strong.[1]

Introduction

We begin our study of business by examining the fundamentals of business and economics in this chapter. First, we introduce the nature of business, including its goals, activities, and participants. Next, we describe the basics of economics and apply them to the United States' economy. Finally, we establish a framework for studying business in this text.

The Nature of Business

business
individuals or organizations who try to earn a profit by providing products that satisfy people's needs

A **business** tries to earn a profit by providing products that satisfy people's needs. The outcome of its efforts are **products** that have both tangible and intangible characteristics that provide satisfaction and benefits. When you purchase a product, what you are buying is the benefits and satisfaction you think the product will provide. A Subway sandwich, for example, may be purchased to satisfy hunger; a Porsche Cayenne sport utility vehicle, to satisfy the need for transportation and the desire to present a certain image.

product
a good or service with tangible and intangible characteristics that provide satisfaction and benefits

Most people associate the word *product* with tangible goods—an automobile, computer, loaf of bread, coat, or some other tangible item. However, a product can also be a service, which results when people or machines provide or process something of value to customers. Dry cleaning, photo processing, a checkup by a doctor, a performance by a movie star or basketball player—these are examples of services. A product can also be an idea. Consultants and attorneys, for example, generate ideas for solving problems.

The Goal of Business

profit
the difference between what it costs to make and sell a product and what a customer pays for it

The primary goal of all businesses is to earn a **profit,** the difference between what it costs to make and sell a product and what a customer pays for it. If a company spends $2.00 to manufacture, finance, promote, and distribute a product that it sells for $2.75, the business earns a profit of 75 cents on each product sold. Businesses have the right to keep and use their profits as they choose—within legal limits—because profit is the reward for the risks they take in providing products. Not all organizations are businesses. **Nonprofit organizations,** such as Greenpeace, Special Olympics, and other charities and social causes, do not have the fundamental purpose of earning profits, although they may provide goods or services.

nonprofit organizations
organizations that may provide goods or services but do not have the fundamental purpose of earning profits

To earn a profit, a person or organization needs management skills to plan, organize, and control the activities of the business and to find and develop employees so that it can make products consumers will buy. A business also needs marketing expertise to learn what products consumers need and want and to develop, manufacture, price, promote, and distribute those products. Additionally, a business needs financial resources and skills to fund, maintain, and expand its operations. Other challenges for businesspeople include abiding by laws and government regulations, acting in an ethical and socially responsible manner, and adapting to economic, technological, and social changes. Even nonprofit organizations engage in management, marketing, and finance activities to help reach their goals.

To achieve and maintain profitability, businesses have found that they must produce quality products, operate efficiently, and be socially responsible and ethical in dealing with customers, employees, investors, government regulators, the community, and society. Because these groups have a stake in the success and outcomes of a business, they are sometimes called **stakeholders.** Many businesses, for example, are concerned about how the production and distribution of their products affect the environment. The New Belgium Brewing Company, based in Fort Collins, Colorado, became the first fully wind-powered brewery in the United States after it invested in wind energy, reducing the firm's emissions by 1,800 metric tons per year. The small business also built a state-of-the-art production facility that employs numerous award-winning environmentally friendly and energy-efficient features. In addition, the brewery contributes $1 per barrel sold to various cultural, social, environmental, and alcohol-awareness programs in the states where it markets its products. Other businesses are concerned about the quality of life in the communities in which they operate. Cummins, Inc., an Indiana-based manufacturing firm with operations around the world, funded the construction of a school in Brazil that serves 800 local children who previously had no school to attend.[2] Others are concerned with promoting business careers among African-American, Hispanic, and Native-American students. The Diversity Pipeline Alliance plans an aggressive advertising campaign to show minority students ages 12 to 24 how a business education can lead to career opportunities.[3] Still other businesses are concerned with social responsibility in times of natural disasters. After wildfires devastated thousands of acres of Colorado forests and destroyed numerous homes, Home Depot gave out thousands of cleanup kits to help homeowners clean up damage caused by smoke, fire, or water. Home Depot also provides how-to clinics to help customers learn how to prepare for natural disasters, such as hurricanes, floods, tornadoes, and ice storms. The Home Depot also publishes a "Hurricane Guide" with the Weather Channel, which contains information on preparing for a hurricane and what to do before, during, and after a hurricane.[4]

stakeholders

groups that have a stake in the success and outcomes of a business

The People and Activities of Business

Figure 1.1 shows the people and activities involved in business. At the center of the figure are owners, employees, and customers; the outer circle includes the primary business activities—management, marketing, and finance. Owners have to put up resources—money or credit—to start a business. Employees are responsible for the work that goes on within a business. Owners can manage the business themselves or hire employees to accomplish this task. The president of General Motors, for example, does not own GM but is an employee who is responsible for managing all the other employees in a way that earns a profit for investors, who are the real owners. Finally, and most importantly, a business's major role is to satisfy the customers who buy its

FIGURE 1.1

Overview of the
Business World

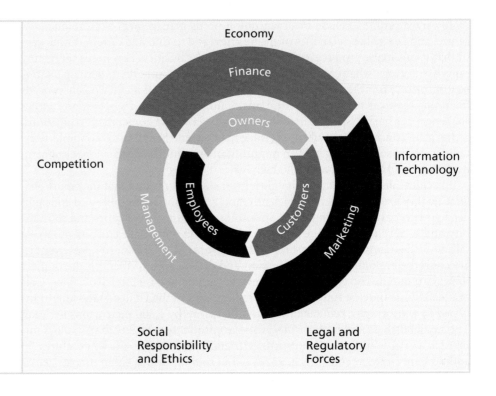

goods or services. Note also that people and forces beyond an organization's control—such as legal and regulatory forces, the economy, competition, technology, and ethical and social concerns—all have an impact on the daily operations of businesses. You will learn more about these participants in business activities throughout this book. Next, we will examine the major activities of business.

Management.   Notice that in Figure 1.1 management and employees are in the same segment of the circle. This is because management involves coordinating employees' actions to achieve the firm's goals, organizing people to work efficiently, and motivating them to achieve the business's goals. At the National Football League, for example, Commissioner Paul Tagliabue managed resources and manpower to boost the organization's revenues from $970 million to $5 billion in 15 years.[5] Management is also concerned with acquiring, developing, and using resources (including people) effectively and efficiently.

A nationally recognized, environmentally efficient wind-powered brewery, New Belgium Brewery in Fort Collins, CO, eliminates 1,800 metric tons of CO_2 emissions per year. (From www.newbelgium.com)

At Yahoo!, the Internet portal, Chief Executive Officer Terry Semel consolidated the rapidly growing firm's businesses and applied strong business and management principles during an economic downturn. Under Semel's leadership, Yahoo's revenues increased by 57 percent and its profits by 470 percent at a time when many other Internet-based firms were failing or struggling to find profits.[6] Production and manufacturing is another element of management. In essence, managers plan, organize, staff, and control the tasks required to carry out the work of the company or nonprofit organization. We will take a closer look at management activities in Parts Three and Four of this text.

To illustrate the importance of management, consider a small hypothetical Mexican restaurant, owned and managed by the Lopez family, which provides traditional home-style recipes and excellent service in the community. Among the many management activities the Lopez family engages in are finding, training, scheduling, and motivating waitstaff and cooks; locating and purchasing high-quality ingredients and equipment; planning daily meals and developing new recipes; and deciding what local community charities it wants to support. If a large corporate restaurant chain, such as Chi Chi's, opens a restaurant nearby, the Lopez family will have to decide how to respond to the new competition—change prices or the menu, advertise, or make some other response. Consequently, making decisions to ensure the business achieves its short- and long-term goals is a vital part of management.

Marketing.   Marketing and consumers are in the same segment of Figure 1.1 because the focus of all marketing activities is satisfying customers. Marketing includes all the activities designed to provide goods and services that satisfy consumers' needs and wants. Marketers gather information and conduct research to determine what customers want. Using information gathered from marketing research, marketers plan and develop products and make decisions about how much to charge for their products and when and where to make them available. For example, when research indicated that an increasing number of Ameri-

Did the "Got Milk?" campaign with famous celebrities and their milk mustaches get you to drink more milk?

cans are following low-carbohydrate diets, like the Atkins and South Beach Diets, many companies responded with new products to satisfy their concerns. The Ruby Tuesday and TGIFriday restaurant chains began offering low-carbohydrate menu items, and Atkins Nutritionals launched an entire product line of low-carb food products.[7] Other food producers have responded to consumer health concerns by modifying their products to make them healthier. PepsiCo, for example, has begun removing trans fats—which have been linked to heart disease—from its Frito-Lay snack foods.[8] Marketers use promotion—advertising, personal selling, sales promotion (coupons, games, sweepstakes, movie tie-ins), and publicity—to communicate the benefits and advantages of their products to consumers and increase sales. Nonprofit organizations also use promotion. For example, the National Fluid Milk Processor Promotion Board's "milk mustache" advertising campaign has featured Pete Sampras, Whoopi Goldberg, Britney Spears, and Elton John, as well as animated "celebrities" such as Garfield, the Rugrats, and Blues Clues.[9] We will examine marketing activities in Part Five of this text.

Finance.   Owners and finance are in the same part of Figure 1.1 because, although management and marketing have to deal with financial considerations, it is the primary responsibility of the owners to provide financial resources for the operation of the business. Moreover, the owners have the most to lose if the business fails to make a profit. Finance refers to all activities concerned with obtaining money and using it effectively. People who work as accountants, stockbrokers, investment advisors, or bankers are all part of the financial world. Owners sometimes have to borrow money to get started or attract additional owners who become partners or stockholders. A mentoring group called 8 Wings helps women entrepreneurs obtain funding by assisting them in perfecting their business plan, preparing their presentation to potential funding sources, and introducing them to potential investors and other business contacts. The 8 Wings partners typically take stock or options in the companies they help.[10] Owners of small businesses in particular often rely on bank loans for funding. Part Six of this text discusses financial management.

Why Study Business?

Studying business can help you develop skills and acquire knowledge to prepare for your future career, regardless of whether you plan to work for a multinational *Fortune* 500 firm, start your own business, work for a government agency, or manage or volunteer at a nonprofit organization. The field of business offers a variety of interesting and challenging career opportunities throughout the world, such as human resources management, information technology, finance, production and operations, wholesaling and retailing, and many more.

Studying business can also help you better understand the many business activities that are necessary to provide satisfying goods and services—and that these activities carry a price tag. For example, if you buy a new compact disc, about half of the price goes toward activities related to distribution and the retailer's expenses and profit margins. The production (pressing) of the CD represents about $1, or a small percentage of its price. Most businesses charge a reasonable price for their products to ensure that they cover their production costs, pay their employees, provide their owners with a return on their investment, and perhaps give something back to their local communities. For example, Russell Simmons, who owns Phat Fashions, the Simmons-Lathan Media Group, and *OneWorld* magazine through his Rush Communications holding company, created the Rush Philanthropic Arts Foundation to donate funds to organizations that help underprivileged youth gain access to the arts.[11] Thus, learning about business can help you become a well-informed consumer and member of society.

Business activities help generate the profits that are essential not only to individual businesses and local economies but also to the health of the global economy. Without profits, businesses find it difficult, if not impossible, to buy more raw materials, hire more employees, attract more capital, and create additional products that in turn make more profits and fuel the world economy. Understanding how our free-enterprise economic system allocates resources and provides incentives for industry and the workplace is important to everyone.

The Economic Foundations of Business

To continue our introduction to business, it is useful to explore the economic environment in which business is conducted. In this section, we examine economic systems, the free-enterprise system, the concepts of supply and demand, and the role of competition. These concepts play important roles in determining how businesses operate in a particular society.

Economics is the study of how resources are distributed for the production of goods and services within a social system. You are already familiar with the types of resources available. Land, forests, minerals, water, and other things that are not made by people are **natural resources. Human resources,** or labor, refers to the physical and mental abilities that people use to produce goods and services. **Financial resources,** or capital, are the funds used to acquire the natural and human resources needed to provide products. Because natural, human, and financial resources are used to produce goods and services, they are sometimes called *factors of production.*

Economic Systems

An **economic system** describes how a particular society distributes its resources to produce goods and services. A central issue of economics is how to fulfill an unlimited demand for goods and services in a world with a limited supply of resources. Different economic systems attempt to resolve this central issue in numerous ways, as we shall see.

Although economic systems handle the distribution of resources in different ways, all economic systems must address three important issues:

1. What goods and services, and how much of each, will satisfy consumers' needs?
2. How will goods and services be produced, who will produce them, and with what resources will they be produced?
3. How are the goods and services to be distributed to consumers?

Communism, socialism, and capitalism, the basic economic systems found in the world today (Table 1.1), have fundamental differences in the way they address these issues.

economics
the study of how resources are distributed for the production of goods and services within a social system

natural resources
land, forests, minerals, water, and other things that are not made by people

human resources
the physical and mental abilities that people use to produce goods and services; also called labor

financial resources
the funds used to acquire the natural and human resources needed to provide products; also called capital

economic system
a description of how a particular society distributes its resources to produce goods and services

TABLE 1.1 Comparison of Communism, Socialism, and Capitalism

	Communism	Socialism	Capitalism
Business ownership	Most businesses are owned and operated by the government.	The government owns and operates major industries; individuals own small businesses.	Individuals own and operate all businesses.
Competition	None. The government owns and operates everything.	Restricted in major industries; encouraged in small business.	Encouraged by market forces and government regulations.
Profits	Excess income goes to the government.	Profits earned by small businesses may be reinvested in the business; profits from government-owned industries go to the government.	Individuals are free to keep profits and use them as they wish.
Product availability and price	Consumers have a limited choice of goods and services; prices are usually high.	Consumers have some choice of goods and services; prices are determined by supply and demand.	Consumers have a wide choice of goods and services; prices are determined by supply and demand.
Employment options	Little choice in choosing a career; most people work for government-owned industries or farms.	Some choice of careers; many people work in government jobs.	Unlimited choice of careers.

Communism.   Karl Marx (1818–1883) first described **communism** as a society in which the people, without regard to class, own all the nation's resources. In his ideal political-economic system, everyone contributes according to ability and receives benefits according to need. In a communist economy, the people (through the government) own and operate all businesses and factors of production. Central government planning determines what goods and services satisfy citizens' needs, how the goods and services are produced, and how they are distributed. However, no true communist economy exists today that satisfies Marx's ideal.

On paper, communism appears to be efficient and equitable, producing less of a gap between rich and poor. In practice, however, communist economies have been marked by low standards of living, critical shortages of consumer goods, high prices, and little freedom. In recent years, Russia, Poland, Hungary, and other Eastern European nations have turned away from communism and toward economic systems governed by supply and demand rather than by central planning. However, their experiments with alternative economic systems have been fraught with difficulty and hardship. China, North Korea, and Cuba continue to apply communist principles to their economies, but these countries are also enduring economic and political change. Consequently, communism is declining and its future as an economic system is uncertain.

Socialism.   Closely related to communism is **socialism,** an economic system in which the government owns and operates basic industries—postal service, telephone, utilities, transportation, health care, banking, and some manufacturing—but individuals own most businesses. Central planning determines what basic goods and services are produced, how they are produced, and how they are distributed. Individuals and small businesses provide other goods and services based on consumer demand and the availability of resources. As with communism, citizens are dependent on the government for many goods and services.

Most socialist nations, such as Sweden, India, and Israel, are democratic and recognize basic individual freedoms. Citizens can vote for political offices, but central government planners usually make decisions about what is best for the nation. People are free to go into the occupation of their choice, but they often work in government-operated organizations. Socialists believe their system permits a higher standard of living than other economic systems, but the difference often applies to the nation as a whole rather than to its individual citizens. Socialist economies profess egalitarianism—equal distribution of income and social services. They believe their economies are more stable than those of other nations. Although this may be true, taxes and unemployment are generally higher in socialist countries. Perhaps as a result, many socialist countries are also experiencing economic turmoil.

Capitalism.   **Capitalism,** or **free enterprise,** is an economic system in which individuals own and operate the majority of businesses that provide goods and services. Competition, supply, and demand determine which goods and services are produced, how they are produced, and how they are distributed. The United States, Canada, Japan, and Australia are examples of economic systems based on capitalism.

There are two forms of capitalism: pure capitalism and modified capitalism. In pure capitalism, also called a **free-market system,** all economic decisions are made without government intervention. This economic system was first described by Adam Smith in *The Wealth of Nations* (1776). Smith, often called the father of capitalism, believed that the "invisible hand of competition" best regulates the economy. He argued that competition should determine what goods and services people need.

---

communism
first described by Karl Marx as a society in which the people, without regard to class, own all the nation's resources

socialism
an economic system in which the government owns and operates basic industries but individuals own most businesses

capitalism, or free enterprise
an economic system in which individuals own and operate the majority of businesses that provide goods and services

free-market system
pure capitalism, in which all economic decisions are made without government intervention

Smith's system is also called *laissez-faire* ("to leave alone") *capitalism* because the government does not interfere in business.

Modified capitalism differs from pure capitalism in that the government intervenes and regulates business to some extent. One of the ways in which the United States and Canadian governments regulate business is through laws. Laws such as the Federal Trade Commission Act, which created the Federal Trade Commission to enforce antitrust laws, illustrate the importance of the government's role in the economy.

Mixed Economies.   No country practices a pure form of communism, socialism, or capitalism, although most tend to favor one system over the others. Most nations operate as **mixed economies,** which have elements from more than one economic system. In socialist Sweden, most businesses are owned and operated by private individuals. In capitalist United States, the federal government owns and operates the postal service and the Tennessee Valley Authority, an electric utility. In Great Britain and Mexico, the governments are attempting to sell many state-run businesses to private individuals and companies. In once-communist Russia, Hungary, Poland, and other Eastern European nations, capitalist ideas have been implemented, including private ownership of businesses.

mixed economies
economies made up of elements from more than one economic system

The Free-Enterprise System

Many economies—including those of the United States, Canada, and Japan—are based on free enterprise, and many communist and socialist countries, such as China and Russia, are applying more principles of free enterprise to their own economic systems. Free enterprise provides an opportunity for a business to succeed or fail on the basis of market demand. In a free-enterprise system, companies that can efficiently manufacture and sell products that consumers desire will probably succeed. Inefficient businesses and those that sell products that do not offer needed benefits will likely fail as consumers take their business to firms that have more competitive products.

A number of basic individual and business rights must exist for free enterprise to work. These rights are the goals of many countries that have recently embraced free enterprise.

1. Individuals must have the right to own property and to pass this property on to their heirs. This right motivates people to work hard and save to buy property.

2. Individuals and businesses must have the right to earn profits and to use the profits as they wish, within the constraints of their society's laws and values.

3. Individuals and businesses must have the right to make decisions that determine the way the business operates. Although there is government regulation, the philosophy in countries like the United States and Australia is to permit maximum freedom within a set of rules of fairness.

4. Individuals must have the right to choose what career to pursue, where to live, what goods and services to purchase, and more. Businesses must have the right to choose where to locate, what goods and services to produce, what resources to use in the production process, and so on.

Without these rights, businesses cannot function effectively because they are not motivated to succeed. Thus, these rights make possible the open exchange of goods and services.

FIGURE 1.2

Equilibrium Price of
Handmade Rugs

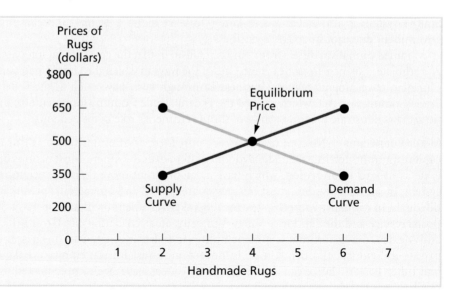

The Forces of Supply and Demand

In the United States and in other free-enterprise systems, the distribution of resources and products is determined by supply and demand. **Demand** is the number of goods and services that consumers are willing to buy at different prices at a specific time. From your own experience, you probably recognize that consumers are usually willing to buy more of an item as its price falls because they want to save money. Consider handmade rugs, for example. Consumers may be willing to buy six rugs at $350 each, four at $500 each, but only two at $650 each. The relationship between the price and the number of rugs consumers are willing to buy can be shown graphically, with a *demand curve* (see Figure 1.2).

Supply is the number of products that businesses are willing to sell at different prices at a specific time. In general, because the potential for profits is higher, businesses are willing to supply more of a good or service at higher prices. For example, a company that sells rugs may be willing to sell six at $650 each, four at $500 each, but just two at $350 each. The relationship between the price of rugs and the quantity the company is willing to supply can be shown graphically with a *supply curve* (see Figure 1.2).

In Figure 1.2, the supply and demand curves intersect at the point where supply and demand are equal. The price at which the number of products that businesses are willing to supply equals the amount of products that consumers are willing to buy at a specific point in time is the **equilibrium price.** In our rug example, the company is willing to supply four rugs at $500 each, and consumers are willing to buy four rugs at $500 each. Therefore, $500 is the equilibrium price for a rug at that point in time, and most rug companies will price their rugs at $500. As you might imagine, a business that charges more than $500 (or whatever the current equilibrium price is) for its rugs will not sell many and might not earn a profit. On the other hand, a business that charges less than $500 accepts a lower profit per rug than could be made at the equilibrium price.

If the cost of making rugs goes up, businesses will not offer as many at the old price. Changing the price alters the supply curve, and a new equilibrium price re-

demand
the number of goods and
services that consumers
are willing to buy at
different prices at a
specific time

supply
the number of products—
goods and services—that
businesses are willing to
sell at different prices at a
specific time

equilibrium price
the price at which the
number of products that
businesses are willing to
supply equals the amount
of products that
consumers are willing to
buy at a specific point in
time

After the U.S. Senate issued dietary recommendations in 1977, telling Americans to eat more chicken and less red meat, per capita beef consumption in the United States began to decline. Over the next 20 years, annual demand for beef declined by as much as 31 percent, lowering the prices received by ranchers as well as at the grocery store.

However, in the late 1990s and early 2000s, the beef market changed dramatically. The price of live cattle increased to more than $1 per pound, while prices closer to 50 cents per pound used to be common. Market analysts credited the price increase to two factors: dietary trends and a decreased supply of cattle. The popularity of low-carb, high-protein diets like the Atkins diet changed the way Americans viewed beef. Once blamed as a source of fat and cholesterol, beef increasingly is seen as a healthy part of a diet that can lead to weight loss. Americans began demanding more beef, including more expensive cuts of beef. However, this rise in demand coincided with a decreased supply of beef, resulting from a prolonged drought in the American rangelands. A five-year drought forced ranchers to reduce their herd size, and the population of cattle in the U.S. reached a seven-year low in 2003. This decrease in supply coupled with the increase in demand resulted in soaring beef prices.

U.S. beef prices fluctuated again after a cow in Washington State tested positive for bovine spongiform encephalopathy (BSE), or "mad cow disease," in December 2003. Although U.S. consumer demand for beef did not immediately decline, more than 50 nations fully or partially banned the import of U.S. beef. The export market previously accounted for approximately 10 percent of U.S. beef sales; the ban on exports resulted in a glut of beef in the domestic market. As a result, the prices ranchers received for live cattle dropped 20 percent in January 2004. Beef prices soon rebounded due to continued strong demand, tight supplies, and the removal of export bans.

After publicity surrounding the mad cow case, grocers and restaurants began to demand more high-end natural organic beef—from cattle raised without artificial growth hormones and locally fed with organic grain or grazed on grassland. At a time when most beef prices were declining, natural beef ranchers reported an increase in demand, pushing organic beef prices up more than $1 per pound above the price of conventional cuts of beef. Natural or organic beef producers such as Coleman Natural Meats and Blue Ridge Premium Beef represent just 1 percent of overall beef production. Beef is an example of an agricultural commodity that experiences unpredictable fluctuations in demand and supply that determine market prices.[12]

Discussion Questions

1. How does the supply of beef influence prices for consumers?
2. What causes the demand for beef to fluctuate so rapidly?
3. What is likely to happen to demand for chicken when the price of beef increases?

---

sults. This is an ongoing process, with supply and demand constantly changing in response to changes in economic conditions, availability of resources, and degree of competition. For example, gasoline prices rose sharply in 2004 in response to a shrinking supply of gasoline and crude oil and rising demand.[13] On the other hand, the world's largest music company, Universal Music Group, slashed the suggested retail price for CDs of popular artists like 50 Cent and Shania Twain to $12.98 in response to declining demand for music CDs. Sales of CDs have declined by 30 percent over the last three years, partly due to increased downloading of music from the Internet.[14] Prices for goods and services vary according to these changes in supply and demand. This concept is the force that drives the distribution of resources (goods and services, labor, money) in a free-enterprise economy.

Critics of supply and demand say the system does not distribute resources equally. The forces of supply and demand prevent sellers who have to sell at higher prices (because their costs are high) and buyers who cannot afford to buy goods at the equilibrium price from participating in the market. According to critics, the wealthy can afford to buy more than they need, but the poor are unable to buy enough of what they need to survive.

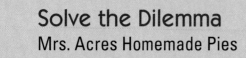

Solve the Dilemma
Mrs. Acres Homemade Pies

Shelly Acres, whose grandmother gave her a family recipe for making pies, loved to cook so she decided to start a business she called Mrs. Acres Homemade Pies. The company produces specialty pies and sells them in local supermarkets and select family restaurants. In each of the first six months, Shelly and three part-time employees sold 2,000 pies for $4.50 each, netting $1.50 profit per pie. The pies were quite successful and Shelly could not keep up with demand. The company's success results from a quality product and productive employees who are motivated by incentives and who enjoy being part of a successful new business.

To meet demand, Shelly expanded operations, borrowing money and increasing staff to four full-time employees. Production and sales increased to 8,000 pies per month, and prof-

its soared to $12,000 per month. However, demand for Mrs. Acres Homemade Pies continues to accelerate beyond what Shelly can supply. She has several options: (1) maintain current production levels and raise prices; (2) expand the facility and staff while maintaining the current price; or (3) contract the production of the pies to a national restaurant chain, giving Shelly a percentage of profits with minimal involvement.

Discussion Questions

1. Explain and demonstrate the relationship between supply and demand for Mrs. Acres Homemade Pies.
2. What challenges does Shelly face as she considers the three options?
3. What would you do in Shelly's position?

The Nature of Competition

competition
the rivalry among businesses for consumers' dollars

Competition, the rivalry among businesses for consumers' dollars, is another vital element in free enterprise. According to Adam Smith, competition fosters efficiency and low prices by forcing producers to offer the best products at the most reasonable price; those who fail to do so are not able to stay in business. Thus, competition should improve the quality of the goods and services available or reduce prices. For example, thanks to smart design and excellent timing, Apple dominates the market for downloadable music with its iTunes online service and iPod MP3 player. However, many companies have set their sights on capturing some of the firm's market share with new products of their own. Wal-Mart and Microsoft have launched online music services, while many rival computer firms have introduced MP3 players with new features and/or lower prices.[15]

Within a free-enterprise system, there are four types of competitive environments: pure competition, monopolistic competition, oligopoly, and monopoly.

pure competition
the market structure that exists when there are many small businesses selling one standardized product

Pure competition exists when there are many small businesses selling one standardized product, such as agricultural commodities like wheat, corn, and cotton. No one business sells enough of the product to influence the product's price. And, because there is no difference in the products, prices are determined solely by the forces of supply and demand.

monopolistic competition
the market structure that exists when there are fewer businesses than in a pure-competition environment and the differences among the goods they sell are small

Monopolistic competition exists when there are fewer businesses than in a pure-competition environment and the differences among the goods they sell is small. Aspirin, soft drinks, and vacuum cleaners are examples of such goods. These products differ slightly in packaging, warranty, name, and other characteristics, but all satisfy the same consumer need. Businesses have some power over the price they charge in monopolistic competition because they can make consumers aware of product differences through advertising. Consumers value some features more than others and are often willing to pay higher prices for a product with the features they want. For example, Advil, a nonprescription pain reliever, contains ibuprofen instead of aspirin. Consumers who cannot take aspirin or who believe ibuprofen is a more effective pain reliever may not mind paying a little extra for the ibuprofen in Advil.

Consider Ethics and Responsibility
Has Wal-Mart Become Too Powerful?

When you purchased school supplies or shopped for items for your home or dorm room, did you consider where to go for the lowest prices? If you did, chances are you went to Wal-Mart, a company that lives obsessively by its low-price mantra and as a result has come to dominate sales in a number of product categories, including home textiles and personal care items. Wal-Mart is often called a "retail giant" or "retail king," but some argue that these are understatements given the enormous influence the company wields. After all, Wal-Mart is not only the largest retailer, with 4,800 stores around the world, but the world's largest company, with $256 billion in revenues in 2003. A basic issue is that Wal-Mart has gotten so big that it is able to do virtually anything it wants in some areas, but this kind of power has enormous ethical and social implications.

Suppliers report that Wal-Mart is able to dictate almost every aspect of their operations—from product design to pricing—in an effort to deliver maximum savings to the consumer. To meet Wal-Mart's demands for lower prices, some suppliers have been forced into laying off employees or moving operations to foreign countries where production costs are cheaper. Companies that balk can risk losing their most lucrative outlet and will find their products quickly replaced by a competitor's on Wal-Mart's shelves. Some suppliers have complained to federal regulators, arguing that Wal-Mart effectively operates as a "monopsony," a competitive condition that exists when one or more companies gain sufficient power to push suppliers' prices down.

Wal-Mart stores can also wreak havoc on businesses and workers in communities. After Wal-Mart entered the Oklahoma City market, 30 supermarkets closed their doors. Indeed, experts project that every Wal-Mart Supercenter that opens in the next five years will result in the closure of two traditional supermarkets. The demise of local businesses means the loss of jobs, and although some workers may be rehired by Wal-Mart, workers at Wal-Mart generally receive lower pay and fewer benefits than workers at other retail stores. Because of the vast Wal-Mart workforce, these policies have been blamed for driving down retail wages across America. Other employment issues that have significant ethical and legal ramifications are allegations that Wal-Mart workers have been forced to work "off the clock" and that it has discriminated against women and minorities in promotions to management positions.

Another consequence of Wal-Mart's dominance is that the company has become, in essence, an arbiter of culture. The retailer is famous for banning music and videos with what it deems objectionable content; it is nonetheless the biggest seller of CDs, videocassettes, and DVDs. Consequently, record companies are producing "sanitized" versions of albums exclusively for Wal-Mart. Other products that Wal-Mart has chosen not to sell are racy, male-oriented magazines such as *Maxim,* and the "morning-after" pill that prevents unwanted pregnancy.

Unquestionably, there are benefits to Wal-Mart's philosophy: It has compelled suppliers to concentrate on efficiency and to innovate with new products (to avoid fewer competitors), it has revived more than one floundering company, and it has directly and indirectly saved consumers an estimated $100 billion a year. But the real costs of Wal-Mart's philosophy have yet to be tallied up. As the world's largest company, it must accept the public scrutiny and social responsibilities that come with the territory.[16]

Discussion Questions
1. When Wal-Mart entered the market, retailing was highly competitive. Evaluate the competitive environment of retailing today.
2. Since Wal-Mart has the largest share of the market for many products, such as personal care products, what effect has this had on companies that manufacture these products for Wal-Mart?
3. Is there a danger of Wal-Mart becoming too powerful in our competitive system?

An **oligopoly** exists when there are very few businesses selling a product. In an oligopoly, individual businesses have control over their products' price because each business supplies a large portion of the products sold in the marketplace. Nonetheless, the prices charged by different firms stay fairly close because a price cut or increase by one company will trigger a similar response from another company. In the airline industry, for example, when one airline cuts fares to boost sales, other airlines quickly follow with rate decreases to remain competitive. Oligopolies exist when it is expensive for new firms to enter the marketplace. Not just anyone can acquire enough financial capital to build an automobile production facility or purchase enough airplanes and related resources to build an airline.

When there is one business providing a product in a given market, a **monopoly** exists. Utility companies that supply electricity, natural gas, and water are monopolies. The

oligopoly
the market structure that exists when there are very few businesses selling a product

monopoly
the market structure that exists when there is only one business providing a product in a given market

economic expansion
the situation that occurs when an economy is growing and people are spending more money; their purchases stimulate the production of goods and services, which in turn stimulates employment

inflation
a condition characterized by a continuing rise in prices

economic contraction
a slowdown of the economy characterized by a decline in spending and during which businesses cut back on production and lay off workers

recession
a decline in production, employment, and income

unemployment
the condition in which a percentage of the population wants to work but is unable to find jobs

government permits such monopolies because the cost of creating the good or supplying the service is so great that new producers cannot compete for sales. Government-granted monopolies are subject to government-regulated prices. Some monopolies exist because of technological developments that are protected by patent laws. Patent laws grant the developer of new technology a period of time (usually 17 years) during which no other producer can use the same technology without the agreement of the original developer. The United States granted the first patent in 1790, and the patent office received an estimated 355,000 patent applications in 2003.[17] This monopoly allows the developer to recover research, development, and production expenses and to earn a reasonable profit. Examples of this type of monopoly are the dry-copier process developed by Xerox and the self-developing photographic technology created by Polaroid. Both companies operated for years without competition and could charge premium prices because no alternative products existed to compete with their products. Through continuous development, Polaroid maintains market dominance. Xerox's patents have expired, however, and many imitators have forced market prices to decline.

Economic Cycles and Productivity

Expansion and Contraction.   Economies are not stagnant; they expand and contract. **Economic expansion** occurs when an economy is growing and people are spending more money. Their purchases stimulate the production of goods and services, which in turn stimulates employment. The standard of living rises because more people are employed and have money to spend. Rapid expansions of the economy, however, may result in **inflation,** a continuing rise in prices. Inflation can be harmful if individuals' incomes do not increase at the same pace as rising prices, reducing their buying power. The Democratic Republic of Congo has the highest inflation rate at 358 percent.[18]

Economic contraction occurs when spending declines. Businesses cut back on production and lay off workers, and the economy as a whole slows down. Contractions of the economy lead to **recession**—a decline in production, employment, and income. Recessions are often characterized by rising levels of **unemployment,** which is measured as the percentage of the population that wants to work but is unable to find jobs. Figure 1.3 shows the overall unemploy-

FIGURE 1.3

Overall Unemployment Rate in the U.S. Civilian Labor Force

Source: "Overall Unemployment Rate in the Civilian Labor Force, 1920–2002," *InfoPlease* (n.d.), www.infoplease.com/ipa/ A0104719.html (accessed February 16, 2004).

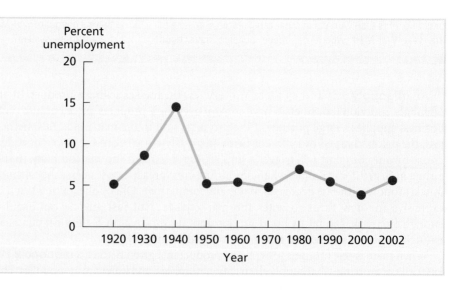

ment rate in the civilian labor force over the past 80 years. Rising unemployment levels tend to stifle demand for goods and services, which can have the effect of forcing prices downward, a condition known as *deflation.* The United States has experienced numerous recessions, the most recent being 1990–1991 and 2001–2002; Japan has also experienced numerous recessions in the last decade. A severe recession may turn into a **depression,** in which unemployment is very high, consumer spending is low, and business output is sharply reduced, such as occurred in the United States in the early 1930s.

Economies expand and contract in response to changes in consumer, business, and government spending. War, too, can affect an economy, sometimes stimulating it (as in the United States during World Wars I and II) and sometimes stifling it (as during the Vietnam and Persian Gulf wars). Although fluctuations in the economy are inevitable and to a certain extent predictable, their effects—inflation and unemployment—disrupt lives and thus governments try to minimize them.

Measuring the Economy.   Countries measure the state of their economies to determine whether they are expanding or contracting and whether corrective action is necessary to minimize the fluctuations. One commonly used measure is **gross domestic product (GDP)**—the sum of all goods and services produced in a country during a year. GDP measures only those goods and services made within a country and therefore does not include profits from companies' overseas operations; it does include profits earned by foreign companies within the country being measured. However, it does not take into account the concept of GDP in relation to population (GDP per capita). Figure 1.4 shows the increase in GDP over several years, while Table 1.2 compares a number of economic statistics for a sampling of countries.

Another important indicator of a nation's economic health is the relationship between its spending and income (from taxes). When a nation spends more than it takes in from taxes, it has a **budget deficit.** In the 1990s, the U.S. government eliminated its long-standing budget deficit by balancing the money spent for social, defense, and other programs with the amount of money taken in from taxes.

depression
a condition of the economy in which unemployment is very high, consumer spending is low, and business output is sharply reduced

gross domestic product (GDP)
the sum of all goods and services produced in a country during a year

budget deficit
the condition in which a nation spends more than it takes in from taxes

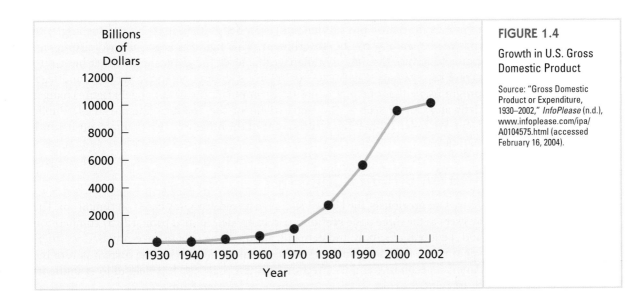

FIGURE 1.4

Growth in U.S. Gross Domestic Product

Source: "Gross Domestic Product or Expenditure, 1930–2002," *InfoPlease* (n.d.), www.infoplease.com/ipa/A0104575.html (accessed February 16, 2004).

TABLE 1.2   A Comparative Economic Analysis of a Sampling of Countries

Country	GDP (in billions of U.S. dollars)	GDP per capita (in U.S. dollars)	Unemployment rate (%)	Inflation rate (%)
Argentina	$403.8	$10,500	21.5	41
Australia	525.5	26,900	6.3	2.8
Brazil	1,376	7,600	6.4	8.3
Canada	934.1	29,300	7.6	2.2
China	5,989	4,700	10*	−0.8
France	1,558	26,000	9.1	1.8
Germany	2,160	26,200	9.8	1.3
India	2,664	2,600	8.8	5.4
Israel	117.4	19,500	10.4	5.7
Japan	3,651	28,700	5.4	−0.9
Mexico	924.4	8,900	3*	6.4
Russia	1,409	9,700	7.9	15
South Africa	427.7	10,000	37**	9.9
United Kingdom	1,528	25,500	5.2	2.1
United States	10,450	36,300	5.8	1.6

* Estimated for urban areas; unemployment rates in rural areas may be higher.

** Includes those no longer looking for jobs.

Source: CIA, "Field Listing," *The World Fact Book 2003* (n.d.), www.cia.gov/cia/publications/factbook/ (accessed January 16, 2004).

In recent years, however, the budget deficit has reemerged and grown to record levels, partly due to defense spending in the aftermath of the terrorist attacks of September 11, 2001. Because Americans do not want their taxes increased, it is difficult for the federal government to bring in more revenue and reduce the deficit. Like consumers and businesses, when the government needs money, it borrows from the public, banks, and other institutions. The national debt (the amount of money the nation owes its lenders) exceeded $7 trillion in 2004,[19] due largely to increased spending by the government. This figure is especially worrisome because, to reduce the debt to a manageable level, the government either has to increase its revenues (raise taxes) or reduce spending on social, defense, and legal programs, neither of which is politically popular. The national debt figure changes daily and can be seen at the Department of the Treasury, Bureau of the Public Debt, Web site. Table 1.3 describes some of the other ways we evaluate our nation's economy.

The American Economy

As we said previously, the United States is a mixed economy based on capitalism. The answers to the three basic economic issues are determined primarily by competition and the forces of supply and demand, although the federal government does intervene in economic decisions to a certain extent. To understand the current state of the American economy and its effect on business practices, it is helpful to examine its history and the roles of the entrepreneur and the government.

Unit of Measure	Description
Trade balance	The difference between our exports and our imports. If the balance is negative, as it has been since the mid-1980s, it is called a trade deficit and is generally viewed as unhealthy for our economy.
Consumer Price Index	Measures changes in prices of goods and services purchased for consumption by typical urban households.
Per capita income	Indicates the income level of "average" Americans. Useful in determing how much "average" consumers spend and how much money Americans are earning.
Unemployment rate	Indicates how many working age Americans are not working who otherwise want to work.*
Inflation	Monitors price increases in consumer goods and services over specified periods of time. Used to determine if costs of goods and services are exceeding worker compensation over time.
Worker productivity	The amount of goods and services produced for each hour worked.

TABLE 1.3

How Do We Evaluate Our Nation's Economy?

*Americans who do not want to work in a traditional sense, such as househusbands/ housewives, are not counted as unemployed.

A Brief History of the American Economy

The Early Economy.   Before the colonization of North America, Native Americans lived as hunter/gatherers and farmers, with some trade among tribes. The colonists who came later operated primarily as an *agricultural economy*. People were self-sufficient and produced everything they needed at home, including food, clothing, and furniture. Abundant natural resources and a moderate climate nourished industries such as farming, fishing, shipping, and fur trading. A few manufactured goods and money for the colonies' burgeoning industries came from England and other countries.

As the nation expanded slowly toward the West, people found natural resources such as coal, copper, and iron ore and used them to produce goods such as horseshoes, farm implements, and kitchen utensils. Farm families who produced surplus goods sold or traded them for things they could not produce themselves, such as fine furniture and window glass. Some families also spent time turning raw materials into clothes and household goods. Because these goods were produced at home, this system was called the domestic system.

The Industrial Revolution.   The 19th century and the Industrial Revolution brought the development of new technology and factories. The factory brought together all the resources needed to make a product—materials, machines, and workers. Work in factories became specialized as workers focused on one or two tasks. As work became more efficient, productivity increased, making more goods available at lower prices. Railroads brought major changes, allowing farmers to send their surplus crops and goods all over the nation for barter or for sale.

Factories began to spring up along the railways to manufacture farm equipment and a variety of other goods to be shipped by rail. Samuel Slater set up the first American textile factory after he memorized the plans for an English factory and emigrated to the United States. Eli Whitney revolutionized the cotton industry with his cotton gin. Francis Cabot Lowell's factory organized all the steps in manufacturing cotton cloth for maximum efficiency and productivity. John Deere's farm equipment increased farm production and reduced the number of farmers required to feed the young nation. Farmers began to move to cities to find jobs in factories and a higher standard of living. Henry Ford developed the assembly-line system to produce automobiles. Workers focused on one part of an automobile and then pushed it to the next stage until it rolled off the assembly line as a finished automobile. Ford's assembly line could manufacture many automobiles efficiently, and the price of his cars was $200, making them affordable to many Americans.

By the 1960s, more and more women were entering the workforce.

The Manufacturing and Marketing Economies. Industrialization brought increased prosperity, and the United States gradually became a *manufacturing economy*—one devoted to manufacturing goods and providing services rather than producing agricultural products. The assembly line was applied to more industries, increasing the variety of goods available to the consumer. Businesses became more concerned with the needs of the consumer and entered the *marketing economy*. Expensive goods such as cars and appliances could be purchased on a time-payment plan. Companies conducted research to find out what products consumers needed and wanted. Advertising made consumers aware of differences in products and prices.

Because these developments occurred in a free-enterprise system, consumers determined what goods and services were produced. They did this by purchasing the products they liked at prices they were willing to pay. The United States prospered, and American citizens had one of the highest standards of living in the world.

The Service and Internet-based Economy. After World War II, with the increased standard of living, Americans had more money and more time. They began to pay others to perform services that made their lives easier. Beginning in the 1960s, more and more women entered the workforce. The profile of the family changed: Today there are more single-parent families and individuals living alone, and in two-parent families, both parents often work. One result of this trend is that time-pressed Americans are increasingly paying others to do tasks they used to do at home, like cooking, laundry, landscaping, and child care. These trends have gradually changed the United States to a *service economy*—one devoted to the production of services that make life easier for busy consumers. Service industries such as restaurants, banking, medicine, child care, auto repair, leisure-related industries, and even education are growing rapidly and may account for as much as 80 percent of the U.S. economy. These trends continue with advanced technology contributing to new service products such as overnight mail, electronic banking, and shopping through cable television networks and the Internet. Table 1.4 shows e-commerce spending in the United States from 2003 to 2008. More about the Internet and e-commerce can be found in Chapter 4.

Did You Know?   60 percent of adult women work.[20]

As this ad demonstrates, e-commerce has made it possible for companies to align shared interests for the sake of new opportunities just about anywhere.

2003	$ 95.7
2004	122.6
2005	149.2
2006	176.8
2007	204.3
2008	229.9

TABLE 1.4

Internet Retail Sales in the United States, 2003–2008* (in billions)

* Totals are estimates or projections.

Source: Forrester Research in "Statistics: International Online Shopper," Shop.org, www.shop.org/learn/stats_intshop_general.html (accessed March 19, 2004)

The Role of the Entrepreneur

An **entrepreneur** is an individual who risks his or her wealth, time, and effort to develop for profit an innovative product or way of doing something. Consider the story of Burt's Bees. Roxanne Quimby, a divorced mother, and Burt Shavitz, a beekeeper, teamed up in 1984 to sell products made from the beeswax of Burt's bees at craft fairs. Quimby grew the small Maine business into a leading natural personal-care products firm by focusing on what customers wanted. After moving the company to North Carolina, Quimby sold 80 percent of Burt's Bees to a private investment firm for $175 million in 2003 and planned to use part of the proceeds to help establish a national park in northern Maine.[21]

entrepreneur
an individual who risks his or her wealth, time, and effort to develop for profit an innovative product or way of doing something

Burt's Bees began as an endeavor to sell products made from beeswax at craft fairs in Maine.

The free-enterprise system provides the conditions necessary for entrepreneurs to succeed. In the past, entrepreneurs were often inventors who brought all the factors of production together to produce a new product. Thomas Edison, whose inventions include the record player and light bulb, was an early American entrepreneur. Henry Ford was one of the first persons to develop mass assembly methods in the automobile industry. Other entrepreneurs, so-called "captains of industry," invested in the country's growth. John D. Rockefeller built Standard Oil out of the fledgling oil industry, and Andrew Carnegie invested in railroads and founded the United States Steel Corporation. Andrew Mellon built the Aluminum Company of America and Gulf Oil. J. P. Morgan started financial institutions to fund the business activities of other entrepreneurs. Although these entrepreneurs were born in another century, their legacy to the American economy lives on in the companies they started, many of which still operate today. Henry Ford's company, for example, celebrated its 100th birthday in 2003 under the leadership of his great grandson William Clay Ford, Jr. Ford Motor Company has grown to the second largest automaker in the world with $162.7 billion in revenues from vehicles with such well-known marques as Jaguar, Volvo, Land Rover, and Astin Martin, as well as Ford, Lincoln, and Mercury.[22]

Entrepreneurs are constantly changing American business practices with new technology and innovative management techniques. Bill Gates, for example, built Microsoft, a software company whose products include MS-DOS (a disk operating system), Word, and Windows, into a multibillion-dollar enterprise. Frederick Smith had an idea to deliver packages overnight, and now his FedEx Company plays an important role in getting documents and packages delivered all over the world for businesses and individuals. Entrepreneurs have been associated with such uniquely American concepts as Dell Computers, Ben & Jerry's, Levi's, Holiday Inns, McDonald's, Dr Pepper, and Wal-Mart. Wal-Mart, founded by entrepreneur Sam Walton, was the first retailer to reach $100 billion in sales in one year and now routinely passes that mark. Wal-Mart has nearly 1.5 million employees and operates 4,800 stores in 10 countries, including Canada and Mexico, which serve more than 138 million shoppers a week.[23] We will examine the importance of entrepreneurship further in Chapter 6.

The Role of Government in the American Economy

The American economic system is best described as modified capitalism because the government regulates business to preserve competition and protect consumers and employees. Federal, state, and local governments intervene in the economy with laws and regulations designed to promote competition and to protect consumers, employees, and the environment. Many of these laws are discussed in Appendix A.

Additionally, government agencies such as the U.S. Department of Commerce measure the health of the economy (GDP, productivity, etc.) and, when necessary, take steps to minimize the disruptive effects of economic fluctuations and reduce unemployment. When the economy is contracting and unemployment is rising, the federal government through the Federal Reserve Board (see Chapter 14) tries to spur growth so that consumers will spend more money and businesses will hire more employees. To accomplish this, it may reduce interest rates or increase its own spending for goods and services. When the economy expands so fast that inflation results, the government may intervene to reduce inflation by slowing down economic growth. This can be accomplished by raising interest rates to discourage spending by businesses and consumers. Techniques used to control the economy are discussed in Chapter 14.

The Role of Ethics and Social Responsibility in Business

In the last few years, you may have read about a number of scandals at a number of well-known corporations, including Enron, WorldCom, Tyco, and Arthur Andersen. In many cases, misconduct by individuals within these firms had an adverse effect on current and retired employees, investors, and others associated with these firms. In some cases, individuals went to jail for their actions. Martha Stewart, for example, was convicted of obstructing justice and lying to federal investigators looking into whether she engaged in insider trading of the stock of ImClone.[24] These scandals undermined public confidence in Corporate America and sparked a new debate about ethics in business. Business ethics generally refers to the standards and principles used by society to define appropriate and inappropriate conduct in the workplace. In many cases, these standards have been codified as laws prohibiting actions deemed unacceptable.

Society is increasingly demanding that businesspeople behave ethically and socially responsibly toward not only their customers but also their employees, investors, government regulators, communities, and the natural environment. Green Mountain Coffee Roasters, for example, has pledged to pay above-market prices for coffee beans to farmer cooperatives in Central and South America in order to help boost the quality of life in those regions. General Mills supports minority-owned suppliers and charities that target women and minorities.[25] Thus, social responsibility relates to the impact of business on society.

One of the primary lessons of the scandals of the early 2000s has been that the reputation of business organizations depends not just on bottom-line profits but also on ethical conduct and concern for the welfare of others. Consider that in the aftermath of these scandals, the reputations of every U.S. company suffered regardless of their association with the scandals.[26] However, there are signs that business ethics is improving. One respected survey

In late 2002-2003, major airlines were still trying to recover from economic pressures and 9/11. Don Carty, then CEO of American Airlines, called on employee unions to accept annual concessions in pay and benefits in order to keep American afloat. But it was later revealed that Carty and other executives not only had kept their own pensions protected, but executive-retention bonuses as well. Carty ceased to be American's CEO in 2003.

reported that observed misconduct in the workplace declined from 31 percent in 2000 to 22 percent in 2003, and that observed pressure to act illegally or unethically fell from 13 percent to 10 percent during the same time period.[27] Although these results suggest that ethics is improving, the fact that employees continue to report observing misconduct and experiencing pressure to engage in unethical or illegal acts remains troubling and suggests that companies need to continue their efforts to raise ethical standards. We take a closer look at ethics and social responsibility in business in Chapter 2.

Can You Learn Business in a Classroom?

Obviously, the answer is yes, or there would be no purpose for this textbook! To be successful in business, you need knowledge, skills, experience, and good judgment. The topics covered in this chapter and throughout this book provide some of the knowledge you need to understand the world of business. The opening vignette at the beginning of each chapter, boxes, examples within each chapter, and the case at the end of each chapter describe experiences to help you develop good business judgment. The "Build Your Skills" exercise at the end of each chapter and the "Solve the Dilemma" box will help you develop skills that may be useful in your future career. However, good judgment is based on knowledge and experience plus personal insight and understanding. Therefore, you need more courses in business, along with some practical experience in the business world, to help you develop the special insight necessary to put your personal stamp on knowledge as you apply it. The challenge in business is in the area of judgment, and judgment does not develop from memorizing an introductory business textbook. If you are observant in your daily experiences as an employee, as a student, and as a consumer, you will improve your ability to make good business judgments.

Figure 1.5 is an overview of how the chapters in this book are linked together and how the chapters relate to the participants, the activities, and the environmental factors found in the business world. The topics presented in the chapters that follow are those that will give you the best opportunity to begin the process of understanding the world of business.

Explore Your Career Options
Changes

The only thing certain anymore is that the world is constantly changing, and this applies to future career options for you and your classmates. The traditional career track that earlier generations followed, in which a person started working at one company upon graduation and worked his or her way up until retirement, is passé. In fact, the average large corporation replaces the equivalent of its entire workforce every four years. Moreover, constantly evolving technology means today's graduates and workers need to be computer literate and able to adapt to new technologies. The globalization of business suggests that you be fluent in a second or even third language, for there is a good chance that you'll be working with people from around the world, and you may even do a stint overseas yourself. Changes in the makeup of the workforce mean more doors opening for women and minorities as companies recognize the need to understand and cater to the desires of a diverse customer base.

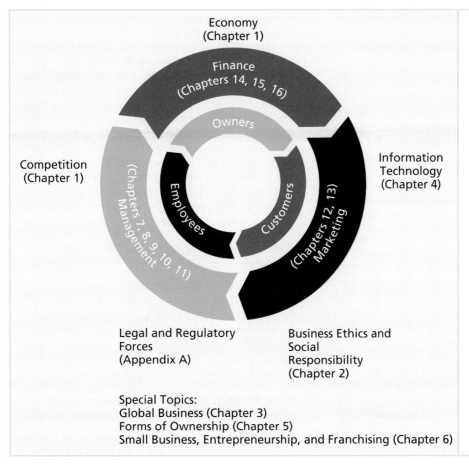

FIGURE 1.5

The Organization of This Book

Economy (Chapter 1)

Finance (Chapters 14, 15, 16)

Owners

Competition (Chapter 1)

(Chapters 7, 8, 9, 10, 11) Management

Employees

Customers

(Chapters 12, 13) Marketing

Information Technology (Chapter 4)

Legal and Regulatory Forces (Appendix A)

Business Ethics and Social Responsibility (Chapter 2)

Special Topics:
Global Business (Chapter 3)
Forms of Ownership (Chapter 5)
Small Business, Entrepreneurship, and Franchising (Chapter 6)

Changes in organizational structure may require you to work in teams, where communication is a crucial skill, or they may leave you out of the corporate hierarchy altogether, and instead put you in an entrepreneurial role as a self-employed contractor or small-business owner.

Because of these and other changes taking place in the business world that we will discuss throughout this book, when you enter the workforce full time, you are far more likely to define yourself by what you do ("I design RISC chips") than by your employer ("I work for Motorola"). And, you're more likely to think in terms of short-term projects, such as launching a product or reengineering a process, rather than a long-term career track like the one your grandfather may have followed.

This business course and textbook, including the boxes, cases, and skills-building exercises, will help you learn the basic knowledge, skills, and trends that you can use whether you work for a corporation or run your own small business, whether you work in upper management or on the shop floor. Along the way, we'll introduce you to some specific careers and offer advice on developing your own job opportunities in career boxes in each chapter. We also present salary range information for different types/levels of jobs. According to the 2000 Census, the average U.S. family earned $63,410 annually, and the breakdown of earnings was:

Less than $15,000	10.4%
$15,000–$34,999	23.3%
$35,000–$49,999	16.8%
$50,000–$74,999	22.0%
$75,000–$99,999	12.3%
$100,000–$149,999	9.7%
$150,000+	5.5%[28]

Review Your Understanding

Define basic concepts such as business, product, and profit.

A business is an organization or individual that seeks a profit by providing products that satisfy people's needs. A product is a good, service, or idea that has both tangible and intangible characteristics that provide satisfaction and benefits. Profit, the basic goal of business, is the difference between what it costs to make and sell a product and what a customer pays for it.

Identify the main participants and activities of business and explain why studying business is important.

The three main participants in business are owners, employees, and customers, but others—government regulators, suppliers, social groups, etc.—are also important. Management involves planning, organizing, and controlling the tasks required to carry out the work of the company. Marketing refers to those activities—research, product development, promotion, pricing, and distribution—designed to provide goods and services that satisfy customers. Finance refers to activities concerned with funding a business and using its funds effectively. Studying business can help you prepare for a career and become a better consumer.

Define economics and compare the four types of economic systems.

Economics is the study of how resources are distributed for the production of goods and services within a social system; an economic system describes how a particular society distributes its resources. Communism is an economic system in which the people, without regard to class, own all the nation's resources. In a socialist system, the government owns and operates basic industries, but individuals own most businesses. Under capitalism, individuals own and operate the majority of businesses that provide goods and services. Mixed economies have elements from more than one economic system; most countries have mixed economies.

Describe the role of supply, demand, and competition in a free-enterprise system.

In a free-enterprise system, individuals own and operate the majority of businesses, and the distribution of resources is determined by competition, supply, and demand. Demand is the number of goods and services that consumers are willing to buy at different prices at a specific time. Supply is the number of goods or services that businesses are willing to sell at different prices at a specific time. The price at which the supply of a product equals demand at a specific point in time is the equilibrium price. Competition is the rivalry among businesses to convince consumers to buy goods or services. Four types of competitive environments are pure competition, monopolistic competition, oligopoly, and monopoly. These economic concepts determine how businesses may operate in a particular society and, often, how much they can charge for their products.

Specify why and how the health of the economy is measured.

A country measures the state of its economy to determine whether it is expanding or contracting and whether the country needs to take steps to minimize fluctuations. One commonly used measure is gross domestic product (GDP), the sum of all goods and services produced in a country during a year. A budget deficit occurs when a nation spends more than it takes in from taxes.

Trace the evolution of the American economy and discuss the role of the entrepreneur in the economy.

The American economy has evolved through several stages: the early economy, the Industrial Revolution, the manufacturing economy, the marketing economy, and the service and Internet-based economy of today. Entrepreneurs play an important role because they risk their time, wealth, and efforts to develop new goods, services, and ideas that fuel the growth of the American economy.

Evaluate a small-business owner's situation and propose a course of action.

The "Solve the Dilemma" box on page 14 presents a problem for the owner of the firm. Should you, as the owner, raise prices, expand operations, or form a venture with a larger company to deal with demand? You should be able to apply your newfound understanding of the relationship between supply and demand to assess the situation and reach a decision about how to proceed.

Revisit the World of Business

1. How would you defend the satellite radio companies' decisions to continue operating despite not showing a profit?

2. Do you see the potential for additional competitors if this product/service offering becomes successful?

3. How would you evaluate XM's and Sirius's strategy of forming exclusive alliances with auto manufacturers?

Learn the Terms

budget deficit   17

business   4

capitalism, or free enterprise   10

communism   10

competition   14

demand   12

depression   17

economic contraction   16

economic expansion   16

economic system   9

economics   9

entrepreneur   21

equilibrium price   12

financial resources   9

free-market system   10

gross domestic product (GDP)   17

human resources   9

inflation   16

mixed economies   11

monopolistic competition   14

monopoly   15

natural resources   9

nonprofit organizations   4

oligopoly   15

product   4

profit   4

pure competition   14

recession   16

socialism   10

stakeholders   5

supply   12

unemployment   16

Check Your Progress

1. What is the fundamental goal of business? Do all organizations share this goal?

2. Name the forms a product may take and give some examples of each.

3. Who are the main participants of business? What are the main activities? What other factors have an impact on the conduct of business in the United States?

4. What are four types of economic systems? Can you provide an example of a country using each type?

5. Explain the terms *supply, demand, equilibrium price,* and *competition.* How do these forces interact in the American economy?

6. List the four types of competitive environments and provide an example of a product of each environment.

7. List and define the various measures governments may use to gauge the state of their economies. If unemployment is high, will the growth of GDP be great or small?

8. Why are fluctuations in the economy harmful?

9. How did the Industrial Revolution influence the growth of the American economy? Why do we apply the term *service economy* to the United States today?

10. Explain the federal government's role in the American economy.

Get Involved

1. Discuss the economic changes occurring in Russia and Eastern European countries, which once operated as communist economic systems. Why are these changes occurring? What do you think the result will be?

2. Why is it important for the government to measure the economy? What kinds of actions might it take to control the economy's growth?

3. Is the American economy currently expanding or contracting? Defend your answer with the latest statistics on GDP, inflation, unemployment, and so on. How is the federal government responding?

Build Your Skills

THE FORCES OF SUPPLY AND DEMAND

Background:
WagWumps are a new children's toy with the potential to be a highly successful product. WagWumps are cute, furry, and their eyes glow in the dark. Each family set consists of a mother, a father, and two children. Wee-Toys' manufacturing costs are about $6 per set, with $3 representing marketing and distribution costs. The wholesale price of a WagWump family for a retailer is $15.75, and the toy carries a suggested retail price of $26.99.

FIGURE 1.6

Equilibrium Price
of WagWumps

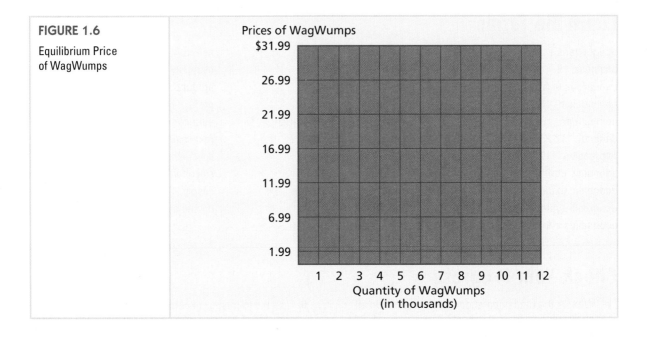

Prices of WagWumps

Quantity of WagWumps
(in thousands)

Task:

Assume you are a decision maker at a retailer, such as Target or Wal-Mart, that must determine the price the stores in your district should charge customers for the WagWump family set. From the information provided above, you know that the SRP (suggested retail price) is $26.99 per set and that your company can purchase the toy set from your wholesaler for $15.75 each. Based on the following assumptions, plot your company's supply curve on the graph provided in Figure 1.6 and label it "supply curve."

Quantity	Price
3,000	$16.99
5,000	21.99
7,000	26.99

Using the following assumptions, plot your customers' demand curve on Figure 1.6, and label it "demand curve."

Quantity	Price
10,000	$16.99
6,000	21.99
2,000	26.99

For this specific time, determine the point at which the quantity of toys your company is willing to supply equals the quantity of toys the customers in your sales district are willing to buy, and label that point "equilibrium price."

e-Xtreme Surfing

- **Bureau of the Public Debt**
  http://www.publicdebt.treas.gov/opd/opdpdodt.htm

- **Entrepreneur Test**
  http://www.liraz.com/webquiz.htm

- **U.S. Department of Commerce**
  www.commerce.gov/

Lists the current public debt, to the penny, and archives past information about the public debt.

Offers a quiz to help you determine whether you have what it takes to become an entrepreneur.

Offers a wealth of information about the state of U.S. economy, including useful statistics and resources.

See for Yourself Videocase

STARBUCKS

Starbucks Corporation was founded in Seattle's open-air farmer's market in 1971. In 1982, Howard Schultz joined Starbucks as director of retail operations and marketing. After visiting Milan, Italy, with its 1,500 coffee bars, Schultz saw the opportunity to develop a similar retail coffee-bar culture in Seattle. He began his own downtown Seattle coffee bar serving Starbucks coffee and espresso beverages. Based on the coffee bar's success, Schultz acquired the assets of Starbucks and began opening stores across the United States in 1987.

Since its start-up in 1971, the company has done things its own way, becoming an industry pioneer in employee management and social responsibility. Starbucks extends health benefits to all employees, including part-timers, and provides a stock option program worth 12 percent of each employee's base pay. This policy has kept employee turnover rates well below those of competitors and granted the company a spot on *Fortune* magazine's annual list of the "Best Places to Work." The company enjoys an excellent reputation in Latin America as a result of its focus on environmental conservation and the welfare of farmers who grow its coffee. Starbucks pays better-than-market-value prices for coffee beans so that Latin American farmers can afford to treat their laborers well. Its efforts have been well rewarded with annual sales in excess of $1 billion as well as growing acceptance around the world.

Starbucks reversed a downward trend in the consumption of gourmet coffee that started in the early 1960s. The Starbucks Coffee bar created a warm environment where people could relax and socialize over coffee and coffee drinks. Starbucks became a stylish environment that attracted younger customers who discovered coffee drinks after years of cola drinks.

In its company operated retail stores, Starbucks sells whole bean coffees and coffee-related accessories and equipment. Starbucks also sells products through its catalog, mail-order service, and the Internet. Starbucks signed joint ventures with Pepsi-Cola to sell a bottled version of the Frappuccino blended beverage and with Dreyer's to sell six flavors of Starbucks Ice Cream and Frozen Novelties. Starbucks Ice Cream became the No. 1 brand of coffee ice cream in the U.S. Starbucks signed an agreement with Kraft Foods to distribute whole bean coffees through 30,000 supermarkets and this market is growing.

The company already has more than 1,500 shops in 28 countries, and it opens an average of three new stores every day somewhere in the world. In Japan alone, it serves more than 2 million customers a week. Starbucks exceeded its goal of opening 4,000 stores by 2001, and has since altered that goal to 10,000 shops by 2005. The company recently opened its first stores in Turkey, Oman, and Chile. In China, a tea-drinking nation, Starbucks hopes to develop coffee drinking among the locals, as well as cater to international customers. Hoping to reach the average consumer, prices have been set very low in comparison to local competition. For instance, a cup of house blend coffee sells for 9 Yuan compared to 22 Yuan ($2.66) for local coffee. Today Starbucks has 500 stores in 12 Asian countries and a total of 1,000 stores in 22 markets outside the U.S. The quality of the product and the brand name has made Starbucks a global product.

The company's goal is to establish Starbucks as the most recognized and respected brand of coffee in the world. To achieve this goal, the company plans to expand retail operations, grow its joint ventures and specialty sales, and leverage the Starbucks brand through the introduction of new products and the development of new ways to distribute its products. Starbucks serves 230 million customers in its stores each week and this figure is growing.

While striving to meet its goal, Starbucks has maintained an excellent reputation for social responsibility and business ethics. Starbucks donated $1 million to the September 11th fund immediately after terrorist attacks in New York and Washington, DC. Cash contributions to this fund to assist victims and their families were accepted at all company-owned Starbucks stores. The company also is committed to a role of environmental leadership in the coffee industry. Starbucks developed a global code of ethics to protect workers who harvest coffee and maintains efforts aimed at increasing the income of small-scale coffee growers. The company provides employees (even part-timers) with the opportunity for stock ownership. In addition, the company supports philanthropic efforts through a nonprofit foundation.[29]

Questions

1. How did Starbucks take a declining product and turn it into a highly successful business concept with few competitors?

2. How has Starbucks been able to sell its brand name through joint ventures with other companies?

3. What is the potential contribution of Starbucks' involvement in activities to support those that produce coffee beans, its own employees, and the communities where it has stores?

Remember to check out our Online Learning Center at www.mhhe.com/ferrell5e.

Chapter 2

Business Ethics and Social Responsibility

OBJECTIVES

After reading this chapter, you will be able to:

- Define business ethics and social responsibility and examine their importance.

- Detect some of the ethical issues that may arise in business.

- Specify how businesses can promote ethical behavior.

- Explain the four dimensions of social responsibility.

- Debate an organization's social responsibilities to owners, employees, consumers, the environment, and the community.

- Evaluate the ethics of a business's decision.

The Home Depot Helps Build Better Communities

The Home Depot employs approximately 300,000 people and operates more than 1,700 stores in all 50 states, the District of Columbia, Puerto Rico, eight Canadian provinces, and Mexico. It also operates four wholly owned subsidiaries: Apex Supply Company, Your Other Warehouse, Maintenance Warehouse, and HD Builder Solutions Group. The company racks up approximately $65 billion in annual sales, dominating the $900 billion worldwide market in home improvement. Home Depot is also the second-largest retailer in the United States. Now the world's largest home-improvement retailer, Home Depot continues to do things on a grand scale, including putting its corporate muscle behind a tightly focused social responsibility agenda.

Home Depot is actively involved in pursuing programs of social responsibility, business ethics, and environmental excellence. From progressive consumer education programs to certified "green" products, the company is dedicated to making a positive impact on society. As a concerned corporate citizen, the company supports organizations such as the World Wildlife Fund and The Nature Conservancy. The company also promotes Energy Star and other energy-efficient merchandise, and it offers advice about energy efficiency in customer clinics. The company sold more than 15 million Energy Star–certified products in 2003, which saved consumers approximately $134 million from their electric bills. In addition, Home Depot recycled thousands of tons of cardboard and 24.5 million wood delivery pallets in the last year.

Building better communities is a central theme for Home Depot, which it demonstrates with its support of nonprofit organizations such as Habitat for Humanity, Rebuilding Together, United Way, and KaBOOM. In 2003, the

continued

company participated in the renovation of 5,300 homes through its partnership with Rebuilding Together, and helped construct 58 playgrounds through Ka-BOOM, the company's largest nonprofit partner. Since 1996, KaBoom has built 152 playgrounds.

Home Depot has developed a strong ethics commitment for its employees and management team. For example, Home Depot is proud of its corporate governance, with 10 out of 11 of its directors being outside the company and independent. While any large corporation will be criticized for not doing more, Home Depot has a commitment to try to be a responsible member of society.[1]

Introduction

As the opening vignette illustrates, Home Depot has taken on the challenge of contributing to society through its business activities. At the other extreme, wrongdoing by some businesses has focused public attention and government involvement to encourage more acceptable business conduct. Any business decision may be judged as right or wrong, ethical or unethical, legal or illegal.

In this chapter, we will take a look at the role of ethics and social responsibility in business decision making. First we define business ethics and examine why it is important to understand ethics' role in business. Next we explore a number of business ethics issues to help you learn to recognize such issues when they arise. Finally, we consider steps businesses can take to improve ethical behavior in their organizations. The second half of the chapter focuses on social responsibility. We survey some important responsibility issues and detail how companies have responded to them.

Business Ethics and Social Responsibility

business ethics
principles and standards that determine acceptable conduct in business

In this chapter, we define **business ethics** as the principles and standards that determine acceptable conduct in business organizations. The acceptability of behavior in business is determined by customers, competitors, government regulators, interest groups, and the public, as well as each individual's personal moral principles and values. For example, Jeffrey K. Skilling, former chief executive officer of Enron, was indicted on charges that he conspired to use fraudulent accounting practices in order to deceive shareholders, creditors, and regulators about the true financial state of the energy company. When Enron's true condition was exposed in 2001, it collapsed under a mountain of debt, resulting in the layoff of thousands of employees and the loss of retirement funds for former employees whose pensions had been invested in the firm's stock. Although Skilling pleaded not guilty to the charges, the ethics of his decision will be judged by a jury.[2]

social responsibility
a business's obligation to maximize its positive impact and minimize its negative impact on society

Many consumers and social advocates believe that businesses should not only make a profit but also consider the social implications of their activities. We define **social responsibility** as a business's obligation to maximize its positive impact and minimize its negative impact on society. Although many people use the terms *social responsibility* and *ethics* interchangeably, they do not mean the same thing. Business ethics relates to an *individual's* or a *work group's* decisions that society evaluates as right or wrong, whereas social responsibility is a broader concept that concerns the impact of the *entire business's* activities on society. From an ethical perspective, for

TABLE 2.1   A Timeline of Ethical and Socially Responsible Concerns

1960s	1970s	1980s	1990s	2000s
• Environmental issues • Civil rights issues • Increased employee-employer tension • Honesty • Changing work ethic • Rising drug use	• Employee militancy • Human rights issues • Covering up rather than correcting issues	• Bribes and illegal contracting practices • Influence peddling • Deceptive advertising • Financial fraud (e.g., savings and loan scandal) • Transparency issues	• Sweatshops and unsafe working conditions in third-world countries • Rising corporate liability for personal damages (e.g., cigarette companies) • Financial mismanagement and fraud	• Cyber crime • Privacy issues • Financial mismanagement • International corruption • Loss of employee privacy • Intellectual property theft

Source: "Business Ethics Timeline," Copyright © 2003, *Ethics Resource Center* (n.d.), www.ethics.org. Used with permission.

example, we may be concerned about a health care organization overcharging the government for Medicare services. From a social responsibility perspective, we might be concerned about the impact that this overcharging will have on the ability of the health care system to provide adequate services for all citizens.

The most basic ethical and social responsibility concerns have been codified as laws and regulations that encourage businesses to conform to society's standards, values, and attitudes. For example, after accounting scandals at a number of well-known firms in the early 2000s shook public confidence in the integrity of Corporate America, the reputations of every U.S. company suffered regardless of their association with the scandals.[3] To help restore confidence in corporations and markets, Congress passed the Sarbanes-Oxley Act, which criminalized securities fraud and stiffened penalties for corporate fraud. At a minimum, managers are expected to obey all laws and regulations. Most legal issues arise as choices that society deems unethical, irresponsible, or otherwise unacceptable. However, all actions deemed unethical by society are not necessarily illegal, and both legal and ethical concerns change over time (see Table 2.1). Business law refers to the laws and regulations that govern the conduct of business. Many problems and conflicts in business can be avoided if owners, managers, and employees know more about business law and the legal system. Business ethics, social responsibility, and laws together act as a compliance system requiring that businesses and employees act responsibly in society. In this chapter, we explore ethics and social responsibility; Appendix A addresses business law, including the Sarbanes-Oxley Act.

The Role of Ethics in Business

You have only to pick up *The Wall Street Journal* or *USA Today* to see examples of the growing concern about legal and ethical issues in business. HealthSouth, for example, has joined the growing list of companies tarnished by accounting improprieties and securities fraud at the turn of the century. Former CEO Richard Scrushy was indicted for allegedly conspiring to inflate the health care firm's reported revenues by $2.7 billion in order to meet shareholder expectations. Although Scrushy pleaded "not guilty" to the 85 criminal charges, 15 former HealthSouth executives have admitted to participating in the deception. If convicted, Scrushy potentially faces

Former U.S. Representative James Trafficant was expelled from Congress and jailed after being convicted of accepting bribes.

650 years in prison, $36 million in fines, and the seizure of $279 million worth of personal assets.[4] Regardless of what an individual believes about a particular action, if society judges it to be unethical or wrong, whether correctly or not, that judgment directly affects the organization's ability to achieve its business goals.[5]

Well-publicized incidents of unethical and illegal activity—ranging from accounting fraud to using the Internet to steal another person's credit-card number, from deceptive advertising of food and diet products to unfair competitive practices in the computer software industry—strengthen the public's perceptions that ethical standards and the level of trust in business need to be raised. Author David Callahan has commented, "Americans who wouldn't so much as shoplift a pack of chewing gum are committing felonies at tax time, betraying the trust of their patients, misleading investors, ripping off their insurance companies, lying to their clients, and much more."[6] Often, such charges start as ethical conflicts but evolve into legal disputes when cooperative conflict resolution cannot be accomplished. For example, Shirley Slesinger Lasswell, whose late husband acquired the rights to Winnie the Pooh and his friends from creator A. A. Milne in 1930, filed a lawsuit against the Walt Disney Company over merchandising rights to the characters. Although Lasswell granted rights to use the character to Walt Disney, she contended that the company cheated her and her family out of millions of dollars in royalties on video sales for two decades. Disney asserted that video sales were not specified in its agreement with Lasswell and declined to pay her a percentage of those sales. A California Superior Court judge dismissed the case after 13 years of negotiations and proceedings, effectively siding with Disney.[7] Indeed, many activities deemed unethical by society have been outlawed through legislation.

However, it is important to understand that business ethics goes beyond legal issues. Ethical conduct builds trust among individuals and in business relationships, which validates and promotes confidence in business relationships. Establishing trust and confidence is much more difficult in organizations that have established reputations for acting unethically. If you were to discover, for example, that a manager had misled you about company benefits when you were hired, your trust and confidence in that company would probably diminish. And, if you learned that a colleague had lied to you about something, you probably would not trust or rely on that person in the future.

Ethical issues are not limited to for-profit organizations. In government, several politicians and some high-ranking officials have been forced to resign in disgrace over ethical indiscretions. For example, James Trafficant of Ohio was expelled from Congress and jailed after being convicted of accepting bribes while serving in the U.S. House of Representatives.[8] Several scientists have been accused of falsifying research data, which could invalidate later research based on their data and jeopardize trust in all scientific research. Bell Labs, for example, fired a scientist for falsifying experiments and misrepresenting data in scientific publications. Jan Hendrik Schon's work on creating tiny, powerful microprocessors seemed poised to advance micro-processor technology and potentially bring yet another Nobel Prize in physics to the award-winning laboratory, a subsidiary of Lucent Technologies.[9] Even sports can be subject to ethical lapses. At many universities, for example, coaches and athletic ad-ministrators have been put on administrative leave after allegations of improper re-cruiting practices by team members came to light.[10] Several other colleges and universities have been put on probation and in some cases given the "death penalty"—complete suspension of their athletic programs—for illegally recruiting or paying players. Thus, whether made in science, politics, or business, most deci-sions are judged as right or wrong, ethical or unethical. Negative judgments can af-fect an organization's ability to build relationships with customers and suppliers, attract investors, and retain employees.[11]

Although we will not tell you in this chapter what you ought to do, others—your superiors, co-workers, and family—will make judgments about the ethics of your ac-tions and decisions. Learning how to recognize and resolve ethical issues is an im-portant step in evaluating ethical decisions in business.

Recognizing Ethical Issues in Business

Learning to recognize ethical issues is the most important step in understanding business ethics. An **ethical issue** is an identifiable problem, situation, or opportu-nity that requires a person to choose from among several actions that may be evalu-ated as right or wrong, ethical or unethical. In business, such a choice often involves weighing monetary profit against what a person considers appropriate conduct. The best way to judge the ethics of a decision is to look at a situation from a customer's or competitor's viewpoint: Should liquid-diet manufacturers make unsubstantiated claims about their products? Should an engineer agree to divulge her former em-ployer's trade secrets to ensure that she gets a better job with a competitor? Should a salesperson omit facts about a product's poor safety record in his presentation to a customer? Such questions require the decision maker to evaluate the ethics of his or her choice.

Many business issues may seem straightforward and easy to resolve, but in reality, a person often needs several years of experience in business to understand what is ac-ceptable or ethical. For example, if you are a salesperson, when does offering a gift—such as season basketball tickets—to a customer become a bribe rather than just a sales practice? Clearly, there are no easy answers to such a question. But the size of the transaction, the history of personal relationships within the particular company, as well as many other factors may determine whether an action will be judged as right or wrong by others.

Ethics is also related to the culture in which a business operates. In the United States, for example, it would be inappropriate for a businessperson to bring an elab-orately wrapped gift to a prospective client on their first meeting—the gift could be viewed as a bribe. In Japan, however, it is considered impolite *not* to bring a gift. In consideration of various cultures in which it operates, including overseas countries, eBay, the online auction site, prohibits the listing of items connected with hate groups, such as Nazis and the Ku Klux Klan. The company also bans the listing of items associated with "notorious individuals who have committed murder within the past 100 years" (for example, Charles Manson).[12] Experience with the culture in which a business operates is critical to understanding what is ethical or unethical.

To help you understand ethical issues that perplex businesspeople today, we will take a brief look at some of them in this section. The vast number of news-format

ethical issue
an identifiable problem, situation, or opportunity that requires a person to choose from among several actions that may be evaluated as right or wrong, ethical or unethical

TABLE 2.2   Types and Incidences of Observed Misconduct

Type of Conduct Observed	Employees Observing It (%)
Abusive or intimidating behavior toward employees	21
Lying to employees, customers, vendors, or the public	19
Withholding needed information from employees, customers, vendors, or the public	18
Discrimination on the basis of race, color, gender, age, or similar categories	13
Stealing, theft, or related fraud	12
Sexual harassment	11
Falsifying financial records and reports	5
Giving or accepting bribes, kickbacks, or inappropriate gifts	4

Source: Copyright © 2003, Ethics Resource Center. Used with permission of the Ethics Resource Center, 1747 Pennsylvania Avenue NW, Suite 400, Washington, DC 20006, www.ethics.org.

investigative programs has increased consumer and employee awareness of organizational misconduct. In addition, the multitude of cable channels and Internet resources has improved the awareness of ethical problems among the general public. The National Business Ethics Survey of 1,500 US employees found that workers witness many instances of ethical misconduct in their organizations (see Table 2.2). The most common types of observed misconduct were lying, withholding information, and abusive/intimidating behavior.[13]

One of the principal causes of unethical behavior in organizations is overly aggressive financial or business objectives. Many of these issues relate to decisions and concerns that managers have to deal with daily. It is not possible to discuss every issue, of course. However, a discussion of a few issues can help you begin to recognize the ethical problems with which businesspersons must deal. Many ethical issues in business can be categorized in the context of their relation with conflicts of interest, fairness and honesty, communications, and business associations.

Conflict of Interest.   A conflict of interest exists when a person must choose whether to advance his or her own personal interests or those of others. For example, a manager in a corporation is supposed to ensure that the company is profitable so that its stockholder-owners receive a return on their investment. In other words, the manager has a responsibility to investors. If she instead makes decisions that give her more power or money but do not help the company, then she has a conflict of interest—she is acting to benefit herself at the expense of her company and is not fulfilling her responsibilities. To avoid conflicts of interest, employees must be able to separate their personal financial interests from their business dealings. For example, federal investigators are looking into whether a $1 million donation by Citigroup to the 92nd St. Y nursery school represents a conflict of interest. Jack Grubman, then an analyst for Salomon Smith Barney, upgraded his rating of AT&T's stock after Sanford Weill, CEO of Citigroup (the parent company of Salomon Smith Barney), agreed to use his influence to help Grubman's twins gain admission to the elite Manhattan nursery school. Grubman denied elevating his rating for AT&T's stock for a quid pro quo, but his children were enrolled.[14]

bribes
payments, gifts, or special favors intended to influence the outcome of a decision

As mentioned earlier, it is considered improper to give or accept **bribes**—payments, gifts, or special favors intended to influence the outcome of a decision. A

Rank	Country	Score*	Rank	Country	Score*
1	Australia	8.5	9	Germany	6.3
2	Sweden**	8.4	9	Singapore	6.3
2	Switzerland	8.4	11	Spain	5.8
4	Austria	8.2	12	France	5.5
5	Canada	8.1	13	United States	5.3
6	Netherlands	7.8	13	Japan	5.3
6	Belgium	7.8	15	Malaysia	4.3
8	United Kingdom	6.9	15	Hong Kong	4.3

TABLE 2.3

Bribe Payers Index

*A perfect score, indicating zero perceived propensity to pay bribes, is 10.0.

**The same number ranking indicates a tie.

Source: "Transparency International Bribe Payers Index 2002," *Transparency International,* May 14, 2002, www.transparency.org/cpi/2002/bpi2002.en.html. Reprinted with permission of Transparency International.

bribe is a conflict of interest because it benefits an individual at the expense of an organization or society. Companies that do business overseas should be aware that bribes are a significant ethical issue and are in fact illegal in many countries. For example, three former executives of IBM Korea went to jail in Seoul after being convicted of using bribes to win orders for computer parts.[15] Bribery is more prevalent in some countries than in others. Transparency International has developed a Bribe Payers Index (Table 2.3) to indicate the degree to which international companies are engaging in paying bribes in specific markets. The index reveals that on a scale of 0 to 10, companies are highly likely to pay bribes to win or retain business in Russia.[16]

Fairness and Honesty.   Fairness and honesty are at the heart of business ethics and relate to the general values of decision makers. At a minimum, businesspersons are expected to follow all applicable laws and regulations. But beyond obeying the law, they are expected not to harm customers, employees, clients, or competitors knowingly through deception, misrepresentation, coercion, or discrimination. Fuji and Kodak, for example, have waged a prolonged legal battle against Jazz Photo Corporation and other firms that recycle disposable cameras by patching them with electrical tape, inserting new film, putting new labels on them, and reselling them for less than Fuji and Kodak's new disposable cameras. Aside from the fact that many consumers may not realize that these "single-use" cameras have been used several times, Fuji contends that the recyclers are violating its patents on disposable cameras. A federal jury sided with Fuji and ordered Jazz Photo to pay the Japanese firm $25 million in damages for lost profits and royalties.[17]

One aspect of fairness relates to competition. Although numerous laws have been passed to foster competition and make monopolistic practices illegal, companies sometimes gain control over markets by using questionable practices that harm competition. Independent ranchers, for example, filed suit against Tyson Foods, accusing the chicken and beef producer of using its contracts with cattle feedyards to illegally depress cattle prices. The federal jury recommended that Tyson pay $1.28 billion in damages; the company planned to appeal the decision.[18]

Another aspect of fairness and honesty relates to disclosure of potential harm caused by product use. Mitsubishi Motors, Japan's number-four automaker, faced criminal charges and negative publicity after executives admitted that the company

What foods come to mind when you think of a healthy diet— whole grains, fresh vegetables, and . . . fried chicken? That's what a short-lived advertising campaign from KFC, previously known as Kentucky Fried Chicken, asked consumers to accept. The ads declared that the Colonel's chicken breast is less fatty than Burger King's Whopper and can work well as part of a healthy, balanced diet. In one commercial, a young man tells a friend that the secret behind his weight loss is eating fried chicken. In another ad, a woman brings home a bucket of chicken and asks her husband, "Remember how we talked about eating better? Well, it starts today." Although the ads carried disclaimers that fried chicken is *not* low in fat, sodium, or cholesterol, the KFC message was clear—fried chicken is good for you, so don't feel guilty about enjoying it.

Critics immediately attacked the campaign, asserting that the ads were misleading and irresponsible. Strong criticism in particular came from the Children's Advertising Review Unit, a watchdog group that condemned the airing of the commercials during children's programming because they were likely to convey the wrong idea about the overall nutritional value of fried chicken to children. After intense scrutiny from the Federal Trade Commission and other consumer interest groups, KFC pulled the ads.

KFC's campaign fueled an ongoing debate surrounding the ethics of marketing the health value of foods to consumers who may be all too eager to believe claims. With the problem of obesity now described as "epidemic" in the United States and with many more Americans trying to lose weight, it's no surprise that fast-food companies are trying to position their products as consistent with a healthy lifestyle. McDonalds has done so by promoting its salads, while Subway adopted Jared Fogle as its "weight-loss hero" in its advertising campaigns. The question is whether marketers that claim to offer "healthy" foods are helping or hindering consumers in achieving their goals to eat better.

There's some evidence to support the benefits of truthful health-food claims. For example, data from the ready-to-eat cereal market shows that allowing manufacturers to make truthful health claims resulted in greater health consciousness and improved diets among consumers, as well as more healthful product innovations in the industry. On the other hand, are manufacturers unfairly capitalizing on the health concerns of consumers, or even perpetuating poor eating habits in some cases? Although KFC offered truthful statements about the fat content of its chicken breasts, its overall message was to promote fried chicken as a healthy product—a statement that any dietician would be quick to debunk. To avoid legal and ethical pitfalls, marketers should ensure that health claims on their food products are not only truthful, but that they also steer clear of the potential to mislead consumers.[19]

Discussion Questions
1. Why is it an ethical issue for KFC to promote "health benefits" of fried chicken?
2. Do you think that the advertising of fast food is contributing to health issues in the United States? Why?
3. How could KFC present more useful health information about its products?

had systematically covered up customer complaints about tens of thousands of defective automobiles over a 20-year period in order to avoid expensive and embarrassing product recalls.[20]

Dishonesty has become a significant problem in the United States. As reported earlier in this chapter, lying was the most observed form of misconduct in the National Business Ethics Survey. Dishonesty is not found only in business, however. A study by the Josephson Institute of Ethics reported that 7 out of 10 students admitted to cheating on a test at least once in the last year, and 92 percent lied to their parents in the past year.[21]

Communications.   Communications is another area in which ethical concerns may arise. False and misleading advertising, as well as deceptive personal-selling tactics, anger consumers and can lead to the failure of a business. Truthfulness about product safety and quality are also important to consumers. Claims about dietary supplements and weight-loss products can be particularly problematic. For example, the Fountain of Youth Group, LLC, and its founder, Edita Kaye, settled charges brought by the Federal Trade Commission that the company made unsubstantiated claims about its weight-loss products. Under the settlement, the firm agreed to stop making specific weight-loss and health claims about its products without competent scientific proof. It was also fined $6 million, but that fine was suspended because the firm lacked the resources to pay it.[22]

Some companies fail to provide enough information for consumers about differences or similarities between products. For example, driven by high prices for medicines, many consumers are turning to Canadian, Mexican, and overseas Internet sources for drugs to treat a variety of illnesses and conditions. However, research suggests that a significant percentage of these imported pharmaceuticals may not actually contain the labeled drug, and the counterfeit drugs could even be harmful to those who take them.[23]

Another important aspect of communications that may raise ethical concerns relates to product labeling. The U.S. Surgeon General currently requires cigarette manufacturers to indicate clearly on cigarette packaging that smoking cigarettes is harmful to the smoker's health. However, labeling of other products raises ethical questions when it threatens basic rights, such as freedom of speech and expression. This is the heart of the controversy surrounding the movement to require warning labels on movies and videogames, rating their content, language, and appropriate audience age. Although people in the entertainment industry believe that such labeling violates their First Amendment right to freedom of expression, other consumers—particularly parents—believe that such labeling is needed to protect children from harmful influences. Similarly, alcoholic beverage and cigarette manufacturers have argued that a total ban on cigarette and alcohol advertisements violates the First Amendment. Internet regulation, particularly that designed to protect children and the elderly, is on the forefront in consumer protection legislation. Because of the debate surrounding the acceptability of these business activities, they remain major ethical issues.

Business Relationships. The behavior of businesspersons toward customers, suppliers, and others in their workplace may also generate ethical concerns. Ethical behavior within a business involves keeping company secrets, meeting obligations and responsibilities, and avoiding undue pressure that may force others to act unethically.

Managers, in particular, because of the authority of their position, have the opportunity to influence employees' actions. For example, a manager can influence employees to use pirated computer software to save costs. The use of illegal software puts the employee and the company at legal risk, but employees may feel pressured to do so by their superior's authority. The National Business Ethics Survey found that employees who feel pressure to compromise ethical standards view supervisors and top managers as the greatest source of such pressure.[24]

It is the responsibility of managers to create a work environment that helps the organization achieve its objectives and fulfill its responsibilities. However, the methods that managers use to enforce these responsibilities should not compromise employee rights.

In May 2002, members of Enron's board of directors were questioned by the U.S. Senate. The company had collapsed after management and accounting leaders inflated profit numbers by $600 million and hid debts and exaggerated revenues in order to continue attracting investors—many of whom were their own employees. The CEO at the time, Kenneth Lay, had received a compensation of $152.7 million in payments and stock—11,000 times the amount of severance paid to the 4,000 laid-off workers after the bankruptcy. Lay chose to invoke the Fifth Amendment when questioned by the Senate.

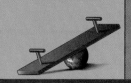

Qwest Communications is the local telephone company for 14 states extending from Minnesota west to Washington and southwest to Arizona and New Mexico. Four former executives of the company—the chief financial officer, a senior vice president, the assistant controller, and a vice president—were indicted on criminal charges of fraud. The four were accused of devising a scheme to create more than $33 million in revenue, violating Securities and Exchange Commission rules by incorrectly reporting a purchase order with the Arizona School Facilities Board. According to the government, Qwest sold equipment to the statewide school computer network, billed the customer, but then held the merchandise for later delivery. According to government officials, the executives took this action to help Qwest meet its numbers during a difficult time for the company. According to the chairman of the SEC, "Simply put, the defendants couldn't make the numbers work, so they cheated." The Justice Department said the company knowingly filed false documents to hide its actions. The SEC also sought civil penalties against eight former employees, including the loss of salaries and bonuses during the time of the alleged misdeed. This was not the first time the company has been in trouble.

In 2002, Qwest chief executive Joseph Nacchio resigned under pressure. In his public testimony, Nacchio said that he talked with founder and director Philip Anschutz about all major decisions. Congressional investigators then interviewed Anschutz about his role in the company's day-to-day affairs. Qwest had been investigated by the Justice Department and the Securities and Exchange Commission and was the subject of congressional hearings into its financial practices. The investigations probed whether Qwest artificially inflated its revenues by swapping network capacity with another scandal-plagued company, Global Crossing Ltd. The company restated its financial reports for 1999 to 2001 because of accounting errors and said it would erase $950 million from improperly booked swaps. Still attempting to clean up its image and its books, Qwest announced in February 2003 that $531 million in revenue that was booked prematurely in the last two years would be deferred.

In 2003, Qwest was fined $20.3 million by California regulators for switching customers' long-distance accounts without their permission (a practice known as "slamming") and adding unauthorized charges to their bills (known as "cramming"). At that time, it was the largest fine ever levied against Qwest by a regulatory agency, but Minnesota officials were considering an even larger one. The administrative judge in California cited 3,583 cases of slamming and 4,871 cases of cramming. Qwest said it had disciplined sales agencies that committed the unlawful practices and had introduced new procedures to prevent them in the future. California utilities commissioners took Qwest's efforts into consideration before levying the fine, but the commission president said, "This company fixed its systems only after regulators began investigating." The commission also required the company to provide refunds to the affected customers within ninety days.[25]

Discussion Questions
1. Why do you think top managers at Qwest would devise a scheme to create nonexistent revenue?
2. Why would a large company switch customers' long-distance accounts without their permission?
3. Discuss why regulation is necessary to keep companies acting responsibly?

Organizational pressures may encourage a person to engage in activities that he or she might otherwise view as unethical, such as invading others' privacy or stealing a competitor's secrets. For example, Betty Vinson, an accounting executive at WorldCom, protested when her superiors asked her to make improper accounting entries in order to cover up the company's deteriorating financial condition. She acquiesced only after being told that it was the only way to save the troubled company. She, along with several other WorldCom accountants, pleaded guilty to conspiracy and fraud charges related to WorldCom's bankruptcy after the accounting improprieties came to light.[26] Or the firm may provide only vague or lax supervision on ethical issues, providing the opportunity for misconduct. Managers who offer no ethical direction to employees create many opportunities for manipulation, dishonesty, and conflicts of interest.

Plagiarism—taking someone else's work and presenting it as your own without mentioning the source—is another ethical issue. As a student, you may be familiar with plagiarism in school; for example, copying someone else's term paper or quoting from a published work or Internet source without acknowledging it. In business,

plagiarism
the act of taking someone else's work and presenting it as your own without mentioning the source

Solve the Dilemma

Customer Privacy

Checkers Pizza was one of the first to offer home delivery service, with overwhelming success. However, the major pizza chains soon followed suit, taking away Checkers's competitive edge. Jon Barnard, Checkers's founder and co-owner, needed a new gimmick to beat the competition. He decided to develop a computerized information database that would make Checkers the most efficient competitor and provide insight into consumer buying behavior at the same time. Under the system, telephone customers were asked their phone number; if they had ordered from Checkers before, their address and previous order information came up on the computer screen.

After successfully testing the new system, Barnard put the computerized order network in place in all Checkers outlets. After three months of success, he decided to give an award to the family that ate the most Checkers pizza. Through the tracking system, the company identified the biggest customer, who had ordered a pizza every weekday for the past three months (63 pizzas). The company put together a program to surprise the family with an award, free-food certificates, and a news story announcing the award. As Barnard began to plan for the event, however, he began to think that maybe the family might not want all the attention and publicity.

Discussion Questions

1. What are some of the ethical issues in giving customers an award for consumption behavior without notifying them first?
2. Do you see this as a potential violation of privacy? Explain.
3. How would you handle the situation if you were Barnard?

Are there any potential legal restrictions or violations that could result from the action?	**TABLE 2.4**
Does your company have a specific code of ethics or policy on the action?	Questions to Consider in Determining Whether an Action Is Ethical
Is this activity customary in your industry? Are there any industry trade groups that provide guidelines or codes of conduct that address this issue?	
Would this activity be accepted by your co-workers? Will your decision or action withstand open discussion with co-workers and managers and survive untarnished?	
How does this activity fit with your own beliefs and values?	

---

an ethical issue arises when an employee copies reports or takes the work or ideas of others and presents it as his or her own. At *USA Today,* for example, an internal investigation into the work of veteran reporter Jack Kelley identified dozens of stories in which Kelley appeared to have plagiarized material from competing newspapers. The investigation also uncovered evidence Kelley fabricated significant portions of at least eight major stories and conspired to cover up his lapses in judgment. The newspaper later apologized to its readers, and Kelley resigned.[27] A manager attempting to take credit for a subordinate's ideas is engaging in another type of plagiarism.

Making Decisions about Ethical Issues

Although we've presented a variety of ethical issues that may arise in business, it can be difficult to recognize specific ethical issues in practice. Whether a decision maker recognizes an issue as an ethical one often depends on the issue itself. Managers, for example, tend to be more concerned about issues that affect those close to them, as well as issues that have immediate rather than long-term consequences. Thus, the perceived importance of an ethical issue substantially affects choices, and only a few issues receive scrutiny, while most receive no attention at all.[28]

Table 2.4 lists some questions you may want to ask yourself and others when trying to determine whether an action is ethical. Open discussion of ethical issues does not eliminate ethical problems, but it does promote both trust and learning in an

FIGURE 2.1

Three Factors that
Influence Business
Ethics

Individual Standards and Values	+	Managers' and Co-workers' Influence	+	Opportunity: Codes and Compliance Requirements	=	Ethical/Unethical Choices in Business

organization.[29] When people feel that they cannot discuss what they are doing with their co-workers or superiors, there is a good chance that an ethical issue exists. Once a person has recognized an ethical issue and can openly discuss it with others, he or she has begun the process of resolving an ethical issue.

Improving Ethical Behavior in Business

Understanding how people make ethical choices and what prompts a person to act unethically may reverse the current trend toward unethical behavior in business. Ethical decisions in an organization are influenced by three key factors: individual moral standards, the influence of managers and co-workers, and the opportunity to engage in misconduct (Figure 2.1). While you have great control over your personal ethics outside the workplace, your co-workers and superiors exert significant control over your choices at work through authority and example. In fact, the activities and examples set by co-workers, along with rules and policies established by the firm, are critical in gaining consistent ethical compliance in an organization. If the company fails to provide good examples and direction for appropriate conduct, confusion and conflict will develop and result in the opportunity for misconduct. If your boss or co-workers leave work early, you may be tempted to do so as well. If you see co-workers making personal long-distance phone calls at work and charging them to the company, then you may be more likely to do so also. In addition, having sound personal values contributes to an ethical workplace.

Because ethical issues often emerge from conflict, it is useful to examine the causes of ethical conflict. Business managers and employees often experience some tension between their own ethical beliefs and their obligations to the organizations in which they work. Many employees utilize different ethical standards at work than they do at home. This conflict increases when employees feel that their company is encouraging unethical conduct or exerting pressure on them to engage in it.

It is difficult for employees to determine what conduct is acceptable within a company if the firm does not have ethics policies and standards. And without such policies and standards, employees may base decisions on how their peers and superiors behave. Professional **codes of ethics** are formalized rules and standards that describe what the company expects of its employees. Codes of ethics do not have to be so detailed that they take into account every situation, but they should provide guidelines and principles that can help employees achieve organizational objectives and address risks in an acceptable and ethical way. The development of a code of ethics should include not only a firm's executives and board of directors, but also legal staff and employees from all areas of a firm.[30] Table 2.5 lists some key things to consider when developing a code of ethics.

Codes of ethics, policies on ethics, and ethics training programs advance ethical behavior because they prescribe which activities are acceptable and which are not, and they limit the opportunity for misconduct by providing punishments for viola-

codes of ethics
formalized rules and standards that describe what a company expects of its employees

TABLE 2.5

Key Things to Consider in Developing a Code of Ethics

- Create a team to assist with the process of developing the code (include management and nonmanagement employees from across departments and functions).
- Solicit input from employees from different departments, functions, and regions to compile a list of common questions and answers to include in the code document.
- Make certain that the headings of the code sections can be easily understood by all employees.
- Avoid referencing specific U.S. laws and regulations or those of specific countries, particularly for codes that will be distributed to employees in multiple regions.
- Hold employee group meetings on a complete draft version (including graphics and pictures) of the text using language that everyone can understand.
- Inform employees that they will receive a copy of the code during an introduction session.
- Let all employees know that they will receive future ethics training which will, in part, cover the important information contained in the code document.

Source: Adapted from William Miller, "Implementing an Organizational Code of Ethics," *International Business Ethics Review* 7 (Winter 2004), pp. 1, 6–10.

tions of the rules and standards. According to the National Business Ethics Survey (NBES), employees in organizations that have written standards of conduct, ethics training, ethics offices or hotlines, and systems for anonymous reporting of misconduct are more likely to report misconduct when they observe it. The survey also found that such programs are associated with higher employee perceptions that they will be held accountable for ethical infractions.[31] The enforcement of such codes and policies through rewards and punishments increases the acceptance of ethical standards by employees.

One of the most important components of an ethics program is a means through which employees can report observed misconduct anonymously. The NBES found that although employees are increasingly reporting illegal and unethical activities they observe in the workplace, 44 percent of surveyed employees indicated they are unwilling to report misconduct because they fear that no corrective action will be taken or that their report will not remain confidential.[32] The lack of anonymous reporting mechanisms may encourage **whistleblowing,** which occurs when an employee exposes an employer's wrongdoing to outsiders, such as the media or government regulatory agencies. However, more companies are establishing programs to encourage employees to report illegal or unethical practices internally so that they can take steps to remedy problems before they result in legal action or generate negative publicity. In recent years, whistleblowers have provided crucial evidence documenting illegal actions at a number of companies. At Enron, for example, Sherron Watkins, a vice president, warned the firm's CEO, Ken Lay, that the energy company was using improper accounting procedures. Soon after, Watkins testified before Congress that Enron had concealed billions of dollars in debt through a complex scheme of off-balance-sheet partnerships.[33] Enron ultimately went bankrupt when its improprieties and high levels of debt were exposed. Unfortunately, whistleblowers are often treated negatively in organizations. The

whistleblowing
the act of an employee exposing an employer's wrongdoing to outsiders, such as the media or government regulatory agencies

Enron executive Sherron Watkins reported financial misconduct as a whistleblower.

government is rewarding firms that encourage employees to report misconduct—with reduced fines and penalties when violations occur.

The current trend is to move away from legally based ethical initiatives in organizations to cultural- or integrity-based initiatives that make ethics a part of core organizational values. Organizations recognize that effective business ethics programs are good for business performance. Firms that develop higher levels of trust function more efficiently and effectively and avoid damaged company reputations and product images. Organizational ethics initiatives have been supportive of many positive and diverse organizational objectives, such as profitability, hiring, employee satisfaction, and customer loyalty.[34] Conversely, lack of organizational ethics initiatives and the absence of workplace values such as honesty, trust, and integrity can have a negative impact on organizational objectives. According to one report on employee loyalty and work practices, 79 percent of employees who questioned their bosses' integrity indicated that they felt uncommitted or were likely to quit soon.[35]

The Nature of Social Responsibility

There are four dimensions of social responsibility: economic, legal, ethical, and voluntary (including philanthropic) (Figure 2.2).[36] Earning profits is the economic foundation of the pyramid in Figure 2.2, and complying with the law is the next step. However a business whose *sole* objective is to maximize profits is not likely to consider its social responsibility, although its activities will probably be legal. (We looked at ethical responsibilities in the first half of this chapter.) Finally, voluntary responsibilities are additional activities that may not be required but which promote hu-

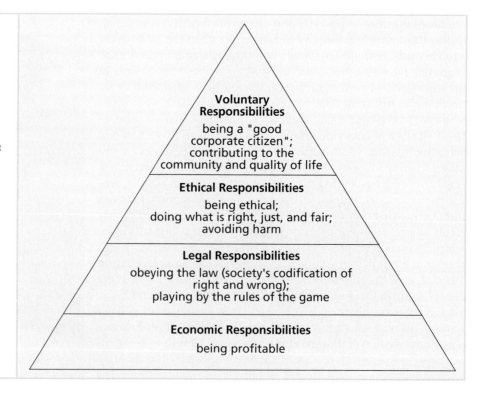

FIGURE 2.2

The Pyramid of Social Responsibility

Source: Reprinted with permission from A. B. Carroll, "The Pyramid of Corporate Social Responsibility: Toward the Moral Management of Organizational Stakeholders," *Business Horizons,* July/August 1991. Copyright © 1991 by the Board of Trustees at Indiana University, Kelley School of Business.

man welfare or goodwill. Legal and economic concerns have long been acknowledged in business, but voluntary and ethical issues are more recent concerns.

Corporate citizenship is the extent to which businesses meet the legal, ethical, economic, and voluntary responsibilities placed on them by their various stakeholders. It involves the activities and organizational processes adopted by businesses to meet their social responsibilities. A commitment to corporate citizenship by a firm indicates a strategic focus on fulfilling the social responsibilities expected of it by its stakeholders. Corporate citizenship involves action and measurement of the extent to which a firm embraces the corporate citizenship philosophy and then follows through by implementing citizenship and social responsibility initiatives. For example, ChevronTexaco, a multinational provider of petroleum and energy products, communicates its values in a document called "The ChevronTexaco Way." This document serves as an ethical foundation and guides the company's conduct around the world. For example, the firm has signed the Global Sullivan Principles, an international, voluntary code of conduct for corporations around the world; contributed to environmental causes such as the World Wildlife Fund and The Nature Conservancy; and donated funds and resources to important social causes around the world. The corporation also publishes a regular report on its social responsibility conduct and initiatives.[37]

corporate citizenship
the extent to which businesses meet the legal, ethical, economic, and voluntary responsibilities placed on them by their stakeholders

Most companies today consider being socially responsible a cost of doing business. Eddie Bauer created a Corporate Social Responsibility (CSR) department to coordinate its social responsibility efforts. The department focuses on five areas: global labor practices, environmental affairs, sustainable business practices, governmental affairs, and public affairs (including philanthropy and volunteerism). The company's good corporate citizenship enhances its bottom line. According to John Thomas, vice president of the CSR department, "Customers are making more learned decisions today on how they shop and who they make their purchases from. Those decisions, I believe, are made on the basis of what a company stands for, what its values are, as well as what its contributions to the community are."[38] *Business Ethics* magazine publishes an annual list of the 100 best American corporate citizens based on service to seven stakeholder groups: stockholders, local communities, minorities, employees, global stakeholders, customers, and the environment. Table 2.6 shows the top 20 from that list.

1	Fannie Mae	11	Imation	**TABLE 2.6**
2	Procter & Gamble	12	IBM	Best Corporate Citizens
3	Intel Corporation	13	Nuveen Investments	
4	St. Paul Companies	14	Herman Miller	
5	Green Mountain Coffee Roasters	15	J. M. Smucker	
6	Deere & Company	16	Safeco	
7	Avon Products	17	Timberland	
8	Hewlett-Packard	18	Zimmer Holdings	
9	Agilent Technologies	19	Cisco	
10	Ecobab	20	3M	

Source: Peter Asmus, with Sandra Waddock and Samuel Graves, "100 Best Corporate Citizens of 2004," *Business Ethics,* (n.d.) www.business-ethics.com/100best.htm (accessed June 9, 2004).

TABLE 2.7	**For:**
The Arguments For and Against Social Responsibility	1. Business helped to create many of the social problems that exist today, so it should play a significant role in solving them, especially in the areas of pollution reduction and cleanup.
	2. Businesses should be more responsible because they have the financial and technical resources to help solve social problems.
	3. As members of society, businesses should do their fair share to help others.
	4. Socially responsible decision making by businesses can prevent increased government regulation.
	5. Social responsibility is necessary to ensure economic survival: If businesses want educated and healthy employees, customers with money to spend, and suppliers with quality goods and services in years to come, they must take steps to help solve the social and environmental problems that exist today.
	Against:
	1. It sidetracks managers from the primary goal of business—earning profits. Every dollar donated to social causes or otherwise spent on society's problems is a dollar less for owners and investors.
	2. Participation in social programs gives businesses greater power, perhaps at the expense of particular segments of society.
	3. Some people question whether business has the expertise needed to assess and make decisions about social problems.
	4. Many people believe that social problems are the responsibility of government agencies and officials, who can be held accountable by voters.

Although the concept of social responsibility is receiving more and more attention, it is still not universally accepted. Table 2.7 lists some of the arguments for and against social responsibility.

Social Responsibility Issues

As with ethics, managers consider social responsibility on a daily basis as they deal with real issues. Among the many social issues that managers must consider are their firms' relations with owners and stockholders, employees, consumers, the environment, and the community.

Social responsibility is a dynamic area with issues changing constantly in response to society's desires. There is much evidence that social responsibility is associated with improved business performance. Consumers are refusing to buy from businesses that receive publicity about misconduct. A number of studies have found a direct relationship between social responsibility and profitability, as well as that social responsibility is linked to employee commitment and customer loyalty—major concerns of any firm trying to increase profits.[39] This section highlights a few of the many social responsibility issues that managers face; as managers become aware of and work toward the solution of current social problems, new ones will certainly emerge.

Relations with Owners and Stockholders.   Businesses must first be responsible to their owners, who are primarily concerned with earning a profit or a return on their investment in a company. In a small business, this responsibility is fairly easy to fulfill because the owner(s) personally manages the business or knows the managers well. In larger businesses, particularly corporations owned by thousands of stockholders, assuring responsibility to the owners becomes a more difficult task.

A business's responsibilities to its owners and investors, as well as to the financial community at large, include maintaining proper accounting procedures, providing all relevant information to investors about the current and projected performance of the firm, and protecting the owners' rights and investments. In short, the business must maximize the owners' investment in the firm.

Employee Relations.   Another issue of importance to a business is its responsibilities to employees, for without employees a business cannot carry out its goals. Employees expect businesses to provide a safe workplace, pay them adequately for their work, and tell them what is happening in their company. They want employers to listen to their grievances and treat them fairly. When employees at Ramtech Building Systems, Inc., approached management with their concerns about cursing used in the company's manufacturing facilities, a Language Code of Ethics was instituted. Many employees indicate that obscene language is common in the workplace, particularly in high-stress jobs. For example, 43 percent of the 12,000 U.S. Postal Service employees surveyed recently reported being cursed at in the workplace.[40] Companies are adjusting their policies and offering training to clean up employee language.

Of a more serious nature, a growing employee-relations concern for multinational companies is the spread of AIDS and its effect on the workforce. Daimler-Chrysler South Africa (DCSA), for example, provides HIV/AIDS testing, free anti-AIDS drugs, and additional treatment and support for its 6,000 South African employees and their families in an effort to combat the disease, which has infected about 9 percent of DCSA's employees there. The company spends an estimated $420,000 a year on antiretroviral drugs. Other German automakers, including Volkswagen and BMW, have launched similar programs to cover their employees in South Africa, where 600 people die every day from the disease. Many U.S. companies have set up AIDS-prevention and treatment programs for their employees in Africa as well. Companies as diverse as Coca-Cola (the largest private employer on the African continent), MTV, American Express, Nike, and ExxonMobil have also joined the Global Business Coalition to help fight the epidemic.[41]

Congress has passed several laws regulating safety in the workplace, many of which are enforced by OSHA. Labor unions have also made significant contributions to achieving safety in the workplace and improving wages and benefits. Most organizations now recognize that the safety and satisfaction of their employees are a critical ingredient in their success, and many strive to go beyond what is expected of them by the law. Healthy, satisfied employees supply more than just labor to their employers, however. Employers are beginning to realize the importance of obtaining input from even the lowest-level employees to help the company reach its objectives.

A major social responsibility for business is providing equal opportunities for all employees regardless of their sex, age, race, religion, or nationality. Women and minorities have been slighted in the past in terms of education, employment, and advancement opportunities; additionally, many of their needs have not been addressed by business. For example, as many as 500,000 female employees of Wal-Mart filed a class-action discrimination lawsuit accusing the giant retailer of paying them lower wages and salaries than it does men in comparable positions. Pretrial proceedings

Home Depot acknowledges the importance of all stakeholders in operating its business.

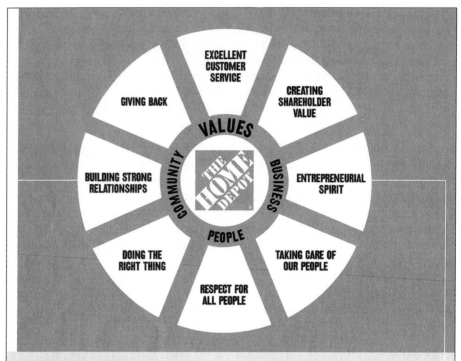

EXCELLENT CUSTOMER SERVICE
Along with our quality products, service, price and selection, we must go the extra mile to give customers knowledgeable advice about merchandise and to help them use those products to their maximum benefit.

CREATING SHAREHOLDER VALUE
The investors who provide the capital necessary to allow our Company to grow need and expect a return on their investment. We are committed to providing it.

ENTREPRENEURIAL SPIRIT
The Home Depot associates are encouraged to initiate creative and innovative ways of serving our customers and improving the business, as well as to adopt good ideas from others.

TAKING CARE OF OUR PEOPLE
The key to our success is treating people well. We do this by encouraging associates to speak up and take risks, by recognizing and rewarding good performance and by leading and developing people so they may grow.

RESPECT FOR ALL PEOPLE
In order to remain successful, our associates must work in an environment of mutual respect where each associate is regarded as part of The Home Depot team.

DOING THE RIGHT THING
We exercise good judgment by "doing the right thing" instead of just "doing things right." We strive to understand the impact of our decisions, and we accept responsibility for our actions.

BUILDING STRONG RELATIONSHIPS
Strong relationships are built on trust, honesty and integrity. We listen and respond to the needs of customers, associates, communities and vendors, treating them as partners.

GIVING BACK
An important part of the fabric of The Home Depot is in giving our time, talents, energy and resources to worthwhile causes in our communities and society.

not only uncovered discrepancies between the pay of men and women but also the fact that men dominate higher-paying store manager positions while women occupy more than 90 percent of cashier jobs, most of which pay about $14,000 a year. Wal-Mart faces fines and penalties in the million of dollars if found guilty of sexual discrimination.[42] Women, who continue to bear most child-rearing responsibilities, often experience conflict between those responsibilities and their duties as employees. Consequently, day care has become a major employment issue for women, and more companies are providing day-care facilities as part of their effort to recruit and advance women in the workforce. In addition, companies are considering alternative scheduling such as flex-time and job sharing to accommodate employee concerns.

Telecommuting has grown significantly over the past 5 to 10 years, as well. Many Americans today believe business has a social obligation to provide special opportunities for women and minorities to improve their standing in society.

Consumer Relations.   A critical issue in business today is business's responsibility to customers, who look to business to provide them with satisfying, safe products and to respect their rights as consumers. The activities that independent individuals, groups, and organizations undertake to protect their rights as consumers are known as **consumerism.** To achieve their objectives, consumers and their advocates write letters to companies, lobby government agencies, make public service announcements, and boycott companies whose activities they deem irresponsible.

Many of the desires of those involved in the consumer movement have a foundation in John F. Kennedy's 1962 consumer bill of rights, which highlighted four rights. The *right to safety* means that a business must not knowingly sell anything that could result in personal injury or harm to consumers. Defective or dangerous products erode public confidence in the ability of business to serve society. They also result in expensive litigation that ultimately increases the cost of products for all consumers. The right to safety also means businesses must provide a safe place for consumers to shop. In recent years, many large retailers have been under increasing pressure to improve safety in their large warehouse-type stores. At Home Depot, for example, three consumer deaths and numerous serious injuries have been caused by falling merchandise. One lawsuit brought against the company over injuries received in one of its stores resulted in a $1.5 million judgment. To help prevent further deaths, injuries, and litigation, Home Depot now has a corporate safety officer and has hired 130 safety managers to monitor store compliance with new safety measures.[43]

The *right to be informed* gives consumers the freedom to review complete information about a product before they buy. This means that detailed information about ingredients, risks, and instructions for use are to be printed on labels and packages. The *right to choose* ensures that consumers have access to a variety of products and services at competitive prices. The assurance of both satisfactory quality and service at a fair price is also a part of the consumer's right to choose. Some consumers are not being given the right to choose. Many are being billed for products and services they never ordered. According to the Federal Trade Commission, complaints about unordered merchandise and services jumped 169 percent over a two-year period. Burdine's, a department store chain, was investigated for failing to notify customers it was enrolling them in a company buying club. Fleet Mortgage was sued for adding fees for unrequested insurance to customers' mortgage bills, and HCI Direct was sued by 11 states for charging customers for panty hose samples they had never ordered.[44] The *right to be heard* assures consumers that their interests will receive full and sympathetic consideration when the government formulates policy. It also assures the fair treatment of consumers who voice complaints about a purchased product.

The role of the Federal Trade Commission's Bureau of Consumer Protection is to protect consumers against unfair, deceptive, or fraudulent practices. The bureau, which enforces a variety of consumer protection laws, is divided into five divisions. The Division of Enforcement monitors compliance with and investigates violations of laws, including unfulfilled holiday delivery promises by online shopping sites, employment opportunities fraud, scholarship scams, misleading advertising for health care products, and more.

consumerism
the activities that independent individuals, groups, and organizations undertake to protect their rights as consumers

Environmental Issues. Environmental responsibility has become a leading issue as both business and the public acknowledge the damage done to the environment in the past. Today's consumers are increasingly demanding that businesses take a greater responsibility for their actions and how they impact the environment.

Organizations such as PETA address animal rights issues.

Animal Rights. One area of environmental concern in society today is animal rights. Probably the most controversial business practice in this area is the testing of cosmetics and drugs on animals who may be injured or killed as a result. Animal-rights activists, such as People for the Ethical Treatment of Animals, say such research is morally wrong because it harms living creatures. Consumers who share this sentiment may boycott companies that test products on animals and take their business instead to companies such as The Body Shop and John Paul Mitchell Systems, which do not use animal testing. However, researchers in the cosmetics and pharmaceutical industries argue that animal testing is necessary to prevent harm to human beings who will eventually use the products. Business practices that harm endangered wildlife and their habitats are another environmental issue.

Pollution. Another major issue in the area of environmental responsibility is pollution. Water pollution results from dumping toxic chemicals and raw sewage into rivers and oceans, oil spills, and the burial of industrial waste in the ground where it may filter into underground water supplies. Fertilizers and insecticides used in farming and grounds maintenance also run off into water supplies with each rainfall. Water pollution problems are especially notable in heavily industrialized areas. Medical waste—such as used syringes, vials of blood, and AIDS-contaminated materials—has turned up on beaches in New York, New Jersey, and Massachusetts, as well as other places. Society is demanding that water supplies be clean and healthful to reduce the potential danger from these substances.

Air pollution is usually the result of smoke and other pollutants emitted by manufacturing facilities, as well as carbon monoxide and hydrocarbons emitted by motor vehicles. In addition to the health risks posed by air pollution, when some chemical compounds emitted by manufacturing facilities react with air and rain, acid rain results. Acid rain has contributed to the deaths of many valuable forests and lakes in North America as well as in Europe. Air pollution may also contribute to global warming, in which carbon dioxide collects in the earth's atmosphere, trapping the sun's heat and preventing the earth's surface from cooling. As a result, the automobile industry is facing increasing pressure to develop affordable, fuel-efficient automobiles that do not contribute to air pollution problems. Toyota, for example, introduced the Prius, a hybrid vehicle that uses electric motors to augment its internal combustion engines, improving its fuel efficiency without a reduction in power. Ford and Dodge also planned to introduce competing hybrid vehicles.[45]

Land pollution is tied directly to water pollution because many of the chemicals and toxic wastes that are dumped on the land eventually work their way into the water supply. Land pollution results from the dumping of residential and industrial waste, strip mining, forest fires, and poor forest conservation. In Brazil and other South American countries, rain forests are being destroyed—at a rate of one acre per minute—to make way for farms and ranches, at a cost of the extinction of the many animals and plants (some endangered species) that call the rain forest home. Large-scale deforestation also depletes the oxygen supply available to humans and other animals.

Related to the problem of land pollution is the larger issue of how to dispose of waste in an environmentally responsible manner. Consumers contribute approximately 1,500 pounds of garbage per person each year to landfills. One specific solid waste problem is being created by rapid innovations in computer hardware that make many computers obsolete after just 18 months. By 2005, 350 million computers will have reached obsolescence, and at least 55 million are expected to end up in landfills.[46] Computers contain such toxic substances as lead, mercury, and polyvinyl chloride, which can leach into the soil and contaminate groundwater when disposed of improperly. Dell Computer, the leading seller of personal computers, has come under increasing criticism from environmental groups for failing to adopt a leadership role in reducing the use of toxic materials in the manufacture of computers and in recycling used computer parts. The company has also encountered criticism for using prison labor to handle the recycling it does do. Several states are considering legislation that would require computers to be recycled at the same levels as in Europe.[47]

Response to Environmental Issues.   Partly in response to federal legislation such as the National Environmental Policy Act of 1969 and partly due to consumer concerns, businesses are responding to environmental issues. Many small and large companies, including Walt Disney Company, Chevron, and Scott Paper, have created a new executive position—a vice president of environmental affairs—to help them achieve their business goals in an environmentally responsible manner. A recent survey indicated that 83.5 percent of *Fortune* 500 companies have a written environmental policy, 74.7 percent engage in recycling efforts, and 69.7 percent have made investments in waste-reduction efforts.[48] Many companies, including Alcoa, Dow Chemical, Phillips Petroleum, and Raytheon, now link executive pay to environmental performance.[49]

> **Did You Know?**   In one year, Americans generated 230 million tons of trash and recycled 23.5 percent of it.[50]

Many firms are trying to eliminate wasteful practices, the emission of pollutants, and/or the use of harmful chemicals from their manufacturing processes. Other companies are seeking ways to improve their products. Utility providers, for example, are increasingly supplementing their services with alternative energy sources, including solar, wind, and geothermal power. In Austin, Texas, local utility customers can even elect to purchase electricity from green sources—primarily wind power—for a few extra dollars a month. The city-owned utility's award-winning GreenChoice program includes many small and large businesses among its customers.[51] Indeed, a growing number of businesses are choosing "green power" sources where available. Kinko's, for example, encourages individual copy-center stores to purchase their electricity from renewable sources, and 45 stores now purchase 100 percent of their electricity from certified green power sources.[52] Many businesses have

The new hybrid gas/electric cars, like the Prius from Toyota in this ad, present a revolutionary response to environmental issues caused by vehicle emissions. Because they are part gas/part electric, give off almost no emissions, and go from zero to 60 in a reasonable amount of time (according to this ad, the Prius does it in just about 10 seconds), they could be the answer to a more environmentally friendly mode of transportation.

turned to *recycling,* the reprocessing of materials—aluminum, paper, glass, and some plastic—for reuse. Such efforts to make products, packaging, and processes more environmentally friendly have been labeled "green" business or marketing by the public and media. Lumber products at Home Depot may carry a seal from the Forest Stewardship Council to indicate that they were harvested from sustainable forests using environmentally friendly methods.[53] Likewise, most Chiquita bananas are certified through the Better Banana Project as having been grown with more environmentally and labor-friendly practices.[54]

It is important to recognize that, with current technology, environmental responsibility requires trade-offs. Society must weigh the huge costs of limiting or eliminating pollution against the health threat posed by the pollution. Environmental responsibility imposes costs on both business and the public. Although people certainly do not want oil fouling beautiful waterways and killing wildlife, they insist on low-cost, readily available gasoline and heating oil. People do not want to contribute to the growing garbage-disposal problem, but they often refuse to pay more for "green" products packaged in an environmentally friendly manner, to recycle as much of their own waste as possible, or to permit the building of additional waste-disposal facilities (the "not in my backyard," or NIMBY, syndrome). Managers must coordinate environmental goals with other social and economic ones.

Community Relations. A final, yet very significant, issue for businesses concerns their responsibilities to the general welfare of the communities and societies in which they operate. Many businesses simply want to make their communities better places for everyone to live and work. The most common way that businesses exercise their community responsibility is through donations to local and national charitable organizations. Corporations contributed more than $12 billion to environmental and social causes last year.[55] For example, Safeway, the nation's fourth-largest grocer, has donated millions of dollars to organizations involved in medical research, such as Easter Seals and the Juvenile Diabetes Research Foundation International. The company's employees have also raised funds to support social causes of interest.[56] Avon's Breast Cancer Awareness Crusade has helped raise $300 million to fund community-based breast cancer education and early detection services. Avon, a marketer of women's cosmetics, is also known for employing a large number of women and promoting them to top management; the firm has more female top managers (86 percent) than any other *Fortune* 500 company.[57] Even small companies participate in philanthropy through

Funded by The Tobacco Tax Initiative, the California Department of Health Services promotes the negative effects of smoking.

donations and volunteer support of local causes and national charities, such as the Red Cross and the United Way.

After realizing that the current pool of prospective employees lacks many basic skills necessary to work, many companies have become concerned about the quality of education in the United States. Recognizing that today's students are tomorrow's employees and customers, firms such as Kroger, Campbell's Soup, Kodak, American Express, Apple Computer, Xerox, and Coca-Cola are donating money, equipment, and employee time to help improve schools in their communities and around the nation. They provide scholarship money, support for teachers, and computers for students, and they send employees out to tutor and motivate young students to stay in school and succeed. Target, for example, contributes significant resources to education, including direct donations of $100 million to schools as well as fund-raising and scholarship programs that assist teachers and students. Through the retailer's Take Charge of Education program, customers using a Target Guest Card can designate a specific school to which Target donates 1 percent of their total purchase. This program is designed to make customers feel that their purchases are benefiting their community while increasing the use of Target Guest Cards.[58]

Hewlett-Packard's Diversity in Education Initiative focuses on math and science in four minority communities and works with students from elementary school to the university level. The program provides hands-on science kits to elementary and middle schools and gives 40 high school students (10 from each community) annual $3,000 college scholarships. A mentor is assigned to each student, who is given a paid summer internship at Hewlett-Packard and taught how to conduct a job search.[59] Although some members of the public fear business involvement in education, others believe that if business wants educated employees and customers in the future, it must help educate them now.

Business is also beginning to take more responsibility for the hard-core unemployed. Some are mentally or physically handicapped; some are homeless. Organizations such as the National Alliance of Businessmen fund programs to train the hard-core unemployed so that they can find jobs and support themselves. In addition to fostering self-support, such opportunities enhance self-esteem and help people become productive members of society.

Explore Your Career Options
Business Ethics

Many career opportunities are emerging today in the field of business ethics and social responsibility. Approximately one-third of *Fortune* 1,000 firms have an ethics officer, a position that most companies have created only in the last few years. The ethics officer is typically responsible for (1) meeting with employees, the board of directors, and top management to discuss and provide advice about ethics issues; (2) distributing a code of ethics; (3) creating and maintaining an anonymous, confidential service to answer questions about ethical issues; (4) taking actions on possible ethics code violations; and (5) reviewing and modifying the code of ethics. Entry-level jobs in ethics involve assisting with communications programs or training.

If you are interested in a career in the area of business ethics and social responsibility, take courses in business ethics, legal environment, and business and society. Many ethics officers have law degrees due to the interrelationship of many legal and ethical issues. Some elective courses in moral philosophy or sociology may also be useful. Subscribe to a magazine such as *Business Ethics,* a popular trade journal that provides information about companies that have ethics programs or are involved with socially responsible activities. By learning more about how real companies are carrying out the ethics/social responsibility function, you will be better prepared to apply for a job and be knowledgeable in matching your interests with a company's needs. Although there are only a small number of jobs available today in this emerging area, you could be in the forefront of a developing concern that has much potential for career advancement. If you prepare yourself properly through education and possibly a part-time job or internship in a large firm with an ethics department, you will greatly enhance the probability of developing a successful career in business ethics and social responsibility.[60]

Review Your Understanding

Define business ethics and social responsibility and examine their importance.

Business ethics refers to principles and standards that define acceptable business conduct. Acceptable business behavior is defined by customers, competitors, government regulators, interest groups, the public, and each individual's personal moral principles and values. Social responsibility is the obligation an organization assumes to maximize its positive impact and minimize its negative impact on society. Socially responsible businesses win the trust and respect of their employees, customers, and society and, in the long run, increase profits. Ethics is important in business because it builds trust and confidence in business relationships. Unethical actions may result in negative publicity, declining sales, and even legal action.

Detect some of the ethical issues that may arise in business.

An ethical issue is an identifiable problem, situation, or opportunity requiring a person or organization to choose from among several actions that must be evaluated as right or wrong. Ethical issues can be categorized in the context of their relation with conflicts of interest, fairness and honesty, communications, and business associations.

Specify how businesses can promote ethical behavior by employees.

Businesses can promote ethical behavior by employees by limiting their opportunity to engage in misconduct. Formal codes of ethics, ethical policies, and ethics training programs reduce the incidence of unethical behavior by informing employees what is expected of them and providing punishments for those who fail to comply.

Explain the four dimensions of social responsibility.

The four dimensions of social responsibility are economic (being profitable), legal (obeying the law), ethical (doing what is right, just, and fair), and voluntary (being a good corporate citizen).

Debate an organization's social responsibilities to owners, employees, consumers, the environment, and the community.

Businesses must maintain proper accounting procedures, provide all relevant information about the performance of the firm to investors, and protect the owners' rights and investments. In relations with employees, businesses are expected to provide a safe workplace, pay employees adequately for their work, and treat them fairly. Consumerism refers to the activities undertaken by independent individuals, groups, and organizations to protect their rights as consumers. Increasingly, society expects businesses to take greater responsibility for the environment, especially with regard to animal rights, as well as water, air, land, and noise pollution. Many businesses engage in activities to make the communities in which they operate better places for everyone to live and work.

Evaluate the ethics of a business's decision.

The "Solve the Dilemma" box on page 41 presents an ethical dilemma at Checkers Pizza. Using the material presented in this chapter, you should be able to analyze the ethical issues present in the dilemma, evaluate Barnard's plan, and develop a course of action for the firm.

Revisit the World of Business

1. Why do you think Home Depot has such a strong commitment to communities?

2. What are the social responsibility benefits to a company that recycles, uses environmentally responsible forest products, and encourages customers to use energy efficient products?

3. Do you think Home Depot would be as successful if it was not involved in social responsibility initiatives? Why or why not?

Learn the Terms

bribes   36
business ethics   32
codes of ethics   42

consumerism   49
corporate citizenship   45
ethical issue   35

plagiarism   40
social responsibility   32
whistleblowing   43

Check Your Progress

1. Define business ethics. Who determines whether a business activity is ethical? Is unethical conduct always illegal?

2. Distinguish between ethics and social responsibility.

3. Why has ethics become so important in business?

4. What is an ethical issue? What are some of the ethical issues named in your text? Why are they ethical issues?

5. What is a code of ethics? How can one reduce unethical behavior in business?

6. List and discuss the arguments for and against social responsibility by business (Table 2.7). Can you think of any additional arguments (for or against)?

7. What responsibilities does a business have toward its employees?

8. What responsibilities does business have with regard to the environment? What steps have been taken by some responsible businesses to minimize the negative impact of their activities on the environment?

9. What are a business's responsibilities toward the community in which it operates?

Get Involved

1. Discuss some recent examples of businesses engaging in unethical practices. Classify these practices as issues of conflict of interest, fairness and honesty, communications, or business relationships. Why do you think the businesses chose to behave unethically? What actions might the businesses have taken?

2. Discuss with your class some possible methods of improving ethical standards in business. Do you think that business should regulate its own activities or

that the federal government should establish and enforce ethical standards? How do you think businesspeople feel?

3. Find some examples of socially responsible businesses in newspapers or business journals. Explain why you believe their actions are socially responsible. Why do you think the companies chose to act as they did?

Build Your Skills

MAKING DECISIONS ABOUT ETHICAL ISSUES

Background:
The merger of Lockheed and Martin Marietta created Lockheed Martin, the number-one company in the defense industry—an industry that includes such companies as McDonnell Douglas and Northrop Grumman.

You and the rest of the class are managers at Lockheed Martin Corporation, Orlando, Florida. You are getting ready to do the group exercise in an ethics training session. The training instructor announces you will be playing *Gray Matters: The Ethics Game.* You are told that *Gray Matters,* which was prepared for your company's employees, is also played at 41 universities, including Harvard University, and at 65 other companies. Although there are 55 scenarios in *Gray Matters,* you will have time during this session to complete only the four scenarios that your group draws from the stack of cards.[61]

Task:
Form into groups of four to six managers and appoint a group leader who will lead a discussion of the case, obtain a consensus answer to the case, and be the one to report the group's answers to the instructor. You will have five minutes to reach each decision, after which time, the instructor will give the point values and rationale for each choice. Then you will have five minutes for the next case, etc., until all four cases have been completed. Keep track of your group's score for each case; the winning team will be the group scoring the most points.

Since this game is designed to reflect life, you may believe that some cases lack clarity or that some of your choices are not as precise as you would have liked. Also, some cases have only one solution, while others have more than one solution. Each choice is assessed points to reflect which answer is the most correct. **Your group's task is to select only one option in each case.**

Your group draws cards 4, 7, 36, and 40.

4

Mini-Case

For several months now, one of your colleagues has been slacking off, and you are getting stuck doing the work. You think it is unfair. What do you do?

Potential Answers

A. Recognize this as an opportunity for you to demonstrate how capable you are.
B. Go to your supervisor and complain about this unfair workload.
C. Discuss the problem with your colleague in an attempt to solve the problem without involving others.
D. Discuss the problem with the human resources department.

7

Mini-Case

You are aware that a fellow employee uses drugs on the job. Another friend encourages you to confront the person instead of informing the supervisor. What do you do?

Potential Answers

A. You speak to the alleged user and encourage him to get help.
B. You elect to tell your supervisor that you suspect an employee is using drugs on the job.
C. You confront the alleged user and tell him either to quit using drugs or you will "turn him in."
D. Report the matter to employee assistance.

36

Mini-Case

You work for a company that has implemented a policy of a smoke-free environment. You discover employees smoking in the restrooms of the building. You also smoke and don't like having to go outside to do it. What do you do?

Potential Answers

A. You ignore the situation.
B. You confront the employees and ask them to stop.
C. You join them, but only occasionally.
D. You contact your ethics or human resources representative and ask him or her to handle the situation.

40

Mini-Case

Your co-worker is copying company-purchased software and taking it home. You know a certain program costs $400, and you have been saving for a while to buy it. What do you do?

Potential Answers

A. You figure you can copy it too since nothing has ever happened to your co-worker.
B. You tell your co-worker he can't legally do this.
C. You report the matter to the ethics office.
D. You mention this to your supervisor.

---

eXtreme Surfing

- **Transparency International**
  www.transparency.org

  Provides a listing of the most corrupt countries in the world.

- **Business for Social Responsibility**
  www.bsr.org

  Offers news and resources about social responsibility in business today as part of a membership organization of global corporations.

- **E-Ethics Center**
  www.e-businessethics.com

  Provides a wealth of information about business ethics, corporate citizenship, organizational compliance, and related topics.

- **Bureau of Consumer Protection**
  www.ftc.gov/bcp/bcp.htm

  Warns consumers information about unfair, deceptive, or fraudulent business practices and offers advice on how to avoid them.

See for Yourself Videocase

MONEY AND ETHICS

Organizational practices and policies often create pressures, opportunities, and incentives that may sway employees to make unethical decisions. We have all seen news articles describing some "decent, hard-working family person" who had a highly ethical personal life yet chose to engage in illegal or unethical conduct in business. Understanding organizational ethics is important in developing ethical leadership. To help gain this understanding, it may be instructive to examine two companies facing ethical and legal issues.

Stew Leonard Makes a Personal Ethical Mistake

The story of Stew Leonard illustrates how one person's misconduct can affect the reputation of a company and destroy years of hard work. Stew Leonard's Farm Fresh Foods began in 1969 as a small dairy store with seven employees. Over the years, the store grew considerably, with over thirty additions. It also expanded beyond the fresh dairy products into meat, fish, produce, bakery, cheeses, and wines. Today, Stew Leonard's has become the World's Largest Dairy Store and a renowned grocery store, with nearly $300 million in annual sales and 2,000 employees. Headquartered in Norwalk, Connecticut, the company also has stores in Danbury, Connecticut, and Yonkers, New York. Where a traditional supermarket might carry an average of 30,000 items, Stew Leonard's stores carry only about 2,000, each individually chosen for its freshness and quality. The company has also remained a family business: the founder's son, Stew Leonard, Jr., is now the company president and CEO, while son Tom Leonard helped to open the Danbury, Connecticut, store.

In every respect, Stew Leonard's has been a model company and was recently named to *Fortune* magazine's "100 Best Companies to Work For." However, Stew Leonard, Sr., brought embarrassment and negative publicity to the company as a result of his personal actions, even though his son took over the company in 1987. After reports that the founder was taking unreported money from the stores to a Caribbean island to avoid federal income taxes, he was convicted of tax invasion and served several years in prison in the 1990s. The publicity surrounding his conviction tarnished the many good things he had achieved in building the business, as well as his own personal reputation.

Prior to his conviction, Stew Leonard, Sr. had been interviewed in numerous publications about the importance of ethics and social responsibility in business and how they had contributed to his own success. Anyone who has spent time in a federal prison will tell you that cheating others to gain more money is not worth it. People who take advantage of others and violate the laws or ethical standards of our society usually have to pay. Although the business Stew Leonard founded continues to do well, his family and business have been tainted by his crime.

Focusing on the Bottom Line Destroys Arthur Andersen

Arthur Andersen LLP was founded in Chicago in 1913 by Arthur Andersen and partner Clarence DeLany. Over a span of nearly ninety years, the Chicago accounting firm became known as one of the "Big Five" largest accounting firms in the United States, together with Deloitte & Touche, PricewaterhouseCoopers, Ernst & Young, and KPMG. For most of those years, the firm's name was nearly synonymous with trust, integrity, and ethics. Such values are crucial for a firm charged with independently auditing and confirming the financial statements of public corporations, on whose accuracy investors depend for investment decisions.

Although Arthur Andersen once exemplified the rock-solid character and integrity that was synonymous with the accounting profession, high-profile bankruptcies of clients such as Enron and WorldCom capped a string of accounting scandals that eventually cost investors nearly $300 billion and hundreds of thousands of people their jobs. As a result, the Chicago-based accounting firm was forced to close its doors after ninety years of business.

During Andersen's last decade, growth became the priority, and the firm's emphasis on recruiting and retaining big clients perhaps came at the expense of quality and independence in its auditing practice. The company developed a major consulting business, which was linked to its auditing practice in a joint cooperative relationship, which may have compromised its auditors' independence, a quality crucial to the execution of a credible audit. The firm's focus on growth also generated a fundamental shift in its corporate culture, to a point where obtaining high-profit consulting business seemed to have been regarded more highly than providing objective auditing services. Those individuals who could deliver the big accounts were often promoted ahead of the practitioners of quality audits.

The company was convicted of obstruction of justice and agreed to cease auditing public corporations in 2002, essentially marking the end of the ninety-year-old accounting institution. Its consulting unit, which had been spun off into a separate entity, called Accenture, was free and clear of all charges. Perhaps understandably, the consulting firm chooses to avoid mentioning its origins and association with Andersen.

A large number of Arthur Andersen's clients were embroiled in the accounting scandals of the early twenty-first century and some sought refuge in bankruptcy court. The scandals helped spur a new focus on business ethics, driven largely by public demands for greater corporate transparency and accountability. In response, Congress passed the Sarbanes-Oxley Act of 2002, which established new guidelines and direction for corporate and accounting responsibility.

Most members of society today are expressing concern for more responsible and ethical conduct in business. The values learned from family, school, and friends may not always provide specific guidelines for complex decisions in the business world. In general, if you are afraid to tell your coworkers or family about what you are doing, have resorted to hiding and destroying information to cover your actions, or have schemed to avoid doing the right thing, then you should recognize that, like Stew Leonard, Sr. and Arthur Andersen, LLP, your actions can not only harm you but also jeopardize all of your good work.[62]

Discussion Questions

1. After becoming so financially successful, why do you think Stew Leonard, Sr. was willing to risk everything by avoiding taxes?

2. What do you think caused Arthur Andersen to focus too much on the bottom line, rather than responsible accounting services?

3. Why do so many ethical problems relate to money and greed?

Remember to check out our Online Learning Center at www.mhhe.com/ferrell5e.

Appendix A

The Legal and Regulatory Environment

Business law refers to the rules and regulations that govern the conduct of business. Problems in this area come from the failure to keep promises, misunderstandings, disagreements about expectations, or, in some cases, attempts to take advantage of others. The regulatory environment offers a framework and enforcement system in order to provide a fair playing field for all businesses. The regulatory environment is created based on inputs from competitors, customers, employees, special interest groups, and the public's elected representatives. Lobbying by pressure groups who try to influence legislation often shapes the legal and regulatory environment.

Sources of Law

Laws are classified as either criminal or civil. *Criminal law* not only prohibits a specific kind of action, such as unfair competition or mail fraud, but also imposes a fine or imprisonment as punishment for violating the law. A violation of a criminal law is thus called a crime. *Civil law* defines all the laws not classified as criminal, and it specifies the rights and duties of individuals and organizations (including businesses). Violations of civil law may result in fines but not imprisonment. The primary difference between criminal and civil law is that criminal laws are enforced by the state or nation, whereas civil laws are enforced through the court system by individuals or organizations.

Criminal and civil laws are derived from four sources: the Constitution (constitutional law), precedents established by judges (common law), federal and state statutes (statutory law), and federal and state administrative agencies (administrative law). Federal administrative agencies established by Congress control and influence business by enforcing laws and regulations to encourage competition and protect consumers, workers, and the environment. The Supreme Court is the ultimate

This ad indicates that lawsuits affect many businesses.

authority on legal and regulatory decisions for appropriate conduct in business.

Courts and the Resolution of Disputes

The primary method of resolving conflicts and business disputes is through **lawsuits,** where one individual or organization takes another to court us-

Marcia & Bill Baker found Heinz was underfilling their 20 oz. ketchup bottles by 1 1/2 oz. Heinz paid civil penalties and costs of $180,000 and had to overfill all ketchup bottles in California by 1/8 oz. for a year.

ing civil laws. The legal system, therefore, provides a forum for businesspeople to resolve disputes based on our legal foundations. The courts may decide when harm or damage results from the actions of others.

Because lawsuits are so frequent in the world of business, it is important to understand more about the court system where such disputes are resolved. Both financial restitution and specific actions to undo wrongdoing can result from going before a court to resolve a conflict. All decisions made in the courts are based on criminal and civil laws derived from the legal and regulatory system.

A businessperson may win a lawsuit in court and receive a judgment, or court order, requiring the loser of the suit to pay monetary damages. However, this does not guarantee the victor will be able to collect those damages. If the loser of the suit lacks the financial resources to pay the judgment— for example, if the loser is a bankrupt business—the winner of the suit may not be able to collect the award. Most business lawsuits involve a request for a sum of money, but some lawsuits request that a

court specifically order a person or organization to do or to refrain from doing a certain act, such as slamming telephone customers.

The Court System

Jurisdiction is the legal power of a court, through a judge, to interpret and apply the law and make a binding decision in a particular case. In some instances, other courts will not enforce the decision of a prior court because it lacked jurisdiction. Federal courts are granted jurisdiction by the Constitution or by Congress. State legislatures and constitutions determine which state courts hear certain types of cases. Courts of general jurisdiction hear all types of cases; those of limited jurisdiction hear only specific types of cases. The Federal Bankruptcy Court, for example, hears only cases involving bankruptcy. There is some combination of limited and general jurisdiction courts in every state.

In a **trial court** (whether in a court of general or limited jurisdiction and whether in the state or the federal system), two tasks must be completed. First, the court (acting through the judge or a jury) must determine the facts of the case. In other words, if there is conflicting evidence, the judge or jury must decide who to believe. Second, the judge must decide which law or set of laws is pertinent to the case and must then apply those laws to resolve the dispute.

An **appellate court,** on the other hand, deals solely with appeals relating to the interpretation of law. Thus, when you hear about a case being appealed, it is not retried, but rather reevaluated. Appellate judges do not hear witnesses but instead base their decisions on a written transcript of the original trial. Moreover, appellate courts do not draw factual conclusions; the appellate judge is limited to deciding whether the trial judge made a mistake in interpreting the law that probably affected the outcome of the trial. If the trial judge made no mistake (or if mistakes would not have changed the result of the trial), the appellate court will let the trial court's decision stand. If the appellate court finds a mistake, it usually sends the case back to the trial court so that the mistake can be corrected. Correction may involve the granting of a new trial. On occasion, appellate courts modify the verdict of the trial court without sending the case back to the trial court.

Martha Stewart is arguably America's most famous home-maker and one of its richest women executives. She left a position as a successful stockbroker to start a gourmet-food shop and catering business that evolved into Martha Stewart Living Omnimedia Inc. (MSLO), a company with interests in publishing, television, merchandising, electronic commerce, and related international partnerships. In 2001, however, Stewart became the center of headlines, speculation, and eventually a much-publicized trial on criminal charges related to her sales of 4,000 shares of ImClone stock one day before that firm's stock price plummeted.

On December 27, 2001, Martha Stewart sold 3,928 shares of ImClone stock, one day before the Food and Drug Administration refused to review ImClone System's cancer drug Erbitux; the company's stock tumbled following the announcement. Stewart later told investigators that she sold the stock after her broker, Peter Bacanovic, informed her that ImClone's stock had fallen below a $60 threshold they had previously arranged. However, Bacanovic's assistant, Douglas Faneuil, who handled the sale for Stewart, later told Merrill Lynch lawyers that Bacanovic had pressured him to lie about the stop-loss order.

In June 2003, a federal grand jury indicted Stewart on charges of securities fraud, conspiracy (together with Peter Bacanovic), making false statements, and obstruction of justice, but not insider trading. The 41-page indictment alleged that she lied to federal investigators about the stock sale, attempted to cover up her activities, and defrauded Martha Stewart Living Omnimedia shareholders by misleading them about the gravity of the situation and thereby keeping the stock price from falling. The indictment further accused Stewart of deleting a computer log of the telephone message from Bacanovic informing her that he thought ImClone's stock "was going to start trading downward." Bacanovic was indicted on similar charges. Both Stewart and Bacanovic pleaded "not guilty" to all charges, but Stewart resigned her positions as chief executive offi-

cer and chairman of the board of Martha Stewart Living Omnimedia just hours after the indictment.

In February 2004, U.S. District Judge Miriam Goldman Cedarbaum threw out the most serious of the charges against Stewart—securities fraud. However, just one week later, a jury convicted Stewart on four remaining charges of making false statements and conspiracy to obstruct justice. Her broker, Peter Bacanovic, was also found guilty on four out of five charges including making false statements, conspiracy to obstruct justice, and perjury. Stewart was sentenced to five months in jail and five months in at-home detention.

Stewart's legal woes did not end with the federal trial. Kmart, with which she had a 17-year partnership to sell an exclusive line of Martha Stewart–branded housewares, filed a complaint in early 2004, accusing Stewart's company of overcharging the discount retailer for the right to sell her Martha Stewart Everyday line of products. MSLO executives denied the accusation as a misunderstanding of the terms of the two firms' contract.

Sources: Krysten Crawford, "Stewart Considers Serving Time Now," CNN/Money, July 20, 2004, http://money.cnn.com; O. C. Ferrell, John Fraedrich, and Linda Ferrell, "Martha Stewart: Insider-Trading Scandal," in *Business Ethics: Ethical Decision Making and Cases,* 6th ed. (Boston: Houghton Mifflin, 2005), pp. 300–6; Sarah Rush, "Kmart Suing Stewart's Company," *The Coloradoan,* February 14, 2004, p. D10; Kara Scannell and Matthew Rose, "Stewart Lawyer Says the Case Wasn't Proved," *The Wall Street Journal,* March 3, 2004, http://online.wsj.com; "Stewart Convicted on All Charges," *CNN/Money,* March 5, 2004, http://money.cnn.com/2004/03/05/news/companies/martha_verdict/

Discussion Questions

1. Why do you think Martha Stewart was convicted of lying about insider trading—a charge that was later thrown out?
2. Do you think the legal system was fair to Martha Stewart given her gender and her celebrity status? Was she used as an example?
3. What do you think Martha Stewart would suggest to others to avoid the legal problems that changed her life?

Alternative Dispute Resolution Methods

Although the main remedy for business disputes is a lawsuit, other dispute resolution methods are becoming popular. The schedules of state and federal trial courts are often crowded; long delays between the filing of a case and the trial date are common. Further, complex cases can become quite expensive to pursue. As a result, many businesspeople are turning to alternative methods of resolving business arguments: mediation and arbitration, the mini-trial, and litigation in a private court.

Mediation is a form of negotiation to resolve a dispute by bringing in one or more third-party mediators, usually chosen by the disputing parties, to help reach a settlement. The mediator suggests different ways to resolve a dispute between the parties. The mediator's resolution is nonbinding—that is, the parties do not have to accept the mediator's suggestions; they are strictly voluntary.

Arbitration involves submission of a dispute to one or more third-party arbitrators, usually chosen by the disputing parties, whose decision usually is final. Arbitration differs from mediation in that an arbitrator's decision must be followed, whereas a mediator merely offers suggestions and facilitates negotiations. Cases may be submitted to arbitration because a contract—such as a labor contract—requires it or because the parties agree to do so. Some consumers are barred from taking claims to court by agreements drafted by banks, brokers, health plans, and others. Instead, they are required to take complaints to mandatory arbitration. Arbitration can be an attractive alternative to a lawsuit because it is often cheaper and quicker, and the parties frequently can choose arbitrators who are knowledgeable about the particular area of business at issue.

A method of dispute resolution that may become increasingly important in settling complex disputes is the **mini-trial,** in which both parties agree to present a summarized version of their case to an independent third party. That person then advises them of his or her impression of the probable outcome if the case were to be tried. Representatives of both sides then attempt to negotiate a settlement based on the advisor's recommendations. For example, employees in a large corporation who believe they have muscular or skeletal stress injuries caused by the strain of repetitive motion in using a computer could agree to a mini-trial to address a dispute related to damages. Although the mini-trial itself does not resolve the dispute, it can help the parties resolve the case before going to court. Because the mini-trial is not subject to formal court rules, it can save companies a great deal of money, allowing them to recognize the weaknesses in a particular case.

In some areas of the country, disputes can be submitted to a private nongovernmental court for resolution. In a sense, a **private court system** is similar to arbitration in that an independent third party resolves the case after hearing both sides of the story. Trials in private courts may be either informal or highly formal, depending on the people involved. Businesses typically agree to have their disputes decided in private courts to save time and money.

Regulatory Administrative Agencies

Federal and state administrative agencies (listed in Table A.1) also have some judicial powers. Many administrative agencies, such as the Federal Trade Commission, decide disputes that involve their regulations. In such disputes, the resolution process is usually called a "hearing" rather than a trial. In these cases, an administrative law judge decides all issues.

Federal regulatory agencies influence many business activities and cover product liability, safety, and the regulation or deregulation of public utilities. Usually, these bodies have the power to enforce specific laws, such as the Federal Trade Commission Act, and have some discretion in establishing operating rules and regulations to guide certain types of industry practices. Because of this discretion and overlapping areas of responsibility, confusion or conflict regarding which agencies have jurisdiction over which activities is common.

Of all the federal regulatory units, the **Federal Trade Commission (FTC)** most influences business activities related to questionable practices that create disputes between businesses and their customers. Although the FTC regulates a variety of business practices, it allocates a large portion of resources to curbing false advertising, misleading pricing, and deceptive packaging and labeling. When it receives a complaint or otherwise has reason to believe that a firm is violating a law, the FTC issues a complaint stating that the business is in violation.

If a company continues the questionable practice, the FTC can issue a cease-and-desist order, which is an order for the business to stop doing whatever has caused the complaint. In such cases, the charged firm can appeal to the federal courts to have the order rescinded. However, the FTC can seek civil penalties in court—up to a maximum penalty of $10,000 a day for each infraction—if a cease-and-desist order is violated. In its battle against unfair pricing, the FTC has issued consent decrees alleging that corporate attempts to engage in price fixing or invitations to competitors to collude are violations even when the competitors in question refuse the invitations. The commission can also require companies

TABLE A.1   Major Regulatory Agencies

Agency	Major Areas of Responsibility
Federal Trade Commission (FTC)	Enforces laws and guidelines regarding business practices; takes action to stop false and deceptive advertising and labeling.
Food and Drug Administration (FDA)	Enforces laws and regulations to prevent distribution of adulterated or misbranded foods, drugs, medical devices, cosmetics, veterinary products, and particularly hazardous consumer products.
Consumer Product Safety Commission (CPSC)	Ensures compliance with the Consumer Product Safety Act; protects the public from unreasonable risk of injury from any consumer product not covered by other regulatory agencies.
Interstate Commerce Commission (ICC)	Regulates franchises, rates, and finances of interstate rail, bus, truck, and water carriers.
Federal Communications Commission (FCC)	Regulates communication by wire, radio, and television in interstate and foreign commerce.
Environmental Protection Agency (EPA)	Develops and enforces environmental protection standards and conducts research into the adverse effects of pollution.
Federal Energy Regulatory Commission (FERC)	Regulates rates and sales of natural gas products, thereby affecting the supply and price of gas available to consumers; also regulates wholesale rates for electricity and gas, pipeline construction, and U.S. imports and exports of natural gas and electricity.
Equal Employment Opportunity Commission (EEOC)	Investigates and resolves discrimination in employment practices.
Federal Aviation Administration (FAA)	Oversees the policies and regulations of the airline industry.
Federal Highway Administration (FHA)	Regulates vehicle safety requirements.
Occupational Safety and Health Administration (OSHA)	Develops policy to promote worker safety and health and investigates infractions.
Securities and Exchange Commission (SEC)	Regulates corporate securities trading and develops protection from fraud and other abuses, provides an accounting oversight board.

to run corrective advertising in response to previous ads considered misleading.

The FTC also assists businesses in complying with laws. New marketing methods are evaluated every year. When general sets of guidelines are needed to improve business practices in a particular industry, the FTC sometimes encourages firms within that industry to establish a set of trade practices voluntarily. The FTC may even sponsor a conference bringing together industry leaders and consumers for the purpose of establishing acceptable trade practices.

Unlike the FTC, other regulatory units are limited to dealing with specific products, services, or business activities. The Food and Drug Administration (FDA) enforces regulations prohibiting the sale and distribution of adulterated, misbranded, or hazardous food and drug products. For example, the FDA outlawed the sale and distribution of most over-the-counter hair-loss remedies after research indicated that few of the products were effective in restoring hair growth.

The Environmental Protection Agency (EPA) develops and enforces environmental protection standards and conducts research into the adverse effects of pollution. The Consumer Product Safety Commission recalls about 300 products a year, ranging from small, inexpensive toys to major appliances. The Consumer Product Safety Commission's web site provides details regarding current recalls.

Important Elements of Business Law

To avoid violating criminal and civil laws, as well as discouraging lawsuits from consumers, employees, suppliers, and others, businesspeople need to be familiar with laws that address business practices.

The Uniform Commercial Code

At one time, states had their own specific laws governing various business practices, and transacting business across state lines was difficult because of the variation in the laws from state to state. To simplify commerce, every state—except Louisiana—has enacted the Uniform Commercial Code (Louisiana has enacted portions of the code). The **Uniform Commercial Code (UCC)** is a set of statutory laws covering several business law topics. Article II of the Uniform Commercial Code, which is discussed in the following paragraphs, has significant impact on business.

Sales Agreements.   Article II of the Uniform Commercial Code covers sales agreements for goods and services but does not cover the sale of stocks and bonds, personal services, or real estate. Among its many provisions, Article II stipulates that a sales agreement can be enforced even though it does not specify the selling price or the time or place of delivery. It also requires that a buyer pay a reasonable price for goods at the time of delivery if the buyer and seller have not reached an agreement on price. Specifically, Article II addresses the rights of buyers and sellers, transfers of ownership, warranties, and the legal placement of risk during manufacture and delivery.

Article II also deals with express and implied warranties. An **express warranty** stipulates the specific terms the seller will honor. Many automobile manufacturers, for example, provide three-year or 36,000-mile warranties on their vehicles, during which period they will fix any and all defects specified in the warranty. An **implied warranty** is imposed on the producer or seller by law, although it may not be a written document provided at the time of sale. Under Article II, a consumer may assume that the product for sale has a clear title (in other words, that it is not stolen) and

New car buyers receive express warranties stating what is covered for repair or replacement over a specific period of time.

that the product will both serve the purpose for which it was made and sold as well as function as advertised.

The Law of Torts and Fraud

A **tort** is a private or civil wrong other than breach of contract. For example, a tort can result if the driver of a Domino's Pizza delivery car loses control of the vehicle and damages property or injures a person. In the case of the delivery car accident, the injured persons might sue the driver and the owner of the company—Domino's in this case—for damages resulting from the accident.

Fraud is a purposeful unlawful act to deceive or manipulate in order to damage others. Thus, in some cases, a tort may also represent a violation of criminal law. Health care fraud has become a major issue in the courts.

An important aspect of tort law involves **product liability**—businesses' legal responsibility for any negligence in the design, production, sale, and consumption of products. Product liability laws have evolved from both common and statutory law. Some states have expanded the concept of product liability to include injuries by products whether or not the producer is proven negligent. Under this strict product liability, a consumer who files suit because of an injury has to prove only that the product was defective, that the defect caused the injury, and that the defect made the product unreasonably dangerous. For example, a carving knife is expected to be sharp and is not considered defective if you cut your finger using it. But an electric knife could be considered defective and unreasonably dangerous if it continued to operate after being switched off.

TABLE A.2 State Court Systems' Reputations for Supporting Business

Most Friendly to Business	Least Friendly to Business
Delaware	Mississippi
Nebraska	West Virginia
Virginia	Alabama
Iowa	Louisiana
Idaho	California
Utah	Texas
New Hampshire	Illinois
Minnesota	Montana
Kansas	Arkansas
Wisconsin	Missouri

Source: U.S. Chamber of Commerce Institute for Legal Reform, in Martin Kasindorf, "Robin Hood Is Alive in Court, Say Those Seeking Lawsuit Limits," *USA Today,* March 8, 2004, p. 4A.

Reforming tort law, particularly in regard to product liability, has become a hot political issue as businesses look for relief from huge judgments in lawsuits. Although many lawsuits are warranted— few would disagree that a wrong has occurred when a patient dies because of negligence during a medical procedure or when a child is seriously injured by a defective toy, and that the families deserve some compensation—many suits are not. Because of multimillion-dollar judgments, companies are trying to minimize their liability, and sometimes they pass on the costs of the damage awards to their customers in the form of higher prices. Some states have passed laws limiting damage awards and some tort reform is occurring at the federal level. Table A.2 lists the state courts systems the U.S. Chamber of Commerce's Institute for Legal Reform has identified as being "friendliest" and "least friendly" to business in terms of juries' fairness, judges' competence and impartiality, and other factors.

The Law of Contracts

Virtually every business transaction is carried out by means of a **contract,** a mutual agreement between two or more parties that can be enforced in a court if one party chooses not to comply with the terms of the contract. If you rent an apartment or house, for example, your lease is a contract. If you have borrowed money under a student loan program, you have a contractual agreement to repay the money. Many aspects of contract law are covered under the Uniform Commercial Code.

A "handshake deal" is in most cases as fully and completely binding as a written, signed contract agreement. Indeed, many oil-drilling and construction contractors have for years agreed to take on projects on the basis of such handshake deals. However, individual states require that some contracts be in writing to be enforceable. Most states require that at least some of the following contracts be in writing:

- Contracts involving the sale of land or an interest in land.
- Contracts to pay somebody else's debt.
- Contracts that cannot be fulfilled within one year.
- Contracts for the sale of goods that cost more than $500 (required by the Uniform Commercial Code).

Only those contracts that meet certain requirements—called *elements*—are enforceable by the courts. A person or business seeking to enforce a contract must show that it contains the following elements: voluntary agreement, consideration, contractual capacity of the parties, and legality.

For any agreement to be considered a legal contract, all persons involved must agree to be bound by the terms of the contract. *Voluntary agreement* typically comes about when one party makes an offer and the other accepts. If both the offer and the acceptance are freely, voluntarily, and knowingly made, the acceptance forms the basis for the contract. If, however, either the offer or the acceptance are the result of fraud or force, the individual or organization subject to the fraud or force can void, or invalidate, the resulting agreement or receive compensation for damages.

The second requirement for enforcement of a contract is that it must be supported by *consideration*—that is, money or something of value must be given in return for fulfilling a contract. As a general rule, a person cannot be forced to abide by the terms of a promise unless that person receives a consideration. The something-of-value could be money, goods, services, or even a promise to do or not to do something.

Contractual capacity is the legal ability to enter into a contract. As a general rule, a court cannot enforce a contract if either party to the agreement lacks contractual capacity. A person's contractual capacity may be limited or nonexistent if he or she is a minor (under the age of 18), mentally unstable, retarded, insane, or intoxicated.

Legality is the state or condition of being lawful. For an otherwise binding contract to be enforceable, both the purpose of and the consideration for the contract must be legal. A contract in which a bank loans money at a rate of interest prohibited by law, a practice known as usury, would be an illegal contract, for example. The fact that one of the parties may commit an illegal act while performing a contract does not render the contract itself illegal, however.

Breach of contract is the failure or refusal of a party to a contract to live up to his or her promises. In the case of an apartment lease, failure to pay rent would be considered breach of contract. The breaching party—the one who fails to comply—may be liable for monetary damages that he or she causes the other person.

The Law of Agency

An **agency** is a common business relationship created when one person acts on behalf of another and under that person's control. Two parties are involved in an agency relationship: The **principal** is the one who wishes to have a specific task accomplished; the **agent** is the one who acts on behalf of the principal to accomplish the task. Authors, movie stars, and athletes often employ agents to help them obtain the best contract terms.

An agency relationship is created by the mutual agreement of the principal and the agent. It is usually not necessary that such an agreement be in writing, although putting it in writing is certainly advisable. An agency relationship continues as long as both the principal and the agent so desire. It can be terminated by mutual agreement, by fulfillment of the purpose of the agency, by the refusal of either party to continue in the relationship, or by the death of either the principal or the agent. In most cases, a principal grants authority to the agent through a formal *power of attorney,* which is a legal document authorizing a person to act as someone else's agent. The power of attorney can be used for any agency relationship, and its use is not limited to lawyers. For instance, in real estate transactions, often a lawyer or real estate agent is given power of attorney with the authority to purchase real estate for the buyer. Accounting firms often give employees agency relationships in making financial transactions.

The Law of Property

Property law is extremely broad in scope because it covers the ownership and transfer of all kinds of real, personal, and intellectual property. **Real property** consists of real estate and everything permanently attached to it; **personal property** basically is everything else. Personal property can be further subdivided into tangible and intangible property. *Tangible property* refers to items that have a physical existence, such as automobiles, business inventory, and clothing. *Intangible property* consists of rights and duties; its existence may be represented by a document or by some other tangible item. For example, accounts receivable, stock in a corporation, goodwill, and trademarks are all examples of intangible personal property. **Intellectual property** refers to property, such as musical works, artwork, books, and computer software, that is generated by a person's creative activities.

Copyrights, patents, and trademarks provide protection to the owners of property by giving them the exclusive right to use it. *Copyrights* protect the ownership rights on material (often intellectual property) such as books, music, videos, photos, and computer software. The creators of such works, or their heirs, generally have exclusive rights to the published or unpublished works for the creator's lifetime, plus 50 years. *Patents* give inventors exclusive rights to their invention for 17 years. The most intense competition for patents is in the pharmaceutical industry. Most patents take a minimum of 18 months to secure.

A *trademark* is a brand (name, mark, or symbol) that is registered with the U.S. Patent and Trademark Office and is thus legally protected from use by any other firm. Among the symbols that have been so protected are McDonald's golden arches and Coca-Cola's distinctive bottle shape. It is estimated that large multinational firms may have as many as 15,000 conflicts related to trademarks. Companies are diligent

TABLE A.3 Types of Bankruptcy	
Chapter 7	Requires that the business be dissolved and its assets liquidated, or sold, to pay off the debts. Individuals declaring Chapter 7 retain a limited amount of exempt assets, the amount of which may be determined by state or federal law, at the debtor's option. Although the type and value of exempt assets varies from state to state, most states' laws allow a bankrupt individual to keep an automobile, some household goods, clothing, furnishings, and at least some of the value of the debtor's residence. All nonexempt assets must be sold to pay debts.
Chapter 11	Temporarily frees a business from its financial obligations while it reorganizes and works out a payment plan with its creditors. The indebted company continues to operate its business during bankruptcy proceedings. Often, the business sells off assets and less-profitable subsidiaries to raise cash to pay off its immediate obligations.
Chapter 13	Similar to Chapter 11 but limited to individuals. This proceeding allows an individual to establish a three- to five-year plan for repaying his or her debt. Under this plan, an individual ultimately may repay as little as 10 percent of his or her debt.

about protecting their trademarks both to avoid confusion in consumers' minds and because a term that becomes part of everyday language can no longer be trademarked. The names *aspirin* and *nylon*, for example, were once the exclusive property of their creators but became so widely used as product names (rather than brand names) that now anyone can use them.

As the trend toward globalization of trade continues, and more and more businesses trade across national boundaries, protecting property rights, particularly intellectual property such as computer software, has become an increasing challenge. While a company may be able to register as a trademark a brand name or symbol in its home country, it may not be able to secure that protection abroad. Some countries have copyright and patent laws that are less strict than those of the United States; some countries will not enforce U.S. laws. China, for example, has often been criticized for permitting U.S. goods to be counterfeited there. Such counterfeiting harms not only the sales of U.S. companies but also their reputations if the knockoffs are of poor quality. Thus, businesses engaging in foreign trade may have to take extra steps to protect their property because local laws may be insufficient to protect them.

The Law of Bankruptcy

Although few businesses and individuals intentionally fail to repay (or default on) their debts, sometimes they cannot fulfill their financial obligations. Individuals may charge goods and services beyond their ability to pay for them. Businesses may take on too much debt in order to finance growth. An option of last resort in these cases is **bankruptcy,** or legal insolvency. For example, Sunbeam filed Chapter 11 bankruptcy in 2001.

Individuals or companies may ask a bankruptcy court to declare them unable to pay their debts and thus release them from the obligation of repaying those debts. The debtor's assets may then be sold to pay off as much of the debt as possible. In the case of a personal bankruptcy, although the individual is released from repaying debts and can start over with a clean slate, obtaining credit after bankruptcy proceedings is very difficult. Although the person or company in debt usually initiates bankruptcy proceedings, creditors may also initiate them. Table A.3 describes the various levels of bankruptcy protection a business or individual may seek.

Laws Affecting Business Practices

One of the government's many roles is to act as a watchdog to ensure that businesses behave in accordance with the wishes of society. Congress has enacted a number of laws that affect business practices; some of the most important of these are summarized in Table A.4. Many state legislatures have enacted similar laws governing business within specific states.

TABLE A.4   Major Federal Laws Affecting Business Practices

Act (Date Enacted)	Purpose
Sherman Antitrust Act (1890)	Prohibits contracts, combinations, or conspiracies to restrain trade; establishes as a misdemeanor monopolizing or attempting to monopolize.
Clayton Act (1914)	Prohibits specific practices such as price discrimination, exclusive dealer arrangements, and stock acquisitions in which the effect may notably lessen competition or tend to create a monopoly.
Federal Trade Commission Act (1914)	Created the Federal Trade Commission; also gives the FTC investigatory powers to be used in preventing unfair methods of competition.
Robinson-Patman Act (1936)	Prohibits price discrimination that lessens competition among wholesalers or retailers; prohibits producers from giving disproportionate services of facilities to large buyers.
Wheeler-Lea Act (1938)	Prohibits unfair and deceptive acts and practices regardless of whether competition is injured; places advertising of foods and drugs under the jurisdiction of the FTC.
Lanham Act (1946)	Provides protections and regulation of brand names, brand marks, trade names, and trademarks.
Celler-Kefauver Act (1950)	Prohibits any corporation engaged in commerce from acquiring the whole or any part of the stock or other share of the capital assets of another corporation when the effect substantially lessens competition or tends to create a monopoly.
Fair Packaging and Labeling Act (1966)	Makes illegal the unfair or deceptive packaging or labeling of consumer products.
Magnuson-Moss Warranty (FTC) Act (1975)	Provides for minimum disclosure standards for written consumer product warranties; defines minimum consent standards for written warranties; allows the FTC to prescribe interpretive rules in policy statements regarding unfair or deceptive practices.
Consumer Goods Pricing Act (1975)	Prohibits the use of price maintenance agreements among manufacturers and resellers in interstate commerce.
Antitrust Improvements Act (1976)	Requires large corporations to inform federal regulators of prospective mergers or acquisitions so that they can be studied for any possible violations of the law.
Trademark Counterfeiting Act (1980)	Provides civil and criminal penalties against those who deal in counterfeit consumer goods or any counterfeit goods that can threaten health or safety.
Trademark Law Revision Act (1988)	Amends the Lanham Act to allow brands not yet introduced to be protected through registration with the Patent and Trademark Office.
Nutrition Labeling and Education Act (1990)	Prohibits exaggerated health claims and requires all processed foods to contain labels with nutritional information.
Telephone Consumer Protection Act (1991)	Establishes procedures to avoid unwanted telephone solicitations; prohibits marketers from using automated telephone dialing system or an artificial or prerecorded voice to certain telephone lines.
Federal Trademark Dilution Act (1995)	Provides trademark owners the right to protect trademarks and requires relinquishment of names that match or parallel existing trademarks.

continued

TABLE A.4 *continued*

Act (Date Enacted)	Purpose
Digital Millennium Copyright Act (1998)	Refined copyright laws to protect digital versions of copyrighted materials, including music and movies.
Children's Online Privacy Protection Act (2000)	Regulates the collection of personally identifiable information (name, address, e-mail address, hobbies, interests, or information collected through cookies) online from children under age 13.
Sarbanes-Oxley Act (2002)	Made securities fraud a criminal offense; stiffened penalties for corporate fraud; created an accounting oversight board; and instituted numerous other provisions designed to increase corporate transparency and compliance.

The **Sherman Antitrust Act,** passed in 1890 to prevent businesses from restraining trade and monopolizing markets, condemns "every contract, combination, or conspiracy in restraint of trade." For example, a request that a competitor agree to fix prices or divide markets would, if accepted, result in a violation of the Sherman Act. Proof of intent plays an important role in attempted monopolization cases under the Sherman Act. Enforced by the Antitrust Division of the Department of Justice, the Sherman Antitrust Act applies to firms operating in interstate commerce and to U.S. firms operating in foreign commerce. The Sherman Antitrust Act, still highly relevant 100 years after its passage, is being copied throughout the world as the basis for regulating fair competition.

Because the provisions of the Sherman Antitrust Act are rather vague, courts have not always interpreted it as its creators intended. The Clayton Act was passed in 1914 to limit specific activities that can reduce competition. The **Clayton Act** prohibits price discrimination, tying and exclusive agreements, and the acquisition of stock in another corporation where the effect may be to substantially lessen competition or tend to create a monopoly. In addition, the Clayton Act prohibits members of one company's board of directors from holding seats on the boards of competing corporations. The act also exempts farm cooperatives and labor organizations from antitrust laws.

In spite of these laws regulating business practices, there are still many questions about the regulation of business. For instance, it is difficult to determine

what constitutes an acceptable degree of competition and whether a monopoly is harmful to a particular market. Many mergers were permitted in the 1990s that resulted in less competition in the banking, publishing, and automobile industries. In some industries, such as utilities, it is not cost-effective to have too many competitors. For this reason, the government permits utility monopolies, although recently, the telephone, electricity, and communications industries have been deregulated. Furthermore, the antitrust laws are often rather vague and require interpretation, which may vary from judge to judge and court to court. Thus, what one judge defines as a monopoly or trust today may be permitted by another judge a few years from now. Businesspeople need to understand what the law says on these issues and try to conduct their affairs within the bounds of these laws.

The Internet: Legal and Regulatory Issues

Our use and dependence on the Internet is increasingly creating a potential legal problem for businesses. With this growing use come questions of maintaining an acceptable level of privacy for consumers and proper competitive use of the medium. Some might consider that tracking individuals who visit or "hit" their Web site by attaching a "cookie" (identifying you as a Web site visitor for potential recontact and tracking your movement throughout the site) is an improper use of the Internet for business

BBB OnLine provides programs and standards that protect the privacy of consumers.

purposes. Others may find such practices acceptable and similar to the practices of non-Internet retailers who copy information from checks or ask customers for their name, address, or phone number before they will process a transaction. There are few specific laws that regulate business on the Internet, but the standards for acceptable behavior that are reflected in the basic laws and regulations designed for traditional businesses can be applied to business on the Internet as well.

The central focus for future legislation of business conducted on the Internet is the protection of personal privacy. The present basis of personal privacy protection is the U.S. Constitution, various Supreme Court rulings, and laws such as the 1971 Fair Credit Reporting Act, the 1978 Right to Financial Privacy Act, and the 1974 Privacy Act, which deals with the release of government records. With few regulations on the use of information by businesses, companies legally buy and sell information on customers to gain competitive advantage. It has been suggested that the treatment of personal data as property will ensure privacy rights by recognizing that customers have a right to control the use of their personal data.

Internet use is different from traditional interaction with businesses in that it is readily accessible, and most online businesses are able to develop databases of information on customers. Congress has restricted the development of databases on children using the Internet. The Children's Online Privacy Protection Act of 2000 prohibits Web sites and Internet providers from seeking personal information from children under age 13 without parental consent.

The Internet has also created a copyright dilemma for some organizations that have found that the Web addresses of other online firms either match or are very similar to their company trademark. "Cyber-squatters" attempt to sell back the registration of these matching sites to the trademark owner. Com-

panies such as Taco Bell, MTC, and KFC have paid thousands of dollars to gain control of domain names that match or parallel company trademarks. The Federal Trademark Dilution Act of 1995 helps companies address this conflict. The act provides trademark owners the right to protect trademarks, prevents the use of trademark-protected entities, and requires the relinquishment of names that match or closely parallel company trademarks. The reduction of geographic barriers, speed of response, and memory capability of the Internet will continue to create new challenges for the legal and regulatory environment in the future.

Legal Pressure for Responsible Business Conduct

To ensure greater compliance with society's desires, both federal and state governments are moving toward increased organizational accountability for misconduct. Before 1991, laws mainly punished those employees directly responsible for an offense. Under new guidelines established by the Federal Sentencing Guidelines for Organizations (FSGO), however, both the responsible employees and the firms that employ them are held accountable for violations of federal law. Thus, the government now places responsibility for controlling and preventing misconduct squarely on the shoulders of top management. The main objectives of the federal guidelines are to train employees, self-monitor and supervise employee conduct, deter unethical acts, and punish those organizational members who engage in illegal acts.

If an organization's culture and policies reward or provide opportunities to engage in misconduct through lack of managerial concern or failure to comply with the seven minimum requirements of the FSGO (provided in Table A.5), then the organization may incur not only penalties but also the loss of customer trust, public confidence, and other intangible assets. For this reason, organizations cannot succeed solely through a legalistic approach to compliance with the sentencing guidelines; top management must cultivate high ethical standards that will serve as barriers to illegal conduct. The organization must want to be a good citizen and

---

TABLE A.5   Seven Steps to Compliance

1. Develop standards and procedures to reduce the propensity for criminal conduct.
2. Designate a high-level compliance manager or ethics officer to oversee the compliance program.
3. Avoid delegating authority to people known to have a propensity to engage in misconduct.
4. Communicate standards and procedures to employees, other agents, and independent contractors through training programs and publications.
5. Establish systems to monitor and audit misconduct and to allow employees and agents to report criminal activity.
6. Enforce standards and punishments consistently across all employees in the organization.
7. Respond immediately to misconduct and take reasonable steps to prevent further criminal conduct.

Source: United States Sentencing Commission, *Federal Sentencing Guidelines for Organizations,* 1991.

---

recognize the importance of compliance to successful workplace activities and relationships.

The federal guidelines also require businesses to develop programs that can detect—and that will deter employees from engaging in—misconduct. To be considered effective, such compliance programs must include disclosure of any wrongdoing, cooperation with the government, and acceptance of responsibility for the misconduct. Codes of ethics, employee ethics training, hotlines (direct 800 phone numbers), compliance directors, newsletters, brochures, and other communication methods are typical components of a compliance program. The ethics component, discussed in Chapter 2, acts as a buffer, keeping firms away from the thin line that separates unethical and illegal conduct.

Despite the existing legislation, a number of ethics scandals in the early 2000s led Congress to pass—almost unanimously—the **Sarbanes-Oxley Act,** which criminalized securities fraud and strengthened penalties for corporate fraud. It also created an accounting oversight board that requires corporations to establish codes of ethics for financial reporting and to develop greater transparency in financial reports to investors and other interested parties. Additionally, the law requires top corporate executives to sign off on their firms' financial reports, and they risk fines and jail sentences if they misrepresent their companies' financial position. Table A.6 summarizes the major provisions of the Sarbanes-Oxley Act.

TABLE A.6   Major Provisions of the Sarbanes-Oxley Act

1. Requires the establishment of a Public Company Accounting Oversight Board in charge of regulations administered by the Securities and Exchange Commission.

2. Requires CEOs and CFOs to certify that their companies' financial statements are true and without misleading statements.

3. Requires that corporate boards of directors' audit committees consist of independent members who have no material interests in the company.

4. Prohibits corporations from making or offering loans to officers and board members.

5. Requires codes of ethics for senior financial officers; code must be registered with the SEC.

6. Prohibits accounting firms from providing both auditing and consulting services to the same client without the approval of the client firm's audit committee.

7. Requires company attorneys to report wrongdoing to top managers and, if necessary, to the board of directors; if managers and directors fail to respond to reports of wrongdoing, the attorney should stop representing the company.

8. Mandates "whistleblower protection" for persons who disclose wrongdoing to authorities.

9. Requires financial securities analysts to certify that their recommendations are based on objective reports.

10. Requires mutual fund managers to disclose how they vote shareholder proxies, giving investors information about how their shares influence decisions.

11. Establishes a 10-year penalty for mail/wire fraud.

12. Prohibits the two senior auditors from working on a corporation's account for more than five years; other auditors are prohibited from working on an account for more than seven years. In other words, accounting firms must rotate individual auditors from one account to another from time to time.

Source: O. C. Ferrell, John Fraedrich, and Linda Ferrell, *Business Ethics: Ethical Decision Making and Cases,* 6th ed. (Boston: Houghton Mifflin, 2005), p. 63.

Chapter 3

Business in a Borderless World

OBJECTIVES

After reading this chapter, you will be able to:

- Explore some of the factors within the international trade environment that influence business.

- Investigate some of the economic, legal-political, social, cultural, and technological barriers to international business.

- Specify some of the agreements, alliances, and organizations that may encourage trade across international boundaries.

- Summarize the different levels of organizational involvement in international trade.

- Contrast two basic strategies used in international business.

- Assess the opportunities and problems facing a small business considering expanding into international markets.

The Porsche Cayenne Becomes a Global Pacesetter

When Wendelin Wiedeking, the chief executive officer of Porsche, decided to take a risk and build a muscular sport utility vehicle (SUV) with distinctive Porsche styling, family shareholders worried the new vehicle might not live up to the company's vaunted sports-car tradition and elite brand image. Porsche's legacy has long been its two-seat sports cars, like the 911 and Boxster. Thus, even Porsche enthusiasts cringed when the company decided to introduce an SUV—despite its top speed of 133 miles per hour, all-wheel drive to defy virtually any terrain, and the performance you would expect from a vehicle sporting the Porsche marque.

The German-based Porsche depends on the North American market for approximately 50 percent of its sales. With a net profit margin of 10.1 percent, Porsche outruns even Japanese brands like Nissan and Toyota, as well as other German rivals such as BMW and DaimlerChrysler. To maintain profits, the company revised everything from manufacturing to marketing. Porsche boosted productivity and profits by slashing production time on various models from 30 to 50 percent.

Part of the secret of the Cayenne's profitability stems from the fact that it shared its development with Volkswagen's Touareg. Although the two vehicles are somewhat similar in appearance, the Porsche looks like—well, a Porsche— particularly in the front with its 911-like grille. However, 90 percent of the basic manufacturing for the Porsche Cayenne—from metal stamping to chassis assembly—has been outsourced to Volkswagen's SUV plant in Slovakia, allowing Porsche to increase production capacity with minimum expenditures.

The good news for Porsche is that only 18 percent of Cayenne buyers had previously owned a Porsche, allowing the company to broaden its customer base. Recognizing that even Porsche buyers have different levels of purchasing power, the company has introduced models ranging from the $47,000 V6 to the Cayenne Turbo, which starts at $90,000 and roars up to $110,000. The Cayenne continues to power record sales and profits at the German automaker, with success made possible through global markets.[1]

Introduction

Consumers around the world can drink Coca-Cola and Pepsi; eat at McDonald's and Pizza Hut; see movies from Mexico, England, France, Australia, and China; and watch CNN and MTV on Toshiba and Sony televisions. The products you consume today are just as likely to have been made in China, Korea, or Germany as in the United States. Likewise, consumers in other countries buy Western electrical equipment, clothing, rock music, cosmetics, and toiletries, as well as computers, robots, and earth-moving equipment.

Many U.S. firms are finding that international markets provide tremendous opportunities for growth. Accessing these markets can promote innovation, while intensifying global competition spurs companies to market better and less expensive products.

> **Did You Know?**   McDonald's serves 46 million customers a day at 31,000 restaurants in 119 countries.[2]

In this chapter, we explore business in this exciting global marketplace. First, we'll look at the nature of international business, including barriers and promoters of trade across international boundaries. Next, we consider the levels of organizational involvement in international business. Finally, we briefly discuss strategies for trading across national borders.

The Role of International Business

international business
the buying, selling, and trading of goods and services across national boundaries

International business refers to the buying, selling, and trading of goods and services across national boundaries. Falling political barriers and new technology are making it possible for more and more companies to sell their products overseas as well as at home. And, as differences among nations continue to narrow, the trend toward the globalization of business is becoming increasingly important. Starbucks, for example, serves 20 million customers a week at more than 6,000 coffee shops in 30 countries.[3] Amazon.com, an online retailer, has nine distribution centers from Nevada to Germany that fill 1.7 million orders a day and ship them to customers in every corner of the world.[4] Businesses from outside the United States are increasingly finding success marketing to Americans. Toyota, for example, now sells more cars and trucks in the United States than it does in Japan, and more than 70 percent of the Japanese firm's profits come from North America.[5] Indeed, most of the world's population and two-thirds of its total purchasing power are outside the United States.

When McDonald's sells a Big Mac in Moscow, Sony sells a stereo in Detroit, or a small Swiss medical supply company sells a shipment of orthopedic devices to a hospital in Monterrey, Mexico, the sale affects the economies of the countries involved. To begin our study of international business, we must first consider some economic issues: why nations trade, exporting and importing, and the balance of trade.

Why Nations Trade

Nations and businesses engage in international trade to obtain raw materials and goods that are otherwise unavailable to them or are available elsewhere at a lower price than that at which they themselves can produce. A nation, or individuals and

Because of saturation of the U.S. market, many businesses that seek additional growth are looking beyond U.S. borders for potential new customers and worldwide sales. This Starbucks in Tokyo was its first to open overseas. What other relatively "new" companies do you think would benefit by capturing international markets?

organizations from a nation, sell surplus materials and goods to acquire funds to buy the goods, services, and ideas its people need. Poland and Hungary, for example, want to trade with Western nations so that they can acquire new technology and techniques to revitalize their formerly communist economies. Which goods and services a nation sells depends on what resources it has available.

Some nations have a monopoly on the production of a particular resource or product. Such a monopoly, or **absolute advantage,** exists when a country is the only source of an item, the only producer of an item, or the most efficient producer of an item. Because South Africa has the largest deposits of diamonds in the world, one company, De Beers Consolidated Mines, Ltd., controls a major portion of the world's diamond trade and uses its control to maintain high prices for gem-quality diamonds. The United States, until recently, held an absolute advantage in oil-drilling equipment. But an absolute advantage not based on the availability of natural resources rarely lasts, and Japan and Russia are now challenging the United States in the production of oil-drilling equipment.

Most international trade is based on **comparative advantage,** which occurs when a country specializes in products that it can supply more efficiently or at a lower cost than it can produce other items. The United States has a comparative advantage in producing agricultural commodities such as corn and wheat. Until recently, the United States had a comparative advantage in manufacturing automobiles, heavy machinery, airplanes, and weapons; other countries now hold the comparative advantage for many of these products. Other countries, particularly India and Ireland, are also gaining a comparative advantage over the United States in the provision of some services, such as call-center operations, engineering, and software programming. As a result, U.S. companies are increasingly **outsourcing,**

absolute advantage
a monopoly that exists when a country is the only source of an item, the only producer of an item, or the most efficient producer of an item

comparative advantage
the basis of most international trade, when a country specializes in products that it can supply more efficiently or at a lower cost than it can produce other items

outsourcing
the transferring of manufacturing or other tasks—such as data processing—to countries where labor and supplies are less expensive

These New Delhi white-collar workers at Wipro Spetramind are 60 percent cheaper than their U.S. counterparts.

or transferring manufacturing and other tasks to countries where labor and supplies are less expensive. Outsourcing has become a controversial practice in the United States because many jobs have moved overseas where those tasks can be accomplished for lower costs.[6]

Trade between Countries

To obtain needed goods and services and the funds to pay for them, nations trade by exporting and importing. **Exporting** is the sale of goods and services to foreign markets. The United States exported more than $1 trillion in goods and services last year.[7] General Motors' operations in China—the fastest growing market in the world—accounted for $1.4 billion worth of North American exports of equipment and components over the last five years. The company expects this number will double as it increases exports of American-made vehicles—including Cadillacs—to China.[8] U.S. businesses export many goods and services, particularly agricultural, entertainment (movies, television shows, etc.), and technological products. **Importing** is the purchase of goods and services from foreign sources. Many of the goods you buy in the United States are likely to be imports or to have some imported components. Sometimes, you may not even realize they are imports. The United States imported more than $1.5 trillion in goods and services last year.[9]

exporting
the sale of goods and services to foreign markets

importing
the purchase of goods and services from foreign sources

balance of trade
the difference in value between a nation's exports and its imports

trade deficit
a nation's negative balance of trade, which exists when that country imports more products than it exports

Balance of Trade

You have probably read or heard about the fact that the United States has a trade deficit, but what is a trade deficit? A nation's **balance of trade** is the difference in value between its exports and imports. Because the United States (and some other nations as well) imports more products than it exports, it has a negative balance of trade, or **trade deficit**. By 2010, the U.S. trade deficit is expected to reach $889.1 billion, with imports of $2,393.7 billion and exports of $3,282.7 billion (see Table 3.1).[10] The trade deficit fluctuates according to such factors as the health of the United States and other economies, productivity, perceived quality, and exchange rates. In 2000, the world economy was healthy and grew at a rapid pace. However, in 2001, that pace had slowed considerably as the United States, Europe, Japan, and some major developing countries experienced rare simultaneous slumps.[11] Trade deficits are harmful because they can mean the failure of businesses, the loss of jobs, and a lowered standard of living.

Of course, when a nation exports more goods than it imports, it has a favorable balance of trade, or trade surplus. Until about 1970, the United States had a trade surplus due to an abundance of natural resources and the relative efficiency of its manufacturing systems. Japan currently has a trade surplus with many of the countries with which it trades. Table 3.2 shows the top 10 countries with which the United States has a trade deficit and a trade surplus.

	1980	1990	2000	2010*	TABLE 3.1
Exports	$333.4	$ 575.7	$ 1,133.2	$ 2,393.7	U.S. Trade Deficit,
Imports	$326.3	$ 632.2	$ 1,532.3	$ 3,282.7	1980–2010 (in billions of dollars)
Trade Surplus/Deficit	$ 7.1	$−56.5	$−399.1	$−889.1	

*Projected.

Source: Exports and Imports of Goods and Services, 1980–2010, *Infoplease.com* (n.d.), www.infoplease.com/ipa/A0855074.html (accessed February 25, 2004). Reprinted with permission of infoplease.com.

The difference between the flow of money into and out of a country is called its **balance of payments.** A country's balance of trade, foreign investments, foreign aid, loans, military expenditures, and money spent by tourists comprise its balance of payments. As you might expect, a country with a trade surplus generally has a favorable balance of payments because it is receiving more money from trade with foreign countries than it is paying out. When a country has a trade deficit, more money flows out of the country than into it. If more money flows out of the country than into it from tourism and other sources, the country may experience declining production and higher unemployment, because there is less money available for spending.

balance of payments
the difference between the flow of money into and out of a country

International Trade Barriers

Completely free trade seldom exists. When a company decides to do business outside its own country, it will encounter a number of barriers to international trade. Any firm considering international business must research the other country's economic, legal, political, social, cultural, and technological background. Such research will help the company choose an appropriate level of involvement and operating strategies, as we will see later in this chapter.

Economic Barriers

When looking at doing business in another country, managers must consider a number of basic economic factors, such as economic development, infrastructure, and exchange rates.

Economic Development.   When considering doing business abroad, U.S. businesspeople need to recognize that they cannot take for granted that other countries offer the same things as are found in *industrialized nations*—economically advanced countries such as the United States, Japan, Great Britain, and Canada. Many countries in Africa, Asia, and South America, for example, are in general poorer and less economically advanced than those in North America and Europe; they are often called *less-developed countries* (LDCs). LDCs are characterized by low per capita income (income generated by the nation's production of goods and services divided by the population), which means that consumers are less likely to purchase nonessential products. Nonetheless, LDCs represent a potentially huge and profitable market for many businesses because they may be buying technology to improve their infrastructures, and much of the population may desire consumer products. For example, cellular and wireless phone technology is reaching many countries at less expense than traditional hard-wired telephone systems. Consequently, opportunities for growth in the cell phone market remain strong in Southeast Asia, Africa, and the Middle East. In Africa, demand for mobile phone service jumped 37 percent in 2003. With experts projecting that sub-Sarahan Africans will spend $3.2 billion a

TABLE 3.2

Top 10 Countries Maintaining Trade Deficits/Surpluses with the United States

	Trade Deficit	Trade Surplus
1.	China	Netherlands
2.	Japan	Hong Kong
3.	Canada	Australia
4.	Germany	Belgium
5.	Mexico	Egypt
6.	Ireland	United Arab Emirates
7.	Venezuela	Panama
8.	France	Jamaica
9.	Republic of Korea	Bermuda
10.	Italy	Byelarus

Source: "Top Ten Countries with Which the U.S. Has a Trade Deficit," www.census. gov/foreign-trade/top/dst / current/deficit.html (accessed February 26, 2004) and "Top Ten Countries with Which the U.S. Has a Trade Surplus," www.census/gov/foreign-trade/top/dst/current/surplus.html (accessed February 26, 2004).

year on wireless services in the next five years, many telecom firms are taking a closer look at the continent's 650 million people.[12] And in war-torn Iraq, many of those same firms are fiercely competing for opportunities to rebuild the nation's telecommunications infrastructure, and WorldCom and Motorola have already won contracts to develop cell phone networks there.[13]

A country's level of development is determined in part by its **infrastructure,** the physical facilities that support its economic activities, such as railroads, highways, ports, airfields, utilities and power plants, schools, hospitals, communication systems, and commercial distribution systems. When doing business in LDCs, for example, a business may need to compensate for rudimentary distribution and communication systems, or even a lack of technology.

Exchange Rates.   The ratio at which one nation's currency can be exchanged for another nation's currency is the **exchange rate.** Exchange rates vary daily and can be found in newspapers and through many sites on the Internet. Familiarity with exchange rates is important because they affect the cost of imports and exports.

Occasionally, a government may alter the value of its national currency. Devaluation decreases the value of currency in relation to other currencies. If the U.S. government were to devalue the dollar, it would lower the cost of American goods abroad and make trips to the United States less expensive for foreign tourists. Thus, devaluation encourages the sale of domestic goods and tourism. Mexico has repeatedly devalued the peso for this reason. Revaluation, which increases the value of a currency in relation to other currencies, occurs rarely.

infrastructure
the physical facilities that support a country's economic activities, such as railroads, highways, ports, airfields, utilities and power plants, schools, hospitals, communication systems, and commercial distribution systems

exchange rate
the ratio at which one nation's currency can be exchanged for another nation's currency

Legal and Political Barriers

A company that decides to enter the international marketplace must contend with potentially complex relationships among the different laws of its own nation, international laws, and the laws of the nation with which it will be trading; various trade restrictions imposed on international trade; and changing political climates. Many companies provide assistance in this area. MyCustoms.com helps companies comply with local trade rules, and NextLinx Corp. provides business advice about international commerce laws.[14]

Laws and Regulations.   The United States has a number of laws and regulations that govern the activities of U.S. firms engaged in international trade. For example, the Webb-Pomerene Export Trade Act of 1918 exempts American firms from antitrust laws if those firms are acting together to enter international trade. This law allows selected U.S. firms to form monopolies to compete with foreign monopolistic organizations, although they are not allowed to limit free trade and competition within the United States or to use unfair methods of competition in international trade. The United States also has a variety of friendship, commerce, and navigation treaties with other nations. These treaties allow business to be transacted between citizens of the specified countries.

Once outside U.S. borders, businesspeople are likely to find that the laws of other nations differ from those of the United States. Many of the legal rights that Americans take for granted do not exist in other countries, and a firm doing business abroad must understand and obey the laws of the host country. Many countries forbid foreigners from owning real property outright; others have strict laws limiting the amount of local currency that can be taken out of the country and the amount of foreign currency that can be brought in.

Some countries have copyright and patent laws that are less strict than those of the United States, and some countries fail to honor U.S. laws. Because copying is a tradition in China and laws protecting copyrights and intellectual property are weak and minimally enforced, the country is flooded with counterfeit videos, movies, CDs, computer software, furniture, and clothing. Bo Concepts, a Danish retail chain, has suffered declining sales in China as a result of domestic firms offering knockoffs of the firm's furniture at discounted prices and mis-using the firm's catalog and brand name.[15] Companies are angry because the counterfeits harm not only their sales, but also their reputations if the knockoffs are of poor quality. Such counterfeiting is not limited to China. In fact, the Business Software Alliance estimates that global losses from software piracy amount to $13 billion a year, including movies, music, and software downloaded from the Internet.[16] In countries where these activities occur, laws against them may not be sufficiently enforced, if counterfeiting is in fact deemed illegal. Thus, businesses engaging in foreign trade may have to take extra steps to protect their products because local laws may be insufficient to do so.

Because laws protecting copyrights and intellectual property are weak in many Southeast Asian countries, like China, counterfeit goods, like these Louis Vuitton handbags, can often be found to purchase on the street.

Tariffs and Trade Restrictions.   Tariffs and other trade restrictions are part of a country's legal structure but may be established or removed for political reasons. An **import tariff** is a tax levied by a nation on goods imported into the country. A *fixed tariff* is a specific amount of money levied on each unit of a product brought into the country, while an *ad valorem tariff* is based on the value of the item. Most countries allow citizens traveling abroad to bring home a certain amount of merchandise without paying an import tariff. A U.S. citizen may bring $200 worth of merchandise into the United States duty free. After that, U.S. citizens must pay an ad valorem tariff based on the cost of the item and the country of origin. Thus, identical items purchased in different countries might have different tariffs.

import tariff
a tax levied by a nation on goods imported into the country

Countries sometimes levy tariffs for political reasons, as when they impose sanctions against other countries to protest their actions. However, import tariffs are more commonly imposed to protect domestic products by raising the price of imported ones. Such protective tariffs have become controversial, as Americans become increasingly concerned over the U.S. trade deficit. Protective tariffs allow more expensive domestic goods to compete with foreign ones. Many advocate the imposition of tariffs on products imported from Japan, particularly luxury automobiles, audio components, and computers. However, Congress fears economic reprisals from Japan if the tariffs are levied on Japanese products.

Critics of protective tariffs argue that their use inhibits free trade and competition. Supporters of protective tariffs say they insulate domestic industries, particularly new ones, against well-established foreign competitors. Once an industry matures, however, its advocates may be reluctant to let go of the tariff that protected it. Tariffs also help when, because of low labor costs and other advantages, foreign competitors can afford to sell their products at prices lower than those charged by domestic companies. Some Americans argue that tariffs should be used to keep domestic wages high and unemployment low.

exchange controls
regulations that restrict the amount of currency that can be bought or sold

Exchange controls restrict the amount of currency that can be bought or sold. Some countries control their foreign trade by forcing businesspeople to buy and sell foreign products through a central bank. If John Deere, for example, receives payments for its tractors in a foreign currency, it may be required to sell the currency to that nation's central bank. When foreign currency is in short supply, as it is in many Third World and Eastern European countries, the government uses foreign currency to purchase necessities and capital goods and produces other products locally, thus limiting its need for foreign imports.

quota
a restriction on the number of units of a particular product that can be imported into a country

A **quota** limits the number of units of a particular product that can be imported into a country. A quota may be established by voluntary agreement or by government decree. After U.S. yarn suppliers complained that cotton yarn (used in underwear, socks, and T-shits) from Pakistan was flooding the market, a quota was imposed. Pakistan complained, and a textile-monitoring panel recommended that the United States lift the restrictions. The United States refused. However, in 2001, the quota was ruled a violation of global trade rules, and the United States was ordered to remove it.[17]

embargo
a prohibition on trade in a particular product

An **embargo** prohibits trade in a particular product. Embargoes are generally directed at specific goods or countries and may be established for political, economic, health, or religious reasons. The United States forbids the importation of cigars from Cuba for political reasons. Health embargoes prevent the importing of various pharmaceuticals, animals, plants, and agricultural products. Muslim nations forbid the importation of alcoholic beverages on religious grounds.

dumping
the act of a country or business selling products at less than what it costs to produce them

One common reason for setting quotas or tariffs is to prohibit **dumping,** which occurs when a country or business sells products at less than what it costs to produce them. The United States, for example, levied extra import duties against some types of Canadian lumber after the U.S. International Trade Commission found evidence that lower prices on the partially subsidized Canadian lumber threatened to harm the domestic lumber industry. However, some of the antidumping tariffs were later found to be in violation of global trade rules, and the United States was ordered to rescind them.[18] A company may dump its products for several reasons. Dumping permits quick entry into a market. Sometimes dumping occurs when the domestic market for a firm's product is too small to support an efficient level of production. In other cases, technologically obsolete products that are no longer

salable in the country of origin are dumped overseas. Dumping is relatively difficult to prove, but even the suspicion of dumping can lead to the imposition of
quotas or tariffs.

Political Barriers.   Unlike legal issues, political considerations are seldom written
down and often change rapidly. Nations that have been subject to economic sanctions for political reasons in recent years include Cuba, Iran, Syria, and North Korea.
While these were dramatic events, political considerations affect international business daily as governments enact tariffs, embargoes, or other types of trade restrictions in response to political events.

Businesses engaged in international trade must consider the relative instability of
countries such as Colombia, Haiti, and Honduras. Political unrest in countries such
as Peru, Somalia, and Russia may create a hostile or even dangerous environment for
foreign businesses. Civil war, as in Chechnya and Bosnia, may disrupt business activities and place lives in danger. And, a sudden change in power can result in a
regime that is hostile to foreign investment. Some businesses have been forced out of
a country altogether, as they were when Fidel Castro closed Cuba to American business. Whether they like it or not, companies are often involved directly or indirectly
in international politics.

Political concerns may lead a group of nations to form a **cartel,** a group of firms
or nations that agrees to act as a monopoly and not compete with each other, to generate a competitive advantage in world markets. Probably the most famous cartel is
OPEC, the Organization of Petroleum Exporting Countries, founded in the 1960s to
increase the price of petroleum throughout the world and to maintain high prices.
By working to ensure stable oil prices, OPEC hopes to enhance the economies of its
member nations.

cartel
a group of firms or nations
that agrees to act as a
monopoly and not
compete with each other,
in order to generate a
competitive advantage in
world markets

Social and Cultural Barriers

Most businesspeople engaged in international trade underestimate the importance
of social and cultural differences; but these differences can derail an important transaction. For example, when Big Boy opened a restaurant in Bangkok, it quickly became popular with European and American tourists, but the local Thais refused to
eat there. Instead, they placed gifts of rice and incense at the feet of the Big Boy statue
(a chubby boy holding a hamburger) because it reminded them of Buddha. In Japan,
customers were forced to tiptoe around a logo painted on the floor at the entrance
to an Athlete's Foot store because in Japan, it is considered taboo to step on a crest.[19]
And in Russia, consumers found the American-style energetic happiness of McDonald's employees insincere and offensive when the company opened its first stores
there.[20] Unfortunately, cultural norms are rarely written down, and what is written
down may well be inaccurate.

Cultural differences include differences in spoken and written language. Although
it is certainly possible to translate words from one language to another, the true
meaning is sometimes misinterpreted or lost. Consider some translations that went
awry in foreign markets. KFC's long-running slogan, "Finger lickin' good," was translated into Chinese as "Eat your fingers off," while Coors' "Turn it loose" campaign
was translated into Spanish as "Drink Coors and get diarrhea." And Parker Pen was
dismayed to learn that "Avoid embarrassment" (from a leaking pen) had been translated into "Avoid pregnancy" in Spanish.[21] Translators cannot just translate slogans,
advertising campaigns, and Web site language; they must know the cultural differences that could affect a company's success.

Understanding the differences among the cultures of countries can be important to a firm. Consider McDonald's, like this one in Manilla, or consider the placement of a McDonald's in India where a cow is considered sacred and no one eats beef. What other cultural differences can you think of that might affect a business like McDonald's? How could they be overcome?

Differences in body language and personal space also affect international trade. Body language is nonverbal, usually unconscious communication through gestures, posture, and facial expression. Personal space is the distance at which one person feels comfortable talking to another. Americans tend to stand a moderate distance away from the person with whom they are speaking. Arab businessmen tend to stand face-to-face with the object of their conversation. Additionally, gestures vary from culture to culture, and gestures considered acceptable in American society—pointing, for example—may be considered rude in others. Table 3.3 shows some of the behaviors considered rude or unacceptable in other countries. Such cultural differences may generate uncomfortable feelings or misunderstandings when businesspeople of different countries negotiate with each other.

Family roles also influence marketing activities. Many countries do not allow children to be used in advertising, for example. Advertising that features people in nontraditional social roles may or may not be successful either. The California Milk Processor Board aired a commercial in which a father and his young daughter shop at a supermarket for sugar, flour, cinnamon, and milk for a cake to be baked when they get home. The ad does not seem unusual except that when it was aired on Spanish-language television, the concept was striking. It is rare for Latino men to appear along with their daughters in Spanish-language ads and even rarer for the commercials to be set outside the home. The Hispanic culture typically reinforces how little boys need their fathers, not how little girls do.[22]

The people of other nations quite often have a different perception of time as well. Americans value promptness; a business meeting scheduled for a specific time seldom starts more than a few minutes late. In Mexico and Spain, however, it is not unusual for a meeting to be delayed half an hour or more. Such a late start might produce resentment in an American negotiating in Spain for the first time.

Companies engaged in foreign trade must observe the national and religious holidays and local customs of the host country. In many Islamic countries, for

Think Globally
Foreign Brands Challenge Coca-Cola and PepsiCo

The Coca-Cola Company and PepsiCo have been locked in a fierce battle for market share in new markets around the world for decades. Now, the two companies face competition from small, regional firms capitalizing on weaknesses in the two giants' marketing strategy.

Coca-Cola has long dominated store shelves and cupboards in Latin America. Mexico, where Coca-Cola has a 70 percent market share, is the second-largest market for soft drinks after the United States and generates annual sales of about $15 billion. However, the company increasingly faces competition from retail private label brands, like Wal-Mart, as well as from regional brands. One of the fastest growing upstarts is Kola Real (officially called Industrias Añaños), which was established in Peru by the Añaños family after they observed routine shortages of Coca-Cola products caused by the hijacking of delivery trucks by local militants. The family initially bottled its Big Cola in recycled beer bottles with hand-pasted labels and hired third-party trucks to deliver it to local stores, allowing it to keep costs low. With an ultra-low pricing strategy, Kola Real's Big Cola soon made sharp inroads into the soft drink markets in Peru, and later into Ecuador, Venezuela, and Mexico. Other regional firms have also debuted in Latin America, including Fiemex SA's El Gallito and the Guadalajara soccer club's Chica Cola.

In Europe and the Middle East, where anti-American sentiment grew after the 2003 war in Iraq, several other brands gained in popularity at the expense of Coca-Cola and PepsiCo., including Iran's ZamZam Cola, France's Mecca Cola, and Britain's Qibla-Cola. Though targeted at Muslim consumers in Arab countries, ZamZam Cola has found new buyers outside of the Arab world. Tawfik Mathlouthi introduced Mecca Cola in France to provide Muslim and non-Muslim consumers there an alternative to products from the U.S.-owned Coca-Cola and PepsiCola. Now available in 54 countries, Mecca Cola generated revenues of 8 million euros ($9 million U.S. dollars) in its first 12 months. Qibla-Cola was founded to give British consumers an alternative to the products of huge multinational corporations; it contributes 10 percent of profits to charitable causes. The company has recently expanded its distribution of cola and flavored carbonated drinks to Canada, Poland, the Netherlands, and Belgium, and has plans to introduce them into Pakistan, Bangladesh, and India as well.

Despite the arrival of so many new regional brands, Coca-Cola insists that sales in the Middle East have actually grown by more than 10 percent, while sales in Europe have risen by 5 to 8 percent. In Latin America, regional brands have hurt PepsiCo far more than Coca-Cola. However, both cola giants have made concessions to retain their appeal. PepsiCo, for example, has twice cut prices in Latin America to better compete with Big Cola, leading to a price war. Although Coca-Cola has not reduced prices in Latin America, it has stepped up retailer promotions, such as offering free cases of product to bodegas. However, two Mexican stores complained to the country's antitrust commission that Coca-Cola has used unfair tactics to get stores to agree not to carry Big Cola, charges that Coca-Cola denies. And in Saudi Arabia, the company recruited Abdul Mejid Abdullah, a popular singer, as a celebrity endorser.[23]

Discussion Questions

1. How do cultural differences influence the consumption of soft drinks?
2. Why are local brands a threat to Coca-Cola and PepsiCo in Latin America, Europe, and the Middle East?
3. Can Kola Real become successful in some regions of the United States?

Region	Gestures Viewed as Rude or Unacceptable
Japan, Hong Kong, Middle East	Summoning with the index finger
Middle and Far East	Pointing with index finger
Thailand, Japan, France	Sitting with soles of shoes showing
Brazil, Germany	Forming a circle with fingers (e.g., the "O.K." sign in the United States)
Japan	Passing an item to someone using only one hand
Buddhist countries	Patting someone on the head

TABLE 3.3

Cultural Behavioral Differences

Source: Adapted from Judie Haynes, "Communicating with Gestures," *EverythingESL* (n.d.), www.everythingesl.net/inservices/body_language.php (accessed March 2, 2004).

Fly-fishing is barely known in Chiang Mai, Thailand, but lure manufacturers have flocked there for some of the world's best fish fly making. "Chiang Mai is to fly tying what Silicon Valley is to computers, " says an executive at Targus Fly & Feather, a Mesa, Arizona, company with large fly-making operations in Thailand. Local residents have a high level of finger dexterity, thanks to centuries of making local handicrafts, and this aptitude is well-suited to fish fly tying. (D. D. Gray, "Thai Town Lures Makers of Fishing Hooks," Seattle Times, April 14, 2003)

example, workers expect to take a break at certain times of the day to observe religious rites. Companies also must monitor their advertising to guard against offending customers. In Thailand and many other countries, public displays of affection between the sexes are unacceptable in advertising messages; in many Middle Eastern nations, it is unacceptable to show the soles of one's feet. In the Muslim world, exposure of a woman's skin, even her arms, is considered offensive.[24]

With the exception of the United States, most nations use the metric system. This lack of uniformity creates problems for both buyers and sellers in the international marketplace. American sellers, for instance, must package goods destined for foreign markets in liters or meters, and Japanese sellers must convert to the English system if they plan to sell a product in the United States. Tools also must be calibrated in the correct system if they are to function correctly. Hyundai and Honda service technicians need metric tools to make repairs on those cars.

The literature dealing with international business is filled with accounts of sometimes humorous but often costly mistakes that occurred because of a lack of understanding of the social and cultural differences between buyers and sellers. Such problems cannot always be avoided, but they can be minimized through research on the cultural and social differences of the host country.

Technological Barriers

Many countries lack the technological infrastructure found in the United States, and some marketers are viewing such barriers as opportunities. For instance, marketers are targeting many countries such as India and China and some African countries where there are few private phone lines. Citizens of these countries are turning instead to wireless communication through cell phones. Technological advances, such as the Internet, are creating additional global marketing opportunities. In some countries, broadband access to the Internet is spreading much faster than in the United States. In fact, 10 nations, including South Korea, Hong Kong, and Canada, outrank the United States in terms of subscribers to broadband Internet access. The growth of high-speed Internet access should facilitate online commerce.[25]

Trade Agreements, Alliances, and Organizations

Although these economic, political, legal, and sociocultural issues may seem like daunting barriers to international trade, there are also organizations and agreements—such as the General Agreement on Tariffs and Trade, the World Bank, and the International Monetary Fund—that foster international trade and can help

Barriers to international trade were significantly reduced by the General Agreement on Tariffs and Trade resulting in an increase in international cargo ship traffic.

companies get involved in and succeed in global markets. Various regional trade agreements, such as the North American Free Trade Agreement and the European Union, also promote trade among member nations by eliminating tariffs and trade restrictions. In this section, we'll look briefly at these agreements and organizations.

General Agreement on Tariffs and Trade (GATT)

During the Great Depression of the 1930s, nations established so many protective tariffs covering so many products that international trade became virtually impossible. By the end of World War II, there was considerable international momentum to liberalize trade and minimize the effects of tariffs. The **General Agreement on Tariffs and Trade (GATT),** originally signed by 23 nations in 1947, provided a forum for tariff negotiations and a place where international trade problems could be discussed and resolved. More than 100 nations abided by its rules. GATT sponsored rounds of negotiations aimed at reducing trade restrictions. The most recent round, the Uruguay Round (1988–1994), further reduced trade barriers for most products and provided new rules to prevent dumping.

The **World Trade Organization (WTO),** an international organization dealing with the rules of trade between nations, was created in 1995 by the Uruguay Round. Key to the World Trade Organization are the WTO agreements, which are the legal ground rules for international commerce. The agreements were negotiated and signed by most of the world's trading nations and ratified by their parliaments. The goal is to help producers of goods and services and exporters and importers conduct their business. In addition to administering the WTO trade agreements, the WTO presents a forum for trade negotiations, monitors national trade policies, provides technical assistance and training for developing countries, and cooperates with other international organizations. Based in Geneva, Switzerland, the WTO has also adopted a leadership role in negotiating trade disputes among nations.[26] For example, the WTO investigated complaints from the European Union and seven countries about a U.S. tariff on imported steel and ultimately ruled the U.S. duties illegal under international trade rules. The United States had imposed the tariffs to protect domestic steel producers from less expensive imported steel, but the WTO found that the United States had failed to prove that its steel industry had been harmed by dumping.[27] Facing the prospect of retaliatory sanctions against American goods, the U.S. dropped the tariffs 16 months early after the ruling.[28]

General Agreement on Tariffs and Trade (GATT) a trade agreement, originally signed by 23 nations in 1947, that provided a forum for tariff negotiations and a place where international trade problems could be discussed and resolved

World Trade Organization international organization dealing with the rules of trade between nations

The North American Free Trade Agreement (NAFTA)

The **North American Free Trade Agreement (NAFTA),** which went into effect on January 1, 1994, effectively merged Canada, the United States, and Mexico into one market of more than 421 million consumers.[29] NAFTA will eliminate virtually all tariffs on goods produced and traded among Canada, Mexico, and the United States to create a free trade area by 2009. The estimated annual output for this trade alliance is $11 trillion.[30] NAFTA makes it easier for U.S. businesses to invest in Mexico and Canada; provides protection for intellectual property (of special interest to high-technology and entertainment industries); expands trade by requiring equal treatment of U.S. firms in both countries; and simplifies country-of-origin rules, hindering Japan's use of Mexico as a staging ground for further penetration into U.S. markets. Although most tariffs on products coming to the United States are being lifted, duties on more sensitive products, such as household glassware, footware, and some fruits and vegetables, are being phased out over a 15-year period.

Canada's 31.9 million consumers are relatively affluent, with a per capita GDP of $28,923.[31] Trade between the United States and Canada totals approximately $411 billion.[32] Currently exports to Canada support approximately 1.5 million U.S. jobs. Canadian investments in U.S. companies are also increasing, and various markets, including air travel, are opening as regulatory barriers dissolve.[33]

With a per capita GDP of $9,146, Mexico's 102 million consumers are less affluent than Canadian consumers. However, they bought $107 billion worth of U.S. products last year, making Mexico the United States' second-largest trading market, after Canada.[34] Many U.S. companies have taken advantage of Mexico's low labor costs and proximity to the United States to set up production facilities, sometimes called *maquiladoras.* Production at the *maquiladoras,* especially in the automotive, electronics, and apparel industries, tripled between 1994 and 2000 as companies as diverse as Ford, John Deere, Motorola, Sara Lee, Kimberly-Clark, and VF Corporation set up facilities in north-central Mexican states. With the *maquiladoras* accounting for roughly half of Mexico's exports, Mexico has risen to become the world's ninth-largest economy.[35]

Mexico's membership in NAFTA links the United States and Canada with other Latin American countries, providing additional opportunities to integrate trade among all the nations in the Western Hemisphere. Indeed, efforts to create a free trade agreement among the 34 nations of North and South America are expected to be completed by 2005. Like NAFTA, the *Free Trade Area of the Americas (FTAA)* will progressively eliminate trade barriers and create the world's largest free trade zone with 800 million people.[36] However, a trade dispute between the United States and Brazil over investment, intellectual property rights, antidumping tariffs, and agriculture subsidies may delay the final agreement.[37]

Despite its benefits, NAFTA has been controversial and disputes continue to arise over the implementation of the trade agreement. Archer Daniels Midland, for example, filed a claim against the Mexican government for losses resulting from a tax on soft drinks containing high fructose corn syrup, which the company believes violates the provisions of NAFTA.[38] While many Americans feared the agreement would erase jobs in the United States, Mexicans have been disappointed that the agreement failed to create more jobs. Moreover, Mexico's rising standard of living has increased the cost of doing business there; some 850 *maquiladoras* have closed their doors and transferred work to China and other nations where labor costs are cheaper. Indeed, China has become the United States' second largest importer.[39]

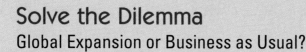

Solve the Dilemma
Global Expansion or Business as Usual?

Audiotech Electronics, founded in 1959 by a father and son, currently operates a 35,000-square-foot factory with 75 employees. The company produces control consoles for television and radio stations and recording studios. It is involved in every facet of production—designing the systems, installing the circuits in its computer boards, and even manufacturing and painting the metal cases housing the consoles. The company's products are used by all the major broadcast and cable networks. The firm's newest products allow television correspondents to simultaneously hear and communicate with their counterparts in different geographic locations. Audiotech has been very successful meeting its customers' needs efficiently.

Audiotech sales have historically been strong in the United States, but recently growth is stagnating. Even though Audiotech is a small, family-owned firm, it believes it should evaluate and consider global expansion.

Discussion Questions
1. What are the key issues that need to be considered in determining global expansion?
2. What are some of the unique problems that a small business might face in global expansion that larger firms would not?
3. Should Audiotech consider a joint venture? Should it hire a sales force of people native to the countries it enters?

Although NAFTA has been controversial, it has become a positive factor for U.S. firms wishing to engage in international marketing. Because licensing requirements have been relaxed under the pact, smaller businesses that previously could not afford to invest in Mexico and Canada will be able to do business in those markets without having to locate there. NAFTA's long phase-in period provides ample time for adjustment by those firms affected by reduced tariffs on imports. Furthermore, increased competition should lead to a more efficient market, and the long-term prospects of including most countries in the Western Hemisphere in the alliance promise additional opportunities for U.S. marketers.

The European Union (EU)

The **European Union (EU),** also called the *European Community* or *Common Market,* was established in 1958 to promote trade among its members, which initially included Belgium, France, Italy, West Germany, Luxembourg, and the Netherlands. East and West Germany united in 1991, and by 1995 the United Kingdom, Spain, Denmark, Greece, Portugal, Ireland, Austria, Finland, and Sweden had joined as well. (Cyprus, Poland, Hungary, the Czech Republic, Slovenia, Estonia, Latvia, Lithuania, Slovakia, and Malta joined in 2004; Romania, Bulgaria, and Turkey have requested membership as well.[40]) Until 1993 each nation functioned as a separate market, but at that time the members officially unified into one of the largest single world markets, which today includes 390 million consumers.

European Union (EU) a union of European nations established in 1958 to promote trade among its members; one of the largest single markets today

To facilitate free trade among members, the EU is working toward standardization of business regulations and requirements, import duties, and value-added taxes; the elimination of customs checks; and the creation of a standardized currency for use by all members. Many European nations (Austria, Belgium, Finland, France, Germany, Ireland, Italy, Luxembourg, the Netherlands, Portugal, and Spain) link their exchange rates together to a common currency, the *euro;* however, several EU members have rejected use of the euro in their countries. Although the common currency requires many marketers to modify their pricing strategies and will subject them to increased competition, the use of a single currency frees companies that sell goods among European countries from the nuisance of dealing with complex exchange rates.[41] The long-term goals are to eliminate all trade barriers within the EU, improve the economic efficiency of the EU nations, and stimulate economic growth, thus making the union's economy more competitive in global markets, particularly against Japan and other Pacific Rim nations, and North America. However, several disputes and debates still divide the member nations, and many barriers to completely free trade remain. Consequently, it may take many years before the EU is truly one deregulated market.

The EU has enacted some of the world's strictest laws concerning antitrust issues, which have had unexpected consequences for some non-European firms. For example, after a five-year investigation, the union fined U.S.-based Microsoft a record 497 million euros ($613 million U.S.) for exploiting its "near-monopoly" in computer operating systems in Europe by including a free media player with Windows to the detriment of software offered by European makers. Microsoft denied the charges and planned to appeal. In addition to the fine, the European Commission insisted that Microsoft release its programming codes to European rivals to allow them to make their competing products compatible with computers relying on Microsoft's Windows operating system.[42]

Asia-Pacific Economic Cooperation (APEC)

Asia-Pacific Economic Cooperation (APEC)
an international trade alliance that promotes open trade and economic and technical cooperation among member nations

The **Asia-Pacific Economic Cooperation (APEC),** established in 1989, promotes open trade and economic and technical cooperation among member nations, which initially included Australia, Brunei Darussalam, Canada, Indonesia, Japan, Korea, Malaysia, New Zealand, the Philippines, Singapore, Thailand, and the United States. Since then the alliance has grown to include China, Hong Kong, Chinese Taipei, Mexico, Papua New Guinea, Chile, Peru, Russia, and Vietnam. The 21-member alliance represents 2.6 billion consumers, has a combined gross domestic product of (US) $19 trillion, and accounts for more than 41 percent of global trade. APEC differs from other international trade alliances in its commitment to facilitating business and its practice of allowing the business/private sector to participate in a wide range of APEC activities.[43]

Despite economic turmoil and a recession in Asia in recent years, companies of the APEC have become increasingly competitive and sophisticated in global business in the last three decades. The Japanese and South Koreans in particular have made tremendous inroads on world markets for automobiles, motorcycles, watches, cameras, and audio and video equipment. Products from Samsung, Sony, Sanyo, Toyota, Daewoo, Mitsubishi, Suzuki, and Toshiba are sold all over the world and have set standards of quality by which other products are often judged. The People's Republic of China, a country of 1.3 billion people, has launched a program of economic reform to stimulate its economy by privatizing many industries, restructuring its banking system, and increasing public spending on infrastructure (including railways and telecommunications).[44] As a result, China has become a manufacturing powerhouse with an economy growing at a rate of more than 10 percent a year.[45] Less visible and sometimes less stable Pacific Rim regions, such as Thailand, Singapore, Taiwan, Vietnam, and Hong Kong, have also become major manufacturing and financial centers.

World Bank

World Bank
an organization established by the industrialized nations in 1946 to loan money to underdeveloped and developing countries; formally known as the International Bank for Reconstruction and Development

The **World Bank,** more formally known as the International Bank for Reconstruction and Development, was established by the industrialized nations, including the United States, in 1946 to loan money to underdeveloped and developing countries.

It loans its own funds or borrows funds from member countries to finance projects ranging from road and factory construction to the building of medical and educational facilities. The World Bank and other multilateral development banks (banks with international support that provide loans to developing countries) are the largest source of advice and assistance for developing nations. The International Development Association and the International Finance Corporation are associated with the World Bank and provide loans to private businesses and member countries.

International Monetary Fund

The **International Monetary Fund (IMF)** was established in 1947 to promote trade among member nations by eliminating trade barriers and fostering financial cooperation. It also makes short-term loans to member countries that have balance-of-payment deficits and provides foreign currencies to member nations. The International Monetary Fund also tries to avoid financial crises and panics by alerting the international community about countries that will not be able to repay their debts. The IMF's Internet site provides additional information about the organization, including news releases, frequently asked questions, and members.

International Monetary Fund (IMF) organization established in 1947 to promote trade among member nations by eliminating trade barriers and fostering financial cooperation

Getting Involved in International Business

Businesses may get involved in international trade at many levels—from a small Kenyan firm that occasionally exports African crafts to a huge multinational corporation such as Shell Oil that sells products around the globe. The degree of commitment of resources and effort required increases according to the level at which a business involves itself in international trade. This section examines exporting and importing, trading companies, licensing and franchising, contract manufacturing, joint ventures, direct investment, and multinational corporations.

Exporting and Importing

Many companies first get involved in international trade when they import goods from other countries for resale in their own businesses. For example, a grocery store chain may import bananas from Honduras and coffee from Colombia. A business may get involved in exporting when it is called upon to supply a foreign company with a particular product. Such exporting enables enterprises of all sizes to participate in international business. Table 3.4 shows the number of U.S. exporters and the export value by company size, while Figure 3.1 shows the major export markets for U.S. companies.

	Number of Exporters	%	Value ($ bil)	%
Small (<100 employees)	212,568	89.2	129.6	20.8
Medium (100–499 employees)	18,168	7.6	52.6	8.4
Large (500 + employees)	7,548	3.2	441.2	70.8

TABLE 3.4

U.S. Exporters and Value by Company Size

Source: "Highlights from a Profile of U.S. Exporting Companies, 2000–2001," U.S. Department of Commerce News, press release, February 20, 2003, www.census.gov/foreign-trade.

FIGURE 3.1

Major Export Markets for U.S. Companies

Source: "Highlights from a Profile of U.S. Exporting Companies, 2000–2001," *U.S. Department of Commerce News,* press release, February 20, 2003, available at www.census.gov/foreign-trade/aip/.

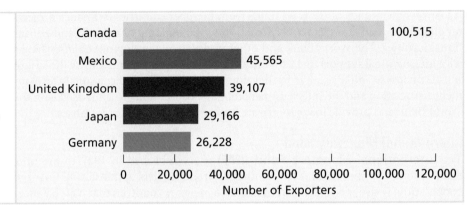

countertrade agreements
foreign trade agreements that involve bartering products for other products instead of for currency

Exporting sometimes takes place through **countertrade agreements,** which involve bartering products for other products instead of for currency. Such arrangements are fairly common in international trade, especially between Western companies and Eastern European nations. An estimated 40 percent or more of all international trade agreements contain countertrade provisions.

Although a company may export its wares overseas directly or import goods directly from their manufacturer, many choose to deal with an intermediary, commonly called an *export agent.* Export agents seldom produce goods themselves; instead, they usually handle international transactions for other firms. Export agents either purchase products outright or take them on consignment. If they purchase them outright, they generally mark up the price they have paid and attempt to sell the product in the international marketplace. They are also responsible for storage and transportation.

An advantage of trading through an agent instead of directly is that the company does not have to deal with foreign currencies or the red tape (paying tariffs and handling paperwork) of international business. A major disadvantage is that, because the export agent must make a profit, either the price of the product must be increased or the domestic company must provide a larger discount than it would in a domestic transaction.

Trading Companies

trading company
a firm that buys goods in one country and sells them to buyers in another country

A **trading company** buys goods in one country and sells them to buyers in another country. Trading companies handle all activities required to move products from one country to another, including consulting, marketing research, advertising, insurance, product research and design, warehousing, and foreign exchange services to companies interested in selling their products in foreign markets. Trading companies are similar to export agents, but their role in international trade is larger. By linking sellers and buyers of goods in different countries, trading companies promote international trade. The best known U.S. trading company is Sears World Trade, which specializes in consumer goods, light industrial items, and processed foods.

Licensing and Franchising

licensing
a trade agreement in which one company—the licensor—allows another company—the licensee—to use its company name, products, patents, brands, trademarks, raw materials, and/or production processes in exchange for a fee or royalty

Licensing is a trade arrangement in which one company—the *licensor*—allows another company—the *licensee*—to use its company name, products, patents, brands, trademarks, raw materials, and/or production processes in exchange for a fee or roy-

1. Subway	**TABLE 3.5**
2. Curves	
3. Quizno's Franchise Co.	Top Ten Global
4. Burger King Corp.	Franchise Operations
5. UPS Store	
6. InterContinental Hotels Group	
7. Domino's Pizza LLC	
8. McDonald's	
9. Jani-King	
10. Kumon Math & Reading Centers	

Source: "Top Ten Global Franchises for 2004," *Entrepreneur,* (n.d.), www.entrepreneur.com/franzone/listings/topglobal/0, 5835,,00.html (accessed March 29, 2004).

alty. The Coca-Cola Company and PepsiCo frequently use licensing as a means to market their soft drinks, apparel, and other merchandise in other countries. Licensing is an attractive alternative to direct investment when the political stability of a foreign country is in doubt or when resources are unavailable for direct investment. Licensing is especially advantageous for small manufacturers wanting to launch a well-known brand internationally. Yoplait is a French yogurt that is licensed for production in the United States.

Franchising is a form of licensing in which a company—the *franchiser*—agrees to provide a *franchisee* a name, logo, methods of operation, advertising, products, and other elements associated with the franchiser's business, in return for a financial commitment and the agreement to conduct business in accordance with the franchiser's standard of operations. Wendy's, McDonald's, Pizza Hut, and Holiday Inn are well-known franchisers with international visibility. Twenty percent of all U.S. franchise systems have foreign operations. The majority of these were located in developed markets such as Canada, Japan, Europe, and Australia.[46] Table 3.5 lists the top ten global franchises as ranked by *Entrepreneur* magazine.

Licensing and franchising enable a company to enter the international marketplace without spending large sums of money abroad or hiring or transferring personnel to handle overseas affairs. They also minimize problems associated with shipping costs, tariffs, and trade restrictions. And, they allow the firm to establish goodwill for its products in a foreign market, which will help the company if it decides to produce or market its products directly in the foreign country at some future date. However, if the licensee (or franchisee) does not maintain high standards of quality, the product's image may be hurt; therefore, it is important for the licensor to monitor its products overseas and to enforce its quality standards.

Contract Manufacturing

Contract manufacturing occurs when a company hires a foreign company to produce a specified volume of the firm's product to specification; the final product carries the domestic firm's

Dominos franchises its pizza business in Asia, serving such toppings as squid, sweet mayonnaise, and duck gizzards.

franchising
a form of licensing in which a company—the franchiser—agrees to provide a franchisee a name, logo, methods of operation, advertising, products, and other elements associated with a franchiser's business, in return for a financial commitment and the agreement to conduct business in accordance with the franchiser's standard of operations

name. Spalding, for example, relies on contract manufacturing for its sports equipment; Reebok uses Korean contract manufacturers to manufacture many of its athletic shoes.

Outsourcing

Earlier, we defined outsourcing as transferring manufacturing or other tasks (such as information technology operations) to companies in countries where labor and supplies are less expensive. Many U.S. firms have outsourced tasks to India, Ireland, Mexico, and the Philippines, where there are many well-educated workers and significantly lower labor costs. Experts estimate that 20 percent of manufacturers and financial-service firms have outsourced some information-technology tasks and project that figure will double by 2006.[47] Bank of America, for example, set up a subsidiary in India to outsource 1,000 back-office support jobs. The bank also contracts with several Indian firms to provide software services. Experts believe that two-thirds of U.S. banks outsource services to China, India, and Russia.[48] Even small firms can outsource. For example, Avalon, an Irish manufacturer of high-end guitars played by musicians like Eric Clapton, contracted with Cort Musical Instruments Company in South Korea to augment the firm's production and help it build a global brand. The outsourcing arrangement helped the small business boost output from 1,500 guitars a year to 8,000 annually, helping it become more competitive with larger manufacturers.[49]

contract manufacturing
the hiring of a foreign company to produce a specified volume of the initiating company's product to specification; the final product carries the domestic firm's name

Although outsourcing has become politically controversial in recent years amid concerns over jobs lost to overseas workers, foreign companies transfer tasks and jobs to U.S. companies—sometimes called *insourcing*—far more often than U.S. companies outsource tasks and jobs abroad.[50] For example, Indian-based Bharti Tele-Ventures, a cell-phone operator, signed a 10-year contract to insource its software, hardware, and other information-technology tasks to IBM in the United States.[51]

Joint Ventures and Alliances

joint venture
the sharing of the costs and operation of a business between a foreign company and a local partner

Many countries, particularly LDCs, do not permit direct investment by foreign companies or individuals. Or, a company may lack sufficient resources or expertise to operate in another country. In such cases, a company that wants to do business in another country may set up a **joint venture** by finding a local partner (occasionally, the host nation itself) to share the costs and operation of the business. General Motors, for example, has a joint venture with Russian automaker Avtovaz in Togliatti, which manufactures four-wheel-drive Chevrolet Nivas and Opel Astras for the Russian market. Demand for the relatively pricey Astra has grown along with Russian household incomes.[52]

strategic alliance
a partnership formed to create competitive advantage on a worldwide basis

In some industries, such as automobiles and computers, strategic alliances are becoming the predominant means of competing. A **strategic alliance** is a partnership formed to create competitive advantage on a worldwide basis. In such industries, international competition is so fierce and the costs of competing on a global basis are so high that few firms have the resources to go it alone, so they collaborate with other companies. An example of such an alliance is New United Motor Manufacturing, Inc. (NUMMI), formed by Toyota and General Motors in 1984 to make automobiles for both firms. This alliance joined the quality engineering of Japanese cars with the marketing expertise and market access of General Motors. Today, NUMMI manufactures the popular Toyota Tacoma compact

Think Globally
India: Beyond Outsourcing

India is not the same place it was five years ago. With the economy growing at 8 percent annually, Indians are excited about job opportunities in their own country, instead of looking for jobs in the United States. No longer limited to credit-card call centers and order-fulfillment operations, India is offering increasingly sophisticated services to business customers around the globe, including consulting, financial analysis, and cutting-edge scientific research. Many American companies have chosen to relocate their operations to India in order to take advantage of cheaper labor, and Indians are performing many jobs once done by Americans. Companies like PeopleSoft, Intel, Microsoft, and General Electric have established operations in India, in addition to many leading pharmaceutical manufacturers, such as Pfizer, Merck, and GlaxoSmithKline.

India is also moving beyond its reputation as a center for outsourcing or "offshoring" industries. Now, India has a growing roster of its own successful blue-chip companies, such as Infosys, Tata Consultancy, and Wipro. Infosys, for example, designs and maintains software for almost 300 *Fortune* 500 companies. These companies and others are moving in to compete with American giants like Accenture and IBM.

India's manufacturing sector is also becoming a global force. Once sluggish and inefficient, the manufacturing industry has benefited from recent economic reforms as well as a plentiful supply of engineering talent and inexpensive labor. Before India's economy began to open up, high tariffs kept out foreign goods and local companies had to seek government approval for almost all elements of their businesses. Much of the economy was dominated by government-run monopolies. An economic crisis in 1991, brought about by skyrocketing oil prices, prompted the government to slash tariffs and eliminate the previously restrictive system.

Consider the effect of these changes on Tata Sons Ltd., a massive conglomerate favored by the government monopoly system. The 1991 reforms fostered local and international competition for Tata, forcing the company to radically restructure in order to compete. The conglomerate had to change old company policies based on nepotism and, for the first time, salaries were tied to performance. Cost-cutting also became a concern in the face of new competition. But instead of backing down, chairman Ratan Tata decided it was time for the company to expand. Tata decided to expand into automobiles, drawing on the available engineering talent to help it succeed. Tata Motors developed its first car, the Indica, for $350 million, about a quarter of the development budget of U.S. and European automakers. When the Indica was launched in 1998 after about three years in development, customer reactions to the first model were not good, However, Tata Motors' management took complaints about the vehicle's poor suspension and lack of after-sales service seriously, and invited customers to help reengineer the Indica. When the new Indica was released in 2001, it quickly became a big seller.[53]

Discussion Questions
1. Why has India been so popular for U.S. companies engaged in outsourcing or offshoring?
2. Why is India's manufacturing sector becoming a global force?
3. What benefits will India gain from developing homegrown industries?

---

pick-up truck as well as the Toyota Corolla, Pontiac Vibe, and a right-hand drive Toyota Voltz for sale in Japan.[54]

Direct Investment

Companies that want more control and are willing to invest considerable resources in international business may consider **direct investment,** the ownership of overseas facilities. Direct investment may involve the development and operation of new facilities—such as when Starbucks opens a new coffee shop in Japan—or the purchase of all or part of an existing operation in a foreign country. General Motors, for example, owns nearly 45 percent of Korean-based Daewoo, 12 percent in Japanese-based Isuzu, and 20 percent of Japanese-based Fuji Heavy Industries.[55]

The highest level of international business involvement is the **multinational corporation (MNC),** a corporation, such as IBM or Exxon Mobil, that operates on

direct investment
the ownership of overseas facilities

multinational corporation (MNC)
a corporation that operates on a worldwide scale, without significant ties to any one nation or region

TABLE 3.6   The Ten Largest Global Corporations

Rank	Company	Country	Industry	Revenues (in millions)
1	Wal-Mart Stores	U.S.	General merchandiser	$246,525
2	General Motors	U.S.	Motor vehicles	$186,763
3	Exxon Mobil	U.S.	Petroleum refining	$182,466
4	Royal Dutch/Shell Group	Netherlands/Britain	Petroleum refining	$179,431
5	BP	Britain	Petroleum refining	$178,721
6	Ford Motor	U.S.	Motor vehicles	$163,871
7	DaimlerChrysler	Germany	Motor vehicles	$141,421
8	Toyota Motor	Japan	Motor vehicles	$131,754
9	General Electric	U.S.	Diversified financials	$131,698
10	Mitsubishi	Japan	Trading	$109,386

Source: "Global 500: The World's Largest Corporations," *Fortune,* July 15, 2003, p. 106. Copyright © 2003 *Time,* Inc. All rights reserved.

a worldwide scale, without significant ties to any one nation or region. Table 3.6 lists the 10 largest multinational corporations. MNCs are more than simple corporations. They often have greater assets than some of the countries in which they do business. General Motors, Exxon Mobil, Ford Motors, and General Electric, for example, have sales higher than the GDP of many of the countries in which they operate. Nestlé, with headquarters in Switzerland, operates more than 300 plants around the world and receives revenues from Europe; North, Central, and South America; Africa; and Asia. The Royal Dutch/Shell Group, one of the world's major oil producers, is another MNC. Its main offices are located in The Hague and London. Other MNCs include BASF, British Petroleum, Cadbury Schweppes, Matsushita, Mitsubishi, Siemens, Texaco, Toyota, and Unilever. Many MNCs have been targeted by antiglobalization activists at global business forums, and some protests have turned violent. The activists contend that MNCs increase the gap between rich and poor nations, misuse and misallocate scarce resources, exploit the labor markets in LDCs, and harm their natural environments.[56]

International Business Strategies

Planning in a global economy requires businesspeople to understand the economic, legal, political, and sociocultural realities of the countries in which they will operate. These factors will affect the strategy a business chooses to use outside its own borders.

Developing Strategies

multinational strategy
a plan, used by international companies, that involves customizing products, promotion, and distribution according to cultural, technological, regional and national differences

Companies doing business internationally have traditionally used a **multinational strategy,** customizing their products, promotion, and distribution according to cultural, technological, regional, and national differences. In France, for example, South Korean–owned AmorePacific Corporation marketed its Lolita Lempicka perfume, with a decidedly French accent. Named for a French fashion designer, the fifth best-selling fragrance in France was formulated by French experts and marketed in a bottle designed by a French artist. Indeed, few French consumers realize the popular perfume is owned by a Korean firm.[57] Many soap and detergent manufacturers have adapted their products to local water conditions, washing equipment, and washing habits. For customers in some less-developed countries, Colgate-Palmolive Co. has developed an inexpensive, plastic, hand-powered washing machine for use in households that have no electricity. Even when products are standardized, advertising often has to be modified to adapt to language and cultural differences. Also, celebrities used in advertising in the United States may be unfamiliar to foreign consumers and thus would not be effective in advertising products in other countries.

More and more companies are moving from this customization strategy to a **global strategy (globalization),** which involves standardizing products (and, as much as possible, their promotion and distribution) for the whole world, as if it were a single entity. Examples of globalized products are American clothing, movies, music, and cosmetics. Exxon Mobil launched a $150 million marketing effort to promote its brands: Exxon, Esso, Mobil, and General. The ads have the same look and feel regardless of the country in which they appear. The ad's message was the same for all countries except the story was told in one of 25 languages.[58]

Before moving outside their own borders, companies must conduct environmental analyses to evaluate the potential of and problems associated with various markets and to determine what strategy is best for doing business in those markets. Failure to do so may result in losses and even negative publicity. Some companies rely on local managers to gain greater insights and faster response to changes within a country. Astute businesspeople today "think globally, act locally." That is, while constantly being aware of the total picture, they adjust their firms' strategies to conform to local needs and tastes.

global strategy (globalization)
a strategy that involves standardizing products (and, as much as possible, their promotion and distribution) for the whole world, as if it were a single entity

Managing the Challenges of Global Business

As we've pointed out in this chapter, many past political barriers to trade have fallen or been minimized, expanding and opening new market opportunities. Managers who can meet the challenges of creating and implementing effective and sensitive business strategies for the global marketplace can help lead their companies to success. Multinational corporations such as General Electric and Ford, which derive a substantial portion of their revenues from international business, depend on savvy managers who can adapt to different cultures. Small businesses, too, can succeed in foreign markets when their managers have carefully studied those markets and prepared and implemented appropriate strategies. Being globally aware is therefore an important quality for today's managers and will become a critical attribute for managers of the 21st century.

Explore Your Career Options
Preparing for the Borderless World

To be a successful businessperson in the twenty-first century, you will need to be globally aware, looking beyond your own region or country to the whole world. Being globally aware requires objectivity, tolerance, and knowledge. Objectivity is crucial in assessing opportunities, evaluating potential markets and opportunities, and resolving problems. Tolerance of cultural differences does not mean that you have to accept as your own the cultural ways of other countries, but it does mean that you must permit others to be different but equal. Being globally aware requires staying informed about social and economic trends because a country's prospects can change, sometimes almost overnight, as social, political, and economic trends change direction or accelerate.

Both trade agreements like NAFTA and new technologies are reducing borders among nations and creating many exciting career opportunities. Most new jobs will have at least some global component. Examples of exciting careers in global business include export and import management, product management and distribution, and advertising. An export manager is responsible for managing all of a large company's exporting activities and supervises the activities of foreign sales representatives who live and work abroad. Since products may be sold in many countries, product management and distribution transcends national boundaries, but may have to be customized for a particular country or region. Students interested in advertising will find an exciting career meeting the challenges of communicating information to people of diverse languages and needs.

While the likelihood of receiving a foreign assignment in your first job is low, the possibility of developing and implementing global strategies is high. Today, many colleges and universities are encouraging study in international business, foreign languages, cross-cultural communications, and related areas to prepare students for the borderless world. In the future, you can expect that it will be a requirement, not an option, to have global business skills.[59]

Review Your Understanding

Explore some of the factors within the international trade environment that influence business.

International business is the buying, selling, and trading of goods and services across national boundaries. Importing is the purchase of products and raw materials from another nation; exporting is the sale of domestic goods and materials to another nation. A nation's balance of trade is the difference in value between its exports and imports; a negative balance of trade is a trade deficit. The difference between the flow of money into a country and the flow of money out of it is called the balance of payments. An absolute or comparative advantage in trade may determine what products a company from a particular nation will export.

Investigate some of the economic, legal-political, social, cultural, and technological barriers to international business.

Companies engaged in international trade must consider the effects of economic, legal, political, social, and cultural differences between nations. Economic barriers are a country's level of development (infrastructure) and exchange rates. Wide-ranging legal and political barriers include differing laws (and enforcement), tariffs, exchange controls, quotas, embargoes, political instability, and war. Ambiguous cultural and social barriers involve differences in spoken and body language, time, holidays and other observances, and customs.

Specify some of the agreements, alliances, and organizations that may encourage trade across international boundaries.

Among the most important promoters of international business are the General Agreement on Tariffs and Trade, the World Trade Organization, the North American Free Trade Agreement, the European Union, the Asia-Pacific Economic Cooperation, the World Bank, and the International Monetary Fund.

Summarize the different levels of organizational involvement in international trade.

A company may be involved in international trade at several levels, each requiring a greater commitment of resources and effort, ranging from importing/exporting to multinational corporations. Countertrade agreements occur at the import/export level and involve bartering products for other products instead of currency. At the next level, a trading company links buyers and sellers in different countries to foster trade. In licensing and franchising, one company agrees to allow a foreign company the use of its company name, products, patents, brands, trademarks, raw materials, and production processes, in exchange for a flat fee or royalty. Contract manufacturing occurs when a company hires a foreign company to produce a specified volume of the firm's product to specification; the final product carries the domestic firm's name. A joint venture is a partnership in which companies from different countries agree to share the costs and operation of the business. The purchase of overseas production and marketing facilities is direct investment. Outsourcing, a form of direct investment, involves transferring manufacturing to countries where labor and supplies are cheap. A multinational corporation is one that operates on a worldwide scale, without significant ties to any one nation or region.

Contrast two basic strategies used in international business.

Companies typically use one of two basic strategies in international business. A multinational strategy customizes products, promotion, and distribution according to cultural, technological, regional, and national differences. A global strategy (globalization) standardizes products (and, as much as possible, their promotion and distribution) for the whole world, as if it were a single entity.

Assess the opportunities and problems facing a small business considering expanding into international markets.

The "Solve the Dilemma" box on page 89 presents a small business considering expansion into international markets. Based on the material provided in the chapter, analyze the business's position, evaluating specific markets, anticipating problems, and exploring methods of international involvement.

Revisit the World of Business

1. Why is a global focus on markets and efficient production locations so important to Porsche?

2. What are the benefits for having Volkswagen as a partner in producing the Porsche Cayenne?

3. Are there any risks for Porsche in having 50 percent of its market in North America?

Learn the Terms

absolute advantage   77
Asia-Pacific Economic Cooperation (APEC)   90
balance of payments   79
balance of trade   78
cartel   83
comparative advantage   77
contract manufacturing   93
countertrade agreements   92
direct investment   95
dumping   82
embargo   82
European Union (EU)   89

exchange controls   82
exchange rate   80
exporting   78
franchising   93
General Agreement on Tariffs and Trade (GATT)   87
global strategy (globalization)   97
import tariff   81
importing   78
infrastructure   80
international business   76
International Monetary Fund (IMF)   91

joint venture   94
licensing   92
multinational corporation (MNC)   95
multinational strategy   96
North American Free Trade Agreement (NAFTA)   88
outsourcing   77
quota   82
strategic alliance   94
trade deficit   78
trading company   92
World Bank   90
World Trade Organization   87

Check Your Progress

1. Distinguish between an absolute advantage and a comparative advantage. Cite an example of a country that has an absolute advantage and one with a comparative advantage.

2. What effect does devaluation have on a nation's currency? Can you think of a country that has devaluated or revaluated its currency? What have been the results?

3. What effect does a country's economic development have on international business?

4. How do political issues affect international business?

5. What is an import tariff? A quota? Dumping? How might a country use import tariffs and quotas to control its balance of trade and payments? Why can dumping result in the imposition of tariffs and quotas?

6. How do social and cultural differences create barriers to international trade? Can you think of any additional social or cultural barriers (other than those mentioned in this chapter) that might inhibit international business?

7. Explain how a countertrade agreement can be considered a trade promoter. How does the World Trade Organization encourage trade?

8. At what levels might a firm get involved in international business? What level requires the least commitment of resources? What level requires the most?

9. Compare and contrast licensing, franchising, contract manufacturing, and outsourcing.

10. Compare multinational and global strategies. Which is best? Under what circumstances might each be used?

Get Involved

1. If the United States were to impose additional tariffs on cars imported from Japan, what would happen to the price of Japanese cars sold in the United States? What would happen to the price of American cars? What action might Japan take to continue to compete in the U.S. automobile market?

2. Although NAFTA has been controversial, it has been a positive factor for U.S. firms desiring to engage in international business. What industries and specific companies have the greatest potential for opening stores in Canada and Mexico? What opportunities exist for small businesses that cannot afford direct investment in Mexico and Canada?

3. Identify a local company that is active in international trade. What is its level of international business involvement and why? Analyze the threats and opportunities it faces in foreign markets, as well as its strengths and weaknesses in meeting those challenges. Based on your analysis, make some recommendations for the business's future involvement in international trade. (Your instructor may ask you to share your report with the class.)

Build Your Skills

GLOBAL AWARENESS

Background:
As American businesspeople travel the globe, they encounter and must quickly adapt to a variety of cultural norms quite different from the United States. When encountering individuals from other parts of the world, the best attitude to adopt is "Here is my way. Now what is yours?" The more you see that you are part of a complex world and that your culture is different from, not better than, others, the better you will communicate and the more effective you will be in a variety of situations. It takes time, energy, understanding, and tolerance to learn about and appreciate other cultures. Naturally you're more comfortable doing things the way you've always done them. Remember, however, that this fact will also be true of the people from other cultures with whom you are doing business.

Task:
You will "travel the globe" by answering questions related to some of the cultural norms that are found in other countries. Form groups of four to six class members and determine the answers to the following questions. Your instructor has the answer key, which will allow you to determine your group's Global Awareness IQ, which is based on a maximum score of 100 points (10 points per question).

Match the country with the cultural descriptor provided.

A. Saudi Arabia
B. Japan
C. Great Britain
D. Germany
E. Venezuela

_____ 1. When people in this country table a motion, they want to discuss it. In America, "to table a motion" means to put off discussion.

_____ 2. In this country, special forms of speech called *keigo* convey status among speakers. When talking with a person in this country, one should know the person's rank. People from this country will not initiate a conversation without a formal introduction.

_____ 3. People from this country pride themselves on enhancing their image by keeping others waiting.

_____ 4. When writing a business letter, people in this country like to provide a great deal of background information and detail before presenting their main points.

_____ 5. For a man to inquire about another man's wife (even a general question about how she is doing) is considered very offensive in this country.

Match the country with the cultural descriptor provided.

    F. China
    G. Greece
    H. Korea
    I. India
    J. Mexico

_____ 6. When in this country, you are expected to negotiate the price on goods you wish to purchase.

_____ 7. While North Americans want to decide the main points at a business meeting and leave the details for later, people in this country need to have all details decided before the meeting ends, to avoid suspicion and distrust.

_____ 8. Children in this country learn from a very early age to look down respectfully when talking to those of higher status.

_____ 9. In this country the husband is the ruler of the household, and the custom is to keep the women hidden.

_____ 10. Many businesspeople from the United States experience frustration because yes does not always mean the same thing in other cultures. For example, the word _yes_ in this country means, "OK, I want to respect you and not offend you." It does not necessarily show agreement.

e-Xtreme Surfing

- **The Universal Currency Calculator**
  www.xe.com/ucc/

  Provides a convenient way to determine how much of a foreign currency you would get in exchange for a specific number of U.S. dollars, or vice versa.

- **The Customs IQ Test**
  www.getcustoms.com/quiz/quiz.html

  Lets you take a number of quizzes to test your understanding of many categories of cultural differences.

- **CIA World Fact Book**
  www.cia.gov/cia/publications/factbook/

  Profiles every country in the world with detailed information about each country's geography, population, government and military, economy, and infrastructure.

- **World Trade Organization (WTO)**
  www.wto.org

  Provides a wealth of information about international trade, including news, statistics, and resources, as well as information about the WTO.

See for Yourself Videocase

BP BUILDS A GLOBAL BRAND

BP was founded by William Knox D'Arcy, shortly after the turn of the twentieth century. He believed that worthwhile oil deposits could be found in Persia (now known as Iran), and for the first six decades of its history, the company focused primarily on oil in the Middle East. Indeed, it was known as the Anglo-Persian Oil Company until 1954 when it changed its name to the British Petroleum Company. Today, London-based BP is one of the world's largest oil and petrochemical groups, with operations in more than 70 countries, more than 103,700 employees, and revenues in excess of $233 billion. Historically, BP's key strengths have been in oil and gas exploration, refining and marketing of petroleum products, and the manufacturing and marketing of chemicals.

In recent years, the company has sought to reinvent and rebrand itself as a single global brand that extends "Beyond Petroleum." This move allows the company to develop visibility for all its goods and services, after many acquisitions brought together the former British Petroleum, Amoco Corporation, Atlantic Richfield (ARCO), and most recently, Burmah Castrol, to craft a unified image. The familiar British Petroleum shield and Amoco torch were replaced with a vibrant sunburst of green, white, and yellow, named after Helios, the sun god of ancient Greece. The logo was designed to signify energy in all its forms, from oil and gas, to solar and wind.

The unified BP brand and logo are intended to show customers that they can get the highest quality goods and services wherever they see the BP sign. The company conducted research to ensure that the new logo communicates this image to all countries and cultures in which BP operates. With around 28,000 sites all over the world, all of the company's customers will see a familiar symbol when refueling and shopping, regardless of the country they visit.

The reinvention of BP also included rebranding the firm as the "green oil company." The firm, which is one of the largest producers of natural gas, is investing in alternative energy sources, such as solar, wind, hydrogen, and new alternative energy technologies. BP is also featuring cleaner-burning fuels and lubricants. Although some environmentalists have questioned the company's reimaging as "Beyond Petroleum," the company maintains that it has a complete commitment to everything green and environmentally responsible. The company has acknowledged problems related to climate change, emissions pollution, and the need for economic sustainability of a global economy based on environmental responsibility.

To support its new unified brand image, the company modernized its entire retail network in a bid to increase its worldwide retail business by more than 10 percent per year. Many retail stores now offer services that allow customers to check weather and traffic conditions, pay without cash or credit cards, or find directions to local destinations. While filling their tanks, customers can use a touch-screen monitor to order sandwiches, pastries, and drinks, which will be waiting for them inside the store. Wherever possible, the company is using solar energy to light the canopy above gas pumps. The move to a global brand, environmental concerns, and increased services is expected to bring a significant increase in sales.

Many people engaged in international business underestimate the importance of social and cultural differences. Although many companies have failed because they poorly communicated the nature and purpose of their business, BP is trying hard to avoid making this mistake. People around the world have many of the same concerns about environmental sustainability and the importance of renewable energy sources. Developing a brand and logo that communicate its commitment to environmental goals has given BP a theme to unite all the different areas of its business around the world. While some may criticize the company for not doing enough in a short period of time, most are willing to reserve judgment to see whether the company is truly committed to moving "beyond petroleum" to sustainable environmental goals and backs them with meaningful actions.[60]

Discussion Questions

1. Is the brand name Beyond Petroleum a true global brand that can unify the various areas of the business? Defend your answer.

2. Evaluate BP's rebranding efforts as a global business strategy.

3. Can you identify any social or cultural barriers related to BP's branding efforts?

Remember to check out our Online Learning Center at www.mhhe.com/ferrell5e.

Chapter 4

Managing Information Technology and E-Business

OBJECTIVES

After reading this chapter, you will be able to:

- Summarize the role and impact of technology in the global economy.

- Specify how information is managed and explain a management information system.

- Describe the Internet and explore its main uses.

- Define e-business and discuss the e-business models.

- Identify the legal and social issues of information technology and e-business.

- Assess the opportunities and problems faced by an individual in an e-business and suggest a course of action.

Reinventing Amazon.com

Amazon.com, one of the few survivors of the dot-com demise, was founded in 1994 by Jeffrey P. Bezos. The company has grown from its garage birthplace into a leading Internet retailer with revenues of $5.3 billion. Although stock shares of the Seattle-based company hit a low of $6 during the dot-com meltdown, they had recovered to as high as $58 by 2004. Bezos even claimed that Amazon had reached a milestone of a full-year profit of $35 million, although some analysts questioned that figure. The company's profit margins have been falling because of continued price cutting and the company's free shipping offer to customers.

For most of its first decade, the company continually reinvented itself. Although the company started out calling itself "the Earth's biggest bookstore," Bezos early on recognized the Internet's potential to link just about anyone to any product without the costly overhead of building multiple stores and employing large numbers of salespersons. Amazon soon branched out into additional product categories, including music, movies, toys, electronics, Web-based services, and auctions, as well as apparel. Amazon's foray into online apparel marketing has been facilitated by relationships with merchants such as eBags, Eddie Bauer, Guess?, OshKosh, and Spiegel. These relationships allow Amazon to charge a sales-based fee to take care of the technology side of the transaction.

Amazon continues to tweak many of its retailing initiatives, such as its effort to have other companies sell their products through Amazon. Now customers see offerings from Amazon and other companies together. Amazon insists that it can earn the same level of profit regardless of which option customers choose. Bezos claims that he knows when to forge ahead or when to pull the plug on new products and ventures.

continued

Enter the World of Business

In the future, Bezos sees Amazon's greatest growth potential in international markets, especially in countries like Germany and Japan where the company already operates. China, with more and more consumers logging onto the Internet, also looms as a tremendous opportunity. Bezos claims that Amazon focuses more on customers than its competitors do, but increasingly sophisticated search engines could make it easier for potential customers to find each other and bypass Amazon. Amazon has always wanted to become an online Wal-Mart or an e-business hub like Yahoo! and other Web portals. Only time will tell whether Amazon can continue to reinvent itself and remain one of the most successful online retailers.[1]

Introduction

information technology (IT) processes and applications that create new methods to solve problems, perform tasks, and manage communication

The technology behind computers, the Internet, and their applications has changed the face of business over the past few decades. **Information technology (IT)** relates to processes and applications that create new methods to solve problems, perform tasks, and manage communication. Information technology has been associated with using computers to obtain and process information as well as using application software and the Internet to organize and communicate information. Information technology's impact on the economy is very powerful especially with regard to productivity, employment, and working environments. Technology has resulted in social issues related to privacy, intellectual property, quality of life, and the ability of the legal system to respond to this environment. Most businesses are using information technology to develop new strategies, enhance employee productivity, and improve services to customers.

In this chapter we first examine the role and impact of technology in our information-driven economy. Next, we discuss the need to manage information. We then analyze management information systems and take a look at information technology applications. Then we provide an overview of the Internet and examine e-business as a strategy to improve business performance and create competitive advantage. Finally, we examine the legal and social issues associated with information technology and e-business.

The Impact of Technology on Our Lives

technology The application of knowledge, including the processes and procedures to solve problems, perform tasks, and create new methods to obtain desired outcomes

Technology relates to the application of knowledge, including the processes and procedures to solve problems, perform tasks, and create new methods to obtain desired outcomes. IT includes intellectual knowledge as well as the computer systems devised to achieve business objectives. Technology has been a driving force in the advancement of economic systems and the quality of life. Today our economic productivity is based more on technology than on any other advance. Information technology is important because our economy is service based. Technology has changed the way consumers take vacations, make purchases, drive cars, and obtain entertainment. Consider the encyclopedia. Thanks to the ever-growing amount of information available on the Internet, sales of traditional hard-bound encyclopedias have plummeted as more people turn to Internet search engines to help them with research for school, work, or fun. Sales of *Encyclopedia Britannica,* first published in

1768, declined by 60 percent in less than a decade, while other publishers went out of business. The firms that survived did so by adapting and providing computerized encyclopedia or online access to encyclopedia content.[2] In the workplace, technology has improved productivity and efficiency, reduced costs, and enhanced customer service. The Homeland Security Department, for example, created a secure Web-based network that lets emergency services share information and coordinate responses to disasters. The Disaster Management Interoperability Services system facilitates vital communications during disasters and may benefit the country during a terrorist attack.[3] The economy of the 21st century is based on these dynamic changes in our society.

Information technology also is changing many traditional products. Reflect.com is an online beauty retailer of cosmetics, hair care, skin care, and fragrance products. Each order to the site is customized for individual skin, hair type, or other preference. From the time Reflect.com receives an order until it is shipped, a flow of information and materials is needed to achieve its one-to-one fulfillment strategy.[4] Keeping pace with new information technology is a challenge for businesses adjusting to new competitive environments.

Information technology has improved global access by linking people in businesses through telecommunications. Satellites permit instant visual and electronic voice connections almost anywhere in the world. The self-sustaining nature of technology acts as a catalyst to spur even faster development. As new innovations are introduced, they stimulate the need for more technology to facilitate further development. Technologies begin a process that creates new opportunities in every industry segment or customer area that is affected.

iPod is a part of the digital music revolution.

Productivity, the amount of output per hour of work, is a key ingredient in determining the standard of living. For the past eight years, the United States has enjoyed significantly faster productivity growth than it did over the preceding two decades. Some analysts believe that the potential gains in productivity from technological advances associated with the computer revolution are far from over.[5] Indeed, experts believe this rapid growth in productivity added an extra $220 billion to the country's gross domestic product over the last three years.[6] For example, the ability to access information in "real time" through the electronic data interface between retailers, wholesalers, and manufacturers has reduced delivery lead times, as well as the hours required to produce and deliver products. Product design times and costs have decreased because technology has minimized the need for architectural drafters and some engineers required for building projects. Consider Buzzsaw.com, which provides a secure, Web-based collaboration and project management service that helps project teams interact, store, manage, and share documents from any Internet connection. This service enhances productivity by reducing costs for architectural firms, builders, engineering companies, and educational institutions as well as those in the hospitality, manufacturing, and retail industries.[7] Medical diagnoses have become faster, more thorough, and more accurate, thanks to access to information and records, hastening treatment and eliminating unnecessary procedures.[8] Some medical services are even offered online to patients.

Managing Information

data
numerical or verbal descriptions related to statistics or other items that have not been analyzed or summarized

knowledge
an understanding of data gained through study or experience

information
meaningful and useful interpretation of data and knowledge that can be used in making decisions

Data refers to numerical or verbal descriptions related to statistics or other items that have not been analyzed or summarized. Data can exist in a variety of forms—as patterns of numbers or letters printed on paper, stored in electronic memory, or accumulated as facts in a person's mind.[9] **Knowledge** is usually referred to as an understanding of data gained through study or experience. **Information** then includes meaningful and useful interpretation of data and knowledge that can be used in making decisions. The less information available, the more risk associated with a decision. For example, when a manager purchases a new computer without conducting any research, the risk of a poor decision is great. A more informed decision could be made after determining existing, and likely, computing needs and the price, capability, and quality of available computers from a number of sources. Information is necessary for good decision making. When information is properly understood, guidelines can be developed that help simplify and improve decisions in future similar circumstances. Therefore, effective information management is crucial.

Businesses often engage in data processing efforts to improve data flow and the usefulness of information. Often, computers are communicating this data without the direct interface or help of an individual. Goods can be ordered when inventories drop or a previous customer can be notified automatically when new product information is available. All of this depends on software and equipment that has been put in place to make data more useful based on established decision criteria.

Management Information Systems

management information system
used for organizing and transmitting data into information that can be used for decision making

Because information is a major business resource, it should be viewed as an asset that must be developed and distributed to managers. Technology has been used to develop systems that provide managers with the information needed to make decisions. A **management information system** (MIS) is used for organizing and transmitting data into information that can be used for decision making. The purpose of the MIS is to obtain data from both internal and external sources to create information that is easily accessible and structured for user-friendly communication to managers. The MIS can range from a simple system in which information is delivered through e-mail to a complex system of records and data that is delivered through sophisticated communications software. At Anheuser-Busch, for example, a system called BudNet compiles information about past sales at individual stores, inventory, competitors' displays and prices, and a host of other information collected by distributors' sales representatives on handheld computers. The system allows company executives to respond quickly to changes in demographic or social trends or competitors' strategies with an appropriate promotional message, package, display, or discount. The system also helps the company pinpoint demo-

Scheid Vineyards produces premium wine grapes and operates approximately 5,600 acres of vineyards, primarily in Monterey County, California. The company sells most of its grape production to wineries producing high-quality table wines, but it also produces a small amount of ultra premium wine under its own label. In 2002, it created "VitWatch," a state-of-the-art information system, which gives clients real-time Web access to their specific vineyard blocks thereby keeping both vitner and client abreast of what is happening "in the field"—literally.

graphic consumption trends, craft promotional messages, and even develop new products such as Michelob Ultra, promoted for its low-carb content.[10]

The MIS breaks down time and location barriers, making information available when and where it is needed to solve problems. An effective MIS can make information available around the globe in seconds, and with wireless communications, it is possible for users to carry the system in a briefcase or pocket. Wireless devices in use today include computers, personal data assistants, cell phones, pagers, and GPS positioning devices found in cars. For example, General Motors provides OnStar Telematics that provide advanced satellite-based communication to pinpoint a car's location. The system can put the car's driver in touch with an adviser for emergency assistance or requests for directions, or connect with an online concierge for entertainment, restaurant, and shopping information. When an airbag deploys in a vehicle equipped with OnStar, the system automatically alerts an adviser, who calls immediately to discern the nature of the emergency.[11]

Collecting Data

To be effective, an MIS must be able to collect data, store and update data, and process and present information. Much of the data that is useful for managers typically comes from sources inside the organization. This internal data can be obtained from company records, reports, and operations. The data may relate to customers, suppliers, expenses, and sales. Information about employees such as salaries, benefits, and turnover can be of great value and is usually incorporated into the system. External sources of data include customers, suppliers, industry publications, the mass media, and firms that gather data for sale.

A **database** is a collection of data stored in one place and accessible throughout the network. A database management program permits participants to electronically store information and organize the data into usable categories that are arranged by decision requirements. For example, if management needs to know the 20 top customers by sales volume, then the system can quickly access the database and print a list of the customers in a matter of moments. This same type of information retrieval can occur throughout the functional areas of the business with the appropriate database management software.

Databases developed by Information Resources, Inc. (IRI) allow businesses to tap into an abundance of information on sales, pricing, and promotion for hundreds of consumer product categories using data from scanners at the checkouts in stores. IRI can track new products to assess their performance and gauge competitors' reactions. Once new products are on store shelves, IRI monitors related information, including the prices and market share of competing products. IRI can also help companies assess customers' reactions to changes in a product's price, packaging, and display. By tracking a product's sales in relation to promotional efforts, the effect of a

database
a collection of data stored in one place and accessible throughout the network

MSN's Internet browser service facilitates consumers' access to and navigation of the Internet.

company's advertising as well as that of competitors can be known.[12] Anheuser-Busch's BudNet system incorporates data purchased from IRI.[13]

The Internet

Internet
global information system
that links many computer
networks together

The **Internet,** the global information system that links many computer networks together, has profoundly altered the way people communicate, learn, do business, and find entertainment. Although many people believe the Internet began in the early 1990s, its origins can actually be traced to the late 1950s (see Table 4.1). Over the last

TABLE 4.1

History of Information
Technology

Year	Event	Significance
1836	Telegraph	The telegraph revolutionized human (tele)communications with Morse code, a series of dots and dashes used to communicate between humans.
1858–1866	Transatlantic cable	Transatlantic cable allowed direct instantaneous communication across the Atlantic Ocean.
1876	Telephone	The telephone created voice communication, and telephone exchanges provide the backbone of Internet connections today.
1957	USSR launches Sputnik	Sputnik was the first artificial earth satellite and the start of global communications.
1962–1968	Packet switching networks developed	The Internet relies on packet switching networks, which split data into tiny packets that may take different routes to a destination.
1971	Beginning of the Internet	People communicate over the Internet with a program to send messages across a distributed network.
1973	Global networking becomes a reality	Ethernet outlined—this is how local networks are basically connected today, and gateways define how large networks (maybe of different architecture) can be connected together.
1991	World Wide Web established	User-friendly interface to World Wide Web established with text-based, menu-driven interface to access Internet resources.
1992	Multimedia changes the face of the Internet	The term "surfing the Internet" is coined.
1993	World Wide Web revolution begins	Mosaic, user-friendly Graphical Front End to the World Wide Web, makes the Internet more accessible and evolves into Netscape.
1995	Internet service providers advance	Online dial-up systems (CompuServe, America Online, Prodigy) begin to provide Internet access.
2000	Broadband connections to the Internet emerge	Provides fast access to multimedia and large text files.
2002	Advances in wireless	Mobile phones, handheld computers, and personal data assistants provide wireless access to the Internet.
2004	Wireless technology expands	Use of radio waves to send e-mail, Web pages, and other information through the air (Wi-Fi).

four decades, the network evolved from a system for government and university researchers into a tool used by millions around the globe for communication, information, entertainment, and e-business. With the development of the **World Wide Web,** a collection of interconnected Web sites or "pages" of text, graphics, audio, and video within the Internet, use of the Internet exploded in the early 1990s.

An **intranet** is a network of computers similar to the Internet that is available only to people inside an organization. Businesses establish intranets to make the MIS available for employees and to create interactive communication about data. The intranet allows employees to participate in creating information useful throughout the organization. The development of an intranet saves money and time because paper is eliminated and data becomes available on an almost instantaneous basis. Over half of all businesses are running some type of intranet. Krispy Kreme, for example, has a network that provides store managers with a wealth of information ranging from instructional videos and ordering recommendations based on each store's past order history to weather forecasts, because consumers are more likely to buy donuts when the temperature falls. Having so much information readily accessible allows employees to focus on customers instead of paperwork.[14]

Some businesses open up their intranets to other selected individuals or companies through an **extranet,** a network of computers that permits selected companies and other organizations to access the same information and may allow different managers in various organizations to collaborate and communicate about the information. For example, one of the most common uses of an extranet is for a company such as Wal-Mart to permit suppliers such as Procter & Gamble or Kraft to access the Wal-Mart MIS to determine inventory levels and product availability. An extranet allows users to share data, process orders, and manage information.

World Wide Web
a collection of interconnected Web sites or pages of text, graphics, audio, and video within the Internet

intranet
a network of computers similar to the Internet that is available only to people inside an organization

extranet
a network of computers that permits selected companies and other organizations to access the same information and may allow collaboration and communication about the information

Country	Users (In Millions)	Estimated Percentage of the Population
Australia	13.1	66.1
United States	185.9	64.0
Canada	20.4	63.5
Japan	78.0	61.3
United Kingdom	34.1	56.8
Germany	41.9	50.8
Israel	3.0	49.8
Chile	5.2	33.5
Russia	22.3	15.4
South Africa	5.2	11.8
Mexico	11.1	10.6
Argentina	4.0	10.4
China	95.9	7.5
India	39.2	3.8
Iraq	0.0125	0.05

TABLE 4.2

Internet Use, by Selected Country

Source: "Population Explosion!" ClickZ, March 12, 2004, www.clickz.com/stats/big_picture/geographics/article.php/151151.

FIGURE 4.1

Leading Internet Activities

Source: "Harris Poll Shows Online Activity Grows, More Use Internet for More Purposes," Harris Interactive, press release, January 21, 2004, www.harrisinteractive.com/news/allnewsbydate.asp?NewsID=753.

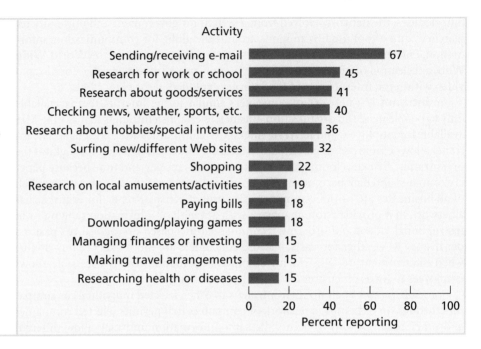

In the next few pages, we will take a brief look at who uses the Internet and ways the Internet is used.

Internet Users

The first Internet users were overwhelmingly male, young, college-educated, and resided in the United States. As access became cheaper and easier, the face of the typical user changed. By 2004, there were more than 945 million Internet users worldwide, and experts projected that figure would grow to nearly 1.5 billion by 2007.[15] The largest expected growth through 2005 is in Asian-speaking countries (34.6 percent), followed by a 27.2 percent growth rate in English-speaking countries. The European nations expect to see a 23.8 percent growth in Internet usage by the end of 2005.[16] Table 4.2 on page 111 shows the percentage of population accessing the Internet in selected countries.

In the United States, about 52 percent of Internet users are women, while only 42 percent of European Internet users are female.[17] One-fifth of American Internet users are between the ages of 2 and 17, who favor sites like DisneyChannel.com and Barbie.com.[18] However, the fastest growing group of Internet users is seniors over age 65, who account for just 7 percent of Internet users but are increasing at a rate of 25 percent annually.[19]

Internet Uses

The Internet is used mainly for communication, information, entertainment, and e-business. The most popular use of the Internet in the United States for both individuals and businesses is communication or e-mail. E-mail is fast, easy to use, and convenient. Figure 4.1 shows the leading online activities by those who say they use the Internet "often" or "very often."

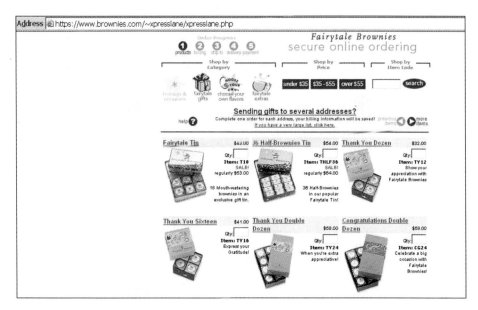

Fairytale Brownies is both a direct mail catalog and an online shopping experience. Childhood friends Eileen Spitalny and David Kravetz set out in 1992 with David's mom's 45-year-old "secret recipe" to create the world's best brownies. In 2003, Bizrate.com recognized brownies.com for its outstanding customer service during the 2003-2004 holiday season with a "Circle of Excellence" Gold award.

An adaptation of e-mail is instant messaging (IM), which allows users to carry on one or more real-time conversations simultaneously. Companies such as America Online, Time Warner Inc., and Yahoo! provide free IM services to more than 100 million people. Like most Internet innovations, IM is letting people communicate faster and more efficiently than ever. Once the realm of teenagers, IM is becoming more widespread in the workplace—though the content is not necessarily work related. Although instant messaging allows employees in large firms to communicate quickly and inexpensively, surveys suggest that most workplace IM deals with gossip and personal communications.[20]

Many users turn to the Net for information on a vast array of topics. Search engines, such as google.com, provide access to information on just about every imaginable subject. The user simply enters a word or phrase, and the search engine returns links to Web sites that potentially contain information the user is seeking. There are also many online reference materials, including encyclopedias, atlases, and almanacs. Other Web sites provide information on one specific topic, such as the weather, tourist/travel information, health/fitness, a particular sport, or any of a limitless number of topics. There are also online publications such as *Business Week, The Wall Street Journal,* the *New York Times,* and hundreds more. There are also sites that provide current and practical information on equipment and technological tools (for example, www.howstuffworks.com). Many businesses provide online information on their products even if they do not sell the products online or sell only a limited amount online. Other sites provide photos (www.photo-vault.com). It is likely there is a site with information on just about anything you can think of.

Other users find entertainment on the Net. You can listen to and download music; read books; track your favorite band, movie star, sports team, or local gas prices; watch video clips; chat about your favorite TV show; play games; build your own crossword puzzles; enter contests and sweepstakes; and find something interesting to do this weekend in your community. At Apple's iTunes Music Store, for example, legal downloads of music (at 99 cents per song) recently topped 1 million per week. And, at RealNetworks, subscribers can trail a celebrity golfer like Annika Sorenstam or Tiger Woods on the course during tournaments or get a front-seat view during a NASCAR race.[22]

Emerging Technologies

The growth of information and communication technologies has exploded in recent years. Consider that the number of subscribers to mobile phone services surpassed the number of fixed-line subscribers in 2002, and cellular has become the dominant technology for voice communications.[23] Indeed, the number of digital photos taken by cell phones has outstripped the number taken by digital cameras. In Japan, for example, camera-phones now account for more than 50 percent of all cell phones sold.[24]

Wireless fidelity (Wi-Fi) networks are changing the way individuals and businesses use the Internet. Wi-Fi sends Web pages and other information to your laptop computer or other electronic device using radio waves. In the not-too-distant future, experts expect Wi-Fi to link all sorts of devices—not just computers, but lamps, stereos, appliances, and more—and to fully integrate the Internet into our lives. For example, Epicurious has modified its Web site to include how-to videos that subscribers can watch while cooking in their kitchens. Wi-Fi is also transforming how companies use the Internet. Some firms use Wi-Fi to replace expensive wired networks or to maintain communications even in hard-to-reach places like warehouses. As such, investments in Wi-Fi can boost productivity and provides a return of 200 percent or more.[25]

Wireless mesh networks are answering the need for more product differentiation and diverse technological advancements. One of the big "killer applications" of wireless technologies will be the establishment of "plug and play" mesh networks, which provide optimized cost, benefit, and reliability ratios. Mesh networks avoid the central switching points found in the current Internet network structure and thus eliminates centralized failure. The mesh networks are self-healing and self-organizing, requiring no manual configuration, thus improving the reliability of communication between points.[26]

Another emerging technology of great importance to business is radio frequency identification (RFID) systems, which use radio waves to identify and track resources and products within the distribution channel. Goods tagged with an RFID tag can be tracked electronically from supplier to factory floor, from warehouse to retail store. Companies are also increasingly employing global positioning systems (GPS) to facilitate shipping and inventory management tasks.[27]

The growth of wireless voice communications and their increasing integration with Internet technologies generates opportunities for further innovations and applications. For example, location-based wireless technologies already aid police and parents in protecting children from kidnapping and other crimes. Multimedia messaging services (MMS) and streaming mobile video raise exciting possibilities for more person-to-person services and even personalized entertainment.[28] However, these possibilities also raise privacy questions, as we shall see later in this chapter.

Paul Easterwood, a recent graduate of Colorado State University in computer science, entered the job market during a slow point in the economy. Tech sector positions were hard to come by, and Paul felt he wouldn't be making anywhere near what he was worth. The only offer he had received was from an entrepreneurial firm, Pentaverate, Inc., that produced freeware. Freeware, or public domain software, is software that is offered to consumers free of charge in exchange for revenues generated later. Makers of freeware (such as Adobe and Netscape) can bring in high profit margins through advertisements, purchases made on the freeware site, or for more specialized software, through tutorials and workshops offered to help end users. Paul did some research and found an article in Worth magazine documenting the enormous success of freeware.

Pentaverate, Inc., offered compensation mainly in the form of stock options, which had the potential to be highly compensatory if the company did well. Paul's job would be to develop freeware that people could download from the Internet and that would generate significant income for Pentaverate, Inc. With this in mind, he decided to accept the position, but he quickly realized he knew very little about business. With no real experience in marketing, Paul was at a loss as to what software he should produce that would make the company money. His first project, IOWatch, was designed to take users on virtual tours of outer space, especially the moons of Jupiter (Paul's favorite subject), by continually searching the Internet for images and video clips associated with the cosmos and downloading them directly to a PC. The images would then appear as soon as the person logged on. Advertisements would accompany each download, generating income for Pentaverate, Inc. However, IOWatch experienced low end-user interest and drew little advertising income as a result. Historically at Pentaverate, Inc., employees were fired after two failed projects.

Desperate to save his job, Paul decides to hire a consultant. He needs to figure out what people might want so that he can design some useful freeware for his second project. He also needs to figure out what went wrong with IOWatch, as he loved the software and can't figure out why it failed. The job market has not improved, so Paul realizes how important it is to be successful in this project.

Discussion Questions

1. As a consultant, what would you do to help Paul figure out what went wrong with IOWatch?
2. What ideas for new freeware can you give Paul? What potential uses will the new software have?
3. How will it make money?

E-Business

Because the phenomenal growth of the Internet and the World Wide Web have provided the opportunity for e-business to grow faster than any other innovation in recent years, we have devoted an entire section to this subject. E-business growth has not been without some setbacks as businesses experimented with new approaches to utilizing information technology and the Internet. Since e-business is based on an interactive model to conduct business, it has expanded the methods for maintaining business relationships. The nature of the Internet has created tremendous opportunities for businesses to forge relationships with consumers and business customers, target markets more precisely, and even to reach previously inaccessible markets. The Internet also facilitates business transactions, allowing companies to network with manufacturers, wholesalers, retailers, suppliers, and outsource firms to serve customers more efficiently.[29] Traditional methods included conducting business personally, through the mail (package document delivery service), and via telephone. The telecommunication opportunities created by the Internet have set the stage for e-business development and growth.

The Nature of E-Business

In general, e-business has the same goal as traditional business. All businesses try to earn a profit by providing products that satisfy people's needs. **E-business** can be distinguished from traditional business as carrying out the goals of business through

e-business
carrying out the goals of business through utilization of the Internet

utilization of the Internet. There are many different areas of e-business that use familiar terms. For example, e-commerce uses the Internet to carry out marketing activities, including buying and selling activities conducted online. These activities include communicating and fostering exchanges and relationships with customers, suppliers, and the public. Dell Computer is one of the most successful e-businesses, making more than $113.4 million a day. Dell operates the highest-volume Internet commerce site in the world. The company's Web site receives more than 1 billion page requests per quarter at 86 country sites in 28 languages and 29 currencies.[30] Other online companies, such as booksellers, other computer dealers, and even some car companies, are trying to duplicate Dell's success.

E-commerce includes activities such as conducting marketing research, providing and obtaining price and product information, and advertising, as well as online selling. Even the U.S. government engages in e-commerce activities—marketing everything from bonds and other financial instruments to oil-drilling leases and wild horses. Procter & Gamble uses the Internet as a fast, cost-effective means for marketing research, judging consumer demand for potential new products by inviting online consumers to sample new prototype products and provide feedback. If a product gets rave reviews from the samplers, the company might decide to introduce it. Procter & Gamble already conducts nearly 100 percent of its concept testing and 40 percent of its 6,000 product tests and other studies online, saving the company significant time and money in getting new products to market.[31]

E-business has changed our economy with companies that could not exist without the technology available through the Internet. For example, DoubleClick is an Internet advertising firm that was founded in 1996 as an agency for advertising for Web sites. The company recognized the value of new information technology and created a priority ad-placement technology, DART, that is used to manage marketing e-mails as well as place banner advertising on Web sites. The firm could not have existed without the development of the Internet.[32]

Many companies that attempted to transact business on the Internet, often called dot-coms, had problems making a profit. Most of the early dot-coms, such as eToys.com, Pets.com, Garden.com, Hardware.com, and BigWords.com, found that no single technology could completely change the nature of business, and many failed. Some dot-coms failed because they thought the only thing that mattered was brand awareness they created through advertising. The reality, however, is that Internet markets are more similar to traditional markets than they are different. Thus, successful e-business strategies, like traditional business strategies, depend on creating products that customers need or want, not merely developing a brand name or reducing the costs associated with online transactions. Consider Amazon.com, which struggled for years to earn a profit, but finally moved into the black in 2003, with profits of $35 million on sales of $5.3 billion.[33] Some of the reasons behind the online retailer's success include the fact that it offers 10 times the selection of a typical "big-box" electronics store and more than 500 top clothing brands. The company's attention to customer satisfaction earned it an 88 on the American Customer Satisfaction Index, the highest score ever recorded on that survey.[34]

Instead of e-business changing all industries, it has had much more impact in certain industries where the cost of business and customer transactions is very high. For example, investment trading is less expensive online because customers can buy and sell investments, such as stocks and mutual funds, on their own. Firms such as E*Trade and Charles Schwab Corp, the biggest online brokerage firm, have been in-

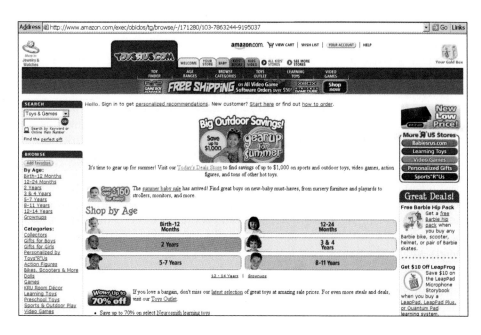

Toysrus.com initially struggled on its own with fulfillment and warehousing issues. In 2000, it partnered with Amazon.com to handle site development, order fulfillment, and customer service, housing both Toysrus.com's and its own inventory in Amazon.com's U.S. distribution centers.

novators in online trading. Traditional brokers such as Merrill Lynch have had to follow these companies and provide online trading for their customers.

E-business can use many benefits of the Internet to reduce the cost of both customer and business transactions. Since the Internet lowers the cost of communication, it can contribute significantly in any industry or activity that depends on the flow of information. Opportunities exist for information-intensive industries such as entertainment, health care, government services, education, and computer services such as software.[35] For example, some insurance companies now pay for doctor–patient e-visits. Help First Group, a Chicago health benefits company, has one of the largest networks of doctors available online. Patients can "talk" with doctors through a special Web page. Help First pays the doctors $25 per e-visit, and the patient pays nothing. Blue Shield of California has created a similar Web site where patients can get online consultation with their own doctors. The patient makes a co-payment just as for a traditional office visit. The future challenge will be finding effective ways to provide online patient service and setting fees that are cost-efficient to the patient and the medical service provider.[36]

A recent trend to help companies control the rising labor costs associated with providing customer service and support is the practice of outsourcing service jobs. The federal government does not keep track of how many U.S. jobs have moved to companies overseas, but there are estimates that 300,000 to 400,000 jobs have gone to places like China, Russia, and India in the last three years. Whether U.S. citizens are aware or not, they may be talking to an employee in India whenever they call the technical support number for Delta Airlines, American Express, Sprint, CitiBank, IBM, or Hewlett-Packard.[37]

In the future, most benefits and significant gains will come from restructuring the way work is done within businesses. While e-business can reduce the cost of both customer and business transactions, it can also improve coordination within and across businesses. E-business systems can become the communications backbone linking traditional relationships and storing employee knowledge in management information systems so that co-workers can access this knowledge instead of starting from ground zero. Leading experts suggest that most e-business benefits will come from changes in business practices and the way organizations function. With the crucial role of communication and information in business, the long-term impact of e-business on economic growth could be substantial.[38]

One area where e-business may have promised too much is in the area of manufacturing. Intranets can be important in reducing inventories and in eliminating costs in purchasing and other supply chain activities, as well as in eliminating unnecessary transactions. The Internet can be useful in determining the cost of components and other supplies and detailed information on customers to help customize products. Still the Internet mainly helps in moving information, while most manufacturing involves making things and motivating employees to maintain quality. Manufacturers still need to move truckloads of materials through congested highways and maintain a labor force that can get the job done. E-business can help manage manufacturing operations but is only one component that can provide quality and productivity.

E-Business Models

There are three major e-business models or markets with unique challenges and opportunities that represent areas with shared characteristics and decisions related to organizational structure, job requirements, and financial needs. The models are based on e-business customer profiles and how the Internet is used to maintain relationships.

business-to-business (B2B)
use of the Internet for transactions and communications between organizations

Busines-to-Business.   **Business-to-business (B2B)** e-business, sometimes called collaborative commerce, is the use of the Internet for transactions and communications between organizations. B2B activities are the largest and fastest growing area of e-business, with one-fourth of all B2B transactions taking place on the Internet. It is estimated that more than $5 trillion of B2B transactions will be done over the Internet by 2006, and the number of businesses engaged in B2B is expected to continue to accelerate at a rapid rate over the next few years.[39] Typical ways that a company might join the B2B world range from the easiest—going online with an electronic catalog—to the more complex—creating a private trading network, using collaborative design, engaging in supply chain management, and creating a public exchange.[40]

Many B2B companies combine these to be successful. For example, Internet infrastructure maker Cisco Systems receives 68 percent of its orders online, and 70 percent of its service calls are resolved online. Cisco is in the process of linking all of its contract manufacturers and key suppliers into an advanced Web supply-chain management system called the e-HUB. This advanced Internet communication system speeds up the information about demand and is distributed to suppliers.[41] Ford Motor Company links 30,000 auto parts suppliers and its 6,900-member dealer network for transactions. Ford expects to save $8.9 billion a year on costs and earn approximately $3 million a year from fees it charges for the use of its supplier network.[42]

The forces unleashed by the Internet are particularly important in B2B relationships, where uncertainties are being reduced by improving the quantity, reliability, and timeliness of information. General Motors, IBM, and Procter & Gamble are learning to consolidate and rationalize their supply chains using the Internet. The Covisint alliance between Ford, General Motors, DaimlerChrysler, Renault, Nissan, Oracle, and Commerce One makes parts from suppliers available through a com-

Growing a Business
eBay Provides Opportunity for Small Business Entrepreneurs

One of the best-known Internet companies is eBay, whose stated mission is "to provide a global platform where practically anyone can trade practically anything." The leading on-line auction site has grown into a community of 62 million registered users around the world who can buy or sell literally anything, from automobiles, boats, and furniture to jewelry, musical instruments, electronics, and collectibles. The auction site, described by CEO Meg Whitman as a "dynamic self-regulating economy," transacts nearly $15 billion in merchandise a year, more than the gross domestic product of many countries, giving it 80 percent of the market. The firm sells more used vehicles than the nation's number-one dealer AutoNation. Unlike many high-tech "dot-com" companies, eBay has been profitable almost from the beginning. The company's revenues totaled $2.17 billion for 2003, up 78 percent from $1.21 in 2002.

Although eBay is known primarily for consumer-to-consumer actions, many small business organizations have discovered they can sell older equipment and excess inventory through eBay. eBay brings together all business-related listings under one designation at www.ebaybusiness.com, which was launched in January 2003. By 2004, there were more than 1 million business-related items listed on eBay.com. After a downturn in the aerospace industry, Reliable Tools Inc. sold a few items on eBay, like a $7,000 2,300-pound milling machine. The California machine-tool shop now sells about $1 million a month, accounting for 75 percent of its business.

For many small businesses, eBay serves as their retail outlet. Today, there are more than 430,000 individuals that sell products full-time or part-time. eBay has also spawned a number of "Trading Assistants," independent companies that act as intermediaries to help consumers and businesses sell goods on the auction site. AuctionDrop, for example, provides six sites in San Francisco where sellers can drop off goods for the small business to auction on eBay and then collects 40 percent of the sales price as a commission, on top of the transaction fee charged by eBay. The company, which handles up to 1,000 items per day, plans to expand to four more locations around the United States.

By providing an easy-to-use site for consumers and businesses to buy and sell goods and remaining proactive, eBay has essentially become the poster child for a successful Internet venture. The benefits to buyers include Judy Branch, owner of Precision Copy in Southern California, who purchased $30,000 in copier equipment with an estimated savings of more than $90,000. With the money saved, she bought two new cars for herself and her husband. With strong leadership from Meg Whitman, Internet insiders believe the company will continue to serve as a model for e-business.[43]

Discussion Questions
1. Why is eBay so valuable for small businesses?
2. Why do you think eBay was successful from its launch and continues to grow?
3. What types of businesses may be threatened by small businesses and entrepreneurs using the Internet?

---

petitive online auction, reducing months of negotiations into a single day. The goal of the alliance is to reduce the time it takes to bring a new vehicle to market from 54 months to 18.[44]

Business-to-Consumer. **Business-to-Consumer (B2C)** e-business means delivering products and services directly to individual consumers through the Internet. The Internet provides an opportunity for mass customization, meaning that individuals can communicate electronically over the Internet and receive responses that satisfy their individual needs. If products and communication can be customized to fit the individual, then long-term relationships can be nurtured. For example, after a consumer makes a purchase at Amazon.com, the site provides recommendations for books, music, DVD, and toys, as well as electronics and software on future site visits by that consumer. Dell Computer is a leading B2C e-business that not only custom-builds computers for consumers but also provides customer service online.

U.S. e-tailers anticipated ringing up $65 billion in sales in 2004—a figure expected to grow by a compound annual growth rate of 17 percent through 2008 to exceed $117 billion. Experts believe the escalation of online retail sales will come primarily from first-time Internet buyers and that the online buying population will continue to grow to include one-half the adult population by 2008.[45]

business-to-consumer (B2C)
delivery of products and services directly to individual consumers through the Internet

Lands' End promotes its online shopping experience by enticing customers with the benefit of not having to stand in line.

Services provided in e-business relationships are often referred to as e-services. E-services are efforts to enhance the value of products through an experience that is created for the consumer. While traditional retailers provide many services, e-business companies have discovered that the unique characteristics of the Internet provide additional opportunities for enhancing the value to the consumer. Some examples of e-services include Map Quest's driving direction service and travel services provided by Travelocity.com and Expedia. According to the Travel Industry Association of America, more than 42 million people booked their travel arrangements online in 2003.[46] The key to the success of e-service sites is creating and nurturing one-to-one relationships with consumers. For example, some e-service travel sites also sell books/maps, apparel, insurance, and bags/luggage.[47]

Consumer-to-Consumer.   One market that is sometimes overlooked is the **consumer-to-consumer (C2C)** market, where consumers market goods and services to each other through the Internet. C2C e-business has become very popular thanks to eBay and other online auctions through which consumers

consumer-to-consumer (C2C)
market in which consumers market goods and services to each other through the Internet

can sell goods, often for higher prices than they might receive through newspaper classified ads or garage sales. Some consumers have even turned their passion for trading online into successful businesses. For example, a collector of vintage guitars might find items in local markets, such as pawnshops or flea markets, and then sell them for a higher price on eBay. Others use Zshops at Amazon.com for selling used items. The growing C2C market may threaten some traditional businesses if consumers find it more efficient to sell their books, CDs, and other used items through online auctions or other C2C venues.[48]

Customer Relationship Management (CRM)[49]

One characteristic of companies engaged in e-business is a renewed focus on building customer loyalty and retaining customers. **Customer relationship management (CRM)** focuses on using information about customers to create strategies that develop and sustain desirable long-term customer relationships. This focus is possible because today's technology helps companies target customers more precisely and accurately than ever before. CRM technology allows businesses to identify specific customers, establish interactive dialogs with them to learn about their needs, and combine this information with their purchase histories to customize products to meet those needs. Procter & Gamble, for example, encourages Oil of Olay customers to join Club Olay, an online community with some 4 million members. In exchange for beauty tips, coupons, and special offers, the Web site collects some information about customers and their use of the skin-care product. The company insists that Club Olay members are 20 percent more loyal to the brand.[50]

customer relationship management (CRM)
focuses on using information about customers to create strategies that develop and sustain desirable long-term customer relationships

Advances in technology and data collection techniques now permit firms to profile customers in real time. The goal is to assess the worth of individual customers and thus estimate their lifetime value (LTV) to the firm. Some customers—those that require considerable coddling or who return products frequently—may simply be too expensive to retain given the low level of profits they generate. Companies can discourage these unprofitable customers by requiring them to pay higher fees for additional services. For example, many banks and brokerages charge sizeable maintenance fees on small accounts. Such practices allow firms to focus their resources on developing and managing long-term relationships with more profitable customers.[51]

CRM focuses on building satisfying relationships with customers by gathering useful data at all customer-contact points—telephone, fax, online, and personal—and analyzing those data to better understand customers' needs and desires. Companies are increasingly automating and managing customer relationships through technology. Indeed, one fast-growing area of CRM is customer-support and call-center software, which helps companies capture information about all interactions with customers and provides a profile of the most important aspects of the customer experience on the Web and on the phone. Customer-support and call-center software can focus on those aspects of customer interaction that are most relevant to performance, such as how long customers have to wait on the phone to ask a question of a service representative or how long they must wait to receive a response from an online request. This technology can also help marketers determine whether call-center personnel are missing opportunities to promote additional products or to provide better service. For example, after buying a new Saab automobile, the customer is supposed to meet a service mechanic who can answer any technical questions about the new car during the first service visit. Saab follows up this visit with a telephone survey to determine whether the new car buyer met the Saab mechanic and to learn about the buyer's experience with the first service call.

Sales automation software can link a firm's sales force to applications that facilitate selling and providing service to customers. Often these applications enable customers to assist themselves instead of using traditional sales and service organizations. At Cisco, for example, 80 percent of all customer-support questions can be answered online through the firm's Web site, eliminating 75,000 phone calls a month.[52] In addition, CRM systems can provide sales managers with information that helps provide the best product solution for customers and thus maximize service. Dell Computer, for example, employs CRM data to identify those customers with the greatest needs for computer hardware and then provides these select customers with additional value in the form of free, secure, customized Web sites. These "premier pages" allow customers—typically large companies—to check their order status, arrange deliveries, and troubleshoot problems. Although Dell collects considerable data about its customers from its online sales transactions, the company avoids selling customer lists to outside vendors.[53]

Legal and Social Issues

The extraordinary growth of information technology, the Internet, and e-business has generated many legal and social issues for consumers and businesses. These issues include privacy concerns, identity theft, and protection of intellectual property and copyrights. Each of these is discussed below, as well as steps taken by individuals, companies, and the government to address the issues.

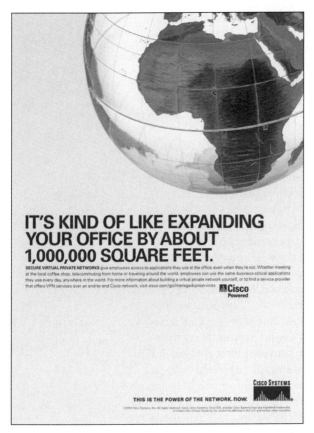

**IT'S KIND OF LIKE EXPANDING
YOUR OFFICE BY ABOUT
1,000,000 SQUARE FEET.**

Cisco Systems is a leader in networking for the Internet. This ad is for its Secure Virtual Private Networks, which allow employees to access company information anywhere in the world. These secure networks reduce risk and protect information from outsiders.

Privacy

Businesses have long tracked consumers' shopping habits with little controversy. However, observing the contents of a consumer's shopping cart or the process a consumer goes through when choosing a box of cereal generally does not result in specific, personally identifying data. Although consumers' use of credit cards, shopping cards, and coupons involves giving up a certain degree of anonymity in the traditional shopping process, consumers can still choose to remain anonymous by paying cash. Shopping on the Internet, however, allows businesses to track consumers on a far more personal level, from their online purchases to the Web sites they favor.[54] Current technology has made it possible to amass vast quantities of personal information, often without consumers' knowledge, and allows for the collection, sharing, and selling of this information to interested third parties. Privacy has, therefore, become one of Web users' biggest concerns.

How is personal information collected on the web? Many sites follow users' online "tracks" by storing a "cookie," or identifying string of text, on their computers. Cookies permit Web site operators to track how often a user visits the site, what he or she looks at while there, and in what sequence. Cookies allow Web site visitors to customize services, such as virtual shopping carts, as well as the particular content they see when they log onto a Web page, but the potential for misuse has left many consumers uncomfortable with this technology.

Some measure of protection of personal privacy is provided by the U.S. Constitution, as well as Supreme Court rulings and federal laws (see Table 4.3). Some of these laws relate specifically to Internet privacy while others protect privacy both on and off the Internet. The U.S. Federal Trade Commission (FTC) also regulates and enforces privacy standards and monitors Web sites to ensure compliance.

Businesses are beginning to recognize that the only way to circumvent further government regulation with respect to privacy is to develop systems and policies to protect consumers' interests. Several nonprofit organizations have also stepped in to help companies develop privacy policies. Among the best known of these are TRUSTe and the Better Business Bureau Online. TRUSTe is a nonprofit organization devoted to promoting global trust in Internet technology. Companies that agree to abide by TRUSTe's privacy standards may display a "trustmark" on their Web sites. Roughly 500 companies display the trustmark seal of approval from TRUSTe.[55] The BBBOnLine program provides verification, monitoring and review, consumer dispute resolution, a compliance seal, enforcement mechanisms, and an educational component. It is managed by the Council of Better Business Bureaus, an organization with considerable experience in conducting self-regulation and dispute-resolution programs, and it employs guidelines and requirements outlined by the Federal Trade Commission and the U.S. Department of Commerce.[56]

TABLE 4.3   Privacy Laws

Act (Date Enacted)	Purpose
Privacy Act (1974)	Requires federal agencies to adopt minimum standards for collecting and processing personal information; limits the disclosure of such records to other public or private parties; requires agencies to make records on individuals available to them on request, subject to certain conditions.
Right to Financial Privacy Act (1978)	Protects the rights of financial-institution customers to keep their financial records private and free from unjust government investigation.
Computer Security Act (1987)	Brought greater confidentiality and integrity to the regulation of information in the public realm by assigning responsibility for standardization of communication protocols, data structures, and interfaces in telecommunications and computer systems to the National Institute of Standards and Technology (NIST), which also announces security and privacy guidelines for federal computer systems.
Computer Matching and Privacy Protection Act (1988)	Amended the Privacy Act by adding provisions regulating the use of computer matching, the computerized comparison of individual information for purposes of determining eligibility for federal benefits programs.
Video Privacy Protection Act (1988)	Specifies the circumstances under which a business that rents or sells videos can disclose personally identifiable information about a consumer or reveal an individual's video rental or sales records.
Telephone Consumer Protection Act (1991)	Regulates the activities of telemarketers by limiting the hours during which they can solicit residential subscribers, outlawing the use of artificial or prerecorded voice messages to residences without prior consent, prohibiting unsolicited advertisements by telephone facsimile machines, and requiring telemarketers to maintain a "do not call list" of any consumers who request not to receive further solicitation.
Driver Privacy Protection Act (1993)	Restricts the circumstances under which state departments of motor vehicles may disclose personal information about any individual obtained by the department in connection with a motor vehicle record.
Fair Credit Reporting Act (amended in 1997)	Promotes accuracy, fairness, and privacy of information in the files of consumer reporting agencies (e.g., credit bureaus); grants consumers the right to see their personal credit reports, to find out who has requested access to their reports, to dispute any inaccurate information with the consumer reporting agency, and to have inaccurate information corrected or deleted.
Children's Online Privacy Protection Act (2000)	Regulates the online collection of personally identifiable information (name, address, e-mail address, hobbies, interests, or information collected through cookies) from children under age 13 by specifying what a Web site operator must include in a privacy policy, when and how to seek consent from a parent, and what responsibilities an operator has to protect children's privacy and safety online.

Spam

Spam, or unsolicited commercial e-mail (UCE), has become a major source of discontent with the Internet. Many Internet users believe spam violates their privacy and steals their resources. Many companies despise spam because it costs them $10 billion a year in lost productivity, new equipment, antispam filters, and manpower. By some estimates, spam accounts for more than 50 percent of corporate e-mail.[57] Spam has been likened to receiving a direct-mail promotional piece with postage due. Some angry recipients of spam have even organized boycotts against companies that advertise in this manner. Other recipients, however, appreciate the opportunity to learn about new products. Table 4.4 lists common reactions to spam.

spam
Unsolicited commercial e-mail

Think Globally
Europe Takes the Lead in Privacy Protection

When General Motors decided to update its electronic corporate phone book, the U.S. automaker learned that Europe's strict privacy laws defined office telephone numbers as "personal information." It took General Motors six months of legal documentation and other paperwork expenses before it could have an internal global electronic company phone book. Tough privacy rules like those established in the European Union (EU) have become the norm in Canada, South America, Australia, and parts of Asia. These laws dictate how companies can transmit personal data to countries that the EU claims lack "adequate" privacy laws, including the United States. The European Union Directive on Data Protection specifically requires companies to explain how collected personal information will be used, to obtain the individual's permission to collect and use the information, and to make customer data files available on request.

Fundamental differences separate U.S. and European regulation of privacy issues. While Europe has defined privacy as a human right, U.S. data-protection laws are often diminished by the free-speech protections granted by the U.S. Constitution. The result has been specific federal laws addressing sensitive areas such as medical and financial records and children's personal data. Some states have sought to go beyond federal regulation. California, for example, passed a law requiring businesses to keep records of all California customers' data shared with third parties—online or offline—for direct marketing purposes. The law requires businesses to tell California customers about all the data, including information relating to income and purchases, that they have shared as well as the names of the third-party users within 30 days of a consumer request for the information. Most U.S. companies set their own standards, where in Europe there is a coordinated comprehensive system for data protection.

In Canada, private industry has taken the lead in creating and developing privacy policies through the Direct Marketing Association of Canada (DMAC). The DMAC's policies resulted in additional Canadian legislation to protect personal privacy. This legislation was inspired by the EU Directive on Data Protection. The challenge for the future is whether the United States will continue with a patchwork of state, federal, and industry specific legislation or match the EU's initiatives on privacy.[58]

Discussion Questions
1. Why do you think the EU's privacy laws are so much stricter than those of the U.S.?
2. What challenges do the EU's strict privacy laws create for American businesses marketing to European consumers?
3. Do you think the U.S. should toughen its privacy laws to be more consistent with the EU? Why or why not?

TABLE 4.4

Common Reactions to Spam

Action	Percent Reporting
Deleted without opening	86
Clicked "remove me"	67
Clicked to get more information	33
Reported to e-mail provider	21
Ordered product	7
Reported to consumer or government agency	7
Provided requested personal information	4
Gave money in response	1

Source: Pew Internet & American Life Project, in Robyn Greenspan, "Spam: Always Annoying, Often Offensive," CyberAtlas, October 22, 2003, http://cyberatlas.internet.com/big_picture/applications/article/0,,1301_3097351,00.html.

Most commercial online services (e.g., America Online) and Internet service providers offer their subscribers the option to filter out e-mail from certain Internet addresses that generate a large volume of spam. Businesses are installing software to filter out spam from outside their networks. Some companies have filed suit against spammers under the Controlling the Assault of Non-Solicited Pornography and Marketing (CAN-SPAM) Law, which went into effect in 2004 and bans fraudulent or deceptive un-

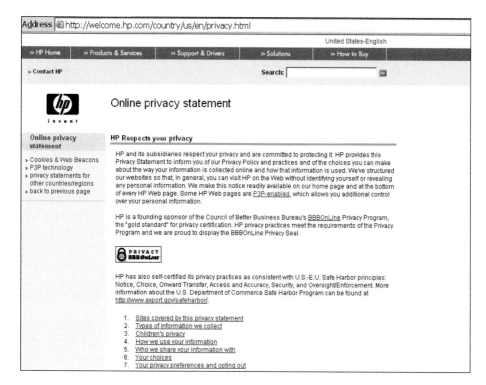

HP provides its Privacy Statement online.

solicited commercial e-mail and requires senders to provide information on how recipients can opt out of receiving additional messages. However, spammers appear to be ignoring the law and finding creative ways to get around spam filters.[59] Although North America is believed to be the source of 80 percent of spam, the European Union ordered eight member nations to enact antispam and privacy-protection legislation. The EU already has strict regulations concerning electronic communications and bans all unsolicited commercial e-mail, but not all member nations have ratified the regulations.[60]

Identity Theft

Another area of growing concern is identity theft, which occurs when criminals obtain personal information that allows them to impersonate someone else in order to use their credit to obtain financial accounts and make purchases. The Federal Trade Commission reported 214,905 consumer complaints about identity theft in 2003, up from 86,212 in 2001. The most common complaints related to credit-card fraud, as well as utility fraud, bank fraud, employment-related fraud, government document fraud, and loan fraud.[61] Because of the Internet's relative anonymity and speed, it fosters legal and illegal access to databases containing Social Security numbers, drivers' license numbers, dates of birth, mothers' maiden names, and other information that can be used to establish a credit card or bank account in another person's name in order to make transactions. One growing scam used to initiate identity theft fraud is the practice of *phishing,* whereby con artists counterfeit a genuine well-known Web site and send out e-mails directing victims to the fake Web site where they find instructions to reveal sensitive information such as credit card numbers. Phishing scams have faked Web sites for PayPal, AOL, and the Federal Deposit Insurance Corporation.[62]

Typically, it takes 14 months before a victim discovers identity theft, and in 45 percent of the cases, it took nearly two years to resolve the theft.[63] According to the

National Fraud Center, arrests for identity theft fraud have increased to nearly 10,000 a year, with losses from such fraud reaching $745 million. To deter identity theft, the National Fraud Center wants financial institutions to implement new technologies, such as digital certificates, digital signatures, and biometrics—the use of finger-printing or retina scanning.[64]

Intellectual Property and Copyrights

In addition to protecting personal privacy, Internet users and others are con-cerned about protecting their rights to property they may create, including songs, movies, books, and software. Such intellectual property consists of the ideas and creative materials developed to solve problems, carry out applications, and edu-cate and entertain others. Intellectual property is generally protected via patents and copyrights. The American Society for Industrial Security estimates that in-tellectual property and proprietary information losses in the United States total more than $59 billion a year.[65] This issue has become a global concern because of disparities in enforcement of laws throughout the world. In fact, the Business Software Alliance estimates that global losses from software piracy amount to $13 billion a year, including movies, music, and software downloaded from the Internet.[66]

U.S. copyright laws protect original works in text form, pictures, movies, com-puter software, musical multimedia, and audiovisual work. Owners of copyrights have the right to reproduce, derive from, distribute and publicly display, and perform the copyrighted works. Copyright infringement is the unauthorized execution of the rights reserved by a copyright holder. Congress passed the Digital Millennium Copy-right Act (DMCA) in 1998 to protect copyrighted materials on the Internet and limit the liability of online service providers.

Taxing the Internet?

An increasingly controversial issue in e-business is whether states should be able to levy a sales tax on Internet sales. The issue of collecting taxes on online pur-chases had been subject to a moratorium that went into effect in 2001. However, many states—facing huge budget deficits—have been lobbying for the right to charge a sales tax on Internet sales originating within their states. A University of Tennessee study suggests that states will miss out on $440 billion worth of tax rev-enue from online sales between 2001 and 2011 if the debate over Internet taxa-tion is not resolved. The goal of the Streamlined Sales Tax Project, which began in 2000, is to simplify sales tax laws and streamline collection procedures across the states and the District of Columbia. One of the project's proposals is to close loopholes that allow online retailers to avoid charging sales tax.[67] This is an issue that is still hotly debated and may ultimately emerge as a national issue rather than a state issue.

The Dynamic Nature of Information Technology and E-Business

As we have pointed out in this chapter, information technology and e-business are having a major effect on the business world and thus your future career. Future leaders of businesses will need more than just a technical understanding of infor-mation technology; they will need a strategic understanding of how information technology and e-business can help make business more efficient and productive. Companies that depend on information technology as their core focus provide examples of how savvy managers can adapt to using our knowledge in this area. Companies such as UPS have found that information systems make their "bricks, mortar, and trucks" world come alive to provide service to customers. Charles Schwab has made stock trading and obtaining securities information more efficient while providing significant savings to customers. Dell Computer and Cisco have found it possible to sell over half their products online. Many medium- and large-sized companies are changing the way they do business in response to the availability of new technologies that facilitate business in a changing world. Small businesses, too, can succeed by using information technology as leverage to implement appropriate strategies. In the future, manufacturing, retailing, health care, and even government will continue to adapt and use information technologies that will improve business operations. Today, technology presents a tremendous range of potential applications that can improve the efficiency of employees and companies while providing better service to customers. With technology changing on an almost daily basis, it is impossible to predict the long-term impact on the global world of business.

Explore Your Career Options
Information Technology Career Options

There is a wide variety of levels of information technology (IT) work, from help-desk call-center technician through chief information officer of a major corporation. People interested in technology can pursue careers in software and database development, telecommunications infrastructure, operations and end-user support, electronic commerce, and management. The main types of IT employers are large corporations and technology service providers such as Internet service providers, consultancies, dotcoms, and high-tech start-ups that operate independently from the Internet.

Although many IT professionals and specialists lost their jobs during the dot-com meltdown at the beginning of the century, demand is once again surging as companies begin to ramp up their IT hiring. Some areas of the United States have been identified as having particularly strong IT hiring markets. The west south-central states (Arkansas, Louisiana, Oklahoma, and Texas) are predicted to show an 8 percent hiring increase, while the east south-central states (Alabama, Kentucky, Mississippi, and Tennessee) are expected to experience a 19 percent increase. Although U.S. companies were expected to create 900,000 new IT jobs in 2001, about 425,000 were expected to remain unfilled because of a shortage of skilled workers. Employ-

ers have a higher demand for certain skills, such as network security and programming in Java and XML. Certain industries present a more dynamic market for IT professionals, including entertainment, food and beverage, health care, pharmaceuticals, and biotechnology.

The Internet contains a wealth of information on IT job prospects, outlook, salaries, and current openings. Some IT job Web sites are www.dice.com, www.hotjobs.com, and www.monster.com. People interested in a future in IT must be prepared to be flexible, adapt, and keep themselves up-to-date on current and expected changes in the world of information technology.

Listed below is the average annual salary for selected computer executives and professionals.

Chief information officer	$128,430
Chief technology officer	$128,164
Internet-technology strategist	$ 98,811
Product manager	$ 88,730
Information security manager	$ 77,959
Database administrator	$ 72,236
Help-desk/technical support manager	$ 64,551
Network administrator	$ 51,265
Help desk/technical support specialist	$ 43,735[68]

Review Your Understanding

Summarize the role and impact of technology in the global economy.

Technology relates to the application of knowledge, including the processes and procedures to solve problems, perform tasks, and create new methods to obtain desired outcomes. It has been a driving force in the advancement of economic systems and improvement in quality of life. Economic productivity is based more on technology than any other advance. Technology has changed the way consumers take vacations, make purchases, drive cars, and obtain entertainment. It has changed many traditional products and has improved global access by linking people through telecommunications.

Specify how information is managed and explain a management information system.

Information includes data and knowledge that can be used in making decisions. Businesses often engage in data processing efforts to improve data flow and the usefulness of information. A management information system (MIS) is used for organizing and transmitting data into information that can be used for decision making. The purpose of the MIS is to obtain data from both internal and external sources to create information that is easily accessible and structured for user-friendly communication to managers. The MIS breaks down time and location barriers, making information available when and where it is needed to solve problems.

Describe the Internet and explore its main uses.

The Internet is a global information system that links many computer networks together. It is used mainly for communication, information, entertainment, and e-business.

Define e-business and discuss the e-business models.

E-business can be distinguished from traditional business as carrying out the goals of business through utilization of the Internet. The three major e-business models are business-to-business (use of the Internet for transactions and communications between organizations), business-to-consumer (delivering products and services directly to individual consumers through utilization of the Internet), and consumer-to-consumer (markets in which consumers market goods and services to each other through utilization of the Internet).

Identify the legal and social issues of information technology and e-business.

The extraordinary growth of information technology, the Internet, and e-business has generated many legal and social issues for consumers and businesses, including concerns about privacy, identity theft, and protection of intellectual property and copyrights.

Assess the opportunities and problems faced by an individual in an e-business and suggest a course of action.

The "Solve the Dilemma" box on page 115 introduced an individual trying to survive in an e-business in today's rapidly changing business environment. Based on the material presented in the chapter, you should be able to evaluate the individual's efforts and suggest an appropriate course of action.

Revisit the World of Business

1. Why do you think Amazon has been so successful?
2. Assess Amazon's plan for growth in the future.
3. Suggest new products that Amazon could sell online.

Learn the Terms

business-to-business (B2B)   118
business-to-consumer (B2C)   119
consumer-to-consumer (C2C)   120
customer relationship
   management   120
data   108

database   109
e-business   115
extranet   111
information   108
information technology (IT)   106
Internet   110

intranet   111
knowledge   108
management information system   108
spam   123
technology   106
World Wide Web   111

Check Your Progress

1. What is information technology? How has technology influenced the economy?

2. Define *data, knowledge,* and *information.* Why is information important in business?

3. What is the purpose of a management information system and how is it used?

4. How has the evolution of the Internet impacted the world?

5. What is an intranet? An extranet? How are they used?

6. What are the four main uses of the Internet? Provide examples of each.

7. What is e-business? Describe the e-business models.

8. What are some of the privacy concerns associated with the Internet and e-business? How are these concerns being addressed in the United States?

9. What is identity theft?

10. Why is protection of intellectual property a concern? Provide an example on the Internet where intellectual property may not be protected or where a copyright has been infringed.

Get Involved

1. Amazon.com is one of the most recognized e-businesses. Visit the site (**www.amazon.com**) and identify the types of products the company sells and explain its privacy policy.

2. Art.com (**www.art.com**) displays and sells art prints via its online store. GE (**www.geappliances.com**) displays its appliances but does not sell them online. Visit the two sites and compare how each company uses the Internet.

3. It has been stated that information technology is to business today what manufacturing was to business during the Industrial Revolution. The information technology revolution requires a strategic understanding greater than learning the latest software or determining which computer is the fastest. Leaders in business can no longer delegate information technology to computer information systems specialists and must be the connectors and the strategists of how information technology will be used in the company. Outline a plan for how you will prepare yourself to function in a business world where information technology knowledge will be important to your success.

Build Your Skills

PLANNING A WEB SITE

Most companies design a Web site that reflects the company's image and goals and strives to ensure consistency in customer service, loyalty, and satisfaction. Many enlist virtual partners, linking their Web site to others where like-minded individuals (i.e., potential customers) might browse. Companies also use various graphics, animation, games, or other interesting information to improve Web site "stickiness" (prolonging the amount of time a user stays at the site).

The U.S. economy surged through the late 1990s as a result of e-commerce. With the coming of the 21st century, however, many dot-coms collapsed. Others, such as E*Trade.com and Amazon.com, survived and continue to compete in the marketplace. Many of the companies that have survived, such as eBay, have done so as a result of catering to a very specific market need that would not be feasible in a "brick and mortar" business (a physical marketplace). This is referred to as being a "niche" player.

As a manager of Biodegradable Packaging Products, Inc., a small business that produces packaging foam from recycled agricultural waste (mostly corn), you want to expand into e-business. It will be important to develop a Web site or to obtain links on existing Web sites to reach potential customers. Your major potential customers are in the business-to-business arena and could include environmentally friendly companies like Tom's of Maine (natural toothpaste) and Celestial Seasonings.

Your task: Plan a Web site that is compatible with your company's current operations by using the form below.

Web site objective _____

URL (Web site name)_____

Overall image and graphic design of your Web site

_____
_____
_____

Images you will use to increase Web site stickiness

_____
_____

Potential virtual partners where your customers may be browsing _____

_____
_____

e-Xtreme Surfing

- **ClickZ**
  www.clickz.com/stats/

  Provides statistics and articles about the the Internet and e-business.

- **TRUSTe**
  www.truste.com

  Promotes global trust in the Internet and and offers a special seal for companies that agree to abide by its privacy standards.

- **Cookie Central**
  www.cookiecentral.com

  Explores how Web sites use cookies to track visitors usage and helps Internet users understand the privacy issues surrounding the use of cookies.

- **Identity Theft**
  www.consumer.gov/idtheft

  Offers information from the Federal Trade Commission about the growing problem of identity theft, including how to recognize it and how to protect yourself from it.

See for Yourself Videocase

GOOGLE: THE SEARCH ENGINE SUCCESS STORY

Google, Inc., has become one of the five most popular Web sites in the world by providing a search engine with an uncanny knack for generating relevant results. The company derived its name from the term *googol,* which refers to the number represented by 1 followed by 100 zeros, to reflect its mission to organize the seemingly infinite amount of information available on the World Wide Web. Google has succeeded where so many other dot-coms have failed by following a conservative strategy; providing a simple, easy-to-use Web site; and developing effective relationships with advertisers. From the beginning, the firm refused to follow the pack of free-spending Internet startups and instead focused on what it does best: providing the most efficient access to information on the Internet. The company can search more than 4 billion documents and return results in less than half a second. It provides 3,000 searches every second of every day, a remarkable 50 percent of all Web searches performed. Google is believed to have sales in excess of $900 million and profits of $150 million in the last year. As Google launches its initial public offering (IPO), it may be valued by the market at $20 billion, a record among Internet companies that have gone public with IPOs.

Google was the brainchild of two Stanford computer science Ph.D. students, Larry Page and Sergey Brin. Page and Brin started their company in September 1998 out of a rented room in a home in Mountain View, California. Their landlady was skeptical at first about whether they could succeed in creating a system for searching the Internet that would be more effective than any other search engine. Later, she ended up quitting her job at Intel to work at Google. Now, instead of a rented room, the company has a four-building campus known as the Googleplex. The company's nearly 2,000 employees enjoy free food, unlimited ice cream, pool and ping-pong tables, and complimentary massages.

If you want to apply for a high-tech position at Google, it takes a degree from MIT, Stanford, CalTech, Carnegie Mellon, or another top engineering school even to get invited for an interview. As you would expect, developing cutting-edge software and building a complex system of computers requires twelve-hour days and networking with others through informal social events and meetings.

Although the company has used a conservative approach to growing its business, licensing, and signing up customers, it has used an unconventional approach to managing people within the organization. Google's corporate culture has been described as chaotic, with an emphasis instead on creativity and openness rather than organization. One CEO who was negotiating a contract with Google reported that interacting with Google is a series of Dilbert-style meetings. People would show up twenty minutes late, requiring repeated presentations, and other people would leave early. During the meeting, Google employees were messaging each other and their friends on Blackberrys and generally engaged in all types of multi-tasking. In addition, outsiders report that it is often hard to figure out who the project manager is on many projects. The founders acknowledge that their company is more disorganized than other dot-coms, but point out that if people aren't prepared in a meeting, it's because they are working around the clock. Even if the company has violated some of the rules of effective human resource management, it has excelled in developing a product that is superior to the competition.

The Google philosophy is that the search is an editorial product, with a clear line between information and ads. This approach has paid off with public trust in the brand and ever-increasing traffic to the site. Now Google is providing new innovations such as Gmail (a free Web-based e-mail service) while competing head-to-head with Yahoo in customized searches. The future of the search industry appears to hinge on customization. Rivals Yahoo and AOL are exploring ways to customize searches for visitors who are willing to provide data about themselves. Some observers believe that search engines in the future will use every bit of personal information you are willing to share, and then provide search results that best match your needs, desires, and location. Although Google has established a strong reputation based on trust and a separation of the search results from advertising, its biggest challenge in the future will be competition with other search engine providers, including Microsoft.

With all of its success, there is no doubt that the founders view this as the right time to cash in. The company is going public, meaning that it is offering its shares of its stock to outsiders in order to secure more resources to continue to grow, innovate, and deal with its strengthening competition. The company plans to raise about $2.7 billion through its IPO, but will yet again violate traditional ways of doing things by auctioning at least some of those shares directly to the public. In doing so, the goal is to shut out large institutional investors, such as mutual fund companies and investment bankers, and thereby shield managers and employees from outside pressures. Founders Page and Brin want to keep the company's focus on innovation and "making the world a better place." The idea of auctioning stock may give the average investor a better chance at buying its stock. Although this approach may alienate some investors desiring a more traditional stock offering, Google has never been a traditional organization, and it wants a different kind of shareholder. The company also plans to contribute as much as one percent of its equity and profits to a foundation that it hopes will tackle some of the world's greatest problems. This approach should be attractive to those who are disgusted with recent corporate scandals, like those at Enron and Worldcom.[69]

Discussion Questions

1. Why do you think that Google has been so successful in quickly gaining the largest share of the search engine market?

2. What do you think about Google's unconventional internal organizational decision making? Would you like to work at a company that was so unstructured on a daily basis?

3. Based on your knowledge about Google, is it the type of company that you would consider investing in by purchasing its stock? Why or why not?

Remember to check out our Online Learning Center at <u>www.mhhe.com/ferrell5e</u>.

National Farm and Garden, Inc.

National Farm and Garden, Inc., (NFG) was incorporated in Nebraska in 1935 and has been a leading supplier of farming equipment for more than 60 years. Over the last five years, however, demand for NFG's flagship product, the Ultra Tiller, has been declining. To make matters worse, NFG's market lead was overtaken by the competition for the first time two years ago.

Last year, NFG expanded its product line with the "Turbo Tiller," a highly advertised and much anticipated upgrade to the Ultra Tiller. The product launch was timed to coincide with last year's fall tilling season. Due to the timing of the release, the research and development process was shortened, and the manufacturing department was pressed to produce high numbers to meet anticipated demand. All responsible divisions approved the product launch and schedule. In order to release the product as scheduled, however, the manufacturing department was forced to employ the safety shield design from the Ultra Tiller. When attached, the shield protects the user from the tilling blades. It is necessary, however, to remove the shield to clean the product. Because of differences between the Ultra and Turbo models, the Turbo's shield is very difficult to reattach after cleaning and the process requires specialized tools. Owners can have the supplier make modifications on site or at the sale location, or leave the shielding off and continue operation. All product documentation warns against operating the tiller without the shielding, and the product itself has three distinct warning labels on it. Modifications are now available that allow for the shield to be removed and replaced quite easily, and these modifications are covered by the factory warranty. However, most owners have elected to operate the Turbo Tiller without the safety shielding after its first cleaning.

Over the last year, a number of farm animals (chickens, cats, a dog, and two goats) have been killed by Turbo Tillers being operated without the guard. Two weeks ago, a seven-year-old Nebraska boy riding on the back of an unshielded tiller fell off. When the tiller caught the sleeve of his shirt, his arm was permanently mangled, requiring amputation. One of the child's parents owns the local newspaper, which ran a story about the accident on the front page. NFG's CEO has called an emergency meeting with the company's divisional vice president, director of product development, director of manufacturing, director of sales, and vice president of public relations to discuss the situation and develop a plan of action.

*This background statement provides information for a role-play exercise designed to help you understand the real world challenge of decision making in business and to integrate the concepts presented previously in this text. If your instructor chooses to utilize this activity, the class will be divided into teams with each team member assigned to a particular role in the fictitious organization. Additional information on each role and instructions for the completion of the exercise will be distributed to individual team members.

Part 2

Starting and Growing a Business

Chapter 5

Options for Organizing Business

OBJECTIVES

After reading this chapter, you will be able to:

- Define and examine the advantages and disadvantages of the sole proprietorship form of organization.

- Identify two types of partnership and evaluate the advantages and disadvantages of the partnership form of organization.

- Describe the corporate form of organization and cite the advantages and disadvantages of corporations.

- Define and debate the advantages and disadvantages of mergers, acquisitions, and leveraged buyouts.

- Propose an appropriate organizational form for a start-up business.

A Company of Companies: Zingerman's Deli

Paul Saginaw and Ari Weinzweig opened Zingerman's Deli in 1982 in Ann Arbor, Michigan. With a reputation for great service and tasty specialty foods, Jewish dishes, and sandwiches, the little deli grew into a local institution with annual sales of $5 million in just eight years. The firm also gained praise for helping to support local charities. Zingerman's became world renowned, thanks to glowing write-ups in the *New York Times, Bon Appetit, Esquire,* and many others.

Despite the accolades, the owners felt the maturing deli had run out of steam in 1992. Employees—frustrated by the lack of advancement opportunities—were leaving, and competitors were beginning to take a bite out of the deli's business. Saginaw and Weinzweig recognized that Zingerman's had arrived at the same crossroads faced by countless other small businesses: remain the same and risk stagnation or grow aggressively and risk sacrificing the qualities that had made the deli so successful. Weinzweig in particular detested the idea of franchising Zingerman's copies in farflung cities where it would be difficult to maintain the firm's reputation for quality. So, they chose a different road for their firm.

After much research and debate, Saginaw and Weinzweig decided in 1994 to create the Zingerman's Community of Businesses (ZCob), a sort of collective of small, independent businesses, all with the Zingerman's name and centralized marketing and administrative functions, but with their own products and identity. Each firm has its own managing partner/owner, who in some cases, came from the deli operations. The first was Zingerman's Bakehouse, which supplies the deli with artisan breads and related products. The second was Zingerman's Training, Inc., which imparts the deli's philosophies to other business owners and managers interested in learning more about its unique training, service concepts, human resources

continued

management, and merchandising. The community also includes a creamery, catering service, sit-down restaurant, and mail-order business.

Although the concept got off to a rough start, ZCoB today includes seven small firms, and there are two more in the planning stages. Together the seven firms bring in a combined $13 million a year in revenues and employ 334 people, many of whom were trained at Zingerman's Training. The company was even named *Inc.* magazine's "Coolest Small Company in America." Not bad for a company in a strong growth mode while retaining all the elements that made it world famous for its unique culture, exceptional service, and products of the highest quality.[1]

Introduction

The legal form of ownership taken by a business is seldom of great concern to you as a customer. When you eat at a restaurant, you probably don't care whether the restaurant is owned by one person (a sole proprietorship), has two or more owners who share the business (a partnership), or is an entity owned by many stockholders (a corporation); all you want is good food. If you buy a foreign car, you probably don't care whether the company that made it has laws governing its form of organization that are different from those for businesses in the United States. You are buying the car because it is well made, fits your price range, or appeals to your sense of style. Nonetheless, a business's legal form of ownership affects how it operates, how much tax it pays, and how much control its owners have.

This chapter examines three primary forms of business ownership—sole proprietorship, partnership, and corporation—and weighs the advantages and disadvantages of each. These forms are the most often used whether the business is a traditional "bricks and mortar" company, an online-only one, or a combination of both. We also take a look at S corporations, limited liability companies, and cooperatives and discuss some trends in business ownership. You may wish to refer to Table 5.1 to compare the various forms of business ownership mentioned in the chapter.

TABLE 5.1 Various Forms of Business Ownership

Structure	Ownership	Taxation	Liability	Use
Sole Proprietorship	1 owner	Individual income taxed	Unlimited	Individual starting a business and easiest way to conduct business
Partnership	2 or more owners	Individual owners' income taxed	Somewhat limited	Easy way for two individuals to conduct business
Corporation	Any number of shareholders	Corporate and shareholder taxed	Limited	A legal entity with shareholders or stakeholders
S Corporation	Up to 75 shareholders	Taxed as a partnership	Limited	A legal entity with tax advantages for restricted number of shareholders
Limited Liability Company	Unlimited number of shareholders.	Taxed as a partnership	Limited	Avoid personal law suits

Sole Proprietorships

Sole proprietorships, businesses owned and operated by one individual, are the most common form of business organization in the United States. Common examples include many restaurants, barber shops, flower shops, dog kennels, and independent grocery stores. Sondra Noffel Biggs opened her own stationery store called Papel (Spanish for "paper") in a high-traffic shopping center in Memphis, Tennessee. Biggs operates the store as a sole proprietorship. Indeed, many sole proprietors focus on services—small retail stores, financial counseling, appliance repair, child care, and the like—rather than on the manufacture of goods, which often requires large amounts of money not available to small businesses.

Sole proprietorships are typically small businesses employing fewer than 50 people. (We'll look at small businesses in greater detail in Chapter 6.) There are nearly 18 million sole proprietorships in the United States (72 percent of all businesses), but they account for just 4 percent of total business sales and 15 percent of total income (see Figure 5.1).[2]

sole proprietorships businesses owned and operated by one individual; the most common form of business organization in the United States

Advantages of Sole Proprietorships

Sole proprietorships are generally managed by their owners. Because of this simple management structure, the owner/manager can make decisions quickly. This is just one of many advantages of the sole proprietorship form of business.

Ease and Cost of Formation.   Forming a sole proprietorship is relatively easy and inexpensive. In some states, creating a sole proprietorship involves merely announcing the new business in the local newspaper. Other proprietorships, such as barber shops and restaurants, may require state and local licenses and permits because of the nature of the business. The cost of these permits may run from $25 to $100. No lawyer is needed to create such enterprises, and the owner can usually take care of the required paperwork.

Of course, an entrepreneur starting a new sole proprietorship must find a suitable site from which to operate the business. Some sole proprietors look no farther than their garage or a spare bedroom that they can convert into a workshop or office. Among the more famous businesses that sprang to life in their founders' garages are Walt Disney, Wham-O, Hewlett-Packard, Apple Computer, and Mattel.[3] Computers,

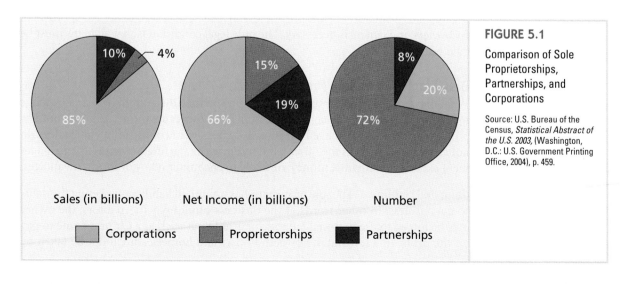

FIGURE 5.1

Comparison of Sole Proprietorships, Partnerships, and Corporations

Source: U.S. Bureau of the Census, *Statistical Abstract of the U.S. 2003,* (Washington, D.C.: U.S. Government Printing Office, 2004), p. 459.

Sales (in billions)   Net Income (in billions)   Number

■ Corporations   ■ Proprietorships   ■ Partnerships

personal copiers, fax machines, and other high-tech gadgets have been a boon for home-based businesses, permitting them to interact quickly with customers, suppliers, and others. Many independent salespersons and contractors can perform their work using a notebook computer as they travel. E-mail and cell phones have made it possible for many proprietorships to develop in the services area. Internet connections also allow small businesses to establish Web sites to promote their products and even to make low-cost long-distance phone calls with voice-over Internet protocol (VOIP) technology.

Secrecy.   Sole proprietorships make possible the greatest degree of secrecy. The proprietor, unlike the owners of a partnership or corporation, does not have to discuss publicly his or her operating plans, minimizing the possibility that competitors can obtain trade secrets. Financial reports need not be disclosed, as do the financial reports of publicly owned corporations.

Distribution and Use of Profits.   All profits from a sole proprietorship belong exclusively to the owner. He or she does not have to share them with any partners or stockholders. The owner decides how to use the profits—for expansion of the business, for salary increases, or for travel to purchase additional inventory or find new customers.

Flexibility and Control of the Business.   The sole proprietor has complete control over the business and can make decisions on the spot without anyone else's approval. This control allows the owner to respond quickly to competitive business conditions or to changes in the economy.

Government Regulation.   Sole proprietorships have the most freedom from government regulation. Many government regulations—federal, state, and local—apply only to businesses that have a certain number of employees, and securities laws apply only to corporations that issue stock. Nonetheless, sole proprietors must ensure that they follow all laws that do apply to their business.

Taxation.   Profits from the business are considered personal income to the sole proprietor and are taxed at individual tax rates. The owner pays one income tax. Another tax benefit is that a sole proprietor is allowed to establish a tax-exempt retirement account or a tax-exempt profit-sharing account. Such accounts are exempt from current income tax, but payments taken after retirement are taxed when they are received.

Closing the Business.   A sole proprietorship can be dissolved easily. No approval of co-owners or partners is necessary. The only legal condition is that all loans must be paid off.

Disadvantages of Sole Proprietorships

What may be seen as an advantage by one person may turn out to be a disadvantage to another. The goals and talents of the individual owner are the deciding factors. For profitable businesses managed by capable owners, many of the following factors do not cause problems. On the other hand, proprietors starting out with little management experience and little money are likely to encounter many of the disadvantages.

Unlimited Liability.   The sole proprietor has unlimited liability in meeting the debts of the business. In other words, if the business cannot pay its creditors, the owner may be forced to use personal, nonbusiness holdings such as a car or a home to pay off the debts. In a few states, however, houses and homesteads cannot be taken by creditors even if the proprietor declares bankruptcy. The more wealth an individual has, the greater is the disadvantage of unlimited liability.

Limited Sources of Funds.   Among the relatively few sources of money available to the sole proprietorship are a bank, friends, family, the Small Business Administration, or his or her own funds. The owner's personal financial condition determines his or her credit standing. Additionally, sole proprietorships may have to pay higher interest rates on funds borrowed from banks than do large corporations because they are considered greater risks. Often the only way a sole proprietor can borrow for business purposes is to pledge a car, a house, other real estate, or other personal assets to guarantee the loan. And if the business fails, the owner may lose the personal assets as well as the business. Publicly owned corporations, in contrast, can not only obtain funds from commercial banks but can sell stocks and bonds to the public to raise money. If a public company goes out of business, the owners do not lose personal assets.

Selecting the sole proprietorship business structure means you are personally liable for your company's liabilities. As a result, you are placing your own assets at risk, and they could be seized to satisfy a business debt or legal claim filed against you.

Limited Skills.   The sole proprietor must be able to perform many functions and possess skills in diverse fields such as management, marketing, finance, accounting, bookkeeping, and personnel. Business owners can rely on specialized professions for advice and services, such as accountants and attorneys. Musicians, for example, can turn to agents for assistance in navigating through the complex maze of the recording business. One start-up firm specializing in this type of assistance for online musicians and bands is the Digital Artists Agency, which researches, markets, and cultivates online music talent in exchange for a commission on their online sales of music, tickets, and merchandise.[4] In the end, however, it is up to the business owner to make the final decision in all areas of the business.

Lack of Continuity.   The life expectancy of a sole proprietorship is directly related to that of the owner and his or her ability to work. The serious illness of the owner could result in failure if competent help cannot be found.

It is difficult to arrange for the sale of a proprietorship and at the same time assure customers that the business will continue to meet their needs. For instance, how does one sell a veterinary practice? A veterinarian's major asset is patients. If the vet dies suddenly, the equipment can be sold but the patients will not necessarily remain loyal to the office. On the other hand, a veterinarian who wants to retire could take in a younger partner and sell the practice to the partner over time. And one advantage to the partnership is that not all the patients are likely to look for a new vet.

Lack of Qualified Employees.   It is usually difficult for a small sole proprietorship to match the wages and benefits offered by a large competing corporation because the proprietorship's level of profits may not be as high. In addition, there is little room for advancement within a sole proprietorship, so the owner may have difficulty attracting and retaining qualified employees. On the other hand, the trend of large corporations to downsize and outsource tasks has created opportunities for small business to acquire well-trained employees.

Taxation.   Although we listed taxation as an advantage for sole proprietorships, it can also be a disadvantage, depending on the proprietor's income. Under current tax rates, sole proprietors pay a higher marginal tax rate than do small corporations on income of less than $75,000. The tax effect often determines whether a sole proprietor chooses to incorporate his or her business.

Partnerships

partnership
a form of business organization defined by the Uniform Partnership Act as "an association of two or more persons who carry on as co-owners of a business for profit"

One way to minimize the disadvantages of a sole proprietorship and maximize its advantages is to have more than one owner. Most states have a model law governing partnerships based on the Uniform Partnership Act. This law defines a **partnership** as "an association of two or more persons who carry on as co-owners of a business for profit." Partnerships are the least used form of business organization, representing just 8 percent of U.S. businesses (see Figure 5.1). Moreover, partnerships account for only 10 percent of sales and 19 percent of income. They are typically larger than sole proprietorships but smaller than corporations.

general partnership
a partnership that involves a complete sharing in both the management and the liability of the business

Types of Partnership

There are two basic types of partnership: general partnership and limited partnership. A **general partnership** involves a complete sharing in the management of a business. In a general partnership, each partner has unlimited liability for the debts of the business. Professionals such as lawyers, accountants, and architects often join together in general partnerships.

limited partnership
a business organization that has at least one general partner, who assumes unlimited liability, and at least one limited partner, whose liability is limited to his or her investment in the business

A **limited partnership** has at least one general partner, who assumes unlimited liability, and at least one limited partner, whose liability is limited to his or her investment in the business. Limited partnerships exist for risky investment projects where the chance of loss is great. The general partners accept the risk of loss; the limited partners' losses are limited to their initial investment. Limited partners do not participate in the management of the business but share in the profits in accordance with the terms of a partnership agreement. Usually the general partner receives a larger share of the profits after the limited partners have received their initial investment back. Popular examples are oil-drilling partnerships and real-estate partnerships.

Ben and Jerry's started as a partnership, then went public, and later was purchased by Unilever.

Articles of Partnership

articles of partnership
legal documents that set forth the basic agreement between partners

Articles of partnership are legal documents that set forth the basic agreement between partners. Most states require articles of partnership, but even if they are not required, it makes good sense for partners to draw them up. Articles of partnership usually list the money or assets that each partner has contributed (called *partnership capital*), state each partner's individual management role or duty, specify how the profits and losses of the partnership will be divided among the partners, and describe how a partner may leave the partnership as well as any other restrictions that might

1. Name, purpose, location	**TABLE 5.2**
2. Duration of the agreement	Issues and Provisions in Articles of Partnership
3. Authority and responsibility of each partner	
4. Character of partners (i.e., general or limited, active or silent)	
5. Amount of contribution from each partner	
6. Division of profits or losses	
7. Salaries of each partner	
8. How much each partner is allowed to withdraw	
9. Death of partner	
10. Sale of partnership interest	
11. Arbitration of disputes	
12. Required and prohibited actions	
13. Absence and disability	
14. Restrictive covenants	
15. Buying and selling agreements	

Source: "Partnership Agreement," State of New Jersey, www.state.nj.us/njbiz/s_step2_partagree.html (accessed March 12, 2004).

apply to the agreement. Table 5.2 lists some of the issues and provisions that should be included in articles of partnership.

Advantages of Partnerships

Law firms, accounting firms, and investment firms with several hundred partners have partnership agreements that are quite complicated in comparison with the partnership agreement among two or three people owning a computer repair shop. The advantages must be compared with those offered by other forms of business organization, and not all apply to every partnership.

Ease of Organization.   Starting a partnership requires little more than drawing up articles of partnership. No legal charters have to be granted, but the name of the business should be registered with the state.

Availability of Capital and Credit.   When a business has several partners, it has the benefit of a combination of talents and skills and pooled financial resources. Partnerships tend to be larger than sole proprietorships and therefore have greater earning power and better credit ratings. Because many limited partnerships have been formed for tax purposes rather than for economic profits, the combined income of all U.S. partnerships is quite low, as shown in

Xcel Energy Corporation strives to build partnerships with minority-owned and women-owned businesses.

Figure 5.1. Nevertheless, the professional partnerships of many lawyers, accountants, and investment banking firms make quite large profits. Goldman Sachs, a large New York investment banking partnership, earns several hundred million dollars in an average year.

Combined Knowledge and Skills.   Partners in the most successful partnerships acknowledge each other's talents and avoid confusion and conflict by specializing in a particular area of expertise such as marketing, production, accounting, or service. The diversity of skills in a partnership makes it possible for the business to be run by a management team of specialists instead of by a generalist sole proprietor. Service-oriented partnerships in fields such as law, financial planning, and accounting may attract customers because clients may think that the service offered by a diverse team is of higher quality than that provided by one person. Larger law firms, for example, often have individual partners who specialize in certain areas of the law—such as family, bankruptcy, corporate, entertainment, and criminal law.

Decision Making.   Small partnerships can react more quickly to changes in the business environment than can large partnerships and corporations. Such fast reactions are possible because the partners are involved in day-to-day operations and can make decisions quickly after consultation. Large partnerships with hundreds of partners in many states are not common. In those that do exist, decision making is likely to be slow.

Regulatory Controls.   Like a sole proprietorship, a partnership has fewer regulatory controls affecting its activities than does a corporation. A partnership does not have to file public financial statements with government agencies or send out quarterly financial statements to several thousand owners, as do corporations such as Eastman Kodak and Ford Motor Co. A partnership does, however, have to abide by all laws relevant to the industry or profession in which it operates as well as state and federal laws relating to hiring and firing, food handling, and so on, just as the sole proprietorship does.

Disadvantages of Partnerships

Partnerships have many advantages compared to sole proprietorships and corporations, but they also have some disadvantages. Limited partners have no voice in the management of the partnership, and they may bear most of the risk of the business while the general partner reaps a larger share of the benefits. There may be a change in the goals and objectives of one partner but not the other, particularly when the partners are multinational organizations. This can cause friction, giving rise to an enterprise that fails to satisfy both parties or even forcing an end to the partnership. Many partnership disputes wind up in court or require outside mediation. For example, a quarrel among the partners who owned the Montreal Expos baseball team moved to U.S. District Court after new general partner Jeffrey Loria moved the team to Florida and renamed it the Florida Marlins. Twelve of the team's limited partners sued Loria, accusing him of buying the Expos with the intent of moving the team, diluting their share in the team, and effectively destroying "the economic viability of baseball in Montreal."[5] In such cases, the ultimate solution may be dissolving the partnership. Major disadvantages of partnerships include the following.

Unlimited Liability.   In general partnerships, the general partners have unlimited liability for the debts incurred by the business, just as the sole proprietor has unlimited liability for his or her business. Such unlimited liability can be a distinct disadvantage to one partner if his or her personal financial resources are greater than those of the others. A potential partner should check to make sure that all partners have comparable resources to help the business in time of trouble. This disadvantage is eliminated for limited partners, who can lose only their initial investment.

Business Responsibility.   All partners are responsible for the business actions of all others. Partners may have the ability to commit the partnership to a contract without approval of the other partners. A bad decision by one partner may put the other partners' personal resources in jeopardy. Personal problems such as a divorce can eliminate a significant portion of one partner's financial resources and weaken the financial structure of the whole partnership.

Life of the Partnership.   A partnership is terminated when a partner dies or withdraws. In a two-person partnership, if one partner withdraws, the firm's liabilities would be paid off and the assets divided between the partners. Obviously, the partner who wishes to continue in the business would be at a serious disadvantage. The business could be disrupted, financing would be reduced, and the management skills of the departing partner would be lost. The remaining partner would have to find another or reorganize the business as a sole proprietorship. In very large partnerships such as those found in law firms and investment banks, the continuation of the partnership may be provided for in the articles of partnership. The provision may simply state the terms for a new partnership agreement among the remaining partners. In such cases, the disadvantage to the other partners is minimal.

Selling a partnership interest has the same effect as the death or withdrawal of a partner. It is difficult to place a value on a partner's share of the partnership. No public value is placed on the partnership, as there is on publicly owned corporations. What is a law firm worth? What is the local hardware store worth? Coming up with a fair value that all partners can agree to is not easy. Selling a partnership interest is easier if the articles of partnership specify a method of valuation. Even if there is not a procedure for selling one partner's interest, the old partnership must still be dissolved and a new one created. In contrast, in the corporate form of business, the departure of owners has little effect on the financial resources of the business, and the loss of managers does not cause long-term changes in the structure of the organization.

Distribution of Profits.   Profits earned by the partnership are distributed to the partners in the proportions specified in the articles of partnership. This may be a disadvantage if the division of the profits does not reflect the work each partner puts into the business. You may have encountered this disadvantage while working on a student group project: You may have felt that you did most of the work and that the other students in the group received grades based on your efforts. Even the perception of an unfair profit-sharing agreement may cause tension between the partners, and unhappy partners can have a negative effect on the profitability of the business.

Limited Sources of Funds.   As with a sole proprietorship, the sources of funds available to a partnership are limited. Because no public value is placed on the business (such as the current trading price of a corporation's stock), potential partners do not know what one partnership share is worth. Moreover, because partnership shares cannot be bought and sold easily in public markets, potential owners may not want to tie up their money in assets that cannot be readily sold on short notice. Accumulating enough funds to operate a national business, especially a business requiring intensive investments in facilities and equipment, can be difficult. Partnerships also may have to pay higher interest rates on funds borrowed from banks than do large corporations because partnerships may be considered greater risks.

Taxation of Partnerships

Partnerships are quasi-taxable organizations. This means that partnerships do not pay taxes when submitting the partnership tax return to the Internal Revenue Service. The tax return simply provides information about the profitability of the organization and the distribution of profits among the partners. Partners must report their share of profits on their individual tax returns and pay taxes at the income tax rate for individuals.

Corporations

When you think of a business, you probably think of a huge corporation such as General Electric, Procter & Gamble, or Sony because most of your consumer dollars go to such corporations. A **corporation** is a legal entity, created by the state, whose assets and liabilities are separate from its owners. As a legal entity, a corporation has many of the rights, duties, and powers of a person, such as the right to receive, own, and transfer property. Corporations can enter into contracts with individuals or with other legal entities, and they can sue and be sued in court.

Corporations account for 85 percent of all U.S. sales and 66 percent of all income. Thus, most of the dollars you spend as a consumer probably go to incorporated businesses (see Figure 5.1). There are almost 5 million corporations, but they account for only 20 percent of all U.S. businesses.[6] Not all corporations are mega-companies like General Mills or Ford Motor; even small businesses can incorporate. As we shall see later in the chapter, many smaller firms elect to incorporate as "S Corporations," which operate under slightly different rules and have greater flexibility than do traditional "C Corporations" like General Mills.

Corporations are typically owned by many individuals and organizations who own shares of the business, called **stock** (thus, corporate owners are often called *shareholders* or *stockholders*). Stockholders can buy, sell, give or receive as gifts, or inherit their shares of stock. As owners, the stockholders are entitled to all profits that are left after all the corporation's other obligations have been paid. These profits may be distributed in the form of cash payments called **dividends.** For example, if a corporation earns $100 million after expenses and taxes and decides to pay the owners $40 million in dividends, the stockholders receive 40 percent of the profits in cash dividends. However, not all after-tax profits are paid to stockholders in dividends. In this example, the corporation retained $60 million of profits to finance expansion.

Creating a Corporation

A corporation is created, or incorporated, under the laws of the state in which it incorporates. The individuals creating the corporation are known as *incorporators.* Each state has a specific procedure, sometimes called *chartering the corporation,* for incorporating a business. Most states require a minimum of three incorporators; thus, many small businesses can be and are incorporated. Another requirement is that the new corporation's name cannot be similar to that of another business. In most states, a corporation's name must end in "company," "corporation," "incorporated," or "limited" to show that the owners have limited liability. (In this text, however, the word *company* means any organization engaged in a commercial enterprise and can refer to a sole proprietorship, a partnership, or a corporation.)

The incorporators must file legal documents generally referred to as *articles of incorporation* with the appropriate state office (often the secretary of state). The articles of incorporation contain basic information about the business. The following

corporation
a legal entity, created by the state, whose assets and liabilities are separate from its owners

stock
shares of a corporation that may be bought or sold

dividends
profits of a corporation that are distributed in the form of cash payments to stockholders

Rated by *Forbes* as one of the top private corporations in the United States, the Longaberger Company is a $1 billion direct sales company based in Newark, Ohio. The company employs over 5,500 people and has nearly 71,000 independent associates who market and sell Longaberger products including baskets, wrought iron, pottery, fabric liners, and accessories.

The company's mission statement—"to stimulate a better quality of life"—is a reflection of entrepreneur-founder Dave Longaberger. The fifth of 12 children, Longaberger was economically disadvantaged, a stutterer, and an epileptic. His problems, however, did not stand in the way of his ambition. He worked in a grocery, shoveled snow, delivered papers, mowed grass, and hauled trash. His family called him the "25-cent millionaire" because he was always making money.

In the early 1970s, Longaberger observed that baskets were becoming very popular. Hoping that consumers would appreciate the handmade craftsmanship and quality in baskets made by his father, Longaberger opened J.W.'s Handwoven Baskets, which later became the Longaberger Company.

Longaberger's hopes were fulfilled. Today, the company is the foremost producer of handmade baskets in the United States. The company has been asked to provide gift baskets for the Blockbuster Entertainment Awards, Academy Awards, NAACP Image Awards, Christmas in Washington, DC, and the Joni Mitchell Tribute. The Longaberger name means quality, and their baskets are made to be handed down from one generation to the next.[7]

Discussion Questions

1. How do you think Longaberger might change if it became a public corporation?
2. What are the advantages for Longaberger maintaining its current product line while remaining a private corporation?
3. Why do you think Longaberger has been so successful?

---

10 items are found in the Model Business Corporation Act, issued by the American Bar Association, which is followed by most states:

1. Name and address of the corporation.
2. Objectives of the corporation.
3. Classes of stock (common, preferred, voting, nonvoting) and the number of shares for each class of stock to be issued.
4. Expected life of the corporation (corporations are usually created to last forever).
5. Financial capital required at the time of incorporation.
6. Provisions for transferring shares of stock between owners.
7. Provisions for the regulation of internal corporate affairs.
8. Address of the business office registered with the state of incorporation.
9. Names and addresses of the initial board of directors.
10. Names and addresses of the incorporators.

Based on the information in the articles of incorporation, the state issues a **corporate charter** to the company. After securing this charter, the owners hold an organizational meeting at which they establish the corporation's bylaws and elect a board of directors. The bylaws might set up committees of the board of directors and describe the rules and procedures for their operation.

corporate charter
a legal document that the state issues to a company based on information the company provides in the articles of incorporation

Types of Corporations

If the corporation does business in the state in which it is chartered, it is known as a *domestic corporation.* In other states where the corporation does business, it is known as a *foreign corporation.* If a corporation does business outside the nation in which it incorporated, it is called an *alien corporation.* A corporation may be privately or publicly owned.

Horizon Dairy became a public corporation by offering stock in order to take advantage of the increased interest in organic products. Pictured here is CEO Barnett Feinblum, cofounder Paul Repetto, and other employees with some of their organic dairy products.

private corporation
a corporation owned by just one or a few people who are closely involved in managing the business

public corporation
a corporation whose stock anyone may buy, sell, or trade

initial public offering (IPO)
selling a corporation's stock on public markets for the first time

A **private corporation** is owned by just one or a few people who are closely involved in managing the business. These people, often a family, own all the corporation's stock, and no stock is sold to the public. Many corporations are quite large, yet remain private, including Cargill, the nation's largest private corporation, which sells nearly $60 billion in agricultural and industrial products every year. Other well-known privately held companies include Publix Super Markets and HE Butt Grocery in the supermarket industry, L. L. Bean and Levi Strauss in the apparel industry, and PricewaterhouseCoopers and Ernst & Young in the accounting and financial services industries.[8] Privately owned corporations are not required to disclose financial information publicly, but they must, of course, pay taxes.

A **public corporation** is one whose stock anyone may buy, sell, or trade. Table 5.3 lists the largest U.S. corporations by revenues. Thousands of smaller public corporations in the United States have sales under $10 million. In large public corporations such as AT&T, the stockholders are often far removed from the management of the company. In other public corporations, the managers are often the founders and the major shareholders. Ford Motor Company, for example, was founded by Henry Ford; his great grandson William Clay Ford Jr. runs the company today.[9] Publicly owned corporations must disclose financial information to the public under specific laws that regulate the trade of stocks and other securities.

A private corporation that needs more money to expand or take advantage of opportunities may have to obtain financing by "going public" through an **initial public offering (IPO),** that is, becoming a public corporation by selling its stock so that it can be traded in public markets. For example, Google, the popular Internet search engine, went public with an initial public offering in 2004.[10] Also, privately owned firms are occasionally forced to go public with stock offerings when a major owner dies and the heirs have enormous estate taxes to pay. The tax payment becomes possible only with the proceeds of the sale of stock. This happened to the brewer Adolph

Rank	Company	Revenues (in billions of dollars)
1.	Wal-Mart Stores	258.7
2.	Exxon Mobil	231.2
3.	General Motors	195.6
4.	Ford Motors	164.5
5.	General Electric	134.2
6.	ChevronTexaco	112.9
7.	ConocoPhilips	99.5
8.	Citigroup	94.7
9.	International Business Machines	89.1
10.	American International Group	81.3
11.	Hewlett-Packard	73.1
12.	Verizon Communications	67.8
13.	Home Depot	64.8
14.	Berkshire Hathaway	63.9
15.	Altria Group	60.7
16.	McKesson	57.1
17.	Cardinal Health	56.8
18.	State Farm Insurance Cos.	56.1
19.	Kroger	53.8
20.	Fannie Mae	53.8

TABLE 5.3

The Largest U.S. Corporations, Arranged by Revenues

Source: "Fortune 500 Largest U.S. Corporations," *Fortune,* April 5, 2004, p. B1. Copyright © 2004 *Time,* Inc. All rights reserved.

Coors, Inc. When Adolph Coors died, his business went public and his family sold shares of stock to the public to pay the estate taxes.

On the other hand, public corporations can be "taken private" when one or a few individuals (perhaps the management of the firm) purchase all the firm's stock so that it can no longer be sold publicly. For example, the founder and CEO of Hollywood Video, Mark Wattles, took the video rental chain private in 2004 by buying up all the stock for $14 a share.[11] Taking a corporation private may be desirable when new owners want to exert more control over the firm or they want to avoid the necessity of public disclosure of future activities for competitive reasons. Taking a corporation private is also one technique for avoiding a takeover by another corporation.

Two other types of corporations are quasi-public corporations and nonprofit corporations. **Quasi-public corporations** are owned and operated by the federal, state, or local government. The focus of these corporations is providing a service to citizens, such as mail delivery, rather than earning a profit. Indeed, many quasi-public corporations operate at a loss. Examples of quasi-public corporations include the National Aeronautics and Space Administration (NASA) and the U.S. Postal Service.

Like quasi-public corporations, **nonprofit corporations** focus on providing a service rather than earning a profit, but they are not owned by a government entity. Organizations like the Children's Television Workshop, the Elks Clubs, the American

quasi-public corporations corporations owned and operated by the federal, state, or local government

nonprofit corporations corporations that focus on providing a service rather than earning a profit but are not owned by a government entity

Habitat for Humanity is a nonprofit, nondenominational Christian housing organization that builds simple, decent, affordable houses in partnership with those who lack adequate shelter. Chosen families work alongside volunteers to build their own home.

board of directors
a group of individuals, elected by the stockholders to oversee the general operation of the corporation, who set the corporation's long-range objectives

Lung Association, the American Red Cross, museums, and private schools provide services without a profit motive. To fund their operations and services, nonprofit organizations solicit donations from individuals and companies and grants from the government and other charitable foundations.

Elements of a Corporation

The Board of Directors. A **board of directors,** elected by the stockholders to oversee the general operation of the corporation, sets the long-range objectives of the corporation. It is the board's responsibility to ensure that the objectives are achieved on schedule. Board members are legally liable for the mismanagement of the firm or for any misuse of funds. An important duty of the board of directors is to hire corporate officers, such as the president and the chief executive officer (CEO), who are responsible to the directors for the management and daily operations of the firm. The role and expectations of the board of directors took on greater significance after the accounting scandals of the early 2000s left many stockholders and other stakeholders demanding greater accountability from boards.[12] As a result, most corporations have restructured how they compensate directors for their time and expertise in serving on a board. Most directors receive annual cash retainers averaging between $35,000 and $40,000, with the chairman of the board receiving an additional average of $7,000 to $10,000. Most companies also provide additional fees and stock options or deferred or restricted stock as part of directors' compensation package.[13]

Directors can be employees of the company (*inside directors*) or people unaffiliated with the company (*outside directors*). Inside directors are usually the officers responsible for running the company. Outside directors are often top executives from other companies, lawyers, bankers, even professors. Directors today are increasingly chosen for their expertise, competence, and ability to bring diverse perspectives to strategic discussions. Outside directors are also thought to bring more independence to the monitoring function because they are not bound by past allegiances, friendships, a current role in the company, or some other issue that may create a conflict of interest. Many of the corporate scandals uncovered in recent years might have been prevented if each of the companies' boards of directors had been better qualified, more knowledgeable, and more independent. A survey by *USA Today* found that corporate boards have considerable overlap. More than 1,000 corporate board members sit on four or more company boards, and of the nearly 2,000 boards of directors, more than 22,000 board members are linked to boards of more than one company.[14] This overlap creates the opportunity for conflicts of interest in decision making and limits the independence of individual boards of directors. For example, the telecommunication firm Verizon, which shares four board members with prescription-drug producer Wyeth, withdrew from nonprofit organization Business for Affordable Medicine, which had been criticized by Wyeth because of its stance on bringing generic drugs to market sooner.[15]

Stock Ownership.   Corporations issue two types of stock: preferred and common.

Owners of **preferred stock** are a special class of owners because, although they generally do not have any say in running the company, they have a claim to any profits before any other stockholders do. Other stockholders do not receive any dividends unless the preferred stockholders have already been paid. Dividend payments on preferred stock are usually a fixed percentage of the initial issuing price (set by the board of directors). For example, if a share of preferred stock originally cost $100 and the dividend rate was stated at 7.5 percent, the dividend payment will be $7.50 per share per year. Dividends are usually paid quarterly. Most preferred stock carries a cumulative claim to dividends. This means that if the company does not pay preferred-stock dividends in one year because of losses, the dividends accumulate to the next year. Such dividends unpaid from previous years must also be paid to preferred stockholders before other stockholders can receive any dividends.

Although owners of **common stock** do not get such preferential treatment with regard to dividends, they do get some say in the operation of the corporation. Their ownership gives them the right to vote for members of the board of directors and on other important issues. Common stock dividends may vary according to the profitability of the business, and some corporations do not issue dividends at all, but instead plow their profits back into the company to fund expansion.

Common stockholders are the voting owners of a corporation. They are usually entitled to one vote per share of common stock. During an annual stockholders' meeting, common stockholders elect a board of directors. Because they can choose the board of directors, common stockholders have some say in how the company will operate. Common stockholders may vote by *proxy,* which is a written authorization by which stockholders assign their voting privilege to someone else, who then votes for his or her choice at the stockholders' meeting. It is a normal practice for management to request proxy statements from shareholders who are not planning to attend the annual meeting. Most owners do not attend annual meetings of the very large companies, such as Westinghouse or Boeing, unless they live in the city where the meeting is held.

Common stockholders have another advantage over preferred shareholders. In most states, when the corporation decides to sell new shares of common stock in the marketplace, common stockholders have the first right, called a *preemptive right,* to purchase new shares of the stock from the corporation. A preemptive right is often included in the articles of incorporation. This right is important because it allows stockholders to purchase new shares to maintain their original positions. For example, if a stockholder owns 10 percent of a corporation that decides to issue new shares, that stockholder has the right to buy enough of the new shares to retain the 10 percent ownership.

Advantages of Corporations

Because a corporation is a separate legal entity, it has some very specific advantages over other forms of ownership. The biggest advantage may be the limited liability of the owners.

Limited Liability.   Because the corporation's assets (money and resources) and liabilities (debts and other obligations) are separate from its owners', in most cases the stockholders are not held responsible for the firm's debts if it fails. Their liability or potential loss is limited to the amount of their original investment. Although a

---

preferred stock
a special type of stock whose owners, though not generally having a say in running the company, have a claim to profits before other stockholders do

common stock
stock whose owners have voting rights in the corporation, yet do not receive preferential treatment regarding dividends

creditor can sue a corporation for not paying its debts, even forcing the corporation into bankruptcy, it cannot make the stockholders pay the corporation's debts out of their personal assets. Occasionally, the owners of a private corporation may pledge personal assets to secure a loan for the corporation; this would be most unusual for a public corporation.

Ease of Transfer of Ownership.   Stockholders can sell or trade shares of stock to other people without causing the termination of the corporation, and they can do this without the prior approval of other shareholders. The transfer of ownership (unless it is a majority position) does not affect the daily or long-term operations of the corporation.

Perpetual Life.   A corporation usually is chartered to last forever unless its articles of incorporation stipulate otherwise. The existence of the corporation is unaffected by the death or withdrawal of any of its stockholders. It survives until the owners sell it or liquidate its assets. However, in some cases, bankruptcy ends a corporation's life. Bankruptcies occur when companies are unable to compete and earn profits. Eventually, uncompetitive businesses must close or seek protection from creditors in bankruptcy court while the business tries to reorganize.

External Sources of Funds.   Of all the forms of business organization, the public corporation finds it easiest to raise money. When a corporation needs to raise more money, it can sell more stock shares or issue bonds (corporate "IOUs," which pledge to repay debt), attracting funds from anywhere in the United States and even overseas. The larger a corporation becomes, the more sources of financing are available to it. We take a closer look at some of these in Chapter 16.

Expansion Potential.   Because large public corporations can find long-term financing readily, they can easily expand into national and international markets. And, as a legal entity, a corporation can enter into contracts without as much difficulty as a partnership.

Disadvantages of Corporations

Corporations have some distinct disadvantages resulting from tax laws and government regulation.

Double Taxation.   As a legal entity, the corporation must pay taxes on its income just like you do. When after-tax corporate profits are paid out as dividends to the stockholders, the dividends are taxed a second time as part of the individual owner's income. This process creates double taxation for the stockholders of dividend-paying corporations. Double taxation does not occur with the other forms of business organization.

Forming a Corporation.   The formation of a corporation can be costly. A charter must be obtained, and this usually requires the services of an attorney and payment of legal fees. Filing fees ranging from $25 to $150 must be paid to the state that awards the corporate charter, and certain states require that an annual fee be paid to maintain the charter.

Disclosure of Information.   Corporations must make information available to their owners, usually through an annual report to shareholders. The annual report contains financial information about the firm's profits, sales, facilities and equipment, and debts, as well as descriptions of the company's operations, products, and plans for the future. Public corporations must also file reports with the Securities and Exchange Commission (SEC), the government regulatory agency that regulates securities such as stocks and bonds. The larger the firm, the more data the SEC requires. Because all reports filed with the SEC are available to the public, competitors can access them. Additionally, complying with securities laws takes time.

> **Did You Know?** The first corporation with a net income of more than $1 billion in one year was General Motors, with a net income in 1955 of $1,189,477,082.[16]

Employee-Owner Separation. Many employees are not stockholders of the company for which they work. This separation of owners and employees may cause employees to feel that their work benefits only the owners. Employees without an ownership stake do not always see how they fit into the corporate picture and may not understand the importance of profits to the health of the organization. If managers are part owners but other employees are not, management-labor relations take on a different, sometimes difficult, aspect from those in partnerships and sole proprietorships. However, this situation is changing as more corporations establish employee stock ownership plans (ESOPs), which give shares of the company's stock to its employees. Such plans build a partnership between employee and employer and can boost productivity because they motivate employees to work harder so that they can earn dividends from their hard work as well as from their regular wages.

Other Types of Ownership

In this section we will take a brief look at joint ventures, S corporations, limited liability companies, and cooperatives—businesses formed for special purposes.

Joint Ventures

A **joint venture** is a partnership established for a specific project or for a limited time. The partners in a joint venture may be individuals or organizations, as in the case of the international joint ventures discussed in Chapter 3. Control of a joint venture may be shared equally, or one partner may control decision making. Joint ventures are especially popular in situations that call for large investments, such as extraction of natural resources and the development of new products. MovieLink, a joint venture of the film studios MGM, Paramount, Sony, Universal, and Warner Bros., was developed as a competitor to Netflix, the popular online movie-rental source.[17]

joint venture
a partnership established for a specific project or for a limited time

S Corporations

An **S corporation** is a form of business ownership that is taxed as though it were a partnership. Net profits or losses of the corporation pass to the owners, thus eliminating double taxation. The benefit of limited liability is retained. Formally known as Subchapter S Corporations, they have become a popular form of business ownership for entrepreneurs and represent almost half of all corporate filings.[18] Accounting Systems, a Fort Collins, Colorado, accounting software firm, elected to incorporate as an S corporation to gain credibility from being incorporated, tax advantages, and limited liability. Advantages of S corporations include the simple method of taxation, the limited liability of shareholders, perpetual life, and the ability to shift income and appreciation to others. Disadvantages include restrictions on the number (75) and types (individuals, estates, and certain trusts) of shareholders and the difficulty of formation and operation.

S corporation
corporation taxed as though it were a partnership with restrictions on shareholders

Thomas O'Grady and Bryan Rossisky have decided to start a small business buying flowers, shrubs, and trees wholesale and reselling them to the general public. They plan to contribute $5,000 each in start-up capital and lease a two-and-one-half-acre tract of land with a small, portable sales office.

Thomas and Bryan are trying to decide what form of organization would be appropriate. Bryan thinks they should create a corporation because they would have limited liability and the image of a large organization. Thomas thinks a partnership would be easier to start and would allow them to rely on the combination of their talents and financial resources. In addition, there might be fewer reports and regulatory controls to cope with.

Discussion Questions

1. What are some of the advantages and disadvantages of Thomas and Bryan forming a corporation?
2. What are the advantages and disadvantages of their forming a partnership?
3. Which organizational form do you think would be best for Thomas and Bryan's company and why?

Limited Liability Companies

limited liability company (LLC)

form of ownership that provides limited liability and taxation like a partnership but places fewer restrictions on members

A **limited liability company (LLC)** is a form of business ownership that provides limited liability, as in a corporation, but is taxed like a partnership. Although relatively new in the United States, LLCs have existed for many years abroad. Professionals such as lawyers, doctors, and engineers often use the LLC form of ownership. Many consider the LLC a blend of the best characteristics of corporations, partnerships, and sole proprietorships. One of the major reasons for the LLC form of ownership is to protect the members' personal assets in case of lawsuits. LLCs are flexible, simple to run, and do not require the members to hold meetings, keep minutes, or make resolutions, all of which are necessary in corporations. For example, Segway, which markets the Segway Human Transporter, is a limited liability company.

Cooperatives

cooperative or co-op

an organization composed of individuals or small businesses that have banded together to reap the benefits of belonging to a larger organization

Another form of organization in business is the **cooperative or co-op,** an organization composed of individuals or small businesses that have banded together to reap the benefits of belonging to a larger organization. Blue Diamond Growers, for example, is a cooperative of California almond growers; Ocean Spray is a cooperative of cranberry farmers. A co-op is set up not to make money as an entity but so that its members can become more profitable or save money. Co-ops are generally expected to operate without profit or to create only enough profit to maintain the co-op organization.

Many cooperatives exist in small farming communities. The co-op stores and markets grain; orders large quantities of fertilizer, seed, and other supplies at discounted prices; and reduces costs and increases efficiency with good management. A co-op can purchase supplies in large quantities and pass the savings on to its members. It also can help distribute the products of its members more efficiently than each could on an individual basis. A cooperative can advertise its members' products and thus generate de-

A group of California almond growers banded together to create the co-op of Blue Diamond Growers.

Jim Farmer, a lifelong livestock producer, wants his son and two daughters to be able to carry on the family farm. To help achieve that goal, he formed the Heartland Farm Foods Co-op with three dozen beef producers to turn 1,000 cattle a year into canned beef. The co-op form of organization is not unusual for small businesses who band together to obtain the benefits of a larger organization. The co-op is not set up to make money as an organization, but rather so that all the ranchers involved can become more profitable, or in this case, continue to maintain a lifestyle that they enjoy. In the face of intense competition from large commercial feedlots, Farmer's idea was to offer a different kind of product and to market and support it through the co-op, which has the support of the Missouri Beef Industry Council and the Missouri Department of Agriculture.

The co-op's canned, precooked product contains just one ingredient—beef, with no preservatives, not even salt. Any harmful bacteria are removed through a pressure-cooking process. Each animal yields 400 to 500 cans of federally inspected beef from cattle raised without steroids, hormone additives, or routine antibiotics. The precooked beef is targeted at outdoor enthusiasts, from hikers and hunters to anglers and campers. Thanks to a shelf life of two to five years, the cans can be stowed in tackle boxes or backpacks, or even stored in storm shelters in case of a disaster.

The co-op has constructed a 4,480-square-foot plant on 10 acres to process the beef. It has disclosed that it anticipates that construction of this facility and first-year operating capital needs are approximately $750,000. Some of these expenses will be partially offset by grants that the co-op has received; co-ops that foster economic development in a region often receive grants or other financial support from state or federal development initiatives.

Currently, Heartland's canned beef can be found only in a few north-central Missouri supermarkets and convenience stores. Retailers sell the product for $4.99 per can. At this price, consumers will surely demand a quality product, but Heartland believes the product's convenience and ingredients should support sales. Although it is too early to know the demand for the product (the U.S. Department of Agriculture has limited information about the market for canned beef.), Heartland's initiative offers an example of creativity in bringing back a product that was once a pantry staple before the era of refrigeration. The cooperative form of organization has made it possible for small ranchers to join together to make this product a reality.[19]

Discussion Questions

1. Why did Heartland Foods employ a cooperative form of organization?
2. What are the advantages for ranchers who belong to the cooperative?
3. Can you think of any other industries where the cooperative form of business ownership would be beneficial?

mand. Ace Hardware, a cooperative of independent hardware store owners, allows its members to share in the savings that result from buying supplies in large quantities; it also provides advertising, which individual members might not be able to afford on their own.

Trends in Business Ownership: Mergers and Acquisitions

Companies large and small achieve growth and improve profitability by expanding their operations, often by developing and selling new products or selling current products to new groups of customers in different geographic areas. Such growth, when carefully planned and controlled, is usually beneficial to the firm and ultimately helps it reach its goal of enhanced profitability. But companies also grow by merging with or purchasing other companies.

A **merger** occurs when two companies (usually corporations) combine to form a new company. An **acquisition** occurs when one company purchases another, generally by buying most of its stock. The acquired company may become a subsidiary of the buyer, or its operations and assets may be merged with those of the buyer. The buying company gains control of the property and assets of the other firm but also assumes its

merger
the combination of two companies (usually corporations) to form a new company

acquisition
the purchase of one company by another, usually by buying its stock

FIGURE 5.2

Trends in Mergers and Acquisitions

Source: U.S. Bureau of the Census, *Statistical Abstract of the United States, 2003* (Washington D.C.: Government Printing Office, 2004), p. 511.

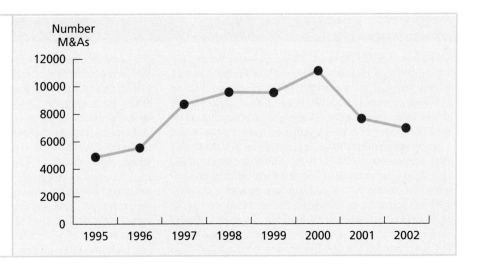

obligations. For example, Cingular Wireless outbid Vodafone Group to acquire AT&T Wireless Services for $47 billion.[20] Acquisitions sometimes involve the purchase of a division or some other part of a company rather than the entire company. The merger and acquisition frenzy seen in the late 1990s is slowing (see Figure 5.2).

When firms that make and sell similar products to the same customers merge, it is known as a *horizontal merger,* as when Martin Marietta and Lockheed, both defense contractors, merged to form Martin Lockheed. Horizontal mergers, however, reduce the number of corporations competing within an industry, and for this reason they are usually reviewed carefully by federal regulators before the merger is allowed to proceed.

When companies operating at different but related levels of an industry merge, it is known as a *vertical merger.* In many instances, a vertical merger results when one corporation merges with one of its customers or suppliers. For example, if Burger King were to purchase a large Idaho potato farm—to ensure a ready supply of potatoes for its french fries—a vertical merger would result.

A *conglomerate merger* results when two firms in unrelated industries merge. For example, the purchase of Sterling Drug, a pharmaceutical firm, by Eastman Kodak, best-known for its films and cameras, represents a conglomerate merger because the two companies are of different industries.

When a company (or an individual), sometimes called a *corporate raider,* wants to acquire or take over another company, it first offers to buy some or all of the other company's stock at a premium over its current price in a *tender offer.* Most such offers are "friendly," with both groups agreeing to the proposed deal, but some are "hostile," when the second company does not want to be taken over. For example, Sanofi-Synthelabo, a French pharmaceutical corporation, made a hostile bid for Aventis, the French-German drug maker. Aventis ultimately accepted a higher, friendlier offer from Sanofi. The merged Sanofi-Aventis will become the world's third-largest pharmaceutical producer, after U.S.-based Pfizer and U.K.-based GlaxoSmithKline.[21]

To head off a hostile takeover attempt, a threatened company's managers may use one or more of several techniques. They may ask stockholders not to sell to the raider; file a lawsuit in an effort to abort the takeover; institute a *poison pill* (in which the firm allows stockholders to buy more shares of stock at prices lower than the current market value) or *shark repellant* (in which management requires a large majority of stockholders to approve the takeover); or seek a *white knight* (a more acceptable firm that is willing to acquire the threatened company). In some cases, management may take the company private or even take on more debt so that the heavy debt obligation will "scare off" the raider. In the case of the initial hostile bid by Sanofi for Aventis, for example, Aventis initially instituted several measures to thwart the takeover attempt, including asking a rival Swiss firm, Novartis, to bid for Aventis. Only when Sanofi significantly raised its offer did Aventis's board of directors recommend that its stockholders accept the revised offer from Sanofi.[22]

In a **leveraged buyout (LBO),** a group of investors borrows money from banks and other institutions to acquire a company (or a division of one), using the assets of the purchased company to guarantee repayment of the loan. In some LBOs, as much as 95 percent of the buyout price is paid with borrowed money, which eventually must be repaid.

With the explosion of mergers, acquisitions, and leveraged buyouts in the 1980s and 1990s, some financial journalists coined the term *merger mania.* Many companies joined the merger mania simply to enhance their own operations by consolidating them with the operations of other firms. Mergers and acquisitions enabled these companies to gain a larger market share in their industries, acquire valuable assets, such as new products or plants and equipment, and lower their costs. Mergers also represent a means of making profits quickly, as was the case during the 1980s when many companies' stock was undervalued. Quite simply, such companies represent a bargain to other companies that can afford to buy them. Additionally, deregulation of some industries has permitted consolidation of firms within those industries for the first time, as is the case in the banking and airline industries.

Some people view mergers and acquisitions favorably, pointing out that they boost corporations' stock prices and market value, to the benefit of their stockholders. In many instances, mergers enhance a company's ability to meet foreign competition in an increasingly global marketplace. And, companies that are victims of hostile takeovers generally streamline their operations, reduce unnecessary staff, cut costs, and otherwise become more efficient operations, which benefits their stockholders whether or not the takeover succeeds.

Critics, however, argue that mergers hurt companies because they force managers to focus their efforts on avoiding takeovers rather than managing effectively and profitably. Some companies have taken on a heavy debt burden to stave off a takeover, later to be forced into bankruptcy when economic downturns left them unable to handle the debt. Mergers and acquisitions also can damage employee morale and productivity, as well as the quality of the companies' products.

Many mergers have been beneficial for all involved; others have had damaging effects for the companies, their employees, and customers. No one can say if mergers will continue to slow, but many experts say the utilities, telecommunications, financial services, natural resources, computer hardware and software, gaming, managed health care, and technology industries are likely targets.

leveraged buyout (LBO) a purchase in which a group of investors borrows money from banks and other institutions to acquire a company (or a division of one), using the assets of the purchased company to guarantee repayment of the loan

Explore Your Career Options
Evaluating a Job Offer

Before you choose to accept or reject any job offer, whether it comes from a sole proprietorship, a partnership, or a corporation, it needs to be properly evaluated.

Most organizations will not expect an immediate decision, so you will have time to consider issues regarding the organization, the job, compensation, and benefits.

Obtaining background information on the organization is important and doing so is generally easy. Factors to consider include the organization's business or activity, as well as its financial condition, age, size, and location. A public company's annual report contains this information and is usually available through the company's public relations office or the company's Web site. Press releases and company brochures or newsletters also can be helpful. Background information on many organizations is available at public libraries through reference directories such as *Dun & Bradstreet's Million Dollar Directory, Standard and Poor's Register of Corporations,* and *Thomas' Register of American Manufacturers.* There also are many sites on the Internet that offer company information, including *Hoover's Online* and the *Thomas Register.* Also, ask yourself whether the organization's business or activity coincides with your interest and values and whether the organization is in an industry with favorable long-term prospects.

Consider the nature of the job offered. Does the work match your interests and make good use of your skills and abilities? Are you comfortable with the hours? Are there opportunities to learn new skills, increase your earnings, and rise to positions of greater responsibility and authority? Ask for an explanation of where the offered job fits into the organization and how you will contribute to overall organizational objectives.

In considering the salary offered, you should have a rough estimate of what the particular type of job should pay. Start with family or friends who may have similar jobs. Ask your college placement director about starting salaries in different industries and for applicants with qualifications such as yours. Consider cost-of-living differences if the job requires relocation to another city. Factor in the offered benefits as they add to base pay. Salary information by occupation can be found on the Web site of the Bureau of Labor Statistics.[23]

Review Your Understanding

Define and examine the advantages and disadvantages of the sole proprietorship form of organization.

Sole proprietorships—businesses owned and managed by one person—are the most common form of organization. Their major advantages are the following: (1) They are easy and inexpensive to form; (2) they allow a high level of secrecy; (3) all profits belong to the owner; (4) the owner has complete control over the business; (5) government regulation is minimal; (6) taxes are paid only once; and (7) the business can be closed easily. The disadvantages include: (1) The owner may have to use personal assets to borrow money; (2) sources of external funds are difficult to find; (3) the owner must have many diverse skills; (4) the survival of the business is tied to the life of the owner and his or her ability to work; (5) qualified employees are hard to find; and (6) wealthy sole proprietors pay a higher tax than they would under the corporate form of business.

Identify two types of partnership and evaluate the advantages and disadvantages of the partnership form of organization.

A partnership is a business formed by several individuals; a partnership may be general or limited. Partnerships offer the following advantages: (1) They are easy to organize; (2) they may have higher credit ratings because the partners possibly have more combined wealth; (3) partners can specialize; (4) partnerships can make decisions faster than larger businesses; and (5) government regula-

tions are few. Partnerships also have several disadvantages: (1) General partners have unlimited liability for the debts of the partnership; (2) partners are responsible for each others' decisions; (3) the death or termination of one partner requires a new partnership agreement to be drawn up; (4) it is difficult to sell a partnership interest at a fair price; (5) the distribution of profits may not correctly reflect the amount of work done by each partner; and (6) partnerships cannot find external sources of funds as easily as can large corporations.

Describe the corporate form of organization and cite the advantages and disadvantages of corporations.

A corporation is a legal entity created by the state, whose assets and liabilities are separate from those of its owners. Corporations are chartered by a state through articles of incorporation. They have a board of directors made up of corporate officers or people from outside the company. Corporations, whether private or public, are owned by stockholders. Common stockholders have the right to elect the board of directors. Preferred stockholders do not have a vote but get preferential dividend treatment over common stockholders.

Advantages of the corporate form of business include: (1) The owners have limited liability; (2) ownership (stock) can be easily transferred; (3) corporations usually last forever; (4) raising money is easier than for other forms of business; and (5) expansion into new businesses is simpler because of the ability of the company to enter into contracts. Corporations also have disadvantages: (1) The company is taxed on its income, and owners pay a second tax on any profits received as dividends; (2) forming a corporation can be expensive; (3) keeping trade secrets is difficult because so much information must be made available to the public and to government agencies; and (4) owners and managers are not always the same and can have different goals.

Define and debate the advantages and disadvantages of mergers, acquisitions, and leveraged buyouts.

A merger occurs when two companies (usually corporations) combine to form a new company. An acquisition occurs when one company buys most of another company's stock. In a leveraged buyout, a group of investors borrows money to acquire a company, using the assets of the purchased company to guarantee the loan. They can help merging firms to gain a larger market share in their industries, acquire valuable assets such as new products or plants and equipment, and lower their costs. Consequently, they can benefit stockholders by improving the companies' market value and stock prices. However, they also can hurt companies if they force managers to focus on avoiding takeovers at the expense of productivity and profits. They may lead a company to take on too much debt and can harm employee morale and productivity.

Propose an appropriate organizational form for a start-up business.

After reading the facts in the "Solve the Dilemma" box on page 152 and considering the advantages and disadvantages of the various forms of business organization described in this chapter, you should be able to suggest an appropriate form for the start-up nursery.

Revisit the World of Business

1. Why do you think Zingerman's Deli was so successful when it first opened?
2. Why do you think most small businesses arrive at a crossroads: remain the same and risk stagnation or grow aggressively and risk sacrificing the qualities that made them successful in the first place?
3. Evaluate Zingerman's implementation of its "community of businesses" concept.

Learn the Terms

acquisition   153
articles of partnership   140
board of directors   148
common stock   149
cooperative (or co-op)   152
corporate charter   145
corporation   144
dividends   144

general partnership   140
initial public offering   146
joint venture   151
leveraged buyout (LBO)   155
limited liability company (LLC)   152
limited partnership   140
merger   153
nonprofit corporations   147

partnership   140
preferred stock   149
private corporation   146
public corporation   146
quasi-public corporations   147
S corporation   151
sole proprietorships   137
stock   144

Check Your Progress

1. Name five advantages of a sole proprietorship.
2. List two different types of partnerships and describe each.
3. Differentiate among the different types of corporations. Can you supply an example of each type?
4. Would you rather own preferred stock or common stock? Why?
5. Contrast how profits are distributed in sole proprietorships, partnerships, and corporations.
6. Which form of business organization has the least government regulation? Which has the most?
7. Compare the liability of the owners of partnerships, sole proprietorships, and corporations.
8. Why would secrecy in operating a business be important to an owner? What form of organization would be most appropriate for a business requiring great secrecy?
9. Which form of business requires the most specialization of skills? Which requires the least? Why?
10. The most common example of a cooperative is a farm co-op. Explain the reasons for this and the benefits that result for members of cooperatives.

Get Involved

1. Select a publicly owned corporation and bring to class a list of its subsidiaries. These data should be available in the firm's corporate annual report, *Standard and Poor's Corporate Records,* or *Moody Corporate Manuals.* Ask your librarian for help in finding these resources.

2. Select a publicly owned corporation and make a list of its outside directors. Information of this nature can be found in several places in your library: the company's annual report, its list of corporate directors, and various financial sources. If possible, include each director's title and the name of the company that employs him or her on a full-time basis.

Build Your Skills

SELECTING A FORM OF BUSINESS

Background:

Ali Bush sees an opportunity to start her own Web site development business. Ali has just graduated from the University of Mississippi with a master's degree in computer science. Although she has many job opportunities outside the Oxford area, she wishes to remain there to care for her aging parents. She already has most of the computer equipment necessary to start the business, but she needs additional software. She is considering the purchase of a server to maintain Web sites for small businesses. Ali feels she has the ability to take this start-up firm and create a long-term career opportunity for herself and others. She knows she can hire Ole Miss students to work on a part-time basis to support her business. For now, as she starts the business, she can work out of the extra bedroom of her apartment. As the business grows, she'll hire the additional full and/or part-time help needed and reassess the location of the business.

Task:

1. Using what you've learned in this chapter, decide which form of business ownership is most appropriate for Ali. Use the tables provided to assist you in evaluating the advantages and disadvantages of each decision.

Sole Proprietorships	
Advantages	**Disadvantages**
•	•
•	•
•	•
•	•
•	•
•	•
•	•

Corporation	
Advantages	**Disadvantages**
•	•
•	•
•	•
•	•
•	•
•	•
•	•

Limited Liability Company	
Advantages	**Disadvantages**
•	•
•	•
•	•
•	•
•	•
•	•

e-Xtreme Surfing

- **<u>Entreworld.org</u>**
  www.entreworld.org

  Provides information about starting and growing a business and includes links to many other helpful Web sites.

- **<u>Inc.</u>**
  www.inc.com

  Offers online access to content of *Inc.* magazine, including information on organizing and growing a business.

- **<u>Hoovers</u>**
  www.hoovers.com

  Supplies capsule information about companies to help you evaluate them whether you are considering a job offer or research a potential investment

See for Yourself Videocase

UNITED FILES FOR BANKRUPTCY

The airline industry has been one of the most turbulent and competitive business areas in our economy. United Airlines is the second largest air carrier in the world, with hubs in Chicago, Denver, San Francisco, Los Angeles, and Washington, D.C., and key international gateways in Tokyo, London, Frankfurt, Miami, and Toronto. The airline flies to 109 destinations in 26 countries and employs 65,000 people worldwide. United customers also have access to more than 700 destinations through alliances with other global airlines. It is owned by UAL Corporation, a holding company.

United likes to think of itself as an industry innovator, offering customer-focused products and services. This customer focus begins at United's Web site, www.united.com, with complete company information and the convenience of United e-tickets for purchasing electronically. In addition, United has implemented easy check-in, gate information displays, and wireless technologies to assist in the travel experience. There are Red Carpet Clubs, international lounges, and United Economy Plus, which provides more legroom than in United's Economy cabin. There are over 40 million members enrolled in United Mileage Plus, named the best frequent flyer program by *Business Traveler International* magazine for four years in a row.

United and its employees are committed to making sure that passengers enjoy safe, seamless travel along with superior customer service. The company recognizes that consumers' expectations change, and the airline industry is highly competitive. There is a continual effort to improve such areas as on-time performance, the check-in process, baggage service, information technology, and a consistent level of quality consumer service in every aspect of travel with United.

United is also committed to helping communities through the United Airlines Foundation, a purely philanthropic organization founded more than 50 years ago. Its mission is to make the United Airlines name and brand synonymous with corporate philanthropy and community involvement. The foundation receives thousands of requests for philanthropic support and assists as many charitable organizations as possible. Its major areas of emphasis include education, health, arts and culture, volunteerism, and diversity.

Although United has maintained an excellent business plan, the airline industry has suffered extreme turbulence over the last few years. When the economy slowed in 2000 in response to a recession in the information technology industry, all airlines experienced a decline in the high-yield travel business. At the same time, labor costs increased dramatically due to various collective bargaining agreements with most of United's employees, which included wage increases. The September 11, 2001 terrorist attack—which involved some United aircraft—also contributed to further significant financial losses. After September 11, United reduced its flight schedule, retired aircraft, curtailed new aircraft deliveries, reduced capital spending, closed several reservation centers, eliminated some commissions paid to travel agencies, and significantly downsized its workforce. The company also attempted to negotiate labor cost reductions with its unions to stave off bankruptcy. Despite these sweeping measures, United continued to deplete its cash reserves, and it was unsuccessful in securing additional financing from the public or private sectors. The Air Transportation Stabilization Board (ATSB) declined United's request for a $1.8 billion federal loan guarantee. Facing debt payments of $875 million coming due, on December 9, 2002, UAL Corporation and its subsidiaries filed voluntary petitions to reorganize their businesses under Chapter 11 of the United States Bankruptcy Code.

As part of the Chapter 11 filing, United arranged for the financing of $1.5 billion so that it could continue operations. Under the bankruptcy arrangement, United was granted a temporary stay from actions to collect on its debts, so that it can continue to pay all of its vendors in full for goods and services provided. Since the filing of the bankruptcy petition, United has made an effort to significantly restructure the company, including lowering labor cost through wage and benefit reductions for union employees, as well as salaried and management employees. The airline also launched new marketing and sales programs, inventory management enhancements, and route and capacity adjustments in order to enhance profitability.

Part of United's campaign to increase profits involved the introduction of a new low-fare airline called Ted. Although it is unusual for companies to introduce new ventures while in bankruptcy, many observers view Ted as United's only hope for surviving its financial crisis. Over the past decade, the growing popularity of smaller, low-fare airlines like Southwest and JetBlue has eroded United's customer base. Hoping to recover some of those customers, United launched Ted in February 2004, promising lower fares to popular leisure destinations like Fort Lauderdale and San Francisco. With hubs in Denver, Chicago, and Washington, D.C., Ted will compete with Frontier, Southwest, and ATA Airlines by offering low-cost tickets on larger, coach-class only planes.

In order to successfully exit Chapter 11 bankruptcy, United must have a plan of reorganization approved by the bankruptcy court. The reorganization plan must detail how United will fulfill its financial obligations, how it has revised its capital structure, and how it will organize its corporate governance after exiting from bankruptcy. The airline must also obtain a federal loan guarantee from the ATSB for about $1.6 billion, so that it can obtain private financing from banks. Initially, United planned to emerge from Chapter 11 during the first half of 2004, but as of this writing, the company still remains in bankruptcy. Observers have speculated that rising costs, particularly the increased price of jet fuel, have interfered with the approval of United's request for a federal loan guarantee.[24]

Discussion Questions

1. United Airlines was forced to file for bankruptcy despite a great business plan and being the second largest air carrier in the world. What could it have done to prevent this situation, if anything?

2. What are the unique aspects of the business environment and competition that make it so difficult for airlines to make a profit?

3. What will be the impact of the introduction of the new low-fare carrier called Ted?

Remember to check out our Online Learning Center at www.mhhe.com/ferrell5e.

Chapter 6

Small Business, Entrepreneurship, and Franchising

OBJECTIVES

After reading this chapter, you will be able to:

- Define entrepreneurship and small business.

- Investigate the importance of small business in the U.S. economy and why certain fields attract small business.

- Specify the advantages of small-business ownership.

- Summarize the disadvantages of small-business ownership and analyze why many small businesses fail.

- Describe how you go about starting a small business and what resources are needed.

- Evaluate the demographic, technological, and economic trends that are affecting the future of small business.

- Explain why many large businesses are trying to "think small."

- Assess two entrepreneurs' plans for starting a small business.

King's Saddlery and King Ropes

King's Saddlery and King Ropes in Sheridan, Wyoming, supplies cowboys around the world with high-quality ropes, saddles, and rodeo gear. Don King, the saddlery's founder, has been making saddles for about 50 years and ropes for more than 30 years. His saddle making has become world renowned and draws such prestigious customers as the Queen of England, former presidents Ronald Reagan and Bill Clinton, and late-night talk-show host David Letterman. Many amateur and professional rodeo cowboys prefer King ropes, and the majority of the world's top calf ropers at the National Finals Rodeo in Las Vegas, Nevada, wield King ropes at the prestigious annual event. Many of the firm's customers have been loyal to the business for many years. Such loyalty can only come from a company that makes every effort to satisfy the needs of demanding customers.

King's Saddlery prides itself on customer service, an attribute that sets it apart from the competition. King's employees are quite knowledgeable about different kinds of rope, allowing them to find just the right product for each customer's problem or task. The materials that go into King Ropes are customized for each purchaser, with much of the work still done by hand. Although such work can be tedious and repetitive, King's employees take pride in doing the job right. All products made and sold by King's are guaranteed, and any product may be returned if the customer is not completely satisfied.

King's Saddlery and King Ropes does a large percentage of its business by mail order, and ships all over the world. Although customers cannot order merchandise online, they can request a catalog by phone. The firm's simple advertisements run semi-annually in trade magazines and seasonally in local newspapers. It also places brochures in local businesses, tourism boards, and gas stations to promote its products as well as the King's Western Museum, located inside the store. The picture-filled brochure provides customers with an interesting explanation of the businesses as well as a unique

continued

souvenir. King's has also received valuable publicity in the form of numerous articles in a variety of publications on topics ranging from Don King himself to saddle making and rope making. Tourist publications, Internet sites, and brochures have highlighted King's as a must-see destination in Sheridan.

King's Saddlery has also received numerous awards and letters expressing thanks for its good business practices and exceptional customer service. In 2004, for example, King's received the Better Business Bureau Torch Award for marketplace ethics. Indeed, the walls of King's Saddlery are festooned with pictures, plaques, and letters from customers, organizations, and suppliers recognizing King's for the extra effort it takes with every single customer. Such effort and care have made King's Saddlery more than just a rope and saddle shop, but also a piece of western cowboy history.[1]

Introduction

Although many business students go to work for large corporations upon graduation, others may choose to start their own business or find employment opportunities in small businesses with 500 or fewer employees. There are nearly 23 million small businesses operating in the United States today.[2] Each small business represents the vision of its entrepreneurial owners to succeed by providing new or better products. Small businesses are the heart of the U.S. economic and social system because they offer opportunities and express the freedom of people to make their own destinies. Today, the entrepreneurial spirit is growing around the world, from Russia and China to Germany, Brazil, and Mexico.

This chapter surveys the world of entrepreneurship and small business. First we define entrepreneurship and small business and examine the role of small business in the American economy. Then we explore the advantages and disadvantages of small-business ownership and analyze why small businesses succeed or fail. Next, we discuss how an entrepreneur goes about starting a small business and the challenges facing small business today. Finally, we look at entrepreneurship in larger businesses.

The Nature of Entrepreneurship and Small Business

enterpreneurship
the process of creating and managing a business to achieve desired objectives

In Chapter 1, we defined an entrepreneur as a person who risks his or her wealth, time, and effort to develop for profit an innovative product or way of doing something. **Entrepreneurship** is the process of creating and managing a business to achieve desired objectives. Many large businesses you may recognize, including Levi Strauss and Co., Procter and Gamble, McDonald's, Dell Computers, Microsoft, and Federal Express, all began as small businesses based on the entrepreneurial visions of their founders. Some entrepreneurs who start small businesses have the ability to see emerging trends; in response, they create a company to provide a product that serves customer needs. For example, rather than inventing a major new technology, an innovative company may take advantage of a new technology to create markets that did not exist before, such as Amazon.com. Or they may offer something familiar but improved or repackaged, such as Starbucks did with its coffee shops. They may innovate by focusing on a particular market segment and delivering a combination of features that consumers in that segment could not find anywhere else (e.g., Lands' End).[3]

Of course, smaller businesses do not have to evolve into such highly visible companies to be successful, but those entrepreneurial efforts that result in rapidly growing businesses become more visible with their success. Entrepreneurs who have achieved success, like Michael Dell and Bill Gates (Microsoft), are the most visible.

The entrepreneurship movement is accelerating with many new, smaller businesses emerging. Technology once available only to the largest firms can now be acquired by a small business. Printers, fax machines, copiers, voice-mail, computer bulletin boards and networks, cellular phones, and even overnight delivery services enable small businesses to be more competitive with today's giant corporations. Small businesses can also form alliances with other companies to produce and sell products in domestic and global markets.

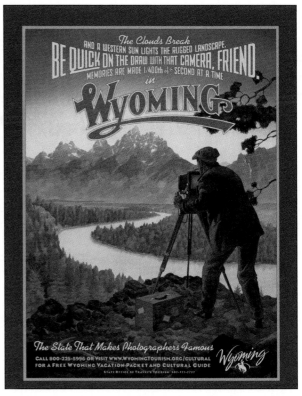

States such as Wyoming and New Mexico compete in a free enterprise system to support small business and entrepreneurship.

What Is a Small Business?

This question is difficult to answer because smallness is relative. In this book, we will define a **small business** as any independently owned and operated business that is not dominant in its competitive area and does not employ more than 500 people. A local Mexican restaurant may be the most patronized Mexican restaurant in your community, but because it does not dominate the restaurant industry as a whole, the restaurant can be considered a small business. This definition is similar to the one used by the **Small Business Administration (SBA),** an independent agency of the federal government that offers managerial and financial assistance to small businesses. On its Web site, the SBA outlines the first steps in starting a small business and offers a wealth of information to current and potential small business owners.

small business
any independently owned and operated business that is not dominant in its competitive area and does not employ more than 500 people

Small Business Administration (SBA)
an independent agency of the federal government that offers managerial and financial assistance to small businesses

The Role of Small Business in the American Economy

No matter how you define small business, one fact is clear: Small businesses are vital to the soundness of the American economy. As you can see in Table 6.1, over 99 percent of all U.S. firms are classified as small businesses, and they employ 50 percent of private workers. Small firms are also important as exporters, representing 97 percent of U.S. exporters of goods and contributing 29 percent of the value of exported goods.[4] In addition, small businesses are largely responsible for fueling job creation and innovation. Small businesses also provide opportunities for minorities and women to succeed in business. Women-owned businesses total 9.1 million, employ 27.5 million, and contribute $3.6 trillion to the economy.[5] Moreover, the number of privately held

TABLE 6.1 Facts About Small Businesses	• Provide about 75% of net new jobs.
	• Represent 99.7% of all employers.
	• Employ 50% of the private workforce.
	• Provide 41% of all sales in the United States.
	• Provide 52% of the private sector output.
	• Represent 97% of all U.S. exporters of goods.
	Source: "Small Business Statistics," Small Business Administration, **www.sba.gov/ aboutsba/sbastats.html** (accessed May 4, 2004).

women-owned businesses grew by 11 percent between 1997 and 2002 during a period when privately owned businesses as a group grew just 6 percent.[6] Minority-owned firms total 3.25 million, employ more than 4.5 million, and account for $517 billion in revenues.[7] Consider the story of Tommy Hodinh, who came to the United States in 1972 as a Vietnamese refugee. After putting himself through college and working at IBM for 15 years, he decided to start his own business. Today MagRabbit, Inc., his software duplication and logistics firm, employs more than 100 and rings up nearly $10 million in annual sales from customers around the world. Hodinh himself has become a source of inspiration for many Asian Americans with an entrepreneurial bent.[8] Or consider Ho-Chunk, Inc., a small corporation owned by the Winnebago tribe, which operates numerous businesses including housing construction, hotels, convenience stores, Web design, tobacco distribution, and community development, as well as several Web-based ventures. The firm not only employs 355 in an area prone to ultrahigh unemployment rates, but is also helping to build new homes and support other new businesses for members of the tribe. Many American Indian tribes are studying the company's operations as a model for their own tribal businesses.[9]

Job Creation.   The energy, creativity, and innovative abilities of small-business owners have resulted in jobs for other people. In fact, in recent years, 75 percent of all new jobs were created by small businesses.[10] Table 6.2 indicates that businesses employing 19 or fewer people account for 89 percent of all businesses, and 99.7 percent of all businesses employ fewer than 500 people.[11]

Many small businesses today are being started because of encouragement from larger ones. Many jobs are being created by big company/small company alliances. Whether through formal joint ventures, supplier relationships, or product or marketing cooperative projects, the rewards of collaborative relationships are creating many jobs for small-business owners and their employees. Some publishing companies, for example, contract out almost all their editing and production to small businesses. Elm Street Publishing Services is a small editing/production house in Hinsdale, Illinois, that provides most services required to turn a manuscript into a bound book.

Innovation.   Perhaps one of the most significant strengths of small businesses is their ability to innovate and bring significant changes and benefits to customers. Small firms produce 55 percent of innovations. Among the important 20th-century innovations by U.S. small firms are the airplane, the audio tape recorder, double-knit fabric, fiber-optic examining equipment, the heart valve, the optical scanner, the pacemaker, the personal computer, soft contact lenses, and the zipper. Paul Moller, an entrepreneur and inventor, may be working on one of the most important 21st century innovations: a flying car. Although currently still in the testing phase, Moller's SkyCar may one day help commuters avoid congested freeways.[12]

Firm Size	Number of Firms	Percentage of All Firms	TABLE 6.2
0–19 employees	5,036,845	89.0	Number of Firms by Employment Size
20–99 employees	518,258	9.2	
100–499 employees	85,304	1.5	
500 or more employees	17,367	0.3	

Source: U.S. Census Bureau **www.census.gov/epcd/www/smallbus.html#EmpSize** (accessed May 4, 2004).

The innovation of successful firms takes many forms. Small businessman Ray Kroc found a new way to sell hamburgers and turned his ideas into one of the most successful fast-food franchises in the world—McDonald's. Small businesses have become an integral part of our lives. John Osher, for example, created a unique spinning electric toothbrush, which became the best-selling toothbrush in the United States in just 15 months. He later sold the company he set up to market Dr. John's SpinBrush to Procter & Gamble for $475 million.[13] They provide fresh ideas and usually have greater flexibility to change than do large companies.

Industries That Attract Small Business

Small businesses are found in nearly every industry, but retailing and wholesaling, services, manufacturing, and high technology are especially attractive to entrepreneurs because they are relatively easy to enter and require low initial financing. Small-business owners also find it easier to focus on a specific group of consumers in these fields than in others, and new firms in these industries suffer less from heavy competition, at least in the early stages, than do established firms.

Retailing and Wholesaling. Retailers acquire goods from producers or wholesalers and sell them to consumers. Main streets, shopping strips, and shopping malls are lined with independent music stores, sporting-goods shops, dry cleaners, boutiques, drugstores, restaurants, caterers, service stations, and hardware stores that sell directly to consumers. Retailing attracts entrepreneurs because gaining experience and exposure in retailing is relatively easy. Additionally, an entrepreneur opening a new retailing store does not have to spend the large sums of money for the equipment and distribution systems that a manufacturing business requires. All that a new retailer needs is a lease on store space, merchandise, enough money to sustain the business, a knowledge about prospective customers' needs and desires, the ability to use promotion to generate awareness, and basic management skills. Some small retailers are taking their businesses online. For example, Holly Thompson and Lucy Smith launched the Button Peddler, an online business that deals in

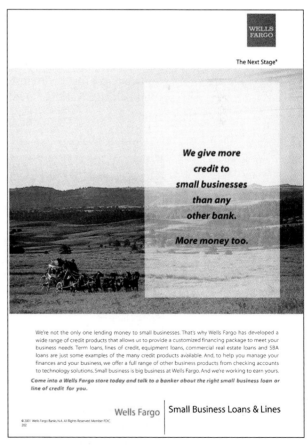

Wells Fargo Bank provides services to small retailers and wholesalers.

specialty buttons. The buttons, made from materials such as rhinestones, shell, and glass, sell from 20 cents to $15. Many of the site's customers are rural seamstresses who don't have access to fabric stores that carry large button selections.[14]

Wholesalers supply products to industrial, retail, and institutional users for resale or for use in making other products. Wholesaling activities range from planning and negotiating for supplies, promoting, and distributing (warehousing and transporting) to providing management and merchandising assistance to clients. Wholesalers are extremely important for many products, especially consumer goods, because of the marketing activities they perform. Although it is true that wholesalers themselves can be eliminated, their functions must be passed on to some other organization such as the producer, or another intermediary, often a small business. Frequently, small businesses are closer to the final customers and know what it takes to keep them satisfied. Some smaller businesses start out manufacturing but find their real niche as a supplier or distributor of larger firms' products.

Services.   Services include businesses that work for others but do not actually produce tangible goods. They represent the fastest growing sector of the U.S. economy, accounting for 60 percent of the nation's economic activity and employing nearly 70 percent of the workforce. Real-estate, insurance, and personnel agencies, barbershops, banks, television and computer repair shops, copy centers, dry cleaners, and accounting firms are all service businesses. Services also attract individuals—such as beauticians, morticians, jewelers, doctors, and veterinarians—whose skills are not usually required by large firms. Many of these service providers are also retailers because they provide their services to ultimate consumers.

Manufacturing.   Manufacturing goods can provide unique opportunities for small businesses. Stoner, Inc., in Quarryville, Pennsylvania, manufactures cleaners, lubricants, and coatings; with just 50 employees, it became the smallest firm to win a Malcolm Baldrige National Quality Award.[15] The award is designed to spur competitive

The Right One online dating service was named the number one services franchise in 2004 by Entrepreneur *magazine. Created in 1990, but franchising since 1999, its Web site touts "Responsible for a marriage a day and a match every 17 minutes."* (**www.therightone.com**)

business practices in American industry, and few companies with 500 or fewer employees have won the award since its inception in 1988. Small businesses can often customize products to meet specific customer needs and wants. Such products include custom artwork, jewelry, clothing, and furniture.

High Technology.   High technology is a broad term used to describe businesses that depend heavily on advanced scientific and engineering knowledge. People who have been able to innovate or identify new markets in the fields of computers, biotechnology, genetic engineering, robotics, and other markets have become today's high-tech giants. Michael Dell, for example, started building personal computers in his University of Texas dorm room at age 19. His Dell Computer is now one of the leading PC companies in the world, with annual sales of over \$431 billion.[16] Apple Computers began in a garage. The Apple prototype was financed by the proceeds Steven Wozniak received from selling his Hewlett-Packard calculator and Steven Jobs got from selling his van. In general, high technology businesses require greater capital and have higher initial start-up costs than do other small businesses. Many of them, nonetheless, started out in garages, basements, kitchens, and dorm rooms.

> **Did You Know?**   39 percent of high-tech jobs are in small businesses.[17]

Advantages of Small-Business Ownership

There are many advantages to establishing and running a small business. These can be categorized as personal advantages and business advantages. Table 6.3 lists some of the traits that can help entrepreneurs succeed.

Independence
Independence is probably one of the leading reasons that entrepreneurs choose to go into business for themselves. Being a small-business owner means being your own boss. Many people start their own businesses because they believe they will do better for themselves than they could do by remaining with their current employer or by changing jobs. They may feel stuck on the corporate ladder and that no business would take them seriously enough to fund their ideas. Sometimes people who venture forth to start their own small business are those who simply cannot work for someone else. Such people may say that they just do not fit the "corporate mold."

More often, small-business owners just want the freedom to choose whom they work with, the flexibility to pick where and when to work, and the option of working in a family setting. The availability of the computer, copy machine, business telephone, and fax machine has permitted many people to work at home. Only a few years ago, most of them would have needed the support that an office provides.

Small business owners, such as florists, play a vital role in the American economy. They offer many opportunities and challenges, including the chance to be one's own boss and provide personal service to customers. The challenges are different from those faced by large businesses.

Growing a Business
Burt's Bees

In 1984, Roxanne Quimby was on her way to her waitress job when she decided to stop at a roadside stand to buy some honey from beekeeper Burt Shavitz. She soon joined forces with Shavitz, and they began to market the honey from Burt's bees to tourists and to make candles and other products out of the beeswax. Quimby made handmade labels and traveled to craft fairs throughout her home state of Maine, marketing their products and closely observing customers' reactions to them. By applying her observations, Quimby learned to develop new products to satisfy a growing niche market for natural beauty products, such as lip balm, soap, and baby products. By 1993, Burt's Bees was bringing in $3 million a year in sales, and Quimby and Shavitz (who has since retired and sold his share in the business to Quimby) decided to move their rapidly growing business to North Carolina. Within another 10 years, the firm had grown to nearly $60 million in sales and provided jobs for 200 full-time and 100 temporary workers.

Today's Burt's Bees beauty and baby products are distributed through 9,000 specialty stores and natural food stores like Whole Foods, as well as online. Burt's Bees does not use advertising for its growing line of products, relying instead on word-of-mouth promotion from satisfied customers and an extensive sampling effort. Every month, Burt's Bees also hosts 10 to 15 special events at retail stores where customers are invited to come and sample and learn about the company's products, giving them a firsthand experience with the products.

When Roxanne Quimby first met Burt Shavitz, she was living a self-sustaining and uncompromising lifestyle in a log cabin in the Maine woods with her three children. While building Burt's Bees, Quimby applied her philosophies and values to the growing company, for example, eschewing wasteful packaging wherever possible, using the best ingredients available, and walking away from potentially lucrative discount store sales when the chain store company asked for concessions that violated her environmental sensibilities. In 2003, Quimby sold 80 percent of Burt's Bees to New York investment firm AEA Investors for $179 million, though she retains 20 percent and remains president and CEO of the firm for now. Quimby plans to give half the proceeds from the sale to a land trust working to create a national park in her beloved Maine. She also plans to keep growing the company, hopefully to a $500 million national brand.[18]

Discussion Questions

1. Why do you think Burt's Bees was able to grow from a tiny company into a national distributor of personal-care products?
2. How has the firm's preference for natural ingredients and environmental consciousness affected its growth?
3. Do you think that Burt's Bees faces major competition from more traditional personal-care products from larger companies like Procter & Gamble?

TABLE 6.3	
Traits Needed to Succeed in Entrepreneurship	Neuroticism—helps entrepreneurs focus on details
	Extroversion—facilitates network building
	Conscientiousness—facilitates planning
	Agreeableness—facilitates networking
	Openness to new ideas

Source: Alex de Noble in Joshua Kurlantzick, "About Face," *Entrepreneur,* January 2004, **www.entrepreneur.com/article/0,4621,312260,00.html.**

Costs

As already mentioned, small businesses often require less money to start and maintain than do large ones. Obviously, a firm with just 25 people in a small factory spends less money on wages and salaries, rent, utilities, and other expenses than does a firm employing tens of thousands of people in several large facilities. And, rather than maintain the expense and staff of keeping separate departments for accounting, advertising, and legal counseling, small businesses can hire other firms (often small businesses themselves) to supply these services as they are needed. Additionally, small-business owners can sometimes rely on friends and family members who volunteer to work to get out a difficult project in order to save money.

Flexibility

With small size comes the flexibility to adapt to changing market demands. Small businesses usually have only one layer of management—the owners. Decisions therefore can be made and carried out quickly. In larger firms, decisions about even routine matters can take weeks because they must pass through two or more levels of management before action is authorized. When McDonald's introduces a new product, for example, it must first research what consumers want, then develop the product and test it carefully before introducing it nationwide, a process that sometimes takes years. An independent snack shop, however, can develop and introduce a new product (perhaps to meet a customer's request) in a much shorter time.

Focus

Small firms can focus their efforts on a few key customers or on a precisely defined market niche—that is, a specific group of customers. Many large corporations must compete in the mass market or for large market segments. Smaller firms can develop products for particular groups of customers or to satisfy a need that other companies have not addressed. For example, Gamblin Artist's Oil Colors, a small paint manufacturer, was started by Robert and Martha Gamblin to "make paint with the artist in mind." A graduate of the San Francisco Art Institute and a painter himself, Robert Gamblin felt he could develop products that artists would use. The company has grown from its modest start in the Gamblins' garage with just three colors of paint. It now sells 87 colors across the United States and abroad, has 20 employees and its own manufacturing facility.[19] By targeting small niches or product needs, small businesses can sometimes avoid fierce competition from larger firms, helping them to grow into stronger companies.

Reputation

Small firms, because of their capacity to focus on narrow niches, can develop enviable reputations for quality and service. A good example of a small business with a formidable reputation is W. Atlee Burpee and Co. which has the country's premier bulb and seed catalog. Burpee has an unqualified returns policy (complete satisfaction or your money back) that demonstrates a strong commitment to customer satisfaction.

Small business owners, such as veterinarians, are concerned with maintaining a high-quality reputation.

Disadvantages of Small-Business Ownership

The rewards associated with running a small business are so enticing that it's no wonder many people dream of it. However, as with any undertaking, small-business ownership has its disadvantages.

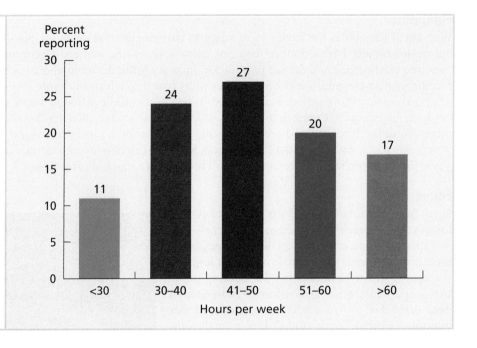

FIGURE 6.1

How Hard Do They
Work?

*Hours worked by small
business owners:*

Source: "21st Annual Small
Business Survey Summary
Report," *Dun & Bradstreet*
(n.d.), **www.sbs.dnb.com/
survey/2002survey.pdf**
(accessed May 4, 2004).

High Stress Level

A small business is likely to provide a living for its owner, but not much more (although there are exceptions as some examples in this chapter have shown). There are always worries about competition, employee problems, new equipment, expanding inventory, rent increases, or changing market demand. In addition to other stresses, small-business owners tend to be victims of physical and psychological stress. The small-business person is often the owner, manager, sales force, shipping and receiving clerk, bookkeeper, and custodian. Figure 6.1 shows the long hours worked by many small-business owners. Many creative persons fail, not because of their business concepts, but rather because of difficulties in managing their business.

High Failure Rate

Despite the importance of small businesses to our economy, there is no guarantee of small-business success. For the past several years, about 9 percent of companies with employees have shut down, and of that 9 percent, virtually all were small companies. But of the companies that close, only about one in seven fails—goes out of business

The failure rate for small businesses is very high.

leaving behind unpaid debts.[20] Table 6.4 shows the total number of companies, number that closed, and number of business bankruptcies over the last decade. Neighborhood restaurants are a case in point. Look around your own neighborhood, and you can probably spot the locations of several restaurants that are no longer in business.

Small businesses fail for many reasons (see Table 6.5). A poor business concept—such as insecticides for garbage cans (research found that consumers are not concerned with insects in their garbage)—will produce disaster nearly every time. Expanding a hobby into a business may work if a genuine market niche exists, but all too often people start such a business without identifying

	1990	1998	2002
Total number of employer companies	5.1 million	5.7 million	5.7 million
Number of employer companies that closed	531,400	524,500	584,500
Number of business bankruptcies	63,912	44,197	38,155

TABLE 6.4

Closed Doors

Source: "Answers to Frequently Asked Questions," Small Business Administration, Office of Advocacy, December 2003; U.S. Census Bureau, **www.ensus.gov/epcd/www/smallbus.html** (accessed May 4, 2004).

- Failing to spend enough time researching the business idea to see if it's viable.
- Miscalculating market size, timing, ease of entry, and potential market share.
- Underestimating financial requirements and timing.
- Overprojecting sales volume and timing.
- Making cost projections that are too low.
- Hiring too many people and spending too much on offices and facilities.
- Lacking a contingency plan for a shortfall in expectations.
- Bringing in unnecessary partners.
- Hiring for convenience rather than skill requirements.
- Neglecting to manage the entire company as a whole.
- Accepting that it's "not possible" too easily rather than finding a way.
- Focusing too much on sales volume and company size rather than profit.
- Seeking confirmation of your actions rather than seeking the truth.
- Lacking simplicity in your vision.
- Lacking clarity of your long-term aim and business purpose.
- Lacking focus and identity.
- Lacking an exit strategy.

TABLE 6.5

Most Common Mistakes Made by Start-up Businesses

Source: John Osher, in Mark Henricks, "What Not to Do," *Entrepreneur,* February 2004, **www.entrepreneur.com/article/0,4621,312661,00.html**.

a real need for the goods or services. Other notable causes of small-business failure include the burdens imposed by government regulation, insufficient funds to withstand slow sales, and vulnerability to competition from larger companies. However, three major causes of small-business failure deserve a close look: undercapitalization, managerial inexperience or incompetence, and inability to cope with growth.

Undercapitalization. The shortest path to failure in business is **undercapitalization,** the lack of funds to operate a business normally. Too many entrepreneurs think that all they need is enough money to get started, that the business can survive on cash generated from sales soon thereafter. But almost all businesses suffer from seasonal variations in sales, which make cash tight, and few businesses make money from the start. Many small rural operations cannot obtain financing within their own communities because small rural banks often lack the necessary financing expertise or assets sizeable enough to counter the risks involved with small business loans. Without sufficient funds, the best small-business idea in the world will fail.

undercapitalization
the lack of funds to operate a business normally

Managerial Inexperience or Incompetence.   Poor management is the cause of many business failures. Just because an entrepreneur has a brilliant vision for a small business does not mean he or she has the knowledge or experience to manage a growing business effectively. A person who is good at creating great product ideas and marketing them may lack the skills and experience to make good management decisions in hiring, negotiating, finance, and control. Moreover, entrepreneurs may neglect those areas of management they know little about or find tedious, at the expense of the business's success.

Inability to Cope with Growth.   Sometimes, the very factors that are advantages turn into serious disadvantages when the time comes for a small business to grow. Growth often requires the owner to give up a certain amount of direct authority, and it is frequently hard for someone who has called all the shots to give up control. Similarly, growth requires specialized management skills in areas such as credit analysis and promotion—skills that the founder may lack or not have time to apply. The founders of many small businesses, including those of Gateway and Dell Computers, found that they needed to bring in more experienced managers to help manage their companies through intense growing pains.

Poorly managed growth probably affects a company's reputation more than anything else, at least initially. And products that do not arrive on time or goods that are poorly made can quickly reverse a company's success.

Starting a Small Business

We've told you how important small businesses are, and why they succeed and fail, but *how do you go about* starting your own business? To start any business, large or small, you must first have an idea. Sam Walton, founder of Wal-Mart stores, had an idea for a discount retailing enterprise and spawned a global retailing empire that changed the way traditional companies look at their business. Next, you need to devise a business plan to guide planning and development in the business. Finally, you must make decisions about form of ownership, the financial resources needed, and whether to buy an existing business, start a new one, or buy a franchise.

The Business Plan

business plan

a precise statement of the rationale for a business and a step-by-step explanation of how it will achieve its goals

A key element of business success is a **business plan**—a precise statement of the rationale for the business and a step-by-step explanation of how it will achieve its goals. The business plan should include an explanation of the business, an analysis of the competition, estimates of income and expenses, and other information. It should establish a strategy for acquiring sufficient funds to keep the business going. Indeed, many financial institutions decide whether to loan a small business money based on its business plan. However, the business plan should act as a guide and reference document—not a shackle to limit the business's flexibility and decision making. Finally, the business plan should be revised periodically to ensure that the firm's goals and strategies can adapt to changes in the environment. Craig Knouf, the CEO of Associated Business Systems, a Portland, Oregon, office-equipment supplier, has revised his business plan more than 120 times since it was founded in 1997. Although most business owners revisit their business plans about once a year, Knouf believes it is necessary to reexamine the business plan at least quarterly.[21] The Small Business Administration Web site provides an overview of a plan for small businesses to use to gain financing. Appendix B presents a comprehensive business plan.

Forms of Business Ownership

After developing a business plan, the entrepreneur has to decide on an appropriate legal form of business ownership—whether it is best to operate as a sole proprietorship, partnership, or corporation—and examine the many factors that affect that decision, which we explored in Chapter 5.

Financial Resources

The old adage "it takes money to make money" holds true in developing a business enterprise. To make money from a small business, the owner must first provide or obtain money (capital) to start the business and keep it running smoothly. Even a small retail store will probably need at least $50,000 in initial financing to rent space, purchase or lease necessary equipment and furnishings, buy the initial inventory of merchandise, and provide working capital. Often, the small-business owner has to put up a significant percentage of the necessary capital. Few new business owners have the entire amount, however, and must look to other sources for additional financing.

Equity Financing.   The most important source of funds for any new business is the owner. Many owners include among their personal resources ownership of a home or the accumulated value in a life-insurance policy or a savings account. A new business owner may sell or borrow against the value of such assets to obtain funds to operate a business. Additionally, the owner may bring useful personal assets—such as a computer, desks and other furniture, a car or truck—as part of his or her ownership interest in the firm. Such financing is referred to as *equity financing* because the owner uses real personal assets rather than borrowing funds from outside sources to get started in a new business. The owner can also provide working capital by reinvesting profits into the business or simply by not drawing a full salary.

Small businesses can also obtain equity financing by finding investors for their operations. They may sell stock in the business to family members, friends, employees, or other investors. **Venture capitalists** are persons or organizations that agree to provide some funds for a new business in exchange for an ownership interest or stock. Venture capitalists hope to purchase the stock of a small business at a low price and then sell the stock for a profit after the business has grown successful. For example, Garage Technology Ventures, which took its name from the fact that so many high-tech start-ups began in garages, invests in emerging technology companies.[22] Individual venture capitalists are sometimes called *angels*. Increasingly, angels are banding together and pooling resources to reduce risk and increase the odds of finding the next Google or Amazon.com.[23] Although these forms of equity financing have helped many small businesses, they require that the small-business owner share the profits of the business—and sometimes control, as well—with the investors.

venture capitalists persons or organizations that agree to provide some funds for a new business in exchange for an ownership interest or stock

Debt Financing.   New businesses sometimes borrow over half of their financial resources. Banks are the main suppliers of external financing to small businesses. On the federal level, the Small Business Administration offers financial assistance to qualifying businesses. More detail on the SBA's loan programs can be found at the SBA Web site. They can also look to family and friends as sources for loans of long-term funds or other assets, such as a computer or an automobile, that are exchanged for an ownership interest in a business. In such cases, the business owner can usually

Solve the Dilemma
The Small-Business Challenge

In October 2001, Jack Gray and his best friend, Bruce McVay, decided to start their own small business. Jack had developed recipes for fat-free and low-fat cookies and muffins in an effort to satisfy his personal health needs. Bruce had extensive experience in managing food-service establishments. They knew that a start-up company needs a quality product, adequate funds, a written business plan, some outside financial support, and a good promotion program. Jack and Bruce felt they had all of this and more and were ready to embark on their new low-fat cookie/muffin store. Each had $35,000 to invest and with their homes and other resources they had borrowing power of an additional $125,000.

However, they still have many decisions to make, including what form or organization to use, how to market their product, and how to determine exactly what products to sell—whether just cookies and muffins or additional products.

Discussion Questions
1. Evaluate the idea of a low-fat cookie and muffin retail store.
2. Are there any concerns in connection with starting a small business that Jack and Bruce have not considered?
3. What advice would you give Jack and Bruce as they start up their business?

structure a favorable repayment schedule and sometimes negotiate an interest rate below current bank rates. If the business goes bad, however, the emotional losses for all concerned may greatly exceed the money involved. Anyone lending a friend or family member money for a venture should state the agreement clearly in writing.

The amount a bank or other institution is willing to loan depends on its assessment of the venture's likelihood of success and of the entrepreneur's ability to repay the loan. The bank will often require the entrepreneur to put up *collateral,* a financial interest in the property or fixtures of the business, to guarantee payment of the debt. Additionally, the small-business owner may have to offer some personal property as collateral, such as his or her home, in which case the loan is called a *mortgage.* If the small business fails to repay the loan, the lending institution may eventually claim and sell the collateral (or the owner's home, in the case of a mortgage) to recover its loss.

Banks and other financial institutions can also grant a small business a *line of credit*—an agreement by which a financial institution promises to lend a business a predetermined sum on demand. A line of credit permits an entrepreneur to take quick advantage of opportunities that require a bank loan. Small businesses may obtain funding from their suppliers in the form of a *trade credit*—that is, suppliers allow the business to take possession of the needed goods and services and pay for them at a later date or in installments. Occasionally, small businesses engage in *bartering*—trading their own products for the goods and services offered by other businesses. For example, an accountant may offer accounting services to an office supply firm in exchange for computer paper and diskettes.

Additionally, some community groups sponsor loan funds to encourage the development of particular types of businesses. State and local agencies may guarantee loans, especially to minority business people or for development in certain areas.

Approaches to Starting a Small Business
Starting from Scratch versus Buying an Existing Business. Although entrepreneurs often start new small businesses from scratch much the way we have discussed in this section, they may elect instead to buy an already existing business. This has

the advantage of providing a network of existing customers, suppliers, and distributors and reducing some of the guesswork inherent in starting a new business from scratch. However, an entrepreneur buying an existing business must also deal with whatever problems the business already has.

Franchising.   Many small-business owners find entry into the business world through franchising. A license to sell another's products or to use another's name in business, or both, is a **franchise.** The company that sells a franchise is the **franchiser.** Dunkin' Donuts, McDonald's, and Jiffy Lube are well-known franchisers with national visibility. The purchaser of a franchise is called a **franchisee.**

The franchisee acquires the rights to a name, logo, methods of operation, national advertising, products, and other elements associated with the franchiser's business in return for a financial commitment and the agreement to conduct business in accordance with the franchiser's standard of operations. Depending on the franchise, the initial fee to join a system varies. In addition, franchisees buy equipment, pay for training, and obtain a mortgage or lease. Table 6.6 shows the name, description, and cost for the top 10 franchises for 2004. The franchisee also pays the franchiser a monthly or annual fee based on a percentage of sales or profits. In return, the franchisee often receives building specifications and designs, site recommendations, management and accounting support, and perhaps most importantly, immediate name recognition. Visit the Web site of the International Franchise Association to learn more on this topic.

The practice of franchising first began in the United States when Singer used it to sell sewing machines in the 19th century. It soon became commonplace in the distribution of goods in the automobile, gasoline, soft drink, and hotel industries. The concept of franchising grew especially rapidly during the 1960s, when it expanded to more diverse industries. Table 6.7 shows the 10 fastest growing franchises and the top 10 new franchises.

franchise
a license to sell another's products or to use another's name in business, or both

franchiser
the company that sells a franchise

franchisee
the purchaser of a franchise

Rank	Franchise Name	Description	Start-Up Costs (thousands of dollars)
1.	Subway	Submarine sandwiches and salads	86–213
2.	Curves	Women's fitness centers	35.6–41.1
3.	The Quizno's Franchise Co.	Submarine sandwiches, soups, salads	208.4–243.8
4.	7-Eleven	Convenience stores	Varies
5.	Jackson Hewitt Tax Service	Tax preparation services	47.4–75.2
6.	The UPS Store	Postal/communication services	141.1–239.7
7.	McDonald's	Hamburgers	506–1.6 million
8.	Jani-King	Commercial cleaning	11.3–34.1
9.	Dunkin' Donuts	Donuts and baked goods	255.7–1.1 million
10.	Baskin Robbins USA Co.	Ice cream and yogurt	145.7–527.8

TABLE 6.6

Top Ten Franchises for 2004

Source: "*Entrepreneur*'s 25th Annual Franchise 500," *Entrepreneur* (n.d.), **www.entrepreneur.com/franchise500** (accessed May 4, 2004).

After an unsuccessful first attempt at franchising, Gary Heavin and his wife started "Curves," a chain of women-only fitness centers. The hook? Fitness, strength training, and weight loss guidance all in 30 minutes. After only eight years, Curves has more than 6,000 locations and was among the top 10 franchises of 2004.

There are both advantages and disadvantages to franchising for the entrepreneur. Franchising allows a franchisee the opportunity to set up a small business relatively quickly, and because of its association with an established brand, a franchise outlet often reaches the breakeven point faster than an independent business would. Franchisees often report the following advantages:

- Management training and support.
- Brand-name appeal.
- Standardized quality of goods and services.
- National advertising programs.
- Financial assistance.
- Proven products and business formats.
- Centralized buying power.
- Site selection and territorial protection.
- Greater chance for success.[24]

However, the franchisee must sacrifice some freedom to the franchiser. Some shortcomings experienced by some franchisees include:

- Franchise fees and profit sharing with the franchiser.
- Strict adherence to standardized operations.
- Restrictions on purchasing.
- Limited product line.
- Possible market saturation.
- Less freedom in business decisions.[25]

Strict uniformity is the rule rather than the exception. Entrepreneurs who want to be their own bosses are often frustrated with a franchise.

Top 10 Fastest-Growing Franchises	Top 10 New Franchises	**TABLE 6.7**
1. Subway	Fiducial Inc.	Fastest Growing and Hottest New Franchises
2. Curves	Comfort Keepers	
3. 7-Eleven	Results! Travel	
4. Kumon Math & Reading Centers	Dippin' Dots Franchising Inc.	
5. Jan-Pro Franchising International Inc.	Cruise Planners	
6. The Quizno's Franchise Co.	Super Wash	
7. Jani-King	Line-X Corp.	
8. Coverall Cleaning Concepts	Tutoring Club Inc.	
9. Liberty Tax Service	Plato's Closet	
10. Jazzercize Inc.	Ident-a-Kid Services of America	

Source: "Fastest Growing Franchises, 2004 Rankings, *Entrepreneur* (n.d.), www.entrepreneur.com/franzone/listings/fastestgrowing/(accessed May 4, 2004); "Top Ten New Franchises for 2004," *Entrepreneur* (n.d.), **www.entrepreneur.com/franzone/listings/topnew/** (accessed May 4, 2004).

Help for Small-Business Managers

Because of the crucial role that small business and entrepreneurs play in the U.S. economy, a number of organizations offer programs to improve the small-business owner's ability to compete. These include entrepreneurial training programs and programs sponsored by the Small Business Administration. Such programs provide small-business owners with invaluable assistance in managing their businesses, often at little or no cost to the owner.

Entrepreneurs can learn critical marketing, management, and finance skills in seminars and college courses. In addition, knowledge, experience, and judgment are necessary for success in a new business. While knowledge can be communicated and some experiences can be simulated in the classroom, good judgment must be developed by the entrepreneur. Local chambers of commerce and the U.S. Department of Commerce offer information and assistance helpful in operating a small business. National publications such as *Inc.* and *Entrepreneur* share statistics, advice, tips, and success/failure stories. Additionally, many urban areas—including Chicago; Jacksonville, Florida; Portland, Oregon; St. Louis, and Nashville—have weekly business journal/newspapers that provide stories on local businesses as well as on business techniques that a manager or small business can use.

The Small Business Administration offers many types of management assistance to small businesses, including counseling for firms in difficulty, consulting on improving operations, and training for owner/managers and their employees. Among its many programs, the SBA funds Small Business Development Centers (SBDCs). These are business clinics, usually located on college campuses, that provide counseling at no charge and training at only a nominal charge. SBDCs are often the SBA's principal means of providing direct management assistance.

The Service Corps of Retired Executives (SCORE) and the Active Corps of Executives (ACE) are volunteer agencies funded by the SBA to provide advice for owners of small firms. Both are staffed by experienced managers whose talents and experience the small firms could not ordinarily afford. SCORE has 10,500 volunteers at 389 U.S. locations and has served 4 million clients since 1964.[26] The SBA also has organized

Derek Su and Ki Shin thought they would use their technical degrees from the University of Texas to do things like design skyscrapers and manage computer systems. Although they did those things for a few years, the two friends gave up their high-tech careers to open a Ben & Jerry's Scoop Shop in their home town of Round Rock, Texas. Su had fallen in love with Ben & Jerry's ice cream on a trip to Las Vegas but was disappointed that he couldn't find a Scoop Shop when he returned home to Central Texas. When he visited Ben & Jerry's Web site, he learned that the socially conscious company wanted to open stores in Texas and was actively recruiting franchisees. Su and Shin thought their recent experience in owning and operating a small bubble tea shop and a coffeeshop made them good candidates for obtaining a Ben & Jerry's franchise. They also thought Ben & Jerry's reputation for social responsibility was a perfect fit for Central Texas, which includes Austin and the University of Texas as well as Round Rock.

After attending an open house in Houston to meet with executives from the company (now owned by the European conglomerate Unilever), Su and Shin flew to company headquarters in Burlington, Vermont, and embarked on Ben & Jerry's rigorous process for obtaining a franchise. The company, which was founded in 1978 by Ben Cohen and Jerry Greenfield and has more than 300 Scoop Shops worldwide, doesn't sell franchises to just anyone. Serious candidates must have good credit, have a minimum net worth of $300,000, pay a franchise fee ranging between $5,000 and $30,000, and provide funds to build their shop. According to Will Patten, Ben & Jerry's director of retail operations, the company looks in particular "for franchisees that buy into our values. . . . We take our franchises very seriously be-cause the franchisee carries the brand." In addition, franchisees pay royalties on sales to the company. Franchisees also undergo training at Ben & Jerry's Scoop "U" in Burlington to learn techniques and policies and gain experience in order to be successful.

The franchise agreement between Su and Shin and Ben & Jerry's grants them the right to open multiple stores in Central Texas. They opened the first in April 2004, the second later that year, and are scouting locations for a third shop. Ben & Jerry's Homemade also plans to open a "PartnerShop" in Austin as part of the company's program to help local nonprofit organizations. That store—one of 15 PartnerShops—will be operated by LifeWorks, an Austin nonprofit that helps at-risk and homeless youth. LifeWorks hopes that store will provide job training opportunities for its clients.

In addition to their prior food-service experience, Su believes their ying/yang personalities will help them succeed. He is the energetic, "big picture" side of the partnership, while Shin is analytical and keeps the partnership focused. With their passion for their product and a good match with their market, Su and Shin have many of the ingredients necessary to become successful franchisees.[27]

Discussion Questions

1. What benefits do Su and Shin gain from buying a well-known franchise instead of starting from scratch?
2. What advantages does Ben & Jerry's Homemade gain from franchising its popular Scoop Shops to people like Derek Su and Ki Shin? What disadvantages does the company face as a result of its franchise program?
3. How can Su and Shin improve their chances of success?

Small Business Institutes (SBIs) on almost 500 university and college campuses in the United States. Seniors, graduate students, and faculty at each SBI provide on-site management counseling.

Finally, the small-business owner can obtain advice from other small-business owners, suppliers, and even customers. A customer may approach a small business it frequents with a request for a new product, for example, or a supplier may offer suggestions for improving a manufacturing process. Networking—building relationships and sharing information with colleagues—is vital for any businessperson, whether you work for a huge corporation or run your own small business. Communicating with other business owners is a great way to find ideas for dealing with employees and government regulation, improving processes, or solving problems. New technology is making it easier to network. For example, some states are setting up computer bulletin boards for the use of their businesses to network and share ideas.

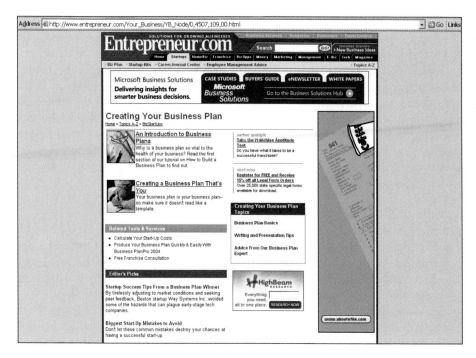

Budding entrepreneurs can find all kinds of helpful information at the entrepreneur.com Web site.

The Future for Small Business[28]

Although small businesses are crucial to the economy, they can be more vulnerable to turbulence and change in the marketplace than large businesses. Next, we take a brief look at the demographic, technological, and economic trends that will have the most impact on small business in the future.

Demographic Trends

America's baby boom started in 1946 and ended in 1964. The earliest boomers are already past 50, and in the next few years, millions more will pass that mark. The boomer generation numbers about 76 million, or 28 percent of U.S. citizens.[29] This segment of the population is probably the wealthiest, but most small businesses do not actively pursue it. Some exceptions, however, include Gold Violin, which sells designer canes and other products online and through a catalog, and LifeSpring, which delivers nutritional meals and snacks directly to the customer. Industries such as travel, financial planning, and health care will continue to grow as boomers age. Many experts think that the boomer demographic is the market of the future.

Another market with huge potential for small business is the echo boomers, also called millennials or Generation Y. Born between 1977 and 1994, there are about 32 million people in the United States in this age group. Typically, they shop frequently and spend lavishly ($187 billion annually) on clothing, entertainment, and food.[30] Companies that have the most success with this group are ones that cater to the teens' and young adults' lifestyles. Some successful small businesses aimed at this market include Alien Workshop (designs and distributes skateboards and apparel), Burton Snowboards (manufactures snowboards and accessories), and Femme Arsenal (develops and distributes cosmetics).

Yet another trend is the growing number of immigrants living in the United States, about 33.1 million. That means that about one in every 9 people living in the United States today was born in another country.[31] This vast number of people provides still another greatly untapped market for small businesses. Retailers who specialize in ethnic products, and service providers who offer bi- or multilingual employees, can find vast potential in this market. Envios, for example, markets money-wiring services to a predominantly Latino immigrant population through 88 stores and independent sales representatives in New York City.[32]

Technological and Economic Trends

Advances in technology have opened up many new markets to small businesses. Although thousands of small dot-coms have failed, experts predict that Internet usage will continue to increase, and one of the hot areas will be the Internet infrastructure area that enables companies to improve communications with employees, suppliers, and customers.

Technological advances and an increase in service exports have created new opportunities for small companies to expand their operations abroad. Changes in communications and technology can allow small companies to customize their services quickly for international customers. Also, free trade agreements and trade alliances are helping to create an environment in which small businesses have fewer regulatory and legal barriers.

In recent years, economic turbulence has provided both opportunities and threats for small businesses. As large information technology companies such as Cisco, Oracle, and Sun Microsystems had to recover from an economic slowdown and an oversupply of Internet infrastructure products, some smaller firms found new niche markets. Smaller companies can react quickly to change and can stay close to their customers. While many well-funded dot-coms were failing, many small businesses were learning how to use the Internet to promote their businesses and sell products online. For example, many arts and crafts dealers and makers of specialty products found they could sell their wares on existing Web sites, such as eBay. Service providers related to tourism, real estate, and construction also found they could reach customers through their own or existing Web sites.

Deregulation of the energy market and interest in alternative fuels and in fuel conservation have spawned many small businesses. Earth First Technologies, Inc., produces clean-burning fuel from contaminated water or sewage. Southwest Windpower, Inc., manufactures and markets small wind turbines for producing electric power for homes, sailboats, and telecommunications. Solar Attic, Inc., has developed a process to recover heat from home attics to use in heating hot water or swimming pools. As entrepreneurs begin to realize that worldwide energy markets are valued in the hundreds of billions of dollars, the number of innovative companies entering this market will increase. In addition, many small businesses have the desire and employee commitment to purchase such environmentally friendly products. New Belgium Brewing Company received the U.S. Environmental Protection Agency and Department of Energy Award for leadership in conservation for making a 10-year commitment to purchase wind energy. The company's employees unanimously agreed to cover the increased costs of wind-generated electricity from the employee profit-sharing program.

The future for small business remains promising. The opportunities to apply creativity and entrepreneurship to serve customers are unlimited. While large organizations such as Wal-Mart, which has more than one million employees, typically must adapt to change slowly, a small business can adapt to customer and community needs and changing trends immediately. This flexibility provides small businesses with a definite advantage over large companies.

Making Big Businesses Act "Small"

The continuing success and competitiveness of small businesses through rapidly changing conditions in the business world have led many large corporations to take a closer look at what makes their smaller rivals tick. More and more firms are emulating small businesses in an effort to improve their own bottom line. Beginning in the 1980s and continuing through the present, the buzzword in business has been to *downsize,* to reduce management layers, corporate staff, and work tasks in order to make the firm more flexible, resourceful, and innovative like a smaller business. Many well-known U.S. companies, including IBM, Gillette, Apple Computer, General Electric, Xerox, and 3M, have downsized to improve their competitiveness, as have German, British, and Japanese firms. Other firms have sought to make their businesses "smaller" by making their operating units function more like independent small businesses, each responsible for its profits, losses, and resources. Of course, some large corporations, such as Southwest Airlines, have acted like small businesses from their inception, with great success.

Trying to capitalize on small-business success in introducing innovative new products, more and more companies are attempting to instill a spirit of entrepreneurship into even the largest firms. In major corporations, **intrapreneurs,** like entrepreneurs, take responsibility for, or "champion," the development of innovations of any kind *within* the larger organization.[33] Often, they use company resources and time to develop a new product for the company.

intrapreneurs
individuals in large firms who take responsibility for the development of innovations within the organizations

Explore Your Career Options
Look to Small Business

Business success is an outgrowth of knowledge and experience. All kinds of life experiences—as a family member, friend, student, employee, or consumer, or in sports or art—are valuable. "The things you know and love and see opportunities in—you ought to pick your business based on that," says Bill Gates, founder of Microsoft.

Because of financial constraints and the lack of experience, most college students cannot start a business immediately after graduation. However, the challenge in starting and running a successful business is to demonstrate good judgment. Someone with a B.S. degree, a $50,000 inheritance, and poor judgment will not succeed as an entrepreneur. On the other hand, a person with $2,000 in savings may end up wealthy because of good business judgment. Steve Jobs and Steve Wozniak started Apple Computer in a garage with only a few thousand dollars. Another high-tech entrepreneur, Michael Dell, started Dell Computers in his University of Texas dorm room. So great was the success of both Apple and Dell that IBM and other large corporations rushed to create new products to compete with them.

It is estimated that 80 percent of new jobs for college graduates will be found in small business. Therefore, knowing about successful small businesses may be the first step in assessing job opportunities. Along with this chapter, reading magazines such as *Inc.* or *Entrepreneur* can provide a good start in learning more about small business opportunities.[34]

Review Your Understanding

Define entrepreneurship and small business.

An entrepreneur is a person who creates a business or product and manages his or her resources and takes risks to gain a profit; entrepreneurship is the process of creating and managing a business to achieve desired objectives. A small business is one that is not dominant in its competitive area and does not employ more than 500 people.

Investigate the importance of small business in the U.S. economy and why certain fields attract small business.

Small businesses are vital to the American economy because they provide products, jobs, innovation, and opportunities. Retailing, wholesaling, services, manufacturing, and high technology attract small businesses because these industries are relatively easy to enter, require relatively low initial financing, and may experience less heavy competition.

Specify the advantages of small-business ownership.

Small-business ownership offers some personal advantages, including independence, freedom of choice, and the option of working at home. Business advantages include flexibility, the ability to focus on a few key customers, and the chance to develop a reputation for quality and service.

Summarize the disadvantages of small-business ownership and analyze why many small businesses fail.

Small businesses have many disadvantages for their owners such as expense, physical and psychological stress, and a high failure rate. Small businesses fail for many reasons: undercapitalization, management inexperience or incompetence, neglect, disproportionate burdens imposed by government regulation, and vulnerability to competition from larger companies.

Describe how you go about starting a small business and what resources are needed.

First, you must have an idea for developing a small business. Next, you need to devise a business plan to guide planning and development of the business. Then you must decide what form of business ownership to use: sole proprietorship, partnership, or corporation. Small-business owners are expected to provide some of the funds required to start their businesses, but funds also can be obtained from friends and family, financial institutions, other businesses in the form of trade credit, investors (venture capitalists), state and local organizations, and the Small Business Administration. In addition to loans, the Small Business Administration and other organizations offer counseling, consulting, and training services. Finally, you must decide whether to start a new business from scratch, buy an existing one, or buy a franchise operation.

Evaluate the demographic, technological, and economic trends that are impacting the future of small business.

Changing demographic trends that represent areas of opportunity for small businesses include more elderly people as baby boomers age, a large group in the 11 to 28 age range known as echo boomers, millennials, or Generation Y, and an increasing number of immigrants to the United States. Technological advances and an increase in service exports have created new opportunities for small companies to expand their operations abroad, while trade agreements and alliances have created an environment in which small business has fewer regulatory and legal barriers. Economic turbulence presents both opportunities and threats to the survival of small businesses.

Explain why many large businesses are trying to "think small."

More large companies are copying small businesses in an effort to make their firms more flexible, resourceful, and innovative, and generally to improve their bottom line. This effort often involves downsizing (reducing management layers, laying off employees, and reducing work tasks) and intrapreneurship, where an employee takes responsibility for (champions) developing innovations of any kind within the larger organization.

Assess two entrepreneurs' plans for starting a small business.

Based on the facts given in the "Solve the Dilemma" box on page 176 and the material presented in this chapter, you should be able to assess the feasibility and potential success of Gray and McVay's idea for starting a small business.

Revisit the World of Business

1. Why do you think King's Saddlery has been so successful as a small business?

2. Is Don King an entrepreneur? What was his vision 50 years ago?

3. How can King's Saddlery continue to be successful as a small business?

Learn the Terms

Check Your Progress

1. Why are small businesses so important to the U.S. economy?

2. Which fields tend to attract entrepreneurs the most? Why?

3. What are the advantages of starting a small business? The disadvantages?

4. What are the principal reasons for the high failure rate among small businesses?

5. What decisions must an entrepreneur make when starting a small business?

6. What types of financing do small entrepreneurs typically use? What are some of the pros and cons of each?

7. List the types of management and financial assistance that the Small Business Administration offers.

8. Describe the franchising relationship.

9. What demographic, technological, and economic trends are influencing the future of small business?

10. Why do large corporations want to become more like small businesses?

Get Involved

1. Interview a local small-business owner. Why did he or she start the business? What factors have led to the business's success? What problems has the owner experienced? What advice would he or she offer a potential entrepreneur?

2. Using business journals, find an example of a company that is trying to emulate the factors that make small businesses flexible and more responsive.

Describe and evaluate the company's activities. Have they been successful? Why or why not?

3. Using the business plan outline in Appendix B, create a business plan for a business idea that you have. (A man named Fred Smith once did a similar project for a business class at Yale. His paper became the basis for the business he later founded: Federal Express!)

Build Your Skills

CREATIVITY

Background:
The entrepreneurial success stories in this chapter are about people who used their creative abilities to develop innovative products or ways of doing something that became the basis of a new business. Of course, being creative is not just for entrepreneurs or inventors; creativity is an important tool to help you find the optimal solutions to the problems you face on a daily basis. Employees rely heavily on their creativity skills to help them solve daily workplace problems.

According to brain experts, the right-brain hemisphere is the source of creative thinking; and the creative part of the brain can "atrophy" from lack of use. Let's see how much "exercise" you're giving your right-brain hemisphere.

Task:

1. Take the following self-test to check your Creativity Quotient.[35]

2. Write the appropriate number in the box next to each statement according to whether the statement describes your behavior always (3), sometimes (2), once in a while (1), or never (0).

	Always 3	Sometimes 2	Once in a While 1	Never 0
1. I am a curious person who is interested in other people's opinions.				
2. I look for opportunities to solve problems.				
3. I respond to changes in my life creatively by using them to redefine my goals and revising plans to reach them.				
4. I am willing to develop and experiment with ideas of my own.				
5. I rely on my hunches and insights.				
6. I can reduce complex decisions to a few simple questions by seeing the "big picture."				
7. I am good at promoting and gathering support for my ideas.				
8. I think further ahead than most people I associate with by thinking long term and sharing my vision with others.				
9. I dig out research and information to support my ideas.				
10. I am supportive of the creative ideas from my peers and subordinates and welcome "better ideas" from others.				
11. I read books and magazine articles to stay on the "cutting edge" in my areas of interest. I am fascinated by the future.				
12. I believe I am creative and have faith in my good ideas.				
Subtotal for each column				
Grand Total				

3. Check your score using the following scale:

   30–36   High creativity. You are giving your right-brain hemisphere a regular workout.

   20–29   Average creativity. You could use your creativity capacity more regularly to ensure against "creativity atrophy."

   10–19   Low creativity. You could benefit by reviewing the questions you answered "never" in the above assessment and selecting one or two of the behaviors that you could start practicing.

   0–9   Undiscovered creativity. You have yet to uncover your creative potential.

e-Xtreme Surfing

- **Small Business Administration**
  www.sba.gov

  Provides statistics, resources, and information links about small business.

- *Entrepreneur*
  www.entrepreneur.com

  Offers online access to content of *Entrepreneur* magazine, including information on starting and growing a business.

- **International Franchise Association**   Supplies information about franchise ownership.
  www.franchise.org

- **SCORE**   Provides free and confidential advice to small business owners.
  www.score.org

See for Yourself Videocase

DALE GRAY AND COMMUNICATION SERVICES, INC.

Dale Gray is president, CEO, and founder of Communication Services, Inc., one of the top 20 companies in the telecommunications industry. Gray is a highly successful entrepreneur and provides one of the best examples of what a person has to do to become a successful businessperson. Dale Gray saw the advantages of establishing and running his own business and now is enjoying all of the fruits of success. Many people in the entrepreneurship movement have seen incredible opportunities in the emerging areas of technology, especially telecommunications. The process of creating and managing a business to achieve objectives takes more than just a business plan, it takes the ability to implement the plan and motivate others to excel.

Dale Gray focused on engineering and business management during the development of his career. He has worked in 10 states for more than 60 government agencies. He provides optimal cost-effective solutions for his clients in the telecommunications industry. By hiring talented people and giving them the tools to succeed, his firm has provided timely solutions with a major focus on repeat business. He employs the best-trained professional surveyors, engineers, and construction personnel who are licensed across the United States. He also maintains partnerships with firms who operate in regions where he does not have construction ability, which strengthens his ability to serve customers nationwide. It is necessary to have staff and partners that are committed to projects from start to finish, with the skills necessary to avoid problems and delays.

His major business has been communication towers. The idea was to provide communications infrastructure from the ground up for cellular, private radio, and other wireless customers. Gray used his experienced professionals to understand every client, every project, and examine things from every angle. The development of communication towers is a complex process involving architectural and engineering licenses, as well as the ability to work with different government entities in gaining access to installing towers in the appropriate location. Gray's specialty is the integration of wireline, fiber, microwave, and wireless systems into an integrated communications network. Some of Dale Gray's clients include Cellular One, Cricket, Lucent Technologies, Motorola, T-Mobile, and the U.S. Border Patrol. Gray also focuses on emergency communication systems. Therefore, the communication systems he develops assist commercial carriers, as well as state and local fire, police, and emergency service agencies. Based on his work in emergency communications networks, he works with governments at all levels. Besides working on projects throughout the United States, he has worked in foreign markets including Russia and Costa Rica.

As you might expect, Gray has a Top Secret-74 security clearance. He is one of four key personnel defined in a contract with the Department of Homeland Security. In other words, Gray is known not only as a successful businessperson, but as someone who is important to national security. He achieved this position of importance through the design and construction of more than 1,000 telecommunications sites, microwave systems, and more than 3,500 miles of fiber optic systems nationwide.

Today, Dale Gray has taken his entrepreneurial skills and built a large successful firm. He has injected the spirit of entrepreneurship and has championed an innovative environment within Communication Services, Inc. When large companies accomplish this level of creativity and responsiveness to customer's needs (acting like an entrepreneur), it is called intrapreneurship. There is no doubt that Dale Gray is one of the best examples of an individual who has a goal and is able to gain the support of an entire organization through his vision and leadership.[36]

Discussion Questions

1. Why do you think that Dale Gray has been so successful as an entrepreneur?

2. While many telecommunications firms have failed over the past few years, explain what might be a key reason why Communication Services, Inc. has continued to succeed.

3. Dale Gray has combined knowledge and experience to stay focused on a growing segment of the telecommunication industry. What are some of the challenges that he might face in the future?

Remember to check out our Online Learning Center at www.mhhe.com/ferrell5e.

Appendix B

The Business Plan

A key element of business success is a *business plan*, a written statement of the rationale for the enterprise and a step-by-step explanation of how it will achieve its goals. A business plan is a blueprint, or written document, that structures all of a firm's activities, including the implementation and control of those activities. It should explain the purpose of the company, evaluate its competition, estimate income and expenses, and indicate a strategy for acquiring sufficient funds to keep the firm going. It should also be formally prepared and contain a detailed statement of how the firm will carry out its strategy. However, a business plan should act as a reference guide, not a shackle that limits the firm's flexibility and decision making.

Developing a business plan is important for both brand new and existing businesses. For a start-up firm, the business plan provides a street map to help it fulfill the entrepreneur's vision. For existing businesses, it is an excellent way for a company to renew its commitment to existing goals and evaluate its merits. Regardless of whether the business plan is for a new or already-existing firm, it should include an executive summary, situation analysis, SWOT (strengths, weaknesses, opportunities, and threats) analysis, business resources, business strategy, financial projections and budgets, and controls and evaluation (Table B.1).

Executive Summary

The executive summary is simply a brief synopsis of the overall business plan. It generally consists of an introduction, highlights of the major aspects of the plan, and implementation considerations. It does not provide detailed information. Rather, the summary should be short and interesting, and it should give the reader an idea of what is contained in the business plan. It is essentially an overview of the plan so that readers can quickly identify the key issues or concerns related to their role in the planning process.

TABLE B.1 The Components of a Business Plan

I. Executive Summary
II. Situation Analysis
A. Competitive forces
B. Economic forces
C. Legal and regulatory forces
D. Technological forces
E. Sociocultural forces
III. SWOT Analysis
A. Strengths
B. Weaknesses
C. Opportunities
D. Threats
IV. Business Resources
A. Financial
B. Human
C. Experience and expertise
V. Business Strategy
A. Objectives
B. Key strategy for using capabilities and resources
VI. Financial Projections and Budgets
VII. Controls and Evaluation
A. Performance standards and financial controls
B. Monitoring procedures
C. Performance analysis

Situation Analysis

The situation analysis examines the difference between the business's current performance and past-stated objectives. In a brand-new firm, it assesses where the entrepreneur is now in his or her development. The situation analysis may also summarize how the current business situation came to be, using data obtained from both the firm's external and internal environment. Depending on the situation, details on the composition of the target market, current marketing objectives and strategies, business trends, and sales and profit history may also be included. The situation analysis enables the entrepreneur either to evaluate the business's current mission or, in instances where a clear vision is nonexistent, to facilitate the articulation of its mission. This situation analysis should include a careful evaluation of the firm's current objectives and performance, as well as specify how performance is to be measured.

A good situation analysis provides input for the next step in the business plan, the SWOT analysis. It is the situation analysis that identifies the issues, concerns, or variables analyzed in the SWOT analysis.

SWOT Analysis

The SWOT (strengths, weaknesses, opportunities, and threats) analysis section of the business plan identifies and articulates all the organization's competitive advantages/strengths as well as its weaknesses in order to develop strategies for capitalizing on the strengths and minimizing the weaknesses. Obviously, if the business is to be successful, its strengths should outweigh its weaknesses. A SWOT analysis also includes a clear assessment of existing and future opportunities and discusses ways of exploiting them. Finally, it examines the threats facing the firm and ranks them in order of their impact on the business.

In analyzing strengths and weaknesses, opportunities and threats, the business plan must address both internal and external elements. Internally, the firm must look at the strengths and weaknesses of its major functional areas—management, operations, finance, and marketing; it must also look at the opportunities and threats related to specific elements in the external environment of the business—the economic, political, legal and regulatory, competitive, technological, and social and cultural factors. The business plan should also include predictions about the future directions of those forces and their possible impact on the implementation of the business plan. Because of the dynamic nature of these factors, managers should periodically review and modify this section of the plan to allow for changes.

The SWOT analysis has gained widespread acceptance because it provides a simple framework for evaluating a company's strategic position. When analyzing the strengths and weaknesses in terms of specific target markets, both quantitative and qualitative variables

identified in the situation analysis should be considered. The firm must focus on those strengths and opportunities that will yield competitive advantage as well as those threats and weaknesses that will erode it. Thus, it is a good idea for the planner to rank the factors under each category according to their impact on the execution of the businesses strategy.

Strengths and Weaknesses

Strengths and weaknesses exist inside the firm or in key relationships between the firm and its suppliers, resellers, and customers. Strengths include any competitive advantage or other distinctive competencies (things that the firm does better than any others) that a company can employ in the marketplace. Strengths exist relative to competitors, such as cheaper access to capital, good relations with vendors and customers, a unique product, or an advantageous location. Thus, strengths specified in a firm's business plan will be specific to that firm and not shared by its competitors. If all of a business's competitors have low production costs, then low cost is not a strength for that business, unless its costs are even lower. A company's distinctive competency can play a key role in positioning it and its products in the minds of customers and so forms a unique strength.

Weaknesses are constraints that limit certain options in the business strategy. A poor image of the firm's products in the minds of consumers is an example of a weakness. It is also true that some weaknesses are less important than others. For example, having higher costs than competitors may not be an issue if cost is not the basis for competition in the industry. The planner must therefore determine which weaknesses have the greatest effect on the firm's competitive position and thus require immediate attention.

In developing a business strategy, a business needs to both capitalize on its skills and talents and ensure that its strategies emphasize these. In order to identify strengths and weaknesses, it is important to have data about current market/product positions, including past performance and expected performance in the next planning period, which should be expressed in the situation analysis.

Opportunities and Threats

The second part of the SWOT analysis addresses external opportunities and threats present in the firm's operating environment. These opportunities and threats exist largely independent of the firm and its operations.

An opportunity is a favorable set of conditions, which limits barriers or provide rewards, that the firm can exploit with a high probability of success. Examples of opportunities include an unmet product need (assuming the firm has the capability to meet that need); a new, lower-cost source of a vital raw material; new technology; or new legislation that opens up a product market or restricts competitors' access to a market. This section of the business plan should place the most attractive opportunities having the greatest potential for success at the head of the list, while those that are less attractive or have a smaller potential for success should receive less emphasis.

Threats relate to barriers or conditions that may prevent the organization from achieving its objectives, ultimately leading to a loss of competitive advantage. Examples include the direct actions of competitors (such as the introduction of a new product or product innovation), adverse governmental legislation, loss of access to cheap capital or other resources, or an economic downturn. This phase of the business plan orders priorities for action in light of the strengths and weaknesses of the firm in dealing with a particular set of external circumstances.

The analysis of the threats and opportunities cannot be completed without the previously mentioned assessment of legal, political, regulatory, technological, competitive, social, and economic factors that will affect the firm's internal strengths and weaknesses. It is also necessary to make predictions about the future. While environmental factors may threaten a firm's ability to achieve its objectives, they may also provide opportunities.

Business Resources

A company's human and financial resources, as well as its experiences and expertise, are major considerations in developing a business plan. The business plan should therefore both outline the human, financial, and physical resources available for accomplishing goals and describe resource constraints that may affect implementation of the plan. This section also describes any distinctive competencies that may give the firm an edge, and it takes into account strengths and weaknesses that may influence the firm's ability to achieve implementation.

Financial resources include all funds available to carry out the plan. It is necessary to detail what funds the firm has at hand and what can be accessed through other sources, such as loans, lines of credit, or additional equity arrangements (such as a venture partner or a public stock offering). Human resources refer to the people that the business has ready to commit to the execution of the plan as well as the quality of that labor force. Physical resources include such things as property, facilities, and equipment required to execute the strategy. This category includes the raw materials available as well as retail outlets and office space. These financial, human, and physical resources comprise the tangible aspects of the firm's resources.

Experience and expertise are intangible aspects, but they are just as crucial to success as the tangible ones. Experience refers to any competence the firm may have developed over time as a result of carrying out activities related to future ones envisioned in the plan. For instance, the firm may have experience marketing home electronics, which may be transferable to marketing computers for home use. Or, the firm may just be further along on the experience curve than its competitors. Expertise is related to experience and includes any proprietary knowledge that the firm may possess, such as patents. Other areas of expertise that represent vital resources include superior knowledge of the market and industry, management wisdom, and competence or scientific knowledge embodied in research and development personnel.

Business Strategy

This section of the business plan spells out the business's objectives and its strategy for achieving them.

Objectives

After taking an inventory of the business's resources and conducting a SWOT analysis, the planner should develop concrete, specific objectives. For example, the plan might specify the firm's objective to become the leader, in terms of market share or sales, in a particular industry, segment, or niche. Or the objective might be to achieve a high return on investment and thus focus on profitability. While a company can have multiple objectives, each should be stated explicitly, in quantifiable terms if possible. For instance, an objective of being the leader in sales should state the level of sales desired and in what time period. A profitability objective should state what return on investment is targeted and within what time period. These objectives will therefore serve as goals to be achieved by the firm and as yardsticks against which to measure its progress. Because most firms have a number of objectives, they should be ranked in order of importance.

Strategy

Once the objectives have been expressed, the business plan should spell out the strategy (or strategies) the firm will use to achieve those objectives. The strategies should be clearly stated in order to guide development of the specific programs and activities that will be used to execute them. For example, if the firm's primary objective is to accumulate market share, it may adopt the strategy of being the lowest-cost producer. Therefore, the implications of being the lowest-cost producer should be specifically stated in the plan. If the major objective is to achieve high returns on investment, the chosen strategy may be a focus strategy, combining a low-cost orientation with some focus on a particular market niche. This strategy would then have to identify the targeted niche, the desired cost levels, and so on, in order to allow formulation of programs and their implementation.

Financial Projections and Budgets

Financial projections and budgets delineate costs and estimates of sales and revenues. This section outlines the returns expected from implementing the business plan. It should estimate the costs of implementing the plan and weigh those costs against the expected revenues. It should also include a budget to allocate resources in order to achieve business objectives. These financial projections and budgets should be sufficiently detailed to identify the source and projected use of funds, broken down according to each activity in the plan. For instance, if employees need addi-

tional training, what will it cost and where will the funds come from? How much will be used in advertising? In reality, budgetary considerations play a key role in the identification of alternative strategies, as well as in the development of plans for those strategies that are identified as most promising.

The financial realities of the organization must be monitored at all times. For example, proposing to expand into new geographic areas or to alter products without specifying the extent and source of the financial resources needed to do so is a waste of time, energy, and opportunity. Even if the funds are available, the expansion must be a "good value" and provide an acceptable return on investment to be part of the final plan.

Controls and Evaluation

This section of the business plan details how the results of the plan will be calculated. It should specify what measures of performance will be used to assess the current achievements and identify internal performance data and external-environmental relationships for diagnosis and evaluation. Next, a schedule should be developed for comparing and monitoring the results achieved with the objectives set forth in the business plan. Finally, the plan may offer guidelines outlining who is responsible for monitoring the program and taking remedial action.

In order for controls to be implemented, the firm must utilize information from the SWOT analysis, look ahead, and determine what will affect the implementation of the business plan during the upcoming planning period. This should create the database for monitoring and evaluating performance and taking corrective action.

I. **EXECUTIVE SUMMARY**

The executive summary is a synopsis of the overall business plan. It is best written after the entire business plan has been completed.

_____
_____
_____
_____
_____

II. **SITUATION ANALYSIS**

The situation analysis examines the difference between the business's current performance and past-stated objectives.

A. Competitive Forces

Who are our major competitors as of today? What are their strengths and weaknesses?

_____
_____
_____

Who are likely to be our major competitors in the future?

_____
_____
_____

(Repeat analysis to examine economic, political, legal and regulatory, technological, and sociocultural forces.)

III. SWOT ANALYSIS

The SWOT analysis identifies and describes the organization's strengths and weaknesses and the opportunities and threats it faces in order to develop strategies for capitalizing on the strengths and opportunities and minimizing the weaknesses and threats.

A. Strengths

Strength 1: _____

How does this strength affect the operations of the company?

_____
_____
_____

How does this strength assist the company in meeting its objectives?

_____
_____
_____

(Repeat this process for all of the strengths that can be identified.)

B. Weaknesses

Weakness 1: _____

How does this weakness affect the operations of the company?

_____
_____
_____

How does this weakness reduce the company's ability to meet its objectives?

_____
_____
_____

(Repeat this process for all of the weaknesses that can be identified.)

C. Opportunities

Opportunity 1: _____

How is this opportunity related to current or future company operations?

_____
_____
_____

What actions must the company take in order to take advantage of this opportunity?

_____
_____
_____

(Repeat this process for all of the opportunities that can be identified.)

D. Threats

Threat 1: _____

How is this threat related to current or future company operations?

_____

_____

What actions must the company take to reduce or eliminate this threat?

_____

_____

_____

(Repeat this process for all of the threats that can be identified.)

IV. BUSINESS RESOURCES
This section outlines the human, financial, and physical resources available for accomplishing goals and describes resource constraints that may affect implementation.

A. Financial Resources
What financial resources are available for accomplishing company goals?

_____

_____

_____

B. Human Resources
Does the company have the personnel needed to implement the goals?

_____

_____

_____

C. Experience and Expertise
Do employees have the experience and expertise needed to successfully achieve stated goals? Will employees require additional training? How will this training be funded?

_____

_____

_____

V. BUSINESS STRATEGY
This section spells out the business's objectives and its strategy for achieving them.

A. Objectives
Objective 1: _____

What is the specific and measurable outcome and timeframe for completing this objective?

_____

_____

_____

How does this objective take advantage of a strength or opportunity?

_____

_____

_____

(Repeat this process for all of the objectives specified.)

B. Strategy for Using Capabilities and Resources
How can the company's strengths be matched to its opportunities to create capabilities?

_____

_____

_____

How can the company convert its weaknesses into strengths?

_____

_____

_____

How can the company convert its threats into opportunities?

_____
_____
_____
_____

VI. FINANCIAL PROJECTIONS AND BUDGETS

Financial projections and budgets delineate costs and estimates of sales and revenues, so this section outlines the returns expected through implementation of the plan and weighs the costs incurred against the expected revenues.

Attach financial projections to this worksheet and develop alternative scenarios.

_____
_____
_____
_____
_____
_____
_____

VII. CONTROLS AND EVALUATION

This section details how the outcomes of the plan will be monitored and measured.

A. Performance Standards and Financial Controls

Activity 1/Budget: _____

Performance Standard: _____

Possible Corrective Action: _____

(Repeat this process for all of the performance measures.)

B. Monitoring Procedures

How will all of the activities be monitored in order to ensure success?

_____
_____
_____

What will be the schedule of the monitoring of activities (i.e., will the monitoring be done weekly, monthly, quarterly, etc.)?

_____
_____
_____

C. Performance Analysis

Currently, how is the company performing in terms of sales volume, market share, and profitability?

_____
_____
_____

How does the company's current performance compare to other firms in the industry?

_____
_____
_____

If the company's performance is declining, are its objectives inconsistent with changes in the external environment?

_____
_____
_____

Is the performance of the industry as a whole improving?

_____
_____

Part 2 Role-Play Exercise*

Human Response, Inc.

Human Response, Inc., (HR) was started in 1996 by Alex Buchfink and his college roommate, Dale Marco. Based in Palo Alto, California, HR specializes in the research of human emotions and associated physiological patterns. The company's mission was to determine whether emotions occurred first, then created physiological responses in the body or whether physiological reactions happened, then were translated into emotions by the brain. Several devices were designed to monitor feelings and record the body's internal reactions to those emotions. Gloves sensed changes through the hands. Jackets absorbed emotions through the skin. Expressive glasses were used by participants to visualize their feelings. Common machines were used to chart the association between feelings, such as anger, fear, and happiness, and physiological responses, such as heart rate, blood pressure, and skin conductivity. The information was stored in databases and compiled with Oracle software.

After understanding the relationship between emotions and other physiological patterns, Alex and Dale proceeded to research how to incorporate those feelings into computer chips. The chips already could absorb and remember the information, so the next step was for the machines to synthesize emotions. When the chip received a familiar signal, it drew the appropriate response from its memory and reacted accordingly. After two years of additional testing, Alex and Dale were able to program the chips to synthesize responses. Imagine a young man who is late for a meeting because he had an argument with his wife before leaving for work. The chip would recognize the man's feelings of tension and anger. By combining situations with natural reactions, the chips create unique responses.

HR not only studies these technologies but has incorporated them into marketable products. One such application is the insertion of the chips into key chains. The Detex key chain senses pulses in the holder's hand and if it detects fear and anxiety (for instance, fear of being mugged), the key chain triggers an alarm that hopefully would defuse the situation. Another product, Auto Wake, would be installed in automobile steering wheels to detect sleepiness in drivers and sound an alarm.

HR is ready to market the products, but suffers from undercapitalization. Its initial funding came from a seed venture capitalist who now owns 20 percent of the partnership. Alex and Dale estimate that money will be gone in three months. They must decide if and how to restructure HR or raise the capital needed to keep the business going and introduce their innovative products. The following options are being considered: approaching additional venture capitalists, incorporating as either a public or private company; forming a limited liability company; and borrowing from banks.

---

*This background statement provides information for a role-play exercise designed to help you understand the real world challenge of decision making in business and to integrate the concepts presented previously in this text. If your instructor chooses to utilize this activity, the class will be divided into teams with each team member assigned to a particular role in the fictitious organization. Additional information on each role and instructions for the completion of the exercise will be distributed to individual team members.

Part 3

Managing for Quality and Competitiveness

Chapter 7

The Nature of Management

OBJECTIVES

After reading this chapter, you will be able to:

- Define management and explain its role in the achievement of organizational objectives.
- Describe the major functions of management.
- Distinguish among three levels of management and the concerns of managers at each level.
- Specify the skills managers need in order to be successful.
- Summarize the systematic approach to decision making used by many business managers.
- Recommend a new strategy to revive a struggling business.

Managing the State of California

Managers try to reach objectives by using resources effectively and efficiently in a changing environment regardless of whether they work in a *Fortune* 500 company or manage a state government. After former California governor Gray Davis was recalled by voters for his alleged support of anti-business legislation, action-movie star Arnold Schwarzenegger was elected to replace him as governor. At the time, California faced a financial crisis with an expected budget deficit of at least $8 billion in 2004. The one-time Mr. Universe and star of movies such as *Terminator* and *Robocop* campaigned on a platform of "bringing jobs back to California" and pledged to open up the books, do an audit, and find wasted resources. To succeed in his new role as manager of the world's fifth largest economy, Schwarzenegger will also have to cut utility rates, gain the support of business, and transform the state's economy into a productive business environment.

Schwarzenegger will have to use his star power and charisma to do whatever it requires to slash billions from the state budget. An equally critical task will be restoring the confidence of the business community that California can once again offer an environment in which corporations can thrive. This task may prove daunting given that the Milken Institute has estimated the cost of doing business in California is 28 percent higher than the national average; only Massachusetts and New York have higher costs. With the state's sky-high energy costs, it will be especially challenging to attract new businesses to California. Schwarzenegger needs to encourage new plant construction to get the utility business out of long-term energy contracts in order to reduce utility prices.

During his gubernatorial campaign, Schwarzenegger crafted the image that he was a self-styled outsider who could help the state get out from under

continued

its real-world problems, much like his muscle-bound movie characters always seem to escape disaster. He will have to use some of that muscle to deal with an out-of-control workers' compensation system, which requires California companies to pay $5.23 for each $100 of payroll, the highest rate in the nation. This is 60 percent higher than in states such as Texas and Nevada that regularly lure California companies to their respective states. In addition, Schwarzenegger will not have to deal with just issues and problems, but develop a strategic plan by which the state can encourage economic development and meet the demands of various stakeholders.[1]

Introduction

For any organization—small or large, for profit or nonprofit—to achieve its objectives, it must have equipment and raw materials to turn into products to market, employees to make and sell the products, and financial resources to purchase additional goods and services, pay employees, and generally operate the business. To accomplish this, it must also have one or more managers to plan, organize, staff, direct, and control the work that goes on.

This chapter introduces the field of management. It examines and surveys the various functions, levels, and areas of management in business. The skills that managers need for success and the steps that lead to effective decision making are also discussed.

The Importance of Management

management
a process designed to achieve an organization's objectives by using its resources effectively and efficiently in a changing environment

managers
those individuals in organizations who make decisions about the use of resources and who are concerned with planning, organizing, staffing, directing, and controlling the organization's activities to reach its objectives

Management is a process designed to achieve an organization's objectives by using its resources effectively and efficiently in a changing environment. *Effectively* means having the intended result; *efficiently* means accomplishing the objectives with a minimum of resources. **Managers** make decisions about the use of the organization's resources and are concerned with planning, organizing, staffing, directing, and controlling the organization's activities so as to reach its objectives. Meg Whitman, president and CEO of eBay, has helped the company become one of the most successful on the Internet.[2] Management is universal. It takes place not only in businesses of all sizes, but also in government, the military, labor unions, hospitals, schools, and religious groups—any organization requiring the coordination of resources.

Every organization, in the pursuit of its objectives, must acquire resources (people, raw materials and equipment, money, and information) and coordinate their use to turn out a final good or service. The manager of a local movie theater, for example, must make decisions about seating, projectors, sound equipment, screens, concession stands, and ticket booths. All this equipment must be in proper working condition. The manager must also make decisions about materials. There must be films to show, popcorn and candy to sell, and so on. To transform the physical resources into final products, the manager must also have human resources—employees to sell the tickets, run the concession stand, run the projector, and maintain the facilities. Finally, the manager needs adequate financial resources to pay for the essential activities; the primary source of funding is the money generated from sales of tickets and snacks. All these resources and activities must be coordinated and controlled if the theater is to earn a profit. Organizations must have adequate resources of all types, and managers must carefully coordinate the use of these resources if they are to achieve the organization's objectives.

Management Functions

To coordinate the use of resources so that the business can develop, make, and sell products, managers engage in a series of activities: planning, organizing, staffing, directing, and controlling (Figure 7.1). Although we describe each separately, these five functions are interrelated, and managers may perform two or more of them at the same time.

Planning

Planning, the process of determining the organization's objectives and deciding how to accomplish them, is the first function of management. Planning is a crucial activity, for it designs the map that lays the groundwork for the other functions. It involves forecasting events and determining the best course of action from a set of options or choices. The plan itself specifies what should be done, by whom, where, when, and how. When McDonald's CEO, Jim Cantalupo, died suddenly of a heart attack in 2004, his successor, Charlie Bell, decided to continue executing a three-year plan Cantalupo had developed to revitalize the fast-food giant. Cantalupo's plans called for sprucing up existing restaurants, extending hours, and boosting service instead of maintaining the company's pace of opening new restaurants. Implementing these plans helped McDonald's boost earnings by 56 percent, with 2.3 million more customers a day.[3] All businesses—from the smallest restaurant to the largest multinational corporation—need to develop plans for achieving success. But before an organization can plan a course of action, it must first determine what it wants to achieve.

Objectives.   Objectives, the ends or results desired by the organization, derive from the organization's **mission,** which describes its fundamental purpose and basic philosophy. A photo lab, for example, might say that its mission is to provide customers with memories. To carry out its mission, the photo lab sets specific objectives relating to its mission, such as reducing development defects to less than 2 percent, introducing a selection of photo albums and frames for customers' use in displaying

planning
the process of determining the organization's objectives and deciding how to accomplish them; the first function of management

mission
the statement of an organization's fundamental purpose and basic philosophy

FIGURE 7.1

The Functions of Management

Managers				
Planning activities to achieve the organization's objectives	**Organizing** resources and activities to achieve the organization's objectives	**Staffing** the organization with qualified people	**Directing** employees' activities toward achievement of objectives	**Controlling** the organization's activities to keep it on course

their photos, providing customers' proofs or negatives over the Internet, providing technical assistance, and so on. Herbal tea marketer Celestial Seasonings says that its mission is "To create and sell healthful, naturally oriented products that nurture people's bodies and uplift their souls."[4]

A business's objectives may be elaborate or simple. Common objectives relate to profit, competitive advantage, efficiency, and growth. Organizations with profit as a goal want to have money and assets left over after paying off business expenses. Objectives regarding competitive advantage are generally stated in terms of percentage of sales increase and market share, with the goal of increasing those figures. The mission of Gillette, for example, "is to build Total Brand Value by innovating to deliver consumer value and customer leadership faster, better and more completely than our competition."[5] Efficiency objectives involve making the best use of the organization's resources. The photo lab's objective of holding defects to less than 2 percent is an example of an efficiency objective. Growth objectives relate to an organization's ability to adapt and to get new products to the marketplace in a timely fashion. The goal at Mercedes-Benz is to decrease the average age of its customers from the mid-50s to the mid-40s. To accomplish this, Mercedes has introduced several models that sell for less than $40,000. Other organizational objectives include service, ethical, and community goals. Starbucks, for example, set an objective of having its employees and customers volunteer 50,000 hours to community organizations. The company exceeded the goal by 60,000 hours.[6] Objectives provide direction for all managerial decisions; additionally, they establish criteria by which performance can be evaluated.

Plans.   There are three general types of plans for meeting objectives—strategic, tactical, and operational. A firm's highest managers develop its **strategic plans,** which establish the long-range objectives and overall strategy or course of action by which the firm fulfills its mission. Strategic plans generally cover periods ranging from 2 to 10 years or even longer. They include plans to add products, purchase companies, sell unprofitable segments of the business, issue stock, and move into international markets. Faced with stiff competition, rising costs, and slowing sales, many companies are closing U.S. plants and moving production to factories abroad. For example, Converse Inc. (sneaker maker), Lionel LLC (producer of model trains), and Zebco (fishing reel manufacturer) all stopped U.S. production in favor of Asian factories.[7] Strategic plans must take into account the organization's capabilities and resources, the changing business environment, and organizational objectives. Plans should be market-driven, matching customers' desire for value with operational capabilities, processes, and human resources.[8]

Tactical plans are short-range plans designed to implement the activities and objectives specified in the strategic plan. These plans, which usually cover a period of one year or less, help keep the organization on the course established in the strategic plan. Because tactical plans permit the organization to react to changes in the environment while continuing to focus on the company's overall strategy, management must periodically review and update them. Declining performance or failure to meet objectives set out in tactical plans may be one reason for revising them. The Walt Disney Company, for example, decided to streamline the organization of its ABC television network subsidiary in response to significant losses of the network's target audience of adults aged 18 to 49.[9]

A retailing organization with a five-year strategic plan to invest $5 billion in 500 new retail stores may develop five tactical plans (each covering one year) specifying

strategic plans
those plans that establish the long-range objectives and overall strategy or course of action by which a firm fulfills its mission

tactical plans
short-range plans designed to implement the activities and objectives specified in the strategic plan

how much to spend to set up each new store, where to locate each new store, and when to open each new store. Tactical plans are designed to execute the overall strategic plan. Because of their short-term nature, they are easier to adjust or abandon if changes in the environment or the company's performance so warrant.

Operational plans are very short term and specify what actions specific individuals, work groups, or departments need to accomplish in order to achieve the tactical plan and ultimately the strategic plan. They may apply to just one month, week, or even day. For example, a work group may be assigned a weekly production quota in order to ensure there are sufficient products available to elevate market share (tactical goal) and ultimately help the firm be number one in its product category (strategic goal). Returning to our retail store example, operational plans may specify the schedule for opening one new store, hiring new employees, obtaining merchandise, training new employees, and opening for actual business.

Another element in planning is the idea of **crisis management** or **contingency planning,** which deals with potential disasters such as product tampering, oil spills, fire, earthquake, computer virus, or even a reputation crisis due to unethical or illegal conduct by one or more employees. Many mutual fund companies, for example, saw their reputations and business suffer as a result of a scandal in the industry when some companies allowed a few large clients special privileges in violation of federal regulations. At Putnam Investments, for example, customers withdrew $61 billion from the company's mutual funds and the company faced numerous lawsuits and federal and state charges of misconduct.[10] Businesses that have contingency plans tend to respond more effectively when problems occur than do businesses who lack such planning.

Many companies, including Ashland Oil, H. J. Heinz, and Johnson & Johnson, have crisis management teams to deal specifically with problems, permitting other managers to continue to focus on their regular duties. Some companies even hold regular disaster drills to ensure that their employees know how to respond when a crisis does occur. Crisis management plans generally cover maintaining business operations throughout a crisis and communicating with the public, employees, and officials about the nature of and the company's response to the problem. Communication is especially important to minimize panic and damaging rumors; it also demonstrates that the company is aware of the problem and plans to respond. The September 11, 2001, terrorist attack on the United States disrupted many business activities. The airlines were especially damaged when many Americans were reluctant to travel. Incidents such as this highlight the importance of tactical planning for crises and the need to respond publicly and quickly when a disaster occurs.

Companies that housed operations in and around the World Trade Center, many of them key players in the financial markets, had to rely on contingency plans after 9/11. Those that could, reassured clients and the world that operations would continue. Many took out patriotic, inspirational ads such as this one from Standard & Poor's.

operational plans
very short-term plans that specify what actions individuals, work groups, or departments need to accomplish in order to achieve the tactical plan and ultimately the strategic plan

crisis management or contingency planning
an element in planning that deals with potential disasters such as product tampering, oil spills, fire, earthquake, computer virus, or airplane crash

Organizing

Rarely are individuals in an organization able to achieve common goals without some form of structure. **Organizing** is the structuring of resources and activities to accomplish objectives in an efficient and effective manner. Managers organize by reviewing plans and determining what activities are necessary to implement them; then, they divide the work into small units and assign it to specific individuals, groups, or departments. As companies reorganize for greater efficiency, more often than not, they are organizing work into teams to handle core processes such as new product development instead of organizing around traditional departments such as marketing and production.

Organizing is important for several reasons. It helps create synergy, whereby the effect of a whole system equals more than that of its parts. It also establishes lines of authority, improves communication, helps avoid duplication of resources, and can improve competitiveness by speeding up decision making. In an effort to reduce costs and improve efficiency, media giant Reuters Group PLC reorganized its product-based divisions into four key customer segments. The new business units are part of the company's strategy to get closer to clients using Internet technologies. The units focus on clients involved in investment banking and brokerage; general banking; asset management; and business and media.[11] Because organizing is so important, we'll take a closer look at it in Chapter 8.

Staffing

Once managers have determined what work is to be done and how it is to be organized, they must ensure that the organization has enough employees with appropriate skills to do the work. Hiring people to carry out the work of the organization is known as **staffing.** Beyond recruiting people for positions within the firm, managers must determine what skills are needed for specific jobs, how to motivate and train employees to do their assigned jobs, how much to pay employees, what benefits to provide, and how to prepare employees for higher-level jobs in the firm at a later date. These elements of staffing will be explored in detail in Chapters 10 and 11.

Another aspect of staffing is **downsizing,** the elimination of significant numbers of employees from an organization, which has been a pervasive and much-talked-about trend. Whether it is called downsizing, rightsizing, trimming the fat, or the new reality in business, the implications of downsizing have been dramatic. Bank of America, for example, cut 12,500 jobs—about 7 percent of its workforce—after it acquired FleetBoston Bank,[12] while Sun Microsystems eliminated 3,300 jobs—about 9 percent of its workforce—as a cost-cutting move.[13] Many firms downsize by outsourcing production, sales, and technical positions to companies in other countries with lower labor costs. Downsizing has helped numerous firms reduce costs quickly and become more profitable (or become profitable after lengthy losses) in a short period of time.

Downsizing and outsourcing, however, have painful consequences. Obviously, the biggest casualty is those who lose their jobs, along with their incomes, insurance, and pensions. Some find new jobs quickly; others do not. Another victim is the morale of the employees at downsized firms who get to keep their jobs. The employees left behind in a downsizing often feel more insecure, angry, and sad, and their productivity may decline as a result, the opposite of the effect sought. Managers can expect that 70 to 80 percent of those surviving a downsize will take a "wait-and-see" attitude and need to be led. Ten to 15 percent will be openly hostile or try to sabotage change in order to return to the way things were before. The remaining 10 to 15 percent will be the leaders who will try proactively to help make the situation work.[14] A survey of workers who remained after a downsizing found that many felt their jobs demanded more time and energy.[15]

After a downsizing situation, an effective manager will promote optimism and positive thinking and minimize criticism and fault-finding. Management should also build teamwork and encourage positive group discussions. Honest communication is important during a time of change and will lead to trust. Truthfulness about what has happened and also about future expectations is essential.

Directing

Once the organization has been staffed, management must direct the employees. **Directing** is motivating and leading employees to achieve organizational objectives. All managers are involved in directing, but it is especially important for lower-level managers who interact daily with the employees operating the organization. For example, an assembly-line supervisor for Frito-Lay must ensure that her workers know how to use their equipment properly and have the resources needed to carry out their jobs, and she must motivate her workers to achieve their expected output of packaged snacks.

directing
motivating and leading employees to achieve organizational objectives

Managers may motivate employees by providing incentives—such as the promise of a raise or promotion—for them to do a good job. But most workers want more than money from their jobs: They need to know that their employer values their ideas and input. Smart managers, therefore, ask workers to contribute ideas for reducing costs, making equipment more efficient, improving customer service, or even developing new products. This participation makes workers feel important, and the company benefits. For example, the Super Service Index (SSI) program at the Kmart Corporation recognizes and rewards employee associates for providing excellent customer service. SSI is a customer feedback program that assigns each store a score that is determined by the number of customers who rate their shopping experience as "excellent." Nearly all Kmart associates participate in the incentive plan. The quarterly bonus is a percentage of associates' earnings and is determined by how much their store has increased its SSI score or maintained an already high score. Associates in 1,290 stores were awarded a total of $18 million in one recent quarter.[16] Recognition and appreciation are often the best motivators for employees. Employees who understand more about their impact on the financial success of the company may be motivated to work harder for that success, and managers who understand the needs and desires of

Eastman Kodak Co., notorious for slow decision making, saw the light thanks to Hewlett Packard's success with all things digital. It was a proverbial "kick in the pants" for a company that held a veritable monopoly on all things photo for a century, and ironic since Kodak created the first digital camera in 1975. Kodak COO Antonio M. Perez plans to concentrate on the digital imaging business, reduce investment in traditional film, and get new products to market by uncovering new uses for nearly 20,000 of Kodak's patents. (Business Week, 5/10/04)

workers can motivate their employees to work harder and more productively. The motivation of employees is discussed in detail in Chapter 10.

Controlling

Planning, organizing, staffing, and directing are all important to the success of an organization, whether its objective is earning a profit or something else. But what happens when a firm fails to reach its goals despite a strong planning effort? **Controlling** is the process of evaluating and correcting activities to keep the organization on course. Control involves five activities: (1) measuring performance, (2) comparing present performance with standards or objectives, (3) identifying deviations from the standards, (4) investigating the causes of deviations, and (5) taking corrective action when necessary.

Controlling and planning are closely linked. Planning establishes goals and standards for performance. By monitoring performance and comparing it with standards, managers can determine whether performance is on target. When performance is substandard, management must determine why and take appropriate actions to get the firm back on course. In short, the control function helps managers assess the success of their plans. When plans have not been successful, the control process facilitates revision of the plans. At Royal Dutch/Shell, for example, gasoline and related petroleum sales are on target, but company executives recognized that Shell is replacing just 60 percent of the oil supplies used to provide that gasoline. To remain competitive with rivals such as ExxonMobil, Shell must boost its replacement ratio to 130 percent over the next 5 years by finding and developing new supplies of petroleum or risk running dry in about 10 years.[17]

controlling
the process of evaluating and correcting activities to keep the organization on course

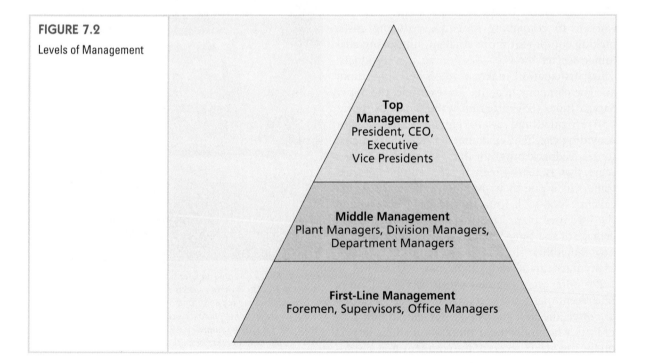

FIGURE 7.2
Levels of Management

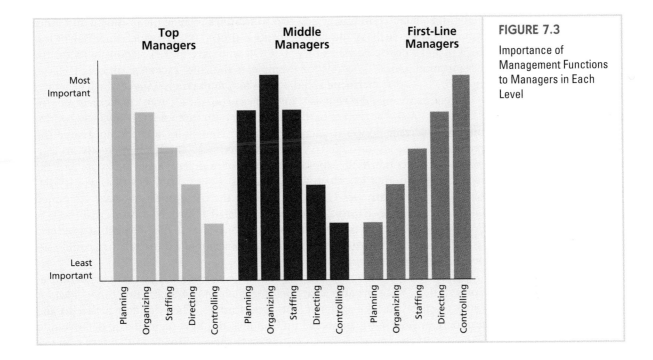

FIGURE 7.3

Importance of
Management Functions
to Managers in Each
Level

The control process also helps managers deal with problems arising outside the firm. For example, if a firm is the subject of negative publicity, management should use the control process to determine why and to guide the firm's response.

Types of Management

All managers—whether the sole proprietor of a small video store or the hundreds of managers of a large company such as Paramount Pictures—perform the five functions just discussed. In the case of the video store, the owner handles all the functions, but in a large company with more than one manager, responsibilities must be divided and delegated. This division of responsibility is generally achieved by establishing levels of management and areas of specialization—finance, marketing, and so on.

Levels of Management

As we have hinted, many organizations have multiple levels of management—top management, middle management, and first-line, or supervisory management. These levels form a pyramid, as shown in Figure 7.2. As the pyramid shape implies, there are generally more middle managers than top managers, and still more first-line managers. Very small organizations may have only one manager (typically, the owner), who assumes the responsibilities of all three levels. Large businesses have many managers at each level to coordinate the use of the organization's resources. Managers at all three levels perform all five management functions, but the amount of time they spend on each function varies, as we shall see (Figure 7.3).

Top Management.　In businesses, **top managers** include the president and other top executives, such as the chief executive officer (CEO), chief financial officer (CFO), and chief operations officer (COO), who have overall responsibility for the organization. Oprah Winfrey, for example, is the chief executive officer of Harpo Inc., which owns *O* magazine and the popular *Oprah Winfrey Show,* which generates $300 million in annual revenues.[18] In public corporations, even chief executive officers have a boss—the firm's board of directors. With technological advances continuing and privacy concerns increasing, some companies are adding a new top management position—chief privacy officer (CPO). There are currently an estimated 2,000 CPOs in U.S. corporations, and that number is expected to rise over the next few years in response to growing concerns about privacy as well as new legislation such as the Sarbanes-Oxley Act. Among the companies that have appointed CPOs are American Express, Citigroup, Hewlett-Packard, Microsoft, and the U.S. Postal Service.[19] In government, top management refers to the president, a governor, or a mayor or city manager; in education, a chancellor of a university or a county superintendent of education.

Top-level managers spend most of their time planning. They make the organization's strategic decisions, decisions that focus on an overall scheme or key idea for using resources to take advantage of opportunities. They decide whether to add products, acquire companies, sell unprofitable business segments, and move into foreign markets. Top managers also represent their company to the public and to government regulators.

Given the importance and range of top management's decisions, top managers generally have many years of varied experience and command top salaries. In addition to salaries, top managers' compensation packages typically include bonuses, long-term incentive awards, stock, and stock options. Michael Dell, for example, earned a $2.5 million bonus in 2003 for helping increase Dell's income by 70.3 percent. The Walt Disney Company's Michael Eisner took home $7.3 million, including a $6.3 million bonus.[21] The average CEO compensation package was $8.1 million in 2003.[22] Table 7.1 lists the 10 highest paid CEOs.

Did You Know?　Women represent only 15.7 percent of corporate officers and just 5.2 percent of all top earners.[20]

TABLE 7.1

The Ten Highest Paid CEOs

Rank	CEO	Company	Total Compensation (in millions of dollars, including salary, bonus, and incentives)
1.	Reuben Mark	Colgate-Palmolive	141.1
2.	Steven P. Jobs	Apple Computer	74.8
3.	George David	United Technologies	70.5
4.	Henry R. Silverman	Cendant	54.4
5.	Sanford I. Weill	Citigroup	54.1
6.	Richard S. Fuld, Jr.	Lehman Bros.	52.9
7.	Lew Frankfort	Coach	45.8
8.	Lawrence J. Ellison	Oracle	40.5
9.	Howard Solomon	Forest Laboratories	36.1
10.	Richard M. Kovacevich	Wells Fargo	35.9

Source: Louis Lavelle, with Jessi Hempel and Diane Brady, "Executive Pay," *Business Week,* April 19, 2004, pp. 106–20.

Some people question the pay disparity between top executives and U.S. workers. According to *Business Week,* the average CEO made 42 times the average blue-collar worker's pay in 1980, 85 times in 1990, and 531 times in 2000.[23] A *Business Week*/Harris poll found that 73 percent of respondents felt that pay for top executives in large U.S. companies was too high.[24] Some CEOs, however, limit the level of compensation that they and other top managers can receive to minimize the disparity between the levels of employees and to show social responsibility with respect to their compensation.

Workforce diversity is an important issue in today's corporations. Effective managers at enlightened corporations have found that diversity is good for workers and for the bottom line. Putting together different kinds of people to solve problems often results in better solutions. Betsy Holden, CEO of Kraft Foods, said, "When we look at the composition of teams within our company, we have found that those with a variety of perspectives are simply the most creative."[25] Managers from companies devoted to workforce diversity devised six rules that make diversity work (see Table 7.2). Diversity is explored in greater detail in Chapter 11.

Rule	Action
1. Search for the best	Invest time and money in "affirmative recruiting."
2. Help newcomers fit in	Emphasize cooperation and teamwork.
3. Educate everyone	Address employees' fears of change and discomfort with people from diverse backgrounds; encourage minority employees to express their views; encourage others to listen.
4. Keep score	Hold managers accountable for diversity goals and progress.
5. Sweat the details	Pay attention to the smaller differences in diverse employees and address concerns.
6. See the future	Invest in potential employees of the future (e.g., develop programs that target minority groups in middle and high schools).

TABLE 7.2

Six Rules That Make Diversity Work

Source: Annie Finnigan, "Different Strokes," *Working Woman,* April 2001, pp. 42–48.

Middle Management.   Rather than making strategic decisions about the whole organization, **middle managers** are responsible for tactical planning that will implement the general guidelines established by top management. Thus, their responsibility is more narrowly focused than that of top managers. Middle managers are involved in the specific operations of the organization and spend more time organizing than other managers. In business, plant managers, division managers, and department managers make up middle management. The product manager for laundry detergent at a consumer products manufacturer, the department chairperson in a university, and the head of a state public health department are all middle managers. The ranks of middle managers have been shrinking as more and more companies downsize to be more productive.

middle managers
those members of an organization responsible for the tactical planning that implements the general guidelines established by top management

First-Line Management.   Most people get their first managerial experience as **first-line managers,** those who supervise workers and the daily operations of the organization. They are responsible for implementing the plans established by middle management and directing workers' daily performance on the job. They spend most of their time directing and controlling. Common titles for first-line managers are foreman, supervisor, and office manager.

Areas of Management

At each level, there are managers who specialize in the basic functional areas of business: finance, production and operations, human resources (personnel), marketing, and administration.

Financial Management.   **Financial managers** focus on obtaining the money needed for the successful operation of the organization and using that money in accordance with organizational goals. Among the responsibilities of financial managers are projecting income and expenses over a specified period, determining short- and long-term financing needs and finding sources of financing to fill those needs, identifying and selecting appropriate ways to invest extra funds, monitoring the flow of financial resources, and protecting the financial resources of the organization. A financial manager at Subway, for example, may be asked to analyze the costs and revenues of a new sandwich product to determine its contribution to Subway's profitability. All organizations must have adequate financial resources to acquire the physical and human resources that are necessary to create goods and services. Consequently, financial resource management is of the utmost importance.

Production and Operations Management.   **Production and operations managers** develop and administer the activities involved in transforming resources into goods, services, and ideas ready for the marketplace. Production and operations managers are typically involved in planning and designing production facilities, purchasing raw materials and supplies, managing inventory, scheduling processes to meet demand, and ensuring that products meet quality standards. Because no business can exist without the production of goods and services, production and operations managers are vital to an organization's success. At Pfizer Global Research, for example, Robert Swanson works as an associate director of logistics and supply chain management, which makes him responsible for transporting and caring for lab equipment, protective gear, chemicals, and maintenance and office supplies and shipping scientific documents, materials, and other equipment to other Pfizer facilities around the world.[26]

Human Resources Management.   **Human resources managers** handle the staffing function and deal with employees in a formalized manner. Once known as personnel managers, they determine an organization's human resource needs; recruit and hire new employees; develop and administer employee benefits, training, and performance appraisal programs; and deal with government regulations concerning employment practices. For example, some companies recognize that their employees' health affects their health care costs. Therefore, more progressive companies provide health care facilities and outside health club memberships, encourage proper nutrition, and discourage smoking in an effort to improve employee health and lower the costs of providing health care benefits. For example, Chrysler's

Top managers use online resources such as ceoexpress.com to gather economic, competitive, and other business information.

human resources managers may develop educational programs to improve employees' health and thereby decrease Chrysler's cost of providing benefits.

Marketing Management.   **Marketing managers** are responsible for planning, pricing, and promoting products and making them available to customers through distribution. The marketing manager who oversees Sony televisions, for example, must make decisions regarding a new television's size, features, name, price, and packaging, as well as plan what type of stores to distribute the television through and the advertising campaign that will introduce the new television to consumers. Within the realm of marketing, there are several areas of specialization: product development and management, pricing, promotion, and distribution. Specific jobs are found in areas such as marketing research, advertising, personal selling, retailing, telemarketing, and Internet marketing.

marketing managers those who are responsible for planning, pricing, and promoting products and making them available to customers

Information Technology (IT) Management.   **Information technology (IT) managers** are responsible for implementing, maintaining, and controlling technology applications in business, such as computer networks. At Google, the online search engine, IT managers oversee an estimated 100,000 computers in at least 12 facilities worldwide, making Google one of the largest distributed networks in the world. The company has more Ph.D.'s per square foot of office space than any other U.S. firm.[27] One major task in IT management is securing computer systems from unauthorized users while making the system easy to use for employees, suppliers, and others who have legitimate reason to access the system. Another crucial task is protecting the systems' data, even during a disaster such as a fire. IT managers are also responsible for teaching and helping employees use technology resources efficiently through training and support. At many companies, some aspects of IT management are outsourced to third-party firms that can perform this function expertly and efficiently.

information technology (IT) managers those who are responsible for implementing, maintaining, and controlling technology applications in business, such as computer networks

Administrative Management.   **Administrative managers** are not specialists; rather they manage an entire business or a major segment of a business, such as the Cadillac Division of General Motors. Such managers coordinate the activities of specialized managers, which in the GM Cadillac Division would include marketing managers, production managers, and financial managers. Because of the broad nature of their responsibilities, administrative managers are often called general managers. However, this does not mean that administrative managers lack expertise in any particular area. Many top executives have risen through the ranks of financial management, production and operations management, or marketing management; but most top managers are actually administrative managers, employing skills in all areas of management.

Skills Needed by Managers

Managers are typically evaluated as to how effective and efficient they are. Managing effectively and efficiently requires certain skills—leadership, technical expertise, conceptual skills, analytical skills, and human relations skills. Table 7.3 describes some of the roles managers may fulfill.

TABLE 7.3   Managerial Roles

Type of Role	Specific Role	Examples of Role Activities
Decisional	Entrepreneur	Commit organizational resources to develop innovative goods and services; decide to expand internationally to obtain new customers for the organization's products
	Disturbance handler	Move quickly to take corrective action to deal with unexpected problems facing the organization from the external environment, such as a crisis like an oil spill, or from the internal environment, such as producing faulty goods or services
	Resource allocator	Allocate organizational resources among different functions and departments of the organization; set budgets and salaries of middle and first-level managers
	Negotiator	Work with suppliers, distributors, and labor unions to reach agreements about the quality and price of input, technical, and human resources; work with other organizations to establish agreements to pool resources to work on joint projects
Informational	Monitor	Evaluate the performance of managers in different functions and take corrective action to improve their performance; watch for changes occurring in the external and internal environment that may affect the organization in the future
	Disseminator	Inform employees about changes taking place in the external and internal environment that will affect them and the organization; communicate to employees the organization's vision and purpose
	Spokesperson	Launch a national advertising campaign to promote new goods and services; give a speech to inform the local community about the organization's future intentions
Interpersonal	Figurehead	Outline future organizational goals to employees at company meetings; open a new corporate headquarters building; state the organization's ethical guidelines and the principles of behavior employees are to follow in their dealings with customers and suppliers
	Leader	Provide an example for employees to follow; give direct commands and orders to subordinates; make decisions concerning the use of human and technical resources; mobilize employee support for specific organizational goals
	Liaison	Coordinate the work of managers in different departments; establish alliances between different organizations to share resources to produce new goods and services

Source: Gareth R. Jones and Jennifer M. George, *Essentials of Contemporary Management* (Boston: McGraw-Hill/Irwin, 2004), p. 14.

Leadership

Leadership is the ability to influence employees to work toward organizational goals. Strong leaders manage and pay attention to the culture of their organizations and the needs of their customers. Table 7.4 offers some tips for successful leadership while Table 7.5 lists the world's 10 most admired companies and their CEOs. The list is compiled for *Fortune* magazine by executives and analysts who grade companies according to nine attributes, including quality of management.

Managers often can be classified into three types based on their leadership style. *Autocratic leaders* make all the decisions and then tell employees what must be done and how to do it. They generally use their authority and economic rewards to get employees to comply with their directions. *Democratic leaders* involve their employees in decisions. The manager presents a situation and encourages his or her subordinates to express opinions and contribute ideas. The manager then considers the employees' points of view and makes the decision. *Free-rein leaders* let their employees work without much interference. The manager sets performance standards and allows employees to find their own ways to meet them. For this style to be effective, employees must know what the standards are, and they must be motivated to attain the standards. The free-rein style of leadership can be a powerful motivator because it demonstrates a great deal of trust and confidence in the employee.

leadership
the ability to influence employees to work toward organizational goals

---

- Build effective and responsive interpersonal relationships.
- Communicate effectively—in person, print, e-mail, etc.
- Build the team and enable employees to collaborate effectively.
- Understand the financial aspects of the business.
- Know how to create an environment in which people experience positive morale and recognition.
- Lead by example.
- Help people grow and develop.

Source: Susan M. Heathfield, "Seven Tips About Successful Management," What You Need to Know About.com (n.d.), **http://humanresources.about.com/cs/managementissues/qt/mgmtsuccess.htm** (accessed April 9, 2004).

TABLE 7.4

Seven Tips for Successful Leadership

Company	Chief Executive Officer
Wal-Mart	H. Lee Scott
Berkshire Hathaway	Warren Buffet
Southwest Airlines	Colleen Barrett
General Electric	Jeffrey Immelt
Dell	Kevin Rollins
Microsoft	Steven A. Balmer
Johnson & Johnson	William C. Weldon
Starbucks	Orin Smith
FedEx	Fred Smith
IBM	Sam Palmisano

Source: Adapted from "World's Most Admired Companies," *Fortune*, March 8, 2004, pp. 80,81.

TABLE 7.5

World's Most Admired Companies and Their CEOs

General Motors (GM) is a global leader in the automobile and truck market, which was expected to exceed 60 million units worldwide in 2004. To carve out a larger piece of this market, GM requires excellence in management, productivity, and skilled employees. In 2003, the company earned $3.8 billion on record revenues of $185.5 billion by effectively leveraging its resources even in a challenging economic and competitive environment around the world. Executives believe that the talent of GM's people to develop new products will help the automaker maintain competitiveness and create financial success. They believe that in the increasingly competitive global marketplace, the winners will be those companies that best combine the efficiencies of global scale with a focus on local markets.

Over the next three years, GM is implementing a plan to redesign 90 percent of its passenger-car lineup with the hope of competing more on distinctive products and less on price. This approach requires developing and bringing to market more "gotta have it" niche models like the stylishly retro Chevy SSR pickup, the reintroduced Pontiac GTO, and Cadillac XLR. With the XLR, the Cadillac subsidiary of GM hopes to reclaim the symbolic title of "standard of the world," and become the ultimate statement of luxury.

General Motors has developed an enviable position in China—the world's fastest-growing automobile market—where its sales increased 46 percent last year. Buick has become a market leader in China with its increasingly sought distinguished vehicles. The company is even exporting some North American Cadillac models to China. It sold 386,000 vehicles in China in 2003, making China GM's fourth-largest market.

GM claims to have a commitment to good corporate citizenship, particularly to its employees around the world. For example, the company fully funded its U.S. salaried and hourly employees pension plans in 2003 at a time when these plans were nearly $18 billion underfunded. Enhancing health care funding for employees is a major concern, and in the last year health care expenses added about $1,400 to the cost of each car and truck the company produced.

The road ahead for General Motors is still challenging, with many twists, turns, and surprises. With competition including Toyota and Ford, as well as a host of others, positioned to challenge GM in most markets, leadership is necessary to create new strategies and provide effective management.[28]

Discussion Questions
1. What challenges do GM's top managers face in maintaining the company's share of automobile and truck sales?
2. What skills should GM's top managers develop to ensure they can face these challenges?
3. What kinds of plans are represented by GM's redesign of 90 percent of its passenger-car lineup?

The effectiveness of the autocratic, democratic, and free-rein styles depends on several factors. One consideration is the type of employees. An autocratic style of leadership is generally needed to stimulate unskilled, unmotivated employees; highly skilled, trained, and motivated employees may respond better to democratic or free-rein leaders. On the other hand, employees who have been involved in decision making generally require less supervision than those not similarly involved. Other considerations are the manager's abilities and the situation itself. When a situation requires quick decisions, an autocratic style of leadership may be best because the manager does not have to consider input from a lot of people. If a special task force must be set up to solve a quality-control problem, a normally democratic manager may give free rein to the task force. Many managers, however, are unable to use more than one style of leadership. Some are unable to allow their subordinates to participate in decision making, let alone make any decisions. Thus, what leadership style is "best" depends on specific circumstances, and effective managers strive to adapt their leadership style as circumstances warrant. Many organizations offer programs to develop leadership. Anne Mulcahy, chief operating officer and president of Xerox, has placed leadership development at the top of her agenda. She utilizes team meetings and retreats with up-and-coming managers to plan strategy and identify talent. Xerox managers have access to online tools designed to help them help themselves. According to Mulcahy, "Leaders must walk the talk, be consistent in the decisions

Managers effectively organize and lead as with this boys' baseball team.

they make, see clearly where they are and where they want to go, and most importantly, empower people to lead themselves."[29]

Technical Expertise

Managers need **technical expertise**, the specialized knowledge and training needed to perform jobs that are related to their area of management. Accounting managers need to be able to perform accounting jobs, and production managers need to be able to perform production jobs. Although a production manager may not actually perform a job, he or she needs technical expertise to train employees, answer questions, provide guidance, and solve problems. Technical skills are most needed by first-line managers and least critical to top-level managers.

Today, most organizations rely on computers to perform routine data processing, simplify complex calculations, organize and maintain vast amounts of information to communicate, and help managers make sound decisions. For this reason, most managers have found computer expertise to be an essential skill.

Conceptual Skills

Conceptual skills, the ability to think in abstract terms, and to see how parts fit together to form the whole, are needed by all managers, but particularly top-level managers. Top management must be able to evaluate continually where the company will be in the future. Conceptual skills also involve the ability to think creatively. Recent scientific research has revealed that creative thinking, which is behind the development of many innovative products and ideas, including fiber optics and compact disks, can be learned. As a result, IBM, AT&T, GE, Hewlett-Packard, Intel, and other top U.S. firms hire creative consultants to teach their managers how to think creatively.

Analytical Skills

Analytical skills refer to the ability to identify relevant issues and recognize their importance, understand the relationships between them, and perceive the underlying causes of a situation. When managers have identified critical factors and causes,

technical expertise
the specialized knowledge and training needed to perform jobs that are related to particular areas of management

conceptual skills
the ability to think in abstract terms and to see how parts fit together to form the whole

analytical skills
the ability to identify relevant issues, recognize their importance, understand the relationships between them, and perceive the underlying causes of a situation

Southwest Airlines has been able to successfully differentiate itself from its competitors by way of no-frills, low-price fares, and a highly diversified workforce. But Southwest also is known for its human relations skills. Humorous flight crews often crack jokes and pull gags on passengers.

they can take appropriate action. All managers need to think logically, but this skill is probably most important to the success of top-level managers.

Human Relations Skills

People skills, or **human relations skills**, are the ability to deal with people, both inside and outside the organization. Those who can relate to others, communicate well with others, understand the needs of others, and show a true appreciation for others are generally more successful than managers who lack human relations skills. People skills are especially important in hospitals, airline companies, banks, and other organizations that provide services. For example, at Southwest Airlines, every new employee attends "You, Southwest and Success," a day-long class designed to teach employees about the airline and its reputation for impeccable customer service. All employees in management positions at Southwest take mandatory leadership classes that address skills related to listening, staying in touch with employees, and handling change without compromising values.

human relations skills
the ability to deal with people, both inside and outside the organization

Where Do Managers Come From?

Good managers are not born; they are made. An organization acquires managers in three ways: promoting employees from within, hiring managers from other organizations, and hiring managers graduating from universities.

Promoting people within the organization into management positions tends to increase motivation by showing employees that those who work hard and are competent can advance in the company. Internal promotion also provides managers who are already familiar with the company's goals and problems. Procter & Gamble prefers to promote managers from within, which creates managers who are familiar with the company's products and policies and builds company loyalty. Promoting from within, however, can lead to problems: It may limit innovation. The new manager may continue the practices and policies of previous managers. Thus it is vital for companies—even companies committed to promotion from within—to hire outside people from time to time to bring new ideas into the organization.

Finding managers with the skills, knowledge, and experience required to run an organization or department is sometimes difficult. At Coca-Cola, for example, the board of directors agonized for months over the best choice to replace former CEO and chairman Douglas Daft upon his retirement. Their search marked the first time in the firm's history that it had sought new leadership from outside the company, although the board concentrated its search among executives experienced with well-known consumer brands.[30] Their ultimate choice wasn't exactly an outsider: E. Neville Isdell had risen through the ranks of Coca-Cola for more than 30 years before leaving to take the reins of another company.[31] Specialized executive employment agencies—sometimes called headhunters, recruiting managers, or executive search firms—can help locate candidates from other companies. The downside is that even though outside people can bring fresh ideas to a company, hiring them may cause resentment among existing employees as well as involve greater expense in relocating an individual to another city or state.

Schools and universities provide a large pool of potential managers, and entry-level applicants can be screened for their developmental potential. People with specialized management skills, such as those with an M.B.A. (Master of Business Administration) degree, may be good candidates.

Some companies offer special training programs for future potential managers. For example, Lehman Brothers Holdings Inc. financed a one-day run through at the Marine Corps base at Quantico, Virginia, for M.B.A. candidates from the University of Pennsylvania's Wharton School of Business. In an effort to acquire leadership skills, student volunteers faced physically daunting tasks, including climbing an 18-foot wall with an 18-degree incline, crossing a rope 20 feet above the ground, crawling facedown under barbed wire through mud, and wading through a four-foot-deep stretch of 50-degree swampy water. The course challenged the students to stay composed in stressful situations, such as rescuing an "injured hostage" in an allotted time and carrying a 20-pound can of "ammunition" across a stream before advancing enemy troops arrived. According to the commanding officer, "The course is designed to take you beyond your self-imposed limits." Top business schools compete to produce the most sought-after graduates. The course at Quantico is designed to develop leadership skills, decisiveness, and teamwork, and Wharton hopes the "taste of life in the trenches" was a valuable experience for the students who participated.[32]

Decision Making

Managers make many different kinds of decisions, such as hours of work, which employees to hire, what products to introduce, and what price to charge for a product. Decision making is important in all management functions and levels, whether the decisions are on a strategic, tactical, or operational level. A systematic approach using these six steps usually leads to more effective decision making: (1) recognizing and defining the decision situation; (2) developing options to resolve the situation; (3) analyzing the options; (4) selecting the best option; (5) implementing the decision; and (6) monitoring the consequences of the decision (Figure 7.4).

Recognizing and Defining the Decision Situation

The first step in decision making is recognizing and defining the situation. The situation may be negative—for example, huge losses on a particular product—or positive—for example, an opportunity to increase sales.

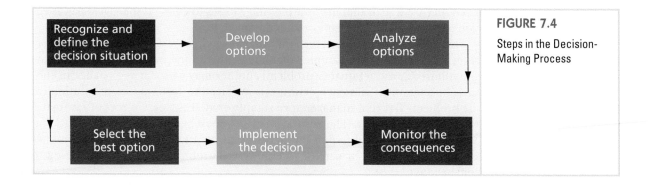

FIGURE 7.4

Steps in the Decision-Making Process

David Neeleman had a dream of a customer-friendly, low-fare airline. After analyzing flight patterns in the New York area, Neeleman decided to base JetBlue at New York City's John F. Kennedy International Airport (JFK). At the time, New Yorkers were limited to low-quality, high-fare airlines, as well as crowds and delays at nearby La Guardia Airport, unless they were willing to venture eight miles further to fly from JFK. Seizing an opportunity to trade off a slightly less convenient location for less competition and better on-time performance, Neeleman secured more than 70 takeoff and landing slots at JFK Airport, enough to accommodate JetBlue's projected growth through 2005. Today, JetBlue serves 25 U.S. cities and has become the number-four airline flying out of New York City.

Neeleman recognized that price is a major consideration for travelers. Major carriers such as Delta typically offer dozens of fares between two locations, depending on time of day and other factors. JetBlue's everyday pricing structure is much simpler and avoids complicated requirements such as Saturday-night stayovers. Fares are based on demand, and JetBlue uses pricing to equalize the loads on the flights so no jet takes off empty while another is completely full. JetBlue's promotional fares are even lower. As a result, JetBlue's flights have an average passenger load of 80 percent of capacity, compared with an industry average of 68.4 percent.

Neeleman and his team made other decisions to set their new airline apart from the competition. Whereas many new carriers buy used jets, JetBlue chose to fly new, state-of-the-art Airbus A320 jets with seat-back personal video screens. JetBlue flies with only 162 seats—instead of the maximum 180 that A320s can hold—which allows passengers more legroom. In addition, the jets are outfitted with roomy leather seats, which cost twice as much as regular seat fabric but last twice as long. More important, passengers feel pampered when they sink into the leather seats and enjoy free satellite television programming, which further differentiates JetBlue from other low-fare airlines.

Another advantage of flying new jets is higher fuel efficiency. A320s can operate on 60 percent of the amount of fuel burned by an equivalent jet built decades before. As a result, JetBlue has not had to raise ticket prices to compensate for rising fuel costs even as the airline expands beyond the East Coast to western destinations such as Long Beach (California) and Seattle. In addition, because JetBlue's technicians work on just one type of jet, they can become more proficient at their maintenance tasks, saving additional time and money.

JetBlue's total costs equal about 6.5 cents per mile—well below the per-mile costs of most major competitors—which helps the airline to keep ticket prices low while delivering a comfortable flying experience. Neeleman's decision to fly from JFK Airport also means JetBlue's on-time record is generally better than that of the big airlines, another important consideration for business travelers and vacationers alike. Not surprisingly, JetBlue became profitable within months after its launch, and Neeleman hopes to keep making sound decisions to keep the airline's revenues and profits soaring.[33]

Discussion Questions

1. How has decision making at JetBlue influenced the start-up's success?
2. How did JetBlue select the best options to gain competitive advantage in its selected markets?
3. What role did implementation play in developing a successful strategy?

Situations calling for small-scale decisions often occur without warning. Situations requiring large-scale decisions, however, generally occur after some warning signals. Effective managers pay attention to such signals. Declining profits, small-scale losses in previous years, inventory buildup, and retailers' unwillingness to stock a product are signals that may warn of huge losses to come. If managers pay attention to such signals, problems can be contained.

Once a situation has been recognized, management must define it. Huge losses reveal a problem—for example, a failing product. One manager may define the situation as a product quality problem; another may define it as a change in consumer preference. These two definitions may lead to vastly different solutions to the problem. The first manager, for example, may seek new sources of raw materials of better quality. The second manager may believe that the product has reached the end of its lifespan and decide to discontinue it. This example emphasizes the importance of carefully defining the problem rather than jumping to conclusions.

Developing Options

Once the decision situation has been recognized and defined, the next step is to develop a list of possible courses of action. The best lists include both standard courses of action and creative ones. As a general rule, more time and expertise are devoted to the development stage of decision making when the decision is of major importance. When the decision is of lesser importance, less time and expertise will be spent on this stage. Options may be developed individually, by teams, or through analysis of similar situations in comparable organizations. Creativity is a very important part of selecting the best option. Creativity depends on new and useful ideas, regardless of where the idea originates or the method used to create the ideas. The best option can range from a required solution to an identified problem to a volunteered solution to an observed problem by an outside work group member.[34]

Analyzing Options

After developing a list of possible courses of action, management should analyze the practicality and appropriateness of each option. An option may be deemed impractical because of a lack of financial resources to implement it, legal restrictions, ethical and social responsibility considerations, authority constraints, technological constraints, economic limitations, or simply a lack of information and expertise to implement the option. For example, a small computer manufacturer may recognize an opportunity to introduce a new type of computer but lack the financial resources to do so. Other options may be more practical for the computer company: It may consider selling its technology to another computer company that has adequate resources or it may allow itself to be purchased by a larger company that can introduce the new technology.

When assessing appropriateness, the decision maker should consider whether the proposed option adequately addresses the situation. When analyzing the consequences of an option, managers should consider the impact the option will have on the situation and on the organization as a whole. For example, when considering a price cut to boost sales, management must consider the consequences of the action on the organization's cash flow and consumers' reaction to the price change.

Selecting the Best Option

When all courses of action have been analyzed, management must select the best one. Selection is often a subjective procedure because many situations do not lend themselves to mathematical analysis. Of course, it is not always necessary to select only one option and reject all others; it may be possible to select and use a combination of several options.

Implementing the Decision

To deal with the situation at hand, the selected option or options must be put into action. Implementation can be fairly simple or very complex, depending on the nature of the decision. Effective implementation of a decision to abandon a product, close a plant, purchase a new business, or something similar requires planning. For example, when a product is dropped, managers must decide how to handle distributors and customers and what to do with the idle production facility. Additionally, they should anticipate resistance from people within the organization (people tend to resist change because they fear the unknown). Finally, management should be ready to deal with the unexpected consequences. No matter how well planned implementation is, unforeseen problems will arise. Management must be ready to address these situations when they occur.

Infinity Computers, Inc., produces notebook computers, which it sells through direct mail catalog companies under the Infinity name and in some retail computer stores under their private brand names. Infinity's products are not significantly different from competitors', nor do they have extra product-enhancing features, although they are very price competitive. The strength of the company has been its CEO and president, George Anderson, and a highly motivated, loyal workforce. The firm's weakness is having too many employees and too great a reliance on one product. The firm switched from the Intel 486 chip to the Pentium chip only after it saw a significant decline in 486 notebook computer sales.

Recognizing that the strategies that initially made the firm successful are no longer working effectively, Anderson wants to reorganize the company to make it more responsive and competitive and to cut costs. The threat of new technological developments and current competitive conditions could eliminate Infinity.

Discussion Questions

1. Evaluate Infinity's current situation and analyze its strengths and weaknesses.
2. Evaluate the opportunities for Infinity, including using its current strategy, and propose alternative strategies.
3. Suggest a plan for Infinity to compete successfully over the next 10 years.

Monitoring the Consequences

After managers have implemented the decision, they must determine whether the decision has accomplished the desired result. Without proper monitoring, the consequences of decisions may not be known quickly enough to make efficient changes. If the desired result is achieved, management can reasonably conclude that it made a good decision. If the desired result is not achieved, further analysis is warranted. Was the decision simply wrong, or did the situation change? Should some other option have been implemented?

If the desired result is not achieved, management may discover that the situation was incorrectly defined from the beginning. That may require starting the decision-making process all over again. Finally, management may determine that the decision was good even though the desired results have not yet shown up or it may determine a flaw in the decision's implementation. In the latter case, management would not change the decision but would change the way in which it was implemented.

The Reality of Management

Management is not a cut-and-dried process. There is no mathematical formula for managing an organization, although many managers passionately wish for one! Management is a widely varying process for achieving organizational goals. Managers plan, organize, staff, direct, and control, but management expert John P. Kotter says even these functions can be boiled down to two basic activities:

1. Figuring out what to do despite uncertainty, great diversity, and an enormous amount of potentially relevant information, and
2. Getting things done through a large and diverse set of people despite having little direct control over most of them.[35]

Managers spend as much as 75 percent of their time working with others—not only with subordinates but with bosses, people outside their hierarchy at work, and people outside the organization itself. In these interactions they discuss anything and everything remotely connected with their business.

Managers spend a lot of time establishing and updating an agenda of goals and plans for carrying out their responsibilities. An **agenda** contains both specific and

agenda
a calender, containing both specific and vague items, that covers short-term goals and long-term objectives

vague items, covering short-term goals and long-term objectives. Like a calendar, an agenda helps the manager figure out what must be done and how to get it done to meet the objectives set by the organization. Technology tools, such as personal digital assistants (PDAs) can help managers manage their agendas, contacts, and time.

Managers also spend a lot of time **networking**—building relationships and sharing information with colleagues who can help them achieve the items on their agendas. Managers spend much of their time communicating with a variety of people and participating in activities that on the surface do not seem to have much to do with the goals of their organization. Nevertheless, these activities are crucial to getting the job done. Networks are not limited to immediate subordinates and bosses; they include other people in the company as well as customers, suppliers, and friends. These contacts provide managers with information and advice on diverse topics. Managers ask, persuade, and even intimidate members of their network in order to get information and to get things done. Networking helps managers carry out their responsibilities. Andrea Nierenberg, independent business consultant and founder of Nierenberg Group Inc., has been called the "queen of networking." She writes three notes a day: one to a client, one to a friend, and one to a prospective client. She maintains a database of 3,000 contacts. However, she believes that it isn't how many people you know, but how many you have helped and who know you well enough to recommend you that really count. Opportunity can knock almost anywhere with such extensive networking. Grateful for numerous referrals to her friends, Nierenberg's dentist introduced her to a Wall Street executive who happened to be in the dentist's office at the same time as Nierenberg. She followed up on the meeting and later landed four consulting projects at the executive's firm.[36]

Finally, managers spend a great deal of time confronting the complex and difficult challenges of the business world today. Some of these challenges relate to rapidly changing technology (especially in production and information processing), increased scrutiny of individual and corporate ethics and social responsibility, the changing nature of the workforce, new laws and regulations, increased global competition and more challenging foreign markets, declining educational standards (which may limit the skills and knowledge of the future labor and customer pool), and time itself—that is, making the best use of it. But such diverse issues cannot simply be plugged into a computer program that supplies correct, easy-to-apply solutions. It is only through creativity and imagination that managers can make effective decisions that benefit their organizations.

> **networking**
> the building of relationships and sharing of information with colleagues who can help managers achieve the items on their agendas

Explore Your Career Options
Management Is Alive and Well

If you've been reading business news over the last several years, you may be a bit skeptical about a career in management. Many companies have sharply reduced their management layers, especially at the middle level. However, management is, and will continue to be, one of the most crucial functions in the survival and growth of every business. Experts project that employment will increase by 21 million jobs—from 144 million to 165 million—between 2002 and 2012. Examples of areas where management jobs will continue to grow at faster-than-average rates include computer and information technology, education, medical and health services, human resources and labor, and marketing. Occupations in the health care and information technology sectors make up the fastest-growing job segments. In the health care industry, for example, job growth will be driven by an aging population, insistence on better care, and breakthroughs in medical technology. The increase in health care workers is part of an overall trend of increasing employment in services, and service jobs in general are expected to increase 40 percent over the next decade. This larger workforce will require more managers to plan, organize, lead, and control their activities and ensure that they continue to increase productivity in the global marketplace.

The median annual salaries for management positions are shown below but, of course, actual salary ranges depend on numerous factors including size of employer, industry sector, and individual experience:

Computer/IT managers	$85,240
Marketing managers	$78,250
Financial managers	$73,340
Human resources/labor managers	$67,710
Production/operations managers	$67,320
Medical/health services managers	$61,370
Administrative managers	$52,500

Companies will continue to recruit and offer positions to candidates with training and experience in how to manage capital and human resources. In order to secure a good job once you graduate, you must have realistic expectations and be adequately prepared to join the working world. This preparation means that you must set realistic goals, adopt positive attitudes, and learn to communicate your skills effectively.[37]

Review Your Understanding

Define management and explain its role in the achievement of organizational objectives.

Management is a process designed to achieve an organization's objectives by using its resources effectively and efficiently in a changing environment. Managers make decisions about the use of the organization's resources and are concerned with planning, organizing, staffing, directing, and controlling the organization's activities so as to reach its objectives.

Describe the major functions of management.

Planning is the process of determining the organization's objectives and deciding how to accomplish them. Organizing is the structuring of resources and activities to accomplish those objectives efficiently and effectively. Staffing obtains people with the necessary skills to carry out the work of the company. Directing is motivating and leading employees to achieve organizational objectives. Controlling is the process of evaluating and correcting activities to keep the organization on course.

Distinguish among three levels of management and the concerns of managers at each level.

Top management is responsible for the whole organization and focuses primarily on strategic planning. Middle management develops plans for specific operating areas and carries out the general guidelines set by top management. First-line, or supervisory, management supervises the workers and day-to-day operations. Managers can also be categorized as to their area of responsibility: finance, production and operations, human resources, marketing, or administration.

Specify the skills managers need in order to be successful.

To be successful, managers need leadership skills (the ability to influence employees to work toward organizational goals), technical expertise (the specialized knowledge and training needed to perform a job), conceptual skills (the ability to think in abstract terms and see how parts fit together to form the whole), analytical skills (the ability to identify relevant issues and recognize their importance, understand the relationships between issues, and perceive the underlying causes of a situation), and human relations (people) skills.

Summarize the systematic approach to decision making used by many business managers.

A systematic approach to decision making follows these steps: recognizing and defining the situation, developing options, analyzing options, selecting the best option, implementing the decision, and monitoring the consequences.

Recommend a new strategy to revive a struggling business.

Using the decision-making process described in this chapter, analyze the struggling company's problems described in "Solve the Dilemma" box on page 200 and formulate a strategy to turn the company around and aim it toward future success.

Revisit the World of Business

1. As governor of California, is Arnold Schwarzenegger a manager?
2. Describe the challenges Schwarzenegger faces as governor of California.
3. What skills can Schwarzenegger bring to his new job? What roles (see Table 7.3) is he likely to fulfill as governor?

Learn the Terms

Check Your Progress

1. Why is management so important, and what is its purpose?

2. Explain why the American Heart Association would need management, even though its goal is not profit related.

3. Why must a company have financial resources before it can use human and physical resources?

4. Name the five functions of management, and briefly describe each function.

5. Identify the three levels of management. What is the focus of managers at each level?

6. In what areas can managers specialize? From what area do top managers typically come?

7. What skills do managers need? Give examples of how managers use these skills to do their jobs.

8. What are three styles of leadership? Describe situations in which each style would be appropriate.

9. Explain the steps in the decision-making process.

10. What is the mathematical formula for perfect management? What do managers spend most of their time doing?

Get Involved

1. Give examples of the activities that each of the following managers might be involved in if he or she worked for the Coca-Cola Company:

   Financial manager
   Production and operations manager
   Personnel manager
   Marketing manager
   Administrative manager
   Information technology manager
   Foreman

2. Interview a small sample of managers, attempting to include representatives from all three levels and all areas of management. Discuss their daily activities and relate these activities to the management functions of planning, organizing, staffing, directing, and controlling. What skills do the managers say they need to carry out their tasks?

3. You are a manager of a firm that manufactures conventional ovens. Over the past several years, sales of many of your products have declined; this year, your losses may be quite large. Using the steps of the decision-making process, briefly describe how you arrive at a strategy for correcting the situation.

Build Your Skills

FUNCTIONS OF MANAGEMENT

Background:
Although the text describes each of the five management functions separately, you learned that these five functions are interre- lated, and managers sometimes perform two or more of them at the same time. Here you will broaden your per- spective of how these functions occur simultaneously in management activities.

Task

1. Imagine that you are the manager in each scenario described in the table below and you have to decide which management function(s) to use in each.

2. Mark your answers using the following codes:

Codes	Management Functions
P	Planning
O	Organizing
S	Staffing
D	Directing
C	Controlling

No.	Scenario	Answer(s)
1	Your group's work is centered around a project that is due in two months. Although everyone is working on the project, you have observed your employees involved in what you believe is excessive socializing and other time-filling behaviors. You decide to meet with the group to have them help you break down the project into smaller subprojects with mini-deadlines. You believe this will help keep the group members focused on the project and that the quality of the finished project will then reflect the true capabilities of your group.	
2	Your first impression of the new group you'll be managing is not too great. You tell your friend at dinner after your first day on the job: "Looks like I got a baby sitting job instead of a management job."	
3	You call a meeting of your work group and begin it by letting them know that a major procedure used by the work group for the past two years is being significantly revamped, and your department will have to phase in the change during the next six weeks. You proceed by explaining to them the reasoning your boss gave you for this change. You then say, "Let's take the next 5 to 10 minutes to let you voice your reactions to this change." After 10 minutes elapse with the majority of comments being critical of the change, you say: "I appreciate each of you sharing your reactions; and I, too, recognize that *all* change creates problems. The way I see it, however, is that we can spend the remaining 45 minutes of our meeting focusing on why we don't want the change and why we don't think it's necessary; or we can work together to come up with viable solutions to solve the problems that implementing this change will most likely create." After about five more minutes of comments being exchanged, the consensus of the group is that the remainder of the meeting needs to be focused on how to deal with the potential problems the group anticipates having to deal with as the new procedure is implemented.	
4	You are preparing for the annual budget allocation meetings to be held in the plant manager's office next week. You are determined to present a strong case to support your department getting money for some high-tech equipment that will help your employees do their jobs better. You will stand firm against any suggestions of budget cuts in your area.	
5	Early in your career you learned an important lesson about employee selection. One of the nurses on your floor unexpectedly quit. The other nurses were putting pressure on you to fill the position quickly because they were overworked even before the nurse left, and then things were really bad. After a hasty recruitment effort, you made a decision based on insufficient information. You ended up regretting your quick decision during the three months of problems that followed until you finally had to discharge the new hire. Since then, you have never let anybody pressure you into making a quick hiring decision.	

e-Xtreme Surfing

- **American Management Association**
  www.amanet.org/index.html

  Provides practical management training and development tools to members worldwide through seminars, conferences, publications, research, and more.

- **Wharton Center for Leadership & Change Management**
  http://leadership.wharton.upenn.edu/

  Offers information on leadership programs from many organizations.

- **CEO Express**
  www.ceoexpress.com/default.asp

  Supplies busy managers with links to a wealth of information including daily news, business research, workplace tools, as well as personal interests.

See for Yourself Videocase

CARLY FIORINA: THE MOST POWERFUL WOMAN IN BUSINESS

Carly Fiorina is chairman and CEO of Hewlett Packard, a leading company in computing and imaging solutions and services. Fiorina is the first female chief executive of a Dow Jones company, but she prefers that people not focus on her gender. Although she has encountered sexism in her career, she never allowed herself to believe the comments that were made to her. She believes that the fast-growing high-tech world simply cannot afford for there to be a glass ceiling for women.

Fiorina has ranked number one on *Fortune's* list of most powerful businesswomen for six years in a row. Other women included in the magazine's list of most powerful women include eBay CEO Meg Whitman, Avon Products chairman and CEO Andrea Jung, Xerox chairman and CEO Anne Mulcahy, and Majorie Magner, chairman and CEO of the Global Consumer Group at Citigroup. Analysts for *Fortune* have found that many fast-track women are not concerned about power, and in fact, many have left their prestigious positions during the past five years. Many of these women say they would not like to be like Carly Fiorina and do not want to run a huge company. Fiorina has not allowed her powerful status to separate her from other employees at HP. When employees land big contracts, she often gives them balloons and flowers, and makes sure that employees who are ill get medical advice and emotional support.

Some view Fiorina's rise to the upper rungs of the corporate ladder as remarkable. Her father was a law professor, and her mother was a painter. Her father's career required the family to move so often that she attended five different high schools. She also has a bachelor of arts degree in medieval history from Stanford University—not the typical degree typical for a CEO of a high-tech firm. After graduating from Stanford, Fiorina entered law school at the University of California at Los Angeles, thinking that she wanted to follow in her father's footsteps. After just one semester, however, she realized she did not enjoy law, and left to pursue other things.

Before joining HP, Fiorina spent nearly 20 years working at AT&T and Lucent Technologies, where she held a number of senior leadership positions. At AT&T, she joined the Network Systems group, which many thought at the time was a career-killing move. But Fiorina thrived and became AT&T's first female officer at the age of 35. By age 40, she was heading AT&T's North American operations. At Lucent, she expanded the company's Internet business and was a key decision maker in implementing its initial public offering and spin-off from AT&T in 1996. In fact, Fiorina stayed up all night with other employees making sure the prospectus for the stock offering was perfect.

After joining HP in 1999, she led a major effort to reinvent the company. Under her leadership, she has emphasized innovation focused on delivering the best total customer experience. Fiorina has many accomplishments at HP, but one of the biggest was her acquisition of Compaq Computer. Critics attacked her plan to acquire the rival computer maker as misguided, and even accused her of potentially destroying the company. She had to fight some board of director's members who were not supportive. Despite the naysayers, Fiorina put the $19 billion deal together, which came in under budget and ahead of schedule, and is anticipated to result in a larger-than-expected cost savings. The merger with Compaq allowed HP to remain in nearly deadlocked with Dell for the number-one spot in the race for global PC market share. Fiorina still needs to prove to HP's shareholders that the company can generate sustained revenue growth. The company has not been able to achieve the same level of sales increases as rival Dell. At this point, merging Compaq with HP has been more of a cost-cutting story and the challenge ahead is to marry HP's corporate culture with Compaq's corporate culture.

There is little question that the Compaq merger is Fiorina's biggest accomplishment thus far, and she has defied all of her critics by showing that she can set tough goals and implement the strategies necessary to accomplish them, even with many obstacles. Fiorina has a skill for winning, which she accomplishes by taking complex ideas and converting them into simple ideas that everyone can understand. Perhaps this is due in part to the days when she was a student of medieval history at Stanford University and had to convert hundreds of pages of writing into crisp, two-page abstracts. She seems to want to get into every aspect of the business, and while at Lucent, she even helped devise the company's logo—a speedily drawn red circle with streaks of white, meant to convey a company blazing into the digital future.

Carly Fiorina strongly supports corporate social responsibility, especially sustaining the environment. She constantly focuses on why companies should commit time and resources to this cause. She outlines the company's ability to meet its commitment in these areas and provides resources to help people with their communication needs around the world. The company has a specific focus on education, and she emphasizes giving back to local communities. The company has developed model programs to help disadvantaged communities with information technology needs in Houston and around the world. Carly Fiorina has become a role model for women who want to be successful in business. She has provided caring leadership, bottom-line results, and a concern for society.[38]

Discussion Questions

1. Why has Carly Fiorina been so successful?

2. What do you think would have happened to Hewlett Packard if Carly Fiorina had not been the company's CEO for the past six years?

3. What do you think Carly Fiorina's greatest accomplishment is at HP, and what do you expect her to do in the future?

Remember to check out our Online Learning Center at www.mhhe.com/ferrell5e.

Chapter 8

Organization, Teamwork, and Communication

OBJECTIVES

After reading this chapter, you will be able to:

- Define organizational structure and relate how organizational structures develop.

- Describe how specialization and departmentalization help an organization achieve its goals.

- Distinguish between groups and teams and identify the types of groups that exist in organizations.

- Determine how organizations assign responsibility for tasks and delegate authority.

- Compare and contrast some common forms of organizational structure.

- Describe how communication occurs in organizations.

- Analyze a business's use of teams.

NASA Looks Inward Before Going Back to the Stars

After the space shuttle *Columbia* broke up on reentry in 2003, killing all seven astronauts on board, the National Aeronautics and Space Agency (NASA) spent more than a year reexamining itself as well as studying the circumstances surrounding the catastrophe in an effort to prevent future accidents in the space program. Barely one year later, NASA was given a new mandate by President George W. Bush to return humans to the moon, even while it continued to oversee the construction of the International Space Station and its ongoing program of unmanned explorations of nearby planets. To address these challenges, NASA was confronted with the need for an attitude adjustment.

In addition to careful analysis of the *Columbia* disaster, NASA employed the consulting firm Behavioral Sciences Technology (BST) to assess what role the agency's values and culture might have played. The consulting firm found that the agency's "can-do" culture may have stifled employees' willingness to speak out about concerns that ultimately led to the destruction of the *Columbia*. Astronaut Jim Wetherbee, a veteran of six shuttle missions, said, "There are a lot of people who won't speak up. They were afraid of being rendered ineffective, which at NASA is the equivalent of being fired." A survey of NASA's 19,000 employees found many who shared that view.

continued

However, the consultants also came to believe that NASA can exploit its "overwhelming drive" to succeed to help make it safer for future missions. BST's CEO, C. Patrick Smith, said, "The most powerful first impression [we had] was how much strength there is in NASA culture. It's in the DNA of people who work at NASA—no task is too big, no task is too challenging." To harness that drive, BST created a 36-month, five-point plan designed to improve communication and decision making, inspire in employees a greater sense of responsibility for mission safety, synchronize NASA's managerial capability with its technological superiority, and apply accountability measures. The consulting firm planned to conduct training—including one-on-one coaching of managers—as well as conduct additional surveys and develop action plans for every one of the agency's employees. BST also recommended training for the 40,000 workers who are employed by contractors working on various NASA projects. NASA director Sean O'Keefe pledged to apply the BST recommendations starting at the very top of the organization in order to make safety one of NASA's guiding values.[1]

Introduction

An organization's structure determines how well it makes decisions and responds to problems, and it influences employees' attitudes toward their work. A suitable structure can minimize a business's costs and maximize its efficiency. For these reasons, many businesses, such as Motorola, Apple Computer, and Hewlett-Packard, have changed their organizational structures in recent years in an effort to enhance their profits and competitive edge.

Because a business's structure can so profoundly affect its success, this chapter will examine organizational structure in detail. First, we discuss how an organization's culture affects its operations. Then we consider the development of structure, including how tasks and responsibilities are organized through specialization and departmentalization. Next, we explore some of the forms organizational structure may take. Finally, we consider communications within business.

Organizational Culture

organizational culture
a firm's shared values, beliefs, traditions, philosophies, rules, and role models for behavior.

One of the most important aspects of organizing a business is determining its **organizational culture,** a firm's shared values, beliefs, traditions, philosophies, rules, and role models for behavior. Also called corporate culture, an organizational culture exists in every organization, regardless of size, organizational type, product, or profit objective. A firm's culture may be expressed formally through its mission statement, codes of ethics, memos, manuals, and ceremonies, but it is more commonly expressed informally. Examples of informal expressions of culture include dress codes (or the lack thereof), work habits, extracurricular activities, and stories. Employees often learn the accepted standards through discussions with co-workers.

The Walt Disney Company focuses on making people happy, and it hires outgoing people for all levels of jobs within the company.

At Southwest Airlines, for example, new employees watch videotapes and attend training sessions that extol the company's policies, philosophies, and culture. This training encourages employees to have fun and to make flying exciting for their passengers. Such activities mark Southwest's culture as fun, casual, and friendly. Disneyland/Disney World and McDonald's have organizational cultures focused on cleanliness, value, and service. At Matsushita, employees sing a company song every morning that translates, "As individuals we will work to improve life and contribute to human progress." The company's president, Kunio Nakamura, also believes the highest paid employee should earn no more than 10 times the lowest paid employee. The effort to hire younger employees and more women is also affecting the Japanese firm's culture.[2] When such values and philosophies are shared by all members of an organization, they will be expressed in its relationships with stakeholders. However, organizational cultures that lack such positive values may result in employees who are unproductive and indifferent and have poor attitudes, which will be reflected externally to customers. Unethical cultures may have contributed to the misconduct at a number of well-known companies, such as Enron and WorldCom, at the turn of the century. At the *USA Today* newspaper, for example, an internal investigation into a reporter's plagiarized and fabricated stories identified the newspaper's organizational culture as one culprit in the scandal, which ultimately resulted in the resignation of the newspaper's editor. Investigators found that careless editing and management, the existence of a "star reporter" system, and a workplace environment of fear discouraged staff members from speaking out about their suspicions about the "Golden Boy" reporter's work.[3]

Organizational culture helps ensure that all members of a company share values and suggests rules for how to behave and deal with problems within the organization. The key to success in any organization is satisfying stakeholders, especially customers. Establishing a positive organizational culture sets the tone for all other decisions, including building an efficient organizational structure.

WorldCom achieved a worldwide presence, acquired telecommunications giant MCI, and ultimately expanded beyond long-distance telephone service to a whole range of telecommunications services. The company seemed poised to become one of the largest telecommunications providers in the world. Instead, it became the largest bankruptcy filing in U.S. history to date and another name on a long roster of those disgraced by accounting scandals.

Unfortunately for thousands of employees and shareholders, WorldCom employed questionable accounting practices and improperly recorded $3.8 billion in capital expenditures, which boosted cash flows and profit. Investors, unaware of the alleged fraud, continued to buy the company's stock, which accelerated the stock's price. WorldCom was already in financial turmoil by 2001, long before the improper accounting practices were disclosed. Declining rates and revenues and an ambitious buying spree had pushed the company deeper into debt. In addition, chief executive Bernard Ebbers received a controversial $408 million loan to cover personal margin calls on loans that were secured by company stock.

Several former WorldCom financial and accounting managers, including David Myers, Buford Yates, Betty Vinson, and Troy Normand, pleaded guilty to securities-fraud charges. According to *The Wall Street Journal,* Betty Vinson, a midlevel accountant for WorldCom, was asked by her superiors to make false accounting entries. She protested a number of times but eventually caved in to help shore up WorldCom's financial condition. For six quarters she made illegal entries, each time hoping it would be the last. At the end of 18 months she had helped falsify at least $3.7 billion in profits. Myers, Yates, Vinson, and Normand claimed that top managers had directed them to cover up WorldCom's deteri-

orating finances. Although they protested that these directions were improper, they say they agreed to follow orders after their superiors told them it was the only way to save the company.

Their story is a cautionary tale for well-meaning, hard-working employees who find themselves directed to do something wrong. When an employee's livelihood is on the line, it's hard to say no to a powerful boss. However, in a speech to Wall Street executives, James Comey, the U.S. attorney prosecuting Vinson's case, said that "just following orders" is never an excuse for breaking the law. Vinson wasn't alone in these predicaments. Investigators hired by the company's new board of directors found that dozens of employees knew about the fraud at WorldCom but were afraid to speak out.

Vinson is awaiting sentencing on charges of conspiracy and securities fraud and preparing her 12-year-old daughter for the possibility that she will go to jail. Former CEO Bernard Ebbers was indicated on securities fraud, conspiracy to commit securities fraud, and making false filings to regulators on March 3, 2004. Scott Sullivan, WorldCom's chief financial officer, pleaded guilty and was expected to cooperate in the case against Ebbers.[4]

Discussion Questions

1. How might WorldCom's culture have contributed to its accounting irregularities?
2. Why do you think employees caved in when their superiors pressured them to engage in what they perceived as unlawful conduct?
3. Why do you think midlevel employees like Betty Vinson, who were "just following orders," wind up pleading guilty to illegal activities while most top managers go free?

Developing Organizational Structure

structure
the arrangement or relationship of positions within an organization

Structure is the arrangement or relationship of positions within an organization. Rarely is an organization, or any group of individuals working together, able to achieve common objectives without some form of structure, whether that structure is explicitly defined or only implied. A professional baseball team such as the Tampa Bay Devil Rays is a business organization with an explicit formal structure that guides the team's activities so that it can increase game attendance, win games, and sell souvenirs such as T-shirts. But even an informal group playing softball for fun has an organization that specifies who will pitch, catch, bat, coach, and so on. Governments and nonprofit organizations also have formal organizational structures to facilitate the achievement of their objectives. Getting people to work together efficiently and coordinating the skills of diverse individuals require careful planning. Developing appropriate organizational structures is therefore a major challenge for managers in both large and small organizations.

An organization's structure develops when managers assign work tasks and activities to specific individuals or work groups and coordinate the diverse activities required to reach the firm's objectives. When Dillard's, for example, has a sale, the store manager must work with the advertising department to make the public aware of the sale, with department managers to ensure that extra salespeople are scheduled to handle the increased customer traffic, and with merchandise buyers to ensure that enough sale merchandise is available to meet expected consumer demand. All the people occupying these positions must work together to achieve the store's objectives.

The best way to begin to understand how organizational structure develops is to consider the evolution of a new business such as a clothing store. At first, the business is a sole proprietorship in which the owner does everything—buys, prices, and displays the merchandise; does the accounting and tax records; and assists customers. As the business grows, the owner hires a salesperson and perhaps a merchandise buyer to help run the store. As the business continues to grow, the owner hires more salespeople. The growth and success of the business now require the owner to be away from the store frequently, meeting with suppliers, engaging in public relations, and attending trade shows. Thus, the owner must designate someone to manage the salespeople and maintain the accounting, payroll, and tax functions. If the owner decides to expand by opening more stores, still more managers will be needed. Figure 8.1 shows these stages of growth with three **organizational charts** (visual displays of organizational structure, chain of command, and other relationships).

Growth requires organizing—the structuring of human, physical, and financial resources to achieve objectives in an effective and efficient manner. Growth necessitates hiring people who have specialized skills. With more people and greater specialization, the organization needs to develop a formal structure to function efficiently. As we shall see, structuring an organization requires that management assign work tasks to specific individuals and departments and assign responsibility for the achievement of specific organizational objectives.

Home Depot's organizational structure begins with CEO Bob Nardelli, to its "Store Manager Council" (pictured here), to its sales associates. The Store Manager Council provides the link for communication between the stores' sales associates and upper management.

organizational chart
a visual display of the organizational structure, lines of authority (chain of command), staff relationships, permanent committee arrangements, and lines of communication

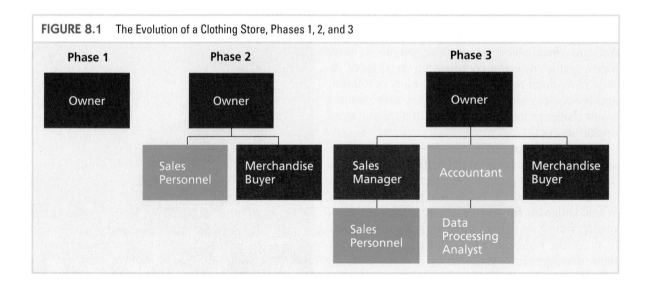

FIGURE 8.1   The Evolution of a Clothing Store, Phases 1, 2, and 3

Assigning Tasks

For a business to earn profits from the sale of its products, its managers must first determine what activities are required to achieve its objectives. At Celestial Seasonings, for example, employees must purchase herbs from suppliers, dry the herbs and place them in tea bags, package and label the tea, and then ship the packages to grocery stores around the country. Other necessary activities include negotiating with supermarkets and other retailers for display space, developing new products, planning advertising, managing finances, and managing employees. All these activities must be coordinated, assigned to work groups, and controlled. Two important aspects of assigning these work activities are specialization and departmentalization.

Specialization

After identifying all activities that must be accomplished, managers then break these activities down into specific tasks that can be handled by individual employees. This division of labor into small, specific tasks and the assignment of employees to do a single task is called **specialization**.

The rationale for specialization is efficiency. People can perform more efficiently if they master just one task rather than all tasks. In *Wealth of Nations*, 18th-century economist Adam Smith discussed specialization, using the manufacture of straight pins as an example. Individually, workers could produce 20 pins a day when each employee produced complete pins. Thus, 10 employees working independently of each other could produce 200 pins a day. However, when one worker drew the wire, another straightened it, a third cut it, and a fourth ground the point, 10 workers could produce 48,000 pins per day.[5] To save money and achieve the benefits of specialization, some companies outsource and hire temporary workers to provide key skills. Many highly skilled, diverse experience workers are available through temp agencies.[6]

Specialization means workers don't waste time shifting from one job to another, and training is easier. However, efficiency is not the only motivation for specialization. Specialization also occurs when the activities that must be performed within an organization are too numerous for one person to handle. Recall the example of the

specialization
the division of labor into small, specific tasks and the assignment of employees to do a single task

clothing store. When the business was young and small, the owner could do everything; but when the business grew, the owner needed help waiting on customers, keeping the books, and managing other business activities.

Overspecialization can have negative consequences. Employees may become bored and dissatisfied with their jobs, and the result of their unhappiness is likely to be poor quality work, more injuries, and high employee turnover. Although some degree of specialization is necessary for efficiency, because of differences in skills, abilities, and interests, all people are not equally suited for all jobs. We examine some strategies to overcome these issues in Chapter 10.

Departmentalization

After assigning specialized tasks to individuals, managers next organize workers doing similar jobs into groups to make them easier to manage. **Departmentalization** is the grouping of jobs into working units usually called departments, units, groups, or divisions. As we shall see, departments are commonly organized by function, product, geographic region, or customer (Figure 8.2). Most companies use more than one departmentalization plan to enhance productivity. For instance, many consumer goods manufacturers have departments for specific product lines (beverages, frozen dinners, canned goods, and so on) as well as departments dealing with legal, purchasing, finance, human resources, and other business functions. Many city governments also have departments for specific services (e.g., police, fire, waste disposal) as well as departments for legal, human resources, and other business functions. Figure 8.3 on page 235 depicts the organizational chart for the city of Corpus Christi, Texas, showing these departments.

departmentalization the grouping of jobs into working units usually called departments, units, groups, or divisions

Functional Departmentalization.   **Functional departmentalization** groups jobs that perform similar functional activities, such as finance, manufacturing, marketing, and human resources. Each of these functions is managed by an expert in the work done by the department—an engineer supervises the production department; a financial executive supervises the finance department. This approach is common in small organizations. A weakness of functional departmentalization is that, because it tends to emphasize departmental units rather than the organization as a whole, decision making that involves more than one department may be slow, and it requires greater coordination. Thus, as business grow, they tend to adopt other approaches to organizing jobs.

functional departmentalization the grouping of jobs tht perform similar functional activities, such as finance, manufacturing, marketing, and human resources

Product Departmentalization.   **Product departmentalization,** as you might guess, organizes jobs around the products of the firm. Procter & Gamble has global units, such as laundry and cleaning products, paper products, and health care products. Each division develops and implements its own product plans, monitors the results, and takes corrective action as necessary. Functional activities—production, finance, marketing, and others—are located within each product division. Consequently, organizing by products duplicates functions and resources and emphasizes the product rather than achievement of the organization's overall objectives. However, it simplifies decision making and helps coordinate all activities related to a product or product group. Kodak, for example, reorganized into special product groups devoted to areas such as digital cameras, online services, or photo kiosks. Chief Operating Officer Antonio Perez hopes this structure will improve communication between engineers and marketers to produce "breakthrough technology" and more rapid product introductions. The arrangement may be paying off: the company introduced six new digital cameras in one month.[7]

product departmentalization the organization of jobs in relation to the products of the firm

FIGURE 8.2

Departmentalization

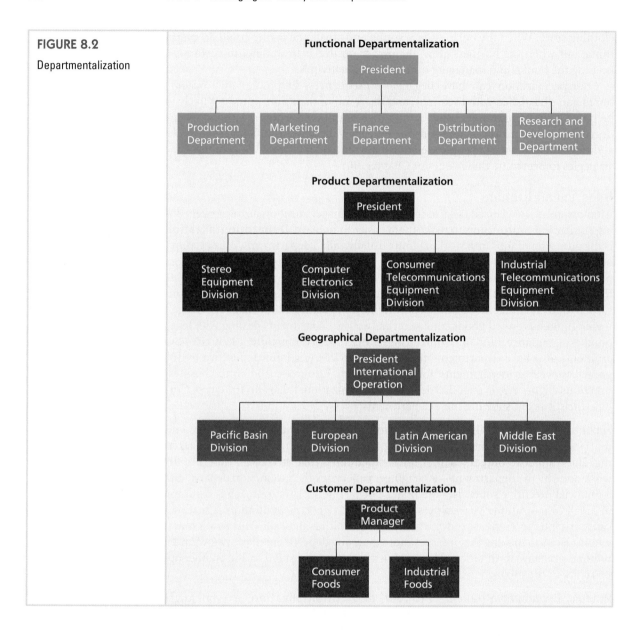

Functional Departmentalization

President

Production Department | Marketing Department | Finance Department | Distribution Department | Research and Development Department

Product Departmentalization

President

Stereo Equipment Division | Computer Electronics Division | Consumer Telecommunications Equipment Division | Industrial Telecommunications Equipment Division

Geographical Departmentalization

President International Operation

Pacific Basin Division | European Division | Latin American Division | Middle East Division

Customer Departmentalization

Product Manager

Consumer Foods | Industrial Foods

---

geographical departmentalization
the grouping of jobs according to geographic location, such as state, region, country, or continent

customer departmentalization
the arrangement of jobs around the needs of various types of customers

Geographical Departmentalization.   **Geographical departmentalization** groups jobs according to geographic location, such as a state, region, country, or continent. FritoLay, for example, is organized into four regional divisions, allowing the company to get closer to its customers and respond more quickly and efficiently to regional competitors. Multinational corporations often use a geographical approach because of vast differences between different regions. Coca-Cola, General Motors, and Caterpillar are organized by region. However, organizing by region requires a large administrative staff and control system to coordinate operations, and tasks are duplicated among the different regions.

Customer Departmentalization.   **Customer departmentalization** arranges jobs around the needs of various types of customers. Banks, for example, typically have

FIGURE 8.3   An Organizational Chart for the City of Corpus Christi

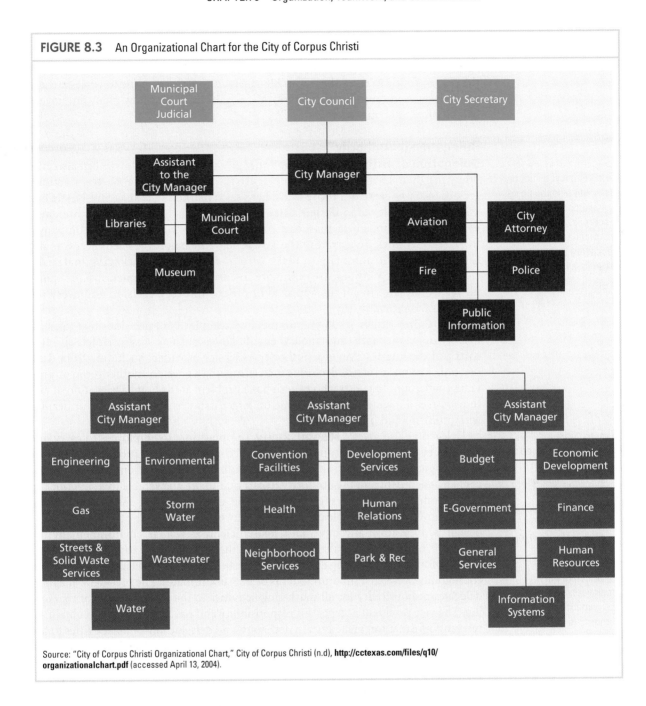

Source: "City of Corpus Christi Organizational Chart," City of Corpus Christi (n.d), **http://cctexas.com/files/q10/ organizationalchart.pdf** (accessed April 13, 2004).

separate departments for commercial banking activities and for consumer or retail banking. This permits the bank to address the unique requirements of each group. Airlines, such as British Airways and Delta, provide prices and services customized for either business/frequent travelers or infrequent/vacationing customers. Customer departmentalization, like geographical departmentalization, does not focus on the organization as a whole and therefore requires a large administrative staff to coordinate the operations of the various groups.

Assigning Responsibility

After all workers and work groups have been assigned their tasks, they must be given the responsibility to carry them out. Management must determine to what extent it will delegate responsibility throughout the organization and how many employees will report to each manager.

Delegation of Authority

delegation of authority
giving employees not only tasks, but also the power to make commitments, use resources, and take whatever actions are necessary to carry out those tasks

Delegation of authority means not only giving tasks to employees but also empowering them to make commitments, use resources, and take whatever actions are necessary to carry out those tasks. Let's say a marketing manager at Nestlé has assigned an employee to design a new package that is less wasteful (more environmentally responsible) than the current package for one of the company's frozen dinner lines. To carry out the assignment, the employee needs access to information and the authority to make certain decisions on packaging materials, costs, and so on. Without the authority to carry out the assigned task, the employee would have to get the approval of others for every decision and every request for materials.

As a business grows, so do the number and complexity of decisions that must be made; no one manager can handle them all. Hotels such as Westin Hotels and Resorts and the Ritz-Carlton give authority to service providers, including front desk personnel, to make service decisions such as moving a guest to another room or providing a discount to guests who experience a problem at the hotel. Delegation of authority frees a manager to concentrate on larger issues, such as planning or dealing with problems and opportunities.

responsibility
the obligation, placed on employees through delegation, to perform assigned tasks satisfactorily and be held accountable for the proper execution of work

Delegation also gives a **responsibility,** or obligation, to employees to carry out assigned tasks satisfactorily and holds them accountable for the proper execution of their assigned work. The principle of **accountability** means that employees who accept an assignment and the authority to carry it out are answerable to a superior for the outcome. Returning to the Nestlé example, if the packaging design prepared by the employee is unacceptable or late, the employee must accept the blame. If the new design is innovative, attractive, and cost-efficient, as well as environmentally responsible, or is completed ahead of schedule, the employee will accept the credit.

accountability
the principle that employees who accept an assignment and the authority to carry it out are answerable to a superior for the outcome

The process of delegating authority establishes a pattern of relationships and accountability between a superior and his or her subordinates. The president of a firm delegates responsibility for all marketing activities to the vice president of marketing. The vice president accepts this responsibility and has the authority to obtain all relevant information, make certain decisions, and delegate any or all activities to his or her subordinates. The vice president, in turn, delegates all advertising activities to the advertising manager, all sales activities to the sales manager, and so on. These managers then delegate specific tasks to their subordinates. However, the act of delegating authority to a subordinate does not relieve the superior of accountability for the delegated job. Even though the vice president of marketing delegates work to subordinates, he or she is still ultimately accountable to the president for all marketing activities.

Degree of Centralization

The extent to which authority is delegated throughout an organization determines its degree of centralization.

Centralized Organizations. In a **centralized organization,** authority is concentrated at the top, and very little decision-making authority is delegated to lower levels. Although decision-making authority in centralized organizations rests with top levels of management, a vast amount of responsibility for carrying out daily and routine procedures is delegated to even the lowest levels of the organization. Many government organizations, including the U.S. Army, the Postal Service, and the IRS, are centralized.

Businesses tend to be more centralized when the decisions to be made are risky and when low-level managers are not highly skilled in decision making. In the banking industry, for example, authority to make routine car loans is given to all loan managers, while the authority to make high-risk loans, such as for a large residential development, may be restricted to upper-level loan officers.

Overcentralization can cause serious problems for a company, in part because it may take longer for the organization as a whole to implement decisions and to respond to changes and problems on a regional scale. McDonald's, for example, was one of the last chains to introduce a chicken sandwich because of the amount of research, development, test marketing, and layers of approval the product had to go through.

Decentralized Organizations. A **decentralized organization** is one in which decision-making authority is delegated as far down the chain of command as possible. Decentralization is characteristic of organizations that operate in complex, unpredictable environments. Businesses that face intense competition often decentralize to improve responsiveness and enhance creativity. Lower-level managers who interact with the external environment often develop a good understanding of it and thus are able to react quickly to changes.

Delegating authority to lower levels of managers may increase the organization's productivity. Decentralization requires that lower-level managers have strong decision-making skills. In recent years the trend has been toward more decentralized organizations, and some of the largest and most successful companies, including GE, Sears, IBM, and J. C. Penney, have decentralized decision-making authority. Nonprofit organizations benefit from decentralization as well. The Salvation Army, a charitable global organization with locations in 100 countries, is highly decentralized. The United States is divided into 50 territories and commands, and each is expected to finance all its activities through local fundraising efforts. The Salvation Army is successful in meeting its goal to help people, with a substantial portion of every $1 spent actually going toward this purpose.[8]

centralized organization a structure in which authority is concentrated at the top, and very little decision-making authority is delegated to lower levels

decentralized organization an organization in which decision-making authority is delegated as far down the chain of command as possible

Bed, Bath & Beyond empowers its store managers who know their customers better than anyone else. Each manager selects about 70 percent of his or her store's merchandise, including linens, appliances, picture frames, and imported olive oil, to ensure they match that store's customers.

FIGURE 8.4

Span of Management: Wide Span and Narrow Span

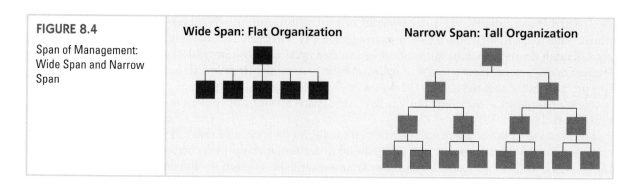

Span of Management

How many subordinates should a manager manage? There is no simple answer. Experts generally agree, however, that top managers should not directly supervise more than four to eight people, while lower-level managers who supervise routine tasks are capable of managing a much larger number of subordinates. For example, the manager of the finance department may supervise 25 employees, whereas the vice president of finance may supervise only five managers. **Span of management** refers to the number of subordinates who report to a particular manager. A *wide span of management* exists when a manager directly supervises a very large number of employees. A *narrow span of management* exists when a manager directly supervises only a few subordinates (Figure 8.4). Wal-Mart, for example, operates with a much broader span of management in its Sam's Clubs and Wal-Mart Superstores than do the Dollar General and Family Dollar discount chains, which employ about four people per store.[9]

Should the span of management be wide or narrow? To answer this question, several factors need to be considered. A narrow span of management is appropriate when superiors and subordinates are not in close proximity, the manager has many responsibilities in addition to the supervision, the interaction between superiors and subordinates is frequent, and problems are common. However, when superiors and subordinates are located close to one another, the manager has few responsibilities other than supervision, the level of interaction between superiors and subordinates is low, few problems arise, subordinates are highly competent, and a set of specific operating procedures governs the activities of managers and their subordinates, a wide span of management will be more appropriate. Narrow spans of management are typical in centralized organizations, while wide spans of management are more common in decentralized firms.

Organizational Layers

Complementing the concept of span of management is **organizational layers,** the levels of management in an organization.

A company with many layers of managers is considered tall; in a tall organization, the span of management is narrow (see Figure 8.4). Because each manager supervises only a few subordinates, many layers of management are necessary to carry out the operations of the business. McDonald's, for example, has a tall organization with many layers, including store managers, district managers, regional managers, and functional managers (finance, marketing, and so on), as well as a chief executive officer and many vice presidents. Because there are more managers in tall organizations

span of management
the number of subordinates who report to a particular manager

organizational layers
the levels of management in an organization

than in flat organizations, administrative costs are usually higher. Communication is slower because information must pass through many layers.

Organizations with few layers are flat and have wide spans of management. When managers supervise a large number of employees, fewer management layers are needed to conduct the organization's activities. Managers in flat organizations typically perform more administrative duties than managers in tall organizations because there are fewer of them. They also spend more time supervising and working with subordinates.

Many of the companies that decentralized during the 1980s and 1990s also flattened their structures and widened their spans of management, often by eliminating layers of middle management. Many corporations, including Avon, AT&T, and Ford Motor Company, did so to reduce costs, speed decision making, and boost overall productivity.

Forms of Organizational Structure

Along with assigning tasks and the responsibility for carrying them out, managers must consider how to structure their authority relationships—that is, what structure the organization itself will have and how it will appear on the organizational chart. Common forms of organization include line structure, line-and-staff structure, multidivisional structure, and matrix structure.

Line Structure

The simplest organizational structure, **line structure,** has direct lines of authority that extend from the top manager to employees at the lowest level of the organization. For example, a convenience store employee may report to an assistant manager, who reports to the store manager, who reports to a regional manager, or, in an independent store, directly to the owner (Figure 8.5). This structure has a clear chain of command, which enables managers to make decisions quickly. A mid-level manager facing a decision must consult only one person, his or her immediate supervisor. However, this structure requires that managers possess a wide range of knowledge and skills. They are responsible for a variety of activities and must be knowledgeable about them all. Line structures are most common in small businesses.

line structure
the simplest organizational structure in which direct lines of authority extend from the top manager to the lowest level of the organization

Line-and-Staff Structure

The **line-and-staff structure** has a traditional line relationship between superiors and subordinates, and specialized managers—called staff managers—are available to assist line managers (Figure 8.6). Line managers can focus on their area of expertise in the operation of the business, while staff managers provide advice and support to line departments on specialized matters such as finance, engineering, human resources, and the law. In the city of Corpus Christi (refer back for Figure 8.3), for example, assistant city managers are line managers who oversee groups of related

line-and-staff structure
a structure having a traditional line relationship between superiors and subordinates and also specialized managers— called staff managers— who are available to assist line managers

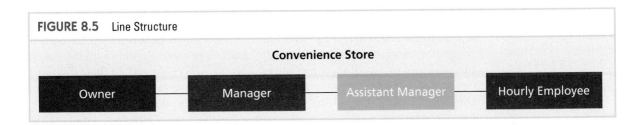

FIGURE 8.5   Line Structure

Convenience Store

Owner — Manager — Assistant Manager — Hourly Employee

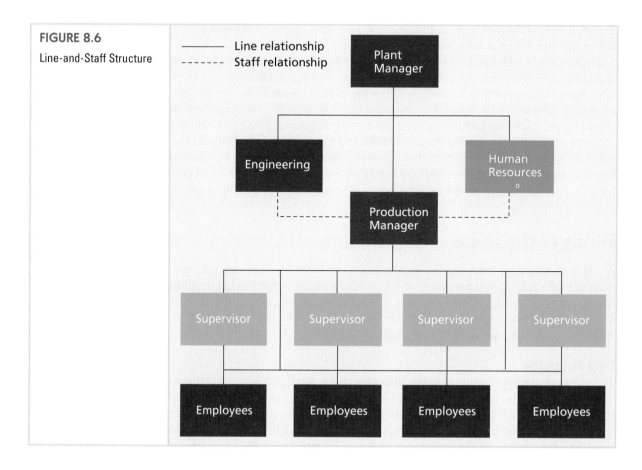

FIGURE 8.6
Line-and-Staff Structure

departments. However, the city attorney, police chief, and fire chief are effectively staff managers who report directly to the city manager (the city equivalent of a business chief executive officer). Staff managers do not have direct authority over line managers or over the line manager's subordinates, but they do have direct authority over subordinates in their own departments. However, line-and-staff organizations may experience problems with overstaffing and ambiguous lines of communication. Additionally, employees may become frustrated because they lack the authority to carry out certain decisions.

Multidivisional Structure

multidivisional structure
a structure that organizes departments into larger groups called divisions

As companies grow and diversify, traditional line structures become difficult to co-ordinate, making communication difficult and decision making slow. When the weaknesses of the structure—the "turf wars," miscommunication, and working at cross-purposes—exceed the benefits, growing firms tend to restructure, often into the divisionalized form. A **multidivisional structure** organizes departments into larger groups called divisions. Just as departments might be formed on the basis of geography, customer, product, or a combination of these, so too divisions can be formed based on any of these methods of organizing. Within each of these divisions, departments may be organized by product, geographic region, function, or some combination of all three. General Motors, for example, operates with divisions structured around its well-known automotive brands (e.g., Chevrolet, Pontiac, and

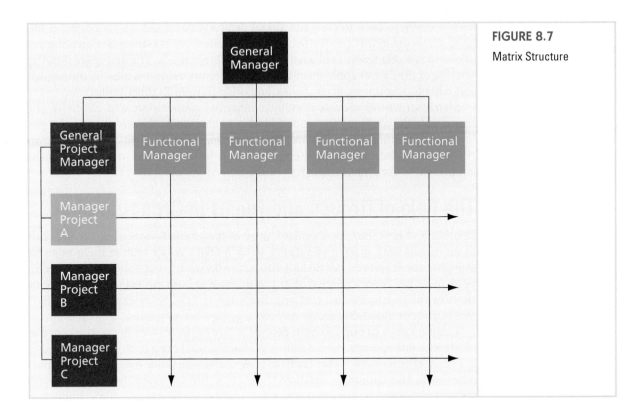

FIGURE 8.7

Matrix Structure

Buick). Within that structure, production and engineering tend to be centralized, while marketing is decentralized under each automotive division. Cadillac, however, operates as a more autonomous division with its own vice president and greater influence on design and engineering than that conferred on other divisions.[10]

Multidivisional structures permit delegation of decision-making authority, allowing divisional and department managers to specialize. They allow those closest to the action to make the decisions that will affect them. Delegation of authority and divisionalized work also mean that better decisions are made faster, and they tend to be more innovative. Most importantly, by focusing each division on a common region, product, or customer, each is more likely to provide products that meet the needs of its particular customers. However, the divisional structure inevitably creates work duplication, which makes it more difficult to realize the economies of scale that result from grouping functions together.

Matrix Structure

Another structure that attempts to address issues that arise with growth, diversification, productivity, and competitiveness, is the matrix. A **matrix structure,** also called a project-management structure, sets up teams from different departments, thereby creating two or more intersecting lines of authority (Figure 8.7). The matrix structure superimposes project-based departments on the more traditional, function-based departments. Project teams bring together specialists from a variety of areas to work together on a single project, such as developing a new fighter jet. In this arrangement, employees are responsible to two managers—functional managers and project managers. Matrix structures are usually temporary: Team mem-

matrix structure
a structure that sets up teams from different departments, thereby creating two or more intersecting lines of authority; also called a project-management structure

bers typically go back to their functional or line department after a project is finished. However, more firms are becoming permanent matrix structures, creating and dissolving project teams as needed to meet customer needs. The aerospace industry was one of the first to apply the matrix structure, but today it is used by universities and schools, accounting firms, banks, and organizations in other industries.

Matrix structures provide flexibility, enhanced cooperation, and creativity, and they enable the company to respond quickly to changes in the environment by giving special attention to specific projects or problems. However, they are generally expensive and quite complex, and employees may be confused as to whose authority has priority—the project manager's or the immediate supervisor's.

The Role of Groups and Teams in Organizations

Regardless of how they are organized, most of the essential work of business occurs in individual work groups and teams, so we'll take a closer look at them now. Although some experts do not make a distinction between groups and teams, in recent years there has been a gradual shift toward an emphasis on teams and managing them to enhance individual and organizational success. Some experts now believe that highest productivity results only when groups become teams.[11]

group
two or more individuals who communicate with one another, share a common identity, and have a common goal

team
a small group whose members have complementary skills; have a common purpose, goals, and approach; and hold themselves mutually accountable

Traditionally, a **group** has been defined as two or more individuals who communicate with one another, share a common identity, and have a common goal. A **team** is a small group whose members have complementary skills; have a common purpose, goals, and approach; and hold themselves mutually accountable.[12] All teams are groups, but not all groups are teams. Table 8.1 points out some important differences between them. Work groups emphasize individual work products, individual accountability, and even individual leadership. Salespeople working independently for the same company could be a work group. In contrast, work teams share leadership roles, have both individual and mutual accountability, and create collective work products. In other words, a work group's performance depends on what its members do as individuals, while a team's performance is based on creating a knowledge center and a competency to work together to accomplish a goal. To sup-

TABLE 8.1	**Working Group**	**Team**
Differences between Groups and Teams	Has strong, clearly focused leader	Has shared leadership roles
	Has individual accountability	Has individual and group accountability
	Has the same purpose as the broader organizational mission	Has a specific purpose that the team itself delivers
	Creates individual work products	Creates collective work products
	Runs efficient meetings	Encourages open-ended discussion and active problem-solving meetings
	Measures its effectiveness indirectly by its effects on others (e.g., financial performance of the business)	Measures performance directly by assessing collective work products
	Discusses, decides, and delegates	Discusses, decides, and does real work together

Source: Robert Gatewood, Robert Taylor, and O. C. Ferrell, *Management: Comprehension Analysis and Application*, 1995, p. 427. Copyright © 1995 Richard D. Irwin, a Times Mirror Higher Education Group, Inc., company. Reproduced with permission of the McGraw-Hill Companies.

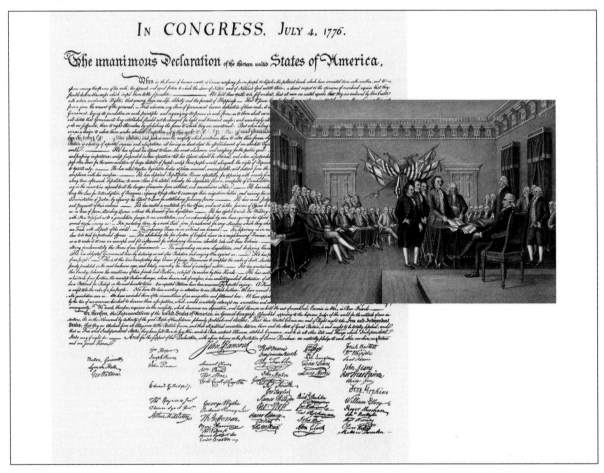

Our country's forefathers, who were charged with the task of coming together to write the Constitution—were they a group or a team? Use the criteria in Table 8.1 to decide.

port sales of its extensive product lines, Procter & Gamble places teams of its employees in key retail customers' headquarters. For instance, Procter & Gamble teams assigned to Dollar General Stores work with the discount retailer to meet its customers' needs and even customize Procter & Gamble products to Dollar General's specification.[13]

The type of groups an organization establishes depends on the tasks it needs to accomplish and the situation it faces. Some specific kinds of groups and teams include committees, task forces, project teams, product-development teams, quality-assurance teams, and self-directed work teams. All of these can be *virtual teams*—employees in different locations who rely on e-mail, audio conferencing, fax, Internet, videoconferencing, or other technological tools to accomplish their goals. One survey found that almost 48 percent of workers have participated in virtual teams.[14]

Committees

A **committee** is usually a permanent, formal group that does some specific task. For example, many firms have a compensation or finance committee to examine the effectiveness of these areas of operation as well as the need for possible changes. Ethics

commitee
a permanent, formal group that performs a specific task

task force
a temporary group of employees responsible for bringing about a particular change

project teams
groups similar to task forces which normally run their operation and have total control of a specific work project

product-development teams
a specific type of project team formed to devise, design, and implement a new product

committees are formed to develop and revise codes of ethics, suggest methods for implementing ethical standards, and review specific issues and concerns.

Task Forces

A **task force** is a temporary group of employees responsible for bringing about a particular change. They typically come from across all departments and levels of an organization. Task force membership is usually based on expertise rather than organizational position. Occasionally, a task force may be formed from individuals outside a company. Such was the case in the task force selected by the Coca-Cola Company and the class representatives in a discrimination lawsuit filed against the company. Creation of the seven-member independent task force was one of the key elements in the settlement between the two parties. The task force will ensure the company's compliance with the settlement agreement and provide oversight of its diversity efforts.[15]

Teams

Teams are becoming far more common in the U.S. workplace as businesses strive to enhance productivity and global competitiveness. In general, teams have the benefit of being able to pool members' knowledge and skills and make greater use of them than can individuals working alone. Team building is becoming increasingly popular in organizations, with 48 percent of executives indicating their companies had team-building training.[16] Teams can also create more solutions to problems than can individuals. Furthermore, team participation enhances employee acceptance of, understanding of, and commitment to team goals. Teams motivate workers by providing internal rewards in the form of an enhanced sense of accomplishment for employees as they achieve more, and external rewards in the form of praise and certain perks. Consequently, they can help get workers more involved. They can help companies be more innovative, and they can boost productivity and cut costs.

Project Teams. **Project teams** are similar to task forces, but normally they run their operation and have total control of a specific work project. Like task forces, their membership is likely to cut across the firm's hierarchy and be composed of people from different functional areas. They are almost always temporary, although a large project, such as designing and building a new airplane at Boeing Corporation, may last for years.

Product-development teams are a special type of project team formed to devise, design, and implement a new product. Sometimes product-development teams exist within a functional

Conflicts can arise for any team—the trick is to make them productive. This ad promotes the American Arbitration Association's mission to train professionals on how to effectively minimize and manage conflict—before the mud starts flying.

Enhancing Business Productivity
War Games to Learn TLC

Teamwork, leadership, and communication skills (or TLC) are especially important in maintaining coordination and commitment to an organization's goals. To help employees become more involved and to boost productivity, many firms, including Domino's Pizza, the Krystal Co., and Captain D's, are sending their managers to Leading Concepts Ranger TLC Experience, a military-style camp run by former Army Rangers. The purpose of the camp is to help managers improve their TLC. Days at the camp begin at the crack of dawn and end around 2 A.M. Much of the intervening time is spent running through the woods and hitting the ground to avoid being hit by "enemy" paint balls. Teams are assigned missions, usually reconnaissance and raids, to recover, food and supplies from the "enemy." Camp participants wear Army fatigues and combat boots and eat army rations. Leading Concepts believes that the war games will help participants develop superior TLC by forcing them to work together to "survive." To keep participants on their toes, leaders are assigned and reassigned at random. Leading Concepts offers different types of programs for team-building and for new or beginning leaders. The Ranger TLC Experience is an advanced leadership and team development program for key leaders and teams, and the Advanced Workshop is exclusively for graduates of the four-day Ranger TLC Experience.

A three-day workshop costs $2,100 per person and includes air travel, local travel, lodging, and food. The camp teaches "soldiers" to step into a new role at a moment's notice.

Over 100 Domino's franchises and about 300 managers from corporate-owned stores have participated in the program. Most Domino's managers who complete the program promise to cross-train their employees as soon as they return to work, and most believe the camp makes them better communicators. The company is hard-pressed to find anyone who doesn't give the experience a positive assessment. The experience motivates managers to work harder, listen more, and be judged as part of a team rather than an individual. According to Domino's national director of corporate training, the program has also slowed turnover. In general, managers link their boot camp experience with increased teamwork and improved productivity.[17]

Discussion Questions

1. Why do you think a "boot camp" exercise can increase teamwork and improve productivity?
2. What do you think employees learn from these military-style exercises?
3. Why do you think the boot camp may be especially appropriate for Domino's managers?

---

area—research and development—but now they more frequently include people from numerous functional areas and may even include customers to help ensure that the end product meets the customers' needs.

Quality-Assurance Teams. **Quality-assurance teams,** sometimes called **quality circles,** are fairly small groups of workers brought together from throughout the organization to solve specific quality, productivity, or service problems. Although the "quality circle" term is not as popular as it once was, the concern about quality is stronger than ever. The use of teams to address quality issues will no doubt continue to increase throughout the business world.

Self-directed Work Teams. A **self-directed work team (SDWT)** is a group of employees responsible for an entire work process or segment that delivers a product to an internal or external customer.[18] Sometimes called self-managed teams or autonomous work groups, SDWTs reduce the need for extra layers of management and thus can help control costs. SDWTs also permit the flexibility to change rapidly to meet the competition or respond to customer needs. The defining characteristic of an SDWT is the extent to which it is empowered or given authority to make and implement work decisions. Thus, SDWTs are designed to give employees a feeling of "ownership" of a whole job. With shared team responsibility for work outcomes, team members often have broader job assignments and cross-train to master other jobs, thus permitting greater team flexibility.

> **quality-assurance teams (or quality circles)**
> small groups of workers brought together from throughout the organization to solve specific quality, productivity, or service problems

> **self-directed work team (SDWT)**
> a group of employees responsible for an entire work process or segment that delivers a product to an internal or external customer

Quest Star (QS), which manufactures quality stereo loudspeakers, wants to improve its ability to compete against Japanese firms. Accordingly, the company has launched a comprehensive quality-improvement program for its Iowa plant. The QS Intracommunication Leadership Initiative (ILI) has flattened the layers of management. The program uses teams and peer pressure to accomplish the plant's goals instead of multiple management layers with their limited opportunities for communication. Under the initiative, employees make all decisions within the boundaries of their responsibilities, and they elect team representatives to coordinate with other teams. Teams are also assigned tasks ranging from establishing policies to evaluating on-the-job safety.

However, employees who are not self-motivated team players are having difficulty getting used to their peers' authority within this system. Upper-level managers face stress and frustration because they must train workers to supervise themselves.

1. What techniques or skills should an employee have to assume a leadership role within a work group?
2. If each work group has a team representative, what problems will be faced in supervising these representatives?
3. Evaluate the pros and cons of the system developed by QS.

Communicating in Organizations

Communication within an organization can flow in a variety of directions and from a number of sources, each using both oral and written forms of communication. The success of communication systems within the organization has a tremendous effect on the overall success of the firm. Communication mistakes can lower productivity and morale.

Alternatives to face-to-face communications—such as meetings—are growing thanks to technology such as voice mail, e-mail, and online newsletters. At Matsushita, for example, company executives are required to file reports to president Kunio Nakamura by mobile e-mail and are provided an Internet-equipped mobile phone for that purpose.[20] At many companies, however, such communications technology has contributed to a state of information overload for employees, who spend more and more time managing e-mail. A growing problem is employees abusing e-mail. In some companies, up to 75 percent of e-mail messages are not business related.[21]

Experts say that managers must (1) plan how they will share important news, (2) repeat important information, and (3) rehearse key presentations. According to one study, 62 percent of executives think employees and companies benefit from fun and humor in communications and management style.[22]

Did You Know? People spend an average of one to one- and-a-half days per week in meetings.[19]

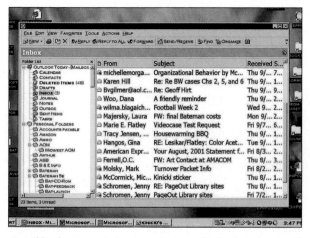

E-mail has become a vital communication tool in business, but not all business e-mail relates to work.

Formal Communication

Formal channels of communication are intentionally defined and designed by the organization. They represent the flow of communication within the formal organizational structure, as shown on organizational charts. Traditionally, formal communication patterns were classified as vertical and horizontal, but with the increased use of teams and matrix structures, formal communication may occur in a number of patterns (Figure 8.8).

Upward communication flows from lower to higher levels of the organization and includes information such as progress reports, suggestions for improvement, inquiries, and grievances. *Downward communication* refers to the traditional flow of information from upper organizational levels to lower levels. This type of communication typically involves directions, the assignment of tasks and responsibilities, performance feedback, and certain details about the organization's strategies and goals. Speeches, policy and procedures manuals, employee handbooks, company leaflets, telecommunications, and job descriptions are examples of downward communication.

Horizontal communication involves the exchange of information among colleagues and peers on the same organizational level, such as across or within departments. Horizontal information informs, supports, and coordinates activities both within the department and with other departments. At times, the business will formally require horizontal communication among particular organizational members, as is the case with task forces or project teams.

With more and more companies downsizing and increasing the use of self-managed work teams, many workers are being required to communicate with others in different departments and on different levels to solve problems and coordinate work. When these individuals from different units and organizational levels communicate, it is *diagonal communication.* At OpenAir.com, Inc., all staff members meet every day at 9:30 A.M. to share information and anecdotes about customer calls from the previous day. No chairs are allowed, and everyone is encouraged to participate. COO Morris Panner says that the communication style "reemphasizes the fact that our company is based on collaboration."[23]

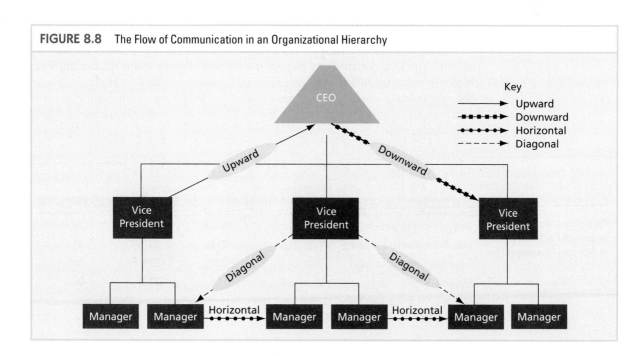

FIGURE 8.8   The Flow of Communication in an Organizational Hierarchy

Informal Communication Channels

Along with the formal channels of communication shown on an organizational chart, all firms communicate informally as well. Communication between friends, for instance, cuts across department, division, and even management-subordinate boundaries. Such friendships and other nonwork social relationships comprise the *informal organization* of a firm, and their impact can be great.

The most significant informal communication occurs through the **grapevine,** an informal channel of communication, separate from management's formal, official communication channels. Grapevines exist in all organizations. Information passed along the grapevine may relate to the job or organization, or it may be gossip and rumors unrelated to either. The accuracy of grapevine information has been of great concern to managers.

Additionally, managers can turn the grapevine to their advantage. Using it as a "sounding device" for possible new policies is one example. Managers can obtain valuable information from the grapevine that could improve decision making. Some organizations use the grapevine to their advantage by floating ideas, soliciting feedback, and reacting accordingly. People love to gossip, and managers need to be aware that grapevines exist in every organization. Managers who understand how the grapevine works also can use it to their advantage by feeding it facts to squelch rumors and incorrect information.

Monitoring Communications

Technological advances and the increased use of electronic communication in the workplace have made monitoring its use necessary for most companies. An American Management Association study found that more than half of the 1,100 employees surveyed believed their employers monitored their e-mail. Such organizational scrutiny of employees' e-mail may be the result of attacks on corporate computer systems, of which 70 percent are conducted from inside the firm.[24] (See Table 8.2.) Failing to monitor employee's use of e-mail and the Internet can be costly. Chevron Corp. agreed to pay $2 million to employees who claimed that unmonitored, sexually harassing e-mail created a threatening environment for them.[25] Instituting practices that show respect for employee privacy but do not abdicate employer responsibility are increasingly necessary in today's workplace. Several Web sites provide model policies and detailed guidelines for conducting electronic monitoring, including the Model Electronic Privacy Act on the American Civil Liberties Union site.

TABLE 8.2

Disciplinary Action for Misuse of Personal Use of Telecom Equipment

	Telephone	E-mail	Internet	Combined
Any disciplinary action	52.8%	54.5%	51.0%	76.4%
Informal reprimand/warning	31.5	24.8	23.0	44.7
Formal reprimand/warning	34.0	38.7	33.6	56.7
Dismissal	10.4	18.6	20.3	30.9

Source: American Management Association, 2001, as reported by Diane E. Lewis, "Devices Keep Close Watch on Workplace," *Boston Globe*, June 24, 2001, p. H9.

Explore Your Career Options
Flexibility First!

Most business school students major in marketing, finance, accounting, management information systems, general management, or sales. Upon graduation, they generally expect to be hired by a company to do more of whatever it is they were trained to do as a student. For example, an accounting major expects to be an accountant. However, depending upon the way the company is organized, the roles played by the employees will differ.

If you are hired by a large, divisionalized company, you might expect to practice your profession among many others doing the same or similar tasks. You are likely to learn one part of the business fairly well but be completely uninformed about other departments or divisions. A wise employee in this situation will learn to request occasional transfers to other divisions to learn all aspects of the corporation, thereby improving his or her usefulness to the company and promotion chances.

On the other hand, if you gain employment in a very small company or in one that is heavily decentralized, you may find that you are expected to do more than the tasks for which you were trained. In many small organizations, employees are often expected to wear many hats in order to make the organization more efficient. For example, it can come as a shock to an accounting graduate to discover that, in addition to accounting, he or she will also be doing bookkeeping, secretarial work and public relations.

Likewise, employees in larger organizations that make heavy use of teams and decentralized decision making may find that the company expects more of them than the skills learned in school. To be an effective team member, you may find that you will not only contribute your skills and expertise, but you will also be expected to learn some engineering, computer science, and marketing to be able to understand the needs and constraints of the other members of the team. Organizational flexibility requires individual flexibility, and those employees willing to take on new domains and challenges will be the employees who survive and prosper in the future.[26]

Review Your Understanding

Define organizational structure and relate how organizational structures develop.

Structure is the arrangement or relationship of positions within an organization; it develops when managers assign work activities to work groups and specific individuals and coordinate the diverse activities required to attain organizational objectives. Organizational structure evolves to accommodate growth, which requires people with specialized skills.

Describe how specialization and departmentalization help an organization achieve its goals.

Structuring an organization requires that management assign work tasks to specific individuals and groups. Under specialization, managers break labor into small, specialized tasks and assign employees to do a single task, fostering efficiency. Departmentalization is the grouping of jobs into working units (departments, units, groups, or divisions). Businesses may departmentalize by function, product, geographic region, or customer, or they may combine two or more of these.

Distinguish between groups and teams and identify the types of groups that exist in organizations.

A group is two or more persons who communicate, share a common identity, and have a common goal. A team is a small group whose members have complementary skills, a common purpose, goals, and approach; and who hold themselves mutually accountable. The major distinction is that individual performance is most important in groups, while collective work group performance counts most in teams. Special kinds of groups include task forces, committees, project teams, product-development teams, quality-assurance teams, and self-directed work teams.

Determine how organizations assign responsibility for tasks and delegate authority.

Delegation of authority means assigning tasks to employees and giving them the power to make commitments, use resources, and take whatever actions are necessary to accomplish the tasks. It lays responsibility on employees to carry out assigned tasks satisfactorily and holds them accountable to a superior for the proper execution of their assigned work. The extent to which authority is delegated throughout an organization determines its degree of centralization. Span of management refers to the number of subordinates who report to a particular manager. A wide span of management occurs in flat organizations; a narrow one exists in tall organizations.

Compare and contrast some common forms of organizational structure.

Line structures have direct lines of authority that extend from the top manager to employees at the lowest level of the organization. The line-and-staff structure has a traditional line relationship between superiors and subordinates, and specialized staff managers are available to assist line managers. A multidivisional structure gathers departments into larger groups called divisions. A matrix, or project-management, structure sets up teams from different departments, thereby creating two or more intersecting lines of authority.

Describe how communication occurs in organizations.

Communication occurs both formally and informally in organizations. Formal communication may be downward, upward, horizontal, and even diagonal. Informal communication takes place through friendships and the grapevine.

Analyze a business's use of teams.

The "Solve the Dilemma" box on page 246 introduced a firm attempting to restructure to a team environment. Based on the material presented in this chapter, you should be able to evaluate the firm's efforts and make recommendations for resolving the problems that have developed.

Revisit the World of Business

1. Which organizational factor contributed most to the *Columbia* disaster at NASA?
2. In what way did the organizational culture contribute to the disaster?
3. How can NASA harness its "can-do" drive to succeed to create safer missions to the moon, Mars, and beyond?

Learn the Terms

accountability   236
centralized organization   237
committee   243
customer departmentalization   235
decentralized organization   237
delegation of authority   236
departmentalization   233
functional departmentalization   233
geographical departmentalization   234
grapevine   248

group   242
line-and-staff structure   239
line structure   239
matrix structure   241
multidivisional structure   240
organizational chart   231
organizational culture   228
organizational layers   238
product departmentalization   233
product-development teams   244

project teams   244
quality-assurance teams (or quality circles)   245
responsibility   236
self-directed work team (SDWT)   245
span of management   238
specialization   232
structure   230
task force   244
team   242

Check Your Progress

1. Identify four types of departmentalization and give an example of each type.
2. Explain the difference between groups and teams.
3. What are self-managed work teams and what tasks might they perform that traditionally are performed by managers?
4. Explain how delegating authority, responsibility, and accountability are related.
5. Distinguish between centralization and decentralization. Under what circumstances is each appropriate?
6. Define span of management. Why do some organizations have narrow spans and others wide spans?
7. Discuss the different forms of organizational structure. What are the primary advantages and disadvantages of each form?

8. Discuss the role of the grapevine within organizations. How can managers use it to further the goals of the firm?

9. How have technological advances made electronic oversight a necessity in many companies?

10. Discuss how an organization's culture might influence its ability to achieve its objectives. Do you think that managers can "manage" the organization's culture?

Get Involved

1. Explain, using a specific example (perhaps your own future business), how an organizational structure might evolve. How would you handle the issues of specialization, delegation of authority, and centralization? Which structure would you use? Explain your answers.

2. Interview the department chairperson in charge of one of the academic departments in your college or university. Using Table 8.1 as a guideline, explore whether the professors function more like a group or a team. Contrast what you find here with what you see on your school's basketball, football, or baseball team.

Build Your Skills

TEAMWORK

Background:
Think about all the different kinds of groups and teams you have been a member of or been involved with. Here's a checklist to help you remember them—with "Other" spaces to fill in ones not listed. Check all that apply.

School Groups/Teams
☐ Sports teams
☐ Cheerleading squads
☐ Musical groups
☐ Hobby clubs
☐ Foreign language clubs
☐ Study groups
☐ Other _____

Community Groups/Teams
☐ Fund-raising groups
☐ Religious groups
☐ Sports teams
☐ Political groups
☐ Boy/Girl Scout Troops
☐ Volunteer organizations
☐ Other _____

Employment Groups/Teams
☐ Problem-solving teams
☐ Work committees
☐ Project teams
☐ Labor union groups
☐ Work crews
☐ Other _____

Task

1. Of those you checked, circle those that you would categorize as a "really great team."

2. Examine the following table[27] and circle those characteristics from columns two and three that were represented in your "really great" team experiences.

Indicator	Good Team Experience	Not-So-Good Team Experience
Members arrive on time?	Members are prompt because they know others will be.	Members drift in sporadically, and some leave early.
Members prepared?	Members are prepared and know what to expect.	Members are unclear what the agenda is.
Meeting organized?	Members follow a planned agenda.	The agenda is tossed aside, and freewheeling discussion ensues.
Members contribute equally?	Members give each other a chance to speak; quiet members are encouraged.	Some members always dominate the discussion; some are reluctant to speak their minds.
Discussions help members make decisions?	Members learn from others' points of view, new facts are discussed, creative ideas evolve, and alternatives emerge.	Members reinforce their belief in their own points of view, or their decisions were made long before the meeting.

Indicator	Good Team Experience	Not-So-Good Team Experience
Any disagreement?	Members follow a conflict-resolution process established as part of the team's policies.	Conflict turns to argument, angry words, emotion, blaming.
More cooperation or more conflict?	Cooperation is clearly an important ingredient.	Conflict flares openly, as well as simmering below the surface.
Commitment to decisions?	Members reach consensus before leaving.	Compromise is the best outcome possible; some members don't care about the result.
Member feelings after team decision?	Members are satisfied and are valued for their ideas.	Members are glad it's over, not sure of results or outcome.
Members support decision afterward?	Members are committed to implementation.	Some members second-guess or undermine the team's decision.

3. What can you take with you from your positive team experiences and apply to a work-related group or team situation in which you might be involved? _____

_____

_____

_____

---

e-Xtreme Surfing

- **Leading Concepts**
  www.leadingconcepts.com/

  Provides information about the company's "boot camp" programs to help companies improve communication and build teamwork.

- **Model Electronic Privacy Act**
  http://archive.aclu.org/issues/worker/legkit2.html

  Offers information from the American Civil Liberties Union about proposed legislation regulating electronic monitoring of employee communications.

- **NASA's organizational chart**
  www.hq.nasa.gov/hq/orgchart.htm

  Presents the organizational chart for the aerospace agency.

See for Yourself Videocase

LEE VAN ARSDALE AND THE DELTA FORCE ILLUSTRATE THE NEED FOR TEAMWORK AND COMMUNICATION

Colonel Lee Van Arsdale is currently the executive director of the University of Nevada, Las Vegas Institute for Security Studies (ISS), which focuses on knowledge related to homeland security. Van Arsdale is involved in teaching, researching, and training related to combating terrorism in a coordinated fashion. Prior to assuming this position, he was president of Unconventional Solutions, Inc., a private security firm specializing in national security and combating terrorism planning and response options.

Colonel Van Arsdale understands the role of teamwork, communication, and organization in attaining goals and objectives. As you might expect from his rank, much of his training and experience comes from the military. Van Arsdale graduated from the United States Military Academy at West Point in 1974, and served in the U.S. Army until his retirement in 1999. During that time, he spent eleven years with the First Special Forces Operational Detachment—Delta (Airborne), where he rose to the position of Sabre Squadron Commander. He served in leadership positions in three combat zones and was decorated for valor with the Silver Star and with the Purple Heart for wounds received in combat. During his final two years in the army, he served as the Counterterrorism/Special Projects Branch Chief, in the Office of the Secretary of Defense. Because of his experience in Operation Just Cause in Panama and his membership in the Delta Force team in Somalia, Colonel Van Arsdale was chosen to be the technical advisor for the movie *Black Hawk Down,* which depicted the rescue of downed helicopter pilots in Somalia and the death of those who tried to rescue the pilots.

Following his military career, Colonel Van Arsdale became a manager at Bechtel Nevada Corporation, a government-contract firm which manages the Nevada Test Site and other Department of Energy facilities. His major focus on this job was Department of Energy emergency response capability, communication technologies, and technologies in support of the federal effort to combat terrorism.

Van Arsdale's success has occurred because of his ability to lead work groups and teams. Teams are small groups whose members have complementary skills, who work with common purpose goals and approach. A key point about team members is that they have both individual and mutual accountability and create collective work products. In other words, an individual's or small group's performance depends on what its members do as individuals while a team's performance is based on creating a knowledge center and a competency to work together to accomplish a goal. *Black Hawk Down* illustrated that teamwork is absolutely necessary when the outcome of an operation is critical.

Special Forces teams are similar to teams in other types of organizations—the difference is that their success can result in either life or death for those involved in carrying out the mission. They need the right people, proper equipment, and of course, the education and training to do their jobs properly. Members of Delta Force are volunteers and are trained to be specialists dealing with areas such as communications, weapons, medics, piloting, etc. The training even addresses how to operate in certain regions of the world, which includes training in language, culture, and how to adapt to various climates. This division of specific tasks handled by highly trained members of the Delta Force provides specialization that is only meaningful with good teamwork.

The Delta Force has an organizational culture with shared values, beliefs, traditions, philosophies, rules, and heroes. The movie *Black Hawk Down* illustrated many of these organizational cultural characteristics of Delta Force. Part of the culture stems from the fact that Delta Force is on call 24/7, 365 days a year. Their planning is done from the bottom up. The team, which may consist of just a few operatives or many more people, is free to decide how to carry out a particular mission. This is similar to empowering employees in a business environment. Most of the principles of management, especially leadership, teamwork, and communication are embedded and understood by Delta Force members. While they may not have learned these concepts out of a textbook, they have mastered these concepts through their military education, training, and experience.

Leaders rely on integrity, trust, and commitment. At times, a leader has to take control while at other times, a leader must simply listen. The heart of teamwork is communications and the ability for each specialist to process and operationalize the information available. Colonel Van Arsdale continues to be a vital resource in the fight against terrorism. From his position at the University of Nevada, Las Vegas, he is assuming a leadership position in helping with homeland security that will hopefully prevent another major terrorist attack on the United States.[28]

Discussion Questions
1. What does the Delta Force teach us about the importance of teamwork within an organization?
2. What are the major differences between implementing a military operation and implementing a business operation?
3. Why do you think Lee Van Arsdale continues to provide leadership and a focused mission to deal with terrorism and homeland security?

Remember to check out our Online Learning Center at www.mhhe.com/ferrell5e.

Chapter 9

Managing Service and Manufacturing Operations

OBJECTIVES

After reading this chapter, you will be able to:

- Define operations management and differentiate between operations and manufacturing.

- Explain how operations management differs in manufacturing and service firms.

- Describe the elements involved in planning and designing an operations system.

- Specify some techniques managers may use to manage the logistics of transforming inputs into finished products.

- Assess the importance of quality in operations management.

- Evaluate a business's dilemma and propose a solution.

Designing Products for a Better Customer Experience

IDEO is a design firm that helps client companies conceive and develop innovative products, environments, and even digital experiences. The Palo Alto–based company also designs consumer experiences and services related to shopping, banking, health care, and wireless communications. The 350-person firm, which has won more design awards over the last decade than any other firm, can have a tremendous impact on the sales of products it had a hand in developing, such as user-friendly computers, PDAs and the Palm V, Polaroid's I-Zone cameras, the Steelcase Leap chair, Oral-B toothbrushes for kids, and even a stand-up toothpaste tube for Crest. Indeed, the company's roster of clients spans the globe, including Hewlett-Packard, AT&T Wireless, Nestlé, Samsung, the BBC, and even NASA.

IDEO, in which furniture-maker Steelcase owns a majority stake, has crafted a set of systematic research methods for understanding the human factors that make products successful—and it does it *fast*. This process places people at the center of the design process and makes the overall product experience the focal point of the design. IDEO employs a five-step process for designing a better consumer experience: observation, brainstorming, rapid prototyping, refining, and implementation. In the first step, IDEO relies on social scientists to better understand consumer experiences with products through observation, interviews, shopping trips, and even storytelling. In the brainstorming phase, designers, engineers, and social scientists interact with the client company to come up with potential solutions—no matter how absurd. The managed chaos of brainstorming

continued

leads to the next step, which involves creating simple working prototypes of the best ideas from the brainstorming session so that everyone can visualize them, understand how they work, and evaluate their pros and cons. This rapid prototyping speeds up innovative decision making. During the refining stage, IDEO narrows the design selections and engages the client to find the best choice. During the final stage, IDEO uses its strong engineering design and understanding of the consumer product experience to develop a final product that satisfies the client. The implementation stage may bring together IDEO's experts in materials science, computer-aided design, and molding, in addition to social scientists such as sociologists, statisticians, and psychologists, to ensure that the final product addresses every issue and creates a satisfying result or experience for the customer.

Although IDEO has traditionally focused on product design, it is now also helping service providers gain valuable insights into how to improve their customer environments. For example, IDEO helped Kaiser Permanente, the nation's largest HMO, realize that it didn't need to make a huge investment in new buildings but instead needed to revamp its patient experience through elements such as more comfortable waiting rooms and larger exam rooms that allowed emergency room patients to have a family member with them. Companies come to IDEO with a problem, and the design firm puts together a team of its experts—both its own and from the client firm—who can focus on a fast implementation of the five-step process to observe and improve the consumer experience.[1]

Introduction

All organizations create products—goods, services, or ideas—for customers. Thus, organizations as diverse as Dell Computer, Campbell Soup, UPS, and a public hospital share a number of similarities relating to how they transform resources into the products we consume. Most hospitals use similar admission procedures, while Burger King and Dairy Queen use similar food preparation methods to make hamburgers. Such similarities are to be expected. But even organizations in unrelated industries take similar steps in creating goods or services. The check-in procedures of hotels and commercial airlines are comparable, for example. The way Subway assembles a sandwich and the way GMC assembles a truck are similar (both use automation and an assembly line). These similarities are the result of operations management, the focus of this chapter.

Here, we discuss the role of production or operations management in acquiring and managing the resources necessary to create goods and services. Production and operations management involves planning and designing the processes that will transform those resources into finished products, managing the movement of those resources through the transformation process, and ensuring that the products are of the quality expected by customers.

The Nature of Operations Management

Operations management (OM), the development and administration of the activities involved in transforming resources into goods and services, is of critical importance. Operations managers oversee the transformation process and the planning and designing of operations systems, managing logistics, quality, and productivity. Quality and productivity have become fundamental aspects of operations management because a company that cannot make products of the quality desired by consumers, using resources efficiently and effectively, will not be able to remain in business. OM is the "core" of most organizations because it is responsible for the creation of the organization's goods or services.

Historically, operations management has been called "production" or "manufacturing" primarily because of the view that it was limited to the manufacture of physical goods. Its focus was on methods and techniques required to operate a factory efficiently. The change from "production" to "operations" recognizes the increasing importance of organizations that provide services and ideas. Additionally, the term *operations* represents an interest in viewing the operations function as a whole rather than simply as an analysis of inputs and outputs.

Today, OM includes a wide range of organizational activities and situations outside of manufacturing, such as health care, food service, banking, entertainment, education, transportation, and charity. Thus, we use the terms **manufacturing** and **production** interchangeably to represent the activities and processes used in making *tangible* products, whereas we use the broader term **operations** to describe those processes used in the making of *both tangible and intangible products.* Manufacturing provides tangible products such as Hewlett-Packard's latest printer, and operations provides intangibles such as a stay at Wyndham Hotels and Resorts.

The Transformation Process

At the heart of operations management is the transformation process through which **inputs** (resources such as labor, money, materials, and energy) are converted into **outputs** (goods, services, and ideas). The transformation process combines inputs in predetermined ways using different equipment, administrative procedures, and technology to create a product (Figure 9.1). To ensure that this process generates

operations management (OM)
the development and administration of the activities involved in transforming resources into goods and services

manufacturing
the activities and processes used in making tangible products; also called production

production
the activities and processes used in making tangible products; also called manufacturing

operations
the activities and processes used in making both tangible and intangible products

inputs
the resources—such as labor, money, materials, and energy—that are converted into outputs

outputs
the goods, services, and ideas that result from the conversion of inputs

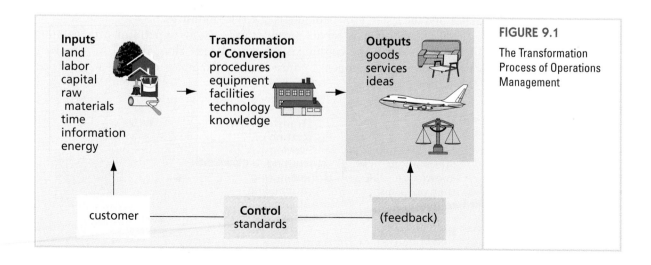

Inputs
land
labor
capital
raw
  materials
time
information
energy

Transformation or Conversion
procedures
equipment
facilities
technology
knowledge

Outputs
goods
services
ideas

customer ——— **Control** standards ——— (feedback)

FIGURE 9.1

The Transformation Process of Operations Management

quality products efficiently, operations managers control the process by taking measurements (feedback) at various points in the transformation process and comparing them to previously established standards. If there is any deviation between the actual and desired outputs, the manager may take some sort of corrective action. All adjustments made to create a satisfying product are a part of the transformation process.

Transformation may take place through one or more processes. In a business that manufactures oak furniture, for example, inputs pass through several processes before being turned into the final outputs—furniture that has been designed to meet the desires of customers (Figure 9.2). The furniture maker must first strip the oak trees of their bark and saw them into appropriate sizes—one step in the transformation process. Next, the firm dries the strips of oak lumber, a second form of transformation. Third, the dried wood is routed into its appropriate shape and made smooth. Fourth, workers assemble and treat the wood pieces, then stain or varnish the piece of assembled furniture. Finally, the completed piece of furniture is stored until it can be shipped to customers at the appropriate time. Of course, many businesses choose to eliminate some of these stages by purchasing already processed materials—lumber, for example—or outsourcing some tasks to third-party firms with greater expertise.

Operations Management in Service Businesses

Different types of transformation processes take place in organizations that provide services, such as airlines, colleges, and most nonprofit organizations. An airline transforms inputs such as employees, time, money, and equipment through processes such as booking flights, flying airplanes, maintaining equipment, and training crews. The output of these processes is flying passengers and/or packages to their destinations. In a nonprofit organization like Habitat for Humanity, inputs such as money, materials, information, and volunteer time and labor are used to transform raw materials into homes for needy families. In this setting, transformation processes include fund-raising and promoting the cause in order to gain new volunteers and donations of supplies, as well as pouring concrete, raising walls, and setting roofs. Transformation processes occur in all organizations, regardless of what they produce or their objectives. For most organizations, the ultimate objective is for the produced outputs to be worth more than the combined costs of the inputs. The service sector represents approximately 80 percent of all employment in the United States, and the fastest growth of jobs is in service industries.[2]

Unlike tangible goods, services are effectively actions or performances that must be directed toward the consumers who use them. Thus, there is a significant customer-contact component to most services. Examples of high-contact services

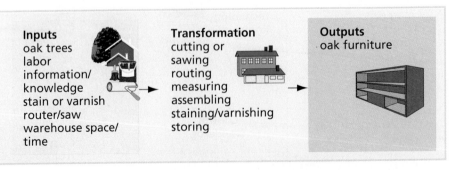

FIGURE 9.2

Inputs, Outputs, and Transformation Processes in the Manufacture of Oak Furniture

Inputs
oak trees
labor
information/
knowledge
stain or varnish
router/saw
warehouse space/
time

Transformation
cutting or
sawing
routing
measuring
assembling
staining/varnishing
storing

Outputs
oak furniture

include health care, real estate, tax preparation, and food service. At the world-renowned Inn at Little Washington, for example, food servers are critical to delivering the perfect dining experience expected by the most discriminating diners. Wait staff are expected not only to be courteous but also to demonstrate a detailed knowledge of the restaurant's offerings, and even to assess the mood of guests in order to respond to diners appropriately.[3] Low-contact services, such as online auction services like eBay, often have a strong high-tech component.

Regardless of the level of customer contact, service businesses strive to provide a standardized process, and technology offers an interface that creates an automatic and structured response. The ideal service provider will be high-tech and high-touch. JetBlue, for example, strives to maintain an excellent Web site; friendly, helpful customer contact; and satellite TV service at every seat on each plane. Thus, service organizations must build their operations around good execution, which comes from hiring and training excellent employees, developing flexible systems, customizing services, and maintaining adjustable capacity to deal with fluctuating demand.[4]

Another challenge related to service operations is that the output is generally intangible and even perishable. Few services can be saved, stored, resold, or returned.[5] A seat on an airline or a table in a restaurant, for example, cannot be sold or used at a later date. Because of the perishability of services, it is can be extremely difficult for service providers to accurately estimate the demand in order to match the right supply of a service. If an airline overestimates demand, for example, it will still have to fly each plane even with empty seats. The flight costs the same regardless of whether it is 50 percent full or 100 percent full, but the former will result in much higher costs per passenger. If the airline underestimates demand, the result can be long lines of annoyed customers or even the necessity of bumping some customers off of an overbooked flight.

Businesses that manufacture tangible goods and those that provide services or ideas are similar yet different. For example, both types of organizations must make design and operating decisions. Most goods are manufactured prior to purchase, but most services are performed after purchase. Flight attendants at Southwest Airlines, hotel service personnel, and even the Tennessee Titans football team engage in performances that are a part of the total product. Though manufacturers and service providers often perform similar activities, they also differ in several respects. We can classify these differences in five basic ways.

Fandango is a leading service operation which provides advance movie tickets, show times, and more on the Internet and by telephone, allowing patrons to bypass the box office line by picking up tickets at the theater. Fandango is also leading the way in new movie-going enhancements with an ongoing test (in select markets) of such advancements as print-at-home ticketing, express theater and concession lines, and more.

Nature and Consumption of Output.   First, manufacturers and service providers differ in the nature and consumption of their output. For example, the term *manufacturer* implies a firm that makes tangible products. A service provider, on the other hand, produces more intangible outputs such as U.S. Postal Service delivery of priority mail or a business stay in a Hyatt hotel. As mentioned earlier, the very nature of the service provider's product requires a higher degree of customer contact. Moreover, the actual performance of the service typically occurs at the point of consumption. At the Hyatt, the business traveler may evaluate in-room communications and the restaurant. Toyota and other automakers, on the other hand, can separate the production of a car from its actual use. Manufacturing, then, can occur in an isolated environment, away from the customer. On the other hand, service providers, because of their need for customer contact, are often more limited than manufacturers in selecting work methods, assigning jobs, scheduling work, and exercising control over operations. At Toyota, for example, any employee who observes a problem can pull a cord and bring the assembly line to a stop to address the issue.[6] The quality of the service experience is often controlled by a service contact employee. However, some hospitals are studying the manufacturing processes and quality control mechanisms applied in the automotive industry in an effort to improve their service quality. By analyzing work processes to find unnecessary steps to eliminate and using teams to identify and address problems as soon as they occur, these hospitals are slashing patient waiting times, decreasing inventories of wheelchairs, readying operating rooms sooner, and generally moving patients through their hospital visit more quickly, with fewer errors, and at a lower cost.[7]

Uniformity of Inputs.   A second way to classify differences between manufacturers and service providers has to do with the uniformity of inputs. Manufacturers typically have more control over the amount of variability of the resources they use than do service providers. For example, each customer calling Fidelity Investments is likely to require different services due to differing needs, whereas many of the tasks required to manufacture a Lincoln Navigator sport utility vehicle are the same across each unit of output. Consequently, the products of service organizations tend to be more "customized" than those of their manufacturing counterparts. Consider, for example, a haircut versus a bottle of shampoo. The haircut is much more likely to incorporate your specific desires (customization) than is the bottle of shampoo.

Uniformity of Output.   Manufacturers and service providers also differ in the uniformity of their output, the final product. Because of the human element inherent in providing services, each service tends to be performed differently. Not all grocery checkers, for example, wait on customers in the same way. If a barber or stylist performs 15 haircuts in a day, it is unlikely that any two of them will be exactly the same. Consequently, human and technological elements associated with a service can result in a different day-to-day or even hour-to-hour performance of that service. The service experience can even vary at McDonald's or Burger King despite the fact that the two chains employ very similar procedures and processes. Moreover, no two customers are exactly alike in their perception of the service experience. Health care offers another excellent example of this challenge. Every diagnosis, treatment, and surgery varies because every individual is different. In manufacturing, the high degree of automation available allows manufacturers to generate uniform outputs and, thus, the operations are more effective and efficient. For example, we would expect every Movado or Rolex watch to maintain very high standards of quality and performance.

Labor Required.   A fourth point of difference is the amount of labor required to produce an output. Service providers are generally more labor-intensive (require more labor) because of the high level of customer contact, perishability of the output (must be consumed immediately), and high degree of variation of inputs and outputs (customization). For example, Adecco provides temporary support personnel. Each temporary worker's performance determines Adecco's product quality. A manufacturer, on the other hand, is likely to be more capital-intensive because of the machinery and technology used in the mass production of highly similar goods. For instance, it would take a considerable investment for Nokia to make a digital phone that has a battery with longer life.

Measurement of Productivity.   The final distinction between service providers and manufacturers involves the measurement of productivity for each output produced. For manufacturers, measuring productivity is fairly straightforward because of the tangibility of the output and its high degree of uniformity. For the service provider, variations in demand (for example, higher demand for air travel in some seasons than in others), variations in service requirements from job to job, and the intangibility of the product make productivity measurement more difficult. Consider, for example, how much easier it is to measure the productivity of employees involved in the production of Intel computer processors as opposed to serving the needs of Prudential Securities' clients.

It is convenient and simple to think of organizations as being either manufacturers or service providers as in the preceding discussion. In reality, however, most organizations are a combination of the two, with both tangible and intangible qualities embodied in what they produce. For example, Porsche provides customer services such as toll-free hotlines and warranty protection, while banks may sell checks and other tangible products that complement their primarily intangible product offering. Thus, we consider "products" to include both tangible physical goods as well as intangible service offerings. It is the level of tangibility of its principal product that tends to classify a company as either a manufacturer or a service provider. From an OM standpoint, this level of tangibility greatly influences the nature of the company's operational processes and procedures.

Planning and Designing Operations Systems

Before a company can produce any product, it must first decide what it will produce and for what group of customers. It must then determine what processes it will use to make these products as well as the facilities it needs to produce them. These decisions comprise operations planning. Although planning was once the sole realm of the production and operations department, today's successful companies involve all departments within an organization, particularly marketing and research and development, in these decisions.

Planning the Product

Before making any product, a company first must determine what consumers want and then design a product to satisfy that want. Most companies use marketing research (discussed in Chapter 12) to determine the kinds of goods and services to provide and the features they must possess. Nissan, for example, conducted intensive market research before launching its first full-size pick-up truck, the Titan. The company interviewed truck buyers about their likes and dislikes and sent researchers to drive competing trucks for a month to learn firsthand about how the large vehicles handle in a variety of situations.[8] Marketing research can also help gauge the demand for a product and how much consumers are willing to pay for it.

Developing a product can be a lengthy, expensive process. For example, in the automobile industry, developing the new technology for night vision, bumper-mounted sonar systems that make parking easier, and a satellite service that locates and analyzes car problems has been a lengthy, expensive process. Most companies work to reduce development time and costs. For example, through Web collaboration, faucet manufacturer Moen has reduced the time required to take an idea to a finished product in stores to just 16 months, a drop of 33 percent.[9] Once management has developed an idea for a product that customers will buy, it must then plan how to produce the product.

Within a company, the engineering or research and development department is charged with turning a product idea into a workable design that can be produced economically. In smaller companies, a single individual (perhaps the owner) may be solely responsible for this crucial activity. Regardless of who is responsible for product design, planning does not stop with a blueprint for a product or a description of a service; it must also work out efficient production of the product to ensure that enough is available to satisfy consumer demand. How does a lawn mower company transform steel, aluminum, and other materials into a mower design that satisfies consumer and environmental requirements? Operations managers must plan for the types and quantities of materials needed to produce the product, the skills and quantity of people needed to make the product, and the actual processes through which the inputs must pass in their transformation to outputs.

Designing the Operations Processes

Before a firm can begin production, it must first determine the appropriate method of transforming resources into the desired product. Often, consumers' specific needs and desires dictate a process. Customer needs, for example, require that all 3/4-inch bolts have the same basic thread size, function, and quality; if they did not, engineers and builders could not rely on 3/4-inch bolts in their construction projects. A bolt manufacturer, then, will likely use a standardized process so that every 3/4-inch bolt produced is like every other one. On the other hand, a bridge often must be customized so that it is appropriate for the site and expected load; furthermore, the bridge must be constructed on site rather than in a factory. Typically, products are designed to be manufactured by one of three processes: standardization, modular design, or customization.

Standardization.   Most firms that manufacture products in large quantities for many customers have found that they can make them cheaper and faster by standardizing designs. **Standardization** is making identical, interchangeable components or even complete products. With standardization, a customer may not get exactly what he or she wants, but the product generally costs less than a custom-designed product. Television sets, ballpoint pens, and tortilla chips are standardized products; most are manufactured on an assembly line. Standardization speeds up production and quality control and reduces production costs. And, as in the example of the 3/4-inch bolts, standardization provides consistency so that customers who need certain products to function uniformly all the time will get a product that meets their expectations. As a result of its entry into the World Trade Organization, China promoted the standardization of agricultural production across the country; the nation saw a 17 percent increase in agricultural export productivity over a 10-month period as a result.[10]

Modular Design.   **Modular design** involves building an item in self-contained units, or modules, that can be combined or interchanged to create different products. Personal computers, for example, are generally composed of a number of com-

standardization
the making of identical interchangeable components or products

modular design
the creation of an item in self-contained units, or modules, that can be combined or interchanged to create different products

ponents—CPU case, motherboard, RAM chips, hard drives, floppy drives, graphics card, etc.—that can be installed in different configurations to meet the customer's needs. Because many modular components are produced as integrated units, the failure of any portion of a modular component usually means replacing the entire component. Modular design allows products to be repaired quickly, thus reducing the cost of labor, but the component itself is expensive, raising the cost of repair materials. Many automobile manufacturers use modular design in the production process.

Customization.   **Customization** is making products to meet a particular customer's needs or wants. Products produced in this way are generally unique. Such products include repair services, photocopy services, custom artwork, jewelry, and furniture, as well as large-scale products such as bridges, ships, and computer software. Although there may be similarities among ships, for example, builders generally design and build each ship to meet the needs of the customer who will use it. Delta Marine Industries, for example, custom-builds each luxury yacht to the customer's exact specifications and preferences for things like helicopter garages, golf courses, and swimming pools. The Seattle-based company has delivered 22 yachts longer than 100 feet since 1990.[11] Likewise, when you go to a printing shop to order business cards, the company must customize the cards with your name, address, and title.

> **customization**
> making products to meet a particular customer's needs or wants

Planning Capacity

Planning the operational processes for the organization involves two important areas: capacity planning and facilities planning. The term **capacity** basically refers to the maximum load that an organizational unit can carry or operate. The unit of measurement may be a worker or machine, a department, a branch, or even an entire plant. Maximum capacity can be stated in terms of the inputs or outputs provided. For example, an electric plant might state plant capacity in terms of the maximum number of kilowatt hours that can be produced without causing a power outage, while a restaurant might state capacity in terms of the maximum number of customers who can be effectively—comfortably and courteously—served at any one particular time. Honda Motor Company's Marysville, Ohio, plant, which produces the Accord sedan, Accord coupe, and Acura TL, has an annual production capacity of 440,000 vehicles.[12]

> **capacity**
> the maximum load that an organizational unit can carry or operate

Efficiently planning the organization's capacity needs is an important process for the operations manager. Capacity levels that fall short can result in unmet demand, and consequently, lost customers. On the other hand, when there is more capacity available than needed, operating costs are driven up needlessly due to unused and often expensive resources. To avoid such situations, organizations must accurately forecast demand and then plan capacity based on these forecasts. Another reason for the importance of efficient capacity planning has to do with long-term commitment of resources. Often, once a capacity decision—such as factory size—has been implemented, it is very difficult to change the decision without incurring substantial costs.

> **Did You Know?**   Hershey's has the production capacity to make 33 million Hershey's kisses per day or more than 12 billion per year.[13]

Planning Facilities

Once a company knows what process it will use to create its products, it then can design and build an appropriate facility in which to make them. Many products are manufactured in factories, but others are produced in stores, at home, or where the product ultimately will be used. Companies must decide where to locate their operations facilities, what layout is best for producing their particular product, and even what technology to apply to the transformation process.

Many firms are developing both a traditional organization for customer contact as well as a virtual organization. Charles Schwab Corporation, a securities brokerage and investment company, maintains traditional offices and has developed complete telephone and Internet services for customers. Through its Web site, investors can obtain personal investment information and trade securities over the Internet without leaving their home or office.

Facility Location.   Where to locate a firm's facilities is a significant question because, once the decision has been made and implemented, the firm must live with it due to the high costs involved. When a company decides to relocate or open a facility at a new location, it must pay careful attention to factors such as proximity to market, availability of raw materials, availability of transportation, availability of power, climatic influences, availability of labor, community characteristics (quality of life), and taxes and inducements. Inducements and tax reductions have become an increasingly important criterion in recent years. Kodak, for example, decided to invest $40 million in a photographic plant expansion in Windsor, Colorado, rather than at its Rochester, New York, headquarters after the Colorado Economic Development Commission offered $120,000 in cash incentives and $24,000 toward job training, and Colorado's Weld County agreed to $600,000 in property tax reductions (over 10 years) and concessions on building permits and inspection fees.[14] The facility-location decision is complex because it involves the evaluation of many factors, some of which cannot be measured with precision. Because of the long-term impact of the decision, however, it is one that cannot be taken lightly.

Facility Layout.   Arranging the physical layout of a facility is a complex, highly technical task. Some industrial architects specialize in the design and layout of certain types of businesses. There are three basic layouts: fixed-position, process, and product.

A company using a **fixed-position layout** brings all resources required to create the product to a central location. The product—perhaps an office building, house, hydroelectric plant, or bridge—does not move. A company using a fixed-position layout may be called a **project organization** because it is typically involved in large, complex projects such as construction or exploration. Project organizations generally make a unique product, rely on highly skilled labor, produce very few units, and have high production costs per unit.

Firms that use a **process layout** organize the transformation process into departments that group related processes. A metal fabrication plant, for example, may have a cutting department, a drilling department, and a polishing department. A hospital may have an X-ray unit, an obstetrics unit, and so on. These types of organizations are sometimes called **intermittent organizations,** which deal with products of a lesser magnitude than do project organizations, and their products are not necessarily unique but possess a significant number of differ-

fixed-position layout
a layout that brings all resources required to create the product to a central location

project organization
a company using a fixed-position layout because it is typically involved in large, complex projects such as construction or exploration

process layout
a layout that organizes the transformation process into departments that group related processes

intermittent organizations
organizations that deal with products of a lesser magnitude than do project organizations; their products are not necessarily unique but possess a significant number of differences

Many firms are concerned with designing their manufacturing facilities to maximize efficiency and profitability.

ences. Doctors, makers of custom-made cabinets, commercial printers, and advertising agencies are intermittent organizations because they tend to create products to customers' specifications and produce relatively few units of each product. Because of the low level of output, the cost per unit of product is generally high.

The **product layout** requires that production be broken down into relatively simple tasks assigned to workers, who are usually positioned along an assembly line. Workers remain in one location, and the product moves from one worker to another. Each person in turn performs his or her required tasks or activities. Companies that use assembly lines are usually known as **continuous manufacturing organizations,** so named because once they are set up, they run continuously, creating products with many similar characteristics. Examples of products produced on assembly lines are automobiles, television sets, vacuum cleaners, toothpaste, and meals from a cafeteria. Continuous manufacturing organizations using a product layout are characterized by the standardized product they produce, the large number of units produced, and the relatively low unit cost of production.

Many companies actually use a combination of layout designs. For example, an automobile manufacturer may rely on an assembly line (product layout) but may also use a process layout to manufacture parts.

Technology.   Every industry has a basic, underlying technology that dictates the nature of its transformation process. The steel industry continually tries to improve steelmaking techniques. The health care industry performs research into medical technologies and pharmaceuticals to improve the quality of health-care service. Two developments that have strongly influenced the operations of many businesses are computers and robotics.

Computers have been used for decades and on a relatively large scale since IBM introduced its 650 series in the late 1950s. The operations function makes great use of computers in all phases of the transformation process. **Computer-assisted design (CAD),** for example, helps engineers design components, products, and processes on the computer instead of on paper. **Computer-assisted manufacturing (CAM)** goes a step further, employing specialized computer systems to actually guide and control the transformation processes. Such systems can monitor the transformation process, gathering information about the equipment used to produce the products and about the product itself as it goes from one stage of the transformation process to the next. The computer provides information to an operator who may, if necessary, take corrective action. In some highly automated systems, the computer itself can take corrective action. At Dell's OptiPlex Plant, electronic instructions are sent to double-decker conveyor belts that speed computer components to assembly stations. Two-member teams are told by computers which PC or server to build, with initial assembly taking only three to four minutes. Then more electronic commands move the products (more than 20,000 machines on a typical day) to a finishing area to be customized, boxed, and sent to waiting delivery trucks. Although the plant covers 200,000 square feet, enough to enclose 23 football fields, it is managed almost entirely by a network of computers.[15]

Using **flexible manufacturing,** computers can direct machinery to adapt to different versions of similar operations. For example, with instructions from a computer, one machine can be programmed to carry out its function for several different versions of an engine without shutting down the production line for refitting.

Robots are also becoming increasingly useful in the transformation process. These "steel-collar" workers have become particularly important in industries such

product layout
a layout requiring that production be broken down into relatively simple tasks assigned to workers, who are usually positioned along an assembly line

continuous manufacturing organizations
companies that use continuously running assembly lines, creating products with many similar characteristics

computer-assisted design (CAD)
the design of components, products, and processes on computers instead of on paper

computer-assisted manufacturing (CAM)
manufacturing that employs specialized computer systems to actually guide and control the transformation processes

flexible manufacturing
the direction of machinery by computers to adapt to different versions of similar operations

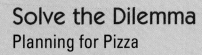

Solve the Dilemma
Planning for Pizza

McKing Corporation operates fast-food restaurants in 50 states, selling hamburgers, roast beef and chicken sandwiches, french fries, and salads. The company wants to diversify into the growing pizza business. Six months of tests revealed that the ideal pizza to sell was a 16-inch pie in three varieties: cheese, pepperoni, and deluxe (multiple toppings). Research found the size and toppings acceptable to families as well as to individuals (single buyers could freeze the leftovers), and the price was acceptable for a fast-food restaurant ($7.99 for cheese, $8.49 for pepperoni, and $9.99 for deluxe).

Marketing and human resources personnel prepared training manuals for employees, advertising materials, and the rationale to present to the restaurant managers (many stores are franchised). Store managers, franchisees, and employees are excited about the new plan. There is just one problem: The drive-through windows in current restaurants are too small for a 16-inch pizza to pass through. The largest size the present windows can accommodate is a 12-inch pie. The managers and franchisees are concerned that if this aspect of operations has been overlooked perhaps the product is not ready to be launched. Maybe there are other problems yet to be uncovered.

Discussion Question

1. What mistake did McKing make in approaching the introduction of pizza?
2. How could this product introduction have been coordinated to avoid the problems that were encountered?
3. If you were an executive at McKing, how would you proceed with the introduction of pizza into the restaurants?

as nuclear power, hazardous-waste disposal, ocean research, and space construction and maintenance, in which human lives would otherwise be at risk. Robots are used in numerous applications by companies around the world. Many assembly operations—cars, television sets, telephones, stereo equipment, and numerous other products—depend on industrial robots. The Robotic Industries Association estimates that about 135,000 robots are now at work in U.S. factories, making the United States the world's second largest user of robotics.[16] Researchers continue to make more sophisticated robots, and some speculate that in the future robots will not be limited to space programs and production and operations, but will also be able to engage in farming, laboratory research, and even household activities. Moreover, robotics are increasingly being used in the medical field. Voice-activated robotic arms operate video cameras for surgeons. Similar technology assists with biopsies, as well as heart, spine, and nervous system procedures. A heart surgeon at London Health Science Centre in Ontario uses a surgical robot to perform bypass operations on patients without opening their chests, except for five tiny incisions, while their hearts continue beating. More than 400 surgeons around the world currently use surgical robots with far fewer postoperative complications than encountered in conventional operations.[17]

computer-integrated manufacturing (CIM)
a complete system that designs products, manages machines and materials, and controls the operations function

When all these technologies—CAD/CAM, flexible manufacturing, robotics, computer systems, and more—are integrated, the result is **computer-integrated manufacturing (CIM),** a complete system that designs products, manages machines and materials, and controls the operations function. Companies adopt CIM to boost productivity and quality and reduce costs. Such technology, and computers in particular, will continue to make strong inroads into operations on two fronts—one dealing with the technology involved in manufacturing and one dealing with the administrative functions and processes used by operations managers. The operations manager must be willing to work with computers and other forms of technology and to develop a high degree of computer literacy.

Managing the Supply Chain

A major function of operations is **supply chain management,** which refers to connecting and integrating all parties or members of the distribution system in order to satisfy customers.[18] Also called logistics, supply chain management includes all the activities involved in obtaining and managing raw materials and component parts, managing finished products, packaging them, and getting them to customers. The supply chain integrates firms such as raw material suppliers, manufacturers, retailers, and ultimate consumers into a seamless flow of information and products.[19] Some aspects of logistics (warehousing, packaging, distributing) are so closely linked with marketing that we will discuss them in Chapter 13. In this section, we look at purchasing, managing inventory, outsourcing, and scheduling, which are vital tasks in the transformation of raw materials into finished goods. To illustrate logistics, consider a hypothetical small business—we'll call it Rushing Water Canoes, Inc.—that manufactures aluminum canoes, which it sells primarily to sporting goods stores and river-rafting expeditions. Our company also makes paddles and helmets, but the focus of the following discussion is the manufacture of the company's quality canoes as they proceed through the logistics process.

When you think about UPS, you usually think of the nice drivers in brown uniforms and brown trucks that deliver packages around the world. In this ad, UPS promotes its "Supply Chain Solutions," its ability to solve logistics and distribution issues for companies, synchronizing "the movement of goods, information, and funds."

Purchasing

Purchasing, also known as procurement, is the buying of all the materials needed by the organization. The purchasing department aims to obtain items of the desired quality in the right quantities at the lowest possible cost. Rushing Water Canoes, for example, must procure not only aluminum and other raw materials, and various canoe parts and components, but also machines and equipment, manufacturing supplies (oil, electricity, and so on), and office supplies in order to make its canoes. People in the purchasing department locate and evaluate suppliers of these items. They must constantly be on the lookout for new materials or parts that will do a better job or cost less than those currently being used. The purchasing function can be quite complex and is one area made much easier and more efficient by technological advances.

Not all companies purchase all the materials needed to create their products. Oftentimes, they can make some components more economically and efficiently than can an outside supplier. Coors, for example, manufactures its own cans at a subsidiary plant. On the other hand, firms sometimes find that it is uneconomical to make or purchase an item, and instead arrange to lease it from another organization. Some airlines, for example, lease airplanes rather than buy them. Whether to purchase, make, or lease a needed item generally depends on cost, as well as on product availability and supplier reliability.

The Coal Creek Coffee Company is a small, privately owned and operated coffeehouse and equipment distributor in Laramie, Wyoming. The small business has more than 25 years of combined experience in the specialty coffee industry and earned the "Best Small Business of the Year Award" in 2002 from the Laramie Economic Development Corporation.

Coal Creek's mission is "simply to provide *Quality, above and beyond all expectations.*" Achieving that quality begins with the finest coffee beans available. In order to comply with Organic Crop Improvement Association (OCIA) standards, Coal Creek must track the coffee beans from the field to its front door and have effective buyer-seller relationships. The company then sample roasts each coffee until it finds the perfect roast profile to bring out that coffee's unique flavors. Coal Creek's wholesale business imports coffee beans internationally and sells them across the United States. In fact, it derives one-quarter of its revenue through wholesale business.

Coal Creek roasts its coffees in a state-of-the-art, gas-fired, dual-blower-design Primo roaster. The 12-kilo machine allows the firm to roast in small batches with minimum cooling times, which helps maintain a high level of consistency while imparting a distinctively sweet, smooth flavor to its artisan coffees.

Coal Creek also sells coffee-making and roasting equipment to established coffeehouses, start-up coffeehouses, and gourmet coffee lovers. For its coffeehouse customers, the company can recommend brewing techniques and equipment and offer advice for beverage service and training. Coal Creek has also built relationships with suppliers of high-quality production equipment, which allows it to place orders on demand and have the orders delivered directly to the customer instead of stocking equipment onsite. One such supplier is the Fregnan family, which has been producing Elektra Italian espresso coffee machines since 1947. Coal Creek chose to work with Elektra because the Fregnan family's commitment to quality meshes well with Coal Creek's own quality philosophies. Coal Creek's owners also prefer to support family-owned businesses, particularly smaller firms that offer high-quality products.[20]

Discussion Questions
1. What does Coal Creek Coffee contribute to supply chain members?
2. Why do you think Coal Creek Coffee selects only the finest coffee beans that comply with organic standards?
3. Why is Coal Creek Coffee so important to start-up coffeehouses?

Managing Inventory

Once the items needed to create a product have been procured, some provision has to be made for storing them until they are needed. Every raw material, component, completed or partially completed product, and piece of equipment a firm uses—its **inventory**—must be accounted for, or controlled. There are three basic types of inventory. *Finished-goods inventory* includes those products that are ready for sale, such as a fully assembled automobile ready to ship to a dealer. *Work-in-process inventory* consists of those products that are partly completed or are in some stage of the transformation process. At McDonald's, a cooking hamburger represents work-in-process inventory because it must go through several more stages before it can be sold to a customer. *Raw materials inventory* includes all the materials that have been purchased to be used as inputs for making other products. Nuts and bolts are raw materials for an automobile manufacturer, while hamburger patties, vegetables, and buns are raw materials for the fast-food restaurant. Our fictional Rushing Water Canoes has an inventory of materials for making canoes, paddles, and helmets, as well as its inventory of finished products for sale to consumers. **Inventory control** is the process of determining how many supplies and goods are needed and keeping track of quantities on hand, where each item is, and who is responsible for it.

Operations management must be closely coordinated with inventory control. The production of televisions, for example, cannot be planned without some knowledge of the availability of all the necessary materials—the chassis, picture tubes, color

inventory
all raw materials, components, completed or partially completed products, and pieces of equipment a firm uses

inventory control
the process of determining how many supplies and goods are needed and keeping track of quantities on hand, where each item is, and who is responsible for it

guns, and so forth. Also, each item held in inventory—any type of inventory—carries with it a cost. For example, storing fully assembled televisions in a warehouse to sell to a dealer at a future date requires not only the use of space, but also the purchase of insurance to cover any losses that might occur due to fire or other unforeseen events.

Inventory managers spend a great deal of time trying to determine the proper inventory level for each item. The answer to the question of how many units to hold in inventory depends on variables such as the usage rate of the item, the cost of maintaining the item in inventory, the cost of paperwork and other procedures associated with ordering or making the item, and the cost of the item itself. Several approaches may be used to determine how many units of a given item should be procured at one time and when that procurement should take place.

The Economic Order Quantity Model.   To control the number of items maintained in inventory, managers need to determine how much of any given item they should order. One popular approach is the **economic order quantity (EOQ) model,** which identifies the optimum number of items to order to minimize the costs of managing (ordering, storing, and using) them.

economic order quantity (EOQ) model a model that identifies the optimum number of items to order to minimize the costs of managing (ordering, storing, and using) them

Just-in-Time Inventory Management.   An increasingly popular technique is **just-in-time (JIT) inventory management,** which eliminates waste by using smaller quantities of materials that arrive "just in time" for use in the transformation process and therefore require less storage space and other inventory management expense. JIT minimizes inventory by providing an almost continuous flow of items from suppliers to the production facility. Many U.S. companies, including General Motors, Hewlett-Packard, IBM, and Harley Davidson, have adopted JIT to reduce costs and boost efficiency.

just-in-time (JIT) inventory management a technique using smaller quantities of materials that arrive "just in time" for use in the transformation process and therefore require less storage space and other inventory management expense

Let's say that Rushing Water Canoes uses 20 units of aluminum from a supplier per day. Traditionally, its inventory manager might order enough for one month at a time: 440 units per order (20 units per day times 22 workdays per month). The expense of such a large inventory could be considerable because of the cost of insurance coverage, recordkeeping, rented storage space, and so on. The just-in-time approach would reduce these costs because aluminum would be purchased in smaller quantities, perhaps in lot sizes of 20, which the supplier would deliver once a day. Of course, for such an approach to be effective, the supplier must be extremely reliable and relatively close to the production facility.

Material-requirements Planning.   Another inventory management technique is **material-requirements planning (MRP),** a planning system that schedules the precise quantity of materials needed to make the product. The basic components of MRP are a master production schedule, a bill of materials, and an inventory status file. At Rushing Water Canoes, for example, the inventory-control manager will look at the production schedule to determine how many canoes the company plans to make. He or she will then prepare a bill of materials—a list of all the materials needed to make that quantity of canoes. Next, the manager will determine the quantity of these items that RWC already holds in inventory (to avoid ordering excess materials) and then develop a schedule for ordering and accepting delivery of the right quantity of materials to satisfy the firm's needs. Because of the large number of parts and materials that go into a typical production process, MRP must be done on a computer. It can be, and often is, used in conjunction with just-in-time inventory management.

material-requirements planning (MRP) a planning system that schedules the precise quantity of materials needed to make the product

The next-day delivery services offered by FedEx and UPS have been a boon to companies practicing just-in-time inventory methods, but some companies are looking for even faster delivery services for an extra edge. San Francisco–based Ensenda has designed a same-day delivery system that is attracting the attention of shippers who are looking for new ways to cut costs and streamline their delivery fleets. Many of these firms outsource the production of some component parts and need to obtain these supplies just-in-time for production. To give them what they need, Ensenda developed a business model based on a system of local delivery networks: The company contracts with small, regionally based couriers to provide same-day delivery in markets where there is sufficient demand for such services. Ensenda's services include ASAP, Priority (delivery in two hours or less), Standard (delivery in four hours or less), Scheduled (same day delivery during a preset time), and Next Day delivery. The company has 10,000 professional delivery personnel, serving more than 210 million people in more than 135 different markets across the United States and Canada. Its biggest customers are Home Depot, Best Buy, Sony, and Crate and Barrel.

Ensuring product deliveries within such tight time frames requires a great deal of collaboration, communication, and flexibility in responding quickly to uncertainties. Ensenda's point-to-point system gives its customers that flexibility to go in any direction. Unlike FedEx's hub-and-spoke approach, which involves having all packages go through a central distribution center before being shipped to their final destination,

Ensenda's network is linked together with a Web-based interface that provides customers with a contact point for all of their shipping.

When LaserNetworks, an office supply company based in Toronto, outsourced the delivery component of its operations to Ensenda, it experienced rapid growth because it was able to pass on the considerable cost savings to its customers in the form of better prices. LaserNetworks has now streamlined its assets in the logistics area to one delivery person and vehicle in each market that it serves. The company believes it has saved more than 20 percent in total cost of shipping from its previous delivery system.

Ensenda benefits from the success and growth of customers like LaserNetworks. Ensenda can also customize services to facilitate the needs of a client in both economic downturns and boom times. Its services mean that its customers do not have to worry about capacity issues, especially the need to provide delivery during overflow peak seasons. They only pay for the delivery service they use, so there is better asset utilization for customers such as LaserNetworks.[21]

Discussion Questions
1. Why does Ensenda contract with small, regionally based couriers to provide its delivery service?
2. Why do firms such as LaserNetworks outsource their delivery services to Ensenda?
3. Why do you think that outsourcing is so widely used by firms to reduce cost and increase services?

Outsourcing

Increasingly, outsourcing has become a component of supply chain management in operations. As we mentioned in Chapter 3, outsourcing refers to the contracting of manufacturing or other tasks to independent companies, often overseas. Many companies elect to outsource some aspects of their operations to companies that can provide these products more efficiently, at a lower cost, and with greater customer satisfaction. Delta Airlines, for example, contracts with Indian-based Wipro to handle its voice and data processing.[22] Many high-tech firms have outsourced the production of memory chips, computers, and telecom equipment to Asian companies.[23] While information technology is often outsourced today, transportation, human resources, services, and even marketing functions can be outsourced. Our hypothetical Rushing Water Canoes might contract with a local janitorial service to clean its offices and with a local accountant to handle routine bookkeeping and tax-preparation functions.

Outsourcing, once used primarily as a cost-cutting tactic, has increasingly been linked with the development of competitive advantage through improved product quality, speeding up the time it takes products to get to the customer, and overall supply-chain efficiencies. Outsourcing allows companies to free up time and resources to focus on what they do best and to create better opportunities to focus on

FIGURE 9.3   A Hypothetical PERT Diagram for a McDonald's Big Mac

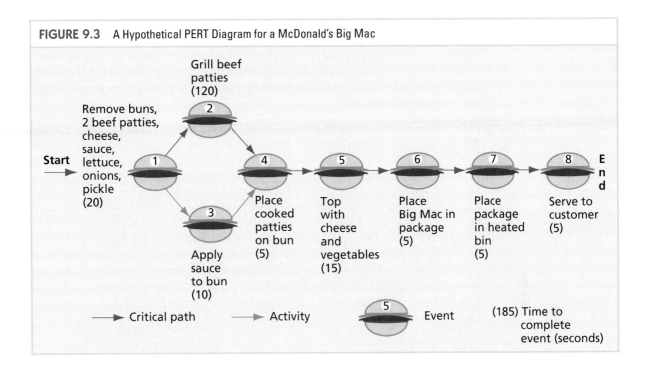

customer satisfaction. Many executives view outsourcing as an innovative way to boost productivity and remain competitive against low-wage offshore factories. However, outsourcing may create conflict with labor and negative public opinion when it results in U.S. workers being replaced by lower-cost workers in other countries.

Routing and Scheduling

After all materials have been procured and their use determined, managers must then consider the **routing,** or sequence of operations through which the product must pass. For example, before employees at Rushing Water Canoes can form aluminum sheets into a canoe, the aluminum must be cut to size. Likewise, the canoe's flotation material must be installed before workers can secure the wood seats. The sequence depends on the product specifications developed by the engineering department of the company.

Once management knows the routing, the actual work can be scheduled. **Scheduling** assigns the tasks to be done to departments or even specific machines, workers, or teams. At Rushing Water, cutting aluminum for the company's canoes might be scheduled to be done by the "cutting and finishing" department on machines designed especially for that purpose.

Many approaches to scheduling have been developed, ranging from simple trial and error to highly sophisticated computer programs. One popular method is the *Program Evaluation and Review Technique (PERT)*, which identifies all the major activities or events required to complete a project, arranges them in a sequence or path, determines the critical path, and estimates the time required for each event. Producing a McDonald's Big Mac, for example, involves removing meat, cheese, sauce, and vegetables from the refrigerator; grilling the hamburger patties; assembling the ingredients; placing the completed Big Mac in its package; and serving it to the customer (Figure 9.3). The cheese, pickles, onions, and sauce cannot be put on before

routing
the sequence of operations through which the product must pass

scheduling
the assignment of required tasks to departments or even specific machines, workers, or teams

the hamburger patty is completely grilled and placed on the bun. The path that requires the longest time from start to finish is called the *critical path* because it determines the minimum amount of time in which the process can be completed. If any of the activities on the critical path for production of the Big Mac fall behind schedule, the sandwich will not be completed on time, causing customers to wait longer than they usually would.

Managing Quality

Quality, like cost and efficiency, is a critical element of operations management, for defective products can quickly ruin a firm. Quality reflects the degree to which a good or service meets the demands and requirements of customers. Customers are increasingly dissatisfied with the quality of service provided by many airlines. There were more than 5,980 air travel complaints last year (see Figure 9.4).[24] Determining quality can be difficult because it depends on customers' perceptions of how well the product meets or exceeds their expectations. For example, the fuel economy of an automobile or its reliability (defined in terms of frequency of repairs) can be measured with some degree of precision. Although automakers rely on their own measures of vehicle quality, they also look to independent sources such as the J. D. Power & Associates annual initial quality survey for confirmation of their quality assessment as well as consumer perceptions of quality. Many people were surprised when J. D. Power ranked Hyundai second behind only Toyota in terms of quality in 2004; for Hyundai executives, the news only substantiated the company's assessment of its long-running initiative to improve quality.[25] How-

FIGURE 9.4

Types and Percentages of Air Travel Complaints in 2003

Source: Office of Aviation Enforcement and Proceedings, *Air Travel Consumer Report*, February 2004, p. 39, available at http://airconsumer.ost.dot.gov/reports/2004/0402atcr.pdf.

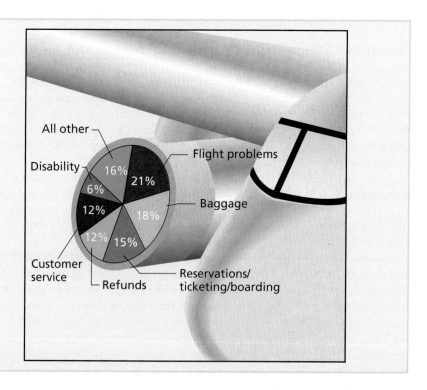

ever, it is more difficult to measure psychological characteristics such as design, color, or status. It is especially difficult to measure these characteristics when the product is a service. A company has to decide exactly which quality characteristics it considers important and then define those characteristics in terms that can be measured.

The Malcolm Baldrige National Quality Award is given each year to companies that meet rigorous standards of quality. The Baldrige criteria are (1) leadership, (2) information and analysis, (3) strategic planning, (4) human resource development and management, (5) process management, (6) business results, and (7) customer focus and satisfaction. The criteria have become a worldwide framework for driving business improvement. Seven companies received the quality award last year: Medrad Inc. (manufacturing), Boeing Aerospace Support (service), Caterpillar Financial Services (service), Stoner Inc. (small business), Community Consolidated School District 15 (education) in Palatine, IL, Baptist Hospital Inc. (health care), and St. Luke's Hospital of Kansas City (health care).[26]

Quality is so important that we need to examine it in the context of operations management. **Quality control** refers to the processes an organization uses to maintain its established quality standards. Dieter Zetsche, DaimlerChrysler CEO, installed the "12 Gates of Quality" to overcome the company's reputation for inconsistent quality. When engineers, planners, marketers, and executives begin planning for a new car model, they must determine 12 benchmarks that must occur prior to the vehicle's launch and assign a deadline to each. Every department working on a project must meet the designated targets before the project can continue into the next phase.[27]

Quality has become a major concern in many organizations, particularly in light of intense foreign competition and increasingly demanding customers. To regain a competitive edge, a number of firms have adopted a total quality management approach. **Total quality management (TQM)** is a philosophy that uniform commitment to quality in all areas of the organization will promote a culture that meets customers' perceptions of quality. It involves coordinating efforts to improve customer satisfaction, increase employee participation and empowerment, form and strengthen supplier partnerships, and foster an organizational culture of continuous quality improvement. TQM requires continuous quality improvement and employee empowerment.

Continuous improvement of an organization's goods and services is built around the notion that quality is free; by contrast, *not* having high-quality goods and services can be very expensive, especially in terms of dissatisfied customers.[28] A primary tool of the continuous improvement process is *benchmarking*, the measuring and evaluating of

quality control
the processes an organization uses to maintain its established quality standards

total quality management (TQM)
a philosophy that uniform commitment to quality in all areas of an organization will promote a culture that meets customers' perceptions of quality

Aimed toward a more mature market, Kellogg's Smart Start promotes the quality and benefits of its cereal by highlighting the antioxidants.

the quality of the organization's goods, services, or processes as compared with the quality produced by the best-performing companies in the industry.[29] Benchmarking lets the organization know where it stands competitively in its industry, thus giving it a goal to aim for over time.

Companies employing total quality management (TQM) programs know that quality control should be incorporated throughout the transformation process, from the initial plans to develop a specific product through the product and production-facility design processes to the actual manufacture of the product. In other words, they view quality control as an element of the product itself, rather than as simply a function of the operations process. When a company makes the product correctly from the outset, it eliminates the need to rework defective products, expedites the transformation process itself, and allows employees to make better use of their time and materials. One method through which many companies have tried to improve quality is **statistical process control,** a system in which management collects and analyzes information about the production process to pinpoint quality problems in the production system.

statistical process control
a system in which management collects and analyzes information about the production process to pinpoint quality problems in the production system

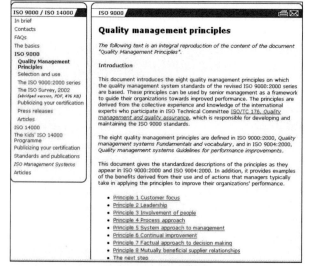

ISO 9000's principles of quality management. (From http://www.iso.ch/isoen/iso9000-14000/iso9000/qmp.html)

Establishing Standards—ISO 9000

Regardless of whether a company has a TQM program for quality control, it must first determine what standard of quality it desires and then assess whether its products meet that standard. Product specifications and quality standards must be set so the company can create a product that will compete in the marketplace. Rushing Water Canoes, for example, may specify that each of its canoes has aluminum walls of a specified uniform thickness, that the front and back of each canoe be reinforced with a specified level of steel, and that each canoe contain a specified amount of flotation material for safety. Production facilities must be designed that can produce products with the desired specifications.

Quality standards can be incorporated into service businesses as well. A hamburger chain, for example, may establish standards relating to how long it takes to cook an order and serve it to customers, how many fries are in each order, how thick the burgers are, or how many customer complaints might be acceptable. Once the desired quality characteristics, specifications, and standards have been stated in measurable terms, the next step is inspection.

ISO 9000
a series of quality assurance standards designed by the International Organization for Standardization (ISO) to ensure consistent product quality under many conditions

The International Organization for Standardization (ISO) has created a series of quality management standards—**ISO 9000**—designed to ensure the customer's quality standards are met. The standards provide a framework for documenting how a certified business keeps records, trains employees, tests products, and fixes defects. To obtain ISO 9000 certification, an independent auditor must verify that a business's factory, laboratory, or office meets the quality standards spelled out by the International Organization for Standardization. The certification process can require significant investment, but for many companies, the process is essential to being able to compete. Thousands of U.S. firms have been certified, and many more are working to meet the standards. Certification has become a virtual necessity for doing business in Europe in some high-technology businesses. ISO 9002 certification was established for service providers.

Inspection

Inspection reveals whether a product meets quality standards. Some product characteristics may be discerned by fairly simple inspection techniques—weighing the contents of cereal boxes or measuring the time it takes for a customer to receive his or her hamburger. As part of the ongoing quality assurance program at Hershey Foods, all wrapped Hershey Kisses are checked, and all imperfectly wrapped kisses are rejected.[30] Other inspection techniques are more elaborate. Automobile manufacturers use automated machines to open and close car doors to test the durability of latches and hinges. The food-processing and pharmaceutical industries use various chemical tests to determine the quality of their output. Rushing Water Canoes might use a special device that can precisely measure the thickness of each canoe wall to ensure that it meets the company's specifications.

Organizations normally inspect purchased items, work-in-process, and finished items. The inspection of purchased items and finished items takes place after the fact; the inspection of work-in-process is preventive. In other words, the purpose of inspection of purchased items and finished items is to determine what the quality level is. For items that are being worked on—an automobile moving down the assembly line or a canoe being assembled—the purpose of the inspection is to find defects before the product is completed so that necessary corrections can be made.

Sampling

An important question relating to inspection is how many items should be inspected. Should all canoes produced by Rushing Water be inspected or just some of them? Whether to inspect 100 percent of the output or only part of it is related to the cost of the inspection process, the destructiveness of the inspection process (some tests last until the product fails), and the potential cost of product flaws in terms of human lives and safety.

Some inspection procedures are quite expensive, use elaborate testing equipment, destroy products, and/or require a significant number of hours to complete. In such cases, it is usually desirable to test only a sample of the output. If the sample passes inspection, the inspector may assume that all the items in the lot from which the sample was drawn would also pass inspection. By using principles of statistical inference, management can employ sampling techniques that assure a relatively high probability of reaching the right conclusion—that is, rejecting a lot that does not meet standards and accepting a lot that does. Nevertheless, there will always be a risk of making an incorrect conclusion—accepting a population that *does not* meet standards (because the sample was satisfactory) or rejecting a population that *does* meet standards (because the sample contained too many defective items).

Sampling is likely to be used when inspection tests are destructive. Determining the life expectancy of light bulbs by turning them on and recording how long they last would be foolish: There is no market for burned-out light bulbs. Instead, a generalization based on the quality of a sample would be applied to the entire population of light bulbs from which the sample was drawn. However, human life and safety often depend on the proper functioning of specific items, such as the navigational systems installed in commercial airliners. For such items, even though the inspection process is costly, the potential cost of flawed systems—in human lives and safety—is too great not to inspect 100 percent of the output.

Explore Your Career Options
A Future in Quality Assurance

In an increasingly competitive global marketplace, quality becomes a key attribute on which companies can differentiate their products from competitors' in the minds and wallets of consumers. Quality has therefore become ever more important in all aspects of business, but particularly in production and operations management. More and more firms are adopting total quality management (TQM) programs to ensure that quality pervades all aspects of their businesses. Many firms are working to satisfy universal quality standards, such as ISO 9000, so that they can compete globally. This has created new career opportunities for students interested in working in TQM and other quality programs.

In the United States, many organizations—including 3M, Du Pont, Eastman Kodak, Kellogg, Union Carbide, and even the U.S. Department of Defense—have obtained ISO 9000 series certification and now require their suppliers to meet ISO 9000 quality standards as well. As a result, companies are experiencing difficulty recruiting graduates who understand the design and implementation of quality-improvement programs.

For these reasons, all students are encouraged to "think quality" when preparing for a business career. Even quality-oriented candidates in fields such as sales, finance, and human resources have the potential to play key roles in the integration of quality throughout their companies. For those who pursue advanced study in TQM in either an undergraduate or graduate program, the prospects for employment and career advancement in the field are promising. The median annual compensation for a quality assurance-control manager is $65,157.[31]

Review Your Understanding

Define operations management and differentiate between operations and manufacturing.

Operations management (OM) is the development and administration of the activities involved in transforming resources into goods and services. Operations managers oversee the transformation process and the planning and designing of operations systems, managing logistics, quality, and productivity. The terms *manufacturing* and *production* are used interchangeably to describe the activities and processes used in making tangible products, whereas *operations* is a broader term used to describe the process of making both tangible and intangible products.

Explain how operations management differs in manufacturing and service firms.

Manufacturers and service firms both transform inputs into outputs, but service providers differ from manufacturers in several ways: They have greater customer contact because the service typically occurs at the point of consumption; their inputs and outputs are more variable than manufacturers', largely because of the human element; service providers are generally more labor-intensive; and their productivity measurement is more complex.

Describe the elements involved in planning and designing an operations system.

Operations planning relates to decisions about what product(s) to make, for whom, and what processes and facilities are needed to produce them. OM is often joined by marketing and research and development in these decisions. Common facility layouts include fixed-position layouts, process layouts, or product layouts. Where to locate operations facilities is a crucial decision that depends on proximity to the market, availability of raw materials, availability of transportation, availability of power, climatic influences, availability of labor, and community characteristics. Technology is also vital to operations, particularly computer-assisted design, computer-assisted manufacturing, flexible manufacturing, robotics, and computer-integrated manufacturing.

Specify some techniques managers may use to manage the logistics of transforming inputs into finished products.

Logistics, or supply chain management, includes all the activities involved in obtaining and managing raw materials and component parts, managing finished products, packaging them, and getting them to customers. The organization must first make or purchase (procure) all the materials it needs. Next, it must control its inventory by determining how many supplies and goods it needs and keeping track of every raw material, component, completed or partially completed product, and piece of equipment, how many of each are on hand, where they are, and who has responsibility for them. Common approaches to inventory control include the economic order quantity (EOQ) model, the just-in-time (JIT) inventory concept, and material-requirements planning (MRP). Logistics also includes routing and scheduling processes and activities to complete products.

Assess the importance of quality in operations management.

Quality is a critical element of OM because low-quality products can hurt people and harm the business. Quality control refers to the processes an organization uses to maintain its established quality standards. To control quality, a company must establish what standard of quality it desires and then determine whether its products meet that standard through inspection.

Evaluate a business's dilemma and propose a solution.

Based on this chapter and the facts presented in the "Solve the Dilemma" box on page 266, you should be able to evaluate the business's problem and propose one or more solutions for resolving it.

Revisit the World of Business

1. Why is IDEO so successful as a design company?
2. Why is it so important to put humans at the center of the design process?
3. Why is it so important to get engineering, sociology, psychology, and statistical experts together in designing a product?

Learn the Terms

capacity   263
computer-assisted design (CAD)   265
computer-assisted manufacturing (CAM)   265
computer-integrated manufacturing (CIM)   266
continuous manufacturing organizations   265
customization   263
economic order quantity (EOQ) model   269
fixed-position layout   264
flexible manufacturing   265

inputs   257
intermittent organizations   264
inventory   268
inventory control   268
ISO 9000   274
just-in-time (JIT) inventory management   269
manufacturing   257
material-requirements planning (MRP)   269
modular design   262
operations   257
operations management (OM)   257

outputs   257
process layout   264
product layout   265
production   257
project organization   264
purchasing   267
quality control   273
routing   271
scheduling   271
standardization   262
statistical process control   274
supply chain management   267
total quality management   273

Check Your Progress

1. What is operations management?
2. Differentiate among the terms *operations, production,* and *manufacturing.*
3. Compare and contrast a manufacturer versus a service provider in terms of operations management.
4. Who is involved in planning products?
5. In what industry would the fixed-position layout be most efficient? The process layout? The product layout? Use real examples.
6. What criteria do businesses use when deciding where to locate a plant?

7. What is flexible manufacturing? How can it help firms improve quality?

8. Define supply chain management and summarize the activities it involves.

9. Describe some of the methods a firm may use to control inventory.

10. When might a firm decide to inspect a sample of its products rather than test every product for quality?

Get Involved

1. Compare and contrast OM at McDonald's with that of Honda of America. Compare and contrast OM at McDonald's with that of a bank in your neighborhood.

2. Find a real company that uses JIT, either in your local community or in a business journal. Why did the company decide to use JIT? What have been the advantages and disadvantages of using JIT for that particular company? What has been the overall effect on the quality of the company's products or services? What has been the overall effect on the company's bottom line?

3. Interview someone from your local Chamber of Commerce and ask him or her what incentives the community offers to encourage organizations to locate there. (See if these incentives relate to the criteria firms use to make location decisions.)

Build Your Skills

REDUCING CYCLE TIME

Background:
An important goal of production and operations management is reducing cycle time—the time it takes to complete a task or process. The goal in cycle time reduction is to reduce costs and/or increase customer service.[32] Many experts believe that the rate of change in our society is so fast that a firm must master speed and connectivity.[33] Connectivity refers to a seamless integration of customers, suppliers, employees, and organizational, production, and operations management. The use of the Internet and other telecommunications systems helps many organizations connect and reduce cycle time.

Task:
Break up into pairs throughout the class. Select two businesses (local restaurants, retail stores, etc.) that both of you frequent, are employed by, and/or are fairly well acquainted with. For the first business, one of you will role play the "manager" and the other will role play the "customer." Reverse roles for the second business you have selected. As managers at your respective businesses, you are to prepare a list of five questions you will ask the customer during the role play. The questions you prepare should be designed to get the customer's viewpoint on how good the cycle time is at your business. If one of the responses leads to a problem area, you may need to ask a follow-up question to determine the nature of the dissatisfaction. Prepare one main question and a follow-up, if necessary, for each of the five dimensions of cycle time:

1. **Speed**—the delivery of goods and services in the minimum time; efficient communications; the elimination of wasted time.

2. **Connectivity**—all operations and systems in the business appear connected with the customer.

3. **Interactive relationships**—a continual dialog exists between operations units, service providers, and customers that permits the exchange of feedback on concerns or needs.

4. **Customization**—each product is tailored to the needs of the customer.

5. **Responsiveness**—the willingness to make adjustments and be flexible to help customers and to provide prompt service when a problem develops.

Begin the two role plays. When it is your turn to be the manager, listen carefully when your partner answers your prepared questions. You need to elicit information on how to improve the cycle time at your business. You will achieve this by identifying the problem areas (weaknesses) that need attention.

After completing both role play situations, fill out the form below for the role play where you were the manager. You may not have gathered enough information to fill in all the boxes. For example, for some categories, the customer may have had only good things to say; for others, the comments may all be negative. Be prepared to share the information you gain with the rest of the class.

I role played the manager at _____ (business). After listening carefully to the customer's responses to my five questions, I determined the following strengths and weaknesses as they relate to the cycle time at my business.

Dimension	Strength	Weakness
Speed		
Connectivity		
Interactive relationships		
Customization		
Responsiveness		

e-Xtreme Surfing

- **Baldrige National Quality Program**
  www.quality.nist.gov

  Offers information about the quality award given out by the U.S. government to reward and publicize excellence by U.S. companies.

- **International Organization for Standardization**
  www.iso.org

  Presents information about 14,000 international standards for business, government, and society, including the ISO 9000 series of quality standards.

- **American Society for Quality (ASQ)**
  www.asq.org

  Provides news, articles, and resources to advance quality improvement and business results for the 104,000 member professional association.

See for Yourself Videocase

NEW BELGIUM ACHIEVES EFFICIENCY WITH SOCIAL RESPONSIBILITY

The idea for New Belgium Brewing Company (NBB) began with a bicycling trip through Belgium on a family vacation. As Jeff Lebesch, an American electrical engineer, cruised around the country on a fat-tired mountain bike, he wondered if he could reproduce the high-quality ales he enjoyed in Belgium back in his home state of Colorado. After returning home, Lebesch began to experiment in his Fort Collins basement. When his home-brewed experiments earned rave reviews from friends, Lebesch and his wife, Kim Jordan, decided to open the New Belgium Brewing Company in 1991. They named their first brew Fat Tire Amber Ale in honor of Lebesch's Belgian biking adventure.

New Belgium's commitment to quality, the environment, and its employees and customers is clearly expressed in its stated purpose: "To operate a profitable brewery which makes our love and talent manifest." The brewery looks for cost-efficient, energy-saving alternatives to conducting business and reducing its impact on the environment. Thus, the company's employee-owners unanimously agreed to invest in a wind turbine, making NBB the first fully wind-powered brewery in the United States. Since the switch from coal power, NBB has reduced its CO_2 emissions by 1,800 metric tons per year. The company further reduces its energy use with a steam condenser that captures and reuses the hot water from boiling the barley and hops in the production process to start the next brew; the steam is redirected to heat the floor tiles and de-ice the loading docks in cold weather. Another way NBB conserves energy is through the use of "sun tubes," which provide natural daytime lighting throughout the brewhouse all year long. NBB also strives to recycle as many supplies as possible, including cardboard boxes, keg caps, office materials, and the amber glass used in bottling. New Belgium has recycled tons of amber glass, cardboard, and shrink-wrap. The brewery also invites local farmers to pick up spent barley and hop grains, free of charge, to feed their pigs. NBB even encourages employees to reduce air pollution through alternative transportation. As an incentive, NBB gives each employee a "cruiser bike"—just like the one on the Fat Tire Amber Ale label—after one year of employment.

Beyond its use of environment-friendly technologies and innovations, New Belgium Brewing Company strives to improve communities and enhance lives through corporate giving, event sponsorship, and philanthropic involvement. The company donates $1 per barrel of beer sold to various cultural, social, environmental, and drug and alcohol awareness programs across the 13 western states in which it distributes beer. Typical grants range from $2,500 to $5,000. Involvement is spread equally among all the states NBB serves, unless a special need requires greater participation or funding. The brewhouse also maintains a community board where organizations can post community involvement activities and proposals. This board allows tourists and employees to see opportunities to help out the community and provides nonprofit organizations with a forum for making their needs known. Organizations can also apply for grants through the New Belgium Brewing Company Web site, which has a link designated for this purpose.

New Belgium's dedication to quality, employees, and the environment has been amply rewarded with both loyal customers and industry awards. It was one of three winners of *Business Ethics* magazine's 2002 Business Ethics Awards for its "dedication to environmental excellence in every part of its innovative brewing process." It won an honorable mention in the National Better Business Bureau's 2002 Torch Award for Outstanding Marketplace Ethics competition and won first place in the Mountain States BBB region. The company has also earned awards for best mid-size

brewmaster at the Great American Beer Festival, while Jeff Lebesch and Kim Jordan were named the recipients of the Rocky Mountain Region Entrepreneur of the Year Award for manufacturing. New Belgium also took home medals for three difference brews: Abbey Belgian Style Ale, Blue Paddle Pilsner, and LaFolie specialty ale.

From cutting-edge environmental programs and high-tech industry advancements to employee-ownership programs and a strong belief in giving back to the community, New Belgium demonstrates its desire to create a living, learning community. NBB would never consider in engaging in some of the controversial and edgy advertising that its national competitors use. According to David Edgar, director of the Institute for Brewing Studies, "They've created a very positive image for their company in the beer-consuming public with smart decision making." Although some members of society do not believe a brewery can be socially responsible, New Belgium has set out to prove that for those who make the choice to drink responsibly, the company can do everything possible to contribute to society.[34]

Discussion Questions

1. Why do you think New Belgium Brewing has focused so much on operating its business in a highly socially responsible manner?

2. Do you think that using wind energy and recycling is something that all companies should implement in an effort to help protect the environment? Why or why not?

3. Do you think it is possible that a company that some members of society would rather not see exist can be a highly ethical and socially responsible business? Defend your answer.

Remember to check out our Online Learning Center at www.mhhe.com/ferrell5e

McDougal Aircraft Company

McDougal is the world's largest manufacturer of airplanes. The company has been in business for 58 years. Of its six divisions, the production of commercial airliners is the largest and comprises 65 percent of the business. Revenue from the manufacture of commercial airliners exceeds $30 billion. The second largest part of the business, representing 20 percent of revenues, involves exclusive contracts with the government to build defense products. McDougal also specializes in the small, but powerful engines used in the automobile industry. These types of products are frequently used in backup generators and temperature regulating equipment.

Although McDougal has the highest brand recognition and sales in the industry, it is not without strong competition. Transportona Industries, an international manufacturer of commercial airplanes, is its largest threat. Transportona recently announced its intent to manufacture a new megaliner, the T600, which will be the largest in the sky and able to carry 600 passengers. The T600 will incorporate several new innovations introduced by the company's research and development efforts. The two full-length decks will enable the company to offer comfortable seating with abundant personal space. Both economy and first-class seats will have access to power sources so passengers can use or charge any electronic device during flight. Most importantly, however, the T600 overcomes the greatest design challenge in large planes. All passengers can be evacuated from the double-decker giant in less than five minutes.

In order to remain competitive, McDougal needs to counter with its own version of the T600. The 838, McDougal's closest equivalent, has been in the research and development phase for the past four years and is still at least two years from the market. The massive new product development effort has drained McDougal of many resources, and the company is starting to suffer financially from a lack of cash. The CEO has been pushing for a downsizing of operations and relocation of the company headquarters for the past two years. Upon analysis of the situation, McDougal managers have determined the two most feasible options: (1) eliminate 700 positions and remain in Chicago, Illinois, its headquarters for over 50 years, or (2) cut the workforce by 300 employees and relocate its headquarters to Denver, Colorado, which has offered many benefits and financial incentives, such as tax reductions for the next 10 years.

A meeting has been scheduled for 2 P.M. tomorrow to analyze the possibilities and select the best option, which will be announced in a press release next week. The CEO, VP of Finance, VP of Human Resources, VP of Marketing, and VP of Ethics and Social Responsibility will consider and debate the benefits and drawbacks of the two options.

---

*This background statement provides information for a role-play exercise designed to help you understand the real world challenge of decision making in business and to integrate the concepts presented previously in this text. If your instructor chooses to utilize this activity, the class will be divided into teams with each team member assigned to a particular role in the fictitious organization. Additional information on each role and instructions for the completion of the exercise will be distributed to individual team members.

Part 4

Creating the Human Resource Advantage

Chapter 10

Motivating the Workforce

OBJECTIVES

After reading this chapter, you will be able to:

- Define human relations and determine why its study is important.

- Summarize early studies that laid the groundwork for understanding employee motivation.

- Compare and contrast the human-relations theories of Abraham Maslow and Frederick Herzberg.

- Investigate various theories of motivation, including theories X, Y, and Z; equity theory; and expectancy theory.

- Describe some of the strategies that managers use to motivate employees.

- Critique a business's program for motivating its sales force.

SAS Makes Work Fun and Rewarding

SAS, the world's largest privately held software company, was one of the few companies that prospered during the 2001–2003 high-tech downturn. When other companies were laying off workers, SAS expanded its workforce by 6 percent in 2001, 8.5 percent in 2002, and 3 percent in 2003. Many credit the company's strong culture with helping to ensure its success. SAS managers work hard to ensure they hire the most talented employees available and then to retain that talent by providing employees with a great working environment and generous benefits. Morale at SAS is high, which translates to higher productivity and employee loyalty. Although typical high-tech companies have employee turnover rates as high as 25 percent a year, SAS's turnover is just 3.8 percent. SAS has also been in the top 10 of *Fortune* magazine's annual list of "100 Best Companies to Work For" in six of the seven years that the list has been published.

SAS begins by choosing impressive locations for its offices instead of the typical science parks and business centers. The company's headquarters are located on a wooded 200-acre campus, in Cary, North Carolina, which includes not only a healthcare center, daycare center, and several gyms, but also an art department that is totally dedicated to campus aesthetics. The company's international locations are also picturesque: the European headquarters in Heidelburg, Germany, overlook the river Neckar and a ruined castle, while the U.K.

continued

offices occupy an Edwardian manorhouse on 110 landscaped acres in Buckinghamshire. Employees like these work settings and find the positive organizational culture motivating.

SAS also takes steps to ensure employees feel valued and secure in the knowledge that the company intends to take care of them for the long term. When other high-tech companies were throwing extravagant parties and offering free gourmet lunches, SAS was concentrating on helping employees build financial and personal security and community. Of course, SAS offers generous monetary incentives for employee performance, including hefty cash bonuses and profit sharing. The company is also committed to long-term employee health and wellness through on-site fitness centers and numerous programs dedicated to work/life balance. SAS has also made a significant effort to reduce employee health care expenses at a time when health care costs are soaring and other companies are cutting benefits. At the Cary facility, for example, all services at the SAS Health Care Center are available 24 hours a day at no cost to full-time employees *and* their immediate family members. The company views the more than $1 million spent on the healthcare facility as a smart investment. The SAS philosophy of treating employees well has obviously paid off and contributes to the company's long-term success.[1]

Introduction

Successful programs such as those used at SAS teach some important lessons about how to interact with and motivate employees to do their best. Because employees do the actual work of the business and influence whether the firm achieves its objectives, most top managers agree that employees are an organization's most valuable resource. To achieve organizational objectives, employees must have the motivation, ability (appropriate knowledge and skills), and tools (proper training and equipment) to perform their jobs. Ensuring that employees have the appropriate knowledge and skills and the proper training is the subject of Chapter 11; this chapter focuses on employee motivation.

We will examine employees' needs and motivation, managers' views of workers, and several strategies for motivating employees. Managers who understand the needs of their employees can help them reach higher levels of productivity and thus contribute to the achievement of organizational goals.

Nature of Human Relations

What motivates employees to perform on the job is the focus of **human relations**, the study of the behavior of individuals and groups in organizational settings. In business, human relations involves motivating employees to achieve organizational objectives efficiently and effectively. The field of human relations has become increasingly important over the years as businesses strive to understand how to boost workplace morale, maximize employees' productivity and creativity, and motivate their ever more diverse employees to be more effective.

Motivation is an inner drive that directs a person's behavior toward goals. A goal is the satisfaction of some need, and a need is the difference between a de-

human relations
the study of the behavior of individuals and groups in organizational settings

motivation
an inner drive that directs a person's behavior toward goals

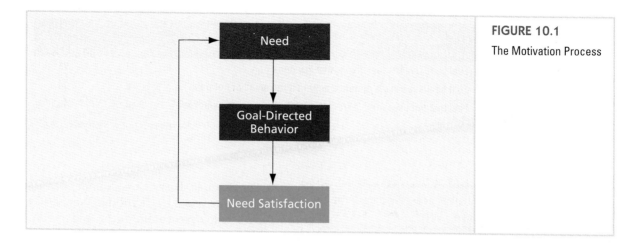

FIGURE 10.1
The Motivation Process

sired state and an actual state. Both needs and goals can be motivating. Motivation explains why people behave as they do; similarly, a lack of motivation explains, at times, why people avoid doing what they should do. A person who recognizes or feels a need is motivated to take action to satisfy the need and achieve a goal (Figure 10.1). Consider a person who feels cold. Because of the difference between the actual temperature and the desired temperature, the person recognizes a need. To satisfy the need and achieve the goal of being warm, the person may adjust the thermostat, put on a sweater, reach for a blanket, start a fire, or hug a friend. Human relations is concerned with the needs of employees, their goals and how they try to achieve them, and the impact of those needs and goals on job performance.

One prominent aspect of human relations is **morale**—an employee's attitude toward his or her job, employer, and colleagues. High morale contributes to high levels of productivity, high returns to stakeholders, and employee loyalty. For example, the Hard Rock Café in San Francisco has one of the lowest turnover rates in the company, partly as a result of caring managers as well as employee benefits such as health and dental insurance, 401(k) plans, tuition reimbursement, bonuses, and prizes like a Rolex watch after 10 years of employment. After 20 years on the job, Hard Rock gives employees a diamond encirclement for the watch face; three San Francisco employees earned the diamond band in 2004.[2] Conversely, low morale may cause high rates of absenteeism and turnover (when employees quit or are fired and must be replaced by new employees).

Respect, involvement, appreciation, adequate compensation, promotions, a pleasant work environment, and a positive organizational culture are all morale

With the explosion of e-mail, some employers are providing employees with PDAs in order for them to stay on top of e-mail while traveling or out of the office. Providing mobile technology improves the company's ability to motivate and lead the employees to effectively do their jobs. What do you think might be some nonmotivating aspects of this scenario?

morale
an employee's attitude toward his or her job, employer, and colleagues

TABLE 10.1

Employee Attitudes Toward Incentives

	Percent Who	
Perception	**Agree**	**Disagree**
Feel bonuses are something they are due	77	23
Feel bonuses have a negative impact if too small or not paid	86	14
Feel that bonuses are a part of the total compensation package	60	40

Source: "2003 Incentive Federation Study Reveals Money Can't Buy Long-Term Motivation," *ClariNet,* September 8, 2003, http://quickstart.clari.net/qs_se/webnews/wed/cy/Bfl-incentive-federation.RPRg_DS8.html.

Did You Know? Absenteeism costs a typical large company more than $3 million a year[3]

The on-site daycare at Procter & Gamble is provided to ease employees' child care concerns, raise morale, and enhance productivity.

boosters. For example, Barry Goss, founder of Professional Project Services in Oak Ridge, New Jersey, acknowledges employee commitment and performance with free dinners at upscale restaurants and weekly e-mails. When the firm nets a big contract, he fetes all 225 employees with a barbeque and beer bash. Such recognition helps improve employees' job satisfaction and morale and helps keep turnover low.[4] Many companies offer a diverse array of benefits designed to improve the quality of employees' lives and increase their morale and satisfaction. As mentioned earlier, many companies offer reward programs to improve morale, lower turnover, and motivate employees. Some of the "best companies to work for" offer on-site day care, concierge services (e.g., dry cleaning, shoe repair, prescription renewal), domestic partner benefits to same-sex couples, and fully paid sabbaticals. Table 10.1 shows employee attitudes towards incentives.

Historical Perspectives on Employee Motivation

Throughout the 20th century, researchers have conducted numerous studies to try to identify ways to motivate workers and increase productivity. From these studies have come theories that have been applied to workers with varying degrees of success. A brief discussion of two of these theories—the classical theory of motivation and the Hawthorne studies—provides a background for understanding the present state of human relations.

Classical Theory of Motivation

The birth of the study of human relations can be traced to time and motion studies conducted at the turn of the century by Frederick W. Taylor and Frank and Lillian Gilbreth. Their studies analyzed how workers perform specific work tasks in an effort to improve the employees' productivity. These efforts led to the application of scientific principles to management.

According to the **classical theory of motivation**, money is the sole motivator for workers. Taylor suggested that workers who were paid more would produce more, an idea that would benefit both companies and workers. To improve productivity, Taylor thought that managers should break down each job into its component tasks (specialization), determine the best way to perform each task, and specify the

classical theory of motivation

theory suggesting that money is the sole motivator for workers

Enhancing Business Productivity
Yum Brands Recognizes Employees for Going the Extra Mile

When Latoya Gardner's Louisville, Kentucky, KFC ran out of crispy strips during lunch, she had to apologize to a customer for the delay. She decided on the spot to offer him a free side item to munch on while the fast-food restaurant fried a new batch of crispy strips. She was quite surprised when the customer returned a short time later and, with much fanfare, handed her a plaque mounted with a seat belt in front of all her co-workers. Unbeknownst to Gardner, her customer was Jonathan Blum, a senior vice president of public affairs for Yum Brands, which owns KFC, Pizza Hut, Taco Bell, and several other restaurant chains. The seat-belt plaque—which symbolizes the roller-coaster nature of the restaurant industry—is just one of several unusual awards the company hands out to employees for taking the initiative to handle a problem.

In addition to the seat-belt plaque, employees have received stickers, pins, stuffed jalapeño pepper toys—for demonstrating a "fire in the belly"—and miniature fans—for "individuals who take leadership in the face of crisis." The most coveted award among Yum's 840,000 employees is a giant set of chattering teeth, the Walking the Talk award. Some awards are delivered to employees by the Random Acts of Recognition Band, complete with musical instruments and noisemakers and often followed by a crowd of cheering employees. The awards are later posted on the walls of the company's hallways. Photos of beaming employees (including Gardner) holding their awards also hang on some executive's office walls.

Recognizing employees who exceed expectations has become a core principle of Yum Brands. The company believes that "catching people doing things right" is vital to motivating employees, which improves productivity, employee retention, and customer satisfaction. At Taco Bell, for example, employee turnover has fallen from 200 percent to 98 percent (the fast-food industry average is 120 percent). Taco Bell has also risen from 14th to 2nd place on *QSM* magazine's annual survey of drive-through effectiveness.

CEO and chairman David Novak launched the unusual award program when he was chief operating officer of Pepsi-Cola North America, which later spun its restaurant business into a separate corporation now called Yum. Novak says, "If you can get your people smiling and feeling good about themselves, that's fundamental to customer satisfaction."[5]

Discussion Questions
1. What role does employee recognition play in improving productivity?
2. What are some other benefits companies derive from acknowledging excellent employees?
3. How could a company such as Wal-Mart apply such principles to enhance productivity?

---

output to be achieved by a worker performing the task. Taylor also believed that incentives would motivate employees to be more productive. Thus, he suggested that managers link workers' pay directly to their output. He developed the piece-rate system, under which employees were paid a certain amount for each unit they produced; those who exceeded their quota were paid a higher rate per unit for all the units they produced.

We can still see Taylor's ideas in practice today in the use of mathematical models, statistics, and incentives. Moreover, companies are increasingly striving to relate pay to performance at both the hourly and managerial level. A survey of 300 business-technology executives by *Optimize* magazine found that their productivity is up 78 percent; about 75 percent of those companies offer formal or informal incentive programs to support productivity increases.[6] Figure 10.2 shows the percentages of companies giving incentives to employees to improve productivity.

More and more corporations are tying pay to performance in order to motivate—even up to the CEO level. For example, Colgate-Palmolive's CEO, Reuben Mark, was granted 4 million stock options 10 years ago that would pay off only if the stock increased 80 percent. Mark was able to cash in the options after Colgate's stock price increased by 286 percent—more than twice the increase of the Standard & Poor 500 Index over the same time frame. The topic of executive pay has become controversial in recent years, and many corporate boards of directors have taken steps to link executive compensation more closely to corporate performance. For example, if

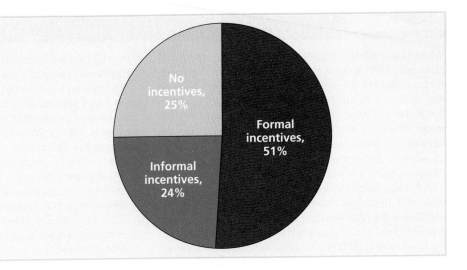

FIGURE 10.2

Companies Giving Employees Incentives to Improve Productivity

Source: Optimize Magazine Productivity 2004 study, in Marianne Kolbasuk McGee, "Behind the Numbers: Employee Productivity Pays Off for Everyone," *Information Week*, February 9, 2004, p. 76.

No incentives, 25%

Formal incentives, 51%

Informal incentives, 24%

Maurice Greenberg, CEO of American International Group (AIG), boosts his company's stock price by 10 percent a year for ten years, he will be able to exercise 750,000 stock options he received in 2003—worth about $66.3 million.[7]

Like most managers of the early 20th century, Taylor believed that satisfactory pay and job security would motivate employees to work hard. However, later studies showed that other factors are also important in motivating workers.

The Hawthorne Studies

Elton Mayo and a team of researchers from Harvard University wanted to determine what physical conditions in the workplace—such as light and noise levels—would stimulate employees to be most productive. From 1924 to 1932, they studied a group of workers at the Hawthorne Works Plant of the Western Electric Company and measured their productivity under various physical conditions.

The employees who participated in the Hawthorne studies responded to the attention they received during the study and thereby improved their performance, not the changing of the physical characteristics of their workplace. Do you think the workers in this photo improved their pace or level of quality as this photo was taken?

What the researchers discovered was quite unexpected and very puzzling: Productivity increased regardless of the physical conditions. This phenomenon has been labeled the Hawthorne effect. When questioned about their behavior, the employees expressed satisfaction because their co-workers in the experiments were friendly and, more importantly, because their supervisors had asked for their help and cooperation in the study. In other words, they were responding to the attention they received, not the changing physical work conditions. The researchers concluded that social and psychological factors could significantly affect productivity and morale. Medtronic, often called the "Microsoft of the medical-device industry," has a built-in psychological factor that influences employee morale. The company makes life-saving medical devices, such as pacemakers, neurostimulators, and stents. New hires at Medtronic receive medallions inscribed with a portion of the firm's mission statement, "alleviate pain, restore health, and extend life." There is an annual party where people whose bodies function thanks to Medtronic devices give testimonials. Obviously, Medtronic employees feel a sense of satisfaction in their jobs. In employee surveys, 86 percent said their work has special meaning and 94 percent felt pride in what they accomplished.[8]

The Hawthorne experiments marked the beginning of a concern for human relations in the workplace. They revealed that human factors do influence workers' behavior and that managers who understand the needs, beliefs, and expectations of people have the greatest success in motivating their workers.

Theories of Employee Motivation

The research of Taylor, Mayo, and many others has led to the development of a number of theories that attempt to describe what motivates employees to perform. In this section, we will discuss some of the most important of these theories. The successful implementation of ideas based on these theories will vary, of course, depending on the company, its management, and its employees. It should be noted, too, that what worked in the past may no longer work today. Good managers must have the ability to adapt their ideas to an ever-changing, diverse group of employees.

Maslow's Hierarchy of Needs

Psychologist Abraham Maslow theorized that people have five basic needs: physiological, security, social, esteem, and self-actualization. **Maslow's hierarchy** arranges these needs into the order in which people strive to satisfy them (Figure 10.3).[9]

Physiological needs, the most basic and first needs to be satisfied, are the essentials for living—water, food, shelter, and clothing. According to Maslow, humans devote all their efforts to satisfying physiological needs until they are met. Only when these needs are met can people focus their attention on satisfying the next level of needs—security.

Security needs relate to protecting yourself from physical and economic harm. Actions that may be taken to achieve security include reporting a dangerous workplace condition to management, maintaining safety equipment, and purchasing insurance with income protection in the event you become unable to work. Once security needs have been satisfied, people may strive for social goals.

Social needs are the need for love, companionship, and friendship—the desire for acceptance by others. To fulfill social needs, a person may try many things: making friends with a co-worker, joining a group, volunteering at a hospital, throwing a party. Once their social needs have been satisfied, people attempt to satisfy their need for esteem.

Esteem needs relate to respect—both self-respect and respect from others. One aspect of esteem needs is competition—the need to feel that you can do something better than anyone else. Competition often motivates people to increase their productivity. Esteem needs are not as easily satisfied as the needs at lower levels in Maslow's hierarchy because they do not always provide tangible evidence of success. However, these needs can be realized through rewards and increased involvement in organizational activities. Until esteem needs are met, people focus their attention on achieving respect. When they feel they have achieved some measure of respect, self-actualization becomes the major goal of life.

Maslow's hierarchy
a theory that arranges the five basic needs of people—physiological, security, social, esteem, and self-actualization—into the order in which people strive to satisfy them

physiological needs
the most basic human needs to be satisfied—water, food, shelter, and clothing

security needs
the need to protect oneself from physical and economic harm

social needs
the need for love, companionship, and friendship—the desire for acceptance by others

esteem needs
the need for respect—both self-respect and respect from others

FIGURE 10.3

Maslow's Hierarchy of Needs

Source: Adapted from Abraham H. Maslow, "A Theory of Human Motivation," *Psychology Review* 50 (1943), pp. 370–396. American Psychology Association.

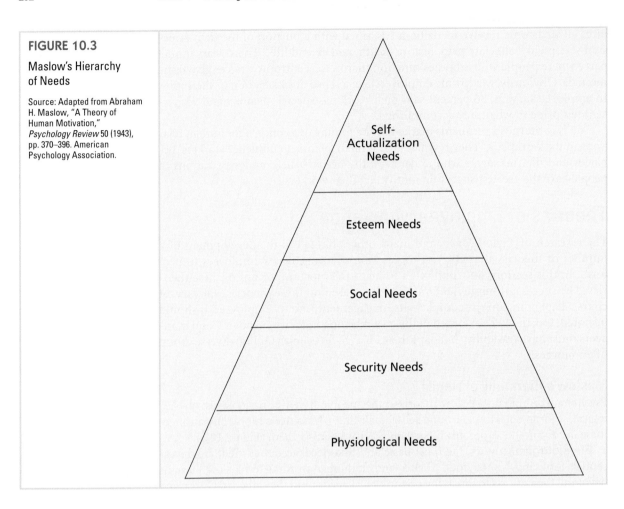

self-actualization needs
the need to be the best one can be; at the top of Maslow's hierarchy

Self-actualization needs, at the top of Maslow's hierarchy, mean being the best you can be. Self-actualization involves maximizing your potential. A self-actualized person feels that she or he is living life to its fullest in every way. For John Grisham, self-actualization might mean being praised as the best writer in the world; for actress Nicole Kidman, it might mean winning an Oscar.

Maslow's theory maintains that the more basic needs at the bottom of the hierarchy must be satisfied before higher-level goals can be pursued. Thus, people who are hungry and homeless are not concerned with obtaining respect from their colleagues. Only when physiological, security, and social needs have been more or less satisfied do people seek esteem. Maslow's theory also suggests that if a low-level need is suddenly reactivated, the individual will try to satisfy that need rather than higher-level needs. Many laid off workers probably shift their focus from high-level esteem needs to the need for security. Almost 10,000 employees in 32 countries in business, government, and nonprofit organizations were surveyed for the Global Employee Relationship Report. Fifty percent of the respondents said they believe their organization cares about developing people for the long term, not just for their current job. Just over half of the employees believed their employers show them genuine care and concern.[10] Managers should learn

Hygiene Factors	Motivational Factors	TABLE 10.2
Company policies	Achievement	Herzberg's Hygiene and Motivational Factors
Supervision	Recognition	
Working conditions	Work itself	
Relationships with peers, supervisors, and subordinates	Responsibility	
Salary	Advancement	
Security	Personal growth	

from Maslow's hierarchy that employees will be motivated to contribute to organizational goals only if they are able to first satisfy their physiological, security, and social needs through their work.

Herzberg's Two-Factor Theory

In the 1950s psychologist Frederick Herzberg proposed a theory of motivation that focuses on the job and on the environment where work is done. Herzberg studied various factors relating to the job and their relation to employee motivation and concluded that they can be divided into hygiene factors and motivational factors (Table 10.2).

Hygiene factors, which relate to the work setting and not to the content of the work, include adequate wages, comfortable and safe working conditions, fair company policies, and job security. These factors do not necessarily motivate employees to excel, but their absence may be a potential source of dissatisfaction and high turnover. Employee safety and comfort are clearly hygiene factors.

Many people feel that a good salary is one of the most important job factors, even more important than job security and the chance to use one's mind and abilities. Salary and security, two of the hygiene factors identified by Herzberg, make it possible for employees to satisfy the physiological and security needs identified by Maslow. However, the presence of hygiene factors is unlikely to motivate employees to work harder.

Motivational factors, which relate to the content of the work itself, include achievement, recognition, involvement, responsibility, and advancement. The absence of motivational factors may not result in dissatisfaction, but their presence is likely to motivate employees to excel. Many companies are beginning to employ methods to give employees more responsibility and control and to involve them more in their work, which serves to motivate them to higher levels of productivity and quality. For example, Song, a discount airline owned by Delta, gave each of its flight attendants four tickets to present to customers who are "nice to one another." Such empowerment makes both passengers and customers happier.[11]

Herzberg's motivational factors and Maslow's esteem and self-actualization needs are similar. Workers' low-level needs (physiological and security) have largely been satisfied by minimum-wage laws and occupational-safety standards set by various government agencies and are therefore not motivators. Consequently, to improve productivity, management should focus on satisfying workers' higher-level needs (motivational factors) by providing opportunities for achievement, involvement, and advancement and by recognizing good performance.

hygiene factors
aspects of Herzberg's theory of motivation that focus on the work setting and not the content of the work; these aspects include adequate wages, comfortable and safe working conditions, fair company policies, and job security

motivational factors
aspects of Herzberg's theory of motivation that focus on the content of the work itself; these aspects include achievement, recognition, involvement, responsibility, and advancement

Premium Standard Farms (PSF) operates a pork-processing plant in Milan, Missouri. Many of the 950 people employed there earn $10 an hour to operate fast-moving disassembly lines. Annual turnover rates of 200 percent in this industry are typical. Striving to improve their company, PSF's management turned to outside help to reduce their turnover rate.

Brad Hill, a senior consultant with the Hay Group in Chicago, began the process with a "design team"—a group of volunteers representing each department. Then he gave a short course on gain sharing and a juggling lesson. Hill says that teaching people to juggle is a great way to show them they can still learn new things about themselves and their jobs. He then guided the team through deciding how they wanted to measure and reward their performance through a compensation plan that is self-funding.

Employees came up with ideas that, when put into practice, saved their company tens of thousands of dollars a month. One employee-initiated change resulted in monthly savings that can run as high as $300,000. The employees are rewarded for their efforts through the incentive program they helped devise.

Hill says his goal is to do more than help workers change how they are paid. He wants to change their attitudes about what they do for a living by giving them more dignity and a sense of purpose. In addition to the meat-packers at PSF, Hill also has helped workers who pour iron at one company and care for the elderly at another.

Hill's methods work. At Premium Standard Farms, annual payouts for last year were projected to exceed $1,000 per employee, and employee retention rates improved by more than half. Hill's idea of instilling in employees a sense of purpose and worth and of getting the respect they deserve lends support to the theories of Herzberg (motivational factors) and Maslow (esteem needs). Now, PSF employees are definitely bringing home more than the bacon.[12]

Discussion Questions

1. Describe the hygiene factors employed at PSF's Milan plant.
2. Describe the motivational factors at work at PSF's Milan plant.
3. Which of Maslow's needs does PSF help employees satisfy?

McGregor's Theory X and Theory Y

In *The Human Side of Enterprise*, Douglas McGregor related Maslow's ideas about personal needs to management. McGregor contrasted two views of management—the traditional view, which he called Theory X, and a humanistic view, which he called Theory Y.

According to McGregor, managers adopting **Theory X** assume that workers generally dislike work and must be forced to do their jobs. They believe that the following statements are true of workers:

1. The average person naturally dislikes work and will avoid it when possible.
2. Most workers must be coerced, controlled, directed, or threatened with punishment to get them to work toward the achievement of organizational objectives.
3. The average worker prefers to be directed and to avoid responsibility, has relatively little ambition, and wants security.[13]

Managers who subscribe to the Theory X view maintain tight control over workers, provide almost constant supervision, try to motivate through fear, and make decisions in an autocratic fashion, eliciting little or no input from their subordinates. The Theory X style of management focuses on physiological and security needs and virtually ignores the higher needs discussed by Maslow.

The Theory X view of management does not take into account people's needs for companionship, esteem, and personal growth, whereas Theory Y, the contrasting view of management, does. Managers subscribing to the **Theory Y** view assume that workers like to work and that under proper conditions employees will

Theory X
McGregor's traditional view of management whereby it is assumed that workers generally dislike work and must be forced to do their jobs

Theory Y
McGregor's humanistic view of management whereby it is assumed that workers like to work and that under proper conditions employees will seek out responsibility in an attempt to satisfy their social, esteem, and self-actualization needs

seek out responsibility in an attempt to satisfy their social, esteem, and self-actualization needs. McGregor describes the assumptions behind Theory Y in the following way:

1. The expenditure of physical and mental effort in work is as natural as play or rest.
2. People will exercise self-direction and self-control to achieve objectives to which they are committed.
3. People will commit to objectives when they realize that the achievement of those goals will bring them personal reward.
4. The average person will accept and seek responsibility.
5. Imagination, ingenuity, and creativity can help solve organizational problems, but most organizations do not make adequate use of these characteristics in their employees.
6. Organizations today do not make full use of workers' intellectual potential.[14]

Obviously, managers subscribing to the Theory Y philosophy have a management style very different from managers subscribing to the Theory X philosophy. Theory Y managers maintain less control and supervision, do not use fear as the primary motivator, and are more democratic in decision making, allowing subordinates to participate in the process. Theory Y managers address the high-level needs in Maslow's hierarchy as well as physiological and security needs. Today, Theory Y enjoys widespread support and may have displaced Theory X.

Theory Z

Theory Z is a management philosophy that stresses employee participation in all aspects of company decision making. It was first described by William Ouchi in his book *Theory Z—How American Business Can Meet the Japanese Challenge.* Theory Z incorporates many elements associated with the Japanese approach to management, such as trust and intimacy, but Japanese ideas have been adapted for use in the United States. In a Theory Z organization, managers and workers share responsibilities; the management style is participative; and employment is long term and often lifelong. Theory Z results in employees feeling organizational ownership. Recent research has found that such feelings of ownership may produce positive attitudinal and behavioral effects for employees.[15] In a Theory Y organization, managers focus on assumptions about the nature of the worker. The two theories can be seen as complementary. Table 10.3 compares the traditional American management style, the Japanese management style, and Theory Z (the modified Japanese management style).

Theory Z
a management philosophy that stresses employee participation in all aspects of company decision making

Variations on Theory Z

Theory Z has been adapted and modified for use in a number of U.S. companies. One adaptation involves workers in decisions through quality circles. Quality circles (also called quality-assurance teams) are small, usually having five to eight members who discuss ways to reduce waste, eliminate problems, and improve quality, communication, and work satisfaction. Such quality teams are a common technique for harnessing the knowledge and creativity of hourly employees to solve problems in companies.

TABLE 10.3   Comparison of American, Japanese, and Theory Z Management Styles

	American	Japanese	Theory Z
Duration of employment	Relatively short term; workers subject to layoffs when business slows	Lifelong; no layoffs	Long term; layoffs rare
Rate of promotion	Rapid	Slow	Slow
Amount of specialization	Considerable; worker develops expertise in one area only	Minimal; worker develops expertise in all aspects of the organization	Moderate; worker learns all aspects of the organization
Decision making	Individual	Consensual; input from all concerned parties is considered	Consensual; emphasis on quality
Responsibility	Assigned to the individual	Shared by the group	Assigned to the individual
Control	Explicit and formal	Less explicit and less formal	Informal but with explicit performance measures
Concern for workers	Focus is on work only	Focus extends to worker's whole life	Focus includes worker's life and family

Source: Adapted from William Ouchi, *Theory Z—How American Business Can Meet the Japanese Challenge,* p. 58. ©1981 by Addison-Wesley Publishing Company, Inc. Reprinted by permission of Perseus Books Publishers, a member of Perseus Books, L.L.C.

Even more involved than quality circles are programs that operate under names such as *participative management, employee involvement,* or *self-directed work teams.* Regardless of the term used to describe such programs, they strive to give employees more control over their jobs while making them more responsible for the outcome of their efforts. Such programs often organize employees into work teams of 5 to 15 members who are responsible for producing an entire product item. Team members are cross-trained and can therefore move from job to job within the team. Each team essentially manages itself and is responsible for its quality, scheduling, ordering and use of materials, and problem solving. Many firms have successfully employed work teams to boost morale, productivity, quality, and competitiveness.

Equity Theory

equity theory
an assumption that how much people are willing to contribute to an organization depends on their assessment of the fairness, or equity, of the rewards they will receive in exchange

According to **equity theory**, how much people are willing to contribute to an organization depends on their assessment of the fairness, or equity, of the rewards they will receive in exchange. In a fair situation, a person receives rewards proportional to the contribution he or she makes to the organization. However, in practice, equity is a subjective notion. Each worker regularly develops a personal input-output ratio by taking stock of his or her contribution (inputs) to the organization in time, effort, skills, and experience and assessing the rewards (outputs) offered by the organization in pay, benefits, recognition, and promotions. The worker compares his or her ratio to the input-output ratio of some other person—a "comparison other," who may be a co-worker, a friend working in another organization, or an "average" of several people working in the organization. If the two ratios are close, the individual will feel that he or she is being treated equitably.

Let's say you have a high-school education and earn $25,000 a year. When you compare your input-output ratio to a co-worker who has a college degree and makes $35,000 a year, you will probably feel that you are being paid fairly. However, if you perceive that your personal input-output ratio is lower than that of your college-educated co-worker, you may feel that you are being treated unfairly and be motivated to seek change. But, if you learn that co-worker who makes $35,000 has only a high-school diploma, you may feel cheated by your employer. To achieve equity, you could try to increase your outputs by asking for a raise or promotion. You could also try to have your co-worker's inputs increased or his or her outputs decreased. Failing to achieve equity, you may be motivated to look for a job at a different company.

Corporate honchos at Booz Allen Hamilton, a global strategy and technology consulting firm, encourage employees to have a life outside of the office. VP Lloyd Howell leaves the office around 5 PM on most Fridays to have a date night with his wife. CEO Ralph Shrader, pictured here, is known to reference his own work/family conflicts in talks to his employees. Motivational opportunities can be organized and promoted by a company, but it can be doubly encouraging for employees to see the effort coming from the top.

Because almost all the issues involved in equity theory are subjective, they can be problematic. Author David Callahan has argued that feelings of inequity may underlie some unethical or illegal behavior in business, such as the $600 million a year stolen from companies by their own employees. Callahan believes that employees who do not feel they are being treated equitably may be motivated to equalize the situation by lying, cheating, or otherwise "improving" their pay, perhaps by stealing.[16] Managers should try to avoid equity problems by ensuring that rewards are distributed on the basis of performance and that all employees clearly understand the basis for their pay and benefits.

Expectancy Theory

Psychologist Victor Vroom described **expectancy theory**, which states that motivation depends not only on how much a person wants something but also on the person's perception of how likely he or she is to get it. A person who wants something and has reason to be optimistic will be strongly motivated. For example, say you really want a promotion. And, let's say because you have taken some night classes to improve your skills, and moreover, have just made a large, significant sale, you feel confident that you are qualified and able to handle the new position. Therefore, you are motivated to try to get the promotion. In contrast, if you do not believe you are likely to get what you want, you may not be motivated to try to get it, even though you really want it.

expectancy theory
the assumption that motivation depends not only on how much a person wants something but also on how likely he or she is to get it

Strategies for Motivating Employees

Based on the various theories that attempt to explain what motivates employees, businesses have developed several strategies for motivating their employees and boosting morale and productivity. Some of these techniques include behavior modification and job design, as well as the already described employee involvement programs and work teams.

Behavior Modification

Behavior modification involves changing behavior and encouraging appropriate actions by relating the consequences of behavior to the behavior itself. The concept of behavior modification was developed by psychologist B. F. Skinner, who showed that there are two types of consequences that can modify behavior—reward and punishment. Skinner found that behavior that is rewarded will tend to be repeated, while behavior that is punished will tend to be eliminated. For example, employees who know that they will receive a bonus, such as an expensive restaurant meal, for making a sale over $2,000 may be more motivated to make sales. Workers who know they will be punished for being tardy are likely to make a greater effort to get to work on time.

However, the two strategies may not be equally effective. Punishing unacceptable behavior may provide quick results but may lead to undesirable long-term side effects, such as employee dissatisfaction and increased turnover. In general, rewarding appropriate behavior is a more effective way to modify behavior.

Job Design

Herzberg identified the job itself as a motivational factor. Managers have several strategies that they can use to design jobs to help improve employee motivation. These include job rotation, job enlargement, job enrichment, and flexible scheduling strategies.

Job Rotation. **Job rotation** allows employees to move from one job to another in an effort to relieve the boredom that is often associated with job specialization. Businesses often turn to specialization in hopes of increasing productivity, but there is a negative side effect to this type of job design: Employees become bored and dissatisfied, and productivity declines. Job rotation reduces this boredom by allowing workers to undertake a greater variety of tasks and by giving them the opportunity to learn new skills. With job rotation, an employee spends a specified amount of time performing one job and then moves on to another, different job. The worker eventually returns to the initial job and begins the cycle again.

Job rotation is a good idea, but it has one major drawback. Because employees may eventually become bored with all the jobs in the cycle, job rotation does not totally eliminate the problem of boredom. Job rotation is extremely useful, however, in situations where a person is being trained for a position that requires an understanding of various units in an organization. Some companies, such as Procter & Gamble, use job rotation to increase functional skills. For example, marketing employees may rotate from growing brands to declining brands, from established markets to new markets, or from global mega-brands to regional small brands.[17] Many executive training programs require trainees to spend time learning a variety of specialized jobs. Job rotation is also used to cross-train today's self-directed work teams.

Job Enlargement. **Job enlargement** adds more tasks to a job instead of treating each task as separate. Like job rotation, job enlargement was developed to overcome the boredom associated with specialization. The rationale behind this strategy is that jobs are more satisfying as the number of tasks performed by an individual increases. Employees sometimes enlarge, or craft, their jobs by noticing what needs to be done and then changing tasks and relationship boundaries to adjust. Individual orientation and motivation shape opportunities to craft new jobs

---

behavior modification
changing behavior and encouraging appropriate actions by relating the consequences of behavior to the behavior itself

job rotation
movement of employees from one job to another in an effort to relieve the boredom often associated with job specialization

job enlargement
the addition of more tasks to a job instead of treating each task as separate

and job relationships.[18] Job enlargement strategies have been more successful in increasing job satisfaction than have job rotation strategies. IBM, AT&T, and Maytag are among the many companies that have used job enlargement to motivate employees.

Job Enrichment.   **Job enrichment** incorporates motivational factors, such as opportunity for achievement, recognition, responsibility, and advancement, into a job. It gives workers not only more tasks within the job but more control and authority over the job. Job enrichment programs enhance a worker's feeling of responsibility and provide opportunities for growth and advancement when the worker is able to take on the more challenging tasks. AT&T and General Foods use job enrichment to improve the quality of work life for their employees. The potential benefits of job enrichment are great, but it requires careful planning and execution.

job enrichment
the incorporation of motivational factors, such as opportunity for achievement, recognition, responsibility, and advancement, into a job

Flexible Scheduling Strategies.   Many U.S. workers work a traditional 40-hour work week consisting of five eight-hour days with fixed starting and ending times. Facing problems of poor morale and high absenteeism as well as a diverse workforce with changing needs, many managers have turned to flexible scheduling strategies such as flextime, compressed work weeks, job sharing, part-time work, and telecommuting. A Hewitt Associates survey of 945 major U.S. employers found that 74 percent offer flexible work options. The most commonly offered arrangements are flextime (59 percent), part-time (48 percent), work-at-home options (36 percent), job sharing (28 percent), compressed work weeks (21 percent), and summer hours (12 percent).[19]

Flextime is a program that allows employees to choose their starting and ending times, as long as they are at work during a specified core period (Figure 10.4). It does not reduce the total number of hours that employees work; instead, it gives employees more flexibility in choosing which hours they work. A firm may specify that employees must be present from 10:00 A.M. to 3:00 P.M. One employee may choose to come in at 7:00 A.M. and leave at the end of the core time, perhaps to attend classes at a nearby college after work. Another employee, a mother who lives in the suburbs, may come in at 9:00 A.M. in order to have time to drop off her children at a day-care center and commute by public transportation to her job. At Cendant Mobility, where the workforce is 70 percent female with an average age of 36, a Flexible Work Options program allows employees to have flexible start and

flextime
a program that allows employees to choose their starting and ending times, provided that they are at work during a specified core period

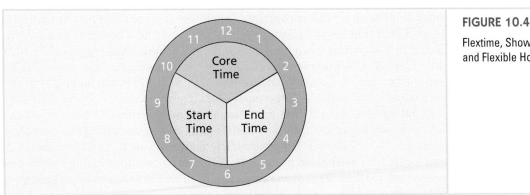

FIGURE 10.4

Flextime, Showing Core and Flexible Hours

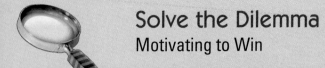
Eagle Pharmaceutical has long been recognized for its innovative techniques for motivating its sales force. It features the salesperson who has been the most successful during the previous quarter in the company newsletter, "Touchdown." The salesperson also receives a football jersey, a plaque, and $1,000 worth of Eagle stock. Eagle's "Superbowl Club" is for employees who reach or exceed their sales goal, and a "Heisman Award," which includes a trip to the Caribbean, is given annually to the top 20 salespeople in terms of goal achievement.

Eagle employs a video conference hook-up between the honored salesperson and four regional sales managers to capture some of the successful tactics and strategies the winning salesperson uses to succeed. The managers summarize these ideas and pass them along to the salespeople they manage. Sales managers feel strongly that programs such as this are important and that, by sharing strategies and tactics with one another, they can be a successful team.

Discussion Questions

1. Which motivational theories are in use at Eagle?
2. What is the value of getting employees to compete against a goal instead of against one another?
3. Put yourself in the shoes of one of the four regional sales managers and argue against potential cutbacks to the motivational program.

---

end times and consolidated schedules. Since implementing the program, turnover has dropped from 30 percent to 9 percent, saving the relocation services firm $8.6 million for each percentage point drop.[20]

Related to flextime are the scheduling strategies of the compressed work week and job sharing. The **compressed work week** is a four-day (or shorter) period in which an employee works 40 hours. Under such a plan, employees typically work 10 hours per day for four days and have a three-day weekend. The compressed work week reduces the company's operating expenses because its actual hours of operation are reduced. It is also sometimes used by parents who want to have more days off to spend with their families.

Job sharing occurs when two people do one job. One person may work from 8:00 A.M. to 12:30 P.M.; the second person comes in at 12:30 P.M. and works until 5:00 P.M. Job sharing gives both people the opportunity to work as well as time to fulfill other obligations, such as parenting or school. Thirty percent of companies allow job sharing.[21] With job sharing, the company has the benefit of the skills of two people for one job, often at a lower total cost for salaries and benefits than one person working eight hours a day would be paid.

Two other flexible scheduling strategies attaining wider use include allowing full-time workers to work part time for a certain period and allowing workers to work at home either full or part time. Employees at some firms may be permitted to work part time for several months in order to care for a new baby or an elderly parent or just to slow down for a little while to "recharge their batteries." By 2020, 40 percent of U.S. workers will be caring for an aging parent, and employees are expected to demand benefits that reflect this major shift.[22] When the employees return to full-time work, they are usually given a position comparable to their original full-time position. Other firms are allowing employees to telecommute or telework (work at home a few days of the week), staying connected via computers, modems, and telephones. Experts estimate that there are 8.7 to 23.5 million U.S. employees who work from home at least one day a month. Although many employees ask for the option of working at home to ease the responsibilities of caring for family members, some have discovered that they are more productive at home

compressed work week
a four-day (or shorter) period during which an employee works 40 hours

job sharing
performance of one full-time job by two people on part-time hours

without the distractions of the workplace. Cigna, Hewlett-Packard, AT&T, and Sun Microsystems have reported significant increases in productivity as well as savings on office space associated with their large telecommuting workforces. At Cigna, for example, 6,000 "E-workers" generated 4–12 percent more output than their co-workers doing similar work in the office.[23] Other employees, however, have discovered that they are not suited for working at home. Still, work-at-home programs do help reduce overhead costs for businesses. For example, some companies used to maintain a surplus of office space but have reduced the surplus through employee telecommuting, "hoteling" (being assigned to a desk through a reservation system), and "hot-desking" (several people using the same desk but at different times).

Companies are turning to flexible work schedules to provide more options to employees who are trying to juggle their work duties with other responsibilities and needs. Preliminary results indicated that flexible scheduling plans increase job satisfaction, which, in turn, leads to increases in productivity. Some recent research, however, has indicated there are potential problems with telecommuting. Some managers are reluctant to adopt the practice because the pace of change in today's workplace is faster than ever, and telecommuters may be

Single working-parent families face a tough challenge in balancing work and home life. For single parents, business travel and other routine demands of a corporate career—including overtime and interoffice transfers—can turn life upside down. Sometimes single parents decline promotions or high-profile assignments to preserve time with their children. In some organizations, experts say, it may be assumed single-mom staffers can't handle new duties because of the responsibilities they're shouldering at home.

left behind or actually cause managers more work in helping them stay abreast of changes. Some employers also worry that telecommuting workers create a security risk by creating more opportunities for computer hackers or equipment thieves. Some employees have found that working outside the office may hurt career advancement opportunities, and some report that instead of helping them balance work and family responsibilities, telecommuting increases the strain by blurring the barriers between the office and home. Co-workers call at all hours, and telecommuters are apt to continue to work when they are not supposed to (after regular business hours or during vacation time).[24]

Importance of Motivational Strategies

Motivation is more than a tool that managers can use to foster employee loyalty and boost productivity. It is a process that affects all the relationships within an organization and influences many areas such as pay, promotion, job design, training opportunities, and reporting relationships. Employees are motivated by the nature of the relationships they have with their supervisors, by the nature of their jobs, and by characteristics of the organization. Motivation tools, then, must be varied as well. Managers can further nurture motivation by being honest, supportive, empathetic, accessible, fair, and open. Motivating employees to increase satisfaction and productivity is an important concern for organizations seeking to remain competitive in the global marketplace.

Explore Your Career Options
Rating Metropolitan Areas

In terms of satisfaction and motivation, where you live can be almost as important as where you work. Obtaining information about various cities can provide fodder for your job hunt and even help you decide to accept or reject a job offer. *Forbes* magazine conducts an annual survey of the "Best Places for Business and Careers." To develop its rankings, the magazine evaluates factors such as expenses related to labor, energy, taxes, and office space; the number of college graduates and Ph.D.'s in the area; job and income growth; migration patterns; crime rates; and culture and leisure activities (e.g., museums, theaters, golf courses, and sports teams). According to the magazine, the 10 best metropolitan areas to work in are

	Metropolitan Area	Job Growth	Income Growth
1.	Madison, Wisconsin	1.5%	4.3%
2.	Raleigh–Durham, North Carolina	1.1	2.4
3.	Austin, Texas	1.7	3.5

	Metropolitan Area	Job Growth	Income Growth
4.	Washington D.C./Northern Virginia	2.1	4.3
5.	Athens, Georgia	1.1	2.9
6.	Provo, Utah	1.5	2.1
7.	Boise, Idaho	2.5	1.9
8.	Huntsville, Alabama	1.2	0.1
9.	Lexington, Kentucky	−0.1	1.8
10.	Richmond, Virginia	1.0	3.2

Salary is certainly an important aspect in any job hunt. Various Web sites will estimate the salaries necessary to live equivalently in two different cities. According to the National Association of Realtors' Salary Calculator site (see e-Xtreme Surfing), if you currently have a job in Atlanta, Georgia, that pays $50,000, you will need a job that pays $76,698 in Boston in order to maintain your standard of living (calculated on May 6, 2004).[25]

Review Your Understanding

Define human relations and determine why its study is important.

Human relations is the study of the behavior of individuals and groups in organizational settings. Its focus is what motivates employees to perform on the job. Human relations is important because businesses need to understand how to motivate their increasingly diverse employees to be more effective, boost workplace morale, and maximize employees' productivity and creativity.

Summarize early studies that laid the groundwork for understanding employee motivation.

Time and motion studies by Frederick Taylor and others helped them analyze how employees perform specific work tasks in an effort to improve their productivity. Taylor and the early practitioners of the classical theory of motivation felt that money and job security were the primary motivators of employees. However, the Hawthorne studies revealed that human factors also influence workers' behavior.

Compare and contrast the human-relations theories of Abraham Maslow and Frederick Herzberg.

Abraham Maslow defined five basic needs of all people and arranged them in the order in which they must be satisfied: physiological, security, social, esteem, and self-actualization. Frederick Herzberg divided characteristics of the job into hygiene factors and motivational factors. Hygiene factors relate to the work environment and must be present for employees to remain in a job. Motivational factors—recognition, responsibility, and advancement—relate to the work itself. They encourage employees to be productive. Herzberg's hygiene factors can be compared to Maslow's physiological and security needs; motivational factors may include Maslow's social, esteem, and self-actualization needs.

Investigate various theories of motivation, including Theories X, Y, and Z; equity theory; and expectancy theory.

Douglas McGregor contrasted two views of management: Theory X (traditional) suggests workers dislike work, while theory Y (humanistic) suggests that workers not only like work but seek out responsibility to satisfy their higher-order needs. Theory Z stresses employee participation in all aspects of company decision making, often through participative management programs and self-directed work teams. According to equity theory, how much people are willing to contribute to an organization depends on their assessment of the fairness, or equity, of the rewards they will receive in exchange. Expectancy theory states that motivation depends not only on how much a person wants something but also on the person's perception of how likely he or she is to get it.

Describe some of the strategies that managers use to motivate employees.

Strategies for motivating workers include behavior modification (changing behavior and encouraging appropriate actions by relating the consequences of behavior to the behavior itself) and job design. Among the job design strategies businesses use are job rotation (allowing employees to move from one job to another to try to relieve the boredom associated with job specialization), job enlargement (adding tasks to a job instead of treating each task as a separate job), job enrichment (incorporating motivational factors into a job situation), and flexible scheduling strategies (flextime, compressed work weeks, job sharing, part-time work, and telecommuting).

Critique a business's program for motivating its sales force.

Using the information presented in the chapter, you should be able to analyze and defend Eagle Pharmaceutical's motivation program in "Solve the Dilemma," box on page 300 including the motivation theories the firm is applying to boost morale and productivity.

Revisit the World of Business

1. Which of Maslow's hierarchy of needs does SAS help employees fulfill? How?
2. Describe the hygiene and motivational factors in effect at SAS.
3. What factors influence the morale of the employees of SAS?

Learn the Terms

behavior modification   298
classical theory of motivation   288
compressed work week   300
equity theory   296
esteem needs   291
expectancy theory   297
flextime   299
human relations   286

hygiene factors   293
job enlargement   298
job enrichment   299
job rotation   298
job sharing   300
Maslow's hierarchy   291
morale   287
motivation   286

motivational factors   293
physiological needs   291
security needs   291
self-actualization needs   292
social needs   291
Theory X   294
Theory Y   294
Theory Z   295

Check Your Progress

1. Why do managers need to understand the needs of their employees?
2. Describe the motivation process.
3. What was the goal of the Hawthorne studies? What was the outcome of those studies?
4. Explain Maslow's hierarchy of needs. What does it tell us about employee motivation?
5. What are Herzberg's hygiene and motivational factors? How can managers use them to motivate workers?
6. Contrast the assumptions of Theory X and Theory Y. Why has Theory Y replaced Theory X in management today?
7. What is Theory Z? How can businesses apply Theory Z to the workplace?
8. Identify and describe four job-design strategies.
9. Name and describe some flexible scheduling strategies. How can flexible schedules help motivate workers?
10. Why are motivational strategies important to both employees and employers?

Get Involved

1. Consider a person who is homeless: How would he or she be motivated and what actions would that person take? Use the motivation process to explain. Which of the needs in Maslow's hierarchy are likely to be most important? Least important?

2. View the video *Cheaper by the Dozen* (1950) and report on how the Gilbreths tried to incorporate their passion for efficiency into their family life.

3. What events and trends in society, technology, and economics do you think will shape human relations management theory in the future?

Build Your Skills

MOTIVATING

Background:
Do you think that, if employers could make work more like play, employees would be as enthusiastic about their jobs as they are about what they do in their leisure time? Let's see where this idea might take us.

Task:
After reading the "Characteristics of PLAY," place a ✔ in column one for those characteristics you have experienced in your leisure time activities. Likewise, check column three for those "Characteristics of WORK" you have experienced in any of the jobs you've held.

All That Apply	Characteristics of PLAY	All That Apply	Characteristics of WORK
	1. New games can be played on different days.		1. Job enrichment, job enlargement, or job rotation.
	2. Flexible duration of play.		2. Job sharing.
	3. Flexible time of when to play.		3. Flextime, telecommuting.
	4. Opportunity to express oneself.		4. Encourage and implement employee suggestions.
	5. Opportunity to use one's talents.		5. Assignment of challenging projects.
	6. Skillful play brings applause, praise, and recognition from spectators.		6. Employee-of-the-month awards, press releases, employee newsletter announcements.
	7. Healthy competition, rivalry, and challenge exist.		7. Production goals with competition to see which team does best.
	8. Opportunity for social interaction.		8. Employee softball or bowling teams.
	9. Mechanisms for scoring one's performance are available (feedback).		9. Profit sharing; peer performance appraisals.
	10. Rules assure basic fairness and justice.		10. Use tactful and consistent discipline.

Discussion Questions

1. What prevents managers from making work more like play?

2. Are these forces real, or imagined?

3. What would be the likely (positive and negative) results of making work more like play?

4. Could others in the organization accept such creative behaviors?

e-Xtreme Surfing

- **International Telework Association & Council**
  www.telecommute.org

  Provides news and resources on teleworking and telecommuting.

- **The Hawthorne Effect**
  www.envisionsoftware.com/articles/
  Hawthorne_Effect.html

  Expands on Flton Mayo's experiments.

- **The Gilbreth Network**
  http://gilbrethnetwork.tripod.com/

  Provides more information about the interesting lives and research of efficiency experts Frank and Lillian Gilbreth.

- **Salary Calculator**
  www.homefair.com/homefair/calc/salcalc.htm

  Helps you estimate the salary you'll need to maintain your standard of living if you move to a new city.

See for yourself Videocase

THE CONTAINER STORE

Kip Tindell and Garrett Boone founded The Container Store in 1978 with the idea of providing products to help people streamline and simplify their lives. At the time, this was an unheard of concept in retail, and Tindell and Boone had to work to persuade many commercial manufacturers to supply them with goods to sell in their store. Ultimately, they were able to create a multifunctional product line that with many items to help consumers save space and time and bring order to their clutter. The Container Store continues its original mission on a much larger scale. Its 31 retail locations range in size from 22,000 to 29,000 square feet, and their shelves are packed with more than 10,000 different products. Each store is divided into "lifestyle sections" such as Closet, Kitchen, Office, and Laundry. Throughout the stores, employees provide unparalleled service, helping customers solve their organizational problems.

In addition to providing solutions for its customers, The Container Store has also been a winner for its employees. The company has appeared many times on *Fortune's* "100 Best Companies to Work For" list. In fact, the company ranked number one on this list in 2000 and 2001; number two in 2002 and 2003; and number three in 2004. The company is guided by values and principles that revolve around the people who operate the business every day—the employees, and it tries to instill the values of pride in ownership, individuality, access to management and information, and having fun.

The Container Store's corporate culture is hard to describe, but easy for employees to understand. For the employees, there are wages above industry average and large merchandise discounts, among other benefits. Employees also receive significant training and other opportunities to extend their education. In a full-time employee's first year, he or she will receive 235 hours of formal training. Employees are encouraged to absorb and share product and company information with each other. In the work environment, they are empowered to make decisions and encouraged to use their intuition and creativity in everything that they do in the work environment. If you work for The Container Store, there is an opportunity for personal growth and the ability to build a career for life.

Motivation is an inner drive that directs people toward achieving a goal, hopefully deriving much satisfaction in that journey toward achievement. The employees at The Container Store have been described as "motivated and enthusiastic." The company reinforces this loyalty by communicating to all stakeholders that its employees are its greatest asset. From a store salesperson to a buyer in an office to a top manager, The Container Store provides respect, appreciation, compensation, and a pleasant work environment. The high morale of The Container Store employees contributes to exceptional levels of productivity and loyalty. In fact, one of The Container Store's business philosophies is that, "One great person equals three good people, so why not hire only great people?" To get great people, The Container Store mainly hires college-educated applicants who were customers first. The company looks for diversity in backgrounds, but is interested only in people who can develop a strong passion for The Container Store.

While earning higher wages, generous merchandise discounts, and a great deal of job security and appreciation is certainly rewarding, most employees would also like to have fun on the job. At The Container Store, many things help provide a pleasant work environment. There is very open communication throughout the company, including the sharing of daily store sales, company goals, and expansion plans. The work attire is casual and comfortable. In addition, The Container Store's employees get to celebrate their 5, 10, 15, and 20th anniversaries. At 10 and 15 years, they and their spouses are invited to the company's headquarters in Dallas, where they are honored by the company's founders at a staff meeting. After the formal recognition, they are invited to the Mansion on Turtle Creek, one of Dallas's foremost restaurants. Although the 26-year-old company hasn't had many retirements, when an employee does retire it creates a buzz throughout the company. When one long-time employee recently retired, the two founders were present for a roast where the retiree was dressed like a queen and her friends and co-workers shared stories about her.

Employees of The Container Store know that personal character and business ethics are important to everyone in the work environment. This is engrained in the company's culture, which encourages people to be the best they can be. The Container Store employee that excels and tries to maximize their potential can achieve some level of self-actualization in their career. Because The Container Store takes care of its employees so well, the employees take care of customers very well. With customer service as The Container Store's core competency, knowledgeable employees are empowered to offer unparalleled customer service that has been recognized in many awards and publications.[26]

Discussion Questions

1. What is the importance of motivational strategies at The Container Store?

2. How does the morale of employees contribute to making service the core competency of The Container Store?

3. What do you feel are the most important aspects of The Container Store work environment that would appeal to you?

Remember to check out our Online Learning Center at www.mhhe.com/ferrell5e.

Chapter 11

Managing Human Resources

OBJECTIVES

After reading this chapter, you will be able to:

- Define human resources management and explain its significance.
- Summarize the processes of recruiting and selecting human resources for a company.
- Discuss how workers are trained and their performance appraised.
- Identify the types of turnover companies may experience, and explain why turnover is an important issue.
- Specify the various ways a worker may be compensated.
- Discuss some of the issues associated with unionized employees, including collective bargaining and dispute resolution.
- Describe the importance of diversity in the workforce.
- Assess an organization's efforts to reduce its workforce size and manage the resulting effects.

The Apprentice: A Novel Approach to Hiring an Employee

Donald Trump, who has been called a "reality tycoon," created the number one new reality television series among adults ages 18 to 49 with *The Apprentice*. The show features 16 contestants vying for a $250,000-a-year management position in the Trump Organization by tackling business challenges ranging from selling lemonade to finding a renter for a penthouse apartment to organizing a Jessica Simpson concert. Each week, one contender is eliminated, with Trump himself telling the contestant, "You're fired!" The show's first season pulled in about 20 million viewers a week, with a median viewer income of $66,495, the highest for a prime-time series on broadcast television.

Of course, *The Apprentice* is a "reality" TV show, not real life. For starters, many believe that Trump is much nicer than the curmudgeon he portrays on the show. Some of the first-season episodes depicted contestants using deceptive practices in order to win their challenge at all costs. Some business-people questioned the firing of leaders for favoring candor over loyalty, saying it damages the trust that is required for success in business, while others complained that female contestants relied overly on sex appeal. Perhaps the biggest issue with the show is that hiring candidates solely for performance might be a short-run approach with potential long-run problems. In the real world, supporting the organization's culture, collaboration, and ethical conduct are also important to success. However, many viewers found real-life lessons in the show, such as the importance of first impressions and of speaking up for yourself.

One reason for the show's popularity is that many people would really like to be hired by Trump, because they see him as one of the best self-promoters of our time. In real life, Trump has managed through his self-promotion,

continued

charisma, painstaking attention to selected detail, personal connections, and a certain amount of drama to convince others that he is the best businessperson ever. This approach has led to wheeling and dealing to create a $6 billion empire of real estate, beauty pageants, and casinos (though some critics and former employees claim his empire is much smaller). There is no doubt that Trump would not be successful without recruiting and hiring highly competent managers for his organizations. Although outsiders have never totally understood his business deals and practices, the loyalty of his employees suggests that he is either very skilled at selecting personnel or there is much more to understand about how he accomplishes his objectives.[1]

Introduction

Of course, most businesses don't have a popular TV show through which to recruit and hire employees, but these are vital tasks in any organization. If a business is to achieve success, it must have sufficient numbers of employees who are qualified to perform the required duties. Thus, managing the quantity (from hiring to firing) and quality (through training, compensating, and so on) of employees is an important business function. Meeting the challenge of managing increasingly diverse human resources effectively can give a company a competitive edge in a cutthroat global marketplace.

This chapter focuses on the quantity and quality of human resources. First we look at how human resources managers plan for, recruit, and select qualified employees. Next we look at training, appraising, and compensating employees, aspects of human resources management designed to retain valued employees. Along the way, we'll also consider the challenges of managing unionized and diverse employees.

The Nature of Human Resources Management

human resources management (HRM)
all the activities involved in determining an organization's human resources needs, as well as acquiring, training, and compensating people to fill those needs

Chapter 1 defined human resources as labor, the physical and mental abilities that people use to produce goods and services. **Human resources management (HRM)** refers to all the activities involved in determining an organization's human resources needs, as well as acquiring, training, and compensating people to fill those needs. Human resources managers are concerned with maximizing the satisfaction of employees and motivating them to meet organizational objectives productively. In some companies, this function is called personnel management.

HRM has increased in importance over the last few decades, in part because managers have developed a better understanding of human relations through the work of Maslow, Herzberg, and others. Moreover, the human resources themselves are changing. Employees today are concerned not only about how much a job pays; they are concerned also with job satisfaction, personal performance, leisure, the environment, and the future. Once dominated by white men, today's workforce includes significantly more women, African-Americans, Hispanics, and other minorities, as well as disabled and older workers. Human resources managers must be aware of these changes and make the best of them to increase the productivity of their employees. Every manager practices some of the functions of human resources management at all times.

Planning for Human Resources Needs

When planning and developing strategies for reaching the organization's overall objectives, a company must consider whether it will have the human resources necessary to carry out its plans. After determining how many employees and what skills are needed to satisfy the overall plans, the human resources department (which may range from the owner in a small business to hundreds of people in a large corporation) ascertains how many employees the company currently has and how many will be retiring or otherwise leaving the organization during the planning period. With this information, the human resources manager can then forecast how many more employees the company will need to hire and what qualifications they must have. HRM planning also requires forecasting the availability of people in the workforce who will have the necessary qualifications to meet the organization's future needs. The human resources manager then develops a strategy for satisfying the organization's human resources needs.

Next, managers analyze the jobs within the organization so that they can match the human resources to the available assignments. **Job analysis** determines, through observation and study, pertinent information about a job—the specific tasks that comprise it; the knowledge, skills, and abilities necessary to perform it; and the environment in which it will be performed. Managers use the information obtained through a job analysis to develop job descriptions and job specifications.

A **job description** is a formal, written explanation of a specific job that usually includes job title, tasks to be performed (for instance, waiting on customers), relationship with other jobs, physical and mental skills required (such as lifting heavy boxes or calculating data), duties, responsibilities, and working conditions. A **job specification** describes the qualifications necessary for a specific job, in terms of education (some jobs require a college degree), experience, personal characteristics (newspaper ads frequently request outgoing, hardworking persons), and physical characteristics. Both the job description and job specification are used to develop recruiting materials such as newspaper and online advertisements.

Recruiting and Selecting New Employees

After forecasting the firm's human resources needs and comparing them to existing human resources, the human resources manager should have a general idea of how many new employees the firm needs to hire. With the aid of job analyses, management can then recruit and select employees who are qualified to fill specific job openings.

Recruiting

Recruiting means forming a pool of qualified applicants from which management can select employees. There are two sources from which to develop this pool of applicants—internal and external.

Internal sources of applicants include the organization's current employees. Many firms have a policy of giving first consideration to their own employees—or promoting from within. The cost of hiring current employees to fill job openings is inexpensive when compared with the cost of hiring from external sources, and it is good for employee morale.

External sources consist of advertisements in newspapers and professional journals, employment agencies, colleges, vocational schools, recommendations from current

job analysis
the determination, through observation and study, of pertinent information about a job—including specific tasks and necessary abilities, knowledge, and skills

job description
a formal, written explanation of a specific job, usually including job title, tasks, relationship with other jobs, physical and mental skills required, duties, responsibilities, and working conditions

job specification
a description of the qualifications necessary for a specific job, in terms of education, experience, and personal and physical characteristics

recruiting
forming a pool of qualified applicants from which management can select employees

The McGraw-Hill Companies has an online database of job offerings called "Strategic Talent Acquisition Resources," or STAR. STAR helps employees manage their careers by alerting them about future opportunities that match their experiences, captures all résumés in a common database so they can be shared nationwide, allows for electronic approvals, and eliminates all paper résumés.

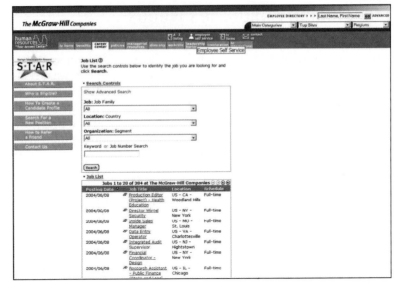

employees, competing firms, unsolicited applications, and online. There are hundreds of Web sites where employers can post job openings and job seekers can post their résumés, including Monster.com, Hotjobs.com, and CareerBuilder.com. Employers looking for employees for specialized jobs can use more focused sites such as Techies.com. Increasingly, companies can turn to their own Web sites for potential candidates: Of the *Fortune* 500 firms, 94 percent provide career Web sites where they recruit, provide employment information, and take applications.[2] Using these sources of applicants is generally more expensive than hiring from within, but it may be necessary if there are no current employees who meet the job specifications or there are better-qualified people outside of the organization. Recruiting for entry-level managerial and professional positions is often carried out on college and university campuses. For managerial or professional positions above the entry level, companies sometimes depend on employment agencies or executive search firms, sometimes called *headhunters*, which specialize in luring qualified people away from other companies.

Selection

selection
the process of collecting information about applicants and using that information to make hiring decisions

Selection is the process of collecting information about applicants and using that information to decide which ones to hire. It includes the application itself, as well as interviewing, testing, and reference checking. This process can be quite lengthy and expensive. At Procter & Gamble, for example, the steps include the application, screening and comprehensive interviews, day visits/site visits, and for those outside the United States, a problem-solving test. According to the company's Web site, "Only the very best candidates will complete the entire process."[3] Such rigorous scrutiny is necessary to find those applicants who can do the work expected and fit into the firm's structure and culture. If an organization finds the "right" employees through its recruiting and selection process, it will not have to spend as much money later in recruiting, selecting, and training replacement employees.

The Application. In the first stage of the selection process, the individual fills out an application form and perhaps has a brief interview. The application form asks for the applicant's name, address, telephone number, education, and previous work expe-

1. Know your aspirations, strengths, and weaknesses—remember, you are selling yourself.	**TABLE 11.1**
2. Know your potential employer—research the organization, industry, and position.	Interviewing Tips
3. Explain how you can help the employer achieve its goals by highlighting your skills and capabilities.	
4. Be organized, speak clearly and confidently, maintain good eye contact, and offer a firm handshake.	
5. Arrive at the interview early, dress professionally, carry an attractive portfolio, pen, and extra copies of your résumé.	
6. Listen carefully and answer questions completely.	

Source: Adapted from "Interviewing Skills," Career Center, Texas A&M University, http://careercenter.tamu.edu/Students/S1/S1B.shtml (accessed May 20, 2004).

rience. The goal of this stage of the selection process is to get acquainted with the applicants and to weed out those who are obviously not qualified for the job. Most companies ask for the following information before contacting a potential candidate: current salary, reason for seeking a new job, years of experience, availability, and level of interest in the position. In addition to identifying obvious qualifications, the application can provide subtle clues about whether a person is appropriate for a particular job. For instance, an applicant who gives unusually creative answers may be perfect for a position at an advertising agency; a person who turns in a sloppy, hurriedly scrawled application probably would not be appropriate for a technical job requiring precise adjustments. Many companies now accept online applications. The online application at Procter & Gamble is designed not only to collect biographical data but to create a picture of the applicant and how the person might contribute within the company. The Web site states that there are no right or wrong answers and indicates that completion takes about 30 to 45 minutes. Applicants also must submit an electronic copy of their résumé.[4]

The Interview.   The next phase of the selection process involves interviewing applicants. Interviews allow management to obtain detailed information about the applicant's experience and skills, reasons for changing jobs, attitudes toward the job, and an idea of whether the person would fit in with the company. Furthermore, the interviewer can answer the applicant's questions about the requirements for the job, compensation, working conditions, company policies, organizational culture, and so on. A potential employee's questions may be just as revealing as his or her answers. Table 11.1 provides some helpful advice for interviewing, while Table 11.2 lists some of the most common questions asked by interviewers.

Testing.   Another step in the selection process is testing. Ability and performance tests are used to determine whether an applicant has the skills necessary for the job. Aptitude, IQ, or personality tests may be used to assess an applicant's potential for a certain kind of work and his or her ability to fit into the organization's culture. One of the most commonly used tests is the Myers-Briggs Type Indicator. Myers-Briggs Type Indicator Test is used over 2.5 million times each year according to a survey by *Workforce Management.* Figure 11.1 shows a few alternative tests, what they attempt to measure and an estimate of the expense per employee. Although polygraph ("lie detector") tests were once a common technique for evaluating the honesty of applicants, in 1988 their use was restricted to specific government jobs and those involving security or access to drugs. Applicants may also undergo physical examinations to determine their suitability for some jobs, and many companies require applicants to be screened for illegal

TABLE 11.2

Top 10 Interview
Questions

1. What are your weaknesses?
2. Why should we hire you?
3. Why do you want to work here?
4. What are your goals?
5. Why did you leave (or why are you leaving) your job?
6. When were you most satisfied in your job?
7. What can you do for us that other candidates can't?
8. What are three positive things your last boss would say about you?
9. What salary are you seeking?
10. If you were an animal, which one would you want to be?

Source: Carole Martin, "Prep for the Top 10 Interview Questions." Copyright © 2004 Monster Worldwide, Inc. All rights reserved. These questions first appeared on Monster.com, the leading online global network for careers.

FIGURE 11.1

Sampling of
Psychological Tests

Source: Paul Kaihla "Getting Inside the Boss's Head," *Business 2.0,* November 2003, Copyright © 2003 *Time* Inc. All rights reserved.

Test/Provider	Purpose	Cost/Person
HCG Cultural Assessment Tool Hagberg Consulting Group Foster City, CA	Determines workplace morale and dysfunction	$15.00–20.00
The Hogan Personality Inventory Hogan Assessment Systems Tulsa, OK	Measures potential employee fit with the company and job	20.00–125.00
The Call Center Solution ePredix Minneapolis, MN	Predicts success in call center jobs and potential for success in upselling	25.00 and up (selection phase)
Sigmaradius 360 Degree Feedback Sigma Assessment Systems Port Huron, MI	Measures managerial effectiveness by evaluating superior's and subordinate's assessment	139.00–199.00

drug use. More than 40 million drug tests are conducted annually by employers, with less than 5 percent yielding a positive result.[5] Drug testing is common among government workers, companies that contract for the government, and in performance-critical industries such as airlines and construction work. However, testing is costly. In just one year, the federal government spent $12 million and found just 153 positives. Some studies have shown that drug testing (1) does not increase productivity, (2) can foster resentment, and (3) may lead highly qualified people to avoid a company.[6] Indeed, the practice of drug testing has spawned a host of products intended to help applicants defeat the tests.[7] Like the application form and the interview, testing serves to eliminate those who do not meet the job specifications.

Reference Checking.   Before making a job offer, the company should always check an applicant's references. Reference checking usually involves verifying educational background and previous work experience. Background checking is important because applicants may misrepresent themselves on their applications or résumés. ADP Screening and Selection Services, which conducts background checks for employers, reported that more than 50 percent of the applicants on whom it conducted background checks had presented false information about themselves on résumés or applications.[8] Consequently, reference checking is a vital, albeit often overlooked, stage in the selection process. Managers charged with hiring should be aware, however, that many organizations will confirm only that an applicant is a former employee, perhaps with beginning and ending work dates, and will not release details about the quality of the employee's work.

Legal Issues in Recruiting and Selecting

Legal constraints and regulations are present in almost every phase of the recruitment and selection process, and a violation of these regulations can result in lawsuits and fines. Therefore, managers should be aware of these restrictions to avoid legal problems. Some of the laws affecting human resources management are discussed below.

Because one law pervades all areas of human resources management, we'll take a quick look at it now. **Title VII of the Civil Rights Act** of 1964 prohibits discrimination in employment. It also created the Equal Employment Opportunity Commission (EEOC), a federal agency dedicated to increasing job opportunities for women and minorities and eliminating job discrimination based on race, religion, color, sex, national origin, or handicap. As a result of Title VII, employers must not impose sex distinctions in job specifications, job descriptions, or newspaper advertisements. Between 75,000 and 90,000 charges of discrimination are filed each year with the EEOC.[9] Sexual harassment cases make up the largest number of claims the EEOC sees each day. Complaints of sexual harassment filed with the EEOC average about 15,000 per year.[10] The Civil Rights Act of 1964 also outlaws the use of discriminatory tests for applicants. Aptitude tests and other indirect tests must be validated; in other words, employers must be able to demonstrate that scores on such tests are related to job performance, so that no one race has an advantage in taking the tests. Almost 40 years after passage of the Civil Rights Act, African-Americans hold 8.2 percent of executive positions, Hispanics comprise 5 percent of the top positions, while women represent 15.7 percent of corporate officers.[11]

Other laws affecting HRM include the Americans with Disabilities Act (ADA), which prevents discrimination against disabled persons. It also classifies people with AIDS as handicapped and, consequently, prohibits using a positive AIDS test as reason to deny an applicant employment. The Age Discrimination in Employment Act specifically outlaws discrimination based on age. Its focus is banning hiring practices that discriminate against people between the ages of 49 and 69, but it also outlaws policies that require employees to retire before the age of 70. Generally, however, when companies need employees, recruiters head to college campuses, and when downsizing is necessary, many

Title VII of the Civil Rights Act
prohibits discrimination in employment and created the Equal Employment Opportunity Commission

Be yourself. Race. Ethnicity. Religion. Nationality. Gender. In the end, there's just one variety of human being. The individual. All six billion of us. **Be bullish.**

ml.com

Merrill Lynch acknowledges individual differences.

older workers are offered early retirement. AARP, the advocacy organization for people 50 and older, found that very few employers consider their companies one of the best for older workers. AARP mailed invitations to 10,000 companies for a chance to compete for a listing in *Modern Maturity* magazine as one of the "best employers for workers over 50." The 35-million-member organization received only 14 applications. Given that nearly 20 percent of the nation's workers will be 55 years old or over by 2015, many companies may need to change their approach toward older workers.[12] The Equal Pay Act mandates that men and women who do equal work must receive the same wage. Wage differences are acceptable only if they are attributed to seniority, performance, or qualifications. Despite these laws, women still earn just 76.2 percent of what men earn in the United States.[13]

Developing the Workforce

orientation
familiarizing newly hired employees with fellow workers, company procedures, and the physical properties of the company

Once the most qualified applicants have been selected and offered positions, and they have accepted their offers, they must be formally introduced to the organization and trained so they can begin to be productive members of the workforce. **Orientation** familiarizes the newly hired employees with fellow workers, company procedures, and the physical properties of the company. It generally includes a tour of the building; introductions to supervisors, co-workers, and subordinates; and the distribution of organizational manuals describing the organization's policy on vacations, absenteeism, lunch breaks, company benefits, and so on. Orientation also involves socializing the new employee into the ethics and culture of the new company. Many larger companies now show videotapes of procedures, facilities, and key personnel in the organization to help speed the adjustment process.

Training and Development

training
teaching employees to do specific job tasks through either classroom development or on-the-job experience

development
training that augments the skills and knowledge of managers and professionals

Although recruiting and selection are designed to find employees who have the knowledge, skills, and abilities the company needs, new employees still must undergo **training** to learn how to do their specific job tasks. *On-the-job training* allows workers to learn by actually performing the tasks of the job, while *classroom training* teaches employees with lectures, conferences, videotapes, case studies, and Web-based training. Employee training expenses are increasing, as a percentage of payroll (up 2.2 percent), per employee (up 12.5 percent), and as a function of total hours of training (up 16 percent).[14] **Development** is training that augments the skills and knowledge of managers and professionals. Training and development are also used to improve the skills of employees in their present positions and to prepare them for increased responsibility and job promotions. Training is therefore a vital function of human resources management. Training and development plans are tailored to meet each employee's needs at Procter & Gamble. In addition to on-the-job training, the company offers one-on-one coaching from managers, peer mentoring, individualized work plans that outline key projects and highlight skills to sharpen, and formal classroom training conducted at the company's "Learning Center" in Cincinnati.[16]

Did You Know?   Internet-based training is expected to grow to be a $10.6 billion market by 2007.[15]

Assessing Performance

Assessing an employee's performance—his or her strengths and weaknesses on the job—is one of the most difficult tasks for managers. However, performance appraisal is crucial because it gives employees feedback on how they are doing and what they

• **Productivity**—rate at which work is regularly produced • **Quality**—accuracy, professionalism, and deliverability of produced work • **Job knowledge**—understanding of the objectives, practices, and standards of work • **Problem solving**—ability to identify and correct problems effectively • **Communication**—effectiveness in written and verbal exchanges • **Initiative**—willingness to identify and address opportunities for improvement • **Adaptability**—ability to become comfortable with change • **Planning and organization skills**—reflected through the ability to schedule projects, set goals, and maintain organizational systems • **Teamwork and cooperation**—effectiveness of collaborations with co-workers • **Judgment**—ability to determine appropriate actions in a timely manner • **Dependability**—responsiveness, reliability, and conscientiousness demonstrated on the job • **Creativity**—extent to which resourceful ideas, solutions, and methods for task completion are proposed • **Sales**—demonstrated through success in selling products, services, yourself, and your company • **Customer service**—ability to communicate effectively with customers, address problems, and offer solutions that meet or exceed their expectations • **Leadership**—tendency and ability to serve as a doer, guide, decision maker, and role model • **Financial management**—appropriateness of cost controls and financial planning within the scope defined by the position	**TABLE 11.3** Performance Characteristics

Source: "Performance Characteristics," Performance Review from **http://www.salary.com/Careerresources/docs/ related_performance_review_ part2_popup.html** (accessed June 12, 2001). Used with permission.

need to do to improve their performance. It also provides a basis for determining how to compensate and reward employees, and it generates information about the quality of the firm's selection, training, and development activities. Table 11.3 identifies 16 characteristics that may be assessed in a performance review.

Performance appraisals may be objective or subjective. An objective assessment is quantifiable. For example, a Westinghouse employee might be judged by how many circuit boards he typically produces in one day or by how many of his boards have defects. A Century 21 real estate agent might be judged by the number of houses she has shown or the number of sales she has closed. A company can also use tests as an objective method of assessment. Whatever method they use, managers must take into account the work environment when they appraise performance objectively.

When jobs do not lend themselves to objective appraisal, the manager must relate the employee's performance to some other standard. One popular tool used in subjective assessment is the ranking system, which lists various performance factors on which the manager ranks employees against each other. Although used by many large companies, ranking systems are unpopular with many employees. Qualitative criteria, such as teamwork and communication skills, used to evaluate employees are generally hard to gauge. Such grading systems have triggered employee lawsuits that allege discrimination in grade/ranking assignments. The charges were brought by older workers at Ford, by blacks and women at Microsoft, and by U.S. citizens at Conoco.[17]

Another performance appraisal method used by many companies is the 360-degree feedback system, which provides feedback from a panel that typically includes superiors, peers, and subordinates. Because of the tensions it may cause, peer appraisal appears to be difficult for many. However, companies that have success with 360-degree feedback tend to be open to learning and willing to experiment and are led by executives who are direct about the expected benefits as well as the challenges.[18] For example, at AAH Pharmaceuticals, one of Great Britain's largest pharmaceutical companies, traditional one-on-one performance evaluations had resulted in conflict, and suggestions for improvements were not always accepted. When the company began to adopt a 360-degree appraisal approach, managers noticed that employees were more likely to accept criticism when it came from several different individuals.[19]

Whether the assessment is objective or subjective, it is vital that the manager discuss the results with the employee, so that the employee knows how well he or she is doing the job. The results of a performance appraisal become useful only when they are communicated, tactfully, to the employee and presented as a tool to allow the employee to grow and improve in his or her position and beyond. Performance appraisals are also used to determine whether an employee should be promoted, transferred, or terminated from the organization.

Turnover

turnover
occurs when employees quit or are fired and must be replaced by new employees

Turnover, which occurs when employees quit or are fired and must be replaced by new employees, results in lost productivity from the vacancy, fees to recruit replacement employees, management time devoted to interviewing, and training costs for new employees. At Wal-Mart, for example, the cost to test, interview, and train a new employee is approximately $2,500.[20] One cause of turnover is job dissatisfaction: A Gallup Poll found that 70 percent of the U.S. workforce is "disengaged"—mentally detached from their current jobs and awaiting new employment opportunities. Part of the reason for this detachment may be overworked employees as a result of downsizing and a lack of training and advancement opportunities.[21] Of course, turnover is not always an unhappy occasion when its takes the form of a promotion or transfer.

promotion
an advancement to a higher-level job with increased authority, responsibility, and pay

A **promotion** is an advancement to a higher-level job with increased authority, responsibility, and pay. In some companies and most labor unions, seniority—the length of time a person has been with the company or at a particular job classification—is the key issue in determining who should be promoted. Most managers base promotions on seniority only when they have candidates with equal qualifications: Managers prefer to base promotions on merit.

transfer
a move to another job within the company at essentially the same level and wage

A **transfer** is a move to another job within the company at essentially the same level and wage. Transfers allow workers to obtain new skills or to find a new position within an organization when their old position has been eliminated because of automation or downsizing.

separations
employment changes involving resignation, retirement, termination, or layoff

Separations occur when employees resign, retire, are terminated, or are laid off. Table 11.4 lists rules for peaceful separations from companies. Employees may be terminated, or fired, for poor performance, violation of work rules, absenteeism, and so on. Businesses have traditionally been able to fire employees *at will*, that is, for any reason other than for race, religion, sex, or age, or because an employee is a union organizer. However, recent legislation and court decisions now require that companies fire employees fairly, for just cause only. Managers must take care, then, to warn

- Leave as soon as practicable after making the decision.
- Prior to leaving, discuss your decision only with those who need to know.
- If asked, be candid about your new job; avoid the appearance of hiding something.
- Prior to leaving, do not disrupt your current employer's business.
- Do not take any documents, computer data, etc. with you.
- Be careful about any paper or electronic trails concerning the process that resulted in your resignation.
- Sign an employment agreement with a new employer only after you have resigned from your current position.
- Do not work for the new employer until after the last day of work at your current job.
- Have the recruiting employer indemnify you regarding judgments, settlements, and attorneys' fees incurred in connection with any litigation initiated by your former employer.
- Specify in a written agreement with your new employer that you will not use or disclose any trade secrets of former employers.

Source: Robert Lenzner and Carrie Shook, "Want to Go Peacefully? Some Rules," *Forbes*, February 23, 1998. Reprinted by permission of *Forbes Magazine*. Copyright 2004 Forbes Inc.

TABLE 11.4

Rules for Peaceful Separations

employees when their performance is unacceptable and may lead to dismissal. They should also document all problems and warnings in employees' work records. To avoid the possibility of lawsuits from individuals who may feel they have been fired unfairly, employers should provide clear, business-related reasons for any firing, supported by written documentation if possible. Employee disciplinary procedures should be carefully explained to all employees and should be set forth in employee handbooks.

Many companies have downsized in recent years, laying off tens of thousands of employees in their effort to become more productive and competitive. Bank of America, for example, cut 12,500 jobs—about 7 percent of its workforce—after it acquired FleetBoston Bank.[22] In the last three years, some 300,000 U.S. jobs have been outsourced to overseas firms with lower labor costs.[23] Layoffs are sometimes temporary; employees may be brought back when business conditions improve. When layoffs are to be permanent, employers often help employees find other jobs and may extend benefits while the employees search for new employment. Such actions help lessen the trauma of the layoffs.

A well-organized human resources department strives to minimize losses due to separations and transfers because recruiting and training new employees is very expensive. Note that a high turnover rate in a company may signal problems either with the selection and training process, the compensation program, or even the type of company. To help reduce turnover, companies have tried a number of strategies. Levi Strauss & Company, for example, provides emergency grants or loans of up to $1,000 to help employees confronted with a car that won't start, a sick child, or other unexpected financial hardship. Kraft Foods allows U.S. workers to share jobs, swap shifts, or to take annual vacations in one-hour increments to help them deal with family emergencies. CVS offers simulated work experience to support new employees coming off welfare who have never held a traditional job.[24] Figure 11.2 shows some of the retention methods used by some businesses to retain frontline employees.

Although the economy is recovering and top companies are seeing increases in profits and stock prices, almost one-third of Americans feel that jobs remain hard to get. The United States seems to be in the midst of a "jobless" recovery. One of the reasons for the lack of jobs, especially in the high-tech industry, is the increasing trend to outsource or offshore jobs to low-wage countries like India and China. High-tech firms, under mounting pressure from key stakeholders to cut costs, can save up to 30 to 40 percent by moving jobs out of the United States.

International Business Machines (IBM), once renowned for offering generous benefits and lifetime employment policies, has not been able to escape the cost-cutting pressure from Wall Street. Analysts estimate that IBM has laid off more than 10,000 workers since 2001, although the company won't confirm that figure. The firm also faces several lawsuits related to its efforts to find cost savings through human resources practices. One case relates to changes the company made to its pension plans in 1995 and 1999, which sharply reduced retirement benefits for the bulk of its workforce. Another suit alleges that IBM is guilty of age discrimination by laying off more older employees because their health and benefits packages cost the company more than those of younger employees.

Job security concerns have harmed morale among the firm's 315,000 employees, a fact not helped by internal company documents leaked to *The Wall Street Journal,* which suggested that the company could save $168 million by shifting several thousand high-paying programming jobs overseas beginning in 2006. A programmer in China with three to five years experience would cost IBM about $12.50/hour in salary and benefits, while a similar employee working in the United States costs the company about $56/hour including benefits.

However, even though IBM is trying to cut employee expenses, a big part of its strategy is to go after specialized lines of business where it can compete on quality rather than price and thus earn higher margins. This strategy creates a need for employees with special skills. Although fewer entry-level jobs may be available, there will still be a premium paid for employees who understand specialized business needs, such as financial services, Linux programming, and other specialized technologies.[25]

Discussion Questions

1. Who are some of the key organizational stakeholders whom IBM would be trying to please by moving jobs to less expensive countries?
2. How would you defend IBM's employment strategy?
3. Are you aware of other companies or industries greatly affected by similar employment strategies?

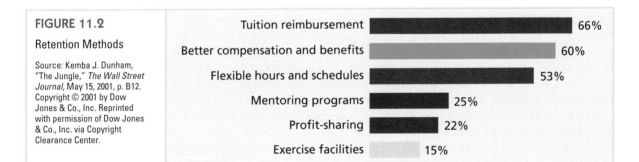

FIGURE 11.2

Retention Methods

Source: Kemba J. Dunham, "The Jungle," *The Wall Street Journal,* May 15, 2001, p. B12. Copyright © 2001 by Dow Jones & Co., Inc. Reprinted with permission of Dow Jones & Co., Inc. via Copyright Clearance Center.

Retention Method	Percentage
Tuition reimbursement	66%
Better compensation and benefits	60%
Flexible hours and schedules	53%
Mentoring programs	25%
Profit-sharing	22%
Exercise facilities	15%

Compensating the Workforce

People don't work for free, and how much they are paid for their work is a complicated issue. Also, designing a fair compensation plan is an important task because pay and benefits represent a substantial portion of an organization's expenses. Wages that are too high may result in the company's products being priced too high, making them uncompetitive in the market. Wages that are too low may damage employee morale and result in costly turnover. Remember that compensation is one of the hygiene factors identified by Herzberg.

	Costco	Sam's Clubs
Number of employees	68,000	102,000
Sales	$34 billion	$35 billion
Average hourly wage	$15.97	$11.52
Percent employees covered by health plans	82%	47%
Turnover (per year)	6%	21%
Profits per employee	$13,647	$11,039

Source: Stanley Holmes and Wendy Zellner, "The Costco Way," *Business Week*, April 12, 2004, pp. 76–77.

TABLE 11.5

Managing the Workforce: Costco versus Sam's Clubs

Designing a fair compensation plan is a difficult task because it involves evaluating the relative worth of all jobs within the business while allowing for individual efforts. Compensation for a specific job is typically determined through a **wage/salary survey,** which tells the company how much compensation comparable firms are paying for specific jobs that the firms have in common. Compensation for individuals within a specific job category depends on both the compensation for that job and the individual's productivity. Therefore, two employees with identical jobs may not receive exactly the same pay because of individual differences in performance.

wage/salary survey
a study that tells a company how much compensation comparable firms are paying for specific jobs that the firms have in common

Financial Compensation

Financial compensation falls into two general categories—wages and salaries. **Wages** are financial rewards based on the number of hours the employee works or the level of output achieved. Wages based on the number of hours worked are called time wages. A cook at Denny's, for example, might earn $5.15 per hour, the minimum wage. Roughly one-fourth of the U.S. workforce between the ages of 18 and 64 earns less than $9.04/hour, a wage that translates into a full-time income of $18,800 a year—the weighted poverty line for a family of four.[26] Table 11.5 compares wage and other information for Costco and Wal-Mart's Sam's Clubs, two well-known membership discount chains. Time wages are appropriate when employees are continually interrupted and when quality is more important than quantity. Assembly-line workers, clerks, and maintenance personnel are commonly paid on a time-wage basis. The advantage of time wages is the ease of computation. The disadvantage is that time wages provide no incentive to increase productivity. In fact, time wages may encourage employees to do less than a full day's work.

wages
financial rewards based on the number of hours the employee works or the level of output achieved

To overcome these disadvantages, many companies pay on an incentive system, using piece wages or commissions. Piece wages are based on the level of output achieved. A major advantage of piece wages is that they motivate employees to supervise their own activities and to increase output. Skilled craftworkers are often paid on a piece-wage basis. At Longaberger, the world's largest maker of handmade baskets, weavers are paid per piece. The 2,500 workers produced 40,000 baskets a day, but productivity varied by as much as 400 percent among the weavers. A team of basket makers was assembled to try to improve productivity and reduce weaver downtime and the amount of leftover materials. After studying the basket makers for 19 days, the team's suggestions were implemented. The changes resulted in $3 million in annual savings for the company.[27]

The other incentive system, **commission,** pays a fixed amount or a percentage of the employee's sales. Karen Sabatini is an automobile salesperson at a Lincoln

commission
an incentive system that pays a fixed amount or a percentage of the employee's sales

Solve the Dilemma
Morale among the Survivors

Medallion Corporation manufactures quality carpeting and linoleum for homes throughout the United States. A recession and subsequent downturn in home sales has sharply cut the company's sales. Medallion found itself in the unenviable position of having to lay off hundreds of employees in the home office (the manufacturing facilities) as well as many salespeople. Employees were called in on Friday afternoon and told about their status in individual meetings with their supervisors. The laid-off employees were given one additional month of work and a month of severance pay, along with the opportunity to sign up for classes to help with the transition, including job search tactics and résumé writing.

Several months after the cutbacks, morale was at an all-time low for the company, although productivity had improved. Medallion brought in consultants, who suggested that the leaner, flatter organizational structure would be suitable for more team activities. Medallion therefore set up task forces and teams to deal with employee concerns, but the diversity of the workforce led to conflict and misunderstandings among team members. Medallion is evaluating how to proceed with this new team approach.

Discussion Questions

1. What did Medallion's HRM department do right in dealing with the employees who were laid off?
2. What are some of the potential problems that must be dealt with after an organization experiences a major trauma such as massive layoffs?
3. What can Medallion do to make the team approach work more smoothly? What role do you think diversity training should play?

Mercury dealership in Garden City, Michigan, just 15 minutes away from Ford's world headquarters. In one year, Sabatini grossed almost $200,000, compared to $40,000 for the average auto salesperson. She earns $250–$300 for every Mercury and $350–$500 for every Lincoln she sells to a Ford employee. She makes $150–$225 on any sale to a non-Ford employee.[28] This method motivates employees to sell as much as they can. Some companies combine payment based on commission with time wages or salaries.

salary
a financial reward calculated on a weekly, monthly, or annual basis

A **salary** is a financial reward calculated on a weekly, monthly, or annual basis. Salaries are associated with white-collar workers such as office personnel, executives, and professional employees. Although a salary provides a stable stream of income, salaried workers may be required to work beyond usual hours without additional financial compensation.

bonuses
monetary rewards offered by companies for exceptional performance as incentives to further increase productivity

In addition to the basic wages or salaries paid to employees, a company may offer **bonuses** for exceptional performance as an incentive to increase productivity further. Many workers receive a bonus as a "thank you" for good work and an incentive to continue working hard. Many owners and managers are recognizing that simple bonuses and perks foster happier employees and reduce turnover. For example, the owner of Ticketcity.com, a small business in Austin, Texas, offers employees tickets to major events like the Super Bowl, Master's golf tournament, and even management retreats. The owner of a DreamMaker remodeling franchise in Peoria, Illinois, provides employees money to use toward new vehicles, takes them on staff outings to sporting games, and funds their retirement plans.[29]

profit sharing
a form of compensation whereby a percentage of company profits is distributed to the employees whose work helped to generate them

Another form of compensation is **profit sharing,** which distributes a percentage of company profits to the employees whose work helped to generate those profits. Some profit-sharing plans involve distributing shares of company stock to employees. Usually referred to as *ESOPs*—employee stock ownership plans—they have been gaining popularity in recent years. One reason for the popularity of ESOPs is the sense of partnership that they create between the organization and employees. Profit sharing can also motivate employees to work hard, because increased productivity and sales mean that the profits or the stock dividends will increase. Many organizations offer employees a stake in the company through stock purchase plans, ESOPs, or stock investments through 401(k) plans. Employees below senior management levels rarely received stock options, until recently. Companies are adopting broad-based stock option plans to build a stronger link between employees' interests and the organization's interests. A study by professors at the Wharton School of the University of Pennsylvania found that companies that paid middle managers 20 percent more in options than comparable companies saw increased performance and stock prices that rose an average 5 percent faster a year. Similar results were seen in companies that paid technical specialists at least 20 percent more in options.[30]

Benefits

Benefits are nonfinancial forms of compensation provided to employees, such as pension plans for retirement; health, disability, and life insurance; holidays and paid days off for vacation or illness; credit union membership; health programs; child care; elder care; assistance with adoption; and more. According to the Bureau of Labor Statistics, employer costs for employee compensation for civilian workers in the United States average $24.59 per hour worked. Wages and salaries account for approximately 71.4 percent of those costs, while benefits account for 28.6 percent. Legally required benefits (Social Security, workers' compensation, and unemployment insurance) average $1.96 per hour, or 8 percent of total compensation.[31] Such benefits increase employee security and, to a certain extent, their morale and motivation.

The Principal Financial Group promotes the advantages of its group benefits plan.

> **benefits**
> nonfinancial forms of compensation provided to employees, such as pension plans, health insurance, paid vacation and holidays, and the like

The Survey of Unit Employment Practices (SULEP) People Report found that, among 75 restaurant industry companies, the average rate of employee turnover in companies that offer basic health, dental, or retirement benefits is 109 percent, compared with 136 percent for companies that do not offer any benefits to their employees.[32] Table 11.6 lists some of the benefits Internet search engine Google offers its employees. Although health insurance is a common benefit for full-time employees, rising health care costs have forced a growing number of employers to trim this benefit. Microsoft, for example, recently reduced its prescription drug benefit, which had cost the company 16 percent of its overall benefit budget, and now requires employees to pay $40 for brand-name prescription drugs for which a generic version is available. The company still provides many generous benefits, including free gym memberships and free drinks on the job.[33]

A benefit increasingly offered is the employee assistance program (EAP). Each company's EAP is different, but most offer counseling for and assistance with those employees' personal problems that might hurt their job performance if not addressed. The most common counseling services offered include drug- and alcohol-abuse

TABLE 11.6

Google's Employees' Benefits

- Health insurance:
  - 100 percent employee medical insurance (spouse and domestic-partner insurance also available)
  - Dental insurance
  - Vision insurance
- Vacation (15 days per year for one–three years' employment; 20 days off for four–five years' employment; 25 days for more than six years' employment)
- Ten paid holidays/year
- Savings plans
  - 401(k) retirement plan, matched by Google up to $2,200/year
  - Flexible spending accounts
- Disability and life insurance
- Employee Assistance Program
- Free lunches, breakfast foods, and snacks
- Massages and gym
- Weekly activities
- Maternity and parental leave
- Adoption assistance
- Tuition reimbursement
- Employee referral plan
- On-site doctor and dentist

Source: "Google's California Benefits," www.google.com/jobs/benefits.html (accessed May 21, 2004). Reprinted with permission of Google, Inc.

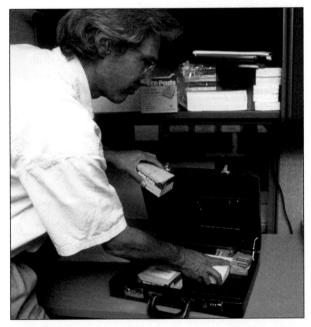

Employees sometimes feel that "borrowing" a few office supplies from their company helps compensate for any perceived inequities in pay or other benefits.

treatment programs, fitness programs, smoking-cessation clinics, stress-management clinics, financial counseling, family counseling, and career counseling. EAPs help reduce costs associated with poor productivity, absenteeism, and other workplace issues by helping employees deal with personal problems that contribute to these issues. For example, exercise and fitness programs reduce health insurance costs by helping employees stay healthy. Family counseling may help workers trying to cope with a divorce or other personal problems better focus on their jobs.

Companies try to provide the benefits they believe their employees want, but diverse people may want different things. In recent years, some single workers have felt that co-workers with spouses and children seem to get "special breaks" and extra time off to deal with family issues. Some companies use flexible benefit programs to allow employees to choose the benefits they would like, up to a specified amount. Over the last two decades, the list of fringe benefits has grown dramatically, and new benefits are being added every year.

In an age when many companies are cutting back health care benefits because of a sluggish economy, many employers are turning to low-cost perks to keep workers happy. In addition to perks like gym facilities and weight-loss programs, an increasing number of companies are even allowing employees to bring their pets to work. An American Animal Hospital Association survey of 1,225 U.S. and Canadian pet owners found that 24 percent of them take their pets to work, and about 5,000 U.S. companies participated in Take Your Dog to Work Day in a recent year.

Having dogs and cats in the workplace can provide many benefits, including a more relaxed and flexible atmosphere, increased staff morale, and even increased employee retention. One company's spokesperson indicated that its pet policy gives employees individual flexibility and shows that the company respects employees enough to let them make choices about their work environment. Companies like Small Dog Electronics, a computer merchant with 27 employees, have even been honored by the American Psychological Association as psychologically healthy workplaces, in part because of their pet-friendly policies.

A pet-friendly workplace can be a definite advantage in recruiting and retaining employees. Small Dog Electronics, for example, boasts an employee turnover rate of 1 percent, compared to its industry average of 11 percent. Even non–pet owners often appreciate the informal, flexible environment that characterizes workplaces with pets. To some extent, being pet-friendly helps define a corporate culture, as it does at AutoDesk, a software provider. Even when it is not possible for employees to bring pets to work every day, some companies allow them to bring their pets to work occasionally for a short period of time.

Many small businesses, particularly retailers, established a pet-friendly policy out of personal necessity. Working couples with long hours may not have an opportunity to spend time with their pets or take care of them properly unless they bring their pets to the office or store. Indeed, many small retailers, such as antique dealers and bookstores, often have a "store cat" or "store dog" who is appreciated as much by customers as by the employees. Although pets are prohibited by law in restaurants in the United States, many European restaurants allow customers to have their dogs right at their tables where food is served.

Although bringing your pet to work can definitely improve morale, there are a few challenges. People with allergies or who are afraid of animals may get distracted from their jobs. Of course, there is always the concern that a dog may bite a person or another dog. However, research by attorneys at Ralston Purina found that lawsuits related to pets in the work environment are quite rare. Individual employees usually prevent problems by exercising common sense and respect for their coworkers and company facilities.[34]

Discussion Questions
1. Why can a nonfinancial benefit, such as being able to bring your dog to work, boost employee morale?
2. What type of businesses are appropriate for a pet-friendly workplace policy?
3. How do you personally feel about having other people's pets in an office where you work or store where you shop?

Managing Unionized Employees

Employees who are dissatisfied with their working conditions or compensation have to negotiate with management to bring about change. Dealing with management on an individual basis is not always effective, however, so employees may organize themselves into **labor unions** to deal with employers and to achieve better pay, hours, and working conditions. Organized employees are backed by the power of a large group that can hire specialists to represent the entire union in its dealings with management. The United Auto Workers, for example, has considerable power in its negotiations with Ford Motor Company and General Motors. Unionized blue-collar workers make 54 percent more than their nonunionized counterparts and are twice as likely to have health insurance and pension plans.[35]

However, union growth has slowed in recent years, and prospects for growth do not look good. One reason is that most blue-collar workers, the traditional members of unions, have already been organized. Factories have become more automated and need fewer blue-collar workers. The United States has shifted from a manufacturing to a service economy, further reducing the demand for blue-collar workers. Moreover, in response to foreign competition, U.S. companies are scrambling to find ways

labor unions
employee organizations formed to deal with employers for achieving better pay, hours, and working conditions

to become more productive and cost efficient. Job enrichment programs and participative management have blurred the line between management and workers. Because workers' say in the way plants are run is increasing, their need for union protection is decreasing.

Nonetheless, labor unions have been successful in organizing blue-collar manufacturing, government, and health care workers, as well as smaller percentages of employees in other industries. In fact, 12.9 percent of all employed Americans are represented by a union.[36] Consequently, significant aspects of HRM, particularly compensation, are dictated to a large degree by union contracts at many companies. Therefore, we'll take a brief look at collective bargaining and dispute resolution in this section.

Collective Bargaining

collective bargaining
the negotiation process through which management and unions reach an agreement about compensation, working hours, and working conditions for the bargaining unit

Collective bargaining is the negotiation process through which management and unions reach an agreement about compensation, working hours, and working conditions for the bargaining unit (Figure 11.3). The objective of negotiations is to reach agreement about a **labor contract,** the formal, written document that spells out the relationship between the union and management for a specified period of time, usually two or three years.

labor contract
the formal, written document that spells out the relationship between the union and management for a specified period of time—usually two or three years

In collective bargaining, each side tries to negotiate an agreement that meets its demands; compromise is frequently necessary. Management tries to negotiate a labor contract that permits the company to retain control over things like work schedules; the hiring and firing of workers; production standards; promotions, transfers, and separations; the span of management in each department; and discipline. Unions tend to focus on contract issues such as magnitude of wages; better pay rates for overtime, holidays, and undesirable shifts; scheduling of pay increases; and benefits. These issues will be spelled out in the labor contract, which union members will vote to either accept (and abide by) or reject.

Many labor contracts contain a *cost-of-living escalator clause (COLA)*, which calls for automatic wage increases during periods of inflation to protect the "real" income of the employees. During tough economic times, unions may be forced to accept *givebacks—*wage and benefit concessions made to employers to allow them to remain competitive or, in some cases, to survive and continue to provide jobs for union workers.

Resolving Disputes

Sometimes, management and labor simply cannot agree on a contract. Most labor disputes are handled through collective bargaining or through grievance procedures. When these processes break down, however, either side may resort to more drastic measures to achieve its objectives.

picketing
a public protest against management practices that involves union members marching and carrying antimanagement signs at the employer's plant

Labor Tactics.   **Picketing** is a public protest against management practices and involves union members marching (often waving antimanagement signs and placards) at the employer's plant. Picketing workers hope that their signs will arouse sympathy for their demands from the public and from other unions. Picketing may occur as a protest or in conjunction with a strike.

strikes
employee walkouts; one of the most effective weapons labor has

Strikes (employee walkouts) are one of the most effective weapons labor has. By striking, a union makes carrying out the normal operations of a business difficult at best and impossible at worst. Strikes receive widespread publicity, but they remain a weapon of last resort. In California, members of the United Food and Commercial Workers (UFCW) went on strike against Albertson's, Ralph's, and Von's supermarkets after they failed to reach agreement on a new contract. The strike, which cost the companies millions of dollars in lost sales and the striking employees significant lost

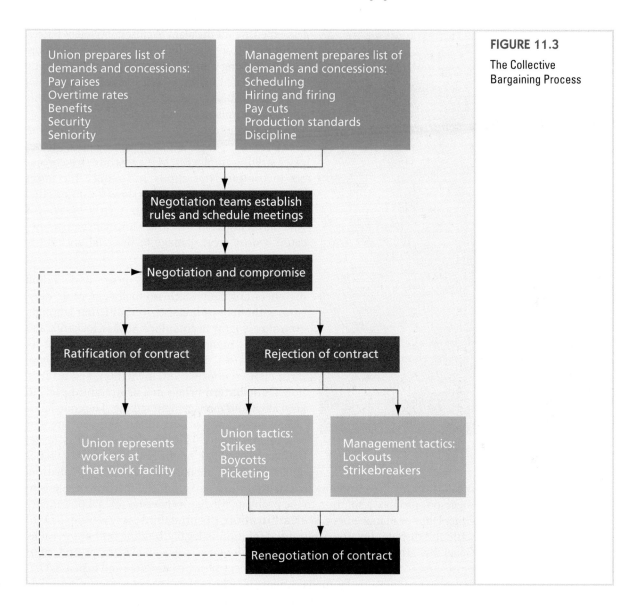

FIGURE 11.3

The Collective Bargaining Process

wages, ended when members agreed to ratify a new contract that gave them bonuses but required them to pay for health insurance for the first time.[37] The threat of a strike is often enough to get management to back down. In fact, the number of worker-days actually lost to strikes is less than the amount lost to the common cold.

A **boycott** is an attempt to keep people from purchasing the products of a company. In a boycott, union members are asked not to do business with the boycotted organization. Some unions may even impose fines on members who ignore the boycott. In order to gain further support for their objectives, a union involved in a boycott may also ask the public—through picketing and advertising—not to purchase the products of the picketed firm.

Management Tactics.   Management's version of a strike is the **lockout;** management actually closes a work site so that employees cannot go to work. Lockouts are used, as a general rule, only when a union strike has partially shut down a plant and it seems

boycott
an attempt to keep people from purchasing the products of a company

lockout
management's version of a strike, wherein a work site is closed so that employees cannot go to work

Striking UFCW members picket Albertson's supermarket.

strikebreakers
people hired by management to replace striking employees; called "scabs" by striking union members

conciliation
a method of outside resolution of labor and management differences in which a third party is brought in to keep the two sides talking

mediation
a method of outside resolution of labor and management differences in which the third party's role is to suggest or propose a solution to the problem

less expensive for the plant to close completely. Fifteen major work stoppages (those involving 1,000 or more workers, lasting a full shift or longer, and including worker-initiated strikes, as well as employer lockouts) began in 2003 and resulted in 131,000 idled workers and about 4 million days of idleness.[38]

Strikebreakers, called "scabs" by striking union members, are people hired by management to replace striking employees. Managers hire strikebreakers to continue operations and reduce the losses associated with strikes—and to show the unions that they will not bow to their demands. Strikebreaking is generally a last-resort measure for management because it does great damage to the relationship between management and labor.

Outside Resolution. Management and union members normally reach mutually agreeable decisions without outside assistance. Sometimes though, even after lengthy negotiations, strikes, lockouts, and other tactics, management and labor still cannot resolve a contract dispute. In such cases, they have three choices: conciliation, mediation, and arbitration. **Conciliation** brings in a neutral third party to keep labor and management talking. The conciliator has no formal power over union representatives or over management. The conciliator's goal is to get both parties to focus on the issues and to prevent negotiations from breaking down. Like conciliation, **mediation** involves bringing in a neutral third party, but the mediator's role is to suggest or propose a solution to the problem. Mediators have no formal power over either labor or management. With **arbitration,** a neutral third party is brought in to settle the dispute, but the arbitrator's solution is legally binding and enforceable. Generally, arbitration takes place on a voluntary basis—management and labor must agree to it, and they usually split the cost (the arbitrator's fee and expenses) between them. Occasionally, management and labor submit to *compulsory arbitration,* in which an outside party (usually the federal government) requests arbitration as a means of eliminating a prolonged strike that threatens to disrupt the economy.

The Importance of Workforce Diversity

Customers, employees, suppliers—all the participants in the world of business—come in different ages, genders, races, ethnicities, nationalities, and abilities, a truth that business has come to label **diversity**. Understanding this diversity means recognizing and accepting differences as well as valuing the unique perspectives such differences can bring to the workplace.

The Characteristics of Diversity
When managers speak of diverse workforces, they typically mean differences in gender and race. While gender and race are important characteristics of diversity, others are also important. We can divide these differences into primary and secondary

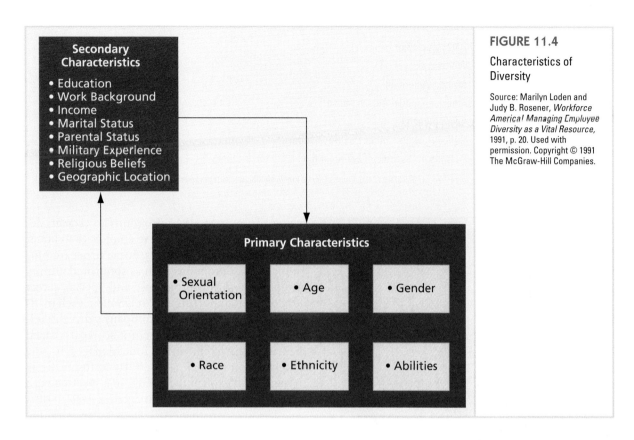

FIGURE 11.4

Characteristics of Diversity

Source: Marilyn Loden and Judy B. Rosener, *Workforce America! Managing Employee Diversity as a Vital Resource,* 1991, p. 20. Used with permission. Copyright © 1991 The McGraw-Hill Companies.

characteristics of diversity. In the lower segment of Figure 11.4, age, gender, race, ethnicity, abilities, and sexual orientation represent *primary characteristics* of diversity which are inborn and cannot be changed. In the upper section of Figure 11.4 are eight *secondary characteristics* of diversity—work background, income, marital status, military experience, religious beliefs, geographic location, parental status, and education—which *can* be changed. We acquire, change, and discard them as we progress through our lives.

Defining characteristics of diversity as either primary or secondary enhances our understanding, but we must remember that each person is defined by the interrelation of all characteristics. In dealing with diversity in the workforce, managers must consider the complete person—not one or a few of a person's differences.

Why Is Diversity Important?

The U.S. workforce is becoming increasingly diverse. Once dominated by white men, today's workforce includes significantly more women, African-Americans, Hispanics, and other minorities, as well as disabled and older workers. By 2010, women's share of the labor force will increase to 47.9 percent.[39] Table 11.7 presents some of the population data from the Census Bureau. It is estimated that within the next 50 years, Hispanics will represent 24 percent of the population, while African-Americans and Asians/Pacific Islanders will comprise 15 percent and 9 percent, respectively.[40] These groups have traditionally faced discrimination and higher unemployment rates and have been denied opportunities to assume leadership roles in corporate America. Consequently, more and more companies are

arbitration
settlement of a labor/management dispute by a third party whose solution is legally binding and enforceable

diversity
the participation of different ages, genders, races, ethnicities, nationalities, and abilities in the workplace

TABLE 11.7	2002 Population	288,368,698
U.S. Census Bureau People Quick Facts	White	75.1%
	African-American	12.3%
	American Indian/Alaska native	0.9%
	Asian persons	3.6%
	Native Hawaiian/other Pacific Islander	0.1%
	Persons of Hispanic or Latino origin	12.5%

Source: "People QuickFacts," U.S. Census Bureau **http://quickfacts.census.gov/qfd/states/00000.html** (accessed May 28, 2004).

Technology solutions can make the difference for the visually impaired, enabling them to operate computers and making the workplace more diverse.

trying to improve HRM programs to recruit, develop, and retain more diverse employees to better serve their diverse customers. Some firms are providing special programs such as sponsored affinity groups, mentoring programs, and special career development opportunities. At US West, each manager's contributions to the company's diversity efforts are measured by a 16-point scorecard called the Diversity Accountability Tool. Managers use the scorecard to rate their own efforts to foster diversity and then explain their score in a meeting with the company's CEO. The manager receives an official diversity score that is one factor in determining the manager's annual bonus. Since the program was instituted, scores have jumped 60 percent.[41] Table 11.8 shows the top 10 companies for minorities according to a study by *Fortune*. Effectively managing diversity in the workforce involves cultivating and valuing its benefits and minimizing its problems.

The Benefits of Workforce Diversity

There are a number of benefits to fostering and valuing workforce diversity, including the following:

1. More productive use of a company's human resources.
2. Reduced conflict among employees of different ethnicities, races, religions, and sexual orientations as they learn to respect each other's differences.
3. More productive working relationships among diverse employees as they learn more about and accept each other.
4. Increased commitment to and sharing of organizational goals among diverse employees at all organizational levels.
5. Increased innovation and creativity as diverse employees bring new, unique perspectives to decision-making and problem-solving tasks.
6. Increased ability to serve the needs of an increasingly diverse customer base.[42]

Companies that do not value their diverse employees are likely to experience greater conflict, as well as prejudice and discrimination. Among individual employ-

Company	% Asian	% Black	% Hispanic	% American Indian	% Total
1. McDonald's	4.0	17.6	27.9	3.0	52.6
2. Fannie Mae	13.6	25.5	4.2	0.4	43.7
3. Denny's	5.3	12.0	29.3	0.1	46.7
4. Union Bank of California	25.7	8.3	21.3	0.5	55.8
5. Sempra Energy	8.6	10.1	28.2	0.8	47.6
6. Southern California-Edison	8.5	8.7	25.5	0.9	43.6
7. SBC Communications	4.7	19.8	12.7	0.6	37.8
8. Freddie Mac	14.4	14.3	3.4	0.3	32.5
9. PepsiCo	2.3	13.7	10.6	0.4	26.9
10. PNM Resources	0.8	1.9	40.8	4.4	47.9

TABLE 11.8

America's 10 Best Companies for Minorities

ees, for example, racial slurs and gestures, sexist comments, and other behaviors by co-workers harm the individuals at whom such behavior is directed. The victims of such behavior may feel hurt, depressed, or even threatened and suffer from lowered self-esteem, all of which harm their productivity and morale. In such cases, women and minority employees may simply leave the firm, wasting the time, money, and other resources spent on hiring and training them. When discrimination comes from a supervisor, employees may also fear for their jobs. A discriminatory atmosphere not only can harm productivity and increase turnover, but it may also subject a firm to costly lawsuits and negative publicity.

Astute businesses recognize that they need to modify their human resources management programs to target the needs of *all* their diverse employees as well as the needs of the firm itself. They realize that the benefits of diversity are long term in nature and come only to those organizations willing to make the commitment. Most importantly, as workforce diversity becomes a valued organizational asset, companies spend less time managing conflict and more time accomplishing tasks and satisfying customers, which is, after all, the purpose of business.

Affirmative Action

Many companies strive to improve their working environment through **affirmative action programs,** legally mandated plans that try to increase job opportunities for minority groups by analyzing the current pool of workers, identifying areas where women and minorities are underrepresented, and establishing specific hiring and promotion goals along with target dates for meeting those goals to resolve the discrepancy. Affirmative action began in 1965 as Lyndon B. Johnson issued the first of a series of presidential directives. It was designed to make up for past hiring and promotion prejudices, to overcome workplace discrimination, and to provide equal employment opportunities for blacks and whites. Since then, minorities have made solid gains.

Legislation passed in 1991 reinforces affirmative action but prohibits organizations from setting hiring quotas that might result in reverse discrimination. Reverse discrimination occurs when a company's policies force it to consider only minorities

affirmative action programs
legally mandated plans that try to increase job opportunities for minority groups by analyzing the current pool of workers, identifying areas where women and minorities are underrepresented, and establishing specific hiring and promotion goals, with target dates, for addressing the discrepancy

or women instead of concentrating on hiring the person who is best qualified. More companies are arguing that affirmative action stifles their ability to hire the best employees, regardless of their minority status. Because of these problems, affirmative action became politically questionable in the mid-1990s.

Explore Your Career Options
How Much Does It Pay?

That's the big question everyone wants to know, whether considering future career options or a specific job in a particular company. While you're not likely to make as much as Donald Trump or Katie Couric, the potential for big bucks is out there, depending on your choice of career, the organization you ultimately work for, *and* how hard you are willing to work.

Experts suggest that you need to earn four times your age ($140,000/year for a 35-year-old, for example) if you want to be able to own a nice house and car, send your kids to college, stay ahead of inflation, and save for a comfortable retirement. Most people never come close to that yardstick, however. The median income for a full-time worker who has a bachelor's degree is $40,415 for women and $56,334 for men.

Clearly, some jobs pay a lot more than others. A CEO of a large corporation can earn millions in salary, benefits, and bonuses; while at the other end of the scale, a preschool teacher might earn just $12,000. Business management, engineers, health professionals, and technology specialists are all hot careers, in terms of both growth potential and pay.

Listed below are some human resource jobs and the median annual income for each:

Labor relations manager	$107,900
Compensation manager	$97,800
Human resources manager	$91,400
Benefits manager	$85,500
Training manager	$78,200
Payroll manager	$70,800

But for many people, money isn't everything. Remember Herzberg's motivation factors? Benefits, job security, desirable working hours, and a satisfying work environment are some of the factors that can help make up for a job that doesn't put you in the same tax bracket as Brad Pitt. The preschool teacher may find molding young minds for $12,000 just as satisfying as the challenge the millionaire CEO enjoys in running a company. And, with companies increasingly opting for limited pay raises in favor of bonuses tied to performance, people working in even fairly low-paying jobs can find themselves earning good money for hard work. The bottom line is that you have to decide what's important to you and go for it.[43]

Review Your Understanding

Define human resources management and explain its significance.

Human resources, or personnel, management refers to all the activities involved in determining an organization's human resources needs and acquiring, training, and compensating people to fill those needs. It is concerned with maximizing the satisfaction of employees and improving their efficiency to meet organizational objectives.

Summarize the processes of recruiting and selecting human resources for a company.

First, the human resources manager must determine the firm's future human resources needs and develop a strategy to meet them. Recruiting is the formation of a pool of qualified applicants from which management will select employees; it takes place both internally and externally. Selection is the process of collecting information about applicants and using that information to decide which ones to hire; it includes the application, interviewing, testing, and reference checking.

Discuss how workers are trained and their performance appraised.

Training teaches employees how to do their specific job tasks; development is training that augments the skills and knowledge of managers and professionals, as well as current employees. Appraising performance involves identifying an employee's strengths and weaknesses on the job. Performance appraisals may be subjective or objective.

Identify the types of turnover companies may experience, and explain why turnover is an important issue.

A promotion is an advancement to a higher-level job with increased authority, responsibility, and pay. A transfer is a move to another job within the company at essentially the same level and wage. Separations occur when employees resign, retire, are terminated, or are laid off. Turnovers due to separation are expensive because of the time, money, and effort required to select, train, and manage new employees.

Specify the various ways a worker may be compensated.

Wages are financial compensation based on the number of hours worked (time wages) or the number of units produced (piece wages). Commissions are a fixed amount or a percentage of a sale paid as compensation. Salaries are compensation calculated on a weekly, monthly, or annual basis, regardless of the number of hours worked or the number of items produced. Bonuses and profit sharing are types of financial incentives. Benefits are nonfinancial forms of compensation, such as vacation, insurance, and sick leave.

Discuss some of the issues associated with unionized employees, including collective bargaining and dispute resolution.

Collective bargaining is the negotiation process through which management and unions reach an agreement on a labor contract—the formal, written document that spells out the relationship written between the union and management. If labor and management cannot agree on a contract, labor union members may picket, strike, or boycott the firm, while management may lock out striking employees, hire strikebreakers, or form employers' associations. In a deadlock, labor disputes may be resolved by a third party—a conciliator, mediator, or arbitrator.

Describe the importance of diversity in the workforce.

When companies value and effectively manage their diverse workforces, they experience more productive use of human resources, reduced conflict, better work relationships among workers, increased commitment to and sharing of organizational goals, increased innovation and creativity, and enhanced ability to serve diverse customers.

Assess an organization's efforts to reduce its workforce size and manage the resulting effects.

Based on the material in this chapter, you should be able to answer the questions posed in the "Solve the Dilemma" box on page 322 and evaluate the company's efforts to manage the human consequences of its downsizing.

Revisit the World of Business

1. What are some of the ethical challenges associated with having employee candidates compete for a job in the Trump organization?

2. Do you feel that tasks such as competing against others in selling lemonade, competitive buying, and organizing celebrity events allow Donald Trump to make an effective hiring decision?

3. What could be done to improve the "realism" of the process so that applicants could better understand what it will be like to work in the Trump Organization?

Learn the Terms

affirmative action programs   331
arbitration   328
benefits   323
bonuses   322
boycott   327

collective bargaining   326
commission   321
conciliation   328
development   316
diversity   328

human resources management (HRM)   310
job analysis   311
job description   311
job specification   311

Check Your Progress

1. Distinguish among job analysis, job descriptions, and job specifications. How do they relate to planning in human resources management?

2. What activities are involved in acquiring and maintaining the appropriate level of qualified human resources? Name the stages of the selection process.

3. What are the two types of training programs? Relate training to kinds of jobs.

4. What is the significance of performance appraisal? How do managers appraise employees?

5. Why does turnover occur? List the types of turnover. Why do businesses want to reduce turnover due to separations?

6. Relate wages, salaries, bonuses, and benefits to Herzberg's distinction between hygiene and motivation factors. How does the form of compensation relate to the type of job?

7. What is the role of benefits? Name some examples of benefits.

8. Describe the negotiation process through which management and unions reach an agreement on a contract.

9. Besides collective bargaining and the grievance procedures, what other alternatives are available to labor and management to handle labor disputes?

10. What are the benefits associated with a diverse workforce?

Get Involved

1. Although many companies screen applicants and test employees for illegal drug use, such testing is somewhat controversial. Find some companies in your community that test applicants and/or employees for drugs. Why do they have such a policy? How do the employees feel about it? Using this information, debate the pros and cons of drug testing in the workplace.

2. If collective bargaining and the grievance procedures have not been able to settle a current labor dispute, what tactics would you and other employees adopt? Which tactics would be best for which situations? Give examples.

3. Find some examples of companies that value their diverse workforces, perhaps some of the companies mentioned in the chapter. In what ways have these firms derived benefits from promoting cultural diversity? How have they dealt with the problems associated with cultural diversity?

Build Your Skills

APPRECIATING AND VALUING DIVERSITY

Background

Here's a quick self-assessment to get you to think about diversity issues and evaluate the behaviors you exhibit that reflect your level of appreciation of other cultures:

Do you . . .	Regularly	Sometimes	Never
1. Make a conscious effort not to think stereotypically?			
2. Listen with interest to the ideas of people who don't think like you do?			
3. Respect other people's opinions, even when you disagree?			
4. Spend time with friends who are not your age, race, gender, or the same economic status and education?			
5. Believe your way is *not* the only way?			
6. Adapt well to change and new situations?			
7. Enjoy traveling, seeing new places, eating different foods, and experiencing other cultures?			
8. Try not to offend or hurt others?			
9. Allow extra time to communicate with someone whose first language is not yours?			
10. Consider the effect of cultural differences on the messages you send and adjust them accordingly?			

Scoring

Number of **Regularly** checks   _____ multiplied by 5 = _____
Number of **Sometimes** checks   _____ multiplied by 3 = _____
Number of **Never** checks   _____ multiplied by 0 = _____
                                                    TOTAL _____

Indications from score

40–50   You appear to understand the importance of valuing diversity and exhibit behaviors that support your appreciation of diversity.

26–39   You appear to have a basic understanding of the importance of valuing diversity and exhibit some behaviors that support that understanding.

13–25   You appear to lack a thorough understanding of the importance of valuing diversity and exhibit only some behaviors related to valuing diversity.

0–12   You appear to lack an understanding of valuing diversity and exhibit few, if any, behaviors of an individual who appreciates and values diversity.

Task:
In a small group or class discussion, share the results of your assessment. After reading the following list of ways you can increase your knowledge and understanding of other cultures, select one of the items that you have done and share how it helped you learn more about another culture. Finish your discussion by generating your own ideas on other ways you can learn about and understand other cultures and fill in those ideas on the blank lines below.

- Be alert to and take advantage of opportunities to talk to and get to know people from other races and ethnic groups. You can find them in your neighborhood, in your classes, at your fitness center, at a concert or sporting event—just about anywhere you go. Take the initiative to strike up a conversation and show a genuine interest in getting to know the other person.

- Select a culture you're interested in and immerse yourself in that culture. Read novels, look at art, take courses, see plays.

- College students often have unique opportunities to travel inexpensively to other countries—for example, as a member of a performing arts group, with a humanitarian mission group, or as part of a college course studying abroad. Actively seek out travel opportunities that will expose you to as many cultures as possible during your college education.

- Study a foreign language.
- Expand your taste buds. The next time you're going to go to a restaurant, instead of choosing that old familiar favorite, use the Yellow Pages to find a restaurant that serves ethnic food you've never tried before.
- Many large metropolitan cities sponsor ethnic festivals, particularly in the summertime, where you can go and take in the sights and sounds of other cultures. Take advantage of these opportunities to have a fun time learning about cultures that are different from yours.

- _____
  _____
- _____
  _____

e-Xtreme Surfing

- **Monster.com**
  www.monster.com

  Provides a wealth of job/career resources for both employers and job seekers; allows job seekers to build and post résumés.

- **Keirsey Temperament Sorter**
  www.advisorteam.com/temperament_sorter/register.asp?partid=1

  Provides a quiz to help you assess your temperament and better understand your traits and motivations.

- **Games2train**
  www.games2train.com/site/default.html

  Offers information about game-based learning and training using video and computer games.

See for Yourself Videocase

HILLERICH & BRADSBY COMPANY: MAKERS OF THE LOUISVILLE SLUGGER

What do Ty Cobb, Babe Ruth, Ted Williams, Joe DiMaggio, Mickey Mantle, Hank Aaron, Johnny Bench, George Brett, and Ken Griffey, Jr. all have in common? They each excelled at their careers in baseball with the help of the Louisville Slugger. The first bat made by Bud Hillerich was for Pete "The Old Gladiator" Browning, a star player with the Louisville Eclipse team in the American Association (forerunner of the National League). When Browning's favorite bat was broken in a game—a game that Hillerich happened to be watching—Hillerich invited Browning to his father's woodworking shop and offered to make him a new bat. After selecting a piece of white ash, the two worked to produce the new bat. When Browning used the bat the next day, he went three for four at bat. The year was 1884, and it took ten more years before a "Louisville Slugger" bat was actually sold. Bud had to work hard to persuade his father that baseball bats could be more lucrative than the roller skids,

bed posts, tenpins, wooden bowling pins, and singing churns that their shop had been producing.

Bud Hellerich recognized the value of working with players to design bats. That process was popular with customers as well as employees. The Louisville Slugger trademark was inscribed on the bat along with the name of the player who endorsed it. Players were not well compensated as endorsers then or now. Babe Ruth, for example, signed an agreement to use a bat for $100. Today, players get no more than $500 or a free set of Powerbilt golf clubs, which Hillerich & Bradsby Company also manufactures.

Hillerich & Bradsby (H&B) is a family business that has been run by a member of the Hillerich family for more than a century. Michael Hillerich IV took over as the fourth-generation president of the company in 2001, replacing his father. As head of the most successful maker of wooden bats with 60 percent of the major league market, 80 percent of the minor league and amateur markets, Michael has stated, "I don't want to be the one who screws this up." A key decision Michael's father made was to bring the business back to Kentucky in 1996 and celebrate the proud history of the company, its employees, and the many users of the Louisville Slugger. The company constructed a corporate complex, manufacturing plant, and museum on Main Street in downtown Louisville, just ten blocks away from where the first "Louisville Slugger" was made in 1884. H&B manufactures more than 1 million wood Louisville Slugger bats every year, and each major league player goes through roughly 90 bats a season. As one of the most visited sites in the central U.S., the company museum is a source of pride, as well as a great escape for workers during the day.

Michael Hillerich understands the importance of keeping his employees happy. As a private, family-run business, Hillerich has a closer relationship with his employees than do executives of large public corporations. That level of closeness along with recognition of commendable performance, improves the overall work environment and worker satisfaction. Hillerich & Bradsby has won the University of Louisville Labor-Management Award for exemplary improvement in employee relations. In the mid-1980s, the company averaged 3,540 grievances a year, but after 1985, the company has racked up a total of 5 (and only 1 reached arbitration). The company is credited with implementing management initiatives such as cross-training, total productive maintenance, self-directed work teams, and just-in-time production.

Hillerich & Bradsby also adheres to the quality philosophies of W. Edwards Deming. In fact, John A. Hillerich serves on the Board of Trustees of the W. Edwards Deming Institute. This dedication to the successful implementation of processes to ensure quality and the desire to share these processes with other companies has proven to be a good strategic move for the company.

To celebrate the rich, proud tradition of the Louisville Slugger and to give the museum another truly rare artifact, John Hillerich IV acquired one of the most famous bats the company ever manufactured: the Louisville Slugger bat that Joe DiMaggio used in his record 56-game hitting streak in 1941—a record many believe will never be beaten and an accomplishment many believe to be the greatest in individual sports. The many generations of leadership and vision have lead to Hillerich & Bradsby's ongoing success.[44]

Discussion Questions

1. Why do you think Hillerich & Bradsby has been successful after so many years and generations of management?

2. What do you perceive to be some of the company's more successful management techniques and why?

3. With so much manufacturing going abroad to generate cost savings and price advantages, how has Hillerich & Bradsby successfully managed their decision to operate out of Louisville?

Remember to check out our Online Learning Center at www.mhhe.com/ferrell5e.

Appendix C

Personal Career Plan

The tools and techniques used in creating a business plan are just as useful in designing a plan to help sell yourself to potential employers. The outline in this appendix is designed to assist you in writing a personalized plan that will help you achieve your career goals. While this outline follows the same general format found in Appendix B, it has been adapted to be more relevant to career planning. Answering the questions presented in this outline will enable you to:

1. Organize and structure the data and information you collect about job prospects, the overall job market, and your competition.
2. Use this information to better understand your own personal strengths and weaknesses, as well as recognize the opportunities and threats that exist in your career development.
3. Develop goals and objectives that will capitalize on your strengths.
4. Develop a personalized strategy that will give you a competitive advantage.
5. Outline a plan for implementing your personalized strategy.

As you work through the following outline, it is very important that you be honest with yourself. If you do not possess a strength in a given area, it is important to recognize that fact. Similarly, do not overlook your weaknesses. The viability of your SWOT analysis and your strategy depend on how well you have identified all of the relevant issues in an honest manner.

I. Summary

If you choose to write a summary, do so after you have written the entire plan. It should provide a brief overview of the strategy for your career. State your career objectives and what means you will use to achieve those objectives.

II. Situation Analysis

A. The External Environment

1. **Competition**
   a) Who are your major competitors? What are their characteristics (number and growth in the number of graduates, skills, target employers)? Competitors to consider include peers at the same college or in the same degree field, peers at different colleges or in different degree fields, and graduates of trade, technical, or community colleges.
   b) What are the key strengths and weaknesses of the total pool of potential employees (or recent college graduates)?
   c) What are other college graduates doing in terms of developing skills, networking, showing a willingness to relocate, and promoting themselves to potential employers?
   d) What are the current trends in terms of work experience versus getting an advanced degree?
   e) Is your competitive set likely to change in the future? If so, how? Who are these new competitors likely to be?

2. **Economic conditions**
   a) What are the general economic conditions of the country, region, state, and local area in which you live or in which you want to relocate?
   b) Overall, are potential employers optimistic or pessimistic about the economy?

c) What is the overall outlook for major job/career categories? Where do potential employers seem to be placing their recruitment and hiring emphasis?

d) What is the trend in terms of starting salaries for major job/career categories?

3. **Political trends**

   a) Have recent elections changed the political landscape so that certain industries or companies are now more or less attractive as potential employers?

4. **Legal and regulatory factors**

   a) What changes in international, federal, state, or local laws and regulations are being proposed that would affect your job/career prospects?

   b) Have recent court decisions made it easier or harder for you to find employment?

   c) Have global trade agreements changed in any way that makes certain industries or companies more or less attractive as potential employers?

5. **Changes in technology**

   a) What impact has changing technology had on potential employers in terms of their need for employees?

   b) What technological changes will affect the way you will have to work and compete for employment in the future?

   c) What technological changes will affect the way you market your skills and abilities to potential employers?

   d) How do technological advances threaten to make your skills and abilities obsolete?

6. **Cultural trends**

   a) How are society's demographics and values changing? What effect will these changes have on your:
      (1) Skills and abilities:
      (2) Career/lifestyle choices:
      (3) Ability to market yourself:
      (4) Willingness to relocate:
      (5) Required minimum salary:

   b) What problems or opportunities are being created by changes in the cultural diversity of the labor pool and the requirements of potential employers?

   c) What is the general attitude of society regarding the particular skills, abilities, and talents that you possess and the career/lifestyle choices that you have made?

B. **The Employer Environment**

   1. **Who are your potential employers?**

      a) Identifying characteristics: industry, products, size, growth, profitability, hiring practices, union/nonunion, employee needs, etc.

      b) Geographic characteristics: home office, local offices, global sites, expansion, etc.

      c) Organizational culture: mission statement, values, priorities, employee training, etc.

      d) In each organization, who is responsible for recruiting and selecting new employees?

   2. **What do your potential employers look for in new employees?**

      a) What are the basic or specific skills and abilities that employers are looking for in new employees?

      b) What are the basic or specific needs that are fulfilled by the skills and abilities that you *currently* possess and that other potential employees currently possess?

      c) How well do your skills and abilities (and those of your competitors) currently meet the needs of potential employers?

      d) How are the needs of potential employers expected to change in the future?

   3. **What are the recent hiring practices of your potential employers?**

      a) How many employees are being hired? What combination of

skills and abilities do these new hires possess?

b) Is the growth or decline in hiring related to the recent expansion or downsizing of markets and/or territories? Changes in technology?

c) Are there major hiring differences between large and small companies? If so, why?

4. **Where and how do your potential employers recruit new employees?**

a) Where do employers make contact with potential employees?

(1) College placement offices:

(2) Job/career fairs:

(3) Internship programs:

(4) Headhunting firms:

(5) Unsolicited applications:

(6) The Internet:

b) Do potential employers place a premium on experience or are they willing to hire new graduates without experience?

5. **When do your potential employers recruit new employees?**

a) Does recruiting follow a seasonal pattern or do employers recruit new employees on an ongoing basis?

C. **Personal Assessment**

1. **Review of personal goals, objectives, and performance**

a) What are your personal goals and objectives in terms of employment, career, lifestyle, geographic preferences, etc.?

b) Are your personal goals and objectives consistent with the realities of the labor market? Why or why not?

c) Are your personal goals and objectives consistent with recent changes in the external or employer environments? Why or why not?

d) How are your current strategies for success working in areas such as course performance, internships, networking, job leads, career development, interviewing skills, etc.?

e) How does your current performance compare to that of your peers

(competitors)? Are they performing well in terms of course performance, internships, networking, job leads, career development, interviewing skills, etc.?

f) If your performance is declining, what is the most likely cause?

g) If your performance is improving, what actions can you take to ensure that your performance continues in this direction?

2. **Inventory of personal skills and resources**

a) What do you consider to be your marketable skills? This list should be as comprehensive as possible and include areas such as interpersonal skills, organizational skills, technological skills, communication skills (oral and written), networking/ teambuilding skills, etc.

b) Considering the current and future needs of your potential employers, what important skills are you lacking?

c) Other than personal skills, what do you consider to be your other career-enhancing resources? This list should be as comprehensive as possible and include areas such as financial resources (to pay for additional training, if necessary), personal contacts or "connections" with individuals who can assist your career development, specific degrees or certificates you hold, and intangible resources (family name, prestige of your educational institution, etc.).

d) Considering the current and future needs of your potential employers, what important resources are you lacking?

III. **SWOT Analysis (your personal strengths and weaknesses and the opportunities and threats that may impact your career)**

A. **Personal Strengths**

1. Three key strengths

a) Strength 1:

b) Strength 2:

c) Strength 3:

2. How do these strengths allow you to meet the needs of your potential employers?

3. How do these strengths compare to those of your peers/competitors? Do these strengths give you an advantage relative to your peers/competitors?

B. Personal Weaknesses

1. Three key weaknesses
   a) Weakness 1:
   b) Weakness 2:
   c) Weakness 3:

2. How do these weaknesses cause you to fall short of meeting the needs of your potential employers?

3. How do these weaknesses compare to those of your peers/competitors? Do these weaknesses put you at a disadvantage relative to your peers/competitors?

C. Career Opportunities

1. Three key career opportunities
   a) Opportunity 1:
   b) Opportunity 2:
   c) Opportunity 3:

2. How are these opportunities related to serving the needs of your potential employers?

3. What actions must be taken to capitalize on these opportunities in the short-term? In the long-term?

D. Career Threats

1. Three key career threats
   a) Threat 1:
   b) Threat 2:
   c) Threat 3:

2. How are these threats related to serving the needs of your potential employers?

3. What actions must be taken to prevent these threats from limiting your capabilities in the short-term? In the long-term?

E. The SWOT Matrix

F. Matching, Converting, Minimizing, and Avoiding Strategies

1. How can you match your strengths to your opportunities to better serve the needs of your potential employers?

2. How can you convert your weaknesses into strengths?

3. How can you convert your threats into opportunities?

4. How can you minimize or avoid those weaknesses and threats that cannot be converted successfully?

IV. Resources

A. Financial

1. Do you have the financial resources necessary to undertake and successfully complete this plan (i.e., preparation/duplication/mailing of a résumé; interviewing costs, including proper attire; etc.)?

B. Human

1. Is the industry in which you are interested currently hiring? Are companies in your area currently hiring?

C. Experience and Expertise

1. Do you have experience from either part-time or summer employment that could prove useful in your current plan?

2. Do you have the required expertise or skills to qualify for a job in your desired field? If not, do you have the resources to obtain them?

V. Strategies

A. Objective(s)

1. Potential employer A:
   a) Descriptive characteristics:
   b) Geographic locations:
   c) Culture/values/mission:
   d) Basic employee needs:
   e) Recruiting/hiring practices:
   f) Employee training/compensation practices:
   g) Justification for selection:

2. Potential employer B:
   a) Descriptive characteristics:
   b) Geographic locations:
   c) Culture/values/mission:
   d) Basic employee needs:
   e) Recruiting/hiring practices:
   f) Employee training/compensation practices:
   g) Justification for selection:

B. Strategy(ies) for Using Capabilities and Resources

1. Strategy A (to meet the needs of potential employer A)

a) Personal skills, abilities, and resources

   (1) Description of your skills and abilities:

   (2) Specific employer needs that your skills/abilities can fulfill:

   (3) Differentiation relative to peers/ competitors (why should *you* be hired?):

   (4) Additional resources that you have to offer:

   (5) Needed or expected starting salary:

   (6) Expected employee benefits:

   (7) Additional employer-paid training that you require:

   (8) Willingness to relocate:

   (9) Geographic areas to target:

   (10) Corporate divisions or offices to target:

   (11) Summary of overall strategy:

   (12) Tactics for standing out among the crowd of potential employees:

   (13) Point of contact with potential employer:

   (14) Specific elements
- (*a*) Résumé:
- (*b*) Internships:
- (*c*) Placement offices:
- (*d*) Job fairs:
- (*e*) Personal contacts:
- (*f*) Unsolicited:

   (15) Specific objectives and budget:

2. Strategy B (to meet the needs of potential employer B)

a) Personal skills, abilities, and resources

   (1) Description of your skills and abilities:

   (2) Specific employer needs that your skills/abilities can fulfill:

   (3) Differentiation relative to peers/ competitors (why should *you* be hired?):

   (4) Additional resources that you have to offer:

   (5) Needed or expected starting salary:

   (6) Expected employee benefits:

   (7) Additional employer-paid training that you require:

   (8) Willingness to relocate:

   (9) Geographic areas to target:

   (10) Corporate divisions or offices to target:

   (11) Summary of overall strategy:

   (12) Tactics for standing out among the crowd of potential employees:

   (13) Point of contact with potential employer:

   (14) Specific elements
- (*a*) Résumé:
- (*b*) Internships:
- (*c*) Placement offices:
- (*d*) Job fairs:
- (*e*) Personal contacts:
- (*f*) Unsolicited:

   (15) Specific objectives and budget:

C. Strategy Summary

   1. How does strategy A (B) give you a competitive advantage in serving the needs of potential employer A (B)?

   2. Is this competitive advantage sustainable? Why or why not?

VI. Financial Projections and Budgets

   A. Do you have a clear idea of your budgetary requirements (e.g., housing, furnishings, clothing, transportation, food, other living expenses)?

   B. Will the expected salaries/benefits from potential employers meet these requirements? If not, do you have an alternative plan (i.e., a different job choice, a second job, requesting a higher salary)?

VII. Controls and Evaluation

   A. Performance Standards

   1. What do you have to offer? Corrective actions that can be taken if your skills, abilities, and resources do not match the needs of potential employers:

   2. Are you worth it? Corrective actions that can be taken if potential employers do not think your skills/abilities are worth your asking price:

3. Where do you want to go?
   Corrective actions that can be taken if potential employers do not offer you a position in a preferred geographic location:
4. How will you stand out among the crowd?
   Corrective actions that can be taken if your message is not being heard by potential employers or is not reaching the right people:

B. **Monitoring Procedures**
   1. What types and levels of formal control mechanisms are in place to ensure the proper implementation of your plan?
      a) Are your potential employers hiring?
      b) Do you need additional training/education?
      c) Have you allocated sufficient time to your career development?
      d) Are your investments in career development adequate?
         (1) Training/education:
         (2) Networking/making contacts:
         (3) Wardrobe/clothing:
         (4) Development of interviewing skills:
      e) Have you done your homework on potential employers?
      f) Have you been involved in an internship program?
      g) Have you attended job/career fairs?
      h) Are you using the resources of your placement center?
      i) Are you committed to your career development?

C. **Performance Analysis**
   1. Number/quality/potential of all job contacts made:
   2. Number of job/career fairs attended and quality of the job leads generated:
   3. Number of résumés distributed:
      a) Number of potential employers who responded:
      b) Number of negative responses:
   4. Number of personal interviews:
   5. Number/quality of job offers:

eQuality Assured

Quality Assured (QA), a nonprofit organization, was started in 1977 to promote the establishment, development, and preservation of high professional standards and audit the social responsibility of companies in the United States. The audits could be used to promote the company's good corporate citizenship and determine areas that need improvement. Of the four issues of social responsibility (voluntary, ethical, legal, and economic), it had always focused most on the voluntary and ethical aspects. During the early years, QA dedicated a majority of its resources to environmental issues and focused on promoting the responsible disposal of wastes and development of recycling programs. But at the end of the 1980s, the focus shifted to meet the changes in the business world. Because consumers had more spending money, more products to choose from, and better information about their options, purchasing power shifted from producers to consumers.

The Internet also caused a shift in the nature of QA's purpose. In fact, the company name was changed to eQuality Assured to reflect the growing impact of technology and the Net in today's society. Most of its efforts now are directed at providing business certifications that are administered over the Internet. eQuality does not administer tests, but instead provides certification based on proven performance standards. Currently, it is trying to develop a national program to certify advertisements directed at children. Working directly with the Children's Advertising Review Unit, eQuality seeks to develop this program within the next month. This deadline is firm and will present some challenges for the organization because it is placing increased pressure on all the workers.

eQuality has a full-time staff of 50 employees. These core workers are responsible for all the functions performed at the organization. Most are not experts on certification, but carry out functional responsibilities such as accounting and technology. Some important tasks include monitoring the business environment, determining which issues need to be addressed, interacting with other nonprofit organizations, recruiting volunteers, and managing all aspects of the projects. Because of the approaching deadline, a majority of the paid staff feels overwhelmed by the workload they have had to assume. Among the staff members are legal counsel, certified public accountant, and a retired professor of management.

As a nonprofit organization, eQuality relies heavily on volunteers. Although the director of human resources was able to recruit a large number of workers, their knowledge and skill level preclude them from assisting with the more important aspects of the certification of advertisements. With a limited number of "busy work" tasks available, the organization has not been able to utilize the volunteers as first anticipated.

In order to get the certification completed by the deadline, the organization must change the fundamental way it is approaching the task. Tomorrow, the director of human resources, chief legal counsel, director of finance, and director of public relations will meet with the executive director of eQuality to determine the best way to proceed. This administrative team will determine the best way to motivate the workers, both paid and volunteer, in order to accomplish the certification program by the deadline.

---

*This background statement provides information for a role-play exercise designed to help you understand the real world challenge of decision making in business and to integrate the concepts presented previously in this text. If your instructor chooses to utilize this activity, the class will be divided into teams with each team member assigned to a particular role in the fictitious organization. Additional information on each role and instructions for the completion of the exercise will be distributed to individual team members.

Part 5

Marketing: Developing Relationships

Chapter 12

Customer-Driven Marketing

OBJECTIVES

After reading this chapter, you will be able to:

- Define marketing and describe the exchange process.

- Specify the functions of marketing.

- Explain the marketing concept and its implications for developing marketing strategies.

- Examine the development of a marketing strategy, including market segmentation and marketing mix.

- Investigate how marketers conduct marketing research and study buying behavior.

- Summarize the environmental forces that influence marketing decisions.

- Assess a company's marketing plans and propose a solution for resolving its problem.

Apple Takes a Bite out of the Music Industry

Credit Steve Jobs with making Apple a brand name that once again turns heads—but this time in the music business. Apple, a pioneer in the computer industry in the 1980s, has long concentrated on developing products that people will want tomorrow and beyond. Now, thanks to the cutting-edge iPod portable digital music player, which runs on both the Macintosh and Microsoft Windows platforms, some analysts credit Jobs with playing a key role in revolutionizing the music business.

Apple's iPod dominates the portable digital music player segment with 50 percent in major markets in mid-2004. Apple has already sold more than 100 million songs through its iTunes Music Store at 99 cents each. Although the company faces new competition from Wal-Mart, Microsoft, and other companies eager to cash in on the rising trend, Apple executives believe their product can maintain a leadership position.

Advertising for the iPod has been more strategic than sizable. The company spent just $10 million advertising iTunes and $9 million for iPods in the first eight months of 2003, a fraction of the $69 million Apple spent on promotions. However, Apple has leveraged its youthful image by entering into cooperative advertising arrangements with Volkswagon, PepsiCo, and BMW.

Perhaps a great deal of Apple's rationale behind a more thoughtful, strategic approach to paid media is the result of the success of its public relations campaign. More than 6,000 articles have been written about the iPod and iTunes service, enabling the company's advertising dollars to reinforce the highly successful publicity and buzz marketing campaigns. Apple has excelled at generating publicity for its products. In 2002, for example, the

continued

 iPod

Welcome to the digital music revolution. 7,500 songs in your pocket.　Works with Mac or PC. Over a million sold. The new iPod.

Enter the World of Business

company gave free Apple computers to all seventh- and eighth-graders in the state of Maine.

The Apple brand has become so desirable that noncompeting firms are asking to link their products and brands with the Apple image. As Apple continues to craft its brand and image, it will likely continue to partner strategically with firms that can leverage their smaller advertising budgets, while remaining sensitive to firms that "fit" with Apple's much valued brand name.[1]

Introduction

Marketing involves planning and executing the development, pricing, promotion, and distribution of ideas, goods, and services to create exchanges that satisfy individual and organizational goals. These activities ensure that the products consumers want to buy are available at a price they are willing to pay and that consumers are provided with information about product features and availability. Organizations of all sizes and objectives engage in these activities.

In this chapter, we focus on the basic principles of marketing. First we define and examine the nature of marketing. Then we look at how marketers develop marketing strategies to satisfy the needs and wants of their customers. Next we discuss buying behavior and how marketers use research to determine what consumers want to buy and why. Finally we explore the impact of the environment on marketing activities.

Nature of Marketing

marketing
a group of activities designed to expedite transactions by creating, distributing, pricing, and promoting goods, services, and ideas

A vital part of any business undertaking, **marketing** is a group of activities designed to expedite transactions by creating, distributing, pricing, and promoting goods, services, and ideas. These activities create value by allowing individuals and organizations to obtain what they need and want. A business cannot achieve its objectives unless it provides something that customers value. McDonald's, for example, introduced an adult "Happy Meal" with a premium salad, water, exercise booklet, and a "stepometer" to satisfy adult consumers' desires to improve their eating habits and health.[2] But just creating an innovative product that meets many users' needs isn't sufficient in today's volatile global marketplace. Products must be conveniently available, competitively priced, and uniquely promoted.

Of all the business concepts covered in this text, marketing may be the hardest for organizations to master. Businesses try to respond to consumer wants and needs and to anticipate changes in the environment. Unfortunately, it is difficult to understand and predict what consumers want: Motives are often unclear; few principles can be applied consistently; and markets tend to fragment, desiring customized products, new value, or better service.[3]

It is important to note what marketing is not: It is not manipulating consumers to get them to buy products they don't want. It is not just selling and advertising; it is a systematic approach to satisfying consumers. Marketing focuses on the many activities—planning, pricing, promoting, and distributing products—that foster exchanges.

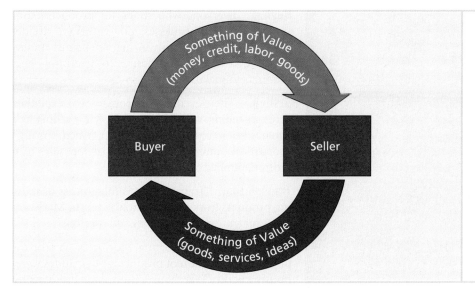

FIGURE 12.1

The Exchange Process:
Giving Up One Thing in
Return for Another

The Exchange Relationship

At the heart of all business is the **exchange**, the act of giving up one thing (money, credit, labor, goods) in return for something else (goods, services, or ideas). Businesses exchange their goods, services, or ideas for money or credit supplied by customers in a voluntary *exchange relationship*, illustrated in Figure 12.1. The buyer must feel good about the purchase, or the exchange will not continue. If your local dry cleaner cleans your nice suit properly, on time, and without damage, you will probably feel good about using its services. But if your suit is damaged or isn't ready on time, you will probably use another dry cleaner next time.

For an exchange to occur, certain conditions are required. As indicated by the arrows in Figure 12.1, buyers and sellers must be able to communicate about the "something of value" available to each. An exchange does not necessarily take place just because buyers and sellers have something of value to exchange. Each participant must be willing to give up his or her respective "something of value" to receive the "something" held by the other. You are willing to exchange your "something of value"—your money or credit—for compact discs, soft drinks, football tickets, or new shoes because you consider those products more valuable or more important than holding on to your cash or credit potential.

When you think of marketing products, you may think of tangible things—cars, stereo systems, or books, for example. What most consumers want, however, is a way to get a job done, solve a problem, or gain some enjoyment. You may purchase a Hoover vacuum cleaner not because you want a vacuum cleaner but because you want clean carpets. Therefore, the tangible product itself may not be as important as the image or the benefits associated with the product. This intangible "something of value" may be capability gained from using a product or the image evoked by it, such as Tommy Hilfiger jeans.

Functions of Marketing

Marketing focuses on a complex set of activities that must be performed to accomplish objectives and generate exchanges. These activities include buying, selling, transporting, storing, grading, financing, marketing research, and risk taking.

exchange

the act of giving up one thing (money, credit, labor, goods) in return for something else (goods, services, or ideas)

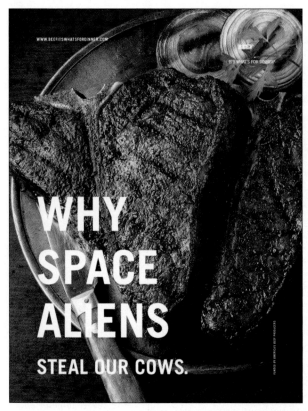

Marketing can be used by industry groups to increase demand for their industry's product—like America's Beef Producers.

Buying.   Everyone who shops for products (consumers, stores, businesses, governments) decides whether and what to buy. A marketer must understand buyers' needs and desires to determine what products to make available.

Selling.   The exchange process is expedited through selling. Marketers usually view selling as a persuasive activity that is accomplished through promotion (advertising, personal selling, sales promotion, publicity, and packaging).

Transporting.   Transporting is the process of moving products from the seller to the buyer. Marketers focus on transportation costs and services.

Storing.   Like transporting, storing is part of the physical distribution of products and includes warehousing goods. Warehouses hold some products for lengthy periods in order to create time utility. Consumers want frozen orange juice year-round, for example, although the production season for oranges is only a few months out of the year. This means that sellers must arrange cold storage for frozen orange juice concentrate all year.

Grading.   Grading refers to standardizing products and displaying and labeling them so that consumers clearly understand their nature and quality. Many products, such as meat, steel, and fruit, are graded according to a set of standards that often are established by the state or federal government.

Financing.   For many products, especially large items such as automobiles, refrigerators, and new homes, the marketer arranges credit to expedite the purchase.

Marketing Research.   Through research, marketers ascertain the need for new goods and services. By gathering information regularly, marketers can detect new trends and changes in consumer tastes.

Risk Taking.   Risk is the chance of loss associated with marketing decisions. Developing a new product creates a chance of loss if consumers do not like it enough to buy it. Spending money to hire a sales force or to conduct marketing research also involves risk. The implication of risk is that most marketing decisions result in either success or failure.

The Marketing Concept

marketing concept
the idea that an organization should try to satisfy customers' needs through coordinated activities that also allow it to achieve its own goals

A basic philosophy that guides all marketing activities is the **marketing concept**, the idea that an organization should try to satisfy customers' needs through coordinated activities that also allow it to achieve its own goals. According to the marketing concept, a business must find out what consumers need and want and then develop the good, service, or idea that fulfills their needs or wants. The business must then get the product to the customer. In addition, the business must continually alter, adapt, and develop products to keep pace with changing consumer needs and wants. McDonald's, as already mentioned, faces increasing pressure to provide more healthful fast-food choices; in addition to introducing its Go Active! Happy Meal, the company has eliminated supersized fries and soft drinks from its menu to address these concerns.[4] Over the years, the fast-food giant has experimented with healthier fare, but consumers often rejected these items. To remain competitive, the company must be prepared to add to or adapt its menu to satisfy customers' desires for new fads or changes in eating habits. Each business must determine how best to implement the marketing concept, given its own goals and resources.

Trying to determine customers' true needs is increasingly difficult because no one fully understands what motivates people to buy things. However, Estée Lauder, founder of her namesake cosmetics company, had a pretty good idea. When a prestigious store in Paris rejected her perfume in the 1960s, she "accidentally" dropped a bottle on the floor where nearby customers could get a whiff of it. So many asked about the scent that Galeries Lafayette was obliged to place an order. Lauder ultimately built an empire using then-unheard-of tactics like free samples and gifts with purchases to market her "jars of hope."[5]

Although customer satisfaction is the goal of the marketing concept, a business must also achieve its own objectives, such as boosting productivity, reducing costs, or achieving a percentage of a specific market. If it does not, it will not survive. For example, Dell could sell computers for $50 and give customers a lifetime guarantee, which would be great for customers but not so great for Dell. Obviously, the company must strike a balance between achieving organizational objectives and satisfying customer needs and wants.

To implement the marketing concept, a firm must have good information about what consumers want, adopt a consumer orientation, and coordinate its efforts throughout the entire organization; otherwise, it may be awash with goods, services, and ideas that consumers do not want or need. Successfully implementing the marketing concept requires that a business view customer value as the ultimate measure of work performance and improving value, and the rate at which this is done, as the measure of success.[6] Everyone in the organization who interacts with customers—*all* customer-contact employees—must know what customers want. They are selling ideas, benefits, philosophies, and experiences—not just goods and services.

Someone once said that if you build a better mousetrap, the world will beat a path to your door. Suppose you do build a better mousetrap. What will happen? Actually, consumers are not likely to beat a path to your door because the market is too competitive. A coordinated effort by everyone involved with the mousetrap is needed to sell the product. Your company must reach out to customers and tell them about your mousetrap, especially how your mousetrap works better than those offered by competitors. If you do not make the benefits of your product widely known, in most cases, it will not be successful. Consider Apple's 74 retail stores, which market computers and electronics in a way unlike any other computer manufacturer or retail store. The upscale stores, located in high-rent shopping districts, show off Apple's products in sparse, stylish settings to encourage consumers to try new things—like making a movie on a computer. The stores also offer special events like concerts and classes to give customers ideas on how to maximize their use of Apple's products.[7] You must also find—or create—stores willing to sell your mousetrap to consumers. You must implement the marketing concept by making a product with satisfying benefits and making it available and visible.

Orville Wright said that an airplane is "a group of separate parts flying in close formation." This is what most companies are trying to accomplish: They are striving for a team effort to deliver the right good or service to customers. A breakdown at any point in the organization—whether it be in production, purchasing, sales, distribution, or advertising—can result in lost sales, lost revenue, and dissatisfied customers.

Evolution of the Marketing Concept

The marketing concept may seem like the obvious approach to running a business and building relationships with customers. However, businesspeople are not always focused on customers when they create and operate businesses. Our society and economic system have changed over time, and marketing has become more important as markets have become more competitive.

The Production Orientation.   During the second half of the 19th century, the Industrial Revolution was well under way in the United States. New technologies, such as electricity, railroads, internal combustion engines, and mass-production techniques, made it possible to manufacture goods with ever increasing efficiency. Together with new management ideas and ways of using labor, products poured into the marketplace, where demand for manufactured goods was strong.

The Sales Orientation.   By the early part of the 20th century, supply caught up with and then exceeded demand, and businesspeople began to realize they would have to "sell" products to buyers. During the first half of the 20th century, businesspeople viewed sales as the major means of increasing profits, and this period came to have a sales orientation. They believed the most important marketing activities were personal selling and advertising. Today some people still inaccurately equate marketing with a sales orientation.

The Marketing Orientation.   By the 1950s, some businesspeople began to recognize that even efficient production and extensive promotion did not guarantee sales. These businesses, and many others since, found that they must first determine what customers want and then produce it rather than making the products first and then trying to persuade customers that they need them. Managers at General Electric first suggested that the marketing concept was a companywide philosophy of doing business. As more organizations realized the importance of satisfying customers' needs, U.S. businesses entered the marketing era, one of marketing orientation.

marketing orientation
an approach requiring organizations to gather information about customer needs, share that information throughout the firm, and use that information to help build long-term relationships with customers

A **marketing orientation** requires organizations to gather information about customer needs, share that information throughout the entire firm, and use that information to help build long-term relationships with customers. Top executives, marketing managers, nonmarketing managers (those in production, finance, human resources, and so on), and customers all become mutually dependent and cooperate in developing and carrying out a marketing orientation. Nonmarketing managers must communicate with marketing managers to share information important to understanding the customer. For example, to respond to the low-carbohydrate diet trend, Ocean Spray introduced Ocean Spray Light Cranberry Juice Cocktail with two-thirds fewer carbs and calories. To develop the product, production and technical managers had to work together to develop the right formula to provide the right taste using the low-calorie sweetener Splenda.

Trying to assess what customers want, difficult to begin with, is further complicated by the rate at which trends, fashions, and tastes can change. Businesses today want to satisfy customers and build meaningful long-term relationships with them. It is more

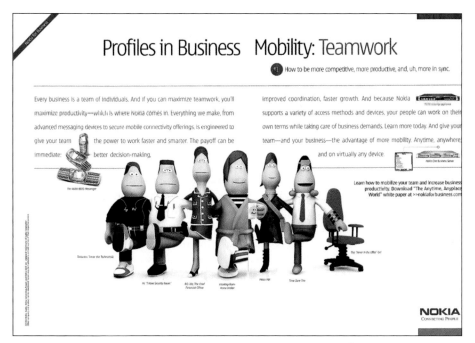

Nokia's first and foremost goal is to sell its products—cell phones, servers, etc. But in this ad, it sells the ability to help a company find solutions. Nokia's marketing orientation is not only for the individual consumer of cell phones, but also an entire company needing solutions to increase business productivity.

efficient to retain existing customers and even increase the amount of business each customer provides the organization than to find new customers. Most companies' success depends on increasing the amount of repeat business. As we saw in Chapter 4, many companies are turning to technologies associated with customer-relationship management to help build relationships and boost business with existing customers.

Communication remains a major element of any strategy to develop and manage long-term customer relationships. By providing multiple points of interactions with customers—that is, Web sites, telephone, fax, e-mail, and personal contact—companies can personalize customer relationships.[8] Saturn provides an example of multiple interactions with customers. The company Web site provides complete product information, and Saturn makes records of each car it sells available to all its dealers. The company also provides special seminars and programs to help educate Saturn buyers about how to take care of their vehicles and get the most enjoyment from them. All Saturn buyers are invited to an annual picnic at the company's Spring Hill, Tennessee, factory. These activities enable Saturn to build a strong relationship with its customers, which hopefully will help it build repeat sales and word-of-mouth advertising. Regardless of the medium through which communication occurs, customers should ultimately be the drivers of marketing strategy because they understand what they want. Customer relationship management systems should ensure that marketers listen to customers to respond to their needs and concerns and build long-term relationships.

Developing a Marketing Strategy

To implement the marketing concept and customer relationship management, a business needs to develop and maintain a **marketing strategy**, a plan of action for developing, pricing, distributing, and promoting products that meet the needs of

marketing strategy
a plan of action for developing, pricing, distributing, and promoting products that meet the needs of specific customers

specific customers. This definition has two major components: selecting a target market and developing an appropriate marketing mix to satisfy that target market.

Selecting a Target Market

market
a group of people who have a need, purchasing power, and the desire and authority to spend money on goods, services, and ideas

target market
a specific group of consumers on whose needs and wants a company focuses its marketing efforts

A **market** is a group of people who have a need, purchasing power, and the desire and authority to spend money on goods, services, and ideas. A **target market** is a more specific group of consumers on whose needs and wants a company focuses its marketing efforts. Nike, for example, introduced a new line of golf clubs targeted at recreational golfers.[9]

Marketing managers may define a target market as a relatively small number of people, or they may define it as the total market (Figure 12.2). Rolls Royce, for example, targets its products at a small, very exclusive, high-income market—people who want the ultimate in prestige in an automobile. General Motors, on the other hand, manufactures vehicles ranging from the Geo Metro to Cadillac to GMC trucks in an attempt to appeal to varied tastes, needs, and desires. Likewise, the Target Corporation not only operates Target discount stores, but also more upscale Marshall Field's and Mervyn's department stores, in order to appeal to diverse target markets.

FIGURE 12.2

Target Market Strategies

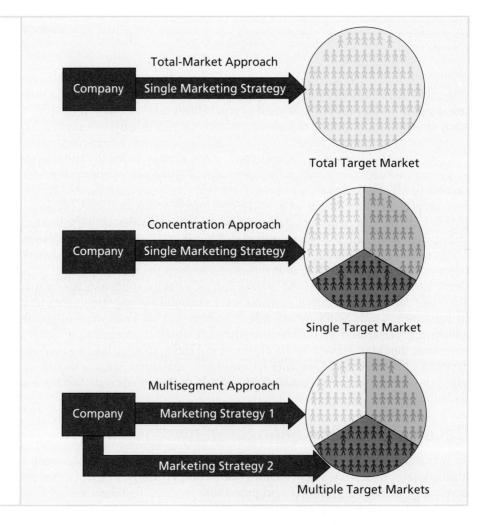

Some firms use a **total-market approach**, in which they try to appeal to everyone and assume that all buyers have similar needs and wants. Sellers of salt, sugar, and many agricultural products use a total-market approach because everyone is a potential consumer of these products. Most firms, though, use **market segmentation** and divide the total market into groups of people who have relatively similar product needs. A **market segment** is a collection of individuals, groups, or organizations who share one or more characteristics and thus have relatively similar product needs and desires. One market segment that many marketers are focusing on is the growing Hispanic population. For example, Procter & Gamble spends more than $46 million a year to promote its products to Hispanic consumers through advertisements on the Univision and Telemundo networks.[10] Table 12.1 shows the buying power and market share percentages of four market segments. Companies use market segmentation to focus their efforts and resources on specific target markets so that they can develop a productive marketing strategy. Two common approaches to segmenting markets are the concentration approach and the multisegment approach.

Market Segmentation Approaches.   In the **concentration approach**, a company develops one marketing strategy for a single market segment. The concentration approach allows a firm to specialize, focusing all its efforts on the one market segment. Porsche, for example, focuses all its marketing efforts toward high-income individuals who want to own high-performance vehicles. A firm can generate a large sales volume by penetrating a single market segment deeply. The concentration approach may be especially effective when a firm can identify and develop products for a particular segment ignored by other companies in the industry.

In the **multisegment approach**, the marketer aims its marketing efforts at two or more segments, developing a marketing strategy for each. Many firms use a multisegment approach that includes different advertising messages for different segments. Coca-Cola, for example, targets teenagers through its Coke Red Lounges, which are teen hangouts in shopping malls with exclusive music, movies, and videos, as well as lots of Coca-Cola products. And, in Britain, the soft-drink giant created a Web site where Internet surfers can mix their own music tracks.[11] Companies also develop product variations to appeal to different market segments. For example, in an effort to appeal to the growing number of children interested in gourmet cooking, Chef Revival U.S.A. launched a children's division that sells child-sized chef's hats, jackets, and kitchen pants in the same designs that a master chef would wear.[12] Many other firms also attempt to use a multisegment approach to market segmentation. The manufacturer of Raleigh bicycles uses a multisegment approach and has designed separate marketing strategies for racers, tourers, commuters, and children.

total-market approach
an approach whereby a firm tries to appeal to everyone and assumes that all buyers have similar needs

market segmentation
a strategy whereby a firm divides the total market into groups of people who have relatively similar product needs

market segment
a collection of individuals, groups, or organizations who share one or more characteristics and thus have relatively similar product needs and desires

concentration approach
a market segmentation approach whereby a company develops one marketing strategy for a single market segment

multisegment approach
a market segmentation approach whereby the marketer aims its efforts at two or more segments, developing a marketing strategy for each

Category	Buying Power (billions)		% Market Share	
	1990	2003	1990	2003
Black	307.8	687.7	7.4	8.4
Hispanic	207.5	652.6	5.0	7.9
Asian	112.9	344.2	2.7	4.2
American Indian	19.2	45.2	0.5	0.5

Source: Jeffrey M. Humphreys, "The Multicultural Economy 2003," *GBEC* 63 (2nd Quarter, 2003), pp. 10, 12, available at www.selig.uqu.edu/forecast/GBEC/GBEC032Q/.

TABLE 12.1

Minority Buying Power by Race, 1990 versus 2003

For the
real meat lover
in the family.

TODAY'S ALPO

With this ad, Alpo targets a premium price dog food market to owners who want the best for their pet.

Niche marketing is a narrow market segment focus when efforts are on one small, well-defined segment that has a unique, specific set of needs. Catering to ice cream "addicts" and people who crave new, exotic flavors, several companies are selling ice cream on the Internet. This niche represents only a fraction of the $20.3 billion a year ice cream business, but online sales at some of the biggest makers increased 30 percent in just one year. Some of the firms focusing on this market are IceCreamSource.com, Nuts About Ice Cream, and Graeter's.[13]

For a firm to successfully use a concentration or multisegment approach to market segmentation, several requirements must be met:

1. Consumers' needs for the product must be heterogeneous.
2. The segments must be identifiable and divisible.
3. The total market must be divided in a way that allows estimated sales potential, cost, and profits of the segments to be compared.
4. At least one segment must have enough profit potential to justify developing and maintaining a special marketing strategy.
5. The firm must be able to reach the chosen market segment with a particular market strategy.

Bases for Segmenting Markets.   Companies segment markets on the basis of several variables:

1. *Demographic*—age, sex, race, ethnicity, income, education, occupation, family size, religion, social class. These characteristics are often closely related to customers' product needs and purchasing behavior, and they can be readily measured. For example, deodorants are often segmented by sex: Secret and Soft n' Dry for women; Old Spice and Mennen for men.
2. *Geographic*—climate, terrain, natural resources, population density, subcultural values. These influence consumers' needs and product usage. Climate, for example, influences consumers' purchases of clothing, automobiles, heating and air conditioning equipment, and leisure activity equipment.
3. *Psychographic*—personality characteristics, motives, lifestyles. Soft-drink marketers provide their products in several types of packaging, including two-liter bottles and cases of cans, to satisfy different lifestyles and motives.
4. *Behavioristic*—some characteristic of the consumer's behavior toward the product. These characteristics commonly involve some aspect of product use.

Developing a Marketing Mix

The second step in developing a marketing strategy is to create and maintain a satisfying marketing mix. The **marketing mix** refers to four marketing activities—product, price, distribution, and promotion—that the firm can control to achieve specific goals within a dynamic marketing environment (Figure 12.3). The buyer or the target market is the central focus of all marketing activities.

Product.   A product—whether a good, a service, an idea, or some combination—is a complex mix of tangible and intangible attributes that provide satisfaction and benefits. A *good* is a physical entity you can touch. A Porsche Cayenne, an Outkast compact disc, a Hewlett-Packard printer, and a kitten available for adoption at an animal shelter are examples of goods. A *service* is the application of human and mechanical efforts to people or objects to provide intangible benefits to customers. Air travel, dry cleaning, haircuts, banking, insurance, medical care, and day care are examples of services. *Ideas* include concepts, philosophies, images, and issues. For instance, an attorney, for a fee, may advise you about what rights you have in the event that the IRS decides to audit your tax return. Other marketers of ideas include political parties, churches, and schools.

A product has emotional and psychological as well as physical characteristics and includes everything that the buyer receives from an exchange. This definition includes supporting services such as installation, guarantees, product information, and promises of repair. Products usually have both favorable and unfavorable attributes; therefore, almost every purchase or exchange involves trade-offs as consumers try to maximize their benefits and satisfaction and minimize unfavorable attributes.

Products are among a firm's most visible contacts with consumers. If they do not meet consumer needs and expectations, sales will be difficult, and product life spans will be brief. The product is an important variable—often the central focus—of the marketing mix; the other variables (price, promotion, and distribution) must be coordinated with product decisions.

Price.   Almost anything can be assessed by a **price**, a value placed on an object exchanged between a buyer and a seller. Although the seller usually establishes the price, it may be negotiated between buyer and seller. The buyer usually exchanges purchasing power—income, credit, wealth—for the satisfaction or utility associated with a product. Because financial

The last time you had this much fun driving a car it cost a quarter and gyrated in front of the supermarket.

The six-speed, 240-horsepower, 0–60 in less than six seconds Honda S2000.   **S2000**   Ⓗ HONDA

Convertible sports cars such as the Honda S2000 appeal to a niche market.

marketing mix
the four marketing activites—product, price, promotion, and distribution—that the firm can control to achieve specific goals within a dynamic marketing environment

Did You Know?   During its first year of operation, sales of Coca-Cola averaged just nine drinks per day for total first-year sales of $50. Today, Coca-Cola products are consumed at the rate of one billion drinks per day.[14]

FIGURE 12.3

The Marketing Mix: Product, Price, Promotion, and Distribution

Marketing Environment

price
a value placed on an object exchanged between a buyer and a seller

price is the measure of value commonly used in an exchange, it quantifies value and is the basis of most market exchanges.

Marketers view price as much more than a way of assessing value, however. It is a key element of the marketing mix because it relates directly to the generation of revenue and profits. Prices can also be changed quickly to stimulate demand or respond to competitors' actions. For example, a price war has developed in the market for high-speed Internet access, with prices for cable-modem service dropping below $20 a month in some areas.[15] McDonald's, Burger King, and other fast-food chains often use price changes to increase store traffic. For example, 99-cent Whoppers at Burger King and 99-cent Big Macs and Egg McMuffins may be offered for a limited time to increase sales, especially among heavy fast-food users.

distribution
making products available to customers in the quantities desired

Distribution.   **Distribution** (sometimes referred to as "place" because it helps to remember the marketing mix as the "4 Ps") is making products available to customers in the quantities desired. McDonald's, for example, expanded distribution by opening restaurants in Wal-Mart stores and in Amoco and Chevron service stations. This practice permits the fast-food giant to share costs with its partners and to reach more customers when and where hunger strikes. McDonald's now operates more than 30,000 restaurants in 119 countries, serving more than 47 million customers a day.[16] Intermediaries, usually wholesalers and retailers, perform many of the activities required to move products efficiently from producers to consumers or industrial buyers. These activities involve transporting, warehousing, materials handling, and inventory control, as well as packaging and communication.

Critics who suggest that eliminating wholesalers and other middlemen would result in lower prices for consumers do not recognize that eliminating intermediaries would not do away with the need for their services. Other institutions would have to perform those services, and consumers would still have to pay for them. In addition, in the absence of wholesalers, all producers would have to deal directly with retailers or customers, keeping voluminous records and hiring people to deal with customers.

promotion
a persuasive form of communication that attempts to expedite a marketing exchange by influencing individuals, groups, and organizations to accept goods, services, and ideas

Promotion.   **Promotion** is a persuasive form of communication that attempts to expedite a marketing exchange by influencing individuals, groups, and organizations to accept goods, services, and ideas. Reebok, for example, held a star-studded party in Manhattan to promote Allen Iverson's Answer 7 and 50 Cent's G6 footwear. The event's highlight was a 6,000-pound half-court basketball court that floated down from the ceiling at midnight.[17] Promotion includes advertising, personal selling, publicity, and sales promotion, all of which we will look at more closely in Chapter 13.

The aim of promotion is to communicate directly or indirectly with individuals, groups, and organizations to facilitate exchanges. When marketers use advertising and other forms of promotion, they must effectively manage their promotional resources and understand product and target-market characteristics to ensure that these promotional activities contribute to the firm's objectives. For example, the *Bakersfield Californian* newspaper used text messaging on cell phones to target 15- to 24-year-olds in a cross-promotion with a local music store. The promotion allowed fans to vote for their favorite new CD listed in World Music's print ads, with participants gaining an opportunity to win gift certificates and other prizes.[18]

Most major companies have set up Web sites on the Internet to promote themselves and their products. The home page for Betty Crocker, for example, offers recipes, meal planning, the company's history, descriptions for its 200 products, online shopping for complementary items such as dinnerware, linens, and gifts, and the ability to print a shopping list based on recipes chosen or ingredients on hand in the consumer's kitchen. The Web sites for The Gap and Old Navy provide consumers with the opportunity to purchase clothing and other items from the convenience of their homes or offices. Some sites, however, simply promote a company's products but do not offer them for sale online.

Marketing Research and Information Systems

Before marketers can develop a marketing mix, they must collect in-depth, up-to-date information about customer needs. **Marketing research** is a systematic, objective process of getting information about potential customers to guide marketing decisions. Such information might include data about the age, income, ethnicity, gender, and educational level of people in the target market, their preferences for product features, their attitudes toward competitors' products, and the frequency with which they use the product. For example, Toyota's marketing research about Generation Y drivers (born between 1977 and 1994) found that they practically live in their cars, and many even keep a change of clothes handy in their vehicles. As a result of this research, Toyota designed its Scion as a "home on wheels" with a 15-volt outlet for plugging in a computer, reclining front seats for napping, and a powerful audio system for listening to MP3 music files, all for a $12,500 price tag.[19] Marketing research is vital because the marketing concept cannot be implemented without information about customers.

A marketing information system is a framework for accessing information about customers from sources both inside and outside the organization. Inside the organization, there is a continuous flow of information about prices, sales, and expenses. Outside the organization, data are readily available through private or public reports and census statistics, as well as from many other sources. Computer networking technology provides a framework for companies to connect to useful databases and customers with instantaneous information about product acceptance, sales performance, and buying behavior. This information is important to planning and marketing strategy development.

marketing research
a systematic, objective process of getting information about potential customers to guide marketing decisions

Embrace Technology
Look-Look.com

Look-Look.com is an online, real-time service that provides accurate and reliable information, research, news, trends, and photos about global trendsetting youths aged 14 to 30. With youth spending estimated at $140 billion annually and growing, many companies are willing to pay an annual subscription fee of about $20,000 for access to this valuable data.

Look-Look pays more than 20,000 handpicked, prescreened young people from all over the world to e-mail information about their styles, trends, opinions, and ideas. These trendsetting young people are forward thinkers, innovative, and influential to their peers. Although trendsetters account for only about 20 percent of the youth population, they influence the other 80 percent. Look-Look also has 20 photographers who travel the globe capturing youth trends in photos.

Look-Look clients have instant access to online surveys and polls and the results. They also can key in research questions and instantly reach a worldwide focus group 24 hours a day. Clients include an apparel company, video game manufacturers, a cosmetics company, beverage firms, and movie studios. Look-Look delivers fast, accurate, and timely information through the Internet and the company's own intranet and database.

Look-Look co-presidents DeeDee Gordon and Sharon Lee believe that full understanding of the youth culture requires a constant dialog with youth—not just once- or twice-a-year focus groups or market research. Look-Look provides information on the latest in fashion, entertainment, technology, activities, eating and drinking habits, health and beauty, mind-set, and City Guide (the best shops, hangouts, and restaurants in selected cities). The "living research" provided by Look-Look means they never stop listening and observing and that their information is alive and always moving. Whether it's cropped cherry red hair, skintight leather hip-huggers, tattoos, or body piercing, Look-Look knows what the youth market likes, and for a fee, they'll help youth marketers stay on top of the latest trends.[20]

Discussion Questions

1. Why does Look-Look.com develop data about trendsetting youths?
2. What types of data does Look-Look.com develop to capture the attitudes, behaviors, and activities of trendsetting youths?
3. How do you think companies use the data from Look-Look.com to develop and improve products for young people?

---

primary data
marketing information that is observed, recorded, or collected directly from respondents

Two types of data are usually available to decision makers. **Primary data** are observed, recorded, or collected directly from respondents. If you've ever participated in a telephone survey about a product, recorded your TV viewing habits for A. C. Nielsen or Arbitron, or even responded to a political opinion poll, you provided the researcher with primary data. Primary data must be gathered by researchers who develop a method to observe phenomena or research respondents. Nissan, for example, sent researchers to Montana to stand in hip waders in cold rivers to ask fly-fishermen about what they like and don't like about pickup trucks. The company also sent researchers to hunting expos, gun shows, and other events frequented by pickup truck owners. The results of their "fishing expedition" helped the company better understand the needs and desires of a highly brand-loyal market in order to develop its first full-size pickup, the Titan.[21] Surveys and focus groups are costly and time-consuming, with costs for a single focus group running as high as $20,000. The state of Nebraska used focus groups as part of its effort to develop a formal marketing campaign. Among other things, focus groups suggested the state promote its history and natural beauty.[22] With surveys, respondents are sometimes untruthful in order to avoid seeming foolish or ignorant.

Some methods for marketing research use passive observation of consumer behavior and open-ended questioning techniques. Called ethnographic or observational research, the approach can help marketers determine what consumers really think about their products and how different ethnic or demographic groups react to them. For example, Best Western International Inc. paid 25 couples over age 55 to videotape themselves on cross-country trips. After viewing the tapes, the hotel chain decided that increasing the discount for senior citizens would not attract new customers in this market segment. The tapes revealed that seniors who asked for a better price at check-in did so not because they couldn't afford a higher rate but because they were after the "thrill of the deal."[23]

Secondary data are compiled inside or outside the organization for some purpose other than changing the current situation. Marketers typically use information compiled by the U.S. Census Bureau and other government agencies, databases created by marketing research firms, as well as sales and other internal reports, to gain information about customers.

secondary data information that is compiled inside or outside an organization for some purpose other than changing the current situation

The marketing of products and collecting of data about buying behavior—information on what people actually buy and how they buy it—represents marketing research of the future. New information technologies are changing the way businesses learn about their customers and market their products. Interactive multimedia research, or *virtual testing*, combines sight, sound, and animation to facilitate the testing of concepts as well as packaging and design features for consumer products. Computerization offers a greater degree of flexibility, shortens the staff time involved in data gathering, and cuts marketing research costs. The evolving development of telecommunications and computer technologies is allowing marketing researchers quick and easy access to a growing number of online services and a vast database of potential respondents. Companies spent $258 million on online research in 2000, and that number was expected to rise to $439 million in 2001.[24] Many companies have created private online communities and research panels that bring consumer feedback into the companies 24 hours a day. Hallmark Cards Inc., for example, hosts an online bulletin board for consumers who can chat about anything from holiday decorating ideas to discussions of ill loved ones. Hallmark monitors the bulletin board and breaks in to steer the conversations in a particular direction or to conduct surveys. The consumers who participate receive Hallmark gifts every month. The payoff for Hallmark has been ideas for new cards and an entire new product line.

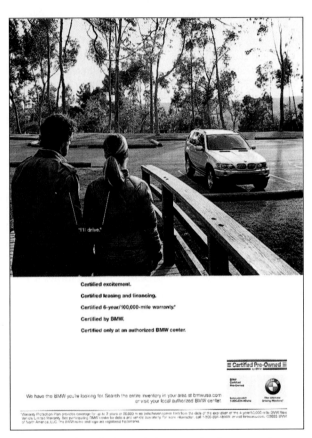

Market research can lead to a whole new market for your product. BMW targets a lower income consumer than its typical high-end one by selling "certified" used BMWs at a lower cost, but still with the BMW brand recognition and expectation.

Other companies are finding that quicker, less-expensive online market research is helping them develop products faster and with greater assurance that the products will be successful. The CEO of Stonyfield Farm (maker of higher-priced yogurt) is convinced that Web feedback saved his company from a multimillion-dollar mistake. The online responses from 105 women caused the company to scrap the name originally planned for its new yogurt from YoFemme (which the respondents did not like) to YoSelf (to which the respondents voted yes).[25]

Solve the Dilemma
Will It Go?

Ventura Motors makes mid-sized and luxury automobiles in the United States. Best-selling models include its basic four-door sedans (priced from $20,000 to $25,000) and two-door and four-door luxury automobiles (priced from $40,000 to $55,000). The success of two-seat sports cars like the Mazda RX-8 started the company evaluating the market for a two-seat sports car priced midway between the moderate and luxury market. Research found that there was indeed significant demand and that Ventura needed to act quickly to take advantage of this market opportunity.

Ventura took the platform of the car from a popular model in its moderate line, borrowing the internal design from its luxury line. The car was designed, engineered, and produced in just over two years, but the coordination needed to bring the design together resulted in higher than anticipated costs. The price for this two-seat car, the Olympus, was set at $32,000. Dealers were anxious to take delivery on the car, and salespeople were well trained on techniques to sell this new model.

However, initial sales have been slow, and company executives are surprised and concerned. The Olympus was introduced relatively quickly, made available at all Ventura dealers, priced midway between luxury and moderate models, and advertised heavily since its introduction.

Discussion Questions

1. What do you think were the main concerns with the Olympus two-door sports coupe? Is there a market for a two-seat, $32,000 sports car when the RX-8 sells for significantly less?
2. Evaluate the role of the marketing mix in the Olympus introduction.
3. What are some of the marketing strategies auto manufacturers use to stimulate sales of certain makes of automobiles?

Buying Behavior

Carrying out the marketing concept is impossible unless marketers know what, where, when, and how consumers buy; marketing research into the factors that influence buying behavior helps marketers develop effective marketing strategies. **Buying behavior** refers to the decision processes and actions of people who purchase and use products. It includes the behavior of both consumers purchasing products for personal or household use as well as organizations buying products for business use. Marketers analyze buying behavior because a firm's marketing strategy should be guided by an understanding of buyers.

Both psychological and social variables are important to an understanding of buying behavior.

Psychological Variables of Buying Behavior

Psychological factors include the following:

- **Perception** is the process by which a person selects, organizes, and interprets information received from his or her senses, as when hearing an advertisement on the radio or touching a product to better understand it.
- Motivation, as we said in Chapter 10, is an inner drive that directs a person's behavior toward goals. A customer's behavior is influenced by a set of motives rather than by a single motive. A buyer of a home computer, for example, may be motivated by ease of use, ability to communicate with the office, and price.
- **Learning** brings about changes in a person's behavior based on information and experience. If a person's actions result in a reward, he or she is likely to behave the same way in similar situations. If a person's actions bring about a negative result, however—such as feeling ill after eating at a certain restaurant—he or she will probably not repeat that action.

buying behavior
the decision processes and actions of people who purchase and use products

perception
the process by which a person selects, organizes, and interprets information received from his or her senses

learning
changes in a person's behavior based on information and experience

- **Attitude** is knowledge and positive or negative feelings about something. For example, a person who feels strongly about protecting the environment may refuse to buy products that harm the earth and its inhabitants.
- **Personality** refers to the organization of an individual's distinguishing character traits, attitudes, or habits. Although market research on the relationship between personality and buying behavior has been inconclusive, some marketers believe that the type of car or clothing a person buys reflects his or her personality.

Social Variables of Buying Behavior

Social factors include **social roles**, which are a set of expectations for individuals based on some position they occupy. A person may have many roles: mother, wife, student, executive. Each of these roles can influence buying behavior. Consider a woman choosing an automobile. Her father advises her to buy a safe, gasoline-efficient car, such as a Volvo. Her teenaged daughter wants her to buy a cool car, such as a Pontiac GTO; her young son wants her to buy a Ford Explorer to take on camping trips. Some of her colleagues at work say she should buy a hybrid vehicle to help the environment. Thus, in choosing which car to buy, the woman's buying behavior may be affected by the opinions and experiences of her family and friends and by her roles as mother, daughter, and employee.

Other social factors include reference groups, social classes, and culture.

- **Reference groups** include families, professional groups, civic organizations, and other groups with whom buyers identify and whose values or attitudes they adopt. A person may use a reference group as a point of comparison or a source of information. A person new to a community may ask other group members to recommend a family doctor, for example.
- **Social classes** are determined by ranking people into higher or lower positions of respect. Criteria vary from one society to another. People within a particular social class may develop common patterns of behavior. People in the upper-middle class, for example, might buy a Lexus or a Cadillac as a symbol of their social class.
- **Culture** is the integrated, accepted pattern of human behavior, including thought, speech, beliefs, actions, and artifacts. Culture determines what people wear and eat and where they live and travel. Many Hispanic Texans and New Mexicans, for example, buy *masa trigo,* a flour mixture used to prepare tortillas, which are basic to Mexican cuisine.

attitude
knowledge and positive or negative feelings about something

personality
the organization of an individual's distinguishing character traits, attitudes, or habits

social roles
a set of expectations for individuals based on some position they occupy

reference groups
groups with whom buyers identify and whose values or attitudes they adopt

Grocery stores often have sections devoted to ethnic foods for Asian, Mexican, or Polish cooking that relates directly to their culture.

social classes
a ranking of people into higher or lower positions of respect

culture
the integrated, accepted pattern of human behavior, including thought, speech, beliefs, actions, and artifacts

Understanding Buying Behavior

Although marketers try to understand buying behavior, it is extremely difficult to explain exactly why a buyer purchases a particular product. The tools and techniques for analyzing consumers are not exact. Marketers may not be able to determine accurately what is highly satisfying to buyers, but they know that trying to understand consumer wants and needs is the best way to satisfy them. In an attempt to better understand consumer behavior, Procter & Gamble sent video crews into about 80 households all around the world. The company, maker of Tide, Crest, Pampers, and many other consumer products, hoped to gain insights into the lifestyles and habits of young couples, families with children, and empty nesters. Participants were taped over a four-day period and were paid about $200–$250 a day. The behaviors caught on tape may lead the company to develop new products or change existing ones to better meet consumers' needs and give the company a competitive advantage over its rivals.[26]

The Marketing Environment

A number of external forces directly or indirectly influence the development of marketing strategies; the following political, legal, regulatory, social, competitive, economic, and technological forces comprise the marketing environment.

- *Political, legal, and regulatory forces*—laws and regulators' interpretation of laws; law enforcement and regulatory activities; regulatory bodies, legislators and legislation, and political actions of interest groups. Specific laws, for example, require that advertisements be truthful and that all health claims be documented.
- *Social forces*—the public's opinions and attitudes toward issues such as living standards, ethics, the environment, lifestyles, and quality of life. For example, social concerns have led marketers to design and market safer toys for children.
- *Competitive and economic forces*—competitive relationships, unemployment, purchasing power, and general economic conditions (prosperity, recession, depression, recovery, product shortages, and inflation).
- *Technological forces*—computers and other technological advances that improve distribution, promotion, and new-product development.

Marketing environment forces can change quickly and radically, which is one reason marketing requires creativity and a customer focus. Because these forces are interconnected, changes in one may cause changes in others. Consider that because of evidence linking children's consumption of soft drinks and fast foods to health issues such as obesity, diabetes, and osteoporosis, marketers of such products have experienced negative publicity and calls for legislation regulating the sale of soft drinks in public schools. When Morgan Spurlock saw an evening news story about two teenagers who unsuccessfully sued McDonald's for their poor health, he decided to make the movie *Super Size Me*. As director, he went on a supersized diet of fast food and gained 25 pounds, suffered from depression, and experienced heart pain.[27] Some companies have responded to these concerns by reformulating products to make them healthier. PepsiCo, for example, has begun removing trans fats—which have been linked to heart disease—from its Frito-Lay snack foods, while the Ruby Tuesday restaurant chain switched to frying with canola oil, which does not contain trans fats, and began offering low-carbohydrate menu items.[28]

Changes in knowledge, attitudes, and consumer behavior may affect an entire industry if product acceptance patterns change as well. This is occurring in the food industry with the growing acceptance of low-carbohydrate diets. The Atkins, South Beach, and other "low-carb" diets have advanced the sales of protein-rich foods while curbing sales of traditionally carbohydrate-rich foods such as breads, pastas, fruit, potatoes, and beans. Roughly 10 percent of the U.S. population follows the Atkins or other low-carb diets, fueling an increase in sales for marketers of eggs, cheese, and meat. The beef industry alone saw sales escalate by 10 percent in 2003.

Some industries have suffered as a result of the "Atkins phenomena," including the orange juice, tortilla, bread, pasta, and wheat industries. Orange juice marketers, for example, attribute a 2.7 percent drop in consumption to the low-carb trend, while the North American Millers Association blame it for dropping annual flour consumption to 137 pounds per person from its peak in 1997 of 147 pounds per person. Dry pasta sales peaked in 2001 and have seen declines in recent years. Negative publicity about the carbohydrate levels of these products has hurt sales. Donut sales have also suffered as evidenced by a decline in Krispy Kreme stores' average weekly sales for the first time since the donut firm went public.

Many other food companies have benefited from the trend by developing and promoting low-carb bagels, tortillas and even beer. In particular, the low-carb craze has created an enormous opportunity for Atkins Nutritionals, which now markets 120 products and licenses numerous other products to dozens of companies. Restaurant chain TGIFriday's, for example, has introduced an Atkins-endorsed menu at restaurants across the United States. In recent years, there has been little growth in the food industry, and Atkins commands the lion's share of that growth.

Public relations has been a key tactic used by the beef industry as well as other low-carb food marketers to capitalize on the trend. Brochures, sponsorships, and scientific reports increase consumers' awareness and acceptance of the benefits of these products as part of a low-carb diet. Consumers are getting their information on the merits of the Atkins diet from books, news stories, and word of mouth. Indeed, publicity has been the main vehicle through which consumers have learned about low-carb food products. All the advertising and public relations has been enhanced by favorable word-of-mouth communication about the benefits and successes of the Atkins diet.[29]

Discussion Questions
1. Why is the low-carb diet an environmental force that influences marketing?
2. How can businesses that view the low-carb diet as a threat respond and maintain their sales?
3. In what industries or types of businesses have the low-carb diet trend required adjustments?

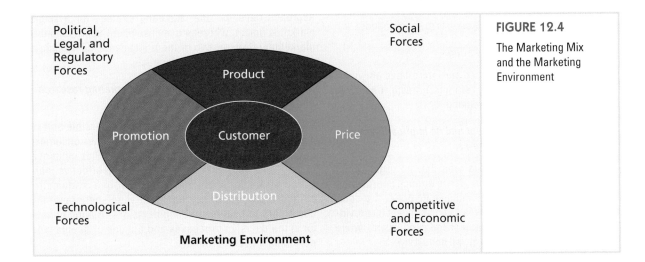

FIGURE 12.4

The Marketing Mix and the Marketing Environment

Although the forces in the marketing environment are sometimes called uncontrollables, they are not totally so. A marketing manager can influence some environmental variables. For example, businesses can lobby legislators to dissuade them from passing unfavorable legislation. Figure 12.4 shows the variables in the marketing environment that affect the marketing mix and the buyer.

Explore Your Career Options
Customer Service in a Service Economy

As you prepare to enter the workplace, you should be aware of how the environment is changing. A major part of your professional development will occur as a result of your ability to respond and adapt to some of these changes. One of the changes that exists today is that we are now living in a service economy. The focus on service means that the jobs available to you will probably require both good product knowledge and an ability to communicate well to customers about how the product can benefit them. Your skills in relating to others are critical to success in your career.

The increased focus on customer service presents opportunities for you in providing superior service to customers. Customer service involves providing what customers need in the best way possible so that they will keep coming back to your company for the products and services they need. Good customer service also helps attract new customers. Typical positions in this area will involve customer service training, customer service management, customer satisfaction, and the like. The average salary for a customer service manager is $57,200. Quality, another major movement, goes hand-in-hand with customer satisfaction. Keeping the company as the number-one choice among customers requires the constant improvement of products and service to ensure that they are of high quality.

To prepare yourself for a career in customer service and customer satisfaction, you may want to major in marketing with a minor in psychology or sociology. Also beneficial will be a class in consumer behavior, as it will enable you to better understand the purchasers.[30]

Review Your Understanding

Define marketing and describe the exchange process.

Marketing is a group of activities designed to expedite transactions by creating, distributing, pricing, and promoting goods, services, and ideas. Marketing facilitates the exchange, the act of giving up one thing in return for something else. The central focus of marketing is to satisfy needs.

Specify the functions of marketing.

Marketing includes many varied and interrelated activities: buying, selling, transporting, storing, grading, financing, marketing research, and risk taking.

Explain the marketing concept and its implications for developing marketing strategies.

The marketing concept is the idea that an organization should try to satisfy customers' needs through coordinated activities that also allow it to achieve its goals. If a company does not implement the marketing concept by providing products that consumers need and want while achieving its own objectives, it will not survive.

Examine the development of a marketing strategy, including market segmentation and marketing mix.

A marketing strategy is a plan of action for creating a marketing mix (product, price, distribution, promotion) for a specific target market (a specific group of consumers on whose needs and wants a company focuses its marketing efforts). Some firms use a total-market approach, designating everyone as the target market. Most firms divide the total market into segments of people who have relatively similar product needs. A company using a concentration approach develops one marketing strategy for a single market segment, whereas a multisegment approach aims marketing efforts at two or more segments, developing a different marketing strategy for each.

Investigate how marketers conduct marketing research and study buying behavior.

Carrying out the marketing concept is impossible unless marketers know what, where, when, and how consumers buy; marketing research into the factors that influence buying behavior helps marketers develop effective marketing strategies. Marketing research is a systematic, objective process of getting information about potential customers to guide marketing decisions. Buying behavior is the decision processes and actions of people who purchase and use products.

Summarize the environmental forces that influence marketing decisions.

There are several forces that influence marketing activities: political, legal, regulatory, social, competitive, economic, and technological.

Assess a company's marketing plans and propose a solution for resolving its problem.

Based on the material in this chapter, you should be able to answer the questions posed in the "Solve the Dilemma" box on page 362 and help the business understand what went wrong and how to correct it.

Revisit the World of Business

1. How has Apple used marketing to make the iPod so successful?
2. With just 10 cents per tune in profits, what are the marketing considerations for making music available for download?
3. What are some of the things Apple does to create publicity about its products?

Learn the Terms

attitude   363
buying behavior   362
concentration approach   355
culture   363
distribution   358
exchange   349
learning   362
market   354
market segment   355
market segmentation   355

marketing   348
marketing concept   350
marketing mix   357
marketing orientation   352
marketing research   359
marketing strategy   353
multisegment approach   355
perception   362
personality   363
price   357

primary data   360
promotion   358
reference groups   363
secondary data   361
social classes   363
social roles   363
target market   354
total-market approach   355

Check Your Progress

1. What is marketing? How does it facilitate exchanges?
2. Name the functions of marketing. How does an organization use marketing activities to achieve its objectives?
3. What is the marketing concept? Why is it so important?
4. What is a marketing strategy?
5. What is market segmentation? Describe three target market strategies.
6. List the variables in the marketing mix. How is each used in a marketing strategy?
7. Why are marketing research and information systems important to an organization's planning and development of strategy?
8. Briefly describe the factors that influence buying behavior. How does understanding buying behavior help marketers?
9. Discuss the impact of technological forces and political and legal forces on the market.

Get Involved

1. With some or all of your classmates, watch several hours of television, paying close attention to the commercials. Pick three commercials for products with which you are somewhat familiar. Based on the commercials, determine who the target market is. Can you surmise the marketing strategy for each of the three?
2. Discuss the decision process and influences involved in purchasing a personal computer.

Build Your Skills

THE MARKETING MIX

Background:
You've learned the four variables—product, promotion, price, and distribution—that the marketer can select to achieve specific goals within a dynamic marketing environment. This exercise will give you an opportunity to analyze the marketing strategies of some well-known companies to determine which of the variables received the most emphasis to help the company achieve its goals.

Task:
In groups of three to five students, discuss the examples below and decide which variable received the most emphasis.

A.   Product

B.   Distribution

C.   Promotion

D.   Price

_____ **1.**   Starbucks Coffee began selling bagged premium specialty coffee through an agreement with Kraft Foods to gain access to more than 30,000 supermarkets.

_____ **2.**   America Online (AOL) offers 24-hour, 9-cents-per-minute long-distance telephone service for AOL Internet customers who will provide their credit card number and receive bills and information about their account online.

_____ **3.**   With 150,000 advance orders, Apple Computer launched the iMac computer with a $100 million advertising budget to obtain first-time computer buyers who could get Internet access by just plugging in the computer.

_____ **4.**   After more than 35 years on the market, WD-40 is in about 80 percent of U.S. households—more than any other branded product. Although WD-40 is promoted as a product that can stop squeaks, protect metal, loosen rusted parts, and free sticky mechanisms, the WD-40 Company has received letters from customers who have sprayed the product on bait to attract fish, on pets to cure mange, and even on people to cure arthritis. Despite more than 200 proposals to expand the WD-40 product line and ideas to change the packaging and labeling, the company stands firmly behind its one highly successful and respected original product.

_____ **5.**   Southwest Airlines makes flying fun. Flight attendants try to entertain passengers, and the airline has an impeccable customer service record. Employees play a key role and take classes that emphasize that having fun translates into great customer service.

_____ **6.**   Hewlett Packard offered a $100 rebate on a $799 HP LaserJet printer when purchased with an HP LaserJet toner cartridge. To receive the rebate, the buyer had to return a mail-in certificate to certify the purchase. A one-page ad with a coupon was used in *USA Today* stating, "We're taking $100 off the top."

_____ **7.**   Denny's, the largest full-service family restaurant chain in the United States, serves more than 1 million customers a day. The restaurants offer the Grand Slam Breakfast for about $3, lunch basket specials for $4–6, and a dinner of prime rib for about $7.

e-Xtreme Surfing

See for Yourself Videocase

FISHING FOR SUCCESS: THE PIKE PLACE FISH MARKET

It has been almost 100 years since the Pike Place Market opened in Seattle. In response to rising produce costs and concerns that farmers were being deprived of their just return by middlemen—a pound of onions rose from 10 cents to $1 in just one year—the market opened so that consumers could buy directly from farmers. On opening day, eight farmers merged on the corner of First and Pike, and more than 10,000 eager buyers showed up to choose from their wares.

Today, the Pike Place Market is much more than its name suggests. Covering roughly nine acres, the market comprises food stores (bakeries, dairies, fish/seafood, commercial produce stands, meat and butcher shops, produce stands, specialty food stores as well as restaurants, cafés, and fast-food businesses) and mercantile shops (antiques and collectibles, art galleries, books, stationery and cards, clothing and shoes, cookware, and flowers) with over 100 vendors operating each day. One of the more popular shops is Uli's Famous Sausage, which produces all-natural sausages made fresh daily. Uli's even offers a "salmon sausage" to hark back to the market's origin. Another popular vendor is the Pike Place Fish Market, which has appeared on numerous cooking television shows. In recent years, retail sales from the Pike Place Market's food stores have exceeded $48.5 million and mercantile sales, more $13 million. Summer season daily visitations are around 27,000 for a weekday and more than 40,000 on Saturdays.

In 1965, John Yokoyama, an employee of a local fish stand inside the market, decided to buy it. He was just 25 years old at the time, and he bought the Pike Place Fish Market to help make the $150 payments on his new Buick Riviera. He thought his income as an owner would be greater than that as an employee. As an owner, Yokoyama brought to the fish market a process and idea for making it a success. He asked, "Who do we want to be?" After talking with employees, one of whom said he wanted the Pike Place Market to be "World Famous," Yokoyama and his employees became committed to this end. "World Famous" was added to all of the shipping boxes. To the employees, "World Famous" meant more than great service, it meant leaving each customer with a true feeling of "being served." The idea was to customize service and relate to each customer one on one.

To get people to notice the fish market, fishmongers stand at the entrance to the market in front of cases of Dungeness crabs and Alaskan sockeye salmon and throw fish from one employee to another. Employees behind the counter banter and shout, "Anyone here to buy some fish?" Tourists and shoppers cheer and cameras flash.

Perhaps the most unique characteristic of Pike Place Fish Market is the fact that, except for a Web site, it has never advertised. If you look on the fish market's Web site, you can read numerous articles that have been written about the company in local newspapers and national newspapers, magazines, and travel guides such as *Frommer's*. The fish market also receives positive publicity every time it is featured on a Food TV channel cooking show. In fact, the company receives more media coverage than most large companies that spend millions on advertising. Such publicity is far more valuable than advertising because it is not a paid placement. The public relations generated is the result of unique, strong business practices that consumers want to read about.

Pike Place Market was featured on the QVC shopping network in a two-hour live broadcast. Of the 13,000 vendors that try to get on QVC every year, just 2–3 percent "make the cut." From Pike Place Market, the featured vendors were Pike Place Fish Market, Uli's Famous Sausage, Seattle's Best Coffee, Chukar Cherry Co., and Ivar's seafood, as well as a couple of cookbooks. Reaching roughly 85 million homes, the coverage generated greater awareness of Seattle's most famous shopping venue and exposed many of the more unique brands available. Inside the market, the Pike Place Fish Market continues to be successful due to the astute marketing and employee-relations decisions made by John Yokoyama. With a vision of what a successful product experience should be, the respect and inclusion of his employees in the venture to help deliver great service, and with a creativity to make his business generate publicity Yokoyama has created a marketing phenomenon in Seattle and truly become "World Famous."[31]

Discussion Questions

1. What do you think is the key marketing variable that contributed to John Yokoyama's success (pricing, product, promotion, or distribution) at the Pike Place Fish Market?

2. Would you recommend that the Pike Place Fish Market engage in advertising? Why or why not?

3. What role do programs like QVC play in helping smaller businesses, such as the Pike Place Fish Market, in reaching their marketing goals?

Remember to check out our Online Learning Center at www.mhhe.com/ferrell5e.

Chapter 13

Dimensions of Marketing Strategy

OBJECTIVES

After reading this chapter, you will be able to:

- Describe the role of product in the marketing mix, including how products are developed, classified, and identified.

- Define price and discuss its importance in the marketing mix, including various pricing strategies a firm might employ.

- Identify factors affecting distribution decisions, such as marketing channels and intensity of market coverage.

- Specify the activities involved in promotion, as well as promotional strategies and promotional positioning.

- Evaluate an organization's marketing strategy plans.

Turkey & Gravy Brings Attention to Small Bottler

Jones Soda Co. manufactures premium soft drinks known for creative flavors, labels, and promotions that clearly differentiate them from mass-market offerings by Coca-Cola and Pepsi. Seattle-based Jones Soda Co. continuously promotes its premium brand and regularly changes flavors and labels, which include photos sent in by customers. Customers can even suggest new flavors to Jones on the company's Web site.

Despite its reputation for curious flavors, Jones's management was surprised by the deluge of publicity generated by the release of a turkey-and-gravy-flavored soft drink near Thanksgiving. The company produced just a few thousand bottles of the seasonal flavor as part of a promotional campaign to draw attention to its other soft drinks. Turkey & Gravy Soda sold out in a matter of hours, perhaps because it seemed fun,

continued

unique, and timely. Although product developers at Jones characterized the product as a sipping soda rather than a thirst-satisfying one, the timing of its holiday release helped fuel its success.

One thing is clear about Turkey & Gravy Soda: people loved talking about the soft drink that was purported to taste like "microwaved Thanksgiving leftovers." In the three weeks following its introduction, the company's president, Peter van Stolk, was contacted more than 500 times by the media, resulting in nearly 100 radio interviews. Even *Business Week* acknowledged the product. Jones was particularly pleased with the radio publicity generated by Turkey & Gravy Soda because the company's target market is teenagers who are known to be devoted radio listeners.

In the case of this novelty product, it is doubtful that paid advertising could have generated nearly as much interest in the curiously flavored soft drink as this buzz marketing approach. Indeed, Turkey & Gravy Soda has been Jones's most successful promotion to date, exceeding the impact of previous promotions associated with flavors such as "Cured Ham" and "Fish-Taco." van Stolk further maximized the public relations impact by mentioning in every radio interview that the company planned to donate all profits from Turkey & Gravy Soda to the Toys for Tots charity. Such creativity in marketing certainly seems to have paid off for Jones Soda: its sales have doubled over the last four years, going from $11 million to $20 million.[1]

Introduction

As Jones Soda Company's success illustrates, creating an effective marketing strategy is important. Getting just the right mix of product, price, promotion, and distribution is critical if a business is to satisfy its target customers and achieve its own objectives (implement the marketing concept).

In Chapter 12, we introduced the concept of marketing and the various activities important in developing a marketing strategy. In this chapter, we'll take a closer look at the four dimensions of the marketing mix—product, price, distribution, and promotion—used to develop the marketing strategy. The focus of these marketing mix elements is a marketing strategy that builds customer relationships and satisfaction.

The Marketing Mix

The key to developing a marketing strategy is maintaining the right marketing mix that satisfies the target market and creates long-term relationships with customers.

To develop meaningful customer relationships, marketers have to develop and manage the dimensions of the marketing mix to give their firm an advantage over competitors. Successful companies offer at least one dimension of value that surpasses all competi-

Did You Know? Domino's Pizza delivery drivers cover 9 million miles a year delivering 400 million pizzas.[2]

tors in the marketplace in meeting customer expectations. However, this does not mean that a company can ignore the other dimensions of the marketing mix; it must maintain acceptable, and if possible distinguishable, differences in the other dimensions as well.

Wal-Mart, for example, emphasizes price ("Always low prices"). Procter & Gamble is well known for its promotion of top consumer brands such as Tide, Cheer, Crest, Ivory, Head & Shoulders, and Folgers. Domino's Pizza is recognized for its superiority in distribution after developing the largest home-delivery pizza company in the world and its innovative new product introductions.

Domino's HeatWave® hot bags changed the face of pizza delivery. While not a new pizza, the bag was a unique innovation that gave Domino's a competitive edge.

Product Strategy

As mentioned previously, the term *product* refers to goods, services, and ideas. Because the product is often the most visible of the marketing mix dimensions, managing product decisions is crucial. In this section, we'll consider product development, classification, mix, life cycle, and identification.

Developing New Products

Each year thousands of products are introduced, but few of them succeed. Coca-Cola, for example, invested more than $50 million to develop and introduce the iFountain, a soft-drink dispenser marketed to restaurants as a "mini-manufacturing plant." Plagued by quality issues, however, the dispensers were installed in relatively few locations, and most of those have since been removed.[3] A firm can take considerable time to get a product ready for the market: It took more than 20 years for the first photocopier, for example. General Motors has trimmed the time required to develop and introduce a new vehicle model from four years to 18 months. The automaker plans to release 29 new models, many with innovative designs, over a 16-month period.[4] Before introducing a new product, a business must follow a multistep process: idea development, the screening of new ideas, business analysis, product development, test marketing, and commercialization.

Idea Development.   New ideas can come from marketing research, engineers, and outside sources such as advertising agencies and management consultants. Microsoft has a separate division—Microsoft Research—where scientists devise technology of the future. The division has 500 full-time employees who work in a university-like research atmosphere. Research teams then present their ideas to Microsoft engineers who are developing specific products. As we said in Chapter 12, ideas sometimes come from customers, too. Other sources are brainstorming and intracompany incentives or rewards for good ideas. New ideas can even create a company. Las Vegas–based Shufflemaster, for example, grew out of entrepreneur Mark Breeding's card-shuffling machine. The Shuffle Master is on 12,000 of the 40,000 tables in casinos around the world.[5]

Coca-Cola's new C2 beverage is its first brand new entry into the market since the introduction of Diet Coke. C2 purports to have half the carbohydrates, calories, and sugar of regular cola, and "all the great taste." It will be the marketer's most expensive advertising push since it rolled out Diet Coke 22 years ago.

New Idea Screening.   The next step in developing a new product is idea screening. In this phase, a marketing manager should look at the organization's resources and objectives and assess the firm's ability to produce and market the product. Important aspects to be considered at this stage are consumer desires, the competition, technological changes, social trends, and political, economic, and environmental considerations. Basically, there are two reasons new products succeed: They are able to meet a need or solve a problem better than products already available or they add variety to the product selection currently on the market. Oscar Mayer's Lunchables have been very successful for both reasons. They solve the everyday problem of what to pack in a lunchbox, and they provide a wide variety of deli meats, sandwiches, tacos, and pizza. Most new-product ideas are rejected during screening because they seem inappropriate or impractical for the organization.

Business Analysis.   Business analysis is a basic assessment of a product's compatibility in the marketplace and its potential profitability. Both the size of the market and competing products are often studied at this point. The most important question relates to market demand: How will the product affect the firm's sales, costs, and profits?

**Market Decisions
Test Market Locations**

FIGURE 13.1

ACNielsen Market
Decisions

Source: "Test Marketing,"
ACNielsen (n.d),
**www.acnielsen.com/services/
testing/test1.htm** (accessed
June 5, 2004). Reprinted with
permission of ACNielsen
Market Decisions.

◆ **Permanent Test Markets
("Data Markets")**

★ **Additional "Custom" Test Markets**

Product Development.   If a product survives the first three steps, it is developed into a prototype that should reveal the intangible attributes it possesses as perceived by the consumer. Product development is often expensive, and few product ideas make it to this stage. New product research and development costs vary. Adding a new color to an existing item may cost $100,000 to $200,000, but launching a completely new product can cost millions of dollars. The Coca-Cola Co. reduced the time and cost of product development research by 50 percent when it created an on-line panel of 100 teenagers and asked them how to remake its Powerade sports drink.[6] During product development, various elements of the marketing mix must be developed for testing. Copyrights, tentative advertising copy, packaging, labeling, and descriptions of a target market are integrated to develop an overall marketing strategy.

Test Marketing.   **Test marketing** is a trial minilaunch of a product in limited areas that represent the potential market. It allows a complete test of the marketing strategy in a natural environment, giving the organization an opportunity to discover weaknesses and eliminate them before the product is fully launched. ACNielsen assists companies in test-marketing their products. Figure 13.1 shows the permanent sites as well as custom locations for test marketing.

test marketing
a trial minilaunch of a product in limited areas that represent the potential market

Commercialization.   **Commercialization** is the full introduction of a complete marketing strategy and the launch of the product for commercial success. During commercialization, the firm gears up for full-scale production, distribution, and promotion. When Volvo launched its second-generation S40 sedan, it employed hip-hop music, video game graphics, and images of the car spinning and crashing (with nary a scratch) to appeal to a younger target market. The car's $24,000 base price also appeals to 25- to 34-year-old drivers. Volvo executives hope these efforts will help the

commercialization
the full introduction of a complete marketing strategy and the launch of the product for commercial success

Newspapers are a convenience product, bought frequently, without a lengthy search, and for relatively immediate consumption.

company keep these younger customers for life by providing larger sedans, SUVs, and sports cars to meet their needs down the road.[7]

Classifying Products

Products are usually classified as either consumer products or industrial products. **Consumer products** are for household or family use; they are not intended for any purpose other than daily living. They can be further classified as convenience products, shopping products, and specialty products on the basis of consumers' buying behavior and intentions.

- *Convenience products,* such as eggs, milk, bread, and newspapers, are bought frequently, without a lengthy search, and often for immediate consumption. Consumers spend virtually no time planning where to purchase these products and usually accept whatever brand is available.

- *Shopping products,* such as furniture, audio equipment, clothing, and sporting goods, are purchased after the consumer has compared competitive products and "shopped around." Price, product features, quality, style, service, and image all influence the decision to buy.

- *Specialty products,* such as ethnic foods, designer clothing and shoes, art, and antiques, require even greater research and shopping effort. Consumers know what they want and go out of their way to find it; they are not willing to accept a substitute.

consumer products
products intended for household or family use

business products
products that are used directly or indirectly in the operation or manufacturing processes of businesses

Business products are used directly or indirectly in the operation or manufacturing processes of businesses. They are usually purchased for the operation of an organization or the production of other products; thus, their purchase is tied to specific goals and objectives. They too can be further classified:

- *Raw materials* are natural products taken from the earth, oceans, and recycled solid waste. Iron ore, bauxite, lumber, cotton, and fruits and vegetables are examples.

- *Major equipment* covers large, expensive items used in production. Examples include earth-moving equipment, stamping machines, and robotic equipment used on auto assembly lines.

- *Accessory equipment* includes items used for production, office, or management purposes, which usually do not become part of the final product. Computers, fax machines, calculators, and hand tools are examples.

- *Component parts* are finished items, ready to be assembled into the company's final products. Tires, window glass, batteries, and spark plugs are component parts of automobiles.

- *Processed materials* are things used directly in production or management operations but not readily identifiable as component parts. Varnish, for example, is a processed material for a furniture manufacturer.
- *Supplies* include materials that make production, management, and other operations possible, such as paper, pencils, paint, cleaning supplies, and so on.
- *Industrial services* include financial, legal, marketing research, security, janitorial, and exterminating services. Purchasers decide whether to provide these services internally or to acquire them from an outside supplier.

Product Line and Product Mix

Product relationships within an organization are of key importance. A **product line** is a group of closely related products that are treated as a unit because of similar marketing strategy. At Colgate-Palmolive, for example, the oral-care product line includes Colgate toothpaste, toothbrushes, and dental floss. A **product mix** is all the products offered by an organization. Figure 13.2 displays a sampling of the product mix and product lines of the Colgate-Palmolive Company.

product line
a group of closely related products that are treated as a unit because of similar marketing strategy, production, or end-use considerations

product mix
all the products offered by an organization

Product Life Cycle

Like people, products are born, grow, mature, and eventually die. Some products have very long lives. Ivory Soap was introduced in 1879 and is still popular. In contrast, a new computer chip is usually outdated within a year because of technological breakthroughs and rapid changes in the computer industry. There are four stages in the life cycle of a product: introduction, growth, maturity, and decline (Figure 13.3). The stage a product is in helps determine marketing strategy.

In the *introductory stage*, consumer awareness and acceptance of the product are limited, sales are zero, and profits are negative. Profits are negative because the firm has spent money on research, development, and marketing to launch the product. During the introductory stage, marketers focus on making consumers aware of the product and its benefits. When Procter & Gamble introduced the Tide Stainbrush to reach the 70 percent of consumers who pretreat stains when doing laundry, it employed press releases as well as television and magazine advertising to make consumers aware of the new product.[8] Sales accelerate as the product enters the growth stage of the life cycle.

In the *growth stage*, sales increase rapidly and profits peak, then start to decline. One reason profits start to decline during the growth stage is that new companies enter the market, driving prices down and increasing marketing expenses. Consider Apple's iPod, the most popular digital music player with 3 million units sold in its first 30 months. Even with the launch of the iPod Mini, Apple faces growing competition from at least 60 new music players from competing firms. Apple executives hope the success of the firm's iTunes online music service, which accounts for 70 percent of all legal music downloads, will help the iPod hold the line against the growing competition.[9] During the growth stage, the firm tries to strengthen its position in the market by emphasizing the product's benefits and identifying market segments that want these benefits.

Sales continue to increase at the beginning of the *maturity stage*, but then the sales curve peaks and starts to decline while profits continue to decline. This stage is characterized by severe competition and heavy expenditures. Automobiles are an example of a mature product; intense competition in the auto industry

FIGURE 13.2   Colgate-Palmolive's Product Mix and Product Lines

← ——————————————— **Product Mix** ——————————————— →

Oral Care	*Personal Care*	*Household Care*	*Pet Nutrition*
Colgate toothpaste	Speed Stick deodorant	Palmolive dishwashing	Science Diet pet foods
	Lady Speed Stick	liquids	Prescription Diet pet
Colgate toothbrushes	deodorant	Ajax	foods
Colgate Simple White	Crystal Clean deodorant		
products	Teen Spirit deodorant	Crystal White	
Colgate dental floss	Irish Spring soaps	Octagon	
		Palmolive dish wipes	
Colgate Oral First Aid	Soft Soap liquid soaps	Palmolive dishwashing	
products	Colgate shaving cream	detergent	
	Skin Bracer aftershave	Murphy's Oil soap	
	Afta aftershave		
	Palmolive Shower Cream	Fabuloso	

(↕ Product Lines)

Source: "Our Products," Colgate-Palmolive (n.d.), **www.colgate.com/app/Colgate/US/Corp/Products.cvsp** (accessed June 5, 2004).

FIGURE 13.3

The Life Cycle of a Product

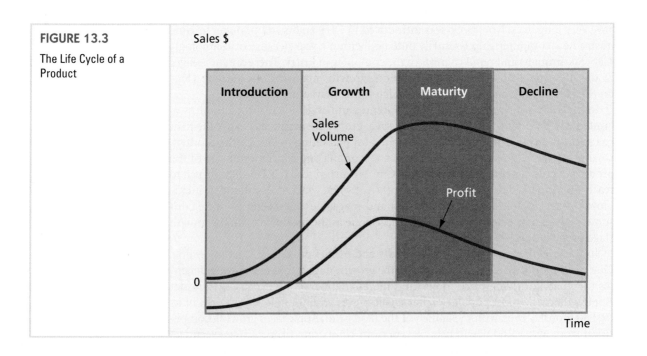

requires Toyota, GM, and other automakers to spend huge sums to make their products stand out in a crowded marketplace.

During the *decline stage,* sales continue to fall rapidly. Profits also decline and may even become losses as prices are cut and necessary marketing expenditures are made. As profits drop, firms may eliminate certain models or items. To reduce ex-

Rank	Brand	2003 Brand Value ($ Billions)
1	Coca-Cola	70.45
2	Microsoft	65.17
3	IBM	51.77
4	GE	42.34
5	Intel	31.11
6	Nokia	29.44
7	Disney	28.04
8	McDonald's	24.70
9	Marlboro	22.18
10	Mercedes	21.37

TABLE 13.1

The 10 Most Valuable Brands in the World

Data: Interbrand

Source: "The 100 Top Brands," *Business Week,* August 4, 2003, via **www.ourfishbowl.com/images/surveys/IB_SV_BIO_8_4_2003.pdf**.

penses and squeeze out any remaining profits, marketing expenditures may be cut back, even though such cutbacks accelerate the sales decline. Finally, plans must be made for phasing out the product and introducing new ones to take its place. In the category of malt-flavored beverages, which were designed to attract women and younger drinkers, 87 million cases were sold in 2002, the peak year. By 2004, Bacardi Silver's sales had dropped by 62.4 percent, Sky Blue's by 58.1 percent, and Smirnoff Ice's, 33 percent. Experts believe the dramatic sales decline signals that only 10 percent, or five individual products, out of the 50 malt-flavored beverages on the market, will survive.[10]

Identifying Products

Branding, packaging, and labeling can be used to identify or distinguish one product from others. As a result, they are key marketing activities that help position a product appropriately for its target market.

Branding.   **Branding** is the process of naming and identifying products. A *brand* is a name, term, symbol, design, or combination that identifies a product and distinguishes it from other products. Consider that Google, iPod, and TiVo are brand names that are used to identify entire product categories, much like Xerox has become synonymous with photocopying and Kleenex with tissues. Protecting a brand name is important in maintaining a brand identity.[11] The world's 10 most valuable brands are shown in Table 13.1. The brand name is the part of the brand that can be spoken and consists of letters, words, and numbers—such as WD-40 lubricant. A *brand mark* is the part of the brand that is a distinctive design, such as the silver star on the hood of a Mercedes or McDonald's golden arches logo. A **trademark** is a brand that is registered with the U.S. Patent and Trademark Office and is thus legally protected from use by any other firm.

branding
the process of naming and identifying products

trademark
a brand that is registered with the U.S. Patent and Trademark Office and is thus legally protected from use by any other firm

Many families appreciate the low prices of generic products.

manufacturer brands
brands initiated and owned by the manufacturer to identify products from the point of production to the point of purchase

private distributor brands
brands, which may cost less than manufacturer brands, that are owned and controlled by a wholesaler or retailer

generic products
products with no brand name that often come in simple packages and carry only their generic name

Two major categories of brands are manufacturer brands and private distributor brands. **Manufacturer brands** are brands initiated and owned by the manufacturer to identify products from the point of production to the point of purchase. Kellogg's, Sony, and Texaco are examples. **Private distributor brands,** which may be less expensive than manufacturer brands, are owned and controlled by a wholesaler or retailer, such as Kenmore appliances (Sears) and Sam's grocery products (Wal-Mart and Sam's Wholesale Club). The names of private brands do not usually identify their manufacturer. The Gap, for example, is repositioning its four-year-old "1969" line of jeans as a premium private-label brand partly by pricing them for $98, double the price of any other Gap jean. Gap managers hope the move will help attract buyers of other high-end jeans from Lucky Brand Dungarees and Diesel USA. Other retailers, including Express and Macy's, are also entering the upscale jeans market with private brands.[12] Manufacturer brands are fighting hard against private distributor brands.

Another type of brand that has developed is **generic products**—products with no brand name at all. They often come in plain simple packages that carry only the generic name of the product—peanut butter, tomato juice, aspirin, dog food, and so on. They appeal to consumers who may be willing to sacrifice quality or product consistency to get a lower price.

Companies use two basic approaches to branding multiple products. In one, a company gives each product within its complete product mix its own brand name. Warner-Lambert, for example, sells many well-known consumer products—Dentyne, Chiclets, Listerine, Halls, Rolaids, and Trident—each individually branded. This branding policy ensures that the name of one product does not affect the names of others, and different brands can be targeted at different segments of the same

Coca-Cola is the most valuable brand in the world.

Coca-Cola's trademark varies from country to country. But the overall look is retained through use of similar letterforms and style, even with different alphabets.

1. Arabic   5. Spanish
2. French   6. Chinese
3. Japanese   7. Hebrew
4. Thai   8. Polish

market, increasing the company's market share (its percentage of the sales for the total market for a product). Another approach to branding is to develop a family of brands with each of the firm's products carrying the same name or at least part of the name. Gillette, Sara Lee, and IBM use this approach.

Packaging. The **packaging,** or external container that holds and describes the product, influences consumers' attitudes and their buying decisions. A survey of over 1,200 consumers found that 40 percent are willing to try a new product based on its packaging.[13] It is estimated that consumers' eyes linger only 2.5 seconds on each product on an average shopping trip; therefore, product packaging should be designed to attract and hold consumers' attention.

A package can perform several functions including protection, economy, convenience, and promotion. Beverage manufacturers have been redesigning their bottles to make them more convenient for consumers and to promote them to certain markets. Scientists videotaped people drinking from different types of bottles and made plaster casts of their hands. They found that the average gulp is 6.44 ounces and that half the population would rather suck liquid through a pop-up

packaging
the external container that holds and describes the product

Packaging can help distinguish a product from its competitors.

top than drink it. Packaging also helps create an overall brand image. Lt. Blender's Margarita in a Bag, for example, is packaged in a unique, strong plastic bag that looks like a hot-water bottle but yields a half gallon of margaritas when liquor is added.[14]

Labeling. **Labeling,** the presentation of important information on the package, is closely associated with packaging. The content of labeling, often required by law, may include ingredients or content, nutrition facts (calories, fat, etc.), care instructions, suggestions for use (such as recipes), the manufacturer's address and toll-free number, Web site, and other useful information. This information can have a strong impact on sales. The labels of many products, particularly food and drugs, must carry warnings, instructions, certifications, or manufacturers' identifications.

Product Quality. **Quality** reflects the degree to which a good, service, or idea meets the demands and requirements of customers. Quality products are often referred to as reliable, durable, easily maintained, easily used, a good value, or a trusted brand name. The level of quality is the amount of quality that a product possesses, and the consistency of quality depends on the product maintaining the same level of quality over time.

Quality of service is difficult to gauge because it depends on customers' perceptions of how well the service meets or exceeds their expectations. In other words, service quality is judged by consumers, not the service providers. A bank may define service quality as employing friendly and knowledgeable employees, but the bank's customers may be more concerned with waiting time, ATM access, security, and statement accuracy. Similarly, an airline traveler considers on-time arrival, on-board food service, and satisfaction with the ticketing and boarding process. The University of Michigan Business School's National Quality Research Center annually surveys customers of more than 200 companies and provides quarterly results for selected industries. The latest results showed that customer satisfaction rose to 67 (out of a possible 100) in nearly all industries covered by the survey, including utilities, hotels, telecommunications, airlines, express mail, and hospitals.[15] Table 13.2 shows the scores for major airlines and the percentage change from 2002. Services are becoming a larger part of international competition.

The quality of services provided by businesses on the Internet can be gauged by consumers on such sites as ConsumerReports.org and BBBOnline. The subscription service offered by ConsumerReports.org provides consumers with a view of e-commerce sites' business, security, and privacy policies. BBBOnline is dedicated to promoting responsibility online. The Web Credibility Project focuses on how health, travel, advocacy, news, and shopping sites disclose business relationships with the companies and products they cover or sell, especially when such relationships pose a potential conflict of interest.[16]

labeling
the presentation of important information on a package

quality
the degree to which a good, service, or idea meets the demands and requirements of customers

	Score*	% Change from Previous Score	TABLE 13.2
Southwest Airlines	75	1.4	Customer Satisfaction
All Others	74	2.8	with Airlines
Continental Airlines	68	0.0	
AMR (American Airlines)	67	6.3	
Delta Air Lines	67	1.5	
USAir Group	64	1.6	
Northwest Airlines	64	−1.5	
UAL (United Airlines)	63	−1.6	

*Possible maximum score is 100.

Source: "First Quarter Scores," ASCI, May 21, 2003, **www.theasci.org/first_quarter.htm#air**.

Pricing Strategy

Previously, we defined price as the value placed on an object exchanged between a buyer and a seller. Buyers' interest in price stems from their expectations about the usefulness of a product or the satisfaction they may derive from it. Because buyers have limited resources, they must allocate those resources to obtain the products they most desire. They must decide whether the benefits gained in an exchange are worth the buying power sacrificed. Almost anything of value can be assessed by a price. Many factors may influence the evaluation of value, including time constraints, price levels, perceived quality, and motivations to use available information about prices.[17] Indeed, consumers vary in their response to price: Some focus solely on the lowest price, while others consider quality or the prestige associated with a product and its price. However, some types of consumers are increasingly "trading up" to more status-conscious products, such as automobiles, home appliances, restaurants, and even pet food, yet remain price-conscious for other products such as cleaning and grocery goods. This trend has benefited marketers such as Starbucks, Sub-Zero, BMW, and Petco—which can charge premium prices for high-quality, prestige products—as well as Sam's Clubs and Costco—which offer basic household products at everyday low prices.[18]

Price is a key element in the marketing mix because it relates directly to the generation of revenue and profits. In large part, the ability to set a price depends on the supply of and demand for a product. For most products, the quantity demanded goes up as the price goes down, and as the price goes up, the quantity demanded goes down. Changes in buyers' needs, variations in the effectiveness of other marketing mix variables, the presence of substitutes, and dynamic environmental factors can influence demand. Consider that gas prices rose dramatically in 2004 in response to tightened petroleum supplies and increasing demand from China and the United States. Sales of large, less fuel-efficient sport utility vehicles began to decline as a result. Of course, price also depends on the cost to manufacture a good or provide a service or idea. A firm may temporarily sell products below cost to match competition, to generate cash flow, or even to increase market share, but in the long run it cannot survive by selling its products below cost.

AFFORDABLE COLOR COPIERS

The Toshiba FC22 color copier boasts our exclusive Color Inline Printing System, which makes it the fastest, smallest and most affordable copier in its class. Delivering an unprecedented 9600x600 dpi color resolution, this champ comes network-capable so you can print remotely and color scan on the fly. In short, it's a whole lot of copier for very little coin. For more information on our copiers, fax machines and printers visit **copiers.toshiba.com**.

TOSHIBA
Don't copy. Lead.

Toshiba positions its copiers based on price.

Price is probably the most flexible variable in the marketing mix. Although it may take years to develop a product, establish channels of distribution, and design and implement promotion, a product's price may be set and changed in a few minutes. Under certain circumstances, of course, the price may not be so flexible, especially if government regulations prevent dealers from controlling prices.

Pricing Objectives

Pricing objectives specify the role of price in an organization's marketing mix and strategy. They usually are influenced not only by marketing mix decisions but also by finance, accounting, and production factors. Maximizing profits and sales, boosting market share, maintaining the status quo, and survival are four common pricing objectives.

Specific Pricing Strategies

Pricing strategies provide guidelines for achieving the company's pricing objectives and overall marketing strategy. They specify how price will be used as a variable in the marketing mix. Significant pricing strategies relate to the pricing of new products, psychological pricing, and price discounting.

Pricing New Products.   Setting the price for a new product is critical: The right price leads to profitability; the wrong price may kill the product. In general, there are two basic strategies to setting the base price for a new product. **Price skimming** is charging the highest possible price that buyers who want the product will pay. The Porsche Cayenne S V8, for example, has a starting price of $56,000, considerably higher than other sport utility vehicles.[19] This strategy allows the company to generate much-needed revenue to help offset the costs of research and development. Conversely, a **penetration price** is a low price designed to help a product enter the market and gain market share rapidly. For example, when Industrias Añaños introduced Kola Real to capitalize on limited supplies of Coca-Cola and Pepsi Cola in Peru, it set an ultralow penetration price to appeal to the poor who predominate in the region. Kola Real quickly secured one-fifth of the Peruvian market and has since made significant gains in Ecuador, Venezuela, and Mexico, forcing larger soft-drink marketers to cut prices.[20] Penetration pricing is less flexible than price skimming; it is more difficult to raise a penetration price than to lower a skimming price. Penetration pricing is used most often when marketers suspect that competitors will enter the market shortly after the product has been introduced.

Psychological Pricing.   **Psychological pricing** encourages purchases based on emotional rather than rational responses to the price. For example, the assumption behind *even/odd pricing* is that people will buy more of a product for $9.99 than $10

price skimming
charging the highest possible price that buyers who want the product will pay

penetration price
a low price designed to help a product enter the market and gain market share rapidly

psychological pricing
encouraging purchases based on emotional rather than rational responses to the price

because it seems to be a bargain at the odd price. The assumption behind *symbolic/ prestige pricing* is that high prices connote high quality. Thus the prices of certain fragrances are set artificially high to give the impression of superior quality. Some over-the-counter drugs are priced high because consumers associate a drug's price with potency.

Price Discounting.   Temporary price reductions, or **discounts,** are often employed to boost sales. Although there are many types, quantity, seasonal, and promotional discounts are among the most widely used. Quantity discounts reflect the economies of purchasing in large volume. Seasonal discounts to buyers who purchase goods or services out of season help even out production capacity. Promotional discounts attempt to improve sales by advertising price reductions on selected products to increase customer interest. Often promotional pricing is geared to increased profits. On the other hand, many companies such as Wal-Mart, Home Depot, and Toys 'Я' Us have shunned promotional price discounts and, with everyday low pricing, are focusing more on relationships with customers. In the airline industry, low-cost airlines like JetBlue, AirTran, Frontier, and America West are competing head-to-head with the major airlines by offering sharply discounted fares. For the Nashville-to-Denver route, for example, Frontier has a three-day advance purchase price of $199, compared to United's $464, although the latter likely will match the discount airline's fare in order to remain competitive. The fare wars sparked by the discounters have led to significant declines on highly competitive routes. On flights from New York's JFK to the West Coast, for example, the entry of JetBlue has forced United and American to reduce fares by as much as 30 percent.[21] Additionally, Web sites like Priceline.com, Orbitz.com, and Travelocity.com help flyers find the lowest fares quickly, forcing airlines to become even more price competitive.

discounts
temporary price reductions, often employed to boost sales

Distribution Strategy

The best products in the world will not be successful unless companies make them available where and when customers want to buy them. In this section, we will explore dimensions of distribution strategy, including the channels through which products are distributed, the intensity of market coverage, and the physical handling of products during distribution.

Marketing Channels

A **marketing channel,** or channel of distribution, is a group of organizations that moves products from their producer to customers. Marketing channels make products available to buyers when and where they desire to purchase them. Organizations that bridge the gap between a product's manufacturer and the ultimate consumer are called *middlemen,* or intermediaries. They create time, place, and ownership utility. Two intermediary organizations are retailers and wholesalers.

Retailers buy products from manufacturers (or other intermediaries) and sell them to consumers for home and household use rather than for resale or for use in producing other products. Toys 'Я' Us, for example, buys products from Mattel and other manufacturers and resells them to consumers. Retailing usually occurs in a store, but the Internet, vending machines, mail-order catalogs, and entertainment, such as going to a Chicago Bulls basketball game, also provide opportunities for retailing. With more than 200 million Americans accessing the Internet, online sales are expected to reach $120 billion in 2004.[22] By bringing together an assortment of

marketing channel
a group of organizations that moves products from their producer to customers; also called a channel of distribution

retailers
intermediaries who buy products from manufacturers (or other intermediaries) and sell them to consumers for home and household use rather than for resale or for use in producing other products

Although studies suggest that Americans still eat 75 percent of their meals at home, they are apparently cooking less. The percentage of American households that cooked two or more times a day dropped from 35.9 percent in 1993 to 32.1 percent in 2001. Today, just over a third of all dinner entrees are completely homemade, and of these, 6.9 percent are sandwiches. As American lifestyles change, food consumption patterns are changing along with them. More families can afford to eat out more because personal income has increased while food prices have declined. Moreover, in families where both parents work full-time, parents would rather spend their spare time enjoying a meal with their families than cleaning up the kitchen. Thus, options like takeout food from a restaurant or prepared food from a supermarket that facilitates family meals have become more desirable. Even busy singles find these options appetizing: daily cooking in single-person households declined from 62.6 percent in 1993 to 57.8 percent in 2001.

Supermarkets have certainly benefited from these trends. Prepared foods from supermarkets, ranging from sushi to cooked-to-order pizza, have become very popular. Americans bought $1.6 billion of hot entrees from supermarkets in 2002, an almost 40 percent increase from 1997. Consequently, supermarkets have expanded the square footage of their prepared foods sections by 168 percent between 1993 and 2002. Natural-food stores have seen a comparable rise in the popularity of prepared foods. The Whole Foods Market chain has seen the biggest growth in its prepared foods category for the past four years. Even small businesses have developed prepared meals for takeout or delivery.

Restaurants have also capitalized on the popularity of eating prepared food at home. Almost all the growth in the restaurant industry in the past 15 years has been in takeout. The National Restaurant Association reports that 60 percent of meals sold by restaurants today are not eaten on-site, compared with a decade ago when most meals were eaten at a restaurant. Outback Steakhouse, for example, offers a takeout option: Customers simply call in their order, and a server will meet them in the parking lot with their food.

Changing consumption patterns will continue to create new opportunities for American businesses and entrepreneurs. If the trends continue, fewer and fewer people will cook at home, creating a need for new services that provide hassle-free, affordable family meals. The opportunities are not limited to just huge supermarket and restaurant chains, but exist for local supermarkets and small restaurants as well. Innovative ideas to help Americans heat without preparing meals are a real market opportunity for entrepreneurs.[23]

Discussion Questions
1. What types of retailers are most benefiting from changes in eating habits?
2. What else could small retailers (restaurants) do to appeal to American diners?
3. What other changes in eating habits could retailers exploit?

products from competing producers, retailers create utility. Retailers arrange for products to be moved from producers to a convenient retail establishment (place utility). They maintain hours of operation for their retail stores to make merchandise available when consumers want it (time utility). They also assume the risk of ownership of inventories (ownership utility). Table 13.3 describes various types of general merchandise retailers.

Today, there are too many stores competing for too few customers, and, as a result, competition between similar retailers has never been more intense. Further, competition between different types of stores is changing the nature of retailing. Supermarkets compete with specialty food stores, wholesale clubs, and discount stores. Department stores compete with nearly every other type of store including specialty stores, off-price chains, category killers, discount stores, and online retailers. Many traditional retailers, such as Wal-Mart and Macy's, have created online shopping sites to retain customers and compete with online-only retailers. One of the best-known online only, or cyber, merchants is Amazon.com. Amazon offers millions of products from which to choose, all from the privacy and convenience of the purchaser's home. In some cases, Web merchants offer wide selections, ultra-convenience, superior service, knowledge, and the best products. More detail on the Internet's effect on marketing was presented in Chapter 4.

wholesalers
intermediaries who buy from producers or from other wholesalers and sell to retailers

Wholesalers are intermediaries who buy from producers or from other wholesalers and sell to retailers. They usually do not sell in significant quantities

TABLE 13.3   General Merchandise Retailers

Type of Retailer	Description	Examples
Department store	Large organization offering wide product mix and organized into separate departments	Macy's, JC Penney, Sears
Discount store	Self-service, general merchandise store offering brand name and private brand products at low prices	Wal-Mart, Target
Supermarket	Self-service store offering complete line of food products and some nonfood products	Kroger, Albertson's, Winn-Dixie
Superstore	Giant outlet offering all food and nonfood products found in supermarkets, as well as most routinely purchased products	Wal-Mart Supercenters
Hypermarket	Combination supermarket and discount store, larger than a superstore	Carrefour
Warehouse club	Large-scale, members-only establishments combining cash-and-carry wholesaling with discount retailing	Sam's Club, Costco
Warehouse showroom	Facility in a large, low-cost building with large on-premises inventories and minimum service	Ikea
Catalog showroom	Type of warehouse showroom where consumers shop from a catalog and products are stored out of buyers' reach and provided in manufacturer's carton	Service Merchandise

Source: William M. Pride and O. C. Ferrell, *Marketing: Concepts and Strategies,* 2003, p. 405. Copyright 2003 by Houghton Mifflin Company. Reprinted with permission.

to ultimate consumers. Wholesalers perform the functions listed in Table 13.4.

Wholesalers are extremely important because of the marketing activities they perform, particularly for consumer products. Although it is true that wholesalers can be eliminated, their functions must be passed on to some other entity, such as the producer, another intermediary, or even the customer. Wholesalers help consumers and retailers by buying in large quantities, then selling to retailers in smaller quantities. By stocking an assortment of products, wholesalers match products to demand.

Supply Chain Management.   In an effort to improve distribution channel relationships among manufacturers and other channel intermediaries, supply chain management creates alliances between channel members. In Chapter 9, we defined supply chain management as connecting and integrating all parties or members of the distribution system in order to satisfy customers. It involves long-term partnerships among marketing channel members working together to reduce costs, waste, and unnecessary movement in the entire marketing channel in order to satisfy customers.[24] It goes beyond traditional channel members (producers, wholesalers, retailers, customers) to include *all* organizations involved in moving products from the producer to the ultimate customer.

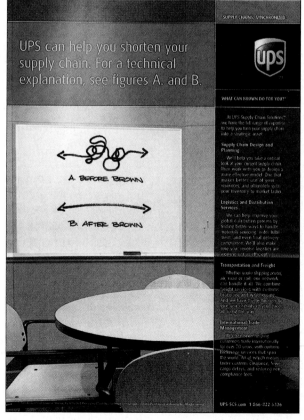

UPS runs a business-to-business ad showcasing its solutions for supply chain management.

TABLE 13.4   Major Wholesaling Functions

Supply Chain Management	Creating long-term partnerships among channel members
Promotion	Providing a sales force, advertising, sales promotion, and publicity
Warehousing, Shipping, and Product Handling	Receiving, storing, and stockkeeping Packaging Shipping outgoing orders Materials handling Arranging and making local and long distance shipments
Inventory Control and Data Processing	Processing orders Controlling physical inventory Recording transactions Tracking sales data for financial analysis
Risk Taking	Assuming responsibility for theft, product obsolescence, and excess inventories
Financing and Budgeting	Extending credit Borrowing Making capital investments Forecasting cash flow
Marketing Research and Information Systems	Providing information about market Conducting research studies Managing computer networks to facilitate exchanges and relationships

Source: William M. Pride and O. C. Ferrell, *Marketing: Concepts and Strategies,* 2003, p. 375. Copyright 2003 by Houghton Mifflin Company. Reprinted with permission.

The focus shifts from one of selling to the next level in the channel to one of selling products *through* the channel to a satisfied ultimate customer. Information, once provided on a guarded, "as needed" basis, is now open, honest, and ongoing. Perhaps most importantly, the points of contact in the relationship expand from one-on-one at the salesperson–buyer level to multiple interfaces at all levels and in all functional areas of the various organizations.

Channels for Consumer Products.   Typical marketing channels for consumer products are shown in Figure 13.4. In Channel A, the product moves from the producer directly to the consumer. Farmers who sell their fruit and vegetables to consumers at roadside stands use a direct-from-producer-to-consumer marketing channel.

In Channel B, the product goes from producer to retailer to consumer. This type of channel is used for products such as college textbooks, automobiles, and appliances. In Channel C, the product is handled by a wholesaler and a retailer before it reaches the consumer. Producer-to-wholesaler-to-retailer-to-consumer marketing channels distribute a wide range of products including refrigerators, televisions, soft drinks, cigarettes, clocks, watches, and office products. In Channel D, the product goes to an agent, a wholesaler, and a retailer before going to the consumer. This long channel of distribution is especially useful for convenience products. Candy and some produce are often sold by agents who bring buyers and sellers together.

Services are usually distributed through direct marketing channels because they are generally produced *and* consumed simultaneously. For example, you cannot take a haircut home for later use. Many services require the customer's presence and participation: The sick patient must visit the physician to receive treatment; the child must be at the day care center to receive care; the tourist must be present to sightsee and consume tourism services.

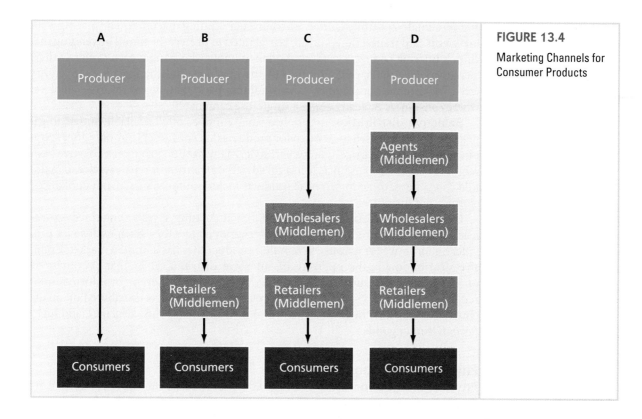

FIGURE 13.4

Marketing Channels for Consumer Products

Channels for Business Products.   In contrast to consumer goods, more than half of all business products, especially expensive equipment or technically complex products, are sold through direct marketing channels. Business customers like to communicate directly with producers of such products to gain the technical assistance and personal assurances that only the producer can offer. For this reason, business buyers prefer to purchase expensive and highly complex mainframe computers directly from IBM, Cray, and other mainframe producers. Other business products may be distributed through channels employing wholesaling intermediaries such as industrial distributors and/or manufacturer's agents.

Intensity of Market Coverage

A major distribution decision is how widely to distribute a product—that is, how many and what type of outlets should carry it. The intensity of market coverage depends on buyer behavior, as well as the nature of the target market and the competition. Wholesalers and retailers provide various intensities of market coverage and must be selected carefully to ensure success. Market coverage may be intensive, selective, or exclusive.

   Intensive distribution makes a product available in as many outlets as possible. Because availability is important to purchasers of convenience products such as bread, milk, gasoline, soft drinks, and chewing gum, a nearby location with a minimum of time spent searching and waiting in line is most important to the consumer. To saturate markets intensively, wholesalers and many varied retailers try to make the product available at every location where a consumer might desire to purchase it. For example, to market its one-time-use Max cameras, Eastman Kodak rolled out

intensive distribution
a form of market coverage whereby a product is made available in as many outlets as possible

10,000 climate-controlled, Internet-connected vending machines. The machines allow credit card transactions and are refrigerated to protect the film. The vending machine's Internet connection allows Kodak to know who bought each camera, where customers live, the specific location of the machine, and the machine's inventory level. The machines are found at zoos, stadiums, parks, hotels, and resorts—all places where consumers typically desire a single-use camera.[25]

<table>
<tr><td>

selective distribution
a form of market coverage whereby only a small number of all available outlets are used to expose products

</td></tr>
</table>

Selective distribution uses only a small number of all available outlets to expose products. It is used most often for products that consumers buy only after shopping and comparing price, quality, and style. Many products sold on a selective basis require salesperson assistance, technical advice, warranties, or repair service to maintain consumer satisfaction. Typical products include automobiles, major appliances, clothes, and furniture.

exclusive distribution
the awarding by a manufacturer to an intermediary of the sole right to sell a product in a defined geographic territory

Exclusive distribution exists when a manufacturer gives an intermediary the sole right to sell a product in a defined geographic territory. Such exclusivity provides an incentive for a dealer to handle a product that has a limited market. Exclusive distribution is the opposite of intensive distribution in that products are purchased and consumed over a long period of time, and service or information is required to develop a satisfactory sales relationship. Products distributed on an exclusive basis include high-quality musical instruments, yachts, airplanes, and high-fashion leather goods.

Physical Distribution

physical distribution
all the activities necessary to move products from producers to customers—inventory control, transportation, warehousing, and materials handling

Physical distribution includes all the activities necessary to move products from producers to customers—inventory control, transportation, warehousing, and materials handling. Physical distribution creates time and place utility by making products available when they are wanted, with adequate service and at minimum cost. Both goods and services require physical distribution. Many physical distribution activities are part of supply chain management, which we discussed in Chapter 9; we'll take a brief look at a few more now.

transportation
the shipment of products to buyers

Transportation.   **Transportation,** the shipment of products to buyers, creates time and place utility for products, and thus is a key element in the flow of goods and services from producer to consumer. The five major modes of transportation used to move products between cities in the United States are railways, motor vehicles, inland waterways, pipelines, and airways.

Railroads offer the least expensive transportation for many products. Heavy commodities, foodstuffs, raw materials, and coal are examples of products carried by railroads. Trucks have greater flexibility than railroads because they can reach more locations. Trucks handle freight quickly and economically, offer door-to-door service, and are more flexible in their packaging requirements than are ships or airplanes. Air transport offers speed and a high degree of dependability but is the most expensive means of transportation; shipping is the least expensive and slowest form. Pipelines are used to transport petroleum, natural gas, semiliquid coal, wood chips, and certain chemicals. Many products can be moved most efficiently by using more than one mode of transportation.

Factors affecting the selection of a mode of transportation include cost, capability to handle the product, reliability, and availability, and, as suggested, selecting transportation modes requires trade-offs. Unique characteristics of the product and consumer desires often determine the mode selected.

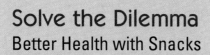

Solve the Dilemma
Better Health with Snacks

Warehousing. **Warehousing** is the design and operation of facilities to receive, store, and ship products. A warehouse facility receives, identifies, sorts, and dispatches goods to storage; stores them; recalls, selects, or picks goods; assembles the shipment; and finally, dispatches the shipment.

Companies often own and operate their own private warehouses that store, handle, and move their own products. They can also rent storage and related physical distribution services from public warehouses. Regardless of whether a private or a public warehouse is used, warehousing is important because it makes products available for shipment to match demand at different geographic locations.

warehousing
the design and operation of facilities to receive, store, and ship products

Materials Handling. **Materials handling** is the physical handling and movement of products in warehousing and transportation. Handling processes may vary significantly due to product characteristics. Efficient materials-handling procedures increase a warehouse's useful capacity and improve customer service. Well-coordinated loading and movement systems increase efficiency and reduce costs.

materials handling
the physical handling and movement of products in warehousing and transportation

Importance of Distribution in a Marketing Strategy

Distribution decisions are among the least flexible marketing mix decisions. Products can be changed over time; prices can be changed quickly; and promotion is usually changed regularly. But distribution decisions often commit resources and establish contractual relationships that are difficult if not impossible to change. As a company attempts to expand into new markets, it may require a complete change in distribution. Moreover, if a firm does not manage its marketing channel in the most efficient manner and provide the best service, then a new competitor will evolve to create a more effective distribution system.

Promotion Strategy

The role of promotion is to communicate with individuals, groups, and organizations to facilitate an exchange directly or indirectly. It encourages marketing exchanges by attempting to persuade individuals, groups, and organizations to accept goods, services, and ideas. Promotion is used not only to sell products but also to influence opinions and attitudes toward an organization, person, or cause. The state of Texas, for example, has successfully used promotion to educate people about the costs of highway litter and thereby reduce littering. Most people probably equate promotion with advertising, but it also includes personal selling, publicity, and sales promotion. The role that these elements play in a marketing strategy is extremely important.

The Promotion Mix

integrated marketing communications
coordinating the promotion mix elements and synchronizing promotion as a unified effort

Advertising, personal selling, publicity, and sales promotion are collectively known as the promotion mix because a strong promotion program results from the careful selection and blending of these elements. The process of coordinating the promotion mix elements and synchronizing promotion as a unified effort is called **integrated marketing communications**. When planning promotional activities, an integrated marketing communications approach results in the desired message for customers. Different elements of the promotion mix are coordinated to play their appropriate roles in delivery of the message on a consistent basis.

advertising
a paid form of nonpersonal communication transmitted through a mass medium, such as television commercials or magazine advertisements

Advertising.   Perhaps the best-known form of promotion, **advertising** is a paid form of nonpersonal communication transmitted through a mass medium, such as television commercials, magazine advertisements or online ads. Commercials featuring celebrities, customers, or unique creations (the Energizer Bunny, for example) serve to grab viewers' attention and pique their interest in a product. Table 13.5 shows companies that spent more than $1 billion on ads in the United States in one year.

advertising campaign
designing a series of advertisements and placing them in various media to reach a particular target market

An **advertising campaign** involves designing a series of advertisements and placing them in various media to reach a particular target audience. The basic content and form of an advertising campaign are a function of several factors. A product's features, uses, and benefits affect the content of the campaign message and individual ads. Characteristics of the people in the target audience—gender, age, education, race, income, occupation, lifestyle, and other attributes—influence both content and form. When Procter & Gamble promotes Crest toothpaste to children,

TABLE 13.5

Ten Leading National Advertisers

Organization	Advertising Expenditures ($ billions)	Sales ($ billions)	Advertising Expenditures as Percentage of Sales
1. General Motors	3.652	138.692	2.6
2. AOL Time Warner	2.923	32.632	9.0
3. Procter & Gamble	2.673	21.198	12.6
4. Pfizer	2.566	20.762	12.4
5. Ford Motor	2.251	108.392	2.1
6. DaimlerChrysler	2.032	72.002	2.8
7. Walt Disney	1.803	20.770	8.7
8. Johnson & Johnson	1.799	22.455	8.0
9. Sears, Roebuck	1.661	37.180	4.5
10. Unilever*	1.640	11.535	14.2

*Based on North American sales.

Source: Reprinted with permission from the June 23, 2003, issue of *Advertising Age.* Copyright © 2005 Crain Communications, Inc.

the company emphasizes daily brushing and cavity control, whereas it promotes tartar control and whiter teeth when marketing to adults. To communicate effectively, advertisers use words, symbols, and illustrations that are meaningful, familiar, and attractive to people in the target audience.

An advertising campaign's objectives and platform also affect the content and form of its messages. If a firm's advertising objectives involve large sales increases, the message may include hard-hitting, high-impact language and symbols. When campaign objectives aim at increasing brand awareness, the message may use much repetition of the brand name and words and illustrations associated with it. Thus, the advertising platform is the foundation on which campaign messages are built.

Advertising media are the vehicles or forms of communication used to reach a desired audience. Print media include newspapers, magazines, direct mail, and billboards, and electronic media include television, radio, and cyber ads. Newspapers, television, and direct mail are the most widely used advertising media. Table 13.6 shows U.S. advertising expenditures by type of media.

Choice of media obviously influences the content and form of the message. Effective outdoor displays and short broadcast spot announcements require concise, simple messages. Magazine and newspaper advertisements can include considerable detail and long explanations. Because several kinds of media offer geographic selectivity, a precise message can be tailored to a particular geographic section of the target audience. For example, a company advertising in *Time* might decide to use one message in the New England region and another in the rest of the nation. A company may also choose to advertise in only one region. Such geographic selectivity lets a firm use the same message in different regions at different times.

The use of online advertising is increasing. However, advertisers are demanding more for their ad dollars and proof that they are working. Certain types of ads are more popular than pop-up ads and banner ads that consumers find annoying. Also increasing in popularity are 6- to 11-minute made-for-the-Web ads called "advertainments." Produced, posted, and promoted by Ford, BMW, Diet Coke and Absolut vodka, the movies feature a product as the star. One BMW movie features a man who

Media	1990	1995	2000	2002
Newspapers	32,281	36,317	49,050	44,030
Magazines	5,803	8,580	12,370	11,000
Television	28,405	36,246	59,231	58,370
Radio	8,726	11,338	19,295	18,880
Yellow Pages	8,926	10,236	13,228	13,780
Outdoor	1,084	1,263	5,176	5,180*
Direct Mail	23,370	32,886	44,591	46,070
Business press	2,875	3,559	4,915	3,980
Internet	NA	NA	4,333	4,880
Miscellaneous	16,170	20,232	31,491	30,730
Total	128,640	160,637	243,680	236,880

TABLE 13.6

U.S. Advertising Expenditures (in millions of dollars)

*Category expanded to more inclusive "out of home"

Source: "Coen Cuts Spending Forecast," *Advertising Age,* June 11, 2001, p. 47; Robert J. Coen, "Coen: Little Ad Growth," *Advertising Age,* May 6, 1991, pp. 1, 16; Robert J. Coen, "Coen's Spending Totals for 2002," *Advertising Age,* **www.adage.com** (accessed June 6, 2004); Robert J. Coen, "U.S. Advertising Volume," *Advertising Age,* May 20, 1996, p. 24.

Responding to Business Challenges
The Perils of Using Celebrities in Advertising

When DaimlerChrysler signed a three-year, $14-million deal with recording artist Céline Dion to promote its automobiles, managers thought they were on to a good thing. The popular French-Canadian diva, who has issued a number of best-selling albums and singles, is adored by millions of fans around the world for her powerful vocals and unabashedly sentimental tunes. To Chrysler managers, she offered a sophisticated and polished image, which seemed the perfect vehicle to steer the company on its "path to premium."

But just a year after signing the deal, Dion's image and voice were conspicuously absent from the company's advertising. Although Dion's partnership with Chrysler helped increase record sales for Dion, it failed to sell cars for Chrysler. Unhappy dealers grumbled that the advertising campaign did more to sell the vocalist than Chrysler cars.

How could such a seemingly brilliant match have failed to ignite sales? Sources suggest that Chrysler's advertising agency had advised Chrysler *against* signing the deal with Dion on the grounds that her devoted audience was older than the buyers Chrysler sought to target. Despite this warning, Chrysler arranged for Dion to star in a number of extravagant commercials and events as part of its "Drive & Love" campaign. The company even sponsored Dion's highly touted Las Vegas show called "A New Day."

Dion's failure to appeal to car buyers as readily as listeners points up some of the pitfalls of using celebrities to endorse products. First, managers impressed by star power may be overeager to sign deals, even when market research suggests that a particular celebrity may not be the best match for a particular product or target market. Moreover, a celebrity with Dion's superstar power can easily eclipse the brand.

Another stumbling block is the possibility that a spokesperson might engage in scandalous or illegal behavior—as in the case of L. A. Lakers guard Kobe Bryant, who was accused of sexually assaulting a 19-year-old woman. Although charges against Bryant were later dropped, the scandal surrounding the charges threatened his endorsement deals with McDonald's, Nike, and Coca-Cola. The fallen-celebrity pitfall is illustrated by another of Chrysler's misfortunes when it struck a deal with Martha Stewart, who was shortly after indicted on charges related to securities fraud. Other problems may arise if celebrities become overexposed by being linked with too many products, or if they become unable to perform and lose their status in their field.[26]

Discussion Questions

1. Who uses celebrities to endorse their products? Which product categories seem to work best with celebrity endorsers?
2. How would you defend the use of a celebrity sponsor?
3. Do we see so many celebrity endorsements that they are losing their impact?

---

drives difficult passengers (in one film, Madonna stars as a difficult, foul-mouthed celebrity) around in flashy BMWs and gives them the ride of their lives. The Ford advertainments feature a Ford vehicle in three different scenarios—the promise of a Ford Focus to a teenager if he can make the team, a shirtless teen boy lying on a Ford Focus, smoking and eyeing a nearby teen girl, and a young man who drives around in a Ford trying to save his goldfish.[27]

Infomercials—typically 30-minute blocks of radio or television air time featuring a celebrity or upbeat host talking about and demonstrating a product—have evolved as an advertising method. Toll-free numbers and Web site addresses are usually provided so consumers can conveniently purchase the product or obtain additional information. Although many consumers and companies have negative feelings about infomercials, apparently they get results.

personal selling
direct, two-way communication with buyers and potential buyers

Personal Selling. **Personal selling** is direct, two-way communication with buyers and potential buyers. For many products—especially large, expensive ones with specialized uses, such as cars, appliances, and houses—interaction between a salesperson and the customer is probably the most important promotional tool.

Personal selling is the most flexible of the promotional methods because it gives marketers the greatest opportunity to communicate specific information that might trigger a purchase. Only personal selling can zero in on a prospect and attempt to persuade that person to make a purchase. Although personal selling has a lot of ad-

The Louisville Zoo advertises on this billboard to increase attendance.

vantages, it is one of the most costly forms of promotion. A sales call on an industrial customer can cost as much as $200 or $300.

There are three distinct categories of salespersons: order takers (e.g., retail sales clerks and route salespeople), creative salespersons (e.g., automobile, furniture, and insurance salespeople), and support salespersons (e.g., customer educators and goodwill builders who usually do not take orders). For most of these salespeople, personal selling is a six-step process:

1. *Prospecting:* Identifying potential buyers of the product.
2. *Approaching:* Using a referral or calling on a customer without prior notice to determine interest in the product.
3. *Presenting:* Getting the prospect's attention with a product demonstration.
4. *Handling objections:* Countering reasons for not buying the product.
5. *Closing:* Asking the prospect to buy the product.
6. *Following up:* Checking customer satisfaction with the purchased product.

Publicity.   **Publicity** is nonpersonal communication transmitted through the mass media but not paid for directly by the firm. A firm does not pay the media cost for publicity and is not identified as the originator of the message; instead, the message is presented in news story form. Obviously, a company can benefit from publicity by releasing to news sources newsworthy messages about the firm and its involvement with the public. Many companies have *public relations* departments to try to gain favorable publicity and minimize negative publicity for the firm.

Although advertising and publicity are both carried by the mass media, they differ in several major ways. Advertising messages tend to be informative, persuasive, or both; publicity is mainly informative. Advertising is often designed to have an immediate impact or to provide specific information to persuade a person to act; publicity describes what a firm is doing, what products it is launching, or other newsworthy information, but seldom calls for action. When advertising is used, the organization must pay for media time and select the media that will best reach target audiences. The mass media willingly carry publicity because they believe it has general public interest. Advertising can be repeated a number of times; most publicity appears in the mass media once and is not repeated.

Advertising, personal selling, and sales promotion are especially useful for influencing an exchange directly. Publicity is extremely important when communication

publicity
nonpersonal communication transmitted through the mass media but not paid for directly by the firm

focuses on a company's activities and products and is directed at interest groups, current and potential investors, regulatory agencies, and society in general.

A variation of traditional advertising is buzz marketing, in which marketers attempt to create a trend or acceptance of a product. Companies seek out trendsetters in communities and get them to "talk up" a brand to their friends, family, coworkers, and others. Toyota, for example, parked its new Scions outside of raves and coffee shops, and offered hip-hop magazine writers the chance for tests drives in order to get the "buzz" going about the new car.[28] Other marketers using the buzz technique include Hebrew National ("mom squads" grilled the company's hot dogs), Hasbro Games (fourth- and fifth-graders tantalized their peers with Hasbro's POX electronic game), and Chrysler (its retro PT Cruiser was planted in rental fleets). The idea behind buzz marketing is that an accepted member of a particular social group will be more credible than any form of paid communication.[29] The concept works best as part of an integrated marketing communication program that also includes traditional advertising, personal selling, sales promotion, and publicity.

A related concept is viral marketing, which describes the concept of getting Internet users to pass on ads and promotions to others. For example, Ebrick offered special discounts to its shoppers and encouraged them to forward the deals to their friends and family.[30]

sales promotion
direct inducements offering added value or some other incentive for buyers to enter into an exchange

Sales Promotion. **Sales promotion** involves direct inducements offering added value or some other incentive for buyers to enter into an exchange. The major tools of sales promotion are store displays, premiums, samples and demonstrations, coupons, contests and sweepstakes, refunds, and trade shows. In 2002, consumers redeemed 3.8 billion coupons, saving an estimated $3 billion. Nearly 80 percent of all consumers use coupons.[31] Sales promotion stimulates customer purchasing and increases dealer effectiveness in selling products. It is used to enhance and supplement other forms of promotion. General Motors, for example, launched an advertising campaign to encourage more prospective buyers to test-drive new vehicles. The "Sleep on It" campaign resulted in more than 350,000 consumers taking GM vehi-

Publicity for a product can be as simple as getting it placed prominently in a movie shot, as in this still from the movie "Malibu's Most Wanted." The Pepsi can is clearly identifiable on the table, with the can turned at just the proper angle for the audience to see the product name.

cles home overnight and ultimately more than 100,000 sales.[32] Test drives allow salespersons to demonstrate vehicles, which can help purchase decisions. Sampling a product may also encourage consumers to buy. PepsiCo, for example, used sampling to promote its Sierra Mist soft drink to reach more than 5 million potential consumers at well-traveled sites such as Times Square and Penn Station.[33] In a given year, almost three-fourths of consumer product companies may use sampling.

Sales promotions are generally easier to measure and less expensive than advertising. Although less than 2 percent of the 248 billion coupons distributed annually are redeemed, offering them in Sunday paper inserts is cheaper than producing a television commercial. Manufacturers typically pay about $7 per 1,000 inserts for a full page to reach 60 million homes, or nearly 60 percent of U.S. households.[34]

Promotion Strategies: To Push or To Pull

In developing a promotion mix, organizations must decide whether to fashion a mix that pushes or pulls the product (Figure 13.5). A **push strategy** attempts to motivate intermediaries to push the product down to their customers. When a push strategy is used, the company attempts to motivate wholesalers and retailers to make the product available to their customers. Sales personnel may be used to persuade intermediaries to offer the product, distribute promotional materials, and offer special promotional incentives for those who agree to carry the product. Chrysler manufacturing plants operate on a push system. They assemble cars according to forecasts of sales demand. Dealers then sell to buyers with the help of incentives and other promotions.[35] A **pull strategy** uses promotion to create consumer demand for a product so that consumers exert pressure on marketing channel members to make it available. For example, when the Coca-Cola Company introduced its new, low-carb, low-carlorie, and low-sugar soft drink Coca-Cola C2, the company gave away

push strategy
an attempt to motivate intermediaries to push the product down to their customers

pull strategy
the use of promotion to create consumer demand for a product so that consumers exert pressure on marketing channel members to make it available

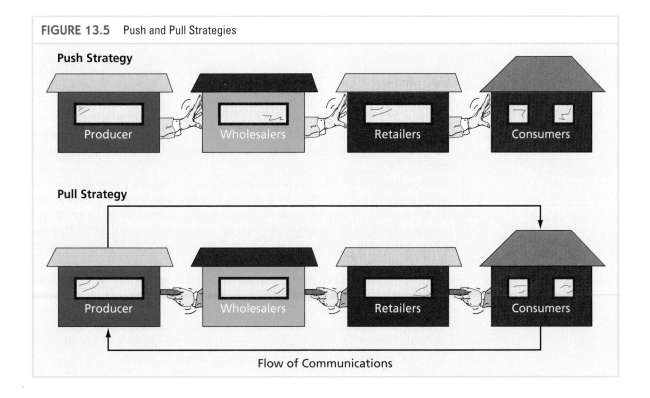

FIGURE 13.5   Push and Pull Strategies

Push Strategy

Producer — Wholesalers — Retailers — Consumers

Pull Strategy

Producer — Wholesalers — Retailers — Consumers

Flow of Communications

samples in Los Angeles, New York, Atlanta, Chicago, and Miami. Coca-Cola employees around the country were also given a case of C2 to share with family and friends.[36] Such sampling prior to a product rollout encourages consumers to request the product from their favorite retailer.

A company can use either strategy, or it can use a variation or combination of the two. The exclusive use of advertising indicates a pull strategy. Personal selling to marketing channel members indicates push strategy. The allocation of promotional resources to various marketing mix elements probably determines which strategy a marketer uses.

Objectives of Promotion

The marketing mix a company uses depends on its objectives. It is important to recognize that promotion is only one element of the marketing strategy and must be tied carefully to the goals of the firm, its overall marketing objectives, and the other elements of the marketing strategy. Firms use promotion for many reasons, but typical objectives are to stimulate demand, to stabilize sales, and to inform, remind, and reinforce customers.

Increasing demand for a product is probably the most typical promotional objective. Stimulating demand, often through advertising and sales promotion, is particularly important when a firm is using a pull strategy.

Another goal of promotion is to stabilize sales by maintaining the status quo—that is, the current sales level of the product. During periods of slack or decreasing sales, contests, prizes, vacations, and other sales promotions are sometimes offered to customers to maintain sales goals. Advertising is often used to stabilize sales by making customers aware of slack use periods. For example, auto manufacturers often provide rebates, free options, or lower-than-market interest rates to stabilize sales and thereby keep production lines moving during temporary slowdowns. A stable sales pattern allows the firm to run efficiently by maintaining a consistent level of production and storage and utilizing all its functions so that it is ready when sales increase.

An important role of any promotional program is to inform potential buyers about the organization and its products. A major portion of advertising in the United States, particularly in daily newspapers, is informational. Providing information about the availability, price, technology, and features of a product is very important in encouraging a buyer to move toward a purchase decision. Nearly all forms of promotion involve an attempt to help consumers learn more about a product and a company.

Promotion is also used to remind consumers that an established organization is still around and sells certain products that have uses and benefits. Often advertising reminds customers that they may need to use a product more frequently or in certain situations. Pennzoil, for example, has run television commercials reminding car owners that they need to change their oil every 3,000 miles to ensure proper performance of their cars.

Reinforcement promotion attempts to assure current users of the product that they have made the right choice and tells them how to get the most satisfaction from the product. Also, a company could release publicity statements through the news media about a new use for a product. Additionally, firms can have salespeople communicate with current and potential customers about the proper use and maintenance of a product—all in the hope of developing a repeat customer.

Promotional Positioning

Promotional positioning uses promotion to create and maintain an image of a product in buyers' minds. It is a natural result of market segmentation. In both promotional positioning and market segmentation, the firm targets a given product or brand at a portion of the total market. A promotional strategy helps differentiate the product and make it appeal to a particular market segment. For example, to appeal to safety-conscious consumers, Volvo heavily promotes the safety and crashworthiness of Volvo automobiles in its advertising. Mazda relied on nostalgia in its advertising of the Miata sports car to appeal to style- and price-conscious baby boomers who want to relive their youth in a British roadster-type automobile. Promotion can be used to change or reinforce an image. Effective promotion influences customers and persuades them to buy.

promotional positioning
the use of promotion to create and maintain an image of a product in buyers' minds

Explore Your Career Options
Diverse Opportunities in Marketing

All organizations need people to perform marketing activities. Whether in manufacturing, financial services, health care, professional services, or nonprofit organizations, companies are constantly seeking individuals who can work to develop new products, use marketing research to stay on top of emerging trends, and, in general, create sales. Broad areas of opportunity in marketing include marketing research, sales, purchasing, advertising, retailing, and direct marketing. Employment of marketing, advertising, and public relations managers is expected to increase faster than average for all occupations through the year 2012. With between one-fourth and one-third of the civilian workforce in the United States employed in marketing-related jobs, it is clear that marketing offers many diverse career opportunities.

With increasing global and domestic competition and more complex products, students with marketing degrees will find excellent job prospects. Service and high-technology firms, in particular, are experiencing rapid growth and have a high demand for marketers to help develop, distribute, and promote new products. A bachelor's degree is generally necessary, but some higher-level positions require a master's or doctorate degree. Students with a bachelor's degree in marketing can expect to start out earning about $29,000, those with advertising degrees, $27,000. With experience and education, top-level advertising executives and marketing managers can expect to reach six-figure salaries, depending on the organization and how many people they supervise.

Listed below are starting salary ranges for selected marketing professionals.

Brand/product manager	$57,000–$86,750
Corporate marketing manager	$47,250–$74,500
Ad agency marketing manager	$47,750–$75,000
Advertising copywriter	$42,500–$59,000
Media buyer	$41,500–$56,000
Ad agency account executive	$38,250–55,000[37]

Review Your Understanding

Describe the role of product in the marketing mix, including how products are developed, classified, and identified.

Products (goods, services, ideas) are among a firm's most visible contacts with consumers and must meet consumers' needs and expectations to ensure success. New product development is a multistep process: idea develop-ment, the screening of new ideas, business analysis, product development, test marketing, and commercialization. Products are usually classified as either consumer or business products. Consumer products can be further classified as convenience, shopping, or specialty products. The business product classifications are raw materials, major equipment, accessory equipment, component parts, processed materials, supplies, and industrial services. Products also can be classified by the stage of the product life cycle (introduction, growth, maturity, and decline). Identifying products includes branding (the process of naming and identifying products); packaging (the product's container); and labeling (information, such as content and warnings, on the package).

Define price and discuss its importance in the marketing mix, including various pricing strategies a firm might employ.

Price is the value placed on an object exchanged between a buyer and a seller. It is probably the most flexible variable of the marketing mix. Pricing objectives include survival, maximization of profits and sales volume, and maintaining the status quo. When a firm introduces a new product, it may use price skimming or penetration pricing. Psychological pricing and price discounting are other strategies.

Identify factors affecting distribution decisions, such as marketing channels and intensity of market coverage.

Making products available to customers is facilitated by middlemen, or intermediaries, who bridge the gap between the producer of the product and its ultimate user. A marketing channel is a group of marketing organizations that directs the flow of products from producers to consumers. Market coverage relates to the number and variety of outlets that make products available to customers; it may be intensive, selective, or exclusive. Physical distribution is all the activities necessary to move products from producers to consumers, including inventory planning and control, transportation, warehousing, and materials handling.

Specify the activities involved in promotion, as well as promotional strategies and promotional positioning.

Promotion encourages marketing exchanges by persuading individuals, groups, and organizations to accept goods, services, and ideas. The promotion mix includes advertising (a paid form of nonpersonal communication transmitted through a mass medium); personal selling (direct, two-way communication with buyers and potential buyers); publicity (nonpersonal communication transmitted through the mass media but not paid for directly by the firm); and sales promotion (direct inducements offering added value or some other incentive for buyers to enter into an exchange). A push strategy attempts to motivate intermediaries to push the product down to their customers, whereas a pull strategy tries to create consumer demand for a product so that consumers exert pressure on marketing channel members to make the product available. Typical promotion objectives are to stimulate demand, stabilize sales, and inform, remind, and reinforce customers. Promotional positioning is the use of promotion to create and maintain in the buyer's mind an image of a product.

Evaluate an organization's marketing strategy plans.

Based on the material in this chapter, you should be able to answer the questions posed in the "Solve the Dilemma" box on page 391 and evaluate the company's marketing strategy plans, including its target market and marketing mix.

Revisit the World of Business

1. How has Jones Soda effectively used public relations?

2. Why would advertising be less effective than public relations for limited-release products like Turkey & Gravy Soda?

3. Jones Soda is a "niche" player in the soft-drink market. How does its product line fit into the competitive field?

Learn the Terms

Check Your Progress

1. What steps do companies generally take to develop and introduce a new product?

2. What is the product life cycle? How does a product's life cycle stage affect its marketing strategy?

3. Which marketing mix variable is probably the most flexible? Why?

4. Distinguish between the two ways to set the base price for a new product.

5. What is probably the least flexible marketing mix variable? Why?

6. Describe the typical marketing channels for consumer products.

7. What activities are involved in physical distribution? What functions does a warehouse perform?

8. How do publicity and advertising differ? How are they related?

9. What does the personal selling process involve? Briefly discuss the process.

10. List the circumstances in which the push and pull promotional strategies are used.

Get Involved

1. Pick three products you use every day (either in school, at work, or for pleasure—perhaps one of each). Determine what phase of the product life cycle each is in. Evaluate the marketer's strategy (product, price, promotion, and distribution) for the product and whether it is appropriate for the life-cycle stage.

2. Design a distribution channel for a manufacturer of stuffed toys.

3. Pick a nearby store, and briefly describe the kinds of sales promotion used and their effectiveness.

Build Your Skills

ANALYZING MOTEL 6'S MARKETING STRATEGY

Background:
Made famous through the well-known radio and TV commercials spoken in the distinctive "down-home" voice of Tom Bodett, the Dallas-based Motel 6 chain of budget motels is probably familiar to you. Based on the information provided below and any personal knowledge you may have about the company, you will analyze the marketing strategy of Motel 6.

Task:
Read the paragraphs below, then complete the questions that follow.

Motel 6 was established in 1962 with the original name emphasizing its low-cost, no-frills approach. Rooms at that time were $6 per night. Today, Motel 6 has more than 760 units, and the average nightly cost is $34. Motel 6 is the largest company-owned and operated lodging chain in the United States. Customers receive HBO, ESPN, free morning coffee, and free local phone calls, and most units have pools and some business services. Motel 6 has made a name for itself by offering clean, comfortable rooms at the lowest prices of any national motel chain and by standardizing both its product offering and its operating policies and procedures. The company's national spokesperson, Tom Bodett, is featured in radio and television commercials that use humorous stories to show why it makes sense to stay at Motel 6 rather than a pricey hotel.

In appealing to pleasure travelers on a budget as well as business travelers looking to get the most for their dollar, one commercial makes the point that all hotel and motel rooms look the same at night when the lights are out—when customers are getting what they came for, a good night's sleep. Motel 6 location sites are selected based on whether they provide convenient access to the highway system and whether they are close to areas such as shopping centers, tourist attractions, or business districts.

1. In SELECTING A TARGET MARKET, which approach is Motel 6 using to segment markets?

    a. concentration approach

    b. multisegment approach

2. In DEVELOPING A MARKETING MIX, identify in the second column of the table what the current strategy is and then identify any changes you think

Motel 6 should consider for carrying it successfully through the next five years.

Marketing Mix Variable	Current Strategy	5-Year Strategy
a. Product		
b. Price		
c. Distribution		
d. Promotion		

e-Xtreme Surfing

- **Product Development & Management Association**
  www.pdma.org

  Provides information about developing and managing new products.

- **Advertising Age**
  www.adage.com

  Offers news and articles about promotion from the magazine.

- **National Retail Federation**
  www.nrf.com

  Presents news, articles, and resources about the retailing industry.

See for Yourself Videocase

HOTEL MONACO

When you think of great hotels you probably think of the Ritz Carlton, Four Seasons, and Biltmore, as well as others. If you travel to Chicago, Denver, New Orleans, Salt Lake City, San Francisco, Seattle, or Washington, D.C., you can add a new name to your list—the Hotel Monaco. Business and leisure travelers sometimes complain that many hotels offer bland and traditional rooms with average services; Hotel Monaco's product and service can be classified as anything but average. In developing the concept for the Hotel Monaco, great attention was paid to providing great service; a unique, worldly and sophisticated décor; and a memorable sensory experience.

How do you create a memorable experience for guests? If you ask the employees of Hotel Monaco, they would first speak to the visual effect. The décor of each Hotel Monaco is vibrant and dynamic, with attractive patterns and original artwork. In terms of sound, upbeat music plays in the lobby, and each room has a portable stereo with a complimentary sample CD. Plush fabrics and interesting textures—from the rich fabrics draping the down comforter to the terry cloth robes and plush towels—appeal to the senses and make you realize the investment in developing a distinctive product. The smells created by the hotels' top-rated restaurants, morning coffee service, Aveda bath products, and spas further add to the inviting and invigorating experience. Guests who are feeling a little stressed and want to relax can go down to the lobby for the complimentary wine happy hour and experience a free "wine hour massage." If they're hungry or thirsty, there are fresh-baked cookies upon check-in, room service, restaurants, the wine hour, as well as in-room coffee and tea service.

In the highly competitive business traveler market, the Hotel Monaco understands its customers' needs. Downtown locations offer two-line phones, in-room fax machines, overnight shoe shines, laundry and valet services, and a complimentary newspaper. For the leisure traveler, spa services, convenient access to local attractions, and attentive service make the hotel very attractive. Guests worried about missing their workout can engage in "Strike a Pose," the nation's first in-room yoga program. The hotel provides complimentary mats, yoga straps, and an instructional CD for sale in the minibar or a 24-hour yoga channel.

How do you make your brand and image distinctive in a very crowded and competitive industry? Just ask Wanda, or Fred or Joe or whatever name you choose to give the goldfish that is delivered to your room upon request. As part of Hotel Monaco's "Pet Companion" program, a goldfish in a bowl will be delivered to your room, day or night. The hotels also offer gourmet dog cookies, clean-up bags, temporary dog tags, one-hour walking services, and dog-sitter services for guests who bring their own pets. Unlike most hotels, Hotel Monaco does not charge a pet deposit.

Major hotels operators recognize that great service is a key differentiating factor in helping potential customers decide which hotel chain to choose. Marriott International spends more than $100 million a year on training with daily 15-minute exercises on the proper method to greet guests and handle complaints. In a survey of *Business Week* subscribers, participants indicated that, after price and location, room quality was very important, as was the quality of the hotel staff and health club. The Hotel Monaco has won many awards and much praise from its customers.

Hotel Monaco's pricing strategy is competitive with hotels providing similar services. It offers a "frequent guest" program that rewards regular guests and personally acknowledges them with in-room freebies. The hotels also offer weekend get-a-way packages periodically, at special prices. Many of Hotel Monaco's customers learn about the property by word-of-mouth. Other than its association with major discount travel sites (such as Expedia, Travelocity, and Orbitz), the hotel does little advertising. With only seven locations nationally, it is difficult to find a mechanism to reach such a diversified target market.

The Hotel Monaco has been very strategic at finding its niche in the luxury hotel market. Understanding the importance of providing a distinctive product, great service, and the right location at a competitive price has been a formula for success.[38]

Discussion Questions

1. How would you compare Hotel Monaco's marketing strategy to that of other hotels that you are familiar with?

2. Why do you think customer loyalty is strong for the Hotel Monaco?

3. Should the Hotel Monaco do more advertising and promotion to reach its target market?

Remember to check out our Online Learning Center at <u>www.mhhe.com/ferrell5e</u>.

RedRiverShops.com

RedRiverShops.com (RRS.com) is a leading online retailer with over 10 million customer accounts in 20 countries and sales of $900 million. RRS.com is among the top five most visited sites on the Web. Product categories include computers, software, music, DVDs, electronics, and sports equipment. RRS.com is the leading online retailer of golf and fishing equipment. RRS.com is organized into three segments: allied electronics, integrated sports, and business-to-consumer auctions. The firm has extensive warehouse and distribution space to store and deliver merchandise to customers. The business-to-consumer auctions allow registered and approved businesses to offer a wide variety of products in an auction format, similar to eBay online auctions.

RRS.com has yet to make a profit due to the high costs of building a distribution system, designing a Web site, implementing customer transaction and service processes, and creating brand awareness through advertising. There is currently $500 million in cash available for operations, but the firm is losing about $50 million per quarter. Since additional financing has not been acquired, RRS.com needs to break even in the next two and a half years. As a publicly held company, RRS.com has been criticized for operating in the "red" for too long. Investment firms have downgraded the stock from a "buy" to a "hold." The board of directors is meeting to consider a proposal from the highly visible president, chief executive officer (CEO) and founder of RRS.com. The CEO has created an opportunity for a possible merger with a major developer of traditional shopping malls. Although unsure if the merger is the right strategy for RRS.com, the CEO views the meeting with the board of directors as the most important aspect in the decision-making process. The CEO respects the ability of the board to make the right recommendation because the members attending the next meeting are company executives with much experience and knowledge in their respective areas of business.

The proposal to be discussed is a merger of RRS.com with American Shopping Malls Properties (ASMP). ASMP is a Houston-based real estate firm that owns 95 shopping malls in 28 states. ASMP is very profitable with $600 million in rental income yielding a bottom line profit of $200 million in the last year. Owners of shopping malls usually earn their revenue from renting space and coordinating the management of the mall. Mall tenants include stores such as Sears, The Gap, and Banana Republic. Merging a popular online retailer and a successful shopping mall could create the ultimate "clicks-and-bricks" marriage. RRS.com could offer Web site exposure for mall tenants that, in many cases, have established national brands by adding these stores to the RRS.com Web site. A joint venture with a mall tenant that sells heavy, durable products, such as washing machines and dryers, could provide an opportunity for RRS.com to offer products that could be delivered and serviced by the mall store. The malls could even be co-branded as RRS.com malls. Co-branding would allow all participating tenants in the malls to have an RRS.com Web site link. This could create a seamless flow between online buying and receiving and returning products in the mall.

It is time for the RRS.com board of directors to meet, discuss, then approve or disapprove the proposed merger. You, as a member of the board, have been assigned a functional role with unique information that can be used in the discussion.

---

*This background statement provides information for a role-play exercise designed to help you understand the real world challenge of decision making in business and to integrate the concepts presented previously in this text. If your instructor chooses to utilize this activity, the class will be divided into teams with each team member assigned to a particular role in the fictitious organization. Additional information on each role and instructions for the completion of the exercise will be distributed to individual team members.

Part 6

Financing the Enterprise

Chapter 14

Money and the Financial System

OBJECTIVES

After reading this chapter, you will be able to:

- Define money, its functions, and its characteristics.

- Describe various types of money.

- Specify how the Federal Reserve Board manages the money supply and regulates the American banking system.

- Compare and contrast commercial banks, savings and loan associations, credit unions, and mutual savings banks.

- Distinguish among nonbanking institutions such as insurance companies, pension funds, mutual funds, and finance companies.

- Investigate the challenges ahead for the banking industry.

- Recommend the most appropriate financial institution for a hypothetical small business.

The Iraqi Dinar in Crisis

In March 2003, a coalition of countries led by the United States invaded Iraq with the purpose of removing Saddam Hussein from power. Following the invasion and the overturn of Hussein's regime, a provisional government was established to help the country get back on its feet. Part of the process of establishing a new government involves revising its monetary system and currency. Saddam Hussein's picture was removed from the Iraqi currency, the dinar, and the currency has been redesigned, with a new form of the dinar introduced into circulation. More than 10,000 tons of old notes with Saddam's portrait were destroyed after the new currency was circulated. The new bills are printed in different colors that are more difficult to counterfeit than the currency from the old regime.

The new Iraqi currency is printed in denominations of 50, 250, 1,000, 5,000, 10,000, and 25,000. Such large denominations are necessary because 250 dinars equaled about 16 cents in U.S. dollars at the time of this writing. Thus, the 10,000 dinar note is worth about U.S. $6.40. Because most Iraqis don't write checks or use credit cards, they sometimes have to carry their money in bags or other containers. Small denominations are more popular because many retailers will not accept larger notes as payment, in part because of rumors that banks in Iraq would no longer accept 10,000-dinar notes. (Likewise, in the U.S., many retailers are reluctant to accept $100 bills because of concerns about counterfeiting

continued

and robbery.) Therefore, the country had to print millions of 250 dinar notes so that Iraqi citizens could spend money to help revive the economy.

As the people of Iraq assume full control of their government and their money, they may decide to design and introduce a brand new currency for Iraq. Some of the issues they will have to address are how to determine the value of the currency and what will be an appropriate exchange rate at this point in the war-torn country's economic recovery. With the absence of many traditional institutions to stabilize the country, the dinar has come to be a focal point of credibility, stability, and confidence. Although many would like to tie the exchange rate of the dinar to the U.S. dollar, few governments have been able to take this approach without some major drawbacks. If the dinar is fixed to the U.S. dollar, the country could suffer even more instability when the U.S. dollar varies against other currencies. Of course, there is the concern that tying the dinar to the U.S. dollar might confirm to many members of the world community that the United States is involved in imperialism.

Money is the common denominator of exchange throughout the modern world. Without money as a measure of value and a medium to accumulate buying power, economic development is difficult. Having money that is accepted with confidence brings stability and provides a foundation for building a stable social structure. The dinar must become such a symbol of exchange that the Iraqi people can trust.[1]

Introduction

finance
the study of money; how it's made, how it's lost, and how it's managed

From Wall Street to Main Street—both overseas and at home—money is the one tool used to measure personal and business income and wealth. Not surprisingly, **finance** is the study of money: how it's made, how it's lost, and how it's managed. This chapter introduces you to the role of money and the financial system in the economy. Of course, if you have a checking account, automobile insurance, a college loan, or a credit card, you already have personal experience with some key players in the financial world.

We begin our discussion with a definition of money and then explore some of the many forms money may take. Next, we examine the roles of the Federal Reserve Board and other major institutions in the financial system. Finally, we explore the future of the finance industry and some of the changes likely to occur over the course of the next several years.

Money in the Financial System

money
anything generally accepted in exchange for goods and services

Strictly defined, **money** is anything generally accepted in exchange for goods and services. Materials as diverse as salt, cattle, fish, rocks, shells, cloth, as well as precious metals such as gold, silver, and copper have long been used by various cultures as money. Most of these materials were limited-supply commodities that had their own value to society (e.g., as a preservative or as jewelry). The supply of these commodities therefore determined the supply of "money" in that society. The next step was the development of "IOUs," or slips of paper that could be exchanged for a specified supply of the underlying commodity. "Gold" notes, for instance, could be exchanged for gold, and the money supply was tied to the amount of gold available. While paper money was first used in North America in 1685 (and even earlier in Europe), the concept of *fiat money*—a paper money not readily convertible to a precious metal such as gold—did not gain full acceptance until the Great Depression in the 1930s. The U.S. abandoned its gold-backed currency standard largely in response to the Great Depression and converted to a fiduciary, or fiat, monetary system. In the United States, paper money is really a government "note" or promise, worth the value specified on the note.

Functions of Money

No matter what a particular society uses for money, its primary purpose is to enable a person or organization to transform a desire into an action. These desires may be for entertainment actions, such as party expenses; operating actions, such as paying for rent, utilities, or employees; investing actions, such as buying property or equipment; or financing actions, such as for starting or growing a business. Money serves three important functions: as a medium of exchange, a measure of value, and a store of value.

Medium of Exchange.   Before fiat money, the trade of goods and services was accomplished through *bartering*—trading one good or service for another of similar value. As any school-age child knows, bartering can become quite inefficient—particularly in the case of complex, three-party transactions involving peanut butter sandwiches, baseball cards, and hair barrettes. There had to be a simpler way, and that was to decide on a single item—money—that can be freely converted to any other good upon agreement between parties.

Measure of Value.   As a measure of value, money serves as a common standard or yardstick of the value of goods and services. For example, $1 will buy a dozen large eggs and $25,000 will buy a nice car in the United States. In Japan, where the currency is known as the yen, these same transactions would cost about 100 yen and 2 million yen, respectively. Money, then, is a common denominator that allows people to compare the different goods and services that can be consumed on a particular income level. While a star athlete and a "burger-flipper" are paid vastly different wages, each uses money as a measure of the value of their yearly earnings and purchases.

Store of Value.   As a store of value, money serves as a way to accumulate wealth (buying power) until it is needed. For example, a person making $500 per week who wants to buy a $500 computer could save $50 per week for each of the next 10 weeks. Unfortunately, the value of stored money is directly dependent on the health of the economy. If, due to rapid inflation, all prices double in one year, then the purchasing power value of the money "stuffed in the mattress" would fall by half. On the other hand, "mattress savings" buy more when prices fall as a result of recessions.

Characteristics of Money

To be used as a medium of exchange, money must be acceptable, divisible, portable, stable in value, durable, and difficult to counterfeit.

Acceptability.   To be effective, money must be readily acceptable for the purchase of goods and services and for the settlement of debts. Acceptability is probably the most important characteristic of money: If people do not trust the value of money, businesses will not accept it as a payment for goods and services, and consumers will have to find some other means of paying for their purchases.

Divisibility.   Given the widespread use of quarters, dimes, nickels, and pennies in the United States, it is no surprise that the principle of divisibility is an important one. With barter, the lack of divisibility often makes otherwise preferable trades impossible, as would be an attempt to trade a steer for a loaf of bread. For money to serve effectively as a measure of value, all items must be valued in terms of comparable units—dimes for a piece of bubble gum, quarters for laundry machines, and dollars (or dollars and coins) for everything else.

Portability.   Clearly, for money to function as a medium of exchange, it must be easily moved from one location to the next. Large colored rocks could be used as money, but you couldn't carry them around in your wallet. Paper currency and metal coins, on the other hand, are capable of transferring vast purchasing power into small, easily carried (and hidden!) bundles. Few Americans realize it, but more U.S. currency is in circulation outside the United States than within. Currently, about $675 billion of U.S. currency is in circulation, and the majority is held outside the United States.[2]

These coins satisfy the need for money to be acceptable, stable, durable, difficult to counterfeit, and especially portable and divisible.

Stability.   Money must be stable and maintain its declared face value. A $10 bill should purchase the same amount of goods or services from one day to the next. The principle of stability allows people who wish to postpone purchases and save their money to do so without fear that it will decline in value. As mentioned earlier, money declines in value during periods of inflation, when economic conditions cause prices to rise. Thus, the same amount of money buys fewer and fewer goods and services. In some countries, particularly in Latin America, people spend their money as fast as they can in order to keep it from losing any more of its value. Instability destroys confidence in a nation's money and its ability to store value and serve as an effective medium of exchange. Ultimately, people faced with spiraling price increases avoid the increasingly worthless paper money at all costs, storing all of their savings in the form of real assets such as gold and land.

Durability.   Money must be durable. The crisp new dollar bills you trade at the music store for the hottest new CD will make their way all around town for about 18 months before being replaced (see Table 14.1). Were the value of an old, faded bill to fall in line with the deterioration of its appearance, the principles of stability and universal acceptability would fail (but, no doubt, fewer bills would pass through the washer!). Although metal coins, due to their much longer useful life, would appear to be an ideal form of money, paper currency is far more portable than metal because of its light weight. Today, coins are used primarily to provide divisibility.

Denomination of Bill	Life Expectancy (Years)
$ 1	1.5
$ 5	2
$ 10	3
$ 20	4
$ 50	9
$100	9

TABLE 14.1

The Life Expectancy of Paper Currency

Source: "How Currency Gets into Circulation," *Federal Reserve Bank of New York* (n.d.), **www.newyorkfed.com/aboutthefed/fedpoint/fed01.html** (accessed June 1, 2004).

Difficulty to Counterfeit.   Finally, to remain stable and enjoy universal acceptance, it almost goes without saying that money must be very difficult to counterfeit—that is, to duplicate illegally. Every country takes steps to make counterfeiting difficult. Most use multicolored money, and many use specially watermarked papers that are virtually impossible to duplicate. Counterfeit bills represent less than .02 percent of the currency in circulation in the United States,[4] but it is becoming increasingly easier for counterfeiters to print money with just a modest inkjet printer. This illegal printing of money is fueled by hundreds of people who often circulate only small amounts of counterfeit bills. To thwart the problem of counterfeiting, the U.S. Treasury Department is in the process of redesigning U.S. bills, starting with the $20 in 2003 and the $50 in 2004. For the first time, U.S. money includes subtle colors in addition to the traditional green, as well as enhanced security features, such as a watermark, security thread, and color-shifting ink.[5]

> **Did You Know?**   Experts estimate that more than $130 million in counterfeit U.S. bills is circulating around the world.[3]

Types of Money

While paper money and coins are the most visible types of money, the combined value of all of the printed bills and all of the minted coins is actually rather insignificant when compared with the value of money kept in checking accounts, savings accounts, and other monetary forms.

You probably have a **checking account** (also called a demand deposit), money stored in an account at a bank or other financial institution that can be withdrawn without advance notice. One way to withdraw funds from your account is by writing a *check,* a written order to a bank to pay the indicated individual or business the amount specified on the check from money already on deposit. Figure 14.1 explains the significance of the numbers found on a typical U.S. check. As legal instruments, checks serve as a substitute for currency and coins and are preferred for many transactions due to their lower risk of loss. If you lose a $100 bill, anyone who finds or steals it can spend it. If you lose a blank check, however, the risk of catastrophic loss is quite low. Not only does your bank

checking account money stored in an account at a bank or other financial institution that can be withdrawn without advance notice; also called a demand deposit

Our new more colorful paper money, like this $50 bill that was released in September 2004, is intended to make counterfeiting more difficult. For example, the "50" in the bottom right-corner is done in "color-shifting" ink. When you tilt the bill in different directions, the number changes between copper and green.

FIGURE 14.1   A Check

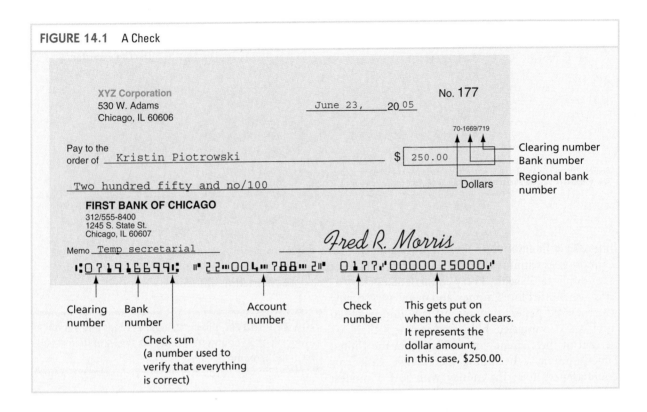

have a sample of your signature on file to compare with a suspected forged signature, but you can render the check immediately worthless by means of a stop-payment order at your bank.

There are several types of checking accounts, with different features available for different monthly fee levels or specific minimum account balances. Some checking accounts earn interest (a small percentage of the amount deposited in the account that the bank pays to the depositor). One such interest-bearing checking account is the *NOW* (*Negotiable Order of Withdrawal*) *account* offered by most financial institutions. The interest rate paid on such accounts varies with the interest rates available in the economy but is typically quite low (ranging between 2 and 5 percent).

Savings accounts (also known as time deposits) are accounts with funds that usually cannot be withdrawn without advance notice and/or have limits on the number of withdrawals per period. While seldom enforced, the "fine print" governing most savings accounts prohibits withdrawals without two or three days' notice. Savings accounts are not generally used for transactions or as a medium of exchange, but their funds can be moved to a checking account or turned into cash.

Money market accounts are similar to interest-bearing checking accounts, but with more restrictions. Generally, in exchange for slightly higher interest rates, the owner of a money market account can write only a limited number of checks each month, and there may be a restriction on the minimum amount of each check.

Certificates of deposit (CDs) are savings accounts that guarantee a depositor a set interest rate over a specified interval of time as long as the funds are not withdrawn before the end of the interval—six months, one year, or seven years, for example. Money may be withdrawn from these accounts prematurely only after paying

savings accounts
accounts with funds that usually cannot be withdrawn without advance notice; also known as time deposits

money market accounts
accounts that offer higher interest rates than standard bank rates but with greater restrictions

certificates of deposit (CDs)
savings accounts that guarantee a depositor a set interest rate over a specified interval as long as the funds are not withdrawn before the end of the period—six months or one year, for example

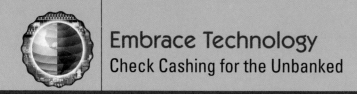

It is estimated that 13 percent of U.S. households do not have checking accounts (or are "unbanked"). Typically, the unbanked consumer cannot cash a payroll check in a regular bank but must turn instead to a check-cashing store, paying a fee of 2 to 3 percent of the check's value plus a transaction fee, in some cases. According to Financial Service Centers of America, a trade group of 3,700 check-cashing stores, more than 180 million checks a year with a total value of $55 billion are cashed in such stores. The large market coupled with technological advances in loss protection has enticed some banks to offer check-cashing services for the unbanked.

Wells Fargo & Co., the nation's fourth largest bank, joined forces with pawnshop operator Cash America International Inc. to develop check-cashing machines targeted to this market. Begun just two years ago, the venture now has more than 1,300 machines in grocery and convenience stores. Users are required to enter personal information before inserting their checks to be scanned. The machines keep track of customers through high-tech biometric photos, which store images of the customer's facial bone structure. The photos are used to protect the company against stolen checks or to alert the system if a person who cashed a bad check attempts to cash another check. The company cashed $1.5 billion in checks in two years.

Union Bank of California has 20 Cash & Save Outlets located inside regular Union Bank branches and in grocery stores. The outlets serve about 143,000 customers. About 85 percent of the checks cashed are payroll checks, and the average check is slightly higher than $300. About 45 percent of the outlet's check-cashing customers eventually convert to regular accounts.

Customers of bank-operated check-cashing stores generally report friendlier environments and lower transaction fees. By embracing technology, many banks have been able to boost their profits while offering a service desired by an underserved market.[6]

Discussion Questions

1. How do these services contribute to our economy?
2. Why do you think so many households do not have checking accounts?
3. What else could businesses do to help the "unbanked" participate in our economy?

---

a substantial penalty. In general, the longer the term of the CD, the higher is the interest rate it earns. As with all interest rates, the rate offered and fixed at the time the account is opened fluctuates according to economic conditions.

Credit cards allow you to promise to pay at a later date by using preapproved lines of credit granted by a bank or finance company. They are a popular substitute for cash payments because of their convenience, easy access to credit, and acceptance by merchants around the world. Indeed, it is difficult today to find stores (and even some governmental services, such as state license plate branches) that do not accept credit cards. The institution issuing the credit card guarantees payment of a credit charge to merchants, less a small transaction fee, typically between 2 and 5 percent of the purchase, and assumes responsibility for collecting the money from the card holder.

credit cards
means of access to preapproved lines of credit granted by a bank or finance company

With few exceptions, credit cards allow cardholders great flexibility in paying off their purchases. Some people always pay off their monthly charges as they come due, but many others take advantage of the option of paying a stated minimum monthly amount with interest charges, based on yearly interest rates, added to the balance until it has been paid in full. Average annual fees for the privilege of carrying specific credit cards are an important source of money for issuing banks and can sometimes reach $60 per year, although bank cards are increasingly available with no annual charge. Credit-card issuers also charge a fee for converting from one nation's currency to another when the card holder uses the card in another country.

Two major credit cards—MasterCard and Visa—represent the vast majority of credit cards held in the United States. Over half of the market is controlled by the industry's "Big Five"—Citigroup, MBNA, First USA, American Express, and Discover.[7] Banks are not the only issuers of credit cards. American Express has long been the dominant card company in the travel and entertainment market, with millions of

THEY BOTH COME WITH AN ESCAPE CLAUSE.
WHERE YOU ESCAPE TO IS UP TO YOU.

**Whether you use the Gold Delta SkyMiles® Credit Card from American Express,
the Gold Delta SkyMiles® Business Credit Card, or both, you can get back on vacation fast.**
Because you can earn 10,000 Bonus Miles with your first purchase. Plus, get Always Double Miles® at gas stations,
home improvement stores and the U.S. Postal Service not to mention on wireless phone bills, Delta purchases and
more. With two Cards and so many ways to earn SkyMiles®, better start planning your escape route today.
Apply now and get an instant decision. Just call 1 800-SKYMILES.

Your next vacation is closer than you think.

*American Express promotes credit cards with Delta SkyMiles as an
added perk.*

debit card

a card that looks like a
credit card but works like
a check; using it results in
a direct, immediate,
electronic payment from
the cardholder's checking
account to a merchant or
third party

cards outstanding. Unlike most bank cards, American Express expects its cardholders to pay their entire balances in full each month.

Major department stores—Sears, JC Penney, Marshall Field's, Saks Fifth Avenue, and others—offer their own credit cards to encourage consumers to spend money in their stores. Unlike the major credit cards discussed above, these "private label" cards are generally accepted only at stores associated with the issuing company.

It is estimated that banks, credit card issuers, and retailers lose more than a billion dollars annually to credit card fraud, which includes lost or stolen cards, counterfeit cards, Internet purchases made with someone else's account number, and identity theft—the most devastating of all credit card frauds. Identity theft (also known as application or true name fraud) involves the assumption of someone else's identity by a criminal who then charges in the victim's name. Another concern is the amount of debt that Americans owe to credit card issuers. In an average month, Americans owe a collective $677 billion in credit card debt, while the British owe $97 billion and the Australians, $19 billion. That works out to about $2,300 for each U.S. man, woman, and child; $1,616 for each Briton, and $950 for each Australian.[8]

A **debit card** looks like a credit card but works like a check. The use of a debit card results in a direct, immediate, electronic payment from the cardholder's checking account to a merchant or other party. While they are convenient to carry and profitable for banks, they lack credit features, offer no purchase "grace period," and provide no hard "paper trail"—all of which kept debit cards from enjoying much popularity with consumers until recently. However, many financial institutions are encouraging customers to use their debit cards to reduce the number of teller transactions and paper-check processing costs. Indeed, debit cards have become the most popular form of payment for grocery and gasoline purchases and at "big-box" retailers like Best Buy.[9]

Traveler's checks, money orders, and cashier's checks are other common forms of "near money." Although each is slightly different from the others, they all share a common characteristic: A financial institution, bank, credit company, or neighborhood currency exchange issues them in exchange for cash and guarantees that the purchased note will be honored and exchanged for cash when it is presented to the institution making the guarantee.

The American Financial System

The U.S. financial system fuels our economy by storing money, fostering investment opportunities, and making loans for new businesses and business expansion as well as for homes, cars, and college educations. This amazingly complex system includes banking institutions, nonbanking financial institutions such as finance companies, and systems that provide for the electronic transfer of funds throughout the world.

FIGURE 14.2   Federal Reserve System

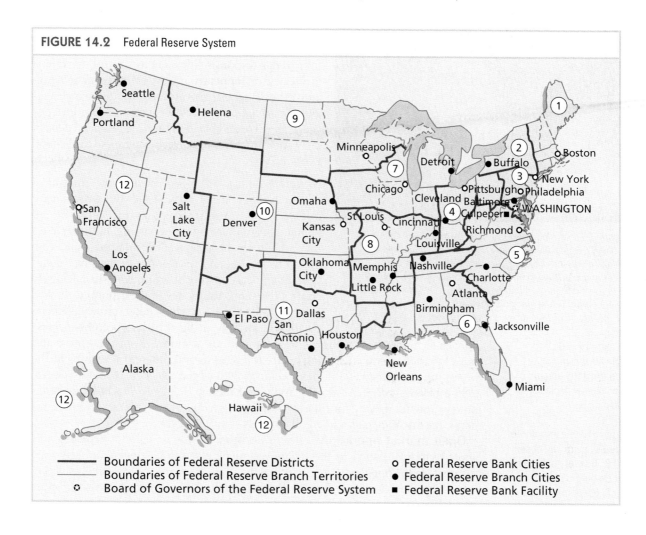

Over the past 20 years, the rate at which money turns over, or changes hands, has increased exponentially. Different cultures place unique values on saving, spending, borrowing, and investing. The combination of this increased turnover rate and increasing interactions with people and organizations from other countries has created a complex money system. First, we need to meet the guardian of this complex system.

The Federal Reserve System

The guardian of the American financial system is the **Federal Reserve Board,** or "the Fed," as it is commonly called, an independent agency of the federal government established in 1913 to regulate the nation's banking and financial industry. The Federal Reserve System is organized into 12 regions, each with a Federal Reserve Bank that serves its defined area (Figure 14.2). All the Federal Reserve banks except those in Boston and Philadelphia have regional branches. The Cleveland Federal Reserve Bank, for example, is responsible for branch offices in Pittsburgh and Cincinnati.

The Federal Reserve Board is the chief economic policy arm of the United States. Working with Congress and the president, the Fed tries to create a positive economic environment capable of sustaining low inflation, high levels of employment, a balance

Federal Reserve Board an independent agency of the federal government established in 1913 to regulate the nation's banking and financial industry

With just a few simple words, Federal Reserve Board Chairman Alan Greenspan has the ability to affect markets and monetary policy across the globe, not just in the United States. His recommendations regarding the U.S. economy can have significant effects on economies in Europe and Japan. Have you ever noticed the stock market on days in which he is supposed to make an announcement? Even days before or just after?

in international payments, and long-term economic growth. To this end, the Federal Reserve Board has four major responsibilities: (1) to control the supply of money, or monetary policy; (2) to regulate banks and other financial institutions; (3) to manage regional and national checking account procedures, or check clearing; and (4) to supervise the federal deposit insurance programs of banks belonging to the Federal Reserve System.

Monetary Policy.   The Fed controls the amount of money available in the economy through **monetary policy.** Without this intervention, the supply of and demand for money might not balance, resulting in either rapid price increases (that is, inflation, in the case of too much money) or economic recession (deflation, in the case of too little money). To effectively control the supply of money in the economy, the Fed must have a good idea of how much money is in circulation at any given time. This has become increas-

monetary policy
means by which the Fed controls the amount of money available in the economy

open market operations
decisions to buy or sell U.S. Treasury bills (short-term debt issued by the U.S. government) and other investments in the open market

ingly challenging because the global nature of our economy means that more and more U.S. dollars are circulating overseas. Using several different measures of the money supply, the Fed establishes specific growth targets which, presumably, ensure a close balance between money supply and money demand. The Fed fine-tunes money growth by using four basic tools: open market operations, reserve requirements, the discount rate, and credit controls (see Table 14.2).

Open market operations refer to decisions to buy or sell U.S. Treasury bills (short-term debt issued by the U.S. government; also called T-bills) and other investments in the open market. The actual purchase or sale of the investments is performed by the New York Federal Reserve Bank. This monetary tool, the most commonly employed of all Fed operations, is performed almost daily in an effort to control the money supply.

TABLE 14.2	**Activity**	**Effect on the Money Supply and the Economy**
Fed Tools for Regulating the Money Supply	Buy government securities	The money supply increases; economic activity increases.
	Sell government securities	The money supply decreases; economic activity slows down.
	Raise discount rate	Interest rates increase; the money supply decreases; economic activity slows down.
	Lower discount rate	Interest rates decrease; the money supply increases; economic activity increases.
	Increase reserve requirements	Banks make fewer loans; the money supply declines; economic activity slows down.
	Decrease reserve requirements	Banks make more loans; the money supply increases; economic activity increases.
	Relax credit controls	More people are encouraged to make major purchases, increasing economic activity.
	Restrict credit controls	People are discouraged from making major purchases, decreasing economic activity.

When the Fed buys securities, it writes a check on its own account to the seller of the investments. When the seller of the investments (usually a large bank) deposits the check, the Fed transfers the balance from the Federal Reserve account into the seller's account, thus increasing the supply of money in the economy and, hopefully, fueling economic growth. The opposite occurs when the Fed sells investments. The buyer writes a check to the Federal Reserve, and when the funds are transferred out of the purchaser's account, the amount of money in circulation falls, slowing economic growth to a desired level.

The second major monetary policy tool is the **reserve requirement,** the percentage of deposits that banking institutions must hold in reserve ("in the vault," as it were). Funds so held are not available for lending to businesses and consumers. For example, a bank holding $10 million in deposits, with a 10 percent reserve requirement, must have reserves of $1 million. If the Fed were to reduce the reserve requirement to, say, 5 percent, the bank would need to keep only $500,000 in reserves. The bank could then lend to customers the $500,000 difference between the old reserve level and the new lower reserve level, thus increasing the supply of money. Because the reserve requirement has such a powerful effect on the money supply, the Fed does not change it very often, relying instead on open market operations most of the time.

reserve requirement
the percentage of deposits that banking institutions must hold in reserve

The third monetary policy tool, the **discount rate,** is the rate of interest the Fed charges to loan money to any banking institution to meet reserve requirements. The Fed is the lender of last resort for these banks. When a bank borrows from the Fed, it is said to have borrowed at the "discount window," and the interest rates charged there are often higher than those charged on loans of comparable risk elsewhere in the economy. This added interest expense, when it exists, serves to discourage banks from borrowing from the Fed.

discount rate
the rate of interest the Fed charges to loan money to any banking institution to meet reserve requirements

When the Fed wants to expand the money supply, it lowers the discount rate to encourage borrowing. Conversely, when the Fed wants to decrease the money supply, it raises the discount rate. The rapid increases in interest rates that occurred in the United States in the mid 1990s were partly the result of a number of increases in the Fed discount rate. Not surprisingly, economists watch changes in this sensitive interest rate as an indicator of the Fed's monetary policy.

The final tool in the Fed's arsenal of weapons is **credit controls**—the authority to establish and enforce credit rules for financial institutions and some private investors. For example, the Fed can determine how large a down payment individuals and businesses must make on credit purchases of expensive items such as automobiles, and how much time they have to finish paying for the purchases. By raising and lowering minimum down-payment amounts and payment periods, the Fed can stimulate or discourage credit purchases of "big ticket" items. The Fed also has the authority to set the minimum down payment investors must use for the credit purchases of stock. Buying stock with credit—"buying on margin"—is a popular investment strategy among individual speculators. By altering the margin requirement (currently set at 50 percent of the price of the purchased stocks), the Fed can effectively control the total amount of credit borrowing in the stock market.

credit controls
the authority to establish and enforce credit rules for financial institutions and some private investors

Regulatory Functions.   The second major responsibility of the Fed is to regulate banking institutions that are members of the Federal Reserve System. Accordingly, the Fed establishes and enforces banking rules that affect monetary policy and the overall level of the competition between different banks. It determines which non-banking activities, such as brokerage services, leasing, and insurance, are appropriate for banks and which should be prohibited. The Fed also has the authority to approve or disapprove mergers between banks and the formation of bank holding companies. Increasingly, mergers between banks are crossing international waters. For example, Frances's BNP Paribas acquired United California Bank and Honolulu-based BancWest Corp., while the Royal Bank of Scotland, through its Citizens Financial Group subsidiary, purchased Pittsburgh's Mellon Financial and Philadelphia's Commonwealth Bancorp.[10] In an effort to ensure that all rules are enforced and that correct accounting procedures are being followed at member banks, surprise bank examinations are conducted by bank examiners each year.

Check Clearing. The Federal Reserve provides national check processing on a huge scale. Divisions of the Fed known as check clearinghouses handle almost all the checks written against a bank in one city and presented for deposit to a bank in a second city. Any banking institution can present the checks it has received from others around the country to its regional Federal Reserve Bank. The Fed passes on the checks to the appropriate regional Federal Reserve Bank, which then sends the checks to the issuing bank for payment. Thanks to technological advancements, the whole process takes a maximum of three days and is often accomplished within 24 hours. While the Fed also handles local checks, the high fees it charges for this service have encouraged the development of private local check clearinghouses in most major cities.

Depository Insurance. The Fed is also responsible for supervising the federal insurance funds that protect the deposits of member institutions. These insurance funds will be discussed in greater detail in the following section.

Banking Institutions

Banking institutions accept money deposits from and make loans to individual consumers and businesses. Some of the most important banking institutions include commercial banks, savings and loan associations, credit unions, and mutual savings banks. Historically, these have all been separate institutions. However, new hybrid forms of banking institutions that perform two or more of these functions have emerged over the last two decades. The following banking institutions all have one thing in common: They are businesses whose objective is to earn money by managing, safeguarding, and lending money to others. Their sales revenues come from the fees and interest that they charge for providing these financial services.

Commercial Banks. The largest and oldest of all financial institutions are **commercial banks,** which perform a variety of financial services. They rely mainly on checking and savings accounts as their major source of funds and use only a portion of these deposits to make loans to businesses and individuals. Because it is unlikely that all the depositors of any one bank will want to withdraw all of their funds at the same time, a bank can safely loan out a large percentage of its deposits. The Fed specifies the minimum amount of deposit reserves that banks must keep on hand to meet the needs of their depositors.

Until recent years, commercial banks primarily made short-term loans (loans that must be repaid within a year or so). Today, however, banks are quite diversified and offer a number of services. Commercial banks make loans for virtually any conceivable legal purpose, from vacations to cars, from homes to college educations. Banks in many states offer *home equity loans,* by which home owners can borrow against the appraised value of their already purchased homes. Banks also issue Visa and MasterCard credit cards and offer CDs and trusts (legal entities set up to hold and man-

commercial banks
the largest and oldest of all financial institutions, relying mainly on checking and savings accounts as sources of funds for loans to businesses and individuals

age assets for a beneficiary). Many banks rent safe-deposit boxes in bank vaults to customers who want to store jewelry, legal documents, artwork, and other valuables. In 1999 Congres passed the Financial Services Modernization Act, also known as the Gramm-Leach-Bliley Bill. This act repealed the Glass Stegal Act, which was enacted in 1929 after the stock market crash and prohibited commercial banks from being in the insurance and investment banking business. This puts U.S. commercial banks on the same competitive footing as European banks and provides a more level playing field for global banking competition. The stimulus for the Gramm-Leach-Bliley Bill was probably the merger of Citibank and Travelers Insurance. With its Salomon Smith Barney investment bank and brokerage units, Travelers Insurance, when combined with Citibank, became the largest financial services company in the United States. As commercial banks and investment banks have merged, the landscape has changed. Consolidation remains the norm in the U.S. banking industry. For example, Banknorth Group, a bank holding company, has acquired more than 24 community banks in New England, making it the second largest banking firm in the United States.[11]

US Bank is a leading commercial bank that focuses on business customers.

Savings and Loan Associations. **Savings and loan associations (S&Ls),** often called "thrifts," are financial institutions that primarily offer savings accounts and make long-term loans for residential mortgages. A mortgage is a loan made so that a business or individual can purchase real estate, typically a home; the real estate itself is pledged as a guarantee (called *collateral*) that the buyer will repay the loan. If the loan is not repaid, the savings and loan has the right to repossess the property. Prior to the 1970s, S&Ls focused almost exclusively on real estate lending and accepted only savings accounts. Today, following years of regulatory changes, S&Ls compete directly with commercial banks by offering many types of services.

savings and loan associations (S&Ls) financial institutions that primarily offer savings accounts and make long-term loans for residential mortgages; also called "thrifts"

Savings and loans have gone through a metamorphosis in the last decade after having almost collapsed in the 1980s. Congress passed legislation that allowed more competition between banks and savings and loans. The problem was the owners and managers of the savings and loans did not know how to behave like a bank, and they did not have the products necessary to compete. Then, Congress passed laws in 1986 that took away many of the tax benefits of owning real estate, which caused investment in real estate to slow considerably and stimulated defaults that were spurred by a poor economy. Developers defaulted on loans, and the S&L managers who had lent the money for these high-risk ventures found themselves holding billions of dollars of virtually unsellable real estate properties.

Despite the efforts of the Federal Savings and Loan Insurance Corporation—which we discuss in more detail shortly—there were not enough funds to bail out the industry. Eventually, the insurance fund ran out of money, and Congress created the Resolution Trust Corporation (RTC) in 1989 to help the industry work its way

Embrace Technology
ING Direct Wants to Be Your Bank

ING Direct has become the largest Internet-based bank in the United States by not acting like a traditional "brick-and-mortar" bank. More than 1.5 million customers leave their money at ING Direct in the United States, and 8 million customers are served by ING Direct in Canada, Australia, France, Spain, Italy, United Kingdom, and Germany. ING Direct's U.S. operations are headquartered in Wilmington, Delaware, with innovative ING Direct cafés in Philadelphia, New York, and Los Angeles, where you can drop by for coffee, call a sales associate, or visit INGdirect.com to learn about the bank and how to use it.

A subsidiary of the Amsterdam-based ING Group, ING Direct has built a reputation as an easy-to-use, reliable bank. It has rejected the notion of building branches with high-service contact on every corner; instead it exploits a range of technological innovations that make it possible to move money around the world electronically. It doesn't shower customers with free toasters and other gifts but rather offers them low-cost, simple banking products. It doesn't spend a lot of time coddling or directly interacting with its customers; such one-on-one service would be expensive and time-consuming. ING instead relies on paperless transactions, which reduce costs and improve speed, efficiency, and service to its clients.

To improve its success, ING studied the lifestyles and habits of its most profitable customers and applied what it learned to targeting prospects with similar behavior. Its ideal customers are savings-minded parents, aged 30 to 50, who are comfortable using the Internet to order products and communicate with others about their buying experiences and what they've learned from searching Internet information resources. The average customer is comfortable but not wealthy, with average deposits of around $14,000.

ING Direct tries to carry out its theme of low-cost, simple transactions by letting savers open accounts with no fees, no minimums, and one of the best rates in the United States. Its mortgages have no application fee, a simple no-hassle application, and great rates that can save customers thousands of dollars on their mortgage compared to the 30-year fixed mortgages offered by traditional banks. Although its operation is simple now, the Amsterdam holding company is suggesting that it might need to provide more services, including online brokerages and other services.[12]

Discussion Questions

1. Why do you think online banking is becoming so popular?
2. Explain why a bank from the Netherlands has been so successful in getting such a large share of the U.S. online banking business.
3. Do you see any major obstacles for ING Direct in competing with U.S. banks in the future?

---

out of trouble. At a cost of hundreds of billions of dollars, the RTC cleaned up the industry and, with its task completed, was dissolved by 1998.

credit union
a financial institution owned and controlled by its depositors, who usually have a common employer, profession, trade group, or religion

Credit Unions. A **credit union** is a financial institution owned and controlled by its depositors, who usually have a common employer, profession, trade group, or religion. The Aggieland Credit Union in College Station, Texas, for example, provides banking services for faculty, employees, and current and former students of Texas A&M University. A savings account at a credit union is commonly referred to as a share account, while a checking account is termed a share draft account. Because the credit union is tied to a common organization, the members (depositors) are allowed to vote for directors and share in the credit union's profits in the form of higher interest rates on accounts and/or lower loan rates.

While credit unions were originally created to provide depositors with a short-term source of funds for low-interest consumer loans for items such as cars, home appliances, vacations, and college, today they offer a wide range of financial services. Generally, the larger the credit union, the more sophisticated its financial service offerings will be.

mutual savings banks
financial institutions that are similar to savings and loan associations but, like credit unions, are owned by their depositors

Mutual Savings Banks. **Mutual savings banks** are similar to savings and loan associations, but, like credit unions, they are owned by their depositors. Among the oldest financial institutions in the United States, they were originally established to provide a safe place for savings of particular groups of people, such as fishermen.

Found mostly in New England, they are becoming more popular in the rest of the country as some S&Ls have converted to mutual savings banks to escape the stigma created by the widespread S&L failures in the 1980s.

Insurance for Banking Institutions.   The **Federal Deposit Insurance Corporation (FDIC),** which insures individual bank accounts, was established in 1933 to help stop bank failures throughout the country during the Great Depression. Today, the FDIC insures personal accounts up to a maximum of $100,000 at nearly 8,000 FDIC member institutions.[13] While most major banks are insured by the FDIC, small institutions in some states may be insured by state insurance funds or private insurance companies. Should a member bank fail, its depositors can recover all of their funds, up to $100,000. Amounts over $100,000, while not legally covered by the insurance, are in fact usually covered because the Fed understands very well the enormous damage that would result to the financial system should these large depositors withdraw their money. The *Federal Savings and Loan Insurance Corporation (FSLIC)* insured thrift deposits prior to its insolvency and failure during the S&L crisis of the 1980s. Now, the insurance functions once overseen by the FSLIC are handled directly by the FDIC through its Savings Association Insurance Fund. The **National Credit Union Association (NCUA)** regulates and charters credit unions and insures their deposits through its National Credit Union Insurance Fund.

When they were originally established, Congress hoped that these insurance funds would make people feel secure about their savings so that they would not panic and withdraw their money when news of a bank failure was announced. The "bank run" scene in the perennial Christmas movie *It's a Wonderful Life,* when dozens of Bailey Building and Loan depositors attempted to withdraw their money (only to have the reassuring figure of Jimmy Stewart calm their fears), was not based on mere fiction. During the Great Depression, hundreds of banks failed and their depositors lost everything. The fact that large numbers of major financial institutions failed in the 1980s and 1990s—without a single major banking panic—underscores the effectiveness of the current insurance system. While the future may yet bring unfortunate surprises, most depositors go to sleep every night without worrying about the safety of their savings.

Nonbanking Institutions

Nonbank financial institutions offer some financial services, such as short-term loans or investment products, but do not accept deposits. These include insurance companies, pension funds, mutual funds, brokerage firms, nonfinancial firms, and finance companies. Table 14.3 lists the top 10 diversified financial services firms,

Federal Deposit Insurance Corporation (FDIC) an insurance fund established in 1933 that insures individual bank accounts

National Credit Union Association (NCUA) an agency that regulates and charters credit unions and insures their deposits through its National Credit Union Insurance Fund

Company	Revenues (in billions)	Company	Revenues (in billions)
General Electric	$134.2	Aon	9.8
Fannie Mae	53.8	Capital One Financial	9.8
American Express	25.9	CIT Group	4.7
Countrywide Financial	13.7	SLM	4.2
Marsh & McLennan	11.6	Arthur J. Gallagher	1.3

TABLE 14.3

Leading Diversified Financial Services Firms

Source: "Fortune 500: Diversified Financial Companies," April 4, 2004. Copyright © 2004 Time Inc. All rights reserved.

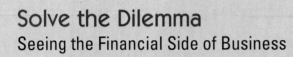
Dr. Stephen Hill, a successful optometrist in Indianapolis, Indiana, has tinkered with various inventions for years. Having finally developed what he believes is his first saleable product (a truly scratch-resistant and lightweight lens), Hill has decided to invest his life savings and open Hill Optometrics to manufacture and market his invention.

Unfortunately, despite possessing true genius in many areas, Hill is uncertain about the "finance side" of business and the various functions of different types of financial institutions in the economy. He is, however, fully aware that he will need financial services such as checking and savings accounts, various short-term investments that can easily and quickly be converted to cash as needs dictate, and sources of borrowing capacity—should the need for either short- or long-term loans arise. Despite having read mounds of brochures from various local and national financial institutions, Hill is still somewhat unclear about the merits and capabilities of each type of financial institution. He has turned to you, his 11th patient of the day for help.

Discussion Questions

1. List the varius types of U.S. financial institutions and the primary function of each.
2. What services of each financial institution is Hill's new company likely to need?
3. Which single financial institution is likely to be best able to meet Hill's small company's needs now? Why?

---

which includes many nonbanking firms, such as manufacturing firms, credit-card issuers, and mortgage providers.

insurance companies
businesses that protect their clients against financial losses from certain specified risks (death, accident, and theft, for example)

Insurance Companies.   **Insurance companies** are businesses that protect their clients against financial losses from certain specified risks (death, injury, disability, accident, fire, theft, and natural disasters, for example) in exchange for a fee, called a premium. Because insurance premiums flow into the companies regularly, but major insurance losses cannot be timed with great accuracy (though expected risks can be assessed with considerable precision), insurance companies generally have large amounts of excess funds. They typically invest these or make long-term loans, particularly to businesses in the form of commercial real estate loans.

pensions funds
managed investment pools set aside by individuals, corporations, unions, and some nonprofit organizations to provide retirement income for members

Pension Funds.   **Pension funds** are managed investment pools set aside by individuals, corporations, unions, and some nonprofit organizations to provide retirement income for members. One type of pension fund is the *individual retirement account (IRA)*, which is established by individuals to provide for their personal retirement needs. IRAs can be invested in a variety of financial assets, from risky commodities such as oil or cocoa to low-risk financial "staples" such as U.S. Treasury securities. The choice is up to each person and is dictated solely by individual objectives and tolerance for risk. The interest earned by all of these investments may be deferred tax-free until retirement.

In 1997, Congress revised the IRA laws and created a Roth IRA. Although similar to a traditional IRA in that investors may contribute $3,000 per year, the money in a Roth IRA is considered an after-tax contribution. When the money is withdrawn at retirement, no tax is paid on the distribution. The Roth IRA is beneficial to young people who can allow a long time for their money to compound and who may be able to have their parents or grandparents fund the Roth IRA with gift money.

Most major corporations provide some kind of pension plan for their employees. Many of these are established with bank trust departments or life insurance companies. Money is deposited in a separate account in the name of each individual employee, and when the employee retires, the total amount in the account can be either withdrawn in one lump sum or taken as monthly cash payments over some defined time period (usually for the remaining life of the retiree).

Social Security, the largest pension fund, is publicly financed. The federal government collects Social Security funds from payroll taxes paid by both employers and employees. The Social Security Administration then takes these monies and makes payments to those eligible to receive Social Security benefits—the retired, the disabled, and the young children of deceased parents.

Mutual Funds.   A **mutual fund** pools individual investor dollars and invests them in large numbers of well-diversified securities. Individual investors buy shares in a mutual fund in the hope of earning a high rate of return and in much the same way as people buy shares of stock. Because of the large numbers of people investing in any one mutual fund, the funds can afford to invest in hundreds (if not thousands) of securities at any one time, minimizing the risks of any single security that does not do well. Mutual funds provide professional financial management for people who lack the time and/or expertise to invest in particular securities, such as government bonds. While there are no hard-and-fast rules, investments in one or more mutual funds are one way for people to plan for financial independence at the time of retirement.

Like most financial institutions, mutual funds are regulated and in recent years have come under closer scrutiny because of a scandal precipitated by questionable activities at some fund companies. The Securities and Exchange Commission (SEC) is developing new rules and reforms "at warp speed" for the $7.5 trillion mutual-fund industry to curtail abuses that gave large traders an advantage over small investors. The problem stems from practices such as late trading and market timing—the rapid buying and selling of fund shares—which can lower the overall performance of a fund and result in higher costs for small investors.[14]

A special type of mutual fund called a *money market fund* invests specifically in short-term debt securities issued by governments and large corporations. Although they offer services such as check-writing privileges and reinvestment of interest income, money market funds differ from the money market accounts offered by banks primarily in that the former represent a pool of funds, while the latter are basically specialized, individual checking accounts. Money market funds usually offer slightly higher rates of interest than bank money market accounts.

Brokerage Firms.   **Brokerage firms** buy and sell stocks, bonds, and other securities for their customers and provide other financial services. Larger brokerage firms like Merrill Lynch, Charles Schwab, and A. G. Edwards offer financial services unavailable at their smaller competitors. Merrill Lynch, for example, offers the Merrill Lynch Cash Management Account (CMA), which pays interest on deposits and allows clients to write checks, borrow money, and withdraw cash much like a commercial bank. The largest of the brokerage firms (including Merrill Lynch) have developed so many specialized services that they may be considered

Mutual funds are considered an excellent method for investing for retirement.

mutual fund
an investment company that pools individual investor dollars and invests them in large numbers of well-diversified securities

brokerage firms
firms that buy and sell stocks, bonds, and other securities for their customers and provide other financial services

financial networks—organizations capable of offering virtually all of the services traditionally associated with commercial banks.

Diversified Firms.   Recently, a growing number of traditionally nonfinancial firms have moved onto the financial field. These firms include manufacturing organizations, such as General Motors and General Electric, that traditionally confined their financial activities to financing their customers' purchases. GE, in particular, has been so successful in the financial arena that its credit subsidiary now accounts for over 30 percent of the company's revenues and earnings. Not every nonfinancial firm has been successful with its financial ventures, however. Sears, the retail giant, once commanded an imposing financial network composed of real estate (Coldwell Banker), credit card (Discover Card), and brokerage (Dean Witter Reynolds) companies, but losses of hundreds of millions of dollars forced Sears to dismantle its network. The very prestigious brokerage firm Morgan Stanley acquired Dean Witter Discover, thus creating one of the largest investment firms in the country—in a league with Smith Barney and Merrill Lynch. Perhaps the moral of the story for firms like Sears is "stick to what you know."

finance companies
business that offer short-term loans at substantially higher rates of interest than banks

Finance Companies.   **Finance companies** are businesses that offer short-term loans at substantially higher rates of interest than banks. Commercial finance companies make loans to businesses, requiring their borrowers to pledge assets such as equipment, inventories, or unpaid accounts as collateral for the loans. Consumer finance companies make loans to individuals. Like commercial finance companies, these firms require some sort of personal collateral as security against the borrower's possible inability to repay their loans. Because of the high interest rates they charge and other factors, finance companies typically are the lender of last resort for individuals and businesses whose credit limits have been exhausted and/or those with poor credit ratings. Major consumer finance companies include Household Finance and Wells Fargo. All finance companies—commercial or consumer—obtain their funds by borrowing from other corporations and/or commercial banks.

Electronic Banking

Since the advent of the computer age, a wide range of technological innovations has made it possible to move money all across the world electronically. Such "paperless" transactions have allowed financial institutions to reduce costs in what has been (and what appears to continue to be) a virtual competitive battlefield. **Electronic funds transfer (EFT)** is any movement of funds by means of an electronic terminal, telephone, computer, or magnetic tape. Such transactions order a particular financial institution to subtract money from one account and add it to another. The most commonly used forms of EFT are automated teller machines, automated clearinghouses, and home banking systems.

electronic funds transfer (EFT)
any movement of funds by means of an electronic terminal, telephone, computer, or magnetic tape

Automated Teller Machines.   Probably the most familiar form of electronic banking is the **automated teller machine (ATM),** which dispenses cash, accepts deposits, and allows balance inquiries and cash transfers from one account to another. ATMs provide 24-hour banking services—both at home (through a local bank) and far away (via worldwide ATM networks such as Cirrus and Plus). Rapid growth, driven by both strong consumer acceptance and lower transaction costs for banks (about half the cost of teller transactions), has led to the installation of hundreds of thousands of ATMs worldwide. Table 14.4 presents some interesting statistics about ATMs.

automated teller machine (ATM)
the most familiar form of electronic banking, which dispenses cash, accepts deposits, and allows balance inquiries and cash transfers from one account to another

<table>
<tr><td>

- An ATM costs between $12,000 and $50,000 depending on the functions it has been designed to perform.
- The top five ATM owners are Bank of America, American Express, Wells Fargo, U.S. Bancorp, and BankOne.
- In 2002, there were 352,000 ATMs in the United States.
- Transactions at these machines totaled $13.9 billion.
- The average ATM user withdraws $67.
- 75% of Americans ages 18–34 use ATMs.
- The average ATM user visits an ATM 10.6 times a month.
- 34.9% of ATM visits are made on the way to work.

Source: "ATM Fact Sheet," *2003 ABA Summary,* American Bankers Association, 2003, www.aba.com; "ATM User Demographics," Strategic Alliance, **www.strategic alliance.com/advertising/demog.php4** (accessed June 5, 2004).

</td><td>

TABLE 14.4

ATM Fact Sheet

</td></tr>
</table>

Automated Clearinghouses. **Automated clearinghouses (ACHs)** permit payments such as deposits or withdrawals to be made to and from a bank account by magnetic computer tape. Most large U.S. employers, and many others worldwide, use ACHs to deposit their employees' paychecks directly to the employees' bank accounts. While direct deposit is used by only 50 percent of U.S. workers, nearly 100 percent of Japanese workers and more than 90 percent of European workers utilize it. The largest user of automated clearinghouses in the United States is the federal government, with 94 percent of federal government employees receiving their pay via direct deposit. And, over 50 percent of all Social Security payments are made through an ACH system.

> **automated clearinghouses (ACHs)** a system that permits payments such as deposits or withdrawals to be made to and from a bank account by magnetic computer tape

The advantages of direct deposits to consumers include convenience, safety, and potential interest earnings. It is estimated that more than four million paychecks are lost or stolen annually, and FBI studies show that 2,000 fraudulent checks are cashed every day in the United States. Checks can never be lost or stolen with direct deposit. The benefits to businesses include decreased check-processing expenses and increased employee productivity. Research shows that businesses that use direct deposit can save more than $1.25 on each payroll check processed. Productivity could increase by $3–5 billion annually if all employees were to use direct deposit rather than taking time away from work to deposit their payroll checks.

Some companies also use ACHs for dividend and interest payments. Consumers can also use ACHs to make periodic (usually monthly) fixed payments to specific creditors without ever having to write a check or buy stamps. The estimated number of bills paid annually by consumers is 20 billion, and the total number paid through ACHs is estimated at only 2.2 billion. The average consumer who writes 10–15 checks each month would save $41–62 annually in postage alone.[15]

Online Banking. With the growth of the Internet, banking activities may now be carried out on a computer at home or at work, or through wireless devices such as cell phones and PDAs anywhere there is a wireless "hot point." Consumers and small businesses can now make a bewildering array of financial transactions at home or on the go 24 hours a day. Functioning much like a vast network of personal ATMs, computer networks such as America Online allow their subscribers to make sophisticated banking transactions, buy and sell stocks and bonds, and purchase products and airline tickets without ever leaving home or speaking to another human being. Many banks allow customers to log directly into their accounts to check balances, transfer money between accounts, view their account statements, and pay bills via home computer or other Internet-enabled devices. Computer and advanced telecommunications technology have revolutionized world commerce. According to the Pew Internet & American Life Project, online banking accelerated by 127 percent between 2000 and 2002, with more than 34 million Americans (30 percent of Internet users) engaging in online banking activities.[16]

Challenge and Change in the Commercial Banking Industry

In the early 1990s, several large commercial banks were forced to admit publicly that they had made some poor loan decisions. Bank failures followed, including that of the Bank of New England, the third-largest bank failure in history. The vibrant economic growth in the 1990s substantially improved what had been a rather bleak picture for many financial institutions. Better management, combined with better regulation and a robust economy, saved commercial banks from the fate of the S&Ls. Indeed, low inflation rates meant low interest rates on deposits, and high employment led to very low loan default rates. Combined, these factors helped to make the 1990s one of the most profitable decades in the history of the banking industry.

The banking industry continued to change in the 2000s, and with the passage of the Gramm-Leach-Bliley Bill, banks are expected to continue their "urge to merge." Now that banks are allowed to offer insurance, brokerage, and investment banking services, there will be a hunt to find likely merger partners that will expand their customer reach and the services they are able to offer. Chase Bank took advantage of the new rules to acquire JP Morgan, which had one of the top 10 investment banks in the United States. On the other side of the coin, even as banks such as Bank America continue to become national banks with offices in more than half the states, small community banks continue to start up to serve the customer who still wants personal service. The ability of these small banks to buy state-of-the-art technology from nonbank service providers allows them to offer Internet banking and many sophisticated services at competitive costs. They also provide a local face and service to the consumer who is more and more likely to be unwelcome at some large banks that cater to corporations and wealthy individuals.

CitiBank is one of the largest international banks in the world and has locations in Asia, Latin America, Europe, and of course North America. People living in Manila can use CitiBank's online banking services from abroad, and CitiBank customers can pay their bills on the Internet while traveling around the world in addition to having access to their money with their CitiBank ATM card. Banking will continue to become more international with large banks such as the Dutch ABN-AMRO bank continuing to acquire banking assets in the United States. For instance in Chicago, ABN-AMRO owns LaSalle Bank, and The Bank of Montreal owns The Harris Bank.

Indeed, the recent trend toward ever bigger banks and other financial institutions is not happening by chance alone. Financial services may be an example of a "natural oligopoly," meaning that the industry may be best served by a few very large firms rather than a host of smaller ones. As the largest U.S. banks merge into even larger international entities, they will erase the relative competitive advantages now enjoyed by the largest foreign banks. It is by no means implausible that the financial services industry of the year 2020 will be dominated by 10 or so internationally oriented "megabanks."

Rapid advances and innovations in technology are challenging the banking industry and requiring it to change. As we said earlier, more and more banks, both large and small, are offering electronic access to their financial services. ATM technology is rapidly changing, with machines now dispensing more than just cash. On-line financial services, ATM technology, and bill presentation are just a few of the areas where rapidly changing technology is causing the banking industry to change as well.

Explore Your Career Options
What Do Economists Do?

Economics is the science of money and its interaction within the general economy. Economists study the ways a society uses scarce resources such as land, labor, raw materials, machinery, and money to produce goods and services. Employed by most major companies and virtually all government agencies, economists conduct research, collect and analyze data, monitor economic trends, and develop forecasts concerning a wide range of economic factors and issues. Within private industry, economists are asked to make predictions concerning the likely economic consequences of various government and/or competitor policies, as well as those of the employing firm.

Commercial banks and other financial institutions are major employers of economists. Indeed, the economic forecasts generated by internal economists play a key role in hosts of financial decisions, from those involving changes in loan rates to the likely future direction of the stock and bond markets, to reasoned conjectures about the direction and impact of expected changes in the money supply and/or government tax policy. While economists can't actually *see* into the future, their estimates about it are frequently so accurate as to suggest otherwise.

The demand for economists is expected to grow about as fast as the average for all occupations through the year 2012. The median annual income for economists is $68,550.[17]

Review Your Understanding

Define money, its functions, and its characteristics.

Money is anything generally accepted as a means of payment for goods and services. Money serves as a medium of exchange, a measure of value, and a store of wealth. To serve effectively in these functions, money must be acceptable, divisible, portable, durable, stable in value, and difficult to counterfeit.

Describe various types of money.

Money may take the form of currency, checking accounts, or other accounts. Checking accounts are funds left in an account in a financial institution that can be withdrawn (usually by writing a check) without advance notice. Other types of accounts include savings accounts (funds left in an interest-earning account that usually cannot be withdrawn without advance notice), money market accounts (an interest-bearing checking account that is invested in short-term debt instruments), certificates of deposit (deposits left in an institution for a specified period of time at a specified interest rate), credit cards (access to a preapproved line of credit granted by a bank or company), and debit cards (means of instant cash transfers between customer and merchant accounts), as well as traveler's checks, money orders, and cashier's checks.

Specify how the Federal Reserve Board manages the money supply and regulates the American banking system.

The Federal Reserve Board regulates the U.S. financial system. The Fed manages the money supply by buying and selling government securities, raising or lowering the discount rate (the rate of interest at which banks may borrow cash reserves from the Fed), raising or lowering bank reserve requirements (the percentage of funds on deposit at a bank that must be held to cover expected depositor withdrawals), and adjusting down payment and repayment terms for credit purchases. It also regulates banking practices, processes checks, and oversees federal depository insurance for institutions.

Compare and contrast commercial banks, savings and loan associations, credit unions, and mutual savings banks.

Commercial banks are financial institutions that take and hold deposits in accounts for and make loans to individuals and businesses. Savings and loan associations are financial institutions that primarily specialize in offering savings accounts and mortgage loans. Credit unions are financial institutions owned and controlled by their depositors. Mutual savings banks are similar to S&Ls except that they are owned by their depositors.

Distinguish among nonbanking institutions such as insurance companies, pension funds, mutual funds, and finance companies.

Insurance companies are businesses that protect their clients against financial losses due to certain circumstances, in exchange for a fee. Pension funds are invest-

ments set aside by organizations or individuals to meet retirement needs. Mutual funds pool investors' money and invest in large numbers of different types of securities. Brokerage firms buy and sell stocks and bonds for investors. Finance companies make short-term loans at higher interest rates than do banks.

Investigate the challenges ahead for the banking industry.

Future changes in financial regulations are likely to result in fewer but larger banks and other financial institutions.

Recommend the most appropriate financial institution for a hypothetical small business.

Using the information presented in this chapter, you should be able to answer the questions in the "Solve the Dilemma" box on page 422 and find the best institution for Hill Optometrics.

Revisit the World of Business

1. What do you feel are the most important functions of money in the recovering Iraqi economy?

2. What can be done to make the Iraqi dinar more acceptable to the country's merchants and stores?

3. What are some of the problems that could develop if the stability of the dinar is not established?

Learn the Terms

automated clearinghouses (ACHs)   425
automated teller machine (ATM)   424
brokerage firms   423
certificates of deposit (CDs)   412
checking account   411
commercial banks   418
credit cards   413
credit controls   417
credit union   420
debit card   414

discount rate   417
electronic funds transfer (EFT)   424
Federal Deposit Insurance Corporation (FDIC)   421
Federal Reserve Board   415
finance   408
finance companies   424
insurance companies   422
monetary policy   416
money   408
money market accounts   412

mutual fund   423
mutual savings banks   420
National Credit Union Association (NCUA)   421
open market operations   416
pension funds   422
reserve requirement   417
savings accounts   412
savings and loan associations (S&Ls)   419

Check Your Progress

1. What are the six characteristics of money? Explain how the U.S. dollar has those six characteristics.

2. What is the difference between a credit card and a debit card? Why are credit cards considerably more popular with U.S. consumers?

3. Discuss the four economic goals the Federal Reserve must try to achieve with its monetary policy.

4. Explain how the Federal Reserve uses open market operations to expand and contract the money supply.

5. What are the basic differences between commercial banks and savings and loans?

6. Why do credit unions charge lower rates than commercial banks?

7. Why do finance companies charge higher interest rates than commercial banks?

8. How are mutual funds, money market funds, and pension funds similar? How are they different?

9. What are some of the advantages of electronic funds transfer systems?

Get Involved

1. Survey the banks, savings and loans, and credit unions in your area, and put together a list of interest rates paid on the various types of checking accounts. Find out what, if any, restrictions are in effect for NOW accounts and regular checking accounts. In which type of account and in what institution would you deposit your money? Why?

2. Survey the same institutions as in question one, this time inquiring as to the rates asked for each of their various loans. Where would you prefer to obtain a car loan? A home loan? Why?

Build Your Skills

MANAGING MONEY

Background:

You have just graduated from college and have received an offer for your dream job (annual salary: $35,000). This premium salary is a reward for your hard work, perseverance, and good grades. It is also a reward for the social skills you developed in college doing service work as a tutor for high school students and interacting with the business community as the program chairman of the college business fraternity, Delta Sigma Pi. You are engaged and plan to be married this summer. You and your spouse will have a joint income of $60,000, and the two of you are trying to decide the best way to manage your money.

Task:

Research available financial service institutions in your area, and answer the following questions.

1. What kinds of institutions and services can you use to help manage your money?

2. Do you want a full service financial organization that can take care of your banking, insurance, and investing needs or do you want to spread your business among individual specialists? Why have you made this choice?

3. What retirement alternatives do you have?

e-Xtreme Surfing

- **Federal Reserve Board**
  www.federalreserve.gov

- **Federal Deposit Insurance Corporation**
  www.fdic.gov

- **National Automated Clearinghouse Association**
  www.nacha.org

Provides news, resources, and information related to the U.S. financial system.

Offers resources, news, and more of interest to consumers.

Presents news, resources, and articles about electronic payment systems.

See for Yourself Videocase

BANK ONE: KEEPING UP WITH GLOBAL TRENDS

Paper money has been used in North America since 1685, when people first began to realize that using paper money as a medium of exchange had several advantages over the barter system. Instead of trading items like furs, grain, or livestock for needed goods or services, people began to use paper money to pay for the things they needed. It was not only more convenient to carry over long distances, but it could also be used as a common measure of value for different goods. As paper money became widely used over time, it took on the characteristics that we value it for today—wide acceptability, easy divisibility, portability, and stability of value.

Part of the convenience of using money in the modern world is that it can be "stored" and accessed in a variety of ways. In the United States, people commonly store their money at commercial banks, credit unions, and savings and loans associations, as well as other banking institutions. Almost 91 percent of Americans have some kind of bank account. Banking institutions accept money deposits from customers into different types of accounts, such as checking, savings, or money market accounts. The banks then use the deposited money as a source of funds to make loans to individuals and businesses. To remain competitive in the global environment, many banks also offer additional financial services such as credit cards, debit cards, investment brokerages, and online banking.

Bank One, one of the largest banks in the United States, started out as a small local bank in Chicago. Opening its doors during the Battle of Gettysburg on July 1, 1863, the bank survived many national changes and tragedies, including the Great Chicago Fire of 1871 and both world wars. It not only survived but thrived by keeping up with the demands of the changing times, and by 2004 had grown to become the sixth largest bank holding company in the U.S., with assets of $320 billion. With 1,845 locations in 14 different states, Bank One served almost 7 million households and 500,000 small businesses in 2004. The company also had international locations in China, Hong Kong, England, Australia, Mexico, South Korea, Taiwan, Japan, and Canada.

By 2004, Bank One was also the number-one issuer of Visa cards, and the third largest credit card issuer in the United States overall. In addition, the bank partnered with many other companies and organizations to offer credit card rewards programs, such as the Audi Visa Signature Card, Southwest Airlines card, Sony card, and even an American Kennel Club card that offers rewards at pet retailers and donations to the AKC with each purchase. In total, Bank One had almost 52 million credit cards in circulation, with more than $74 billion in managed receivables for these cards.

Despite Bank One's growth and success, it agreed to merge with J. P. Morgan Chase on July 1, 2004, in order to remain competitive in today's banking market. The merger resulted in the creation of the second largest bank in the United States, with $1.1 trillion in assets. The two firms decided that the Bank One name would no longer be used after the merger, and the entire company would henceforth be referred to by the well-recognized J.P. Morgan Chase moniker. The new Chase has the benefit of the best of both worlds in banking and financial services: While Bank One was an industry leader in commercial banking services, J. P. Morgan Chase was a leading global firm in investment banking and financial services for consumers and businesses. This new powerful combination is expected to result in a "bigger, better, stronger" bank with a greater variety of services available to its customers, allowing them to manage their bank accounts *and* investments through one firm.

The modern banking industry has become extremely competitive, and the market is dominated by large and powerful conglomerates like the newly created J. P. Morgan Chase brand name. In order to remain competitive, banks today have to do more than ever to attract and retain customers, as well as get customers to invest a larger percentage of their money. The following are some of the major issues that banks must consider in order to remain competitive:

- Finding ways to increase the share of total investments from existing customers

- Finding innovative ways to boost employee productivity in order to increase profitability

- Outsourcing, or offshoring, some operations to lower-cost locations like India or China to reduce operating costs

- Confronting new regulatory changes as a result of the Sarbanes-Oxley Act and changes to International Financial Reporting Standards

- Strengthening corporate governance and internal controls, as well as enhancing disclosures to investors

- Investing in new technology in order to reduce costs, improve efficiency, and offer innovative services to customers

With the combined talents of Bank One and J. P. Morgan Chase, the newly created Chase company should have the strength to meet these challenges.[18]

Discussion Questions

1. What role do banks like Bank One provide with regard to the functions and characteristics of money?

2. Why do you think it was so beneficial for Bank One and J. P. Morgan Chase to merge in today's competitive financial industry?

3. What advantages do consumers and business customers gain from being able to conduct all their banking activities at one location? Can you think of any disadvantages?

Remember to check out our Online Learning Center at www.mhhe.com/ferrell5e.

Chapter 15

Accounting and Financial Statements

OBJECTIVES

After reading this chapter, you will be able to:

- Define accounting and describe the different uses of accounting information.

- Demonstrate the accounting process.

- Decipher the various components of an income statement in order to evaluate a firm's "bottom line."

- Interpret a company's balance sheet to determine its current financial position.

- Analyze financial statements, using ratio analysis, to evaluate a company's performance.

- Assess a company's financial position using its accounting statements and ratio analysis.

The Public Company Accounting Oversight Board

The Financial Accounting Standards Board has been establishing standards for financial accounting and reporting in the private sector since 1973. Its main mission is to provide guidance for responsible accounting methods, reporting, and policies to protect investors, lenders, and the public. In response to public outrage surrounding corporate accounting scandals at Enron, WorldCom, and many other firms, in which investors and employees lost much of their savings, Congress passed the Sarbanes-Oxley Act in 2002 to restore stakeholder confidence in business financial reporting. Among its many provisions, the Sarbanes-Oxley Act established oversight of public corporate governance and financial reporting obligations and redesigned accountability and ethics standards for corporate officers, auditors, and analysts. While the oversight of accounting had to some extent been an industry self-regulatory function, the passage of the Sarbanes-Oxley Act and the establishment of the accounting oversight board placed more government control over the accounting industry and the public firms they serve.

The Sarbanes-Oxley Act established the Public Company Accounting Oversight Board (PCAOB), which oversees the audit of public companies in order to protect the interests of investors and further the public interest in the preparation of informative, accurate, and independent audit reports for companies. The duties of the PCAOB include registration of public accounting firms; establishment of auditing, quality control, ethics, independence, and other standards relating to preparation of audit reports; inspection of accounting firms; investigations, disciplinary proceedings, and imposition of sanctions; and enforcement of compliance with accounting rules of the board, professional standards and securities laws relating to the preparation and issuance of audit reports and obligations and liabilities of accountants.

continued

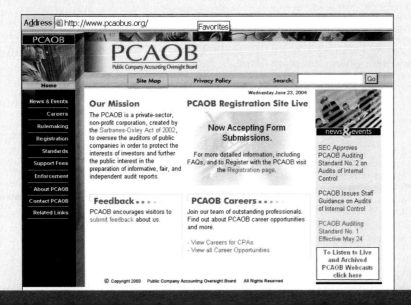

The oversight board reports to the Securities and Exchange Commission (SEC) on an annual basis that includes any new established rules and any final disciplinary rulings. The board works with designated professional groups of accountants and other standard-setting advisory groups to establish auditing, quality control, ethics, and independence rules. It is important to note that the board has the authority to amend, modify, repeal, and reject any standards suggested by these groups. The board is accountable to the SEC, which reviews its standard-setting activity each year. While the creation of an oversight board is a good starting point in obtaining compliance with expected behavior, the Sarbanes-Oxley Act also places accountability among corporate leaders, auditors, security analysts, employees, and attorneys.[1]

Introduction

Accounting, the financial "language" that organizations use to record, measure, and interpret all of their financial transactions and records, is very important in business. All businesses—from a small family farm to a giant corporation—use the language of accounting to make sure they use their money wisely and to plan for the future. Nonbusiness organizations such as charities and governments also use accounting to demonstrate to donors and taxpayers how well they are using their funds and meeting their stated objectives.

This chapter explores the role of accounting in business and its importance in making business decisions. First, we discuss the uses of accounting information and the accounting process. Then, we briefly look at some simple financial statements and accounting tools that are useful in analyzing organizations worldwide.

The Nature of Accounting

accounting
the recording, measurement, and interpretation of financial information

Simply stated, **accounting** is the recording, measurement, and interpretation of financial information. Large numbers of people and institutions, both within and outside businesses, use accounting tools to evaluate organizational operations. The Financial Accounting Standards Board has been establishing standards of financial accounting and reporting in the private sector since 1973. Its mission is to establish and improve standards of financial accounting and reporting for the guidance and education of the public, including issuers, auditors, and users of financial information. However, the accounting scandals at the turn of the century resulted when many accounting firms and businesses failed to abide by generally accepted accounting principles. More than 1,000 firms ultimately reported flaws in their financial statements between 1997 and 2002; in 2002 alone, a record 330 companies chose to restate their earnings to avoid further questions.[2] Consequently, the federal government has taken a greater role in making rules, requirements, and policies for accounting firms and businesses through the Securities and Exchange Commission's Public Company Accounting Oversight Board. For example, Ernst & Young, a leading accounting firm, was barred from undertaking new audit clients for six months as penalty for abusing the agency's auditor-independence rules.[3]

To better understand the importance of accounting, we must first understand who prepares accounting information and how it is used.

The Enron Corporation, which once ranked among the top *Fortune* 500 companies, collapsed in 2001 under a mountain of debt that had been concealed through a complex scheme of off-balance-sheet partnerships. Forced to declare bankruptcy, the energy firm laid off thousands of employees; thousands more lost their retirement savings, which had been invested in Enron stock. The company's shareholders lost tens of billions of dollars after the stock price plummeted. The scandal surrounding Enron's demise engendered a global loss of confidence in corporate ethics that continues to plague markets and eventually triggered tough new scrutiny of financial reporting practices, including the 2002 Sarbanes-Oxley Act.

Andy Fastow, Enron's former chief financial officer, pleaded guilty to fraud charges in a Houston courtroom in 2004, stating, "While CFO, I and other members of Enron's senior management fraudulently manipulated Enron's publicly reported financial results. I also engaged in schemes to enrich myself and others at the expense of Enron's shareholders and in violation of my duty of honest services to those shareholders." In a plea bargain, Fastow agreed to serve 10 years in prison; forfeit $23.8 million, including homes in Galveston and Vermont; and forfeit claims on another $6 million held by third parties. His wife, Lea Fastow, pleaded guilty to one count of filing a false tax report for failing to report $47,800 in income on her 2000 personal taxes, part of more than $204,000 undeclared over four years. Lea Fastow tried to conceal improper income from Enron side deals as if they were gifts of less than $10,000, which need not be reported. Lea Fastow agreed to serve five months in prison and five months under house confinement. Lea Fastow's attorney said the couple insisted on the five-month sentence to ensure that their two young sons have at least one parent at home.

Andy and Lea Fastow are not the only two people who destroyed their lives through misconduct. Many other individuals survived the scandal, but the events of Enron changed their lives forever. Sherron Watkins tried to communicate about misconduct with Ken Lay, Enron's chairman, but was brushed aside. Lay, Enron's team of attorneys, and its accountants decided nothing was wrong in the company's accounting methods. Later, Watkins went on to become one of three women chosen as *Time* magazine's "People of the Year" for blowing the whistle on Enron's deception.

Even though Enron had a code of ethics and was a member of the Better Business Bureau, the company was devastated by unethical activities and corporate scandal. According to Lynn Brewer, former Enron executive and author of *House of Cards: Confessions of an Enron Executive,* many Enron managers and employees knew the company was involved in illegal and unethical activities. Many executives, employees, and board members at Enron did not know or seem to care how decisions were made and disregarded the importance of an ethical corporate culture.[4]

Discussion Questions
1. What role did accounting play in the Enron scandal?
2. How could accountants have mitigated the magnitude of the scandal?
3. What ethical duties do accountants owe to their client companies? To the investors and employees of those companies? To society at large?

Accountants

Many of the functions of accounting are carried out by public or private accountants.

Public Accountants. Individuals and businesses can hire a **certified public accountant (CPA),** an individual who has been certified by the state in which he or she practices to provide accounting services ranging from the preparation of financial records and the filing of tax returns to complex audits of corporate financial records. Certification gives a public accountant the right to express, officially, an unbiased opinion regarding the accuracy of the client's financial statements. Most public accountants are either self-employed or members of large public accounting firms such as Ernst & Young, KPMG, Deloitte & Touche, and PricewaterhouseCoopers, together referred to as "the Big Four." In addition, many CPAs work for one of the second-tier accounting firms that are about one-third the size of the Big Four firms, as illustrated in Table 15.1. The accounting scandals at the turn of the century, combined with more stringent accounting requirements legislated by the Sarbanes-Oxley Act, have increased job prospects for accountants and students with

certified public accountant (CPA) an individual who has been state certified to provide accounting services ranging from the preparation of financial records and the filing of tax returns to complex audits of corporate financial records

TABLE 15.1

Leading Accounting Firms

Company	Revenues ($ millions)	Partners
"Big Four"		
PricewaterhouseCoopers	13.78	7,020
Deloitte & Touche	12.50	6,714
KPMG	10.72	6,600
Ernst & Young	10.12	6,131
Second-Tier Firms		
BDO Sideman	2.40	2,182
Grant Thornton	1.84	2,256
McGladrey & Pullen	1.83	2,245

Source: John Goff, "They Might Be Giants," *CFO,* January 2004, p. 47. © 2003 CCH Incorporated. All rights reserved. Reprinted with permission from Public Accounting Report 2003.

accounting degrees as companies and accounting firms hire more auditors to satisfy the law and public demand for greater transparency.[5]

A growing area for public accountants is *forensic accounting,* which involves analyzing financial documents in search of fraudulent entries or financial misconduct. Functioning as much like detectives as accountants, forensic accountants have been used since the 1930s. In the wake of the accounting scandals of the early 2000s, many auditing firms are rapidly adding or expanding forensic or fraud-detection services. Additionally, many forensic accountants root out evidence of "cooked books" for federal agencies like the Federal Bureau of Investigation or the Internal Revenue Service. The Association of Certified Fraud Examiners, which certifies accounting professionals as *Certified Fraud Examiners (CFEs),* has grown to more than 27,000 members.[7]

Did You Know? Corporate fraud costs are estimated at $600 billion annually.[6]

Private Accountants. Large corporations, government agencies, and other organizations may employ their own **private accountants** to prepare and analyze their financial statements. With titles such as controller, tax accountant, or internal auditor, private accountants are deeply involved in many of the most important financial decisions of the organizations for which they work. Private accountants can be CPAs and may become **certified management accountants (CMAs)** by passing a rigorous examination by the Institute of Management Accountants.

private accountants
accountants employed by large corporations, government agencies, and other organizations to prepare and analyze their financial statements

certified management accountants (CMAs)
private accountants who, after rigorous examination, are certified by the National Association of Accountants and who have some managerial responsibility

Accounting or Bookkeeping?

The terms *accounting* and *bookkeeping* are often mistakenly used interchangeably. Much narrower and far more mechanical than accounting, bookkeeping is typically limited to the routine, day-to-day recording of business transactions. Bookkeepers are responsible for obtaining and recording the information that accountants require to analyze a firm's financial position. They generally require less training than accountants. Accountants, on the other hand, usually complete course work beyond their basic four- or five-year college accounting degrees. This additional training allows accountants not only to record financial information, but to understand, interpret, and even develop the sophisticated accounting systems necessary to classify and analyze complex financial information.

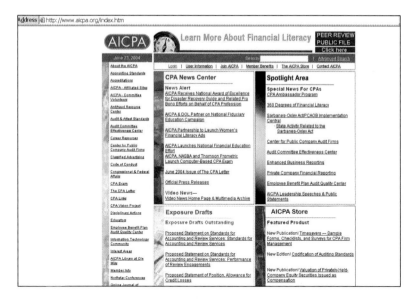

The American Institute of Certified Public Accountants (AICPA) is the premier national professional association for CPAs in the United States.

Source: Copyright © 2004 by the American Institute of Certified Public Accountants, Inc. Reprinted with permission.

The Uses of Accounting Information

Accountants summarize the information from a firm's business transactions in various financial statements (which we'll look at in a later section of this chapter) for a variety of stakeholders, including managers, investors, creditors, and government agencies. Many business failures may be directly linked to ignorance of the information "hidden" inside these financial statements. Likewise, most business successes can be traced to informed managers who understand the consequences of their decisions. While maintaining and even increasing short-run profits is desirable, the failure to plan sufficiently for the future can easily lead an otherwise successful company to insolvency and bankruptcy court.

Basically, managers and owners use financial statements (1) to aid in internal planning and control and (2) for external purposes such as reporting to the Internal Revenue Service, stockholders, creditors, customers, employees, and other interested parties. Figure 15.1 shows some of the users of the accounting information generated by a typical corporation.

Internal Uses.   **Managerial accounting** refers to the internal use of accounting statements by managers in planning and directing the organization's activities. Perhaps management's greatest single concern is **cash flow,** the movement of money through an organization over a daily, weekly, monthly, or yearly basis. Obviously, for any business to succeed, it needs to generate enough cash to pay its bills as they fall due. However, it is not at all unusual for highly successful and rapidly growing companies to struggle to make payments to employees, suppliers, and lenders because of an inadequate cash flow. One common reason for a so-called "cash crunch," or shortfall, is poor managerial planning.

Managerial accountants also help prepare an organization's **budget,** an internal financial plan that forecasts expenses and income over a set period of time. It is not unusual for an organization to prepare separate daily, weekly, monthly, and yearly budgets. Think of a budget as a financial map, showing how the company expects to move from Point A to Point B over a specific period of time. While most companies prepare *master budgets* for the entire firm, many also prepare budgets for

managerial accounting
the internal use of accounting statements by managers in planning and directing the organization's activities

cash flow
the movement of money through an organization over a daily, weekly, monthly, or yearly basis

budget
an internal financial plan that forecasts expenses and income over a set period of time

FIGURE 15.1   The Users of Accounting Information

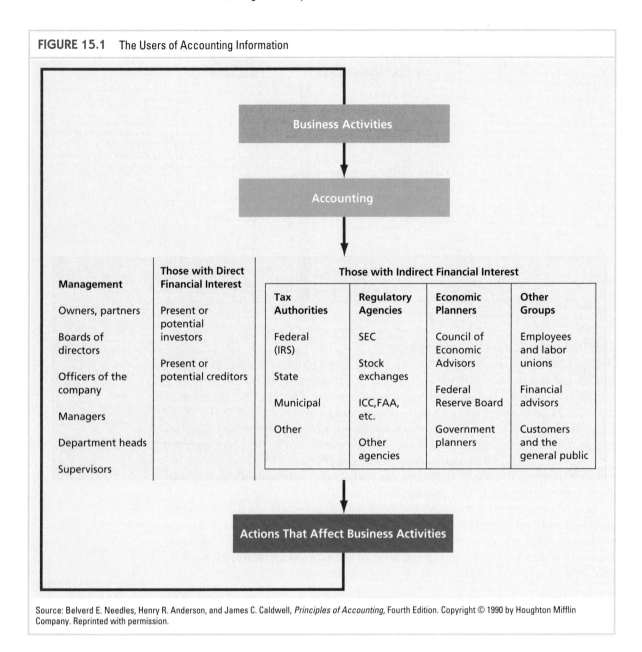

Source: Belverd E. Needles, Henry R. Anderson, and James C. Caldwell, *Principles of Accounting,* Fourth Edition. Copyright © 1990 by Houghton Mifflin Company. Reprinted with permission.

smaller segments of the organization such as divisions, departments, product lines, or projects. "Top-down" master budgets begin at the top and filter down to the individual department level, while "bottom-up" budgets start at the department or project level and are combined at the chief executive's office. Generally, the larger and more rapidly growing an organization, the greater will be the likelihood that it will build its master budget from the ground up.

Regardless of focus, the major value of a budget lies in its breakdown of cash inflows and outflows. Expected operating expenses (cash outflows such as wages, materials costs, and taxes) and operating revenues (cash inflows in the form of payments from customers) over a set period of time are carefully forecast and subsequently compared with actual results. Deviations between the two serve as a "trip wire" or "feedback loop" to launch more detailed financial analyses in an effort to pinpoint trouble spots and opportunities.

External Uses. Managers also use accounting statements to report the business's financial performance to outsiders. Such statements are used for filing income taxes, obtaining credit from lenders, and reporting results to the firm's stockholders. They become the basis for the information provided in the official corporate **annual report,** a summary of the firm's financial information, products, and growth plans for owners and potential investors. While frequently presented between slick, glossy covers prepared by major advertising firms, the single most important component of an annual report is the signature of a certified public accountant attesting that the required financial statements are an accurate reflection of the underlying financial condition of the firm. Financial statements meeting these conditions are termed *audited.* The primary external users of audited accounting information are government agencies, stockholders and potential investors, and lenders, suppliers, and employees.

Federal, state, and local governments (both domestic and overseas) require organizations to file audited financial statements concerning taxes owed and paid, payroll deductions for employees, and, for corporations, new issues of securities (stocks and bonds). Even nonprofit corporations and other nonbusiness organizations may be required to file regular financial statements. NASA, the federal space agency, has been criticized for not managing costs and for failing to adequately document them. PricewaterhouseCoopers, which audited the agency's financial statements, found numerous reporting errors and discrepancies as well as a $204 million line item labeled simply "Other" that the agency could not explain or support in a 2003 quarterly statement.[8] Like individuals, well-managed companies generally try to minimize their taxable income by using accepted accounting practices. Usually, accounting practices that reduce taxes also reduce reported profits. By reducing taxes, the firm increases the cash available to the firm that can be used for many purposes, such as plant expansion, debt retirement, or repurchase of common stock.

A corporation's stockholders use financial statements to evaluate the return on their investment and the overall quality of the firm's management team. As a result, poor financial statements often result in changes in top management. Potential investors study the financial statements in a firm's annual report to determine whether the company meets their investment requirements and whether the returns from a given firm are likely to compare favorably with other similar companies.

Banks and other lenders look at financial statements to determine a company's ability to meet current and future debt obligations if a loan or credit is granted. To

Accountants use the most up-to-date software to stay in compliance with disclosure procedures.

annual report
summary of a firm's financial information, products, and growth plans for owners and potential investors

In 1961, Calisto Tanzi took over his father's small salami and tomato purée factory in Collecchio, Italy. Two years later, he adopted a revolutionary heat-treating process for dairy products, which allowed him to launch the world's first shelf-stable milk. This product, known as Parmalat, became the basis for a global dairy empire. Today, Parmalat employs 36,000 people worldwide, including 3,100 in the United States, and it conducts business in 30 countries across five continents. Despite the success of the company, Tanzi was not one to flaunt his wealth, and he was respected by other residents of Parma. He continued to live in a modest one-story villa outside Parma, where his family regularly attended church and Tanzi donated money to restore a local cathedral and opera house.

The community was shocked when this low-key, highly respected businessman was accused of massive accounting fraud. Arrested on December 27, 2003, Tanzi admitted that he knew that the company's accounts were being falsified. He also told prosecutors that he took money from Parmalat to help his family's failing travel business. An estimated total of $10 billion is missing from the company's books, and the company's debt has reached $17.6 billion. In addition to Tanzi, 10 other suspects have been arrested, including former chief financial officer Fausto Tonna.

Italian authorities have also met with financial institutions involved with Parmalat, including leading U.S. banks like Citigroup and Bank of America. American financial involvement in the Parmalat scandal extends even farther, with insurance companies and other institutions holding more than 60 percent of Parmalat's $10 billion bond debt. AFLAC, for example, held

$383.6 million in Parmalat bonds and lost $257 million when it sold the investment in December 2003. Parmalat, its banks, and its auditors have also been sued by an Alaskan carpenters' pension fund that claims the company victimized investors with its multibillion-dollar scam.

The fraud accusations have Parmalat's U.S. employees worried about the future of their jobs. After its top executives were arrested in December 2003, Parmalat filed for bankruptcy protection in Italy. However, it has not filed for bankruptcy protection in the United States and says its North American division will continue operating normally and is not for sale. The firm also affirmed that the U.S. division, which operates independently, will continue to meet its obligations to suppliers and customers. Despite these declarations, many speculate that Parmalat will eventually have to divest some of its U.S. assets. This is a major concern to the thousands of dairy farms in the United States that supply milk to Parmalat's six U.S. plants. Many of these suppliers are looking for other companies to turn to in case Parmalat North America fails.[9]

Discussion Questions

1. Investors, like large pension funds, banks, and individual investors, depend on auditors to accurately present a company's financial picture. Why was the fraud at Parmalat not discovered for so long?
2. What should auditors have done to prevent (or at least mitigate) the financial damage to the company, its suppliers, and its investors?
3. Could the Parmalat scandal have occurred in the United States today?

determine this ability, a lender examines a firm's cash flow to assess its ability to repay a loan quickly with cash generated from sales. A lender is also interested in the company's profitability and indebtedness to other lenders. Short-term creditors focus on a firm's ability to pay off loans quickly; long-term lenders focus on profitability and indebtedness.

Labor unions and employees use financial statements to establish reasonable expectations for salary and other benefit requests. Just as firms experiencing record profits are likely to face added pressure to increase employee wages, so too are employees unlikely to grant employers wage and benefit concessions without considerable evidence of financial distress.

The Accounting Process

Many view accounting as a primary business language. It is of little use, however, unless you know how to "speak" it. Fortunately, the fundamentals—the accounting equation and the double-entry bookkeeping system—are not difficult to learn. These two concepts serve as the starting point for all currently accepted accounting principles.

The Accounting Equation

Accountants are concerned with reporting an organization's assets, liabilities, and owners' equity. To help illustrate these concepts, consider a hypothetical floral shop called Anna's Flowers, owned by Anna Rodriguez. A firm's economic resources, or items of value that it owns, represent its **assets**—cash, inventory, land, equipment, buildings, and other tangible and intangible things. The assets of Anna's Flowers include counters, refrigerated display cases, flowers, decorations, vases, cards, and other gifts, as well as something known as "goodwill," which in this case is Anna's reputation for preparing and delivering beautiful floral arrangements on a timely basis. **Liabilities,** on the other hand, are debts the firm owes to others. Among the liabilities of Anna's Flowers are a loan from the Small Business Administration and money owed to flower suppliers and other creditors for items purchased. The **owners' equity** category contains all of the money that has ever been contributed to the company that never has to be paid back. The funds can come from investors who have given money or assets to the company, or it can come from past profitable operations. In the case of Anna's Flowers, if Anna were to sell off, or liquidate, her business, any money left over after selling all the shop's assets and paying off its liabilities would comprise her owner's equity. The relationship between assets, liabilities, and owners' equity is a fundamental concept in accounting and is known as the **accounting equation:**

$$\text{Assets} = \text{Liabilities} + \text{Owners' equity}$$

Double-Entry Bookkeeping

Double-entry bookkeeping is a system of recording and classifying business transactions in separate accounts in order to maintain the balance of the accounting equation. Returning to Anna's Flowers, suppose Anna buys $325 worth of roses on credit from the Antique Rose Emporium to fill a wedding order. When she records this transaction, she will list the $325 as a liability or a debt to a supplier. At the same time, however, she will also record $325 worth of roses as an asset in an account known as "inventory." Because the assets and liabilities are on different sides of the accounting equation, Anna's accounts increase in total size (by $325) but remain in balance:

$$\text{Assets} = \text{Liabilities} + \text{Owners' equity}$$
$$\$325 = \$325$$

Thus, to keep the accounting equation in balance, each business transaction must be recorded in two separate accounts.

In the final analysis, all business transactions are classified as either assets, liabilities, or owners' equity. However, most organizations further break down these three accounts to provide more specific information about a transaction. For example, assets may be broken down into specific categories such as cash, inventory, and equipment, while liabilities may include bank loans, supplier credit, and other debts.

Figure 15.2 shows how Anna used the double-entry bookkeeping system to account for all of the transactions that took place in her first month of business. These transactions include her initial investment of $2,500, the loan from the Small Business Administration, purchases of equipment and inventory, and the purchase of roses on credit. In her first month of business, Anna generated revenues of $2,000 by selling $1,500 worth of inventory. Thus, she deducts, or (in accounting notation that is appropriate for assets) *credits,* $1,500 from inventory and adds, or *debits,* $2,000 to

assets
a firm's economic resources, or items of value that it owns, such as cash, inventory, land, equipment, buildings, and other tangible and intangible things

liabilities
debts that a firm owes to others

owners' equity
equals assets minus liabilities and reflects historical values

accounting equation
assets equal liabilities plus owners' equity

double-entry bookkeeping
a system of recording and classifying business transactions that maintains the balance of the accounting equation

FIGURE 15.2 The Accounting Equation and Double-Entry Bookkeeping for Anna's Flowers

	Assets			=	Liabilities	+	Owners' Equity
	Cash	Equipment	Inventory		Debts to suppliers	Loans	Equity
Cash invested by Anna	$2,500.00						$2,500.00
Loan from SBA	$5,000.00					$5,000.00	
Purchase of furnishings	–$3,000.00	$3,000.00					
Purchase of inventory	–$2,000.00		$2,000.00				
Purchase of roses			$325.00		$325.00		
First month sales	$2,000.00		–$1,500.00				$500.00
Totals	$4,500.00	$3,000.00	$825.00		$325.00	$5,000.00	$3,000.00
	$8,325			=	$5,325	+	$3,000
	$8,325 Assets			=	$8,325 Liabilities + Owners' Equity		

the cash account. The difference between Anna's $2,000 cash inflow and her $1,500 outflow is represented by a credit to owners' equity, because it is money that belongs to her as the owner of the flower shop.

The Accounting Cycle

accounting cycle
the four-step procedure of an accounting system: examining source documents, recording transactions in an accounting journal, posting recorded transactions, and preparing financial statements

In any accounting system, financial data typically pass through a four-step procedure sometimes called the **accounting cycle.** The steps include examining source documents, recording transactions in an accounting journal, posting recorded transactions, and preparing financial statements. Figure 15.3 shows how Anna works through them. Traditionally, all of these steps were performed using paper, pencils, and erasers (lots of erasers!), but today the process is often fully computerized.

Step One: Examine Source Documents. Like all good managers, Anna Rodriguez begins the accounting cycle by gathering and examining source documents—checks, credit-card receipts, sales slips, and other related evidence concerning specific transactions.

journal
a time-ordered list of account transactions

Step Two: Record Transactions. Next, Anna records each financial transaction in a **journal,** which is basically just a time-ordered list of account transactions. While most businesses keep a general journal in which all transactions are recorded, some classify transactions into specialized journals for specific types of transaction accounts.

ledger
a book or computer file with separate sections for each account

Step Three: Post Transactions. Anna next transfers the information from her journal into a **ledger,** a book or computer program with separate files for each account. This process is known as *posting.* At the end of the accounting period (usually yearly,

FIGURE 15.3 The Accounting Process for Anna's Flowers

Step 1:
Source documents show that a transaction took place.

Receipt Anna's Flowers	
July 7 Wedding floral arrangements	$500.00
Consultation services	250.00

Step 2:
The transaction is recorded in the journal.

Assets		
	Cash	
July 7 Brown wedding		$750.00

Step 3:
The transaction is posted to the general ledger under the appropriate account (asset, liability, or some further breakdown of these main accounts).

Date		Explanation	PR	Debit	Credit	Balance Debit	Balance Credit
2005							
July	1		1	2,000		2,000	
	3		1		1,250		1,250
	4		1				
	7	Brown wedding	1		750		750
	14		1				

Step 4: At the end of the accounting period, the ledger is used to prepare the firm's financial statements.

Anna's Flowers
Income Statement
December 31, 2005

Revenues:		
Net sales		$123,850
Consulting		73,850
Total revenues		$197,700
Expenses:		
Cost of goods sold	$72,600	
Selling expenses	37,700	
General and admin.	18,400	
Other expenses	5,600	
Total expenses		134,300
Net income		$ 63,400

Anna's Flowers
Balance Sheet
December 31, 2005

Assets
Current assets:
Cash	$17,850	
Accounts receivable	10,200	
Merch. Inventory	8,750	
Tot. assets		$36,800
Property and Equipment
Equipment	11,050	
Office building	73,850	
Tot. prop. & equip.		84,900
Total assets		$121,700

Liabilities and Owner's Equity
Current liabilities
| Accounts payable | $12,600 | |
| Tot. cur. liabilities | | 12,600 |
Long-term liabilities
| Mortgage payable | | 23,600 |
| Total liabilities | | 36,200 |
Owner's equity:
| **Anna Rodriguez, capital** | | $ 85,500 |
Tot. liabilities and owners' equity $ 121,700

Anna's Flowers
Annual Budget
for 2005

	Sales	Consulting	Total
January	10,500	4,500	15,000
February	10,000	5,500	15,500
March	10,800	5,700	16,500
April	10,100	6,050	16,150
May	12,000	6,000	18,000
June	12,100	6,250	18,350
July	13,000	6,600	19,600
August	9,950	6,000	15,950
September	9,700	6,200	15,900
October	9,900	7,000	16,900
November	8,500	7,150	15,650
December	7,300	6,900	14,200
Annual	$123,850	$73,850	$197,700

Grant Thorton provides comprehensive accounting services such as financial statements.

but occasionally quarterly or monthly), Anna prepares a *trial balance,* a summary of the balances of all the accounts in the general ledger. If, upon totalling, the trial balance doesn't (that is, the accounting equation is not in balance), Anna or her accountant must look for mistakes (typically an error in one or more of the ledger entries) and correct them. If the trial balance is correct, the accountant can then begin to prepare the financial statements.

Step Four: Prepare Financial Statements. The information from the trial balance is also used to prepare the company's financial statements. In the case of public corporations and certain other organizations, a CPA must *attest,* or certify, that the organization followed generally accepted accounting principles in preparing the financial statements. When these statements have been completed, the organization's books are "closed," and the accounting cycle begins anew for the next accounting period.

Financial Statements

The end results of the accounting process are a series of financial statements. The income statement, the balance sheet, and the statement of cash flows are the best-known examples of financial statements. These statements are provided to stockholders and potential investors in a firm's annual report as well as to other relevant outsiders such as creditors, government agencies, and the Internal Revenue Service.

It is important to recognize that not all financial statements follow precisely the same format. The fact that different organizations generate income in different ways suggests that when it comes to financial statements, one size definitely does not fit all. Manufacturing firms, service providers, and nonprofit organizations each use a different set of accounting principles or rules upon which the public accounting profession has agreed. As we have already mentioned, these are sometimes referred to as *generally accepted accounting principles (GAAP).* Each country has a different set of rules that the businesses within that country are required to use for their accounting process and financial statements. Moreover, as is the case in many other disciplines, certain concepts have more than one name. For example, *sales* and *revenues* are often interchanged, as are *profits, income,* and *earnings.* Table 15.2 lists a few common equivalent terms that should help you decipher their meaning in accounting statements.

The Income Statement

The question, "What's the bottom line?" derives from the income statement, where the bottom line shows the overall profit or loss of the company after taxes.

Term	Equivalent Term	
Revenues	Sales	**TABLE 15.2**
	Goods or services sold	Equivalent Terms
Gross profit	Gross income	in Accounting
	Gross earnings	
	Gross margin	
Operating income	Operating profit	
	Earnings before interest and taxes (EBIT)	
	Income before interest and taxes (IBIT)	
Income before taxes (IBT)	Earnings before taxes (EBT)	
	Profit before taxes (PBT)	
Net income (NI)	Earnings after taxes (EAT)	
	Profit after taxes (PAT)	
Income available to common stockholders	Earnings available to common stockholders	

Thus, the **income statement** is a financial report that shows an organization's profitability over a period of time, be that a month, quarter, or year. By its very design, the income statement offers one of the clearest possible pictures of the company's overall revenues and the costs incurred in generating those revenues. Other names for the income statement include profit and loss (P&L) statement or operating statement. A sample income statement with line-by-line explanations is presented in Figure 15.4, while Figure 15.5 presents the income statement of Starbucks. The income statement indicates the firm's profitability or income (the bottom line), which is derived by subtracting the firm's expenses from its revenues.

income statement
a financial report that shows an organization's profitability over a period of time—month, quarter, or year

Revenue.   **Revenue** is the total amount of money received (or promised) from the sale of goods or services, as well as from other business activities such as the rental of property and investments. Nonbusiness entities typically obtain revenues through donations from individuals and/or grants from governments and private foundations. Starbucks' income statement (see Figure 15.5) shows one main source of income: sales of Starbucks' products.

revenue
the total amount of money received from the sale of goods or services, as well as from related business activities

For most manufacturing and retail concerns, the next major item included in the income statement is the **cost of goods sold,** the amount of money the firm spent (or promised to spend) to buy and/or produce the products it sold during the accounting period. This figure may be calculated as follows:

cost of goods sold
the amount of money a firm spent to buy or produce the products it sold during the period to which the income statement applies

Cost of goods sold = Beginning inventory + Interim purchases − Ending inventory

Let's say that Anna's Flowers began an accounting period with an inventory of goods for which it paid $5,000. During the period, Anna bought another $4,000 worth of goods, giving the shop a total inventory available for sale of $9,000. If, at the end of the accounting period, Anna's inventory was worth $5,500, the cost of goods sold

---

FIGURE 15.4   Sample Income Statement

The following exhibit presents a sample income statement with all the terms defined and explained.

**Company Name
for the Year Ended
December 31**

Revenues (sales)	Total dollar amount of products sold (includes income from other business services such as rental-lease income and interest income).
Less: Cost of goods sold	The cost of producing the goods and services, including the cost of labor and raw materials as well as other expenses associated with production.
Gross profit	The income available after paying all expenses of production.
Less: Selling and administrative expense	The cost of promoting, advertising, and selling products as well as the overhead costs of managing the company. This includes the cost of management and corporate staff. One non-cash expense included in this category is depreciation, which approximates the decline in the value of plant and equipment assets due to use over time. In most accounting statements, depreciation is not separated from selling and administrative expenses. However, financial analysts usually create statements that include this expense.
Income before interest and taxes (operating income or EBIT)	This line represents all income left over after operating expenses have been deducted. This is sometimes referred to as operating income since it represents all income after the expenses of operations have been accounted for. Occasionally, this is referred to as EBIT, or earnings before interest and taxes.
Less: Interest expense	Interest expense arises as a cost of borrowing money. This is a financial expense rather than an operating expense and is listed separately. As the amount of debt and the cost of debt increase, so will the interest expense. This covers the cost of both short-term and long-term borrowing.
Income before taxes (earnings before taxes—EBT)	The firm will pay a tax on this amount. This is what is left of revenues after subtracting all operating costs, depreciation costs, and interest costs.
Less: Taxes	The tax rate is specified in the federal tax code.
Net income	This is the amount of income left after taxes. The firm may decide to retain all or a portion of the income for reinvestment in new assets. Whatever it decides not to keep it will usually pay out in dividends to its stockholders.
Less: Preferred dividends	If the company has preferred stockholders, they are first in line for dividends. That is one reason why their stock is called "preferred."
Income to common stockholders	This is the income left for the common stockholders. If the company has a good year, there may be a lot of income available for dividends. If the company has a bad year, income could be negative. The common stockholders are the ultimate owners and risk takers. They have the potential for very high or very poor returns since they get whatever is left after all other expenses.
Earnings per share	Earnings per share is found by taking the income available to the common stockholders and dividing by the number of shares of common stock outstanding. This is income generated by the company for each share of common stock.

---

gross income (or profit)
revenues minus the cost
of goods sold required to
generate the revenues

during the period would have been $3,500 ($5,000 + $4,000 − $5,500 = $3,500). If Anna had total revenues of $10,000 over the same period of time, subtracting the cost of goods sold ($3,500) from the total revenues of $10,000 yields the store's **gross income or profit** (revenues minus the cost of goods sold required to generate the revenues): $6,500. For Starbucks, cost of goods sold was more than $1 billion in 2003.

FIGURE 15.5   2003 Income Statement for Starbucks (all figures in thousands of dollars, except per share data)

Fiscal Year Ended	Sept 28, 2003	Sept 29, 2002	Sept 30, 2001
Net revenues:			
Retail	$ 3,449,624	$ 2,792,904	$ 2,229,394
Specialty	625,898	496,004	419,386
Total net revenues	4,075,522	3,288,908	2,648,980
Cost of sales including occupancy costs	1,685,928	1,350,011	1,112,785
Store operating expenses	1,379,574	1,109,782	867,957
Other operating expenses	141,346	106,084	72,406
Depreciation and amortization expenses	237,807	205,557	163,501
General and administrative expenses	244,550	234,581	179,852
Income from equity investees	38,396	33,445	27,740
Operating income	424,713	316,338	280,219
Interest and other income, net	11,622	9,300	10,768
Internet-related investment losses	–	–	2,940
Gain on sale of investment	–	13,361	–
Earnings before income taxes	436,335	338,999	288,047
Income taxes	167,989	126,313	107,712
Net earnings	$ 268,346	$ 212,686	$ 180,335
Net earnings per common share – basic	$ 0.69	$ 0.55	$ 0.47
Net earnings per common share – diluted	$ 0.67	$ 0.54	$ 0.46
Weighted average shares outstanding:			
Basic	390,753	385,575	380,566
Diluted	401,648	397,526	394,349

Source: *Starbucks 2003 Annual Report,* p. 24, available at **www.starbucks.com/aboutus/Annual_Report_2003_part2.pdf** (accessed June 14, 2004).

Expenses.   **Expenses** are the costs incurred in the day-to-day operations of an organization. Three common expense accounts shown on income statements are (1) selling, general, and administrative expenses, (2) research, development, and engineering expenses, and (3) interest expenses (remember that the costs directly attributable to selling goods or services are included in the cost of goods sold). Selling expenses include advertising and sales salaries. General and administrative expenses include salaries of executives and their staff and the costs of owning and maintaining the general office. Research and development costs include scientific, engineering, and marketing personnel and the equipment and information used to design and build prototypes and samples. Interest expenses include the direct costs of borrowing money.

The number and type of expense accounts vary from organization to organization. Included in the general and administrative category is a special type of expense known as **depreciation,** the process of spreading the costs of long-lived assets such

expenses
the costs incurred in the day-to-day operations of an organization

depreciation
the process of spreading the costs of long-lived assets such as buildings and equipment over the total number of accounting periods in which they are expected to be used

as buildings and equipment over the total number of accounting periods in which they are expected to be used. Consider a manufacturer that purchases a $100,000 machine expected to last about 10 years. Rather than showing an expense of $100,000 in the first year and no expense for that equipment over the next nine years, the manufacturer is allowed to report depreciation expenses of $10,000 per year in each of the next 10 years because that better matches the cost of the machine to the years the machine is used. Each time this depreciation is "written off" as an expense, the book value of the machine is also reduced by $10,000. The fact that the equipment has a zero value on the firm's balance sheet when it is fully depreciated (in this case, after 10 years) does not necessarily mean that it can no longer be used or is economically worthless. Indeed, in some industries, machines used every day have been reported as having no book value whatsoever for over 30 years.

net income
the total profit (or loss) after all expenses including taxes have been deducted from revenue; also called net earnings

Net Income.   **Net income** (or net earnings) is the total profit (or loss) after all expenses including taxes have been deducted from revenue. Generally, accountants divide profits into individual sections such as operating income and earnings before interest and taxes. Starbucks, for example, lists earnings before income taxes, net earnings, and earnings per share of outstanding stock (see Figure 15.5). Like most companies, Starbucks presents not only the current year's results but also the previous two years' income statements to permit comparison of performance from one period to another.

Temporary Nature of the Income Statement Accounts.   Companies record their operational activities in the revenue and expense accounts during an accounting period. Gross profit, earnings before interest and taxes, and net income are the results of calculations made from the revenues and expenses accounts; they are not actual accounts. At the end of each accounting period, the dollar amounts in all the revenue and expense accounts are moved into an account called "Retained Earnings," one of the owners' equity accounts. Revenues increase owners' equity, while expenses decrease it. The resulting change in the owners' equity account is exactly equal to the net income. This shifting of dollar values from the revenue and expense accounts allows the firm to begin the next accounting period with zero balances in those accounts. Zeroing out the balances enables a company to count how much it has sold and how many expenses have been incurred during a period of time. The basic accounting equation (assets = liabilities + owners' equity) will not balance until the revenue and expense account balances have been moved or "closed out" to the owners' equity account.

One final note about income statements: You may remember from Chapter 5 that corporations may choose to make cash payments called dividends to shareholders out of their net earnings. When a corporation elects to pay dividends, it decreases the cash account (in the assets category) as well as a capital account (in the owners' equity category). During any period of time, the owners' equity account may change because of the sale of stock (or contributions/withdrawals by owners), the net income or loss, or from the dividends paid.

The Balance Sheet

balance sheet
a "snapshot" of an organization's financial position at a given moment

The second basic financial statement is the **balance sheet,** which presents a "snapshot" of an organization's financial position at a given moment. As such, the balance sheet indicates what the organization owns or controls and the various sources of the funds used to pay for these assets, such as bank debt or owners' equity.

The balance sheet takes its name from its reliance on the accounting equation: Assets *must* equal liabilities plus owners' equity. Figure 15.6 provides a sample balance sheet with line-by-line explanations. Unlike the income statement, the balance sheet does not represent the result of transactions completed over a specified accounting period. Instead, the balance sheet is, by definition, an accumulation of all financial transactions conducted by an organization since its founding. Following long-established traditions, items on the balance sheet are listed on the basis of their original cost less accumulated depreciation, rather than their present values.

Balance sheets are often presented in two different formats. The traditional balance sheet format placed the organization's assets on the left side and its liabilities and owners' equity on the right. More recently, a vertical format, with assets on top followed by liabilities and owners' equity, has gained wide acceptance. Starbucks' balance sheet for 2002 and 2003 is presented in Figure 15.7 on page 452. In the sections that follow, we'll briefly describe the basic items found on the balance sheet; we'll take a closer look at a number of these in Chapter 16.

Assets.   All asset accounts are listed in descending order of *liquidity*—that is, how quickly each could be turned into cash. **Current assets,** also called short-term assets, are those that are used or converted into cash within the course of a calendar year. Thus, cash is followed by temporary investments, accounts receivable, and inventory, in that order. **Accounts receivable** refers to money owed the company by its clients or customers who have promised to pay for the products at a later date. Accounts receivable usually includes an allowance for bad debts that management does not expect to collect. The bad-debts adjustment is normally based on historical collections experience and is deducted from the accounts receivable balance to present a more realistic view of the payments likely to be received in the future, called net receivables. Inventory may be held in the form of raw materials, work-in-progress, or finished goods ready for delivery.

Long-term, or fixed, assets represent a commitment of organizational funds of at least one year. Items classified as fixed include long-term investments, plant and equipment, and intangible assets, such as corporate "goodwill," or reputation, as well as patents and trademarks.

Liabilities.   As seen in the accounting equation, total assets must be financed either through borrowing (liabilities) or through owner investments (owners' equity). **Current liabilities** include a firm's financial obligations to short-term creditors, which must be repaid within one year, while long-term liabilities have longer repayment terms. **Accounts payable** represents amounts owed to suppliers for goods and services purchased with credit. For example, if you buy gas with a Texaco credit card, the purchase represents an account payable for you (and an account receivable for Texaco). Other liabilities include wages earned by employees but not yet paid and taxes owed to the government. Occasionally, these accounts are consolidated into an **accrued expenses** account, representing all unpaid financial obligations incurred by the organization.

Owners' Equity.   Owners' equity includes the owners' contributions to the organization along with income earned by the organization and retained to finance continued growth and development. If the organization were to sell off all of its assets and pay off all of its liabilities, any remaining funds would belong to the owners. Not

current assets
assets that are used or converted into cash within the course of a calendar year

accounts receivable
money owed a company by its clients or customers who have promised to pay for the products at a later date

current liabilities
a firm's financial obligations to short-term creditors, which must be repaid within one year

accounts payable
the amount a company owes to suppliers for goods and services purchased with credit

accrued expenses
all unpaid financial obligations incurred by an organization

FIGURE 15.6   Sample Balance Sheet

The following exhibit presents a balance sheet in word form with each item defined or explained.

Typical Company
December 31

Assets	This is the major category for all physical, monetary, or intangible goods that have some dollar value.
Current assets	Assets that are either cash or are expected to be turned into cash within the next 12 months.
Cash	Cash or checking accounts.
Marketable securities	Short-term investments in securities that can be converted to cash quickly (liquid assets)
Accounts receivable	Cash due from customers in payment for goods received. These arise from sales made on credit.
Inventory	Finished goods ready for sale, goods in the process of being finished, or raw materials used in the production of goods.
Prepaid expense	A future expense item that has already been paid, such as insurance premiums or rent.
Total current assets	The sum of the above accounts.
Fixed assets	Assets that are long term in nature and have a minimum life expectancy that exceeds one year.
Investments	Assets held as investments rather than assets owned for the production process. Most often the assets include small ownership interests in other companies.
Gross property, plant, and equipment	Land, buildings, and other fixed assets listed at original cost.
Less: Accumulated depreciation	The accumulated expense deductions applied to all plant and equipment over their life. Land may not be depreciated. The total amount represents in general the decline in value as equipment gets older and wears out. The maximum amount that can be deducted is set by the U.S. Federal Tax Code and varies by type of asset.
Net property, plant, and equipment	Gross property, plant, and equipment minus the accumulated depreciation. This amount reflects the book value of the fixed assets and not their value if sold.
Other assets	Any other asset that is long term and does not fit into the above categories. It could be patents or trademarks.
Total assets	The sum of all the asset values.

---

surprisingly, the accounts listed as owners' equity on a balance sheet may differ dramatically from company to company. As mentioned in Chapter 5, corporations sell stock to investors, who become the owners of the firm. Many corporations issue two, three, or even more different classes of common and preferred stock, each with different dividend payments and/or voting rights. Since each type of stock issued represents a different claim on the organization, each must be represented by a separate owners' equity account, called contributed capital.

The Statement of Cash Flow

statement of cash flow explains how the company's cash changed from the beginning of the accounting period to the end

The third primary financial statement is called the **statement of cash flow,** which explains how the company's cash changed from the beginning of the accounting period to the end. Cash, of course, is an asset shown on the balance sheet, which provides a snapshot of the firm's financial position at one point in time. However, many investors and other users of financial statements want more information about the cash flowing into and out of the firm than is provided on the balance sheet to better understand the company's financial health. The statement of cash flow takes the cash

---

FIGURE 15.6   Sample Balance Sheet *(continued)*

Liabilities and Stockholders' Equity	This is the major category. Liabilities refer to all indebtedness and loans of both a long-term and short-term nature. Stockholders' equity refers to all money that has been contributed to the company over the life of the firm by the owners.
Current liabilities	Short-term debt expected to be paid off within the next 12 months.
Accounts payable	Money owed to suppliers for goods ordered. Firms usually have between 30 and 90 days to pay this account, depending on industry norms.
Wages payable	Money owned to employees for hours worked or salary. If workers receive checks every two weeks, the amount owed should be no more than two weeks' pay.
Taxes payable	Firms are required to pay corporate taxes quarterly. This refers to taxes owed based on earnings estimates for the quarter.
Notes payable	Short-term loans from banks or other lenders.
Other current liabilities	The other short-term debts that do not fit into the above categories.
Total current liabilities	The sum of the above accounts.
Long-term liabilities	All long-term debt that will not be paid off in the next 12 months.
Long-term debt	Loans of more than one year from banks, pension funds, insurance companies, or other lenders. These loans often take the form of bonds, which are securities that may be bought and sold in bond markets.
Deferred income taxes	This is a liability owed to the government but not due within one year.
Other liabilities	Any other long-term debt that does not fit the above two categories.
Stockholders' equity	The following categories are the owners' investment in the company.
Common stock	The tangible evidence of ownership is a security called common stock. The par value is stated value and does not indicate the company's worth.
Capital in excess of par (a.k.a. contributed capital)	When shares of stock were sold to the owners, they were recorded at the price at the time of the original sale. If the price paid was $10 per share, the extra $9 per share would show up in this account at 100,000 shares times $9 per share, or $900,000.
Retained earnings	The total amount of earnings the company has made during its life and not paid out to its stockholders as dividends. This account represents the owners' reinvestment of earnings into company assets rather than payments of cash dividends. This account does not represent cash.
Total stockholders' equity	This is the sum of the above equity accounts representing the owner's total investment in the company.
Total liabilities and stockholders' equity	The total short-term and long-term debt of the company plus the owner's total investment. This combined amount *must* equal total assets.

balance from one year's balance sheet and compares it to the next while providing detail about how the firm used the cash. Figure 15.8 presents Starbucks' statement of cash flows.

The change in cash is explained through details in three categories: cash from (used for) operating activities, cash from (used for) investing activities, and cash from (used for) financing activities. *Cash from operating activities* is calculated by combining the changes in the revenue accounts, expense accounts, current asset accounts, and current liability accounts. This category of cash flows includes all the accounts on the balance sheet that relate to computing revenues and expenses for the accounting period. If this amount is a positive number, as it is for Starbucks, then the business is making extra cash that it can use to invest in increased

FIGURE 15.7   Balance Sheet for Starbucks (in thousands of dollars, except per share data)

Fiscal Year Ended	Sept 28, 2003	Sept 29, 2002
ASSETS		
Current assets:		
Cash and cash equivalents	$ 200,907	$ 99,677
Short-term investments – Available-for-sale securities	128,905	217,302
Short-term investments – Trading securities	20,199	10,360
Accounts receivable, net of allowances of $4,809 and $3,680, respectively	114,448	97,573
Inventories	342,944	263,174
Prepaid expenses and other current assets	55,173	42,351
Deferred income taxes, net	61,453	42,206
Total current assets	924,029	772,643
Long-term investments – Available-for-sale securities	136,159	–
Equity and other investments	144,257	102,537
Property, plant and equipment, net	1,384,902	1,265,756
Other assets	52,113	43,692
Other intangible assets	24,942	9,862
Goodwill	63,344	19,902
TOTAL ASSETS	$ 2,729,746	$ 2,214,392
LIABILITIES AND SHAREHOLDERS' EQUITY		
Current liabilities:		
Accounts payable	$ 168,984	$ 135,994
Accrued compensation and related costs	152,608	105,899
Accrued occupancy costs	56,179	51,195
Accrued taxes	54,934	54,244
Other accrued expenses	101,800	72,289
Deferred revenue	73,476	42,264
Current portion of long-term debt	722	710
Total current liabilities	608,703	462,595
Deferred income taxes, net	33,217	22,496
Long-term debt	4,354	5,076
Other long-term liabilities	1,045	1,036
Shareholders' equity:		
Common stock and additional paid-in capital – Authorized. 600,000,000 shares; issued and outstanding, 393,692,536 and 388,228,592 shares, respectively, (includes 1,697,100 common stock units in both periods)	959,103	891,040
Other additional paid-in-capital	39,393	39,393
Retained earnings	1,069,683	801,337
Accumulated other comprehensive income/(loss)	14,248	(8,581)
Total shareholders' equity	2,082,427	1,723,189
TOTAL LIABILITIES AND SHAREHOLDERS' EQUITY	$ 2,729,746	$ 2,214,392

Source: *Starbucks 2003 Annual Report,* p. 24, available at **www.starbucks.com/aboutus/Annual_Report_2003_part2.pdf** (accessed June 14, 2004).

FIGURE 15.8 Starbucks' Statement of Cash Flow (in thousands)

Fiscal Year Ended	Sept 28, 2003	Sept 29, 2002	Sept 30, 2001
OPERATING ACTIVITIES:			
Net earning	$ 268,346	$ 212,686	$ 180,335
Adjustments to reconcile net earnings to net cash provided by operating activities:			
Depreciation and amortization	259,271	221,141	177,087
Gain on sale of investment	–	(13,361)	–
Internet-related investment losses	–	–	2,940
Provision for impairments and asset disposals	7,784	26,852	11,044
Deferred income taxes, net	(5,932)	(6,088)	(6,068)
Equity in income of investees	(22,813)	(19,584)	(14,838)
Tax benefit from exercise of non-qualified stock options	36,590	44,199	30,899
Net accretion of discount and amortization of premium on marketable securities	5,996	–	–
Cash provided/(used) by changes in operating assets and liabilities:			
Inventories	(64,768)	(41,379)	(19,704)
Prepaid expenses and other current assets	(12,861)	(12,460)	(10,919)
Accounts payable	24,990	5,463	54,117
Accrued compensation and related costs	42,132	24,087	12,098
Accrued occupancy costs	4,293	15,343	6,797
Deferred revenue	30,732	15,321	19,594
Other operating assets and liabilities	(7,313)	5,465	12,923
Net cash provided by operating activities	566,447	477,685	456,305
INVESTING ACTIVITIES:			
Purchase of available-for-sale securities	(323,331)	(339,968)	(184,187)
Maturity of available-for-sale securities	180,687	78,349	93,300
Sale of available-for-sale securities	88,889	144,760	46,931
Purchase of Seattle Coffee Company: net of cash acquired	(69,928)	–	–
Net additions to equity, other investments and other assets	(47,259)	(15,841)	(17,424)
Distributions from equity investees	28,966	22,834	16,863
Net additions to property, plant and equipment	(357,282)	(375,474)	(384,215)
Net cash used by investing activities	(499,258)	(485,340)	(428,532)
FINANCING ACTIVITIES:			
Proceeds from issuance of common stock	107,183	107,467	59,639
Principal payments on long-term debt	(710)	(697)	(685)
Repurchase of common stock	(75,710)	(52,248)	(49,788)
Net cash provided by financing activities	30,763	54,522	9,166
Effect of exchange rate changes on cash and cash equivalents	3,278	1,560	(174)
Net increase in cash and cash equivalents	101,230	48,427	36,765
CASH AND CASH EQUIVALENTS:			
Beginning of period	99,677	51,250	14,485
End of the period	$ 200,907	$ 99,677	$ 51,250
SUPPLEMENTAL DISCLOSURE OF CASH FLOW INFORMATION:			
Cash paid during the year for:			
Interest	$ 265	$ 303	$ 432
Income taxes	$ 140,107	$ 105,339	$ 47,690

Source: *Starbucks 2003 Annual Report,* p. 25, available at **www.starbucks.com/aboutus/Annual_Report_2003_part2.pdf**
(accessed June 14, 2004).

long-term capacity or to pay off debts such as loans or bonds. A negative number may indicate a business that is still in a growing stage or one that is in a declining position with regards to operations.

Cash from investing activities is calculated from changes in the long-term or fixed asset accounts. If this amount is negative, as is the case with Starbucks, the company is purchasing long-term assets for future growth. A positive figure indicates a business that is selling off existing long-term assets and reducing its capacity for the future.

Finally, *cash from financing activities* is calculated from changes in the long-term liability accounts and the contributed capital accounts in owners' equity. If this amount is negative, the company is likely paying off long-term debt or returning contributed capital to investors. As in the case of Starbucks, if this amount is positive, the company is either borrowing more money or raising money from investors by selling more shares of stock.

Ratio Analysis: Analyzing Financial Statements

ratio analysis
calculations that measure an organization's financial health

The income statement shows a company's profit or loss, while the balance sheet itemizes the value of its assets, liabilities, and owners' equity. Together, the two statements provide the means to answer two critical questions: (1) How much did the firm make or lose? and (2) How much is the firm presently worth based on historical values found on the balance sheet? **Ratio analysis,** calculations that measure an organization's financial health, brings the complex information from the income statement and balance sheet into sharper focus so that managers, lenders, owners, and other interested parties can measure and compare the organization's productivity, profitability, and financing mix with other similar entities.

As you know, a ratio is simply one number divided by another, with the result showing the relationship between the two numbers. Financial ratios are used to weigh and evaluate a firm's performance. Interestingly, an absolute value such as earnings of $70,000 or accounts receivable of $200,000 almost never provides as much useful information as a well-constructed ratio. Whether those numbers are good or bad depends on their relation to other numbers. If a company earned $70,000 on $700,000 in sales (a 10 percent return), such an earnings level might be quite satisfactory. The president of a company earning this same $70,000 on sales of $7 million (a 1 percent return), however, should probably start looking for another job!

Looking at ratios in isolation is probably about as useful and exciting as staring at a blank wall. It is the relationship of the calculated ratios to both prior organizational performance and the performance of the organization's "peers," as well as its stated goals, that really matters. Remember, while the profitabil-

CPA assists customers with financial analysis.

ity, asset utilization, liquidity, debt ratios, and per share data we'll look at here can be very useful, you will never see the forest by looking only at the trees.

Profitability Ratios

Profitability ratios measure how much operating income or net income an organization is able to generate relative to its assets, owners' equity, and sales. The numerator (top number) used in these examples is always the net income after taxes. Common profitability ratios include profit margin, return on assets, and return on equity. The following examples are based on the 2003 income statement and balance sheet for Starbucks, as shown in Figures 15.5 and 15.7. Except where specified, all data are expressed in millions of dollars.

The **profit margin,** computed by dividing net income by sales, shows the overall percentage profits earned by the company. It is based solely upon data obtained from the income statement. The higher the profit margin, the better the cost controls within the company and the higher the return on every dollar of revenue. Starbucks' profit margin is calculated as follows:

$$\text{Profit margin} = \frac{\text{Net income}}{\text{Sales}} \quad \frac{\$268.346}{\$4,075.522} = 6.58\%$$

Thus, for every \$1 in sales, Starbucks generated profits of more than 6 cents.

Return on assets, net income divided by assets, shows how much income the firm produces for every dollar invested in assets. A company with a low return on assets is probably not using its assets very productively—a key managerial failing. By its construction, the return on assets calculation requires data from both the income statement and the balance sheet.

$$\text{Return of Assets} = \frac{\text{Net income}}{\text{Assets}} \quad \frac{\$268.346}{\$2,729.746} = 9.83\%$$

In the case of Starbucks, every \$1 of assets generated a return of 9.83 percent, or profits of nearly 10 cents.

Stockholders are always concerned with how much money they will make on their investment, and they frequently use the return on equity ratio as one of their key performance yardsticks. **Return on equity** (also called return on investment [ROI]), calculated by dividing net income by owners' equity, shows how much income is generated by each \$1 the owners have invested in the firm. Obviously, a low return on equity means low stockholder returns and may indicate a need for immediate managerial attention. Because some assets may have been financed with debt not contributed by the owners, the value of the owners' equity is usually considerably lower than the total value of the firm's assets. Starbucks' return on equity is calculated as follows:

$$\text{Return on Equity} = \frac{\text{Net income}}{\text{Equity}} \quad \frac{\$268.346}{\$2,082.427} = 12.89\%$$

Asset Utilization Ratios

Asset utilization ratios measure how well a firm uses its assets to generate each \$1 of sales. Obviously, companies using their assets more productively will have higher returns on assets than their less efficient competitors. Similarly, managers

---

profitability ratios ratios that measure the amount of operating income or net income an organization is able to generate relative to its assets, owners' equity, and sales

profit margin net income divided by sales

return on assets net income divided by assets

return on equity net income divided by owner's equity; also called return on investment (ROI)

asset utilization ratios ratios that measure how well a firm uses its assets to generate each \$1 of sales

can use asset utilization ratios to pinpoint areas of inefficiency in their operations. These ratios (receivables turnover, inventory turnover, and total asset turnover) relate balance sheet assets to sales, which are found on the income statement.

receivables turnover
sales divided by accounts receivable

The **receivables turnover,** sales divided by accounts receivable, indicates how many times a firm collects its accounts receivable in one year. It also demonstrates how quickly a firm is able to collect payments on its credit sales. Obviously, no payments mean no profits. Starbucks collected its receivables 35.6 times per year.

$$\text{Receivable turnover} = \frac{\text{Sales}}{\text{Receivables}} \quad \frac{\$4,075.522}{\$114.448} = 35.61 \times$$

inventory turnover
sales divided by total inventory

Inventory turnover, sales divided by total inventory, indicates how many times a firm sells and replaces its inventory over the course of a year. A high inventory turnover ratio may indicate great efficiency but may also suggest the possibility of lost sales due to insufficient stock levels. Starbucks' inventory turnover indicates that it replaced its inventory nearly 12 times per year.

$$\text{Inventory turnover} = \frac{\text{Sales}}{\text{Inventory}} \quad \frac{\$4,075.522}{\$342.944} = 11.88 \times$$

total asset turnover
sales divided by total assets

Total asset turnover, sales divided by total assets, measures how well an organization uses all of its assets in creating sales. It indicates whether a company is using its assets productively. Starbucks generated $1.49 in sales for every $1 in total corporate assets.

$$\text{Total asset turnover} = \frac{\text{Sales}}{\text{Total assets}} \quad \frac{\$4,075.522}{\$2,729.746} = 1.49 \times$$

Liquidity Ratios

liquidity ratios
ratios that measure the speed with which a company can turn its assets into cash to meet short-term debt

Liquidity ratios compare current (short-term) assets to current liabilities to indicate the speed with which a company can turn its assets into cash to meet debts as they fall due. High liquidity ratios may satisfy a creditor's need for safety, but ratios that are too high may indicate that the organization is not using its current assets efficiently. Liquidity ratios are generally best examined in conjunction with asset utilization ratios because high turnover ratios imply that cash is flowing through an organization very quickly—a situation that dramatically reduces the need for the type of reserves measured by liquidity ratios.

current ratio
current assets divided by current liabilities

The **current ratio** is calculated by dividing current assets by current liabilities. Starbucks's current ratio indicates that for every $1 of current liabilities, the firm had $1.52 of current assets on hand.

$$\text{Current ratio} = \frac{\text{Current assets}}{\text{Current liabilities}} \quad \frac{\$924.029}{\$608.703} = 1.52 \times$$

quick ratio (acid test)
a stringent measure of liquidity that eliminates inventory

The **quick ratio** (also known as the **acid test**) is a far more stringent measure of liquidity because it eliminates inventory, the least liquid current asset. It measures how well an organization can meet its current obligations without resorting to the sale of its inventory. In 2003, Starbucks had just $.95 invested in current assets (after subtracting inventory) for every $1 of current liabilities.

$$\text{Quick ratio} = \frac{\text{Current assets} - \text{Inventory}}{\text{Current liabilities}} \quad \frac{\$581.085}{\$608.703} = 0.95 \times$$

You have just been promoted from vice president of marketing of BrainDrain Corporation to president and CEO! That's the good news. Unfortunately, while you know marketing like the back of your hand, you know next to nothing about finance. Worse still, the "word on the street" is that BrainDrain is in danger of failure if steps to correct large and continuing financial losses are not taken immediately. Accordingly, you have asked the vice president of finance and accounting for a complete set of accounting statements detailing the financial operations of the company over the past several years.

Recovering from the dual shocks of your promotion and feeling the weight of the firm's complete accounting report for the very first time, you decide to attack the problem systematically and learn the "hidden secrets" of the company, statement by statement. With Mary Pruitt, the firm's trusted senior financial analyst, by your side, you delve into the accounting statements as never before. You resolve to "get to the bottom" of the firm's financial problems and set a new course for the future—a course that will take the firm from insolvency and failure to financial recovery and perpetual prosperity.

Discussion Questions

1. Describe the three basic accounting statements. What types of information does each provide that can help you evaluate the situation?

2. Which of the financial ratios are likely to prove to be of greatest value in identifying problem areas in the company? Why? Which of your company's financial ratios might you expect to be especially poor?

3. Discuss the limitations of ratio analysis.

Debt Utilization Ratios

Debt utilization ratios provide information about how much debt an organization is using relative to other sources of capital, such as owners' equity. Because the use of debt carries an interest charge that must be paid regularly regardless of profitability, debt financing is much riskier than equity. Unforeseen negative events such as recessions affect heavily indebted firms to a far greater extent than those financed exclusively with owners' equity. Because of this and other factors, the managers of most firms tend to keep debt-to-asset levels below 50 percent. However, firms in very stable and/or regulated industries, such as electric utilities, often are able to carry debt ratios well in excess of 50 percent with no ill effects.

debt utilization ratios ratios that measure how much debt an organization is using relative to other sources of capital, such as owners' equity

The **debt to total assets ratio** indicates how much of the firm is financed by debt and how much by owners' equity. To find the value of Starbucks' total debt, you must add current liabilities to long-term debt and other liabilities.

debt to total assets ratio a ratio indicating how much of the firm is financed by debt and how much by owners' equity

$$\text{Debt to total assets} = \frac{\text{Total debt}}{\text{Total assets}} \quad \frac{\$647.319}{\$2,729.746} = 23.71\%$$

Thus, for every \$1 of Starbucks' total assets, 23.7 percent is financed with debt. The remaining 76.3 percent is provided by owners' equity.

The **times interest earned ratio,** operating income divided by interest expense, is a measure of the safety margin a company has with respect to the interest payments it must make to its creditors. A low times interest earned ratio indicates that even a small decrease in earnings may lead the company into financial straits. We cannot calculate a times interest earned ratio for Starbucks because it had so little debt that its interest expense was less than the interest income earned on short-term investments. Starbucks therefore shows net interest income on its income statement instead of a net interest expense. For most companies, however, the times interest earned ratio is calculated as follows:

times interest earned ratio operating income divided by interest expense

$$\text{Times interest earned} = \frac{\text{Income before interest and taxes}}{\text{Interest expense}}$$

Per Share Data

per share data
data used by investors to
compare the performance
of one company with
another on an equal, per
share basis

Investors may use **per share data** to compare the performance of one company with another on an equal, or per share, basis. Generally, the more shares of stock a company issues, the less income is available for each share.

Earnings per share is calculated by dividing net income or profit by the number of shares of stock outstanding. This ratio is important because yearly changes in earnings per share, in combination with other economywide factors, determine a company's overall stock price. When earnings go up, so does a company's stock price—and so does the wealth of its stockholders.

earnings per share
net income or profit
divided by the number of
stock shares outstanding

$$\text{Earnings per share} = \frac{\text{Net income}}{\text{Number of shares outstanding}}$$

$$\begin{array}{cc} 2002 & 2003 \\ \dfrac{\$212.686}{385.575} = \$.55 & \dfrac{\$268.346}{390.753} = \$.69 \end{array}$$

Starbucks' basic earnings per share increased from $.55 in 2002 to $.69 in 2003. Notice that Starbucks lists diluted earnings per share of $.67 for 2003 and $.54 for 2002. You can see from the income statement that diluted earnings per share include more shares than the basic calculation; this is because diluted shares include potential shares that could be issued due to the exercise of stock options or the conversion of certain types of debt into common stock.

dividends per share
the actual cash received
for each share owned

Dividends per share is the actual before-tax cash payment received for each share owned. This ratio, obviously closely related to the earnings per share, is simply another way to analyze the overall return resulting from a stockholder's total investment. Since Starbucks paid no dividend in 2003, this calculation does not apply.

$$\text{Dividends per share} = \frac{\text{Total dividends paid}}{\text{Number of shares outstanding}} \quad \frac{\$0}{390.753} = \$0$$

Industry Analysis

Numbers in a vacuum are not particularly useful for measuring an organization's performance. While comparing a firm's performance to previous years is an excellent

TABLE 15.3		Starbucks (SBUX)	Diedrich Coffee (DDRX)	Green Mountain Coffee Roasters (GMRC)
Industry Analysis	Profit margin	6.58%	− 1.82%	5.37%
	Return on assets	9.83%	− 3.70%	10.45%
	Return on equity	12.89%	− 5.88%	17.83%
	Receivable turnover	35.61X	18.33X	9.19X
	Inventory turnover	11.88X	18.33X	15.64X
	Total asset turnover	1.49X	2.04X	1.95X
	Current ratio	1.52X	1.29X	16.93X
	Quick ratio	0.95X	0.86X	1.13X
	Debt to total assets	23.71%	37.04%	41.41%

Source: *2003 Annual Report,* Diedrich Coffee, **www.corporate-ir.net/ireye/ir_site.zhtml?ticker=ddrx&script=950**; *2003 Annual Report,* Green Mountain Coffee Roasters, **www.greenmountaincoffee.com/investor_services/scripts/annual_report.asp**; *Starbucks 2003 Annual Report,* **www.starbucks.com/aboutus/Annual_Report_2003_part2.pdf**.

gauge of whether corporate operations are improving or deteriorating, another way to analyze a firm is to compare its performance with competitors in its industry. Table 15.3 compares various ratios for Starbucks—which has 7,500 coffee shops around the world—with two competitors in the coffee industry—Diedrich Coffee (which owns 400 Diedrich Coffee, Gloria Jean's, and Coffee People shops) and Green Mountain Coffee Roasters.[10] While Starbucks and Diedrich Coffee are direct competitors in the coffee retail market, Green Mountain is an indirect competitor as a supplier and wholesaler of coffee and related products. They all compete for dollars spent by consumers on coffee products. Starbucks dominates the other two companies in size and sales, but not necessarily in performance, as indicated by the ratio analyses in Table 15.3. While Starbucks has the strongest profit margin and receivables turnover, Diedrich Coffee seems to be doing a better job of managing other assets. Green Mountain has the highest returns on assets and equity and seems to be doing an excellent job of managing its current liabilities, but it has the highest debt-to-total-assets ratio.

Explore Your Career Options
More Power to the Accountants

Perhaps no single area of business study offers better short- and long-term business opportunities than does accounting. Whether employed by private companies, public accounting firms, or government agencies, accountants probably learn and "know the numbers" of their organizations better than any other group of employees. If knowledge is power, then accountants are powerful people. And CPAs and CMAs, by virtue of their advanced study and higher prestige, are far and away the most powerful accountants.

Accountants prepare, analyze, and verify financial reports and taxes and monitor the systems that furnish this information to managers in all business, nonprofit, and government organizations. Management accountants are employed by private businesses to prepare, analyze, and interpret the financial information corporate executives need to make sound decisions. Public accountants and private internal auditors, on the other hand, specialize in the verification of corporate and personal financial records and in the preparation of tax filings. The increasing computerization of accounting means that accountants are frequently the most computer-literate employees not directly involved with the design and maintenance of an organization's computer systems.

As more states have increased the CPA collegiate hour requirement beyond 120–150 hours, the number of "accounting majors" meeting the new requirements has declined. With industry demand high and increasing, and the number of qualified accountants holding steady or even decreasing, accounting salaries (particularly for CPAs and CMAs) continue to rise from what are already high levels when compared with other business degrees.

According to Robert Half International, projected annual salaries for first-year accountants range from $35,750 to $42,500 at large public accounting firms, and from $29,500 to $38,250 at medium or small ones. In the corporate arena, first-year CMA salaries range from $28,500 to $39,750. In the fast-growing area of forensic accounting, starting salaries range from $25,000 to $40,000, but CFEs with several years' experience can earn $70,000 to as much as $150,000 in the private sector.[11]

Review Your Understanding

Define accounting and describe the different uses of accounting information.

Accounting is the language businesses and other organizations use to record, measure, and interpret financial transactions. Financial statements are used internally to judge and control an organization's performance and to plan and direct its future activities and measure goal attainment. External organizations such as lenders, governments, customers, suppliers, and the Internal Revenue Service are major consumers of the information generated by the accounting process.

Demonstrate the accounting process.

Assets are an organization's economic resources; liabilities, debts the organization owes to others; owners' equity, the difference between the value of an organization's assets and liabilities. This principle can be expressed as the accounting equation: Assets = Liabilities + Owners' equity. The double-entry bookkeeping system is a system of recording and classifying business transactions in accounts that maintain the balance of the accounting equation. The accounting cycle involves examining source documents, recording transactions in a journal, posting transactions, and preparing financial statements on a continuous basis throughout the life of the organization.

Decipher the various components of an income statement in order to evaluate a firm's "bottom line."

The income statement indicates a company's profitability over a specific period of time. It shows the "bottom line," the total profit (or loss) after all expenses (the costs incurred in the day-to-day operations of the organization) have been deducted from revenue (the total amount of money received from the sale of goods or services and other business activities). The cash flow statement details how much cash is moving through the firm and thus adds insight to a firm's "bottom line."

Interpret a company's balance sheet to determine its current financial position.

The balance sheet, which summarizes the firm's assets, liabilities, and owners' equity since its inception, portrays its financial position as of a particular point in time. Major classifications included in the balance sheet are current assets (assets that can be converted to cash within one calendar year), fixed assets (assets of greater than one year's duration), current liabilities (bills owed by the organization within one calendar year), long-term liabilities (bills due more than one year hence), and owners' equity (the net value of the owners' investment).

Analyze financial statements, using ratio analysis, to evaluate a company's performance.

Ratio analysis is a series of calculations that brings the complex information from the income statement and balance sheet into sharper focus so that managers, lenders, owners, and other interested parties can measure and compare the organization's productivity, profitability, and financing mix with other similar entities. Ratios may be classified in terms of profitability (measure dollars of return for each dollar of employed assets), asset utilization (measure how well the organization uses its assets to generate $1 in sales), liquidity (assess organizational risk by comparing current assets to current liabilities), debt utilization (measure how much debt the organization is using relative to other sources of capital), and per share data (compare the performance of one company with another on an equal basis).

Assess a company's financial position using its accounting statements and ratio analysis.

Based on the information presented in the chapter, you should be able to answer the questions posed in the "Solve the Dilemma" box on page 457 to formulate a plan for determining BrainDrain's bottom line, current worth, and productivity.

Revisit the World of Business

1. Why do you think the Financial Accounting Standards Board failed to prevent the WorldCom and Enron accounting scandals?

2. How do you feel about the government playing a much stronger role in the regulation of accounting?

3. Even after the accounting oversight board began to make rules and policies for the accounting industry, some companies continue to violate the rules. What does this suggest to you?

Learn the Terms

accounting   434
accounting cycle   442
accounting equation   441
accounts payable   449
accounts receivable   449

accrued expenses   449
annual report   439
asset utilization ratios   455
assets   441
balance sheet   448

budget   437
cash flow   437
certified management accountants (CMAs)   436
certified public accountant (CPA)   435

Check Your Progress

1. Why are accountants so important to a corporation? What function do they perform?

2. Discuss the internal uses of accounting statements.

3. What is a budget?

4. Discuss the external uses of financial statements.

5. Describe the accounting process and cycle.

6. The income statements of all corporations are in the same format. True or false? Discuss.

7. Which accounts appear under "current liabilities"?

8. Together, the income statement and the balance sheet answer two basic questions. What are they?

9. What are the five basic ratio classifications? What ratios are found in each category?

10. Why are debt ratios important in assessing the risk of a firm?

Get Involved

1. Go to the library or the Internet and get the annual report of a company with which you are familiar. Read through the financial statements, then write up an analysis of the firm's performance using ratio analysis. Look at data over several years and analyze whether the firm's performance is changing through time.

2. Form a group of three or four students to perform an industry analysis. Each student should analyze a company in the same industry, and then all of you should compare your results. The following companies would make good group projects:

Automobiles: DaimlerChrysler, Ford, General Motors

Computers: Apple, IBM, Dell

Brewing: Anheuser-Busch, Adolph Coors, G. Heileman

Chemicals: Du Pont, Dow Chemical, Monsanto

Petroleum: Chevron, ExxonMobil, Amoco

Pharmaceuticals: Merck, Lilly, UpJohn

Retail: Sears, J. C. Penney, Kmart, The Limited

Build Your Skills

FINANCIAL ANALYSIS

Background:

The income statement for Western Grain Company, a producer of agricultural products for industrial as well as consumer mar-

kets, is shown below. Western Grain's total assets are $4,237.1 million, and its equity is $1,713.4 million.

Consolidated Earnings and Retained Earnings Year Ended December 31

(Millions)	2002
Net sales	$6,295.4
Cost of goods sold	2,989.0
Selling and administrative expense	2,237.5
Operating profit	1,068.9
Interest expense	33.3
Other income (expense), net	(1.5)
Earnings before income taxes	1,034.1
Income taxes	353.4

Net earnings	680.7
(Net earnings per share)	$2.94
Retained earnings, beginning of year	3,033.9
Dividends paid	(305.2)
Retained earnings, end of year	$3,409.4

Task:

Calculate the following profitability ratios: profit margin, return on assets, and return on equity. Assume that the industry averages for these ratios are as follows: profit margin, 12%; return on assets, 18%; and return on equity, 25%. Evaluate Western Grain's profitability relative to the industry averages. Why is this information useful?

e-Xtreme Surfing

- **Financial Accounting Standards Board**
  www.fasb.org

- **Public Company Accounting Oversight Board**
  www.pcaobus.org

- *Forbes* **Factbox**
  www.forbes.com/home_europe/newswire/
  2004/01/12/ntr1207517.html

Provides news, resources, and information about generally accepted accounting principles.

Offers resources, news, and information rules and standards of accounting.

Provides a "scorecard" with information about recent accounting scandals.

See for Yourself Videocase

AON MANAGES A DIVERSE ARRAY OF GOODS AND SERVICES

Although you may not have never heard the name, Aon is the largest reinsurance broker in the world, the second largest insurance brokerage, and the third largest employee benefits consultant. Headquartered in Chicago, Aon has offices in more than 120 countries and employs 54,000 people in 600 offices. It is ranked 199th in revenue on the *Fortune* 500, and it does business with 85 percent of the companies in the *Fortune* 500 and the *Fortune* Global 500. The Aon Corporation has annual revenues approaching $10 billion.

Aon is a Gaelic word for "oneness," a concept that is an important part of the company's strategy. Its primary goal is to be the world's most responsive and client-focused insurance company in the world. To achieve this goal, the company integrates thousands of top professionals who work in hundreds of disciplines to provide the best and most customized service possible to their clients. Aon knows that its clients want services that are uniquely tailored to their needs, but they also want those services to be provided by professionals who are experts in their areas. Aon has therefore built a worldwide network of experts and linked them with leading technology so that the company can remain flexible enough to provide customized service while maintaining a large population of specialized employees.

The Aon Corporation has three major business segments: risk and insurance brokerage services, human capital consulting, and specialty insurance underwriting. It offers a diverse array of services to both business and consumer markets. For businesses, Aon offers insurance products like property and liability insurance, and they can consult with Aon about their needs for human resource management and benefits, outsourcing management, and the establishment of warranties on goods and services. Aon also specializes in crisis-management programs, helping companies prepare for potential disasters like product contaminations or recalls, terrorist attacks, natural disasters, and emergency evacuations. Aon has even formed a strategic alliance with the Giuliani Group, run by former New York City Mayor Rudolph Giuliani and other members of his administration, to provide crisis consulting services for major corporations.

For individual consumers, Aon offers traditional insurance products such as life, health, and property insurance, in addition to a line of specialty insurance services and private risk management. If you have a particularly valuable item—say, an art collection or a prize-winning racehorse—Aon specialists can design an insurance product especially for your needs. Or, if you are an important political figure or employed in a dangerous line of work, Aon can provide you with insurance to protect against kidnapping, ransom, and extortion.

With so many offices and so many different products, another function becomes critical at Aon: accounting. Every day, Aon receives financial data from its offices around the globe. Because the company is based in the United States, this data must be compiled and translated into U.S. dollars before it can be published in financial statements. An enormous amount of data must be processed before finalized financial statements can be presented to managers, executives, and regulatory agencies. At a multinational firm like Aon, a large staff of accountants is required to complete the accounting cycle. Source documents from each office must be examined and a countless number of transactions recorded and posted. Of course, most of this is accomplished with the assistance of computers, but skilled accountants are still needed to complete the process. Finally, all of this information must be distilled down into precise, accurate financial statements which present information according to the generally accepted accounting principles (GAAP).

Properly prepared financial statements are essential to the survival and reputation of any firm. They can serve as a form of protection for a company if, for instance, the company is accused of misconduct and comes under investigation. In fact, Aon and several other major insurance firms, including Aetna and MetLife, were subpoenaed by the New York attorney general in April 2004 as part of an investigation into possible conflicts of interest over fees charged to insurance companies by insurance brokers. Although Aon and other insurance brokers help their clients choose appropriate insurance policies, the actual policies themselves are often underwritten by other insurance firms. These other insurers pay fees to Aon in return for Aon selling their products. The New York attorney general opened his investigation based on the suspicion that the collection of these fees might represent a conflict of interest on the part of the insurance brokerages. At the time of this writing, the investigation was still underway, and Aon was fully cooperating with the attorney general's office. Aon representatives insist that the collection of these fees has been standard practice for some time and that the company has openly disclosed the amount of fees it received. Such fees accounted for about $200 million in revenue for Aon in 2003, or about 3.5 percent of the company's total brokerage revenue. Only time will tell if Aon's financial statements hold up to close scrutiny and aid in the company's defense against this investigation.[12]

Discussion Questions

1. What role does accounting play at Aon?

2. How can Aon's financial documents help the company defend itself against conflict-of-interest charges?

3. Aon advises other companies how to handle crisis situations. How can the company's crisis-management consulting services help in its present situation?

Remember to check out our Online Learning Center at <u>www.mhhe.com/ferrell5e</u>.

Chapter 16

Financial Management and Securities Markets

OBJECTIVES

After reading this chapter, you will be able to:

- Describe some common methods of managing current assets.

- Identify some sources of short-term financing (current liabilities).

- Summarize the importance of long-term assets and capital budgeting.

- Specify how companies finance their operations and manage fixed assets with long-term liabilities, particularly bonds.

- Discuss how corporations can use equity financing by issuing stock through an investment banker.

- Describe the various securities markets in the United States.

- Critique the short-term asset and liabilities position of a small manufacturer and recommend corrective action.

Hershey Foods Corporation Stock Provides a Social Contribution

Hershey Foods is the leading North American producer of quality chocolate and candy products, including such much-loved brands as Hershey's milk-chocolate bar, Hershey's syrup, Hershey's cocoa, Almond Joy, Mr. Goodbar, Hershey's Kisses, Kit Kat, and Reese's peanut butter cups. A century after its founding, the company continues to operate by the values of its founder. Milton Hershey was born in 1857 and was of Pennsylvania Dutch descent. He became an apprentice to a candy maker in 1872, at age 15. By age 30, he had founded the Lancaster Caramel Company. After visiting the Chicago Exhibition in 1893, he became very interested in a new chocolate-making machine. He sold his caramel factory and built a large chocolate factory in Derry Church, Pennsylvania, in 1905; the city was renamed Hershey in 1906. Hershey pioneered modern confectionery mass-production techniques by developing much of the machinery for making and packaging his milk-chocolate products. The Hershey Foods Corporation as it exists today was organized under the laws of the state of Delaware on October 24, 1927, as a successor to the original business founded in 1894 by Milton Hershey. The company's stock was first publicly traded on December 1, 1927, and investors can still purchase shares today.

Milton Hershey was not only interested in innovative candy making; he also wanted to help the members of his community. An example of his concern for the community was the founding of a home and school for orphan children, the Hershey Industrial School (now called the Milton Hershey School), in 1909. Many of the children who attended the school became Hershey employees,

continued

including former Hershey chairman William Dearden (1976–1984). Today the 10,000-acre campus houses and provides education for nearly 1,300 financially and socially disadvantaged children. Although Hershey remains a public corporation, the Milton Hershey School Trust, which financially supports the school, owns about 32 percent of Hershey Foods' total equity and has 77 percent of voting control. The Milton Hershey School Trust also owns 100 percent of the Hershey Entertainment and Resort Company, which operates a number of Hershey's non-chocolate properties, including the Hershey Park® theme park, the Dutch Wonderland theme park for younger children, the Hershey Hotel, the Hershey Lodge and Convention Center, the Hershey Bears minor league hockey team, Hershey's zoo, a four-course golf club, an outdoor sports stadium, and an indoor sports arena. Because of Milton Hershey's original funding and the wise investment management by the trust managers, the assets of the Milton Hershey School Trust have grown to a value of over $5 billion. Milton Hershey was a visionary in terms of using a public corporation to support his philanthropic dreams.[1]

Introduction

While it's certainly true that money makes the world go 'round, financial management is the discipline that makes the world turn more smoothly. Indeed, without effective management of assets, liabilities, and owners' equity, all business organizations are doomed to fail—regardless of the quality and innovativeness of their products. Financial management is the field that addresses the issues of obtaining and managing the funds and resources necessary to run a business successfully. It is not limited to business organizations: All organizations, from the corner store to the local nonprofit art museum, from giant corporations to county governments, must manage their resources effectively and efficiently if they are to achieve their objectives.

In this chapter, we look at both short- and long-term financial management. First, we discuss the management of short-term assets, which companies use to generate sales and conduct ordinary day-to-day business operations. Next we turn our attention to the management of short-term liabilities, the sources of short-term funds used to finance the business. Then, we discuss the management of long-term assets such as plant and equipment and the long-term liabilities such as stocks and bonds used to finance these important corporate assets. Finally, we look at the securities markets, where stocks and bonds are traded.

Managing Current Assets and Liabilities

Managing short-term assets and liabilities involves managing the current assets and liabilities on the balance sheet (discussed in Chapter 15). Current assets are short-term resources such as cash, investments, accounts receivable, and inventory. Current liabilities are short-term debts such as accounts payable, accrued salaries, accrued taxes, and short-term bank loans. We use the terms *current* and *short term* interchangeably because short-term assets and liabilities are usually replaced by new

Many small businesses that are seasonal in nature have difficult financing problems. This is particularly true of retail nursery (plants) stores, greeting-card shops, boating stores, and so on. The problem is that each of these businesses has year-round fixed commitments, but the business is seasonal. For example, Calloway's Nursery, located in the Dallas–Ft. Worth metroplex, does approximately half of its business in the April to June quarter, yet it must make lease payments for its 27 retail outlets in Dallas, Ft. Worth, Houston, and San Antonio every month of the year. The problem is compounded by the fact that during seasonal peaks it must compete with large national chains such as Kmart and Home Depot that can easily convert space allocated to nursery products to other purposes when winter comes. While Calloway's Nursery can sell garden-related arts and crafts in its off-season, the potential volume is small compared to the boom period of April to June.

The obvious answer to seasonal working capital problems is sufficient financial planning to ensure that profits produced during the peak season are available to cover losses during the off-season. Calloway's and many other small firms predict at the beginning of their fiscal period the movement of cash flow for every week of the year. This includes the expansion and reduction of the workforce during peak and slow periods and the daily tracking of inventory. However, even such foresight cannot fully prepare a firm for an unexpected situation, such as a freeze, a flood, the entrance of a new competitor in the marketplace, or a zoning change that redirects traffic.

Thus, the answer lies not just in planning but in *flexible* planning. If sales are down by 10 percent, then a similar reduction in employees, salaries, fringe benefits, inventory, and other areas must take place. Plans for expansion must be changed into plans for contraction.[2]

Discussion Questions
1. Why is it challenging for businesses whose primary sales are seasonal to maintain year-round financing?
2. What tools can small businesses with seasonal sales utilize for year-round financial management?
3. What other types of businesses might face seasonal financing issues like Calloway's Nursery?

---

assets and liabilities within three or four months, and always within a year. Managing short-term assets and liabilities is sometimes called **working capital management** because short-term assets and liabilities continually flow through an organization and are thus said to be "working."

working capital management
the managing of short-term assets and liabilities

Managing Current Assets

The chief goal of financial managers who focus on current assets and liabilities is to maximize the return to the business on cash, temporary investments of idle cash, accounts receivable, and inventory.

Managing Cash. A crucial element facing any financial manager is effectively managing the firm's cash flow. Remember that cash flow is the movement of money through an organization on a daily, weekly, monthly, or yearly basis. Ensuring that sufficient (but not excessive) funds are on hand to meet the company's obligations is one of the single most important facets of financial management.

Idle cash does not make money, and corporate checking accounts typically do not earn interest. As a result, astute money managers try to keep just enough cash on hand, called **transaction balances,** to pay bills—such as employee wages, supplies, and utilities—as they fall due. To manage the firm's cash and ensure that enough cash flows through the organization quickly and efficiently, companies try to speed up cash collections from customers.

To accelerate the collection of payments from customers, some companies have customers send their payments to a **lockbox,** which is simply an address for receiving payments, instead of directly to the company's main address. The manager of the lockbox, usually a commercial bank, collects payments directly from the lockbox several times a day and deposits them into the company's bank account. The bank

transaction balances
cash kept on hand by a firm to pay normal daily expenses, such as employee wages and bills for supplies and utilities

lockbox
an address, usually a commercial bank, at which a company receives payments in order to speed collections from customers

can then start clearing the checks and get the money into the company's checking account much more quickly than if the payments had been submitted directly to the company. However, there is no free lunch: The costs associated with lockbox systems make them worthwhile only for those companies that receive thousands of checks from customers each business day.

Large firms with many stores or offices around the country, such as Household International (parent company of the well-known finance company, Household Finance), frequently use electronic funds transfer to speed up collections. Household Finance's local offices deposit checks received each business day into their local banks and, at the end of the day, Household's corporate office initiates the transfer of all collected funds to its central bank for overnight investment. This technique is especially attractive for major international companies, which face slow and sometimes uncertain physical delivery of payments and/or less-than-efficient check-clearing procedures.

More and more companies are now using electronic funds transfer systems to pay and collect bills online. It is interesting that companies want to collect cash quickly but pay out cash slowly. When companies use electronic funds transfers between buyers and suppliers, the speed of collections and disbursements increases to one day. Only with the use of checks can companies delay the payment of cash quickly and have a three-or four-day waiting period until the check is presented to their bank and the cash leaves their account.

Investing Idle Cash.   As companies sell products, they generate cash on a daily basis, and sometimes cash comes in faster than it is needed to pay bills. Organizations often invest this "extra" cash, for periods as short as one day (overnight) or for as long as one year, until it is needed. Such temporary investments of cash are known as **marketable securities.** Examples include U.S. Treasury bills, certificates of deposit, commercial paper, and Eurodollar loans. Table 16.1 summarizes a number of different marketable securities used by businesses and some sample interest rates on these investments as of June 2004. The safety rankings are relative. While all of the listed securities are very low risk, the U.S. government securities are the safest.

Many large companies invest idle cash in U.S. **Treasury bills (T-bills),** which are short-term debt obligations the U.S. government sells to raise money. Issued weekly by the U.S. Treasury, T-bills carry maturities of between one week to one year. U.S. T-bills are generally considered to be the safest of all investments and are called risk free because the U.S. government will not default on its debt.

Commercial certificates of deposit (CDs) are issued by commercial banks and brokerage companies. They are available in minimum amounts of $100,000 but

marketable securities
temporary investment of "extra" cash by organizations for up to one year in U.S. Treasury bills, certificates of deposit, commercial paper, or Eurodollar loans

Treasury bills (T-bills)
short-term debt obligations the U.S. government sells to raise money

commercial certificates of deposit (CDs)
certificates of deposit issued by commercial banks and brokerage companies, available in minimum amounts of $100,000, which may be traded prior to maturity

---

TABLE 16.1

Short-Term Investment Possibilities for Idle Cash

Type of Security	Maturity	Seller of Security	Interest Rate 6/10/04	Safety Level
T-bills	90 days	U.S. government	1.27%	Excellent
Commercial paper	90 days	Major corporations	1.36%	Very good
CDs	90 days	U.S. commercial banks	1.43%	Very good
CDs	180 days	U.S. commercial banks	1.74%	Very good
Eurodollars	90 days	European banks	1.42%	Good
Treasury notes	1 year	U.S. government	2.14%	Excellent

Source: "Selected Interest Rates," Federal Reserve, release: June 14, 2004, **www.federal reserve.gov/release/h15/current/**.

are typically in units of $1 million for large corporations investing excess cash. Unlike consumer CDs (discussed in Chapter 14), which must be held until maturity, commercial CDs may be traded prior to maturity. Should a cash shortage occur, the organization can simply sell the CD on the open market and obtain needed funds.

One of the most popular short-term investments for the largest business organizations is **commercial paper**—a written promise from one company to another to pay a specific amount of money. Since commercial paper is backed only by the name and reputation of the issuing company, sales of commercial paper are restricted to only the largest and most financially stable companies. As commercial paper is frequently bought and sold for durations of as short as one business day, many "players" in the market find themselves buying commercial paper with excess cash on one day and selling it to gain extra money the following day.

Some companies invest idle cash in international markets such as the **Eurodollar market,** a market for trading U.S. dollars in foreign countries. Because the Eurodollar market was originally developed by London banks, any dollar-denominated deposit in a non-U.S. bank is called a Eurodollar deposit, regardless of whether the issuing bank is actually located in Europe, South America, or anyplace else. For example, if you travel overseas and deposit $1,000 in a German bank, you will have "created" a Eurodollar deposit in the amount of $1,000. Since the U.S. dollar is accepted by most countries for international trade, these dollar deposits can be used by international companies to settle their accounts. The market created for trading such investments offers firms with extra dollars a chance to earn a slightly higher rate of return with just a little more risk than they would face by investing in U.S. Treasury bills.

Maximizing Accounts Receivable.   After cash and marketable securities, the balance sheet lists accounts receivable and inventory. Remember that accounts receivable is money owed to a business by credit customers. For example, if you charge your Shell gasoline purchases, until you actually pay for them with cash or a check, they represent an account receivable to Shell. Many businesses make the vast majority of their sales on credit, so managing accounts receivable is an important task.

Each credit sale represents an account receivable for the company, the terms of which typically require customers to pay the full amount due within 30, 60, or even 90 days from the date of the sale. To encourage quick payment, some businesses offer some of their customers discounts of between 1 to 2 percent if they pay off their balance within a specified period of time (usually between 10 and 30 days). On the other hand, late payment charges of between 1 and 1.5 percent serve to discourage slow payers from sitting on their bills forever. The larger the early payment discount offered, the faster customers will tend to pay their accounts. Unfortunately, while discounts increase cash flow, they also reduce profitability. Finding the right balance between the added advantages of early cash receipt and the disadvantages of reduced profits is no simple matter. Similarly, determining the optimal balance between the higher sales likely to result from extending credit to customers with less than sterling credit ratings and the higher bad-debt losses likely to result from a more lenient credit policy is also challenging. Information on company credit ratings is provided by local credit bureaus, national credit-rating agencies such as Dun and Bradstreet, and industry trade groups.

Optimizing Inventory.   While the inventory that a firm holds is controlled by both production needs and marketing considerations, the financial manager has to coordinate inventory purchases to manage cash flows. The object is to minimize the firm's investment in inventory without experiencing production cutbacks as a result of critical materials shortfalls or lost sales due to insufficient finished goods inventories. Every

commercial paper
a written promise from one company to another to pay a specific amount of money

Eurodollar market
a market for trading U.S. dollars in foreign countries

Automakers typically try to keep a 60-day supply of unsold cars on their lots. What might be the difference between a Honda lot and an Oldsmobile lot? Why?

dollar invested in inventory is a dollar unavailable for investment in some other area of the organization. Optimal inventory levels are determined, in large part, by the method of production. If a firm attempts to produce its goods just in time to meet sales demand, the level of inventory will be relatively low. If, on the other hand, the firm produces materials in a constant, level pattern, inventory increases when sales decrease and decreases when sales increase. One way that companies are attempting to optimize inventory is through the use of radio frequency identification (RFID) technology.

The automobile industry is an excellent example of an industry driven almost solely by inventory levels. Because it is inefficient to continually lay off workers in slow times and call them back in better times, Ford, General Motors, and Chrysler try to set and stick to quarterly production quotas. Automakers typically try to keep a 60-day supply of unsold cars. During particularly slow periods, however, it is not unusual for inventories to exceed 100 days of sales. When sales of a particular brand fall far behind the average and inventories build up, production of that model may be canceled, as General Motors did with its Oldsmobile marque. Before eliminating a brand outright, however, automakers typically try to "jump-start" sales by offering rebates, special financing incentives, or special lease terms—all of which GM tried without success.

Although less publicized, inventory shortages can be as much of a drag on potential profits as too much inventory. Not having an item on hand may send the customer to a competitor—forever. Complex computer inventory models are frequently employed to determine the optimum level of inventory a firm should hold to support a given level of sales. Such models can indicate how and when parts inventories should be ordered so that they are available exactly when required—and not a day before. Developing and maintaining such an intricate production and inventory system is difficult, but it can often prove to be the difference between experiencing average profits and spectacular ones.

Managing Current Liabilities

While having extra cash on hand is a delightful surprise, the opposite situation—a temporary cash shortfall—can be a crisis. The good news is that there are several potential sources of short-term funds. Suppliers often serve as an important source through credit sales practices. Also, banks, finance companies, and other organizations offer short-term funds through loans and other business operations.

Accounts Payable.   Remember from Chapter 15 that accounts payable is money an organization owes to suppliers for goods and services. Just as accounts receivable must be actively managed to ensure proper cash collections, so too must accounts payable be managed to make the best use of this important liability.

trade credit
credit extended by suppliers for the purchase of their goods and services

The most widely used source of short-term financing, and therefore the most important account payable, is **trade credit**—credit extended by suppliers for the purchase of their goods and services. While varying in formality, depending on both the organizations involved and the value of the items purchased, most trade credit agreements offer discounts to organizations that pay their bills early A supplier, for example, may offer trade terms of "1/10 net 30," meaning that the purchasing organization may take a 1 percent discount from the invoice amount if it makes payment by the 10th day after receiving the bill. Otherwise, the entire amount is due within 30 days. For example, pretend that you are the financial manager in charge of payables. You owe Ajax Company $10,000, and it offers trade terms of 2/10 net 30. By paying the amount due within 10 days, you can save 2 percent of $10,000, or $200. Assume you place orders with Ajax once per month and have 12 bills of $10,000 each per year. By taking the discount every time, you will save 12 times $200, or $2,400, per year. Now assume you are the financial manager of Gigantic Corp., and it has monthly payables of $100 million per month. Two percent of $100 million is $2 million per month. Failure to take advantage of such trade discounts can, in many cases, add up to large opportunity losses over the span of a year.

Bank Loans.   Virtually all organizations—large and small—obtain short-term funds for operations from banks. In most instances, the credit services granted these firms take the form of a line of credit or fixed dollar loan. A **line of credit** is an arrangement by which a bank agrees to lend a specified amount of money to the organization upon request—provided that the bank has the required funds to make the loan. In general, a business line of credit is very similar to a consumer credit card, with the exception that the preset credit limit can amount to millions of dollars.

In addition to credit lines, banks also make **secured loans**—loans backed by collateral that the bank can claim if the borrowers do not repay the loans—and **unsecured loans**—loans backed only by the borrowers' good reputation and previous credit rating. Both individuals and businesses build their credit rating from their history of borrowing and repaying borrowed funds on time and in full. The three national credit-rating services are Equifax, TransUnion, and Experian. A lack of credit history or a poor credit history can make it difficult to get loans from financial institutions. The *principal* is the amount of money borrowed; *interest* is a percentage of the principal that the bank charges for use of its money. As we mentioned in Chapter 14, banks also pay depositors interest on savings accounts and some checking accounts. Thus, banks charge borrowers interest for loans and pay interest to depositors for the use of their money. In addition, these loans may include origination fees.

The **prime rate** is the interest rate commercial banks charge their best customers (usually large corporations) for short-term loans. While, for many years, loans at the prime rate represented funds at the lowest possible cost, the rapid development of the market for commercial paper has dramatically reduced the importance of commercial banks as a source of short-term loans. Today, most "prime" borrowers are actually small- and medium-sized businesses.

The interest rates on commercial loans may be either fixed or variable. A variable, or floating-rate loan offers an advantage when interest rates are falling but represents a distinct disadvantage when interest rates are rising. Between 1999 and 2004, interest rates plummeted, and borrowers refinanced their loans with low-cost fixed-rate loans. Nowhere was this more visible than in the U.S. mortgage markets, where homeowners lined up to refinance their high-percentage home mortgages with lower-cost loans, in some cases as low as 5 percent on a 30-year loan. Individuals and corporations have the same motivation: to minimize their borrowing costs.

Nonbank Liabilities.   Banks are not the only source of short-term funds for businesses. Indeed, virtually all financial institutions, from insurance companies to pension funds, from money market funds to finance companies, make short-term loans to many organizations. The largest U.S. companies also actively engage in borrowing money from the Eurodollar and commercial paper markets. As noted above, both of these funds' sources are typically slightly less expensive than bank loans.

---

line of credit
an arrangement by which a bank agrees to lend a specified amount of money to an organization upon request

secured loans
loans backed by collateral that the bank can claim if the borrowers do not repay them

unsecured loans
loans backed only by the borrowers' good reputation and previous credit rating

prime rate
the interest rate that commercial banks charge their best customers (usually large corporations) for short-term loans

factor
a finance company to which businesses sell their accounts receivable—usually for a percentage of the total face value

In some instances, businesses actually sell their accounts receivable to a finance company known as a **factor,** which gives the selling organizations cash and assumes responsibility for collecting the accounts. For example, a factor might pay $60,000 for receivables with a total face value of $100,000 (60 percent of the total). The factor profits if it can collect more than what it paid for the accounts. Because the selling organization's customers send their payments to a lockbox, they may have no idea that a factor has bought their receivables.

Additional nonbank liabilities that must be efficiently managed to ensure maximum profitability are taxes owed to the government and wages owed to employees. Clearly, businesses are responsible for many different types of taxes, including federal, state, and local income taxes, property taxes, mineral rights taxes, unemployment taxes, Social Security taxes, workers' compensation taxes, excise taxes, and even more! While the public tends to think that the only relevant taxes are on income and sales, many industries must pay other taxes that far exceed those levied against their income. Taxes and employees' wages represent debt obligations of the firm, which the financial manager must plan to meet as they fall due.

Managing Fixed Assets

Up to this point, we have focused on the short-term aspects of financial management. While most business failures are the result of poor short-term planning, successful ventures must also consider the long-term financial consequences of their actions. Managing the long-term assets and liabilities and the owners' equity portion of the balance sheet is important for the long-term health of the business.

long-term (fixed) assets
production facilities (plants), offices, and equipment—all of which are expected to last for many years

Long-term (fixed) assets are expected to last for many years—production facilities (plants), offices, equipment, heavy machinery, furniture, automobiles, and so on. In today's fast-paced world, companies need the most technologically advanced, modern facilities and equipment they can afford. The tremendous competition faced by the U.S. automotive industry in the 1970s and 1980s from producers overseas was due, in large part, to inefficient fixed assets. When General Motors tried to close an outmoded plant in the late 1990s, the United Automobile Workers Union went on strike. Clearly, balancing the management of long-term assets with employee morale and stockholder returns is not a simple task. After a costly strike, General Motors settled with the union, and financial analysts did not think that General Motors made much headway in getting the union's approval to close old factories.

But modern and high-tech equipment carry high price tags, and the financial arrangements required to support these investments are by no means trivial. Obtaining major long-term financing can be challenging for even the most profitable organizations. For less successful firms, such challenges can prove nearly impossible. We'll take a closer look at long-term financing in a moment, but first let's address some issues associated with fixed assets, including capital budgeting, risk assessment, and the costs of financing fixed assets.

Although improving or moving the location of a fixed asset, such as a factory, seems like a beneficial objective for the future, worker relations, not to mention financing, are often large hurdles to completion.

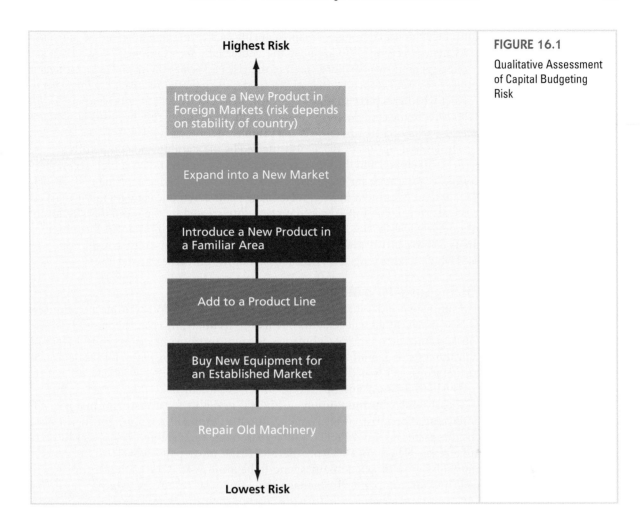

FIGURE 16.1

Qualitative Assessment of Capital Budgeting Risk

Capital Budgeting and Project Selection

One of the most important jobs performed by the financial manager is to decide what fixed assets, projects, and investments will earn profits for the firm beyond the costs necessary to fund them. The process of analyzing the needs of the business and selecting the assets that will maximize its value is called **capital budgeting,** and the capital budget is the amount of money budgeted for investment in such long-term assets. But capital budgeting does not end with the selection and purchase of a particular piece of land, equipment, or major investment. All assets and projects must be continually reevaluated to ensure their compatibility with the organization's needs. If a particular asset does not live up to expectations, then management must determine why and take necessary corrective action. JC Penney, for example, sold its Eckerd drugstore chain subsidiary for $4.5 billion in order to focus on its core department store, catalog, and Internet businesses.[3]

capital budgeting the process of analyzing the needs of the business and selecting the assets that will maximize its value

Assessing Risk

Every investment carries some risk. Figure 16.1 ranks potential investment projects according to estimated risk. When considering investments overseas, risk assessments must include the political climate and economic stability of a region. The decision to introduce a product or build a manufacturing facility in England would be much less risky than a decision to build one in the Middle East, for example.

Not apparent from Figure 16.1 are the risks associated with time. The longer a project or asset is expected to last, the greater its potential risk because it is hard to predict whether a piece of equipment will wear out or become obsolete in 5 or 10 years. Predicting cash flows one year down the road is difficult, but projecting them over the span of a 10-year project is a gamble.

The level of a project's risk is also affected by the stability and competitive nature of the marketplace and the world economy as a whole. IBM's latest high-technology computer product is far more likely to become obsolete overnight than is a similar $10 million investment in a manufacturing plant. Dramatic changes in the marketplace are not uncommon. Indeed, uncertainty created by the rapid devaluation of Asian currencies in the late 1990s wrecked a host of assumptions in literally hundreds of projects worldwide. Financial managers must constantly consider such issues when making long-term decisions about the purchase of fixed assets.

Pricing Long-Term Money

The ultimate profitability of any project depends not only on accurate assumptions of how much cash it will generate but also on its financing costs. Because a business must pay interest on money it borrows, the returns from any project must cover not only the costs of operating the project but also the interest expenses for the debt used to finance its construction. Unless an organization can effectively cover all of its costs—both financial and operating—it will eventually fail.

Clearly, only a limited supply of funds is available for investment in any given enterprise. The most efficient and profitable companies can attract the lowest-cost funds because they typically offer reasonable financial returns at very low relative risks. Newer and less prosperous firms must pay higher costs to attract capital because these companies tend to be quite risky. One of the strongest motivations for companies to manage their financial resources wisely is that they will, over time, be able to reduce the costs of their funds and in so doing increase their overall profitability.

In our free-enterprise economy, new firms tend to enter industries that offer the greatest potential rewards for success. However, as more and more companies enter an industry, competition intensifies, eventually driving profits down to average levels. The digital music player market of the early 2000s provides an excellent example of the changes in profitability that typically accompany increasing competition. When Apple introduced its iPod player, it earned very high returns, boosted by paid music downloads from its iTunes online service. Early on, Apple dominated the market with a 40 percent share of digital music player sales and 70 percent of legal paid music downloads. These high returns, coupled with the growing interest in music downloads, spurred competing firms like Dell, Samsung, Creative, and Rio Nitrus to introduce players with new features or lower prices. Creative, for example, markets a 40-gigabyte player for $200 less than the 40-gigabyte iPod. It is difficult to maintain market dominance in the consumer electronics industry for extended periods of time. Some have even suggested that Apple spin off its iPod business through an initial public offering.[4] The same is true in the personal computer market. With increasing competition, prices have fallen dramatically since the 1990s. Even Dell and Gateway, with their low-cost products, have moved into other markets such as servers and televisions in order to maintain growth in a maturing market. Weaker companies have failed, leaving the most efficient producers/marketers scrambling

Glasspray Corporation is a small firm that makes industrial fiberglass spray equipment. Despite its size, the company supplies to a range of firms from small mom-and-pop boatmakers to major industrial giants, both overseas and here at home. Indeed, just about every molded fiberglass resin product, from bathroom sinks and counters to portable spas and racing yachts, is constructed with the help of one or more of the company's machines.

Despite global acceptance of its products, Glasspray has repeatedly run into trouble with regard to the management of its current assets and liabilities as a result of extremely rapid and consistent increases in year-to-year sales. The firm's president and founder, Stephen T. Rose, recently lamented the sad state of his firm's working capital position: "Our current assets aren't, and our current liabilities are!" Rose shouted in a recent meeting of the firm's top officers. "We can't afford any more increases in sales! We're selling our way into bankruptcy! Frankly, our *working* capital doesn't!"

Discussion Questions
1. Normally, rapidly increasing sales are a good thing. What seems to be the problem here?
2. List the important components of a firm's working capital. Include both current assets and current liabilities.
3. What are some management techniques applied to current liabilities that Glasspray might use to improve its working capital position?

for market share. The expanded market for personal computers dramatically reduced the financial returns generated by each dollar invested in productive assets. The "glory days" of the personal computer industry—the time in which fortunes could be won and lost in the space of an average-sized garage—have long since passed into history. Personal computers have essentially become commodity items, and profit margins for companies in this industry have shrunk as the market becomes mature and new PC versions do little to unleash new demand for the product. With sales falling and profits falling faster, Hewlett-Packard and Compaq merged to gain the economies of scale that saved money and created efficiencies.

Financing with Long-Term Liabilities

As we said earlier, long-term assets do not come cheap, and few companies have the cash on hand to open a new store across town, build a new manufacturing facility, research and develop a new life-saving drug, or launch a new product worldwide. To develop such fixed assets, companies need to raise low-cost long-term funds to finance them. Two common choices for raising these funds are attracting new owners (*equity financing*), which we'll look at in a moment, and taking on long-term liabilities (*debt financing*), which we'll look at now.

Long-term liabilities are debts that will be repaid over a number of years, such as long-term bank loans and bond issues. These take many different forms, but in the end, the key word is *debt*. Companies may raise money by borrowing it from commercial banks or other financial institutions in the form of lines of credit, short-term loans, or long-term loans. Many corporations acquire debt by borrowing money from pension funds, mutual funds, or life-insurance funds.

Companies that rely too heavily on debt can get into serious trouble should the economy falter; during these times, they may not earn enough operating income to make the required interest payments (remember the times-interest-earned ratio in Chapter 15). In severe cases when the problem persists too long, creditors will not restructure loans but will instead sue for the interest and principal owed and force the company into bankruptcy.

long-term liabilities
debts that will be repaid over a number of years, such as long-term loans and bond issues

An IBM bond certificate.

Bonds: Corporate IOUs

bonds
debt instruments that larger companies sell to raise long-term funds

Aside from loans, much long-term debt takes the form of **bonds,** which are debt instruments that larger companies sell to raise long-term funds. In essence, the buyers of bonds (bondholders) loan the issuer of the bonds cash in exchange for regular interest payments until the loan is repaid on or before the specified maturity date. The bond itself is a certificate, much like an IOU, that represents the company's debt to the bondholder. Bonds are issued by a wide variety of entities, including corporations; national, state, and local governments; public utilities; and nonprofit corporations. Most bondholders need not hold their bonds until maturity; rather, the existence of active secondary markets of brokers and dealers allows for the quick and efficient transfer of bonds from owner to owner.

The bond contract, or *indenture,* specifies all of the terms of the agreement between the bondholders and the issuing organization. The indenture, which can run more than 100 pages, specifies the basic terms of the bond, such as its face value, maturity date, and the annual interest rate. Figure 16.2 briefly explains how to determine these and more things about a bond from a bond quote, as it might appear in *The Wall Street Journal.* The face value of the bond, its initial sales price, is typically $1,000. After this, however, the price of the bond on the open market will fluctuate along with changes in the economy (particularly, changes in interest rates) and in the creditworthiness of the issuer. Bondholders receive the face value of the bond along with the final interest payment on the maturity date. The annual interest rate (often called the *coupon rate*) is the guaranteed percentage of face value that the company will pay to the bond owner every year. For example, a $1,000 bond with a coupon rate of 7 percent would pay $70 per year in interest. In most cases, bond indentures specify that interest payments be made every six months. In the example above, the $70 annual payment would be divided into two semiannual payments of $35.

In addition to the terms of interest payments and maturity date, the bond indenture typically covers other important areas, such as repayment methods, interest payment dates, procedures to be followed in case the organization fails to make the interest payments, conditions for the early repayment of the bonds, and any conditions requiring the pledging of assets as collateral.

Bonds	Cur Yld	Vol	Close	Net Chg	FIGURE 16.2
ATT 8⅛ 22	7.9	121	102½	. . . .	A Basic Bond Quote
FordCr 6⅜ 08	6.4	45	100	−⅛	
IBM 7½ 13	6.7	2	112	+1½	
(1) (2) (3)	(4)	(5)	(6)	(7)	

(1) **Bond**—the name or abbreviation of the name of the company issuing the bond; in this case, IBM.

(2) **Annual Interest Rate**—the annual percentage rate specified on the bond certificate: IBM's is 7.5 percent so a $1,000 bond will earn $75 per year in interest.

(3) **Maturity date**—the bond's maturity date; the year in which the issuer will repay bondholders the face value of each bond; 2013.

(4) **Current yield**—percentage return from interest, based on the closing price (column 6); if you buy a bond with a $1,000 par value at today's closing price of 112.00 ($1,120) and receive $75 per year, your cash return will be 6.7 percent.

(5) **Volume**—the number of bonds trading during the day; 2.

(6) **Close**—the closing price; 112.00 = 112 percent of $1,000 per value or $1,120 per bond.

(7) **Change**—change in the price from the close of the previous trading day; IBM's went up 1½ percent of its $1,000 per value or $15.00 per bond.

Types of Bonds

Not surprisingly, there are a great many different types of bonds. Most are **unsecured bonds,** meaning that they are not backed by specific collateral; such bonds are termed *debentures*. **Secured bonds,** on the other hand, are backed by specific collateral that must be forfeited in the event that the issuing firm defaults. Whether secured or unsecured, bonds may be repaid in one lump sum or with many payments spread out over a period of time. **Serial bonds,** which are different from secured bonds, are actually a sequence of small bond issues of progressively longer maturity. The firm pays off each of the serial bonds as they mature. **Floating-rate bonds** do not have fixed interest payments; instead, the interest rate changes with current interest rates otherwise available in the economy.

In recent years, a special type of high-interest-rate bond has attracted considerable attention (usually negative) in the financial press. High-interest bonds, or **junk bonds** as they are popularly known, offer relatively high rates of interest because they have higher inherent risks. Historically, junk bonds have been associated with companies in poor financial health and/or start-up firms with limited track records. In the mid-1980s, however, junk bonds became a very attractive method of financing corporate mergers; they remain popular today with many investors as a result of their very high relative interest rates. But higher risks are associated with those higher returns (upwards of 12 percent per year in some cases) and the average investor would be well-advised to heed those famous words: Look before you leap!

Financing with Owners' Equity

A second means of long-term financing is through equity. Remember from Chapter 15 that owners' equity refers to the owners' investment in an organization. Sole proprietors and partners own all or a part of their businesses outright, and their equity

unsecured bonds
debentures, or bonds that are not backed by specific collateral

secured bonds
bonds that are backed by specific collateral that must be forfeited in the event that the issuing firm defaults

serial bonds
a sequence of small bond issues of progressively longer maturity

floating-rate bonds
bonds with interest rates that change with current interest rates otherwise available in the economy

junk bonds
a special type of high-interest-rate bond that carries higher inherent risks

FIGURE 16.3

A Basic Stock Quote

Source: Data from *The Wall Street Journal,* June 16, 2004.

1		2	3	4	5	6	7	8
52 weeks					Yld			Net
Hi	Lo	Stock	Sym	Div	%	Vol	Close	Chg
78.56	49.60	Nike	NKE	.80	1.1	11,527,000	71.68	.45
42.95	31.50	Reebok	RBK	.30	.8	8,715,000	35.81	.21
67.50	41.88	Timberland	TBL	-0-	N/A	2,055,000	63.83	.47

1. The **52-week high and low**—the highest and lowest prices, respectively, paid for the stock in the last year; for Nike stock, the highest was $78.56 and the lowest price, $49.60
2. **Stock**—the name of the issuing company. When followed by the letters "pf," the stock is preferred stock.
3. **Symbol**—the ticker tape symbol for the stock; NKE.
4. **Dividend**—the annual cash dividend paid to stockholders; Nike paid a dividend of $.80 per share of stock outstanding.
5. **Dividend yield**—the dividend return on one share of common stock; 1.1%.
6. **Volume**—the number of shares traded on this day; 11,527,000.
7. **Close**—Nike's last sale of the day was for $71.68.
8. **Net Change**—the difference between the previous day's close and the close on the day being reported; Nike was up $.45.

includes the money and assets they have brought into their ventures. Corporate owners, on the other hand, own stock or shares of their companies, which they hope will provide them with a return on their investment. Stockholders' equity includes common stock, preferred stock, and retained earnings.

Common stock (introduced in Chapter 5) is the single most important source of capital for most new companies. On the balance sheet, the common stock account is separated into two basic parts—common stock at par and capital in excess of par. The *par value* of a stock is simply the dollar amount printed on the stock certificate and has no relation to actual *market value*—the price at which the common stock is currently trading. The difference between a stock's par value and its offering price is called *capital in excess of par.* Except in the case of some very low-priced stocks, the capital in excess of par account is significantly larger than the par value account. Figure 16.3 briefly explains how to gather important information from a stock quote, as it might appear in *The Wall Street Journal* or on the NASDAQ Web site.

Preferred stock was defined in Chapter 5 as corporate ownership that gives the stockholder preference in the distribution of the company's profits but not the voting and control rights accorded to common stockholders. Thus, the primary advantage of owning preferred stock is that it is a safer investment than common stock.

All businesses exist to earn profits for their owners. Without the possibility of profit, there can be no incentive to risk investors' capital and succeed. When a corporation has profits left over after paying all of its expenses and taxes, it has the choice of retaining all or a portion of its earnings and/or paying them out to its shareholders in the form of dividends. **Retained earnings** are reinvested in the assets of the firm and belong to the owners in the form of equity. Retained earnings are an important source of funds and are, in fact, the only long-term funds that the company can generate internally.

When the board of directors distributes some of a corporation's profits to the owners, it issues them as cash dividend payments. But not all firms pay dividends.

retained earnings
earnings after expenses and taxes that are reinvested in the assets of the firm and belong to the owners in the form of equity

Ticker Symbol	Company Name	Price per Share	Dividend per Share	Dividend Yield	P-E Ratio	TABLE 16.2
AXP	American Express	51.22	.40	0.8	21	
BKHA	Berkshire Hathaway	89,425	-0-	NA	17	Estimated Common Stock Price-Earnings Ratio and Dividends for Selected Companies
CPB	Campbell Soup	25.95	.63	2.4	16	
F	Ford	15.41	.40	2.6	18	
GPS	The Gap	24.66	.09	0.4	21	
G	Gillette	43.29	.65	1.5	29	
HSY	Hershey Foods	92.03	1.58	1.7	25	
HD	Home Depot	35.77	.34	1.0	18	
NKE	Nike	71.68	.80	1.1	22	
LUV	Southwest Airlines	15.41	.02	0.1	29	

Source: Data from *The Wall Street Journal,* June 16, 2004.

Many fast-growing firms retain all of their earnings because they can earn high rates of return on the earnings they reinvest. Companies with fewer growth opportunities typically pay out large proportions of their earnings in the form of dividends, thereby allowing their stockholders to reinvest their dividend payments in higher-growth companies. Table 16.2 presents a sample of companies and the dividend each paid on a single share of stock. As shown in the table, when the dividend is divided by the price the result is the **dividend yield**. The dividend yield is the cash return as a percentage of the price but does not reflect the total return an investor earns on the individual stock. If the dividend yield is 3.1 percent on Campbell Soup and the stock price increases by 10 percent from $28.62 to $31.48, then the total return would be 13.1 percent. It is not clear that stocks with high dividend yields will be preferred by investors to those with little or no dividends. Most large companies pay their stockholders dividends on a quarterly basis.

Investment Banking

A company that needs more money to expand or take advantage of opportunities may be able to obtain financing by issuing stock. The first-time sale of stocks and bonds directly to the public is called a *new issue.* Companies that already have stocks or bonds outstanding may offer a new issue of stock to raise additional funds for specific projects. When a company offers its stock to the public for the very first

A General Mills stock certificate.

dividend yield the dividend per share divided by the stock price

primary market
the market where firms raise financial capital

secondary markets
stock exchanges and over-the-counter markets where investors can trade their securities with others

investment banking
the sale of stocks and bonds for corporations

securities markets
the mechanism for buying and selling securities

time, it is said to be "going public," and the sale is called an *initial public offering.*

New issues of stocks and bonds are sold directly to the public and to institutions in what is known as the **primary market**—the market where firms raise financial capital. The primary market differs from **secondary markets,** which are stock exchanges and over-the-counter markets where investors can trade their securities with other investors rather than the company that issued the stock or bonds. Primary market transactions actually raise cash for the issuing corporations, while secondary market transactions do not.

Investment banking, the sale of stocks and bonds for corporations, helps such companies raise funds by matching people and institutions who have money to invest with corporations in need of resources to exploit new opportunities. Corporations usually employ an investment banking firm to help sell their securities in the primary market. An investment banker helps firms establish appropriate offering prices for their securities. In addition, the investment banker takes care of the myriad details and securities regulations involved in any sale of securities to the public.

Just as large corporations such as IBM, General Motors, and Microsoft have a client relationship with a law firm and an accounting firm, they also have a client relationship with an investment banking firm. An investment banking firm such as Merrill Lynch, Goldman Sachs, or Morgan Stanley can provide advice about financing plans, dividend policy, or stock repurchases, as well as advice on mergers and acquisitions. Many now offer additional banking services, making them "one-stop shopping" banking centers. When Chrysler merged with Daimler-Benz, both companies used investment bankers to help them value the transaction. Each firm wanted an outside opinion about what it was worth to the other. Sometimes mergers fall apart because the companies cannot agree on the price each company is worth or the structure of management after the merger. The advising investment banker, working with management, often irons out these details. Of course, investment bankers do not provide these services for free. They usually charge a fee of between 1 and 1.5 percent of the transaction. A $20 billion merger can generate between $200 and $300 million in investment banking fees. The merger mania of the late 1990s allowed top investment bankers to earn huge sums. Unfortunately, this type of fee income is dependent on healthy stock markets, which seem to stimulate the merger fever among corporate executives.

The Securities Markets

Securities markets provide a mechanism for buying and selling securities. They make it possible for owners to sell their stocks and bonds to other investors. Thus, in the broadest sense, stocks and bonds markets may be thought of as providers of liquidity—the ability to turn security holdings into cash quickly and at minimal ex-

FBR ranks No. 1 among all investment banks.

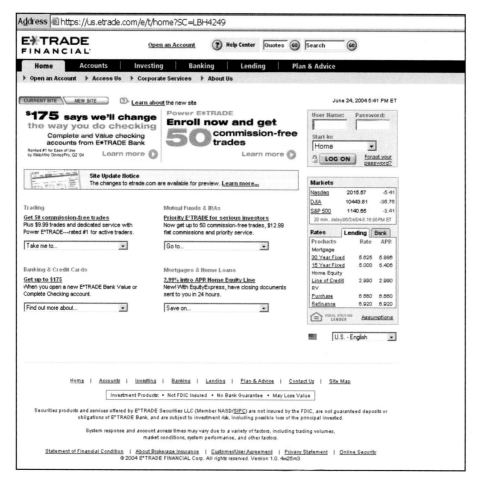

pense and effort. Without liquid securities markets, many potential investors would sit on the sidelines rather than invest their hard-earned savings in securities. Indeed, the ability to sell securities at well-established market prices is one of the very pillars of the capitalistic society that has developed over the years in the United States.

Unlike the primary market, in which corporations sell stocks directly to the public, secondary markets permit the trading of previously issued securities. There are many different secondary markets for both stocks and bonds. If you want to purchase 100 shares of Du Pont common stock, for example, you must purchase this stock from another investor or institution. It is the active buying and selling by many thousands of investors that establishes the prices of all financial securities. Secondary market trades may take place on organized exchanges or in what is known as the over-the-counter market. Many brokerage houses exist to help investors with financial decisions, and many offer their services through the Internet. One such broker is Paine Webber. Its site offers a wealth of information and provides educational material to individual investors.

Organized Exchanges

Organized exchanges are central locations where investors buy and sell securities. Buyers and sellers are not actually present on the floor of the exchange; instead, they are represented by brokers, who act as agents and buy and sell securities according to investors' wishes for a fee. The New York Stock Exchange (NYSE), the largest and

organized exchanges
central locations where investors buy and sell securities

Embrace Technology
Google's Dutch Auction

When Google, one of the hottest high-tech stocks in years, went public in 2004, it did so through an unusual "Dutch auction." Initial public offering (IPO) stocks are traditionally distributed to a select few people chosen by investment bankers, who then sell the stocks through organized or over-the-counter stock exchanges. Google managers, however, decided to set the price of the IPO stock through a Dutch auction to give ordinary investors a better opportunity to buy the stock. In a traditional auction, the price escalates until one bidder remains; in a Dutch auction, the auctioneer sets a high price and continues to lower it until someone bids on the item for sale. If a company is using a Dutch auction for its initial public offering, the auctioneer begins by calling out a prohibitively high price per share that is unlikely to attract bids. The price is progressively lowered until someone decides to bid for a few shares. Then, the auctioneer continues to lower the price until more people buy shares. Google's approach to going public may alienate some traditional investors seeking a more traditional stock-purchasing approach. However, it may appeal to smaller investors who value transparency and do not want to be a part of corporate scandals that were associated with favors granted to some corporate executives purchasing IPO stocks.

Google planned to auction shares to raise up to $2.7 billion in capital. One of the IPO's underwriters, Crédit Suisse First Boston (CSFB), indicated that the process for buying the shares in the Google auction required that potential bidders (1) open an account with one of two underwriters, CSFB or Morgan Stanley; (2) obtain a copy of Google's IPO prospectus detailing the risks of the investment; (3) obtain a unique bidder ID before the start of the auction; and (4) after the auction starts, make a bid including the number of shares they want and the price they are willing to pay.

The final IPO price was determined after the auction closed. The underwriters calculated the price by analyzing all of the bids and identifying the price at or above which all of the shares could be sold. The IPO price was determined by the lowest price bid on any of the 150 million shares offered to investors. In other words, all bidders pay the same price, even though they may have placed a higher bid. This type of auction should eliminate the quick run-up in share prices experienced by tech stocks in the early 2000s. In other words, the buyers of Google are making a commitment to owning Google stock and will not be able to take advantage of acquiring stocks and selling them the next day for a huge gain. Google's executives want the firm to be a socially responsible company and to resist pressures from Wall Street to maintain continual short-term gains. Their goal is not to focus on short-term growth but on attracting investors who desire long-term performance.[6]

Discussion Questions

1. Why do you think Google used a Dutch auction for its IPO?
2. Google became successful as a private company but found that it needed to go public to gain additional funding to remain competitive. Do you feel there were any options other than selling stock?
3. Assess the use of a Dutch auction in helping to establish the integrity and corporate culture of a company like Google.

---

most important of all the exchanges in the United States, is located at the corner of Broad and Wall streets in New York City (hence reference to the financial community by the media as "Wall Street"). The American Stock Exchange (AMEX) trades smaller companies than NYSE. Chicago, Boston, Baltimore, Cincinnati, and other cities have regional exchanges. Internationally, the London Stock Exchange, the Paris Bourse, and the Tokyo Stock Exchange are among the many vital organized exchanges that provide venues for trading domestic and international securities.

The Over-the-Counter Market

over-the-counter (OTC) market

a network of dealers all over the country linked by computers, telephones, and Teletype machines

Unlike the organized exchanges, the **over-the-counter (OTC) market** is a network of dealers all over the country linked by computers, telephones, and Teletype machines. It has no central location. While many very small new companies are traded on the OTC market, many very large and well-known concerns trade there as well. Indeed, thousands of shares of the stocks of companies such as Apple Computer, Intel, and Microsoft are traded on the OTC market every day. Further, since most corporate bonds and all U.S. securities are traded over the counter, the OTC market regularly accounts for the largest total dollar value of all of the secondary markets.

3M	ExxonMobil	McDonald's	TABLE 16.3
Alcoa	General Electric	Merck	
Altria	General Motors	Microsoft	The 30 Stocks in the Dow Jones Industrial Average
American Express	Hewlett-Packard	Pfizer	
American International Group	Home Depot	Procter & Gamble	
Boeing	Honeywell	SBC Communications	
Caterpillar	IBM	United Technologies	
Citigroup	Intel	Verizon	
Coca-Cola	Johnson & Johnson	Wal-Mart	
Du Pont	JP Morgan Chase	Walt Disney	

Measuring Market Performance

Investors, especially professional money managers, want to know how well their investments are performing relative to the market as a whole. Financial managers also need to know how their companies' securities are performing when compared with their competitors'. Thus, performance measures—averages and indexes—are very important to many different people. They not only indicate the performance of a particular securities market but also provide a measure of the overall health of the economy.

Indexes and averages are used to measure stock prices. An *index* compares current stock prices with those in a specified base period, such as 1944, 1967, or 1977. An *average* is the average of certain stock prices. The averages used are usually not simple calculations, however. Some stock market averages (such as the Standard and Poor's Composite Index) are weighted averages, where the weights employed are the total market values of each stock in the index (in this case 500). The Dow Jones Industrial Average is a price-weighted average. Regardless of how constructed, all market averages of stocks move closely together over time.

Many investors follow the activity of the Dow Jones Industrial Average very closely to see whether the stock market has gone up or down. Table 16.3 lists the 30 companies that currently make up the Dow. Although these companies are only a small fraction of the total number of companies listed on the New York Stock Exchange, because of their size they account for about 25 percent of the total value of the NYSE.

The numbers listed in an index or average that tracks the performance of a stock market are expressed not as dollars but as a number on a fixed scale. If you know, for example, that the Dow Jones

Smith Barney Citigroup provides brokerage accounts and many other financial services.

FIGURE 16.4   The Long Ride

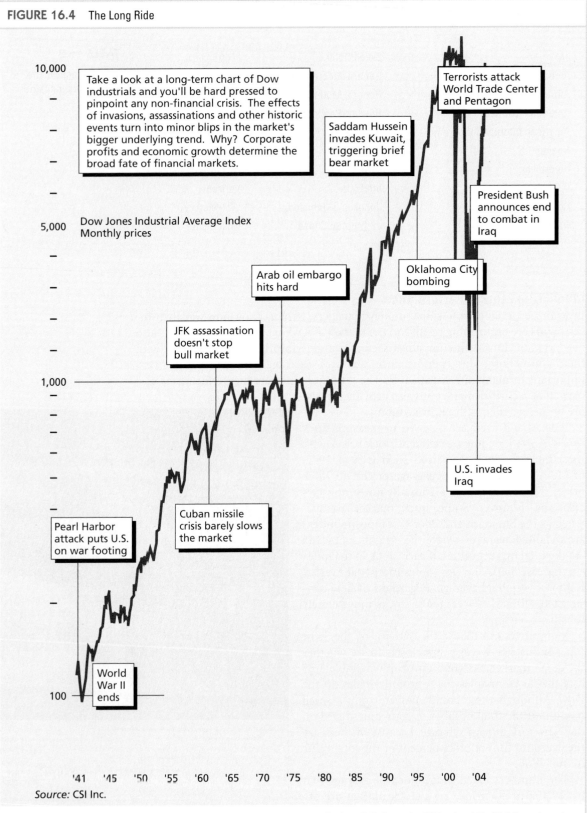

Take a look at a long-term chart of Dow industrials and you'll be hard pressed to pinpoint any non-financial crisis. The effects of invasions, assassinations and other historic events turn into minor blips in the market's bigger underlying trend. Why? Corporate profits and economic growth determine the broad fate of financial markets.

Dow Jones Industrial Average Index Monthly prices

Saddam Hussein invades Kuwait, triggering brief bear market

Terrorists attack World Trade Center and Pentagon

President Bush announces end to combat in Iraq

Arab oil embargo hits hard

Oklahoma City bombing

JFK assassination doesn't stop bull market

U.S. invades Iraq

Pearl Harbor attack puts U.S. on war footing

Cuban missile crisis barely slows the market

World War II ends

Source: CSI Inc.

Source: Ken Hoover, "It Takes More Than a Crisis to Change Market's Trend," *Investor's Business Daily*, September 2001, p. 4, and *The Wall Street Journal*. Reprinted with permission.

Industrial Average climbed from 860 in August 1982 to a high of 11,497 at the beginning of 2000, you can see clearly that the value of the Dow Jones Average increased more than 10 times in this 19-year period, making it one of the highest rate of return periods in the history of the stock market. With U.S. interest rates at modest levels and inflation at 30 year lows, many people think that as long as U.S. companies can continue to produce rising earnings, stock prices will continue to climb. If inflation rises and interest rates go up, and if corporate earnings slow down or decline, the market will most likely be in for a tumble.

A period of large increases in stock prices is known as a *bull market,* with the bull symbolizing an aggressive, charging market and rising stock prices. The bull market of the 1990s was one of the strongest on record, with the Dow Jones Industrial Average rising from 3,300 in April 1992 to over 11,000 in 2000. A declining stock market is known as a *bear market,* with the bear symbolizing sluggish, retreating activity. When stock prices decline very rapidly, the market is said to *crash.* The worst point loss in history (684.81 points) occurred on September 17, 2001, after markets were closed for four days following the terrorist attacks on September 11 that destroyed the World Trade Center and portions of the Pentagon.[7] The stock market—and indeed all of American industry—occasionally stumbles, but it eventually returns to its long-term pattern of growth. (See Figure 16.4.)

In order for investors to make sound financial decisions, it is important that they stay in touch with business news, markets, and indexes. Of course, business and investment magazines, such as *Business Week, Fortune,* and *Money,* offer this type of information. Many Internet sites, including the CNN/*Money, Business Wire, USA Today,* other online newspapers, and *PR Newswire,* offer this information, as well. Many sites offer searchable databases of information by topic, company, or keyword. However investors choose to receive and review business news, doing so is a necessity in today's market.

Explore Your Career Options
Financial Management

Practically every organization—whether in manufacturing, communications, finance, education, health care, or government—has one or more financial managers and/or financial analysts. Working under titles such as treasurer, controller, cash manager, or financial analyst, these financial managers and analysts prepare and interpret the financial reports required by organizations seeking to ensure that the resources under their control are optimally employed.

Financial management differs from accounting chiefly by its differential focus. By nature, accounting is based almost exclusively on summaries of past organizational transactions and prior account history. In contrast, financial management, despite its frequent reliance on many accounting statements, primarily looks forward. The question, "Where should we go from here?"

could serve as the creed of most financial analysis. Should a new project be implemented? Should a new stock issue be sold? Should dividends be increased? How should the firm invest its excess cash? These and countless other forward-looking questions are addressed by legions of financial managers and analysts every business day.

The employment of financial managers and analysts is expected to increase about as fast as the average for all occupations through the year 2012. Unfortunately, like other managerial occupations, the number of applicants for financial management positions is expected to exceed the number of job openings, resulting in increased competition for superior positions. However, those finding employment as financial managers are likely to enjoy considerable economic rewards.[8]

Review Your Understanding

Describe some common methods of managing current assets.

Current assets are short-term resources such as cash, investments, accounts receivable, and inventory, which can be converted to cash within a year. Financial managers focus on minimizing the amount of cash kept on hand and increasing the speed of collections through lockboxes and electronic funds transfer and investing in marketable securities. Marketable securities include U.S. Treasury bills, certificates of deposit, commercial paper, and money market funds. Managing accounts receivable requires judging customer creditworthiness and creating credit terms that encourage prompt payment. Inventory management focuses on determining optimum inventory levels that minimize the cost of storing and ordering inventory without sacrificing too many lost sales due to stockouts.

Identify some sources of short-term financing (current liabilities).

Current liabilities are short-term debt obligations that must be repaid within one year, such as accounts payable, taxes payable, and notes (loans) payable. Trade credit is extended by suppliers for the purchase of their goods and services. A line of credit is an arrangement by which a bank agrees to lend a specified amount of money to a business whenever the business needs it. Secured loans are backed by collateral; unsecured loans are backed only by the borrower's good reputation.

Summarize the importance of long-term assets and capital budgeting.

Long-term, or fixed, assets are expected to last for many years, such as production facilities (plants), offices, and equipment. Businesses need modern, up-to-date equipment to succeed in today's competitive environment. Capital budgeting is the process of analyzing company needs and selecting the assets that will maximize its value; a capital budget is the amount of money budgeted for the purchase of fixed assets. Every investment in fixed assets carries some risk.

Specify how companies finance their operations and manage fixed assets with long-term liabilities, particularly bonds.

Two common choices for financing are equity financing (attracting new owners) and debt financing (taking on long-term liabilities). Long-term liabilities are debts that will be repaid over a number of years, such as long-term bank loans and bond issues. A bond is a long-term debt security that an organization sells to raise money. The bond indenture specifies the provisions of the bond contract—maturity date, coupon rate, repayment methods, and others.

Discuss how corporations can use equity financing by issuing stock through an investment banker.

Owners' equity represents what owners have contributed to the company and includes common stock, preferred stock, and retained earnings (profits that have been reinvested in the assets of the firm). To finance operations, companies can issue new common and preferred stock through an investment banker that sells stocks and bonds for corporations.

Describe the various securities markets in the United States.

Securities markets provide the mechanism for buying and selling stocks and bonds. Primary markets allow companies to raise capital by selling new stock directly to investors through investment bankers. Secondary markets allow the buyers of previously issued shares of stock to sell them to other owners. The major secondary markets are the New York Stock Exchange, the American Stock Exchange, and the over-the-counter market. Investors measure stock market performance by watching stock market averages and indexes such as the Dow Jones Industrial Average and the Standard and Poor's (S&P) Composite Index.

Critique the short-term asset and liabilities position of a small manufacturer and recommend corrective action.

Using the information presented in this chapter, you should be able to "Solve the Dilemma" on page 475 presented by the current bleak working capital situation of Glasspray Corporation.

Revisit the World of Business

1. Do you think that Milton Hershey made the right decision in leaving his foundation the controlling voting interest in the Hershey Foods Corporation?

2. Is Hershey Foods' example of founders willing stock for philanthropic purposes something that

you believe that companies could do today? Why or why not?

3. Knowing that a large share of Hershey's profits support philanthropic causes, would you be more likely to purchase the company's stock?

Learn the Terms

Check Your Progress

1. Define working capital management.
2. How can a company speed up cash flow? Why should it?
3. Describe the various types of marketable securities.
4. What does it mean to have a line of credit at a bank?
5. What are fixed assets? Why is assessing risk important in capital budgeting?
6. How can a company finance fixed assets?
7. What are bonds and what do companies do with them?
8. How can companies use equity to finance their operations and long-term growth?
9. What are the functions of securities markets?
10. Define bull and bear markets.

Get Involved

1. Using your local newspaper or *The Wall Street Journal,* find the current rates of interest on the following marketable securities. If you were a financial manager for a large corporation, which would you invest extra cash in? Which would you invest in if you worked for a small business?

   a. Three-month T-bills

   b. Six-month T-bills

   c. Commercial certificates of deposit

   d. Commercial paper

   e. Eurodollar deposits

   f. Money market deposits

2. Select five of the Dow Jones Industrials from Table 16.3. Look up their earnings, dividends, and prices for the past five years. What kind of picture is presented by this information? Which stocks would you like to have owned over this past period? Do you think the next five years will present a similar picture?

Build Your Skills

CHOOSING AMONG PROJECTS

Background:

As the senior executive in charge of exploration for High Octane Oil Co., you are constantly looking for projects that will add to the company's profitability—without increasing the company's risk. High Octane Oil is an international oil company with operations in Latin America, the Middle East, Africa, the United States, and Mexico. The company is one of the world's leading experts in deep-water exploration and drilling. High Octane currently produces 50 percent of its oil in the United States, 25 percent in the Middle East, 5 percent in Africa, 10 percent in Latin America, and 10 percent in Mexico. You are considering six projects from around the world.

Project 1—Your deep-water drilling platform in the Gulf of Mexico is producing at maximum capacity from the Valdez oil field, and High Octane's geological engineers think there is a high probability that there is oil in the Sanchez field, which is adjacent to Valdez. They recommend drilling a new series of wells. Once commercial quantities of oil have been discovered, it will take two more years to build the collection platform and pipelines. It will be four years before the discovered oil gets to the refineries.

Project 2—The Brazilian government has invited you to drill on some unexplored tracts in the middle of the central jungle region. There are roads to within 50 miles of the tract and British Petroleum has found oil 500 miles away from this tract. It would take about three years to develop this property and several more years to build pipelines and pumping stations to carry the oil to the refineries. The Brazilian government wants 20 percent of all production as its fee for giving High Octane Oil Co. the drilling rights or a $500 million up-front fee and 5 percent of the output.

Project 3—Your fields in Saudi Arabia have been producing oil for 50 years. Several wells are old, and the pressure has diminished. Your engineers are sure that if you were to initiate high-pressure secondary recovery procedures, you would increase the output of these existing wells by 20 percent. High-pressure recovery methods pump water at high pressure into the underground limestone formations to enhance the movement of petroleum toward the surface.

Project 4—Your largest oil fields in Alaska have been producing from only 50 percent of the known deposits. Your geological engineers estimate that you could open up 10 percent of the remaining fields every two years and offset your current declining production from existing wells. The pipeline capacity is available and, while you can only drill during six months of the year, the fields could be producing oil in three years.

Project 5—Some of High Octane's west Texas oil fields produce in shallow stripper wells of 2,000- to 4,000-foot depths. Stripper wells produce anywhere from 10 to 2,000 barrels per day and can last for six months or 40 years. Generally, once you find a shallow deposit, there is an 80 percent chance that offset wells will find more oil. Because these wells are shallow, they can be drilled quickly at a low cost. High Octane's engineers estimate that in your largest tract, which is closest to the company's Houston refinery, you could increase production by 30 percent for the next 10 years by increasing the density of the wells per square mile.

Project 6—The government of a republic in Russia has invited you to drill for oil in Siberia. Russian geologists think that this oil field might be the largest in the world, but there have been no wells drilled and no infrastructure exists to carry oil if it should be found. The republic has no money to help you build the infrastructure but if you find oil, it will let you keep the first five years' production before taking its 25 percent share. Knowing that oil fields do not start producing at full capacity for many years after initial production, your engineers are not sure that your portion the first five years of production will pay for the infrastructure they must build to get the oil to market. The republic also has been known to have a rather unstable government, and the last international oil company that began this project left the country when a new government demanded a higher than originally agreed-upon percentage of the expected output. If this field is in fact the largest in the world, High Octane's supply of oil would be ensured well into the 21st century.

Task:

1. Working in groups, rank the six projects from lowest risk to highest risk.

2. Given the information provided, do the best you can to rank the projects from lowest cost to highest cost.

3. What political considerations might affect your project choice?

4. If you could choose one project, which would it be and why?

5. If you could choose three projects, which ones would you choose? In making this decision, consider which projects might be highly correlated to High Octane Oil's existing production and which ones might diversify the company's production on a geographical basis.

e-Xtreme Surfing

- **CNN/Money**
  http://money.cnn.com
  Provides financial news and research about stock/bond markets and individual stocks/bonds.

- **Yahoo! Finance**
  http://finance.yahoo.com
  Provides financial news and research about stock/bond markets and individual stocks/bonds.

- **Motley Fool**
  www.fool.com
  Provides news, articles, and resources about the financial world, personal finance, and corporate information.

See for Yourself Videocase

THE NEW YORK STOCK EXCHANGE UNDERGOES GOVERNANCE REFORM

Located at the corner of Broad and Wall Streets in New York City, the New York Stock Exchange (NYSE) is the largest and most important organized securities exchange in the United States. It is also the world's largest equities market—more capital is raised at the NYSE than in any other equities market in the world. Many different groups trade securities on the NYSE, including companies that are listed on the exchange, individual investors, and institutional investors such as mutual fund companies and pension funds. More than 2,700 companies are listed on the NYSE, with a combined total of 350 billion shares available for trading. These shares have a combined value of over $15 trillion, more than three times the value of shares being traded on any other organized exchange. During any given day, an average of 1 billion of these shares are bought and sold on the exchange.

Although it may be hard to believe, this large and powerful organization had humble beginnings. The NYSE dates back to 1792, when 24 well-known merchants of the time met on Wall Street to sign the Buttonwood Agreement, which established a market for trading securities on a common commission basis. A total of just five securities were traded on the NYSE in 1792; three were government bonds, and two were bank stocks. However, by 1824, annual trading volume had already reached 380,000 shares.

The NYSE also has a long history of evolving regulations and governance procedures. The NYSE adopted its first constitution in 1817. This constitution laid out rules for the conduct of business. The primary governing body of the exchange was the Governing Committee, and a member of the exchange held the unpaid position of president and chief executive. The NYSE first underwent major reforms in 1938, when the first full-time paid president and chief executive officer was appointed and a 33-member Board of Governors was created. The Board of Governors also had a chairman who was responsible for presiding over meetings of the board. This Board of Governors was replaced by a 21-member Board of Directors with 10 public members in 1972. At this time, the chairman of the Board of Directors was also made the full-time paid chief executive officer of the NYSE.

The positions of chairman and chief executive officer continued to be occupied by one person until December 2003, when the NYSE again underwent major reforms. These reforms, precipitated by public outcry against the high level of executive compensation at the NYSE, were highly publicized by news media and resulted in some negative publicity for the exchange. Early in 2003, lawmakers and regulators had begun to pressure the NYSE to re-examine its corporate governance policies in response to the corporate reform initiatives sparked by the Sarbanes-Oxley Act of 2002 and other new business regulations. The NYSE promised to disclose the salaries of its top executives, which it did in August 2003. Regulators and the public alike were shocked to learn that the annual salary of NYSE chairman and CEO, Richard Grasso, was $1.4 million with a minimum annual bonus of $1 million. Additionally, the NYSE had paid Grasso a lump sum of $139.5 million in deferred savings, past bonuses, and retirement benefits.

The NYSE board of directors was sharply criticized for Grasso's pay package, which many said resembled that of a CEO of a *Fortune* 500 company and was inappropriate for a nonprofit organization like the NYSE. The public outcry against Grasso became so strident that he stepped down from his position in September 2003, and was replaced by interim chairman John Reed. A former co-CEO of Citigroup, Reed agreed to take over temporarily as chairman for a nominal salary of $1. Widely recognized as a no-nonsense leader with character, integrity, and ethics, Reed immediately began proposing reforms to the NYSE board. In a letter to the members of the NYSE board of directors, Reed stated that his priorities were to re-establish trust and confidence in the NYSE, as well as to ensure that the NYSE continued to serve its many constituencies well.

One of Reed's greatest challenges was creating a new, more independent board of directors. Under Chairman Richard Grasso, the NYSE board had grown to include 27 members, many of whom were accused of having conflicts of interest because of their involvement with companies on Wall Street. Reed proposed that the board should consist of eight independent members, with a 20-plus-member advisory board that could include Wall Street executives. This proposal was approved by both members of the NYSE and the Securities and Exchange Commission (SEC). Following a suggestion from the SEC, Reed also decided to split the roles of chairman and CEO, effective upon his relinquishing the post. These reforms were designed to create a more independent governance board that would better serve the needs of stockholders and help restore investor confidence, in place of the former board which was accused of being self-serving.

Although these reforms were unanimously approved by the SEC, many felt that Reed's reforms do not go far enough. Many of the nation's large pension funds, which control billions of dollars worth of investments, are calling for even more reforms. These powerful institutional investors would like to see a better division of the NYSE's regulatory and market functions, as well as the elimination of many market trading rules which they view as outdated.

Although interim chairman Reed's reforms have greatly improved the corporate governance of the NYSE, more reforms may be yet to come.[9]

Discussion Questions

1. Do you think former Chairman/CEO Richard Grasso's compensation package was excessive given his responsibilities as head of the world's largest stock exchange?

2. Why was it necessary to reform the NYSE's governance procedures and to make its governing board more independent?

3. Do you agree with institutional investors' concerns that Reed's reforms have not gone far enough? Why or why not?

Remember to check out our Online Learning Center at www.mhhe.com/ferrell5e.

Part Six Role-Play Exercise*

Dana Fashion Designs, Inc.

Dana Fashion Designs, Inc., (DFD) is an international corporation that manufactures high-quality custom clothing. The apparel is priced to reflect the customer-oriented sales process. DFD custom designs all clothing to meet the fashion requirements of its target market, the upper middle class that considers fashion important. Typically, a customer would visit its exclusive retail establishments to inquire about clothing. The salesperson would take the measurements of the customer and input them into the company's computer system, which were then accessible from any DFD store or factory nationwide. Scanners are used to survey the customer's body and transfer the measurements into the BodyContour Pro Network (BCPN) software, which compares the digitized and manual measurements to create the customer's exact measurements. The customer would then begin the designing process. With the salesperson's assistance, the customer custom designs any garment on the BCPN. Each article is unique to its designer's wishes. The software combines the customer's specifications of garment type, style, color, and so on with preprogrammed patterns to create a feasible combination of creativity and factory efficiency. After completion, the garment is created by the factory, and within three weeks, the customer has custom clothing. Sizes are stored in the system to reduce the preparation time for repeat customers.

After six years in business, the company started to face a decline in sales volume. The company marketed its product as an "experience." Customers could experience the delight of creating their own attire. Because DFD focuses on the upper-middle-class market, it is subject to major fluctuations in the economy. Donnie Mitchel, the company's CEO, suspects the decrease in sales is a direct reflection of the current economic slump.

Earlier this year, the stock market began to fluctuate with a 25 percent drop in major stock indices. The United States experienced a bull market for many years, so most consumers and companies were not expecting the sudden drop in market confidence. High-technology stock prices plummeted, and price/earnings ratios fell. After a year of reduced growth, the Federal Reserve decided to reduce the interest rate to stimulate the economy. The Conference Board, a New York research group, said the index of consumer confidence had dropped 20 percent in the last three months based on its perceptions of the economic outlook. The Fed's efforts were not improving the stock or bond markets. Eventually, the executive branch stepped in and decided to lower the tax rates. Surely, these measures combined would improve the economy in the long run. But what about the short term?

The management team at DFD is concerned about its ability to meet current liabilities. In addition to short-term debt, the company used a significant amount of long-term debt financing. How would the company be able to make its interest payments while still covering its accounts payable, accrued wages, and utilities payable? DFD needed to cut costs immediately or face serious bankruptcy potential. Where should these cuts be made?

Mitchel called an emergency meeting with the heads of the marketing, finance, production, and human resource departments to discuss the company's options. He asked each department to consider methods to improve its efficiency and reduce costs. Tomorrow morning, the department heads will discuss what they think the company should do to recover from the downturn in the economy.

*This background statement provides information for a role-play exercise designed to help you understand the real world challenge of decision making in business and to integrate the concepts presented previously in this text. If your instructor chooses to utilize this activity, the class will be divided into teams with each team member assigned to a particular role in the fictitious organization. Additional information on each role and instructions for the completion of the exercise will be distributed to individual team members.

Appendix D

Personal Financial Planning*

The Financial Planning Process

Personal financial planning is the process of managing your finances so that you can achieve your financial goals. By anticipating future needs and wants, you can take appropriate steps to prepare for them. Your needs and wants will undoubtedly change over time as you enter into various life circumstances. Although financial planning is not entirely about money management, a large part of this process is concerned with decisions related to expenditures, investments, and credit.

Although every person has unique needs, everyone can benefit from financial planning. Even if the entire financial plan is not implemented at once, the process itself will help you focus on what is important. With a little forethought and action, you may be able to achieve goals that you previously thought were unattainable. Figure D.1 shows how teens handle finances.

The steps in development and implementation of an effective financial plan are:

- Evaluate your financial health.
- Set short-term and long-term financial goals.
- Create and adhere to a budget.
- Manage credit wisely.
- Develop a savings and investment plan.
- Evaluate and purchase insurance.
- Develop an estate plan.
- Adjust your financial plan to new circumstances.

Evaluate Your Financial Health

Just as businesses make use of financial reports to track their performance, good personal financial planning requires that individuals keep track of their income and expenses and their overall finan-

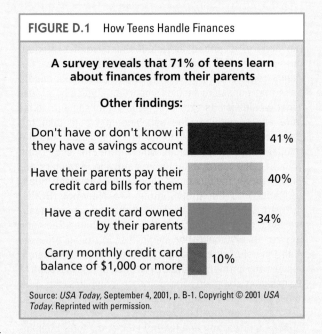

FIGURE D.1   How Teens Handle Finances

A survey reveals that 71% of teens learn about finances from their parents

Other findings:

Don't have or don't know if they have a savings account — 41%

Have their parents pay their credit card bills for them — 40%

Have a credit card owned by their parents — 34%

Carry monthly credit card balance of $1,000 or more — 10%

Source: *USA Today,* September 4, 2001, p. B-1. Copyright © 2001 *USA Today.* Reprinted with permission.

cial condition. Several software packages are readily available to help track personal finances (e.g., Quicken and Microsoft Money), but all that is really needed is a simple spreadsheet program. This appendix includes some simple worksheets that can be reproduced to provide a starting point for personal financial planning. Comprehensive financial planning sites are also available on the Internet. For example, **http://www.moneycentral.msn. com** and **http://www.smartmoney.com** both provide information and tools to simplify this process.

While it is possible to track all kinds of information over time, the two most critical elements of your finances are your personal net worth and your personal cash flow. The information necessary for these two measures is often required by lending institutions on loan applications, so keeping it up-to-date can save you time and effort later.

*This appendix was contributed by Dr. Vickie Bajtelsmit.

TABLE D.1   Personal Net Worth

Assets	$	Liabilities	$
Checking accounts	_____	Credit cards balances (list)	
Savings accounts	_____	1 _____	_____
Money market accounts	_____	2 _____	_____
Other short-term investment	_____	3 _____	_____
		Personal Loans	_____
Market value of investments (stocks, bonds,	_____	Student loans	_____
mutual funds)		Car Loans	_____
Value of retirement funds	_____	Home mortgage balance	_____
College savings plan	_____	Home equity loans	_____
Other savings plans	_____	Other real estate loans	_____
Market value of real estate	_____	Alimony/child support owed	_____
Cars	_____	Taxes owed (above withholding)	_____
Home furnishings	_____	Other investment loans	_____
Jewelry/art/collectibles	_____	Other liabilities/debts	_____
Clothing/personal assets	_____		
Other assets	_____		
TOTAL ASSETS	_____	TOTAL LIABILITIES	_____
	PERSONAL NET WORTH = TOTAL ASSETS MINUS TOTAL LIABILITIES = $_____		

The Personal Balance Sheet

For businesses, net worth is usually defined as *assets minus liabilities,* and this is no different for individuals. **Personal net worth** is simply the total value of all personal assets less the total value of unpaid debts or liabilities. Although a business could not survive with a negative net worth since it would be technically insolvent, many students have negative net worth. As a student, you probably are not yet earning enough to have accumulated significant assets, such as a house or stock portfolio, but you are likely to have incurred various forms of debt, including student loans, car loans, and credit card debt.

At this stage in your life, negative net worth is not necessarily an indication of poor future financial prospects. Current investment in your "human capital" (education) is usually considered to have a resulting payoff in the form of better job opportunities and higher potential lifetime income, so this "upside-down" balance sheet should not stay that way forever. Unfortunately, there are many people in the United States who have negative net worth much later in

their lives. This can result from unforeseen circumstances, like divorce, illness, or disability, but the easy availability of credit in the last couple of decades has also been blamed for the heavy debt loads of many American families. No matter the immediate trigger, it is usually poor financial planning—the failure to prepare in advance for those unforeseen circumstances—that makes the difference between those who fail and those who survive. It is interesting to note that we could say the exact same thing about business failures. Most are attributable to poor financial planning. If your net worth is negative, you should definitely include debt reduction on your list of short and/or long-term goals.

You can use Table D.1 to estimate your net worth. On the left-hand side of the balance sheet, you should record the value of *assets,* all the things you own that have value. These include checking and savings account balances, investments, furniture, books, clothing, vehicles, houses, and the like. As with business balance sheets, assets are usually arranged from most liquid (easily convertible to cash) to least liquid. If you are a young student, it should not be surprising to find that you have little, if anything, to put on this side of your balance sheet. You should note that balance sheets are sensitive to the point in time chosen for evaluation. For example, if you always get paid on the first day of the month, your checking balance will be greatest at that point but will quickly be depleted as you pay for rent, food, and other needs. You may want to use your average daily balance in checking and savings accounts as a more accurate reflection of your financial condition. The right-hand side of the balance sheet is for recording *liabilities,* amounts of money that you owe to others. These include bank loans, mortgages, credit card debt, and other personal loans and are usually listed in order of how soon they must be paid back to the lender.

The Cash Flow Statement

Businesses forecast and track their regular inflows and outflows of cash with a cash budget and summarize annual cash flows on the statement of cash flows. Similarly, individuals should have a clear understanding of their flow of cash as they budget their expenditures and regularly check to be sure that they are sticking to their budget.

What is cash flow? Anytime you receive cash or pay cash (including payments with checks), the dollar amount that is moving from one person to another is a **cash flow.** For students, the most likely cash inflows will be student loans, grants, and income from part-time jobs. Cash outflows will include rent, food, gas, car payments, books, tuition, and personal care expenses. Although it may seem obvious that you need to have enough inflows to cover the outflows, it is very common for people to estimate incorrectly and overspend. This may result in hefty bank overdraft charges or increasing debt as credit lines are used to make up the difference. Accurate forecasting of cash inflows and outflows allows you to make arrangements to cover estimated shortfalls before they occur. For students, this can be particularly valuable when cash inflows primarily occur at the beginning of the semester (e.g., student loans) but outflows are spread over the semester.

How should you treat credit card purchases on your cash flow worksheet? Since credit purchases do not require payment of cash *now,* your cash flow statement should not reflect the value of the purchase as an outflow until you pay the bill. Take for example the purchase of a television set on credit. The $500 purchase will increase your assets and your liabilities by $500 but will only result in a negative cash flow of a few dollars per month, since payments on credit cards are cash outflows when they are made. If you always pay your credit card balances in full each month, the purchases are really the same thing as cash, and your balance sheet will never reflect the debt. But if you purchase on credit and only pay minimum balances, you will be living beyond your means, and your balance sheet will get more and more "upside down." A further problem with using credit to purchase assets that decline in value is that the liability may still be there long after the asset you purchased has no value.

Table D.2 can be used to estimate your cash flow. The purpose of a cash flow worksheet for your financial plan is to heighten your awareness of where the cash is going. Many people are surprised to find that they are spending more than they make (by using too much credit) or that they have significant "cash leakage"—those little expenditures that add up to a lot without their even noticing. Examples include afternoon lattes or snacks, too many nights out at the local pub, eating lunch at the Student Center instead of packing a bag, and regularly paying for parking (or parking tickets) instead of biking or riding the bus to school. In many cases, plugging the little leaks can free up enough cash to make a significant contribution toward achieving long-term savings goals.

Set Short-Term and Long-Term Financial Goals

Just as a business develops its vision and strategic plan, individuals should have a clear set of financial goals. This component of your financial plan is the road map that will lead you to achieving your short-term and long-term financial goals.

Short-term goals are those that can be achieved in two years or less. They may include saving for particular short-term objectives, such as a new car, a down payment for a home, a vacation, or other major consumer purchase. For many people, short-term financial goals should include tightening up on household spending patterns and reducing outstanding credit.

Long-term goals are those that require substantial time to achieve. Nearly everyone should include retirement planning as a long-term objective. Those who have or anticipate having children will probably consider college savings a priority. Protection of

TABLE D.2 Personal Cash Flow

Cash Inflows	Monthly	Annual
Salary/wage income (gross)	$_____	$_____
Interest/dividend income	_____	_____
Other income (self-employment)	_____	_____
Rental income (after expenses)	_____	_____
Capital gains	_____	_____
Other income	_____	_____
Total income	_____	_____

Cash Outflows	Monthly	Annual
Groceries	$_____	$_____
Housing	_____	_____
Mortgage or rent	_____	_____
House repairs/expenses	_____	_____
Property taxes	_____	_____
Utilities	_____	_____
Heating	_____	_____
Electric	_____	_____
Water and sewer	_____	_____
Cable/phone/satellite/Internet	_____	_____
Car loan payments	_____	_____
Car maintenance/gas	_____	_____
Credit card payments	_____	_____
Other loan payments	_____	_____
Income and payroll taxes	_____	_____
Other taxes	_____	_____
Insurance	_____	_____
Life	_____	_____
Health	_____	_____
Auto	_____	_____
Disability	_____	_____
Other insurance	_____	_____
Clothing	_____	_____
Gifts	_____	_____
Other consumables (TVs,etc)	_____	_____
Child care expenses	_____	_____
Sports-related expenses	_____	_____
Health club dues	_____	_____
Uninsured medical expenses	_____	_____
Education	_____	_____
Vacations	_____	_____
Entertainment	_____	_____
Alimony/child support	_____	_____
Charitable contributions	_____	_____
Required pension contributions	_____	_____
Magazine subscriptions/books	_____	_____
Other payments/expenses	_____	_____
Total Expenses	$_____	$_____

NET PERSONAL CASH FLOW = TOTAL INCOME − TOTAL EXPENSES = $_____

loved ones from the financial hazards of your unexpected death, illness, or disability is also a long-term objective for many individuals. If you have a spouse or other dependents, having adequate insurance and an estate plan in place should be part of your long-term goals.

Create and Adhere to a Budget

Whereas the cash flow table you completed in the previous section tells you what you are doing with your money currently, a **budget** shows what you plan to do with it in the future. A budget can be for any period of time, but it is common to budget in monthly and/or annual intervals.

Developing a Budget

You can use the cash flow worksheet completed earlier to create a budget. Begin with the amount of income you have for the month. Enter your nondiscretionary expenditures (i.e., bills you *must* pay, such as tuition, rent, and utilities) on the worksheet and determine the leftover amount. Next list your discretionary expenditures, such as entertainment and cable TV, in order of importance. You can then work down your discretionary list until your remaining available cash flow is zero.

An important component of your budget is the amount that you allocate to savings. If you put a high priority on saving and you do not use credit to spend beyond your income each month, you will be able to accumulate wealth that can be used to meet your short-term and long-term financial goals. In the best-seller *The Millionaire Next Door,* authors Thomas J. Stanley and William D. Danko point out that most millionaires have achieved financial success through hard work and thriftiness as opposed to luck or inheritance. You cannot achieve your financial goals unless your budget process places a high priority on saving and investing.

Tracking Your Budgeting Success

Businesses regularly identify budget items and track their variance from budget forecasts. People who follow a similar strategy in their personal finances are better able to meet their financial goals as well. If certain budgeted expenses routinely turn out to be under or over your previous estimates, then it is important to either revise the budget estimate or develop a strategy for reducing that expense.

College students commonly have trouble adhering to their budget for food and entertainment expenses. A strategy that works fairly well is to limit yourself to cash payments. At the beginning of the week, withdraw an amount from checking that will cover your weekly budgeted expenses. For the rest of the week, leave your checkbook, ATM card, and credit cards at home. When the cash is gone, don't spend any more. While this is easier said than done, after a couple of weeks, you will learn to cut down on the cash leakage that inevitably occurs without careful cash management.

Manage Credit Wisely

One of the cornerstones of your financial plan should be to keep credit usage to a minimum and to work at reducing outstanding debt. The use of credit for consumer and home purchases is well entrenched in our culture and has arguably fueled our economy and enabled Americans to better their standard of living as compared to earlier generations. Nevertheless, credit abuse is a serious problem in this country, and the economic downturn of 2001 doubtless pushed many households over the edge into bankruptcy as a result.

To consider the pros and cons of credit usage, compare the following two scenarios. In the first case, Joel takes an 8 percent fixed-rate mortgage to purchase a house to live in while he is a college student. The mortgage payment is comparable to alternative monthly rental costs, and his house appreciates 20 percent in value over the four years he is in college. At the end of college, Joel will be able to sell his house and reap the return, having invested only a small amount of his own cash. For example, if he made an initial 5 percent down payment on a $100,000 home that is now worth $120,000 four years later, he has earned $12,800 (after a 6 percent commission to the real estate agent) on an investment of $5,000. This amounts to a sizable return on investment of more than 250 percent over four years. This example is oversimplified in that we did not take into account the principal that has been repaid over the four years, and we did not consider the mortgage payment costs or the tax deductibility of interest paid during that time. However, the point is still clear; borrowing money to buy an asset that appreciates in value by more than the cost of the debt is a terrific way to invest.

In the second case, Nicole uses her credit card to pay for some of her college expenses. Instead of paying off the balance each month, Nicole makes only the minimum payment and incurs 16 percent interest costs. Over the course of several years of college, Nicole's credit card debt is likely to amount to several thousand dollars, typical of college graduates in the United States. The beer and pizza Nicole purchased have long ago been digested, yet the debt remains, and the payments continue. If Nicole continues making minimum payments, it will take many years to pay back that original debt, and in the meantime the interest paid will far exceed the original amount borrowed. Credit card debt in the amount of $1,000 will usually require a minimum payment of at least $15 per month. At this payment level, it will take 166 months (almost 14 years) to pay the debt in full, and the total interest paid will be more than $1,400!

So when is borrowing a good financial strategy? A rule of thumb is that you should borrow only to buy assets that will appreciate in value or when your financing charges are less than what you are earning on the cash that you would otherwise use to make the purchase. This rule generally will limit your borrowing to home purchases and investments.

Use and Abuse of Credit Cards

Credit cards should be used only as a cash flow management tool. If you pay off your balance every month, you avoid financing charges (assuming no annual fee), you have proof of expenditures, which may be necessary for tax or business reasons, and you may be able to better match your cash inflows and outflows over the course of the month. There are several aspects of credit cards that you should be familiar with.

- *Finance charges.* Credit card companies make money by lending to you at a higher rate than it costs them to obtain financing. Since many of their customers don't pay back their debts in a timely fashion (default), they must charge enough to cover the risk of default as well. Interest is usually calculated on the average daily balance over the month, and payments are applied to old debts first. Although there are "teaser" rates that may be less than 5 percent, most credit cards regularly charge 8 to 24 percent annual interest. The low introductory rates are subject to time limitations (often six months or less), and they revert to the higher rates if you don't pay on time.

- *Annual fee.* Many credit cards assess an annual fee that may be as low as $15 or as much as $100 per year. If you regularly carry a very low balance, this amounts to the equivalent of a very high additional interest charge. For example, a $50 annual fee is the equivalent of an additional 5 percent on your annual interest rate if your balance is $1,000. Since the cards with fees do not generally provide you with different services, it is best to choose no-annual-fee credit cards.

- *Credit line.* The credit line is the maximum you are allowed to borrow. This may begin with a small amount for a new customer, perhaps as low as $300. As the customer shows the ability and intent to repay (by doing so in a timely fashion), the limit can increase to many thousands of dollars.

- *Grace period.* The grace period for most credit cards is 25 days. This may amount to twice as long a period of free credit depending on when your purchase date falls in the billing cycle. For example, if you used your card on January 1 and your billing cycle goes from the 1st to the 31st, then the bill for January purchases will arrive the first week in February and will be due on February 25. If you pay it in full on the last possible day, you will have had 55 days of free credit. Keep in mind that the lender considers the bill paid when the check is *received,* not when it is mailed.

- *Fees and penalties.* In addition to charging interest and annual fees, credit card companies charge extra for late payments and for going over the stated limit on the card. These fees have been on the rise in the last decade and $25 or higher penalties are now fairly common.

- *ATM withdrawals.* Most credit cards can be used to obtain cash from ATMs. Although this may be convenient, it contributes to your increasing credit card balance and may result in extra expenditures that you would otherwise have avoided. In addition, these withdrawals may have hidden costs. Withdrawing cash from a machine that is not owned by your credit card lender will usually cause you to incur a fee of $1 or $1.50. The effective interest that this represents can be substantial if you are withdrawing small amounts of cash. A $1 charge on a withdrawal of $50 is the equivalent of 2 percent interest in addition to any interest you might pay to the credit card lender.

TABLE D.3   How Much Will It Take to Pay That Debt?

Months to Pay	Interest Rate	Amount of Debt			
		$1,000	$2,500	$5,000	$10,000
12	15%	$90.26	$225.65	$451.29	$902.58
	18%	$91.68	$229.20	$458.40	$916.80
	21%	$93.11	$232.78	$465.57	$931.14
24	15%	$48.49	$121.22	$242.43	$484.87
	18%	$49.92	$124.81	$249.62	$499.24
	21%	$51.39	$128.46	$256.93	$513.86
36	15%	$34.67	$86.66	$173.33	$346.65
	18%	$36.15	$90.38	$180.76	$361.52
	21%	$37.68	$94.19	$188.38	$376.75
48	15%	$27.83	$69.58	$139.15	$278.31
	18%	$29.37	$73.44	$146.87	$293.75
	21%	$30.97	$77.41	$154.83	$309.66
60	15%	$23.79	$59.47	$118.95	$237.90
	18%	$25.39	$63.48	$126.97	$253.93
	21%	$27.05	$67.63	$135.27	$270.53
72	15%	$21.15	$52.86	$105.73	$211.45
	18%	$22.81	$57.02	$114.04	$228.08
	21%	$24.54	$61.34	$122.68	$245.36

• *Perks.* Most credit cards provide a number of additional services. These may include a limitation on your potential liability in the event your card is lost or stolen or trip insurance. Some cards promise "cash back" in the form of a small rebate based on dollar volume of credit purchases. Many credit card companies offer the opportunity to participate in airline mileage programs. The general rule of thumb is that none of these perks is worth the credit card interest that is charged. If, however, you use your credit card as a cash management tool only, paying off your balance every month, then these perks are truly free to you.

Student Loans

Student loans are fairly common in today's environment of rising college tuition and costs. These loans can be a great deal, offering lower interest rates than other loans and terms that allow deferral of repayment until graduation. Furthermore, the money is being borrowed to pay for an asset that is expected to increase in value—your human capital. Don't underestimate, however, the monthly payments that will be required upon graduation. Students today graduate with average student loan debt of more than $19,000. Table D.3 shows the monthly payments required to repay the debt under various term and interest scenarios. For larger outstanding debt amounts, new college graduates in entry-level positions find that it is difficult to make the necessary payments without help.

Develop a Savings and Investment Plan

The next step to achieving your financial goals is to decide on a savings plan. A common recommendation of financial planners is to "pay yourself first." What this means is that you begin the month by setting aside an amount of money for your savings and investments, as compared to waiting until the end of the month and seeing what's left to save or invest. The budget is extremely important for deciding on a rea-

Elizabeth Handlin began by educating Chicago consumers about managing their personal finances free of charge. Her "Money Smart Week" will be stretching to Detroit this year—all with hopes of becoming a nationwide movement. Handlin's dream is for financial literacy for all Americans.

sonable dollar amount to apply to this component of your financial plan.

As students, you might think that you cannot possibly find any extra dollars in your budget for saving, but, in fact, nearly everyone can stretch their budget a little. Some strategies for students might include taking public transportation several times a week and setting aside the gas or parking dollars you would have spent, buying regular coffees instead of Starbucks lattes, or eating at home one more night per week.

Understanding the Power of Compounded Returns

Even better, if you are a college student living on a typically small budget, you should be able to use this experience to help jump-start a viable savings program after graduation. If you currently live on $10,000 per year and your first job pays $30,000, it should be easy to "pay yourself" $2,000 or more per year. Putting the

current maximum of $3,000 in an individual retirement account (IRA) will give you some tax advantages and can result in substantial wealth accumulation over time. An investment of only $2,000 per year from age 22 to retirement at 67 at 6 percent return per year will result in $425,487 at the retirement date. An annual contribution of $5,000 for 45 years will result in retirement wealth of about $1 million, not considering any additional tax benefits you might qualify for. If you invest that $5,000 per year for only 10 years and discontinue your contributions, you will still have about half a million dollars at age 67. And that assumes only a 6 percent return on investment!

What happens if you wait 10 years to start, beginning your $5,000 annual savings at age 32? By age 67, you will have only about a half million. Thirty-five years of investing instead of 45 doesn't sound like a big difference, but it cuts your retirement wealth in half. These examples illustrate an important point about long-term savings and wealth accumulation—the earlier you start, the better off you will be.

The Link between Investment Choice and Savings Goals

Once you have decided how much you can save, your choice of investment should be guided by your financial goals and the investment's risk and return and whether it will be long-term or short-term.

In general, investments differ in risk and return. The types of risk that you should be aware of are:

- Liquidity risk—How easy/costly is it to convert the investment to cash without loss of value?
- Default risk—How likely are you to receive the promised cash flows?
- Inflation risk—Will changes in purchasing power of the dollar over time erode the value of future cash flows your investment will generate?
- Price risk—How much might your investment fluctuate in value in the short run and the long run?

In general, the riskier an investment, the higher the return it will generate to you. Therefore, even though individuals differ in their willingness to take risk, it is important to invest in assets that expose you to at least moderate risk so that you can accumulate sufficient wealth to fund your long-term goals. To illustrate this more clearly, consider a $1 investment made in 1926. If this dollar had been invested in short-term Treasury bills, at the end of 2000 it would have grown to only $16.57. If the dollar had been invested in the S&P 500 index, which includes a diversified mix of stocks, the investment would be worth $2,586 in 2000, almost 200 times more than an investment in Treasury bills. But this gain was not without risk. In some of those 70 years, the stock market lost money and your investment would have actually declined in value.

Short-Term versus Long-Term Investment

Given the differences in risk exposure across investments, your investment time horizon plays an important role in choice of investment vehicle. For example, suppose you borrow $5,000 on a student loan today but the money will be needed to pay tuition six months from now. Since you cannot afford to lose *any* of this principal in the short run, your investment should be in a low-risk security such as a bank certificate of deposit. These types of accounts promise that the original $5,000 principal plus promised interest will be available to you when your tuition is due. During the bull market of the 1990s, many students were tempted to take student loans and invest in the stock market in the hopes of doubling their money (although this undoubtedly violated their lender's rules). However, in the recent bear market, this strategy might have reduced the tuition funds by 20 percent or more.

In contrast to money that you are saving for near-term goals, your retirement is likely to be many decades away, so you can afford to take more risk for greater return. The average return on stocks over the last 25 years has been around 17 percent. In contrast, the average return on long-term corporate bonds, which offer regular payments of interest to investors, has been around 10 percent. Short-term, low-risk debt securities have averaged 7 percent. The differences in investment returns between these three categories is explainable based on the difference in risk imposed on the owners. Stock is the most risky. Corporate bonds with their regular payments of interest are less risky to you since you do not have to wait until you sell your investment to get some of your return on the investment. Since they are less risky, investors expect a lower percentage return.

Investment Choices

There are numerous possible investments, both domestic and international. The difficulty lies in deciding which ones are most appropriate for your needs and risk tolerance.

Savings Accounts and Certificates of Deposit.   The easiest parking spot for your cash is in a savings account. Unfortunately, investments in these low-risk (FDIC-insured), low-return accounts will barely keep up with inflation. If you have a need for liquidity but not necessarily immediate access to cash, a certificate of deposit wherein you promise to leave the money in the bank for six months or more will give you a slightly higher rate of return.

Bonds.   Corporations regularly borrow money from investors and issue bonds, which are securities that contain the firm's promise to pay regular interest and to repay principal at the end of the loan period, often 20 or more years in the future. These investments provide higher return to investors than short-term, interest-bearing accounts, but they also expose investors to price volatility, liquidity, and default risk.

A second group of bonds are those offered by government entities, commonly referred to as municipal bonds. These are typically issued to finance government projects, such as roads, airports, and bridges. Like corporate bonds, municipal bonds will pay interest on a regular basis, and the principal amount will be paid back to the investor at the end of a stated period of time, often 20 or more years. This type of bond has fewer interested investors and therefore has more liquidity risk.

Stocks.   A share of stock represents proportionate ownership interest in a business. Stockholders are thus exposed to all the risks that impact the business environment—interest rates, competition from other firms, input and output price risk, and others. In return for being willing to bear this risk, shareholders may receive dividends and/or capital appreciation in the value of their share(s). In any given year, stocks may fare better or worse than other investments, but there is substantial evidence that for long holding periods (20-plus years) stocks tend to outperform other investment choices.

Mutual Funds.   For the novice investor with a small amount of money to invest, the best choice is mutual funds. A mutual fund is a pool of funds from many investors that is managed by professionals who allocate the pooled dollars among various investments that meet the requirements of the mutual fund investors. There are literally thousands of these funds from which to choose, and they differ in type of investment (bonds, stocks, real estate, etc.), management style (active versus passive), and fee structure. Although even small investors have access to the market for individual securities, professional investors spend 100 percent of their time following the market and are likely to have more information at their disposal to aid in making buy and sell decisions.

Purchase of a Home. For many people, one of the best investments is the purchase of a home. With a small up-front investment (your down payment) and relatively low borrowing costs, modest appreciation in the home's value can generate a large return on investment. This return benefits from the tax deductibility of home mortgage interest and capital gains tax relief at the point of sale. And to top it off, you have a place to live and thus save any additional rental costs you would incur if you invested your money elsewhere. There are many sources of information about home ownership for investors on the Internet. How much house can you afford? What mortgage can you qualify for? How much difference does investment choice make?

Everyone needs to have a place to live, and two-thirds of Americans own their own homes. Nevertheless, owning a home is not necessarily the best choice for everyone. The decision on when and how to buy a house and how much to spend must be made based on a careful examination of your ability to pay the mortgage and to cover the time and expense of maintenance and repair. A home is probably the largest purchase you will ever make in your life. It is also one of the best investments you can make. As in the example given earlier, the ability to buy with a small down payment and to deduct the cost of interest paid from your taxable income provides financial benefits that are not available with any other investment type.

Few people could afford to buy homes at young ages if they were required to pay the full purchase price on their own. Instead, it is common for people to borrow most of the money from a financial institution and pay it back over time. The process of buying a home can begin with your search for the perfect home or it can begin with a visit to your local lender, who can give you an estimate of the amount of mortgage for which you can qualify. Mortgage companies and banks have specific guidelines that help them determine your creditworthiness. These include consideration of your ability and willingness to repay the loan in a timely fashion,

as well as an estimate of the value of the house that will be the basis for the loan.

A **mortgage** is a special type of loan that commonly requires that you make a constant payment over time to repay the lender the original money you borrowed (**principal**) together with **interest,** the amount that the lender charges for your use of its money. In the event that you do not make timely payments, the lender has the right to sell your property to get its money back (a process called **foreclosure).**

Mortgage interest rates in the last decade have ranged from 5 to 10 percent per year, depending on the terms and creditworthiness of the borrower. There are many variations on mortgages, some that lock in an interest rate for the full term of the loan, often 30 years, and others that allow the rate to vary with market rates of interest. In low-interest-rate economic circumstances, it makes sense to lock in the mortgage at favorable low rates.

Several measures are commonly applied to assess your *ability to repay* the loan. In addition to requiring some work history, most lenders will apply two ratio tests. First, the ratio of your total mortgage payment (including principal, interest, property taxes, and homeowners insurance) to your gross monthly income can be no more than a prespecified percentage that varies from lender to lender but is rarely greater than 28 percent. Second, the ratio of your credit payments (including credit cards, car loan or lease payments, and mortgage payment) to your gross monthly income is limited to no more than 36 percent. More restrictive lenders will have lower limits on both of these ratios.

Lenders also consider your *willingness to repay* the loan by looking at how you have managed debt obligations in the past. The primary source of information will be a credit report provided by one of the large credit reporting agencies. Late payments and defaulted loans will appear on that report and may result in denial of the mortgage loan. Most lenders, however, will overlook previously poor credit if more recent credit management shows a change in behavior. This can be helpful to college students who had trouble paying bills before they were gainfully employed.

The value of the home is important to the lender since it is the **collateral** for the loan; that is, in the event that you default on the loan (don't pay), the lender has the right to take the home in payment of the loan. To ensure that they are adequately covered, lenders will rarely lend more than 95 percent of the appraised value of the home. If you borrow more than 80 percent of the value, you will usually be required to pay a mortgage insurance premium with your regular payments. This will effectively increase the financing costs by ½ percent per year.

To illustrate the process of buying a home and qualifying for a mortgage, consider the following example. Jennifer graduated from college two years ago and has saved $7,000. She intends to use some of her savings as a down payment on a home. Her current salary is $36,000. She has a car payment of $250 per month and credit card debt that requires a minimum monthly payment of $100 per month. Suppose that Jennifer has found her dream home, which has a price of $105,000. She intends to make a down payment of $5,000 and borrow the rest. Can she qualify for the $100,000 loan at a rate of 7 percent?

Using Table D.4, her payment of principal and interest on a loan of $100,000 at 7 percent annual interest will be $665. With an additional $150 per month for property taxes and insurance (which may vary substantially in different areas of the country), her total payment will be $815. Since her gross monthly income is $3,000, the ratio of her payment to her income is 27 percent. Unless her lender has fairly strict rules, this should be acceptable. Her ratio of total payments to income will be ($815 + $250 + $150)/$3,000 = 40.5 percent. Unfortunately, Jennifer will not be able to qualify for this loan in her current financial circumstances.

So what can she do? The simplest solution is to use some of her remaining savings to pay off her credit card debt. By doing this, her debt ratio will drop to 35.5 percent and she will be accomplishing another element of good financial planning—reducing credit card debt and investing in assets that increase in value.

Planning for a Comfortable Retirement

Although it may seem like it's too early to start thinking about retirement when you are still in college, this is actually the best time to do so. In the investment section of this Appendix, you learned about the power of compound interest over long periods of time. The earlier you start saving for long-term goals, the easier it will be to achieve them.

How Much to Save. There is no "magic number" that will tell you how much to save. You must determine, based on budgeted income and expenses, what

TABLE D.4 Calcualting Monthly Mortgage Payments (30 year loan, principal and interest only)

Annual Interest %	Amount Borrowed			
	$75,000	$100,000	$125,000	$150,000
6.0	$450	$600	$749	$899
6.5	$474	$632	$790	$948
7.0	$499	$665	$832	$998
7.5	$524	$699	$874	$1,049
8.0	$550	$734	$917	$1,101
8.5	$577	$769	$961	$1,153
9.0	$603	$805	$1,006	$1,207
9.5	$631	$841	$1,051	$1,261
10.0	$658	$878	$1,097	$1,316

amount is realistic to set aside for this important goal. Several factors should help to guide this decision:

- Contributions to qualified retirement plans can be made before tax. This allows you to defer the payment of taxes until you retire many years from now.

- Earnings on retirement plan assets are tax deferred. If you have money in nonretirement vehicles, you will have to pay state and federal taxes on your earnings, which will significantly reduce your ending accumulation.

- If you need the money at some time before you reach age 59½, you will be subject to a withdrawal penalty of 10 percent, and the distribution will also be subject to taxes at the time of withdrawal.

In planning for your retirement needs, keep in mind that inflation will erode the purchasing power of your money. You should consider your ability to replace preretirement income as a measure of your success in retirement preparation. You can use the Social Security Administration Web site (**www.ssa.gov**) to estimate your future benefits from that program. In addition, most financial Web sites provide calculators to aid you in forecasting the future accumulations of your savings.

Employer Retirement Plans. Many employers offer retirement plans as part of their employee benefits package. **Defined benefit plans** promise a specific benefit at retirement (e.g., 60 percent of final salary).

More commonly, firms offer **defined contribution plans,** where they promise to put a certain amount of money into the plan in your name every pay period. The plan may also allow you to make additional contributions or the employer may base its contribution on your contribution (e.g., by matching the first 3 percent of salary that you put in). Employers also may make it possible for their employees to contribute additional amounts toward retirement on a tax-deferred basis. Many plans now allow employees to specify the investment allocation of their plan contributions and to shift account balances between different investment choices.

Some simple rules to follow with respect to employer plans include the following:

- If your employer offers you the opportunity to participate in a retirement plan, you should do so.

- If your employer offers to match your contributions, you should contribute as much as is necessary to get the maximum match, if you can afford to. Every dollar that the employer matches is like getting a 100 percent return on your investment in the first year.

- If your plan allows you to select your investment allocation, do not be too conservative in your choices if you still have many years until retirement.

Individual Retirement Accounts (IRAs).   Even if you do not have an employer-sponsored plan, you can contribute to retirement through an individual retirement account (IRA). There are two types of IRAs with distinctively different characteristics (which are summarized in Table D.5). Although previously subject to a $2,000 maximum annual contribution limit, tax reform in 2001 increases that limit gradually to $5,000 by 2008. The critical difference between Roth IRAs and traditional IRAs is the taxation of contributions and withdrawals. Roth IRA contributions are taxable, but the withdrawals are tax-free. Traditional IRAs are deductible, but the withdrawals are taxable. Both types impose a penalty of 10 percent for withdrawal before the qualified retirement age of 59½, subject to a few exceptions.

Social Security.   Social security is a public pension plan sponsored by the federal government and paid for by payroll taxes equally split between employers and employees. In addition to funding the retirement portion of the plan, Social Security payroll taxes pay

TABLE D.5   Comparing Individual Retirement Account Options

	Roth IRA	Traditional IRA
2003–2005 allowable contribution	$3,000	$3,000
Contributions deductible from current taxable income	No	Yes
Current tax on annual investment earnings	No	No
Tax due on withdrawal in retirement	No	Yes
10% penalty for withdrawal before age 59½	Yes	Yes
Mandatory distribution before age 70½	No	Yes
Tax-free withdrawals allowed for first-time homebuyers	Yes	No

for Medicare insurance (an old-age health program), disability insurance, and survivors benefits for the families of those who die prematurely.

The aging of the U.S. population has created a problem for funding the current Social Security system. Whereas it has traditionally been a pay-as-you-go program, with current payroll taxes going out to pay current retiree benefits, the impending retirement of baby boomers is forecast to bankrupt the system early in this century if changes are not made in a timely fashion. To understand the problem, consider that when Social Security began, there were 17 workers for each retiree receiving benefits. There are currently fewer than four workers per beneficiary. After the baby boom retirement, there will be only two workers to pay for each retiree. Obviously, that equation cannot work.

Does that mean that Social Security will not be around when you retire? Contrary to popular belief, it is unlikely that this will happen. There are simply too many voters relying on the future of Social Security for Congress to ever take such a drastic action. Instead, it is likely that the current system will be revised to help it balance. Prior to the heavy declines in the stock market in 2001, there was some general support for a plan that would divert some of the current payroll taxes to fund individual retirement accounts that could be invested in market assets. In addition, it seems likely that the retirement age will increase gradually to age 67. Other possible changes are to increase payroll taxes or to limit benefits payable to wealthier individuals. The proposed solutions are all complicated by the necessity of providing a transition program for those who are too old to save significant additional amounts toward their retirement.

Evaluate and Purchase Insurance

The next step in personal financial planning is the evaluation and purchase of insurance. Insurance policies are contracts between you and an insurance company wherein the insurer promises to pay you money in the event that a particular event occurs. Insurance is important, not only to protect your own assets from claims but also to protect your loved ones and dependents. The most common types of insurance for individuals are identified and briefly described below.

Automobile Insurance

In most states, drivers are required by law to carry a minimum amount of **auto liability insurance.** In the event that you are in a car accident, this coverage promises to pay claims against you for injuries to persons or property, up to a maximum per person and per accident. The basic liability policy will also cover your own medical costs. If you want to insure against damage to your own vehicle, you must purchase an additional type of coverage called **auto physical damage insurance.** If you have a car loan, the lender will require that you carry this type of insurance, since the value of the car is the collateral for that loan and the lender wants to be sure that you can afford to fix any damage to the vehicle following an accident. The minimum limits in most states are too low to cover typical claim levels. Good financial planning requires that you pay for insurance coverage with much higher limits.

Auto physical damage insurance coverage is always subject to a **deductible.** A deductible is an amount that you must pay before the insurance company will pay. To illustrate this, suppose your policy has a $250 deductible. You back into your garage door and damage your bumper, which will cost $750 to fix. The insurer will only pay $500, since you are responsible for the first $250. Once you receive the check from the insurer, you are free to try to get it fixed for less than the full $750.

Homeowners/Renters Insurance

Homeowners insurance provides coverage for liability and property damage in your home. For example, if someone slips and falls on your front steps and sues you for medical expenses, this insurance policy will pay the claim (or defend you against the claim if the insurer thinks it is not justified). If your house and/or property are damaged in a fire, the insurance will pay for lost property and the costs of repair. It is a good idea to pay extra for replacement cost insurance, since otherwise the insurance company is only obligated to pay you the depreciated value, which won't be enough to replace your belongings.

Renters insurance is similar to homeowners in that it covers you for liability on your premises (e.g., if your dog bites someone) and for damage to your personal property. Since you do not own the house, your landlord needs to carry separate insurance for his building. This insurance is very cheap and is well worth the cost, since your landlord's insurance will not pay anything to you in the event that the house burns down and you lose all your belongings.

Life Insurance

As compared to other types of insurance, the primary purpose of life insurance is to provide protection for others. **Life insurance** pays a benefit to your designated beneficiary (usually your spouse or other family members) in the event that you die during the coverage period. Life insurance premiums will depend on the face amount of the policy, your age and health, your habits (smoker versus nonsmoker), and the type of policy (whether it includes an investment component in addition to the death benefit).

The simplest type of life insurance is **term insurance.** This policy is usually for one year and the insurer promises to pay your designated beneficiary only the face amount of the policy in the event that you die during the year of coverage. Since the probability of dying at a young age is very small, the cost of providing this promise to people in their 20s and 30s is very inexpensive, and premiums are fairly low. Term insurance becomes more expensive at older ages, since the probability of dying is much higher and insurers must charge more.

Other types of life insurance usually fall into a category often called **permanent insurance,** since they are designed to provide you with insurance protection over your lifetime. In order to provide lifetime coverage at a reasonable cost, premiums will include an investment component. While there are many variations, typically in the early years of the policy you are paying a lot more than the actual cost of providing the death protection. The insurer takes that extra and invests it so that when you are older, the company has sufficient funds to cover your death risk. The primary difference between different types of permanent insurance is the way that they treat the investment component. Some policies allow the buyer to direct the investment choice and others do not.

Health Insurance

Health insurance pays the cost of covered medical expenses during the policy period, which is usually six months or one year. Most health insurance is provided under group policies through employers, but it is possible to purchase an individual policy. Since those who want to buy individual insurance are likely to be people who anticipate medical expenses, individual policies can be very expensive and are usually subject to exclusions, high coinsurance (the percentage of each dollar of expenses that you must pay out of pocket), and deductibles (the amount you must pay in full before the insurance pays).

From a financial-planning perspective, the type of health coverage that is most important is that which will protect you and your family from unexpected large medical costs. The usual checkups, shots, and prescription drugs are all budgetable expenses so need not be insured. At a minimum, you should have a policy that covers hospitalization and care for major disease or injury. This can be accomplished at relatively low cost by contracting for a large deductible (e.g., you pay the first $1,000 of costs per year).

The two main types of health insurance plans are *fee-for-service* and *managed care.* In a fee-for-service arrangement, the insurer simply pays for whatever covered medical costs you incur, subject to the deductible and coinsurance. Blue Cross and Blue Shield plans are the best known of this type. Managed care includes health maintenance organizations (HMOs) and preferred provider organizations (PPOs). In these health insurance arrangements, your health insurer pays all your costs (subject sometimes to small co-pays for office visits), but the care you receive is determined by your physician, who has contracted with the health insurer and has incentives to control overall costs. You are often limited in your choice of physician and your ability to seek specialist care under these plans.

Disability Insurance

One of the most overlooked types of insurance is **disability insurance,** which pays replacement income to you in the event you are disabled under the definition in your policy. Since one in three people will be disabled for a period of three months or more during their lifetime, disability insurance should be a component of the financial plan for anyone without sufficient financial resources to weather a period of loss of income.

Develop an Estate Plan

As with retirement planning, it is difficult to think about estate planning when you are young. In fact, you probably don't need to think much about it yet. If you have no dependents, there is little point in doing so. However, if you are married or have other dependents, you should include this as a necessary part of your financial plan. The essential components of an **estate plan** are:

- Your will, including a plan for guardianship of your children.
- Minimization of taxes on your estate.
- Protection of estate assets.

Estate planning is a complicated subject that is mired in legal issues. As such, appropriate design and implementation of an estate plan requires the assistance of a qualified professional.

The Importance of Having a Will

There are several circumstances that necessitate having a will. If you have a spouse and/or dependent children, if you have substantial assets, or if you have specific assets that you would like to give to certain individuals in the event of your death, you *should* have a will. On the other hand, if you are single with no assets or obligations (like many students), a will is probably not necessary—yet.

Having a valid will makes the estate settlement simpler for your spouse. If your children are left parentless, will provisions specify who will take guardianship of the children and direct funds for their support. You might also like to include a *living will,* which gives your family directions for whether to keep you on life support in the event that an illness or injury makes it unlikely for you to survive without extraordinary interventions. Lastly, you may want to make a will so that you can give your CD collection to your college roommate or Grandma's china to your daughter. Absent such provisions, relatives and friends have been known to take whatever they want without regard to your specific desires.

Avoiding Estate Taxes

As students, it will likely be many years before you will have accumulated a large enough estate (all your "worldly possessions") to have to worry about estate taxes. Although recent tax law changes have effectively eliminated the estate tax through 2009, the law includes a provision that reinstates current tax laws in 2010. Since no one can predict the date of his or her death, this implies that estate tax planning should be done assuming the worst-case scenario. Current estate taxes can take a big bite (more than half) out of your family's inheritance for wealthy taxpayers. Thus, much of estate planning is actually tax-avoidance

planning. Professionals can help set up trust arrangements that allow all or part of your estate to pass to your heirs without incurring taxes.

Adjust Your Financial Plan to New Circumstances

Finally, to ensure the success of your overall financial plan, it is vital that you evaluate it on a periodic basis and adjust it to accommodate changes in your life, such as marriage, children, or the addition or deletion of a second income from your spouse. Your plan also must be adjusted as your financial goals change (e.g., desires to own a home, make a large purchase, or retire at an early age). Whatever your goals may be, the information and worksheets provided here will help with your personal financial planning.

Gender Differences Create Special Financial Planning Concerns

Although most people would agree that there are some essential differences between men and women, it is not as clear why their financial planning needs should be different. After all, people of both sexes need to invest for future financial goals like college educations for their children and retirement income for themselves. In the last few years, professionals have written articles considering this subject. The results are both controversial and eye-opening.

- Even though 75 percent of women in the United States are working, they still have greater responsibility for household chores, child care, and care of aging parents than their husbands. This leaves less time for household finances.
- Women still earn much less than men, on average.
- Women are much less likely to have a pension sponsored through their employer. Only one-third of all working women have one at their current employer.
- Women are more conservative investors than men. Although there is evidence that women are gradually getting smart about taking a little more risk in their portfolios, on average they allocate half as much as men do to stocks.
- Most women will someday be on their own, either divorced or widowed.

Since women live an average of five years longer than men, they actually need to have saved more to provide a comparable retirement income. The combined impact of the above research findings makes it difficult but not impossible for women to save adequately for retirement. Much of the problem lies in education. Women need to be better informed about investing in order to make choices early in life that will pay off in the end. If they don't take the time to become informed about their finances or can't due to other obligations, in the end they will join the ranks of many women over age 65 who are living in poverty. But when women earn less, they don't have access to an employer pension, and they invest too conservatively, it is no surprise that women have so little wealth accumulation.

In her book, *The Busy Woman's Guide to Financial Freedom,* Dr. Vickie Bajtelsmit, an associate professor at Colorado State University, provides a road map for women who are interested in taking charge of their financial future. With simple-to-follow instructions for all aspects of financial planning, from investing to insurance to home buying, the book provides information for women to get on the right financial track.

THE
Busy Woman's Guide
TO
FINANCIAL
FREEDOM

VICKIE L. BAJTELSMIT

Glossary

A

absolute advantage a monopoly that exists when a country is the only source of an item, the only producer of an item, or the most efficient producer of an item

accountability the principle that employees who accept an assignment and the authority to carry it out are answerable to a superior for the outcome

accounting the recording, measurement, and interpretation of financial information

accounting cycle the four-step procedure of an accounting system: examining source documents, recording transactions in an accounting journal, posting recorded transactions, and preparing financial statements

accounting equation assets equal liabilities plus owners' equity

accounts payable the amount a company owes to suppliers for goods and services purchased with credit

accounts receivable money owed a company by its clients or customers who have promised to pay for the products at a later date

accrued expenses all unpaid financial obligations incurred by an organization

acquisition the purchase of one company by another, usually by buying its stock

administrative managers those who manage an entire business or a major segment of a business; they are not specialists but coordinate the activities of specialized managers

advertising a paid form of nonpersonal communication transmitted through a mass medium, such as television commercials or magazine advertisements

advertising campaign designing a series of advertisements and placing them in various media to reach a particular target market

affirmative action programs legally mandated plans that try to increase job opportunities for minority groups by analyzing the current pool of workers, identifying areas where women and minorities are underrepresented, and establishing specific promotion goals, with target dates, for addressing the discrepancy

agenda a calender, containing both specific and vague items, that covers short-term goals and long-term objectives

analytical skills the ability to identify relevant issues, recognize their importance, understand the relationships between them, and perceive the underlying causes of a situation

annual report summary of a firm's financial information, products, and growth plans for owners and potential investors

arbitration settlement of a labor/management dispute by a third party whose solution is legally binding and enforceable

articles of partnership legal documents that set forth the basic agreement between partners

Asia-Pacific Economic Cooperation (APEC) an international trade alliance that promotes open trade and economic and technical cooperation among member nations

asset utilization ratios ratios that measure how well a firm uses its assets to generate each $1 of sales

assets a firm's economic resources, or items of value that it owns, such as cash, inventory, land, equipment, buildings, and other tangible and intangible things

attitude knowledge and positive or negative feelings about something

automated clearinghouses (ACHs) a system that permits payments such as deposits or withdrawals to be made to and from a bank account by magnetic computer tape

automated teller machine (ATM) the most familiar form of electronic banking, which dispenses cash, accepts deposits, and allows balance inquiries and cash transfers from one account to another

B

balance of payments the difference between the flow of money into and out of a country

balance of trade the difference in value between a nation's exports and its imports

balance sheet a "snapshot" of an organization's financial position at a given moment

behavior modification changing behavior and encouraging appropriate actions by relating the consequences of behavior to the behavior itself

benefits nonfinancial forms of compensation provided to employees, such as pension plans, health insurance, paid vacation and holidays, and the like

board of directors a group of individuals, elected by the stockholders to oversee the general operation of the corporation, who set the corporation's long-range objectives

bonds debt instruments that larger companies sell to raise long-term funds

bonuses monetary rewards offered by companies for exceptional performance as incentives to further increase productivity

boycott an attempt to keep people from purchasing the products of a company

branding the process of naming and identifying products

bribes payments, gifts, or special favors intended to influence the outcome of a decision

brokerage firms firms that buy and sell stocks, bonds, and other securities for their customers and provide other financial services

budget an internal financial plan that forecasts expenses and income over a set period of time

budget deficit the condition in which a nation spends more than it takes in from taxes

business individuals or organizations who try to earn a profit by providing products that satisfy people's needs

business ethics principles and standards that determine acceptable conduct in business

business plan a precise statement of the rationale for a business and a step-by-step explanation of how it will achieve its goals

business products products that are used directly or indirectly in the operation or manufacturing processes of businesses

business-to-business (B2B) use of the Internet for transactions and communications between organizations

business-to-consumer (B2C) delivery of products and services directly to individual consumers through the Internet

buying behavior the decision processes and actions of people who purchase and use products

C

capacity the maximum load that an organizational unit can carry or operate

capital budgeting the process of analyzing the needs of the business and selecting the assets that will maximize its value

capitalism, or free enterprise an economic system in which individuals own and operate the majority of businesses that provide goods and services

cartel a group of firms or nations that agrees to act as a monopoly and not compete with each other, in order to generate a competitive advantage in world markets

cash flow the movement of money through an organization over a daily, weekly, monthly, or yearly basis

centralized organization a structure in which authority is concentrated at the top, and very little decision-making authority is delegated to lower levels

certificates of deposit (CDs) savings accounts that guarantee a depositor a set interest rate over a specified interval as long as the funds are not withdrawn before the end of the period

certified management accountants (CMAs) private accountants who, after rigorous examination, are certified by the National Association of Accountants and who have some managerial responsibility

certified public accountant (CPA) an individual who has been state certified to provide accounting services ranging from the preparation of financial records and the filing of tax returns to complex audits of corporate financial records

checking account money stored in an account at a bank or other financial institution that can be withdrawn without advance notice; also called a demand deposit

classical theory of motivation theory suggesting that money is the sole motivator for workers

codes of ethics formalized rules and standards that describe what a company expects of its employees

collective bargaining the negotiation process through which management and unions reach an agreement about compensation, working hours, and working conditions for the bargaining unit

commercial banks the largest and oldest of all financial institutions, relying mainly on checking and savings accounts as sources of funds for loans to businesses and individuals

commercial certificates of deposit (CDs) certificates of deposit issued by commercial banks and brokerage companies, available in minimum amounts of $100,000, which may be traded prior to maturity

commercial paper a written promise from one company to another to pay a specific amount of money

commercialization the full introduction of a complete marketing strategy and the launch of the product for commercial success

commission an incentive system that pays a fixed amount or a percentage of the employee's sales

commitee a permanent, formal group that performs a specific task

common stock stock whose owners have voting rights in the corporation, yet do not receive preferential treatment regarding dividends

communism first described by Karl Marx as a society in which the people, without regard to class, own all the nation's resources

comparative advantage the basis of most international trade, when a country specializes in products that it can supply more efficiently or at a lower cost than it can produce other items

competition the rivalry among businesses for consumers' dollars

compressed work week a four-day (or shorter) period during which an employee works 40 hours

computer-assisted design (CAD) the design of components, products, and processes on computers instead of on paper

computer-assisted manufacturing (CAM) manufacturing that employs specialized computer systems to actually guide and control the transformation processes

computer-integrated manufacturing (CIM) a complete system that designs products, manages machines and materials, and controls the operations function

concentration approach a market segmentation approach whereby a company develops one marketing strategy for a single market segment

conceptual skills the ability to think in abstract terms and to see how parts fit together to form the whole

conciliation a method of outside resolution of labor and management differences in which a third party is brought in to keep the two sides talking

consumer products products intended for household or family use

consumer-to-consumer (C2C) market in which consumers market goods and services to each other through the Internet

consumerism the activities that independent individuals, groups, and organizations undertake to protect their rights as consumers

continuous manufacturing organizations companies that use continuously running assembly lines, creating products with many similar characteristics⁺

contract manufacturing the hiring of a foreign company to produce a specified volume of the initiating company's product to specification; the final product carries the domestic firm's name

controlling the process of evaluating and correcting activities to keep the organization on course

cooperative or co-op an organization composed of individuals or small businesses that have banded together to reap the benefits of belonging to a larger organization

corporate charter a legal document that the state issues to a company based on information the company provides in the articles of incorporation

corporate citizenship the extent to which businesses meet the legal, ethical, economic, and voluntary responsibilities placed on them by their stakeholders

corporation a legal entity, created by the state, whose assets and liabilities are separate from its owners

cost of goods sold the amount of money a firm spent to buy or produce the products it sold during the period to which the income statement applies

countertrade agreements foreign trade agreements that involve bartering products for other products instead of for currency

credit cards means of access to preapproved lines of credit granted by a bank or finance company

credit controls the authority to establish and enforce credit rules for financial institutions and some private investors

credit union a financial institution owned and controlled by its depositors, who usually have a common employer, profession, trade group, or religion

crisis management or contingency planning an element in planning that deals with potential disasters such as product tampering, oil spills, fire, earthquake, computer virus, or airplane crash

culture the integrated, accepted pattern of human behavior, including thought, speech, beliefs, actions, and artifacts

current assets assets that are used or converted into cash within the course of a calendar year

current liabilities a firm's financial obligations to short-term creditors, which must be repaid within one year

current ratio current assets divided by current liabilities

customer departmentalization the arrangement of jobs around the needs of various types of customers

customer relationship management (CRM) focuses on using information about customers to create strategies that develop and sustain desirable long-term customer relationships

customization making products to meet a particular customer's needs or wants

D

data numerical or verbal descriptions related to statistics or other items that have not been analyzed or summarized

database a collection of data stored in one place and accessible throughout the network

debit card a card that looks like a credit card but works like a check; using it results in a direct, immediate, electronic payment from the cardholder's checking account to a merchant or third party

debt to total assets ratio a ratio indicating how much of the firm is financed by debt and how much by owners' equity

debt utilization ratios ratios that measure how much debt an organization is using relative to other sources of capital, such as owners' equity

decentralized organization an organization in which decision-making authority is delegated as far down the chain of command as possible

delegation of authority giving employees not only tasks, but also the power to make commitments, use resources, and take whatever actions are necessary to carry out those tasks

demand the number of goods and services that consumers are willing to buy at different prices at a specific time

departmentalization the grouping of jobs into working units usually called departments, units, groups, or divisions

depreciation the process of spreading the costs of long-lived assets such as buildings and equipment over the total number of accounting periods in which they are expected to be used

depression a condition of the economy in which unemployment is very high, consumer spending is low, and business output is sharply reduced

development training that augments the skills and knowledge of managers and professionals

direct investment the ownership of overseas facilities

directing motivating and leading employees to achieve organizational objectives

discount rate the rate of interest the Fed charges to loan money to any banking institution to meet reserve requirements

discounts temporary price reductions, often employed to boost sales

distribution making products available to customers in the quantities desired

diversity the participation of different ages, genders, races, ethnicities, nationalities, and abilities in the workplace

dividend yield the dividend per share divided by the stock price

dividends profits of a corporation that are distributed in the form of cash payments to stockholders

dividends per share the actual cash received for each share owned

double-entry bookkeeping a system of recording and classifying business transactions that maintains the balance of the accounting equation

downsizing the elimination of a significant number of employees from an organization

dumping the act of a country or business selling products at less than what it costs to produce them

E

e-business carrying out the goals of business through utilization of the Internet

earnings per share net income or profit divided by the number of stock shares outstanding

economic contraction a slowdown of the economy characterized by a decline in spending and during which businesses cut back on production and lay off workers

economic expansion the situation that occurs when an economy is growing and people are spending more money; their purchases stimulate the production of goods and services, which in turn stimulates employment

economic order quantity (EOQ) model a model that identifies the optimum number of items to order to minimize the costs of managing (ordering, storing, and using) inventory

economic system a description of how a particular society distributes its resources to produce goods and services

economics the study of how resources are distributed for the production of goods and services within a social system

electronic funds transfer (EFT) any movement of funds by means of an electronic terminal, telephone, computer, or magnetic tape

embargo a prohibition on trade in a particular product

entrepreneur an individual who risks his or her wealth, time, and effort to develop for profit an innovative product or way of doing something

enterpreneurship the process of creating and managing a business to achieve desired objectives

equilibrium price the price at which the number of products that businesses are willing to supply equals the amount of products that consumers are willing to buy at a specific point in time

equity theory an assumption that how much people are willing to contribute to an organization depends on their assessment of the fairness, or equity, of the rewards they will receive in exchange

esteem needs the need for respect—both self-respect and respect from others

ethical issue an identifiable problem, situation, or opportunity that requires a person to choose from among several actions that may be evaluated as right or wrong, ethical or unethical

Eurodollar market a market for trading U.S. dollars in foreign countries

European Union (EU) a union of European nations established in 1958 to promote trade among its members; one of the largest single markets today

exchange the act of giving up one thing (money, credit, labor, goods) in return for something else (goods, services, or ideas)

exchange controls regulations that restrict the amount of currency that can be bought or sold

exchange rate the ratio at which one nation's currency can be exchanged for another nation's currency

exclusive distribution the awarding by a manufacturer to an intermediary of the sole right to sell a product in a defined geographic territory

expectancy theory the assumption that motivation depends not only on how much a person wants something but also on how likely he or she is to get it

expenses the costs incurred in the day-to-day operations of an organization

exporting the sale of goods and services to foreign markets

extranet a network of computers that permits selected companies and other organizations to access the same information and may allow collaboration and communication about the information

F

factor a finance company to which businesses sell their accounts receivable—usually for a percentage of the total face value

Federal Deposit Insurance Corporation (FDIC) an insurance fund established in 1933 that insures individual bank accounts

Federal Reserve Board an independent agency of the federal government established in 1913 to regulate the nation's banking and financial industry

finance companies business that offer short-term loans at substantially higher rates of interest than banks

finance the study of money; how it's made, how it's lost, and how it's managed

financial managers those who focus on obtaining needed funds for the successful operation of an organization and using those funds to further organizational goals

financial resources the funds used to acquire the natural and human resources needed to provide products; also called capital

first-line managers those who supervise both workers and the daily operations of an organization

fixed-position layout a layout that brings all resources required to create the product to a central location

flexible manufacturing the direction of machinery by computers to adapt to different versions of similar operations

flextime a program that allows employees to choose their starting and ending times, provided that they are at work during a specified core period

floating-rate bonds bonds with interest rates that change with current interest rates otherwise available in the economy

franchise a license to sell another's products or to use another's name in business, or both

franchisee the purchaser of a franchise

franchiser the company that sells a franchise

franchising a form of licensing in which a company—the franchiser—agrees to provide a franchisee a name, logo, methods of operation, advertising, products, and other elements associated with a franchiser's business, in return for a financial

free-market system pure capitalism, in which all economic decisions are made without government intervention

functional departmentalization the grouping of jobs tht perform similar functional activities, such as finance, manufacturing, marketing, and human resources

G

General Agreement on Tariffs and Trade (GATT) a trade agreement, originally signed by 23 nations in 1947, that provided a forum for tariff negotiations and a place where international trade problems could be discussed and resolved

general partnership a partnership that involves a complete sharing in both the management and the liability of the business

generic products products with no brand name that often come in simple packages and carry only their generic name

geographical departmentalization the grouping of jobs according to geographic location, such as state, region, country, or continent

global strategy (globalization) a strategy that involves standardizing products (and, as much as possible, their promotion and distribution) for the whole world, as if it were a single entity

grapevine an informal channel of communication, separate from management's formal, official communication channels

gross domestic product (GDP) the sum of all goods and services produced in a country during a year

gross income (or profit) revenues minus the cost of goods sold required to generate the revenues

group two or more individuals who communicate with one another, share a common identity, and have a common goal

H

human relations the study of the behavior of individuals and groups in organizational settings

human relations skills the ability to deal with people, both inside and outside the organization

human resources the physical and mental abilities that people use to produce goods and services; also called labor

human resources management (HRM) all the activities involved in determining an organization's human resources needs, as well as acquiring, training, and compensating people to fill those needs

human resources managers those who handle the staffing function and deal with employees in a formalized manner

hygiene factors aspects of Herzberg's theory of motivation that focus on the work setting and not the content of the work; these aspects include adequate wages, comfortable and safe working conditions, fair company policies, and job security

I

import tariff a tax levied by a nation on goods imported into the country

importing the purchase of goods and services from foreign sources

income statement a financial report that shows an organization's profitability over a period of time—month, quarter, or year

inflation a condition characterized by a continuing rise in prices

information meaningful and useful interpretation of data and knowledge that can be used in making decisions

information technology (IT) processes and applications that create new methods to solve problems, perform tasks, and manage communication

information technology (IT) managers those who are responsible for implementing, maintaining, and controlling technology applications in business, such as computer networks

infrastructure the physical facilities that support a country's economic activities, such as railroads, highways, ports, airfields, utilities and power plants, schools, hospitals, communication systems, and commercial distribution systems

initial public offering (IPO) selling a corporation's stock on public markets for the first time

inputs the resources—such as labor, money, materials, and energy—that are converted into outputs

insurance companies businesses that protect their clients against financial losses from certain specified risks (death, accident, and theft, for example)

integrated marketing communications coordinating the promotion mix elements and synchronizing promotion as a unified effort

intensive distribution a form of market coverage whereby a product is made available in as many outlets as possible

intermittent organizations organizations that deal with products of a lesser magnitude than do project organizations; their products are not necessarily unique but possess a significant number of differences

international business the buying, selling, and trading of goods and services across national boundaries

International Monetary Fund (IMF) organization established in 1947 to promote trade among member nations by eliminating trade barriers and fostering financial cooperation

Internet global information system that links many computer networks together

intranet a network of computers similar to the Internet that is available only to people inside an organization

intrapreneurs individuals in large firms who take responsibility for the development of innovations within the organizations

inventory all raw materials, components, completed or partially completed products, and pieces of equipment a firm uses

inventory control the process of determining how many supplies and goods are needed and keeping track of quantities on hand, where each item is, and who is responsible for it

inventory turnover sales divided by total inventory

investment banking the sale of stocks and bonds for corporations

ISO 9000 a series of quality assurance standards designed by the International Organization for Standardization (ISO) to ensure consistent product quality under many conditions

J

job analysis the determination, through observation and study, of pertinent information about a job—including specific tasks and necessary abilities, knowledge, and skills

job description a formal, written explanation of a specific job, usually including job title, tasks, relationship with other jobs, physical and mental skills required, duties, responsibilities, and working conditions

job enlargement the addition of more tasks to a job instead of treating each task as separate

job enrichment the incorporation of motivational factors, such as opportunity for achievement, recognition, responsibility, and advancement, into a job

job rotation movement of employees from one job to another in an effort to relieve the boredom often associated with job specialization

job sharing performance of one full-time job by two people on part-time hours

job specification a description of the qualifications necessary for a specific job, in terms of education, experience, and personal and physical characteristics

joint venture a partnership established for a specific project or for a limited time

joint venture the sharing of the costs and operation of a business between a foreign company and a local partner

journal a time-ordered list of account transactions

junk bonds a special type of high-interest-rate bond that carries higher inherent risks

just-in-time (JIT) inventory management a technique using smaller quantities of materials that arrive "just in time" for use in the transformation process and therefore require less storage space and other inventory management expense

K

knowledge an understanding of data gained through study or experience

L

labeling the presentation of important information on a package

labor contract the formal, written document that spells out the relationship between the union and management for a specified period of time—usually two or three years

labor unions employee organizations formed to deal with employers for achieving better pay, hours, and working conditions

leadership the ability to influence employees to work toward organizational goals

learning changes in a person's behavior based on information and experience

ledger a book or computer file with separate sections for each account

leveraged buyout (LBO) a purchase in which a group of investors borrows money from banks and other institutions to acquire a company (or a division of one), using the assets of the purchased company to guarantee repayment of the loan

liabilities debts that a firm owes to others

licensing a trade agreement in which one company—the licensor—allows another company—the licensee—to use its company name, products, patents, brands, trademarks, raw materials, and/or production processes in exchange for a fee or royalty

limited liability company (LLC) form of ownership that provides limited liability and taxation like a partnership but places fewer restrictions on members

limited partnership a business organization that has at least one general partner, who assumes unlimited liability, and at least one limited partner, whose liability is limited to his or her investment in the business

line of credit an arrangement by which a bank agrees to lend a specified amount of money to an organization upon request

line structure the simplest organizational structure in which direct lines of authority extend from the top manager to the lowest level of the organization

line-and-staff structure a structure having a traditional line relationship between superiors and subordinates and also specialized managers—called staff managers—who are available to assist line managers

liquidity ratios ratios that measure the speed with which a company can turn its assets into cash to meet short-term debt

lockbox an address, usually a commercial bank, at which a company receives payments in order to speed collections from customers

lockout management's version of a strike, wherein a work site is closed so that employees cannot go to work

long-term (fixed) assets production facilities (plants), offices, and equipment—all of which are expected to last for many years

long-term liabilities debts that will be repaid over a number of years, such as long-term loans and bond issues

M

management a process designed to achieve an organization's objectives by using its resources effectively and efficiently in a changing environment

management information system used for organizing and transmitting data into information that can be used for decision making

managerial accounting the internal use of accounting statements by managers in planning and directing the organization's activities

managers those individuals in organizations who make decisions about the use of resources and who are concerned with planning, organizing, staffing, directing, and controlling the organization's activities to reach its objectives

manufacturer brands brands initiated and owned by the manufacturer to identify products from the point of production to the point of purchase

manufacturing the activities and processes used in making tangible products; also called production

market a group of people who have a need, purchasing power, and the desire and authority to spend money on goods, services, and ideas

market segment a collection of individuals, groups, or organizations who share one or more characteristics and thus have relatively similar product needs and desires

market segmentation a strategy whereby a firm divides the total market into groups of people who have relatively similar product needs

marketable securities temporary investment of "extra" cash by organizations for up to one year in U.S. Treasury bills, certificates of deposit, commercial paper, or Eurodollar loans

marketing a group of activities designed to expedite transactions by creating, distributing, pricing, and promoting goods, services, and ideas

marketing channel a group of organizations that moves products from their producer to customers; also called a channel of distribution

marketing concept the idea that an organization should try to satisfy customers' needs through coordinated activities that also allow it to achieve its own goals

marketing managers those who are responsible for planning, pricing, and promoting products and making them available to customers

marketing mix the four marketing activites—product, price, promotion, and distribution—that the firm can control to achieve specific goals within a dynamic marketing environment

marketing orientation an approach requiring organizations to gather information about customer needs, share that information throughout the firm, and use that information to help build long-term relationships with customers

marketing research a systematic, objective process of getting information about potential customers to guide marketing decisions

marketing strategy a plan of action for developing, pricing, distributing, and promoting products that meet the needs of specific customers

Maslow's hierarchy a theory that arranges the five basic needs of people—physiological, security, social, esteem, and self-actualization—into the order in which people strive to satisfy them

material-requirements planning (MRP) a planning system that schedules the precise quantity of materials needed to make the product

materials handling the physical handling and movement of products in warehousing and transportation

matrix structure a structure that sets up teams from different departments, thereby creating two or more intersecting lines of authority; also called a project-management structure

mediation a method of outside resolution of labor and management differences in which the third party's role is to suggest or propose a solution to the problem

merger the combination of two companies (usually corporations) to form a new company

middle managers those members of an organization responsible for the tactical planning that implements the general guidelines established by top management

mission the statement of an organization's fundamental purpose and basic philosophy

mixed economies economies made up of elements from more than one economic system

modular design the creation of an item in self-contained units, or modules, that can be combined or interchanged to create different products

monetary policy means by which the Fed controls the amount of money available in the economy

money anything generally accepted in exchange for goods and services

money market accounts accounts that offer higher interest rates than standard bank rates but with greater restrictions

monopolistic competition the market structure that exists when there are fewer businesses than in a pure-competition environment and the differences among the goods they sell are small

monopoly the market structure that exists when there is only one business providing a product in a given market

morale an employee's attitude toward his or her job, employer, and colleagues

motivation an inner drive that directs a person's behavior toward goals

motivational factors aspects of Herzberg's theory of motivation that focus on the content of the work itself; these aspects include achievement, recognition, involvement, responsibility, and advancement

multidivisional structure a structure that organizes departments into larger groups called divisions

multinational corporation (MNC) a corporation that operates on a worldwide scale, without significant ties to any one nation or region

multinational strategy a plan, used by international companies, that involves customizing products, promotion, and distribution according to cultural, technological, regional and national differences

multisegment approach a market segmentation approach whereby the marketer aims its efforts at two or more segments, developing a marketing strategy for each

mutual fund an investment company that pools individual investor dollars and invests them in large numbers of well-diversified securities

mutual savings banks financial institutions that are similar to savings and loan associations but, like credit unions, are owned by their depositors

N

National Credit Union Association (NCUA) an agency that regulates and charters credit unions and insures their deposits through its National Credit Union Insurance Fund

natural resources land, forests, minerals, water, and other things that are not made by people

net income the total profit (or loss) after all expenses including taxes have been deducted from revenue; also called net earnings

networking the building of relationships and sharing of information with colleagues who can help managers achieve the items on their agendas

nonprofit corporations corporations that focus on providing a service rather than earning a profit but are not owned by a government entity

nonprofit organizations organizations that may provide goods or services but do not have the fundamental purpose of earning profits

North American Free Trade Agreement (NAFTA) agreement that eliminates most tariffs and trade restrictions on agricultural and manufactured products to encourage trade among Canada, the United States, and Mexico

O

oligopoly the market structure that exists when there are very few businesses selling a product

open market operations decisions to buy or sell U.S. Treasury bills (short-term debt issued by the U.S. government) and other investments in the open market

operational plans very short-term plans that specify what actions individuals, work groups, or departments need to accomplish in order to achieve the tactical plan and ultimately the strategic plan

operations the activities and processes used in making both tangible and intangible products

operations management (OM) the development and administration of the activities involved in transforming resources into goods and services

organizational chart a visual display of the organizational structure, lines of authority (chain of command), staff relationships, permanent committee arrangements, and lines of communication

organizational culture a firm's shared values, beliefs, traditions, philosophies, rules, and role models for behavior

organizational layers the levels of management in an organization

organized exchanges central locations where investors buy and sell securities

organizing the structuring of resources and activities to accomplish objectives in an efficient and effective manner

orientation familiarizing newly hired employees with fellow workers, company procedures, and the physical properties of the company

outputs the goods, services, and ideas that result from the conversion of inputs

outsourcing the transferring of manufacturing or other tasks—such as data processing—to countries where labor and supplies are less expensive

over-the-counter (OTC) market a network of dealers all over the country linked by computers, telephones, and Teletype machines

owners' equity equals assets minus liabilities and reflects historical values

P

packaging the external container that holds and describes the product

partnership a form of business organization defined by the Uniform Partnership Act as "an association of two or more persons who carry on as co-owners of a business for profit"

penetration price a low price designed to help a product enter the market and gain market share rapidly

pensions funds managed investment pools set aside by individuals, corporations, unions, and some nonprofit organizations to provide retirement income for members

per share data data used by investors to compare the performance of one company with another on an equal, per share basis

perception the process by which a person selects, organizes, and interprets information received from his or her senses

personal selling direct, two-way communication with buyers and potential buyers

personality the organization of an individual's distinguishing character traits, attitudes, or habits

physical distribution all the activities necessary to move products from producers to customers—inventory control, transportation, warehousing, and materials handling

physiological needs the most basic human needs to be satisfied—water, food, shelter, and clothing

picketing a public protest against management practices that involves union members marching and carrying antimanagement signs at the employer's plant

plagiarism the act of taking someone else's work and presenting it as your own without mentioning the source

planning the process of determining the organization's objectives and deciding how to accomplish them; the first function of management

preferred stock a special type of stock whose owners, though not generally having a say in running the company, have a claim to profits before other stockholders do

price a value placed on an object exchanged between a buyer and a seller

price skimming charging the highest possible price that buyers who want the product will pay

primary data marketing information that is observed, recorded, or collected directly from respondents

primary market the market where firms raise financial capital

prime rate the interest rate that commercial banks charge their best customers (usually large corporations) for short-term loans

private accountants accountants employed by large corporations, government agencies, and other organizations to prepare and analyze their financial statements

private corporation a corporation owned by just one or a few people who are closely involved in managing the business

private distributor brands brands, which may cost less than manufacturer brands, that are owned and controlled by a wholesaler or retailer

process layout a layout that organizes the transformation process into departments that group related processes

product a good or service with tangible and intangible characteristics that provide satisfaction and benefits

product departmentalization the organization of jobs in relation to the products of the firm

product-development teams a specific type of project team formed to devise, design, and implement a new product

product layout a layout requiring that production be broken down into relatively simple tasks assigned to workers, who are usually positioned along an assembly line

product line a group of closely related products that are treated as a unit because of similar marketing strategy, production, or end-use considerations

product mix all the products offered by an organization

production and operations managers those who develop and administer the activities involved in transforming resources into goods, services, and ideas ready for the marketplace

production the activities and processes used in making tangible products; also called manufacturing

profit margin net income divided by sales

profit sharing a form of compensation whereby a percentage of company profits is distributed to the employees whose work helped to generate them

profit the difference between what it costs to make and sell a product and what a customer pays for it

profitability ratios ratios that measure the amount of operating income or net income an organization is able to generate relative to its assets, owners' equity, and sales

project organization a company using a fixed-position layout because it is typically involved in large, complex projects such as construction or exploration

project teams groups similar to task forces which normally run their operation and have total control of a specific work project

promotion a persuasive form of communication that attempts to expedite a marketing exchange by influencing individuals, groups, and organizations to accept goods, services, and ideas

promotion an advancement to a higher-level job with increased authority, responsibility, and pay

promotional positioning the use of promotion to create and maintain an image of a product in buyers' minds

psychological pricing encouraging purchases based on emotional rather than rational responses to the price

public corporation a corporation whose stock anyone may buy, sell, or trade

publicity nonpersonal communication transmitted through the mass media but not paid for directly by the firm

pull strategy the use of promotion to create consumer demand for a product so that consumers exert pressure on marketing channel members to make it available

purchasing the buying of all the materials needed by the organization; also called procurement

pure competition the market structure that exists when there are many small businesses selling one standardized product

push strategy an attempt to motivate intermediaries to push the product down to their customers

Q

quality control the processes an organization uses to maintain its established quality standards

quality the degree to which a good, service, or idea meets the demands and requirements of customers

quality-assurance teams (or quality circles) small groups of workers brought together from throughout the organization to solve specific quality, productivity, or service problems

quasi-public corporations corporations owned and operated by the federal, state, or local government

quick ratio (acid test) a stringent measure of liquidity that eliminates inventory

quota a restriction on the number of units of a particular product that can be imported into a country

R

ratio analysis calculations that measure an organization's financial health

receivables turnover sales divided by accounts receivable

recession a decline in production, employment, and income

recruiting forming a pool of qualified applicants from which management can select employees

reference groups groups with whom buyers identify and whose values or attitudes they adopt

reserve requirement the percentage of deposits that banking institutions must hold in reserve

responsibility the obligation, placed on employees through delegation, to perform assigned tasks satisfactorily and be held accountable for the proper execution of work

retailers intermediaries who buy products from manufacturers (or other intermediaries) and sell them to consumers for home and household use rather than for resale or for use in producing other products

retained earnings earnings after expenses and taxes that are reinvested in the assets of the firm and belong to the owners in the form of equity

return on assets net income divided by assets

return on equity net income divided by owner's equity; also called return on investment (ROI)

revenue the total amount of money received from the sale of goods or services, as well as from related business activities

routing the sequence of operations through which the product must pass

S

S corporation corporation taxed as though it were a partnership with restrictions on shareholders

salary a financial reward calculated on a weekly, monthly, or annual basis

sales promotion direct inducements offering added value or some other incentive for buyers to enter into an exchange

savings accounts accounts with funds that usually cannot be withdrawn without advance notice; also known as time deposits

savings and loan associations (S&Ls) financial institutions that primarily offer savings accounts and make long-term loans for residential mortgages; also called "thrifts"

scheduling the assignment of required tasks that is given to departments or even specific machines, workers, or teams

secondary data information that is compiled inside or outside an organization for some purpose other than changing the current situation

secondary markets stock exchanges and over-the-counter markets where investors can trade their securities with others

secured bonds bonds that are backed by specific collateral that must be forfeited in the event that the issuing firm defaults

secured loans loans backed by collateral that the bank can claim if the borrowers do not repay them

securities markets the mechanism for buying and selling securities

security needs the need to protect oneself from physical and economic harm

selection the process of collecting information about applicants and using that information to make hiring decisions

selective distribution a form of market coverage whereby only a small number of all available outlets are used to expose products

self-actualization needs the need to be the best one can be; at the top of Maslow's hierarchy

self-directed work team (SDWT) a group of employees responsible for an entire work process or segment that delivers a product to an internal or external customer

separations employment changes involving resignation, retirement, termination, or layoff

serial bonds a sequence of small bond issues of progressively longer maturity

small business any independently owned and operated business that is not dominant in its competitive area and does not employ more than 500 people

Small Business Administration (SBA) an independent agency of the federal government that offers managerial and financial assistance to small businesses

social classes a ranking of people into higher or lower positions of respect

social needs the need for love, companionship, and friendship—the desire for acceptance by others

social responsibility a business's obligation to maximize its positive impact and minimize its negative impact on society

social roles a set of expectations for individuals based on some position they occupy

socialism an economic system in which the government owns and operates basic industries but individuals own most businesses

sole proprietorships businesses owned and operated by one individual; the most common form of business organization in the United States

spam Unsolicited commercial e-mail

span of management the number of subordinates who report to a particular manager

specialization the division of labor into small, specific tasks and the assignment of employees to do a single task

staffing the hiring of people to carry out the work of the organization

stakeholders groups that have a stake in the success and outcomes of a business

standardization the making of identical interchangeable components or products

statement of cash flow explains how the company's cash changed from the beginning of the accounting period to the end

statistical process control a system in which management collects and analyzes information about the production process to pinpoint quality problems in the production system

stock shares of a corporation that may be bought or sold

strategic alliance a partnership formed to create competitive advantage on a worldwide basis

strategic plans those plans that establish the long-range objectives and overall strategy or course of action by which a firm fulfills its mission

strikebreakers people hired by management to replace striking employees; called "scabs" by striking union members

strikes employee walkouts; one of the most effective weapons labor has

structure the arrangement or relationship of positions within an organization

supply chain management connecting and integrating all parties or members of the distribution system in order to satisfy customers

supply the number of products—goods and services—that businesses are willing to sell at different prices at a specific time

T

tactical plans short-range plans designed to implement the activities and objectives specified in the strategic plan

target market a specific group of consumers on whose needs and wants a company focuses its marketing efforts

task force a temporary group of employees responsible for bringing about a particular change

team a small group whose members have complementary skills; have a common purpose, goals, and approach; and hold themselves mutually accountable

technical expertise the specialized knowledge and training needed to perform jobs that are related to particular areas of management

technology The application of knowledge, including the processes and procedures to solve problems, perform tasks, and create new methods to obtain desired outcomes

test marketing a trial minilaunch of a product in limited areas that represent the potential market

Theory X McGregor's traditional view of management whereby it is assumed that workers generally dislike work and must be forced to do their jobs

Theory Y McGregor's humanistic view of management whereby it is assumed that workers like to work and that under proper conditions employees will seek out

responsibility in an attempt to satisfy their social, esteem, and self-actualization

Theory Z a management philosophy that stresses employee participation in all aspects of company decision making

times interest earned ratio operating income divided by interest expense

Title VII of the Civil Rights Act prohibits discrimination in employment and created the Equal Employment Opportunity Commission

top managers the president and other top executives of a business, such as the chief executive officer (CEO), chief financial officer (CFO), and chief operations officer (COO), who have overall responsibility for the organization

total asset turnover sales divided by total assets

total quality management (TQM) a philosophy that uniform commitment to quality in all areas of an organization will promote a culture that meets customers' perceptions of quality

total-market approach an approach whereby a firm tries to appeal to everyone and assumes that all buyers have similar needs

trade credit credit extended by suppliers for the purchase of their goods and services

trade deficit a nation's negative balance of trade, which exists when that country imports more products than it exports

trademark a brand that is registered with the U.S. Patent and Trademark Office and is thus legally protected from use by any other firm

trading company a firm that buys goods in one country and sells them to buyers in another country

training teaching employees to do specific job tasks through either classroom development or on-the-job experience

transaction balances cash kept on hand by a firm to pay normal daily expenses, such as employee wages and bills for supplies and utilities

transfer a move to another job within the company at essentially the same level and wage

transportation the shipment of products to buyers

Treasury bills (T-bills) short-term debt obligations the U.S. government sells to raise money

turnover occurs when employees quit or are fired and must be replaced by new employees

U

undercapitalization the lack of funds to operate a business normally

unemployment the condition in which a percentage of the population wants to work but is unable to find jobs

unsecured bonds debentures, or bonds that are not backed by specific collateral

unsecured loans loans backed only by the borrowers' good reputation and previous credit rating

V

venture capitalists persons or organizations that agree to provide some funds for a new business in exchange for an ownership interest or stock

W

wage/salary survey a study that tells a company how much compensation comparable firms are paying for specific jobs that the firms have in common

wages financial rewards based on the number of hours the employee works or the level of output achieved

warehousing the design and operation of facilities to receive, store, and ship products

whistleblowing the act of an employee exposing an employer's wrongdoing to outsiders, such as the media or government regulatory agencies

wholesalers intermediaries who buy from producers or from other wholesalers and sell to retailers

working capital management the managing of short-term assets and liabilities

World Bank an organization established by the industrialized nations in 1946 to loan money to underdeveloped and developing countries; formally known as the International Bank for Reconstruction and Development

World Trade Organization international organization dealing with the rules of trade between nations

World Wide Web a collection of interconnected Web sites or pages of text, graphics, audio, and video within the Internet

Notes

Chapter 1

1. Robert Barker, "Satellite Radio: Clear Growth, Far-Off Profits," *BusinessWeek,* February 2, 2004, p. 91; Paul Keegan, "The Real Information Superhighway," *Business 2.0,* www.business2.com; Paul R. LaMonica, "Satellite Radio Ga-Ga," *Business 2.0,* February 3, 2004, www.business2.com; Mike Langberg, "Satellite Radio Ready to Hit the Mainstream," *Silicon Valley.com,* July 3, 2003, www.siliconvalley.com/mld/siliconvalley/business/technology/personal_technology/6225 804.htm; Gary Martin, "Clear Channel Accused of Stifling Competition, Bullying Musicians," *Austin American-Statesman,* January 31, 2003, www.austin360.com/statesman/; Sam Silverstein, "Satellite Radio: Business Is Booming," *Space News,* November 12, 2003, www.space.com/businesstechnology/technology/satcom_radio_industry_031112.html; "Sky-High Stakes for Satellite Radio," *BusinessWeek Online,* September 4, 2003, www.businessweek.com/technology/content/sep2003/tc2003094_0275_tc127.htm.

2. Peter Asmus, with Sandra Waddock and Samuel Graves, "100 Best Corporate Citizens of 2003," *Business Ethics* (n.d.), www.business-ethics.com/100best.htm#100%20Best%20Corporate%20Citizens%20of%202003 (accessed January 12, 2004).

3. Kemba J. Dunham, "The Jungle," *The Wall Street Journal,* May 1, 2001, p. B10.

4. "The Home Depot Social Responsibility Report 2000," Home Depot (n.d.), www.homedepot.com (accessed August 27, 2001); "Preparing and Responding to Disasters," Home Depot (n.d.), www.homedepot.com/HDUS/EN_US/corporate/corp_respon/prepare_respond.shtml (accessed March 5, 2004).

5. "Paul Tagliabue: National Football League," *BusinessWeek,* January 12, 2004, p. 66.

6. "Terry Semel: Yahoo," *BusinessWeek,* January 12, 2004, p. 64.

7. Brian Grow with Gerry Khermouch, "The Low-Carb Food Fight Ahead," *BusinessWeek,* December 22, 2003, p. 48; "Ruby Tuesday to Use Healthier Oil, Offer Low-Carb Items," *USA Today,* November 11, 2003, www.usatoday.com/money/industries/food/2003-11-11ruby-tuesday_x.htm.

8. "Coke Chief Wants Anti-Obesity Effort," *CNN/Money,* December 9, 2003, www.cnn.com.

9. "Got Milk," National Fluid Milk Processor Promotion Board (n.d.), www.whymilk.com (accessed March 5, 2004).

10. Toddi Guttner, "In the Venture Drought, an Oasis," *BusinessWeek,* July 16, 2001, pp. 86E2, 86E4.

11. Susan Berfield, with Diane Brady and Tom Lowry, "The CEO of Hip Hop," *BusinessWeek,* October 27, 2003, pp. 90–98.

12. "Cattlemen Credit Atkins Diet for High Demand in Beef," *The [Fort Collins] Coloradoan,* November 17, 2003, p. E4; Blaine Harden, "Low-Carb Diet Fad, Thinner Herds Fatten Wallets of Ranchers," *The Wall Street Journal,* December 23, 2003, http://online.wsj.com/; Scott Kilman and Tamsin Carlisle, "U.S. Meatpackers Lay Off Workers amid Export Ban," *The Wall Street Journal,* January 12, 2004, http://online.wsj.com/; Sue Kirchhoff, "Natural Beef Industry Might See Boost from Mad Cow Fears," *USA Today,* January 12, 2004, p. 1B, 2B; "Strong Demand, Limited Supply Push Beef Prices Higher," National Cattlemans Beef Association, June 2, 2004, www.beefusa.ovg/dsp/dsp_Topiccfm?_Topic127.

13. James R. Healey, "Gasoline Supplies Likely to Shrink, Prices Rise," *USA Today,* February 26, 2004, p. 1B.

14. Michael McCarthy and Theresa Howard, "Universal Music Slashes CD, Cassette Prices," *USA Today,* September 4, 2003, p. 1B.

15. Ronald Grover and Tom Lowry, "Show Time!" *BusinessWeek,* February 2, 2004, pp. 56–64.

16. Anthony Bianco and Wendy Zellner, "Is Wal-Mart Too Powerful?" *BusinessWeek,* October 6, 2003, pp. 102–10; Cora Daniels, "Women vs. Wal-Mart," *Fortune,* July 21, 2003, pp. 79–82; Karen Dybis, "Savvy Shoppers Speeding Supermarket Shakeout," *The Coloradoan,* February 22, 2004, p. E4; Charles Fishman, "The Wal-Mart You Don't Know: Why Low Prices Have a High Cost," *Fast Company,* December 2003, pp. 70–80; Daren Fonda, "Will Wal-Mart Steal Christmas?" *Time,* December 8, 2003, pp. 54–56; "Wal-Mart Stores, Inc.," Hoover's, www.hoover.com, (accessed June 7, 2004); John R. Wilke, "How Driving Prices Lower Can Violate Antitrust Statutes," *The Wall Street Journal,* January 27, 2004, http://online.wsj.com.

17. "Table 2: Patent Applications Filed," in United States Patent and Trademark Office, *United States Patent and Trademark Office Performance and Accountability Report Fiscal Year 2003,* (n.d.), www.uspto.gov/web/offices/com/annual/2003/060402_table2.html (accessed March 9, 2004).

18. "Country Statistics at a Glance," *Fact Monster from InfoPlease,* http://fekids.factmonster.com/ipka/A0762380.html (accessed February 16, 2004).

19. "The Debt to the Penny," *Bureau of the Public Debt, United States Treasury* (n.d.), www.publicdebt.treas.gov/opd/opdpenny.htm (accessed February 23, 2004).

20. "Women in the Labor Force, 1900–2002," *InfoPlease* (n.d.), www.infoplease.com/ipa/A0104673.html (accessed March 9, 2004).

21. Susan Donovan, "How I Did It: Roxanne Quimby," *Inc.,* January 2004, www.inc.com.

22. David Kiley, "Ford Family Celebrates 100 Years of Cars," *USA Today,* June 10, 2003, pp. 1B, 2B.

23. Anthony Bianco and Wendy Zellner, "Is Wal-Mart Too Powerful?" *BusinessWeek,* October 6, 2003, pp. 100–10.

24. "Stewart Convicted on All Charges," *CNN/Money,* March 5, 2004, www.money.cnn.com.

25. Asmus, "100 Best Corporate Citizens of 2003."

26. Ronald Alsop, "Corporate Scandals Hit Home," *The Wall Street Journal,* February 18, 2004, http://online.wsj.com.

27. 2003 National Business Ethics Survey (n.d.), **www.ethics.org/nbes/2003/1003nbes_summary.html** (accessed January 6, 2004).

28. Census 2000 Supplementary Survey presented in *USA Today* Snapshot, *USA Today,* August 24, 2001, p. A1; Maggie Jones, "25 Hottest Careers for Women," *Working Women,* July 1995, pp. 31–33; "Reversing the Decline in Corporate Loyalty," PR Newswire (n.d.); Thomas A Stewart, "Planning a Career in a World Without Managers," *Fortune,* March 20, 1994, pp. 72–80.

29. "The Company," Starbucks (n.d.), **www.starbucks.com/aboutus/overview.asp** (accessed March 8, 2004); Cora Daniels, "Mr. Coffee," *Fortune,* April 14, 2003, pp. 139, 140; Keith Johnson, "Starbucks Enters Market in Spain as Part of Broad Global Expansion," *The Wall Street Journal,* April 11, 2002, **http://online.wsj.com;** Ariff Kachra and Mary Crossan, "Starbucks," in Michael A. Hitt, R. Duane Ireland, and Robert E. Hoskisson, *Strategic Management Competitiveness and Globalization,* 4th ed. (2001), pp. 569–85; "Starbucks Out to Promote Coffee-Drinking in China," *The Nation,* January 12, 1999, p. B3; "Starbucks Steaming Toward Long-Term Profitability and Growth Internationally," *Business Wire,* June 20, 2003, via **www.findarticles.com/cf_0/mEIN/2003_June_20/103773499/print.jhtml**; "Starbucks Timeline and History," *Starbucks* (n.d.), **www.starbucks.com/aboutus/timeline.asp**, (accessed March 8, 2004).

Chapter 2

1. "Environmental Responsibility," The Home Depot, **www.homedepot.com/HDUS/EN_US/corporate/corp_respon/environmental.shtml** (accessed April 29, 2004); The Home Depot, *Annual Report 2003,* pp. 10–11; Debbie Thorne McAlister, Linda Ferrell, and O.C. Ferrell, *Business and Society: A Strategic Approach to Social Responsibility,* 2nd ed. (Boston: Houghton Mifflin, 2005), pp. 431–36.

2. Alexei Barrionuevo, "Former Enron CEO Skilling Is Charged; Pleads Not Guilty," *The Wall Street Journal,* February 19, 2004, **http://online.wsj.com.**

3. Ronald Alsop, "Corporate Scandals Hit Home," *The Wall Street Journal,* February 18, 2004, **http://online.wsj.com.**

4. Greg Farrell, "Scrushy Sticks to His Defense: They're All Lying," *USA Today,* November 5, 2003, pp. 1B, 2B.

5. O. C. Ferrell, John Fraedrich, Linda Ferrell, *Business Ethics: Ethical Decision Making and Cases,* 6th ed. (Boston: Houghton Mifflin, 2005), p. 7.

6. David Callahan, as quoted in Archie Carroll, "Carroll: Do We Live in a Cheating Culture?" *Athens Banner-Herald,* February 21, 2004, **www.onlineathens.com/stores/022204/bus_20040222028.shtml.**

7. Devon Leonard, "The Curse of Pooh," *Fortune,* January 20, 2003, pp. 85–92; "Pooh Suit against Disney Dismissed," *CNN,* March 29, 2004, **www.cnn.com.**

8. Jeffrey M. Jones, "Effects of Year's Scandals Evident in Honesty and Ethics Ratings, Gallup Organization, press release, December 4, 2002, **www.gallup.com/poll/releases/pr021204.asp.**

9. Charles Piller "Bell Labs Says Its Physicist Faked Groundbreaking Data," *Austin American-Statesman,* September 26, 2002, **www.austin360.com/statesman.**

10. "Colorado Places Barnett on Administrative Leave," *SI.com,* February 19, 2004, **http://sportsillustrated.cnn.com/.**

11. Ferrell, Fraedrich, Ferrell, *Business Ethics.*

12. "eBay Bans Items Connected to Hate Groups," *The Wall Street Journal,* May 4, 2001, p. B6.

13. "Major Survey of America's Workers Finds Substantial Improvements in Ethics," Ethics Resource Center, press release, May 21, 2003, **www.ethics.org/releases/nr_20030521_nbes.html.**

14. Emily Nelson and Laurie P. Cohen, "Why Grubman Was so Keen to Get His Twins into the Y," *The Wall Street Journal,* November 15, 2002, **http://online.wsj.com.**

15. "Three Ex-IBM Korea Officials Are Sentenced," *The Wall Street Journal,* February 18, 2004, **http://online.wsj.com.**

16. "Russian, Chinese, Taiwanese and S. Korean Companies Widely Seen Using Bribes in Developing Countries," Transparency International, press release, May 14, 2002, **www.transparency.org/pressreleases_archive/2002/2002.05.14.bpi.en.html.**

17. James Bandler, "Two Big Film Makers Strive to Crush Renegade Recycler," *The Wall Street Journal,* December 4, 2002, **http://online.wsj.com.**

18. "Big Beef with Tyson," *BusinessWeek,* March 1, 2004, p. 45.

19. "About KFC: KFC Sets the Record Straight," KFC, press release, October 28, 2003, **www.kfc.com/about/pr/102803.htm;** K. MacArthur, "KFC Pulls Controversial Health-Claim Chicken Ads," *Advertising Age,* November 18, 2003, **www.adage.com/news.cms?newsId=39220;** A. D. Mathios and P. Ippolito, "Health Claims in Food Advertising and Labeling: Disseminating Food Information to Consumers," in Elizabeth Frazao (ed.) *America's Eating Habits: Changes and Consequences,* Agriculture Information Bulletin No. 750, USDA Economic Research Service, Food and Rural Economics Division, 1999, pp. 189–212, available at **www.ers.usda.gov/publications/aib750/aib750k.pdf;** A. W. Matthews and B. Steinberg, "FTC Examines Health Claims in KFC's Ads," *The Wall Street Journal,* November 19, 2003, pp. B1, B2; Ira Teinowitz, "CARU'S Role in KFC Advertising Debacle Revealed: Children's Marketing Watchdog Releases Fried Chicken Case File," *Advertising Age,* December 05, 2003, **www.adage.com/news.cms?newsId=39339.**

20. Yuri Kageyama, "Mitsubishi Motors Says Massive Defect Cover-ups Were Intentional," *Boston Globe,* August 22, 2000, **www.boston.com;** "Mitsubishi Cover-up May Bring Charges," *Detroit News,* August 23, 2000, **www.det-news.com/2000/autos/0008/23/b03-109584.htm.**

21. Gisele Durham, "Study Finds Lying, Cheating in Teens," *AOL News,* October 16, 2000, **www.aol.com.**

22. "The 'Skinny Pills' Do Not Make You Skinny, Says the FTC," Federal Trade Commission, press release, February 4, 2004, **www.ftc.gov/opa/2004/02/skinnypill.htm.**

23. "Campaign Warns about Drugs from Canada," *CNN,* February 5, 2004, **www.cnn.com;** Gardiner Harris and Monica Davey, "FDA Begins Push to End Drug Imports," *The New York Times,* January 23, 2004, p. C1.

24. *2000 National Business Ethics Survey* (Washington D.C.: Ethics Resource Center, 2000), p. 33.

25. Andrew Backover, "Write-Down by Qwest Grows to $40.8 Billion," *USA Today,* October 29, 2002, p. B1; Andrew Backover and Greg Farrell, "Qwest Execs Charged with Fraud," *USA Today,* February 26, 2003, p. B1; "Ex-Qwest Execs Indicted,"

CNN/Money, February 25, 2003, **http://money.cnn.com/2003/ 02/25/technology/qwest/index.htm;** "Feds Indict Four ex-Qwest Executives," *MSNBC,* February 25, 2003, **www.msnbc.com/ news/876997.asp;** Kris Hudson, "Qwest Assessed $20 Million Fine," *Denver Post,* October 25, 2002; "Qwest's Anschutz to Face Second Questioning—WSJ," *Reuters,* October 8, 2002.

26. Susan Pullman, "Ordered to Commit Fraud, A Staffer Balked, Then Caved," *The Wall Street Journal,* June 23, 2003, **http://online.wsj.com.**

27. Blake Morrison, "Ex-USA Today Reporter Faked Major Stories," *USA Today,* March 19, 2004, **www.usatoday.com/.**

28. Thomas M. Jones, "Ethical Decision Making by Individuals in Organizations: An Issue-Contingent Model," *Academy of Management Review* 2 (April 1991), pp. 371–73.

29. Sir Adrian Cadbury, "Ethical Managers Make Their Own Rules," *Harvard Business Review* 65 (September–October 1987), p. 72.

30. Ferrell, Fraedrich, and Ferrell, pp. 174–75.

31. Ethics Resource Center.

32. Ethics Resource Center, "2003 National Business Ethics Survey: Executive Summary" (n.d.), **www.ethic.org/nbes2003/ 2003nbes_summary.html** (accessed March 3, 2004).

33. Richard Lacavo and Amanda Ripley, "Persons of the Year 2002—Cynthia Cooper, Coleen Rowley, and Sherron Watkins," *Time,* December 22, 2002, **www.time.com/personof theyear/2002.**

34. Ferrell, Fraedrich, and Ferrell, p. 13.

35. John Galvin, "The New Business Ethics," *SmartBusinessMag.com,* June 2000, p. 99.

36. Archie B. Carroll, "The Pyramid of Corporate Social Responsibility: Toward the Moral Management of Organizational Stakeholders," *Business Horizons* 34 (July/Aug. 1991), p. 42.

37. "Social Responsibility," ChrevronTexaco (n.d.), **www.chevrontexaco.com/social_responsibility/** (accessed April 6, 2004).

38. Mary Miller, "A New Job Title to Love," *Business Ethics,* Summer 2001, p. 12.

39. Ferrell, Fraedrich, and Ferrell, pp. 13–19.

40. Rachel Emma Silverman, "On-the-Job Cursing: Obscene Talk Is Latest Target of Workplace Ban," *The Wall Street Journal,* May 8, 2001, p. B12.

41. "Business Discover the Value in Fighting AIDS," *Milwaukee Journal Sentinel,* March 14, 2004, via World Business Council for Sustainable Development, **www.wbcsd.org/Plugins/DocSearch/ details.asp. . .;** Lucia Mutikani, "German Automakers Tackle S. Africa AIDS Scourge," Reuters News Service, as reported in *Forbes,* January 22, 2004, **www.forbes.com/business/newswire/ 2004/01/22/rtr1221795.html.**

42. Wendy Zellner, "No Way to Treat a Lady?" *BusinessWeek,* March 3, 2003, pp. 63–66.

43. Chad Terhune, "Jury Says Home Depot Must Pay Customer Hurt by Falling Merchandise $1.5 Million," *The Wall Street Journal,* July 16, 2001, p. A14.

44. Charales Haddad and Brian Grow, "Wait a Second—I Didn't Order That!" *BusinessWeek,* July 16, 2001, p. 45.

45. Lawrence Ulrich, "The New Green Machines," *Money* 32 (July 2003), pp. 117–19.

46. John Yaukey, "Discarded Computers Create Waste Problem, *USA Today* (n.d.), **www.usatoday.com/news/ndsmon14.htm** (accessed October 13, 2000.)

47. Andrew Park, "Stemming the Tide of Tech Trash," *BusinessWeek,* October 7, 2002, pp. 36A–36F.

48. Alan K. Reichert, Marion S. Webb, and Edward G. Thomas, "Corporate Support for Ethical and Environmental Policies: A Financial Management Perspective," *Journal of Business Ethics* 25 (2000), pp. 53–64.

49. "Trend Watch," *Business Ethics,* March/April 2001, p. 8.

50. Amy Standen, "Bulging at the Waste," *Terrain,* Winter 2003, **www.ci.sf.ca.us/sfenvironment/articles_pr/2003/article/11000 3_2.htm.**

51. "GreenChoice: The #1 Green Power Program in America," Austin Energy (n.d.), **www.austinenergy.com/Energy%20Efficiency/Programs/ Green%20Choice/index.htm** (accessed February 24, 2004).

52. "Kinko's Increases Green Power Use Nearly 80 Percent with Agreements in Four New States," Kinko's, press release, October 20, 2003, **www.kinkos.com/about_us/newsroom/pr_oct202003.php.**

53. "Certification," Home Depot (n.d.), **www.homedepot.com/ HDUS/EN_US/corporate/corp_respon/certification.shtml** (accessed April 6, 2004).

54. "Yes, We Have No Bananas: Rainforest Alliance Certifies Chiquita Bananas," *AgJournal* (n.d.), **www.agjournal.com/ story.cfm?story_id=1047** (accessed April 6, 2004).

55. "Charity Holds Its Own in Tough Times (Giving USA 2003: The Annual Report on Philanthropy for the Year 2002)," American Association of Fundraising Council, press release, June 23, 2003, **http://aafrc.org/press_releases/trustreleases/ charityholds.html.**

56. Mark Calvey, "Profile: Safeway's Grants Reflect Its People," *San Francisco Business Times,* July 14, 2003, **http://sanfrancisco. bizjournals.com/sanfrancisco/stories/2003/07/14/focus9.html.**

57. "About Avon," Avon (n.d.), **www.avoncompany.com/about/** (accessed February 25, 2004; "The Avon Breast Cancer Crusade," Avon (n.d.), **www.avoncompany.com/women/avoncrusade/** (accessed February 25, 2004).

58. "Take Charge of Education," Target (n.d.), **http://target.com/ common/page.jhtml;jsessionid=GWORM5AQSLBLDLARAAV WW4FMCEACU1IX?content=target_cg_take_charge_of_ education** (accessed February 25, 2004).

59. Tim Klusmann, "The 100 Best Corporate Citizens," *Business Ethics,* March/April 2000, p. 13.

60. Susan Gains, "Holding Out Halos," *Business Ethics* 8 (March/April 1994), p. 21; Judith Kamm, "Ethics Officers: Corporate America's Newest Profession," *Ethics, Easier Said Than Done,* Summer 1993, Josephson Institute, p. 38; Robert Levering and Milton Moskowitz, *The 100 Best Companies to Work for in America* (New York: The Penguin Group, 1994), p. 123; Allynda Wheat, "Keeping an Eye on Corporate America," *Fortune,* November 24, 2002, pp. 44–45.

61. Permission granted by the author of *Gray Matters,* George Sammet, Jr., Vice President, Office of Corporate Ethics, Lockheed

Martin Corporation, Orlando, Florida, to use these portions of *Gray Matters: The Ethics Game* © 1992. If you would like more information about the complete game, call 1-800-3ETHICS.

62. "Company Background," Stew Leonard's Farm Fresh Foods, (n.d.). **www.stewleonards.com/html/about.cfm** (accessed June 2, 2004); Heather Stein, "Arthur Andersen: Questionable Accounting Practices," in Debbie Thorne McAlister, O. C. Ferrell, and Linda Ferrell, *Business and Society*, 2nd ed, (Boston: Houghton Mifflin, 2005), pp. 474–482.

Chapter 3

1. "Cayenne," Porsche North America (n.d.), **www3.us.porsche. com/English/usa/cayenne/cayennev6/default.htm** (accessed April 29, 2004); Gail Edmondson, "This SUV Can Tow an Entire Carmaker," *BusinessWeek,* January 19, 2004, pp. 40–41; Don Hammonds, "Porsche's First SUV Is Fast, Rugged and a Bit Too Sensitive," *Pittsburg Post-Gazette*, December 5, 2003, **www.post-gazette.com/pg/pp/03339/247473.stm.**

2. Grainger David, "Can McDonald's Cook Again," *Fortune,* April 14, 2003, p. 122; McDonald's (n.d.), **www.mcdonalds.com/corp.html** (accessed March 22, 2004).

3. Cora Daniels, "Mr. Coffee," *Fortune,* April 14, 2003, pp. 139–40.

4. Robert D. Hof, "Reprogramming Amazon," *BusinessWeek,* December 22, 2003, pp. 82–86.

5. Alex Taylor III, "The Americanization of Toyota," *Fortune,* December 8, 2003, pp. 165–70.

6. Jyoti Thottam, "Is Your Job Going Abroad?" *Time,* March 1, 2004, pp. 27–36.

7. "U.S. International Trade in Goods and Services," U.S. Department of Commerce, news release, March 10, 2004, p. 4, available at **www.bea.doc.gov/bea/newsrel/archive/2004/trad0104.htm.**

8. "Shareholder News," *General Motors,* newsletter, March 2004.

9. "U.S. International Trade in Goods and Services."

10. "Exports and Imports of Goods and Services, 1980–2010," *Infoplease* (n.d.), **www.infoplease.com/ipa/A0855074.html** (accessed February 25, 2004).

11. Joseph Kahn and Edmund L. Andrews, "Across World, Economy Lags in All Regions," *The [Memphis] Commercial Appeal*, August 20, 2001, p. A1.

12. Andy Reinhardt, "A Wide-Open Wireless Frontier," *BusinessWeek,* February 9, 2004, p. 16.

13. Elisa Batista, "Telcos Duke It Out over Iraq," *Wired News,* June 27, 2003, **www.wired.com/news/politics/0,1283,59410,00.html;** Ben Charny, "Study: Cell Phone Use to Double," *clnet,* August 2003, **http://news.com.com/2100-1039_3-5060745.html.**

14. J. Bonasia, "For Web, Global Reach Is Beauty—and Challenge," *Investor's Business Daily,* June 13, 2001, p. A6.

15. Pamela Yatsko, "Knocking Out the Knockoffs," *Fortune,* October 1, 2000, pp. 213–18.

16. Douglas Heingartner, "Software Piracy Is in Resurgence," New York Times News Service, *Naples Daily News,* January 20, 2004, **www.naplesnews.com/npdn/business/article/0,2071,NPDN_14901_2588425,00.html.**

17. Helene Cooper, "WTO Rules Against U.S.'s Quota on Yarn from Pakistan in Latest Textiles Setback," *The Wall Street Journal,* April 27, 2001, p. A4.

18. "WTO Panel Rules U.S. Duties on Canadian Lumber Are Illegal," *The Wall Street Journal,* March 22, 2004, **http://online.wsj.com.**

19. Julie Bennett, "Product Pitfalls Proliferate in Global Cultural Maze," *The Wall Street Journal,* May 14, 2001, p. B11.

20. Greg Botelho, "2003 Global Influentials: Selling to the World," *CNN,* December 9, 2003, **www.cnn.com.**

21. Anton Piësch, "Speaking in Tongues," *Inc.,* 25 (June 2003), p. 50.

22. Sydney B. Leavens, "Father-Daughter Ad Breaks Latino Mold," *The Wall Street Journal,* p. B7.

23. Janet Guyon, "Brand America," *Fortune,* October 27, 2003, pp. 179–82; David Luhnow and Chad Terhune, "Latin Pop: A Low-Budget Cola Shakes Up Markets South of the Border," *The Wall Street Journal,* October 27, 2003, pp. A1, A18; Arundhati Parmar, "Drink Politics," *Marketing News,* February 15, 2004, pp. 1, 11.

24. Bonasia, "For Web Global Reach Is Beauty—and Challenge."

25. Jim Hopkins, "Other Nations Zip by USA in High-Speed Net Race," *USA Today,* January 19, 2004, pp. 1B, 2B.

26. "What Is the WTO," World Trade Organization (n.d.), **www.wto.org** (accessed February 25, 2004).

27. "WTO: U.S. Steel Duties Are Illegal," *USA Today,* November 10, 2003, **http://usatoday.com.**

28. "Bush Ends Steel Tariffs," *CNNMoney,* December 4, 2003, **http://cnnmoney.com.**

29. Geri Smith and Cristina Lindblad, "Mexico: Was NAFTA Worth It?" *BusinessWeek,* December 22, 2003, pp. 66–72.

30. Bureau of the Census, *Statistical Abstract of the United States, 2003* (Washington D.C.: Government Printing Office, 2004), pp. 842–44, 852; "NAFTA: A Decade of Strengthening a Dynamic Relationship," U.S. Department of Commerce, pamphlet, 2003, available at **www.ustr.gov.**

31. Bureau of the Census, *Statistical Abstract,* pp. 842, 852.

32. "Canada-U.S. Trade Statistics," Canada Customs and Revenue Agency, September 2002, **www.ccra-adrc.gc.ca/newsroom/factsheets/2002/sep/stats-e.html.**

33. William C. Symonds, "Meanwhile, to the North, NAFTA Is a Smash," *BusinessWeek,* February 27, 1995, p. 66.

34. Bureau of the Census, pp. 843, 852; "NAFTA: A Decade of Strengthening a Dynamic Relationship."

35. Smith and Lindblad, "Mexico: Was NAFTA Worth It?"; Cheryl Farr Leas, "The Big Boom," *Continental,* April 2001, pp. 85–94.

36. "Antecedents of the FTAA Process," Free Trade Area of the Americas (n.d.), **www.ftaa-alca.org/View_e.asp** (accessed February 25, 2004); "FTAA Fact Sheet," Market Access and Compliance, U.S. Department of Commerce (n.d.), **www.mac.doc.gov/ftaa2005/ftaa_fact_sheet.html** (accessed November 3, 2003).

37. "U.S.-Brazil Split May Doom Americas Free-Trade Zone," *The Wall Street Journal,* November 7, 2003, **http://online.wsj.com.**

38. "Archer Daniels to File NAFTA Claim Against Mexico," *Inbound Logistics,* October 2003, p. 30.

39. Smith and Lindblad.

40. "The European Union at a Glance," Europa (European Union online) (n.d.), **http://europa.eu.int/abc/index_en.htm#** (accessed February 26, 2004).

41. Stanley Reed, with Ariane Sains, David Fairlamb, and Carol Matlack, "The Euro: How Damaging a Hit?" *Business Week,* September 29, 2003, p. 63; "The Single Currency," *CNN* (n.d.), **www.cnn.com/SPECIALS/2000/eurounion/story/currency/** (accessed July 3, 2001).

42. "Microsoft Hit by Record EU Fine," *CNN,* March 24, 2004, **www.cnn.com.**

43. "About APEC," Asia-Pacific Economic Cooperation (n.d.), **www.apecsec.org.sg/apec/about_apec.html** (accessed February 26, 2004).

44. Smith and Lindblad.

45. Clay Chandler, "China Is Too Darn Hot!" *Fortune,* November 10, 2003, pp. 39–40; Clay Chandler, "How to Play the China Boom," *Fortune,* December 22, 2003, pp. 141, 142.

46. Brad Fishman, "International Trade Shows: The Smartest Ticket for Overseas Research," International Franchise Association (n.d.), **www.franchise.org/news/fw/april03c.asp** (accessed July 27, 2001).

47. Tim Annett, Yu Wong, and Deborah Creighton, "Understanding Outsourcing: An Online Journal Roundtable," *The Wall Street Journal,* March 1, 2004, **http://online.wsj.com.**

48. "Bank of America to Outsource 1,000 Jobs to India," [Albany] *Business Review,* February 18, 2004, **www.bizjournals.com/albany/stories/2004/02/16/daily18.html.**

49. Nick Easen, "Firms Get Savvy About Outsourcing," *CNNMoney,* February 18, 2004, **www.cnn.com.**

50. Walter B. Wriston, "Ever Heard of Insourcing?" commentary, *The Wall Street Journal,* March 24, 2004, p. A20.

51. "Bharti of India Will Outsource IT Needs to IBM," *The Wall Street Journal,* March 29, 2004, **http://online.wsj.com.**

52. Jason Bush, "GM: On the Road to Russia," *BusinessWeek,* January 19, 2004, p. 14.

53. James Cox, "As Economy Expands, India on 'Verge of Something Big,'" *USA Today,* February 9, 2004, pp. 1B–2B; Joanna Slater and Jay Solomon, "With a Small Car, India Takes Big Step onto Global Stage," *The Wall Street Journal,* February 5, 2004, pp. 1A, 9A.

54. "What We're About," NUMMI (n.d.), **www.nummi.com/co_info.html** (accessed February 26, 2004).

55. Joann Muller, "Global Motors," *Forbes,* January 12, 2004, pp. 62–68.

56. O. C. Ferrell, John Fraedrich, and Linda Ferrell, *Business Ethics,* 6th ed. (Boston: Houghton Mifflin, 2005), pp. 227–30.

57. Kim Jung Min, "Asian Company's Perfume Passes French Smell Test," *The Wall Street Journal,* March 19, 2004, **http://online.wsj.com.**

58. Vanessa O'Connell, "Exxon 'Centralizes' New Global Campaign," *The Wall Street Journal,* July 11, 2001, p. B6.

59. Philip R. Cateora, *International Marketing,* 8th ed. (Homewood, IL: Richard D. Irwin, 1993), pp. 25–26; "NAFTA: Exports, Jobs, Wages, and Investment," *Business America,* October 18, 1993, p. 3; *VGM's Handbook of Business & Management Careers,* Annette Selden, ed. (Lincolnwood, IL: VGM Career Horizons, 1993), pp. 43–44.

60. Erik Assadourian, "How Serious is BP?" *World Watch,* 17 (May/June 2004): 28–29; "BP Amoco Unveils New Global Brand to Drive Growth," BP Australia, press release, July 24, 2000, **www.bp.com.au/news_information/press_release/previous/brand.asp;** "BP at a Glance," BP, (n.d.) **www.bp.com/sectiongenericaricle.do?categoryID=3&contentID= . . .** (accessed June 2, 2004); "History of BP," BP, (n.d.) **www.bp.com/sectiongenericarticle.do?categoryId=2010123&contentId= 201440,** (accessed June 2, 2004).

Chapter 4

1. "Amazon Seeing Growth in Apparel Store," *Puget Sound Business Journal,* Mar. 9, 2004, **http://seattle.bizjournals.com/seattle/stores/2004/03/08/daily13.html;** Allison Linn, "Amazon.com Aims for Post-Boom Success," *Contra Costa Times,* Mar. 23, 2004, **www.contracostatimes.com/mld/cctimes/8254499.htm;** David Stires, "Amazon's Secret," *Fortune,* Apr. 19, 2004, p. 144.

2. "Encyclopedias Gather Dust as Research Moves Online," *CNN,* March 11, 2004, **www.cnn.com.**

3. Catherine Yang, "Homeland Security Dept.," *Business Week,* November 24, 2003, p. 85.

4. "Reflect.com Gets a Makeover," *Inbound Logistics,* August 2001, p. 62.

5. Roger W. Ferguson, Jr., "Remarks by Vice Chairman Roger W. Ferguson, Jr.," American Economic Association meeting, January 4, 2004, San Diego, California, available at **www.federalreserve.gov/boarddocs/speeches/2004/200401042/default.htm.**

6. Michael J. Mandel, "Productivity: Who Wins, Who Loses," *Business Week,* March 22, 2004, pp. 44–46.

7. "Overview," Autodesk (n.d.), **http://usa.autodesk.com/adsk/servlet/index?siteID=123112&id=2387111** (accessed March 2, 2004).

8. Alan Greenspan, "Remarks to the Economic Club of New York," January 13, 2000, Federal Reserve Board, available at **www.federalreserve.gov/boarddocs/speeches/2000/200001132.htm.**

9. "Data," *Webopedia,* October 28, 2003, **www.webopedia.com/TERM/D/data.html.**

10. Kevin Kelleher, "66,207,896 Bottles of Beer on the Wall," *Business 2.0,* via CNN, February 25, 2004, **www.cnn.com.**

11. "What Is OnStar?" OnStar (n.d.), **www.onstar.com** (accessed March 2, 2004).

12. "About IRI," Information Resources Inc. (n.d.), **www.infores.com/public/global/about/default.htm** (accessed April 23, 2004); "On-line Purchases of Consumer Packaged Goods on the Rise," study by Information Resources, Inc., *DSN Retailing Today,* June 4, 2001.

13. Kelleher, "66,207,896 Bottles of Beer on the Wall."

14. "Krispy Kreme's Secret Ingredient," *Business 2.0,* September 2003, p. 36.

15. "Population Explosion," ClickZ, March 12, 2004, **www.clickz.com/stats/big_picture/geographics/article.php/151151.**

16. "World E-Commerce Growth Projections and Online Language Use Projections for 2004–2005," Translate to Success, **www.translate-to-success.com/e-commerce-growth-projections.html** (accessed March 2, 2004).

17. Robyn Greenspan, "Europe, U.S. on Different Sides of Gender Divide," ClickZ, October 21, 2003, **www.clickz.com/stats/big_picture/demographics/article.php/5901_3095681.**

18. "2 in 10 Are Connected Kids," ClickZ, November 18, 2003, **www.clickz.com/stats/big_picture/demographics/article.php/3110071.**

19. Robyn Greenspan, "Senior Surfing Surges," ClickZ, November 28, 2003, **www.clickz.com/stats/big_picture/demographics/article.php/3111871.**

20. "Survey: Forget Work, IM Is for Flirting, Gossip," *CNN,* September 16, 2003, **www.cnn.com.**

21. "S&P500," *Business Week,* April 5, 2004, p. 157.

22. Byron Acohido, "Golf Fever Proves Fans Will Pay to Log On," *USA Today,* May 23, 2003, p. 1B.

23. "Shaping the Future Mobile Information Society," International Telecommunication Union (n.d.), **www.itu.int/osg/spu/ni/futuremovile** (accessed March 21, 2004).

24. Robyn Greenspan, "Phones Surpass Cameras for Digital Images," ClickZ, March 19, 2004, **www.clickz.com/stats/big_picture/hardware/article.php/3328741.**

25. Michelle Kesser, "Wi-Fi Changes Virtually Everything," *USA Today,* February 19, 2004, pp. 1B, 2B.; "Wi-Fi," *Webopedia* (n.d.), **www.webopedia.com/TERM/W/Wi_Fi.html** (accessed March 2, 2004).

26. Bob Jordan, "Wireless Mesh Networks Boost Reliability," NetworkWorldFusion, November 10, 2003, **www.nwfusion.com/news/tech/2003/1110techupdate.html;** Alexander Linden, "Predicts 2004: Emerging Technologies," Gartner Research, December 12, 2003, **www4.gartner.com/DisplayDocument?doc_cd=118940.**

27. Rachel Gecker, "A Walk on the Wireless Side," *Inbound Logistics,* March 2004, pp. 62–72.

28. "Shaping the Future Mobile Information Society."

29. William M. Pride and O. C. Ferrell, *Marketing Concepts and Strategies,* 13th ed. (Boston: Houghton Mifflin, 2005).

30. "Dell at a Glance," Dell (n.d.), **www1.us.dell.com/content/topics/global.aspx/corp/background/en/facts?c=us&l+en&....** (accessed March 3, 2004).

31. John Gaffney, "How Do You Feel about a $44 Tooth-Bleaching Kit?" *Business 2.0,* October 2001, p. 126; Stephanie Stahl and John Soat, "Feeding the Pipeline: Procter & Gamble Uses IT to Nurture New Product Ideas," *Information Week,* February 24, 2003, **www.informationweek.com/story/showArticle.jhtml;jsessionid=4SA2E1BSJYSZCQSNDBGCKHY?articleID=8700568&pgno=1.**

32. "About DoubleClick," DoubleClick (n.d.), **www.doubleclick.com/us/about_doubleclick/** (accessed April 28, 2004); Julia Angwin, "DoubleClick Stays Two Steps Ahead of Rivals," *The Wall Street Journal,* April 26, 2001, p. B6.

33. "Amazon.com Announced Record Free Cash Flow Fueled by Lower Prices and Year-Round Free Shipping," Amazon.com, press release, January 27, 2004.

34. "To Our Shareholders," Amazon.com (n.d.), **http://media.corporate-ir.net/media_files/irol/97/97664/reports/8k_041103/v89126exv99w1.htm** (accessed March 21, 2004).

35. Michael J. Mandel and Robert D. Hof, "Rethinking the Internet," *Business Week,* March 26, 2001, p. 118.

36. Julie Appleby, "Insurer Embraces Doctor-Patient e-visits," *The Coloradoan,* April 24, 2001, p. E-1.

37. "60 Minutes: Out of India," CBS, January 11, 2004, **www.cbsnews.com/stories/2003/12/23/60minutes/main590004.shtml.**

38. Mandel and Hof, "Rethinking the Internet."

39. Rob Preston, "What Internet Slowdown?" *Network Computing,* March 21, 2003, **www.nwc.com/1405/1405colpreston.html.**

40. "How It Works," *The Wall Street Journal,* May 21, 2001, p. R8.

41. Mandel and Hof.

42. *Business Week,* special supplement, February 28, 2000, p. 74.

43. Karen Bannan, "Sole Survivor," *Sales & Marketing Management,* July 2001, pp. 36–41; "Company Overview," *eBay* (n.d.), **http://pages.ebay.com/community/aboutebay/overview/index.html** (accessed April 15, 2004); "eBay Inc. Announces Fourth Quarter and Full Year 2003 Financial Results," eBay, press release, January 21, 2004, **http://investor.ebay.com/news/Q403/EBAY012104-712351.pdf;** "Small Businesses Come to eBay in Record Numbers," eBay, press release, February 23, 2004, **http://investor.ebay.com/ReleaseDetail.cfm?ReleaseID=130974;** Lizette Wilson, "Businesses Build Profits Helping Others Use EBay," *San Francisco Business Times,* May 26, 2002, **http://sanfrancisco.bizjournals.com/sanfrancisco/stories/2003/05/26/story8.html.**

44. "Covisint Parts Exchange Officially Opens for Business," *Bloomberg Newswire,* December 11, 2000, via **www.aol.com.**

45. Laura Rush, "E-Commerce Growth Will Impact SMBs," *InternetNews.com,* January 23, 2004, **www.internetnews.com/stats/article/php/3303241.**

46. *The Ticket,* newsletter, March 2004, **www.travelskills.com/tktarchive/2004/mar.html**

47. Tessa Romita, "Sky's the Limit for Airlines Online," *Business2.com,* January 23, 2001, p. 4.

48. Adapted from Judy Strauss and Raymond Frost, *Emarketing,* 2nd ed. (Upper Saddle River, NJ: Prentice-Hall, 2001).

49. Adapted from William M. Pride and O. C. Ferrell, *Marketing,* 13th ed. (Boston: Houghton Mifflin, 2005).

50. Stahl and Soat, "Feeding the Pipeline."

51. O. C. Ferrell, Michael D. Hartline, and George H. Lucas, Jr., *Marketing Strategy* (Fort Worth, TX: Dryden, 2002), p. 97.

52. "Better Relationships, Better Business," *Business Week,* Special Advertising Section, April 29, 2002.

53. Edward Prewitt, "How to Build Customer Loyalty in an Internet World," *CIO,* January 1, 2002, **www.cio.com/archive/010102/loyalty_content.html.**

54. Eve M. Caudill and Patrick E. Murphy, "Consumer Online Privacy: Legal and Ethical Issues," *Journal of Public Policy & Marketing,* 19 (Spring 2000), pp. 7–12.

55. TRUSTe (n.d.), **www.truste.org/** (accessed April 28, 2004).

56. Better Business Bureau Online (n.d.), **www.bbbonline.org/** (accessed April 28, 2004).

57. Jon Swartz, "Spam Fighters Win Battles, But the War Rages On," *USA Today*, August 11, 2003, pp. 1B, 2B.

58. "European Union Directive on Privacy," *Banking and Financial Services Policy Report*, December 2002, pp. 1–5; David Scheer, "Europe's New High-Tech Role: Playing Privacy Cop to the World," *The Wall Street Journal*, October 10, 2003; **http://online.wsj.com;** Deborah L. Venice, "New California Privacy Law Appears Redundant to DMers," *Marketing News*, October 27, 2003, p. 9.

59. Tim Hanrahan and Jason Fry, "Spammers, Human Mind Do Battle Over Spelling," *The Wall Street Journal*, February 9, 2004, **http://online.wsj.com.**

60. "EU Orders Anti-Spam Legislation," *CNN*, April 1, 2004, **www.cnn.com.**

61. Federal Trade Commission, "National and State Trends in Fraud and Identity Theft," *Consumer Sentinel*, January 22, 2004, available at **www.consumer.gov/sentinel/pubs/Top10Fraud.pdf.**

62. Andrea Chipman, "Stealing You," *The Wall Street Journal*, April 26, 2004, **http://online.wsj.com.**

63. Christine Dugas, "Identity Theft on the Rise," *USA Today*, May 11, 2001, p. 3B.

64. Jack McCarthy, "National Fraud Center: Internet Is Driving Identity Theft," *CNN*, March 20, 2000, **www.cnn.com.**

65. Juan Carlos Perez, "Biggest Security Threat? Insiders," *PC World*, October 2, 2002, **www.pcworld.com/news/article/0,aid,105528,00.asp.**

66. Douglas Heingartner, "Software Piracy Is in Resurgence," New York Times News Service, *Naples Daily News*, January 20, 2004, **www.naplesnews.com/npdn/business/article/0,2071,NPDN_14901_2588425,00.html.**

67. "Coming to a State Near You: Internet Sales Taxes," *CIO*, April 15, 2003, **www.cio.com/archive/041503/tl_tax.html.**

68. "Computer Executives and Professionals, *Career Journal*, **www.careerjournal.com/salaryhiring/industries/computers/20031125-computer-tab.html** (accessed April 29, 2004); "Tech Hiring: No Longer an Oxymoron," *Business Week Online*, February 4, 2004, **www.businessweek.com/technology/content/feb2004/tc2004024_4516_tc044.htm;** Mark Watson, "Book Touts Memphis as Haven for IT Work," *Commercial Appeal*, September 9, 2001, pp. C1, C3; Mark Watson, "More IT Jobs on the Way, Study Says," *Commercial Appeal*, September 9, 2001, pp. C1, C3.

69. Michael Bazeley, "Google Going Public," *[Fort Collins] Coloradoan*, Apr. 30, 2004, p. D8; "Corporate Information," Google, **www.google.com/corporate/,** (accessed June 3, 2004); Ben Elgin, Jay Greene, and Steve Hamm, "Google: Why the World's Hottest Tech Company Will Struggle to Keep its Edge," *Business Week*, May 3, 2004, pp. 82–89; Jefferson Graham, "The Search Engine that Could," *USA Today*, Aug. 23, 2003, p. 1D; Fred Vogelstein, "Can Google Grow Up?" *Fortune*, Dec. 8, 2003, pp. 102–112.

Chapter 5

1. Bo Burlingham, "The Coolest Small Company in America," *Inc.*, 25 (January 2003), pp. 64–74; Zingerman's, (n.d.), **www.zingermans.com/** (accessed February 13, 2004).

2. U.S. Bureau of the Census, *Statistical Abstract of the U.S., 2003* (Washington D.C.: U.S. Government Printing Office, 2004), p. 495.

3. Maggie Overfelt, "Start-Me-Up: The California Garage," *Fortune Small Business*, July/Aug. 2003, **www.fortune.com/fortune/smallbusiness/articles/0,15114,475872,00.html.**

4. "1: Digital Artists Agency," *Business 2.0*, April 2004, p. 90.

5. Alexis Muellner, "Marlins Partners in Dispute, Still Want Rings," *South Florida Business Journal*, February 27, 2004, **www.bizjournals.com/southflorida/stories/2004/03/01/story5.html.**

6. U.S. Census Bureau, *Statistical Abstract.*

7. "Longaberger: The Nation's Premier Maker of Handcrafted Baskets," Longaberger (n.d.), **www.longaberger.com** (accessed March 12, 2004); "Fast Facts about the Longaberger Company," Longaberger (n.d.), **www.longaberger.com** (accessed March 12, 2004); "The 2001 Blockbuster Entertainment Awards—Longaberger Is Official Basketmaker to the Stars," Longaberger, press release, **www.longaberger/data/ourStory/blockbuster.txt** (accessed July 27, 2001).

8. "America's Largest Private Companies," *Forbes*, November 6, 2003, **www.forbes.com/maserati/privates2003/privateland.html.**

9. David Kiley, "Ford Family Celebrates 100 Years of Cars," *USA Today*, June 10, 2003, pp. 1B, 2B.

10. Kevin J. Delaney and Robin Sidel, "Google IPO Aims to Change the Rules," *The Wall Street Journal*, April 30, 2004, **http://online.wsj.com.**

11. Merissa Marr, "Video Chain CEO to Take Company Private in Buyout," *The Wall Street Journal*, March 30, 2004, **http://online.wsj.com.**

12. O. C. Ferrell, John Fraedrich, and Linda Ferrell, *Business Ethics: Ethical Decision Making and Cases*, 6th ed. (Boston: Houghton Mifflin, 2005), p. 84.

13. Michael Powers and Gerard Leider, "Director Compensation: Balancing Economic Pressures with the Critical Need for Qualified Candidates," *Journal of Compensation and Benefits* (n.d.), available at Hewitt, **was4.hewitt.com/hewitt/resource/articleindex/talent/pdf/director_compensation.pdf** (accessed April 29, 2004).

14. Matt Krantz, "Web of Board Members Ties Together Corporate America," *USA Today*, November 23, 2002, pp. 1B, 3B.

15. Ibid.

16. Joseph Nathan Kane, *Famous First Facts*, 4th ed. (New York: The H. W. Wilson Company, 1981), p. 202.

17. Eric J. Savitz, "Movie Madness," *Barron's*, February 23, 2004, **http://online.wsj.com/barrons/.**

18. Robert D. Hisrich and Michael P. Peters, *Entrepreneurship*, 5th ed. (Boston: McGraw-Hill, 2002), pp. 315–16.

19. "Farmers Offering up Beef in a Can," *CNN*, March 22, 2004, **www.cnn.com/2004/US/Midwest/03/22/canned.beef.asp;** Jim Suhr, "Farmers Form Canned-Beef Co-op," *Courier-Journal*, March 28, 2004, **www.courier-jounal.com/business/news2004/03/28/E7-beefcan28–4323.html;** Jim Suhr, "Livestock Farmer Hopes Canned Beef Will Catch On," *The Coloradoan*, March 28, 2004, p. E2.

20. Roger O. Crockett, "How the Cingular Deal Helps Verizon," *Business Week*, March 1, 2004, pp. 36–37.

21. "Aventis Accepts Higher, Friendly Sanofi Bid," Dow Jones Newswire, April 26, 2004, via *The Wall Street Journal,* **http://online.wsj.com.**

22. Ibid.

23. U.S. Department of Labor, "Evaluating a Job Offer," *2004–05 Occupational Outlook Handbook,* **http://stats.bls.gov/oco/oco20046.htm** (accessed March 12, 2004).

24. "About United," United Airlines, (n.d.) **www.united.com/page/middlepage/0,6823,1276,00.html,** (accessed June 3, 2004); Marilyn Adams, "Meet Ted, United's Scrappy Champion in Low-Fare Flight," USA Today, Feb. 11, 2004, p. 1B; Marilyn Adams, "Fuel Prices Muddle United's Recovery," USA Today, June 1, 2004, p. 2B; United Airlines 2003 Annual Report, available at **www.united.com/page/framedpage/0,6837,1379,00.html.**

Chapter 6

1. Better Business Bureau Marketplace Ethics Torch Award Competition Project: King's Saddlery and King Ropes, 2004; Interviews with Bruce King and Mary King by Krista Ocker, Stacie Bergstrom, Kim Nissen, and Wendy Gleckler, for Linda Ferrell, University of Wyoming, Marketing Ethics class, November 7, 2003.

2. "Small Business Statistics," Small Business Administration (n.d.), **www.sba.gov/aboutsba/sbastats.html** (March 16, 2004).

3. "The Power of Innovation," *Inc. State of Small Business,* 23, no. 7. (2001), p. 103.

4. "Small Business Statistics," Small Business Administration.

5. "About Us," SBA Online Women's Business Center (n.d.), **www.onlinewbc.gov/about_us.html** (accessed March 16, 2004).

6. Joshua Kurlantzick, "About Face," *Entrepreneur,* January 2004, **www.entrepreneur.com/article/0,4621,312260,00.html.**

7. "Minorities in Business, 2001," Small Business Administration (n.d.), **www.sba.gov/advo/stats/min01.htm** (accessed March 16, 2004).

8. Kurlantzwick, "About Face."

9. Patrick J. Sauer, "Lance Morgan: Ho-Chunk," *Inc.,* April 2004, p. 116.

10. "Small Business Statistics."

11. "Statistics about Business Size (including Small Business)," U.S. Census Bureau, **www.census.gov/epcd/www/smallbus.html#EMpSize** (accessed May 3, 2004).

12. Kevin Many, "He Has a Vision, but Does He Have the Wright Stuff?" *USA Today,* March 30, 2004, p. 1B.

13. Mark Enricks, "What Not to Do," *Entrepreneur,* February 2004, **www.entrepreneur.com/article/0,4621,312661,00.html.**

14. Linda A. Moore, "Mom, Daughter Button Up New Family Business at Home, Online," *Commercial Appeal,* March 6, 2001, p. B6.

15. "Malcolm Baldrige National Quality Award: 2003 Award Recipient, Small Business Category," National Institute of Standards and Technology (n.d.), **www.nist.gov/public_affairs/releases/stoner.htm** (accessed May 4, 2004).

16. "Dell at a Glance," Dell (n.d.), **www1.us.dell.com/content/topics/global.aspx/corp/background/en/facts?c=us&l=en&s=corp&~section=000&~ck=mn** (accessed May 4, 2004).

17. "Small Business Statistics."

18. Susan Donovan, "How I Did It: Roxanne Quimby," *Inc.,* January 2004, **http://pf.inc.com/magazine/20040101/howididit.html;** "Hands on Marketing: Roxanne Quimby, CEO of Burt's Bees, Feels the Best Way to Sell Her Products Is by Putting It in Your Hands," *Inc.,* January 2004, **http://pf/inc.com/articles/2004/01/handsonmarketing.html;** "In Depth. Largest Triangle Deals of 2003," *Triangle Business Journal,* February 6, 2004, **www.bizjournals.com/triangle/stories/2004/02/09/focus6.html;** "Our Story," Burt's Bees, **www.burtsbees.com/** (accessed March 17, 2004).

19. Jane Applegate, "Just-in-time Can Work on Small-Business Scale," *Indianapolis Star,* May 28, 2001, p. G4.

20. "End Game," *Inc. State of Small Business,* 23, no. 7 (2001), p. 56.

21. Nicole Gull, "Plan B (and C and D and . . .)," *Inc.,* March 2004, p. 40.

22. "About Us," Garage Technology Ventures, **www.garage.com/about/index.shtml** (accessed March 16, 2004).

23. Susan McGee, "A Chorus of Angels," *Inc.,* January 2004, **www.inc.com/magazine/20040101/finance.html.**

24. Thomas W. Zimmerer and Norman M. Scarborough, *Essentials of Entrepreneurship and Small Business Management,* 4th ed. (Upper Saddle River, NJ: Pearson Prentice Hall, 2005), pp. 118–24.

25. Zimmerer and Scarborough, *Essentials of Entrepreneurship and Small Business Management.*

26. "What Is the SCORE Association?" SCORE (n.d.), **www.score.org** (accessed March 16, 2004).

27. Ricardo Gándara, "Conquering Austin with Coffee, Tea, and Ice Cream," *Austin American-Statesman,* April 14, 2004, **www.statesman.com;** Giselle Greenwood, "The Scoop: Ben & Jerry's Opening in Central Texas," *Austin Business Journal,* January 23, 2004, **http://austin.bizjournals.com/austin/stories/2004/01/26/story8.html;** "Most Commonly Asked Questions about a Ben & Jerry's Franchise Scoop Shop," Ben & Jerry's (n.d.), **www.benjerry.com/scoop_shops/franchise_info/faqs.html** (accessed May 4, 2004).

28. Adapted from "Tomorrow's Entrepreneur," *Inc. State of Small Business,* 23, no. 7 (2001), pp. 80–104.

29. "The Boomer Stats," Baby Boomer HQ, **www.bbhq.com/bomrstat.htm** (accessed March 17, 2004).

30. Michael J. Weiss, "To Be About to Be," *American Demographics,* 25 (September 2003), pp. 29–36.

31. "Current Numbers," Center for Immigration Studies (n.d.), **www.cis.org/topics/currentnumbers.html** (accessed May 5, 2004).

32. "Envios R. D./Pronto Envios," *Inc.* (n.d.), **www.inc.com/magazine/inner100/profiles/envios.html** (accessed May 5, 2004).

33. Gifford Pinchott III, *Intrapreneuring* (New York: Harper & Row, 1985), p. 34.

34. "How Can Somebody Not Be Optimistic?" *Business Week/Reinvesting America 1992,* special issue, p. 185; Mark Memmott, "Cutbacks Create Fierce Undertow," *USA Today,* October 20, 1993, p. B1.

35. Adapted from Carol Kinsey Goman, *Creativity in Business: A Practical Guide for Creative Thinking,* Crisp Publications, Inc. 1989, pp. 5–6. © Crisp Publications, Inc. 1200 Hamilton Court, Menlo Park, CA 94025.

36. Communication Services, Inc., brochure, available at **www.com-serv.com/Brochure.PDF,** (accessed June 3, 2004); "The Company," Communication Services, Inc., **www.com-serv.com/index.htm** (accessed June 3, 2004); "Key Personnel," Communication Services, Inc., (n.d.) **www.com-serv.com/index.htm** (accessed June 3, 2004).

Chapter 7

1. Ronald Grover and Christopher Palmeri, "Something's Got to Give," *Business Week,* October 20, 2003, p. 36; J. D. Heyman, Lorenzo Benet, Michael Fleeman, Lyndon Stambler, Frank Swertlow, and Macon Morehouse, "Arnie Does It!" *People,* October 20, 2003, p. 108; Shawn Tully, "Time For Some Muscle," *Fortune,* October 27, 2003, p. 47.

2. "Most Powerful Women," *Fortune,* **www.fortune.com/indexw.jhtml;jessionid-HCAOKUJFQYGNQQAMEHSSFE0ABQQ4MIV0?channel=list.jhtml&list_frag=survey_results.jhtml**&pers (accessed July 3, 2001); "The 50 Most Powerful Women in American Business, *Fortune,* October 13, 2003, pp. 103–14.

3. David Stires, "McDonald's Keeps Right on Cookin'," *Fortune,* May 17, 2004, p. 174.

4. "Our Mission," Celestial Seasonings, **www.celestialseasonings.com/whoweare/corporatehistory/mission.php** (accessed May 14, 2004).

5. Gillette (n.d.), **www.gillette.com/company/ourvision.asp** (accessed May 14, 2004).

6. "Starbucks Make Your Mark Program in September Exceeds Program Goals," Starbucks, press release, November 7, 2003, via **www.socialfunds.com/news/release.cgi/2250.html.**

7. Kelly Kurt, "Tulsa Bids Zebco Fishing Reels Farewell," *Chicago Tribune,* March 11, 2001, section 5, p. 7.

8. G. Tomas, M. Hult, David W. Cravens, and Jagdish Sheth, "Competitive Advantage in the Global Marketplace: A Focus on Marketing Strategy," *Journal of Business Research* 51 (January 2001), p. 1.

9. Gary Levin, "ABC Reshuffles Management as Ratings Slump," *USA Today,* April 21, 2004, p. B1.

10. Christine Dugas, "Putnam Targets Its Cutthroat Culture," *USA Today,* April 15, 2004, pp. B1, B2.

11. Stephanie Gruner, "Reuters Reorganized into Four Segments, Shifts Management," *The Wall Street Journal,* June 8, 2001, p. B6.

12. Sasha Talcott, "Bank of America to Cut 12,500 Jobs," *Boston Globe,* April 6, 2004, **www.boston.com/news/nation/articles/2004/04/06/bank_of_america_to_cut_12500_jobs/.**

13. "Sun Cuts 3,300 Jobs, Lowers Outlook," *Yahoo! News,* April 2, 2004, **http://story.news.yahoo.com/news?tmpl=story&ncid=&e=6&u=/ap/20040402/ap_on_hi_te/sun_microsystems_1.**

14. John Shepler, "Managing After Downsizing," JohnShepler.com (n.d.), **www.johnshepler.com/articles/managedown.html** (accessed May 18, 2004).

15. "The Big Picture," *Business Week,* July 16, 2001, p. 12.

16. "Kmart Rewards Store Associates with $18 Million in Cash Bonuses," Kmart, press release, June 4, 2001, **www.bluelight.com.**

17. Janet Guyon, "Now If only Shell Could Find Some Oil . . . ," *Fortune,* May 17, 2004, p. 38.

18. "Most Powerful Black Executives: Oprah Winfrey," *Fortune* (n.d.), **www.fortune.com/fortune/blackpower/snapshot/0,15307,10,00.html** (accessed April 9, 2004).

19. Steve Ulfelder, "Chief Privacy Officers: Hot or Not?" *Computer World,* March 15, 2004, **www.computerworld.com/securitytopics/security/story/0,10801,91168p3,00.html;** Steve Ulfelder, "CPOs on the Rise?" *Computer World,* March 15, 2004, **www.computerworld.com/securitytopics/security/story/0,10801,91166,00.html.**

20. "2002 Catalyst Census of Women Corporate Officers and Top Earners," Catalyst (n.d.), **www.catalystwomen.org/press_room/factsheets/COTE%20Factsheet%202002.pdf.** (accessed April 9, 2004).

21. Louis Lavelle with Michael Arndt, "Living Large in the Corner Office," *Business Week,* February 23, 2004, p. 47.

22. Louis Lavelle, with Jessi Hempel and Diane Brady, "Executive Pay," *Business Week,* April 19, 2004, pp. 106–20.

23. "2002 Trends in CEO Pay," AFL-CIO, **www.aflcio.org/corporateamerica/paywatch/pay/** (accessed April 9, 2004).

24. Michael Arndt, Wendy Zellner, and Peter Coy, "Too Much Corporate Power," *Business Week,* September 11, 2000, p. 148.

25. Annie Finnigan, "Different Strokes," *Working Woman,* April 2001, p. 44.

26. "Developing Colleagues with Passion," *Inbound Logistics,* April 2004, p. 14.

27. David LaGesse, "The World According to Google," *U.S. News & World Report,* May 10, 2004, pp. 45–47.

28. *General Motors Annual Report 2003,* pp. 3–7 David Kiley, "GM Tries to Cut Cord on Costly Rebates," *USA Today,* January 23, 2004, pp. 1B, 2B; Chris Isidore, "GM Execs: No Let Up on Incentives," *CNN/Money,* January 5, 2003, via Lexis-Nexis Academic Database; "North America Exports to China to Nearly Double," GM, shareholder newsletter, 10 (March 2004).

29. John Joseph, "Developing Leadership: Anne Mulcahy, President of Xerox Corporation," *Wharton Leadership Digest,* June 2001, p. 32.

30. Chad Terhune and Joann S. Lublin, "Coca-Cola Considers 4 Outsiders as Search for New CEO Intensifies," *The Wall Street Journal,* April 9, 2004, **http://online.wsj.com.**

31. "Coca-Cola Names E. Neville Isdell Chairman and Chief Executive Officer Elect," Coca-Cola, press release, May 4, 2004, **www2.coca-cola.com/presscenter/pc_include/.**

32. Kara Scannell, "The Few . . . The Proud. The . . . M.B.A.s (?!)," *The Wall Street Journal,* June 5, 2001, pp. C1, C18.

33. "Blue Skies: Is JetBlue the Next Great Airline—or Just a Little Too Good to Be True?" *Time,* July 30, 2001, pp. 241; J. K. Dineen, "JetBlue Offering $99 Nonstop Coast-to-Coast Flights," *New York Daily News,* August 15, 2001, **www.nydailynews.com;** "Fact Sheet," JetBlue, **www.jetblue.com/learnmore/factsheet.html** (accessed April 9, 2004); Dan Reed, "JetBlue Gains on Its Competition," *USA Today,* August 13, 2003, p. 3B; Darren Shannon, "Three of a Kind," *Travel Agent,* July 23, 2001, p. 601.

34. Kerrie Unsworth, "Unpacking Creativity," *Academy of Management Review*, 26 (April 2001), pp. 289–97.

35. *Harvard Business Review* 60 (November–December 1982), p. 160.

36. Kris Maher, "The Jungle," *The Wall Street Journal*, May 29, 2001, p. B16.

37. Bureau of Labor Statistics, U.S. Department of Labor, *Occupational Outlook Handbook*, 2004–2005 ed., **www.bls.gov/ oco/home.htm** (accessed May 18, 2004); "The Fogelman News: Student Edition," *Special/Career Week*, 1995; Managing Your Career, The College Edition of the National Business Employment Weekly," *The Wall Street Journal*, Spring 1994; "A Unifi Survey of Total Compensation for Middle Management: 2000," PricewaterhouseCoopers LLP, Unifi Network Survey Unit, Westport, Conn., **www.careerjournal.com/salaries/industries/ middlemanagers/20010308-middle-tab.html** (accessed July 4, 2001).

38. Peter Burrows, "HP's Carly Fiorina: The Boss," *Business Week*, August 2, 1999, **www.businessweek.com:/1999/99_31/ b3640001.htm?sciptFramed;** "Carleton S. Fiorina, Executive Team Biography," HP, (n.d.) **www.hp.com/hpino/execteam/ bios/fiorina.html (accessed March 4, 2004); "Carly Most Powerful Woman-Again,"** *CNN Money*, **September 29, 2003, http://money.cnn.com/2003/09/29/technology/fortune_women;** Amy Tsao and Jane Black, "Where Will Carly Fiorina Take HP?" *Business Week*, May 29, 2003, **www.businessweek.com:/ print/technology/content/may2003/tc20030529_9712.**

Chapter 8

1. David Ballingrud, "One Year Later: NASA's Cautious Re-Entry," *St. Petersburg Times*, February 1, 2004, **www.globalsecurity.org/org/news/2004/040201-nasa-reentry.htm;** Michael Coren, "NASA's 'Can Do' Culture to Help Fuel Reform," *CNN*, April 15, 2004, **www.cnn.com;** Ralph Vartabedian and Peter Pae, "NASA Faces Major Reorganization," *Los Angeles Times*, via ContraCosta Times.com, January 15, 2004, **www.contracostatimes.com/mld/cctimes/news/ 7715819.htm.**

2. Benjamin Fulford, "The Tortoise Jumps the Hare," *Forbes*, February 2, 2004, pp. 53–56.

3. "USA Today Culture Enabled Fabrications, Report Says," *The Wall Street Journal*, April 22, 2004, **http://online.wsj.com.**

4. O. C. Ferrell, John Fraedrich, and Linda Ferrell, *Business Ethics: Ethical Decision Making and Cases* (Boston: Houghton Mifflin, 2005), pp. 248, 274; Mary Flood and Michael Hedges, "Fastow Accepts Prison Time in Plea Bargain," *Houston Chronicle*, January 28, 2004, **www.chron.com/cs/CDA/printstory.hts/ business/2354675;** Susan Pulliam, "Ordered to Commit Fraud, A Staffer Balked, Then Caved," *The Wall Street Journal*, June 23, 2003, **http://online.wsj.com/article/0,,SB105631811322355600, 00.html,** Susan Pulliam, Almar Latour, and Ken Brown, "U.S. Indicts WorldCom Chief Ebbers," *The Wall Street Journal*, March 3, 2004, **http://online.wsj.com;** Sherron S. Watkins, "Ethical Conflicts at Enron: Moral Responsibility in Corporate Capitalism," *California Management Review* 45 (Summer 2003), pp. 6–19.

5. Adam Smith, *Wealth of Nations* (New York: Modern Library, 1937; originally published in 1776).

6. Jyoti Thottam, "When Execs Go Temp," *Time*, April 26, 2004, pp. 40–41.

7. Faith Arner, with Rachel Tiplady, "No Excuse Not to Succeed," *Business Week*, May 10, 2004, pp. 96, 98.

8. Susan Lee and Ashlea Ebeling, "Can You Top This for Cost-Efficient Management?" *Forbes*, April 20, 1998, pp. 207–12.

9. Robert Berner and Brian Grow, "Out-Discounting the Discounter," *Business Week*, May 10, 2004, pp. 78–79.

10. Jerry Flint, "When Car Guys Ran GM," *Forbes*, April 19, 2004, p. 77.

11. Jon R. Katzenbach and Douglas K. Smith, "The Discipline of Teams," *Harvard Business Review* 71 (March–April 1993), pp. 111–20.

12. Ibid.

13. Berner and Grow, "Out-Discounting the Discounter."

14. Darryl Haralson and Adrienne Lewis, "USA Today Snapshots," *USA Today*, April 26, 2001, p. B1.

15. "Coca-Cola Task Force Named," PRNewswire, press release, July 2, 2001, via **www.prnewswire.com/cgi-bin/ stories.pl?_ACCT=104&STORY=/www/story/07-02-01/ 0001525462&EDATE=.**

16. Julia Chang, "A View from the Top," *Sales & Marketing Management*, February 2004, p. 19.

17. "Breaking into the Quick Serve Industry," Leading Concepts, press release, January 2001, **www.leadingconcpets.com/ prjan01.html** (accessed July 12, 2001); Dina Berta, "Managers Sharpen Leadership Skills While 'in the Trenches,'" *Nation's Restaurant News*, March 2001, via **www.leadingconcepts.com/ bertastory.htm;** Leading Concepts (n.d.), **www. leadingconcepts.com** (accessed April 16, 2004); Linda S. Morris, "Leading the Way," *Business First*, March 30, 2001, **http:// louisville.bentral.com/louisville/stories/2001/0402/smallb1. html;** L. M. Sixel, "Atten-hut! Military Style Business Books Storm Shelves," *Houston Chronicle*, February 12, 2004, **www.chron.com/cs/CDA/story.hts/business/sixel/2400831.**

18. Richard S. Wellins, William C. Byham, and Jeanne M. Wilson, *Empowered Teams: Creating Self-Directed Work Groups That Improve Quality, Productivity, and Participation* (San Francisco: Jossey-Bass Publishers, 1991), p. 5.

19. Peg Kelly, "Vampire Meetings and How to Slay Them," *WebPro News*, January 7, 2003, **www.webpronews.com/articles/ 2003/0102pk.html.**

20. Fulford, "The Tortoise Jumps Over the Hare."

21. "Personal Use Abuse," *Internet Works* 66 (January 2003), **www.iwks.com.**

22. "New Products Add Fun and Humor to Employee Communications and Training," PRNewswire, press release, June 5, 2001, via **www.prnewswire.com.**

23. Erika Germer, "Huddle Up," *Fast Company*, December 2000, p. 86.

24. Olga Kharif, "Ever-Sharper Eyes Watch You Work," *Business Week*, July 22, 2003, **www.businessweek.com.**

25. "Privacy (Employee)," Business for Social Responsibility, **www.bsr.org/CSRResources/IssueBriefDetail.cfm? DocumentID=538** (accessed May 20, 2004).

26. Robert Gatewood, Robert Taylor, and O. C. Ferrell, *Management: Comprehension, Analysis, and Application* (Homewood, IL: Austen Press, 1995), pp. 361, 365–66.

27. Michael D. Maginn, *Effective Teamwork,* 1994, p. 10. © 1994 Richard D. Irwin, a Times Mirror Higher Education Group, Inc., company.

28. Biography of Lee Van Arsdale, University of Nevada, Las Vegas Institute for Security Studies, (n.d.) **http://edoutreach. unlv.edu/iss/pdfs/Lee_CV.pdf** (accessed June 3, 2004); "Mission Statement," University of Nevada, Las Vegas Institute for Security Studies, (n.d.) **http://edoutreach.unlv.edu/iss/** (accessed June 3, 2004).

Chapter 9

1. "About Us," IDEO (n.d.), **www.ideo.com/about** (accessed May 12, 2004); Bruce Nussbaum, "The Power of Design," *Business Week,* May 17, 2004, pp. 88–94; Daniel H. Pink, "Out of the Box," *Fast Company,* October 2003, pp. 104–06.

2. Valerie A. Zeithaml and Mary Jo Bitner, *Services Marketing,* 3rd ed. (Boston: McGraw-HillIrwin, 2003), p. 7.

3. Tahl Raz, "A Recipe for Perfection," *Inc.,* July 2003, pp. 36–38.

4. Leonard L. Berry, *Discovering the Soul of Service* (New York: The Free Press, 1999), pp. 86–96.

5. Zeithaml and Bitner, *Services Marketing,* pp. 3, 22.

6. Bernard Wysocki Jr., "To Fix Health Care, Hospitals Take Tips from the Factory Floor," *The Wall Street Journal,* April 9, 2004, **http://online.wsj.com.**

7. Ibid.

8. Jean Halliday, "Nissan Delves into Truck Owner Psyche," *Advertising Age,* December 1, 2003, p. 11.

9. Faith Keenan, "Opening the Spigot," *Business Week e.biz,* June 4, 2001, **www.businessweek.com/magazine/content/ 01_23/b3735616.htm.**

10. "Agricultural Export Benefits from Standardized Production," China.org, December 24, 2003, **www.china.org.cn/ english/2003/Dec/83203.htm.**

11. Stanley Holmes, "Boats as Big as the Ritz," *Business Week,* April 26, 2004, **www.businessweek.com.**

12. "Overview of Assembly," Honda (n.d.), **www. hondacorporate.com/america/index.html?subsection = manufacturing** (accessed May 13, 2004).

13. "Hershey's Chocolate Kisses," Hershey (n.d.), **www.hersheys.com/products/kisses.shtml** (accessed April 21, 2004).

14. Gargi Chakrabarty, "Kodak Picks Weld," *Rocky Mountain News,* March 23, 2004, **www.rockymountainnews.com/ drmn/cda/article_print/1,1983,DRMN_4_2750621....**

15. Stacy Perman, "Automate or Die," *eCompany,* July 2001, p. 62.

16. "North American Robot Orders Jump 19% in 2003," Robotic Industries Association, press release, February 13, 2004, **www.roboticsonline.com/public/articles/articlesdetails.cfm? id=1361.**

17. David Noonan, "The Ultimate Remote Control," *Newsweek,* via **www.msnbc.com/news/588560.asp** (accessed July 18, 2001).

18. O. C. Ferrell and Michael D. Hartline, *Marketing Strategy* (Mason, OH: South-Western, 2005), p. 215.

19. Ibid.

20. "About Coal Creek & Our Coffee," Coal Creek Coffee (n.d.), **www.coalcreekcoffee.com/AboutUs.aspx** (accessed February 19, 2004); "Coal Creek Coffee Company," Better Business Bureau Market Place Ethics Torch Award Nomination; "The Philosophy," Elektra (n.d.), **www.elektrasrl.com/uk/ companydiray/companydiary4.asp** (accessed February 19, 2004); Mike Ferguson, "Honoring Excellence in Specialty Coffee Retailing." *Fresh Cup,* October 2003, pp. 69–69; research assistance provided by Stephanie Anderson, Jesse Jorgensen, Molly Meeker, and Josh Saenger for Linda Ferrell, Assistant Professor of Marketing University of Wyoming.

21. Joseph O'Reilly, "LaserNetworks Banks on Same-Day Delivery," *Inbound Logistics,* April 2004, pp. 74–77.

22. Jyoti Thottam, "Is Your Job Going Abroad?" *Time,* March 1, 2004, pp. 28–34.

23. Bruce Nussbaum, "Where Are the Jobs?" *Business Week,* March 22, 2004, pp. 36–37.

24. Office of Aviation Enforcement & Proceedings, *Air Travel Consumer Report,* February 2004, p. 39, via **http://airconsumer. ost.dot.gov/reports/2004/0402atcr.pdf.**

25. Moon Ihlwan, with Larry Armstrong and Michael Eidam, "Hyuandai: Kissing Clunkers Goodbye," *Business Week,* May 17, 2004, p. 45.

26. "President and Commerce Secretary Announce Recipients of Nation's Highest Honor in Quality and Performance Excellence," National Institute of Standards and Technology, press release, November 24, 2003, **www.nist.gov/public_affairs/releases/ 2003baldrigewinners.htm.**

27. James R. Healey and David Kiley, "Surprise, Chrysler Loves Its German Boss," *USA Today,* May 3, 2001, p. 2B.

28. Philip B. Crosby, *Quality Is Free: The Art of Making Quality Certain* (New York: McGraw-Hill, 1979), pp. 9–10.

29. Nigel F. Piercy, *Market-Led Strategic Change* (Newton, MA: Butterworth-Heinemann, 1992), pp. 374–385.

30. "Hershey's Chocolate Kisses," Hershey.

31. T. E. Benson, "Quality Goes International," *Industry Week,* August 19, 1991, pp. 54–57; A. F. Borthick and H. P. Roth, "Will Europeans Buy Your Company's Products?" *Business Credit,* November/December 1992, pp. 23–24; S. J. Harrison and R. Stupak, "Total Quality Management: The Organizational Equivalent of Truth in Public Administration Theory and Practice," *Public Administration Quarterly,* 6 (1992), pp. 416–29; C. W. L. Hart and P. E. Morrison, "Students Aren't Learning Quality Principles in Business Schools," *Quality Progress,* January 1992, pp. 25–27; D. Marquardt, "Vision 2000: The Strategy for the ISO 9000 Series of Standards in the 90's," *Quality Progress,* May 1991, pp. 25–31; "Manufacturing Professionals & Managers: Median Annual Total Income," *Career Journal* (n.d.), **www.careerjournal.com/ salaryhiring/industries/manufacturing/20030827- manu-tab.html** (accessed April 22, 2004).

32. James Wetherbe, "Principles of Cycle Time Reduction," *Cycle Time Research,* 1995, p. iv.

33. Stan Davis and Christopher Meyer, *Blur: The Speed of Change in the Connected Economy* (Reading, MA: Addison-Wesley, 1998), p. 5.

34. Nikole Haiar and O. C. Ferrell, "New Belgium Brewing Company: Environmental and Social Concerns," in Debbie

Thorne McAlister, O. C. Ferrell, and Linda Ferrell, *Business and Society,* 2nd ed. (Boston: Houghton Mifflin Company, 2005) pp. 437–441; New Belgium Brewing Company, **www.newbelgium.com,** (accessed June 8, 2004); "New Belgium Brewing Wins Ethics Award," *Denver Business Journal,* January 2, 2003, **http://denver.bizjournals.com/denver/ stories/2002/12/30/daily21.html;** Greg Owsley, New Belgium Brewing Company, personal interview with O. C. Ferrell, April 19, 2004.

Chapter 10

1. "Case Study: SAS Institute," *Financial Times,* April 29, 2004, via Lexis-Nexis Academic Database; Kevin Maney, "SAS Workers Won When Greed Lost," *USA Today,* April 22, 2004, pp. B1–B2; "SAS Again in Top Ten of Fortune's List of 100 Best Companies to Work For," SAS, press release, January 6, 2004, **www.sas.com/news/preleases/010604/news2.html**; "SAS Responds to Rising Health Care Costs with Health Care Center Expansion; Commitment to Workforce Health Remains an Important Part of Overall Business Strategy," *Business Wire,* January 23, 2003, via Lexis-Nexis Academic Database.

2. Wade Daniels, "Kelly Marshall: Not Just Another Starstruck Fan, GM Keeps Her Casual Cool at this Celebrity-Focused Restaurant—Hard Rock Café," *Nation's Restaurant News,* January 26, 2004, via **http://findarticles.com**.

3. "The Flip Side of Productivity," *Ceredian,* newsletter, Spring 2004, **www.ceredian.com/myceredian/article/ 1,2481,11337–53923,00.html**.

4. Jess McCuan, "Guard Your Exits," *Inc.,* April 2004, pp. 44+.

5. Rachel King, "Great Things Are Starting at Yum," *Workforce Management,* November 2003, **www.workforce.com/ section/06/feature/23/54/58/**; Curtis Sittenfeld, "Great Job! Here's a Seat Belt!" *Fast Company,* January 2004, p. 29.

6. Marianne Kolbasuk McGee, "Behind the Numbers: Employee Productivity Pays Off for Everyone," *Information Week,* February 9, 2004, p. 76.

7. Louis Lavelle, with Jessi Hempel and Diane Brady, "Executive Pay," *Business Week,* April 19, 2004, **www.businessweek.com**.

8. "Our Mission," Medtronic, (n.d.), **www.medtronic.com/ corporate/mission.html** (accessed May 19, 2004); David Whitford, "A Human Place to Work," *Fortune,* January 8, 2001, **www.fortune.com/indext.jhtml**.

9. Abraham Maslow, *Motivation and Personality* (New York: Harper & Row, 1954).

10. "Global Workforce Study Ranks Employees Low on Loyalty, Commitment to Employers," *SHRM HR News,* September 25, 2000, **www.shrm.org/hrnews/articles/default.asp?page = bna0925c.htm**.

11. "Airline to Give Free Tickets for Being Nice," *CNN,* May 19, 2004, **www.cnn.com**.

12. Rekha Balue, "Bonuses Aren't Just for the Bosses," *Fast Company,* December 2000, pp. 74, 76; Premium Standard Farms (n.d.), **www.psfarms.com** (accessed May 25, 2004).

13. Douglas McGregor, *The Human Side of Enterprise* (New York: McGraw-Hill, 1960), pp. 33–34.

14. Ibid, pp. 47–48.

15. Jon L. Pierce, Tatiana Kostova, and Kurt T. Kirks, "Toward a Theory of Psychological Ownership in Organizations, *Academy of Management Review* 26, no. 2 (2001), p. 298.

16. Archie Carroll, "Carroll: Do We Live in a Cheating Culture?" *Athens Banner-Herald,* February 21, 2004, **www.onlineathens.com/ stories/022204/bus_20040222028.shtml**.

17. "FAQs," Procter & Gamble (n.d.), **www.pg.com/jobs/jobs_us/ faqs/index.jhtml** (accessed May 25, 2004).

18. Amy Wrzesniewski and Jen E. Dutton, "Crafting a Job: Revisioning Employees as Active Crafters of Their Work," *Academy of Management Review* 26, no. 2 (2001), p. 179.

19. "Hewitt Study Shows Work/Life Balance Benefits Hold Steady Despite Recession," Hewitt Associates, press release, May 13, 2002, **http://was4.hewitt.com/hewitt/resource/newsroom/ pressrel/2002/05–13–02.htm**.

20. Eilene Zimmerman, "The Joy of Flex," *Workforce Management* 83 (March 2004), p. 38.

21. Adam Geller, "Employers Cut 'Work/Life' Programs," *Sun,* October 23, 2003, **www.thesunlink.com/redesign/ 2003–10–23/business/290909.shtml**.

22. Larry Muhammad, "Help for the Helpers," *[Louisville] Courier-Journal,* April 20, 2004, **www.courier-journal.com/features/ 2004/04/20/helpers.html**.

23. Doug Bartholomew, "Your Place or Mine?" *CFO,* March 15, 2004, **www.cfo.com/article/1,5309,12605,00.html**.

24. Stephanie Armour, "Telecommuting Gets Stuck in the Slow Lane," *USA Today,* June 25, 2001, pp. 1A, 2A.

25. Kurt Badenhausen, "Closer to Home," *Forbes,* May 24, 2004, pp. 15, 151; "The Salary Calculator," Realtor.com, **www.homefair.com/homefair/calc/salcalc.html** (accessed May 6, 2004).

26. "Guided by Principles: Focus on The Container Store," Family Edge, **www.familyedge.com/cgi-bin/kidsedge/scripts/ article.jsp?BV_SessionID = @@@@1643708281. 1086389215@@@@&BV_EngineID = ccceadclijmfemjcfngcfkmdfhfdhji.0&ed_name = pe_wp_ffc_019;** (accessed June 4, 2004); Jennifer Koch Laabs, "Thinking Outside the Box at The Container Store," *Workforce,* March 2001, via **www.findarticles.com/cf_dls/m0FXS/3_80/ 71836861/p1/article.jhtml;** "Learn about Us," The Container Store, **www.thecontainerstore.com/learn/index.jhtml,** (accessed June 4, 2004); Joe Mullich, "They've Got the Gold Watch Blues," *Workforce Management,* **www.workforce.com/section/02/feature/23/55/01/** (accessed June 4, 2004).

Chapter 11

1. Del Jones, "Experts Agree: Finalists Have Right Stuff," *USA Today,* April 9, 2004, p. 5B; Del Jones, "Trump Picks Bill to Be His Apprentice," *USA Today,* April 16, 2004, p. 1B; Patricia Kitchen, "Lessons from 'The Apprentice,'" *Austin American-Statesman,* April 14, 2004, **www.statesman.com;** Daniel Roth, "The Trophy Life," *Fortune,* April 19, 2004, p. 70; Jeffrey Sonnenfeld, "Trump Needs to Face a Few Non-Realities," *The Wall Street Journal,* March 19, 2004, p. A15.

2. Drew Robb, "Career Portals Boost Online Recruiting," *HR Magazine* 49 (April 2004), pp. 111+.

3. "US Jobs," Procter & Gamble (n.d.), **www.pg.com/jobs/jobs_us/recruitsoft/index.jhtml** (accessed May 7, 2004).

4. Ibid.

5. Adam Geller, "Cheating Is Employed in Worker Drug Tests," *Detroit News,* March 28, 2004, **www.detnews.com/2004/business/0403/29/c04-105176.htm.**

6. Lewis L. Malby, "Drug Testing: A Bad Investment," *Business Ethics,* March/April 2001, p. 7.

7. Geller, "Cheating Is Employed in Worker Drug Tests."

8. "Resume Fraud Gets Slicker and Easier," *CNN,* March 11, 2004, **www.cnn.com.**

9. "Charge Statistics FY 1992 through FY 2003," Equal Employment Opportunity Commission (n.d.), **www.eeoc.gov/stats/charges.html** (accessed May 28, 2004).

10. "Sexual Harassment Charges EEOC & FEPAs Combined: FY 1992 – FY 2003," Equal Employment Opportunity Commission (n.d.), **www.eeoc.gov/stats/harass.html** (accessed May 28, 2004).

11. Annie Finnigan, "Different Strokes," *Working Woman,* April 2001, p. 42; Linda Tischler, "Where Are the Women?" *Fast Company,* February 2004, pp. 52–60.

12. Sue Shellenberger, "Work and Family," *The Wall Street Journal,* May 23, 2001, p. B1.

13. "Women Still Lag White Males in Pay," *CNN,* April 23, 2004, **www.cnn.com.**

14. "Employee Training Expenditures on the Rise," *American Salesman* 49 (January 2004), p. 26.

15. "By The Numbers," DMN (n.d.), **www.avvideo.com/articles/viewarticle.jsp?id=22469** (accessed May 28, 2004).

16. "FAQs," Procter & Gamble (n.d.), **www.pg.com/jobs/jobs_us/faqs/index.jhtml** (accessed May 7, 2004).

17. Matthew Boyle, "Performance Reviews: Perilous Curves Ahead," *Fortune,* May 28, 2001, pp. 187–88.

18. Maury A. Peiperl, "Getting 360-Degree Feedback Right," *Harvard Business Review,* January 2001, pp. 142–48.

19. Nathalie Towner, "Turning Appraisals 360 Degrees," *Personnel Today,* February 2, 2004, p. 18.

20. Stanley Holmes and Wendy Zellner, "Commentary: The Costco Way," *Business Week,* April 12, 2004, **www.businessweek.com.**

21. Anne Fisher, "Workplace: Turning Clock Watchers into Stars," *Fortune,* March 8, 2004, **www.fortune.com.**

22. Sasha Talcott, "Bank of America to Cut 12,500 Jobs," *Boston Globe,* April 6, 2004, **www.boston.com/news/nation/articles/2004/04/06/bank_of_america_to_cut_12500_jobs/.**

23. Bruce Nussbaum, "Where Are the Jobs?" *Business Week,* March 22, 2004, p. 37.

24. Aaron Bernstein and Louise Lee, "Smart Ways to Help Low-Wage Workers," *Business Week,* April 21, 2004, **www.businessweek.com.**

25. William M. Bulkeley, "IBM Documents Give Rare Look at Sensitive Plans on 'Offshoring,'" *The Wall Street Journal,* January 19, 2004, **http://online.wsj.com;** Richard J. Newman, "Big Worker Blues," *U.S. News & World Report,* February 9, 2004, pp. 36–39.

26. "The Working Poor: We Can Do Better," *Business Week,* May 31, 2004, **www.businessweek.com.**

27. David Kiley, "Crafty Basket Makers Cut Downtimes, Waste," *USA Today,* May 10, 2001, p. C1.

28. Ed Henry, "The Personal Touch," *Kiplinger's,* June 2001, p. 87.

29. Kemp Powers, "Happy Employees," *Fortune,* March 25, 2004, **www.fortune.com.**

30. Winston Wood, "Work Week," *The Wall Street Journal,* May 1, 2001, p. A1.

31. "Employer Costs for Employee Compensation—December 2003," Bureau of Labor Statistics, press release, February 26, 2004, **www.bls.gov/news.release/ecec.nr0.htm.**

32. Marilyn Odesser-Torpey, "The Benefits Advantage," *QSR* (n.d.), **www.qsrmagazine.com/issue/62/benefits.phtml** (accessed May 7, 2004).

33. "Microsoft Reins in Benefits," *Austin American-Statesman,* May 21, 2004, **www.statesman.com.**

34. "Employers Reap Awards and Rewards for Psychologically Healthy Workplaces," *Employee Benefit News,* April 15, 2004, **www.benefitnews.com/pfv.cfm?id=5832;** Susan McCullough, "Pets Go to the Office," *HR Magazine* 43 (June 1998), pp. 162–68; "Pets Provide Relief to Workplace Stress," *BenefitNews Connect,* July 1, 2003, **www.benefitnews.com/detail.cfm?id=4736;** Sharda Prashad, "Taking Your Best Friend to Work," *Toronto Star,* December 13, 2003, p. C11.

35. Michelle Conlin and Aaron Bernstein, "Working . . . and Poor," *Business Week,* May 31, 2004, **www.businessweek.com.**

36. "Union Members in 2003," Bureau of Labor Statistics, press release, January 21, 2004, **www.bls.gov/news.release/union2.nr0.htm.**

37. "5-Month Grocery Strike Draws to an End," *CNN,* March 1, 2004, **www.cnn.com.**

38. "Collective Bargaining," Bureau of Labor Statistics, **http://data.bls.gov/cgi-bin/surveymost?ws** (accessed May 28, 2004).

39. "Characteristics of the Civilian Labor Force, 1990–2010," *InfoPlease* (n.d.), **www.infoplease.com/ipa/A0904534.html** (accessed May 28, 2004).

40. Finnigan, "Different Strokes," p. 44.

41. Feliciano Garcia, "US West Has the Tool," *Fortune,* July 10, 2000, p. 198.

42. Taylor H. Cox, Jr., "The Multicultural Organization," *Academy of Management Executives* 5 (May 1991), pp. 34–47; Marilyn Loden and Judy B. Rosener, *Workforce America! Managing Employee Diversity as a Vital Resource* (Homewood, IL: Business One Irwin, 1991).

43. "Human Resources Managers," *CareerJournal* (n.d.), **www.careerjournal.com/salaryhiring/industries/hr/20040127-hr-tab.html** (accessed May 7, 2004); "Median Annual Income, by Level of Education, 1990–2000, *InfoPlease* (n.d.), **www.infoplease.com/ipa/A0883617.html** (accessed May 7, 2004).

44. Monte Burke, "Carry a Big Stick," *Forbes,* April 14, 2003, pp. 220–222; Mark Bechtel and Sridhar Pappu, "Go Figure," *Sports Illustrated,* May 10, 2004, p. 18; "Company History," Louisville Slugger Museum, Hillerich & Bradsby Company, **www.sluggermuseum.org/education/index.html?step=2&id=4038** (accessed June 6, 2004); "Louisville Slugger

Museum to Display DiMaggios 56 Game Winning Streak Bat," WAVE, Louisville, Kentucky, April 27, 2004, **www.wave3.com/ Global/story.asp?S=1820473&nav=0RZFMeAu;** "Hillerich & Bradsby Steelworkers Earn University of Louisville Labor-Management Award," Labor-Management Center, University of Louisville, press release, April 17, 1996, **www.louisville.edu/ cbpa/lmc/award/award.96.html;** "The W. Edwards Deming Institute Board of Trustees," W. Edwards Deming Institute, **www.deming.org/instituteinfo/boardmembers01.html** (accessed June 6, 2004).

Chapter 12

1. Apple, **www.apple.com** (accessed May 10, 2004); Peter Burrows, "Show Time!" *Business Week,* February 2, 2004, pp. 57–64; Alice Z. Cuneo, "Marketer of the Year: Apple," *Advertising Age,* December 15, 2003, **www.adage.com;** Scott Donaton, "A Marketing Tale of the Great and the Desperate," *Advertising Age,* December 15, 2003, **www.adage.com.**

2. "McDonald's Adult Happy Meal Arrives," *CNN/Money,* May 11, 2004, **http://money.cnn.com.**

3. "Winning Ideas in Marketing," *Fortune,* May 15, 1995, p. 201.

4. "McDonald's Adult Happy Meal Arrives."

5. "Beauty Queen," *People,* May 10, 2004, p. 187.

6. Michael Treacy and Fred Wiersema, *The Discipline of Market Leaders* (Reading, MA: Addison Weslsey, 1995), p. 176.

7. Peter Burrows, "Show Time!" *Business Week,* February 2, 2004, pp. 57–64.

8. Venky Shankar, "Multiple Touch Point Marketing," American Marketing Association Faculty Consortium on Electronic Commerce, Texas A&M University, July 14–17, 2001.

9. Stephanie Kang, "The Swoosh Finds Its Swing, Targeting Weekend Golfers," *The Wall Street Journal,* April 8, 2004, p. B1.

10. Eduardo Porter, "Hispanic Marketers Try to Push Ad Spending Aimed at Latinos," *The Wall Street Journal,* April 24, 2001, **http://interactive.wsj.com.**

11. Dean Foust, with Brian Grow, "Coke: Wooing the TiVo Generation," *Business Week,* March 1, 2004, p. 77.

12. Pooja Bhatia, "The Pint-Size Gourmet," *The Wall Street Journal,* April 27, 2001, pp. W1, W4.

13. Charles Passy, "Your Scoop Is in the Mail," *The Wall Street Journal,* May 25, 2001, pp. W1, W6.

14. The Coca-Cola Company, **www.questions.coca-cola.com/ vrep/CokeSay.htm** (accessed June 2, 2004).

15. Jon Swartz, "Price War Looms for High-Speed Net Access," *USA Today,* November 14, 2003, p. 1B.

16. Grainger David, "Can McDonald's Cook Again," *Fortune,* April 14, 2003, p. 122; "McDonald's Worldwide Corporate Site," McDonald's (n.d.), **www.mcdonalds.com/corporate/index.html** (accessed June 2, 2004).

17. Theresa Howard, "Marketing Parties' Pizazz Pulls Plenty," *USA Today,* November 19, 2003, **http://usatoday.com.**

18. "Californian' Targets Youth with Text Messaging," *Yahoo! News,* November 20, 2003, **http://news.yahoo.com.**

19. Michael J. Weiss, "To Be About to Be," *American Demographics* 25 (September 2003): pp. 29–36.

20. Sarah Moore, "On Your Markets," *Working Woman,* February 2001, p. 26; "Quest for Cool," *Time,* September 2003, via **www.look-look.com/looklook/html/Test_Drive_ Press_Time.html;** "What We Do," Look-Look.com (n.d.), **www.look-look.com/dynamic/looklook/jsp/What_We_Do.jsp** (accessed May 11, 2004); "Who We Are," Look-Look.com (n.d.), **www.look-look.com/looklook/html/Test_Drive_Who_ We_Are.html#Methodology** (accessed May 11, 2004).

21. Jean Halliday, "Nissan Delves into Truck Owner Psyche," *Advertising Age,* December 1, 2003, p. 11.

22. "Focus Groups in Nebraska Help Market Tourism," *Marketing News,* January 6, 2003, p. 5.

23. Gerry Khermouch, "Consumers in the Mist," *Business Week,* February 26, 2001, p. 92.

24. Faith Keenan, "Friendly Spies on the Net," *Business Week e.biz,* July 9, 2001, pp. EB 26–28.

25. Ibid.

26. Emily Nelson, "P&G Checks Out Real Life," *The Wall Street Journal,* May 17, 2001, p. B1.

27. Karen Valby, "The Man Who Ate Too Much," *Entertainment Weekly,* May 21, 2004, p. 45.

28. "Coke Chief Wants Anti-Obesity Effort," *CNN/Money,* December 9, 2003, **www.cnn.com;** "Ruby Tuesday to Use Healthier Oil, Offer Low-Carb Items," *USA Today,* November 11, 2003, **www.usatoday.com/money/industries/food/ 2003-11-11ruby-tuesday_x.htm.**

29. Brian Grow and Gerry Khermouch, "The Low-Carb Food Fight Ahead," *Business Week,* December 22, 2003, **www.businessweek.com;** Kate MacArthur, "Miller Lite Ads Turn Tables on Coors," *Advertising Age,* **www.adage.com** (accessed December 22, 2003); Chad Terhune, "Krispy Kreme Issues Profit Warning," *The Wall Street Journal,* May 10, 2004, **http://online.wsj.com;** Andrea K. Walker, "Low-Carb Product Craze Puts Bread Industry on Defensive," *Austin American-Statesman,* December 17, 2003, **www.statesman.com.**

30. "Customer Service Professionals, Average Base Salary," CareerJournal.com (n.d.), **www.careerjounral.com/salaryhiring/ industries/sales/20040223-customer-tab.html** (accessed May 11, 2004); Donna J. Yena, *Career Directions,* 2nd ed. (Burr Ridge, IL: Richard D. Irwin, 1993).

31. "About the Market," Pike Place Market, **www.pikeplacemarket.com/about** (accessed June 5, 2004); Rekka Balu, "A New Fish-Economy Story," *Fast Company,* October 2000, p. 46; Jake Batsell, "Cable Network QVC Pitches Pike Place Market Specialities," *Seattle Times,* May 10, 2003, **www.seattletimes.nwsource.com/cgi-bin/PrintStory.pl? document_id = 134711901&zsection;** Hsiao-Ching Chou, "Shopping at the Market is an Experience All Its Own," *Seattle Post Intelligencer,* May 14, 2003, **www.seattlepi.com/food/ 121790_bestnw03_pikefood.html;** Stewart Emmrich, "Journey: 36 Hours Seattle," *New York Times,* August 22, 2003, **www.travel2.nytimes.com/mem/travel/article-printpage.html?** res = 9C01E5DD1639F931A15; Susan Phinney, "Pike Place Market Is a Unique Bazaar with Global Goods both Quirky and Classic," *Seattle Post Intelligencer,* May 14, 2003, **www.seattlepi. nwsource.com/lifestyle/121791_bestnw03_pikeshop.html.**

Chapter 13

1. Edward Popper, "Talking Turkey about Pop Culture," *Business Week*, November 25, 2003, **www.businessweekonline.com**; "The Jones Soda Story," Jones Soda, **www.jonessoda.com** (accessed December 22, 2003); "Jones Soda Swamped with Requests for Turkey & Gravy Soda," Jones Soda, **www.jonessoda.com** (accessed December 22, 2003).

2. "Pizza Particulars," Domino's Pizza (*n.d.*), **www.dominos.com/** (accessed May 11, 2004).

3. Elliot Blair Smith, Theresa Howard, and Edward Iwata, "Fountain Dispenses Problems," *USA Today,* May 28, 2003, pp. 1B, 2B.

4. Steve Rosenbush, "At GM, Tech Is Steering," *Business Week,* May 27, 2004, **www.businessweek.com**.

5. Amy Barrett, with Christopher Palmeri and Stephanie Anderson Forest, "Hot Growth Companies," *Business Week,* June 7, 2004, pp. 86–90.

6. Faith Keenan, "Friendly Spies on the Net," *Business Week e.biz,* July 9, 2001, p. EB27.

7. Thomas Mucha, "Volvo, Keepin' It Real," *Business2.0,* April 29, 2004, **www.business2.com**.

8. "Tide Unveils Milestone in Fabric Care with New Tide Stainbrush," Procter & Gamble, press release, February 13, 2004, **www.pg.com/news/**.

9. Peter Burrows, with Tom Lowry, "Commentary: Rock on, iPod," *Business Week,* June 7, 2004, **www.businessweek.com**.

10. Thomas Mucha, "Alcopops Lose Their Fizz," *Business2.0,* June 2004, **www.business2.com**.

11. Eric Wellweg, "Test Time for TiVo," *Business2.0,* May 24, 2004, **www.business2.com**.

12. Robert Berner, "Race You to the Top of the Clothing Market," *Business Week,* December 8, 2003, **www.businessweek.com**.

13. Alessandra Galloni, "Advertising," *The Wall Street Journal,* June 1, 2001, p. B6.

14. Bill Barol, "Sweet Things, Small Packages," *Fortune,* March 5, 2004, **www.fortune.com**.

15. Patrick Barta and Christina Binkley, "US Travelers' Satisfactions with Hotels, Airlines, Rises," *The Wall Street Journal,* May 21, 2003.

16. Stephanie Miles, "Consumer Groups Want to Rate the Web," *The Wall Street Journal,* June 21, 2001, p. B13.

17. Rajneesh Suri and Kent B. Monroe, "The Effects of Time Constraints on Consumers' Judgments of Prices and Products," *Journal of Consumer Research* 30 (June 2003), pp. 92+.

18. Linda Tischler, "The Price Is Right," *Fast Company,* November 2003, pp. 83+.

19. Gail Edmondson, "This SUV Can Tow an Entire Carmaker," *Business Week,* January 19, 2004, pp. 40, 41.

20. David Luhnow and Chad Terhune, "Latin Pop: A Low-Budget Cola Shakes Up Markets South of the Border," *The Wall Street Journal,* October 27, 2003, pp. A1, A18.

21. Shawn Tully, "Airlines: Why the Big Boys Won't Come Back," *Fortune,* June 1, 2004, **www.fortune.com**.

22. "E-Commerce Takes Off," *The Economist,* May 15, 2004, p. 9.

23. Jerry Adler, "Takeout Nation," *Newsweek,* February 9, 2004, pp. 52–54; Dina El Boghdady, "Takeout: They Take Out to You: More Casual Dining Restaurants Begin Offering Curbside Service," *Washington Post,* September 13, 2003, p. E01; Marguerite Higgins, "Fast-Food Industry Responds to Fat Charges; Study Shows Americans Eat Most Meals at Home, Consume Larger Portions," *Washington Times,* July 3, 2003, p. C10; Michael Lawrence, "Cooking Trends in the United States: Are We Really Becoming a Fast Food Country," **www.eia.doe.gov/emeu/recs/cookingtrends/cooking.html** (accessed February 12, 2004).

24. O. C. Ferrell and Michael D. Hartline, *Marketing Strategy* (Mason, OH: South-Western, 2005), p. 215.

25. Todd Wasserman, "Kodak Rages in Favor of the Machines," *BrandWeek,* February 26, 2001, p. 6.

26. "Chrysler: Drive & Love," DaimlerChrysler, **www.chrysler.com/celine/celine.html** (accessed December 11, 2003); David Kiley, "Chrysler Bets Big on Dion's Auto Endorsement Deal," *USA Today,* June 8, 2003, **http://advertising.about.com/library/weekly/aa072903a.htm**; "Kobe Bryant's Endorsement Deals," *About Advertising,* **http://advertising.about.com/library/weekly/aa072903a.htm** (accessed December 10, 2003); Jason Stein, "Inside Chrysler's Céline Dion Advertising Disaster: Selling the Celebrity Instead of the Product," *Advertising Age,* November 24, 2003, **www.adage.com/news.cms?newsId=39262**.

27. Jefferson Graham, "Web Pitches, That's 'Advertainment'," *USA Today,* June 26, 2001, p. 3D.

28. Michael J. Weiss, "To Be About to Be," *American Demographics* 25 (September 2003), pp. 29–36.

29. Gerry Khermouch and Jeff Green, "Buzz Marketing," *Business Week,* July 30, 2001, pp. 50–56.

30. Olga Kharif, "An Epidemic of 'Viral Marketing'," *Business Week,* August 30, 2001, **www.businessweek.com**.

31. "September Is National Coupon Month," Promotion Marketing Association, press release, September 2, 2003, **www.couponmonth.com/pages/news.htm**.

32. Jean Halliday, "GM's 'Sleep on It' Test Drives: Christopher 'C. J.' Fraleigh," *Advertising Age,* November 17, 2003, p. S-8.

33. Kate MacArthur, "Sierra Mist: Cie Nicholson," *Advertising Age,* November 17, 2003, p. S-2.

34. Renae Merle, "U.S. Slowdown Is Good News for Coupon Seller Valassis," *The Wall Street Journal,* May 1, 2001, p. B2.

35. Michelle Maynard, "Amid the Turmoil, A Rare Success at DaimlerChrysler," *Fortune,* January 22, 2001, p. 112.

36. "Coca-Cola Unveils U.S. Launch Plans for Its New Lower-Carb, Lower-Cal Cola, Coca-Cola C2," Coca-Cola, press release, May 24, 2004, **www2.coca-cola.com/presscenter/**.

37. Bureau of Labor Statistics, U.S. Department of Labor, *Occupational Outlook Handbook,* 2004–2005 ed., **www.bls.gov/oco/ocos020.htm** (accessed June 7, 2004); "Advertising and Marketing Professionals Annual Average Starting Salary Range," CareerJournal.com (n.d.), **www.careerjournal.com/salaryhiring/industries/sales/20040109-adv-mrk-tab.html** (accessed May 12, 2004).

38. "Goldfish Companions at the Luxury Hotel Monaco," "Pets and Their Owners Travel in Style at the Hotel Monaco," and "The Story," Hotel Monaco, (n.d.), **www.hotelmonaco.com** (accessed June 5, 2004); "It's Not a Stretch: Hotels Going Yoga," *USA Today,* December 12, 2003, p. 10D; Christopher Palmeri,

"Home Sweet Hotel," *Business Week,* October 27, 2003, **www.busniessweek.com/print/magazine/content/03_43/b3855150.htm?mz.**

Chapter 14

1. James Cox, "Economy in Iraq Grows," *USA Today,* February 19, 2004, **www.usatoday.com/money/world/2004–02–19-iraqecon_x.htm;** Jeffrey Frankel, "Iraq's Currency Solution: the Importance of Adding Oil to the Equation," *The International Economy,* Fall 2003, via **http://articles.findarticles.com/p/articles/mi_m2633/is_4_17/ai_111013458;** Charlie Keenan, "A Face Lift for Iraqi Currency," *Scholastic Teachers,* **http://teacher.scholastic.com/scholasticnews/indepth/iraq/life_today/index.asp?article=currency** (accessed June 3, 2004); Karl Penhaul, "Saddam-Free Iraq Cash Now Official," *CNN,* January 16, 2004, **www.cnn.com/2004/WORLD/meast/01/15/sprj.nirq.currency/.**

2. "How Currency Gets into Circulation," Federal Reserve Bank of New York (n.d.), **www.newyorkfed.org/aboutthefed/fedpoint/fed01.html** (accessed June 1, 2004).

3. Barbara Hagenbaugh, "It's Too Easy Being Green," *USA Today,* May 13, 2003, **www.usatoday.com/.**

4. Ibid.

5. "U.S. Unveils New $50 Note with Background Colors," Bureau of Engraving and Printing, U.S. Department of the Treasury, press release, April 26, 2004, **www.moneyfactory.com/newmoney/main.cfm/media/.**

6. Calmetta Coleman, "Altering Course, Banks Welcome Check Cashers," *The Wall Street Journal,* July 6, 2001, p. B1; "Innovations in Personal Finance for the Unbanked: Emerging Practices from the Field; Case Study: Cash & Save—Union Bank of California," Fannie Mae Foundation, **www.fanniemaefoundation.org/programs/pdf/fscs_CashSave.pdf** (accessed June 9, 2004).

7. Emily Thornton, Heather Timmons, and Joseph Weber, "Who Will Hold the Cards," *Business Week,* March 19, 2001, p. 90.

8. "Card Debt," Card Trak, May 2004, **http://cardweb.com/cardtrak/pastissues/may2004.html.**

9. David Breitkopf, "MasterCard, Pulse Report Wider Use of Debit Cards," *American Banker,* May 17, 2004, p. 5.

10. Ian Rowley, "Banking on U.S. Acquisitions," *CFO,* February 2003, pp. 79–80.

11. Daniel Kruger, "Banknorth: Circuit Rider," *Forbes,* January 12, 2004, p. 151.

12. "About Us," ING Direct, **http://home.ingdirect.com/about/corporate_content.html,** (accessed June 8, 2004); "ING Direct Bank Does One Thing Noticeably Well," ING Direct, news release, March 7, 2004, **http://home.ingdirect.com/about/aboutus_news.html#03072004;** Matthew Swibel, "Where Money Doesn't Talk," *Forbes,* May 24, 2004, p. 176.

13. "FDIC: Statistics on Banking," FDIC, **www.fdic.gov/bank/statistical** (accessed June 10, 2004).

14. Judith Burns, "Mutual Fund Reforms 'at Warp Speed'—SEC Chmn Donaldson," *The Wall Street Journal,* May 13, 2004, **http://online.wsj.com.**

15. NACHA, news release, April 23, 2001, **www.nacha.org/news/news/pressreleases/2001/PR042301b/pr042301b.htm** (accessed September 6, 2001).

16. Mary Madden, with Lee Rainie, "America's Online Pursuits," December 22, 2003, Pew Internet & American Life Project, available at **www.pewinternet.org.**

17. Department of Labor, Bureau of Labor Statistics, *Occupational Outlook Handbook 2004–2005,* **www.bls.gov/oco/oco5055.htm** (accessed June 1, 2004).

18. "2001 Survey of Consumer Finances," Federal Reserve Board, 2003, **www.federalreserve.gov/pubs/oss/oss2/2001/scf2001home.html** (accessed June 21, 2004); "Chase Selected as Brand Name for Consumer and Commercial Banking Businesses after Merger of JPMorgan Chase and Bank One," Bank One, press release, June 8, 2004, **www.shareholder.com/one/news/20040608–136759.cfm?categoryis=;** "JPMorgan Chase and Bank One Set July 1 to Merge," Bank One, press release, June 14, 2004, **www.shareholder.com/one/news/20040614–137038.cfm?categoryis=;** Pat Quinn, "Editorial: What's in the Bank One Merger for Us?" *Chicago Sun-Times,* May 11, 2004, p. 36, accessed via Lexis-Nexis Academic Database; "Top Ten Global Banking Issues for 2004," Deloitte Global Banking Industry Outlook, **www.deloitte.com/dtt/research/0,2310,cid=35348&pv=Y,00.html** (accessed June 21, 2004).

Chapter 15

1. Liza Hunn, "Significant Provisions of the Sarbanes-Oxley Act of 2002," unpublished research paper, Colorado State University, 2004; Sarbanes-Oxley Act of 2002.

2. "Post-Enron Restatements Hit Record," *MSNBC,* January 21, 2003, **www.msnbc.com/news/862325.asp.**

3. "Break up the Big Four?" *CFO,* June 1, 2004, **www.cfo.com/article/1,5309,14007%7C%7CM%7C926,00.html.**

4. O. C. Ferrell, John Fraedrich, and Linda Ferrell, *Business Ethics: Ethical Decision Making and Cases* (Boston: Houghton Mifflin, 2005), pp. 248–56; Mary Flood and Michael Hedges, "Fastow Accepts Prison Time in Plea Bargain," *Houston Chronicle,* January 28, 2004, **www.chron.com/cs/CDA/printstory.hts/business/2354675;** Susan Pulliam, "Ordered to Commit Fraud, a Staffer Balked, Then Caved," *The Wall Street Journal,* June 23, 2003, **http://online.wsj.com/article/0,,SB105631811322355600,00.html;** Sherron S. Watkins, "Ethical Conflicts at Enron: Moral Responsibility in Corporate Capitalism," *California Management Review* 45 (Summer 2003), pp. 6–19.

5. Ken Rankin, "Silver Linings: Scandals May Create Job Security for CPAs," *Accounting Today,* May 17–June 6, 2004, **www.webcpa.com.**

6. Kris Frieswick, "How Audits Must Change," *CFO,* July 2003, p. 44.

7. Peter Vogt, "Forensic Accounting Emerges as a Hot Field," *The Wall Street Journal's College Journal* (n.d.), **www.collegejournal.com/salarydata/accounting/20030410-vogt.html** (accessed June 14, 2004).

8. Kris Frieswick, "NASA, We Have a Problem," *CFO,* May 2004, pp. 54–64.

9. Paul Davidson, "Parmalat's American Workers Uneasy, While Investors Are Angry," *USA Today,* January 14, 2004, pp. 1B–2B; Ellen Hale, "Italians Struggle to Grasp Fall of Beloved Parmalat," *USA Today,* January 6, 2004, pp. 1B–2B; "History of Parmalat," Parmalat (n.d.), **www.parmalat-asia.com/content/history.asp** (accessed March 4, 2004); Kevin McCoy, "Alaskan Pension Fund

Files Fraud Suit Against Parmalat," *USA Today,* January 6, 2004, p. 2B; Kevin McCoy, "SEC Chief Says Parmalat Case Might Ensnare Bankers," *USA Today,* January 27, 2004, p. 1B.

10. Hoover's, **www.hoovers.com** (accessed June 18, 2004).

11. "Accounting," *The Wall Street Journal's College Journal* (n.d.), **www.collegejournal.com/salarydata/accounting/** (accessed June 14, 2004); Peter Vogt, "Forensic Accounting Emerges as a Hot Field," *The Wall Street Journal's College Journal* (n.d.), **www.collegejournal.com/salarydata/accounting/20030410-vogt.html** (accessed June 14, 2004).

12. "About Aon," Aon, (n.d.) **www.aon.com/about/** (accessed June 22, 2004); "Insurers Subpoenaed over Broker Fees," *Los Angeles Times,* June 12, 2004, p. C3, accessed via Lexis-Nexis Academic Database; Helen Stock and David Plumb, "Aon Defends Fees it Charges Insurers," *Chicago Sun-Times,* May 5, 2004, p. 82, accessed via Lexis-Nexis Academic Database.

Chapter 16

1. "About Hershey Trust Company," Hershey Trust (n.d.), **www.hersheytrust.com/cornerstones/about.shtml** (accessed June 10, 2004); O. C. Ferrell, "Hershey Foods' Ethics and Social Responsibility," case developed for classroom use, Colorado State University, revised edition 2004; "Frequently Asked Questions," Hershey Foods (n.d.), **www.hersheyinvestorrelations.com/ireye/ir_site.zhtml?ticker=HSY&script=1801** (accessed June 10, 2004); William C. Smith, "Seeing to the Business of Fun: Franklin A. Miles Jr., Hershey Entertainment & Resorts Co.," *National Law Journal* December 22, 2003, p. 8.

2. Stanley R. Block and Geoffrey A. Hirt, *Foundations of Financial Management* (Burr Ridge, IL: McGraw-Hill, 2002); Calloway's Nursery (n.d.), **www.calloways.com/index_main.html** (accessed June 16, 2004).

3. "JCPenney Agrees to Sell Eckerd Drugstores for $4.525 Billion," JC Penney, press release, April 5, 2004, **www.jcpenney.net/company/press/eckerdsale.htm.**

4. Alex Salkever, "It's Time for an iPod IPO," *Business Week,* May 5, 2004, **www.businessweek.com.**

5. "Company Research," *The Wall Street Journal,* **http://online.wsj.com** (accessed June 17, 2004); Selena Maranjian, "The Math of the Dow," Motley Fool, January 29, 2004, **http://netscape.fool.com/News/mft/2004/mft04012904.htm.**

6. Michael Bazeley, "Google Going Public: Not Selling Out," *The* [Fort Collins] *Coloradoan,* April 30, 2004, p. D8; Les Christie, "The ABCs of a Unique IPO," *CNNMoney,* April 29, 2004, **http://money.cnn.com/2004/04/29/technology/googleauction/;** Bruce Gottlieb, "Explainer: What Is a Dutch Auction IPO?" *MSN Slate* (n.d.), **http://slate.msn.com/toolbar.aspx?action=print&id=1002736** (accessed June 10, 2004).

7. "Dow Data, 2000–2009," Dow Jones Indexes (n.d.), **www.djindexes/jsp/avgDecades.jsp?decade=2000** (accessed June 18, 2004).

8. Adapted from "Financial Managers," *Occupational Outlook Handbook, 2004–2005,* Bureau of Labor Statistics, U.S. Department of Labor, **www.bls.gov/oco/ocos010.htm** (accessed June 18, 2004).

9. "Historical Perspective," New York Stock Exchange, (n.d.) **www.nyse.com/about/p1020656067652.html?displayPage=%2Fabout%2F1022221392718.html** (accessed June 23, 2004); "NYSE at a Glance," New York Stock Exchange, Topic Outline Brochure, (n.d.) available at **www.nyse.com/pdfs/atAGlance.pdf** (accessed June 23, 2004); Adam Shell, "NYSE Reveals Grasso's Payout: $139.5M," *USA Today,* August 28, 2003, p. 1B, accessed via Lexis-Nexis Academic Database; Gary Strauss and Thor Valdmanis, "Interim Chief Reed Tackles NYSE Reform Right Away," *USA Today,* September 29, 2003, p. 3B, accessed via Lexis-Nexis Academic Database; Thor Valdmanis, "SEC Votes to Bless Reform," *USA Today,* December 18, 2003, p. 1B, accessed via Lexis-Nexis Academic Database.

Photo Credits

Chapter 1
Photo 1.1, page 3, Courtesy Sirius Satellite Radio, Inc.

Photo 1.2, page 6, Courtesy New Belgium Brewery Co., Inc.; Photo: Craig Demartino.

Photo 1.3, page 7, Courtesy National Fluid Milk Processor Promotion Board; Agency: Lowe Worldwide, Inc.

Photo 1.4, page 20, ©Bettmann/CORBIS.

Photo 1.5, page 21, Courtesy IBM.

Photo 1.6, page 22, Courtesy Burt's Bees, Inc.; Agency: Behrman Communications.

Photo 1.7, page 23, AP Photo/David Adame.

Chapter 2
Photo 2.1, page 31, Courtesy Home Depot.

Photo 2.2, page 34, AP Photo/Haraz Ghanbari.

Photo 2.3, page 39, AP Photo/Kenneth Lambert.

Photo 2.4, page 43, Mark Wilson/Getty Images.

Photo 2.5, page 48, Home Depot.

Photo 2.6, page 50, Courtesy PETA.

Photo 2.7, page 52, Courtesy Toyota Motor Sales, U.S.A., Inc.; Agency: Saatchi & Saatchi.

Photo 2.8, page 53, Courtesy California Department of Health Services.

Appendix A
Photo A-1, page 60, Courtesy LitigationFairness.org.

Photo A-2, page 61, ©2001 Steve Labadessa.

Photo A-3, page 65, ©Brent Jones.

Photo A-4, page 71, Courtesy of Council of Better Business Bureau, Inc.

Chapter 3
Photo 3.1, page 75, Photo by Porsche AG via Getty Images.

Photo 3.2, page 77, AP Photo/Koji Sasahara.

Photo 3.3, page 78, Aurora & Quanta Productions/Photo by: Samuel Zuder.

Photo 3.4, page 81, ©Reuters/CORBIS.

Photo 3.5, page 84, ©Paul A. Souders/CORBIS.

Photo 3.6, page 86, AP Photo/Apichart Weerawong.

Photo 3.7, page 87, ©2001 PhotoDisc, Inc.

Photo 3.8, page 93, Courtesy Higa Industries, Domino's Pizza Division.

Chapter 4
Photo 4.1, page 105, Photo/Stephen Chernin.

Photo 4.2, page 107, AP Photo/Paul Sakuma.

Photo 4.3, page 108, Courtesy of Scheid Vineyards, Inc.

Photo 4.4, page 109, Courtesy Microsoft Corporation.

Photo 4.5, page 113, Reprinted with permission of Fairytale Brownies, Inc.

Photo 4.6, page 117, Copyright © 2004 Amazon.com, Inc. All Rights Reserved.

Photo 4.7, page 120, © 2004 Lands' End, Inc. Used with permission.

Photo 4.8, page 122, Courtesy Cisco Systems, Inc.; Agency: Ogilvy & Mather/Los Angeles.

Photo 4.9, page 125, http://welcome,hp.com/country/us/en/privacy.html

Chapter 5
Photo 5.1, page 135, Photo by: Erica Perrault.

Photo 5.2, page 139, PhotoLink/Getty Images.

Photo 5.3, page 140, AP Photo/Dawn Villella.

Photo 5.4, page 141, Courtesy Xcel.

Photo 5.5, page 146, © John Hatch.

Photo 5.6, page 148, © GMAC Financial Services.

Photo 5.7, page 152, Courtesy Almond Board of California.

Chapter 6
Photo 6.1, page 163, Courtesy Don King Museum.

Photo 6.2, page 165, Courtesy Wyoming Travel & Tourism.

Photo 6.3, page 167, ©Wells Fargo.

Photo 6.4, page 168, Reprinted with permission.

Photo 6.5, page 169, Scott T. Baxter/Getty Images.

Photo 6.6, page 171, ZiggyKaluzny/Stone.

Photo 6.7, page 172, ©Brent Jones.

Photo 6.8, page 178, Curves International Inc. 2003.

Photo 6.9, page 181, Reprinted with permission from Entrepreneur.com.

Chapter 7
Photo 7.1, page 199, Photo by Justin Sullivan/Getty Images.

Photo 7.2, page 203, Courtesy Standard's & Poor.

Photo 7.3, page 205, AP Photo/Kevin Rivoli.

Photo 7.4, page 211, Reprinted with permission of CEO Express Company.

Photo 7.5, page 215, Courtesy John Biernat.

Photo 7.6, page 216, Courtesy Southwest Airlines.

Chapter 8
Photo 8.1, page 227, Photo by Consolidated News Pictures/Getty Images.

Photo 8.2, page 231, Courtesy The Home Depot, Inc.

Photo 8.3, page 229, ©Frank Trapper/Corbis.

Photo 8.4a, page 243, Stock Montage.

Photo 8.4b, page 243, Stock Montage.

Photo 8.5, page 237, ©Mark Peterson/Corbis.

Photo 8.6, page 244, Reprinted with permission from the American Arbitration Association.

Photo 8.7, page 246, © The McGraw-Hill Companies.

Chapter 9

Photo 9.1, page 255, © IDEO.

Photo 9.2, page 259, Copyright © 2004 Fandango. All Rights Reserved.

Photo 9.3, page 264, John A. Rizzo/Getty Images.

Photo 9.4, page 267, Courtesy United Parcel Service of America, Inc.

Photo 9.5, page 273, Kellogg's® and package design are registered trademarks of Kellogg Company. All rights reserved. Used with permission.

Photo 9.6, page 274, Reprinted with permission of International Organization for Standardization, www.iso.org.

Chapter 10

Photo 10.1, page 285, Courtesy SAS Institute, Inc.

Photo 10.2, page 287, Courtesy Verizon Wireless.

Photo 10.3, page 288, Royalty-Free/Corbis.

Photo 10.4, page 290, Getty Images.

Photo 10.5, page 297, Courtesy Booz-Allen Hamilton Inc.

Photo 10.6, page 301, Tony May/Getty Images.

Chapter 11

Photo 11.1, page 309, © Mark Burnett Productions, Inc.

Photo 11.2, page 312, Reprinted with permission of the McGraw-Hill Companies.

Photo 11.3, page 315, ©2001 Merrill Lynch.

Photo 11.4, page 323, ©Principal Financial Group.

Photo 11.5, page 324, Michael Newman/PhotoEdit.

Photo 11.6, page 328, Courtesy UFCW News Service.

Photo 11.7, page 330, Michael Newman/PhotoEdit.

Chapter 12

Photo 12.1, page 347, Courtesy Apple Computer.

Photo 12.2, page 350, Courtesy of the Cattlemen's Beef Board.

Photo 12.3, page 353, Courtesy Nokia America.

Photo 12.4, page 356, Courtesy Nestle Purina PetCare Company.

Photo 12.5, page 357, Produced by Rubin Postaer for American Honda, Inc.; Torfi Pictures.

Photo 12.6, page 361, ©2004 BMW of North America, LLC, used with permission. The BMW name and logo are registered trademarks.

Photo 12.7, page 363, Kayte M. Beioma/PhotoEdit.

Chapter 13

Photo 13.1, page 371, Courtesy Jones Soda Co.

Photo 13.2, page 373, Courtesy Domino's Pizza, Inc.

Photo 13.3, page 374, Courtesy The Coca-Cola Company.

Photo 13.4, page 376, Photodisc/Getty Images.

Photo 13.5, page 380, Cathy Melloan/PhotoEdit.

Photo 13.6, page 381, Courtesy The Coca-Cola Company.

Photo 13.7, page 382, ©M. Hruby.

Photo 13.8, page 384, ©2001 Toshiba America Business Solutions, Inc. Electronic Imaging Division.

Photo 13.9, page 387, Courtesy United Parcel Service of America, Inc.

Photo 13.10, page 395, Courtesy Louisville Zoo.

Photo 13.11, page 396, ©Shooting Star.

Chapter 14

Photo 14.1, page 407, AFP/Getty Images.

Photo 14.2, page 410, Royalty Free/Corbis.

Photo 14.3, page 411, U.S. Department of Treasury via Getty Images.

Photo 14.4, page 414, Courtesy Delta Air Lines, Inc.

Photo 14.5, page 416, Photo by Mark Wilson/Getty Images.

Photo 14.6, page 419, Courtesy of U.S. Bank and Virtual Creative, Inc.

Photo 14.7, page 423, Courtesy Franklin Resources, Inc.

Chapter 15

Photo 15.1, page 433, Reprinted with permission of Public Company Accounting Oversight Board.

Photo 15.2, page 437, Copyright © 2004 by the American Institute of Certified Public Accountants, Inc. Reprinted with permission.

Photo 15.3, page 439, SAS and all other SAS Institute Inc. product or service names are registered trademarks or trademarks of SAS Institute Inc. in the USA and other countries. ® indicates USA registration. Other brand and product names are trademarks of their respective companies. Copyright ©2003. SAS Institute Inc. Cary, NC, USA. All rights reserved.

Photo 15.4, page 444, Courtesy Grant Thornton.

Photo 15.5, page 454, Courtesy American Institute of CPA.

Chapter 16

Photo 16.1, page 465, Courtesy Milton Hershey School.

Photo 16.2, page 470, Thinkstock/Getty Images.

Photo 16.3, page 472, AP Photo/Charlie Neibergall.

Photo 16.4, page 476, Courtesy International Business Machines Corporation.

Photo 16.5, page 479, Courtesy General Mills.

Photo 16.6, page 480, Courtesy Friedman, Billings, Ramsey Group, Inc.

Photo 16.7, page 481, Reprinted with permission of E*Trade Financial.

Photo 16.8, page 483, Courtesy Citigroup Global Markets Holdings, Inc.

Appendix D

Photo D-1, page 499, Courtesy Elizabeth Handlin; June 2004 Smart Money Magazine.

Name Index

Company Index

Subject Index